THE COMMON LAW OF EUROPE CASEBOOKS
TORT LAW

COMMON LAW OF EUROPE CASEBOOKS

Tort Law

Walter van Gerven
Jeremy Lever
Pierre Larouche

·HART·
PUBLISHING
OXFORD AND PORTLAND, OREGON
2000

Hart Publishing
Oxford and Portland, Oregon

Published in North America (US and Canada) by
Hart Publishing c/o
International Specialized Book Services
5804 NE Hassalo Street
Portland, Oregon
97213-3644
USA

Distributed in the Netherlands, Belgium and Luxembourg by
Intersentia, Churchillaan 108
B2900 Schoten
Antwerpen
Belgium

Hart Publishing Ltd is a specialist legal publisher based in Oxford, England.
To order further copies of this book or to request a list of other
publications please write to:

Hart Publishing Ltd, Salter's Boatyard, Folly Bridge,
Abingdon Road, Oxford OX1 4LB
Telephone: +44 (0)1865 245533 or Fax: +44 (0)1865 794882
e-mail: mail@hartpub.co.uk
www.hartpub.co.uk

British Library Cataloguing in Publication Data
Data Available
ISBN 1 84113 139 3 (paper)

Typeset by Hope Services (Abingdon) Ltd.
Printed in Great Britain on acid-free paper
by Biddles Ltd, Guildford and King's Lynn.

Foreword

The present book, which contains cases and other material on *Tort Law*, is part of the series of *Casebooks for the Common Law of Europe* of which the first undersigned is the General Editor. Other casebooks on which work is being done relate to *Contracts* and to *Judicial Review of Administrative Action*. The objective of this book, and of the whole series, is to help to uncover common roots, notwithstanding differences in approach, of the European legal systems with a view to strengthening the common legal heritage of Europe, not to strangling its diversity. The authors hope that the book will be used as teaching material in universities and other institutions throughout Europe and elsewhere in order to familiarize future generations of lawyers with each others' legal systems and to assess and facilitate the impact of European supranational legal systems on the development of national laws, and *vice versa*.

It is not the intention of this book, or of the series as a whole, to unify the existing laws of tort or of the other areas of law that are to be covered. That would not be possible, nor would it be desirable. For indeed, the diversity of European legal systems reflects not only a variety of legal cultures—which are bound to converge in step with European integration—but also and perhaps mostly a variety of value judgments or policy choices which find their expression in the legal systems. In their effort to uncover common roots, the authors do not wish to express any preference for the solution embodied in one or the other legal system, where that would imply endorsing the underlying value judgment over alternative judgments. In the absence of a common European legislature (outside the limited areas for which national competences have been transferred to the European Union), there is indeed no authoritative source, other than national legislation or case law, from which a common understanding as to the fundamental value judgments underlying national law can be derived. Although that should not prevent legal writers from expressing their own personal preferences, we would prefer not to do that, or to do it only exceptionally, in a book like the present one which is intended to inquire into the common core of principles in the national and supranational legal orders existing within the European Union.

Parts of this book were published in 1998 in a separate volume under the title *Tort Law: Scope of Protection* (hereafter: the previous book). The present casebook is complete. It comprises nine chapters: I. General Topics; II. Scope of Protection; III. Liability for One's Own Conduct; IV. Causation; V. Liability for the Conduct of Others; VI. Liability not Based on Conduct; VII. Defences; VIII. Remedies; IX. Impact of Supranational and International Law. The parts published in the previous book are now updated and integrated in the present volume, mainly in Chapter II but also to some extent in Chapters I, III, VI and IX.

In order to keep the present book within acceptable limits of size and price, some relevant material has not been included, but is being reproduced on our Internet site, at

<http://www.rechten.unimaas.nl/casebook>. However, all of the material, whether on paper or on the Internet, is listed in the Table of Contents, indicating for each document where it can be found. All of the material has also been taken into account in drawing up the Comparative Overviews included in the present book. To make referencing possible, all of the material, whether in the book or on the Internet, has been numbered consecutively. As with the previous book, the original language version of the translated material—both that included in the book and that available in electronic format—can also be found on the Internet site referred to above.

Selecting and presenting documents from various legal systems are not an easy task and errors will not always have been avoided. For English law, all authors had the benefit of direct input from an English lawyer, thanks to the presence in our team of Jeremy Lever. As for German and French law, Professor Christian von Bar (Professor of Comparative Law at the University of Osnabrück and Director of the Institute of Private International and Comparative Law) and Professor Geneviève Viney (Professor at Paris I, Sorbonne) generously agreed, notwithstanding the heavy workload imposed by their own academic work, to supply advice and comments for which the authors are extremely grateful.

The authors regret very much that, due to lack of time and of human resources, they could not include much material from national legal systems other than the English, French and German legal systems, representing the three major European "legal families", but they have included material from the two European supranational legal orders, that of the European Union and that of the European Convention on Human Rights (however, the documents from the "Nordic" legal family and other national legal orders, including some from outside Europe, which were reproduced in the previous book, remain available on the Internet site of the project). Fortunately this important gap is made good by Professor C. von Bar's work *The Common European Law of Torts* (see Table of Frequently Cited Works). In that impressive work, numerous references to the legal systems of all EU Member States can be found with regard to all of the subjects treated in the present book (and many more). On this occasion we would also like to draw attention to another *magnum opus*, Professor R. Zimmermann's *The Law of Obligations. Roman Foundations of the Civilian Tradition* (Oxford: Clarendon, 1996). The book gives many insights into the origin of the establishment in Europe of an ius commune under the influence of roman law under which "Law professors moved freely from a chair in one country to one in another; the same textbooks were used at Pavia or Bologna as much as at Halle, Alcalà or Oxford . . ." (at x). It shows how "the 'European' ius commune and the 'English' common law were (and are) not really so radically distinct as is often suggested" (at xi). It provides an illustration of how the past and the future may meet in a newly emerging ius commune, to which the present book wishes to make a modest contribution.

Many have contributed to the preparation and publication of this book (which proved to be a difficult and immense task). The editors, and also the main authors, are the undersigned: Walter van Gerven (Professor, K.U. Leuven, U. Maastricht and King's College, formerly Advocate General at the European Court of Justice), Jeremy Lever, QC (Senior Dean of All Souls College, Oxford University) and Pierre Larouche (Post-Doctoral Researcher, U. Maastricht). They have divided the work between them as follows: Jeremy Lever, apart from monitoring the English materials as to contents, invested considerable energy in relation to the drafting of the English in the sections dealing with non-English systems (albeit that the volume of work was such that a small proportion of the final work could not be reviewed by him). Pierre Larouche is the author of Chapters IV, V and VI and was responsible for the formatting of the book and the Internet site. Walter van Gerven, apart from being responsible for the concept and structure of the project, is the main author of most of the parts published in the previous book (Pierre Larouche being the co-author or author of the other parts) and co-authored and/or supervised the work on the other Chapters in the new book. That has not prevented all three of them of working closely together and supervising, and updating, each other's work.

Others have contributed to one or more chapters: Bart De Temmerman (referendaris at the Belgian Court of Cassation and former Researcher at the K.U. Leuven) is the main author of Chapter VIII, Ignace Claeys (Researcher at the Belgian Research Fund) and Jan Wouters (Professor, K.U. Leuven) have contributed, as co-authors, to Chapters I and III respectively, Sofie Covemaeker (Research Assistant, K.U. Leuven) and Sophie Stijns (Associate Professor, K.U. Leuven) have contributed to Chapter VII. Madeleine Van Rossum (Associate Professor, U. Maastricht) has worked on Chapter IV. Yvonne Salmon (Oxford) has worked on various chapters, mainly Chapters VII and VIII. As for the previous book, Adriana Alvarez (U. Maastricht) coordinated much of the work, notwithstanding her own time-consuming commitments in the financial sector. Iris Vervoort (K.U. Leuven) assisted the editors in the immensely difficult work of preparing the tables and the index and Linda Mees (K.U. Leuven) supplied the logistic support to finalize the materials in due time.

Many helped in preparing translations of the French, German and other non-English material in the book or on the Internet site. Their names are mentioned under each of the translated documents.

The editors are grateful to all those, mentioned and not mentioned above, who provided help in various ways with the preparation of this book and to Richard Hart of Hart Publishing who provided advice and put the book in final shape.

This book has been made possible thanks to continuing financial support from the University of Maastricht and, at the beginning, from the European Commission, and thanks to the no less important moral support from Appie Luermans, Director of the Law Faculty of the U. Maastricht. As appears from the foregoing, substantial personnel support has been supplied by the U. Maastricht and by the K.U. Leuven. The series Casebooks for a Common Law of Europe, of which this book is part, has its home base at METRO, the Maastricht Institute for Transnational Legal Research of the University of Maastricht, which kindly hosts our Internet site <**http://www.rechten.unimaas.nl/casebook**>.

The materials in the book have been updated until 1 January 2000 (but exceptionally further developments have been incorporated).

Walter van Gerven
Jeremy Lever
Pierre Larouche

Table of Contents

(@ = Materials available on Internet)

CONTENTS

CHAPTER TWO
SCOPE OF PROTECTION

CONTENTS

CONTENTS

CHAPTER THREE
LIABILITY FOR ONE'S OWN CONDUCT

**CHAPTER FOUR
CAUSATION**

CHAPTER FIVE
LIABILITY FOR THE CONDUCT OF OTHERS

**CHAPTER SIX
LIABILITY NOT BASED ON CONDUCT**

**CHAPTER SEVEN
DEFENCES**

CHAPTER EIGHT
REMEDIES

CONTENTS

CHAPTER NINE
IMPACT OF SUPRANATIONAL AND INTERNATIONAL LAW

CONTENTS

CONTENTS

Guide to the Reader

The following paragraphs provide some practical guidance to the reader of this book.

Structure of the book

As mentioned in the Foreword, this book comprises nine Chapters, each of which is divided into sections, which are in turn divided into a number of subsections (some subsections are further split into parts). Each of the subsections comprises first an Introductory Note, which gives an overview of the issues and of the materials included therein (the Introductory Notes are sub-divided with letters, e.g. a), b)). Materials are presented after the Introductory Note, either individually or together, where they bear on the same point. Annotations (sub-divided with arabic numerals, e.g. (1), (2)) follow each document or group of documents. For cases, a summary of the facts and of the holdings of the courts which have decided on the case is provided before the excerpts from the judgment itself.

Foreign words and expressions

The authors have purposely left foreign words or expressions in the original language (for example *Recht am Gewerbebetrieb*, *obligation de moyens*) designating legal concepts which cannot meaningfully be rendered in English, either because they cannot adequately be translated by a crisp phrase or expression or because the most appropriate translation would itself be a term which the common law infuses with specific meaning. Thus it was thought more efficient to keep the foreign words in, so that at least the readers who know the foreign system in question would recognize the concept, while including a brief explanatory note for other readers. That note has generally been added where the foreign word or expression is used for the first time. Some notes have also been made for English words which have a specific meaning in the English common law which the foreign reader may not be expected to know. All the words and expressions for which a note has been made are indicated in the subject-matter index, and so is the reference to the page where the note can be found.

For countries with more than one official language (e.g. Belgium, Switzerland), some official names have been translated into English.

Lower courts

Furthermore, the authors have also intentionally removed references to the specific designation of the lower courts in the presentation of the cases excerpted in this book, considering that this book does not purport to deal with the comparative structure of courts. For each case, only the actual court whose judgment is reproduced is identified by its official name (usually a supreme court). Since most of the legal systems studied here have a three-tiered court structure, the lower courts have been referred to simply as the "court of first instance" and the "court of appeal".

Cross-references

Two numbering systems run in parallel throughout the book for ease of cross-reference.

First of all, cross-references in normal typeface point to the numbering of the subdivisions of this book. That numbering can be found on the top right-hand corner of the odd-numbered pages, within square brackets. For instance, a cross-reference to "2.3.2., Introductory Note under a)" refers to paragraph a) of the Introductory Note to Subsection 2 of Section 3 of Chapter II. By looking at the number on the top left-hand corner of even-numbered pages, the reader can quickly find Subsection 2 of Section 3 of Chapter II ("2.3.2.") and then locate paragraph a) of the Introductory Note. Similarly, "1.4.1.A." refers to part A. of Subsection 1 of Section 4 of Chapter I.

Secondly, all materials included in the book have been numbered, and these numbers have been indicated on the top right-hand corner of odd-numbered pages (where those include materials). Documents have been numbered consecutively for each chapter; a document number comprises the chapter number, an indication of the origin of the document and the sequential number of the document within the chapter. Cross-references in bold denote that numbering system. For instance, a cross-reference to "**9.EC.6.**, Note (1)" refers to Note (1) under document number 6 of Chapter IX. "EC" indicates that the document comes from the EC legal system. By looking at the numbering on the top left-hand corner of even-numbered pages, the reader can quickly find document **9.EC.6.** (the *Brasserie du Pêcheur* case) and then locate Note (1) thereunder. Similarly, "**7.F.6.**" refers to document number 6 of Chapter VII, which comes from the French legal system.

Tables and indexes

The following tables and indexes have been included for the convenience of the reader:

– a subject-matter index;
– a table of cases, where cases which are excerpted in the book are highlighted;
– a table of legislative instruments, where instruments which are included in the book are highlighted;
– a table of abbreviations;
– a table of frequently cited works.

Citation and style conventions

In general, citation of legislative materials or cases has been made according to the format commonly used in the legal system in question; some information has been added where it was thought useful for foreign readers. Doctrinal works (monographs and articles) have been cited as far as possible according to a uniform format based on the standard format used in English-speaking countries.

In particular, it should be noted that (i) the standard reference for serials (case reports or periodicals) contains a year and/or volume number and a page reference to the beginning of the document, unless otherwise indicated in the table of abbreviations, (ii) pinpoint references (indicated by "at . . .") are to page numbers unless otherwise indicated, (iii) an indication has been inserted where references have been omitted from within excerpts, (iv) references to currency units have been made using the standard ISO three-letter code (see the table of abbreviations) and (v) periods have largely been removed from citations and abbreviations.

The authors wish to express the hope that readers will find this book practical and pleasant to use. They are grateful for any suggestions or comments from readers in this respect.

Table of Frequently Cited Works

The works mentioned below are referred to frequently in this book and have accordingly been abbreviated as follows:

Akkermans

A.J. Akkermans, *Proportionele aansprakelijkheid bij onzeker causaal verband* (Deventer: Tjeenk Willink, 1997), to be published in English as *Proportional liability in circumstances of uncertain causation* (Deventer: Kluwer Law International, 2000)

Bénac-Schmidt/Larroumet

F. Bénac-Schmidt and C. Larroumet, in *Encyclopédie Dalloz—Civil*, v° "Responsabilité du fait d'autrui" (in Chapter V) and "Responsabilité des choses inanimées" (in Chapter VI)

Boré

L. Boré, *La défense des intérêts collectifs par les associations devant les juridictions administratives et judiciaires* (Paris: LGDJ, 1997)

Clerk & Lindsell on Torts

M.R. Brazier, (gen. ed.), *Clerk & Lindsell on Torts*, 17th edn. (London: Sweet & Maxwell, 1995)

Dejean de la Bâtie

N. Dejean de la Bâtie, *Aubry & Rau—Droit civil français*, Vol. VI–2, 8th edn. (Paris: Librairies Techniques, 1989)

Goubeaux

G. Goubeaux, *Traité de droit civil—Les personnes* (Paris: LGDJ, 1989)

Gour

C. Gour, in *Encyclopédie Dalloz—Responsabilité de la puissance publique*, v° "Faute de service"

Hart and Honoré

H.L.A. Hart and T. Honoré, *Causation in the Law*, 2nd edn. (Oxford: Clarendon, 1985)

Heukels and McDonnell

T. Heukels and A. McDonnell, (eds.), *The Action for Damages in Community law* (The Hague: Kluwer Law International, 1997)

Honoré

A.M. Honoré, *Causation and Remoteness of Damage*, in A. Tunc, (ed.), *International Encyclopedia of Comparative Law*, Vol. XI, Chapter 7 (Tübingen: Mohr, 1971)

Howells

G. Howells, *Comparative Product Liability* (Aldershot: Darthmouth, 1993)

Jourdain

P. Jourdain, in *Juris-Classeur Civil*, v° "Art. 1382 à 1386" (referred to with fascicule number and page)

teur d'un principe général de responsabilité (Brussel: Bruylant, 1998).

Soergel (contributor)
  (with section number)
H.T. Soergel and W. Siebert, *Bürgerliches Gesetzbuch mit Einführungsgesetz und Nebengesetzen*, 12th edn. (Stuttgart: Kohlhammer, 1987).

Stapleton
J. Stapleton, *Product Liability* (London: Butterworths, 1994)

Starck, Roland and Boyer
B. Starck, H. Roland and L. Boyer, *Obligations. 1. Responsabilité délictuelle*, 5th edn. (Paris: Editions Litec, 1996)

Staudinger (contributor)
  (with section number)
J. von Staudingers Kommentar zum Bürgerlichen Gesetzbuch, 13th edn. (except for Schäfer, §823 and Medicus, §249, cited to the 12th edn.) (Berlin: Sellier—de Gruyter)

Truchet
D. Truchet, in *Encyclopédie Dalloz—Responsabilité de la puissance publique*, v° "Hôpitaux"

Viney and Jourdain, *Conditions*
G. Viney and P. Jourdain, *Traité de droit civil—Les conditions de la responsabilité*, 2nd edn. (Paris: LGDJ, 1998)

Viney, *Introduction*
G. Viney, *Traité de droit civil—Introduction à la responsabilité* (Paris: LGDJ, 1995)

Viney, *Effets*
G. Viney, *Traité de droit civil—Les obligations: la responsabilité: effets* (Paris: LGDJ, 1988)

von Bar I
C. von Bar, *The common European Law of Torts*, Vol. I (München: Beck, 1998)

von Bar II
C. von Bar, *Gemeineuropäisches Deliktsrecht*, Vol. II (München: Beck, 1999)

Weir
T. Weir, *A Casebook on Tort*, 8th edn. (London: Sweet & Maxwell, 1996)

Zweigert and Kötz
K. Zweigert and H. Kötz, *Introduction to Comparative Law*, 3rd rev. edn., transl. by T. Weir (Oxford: Clarendon, 1998)

Table of Abbreviations

Unless otherwise indicated below references to periodicals are made to the year and/or volume number and to the page number.

§	Paragraph (section number for German, Austrian and Scandinavian legislation)
AA	Ars Aequi (Netherlands)
ABGB	Allgemeines Bürgerliches Gesetzbuch (Civil Code—Austria)
AC	Appeal Cases (UK)
	Arresten van het Hof van Cassatie (Belgium)
AcP	Archiv für die civilistische Praxis (Germany)
AG	Aktiengesellschaft (public limited company—Germany)
AGBG	Gesetz zur Regelung des Rechts der Allgemeinen Geschäfts-bedingungen (Act on Standard Contractual Terms—Germany)
AJCL	American Journal of Comparative Law
AJDA	Les actualités juridiques—Droit administratif (France)
AK	Astikos Kodikas (Civil Code—Greece)
All ER	All England Reports (UK)
ALI	American Law Institute
ALR	Australian Law Reports (Australia)
AMG	Arzneimittelgesetz (Drug Act—Germany)
App.Cas.	Law Reports Appeal Cases, House of Lords (UK)
Arr. Verbr.	Arresten van het Hof van Verbreking (Belgium)
Art.	Article(s)
AtomG	Atomgesetz (Germany)
Aust LJ	Australian Law Journal (Australia)
B&S	Best & Smith's Queen's Bench Reports (UK)
BAG	Bundesarbeitsgericht (Germany)
BBergG	Bundesbergbaugesetz (Federal Mining Act—Germany)
BEF	Belgian Francs
BGB	Bürgerliches Gesetzbuch (Civil Code—Germany)
BGBl.	Bundesgesetzblatt (Germany), with reference to number of part and page number
BGH	Bundesgerichtshof (Germany)
BGH-GS	Bundesgerichtshof (Germany)—Großer Senat für Zivilsachen

BGHSt.	Entscheidungen des Bundesgerichtshofes in Strafsachen (Germany)
BGHZ	Entscheidungen des Bundesgerichtshofes in Zivilsachen (Germany)
Bing NC	Bingham, New Cases, English Common Pleas (UK)
BNatSchG	Bundesnaturschutzgesetz (Federal Act on Nature Protection—Germany)
BNotO	Bundesnotarordnung (Germany)
BPflV	Bundespflegesatzverordnung (Germany)
BS/MB	Belgisch Staatsblad/Moniteur belge (Belgium)
BT Drucks	Drucksachen des Deutschen Bundestages (Germany)
Bull.civ.	Bulletin des arrêts de la Cour de cassation, chambres civiles (France), with reference to part of reporter and sequential number of cases
Bull.crim.	Bulletin des arrêts de la Cour de cassation, chambre criminelle (France), with reference to sequential number of case
BVerfG	Bundesverfassungsgericht (Germany)
BVerfGE	Entscheidungen des Bundesverfassungsgerichtes (Germany)
BW	Burgerlijk Wetboek (Civil Code—Netherlands, Belgium)
c.	chapter(s)
C & P	Carrington & Payne's Nisi Prius Reports
CA	Court of Appeal (UK)
	Quebec Court of Appeal (Canada)
CAA	Cour administrative d'appel (France), with location
CAD	Canadian Dollar
Camb LJ	Cambridge Law Journal (UK)
Cass.	Cour de cassation (France), as the case may be :
Ass. plén.	Plenary Assembly (since 1967)
Ch. mixte	Mixed Chambers
Ch. réun.	Joined Chambers (until 1967)
civ.	Civil Chamber (with chamber number after 1952)
comm.	Commercial Chamber
crim.	Criminal Chamber
Req.	Motions Chamber
Soc.	Social Chamber
C.civ.	Code civil (Civil Code—France, Belgium)
CCP	Code of Civil Procedure of Quebec (Canada)
CDE	Cahiers de droit européen
CÉ	Conseil d'État (France)
CFI	Court of First Instance of the Court of Justice of the European Communities
Ch	Law Reports, Chancery (UK)
ChD	Chancery Division of the High Court (UK)
Chron	Chroniques
C.i.c.	*culpa in contrahendo*

Cir.	Circuit Court (UK)
CJ	Chief Justice (UK)
CLR	Commonwealth Law Reports (Australia)
Cm.	Command paper (UK)
CMLRep	Common Market Law Reports
CMLRev	Common Market Law Review
Cmnd	Command Papers, 5th series (UK)
Co	Company
Com	Commentaire
COM	Document of the European Commission, with reference to year and serial number
Cons LJ	Consumer Law Journal
Corp	Corporation
CrimLR	Criminal Law Review
Ct	Court
Curr Legal Prob	Current Legal Problems (UK)
D	Recueil Dalloz et Sirey (France), with reference to name of part and page number
DA	Recueil analytique Dalloz (France)
DAR	Deutsches Autorecht (Germany)
DB	Der Betrieb (Germany)
DC	Divisional Court (UK)
	Recueil critique Dalloz (France)
DEM	Deutschmark
DH	Recueil hebdomadaire Dalloz (France)
DJZ	Deutsche Juristenzeitung (Germany)
DLR	Dominion law reports (Canada)
Doct	Doctrine
DP	Recueil périodique et critique Dalloz (France, until 1940), with reference to number of part and page number
DR	Deutsches Recht (Germany)
East	East's Term Reports, King's Bench (UK)
EC	European Community
	Treaty establishing the European Community
ECC	European Commercial Cases
ECHR	European Convention on Human Rights
ECJ	Court of Justice of the European Communities
ECR	Reports of Cases before the Court of Justice of the European Communities and the Court of First Instance
ECtHR	European Court of Human Rights
ECU	European Currency Unit
ed.	editor
edn.	edition
EEC	European Economic Community (Common Market)
EGLR	Estates Gazette Law Reports (UK)

EHRR	European Human Rights Reports
El & Bl	Ellis & Blackburn's Queen's Bench Reports (UK)
ELRev	European Law Review
ER	English Reports (UK)
ETS	European Treaty Series
EU	European Union
	Treaty on European Union
EuGRZ	Europäische Grundrechte Zeitschrift
Eur.RPrivL.	European Review of Private Law
EuZW	Europäische Zeitschrift für Wirtschaftsrecht (Germany)
eV	eingetragener Verein (private limited company—Germany)
Ex	Court of Exchequer (UK)
Ex.Ch.	Court of Exchequer Chamber (UK)
Ex. p.	ex parte
F	Federal Reporter (USA)
F 2d	Federal Reporter, Second Series (USA)
Fam. Law	Family Law (UK)
Fasc.	Fascicule (Fr.), part or issue of a periodical or book
FLR	Family Law Reports (UK)
Foro it.	Il Foro Italiano (Italy)
FRF	French Franc
FSR	Fleet Street Reports (UK)
FS	Festschrift
GA	Goltdammer's Archiv für Strafrecht (Germany)
Gaz.Pal.	Gazette du Palais (France), with reference to name of part and page number
GBP	UK Sterling Pound
gen. ed.	general editor
GenTG	Gentechnikgesetz (Genetic Engineering Act—Germany)
GG	Grundgesetz (Constitution/Basic Law—Germany)
Giur. It.	Giurisprudenza italiana (Italy)
GmbH	Gesellschaft mit beschränkter Haftung (limited liability company—Germany)
GRD	Greek Drachmas
H&C	Hurlston & Coltman's Exchequer Reports
HaftpflG	Haftsplichtgesetz (Civil liability Act—Germany)
HC	High Court (UK)
HD	Högsta domstolen (Sweden)
HGB	Handelsgesetzbuch (Commercial Code—Germany)
HL	House of Lords (UK)
HLR	Housing Law Reports (UK)
HR	Hoge Raad (Netherlands)
ICJ	International Court of Justice
ICJ Rep	Reports of Judgments, Advisory Opinions and Orders (International Court of Justice)

ICLQ	International and Comparative Law Quarterly (UK)
ICR	Industrial Cases Reports (UK)
ILC	International Law Commission of the United Nations
ILM	International Legal Materials (USA)
ILRM	Irish Law Reports Monthly (Ireland)
Imm. AR	Immigration appeal reports
Int'l J of Semiotics of Law	International Journal of Semiotics of Law
Int'l Rev. L. Econ.	International Review of Law and Economics
I.P.P.	incapacité permanente partielle
IPRax	Praxis des internationalen Privat- und Verfahrensrecht (Germany)
IR	Irish Reports (Ireland)
	Information rapides
J	Justice (UK, Ireland)
JA	Justice of Appeal (Canada)
JBl.	Juristische Blätter (Austria)
JCP	Semaine Juridique or Juris-classeur périodique, General Edition (France), with reference to number of part and sequential number of document
JCP(E)	Juris-classeur périodique, Edition Entreprise (France), with reference to number of part and sequential number of document
JE	Jurisprudence-Express (Canada)
JJ	Justices (UK, Ireland)
J Law & Econ (ns)	Journal of Law and Economics (new series) (USA)
J Leg Stud	Journal of Legal Studies (USA)
JLSS	Journal of the Law Society of Scotland (UK)
JO	Journal Officiel (Official Gazette—France)
Jour. Soc. lég. comp.	Journées de la Société de législation comparée (France)
JR	Juristische Rundschau (Germany)
JT	Journal des tribunaux (Belgium)
Jur	Jurisprudence
JuS	Juristische Schulung (Germany)
JZ	Juristenzeitung (Germany)
KB	King's Bench (UK)
	Koninklijk Besluit (Belgium)
KBD	King's Bench Division (UK)
KCLJ	King's College Law Journal (UK)
KIR	Knight's Industrial Reports
KKO	Korkein oikeus (Finland)
LC	Lord Chancellor (UK)
LCJ	Lord Chief Justice (UK)
Ld.Raym.	Lord Raymond's King's Bench Reports
Leb.	Recueil des décisions du Conseil d'État (Recueil Lebon—France)

Lég	Législation
LJ	Lord Justice (UK)
LJJ	Lord Justices (UK)
Lloyd's Rep	Lloyd's List Law Reports
LM	Lindenmaier-Möhring, Nachschlagewerk des Bundes-gerichtshofes (Collection of Decisions of the Federal Supreme Court, together with comments—Germany)
LNTS	League of Nations Treaty Series
LQR	Law Quarterly Review (UK)
LR	Law Reports (UK)
LT	Law Times
Ltd.	limited
LuftVG	Luftverkehrgesetz (Air Traffic Act—Germany)
M & R	Milieu en Recht (Netherlands)
M & W	Meeson & Welsby's Exchequer Reports
Macq	Macqueen's Scots Appeal Cases
MDR	Monatschrift für Deutsches Recht (Germany)
Mer	Merivale's Reports
MJ	Maastricht Journal of European and Comparative Law (Netherlands)
Mod.	Modern Reports
Mod LR	Modern Law Review (UK)
m.p.h.	miles per hour
MR	Master of the Rolls (UK)
NBW	Nieuw Burgerlijk Wetboek (New Civil Code—Netherlands)
NE	North Eastern Reporter (USA)
N.I.	Northern Ireland Reports
NILR	Netherlands International Law Review (Netherlands)
NJ	Nederlandse Jurisprudentie (Netherlands), with reference to sequential number of cases
NJA	Nytt Juridiskt Arkiv (Sweden)
NJB	Nederlands Juristenblad (Netherlands)
NJW	Neue Juristische Wochenschrift (Germany)
NJW-RR	Neue Juristische Wochenschrift—Rechtsprechungs-Report Zivilrecht (Germany)
No.	number
NTBR	Kwartaalbericht Nieuw BW (Netherlands)
N.V.	Naamloze Vennootschap (limited liability company—Belgium)
NW	North Western Reporter (USA)
NY	New York Court of Appeals Reports (USA)
NZV	Neue Zeitschrift für Verkehrsrecht (Germany)
OGH	Oberster Gerichtshof (Austria)
OJ	Official Journal of the European Communities, with reference to series, issue number and page number

OJ C	Official Journal of the European Communities, Cases
OJ L	Official Journal of the European Communities, Legislation
OJLS	Oxford Journal of Legal Studies (UK)
ØLD	Østre Landsrets Dom (Denmark)
OLG	Oberlandesgericht (Germany), with location
OLRC	Ontario Law Reform Commission (Canada)
OUP	Oxford University Press (UK)
P	Pacific Reporter
P 2d	Pacific Reporter, Second Series
Pan	Panorama
para.	paragraph(s)
Pas.	Pasicrisie/Pasinomie (Belgium), with reference to number of part and page number
PC	Judicial Committee of the Privy Council (UK)
PCIJ	Permanent Court of International Justice
Plc.	Public Limited Company
ProdHaftG	Produkthaftungsgesetz (Product Liability Act—Germany)
Pt	part
PTE	Portuguese Escudo
Pub L	Public Law (UK)
QB	Queen's Bench Reports (UK)
QBD	Queen's Bench Division of the High Court (UK)
RCJB	Revue critique de jurisprudence belge (Belgium)
Rec.	Recueil des décisions du Conseil d'État (France)
Rep. Not. Defr.	Répertoire du notariat Defrénois (France)
Resp.Ass.	Responsabilité civile et assurances (France)
RFDA	Revue française de droit administratif (France)
RG	Reichsgericht (Germany)
RGAR	Revue générale des assurances et des responsabilités (Belgium), with reference to sequential number of case
RGBl.	Reichsgesetzblatt (Germany)
RGRK	Reichsgerichtskommentar (Germany)
RGZ	Entscheidungen des Reichsgerichtes (Germany)
RHDI	Revue hellénique de droit international (Greece)
RIAA	Report of International Arbitral Awards
RIW	Recht der internationalen Wirtschaft
RJQ	Recueil de jurisprudence du Quebec (Canada)
RLF	retrolental fibroplasia
RM Themis	Rechtsgeleerd Magazijn Themis (Netherlands)
RPC	Reports of Patent, Design and Trade Mark Cases
RSC	Rules of the Supreme Court (UK)
RSQ	Revised Statutes of Quebec (Canada)
RTDciv.	Revue trimestrielle de droit civil (France)
RTR	Road Traffic Reports (UK)
RvdW	Rechtspraak van de Week (Netherlands)

RW	Rechtskundig Weekblad (Belgium)
s.	section(s)
S	Recueil Sirey (France, until 1962), with reference to number of part and page number
S.A.	Société Anonyme (France)
Salk	Salkeld's King's Bench Reports
SBC	Statutes of British Columbia (Canada)
SCR	Supreme Court Reports (Canada)
SEK	Swedish Krone
Ser.	Series
SI	Statutory Instrument
SKL	Skadeståndslag (Tort Law Act—Sweden, Finland)
SLT Rep.	Scottish Law Times Reports (UK)
SO	Statutes of Ontario (Canada)
Somm	Sommaires
Starkie	Starkie's Nisi Prius Reports
StGB	Strafgesetzbuch (Criminal Code—Germany)
StPO	Strafprozeßordnung (Ordinance of Criminal Procedure—Germany)
St R&O	Statutory Rules and Orders
StVG	Straßenverkehrgesetz (Road Traffic Act—Germany)
StVO	Straßenverkehrsordnung (Road Traffic Regulations—Germany)
StVZO	Straßenverkehrs-Zulassungs-Ordnung (Road Traffic Licensing Ordinance—Germany)
sub nom.	sub nomine
Sup Ct	Supreme Court (Ireland)
	Quebec Superior Court (Canada)
TBBR	Tijdschrift voor Belgisch burgerlijk recht (Belgium)
TBP	Tijdschrift voor bestuurswetenschappen en publiek recht (Belgium)
Texas LR	Texas Law Review (USA)
TGI	Tribunal de grande instance (France), with reference to location
TLR	Times Law Reports
TR	Durnford & East's Term Reports
TvC	Tijdschrift voor Consumentenrecht (Netherlands)
TVVS	Maandblad voor ondernemingsrecht en rechtspersonen (Netherlands)
UfR	Ugeskrift for Retsvoesen (Denmark)
UHG	Umweltshaftungsgesetz (Environmental Liability Act—Germany)
UNTS	United Nations Treaty Series
US	United States Supreme Court Reports (USA)
USD	United States Dollar

UWG	Gesetz gegen unlauteren Wettbewerb (the Act on Unfair Competition—Germany)
v°	verbo, part of an encyclopaedic work
Va J. Int'l L.	Virginia Journal of International Law (USA)
VersR	Versicherungsrecht (Germany)
W.Bl.	Sir William Blackstone's King's Bench Reports
WHG	Wasserhaushaltsgesetz (Water Resources Act—Germany)
WLR	Weekly Law Reports (UK)
WPNR	Weekblad voor privaatrecht, notariaat en registratie (Netherlands)
W.Rob.(Adm.)	W. Robinson's Admiralty Reports
WTO	World Trade Organization
WWR	Western Weekly Law Reports (Canada)
Yale LJ	Yale Law Journal (USA)
Yale U. Press	Yale University Press
YEL	Yearbook of European Law
ZEuP	Zeitschrift für Europäisches Privatrecht
ZIP	Zeitschrift für Wirtschaftsrecht (Germany)
ZPO	Zivilprozeßordnung (Ordinance on Civil Procedure—Germany)
ZRP	Zeitschrift für Rechtspolitik (Germany)
ZZP	Zeitschrift für Zivilprozess (Germany)

Table of Cases

The following table contains all cases referred to in this book.
Cases in **bold** are excerpted at the page number indicated in **bold**.

The Internet site (http://www.rechten.unimaas.nl/ casebook) contains a table of the cases referred to therein. In the following table, an "@" indicates that the case is also referred to in the materials posted on the Internet.

European Jurisdictions

Table of Legislative Instruments

The following table contains the legislative instruments (legislative acts, EC legislation, treaties) referred to in this book. Instruments in **bold** are excerpted at the page number indicated in **bold**.

The Internet site (http://www.rechten.unimaas.nl/ casebook) contains a table of the legislative instruments referred to therein. In the following table, an "@" indicates that the instrument is also referred to in the materials posted on the Internet.

European legislation

European Community (in chronological order)
ECSC Treaty

General Introduction

Persons living together in society are almost bound on occasions to cause each other harm. As set out in Chapter One, the law of tort is concerned with the prevention of such harm, as far as practicable, and if it should occur, with the allocation of the loss. Such loss may take many forms: personal injury, that is injury to bodily integrity and health, often giving rise to pain and suffering and material loss (e.g. medical expenses, loss of income); damage to physical property which may give rise to material loss directly consequential thereon (e.g. loss of profit on sale of destroyed goods belonging to the plaintiff) as well as so-called "pure economic loss" (e.g. loss not accompanying harm to the person or property of the plaintiff); injury to reputation or, more generally, to personality rights; infringement of intellectual property rights.

Anyone who suffers damage may look to the law for redress, which in earlier days meant looking for a private law remedy in contract or tort. This division between contract and tort is in itself an impediment to comparison, as it creates important differences between legal systems. For, indeed, the distinction between contractual and tortious liability is not consistently drawn: whereas some legal systems use contract law techniques to protect the interests of third parties by drawing them within the protective ambit of a contract, those techniques do not exist in other legal systems, or within narrow limits only, thus leaving third parties "unprotected", at least under the rules of private law, if tort law is of no assistance to them—except for the traditionally limited set of cases where an alternative remedy is available in quasi-contract or for unjust enrichment or restitution or in property law. As far as tort rules themselves are concerned, basic differences in approach between the legal systems are apparent: some of them take an outright "pro-victim" approach whereas others seek rather to keep the imposition of burdens on individual defendants within limits. Further, in more recent times the growth of private insurance and the development of social security systems, while it is a general trend, have nonetheless taken place at a varying pace from country to country. Accordingly, the compensatory function of tort law nowadays varies even more in significance from one country to another.

All of this makes it extremely difficult to assess the overall ability of a legal system to solve the complex problem of loss allocation. It also makes it hazardous to compare the various legal systems as regards the efficiency of tort law. Obviously, the "law and economics" approach may help in the search for the most efficient way to prevent and allocate losses; either through tort or contract laws, insurance or social security schemes. One may safely say though, that on any view of efficiency, the most efficient system will consist of a mix of techniques, the composition of which will vary according to the general perception of the particular society regarding the extent to which losses falling on the shoulders of one person should be shifted onto others or onto the community at large.

BASIC DIFFERENCES IN APPROACH BETWEEN THE LEGAL SYSTEMS

This casebook deals with the main topics usually associated with the law of tort or delict. Before going into these topics, it might be useful to give a quick overview of the basic approach and structure of the law of tort or delict in the legal systems studied here.

Differences in approach between the three major systems

English law today still resembles Roman law in retaining specific heads of tortious liability (and specific forms of redress related thereto)—the "pigeon-hole" approach as it is often irreverently called—while Continental legal systems have moved away from that approach.[1] In the course of English legal history the various heads of tortious liability have gained specific names, such as trespass to the person (and the more specific torts of assault, battery and false imprisonment which developed out of that form of trespass), trespass to land and nuisance (whose pedigree is as long as that of trespass to the person) and "the action on the case" (from which the more modern—and now more general—tort of negligence developed in the course of the nineteenth century).[2] It is important to appreciate that an English common lawyer still thinks in terms of these old forms of tortious liability.

The various heads of tortious liability under English common law are not meant to be all-encompassing: some forms of injurious conduct, although they may be thought of as wrong, will fall outside any known head of tortious liability. Among gaps of that sort, the most important one nowadays is found in the realm of personality rights, where English common law does not recognize any general personality right or right to privacy, instead leaving one with the limited protection afforded by a series of "narrower" torts (such as libel and malicious falsehood, to name the main ones). In addition to these gaps in the overall tort law, the main tort, negligence, is itself limited in scope by the notion of "duty of care". Thus, as one of the conditions for liability in negligence, the plaintiff must show that the defendant owed a duty of care to the plaintiff. As will be seen below, the notion of duty of care in practice is closely linked to the kind of prejudice suffered by the plaintiff, so that a certain hierarchization of protected interests, not unlike that of German law, can be discerned in English common law.

In marked contrast to the piecemeal approach of English law, the **French** *Code civil* (C.civ.) of 1804, in the spirit of the French Revolution, sought to eradicate the feudal institutions of the past[3] and did away with the different heads of tort by laying down, in the celebrated general clause of Article 1382 C.civ. that "anyone who, through his act, causes damage to another by his fault shall be obliged to compensate the damage"; Article 1383 then goes on to provide that "everyone is responsible for the damage caused not only by his act but also by his negligence or carelessness".[4] These general clauses are

---

[1] See further R. Zimmermann, *The Law of Obligations, Roman Foundations of the Civilian Tradition* (Clarendon Press: Oxford, 1995) at 907–8.

[2] *Infra*, Chapter I, **1.E.20.–21.**

[3] Zweigert and Kötz at 74.

[4] Thus making liability for omissions almost self-evident: *infra*, Chapter III, 3.1.1.

complemented by a few rules, contained in Article 1384–1386, on liability for other persons, things or animals under one's supervision or guardianship. Accordingly, all forms of socially unacceptable behaviour, because of their wrongful or dangerous character, can in principle lead to tortious liability; all kinds of injury caused by such behaviour to primary and secondary victims, including dependants, can then be recovered.[5]

Yet another approach can be seen in the **German *Bürgerliches Gesetzbuch*** (BGB), which symbolically entered into force on 1 January 1900. The BGB "is the child of the deep, exact, and abstract learning of the German Pandectist School" and of the Enlightenment.[6] The structure of the BGB is very remarkable, in that the general is constantly treated before the specific, at every level of the BGB structure. The BGB opens in Book One with a General Part *(Allgemeiner Teil)*. Book 2 deals more specifically with Obligations (*Schuldverhältnisse*). The first six parts of Book 2 concern general issues relating to Obligations, and only at the very end of the seventh part of Book 2 can provisions on tortious liability be found under the heading "*Unerlaubte Handlungen*" (Impermissible Behaviour, §§ 823 ff). The BGB steers a middle course between the English and French legal systems by breaking with a tradition of specific heads of liability, on the one hand, while, on the other hand and after much learned discussion, not including a general clause. Instead, the BGB sets out three more limited but still broad heads of tortious liability in §§ 823 and 826 BGB[7] which are then complemented, as under French law, by provisions relating to liability for acts of other persons and for things. Unlike the French *Code civil*, the BGB also contains provisions on the tort liability of civil servants (§ 839 BGB). The overall objective of the drafters of the BGB in not following the French example was to limit liability in respect of both the class of claimants and the kinds of damage eligible for compensation. The technique used first and foremost was to restrict the set of legal interests protected by the main broad head of § 823(1) BGB. Accordingly, § 823(1) BGB enables recovery only for injury either to one of a limitative list of "rights" enumerated therein (life, body, health, freedom, ownership) or to "another right" (*ein sonstiges Recht*), provided, that the injury to the victim was caused "wilfully or negligently" (*vorsätzlich oder fahrlässig*). This limitative approach is, however, partially offset by the two other broad heads of liability, namely § 823(2) BGB, which enables recovery for injury resulting from a breach of a protective statutory provision, and § 826 BGB, which enables recovery for injury resulting from conduct *contra bonos mores*.

Table 1 on p. 4 gives a simplified overview of the respective approaches of German, English and French law to protected interests, as it has been outlined in the preceding paragraph.

Differences in approach among the other legal systems[8]

The differences in approach between the German, English and French tort law systems are also reflected in the other countries which follow one or several of these major systems. Not infrequently, the rules in those other countries either bear some resemblance to

---

[5] With the limited proviso that the protected interest must not be "illicit", see *infra*, Chapter I, 1.4.2.
[6] See Zweigert and Kötz at 137–8.
[7] *Infra*, Chapter I, **1.G.27.** Two more specific heads of liability are set out in §§ 824 and 825 BGB.
[8] Apart from a few exceptions (see the discussion of class actions in North America, *infra*, Chapter II, 2.5.2.B.), this work is limited to the legal systems of EU Member States.

Table 1: Overview of English, French and German law approaches to protected interests

English law	French law	German law
A series of circumscribed torts (some cases of injurious behaviour do not fall within any tort)	One general clause applicable to all situations	Three broad clauses, each applicable to a large but limited set of situations (and some specific clauses)
The most general tort (negligence) requires proof of a duty of care owed by the defendant to the plaintiff	No limitation of protected interests	The most general heading (§ 823(1) BGB) protects only the legal rights listed therein

the "general clause" approach of the French *Code civil* at first glance, whereas upon closer examination they appear to reflect rather the restrictive "protected rights" approach of the German BGB, or vice versa.

The **Nordic** legal systems (Denmark, Finland, Iceland, Norway and Sweden) take a special place in this regard. They "cannot be allocated to the Common law" as they have historically been quite independent of medieval English law.[9] Nor can they be brought under the same heading as the legal systems of Continental Europe, as they have been less imbued with Roman law and have relied less on comprehensive codification as the primary means of ordering private law.[10] On the other hand, conditions for achieving harmony, if not unity, between the laws of the Nordic countries were particularly propitious. As Zweigert and Kötz put it, "[t]heir historical development was very similar, their cultural links were very close, their languages [except Finnish] were very alike, there were no serious political differences, their population and economic power were approximately equivalent, and they were all . . . on the edge of Europe".[11]

In many areas, Nordic co-operation led to uniform law, such as the law of contracts and of other legal transactions concerning property and obligations, which came into force in Sweden, Denmark and Norway between 1915 and 1918 and in Finland in 1929. That uniform law, again in the words of Zweigert and Kötz, "confines itself to a few problems of proven practical importance, with rules concerning the *conclusion of contracts, agency, and the invalidity of legal acts*. It is very clear that the draftsmen kept an eye on the general private law doctrines of the German Pandectist School as well as the texts of the German and Swiss codes, but thanks to those twin virtues of Scandinavian jurists, namely reasonableness and realism, the Act shows no signs of that exaggerated passion for putting general rules 'right out front' which we find in the BGB".[12] No uniform law was

---

[9] Zweigert and Kötz at 277.
[10] Ibid.
[11] Ibid. at 284.
[12] Ibid. at 281–2.

achieved, however, in the area of tort law. After the proposals of the Danish scholar A. Vinding Kruse for a Nordic Civil Code (first draft in 1948, second draft in 1962) failed, special legislation on civil liability was enacted in Norway in 1969, in Sweden in 1972, in Finland in 1974 and in Denmark in 1984.

As a general feature, the tort law of the three Nordic countries now belonging to the European Union (Denmark, Finland and Sweden) rests on the wrongdoer's liability for his or her own fault—the 'culpa' rule laid down in Finland and Sweden in quasi-identical legislative provisions and in Denmark in case law and customary law.[13]

Scottish and **Irish** law belong to the common law world,[14] although Scots law has notable "civilian" (i.e. Romanistic) aspects which set it somewhat apart: "Scots law has so far managed to maintain its independence in the heartland of private law".[15] Thus, for instance: "[i]n Scotland almost the whole of the law of delict is covered by general liability for *culpa* (which developed from the *actio legis Aquiliae*) and the *actio iniuriarum*; here, in contrast to English law with its great profusion of separate torts . . ., the law of Scotland operates with only a few high-level principles and concepts, thereby demonstrating that inner economy which 'civilian' legal thought regards as a virtue".[16] Compensation for personal injuries as a consequence of death, or interference with bodily integrity, is governed in Scotland by the Damages Act 1976.[17] Notwithstanding these differences Scots law on delictual liability remains very close to English tort law, or vice versa.[18] In Ireland, the Civil Liability Act 1961 governs large parts of tort law.[19] Whereas Irish courts follow by and large the case law of English courts,[20] that is not necessarily so in areas involving constitutional rights enshrined at Article 40–44 of the Irish Constitution.[21]

The French *Code civil* was the great model for a whole range of civil codes.[22] In countries such as **Belgium** and **Luxembourg**, the civil code is still more or less identical to the *Code civil*, although with the passage of time many legislative modifications have given it a distinctive touch, especially in Belgium (in contract and tort law less than in other fields such as family law). Judicial interpretation of the Belgian Civil Code has also taken its own path, often led to do so by doctrinal writings that seek inspiration in the new Dutch

---

[13] von Bar I at 268–9, para. 243; see also *infra*, Chapter I, **1.SCAN.29.**

[14] For an overview of the main legal systems which form part of the Anglo-American legal family, see Zweigert and Kötz at 180–275.

[15] Zweigert and Kötz at 203.

[16] Ibid. at 203–4.

[17] von Bar I at 265, para. 240.

[18] See von Bar I at 319–22, para. 299–301, where some of the differences, amongst which the non-acceptance in Scotland of the rule in *Rylands* v. *Fletcher*, discussed *infra*, Chapter II, 2.3.1., are mentioned. In some instances, it is more correct to say that English law comes close to Scots law: indeed, as von Bar I points out at 319–20, para. 299, some leading cases decided by the House of Lords are Scots cases, such as *Donoghue* v. *Stevenson*, *infra*, Chapter I, **1.E.23.**, *Bourhill* v. *Young* [1943] AC 92, [1942] All ER 396 and *Smith* v. *Littlewoods Organisation Ltd*, *infra*, Chapter III, **3.E.5.** For a recent overview of the Scottish law of delict, see C. Willett and A. O'Donnell, *Scottish Business Law*, 2nd edn. (London: Blackstone, 1996) at 111 ff.

[19] No. 41, as amended by the Civil Liability (Amendment) Act 1964, No. 17.

[20] Albeit not always wholeheartedly, as in the case of *John C. Doherty Timber Ltd* v. *Drohedie Harbour Commissioners* [1993] ILRM 401, [1993] 1 IR 315, Sup. Ct., where the overruling of *Anns* v. *London Merton Borough Council* [1978] AC 728, HL by *Murphy* v. *Brentwood District Council* [1991] 1 AC 398, [1990] 2 All ER 269, HL (*infra*, 1.4.1.B.) was discussed.

[21] See *infra*, Chapter II, **2.IRL.33.**

[22] On the reception of the *Code civil*, see Zweigert and Kötz at 98–118.

Burgerlijk Wetboek and Anglo-American law, since many academics were trained in the USA in the post-war era. The French *Code civil* also influenced the Dutch, Italian, Portuguese and Spanish Civil Codes at the outset. Yet of those countries, only **Spain** has remained consistently within the French legal family, although even in Spain regional customary and statutory rules have had a large impact in various parts of the country.[23] Thus, Article 1902 of the Spanish *Codigo civil* of 1889 merges Article 1382 and 1383 of the *Code civil* into one provision, which for the remainder is a copy of the French code.[24]

In the other three legal systems just mentioned, subsequent enactments have broken the bond with French law. In **Italy**, that happened with the enactment of the *Codice civile*, which came into force on 21 April 1942. Notwithstanding fundamental differences (particularly in the area of matrimonial law) and the inclusion of commercial law in the *Codice civile*, the basic principles of the law of obligations are similar in Italy and France.[25] In the area of tort law however, the Italian Code lies somewhere between French and German law. Thus, the main provision, Article 2043 of the *Codice civile*, is a general provision like that of Article 1382 and 1383 C.civ. It refers however not only to "fault" but also to "illegality" (although illegality relates not to fault but to damage: *danno ingiusto*). This additional concept was at the outset understood to limit compensation to *lesione di un diritto assoluto* (infringement of an absolute right) only; later it was also extended to *lesione di un interesse giuridicamente rilevante* (infringement of a relevant legal interest).[26] Moreover, in the provisions following Article 2043, matters such as defences and imputability are extensively regulated, alongside liability for others, dangerous activities, animals, buildings and motor vehicles (Article 2044 ff. of the *Codice civile*).

In **Portugal** the *Código Civil* of 1867, which belonged to the generation of "learned" codes, was replaced on 1 June 1967 by a new and—from the point of view of both form and substance—much improved code. The new code is "remarkable for the intelligent attention it pays to foreign legislation—especially German, Swiss, and Italian—to the point where one may wonder whether Portuguese private law ought still to be included in the Romanistic legal family".[27] That is apparent especially in the formulation of the general principle of tortious liability in Article 483(1), which merges § 823 (1) and (2) BGB into one (the *Código Civil* contains no provision similar to § 826 BGB, however). It can also be noted that, under Article 486, pure omissions give rise to liability only when there is a duty to act pursuant to law or contract. However, thanks to a broad interpretation of Article 493(1) relating to liability for things and to the absence in Article 483(1) of a limitative enumeration of protected rights (as in § 823(1) BGB), many legal interests, especially in the field of personality rights and privacy, have been included by the courts in the scope of protection of tort law, turning the provisions of the *Código Civil* into a kind of general principle.[28]

The most recent Civil Code is the **Dutch** *Burgerlijk Wetboek* (BW), the section of which relating to obligations came into force on 1 January 1992. The BW, like the BGB, is char-

---

[23] Zweigert and Kötz at 107.
[24] von Bar I at 23, para. 15.
[25] Zweigert and Kötz at 105.
[26] von Bar I at 31, para. 21, with reference to the case law of the *Corte di Cassazione*; see also G. Visintini, *Trattato breve della responsabilità civile* (Milano: Cedam, 1996) at 343–8.
[27] Zweigert and Kötz at 108.
[28] von Bar I at 33–7, para. 22–3.

acterized by its learned character, due to more than four decades of extensive comparative law research by the drafting commission, as well as thorough discussions not only in the Legislature and in legal writing, but also in the case law of the Hoge Raad in particular (in anticipation of the new BW). Given the substantial comparative input and because commercial law and to a large extent consumer law were included in the BW, Dutch law has moved away from the French legal tradition without, however, getting closer to any other legal family.[29] In tort law, the evolution is perhaps less discernible, since Article 6:162 BW builds on its predecessor Article 1401 of the old BW, which was still very much influenced by the French *Code civil* (but for the distinction it makes between fault and illicitness), and on Hoge Raad case law, starting with *Lindenbaum/Cohen*.[30] For liability in tort to arise under Article 6:162 BW, there must be an unlawful act which can be imputed to someone and which caused damage to someone else (para. 1). For conduct to be unlawful, it must infringe a subjective right or violate a statutory duty or an unwritten rule on proper social conduct, unless there is a ground of justification (para. 2). For an unlawful act to be imputable to the tortfeasor, it must be due to his or her fault or to a cause for which he or she is accountable according to prevailing opinions in society (para. 3). According to Article 6:163 BW, no liability arises if the infringed rule is not intended to protect the injured person against the damage that he or she suffered. As in German law, further restrictions are contained in the provisions on obligations in general (Article 6:95 and 6:106 to 6:110 BW).[31]

The **Austrian**, **Swiss** and **Greek** legal systems clearly belong to the German legal family, although the **Austrian** *Allgemeines Bürgerliches Gesetzbuch* of 1811 long predates the German BGB. It was the third of the great codes which came into force in Europe at the end of the eighteenth and the beginning of the nineteenth century, after the Prussian *Landesrecht* and the French *Code civil*.[32] Later, under the influence of the pro-German school led by J. Unger, close ties were established between Austrian law and German Pandectist doctrines. From then on, Austrian and German legal scholars have worked closely together.[33] The ABGB contains at § 1295 a general liability clause, which is applicable in both contract and tort law. It entitles anyone who suffered harm to claim compensation from the person who was at fault in causing it. In 1916, a second paragraph modelled on § 826 BGB was added to § 1295, in the course of a general legislative enactment designed to remedy the many defects which came to light after the enactment of the German BGB. More than any other code, the ABGB rests on fault-based liability, even in the areas of liability for things and other persons, although modern developments outside the framework of the ABGB in the area of accident law have introduced some elements of no-fault liability.[34]

The **Swiss** Civil Code of 1907 has been supplemented with a Code of Obligations. It added to the group of European private law codes "a powerful new voice representing the particular style of Swiss legal thinking".[35] The Swiss Codes improve on the German BGB

---

[29] Zweigert and Kötz at 102–3.
[30] HR, 31 January 1919, NJ 1919, 161.
[31] See *infra*, Chapter II, 2.1.4., Introductory Note under c).
[32] Zweigert and Kötz at 158.
[33] Ibid. at 162.
[34] Ibid. at 165.
[35] Ibid. at 171.

by avoiding overly complex language and technique, sophisticated structures and extreme conceptualism. The Swiss Codes are readable and easily understood, they have an open structure and were deliberately left incomplete so as to allow courts to operate within the Codes' open structures by using standards of appropriateness, reasonableness and equity.[36] Typical of the Swiss Civil Code is its famous Article 1(2) which provides that: "In the absence of an applicable legal provision, the court shall rule on the basis of customary law or, in the absence of custom, on the basis of the rules which the court would enact if it had a legislative function". The extensive use of general clauses to be filled out by the courts characterizes the Swiss Codes; on this point the Swiss stray from the dominant conceptions regarding the position of the judge in Germany, at least at the time the BGB was enacted[37] and, we would add, perhaps even today. That is particularly apparent in tort law, as laid down in Article 41 to 61 of the Code of Obligations. Following the general words of Article 41, which does not contain a limitative enumeration of protected rights, many provisions give considerable leeway to the court, such as Article 43(1) on adapting compensation to the circumstances of the case and Article 49(1) on defining the interests of the injured person that deserve protection.

Finally, the **Greek** Civil Code of 1940 reflects the BGB in its structure, but at the same time takes account of subsequent developments in Germany.[38] The provisions on tort are a mixture, nonetheless, of French, Swiss and German rules. Article 914 of the Greek Civil Code is a general clause similar to Article 1382 C.civ. and Article 41(1) of the Swiss Code of Obligations, but at the same time it includes some special tort headings, as found in §§ 824–6 BGB.[39] Case law has turned Article 914 into more of a general clause.[40]

We shall not be able to devote much space in this work to the "other" legal systems. Nonetheless, as far as the *a priori* hierarchization of protected interests is concerned (Chapter II), we have referred to some materials from these other legal systems, when they represent a special development in a specific area of tort law. Some of these materials are included in this casebook, but the reader will find other materials on our website (<http://www.rechten.unimaas.nl/casebook>). Beyond that, an impressive amount of information on the law of tort or delict in the EU Member States can be found in C. von Bar's *Gemeineuropäisches Deliktsrecht*,[41] available in English as *The Common European Law of Torts*.[42]

HARMONIZATION OF TORT LAW AT THE SUPRANATIONAL LEVEL IN EUROPE

Codification of legal rules, whether through unification or harmonization, has no doubt many advantages for a domestic legal order. At the same time, however, there is no denying that in Europe codification was often linked with the awakening of a national legal conscience and was thus responsible for de-unification, or de-harmonization, between the

---

[36] Zweigert and Kötz at 171–2.
[37] Ibid. at 174.
[38] Ibid. at 155–6.
[39] Ibid.
[40] von Bar I at 28–9, para. 19.
[41] C. von Bar, *Gemeineuropäisches Deliktsrecht* (Munich: Beck, 1996 (Vol. I) and 1999 (Vol. II)).
[42] C. von Bar, *The Common European Law of Torts* (Oxford: OUP, 1998 (Vol. I) and forthcoming (Vol. II)).

legal orders. Whilst the common law is still able, because of the absence of local codifications which would mask a common heritage, to keep different legal systems in different parts of the world in step with each other around a legal core, the codification movement on the European Continent has done a lot to undo the *ius commune* which previously existed.[43] The harmonization of legal rules which necessarily comes with large integration processes, particularly within the European Union but also within the Council of Europe, will not in and of itself suffice to forge a new *ius commune*. Indeed, harmonization is limited by jurisdictional issues (nowadays enshrined in the principle of subsidiarity). Secondly and by the same token, harmonization measures, limited as they are, focus on *very* specific areas of the law (incremental approach), and in fact cut through areas of law which were previously subject to unitary rules at the national level. In other words, harmonization between the legal systems simultaneously implies a de-harmonization of legal rules within each of the systems. That is true for harmonization through both legislative measures, mainly at European Community level,[44] and decisions of the European Court of Justice concerning the interpretation of supranational legal rules.

In the area of tort law, both forms of harmonization, legislative and judicial, have had a significant impact (even though judicial harmonization has been limited so far to the extra-contractual liability of public bodies). In that regard, it is important to emphasize that in this casebook both the tort regime applying to private persons and that applying to public bodies (such as Community institutions, the Member States and their respective civil servants) will be taken into account. That may surprise lawyers from the Romanistic and Germanic legal traditions, because of the distance which usually separates private and public law, including tort law, on the Continent. There are two reasons why we have included both tort regimes, however. First, the distinction between those two regimes does not make much sense to common lawyers since, to take English law as an example, the rules of tort law are equally applicable to "private" and "public" torts, with the exception of the—anomalous—tort of "misfeasance in public office". And indeed, many of the leading English cases reprinted below concern acts or omissions of public authorities. Moreover, on the Continent as well some legal systems, like the Belgian and Dutch ones, apply the same tort rules to private and public torts. The second reason why both regimes are covered is that precisely in the area of tort liability of public bodies there is a discernible tendency for the legal systems of European Union Member States to converge. As we shall see, that is to a large extent a consequence of Community law, which requires that the legal systems of the Member States provide remedies that allow persons to secure effectively the rights which Community law confers upon them.[45] It is not to be excluded that sooner or later that requirement will also apply between private persons as regards breaches by private persons of provisions of Community law which directly impose obligations upon them, such as for instance Article 81 and 82 EC.

Harmonization of tort rules by way of legislation, or rather multinational treaties, has occurred mainly at the level of the Council of Europe or the United Nations Economic

---

[43] See further ibid. at 383, para. 368, who mentions that some parts of the BGB were even written as sort of an "anti-*Code civil*".

[44] See P.C. Müller-Graf, "Private Law Unification by Means other than of Codification" in A.S. Hartkamp *et al.*, (eds.), *Towards a European Civil Code*, 2nd edn. (Nijmegen: Ars Aequi Libri, 1998) at 71.

[45] *Infra*, Chapter IX, 9.1.

Commission for Europe. Harmonization has so far been limited to specific or even peripheral matters, such as the multinational treaties concerning transport of goods by air, road, rail or ship, or concerning compulsory insurance for transport of goods by lorry.[46] More central to tort law are the treaties relating to environmental protection against escape of radioactive materials from nuclear power stations, pollution of the sea by oil and more generally environmental liability.[47]

In the European Union, harmonization is brought about mainly by way of directives. As far as rules of tortious liability are concerned, harmonization directives have been enacted or proposed:

– in the field of **motor vehicle insurance**, with the aims first of creating a harmonized system of compulsory liability insurance to facilitate free movement and guarantee compensation to persons injured in another Member State, and secondly of assuring mutual recognition of insurance obtained in another Member State;[48]
– in the field of **consumer law**, where Directive 85/374 of 25 July 1985 on liability for defective products is, so far, the most important enactment in the area of tortious liability;[49] and
– in the field of **environmental liability** where harmonization is now carried out within the framework of Article 174 EC, which provides amongst other guiding principles, that "the polluter should pay".[50]

Judicial harmonization of tort rules occurs mainly in connection with the preliminary rulings of the European Court of Justice pursuant to Article 234 EC. As demonstrated elsewhere,[51] the case law of the Court plays an important role in the area of tortious liability of public bodies because adequate compensation is one of the remedies which the Member States must ensure to individuals in order to guarantee an effective legal protection of the rights which they derive from Community law. Judicial harmonization of tort rules also occurs as a consequence of the role played by the European Court of Human Rights in examining the compatibility of national measures with the provisions of the ECHR and its Protocols.[52]

The direct significance of Community law for the growing convergence between national legal systems and the emergence of a *ius commune* should not be overestimated.[53]

---

[46] For an overview see von Bar I at 390–5, para. 374–8.

[47] For an overview see von Bar I at 395–400, para. 379–83. See in this respect the far-reaching European Convention on Civil Liability for Damage resulting from Activities Dangerous to the Environment of 21 June 1993, *infra*, Chapter VI, **6.CE.43.**, which is not in force.

[48] Directives 72/166, 84/5 and 90/232, *infra*, Chapter VI, **6.EC.23.–25.** For a full discussion, see R. Merkin and A. Rodger, *EC Insurance Law* (London: Longman, 1997) at 51 ff.

[49] *Infra*, Chapter VI, **6.EC.35.** See von Bar I at 404–7, para. 390–3.

[50] von Bar I at 401–3, para. 387–9. See *infra*, Chapter VI, 6.4.3.

[51] W. van Gerven, "Bridging the Unbridgeable: Community and National tort laws after *Francovich* and *Brasserie*" (1996) 45 ICLQ 507.

[52] See *infra*, Chapter IX, 9.2. For a general overview of the significance of ECtHR case law for the emergence of a *ius commune*, see A.W. Heringa, "The 'Consensus Principle'. The role of 'common law' in the ECHR case-law" (1996) 3 MJ 108.

[53] See W. van Gerven, "Community and national legislators, regulators, judges, academics and practitioners: living together apart?" in B. Markesinis, (ed.), *Law Making, Law Finding, and Law Shaping: The Diverse Influences—Clifford Chance Lectures, Vol. II* (New York: Oxford University Press, 1997) 13 and von Bar I, who tries at 407, para. 394 to find some common ground in the directives enacted so far in the area of tort law.

The indirect impact of Community law may be greater in the long run. First, Community law shows how common rules can and should be integrated in divergent legal systems, for instance through the interpretation of national law in conformity with Community law. Secondly, in areas such as tort law which are crucial to Community law because of the compensation remedy which must be made available to individuals, there will be a drive towards increased and harmonized legal protection in areas of domestic law which are not covered by Community law.[54] All this may cause lawyers from different countries to get more and more used to working with common rules and, in the process, to observe that any differences in mentality among them are inclined to be reduced because of numerous contacts between members of the same profession, teachers and students who become increasingly aware that they have a future in common.[55] However that may be, comparative research trying to uncover similarities and differences between legal systems remains of great importance. It is even more important to prepare common teaching materials allowing students of the law and their teachers, regardless of age or nationality, to discuss common points of interest and thereby bring about a convergence of mentalities. That is what this series of casebooks is about.

CONSEQUENCES OF THE DIFFERENCES IN APPROACH FOR THE STRUCTURE OF THE PRESENT BOOK

Given the differences between legal systems, structuring a casebook such as this one was not without difficulties. Basically, we had to reconcile two conflicting objectives. One is to respect as much as possible the identity and structure, the genius and style of each of the legal systems—that is, in the first place, those of France, Germany and England. The other objective is to make those systems comparable by identifying similar cases and issues (leading to similar or contrasting solutions and principles) within each legal system and then bringing them together so as to allow similarities and differences to appear. It may be that the need to follow such a harmonized structure has led us in our description of the systems to distort the traditional categories and concepts that they use, but it is to be hoped that that has not occurred to the point where the characteristics of each system become unrecognizable.

For instance, as to English law, it was most troublesome to bring specific torts under one or another sub-division, since the old common law torts do not easily lend themselves to classification, particularly when they are seen in conjunction with the expanding and therefore overlapping "modern" tort of negligence. But the latter tort is also difficult to categorize because the standard of proximity or remoteness that determines the limits of liability is defined, if at all, in relation to classes of persons, and categories of behaviour

---

[54] See further W. van Gerven, "Bridging the unbridgeable: Community and National tort laws after *Francovich* and *Brasserie*" (1996) 45 ICLQ 507 at 537 ff.

[55] But see P. Legrand, "European Legal Systems Are Not Converging" (1996) 45 ICLQ 52, whose analysis is, in our view, based on an overly generalized view of differences between large legal families, which are presented as monolithic and static entities. That analysis disregards the convergence of mentalities which is the consequence of living together under the same *acquis communautaire* within the European Union, therefore sharing not only a common past but also, and most importantly, a common future. See also B. De Witte, "The Convergence Debate" (1996) 3 MJ 105.

(such as deeds, words and omissions), in a way that makes comparison with other legal systems difficult, to say the least.

Furthermore, the fact that each legal system has created—with large differences in emphasis and at a different pace—specific regimes of liability not based on conduct has not made things easier, particularly because the specific regimes are often found not in legislative measures but, at least at the outset, in generous interpretations of vague and flexible *Code civil* provisions, as in France, or of old common law torts such as nuisance and the rule in *Rylands* v. *Fletcher*, as in England. Such regimes of liability not based on conduct are discussed in Chapter VI.

When dealing with each topic, we shall present the legal systems under study in the most appropriate order, which will not always be the same from one topic to another. Sometimes we shall start with the legal system which offers the widest protection, sometimes with the one offering the most restrictive protection and then contrast it with the least restrictive system, sometimes with a legal system that shows an interesting development. Materials from the legal orders of the European Community and the ECHR will be included mainly in order to point out how they may encourage convergence. They are dealt with in Chapter IX. Some EC materials are discussed in Chapter VI, according to the specific topic to which they relate.

So far as possible, we shall try to avoid imposing our own views on the user of the book. That holds true in particular for our personal opinion on the fundamental choice facing those drafting or interpreting tort rules, namely whether they should apply a victim-minded approach or a defendant-minded approach.

CHAPTER ONE
GENERAL TOPICS

1.1. MEANING OF TORT LAW

Introductory Note

The concept of tort does not readily lend itself to a clear-cut definition. Many authors take as a starting point the proposition that the loss rests where it falls,[1] and that it is for the rules of tort to determine the special circumstances under which loss will be shifted to a person other than the injured person. Traditionally fault has been seen as such a special circumstance, albeit subject, in some legal systems, to restrictions as to the class of interests which tort law aims to protect. Other circumstances, which can be brought under the general heading of liability not based on conduct (often based on risk), have also been deemed to justify, under certain conditions, that harm be shifted from the injured onto another person. Tort law then consists of a body of rules determining the circumstances, and conditions, under which harm suffered by a victim will be borne by another person, most frequently, the perpetrator of the harm.[2]

Tort law is therefore about (re-)distribution of losses and in consequence allocation of risks. Reduced to its bare essentials, it strikes a balance between the respective interests of the victim and the injurer, taking into account broader social interests as well. The victim is primarily interested in the protection of his or her physical integrity and property but also, where feasible, of his or her economic interests and prospects. The injurer, in turn, is interested in his or her freedom to engage in certain activities without being obstructed by the threat of potential liability. Lastly, society is interested in achieving distributive justice in a cost-efficient way, without stifling economic initiative.[3] As set out in the third excerpt, the balancing of these interests is reflected in the way in which a legal system arranges three basic elements of tort law: sanctioned behaviour on the part of the perpetrator of the harm, protected interests on the part of the injured person and corrective remedies for damage caused by the perpetrator of harm to the injured person.

---

[1] Asser-Hartkamp, *Verbintenissenrecht—Vol. III: De verbintenis uit de wet*, 10th edn. (Deventer: Tjeenk Willink, 1998) at 12, para. 12; Prosser/Keeton, *The Law of Torts*, 5th edn. (St. Paul: West Publishing, 1984) at 20.

[2] On the Continent, tort law is often referred to as *Deliktsrecht*, or *responsabilité délictuelle*, an expression which refers to fault as the major circumstance to shift the loss to another person, and which is therefore not necessarily apt to include rules based on other circumstances, such as the creation of risk. In order to include these rules the term *extra- contractual liability* is often used (or "non-contractual liability", as in Article 288 (2) EC) in contradistinction to liability arising from the non-performance of contractual obligations.

[3] See G. Calabresi, *The Costs of Accidents* (New Haven: Yale U. Press, 1970) at 16.

B. Starck, H. Roland and L. Boyer   **1.F.1., 1.G.2., 1.E.3.**
Obligations, Vol. 1: Responsabilité délictuelle[4]
and
K. Larenz and C.W. Canaris, *Lehrbuch des Schuldrechts*[5]
and
P. Cane, *The Anatomy of Tort Law*[6]

1. B. Starck, H. Roland and L. Boyer, *Obligations, Vol. 1: Responsabilité délictuelle*
1.F.1.

"To the question '*why* must the person who caused the damage be ordered to compensate the victim?', the answer was given without hesitation; because he has committed a fault, and only in that case. It was not required that the fault be intentional; even an unintentional fault was enough to order the person who caused the damage to make it good, and even the *lightest fault* (*levissima culpa*) sufficed.

What was the justification for this position? . . .

It was not only the *Code civil* which was invoked to that end, but also concepts of a moral nature. It was argued that civil liability was but one particular aspect of moral responsibility . . . The latter cannot be envisaged in the absence of fault. Therefore this doctrine claims that, if one were to order a person who caused an injury without committing a fault to make good the injury, one would be punishing an innocent individual.

Risk theory was put forward as early as the late 19th century in France under the aegis of Saleilles, as well as in some other countries. It subsequently underwent various modifications and variants of the theory appeared . . .

While the necessity of an alliance between fault and risk seems to be in keeping with the rules of positive law (legislation and case law), it remains to be explained how these two foundations of civil liability are going to interact with one another. Without going into the details of a complicated debate, the following are the two main theories:

a) According to some authors . . . fault remains the main basis for civil liability: 'the fairer source'. *Risk comes into play only in a subsidiary capacity*, when fairness requires to go to the aid of the victim. In leaving the leading role to fault, these authors intend to pay tribute to the moral concepts upon which civil liability is meant to rest, explaining in this way the persistence of the notion of fault in legislation and case law; by greeting risk nonetheless, they believe they are providing a basis for the many cases of no-fault liability . . .

b) According to Josserand . . . and many other authors, civil liability has two poles of attraction, namely fault and risk: neither has pre-eminence over the other, *they are on the same level*. It then becomes necessary to define their respective fields . . .

The rights of the victim are not the only ones at stake . . . The person who acts and who, in acting, causes injury to another may also invoke rights: one cannot live in society without taking action and, to that end, everyone has at his disposal various rights and freedoms. Ordering someone to make good the harmful consequences of his actions amounts to *restricting or taking away* his freedom to act.

---

[4] 5th edn. (Paris: Litec, 1996) at 19 and 41, para. 29–30 and 68 (footnotes omitted). Translation by A. Dumas-Eymard.
 [5] Vol. II, Pt 2, 13th edn. (München: Beck, 1994) at 350–352 (footnotes omitted). Translation by M. Jelbert.
 [6] (Oxford: Hart Publishing, 1997) at 13–15.

If one thinks about this carefully, one realises that the issue of civil liability is one of *conflicting rights*. On the one hand, *the right to act*, thanks to the various prerogatives (*subjective rights*) at our disposal and, on the other hand, *the right to security*, which belongs to each of us.

Therefore the crux of the matter is to decide how to reconcile these conflicting rights and, if need be, to determine which of the two must give way to the other."

2. K. Larenz and C.W. Canaris, *Lehrbuch des Schuldrechts*   1.G.2.

"The basic problem of any tort regulation lies in the *conflict between the protection of legal interests* (Güterschutz) *and freedom of action*. However desirable it may be, from the point of view of the victim, that the injurer would have to compensate the victim for the injury suffered, it must be seen that, by the same token, considerable limits are imposed on the personal and economic development of the injurer. This creates an inherent danger, which is all the more serious as the mere possibility of becoming entangled in liability [claims] can keep citizens from engaging in such activities as are *lawful* or indeed socially desirable, on account of the uncertainty associated with the evaluation of the risk involved . . . The aim is accordingly to resolve conflicts of that kind in the light of the criteria of the 'most considerate balance' or the 'practical concordance' . . . The legislature quite rightly saw the task of the law of tort as 'the delineation of the respective spheres of rights of individuals, within which each may take advantage of his or her personal freedom and pursue his or her interests' . . . It sought to discharge the bulk of that task through *two fundamental decisions*: liability was based on the fault principle, and relatively firm and precise heads of liability were formulated . . .

Therefore, in order for anyone to hold another person liable to repair harm, a *specific [legal] basis* is always required. Without such a specific basis, a liability claim would be arbitrary and unworthy of any legal recognition from the outset, since imposing liability represents an infringement upon the freedom and the estate (*Vermögen*) of the person who is made liable, and therefore requires legitimation. Accordingly, the starting point is the principle '*casum sentit dominus*', according to which the consequences of a chance event are to be borne by the person affected by them. Contrary to a widespread misconception, that principle is in no way a solution of last resort; on the contrary, it reflects elementary justice, since it is derived from the self-evident truth that everyone must bear the "general risk associated with existence" (*allgemeines Lebensrisiko*) and cannot simply pass it on to other individuals . . .

According to the BGB, the obligation to make reparation for damages can find its basis in a *fault* (*Verschulden*) on the part of the person against whom a claim is made. In the BGB, that basis comes to bear first and foremost in § 823(1) BGB, which requires intentional or negligent conduct as a condition for the liability of the person who violated [one of the protected interests listed therein]. The other provisions of tort law are also based on the fault principle, albeit at times in other ways. From the point of view of legal ethics, [reliance on fault as a basis for liability] finds its legitimation in the principles of autonomy and self-determination . . .

The concept of fault only makes sense where the legal system disapproves of the conduct in question. Consequently, fault in and of itself is not sufficient ground for liability, as is very clearly shown in cases of deliberate action. If, for example, a firm 'stole' an order away from a competitor because it made a more favourable offer, it inflicted harm on that competitor knowingly and therefore deliberately, but not culpably—except in the event of an infringement of the Act on Unfair Competition (UWG)—because such behaviour is not unlawful (and even desirable in a market economy). Fault is therefore preceded by *unlawfulness*, without which the law of tort (*unerlaubte Handlungen*) cannot be structured consistently. The law of tort therefore rests on the *principle of liability for fault in an unlawful course of conduct* . . .

On the other hand, there are a number of regimes of (mere) *risk-based liability* (*Gefährdungshaftung*) . . . In order for liability to arise, they require neither fault nor . . . unlawfulness . . .

15

They are clearly different, both in theory and practice—despite overlaps—from liability for fault in an unlawful course of action . . . "

3. P. Cane, *The Anatomy of Tort Law*   **1.E.3.**

"This analysis of the law of tort will be built on three basic concepts: sanctioned conduct, protected interests and sanctions. Let us look briefly at each of these concepts. First, sanctioned conduct. Tort law is concerned with people's responsibility for their acts and omissions. And because it deals with interactions between people, it contains principles relevant not only to the conduct of injurers but also to the conduct of victims. For example, in the tort of negligence, not only is there a principle that people should take reasonable care not to injure others but there is also a principle that people should take reasonable care for their own safety. Every cause of action in tort has elements concerned with the conduct of the interacting parties . . .

The second basic component of the correlative analysis of the law of tort is 'protected interests'. For instance, tort law protects a person's interest in maintaining a good reputation, in being healthy in mind and body, in not having tangible property damages, and so on. The law of tort protects people's interests by sanctioning conduct which interferes with or damages those interests. Just as tort law is concerned with the conduct of victims as well as that of injurers, it is, conversely, also concerned with the interests of injurers as well as those of victims. But whereas, in relation to victims, the law of tort offers positive protection to a wide range of tangible and intangible assets by granting remedies of various sorts, to injurers the law offers negative protection . . . Because the imposition of tort liability on a person significantly impinges on that person's freedom of action and reduces their financial wealth, the law, to be fair, must strike a balance between the interests of victims and the interests of injurers. This it does negatively by limiting the definition of 'protected interests' and of 'sanctioned conduct' and by protecting certain interests only from interference or damage resulting from certain types of sanctioned conduct . . .

The selection of sanctions (which form the third basic component of the correlative analysis of tort law) is important in balancing the interests of victims and injurers. As we will see, a variety of sanctions are available in tort law, but not all of these sanctions are necessarily available to sanction all the types of conduct which fall within the purview of tort law, nor are they all available to protect all the types of interests which fall within the purview of tort law. The sanctions attaching to causes of action in tort express and give effect to the balance struck by the law between the positions of the two parties to each cause of action. We cannot give a full account of the interests protected and the conduct sanctioned by tort law without also giving an account of how those interests are protected and that conduct is sanctioned because sanctions are the means by which tort law gives practical expression to the balance it strikes between responsibility and freedom . . . "

Notes

(1) Tort law is mainly about payment of money—that is when no more direct form of reparation ("in kind") is possible, or appropriate—by someone whom the law holds liable for harm sustained by another person, to that other person. As the excerpts indicate, in situations other than contractual situations, one will be held liable to make good harm suffered by another only where special circumstances justify a departure from the general proposition that everyone is expected himself or herself to bear the harmful consequences of the vicissitudes of life. To determine those circumstances, the law looks mainly at wrongful conduct that can be attributed to the perpetrator of harm, or to someone or something for which he or she is responsible, but will also take into account wrongful conduct on the part of the victim, which the perpetrator can plead to negate or reduce his liability.

(2) Burdening a perpetrator of harm with a duty to make reparation is tantamount to limiting his freedom to act. That in itself needs justification especially when one's conduct is not only useful for one's own purposes but also for society as a whole. The imposition of tort liability thus implies a balancing act whereby the interest of the victim in seeing his or her position restored, and the interest of society in ensuring that injury is made good, will be weighed against the interest of the perpetrator and of society in not having too many restrictions imposed on people's freedom of action. The elements which tort law uses to give effect to such balancing act are: wrongful conduct of the injurer (but also of the victim) or other event triggering liability, the rights or interests of the victim (but also of the injurer) which need legal protection, and the kind and extent of the remedy deployed to make good the interference with the victim's protected rights or interests.

(3) The balancing approach described above will be viewed by many as too imprecise. In the last decades, a more sophisticated view has been put forward through the economic analysis of the law. That analysis "sees the legal system as a potential means of enhancing the efficient allocation of society's resources" in that law can provide incentives to complement the allocative mechanisms of the market.[7] A crucial idea in the economic analysis of law is the Coase theorem,[8] according to which the assignment, through law, of rights and liabilities—for reasons such as those mentioned in the previous paragraphs— has no implications for economic efficiency, as long as the parties involved in a particular dispute can bargain with *zero transaction costs* to resolve that dispute.[9] In general "transaction costs include the costs of identifying the parties with whom one has to bargain, the costs of getting together with them, the costs of the bargaining process itself, and the costs of enforcing any bargain reached".[10] Obviously, in many conflict situations there *are* transaction costs. In that case, economic efficiency will not occur under *any* legal rule, but only under the rule which, under the circumstances, *minimizes* the effect of transaction costs.[11]

(4) In his book *The Costs of Accidents*,[12] G. Calabresi applied economic analysis to the area of accidents. Instead of viewing tort law in the conventional way as a means of satisfying the claims of individual victims for compensation for their injuries, he insisted that a "principal function of accident law is to reduce the sum of the costs of accidents and the costs of avoiding accidents".[13] Therefore, the costs of avoidance and the costs of administering compensation systems must be taken into account, just as much as the injuries and economic losses sustained by victims. Costs can be avoided through a variety of means and a variety of systems of compensation: it is the purpose of economic analysis

---

[7] See Markesinis and Deakin at 23–4 for an overview of the economic analysis of tort law.

[8] The Coase theorem was named after Ronald Coase, who enunciated it in his seminal article "The Problem of Social Cost" (1960) 3 J Law & Econ (ns) 1.

[9] Under the Coase theorem the parties involved are assumed to be "economic operators" who will be exclusively motivated by profit maximization or loss minimization, which will not necessarily be so with individuals. Even under the limited conditions in which the Coase theorem is valid, its usefulness to the lawyer is limited, since it tells one nothing about the allocation of risk and cost that will be perceived by society to be fair. See also the remarks of Calabresi at Note (5) below.

[10] A. Mitchell Polinsky, *An Introduction to Law and Economics* (Boston: Little, Brown and Co., 1989) at 12.

[11] These effects include the actual incurring of transaction costs and the inefficient choices induced by a desire to avoid transaction costs: Polinsky, ibid. at 13.

[12] (New Haven: Yale U. Press, 1970). See also *infra*, **1.US.10.**

[13] Ibid. at 26. See *infra*, **1.US.10.**

to "indicate the questions we must ask in deciding whether one system is preferable to another".[14] Seen from that viewpoint fault-based liability is not necessarily the best system.

(5) The law of tort has proven to be an excellent branch of the law for the application of economic analysis.[15] However, not all areas of tort law have provided as fertile a ground; for instance, in liability for personal injuries, the protection of the interests of the victim "stands as a goal in its own right, leaving perhaps only a secondary role for cost-benefit analysis of the wider effects of a particular liability rule".[16] In such area, judgments " . . . are likely to take into account a number of policy factors, of which cost-benefit analysis will be only one. In the case of economic loss, however, there will be much less justification for imposing tort liability if its effect is to impose wider costs on society".[17] As G. Calabresi wrote: "[A]n economically optimal system of reducing accident costs [may] be totally or partially unacceptable because it strikes us as unfair . . . Justice must ultimately have its due . . . ".[18]

(6) The economic analysis of the law was at the origin of a vast movement mainly in the USA, but also in Europe. It is impossible to go into it in any depth. Three excerpts from legal writing are included further below; the first two present the "law and economics" approach, and the third one is more critical.[19]

1.2. FUNCTIONS OF TORT LAW

Legal writing has analyzed the functions for which tort law is said to be an adequate tool.[20] It has identified the following as the main functions of tort law, in cooperation with other compensatory systems (mainly private insurance and social security): (1) compensation; (2) loss shifting (and spreading); (3) deterrence; and (4) avoidance of economically inefficient behaviour. Those functions are interdependent in that no one function can, in itself, fully explain tort law.[21]

---

[14] Ibid. at 312–318.

[15] See R.A. Posner, "A Theory of Negligence" (1972) 1 J Leg Stud 29. See also *infra*, **1.US.11.**

[16] B.S. Markesinis and S.F. Deakin, *Tort Law*, 3rd edn. (Oxford: Clarendon, 1994) at 30, with a reference to Professor Fleming's article "Is there a Future for Tort" (1984) 58 Aust LJ 131 at 135.

[17] Ibid.

[18] See the excerpt *infra*, **1.US.10.**

[19] See *infra*, **1.US.10.–11., 1.E.12.**

[20] For a comparative account see among others A. Tunc, "Introduction" in *International Encyclopedia of Comparative Law—Vol. XI/1: Torts* (Tübingen: Mohr, 1974) at 87–107. For a comparative view on French law (by A. Tunc), German law (by E. Deutsch) and Swiss law (by W. Yung), see F.-E. Klein, (ed.), *Colloque franco-germano-suisse sur les fondements et les fonctions de la responsabilité civile* (Basel: Helbing und Lichtenhahn, 1973). See also for France: Viney, *Introduction* at 57–69; for Germany: E. Deutsch, "Die Zwecke des Haftungsrechts" JZ 1971, 244; Markesinis at 909 ff; and for the common law: P.S. Atiyah, *The Damages Lottery* (Oxford: Hart Publishing, 1997) at 159–172; P. Cane, *The Anatomy of Tort Law* (Oxford: Hart Publishing, 1997) at 205–238; Markesinis and Deakin at 36–41; Salmond and Heuston at 23–25.

[21] See E. Deutsch, ibid.; G.T. Schwarz, "Mixed Theories of Tort Law: Affirming Both Deterrence and Corrective Justice" (1997) 75 Texas LR 1834; P. Cane, ibid. at 224–225; *Clerk & Lindsell on Torts* at 3, para. 1–03 ("multi-purpose functions").

In addition to the functions enumerated above, civil liability may have other less apparent purposes, such as appeasement or satisfaction of the victim or judicial recognition of his or her right, through the award of nominal damages or a *franc symbolique*. Furthermore, the functions of compensation and deterrence may be understood to include the prevention of unjust enrichment of the wrongdoer (eg by the award of restitutionary damages).[22] These other functions are discussed in Chapter VIII on Remedies.[23]

A theory of the functions of tort is of limited value as none of the functions enumerated, with the arguable exception of the fourth, is able to lead to concrete answers to questions as to when a victim should be compensated, the injurer deterred or the harm insured. Such a theory does, however, point to the strengths and weaknesses of tort law relative to other legal institutions such as criminal law, contract law, the law of restitution, administrative regulation, social security and private insurance, all of which pursue some of the aims which are also pursued by tort law, albeit in a different manner and with a different effect.[24] Above all, the theory can serve as a useful device to look beyond the conceptualism of the various legal systems and to discover whether different concepts in reality conceal the pursuit of similar functions.

1.2.1. COMPENSATION AND ITS DIFFERENT MEANINGS

Introductory Note

Although we often speak of tort as a system of *liability* of the injurer,[25] compensation of the injured is generally viewed as the prime function of tort:[26] tort aims to compensate the victim for the harm done to him or her. This focus on the victim explains why the degree of blameworthiness of the conduct of the injurer has no effect, in principle, on the amount of damages to be awarded; while even the slightest fault can lead to a heavy burden of damages, the most despicable act can lead to the award of only very small damages. It is this corrective or compensatory function of tort which distinguishes it from criminal law: the latter aims to punish the criminal, even where no harm has occurred,[27] and is linked primarily to the gravity of the culprit's fault.[28] However, in certain legal systems (albeit only under limited circumstances) tort rules also strive for punishment by allowing punitive or exemplary damages.[29] Moreover, some heads of compensation, e.g. damages for pain and suffering, are awarded not as an equivalent but as a substitute or solace for what has been lost.[30]

---

[22] See further Markesinis and Deakin at 38–41.
[23] *Infra*, Chapter VIII, 8.1.
[24] For a thorough comparative law analysis of the interplay between tort law and neighbouring branches of not only private law but also constitutional and criminal law, see von Bar I at 423 ff. and 569 ff. respectively.
[25] See Rogers at 29.
[26] See among others Viney, *Introduction* at 58; Salmond and Heuston at 24.
[27] See among others *Clerk & Lindsell on Torts* at 13, para. 1–14.
[28] Viney, *Introduction* at 64.
[29] See *infra*, Chapter VIII, 8.1.
[30] See Atiyah, *supra*, **1.E.4.**

Notwithstanding its emphasis on the victim, tort law does not always fulfil its compensatory aim. For example, a victim can be left without compensation if his injurer has an empty pocket. Or, because of the large costs and the lapse of time involved in litigation, parties may settle for a smaller amount than the actual harm suffered.[31] The assessment of damages is often indeterminate in nature. The victim is sometimes not in a position to bring forward satisfactory evidence of all elements of liability. Those disadvantages make some legal writers regard tort as a "forensic lottery"[32] or a "damages lottery",[33] which makes of tort a prohibitively expensive system, at least in the field of accidental injury.

A legal system should not be a lottery and the compensatory function is no longer the monopoly of tort. Social security and private insurance are two other means of compensating the victim, which raises the question of even whether tort is an appropriate way to achieve compensation at all. The main element in its favour is that, as a rule, it leads to full compensation and that it can thus be used as a remedy to complement other compensation mechanisms which, because of economic restraints, can offer partial compensation only.[34]

P.S. Atiyah, Accidents, Compensation and the Law[35]   1.E.4.

"What is compensation for? What objectives does a compensation system have? What indeed, *is* compensation? It seems that the notion of compensation embraces at least three distinct ideas. Sometimes, compensation is granted as an equivalent for what has been lost; sometimes, it is granted as a substitute or solace for what has been lost; and sometimes it is granted not because of what has been lost, but because of what the victim has never had in comparison with others in a similar situation. Let us take these ideas in turn and elaborate on them.

Compensation as an equivalent for what has been lost

This is the simplest and most straightforward case (which we may call 'equivalence compensation'), but even here we can distinguish at least three types of case, according to the kind of 'loss'. First, a person may 'lose' (in the sense of being physically deprived of) money or other valuable property which can be replaced with money. A person's car is wrecked in an accident, and he wants compensation to enable him to buy an equivalent car or his house is destroyed by fire, and he must rebuild or buy a new house. In this type of case the purpose of compensation seems self-evident— we are simply restoring what has been taken away; we are restoring the *status quo*; trying to avoid the dislocation caused by change.

The second type of equivalence compensation is designed to compensate, not for physical deprivation of property, but for costs which are incurred by the victim. These may take varied forms, from payment of medical expenses to payment of the cost of hospital visits . . .

The third type of equivalence compensation is compensation for lost expectations. Predominant here is the entire problem of income losses which to a very large extent lies at the heart of all the

---

[31] See Atiyah, *infra*, **1.E.4.** See also Rogers at 34–36.

[32] T.G. Ison, *The Forensic Lottery—A critique on Tort Liability as a system of Personal Injury Compensation* (London: Staples Press, 1967) at 108: "[We] should abandon any plan by which compensation depends on the cause of the disability"; Viney, *Introduction* at 61, para. 37 speaks of a "loterie judiciaire".

[33] P.S. Atiyah, *The Damages Lottery* (Oxford: Hart, 1997).

[34] Viney, *Introduction* at 59–60 and 62, para. 36 and 38.

[35] (London: Weidenfeld and Nicolson, 1978) at 480–485 (footnotes omitted).

systems of compensation operating today. When a person is sick, or injured or disabled, so that he is unable to work, or when a person is killed or dies, leaving dependants who would have been maintained by his earnings, compensation for lost income is instinctively felt to be required. It will be noticed that this form of compensation differs from compensation for an actual deprivation . . . for in this kind of case the victim never had what he is being compensated for losing . . .

Substitute (or solace) compensation

In the second type of case, compensation is awarded not as an equivalent but as a substitute or solace for what has been lost. Since it is almost impossible in any modern legal system to award compensation in any form other than money, it follows that giving compensation for 'losses' which cannot be replaced by money must have a different purpose from that involved in giving compensation for things that can be replaced by money. The object here cannot be to replace what has been lost by some equivalent but to enable the victim to obtain a substitute, or alternatively to solace him . . . for what has happened. This type of compensation is associated almost exclusively with bodily injury which (quite apart from any claims to equivalence compensation to which it may give rise) may also call for compensation under the tort system . . .

What is this form of compensation really for? It does not give the victim back what he has 'lost', nor does it in any way deal with the problem of disappointed expectations. It does, of course, quite often enable the victim to obtain in some broad sense a substitute for what he has lost. The man who is blinded and can no longer watch television may be enabled to buy a gramophone and a collection of records to give him an alternative form of pleasure. The man who loses a leg and can no longer go for a country walk may be enabled to buy a car and savour the pleasures of the countryside in a different way. What we are doing here is trying to provide some other pleasure to the victim in lieu of those he can no longer enjoy—what we might call 'substitute compensation'. There is, it will be noticed, still some element of 'loss' in this type of compensation, though not necessarily in the crude sense of physical deprivation: we are substituting, or enabling the victim to substitute a new pleasure for the lost one . . .

But there is also another type of case in which compensation is given not as a substitute for pleasures forgone, but as a solace for pain inflicted or endured. Damages for pain and suffering, for mental distress, for the loss of child or parent (if awardable at all) are not really awarded for 'losses' at all, certainly not for losses in the sense of property deprivation in which we usually use the term. Compensation here is merely a solace for unpleasantness and misfortune . . .

Equalization compensation

We have already suggested in an earlier chapter that there are circumstances in which we use the notion of compensation in order to justify a sort of egalitarianism. For example when we talk of compensating children born with deformities as a result of prenatal injuries, such as those involved in the thalidomide tragedies, we are (it seems) moved primarily by a desire to equalize the position of these children as compared with normal children . . . "

Note
See *infra*, under **1.US.10.–11., 1.E.12.**

1.2.2. FROM LOSS-SHIFTING TO LOSS-SPREADING

Introductory Note

Tort rules merely shift losses from one individual to another. In combination with private insurance and social security techniques they now also distribute losses amongst many and collectivize them.[36] Depending on whether risks should be spread over a large group of citizens, or rather over the beneficiaries of a certain kind or sector of activity only, social security or private insurance respectively will be chosen as a loss-spreading technique.

In addition to social security or private insurance, the workings of the market can also have as an effect that losses are spread, but then as a direct result of passing on the costs involved in the application of tort law (and of insurance and social security). The potential civil liability that weighs upon suppliers of goods or services is a cost which will be reflected in the price of the product or the service that they sell.[37] The question is then not simply who will carry the burden of liability but who will be in the best position to pass it "on to the public by way of increased prices".[38] Product liability is an example of such a technique: the cost of liability, including the burden of taking precautions and of taking insurance, is included in the price of the product, just like other manufacturing or marketing costs.[39]

The ability of private insurance, social security and the market to shift and spread losses from one individual to another individual or to groups of individuals is of great significance for the development of tort law. Insurance, more particularly, has not only encroached upon the quasi-monopoly of tort law as a compensation system, it has also influenced the constitutive elements of tort law itself. On the one hand, insurance or insurability has been an important factor under a system of fault-based liability; a court may find it easier to impose liability on a defendant who is or should be insured. On the other hand, the wider availability of insurance also had profound consequences for the general discussion on the appropriate basis for civil liability, i.e. fault or another basis such as risk.

The three following excerpts describe how private insurance and social security have become complementary to tort law; they show a parallel development in the three legal systems under review.

---

[36] Viney, *Introduction* at 99, para. 61; E. Deutsch, "Die Zwecke des Haftungsrechts" JZ 1971, 244 at 245.

[37] See P. Cane, *The Anatomy of Tort Law* (Oxford: Hart Publishing, 1997) at 228; Viney, *Introduction* at 63, para. 38.

[38] See R.F.V. Heuston (intervention in debate) in F.-E. Klein, (ed.), *Colloque franco- germano-suisse sur les fondements et les fonctions de la responsabilité civile* (Basel: Helbing und Lichtenhahn, 1973) at 242.

[39] See further J. Stapleton, *Product Liability* (London: Butterworths, 1994).

G. Viney, *Introduction à la responsabilité*[40]   **1.F.5, 1.G.6, 1.E.7.**
and
B.S. Markesinis, *The German Law of Obligations, Vol. II*
The Law of Torts: A Comparative Introduction[41]
and
W.V.H. Rogers, *Winfield and Jolowicz on Tort*[42]

1. G. Viney, *Introduction à la responsabilité*   **1.F.5.**

"19. The growth of civil liability insurance
Since the beginning of the 20th century, the growth of civil liability insurance has been spectacular in all industrialised countries . . .

[T]he legislature has intervened directly in many instances to impose compulsory insurance against civil liability; this duty arises in particular today with respect to persons using motor vehicles on public roads, hunters or persons who practise a dangerous sport. This duty falls, moreover, on those who exercise certain professional or profit-making activities. It is important to note that in the case of insurance of motor vehicles and the insurance of hunting, the legal obligation to take out liability insurance is complemented by the setup of a 'guarantee fund'. The role of the fund consists of taking into charge the compensation of damages the author of which is unidentified or is uninsured.

Furthermore, it happens nowadays that even outside of cases in which the legislator has created an obligation to take out insurance, the courts determine that there is, on the part of the person who caused the damage, negligence in having failed to take out an insurance policy (*imprudence fautive à ne pas avoir pris d'assurance*)—notably if professional usage requires such insurance to be taken out . . .

25. The connection between the growth of insurance and the decline of fault
In the context of a generalisation of this form of insurance, the financial consequences of a finding of liability normally rest upon the insurer. This removes *a priori* the justification for requiring fault on the part of the person who is found liable. *From the moment where liability becomes a mere basis for insurance*, there is no longer in fact any reason to ask, in each instance of damage, whether the injury was due to fault or not. Nor is there any need to designate the person who actually committed the fault as 'responsible' (that is responsible for providing insurance cover for such injury). The normal and logical process consists rather in imputing this responsibility to the person *who was best placed, before the injury, to enter into an insurance contract intended to cover the risk*. For this reason, we believe that this notion of *ability to obtain insurance coverage* is not unfamiliar to the organisation of systems of objective responsibility that we have just summarised . . .

As for the legal regimes of objective liability (*responsabilité de plein droit*), their structure sometimes reveals an obvious link with insurance. Thus, for example, the entity to which the responsibility for nuclear accidents has been assigned is, according to the Convention of Paris, 'the person who, by decision of the competent public authority, is bound to have sufficient insurance cover to support the legal duty of reparation to the public'. By the same token, the Brussels Convention of 29 November 1969 and the Act of 26 May 1977 impose upon the owner of the vessel transporting hydrocarbons both the statutory responsibility for the consequences of maritime pollution that the

---

[40] 2nd edn. (Paris: LGDJ, 1995) at 24–6, 35–6 and 41–2, para. 19, 25 and 28–1 (footnotes omitted). Translation by A. Dumas-Eymard.

[41] 3rd edn. (Oxford: Clarendon, 1997) at 909–911.

[42] (London: Sweet & Maxwell, 1998) at 20–22 and 24 (footnotes omitted).

vessel may cause, and the duty to take out insurance to guarantee the due discharge of that responsibility. The Act of 4 January 1978 similarly makes building contractors objectively liable for defective buildings and imposes upon them the obligation to take out a professional liability policy that covers that strict liability.

Similarly, in the Act of 5 July 1985 aiming at the improvement of the position of victims of traffic accidents, we find again this process of 'predetermination' of the person upon whom the obligation to compensate is placed, by way of identifying the person who must be insured, even if this process is not formally explained in the Act. Whereas the duty of compensation is placed upon the driver and the keeper (*gardien*) of the vehicle involved in the accident, the discharge of that duty is now guaranteed by compulsory insurance, even in the case of theft or other misappropriation of the vehicle. It is thus the insurer, rather than the driver or the keeper of the vehicle, who truly owes the duty of compensation . . .

28–1. The development of social insurance and Social Security

However, the movement towards socialisation has been supported above all by other institutions which are completely foreign to liability. Notably, *direct insurance of persons or things*, which consists in transferring to a mutual insurance system certain risks (notably for accidents, illness, destruction of property . . .) to which each participant in the system is exposed, permits the cost of compensation to be spread between all those who are so exposed. This form of insurance at first developed spontaneously. However, its advantages soon became obvious, notably in relation to the risks of accidents and of illnesses that are liable to affect wage-earners in their earning capacity. Therefore, it was not long before the legislator made this form of insurance compulsory . . .

However, it is important to note that the benefits paid by social security only ever compensate partially the injuries suffered and that both the methods and the goals of social security are clearly different from those of civil liability.

Moreover, however extensive it may be, social security provides a remedy only for injury to persons: it does not cover all social risks. Consequently, other forms of compensation exist side by side with social security, *which organize, according to various methods, the sharing of certain risks* [emphasis added]."

2. B.S. Markesinis, *The German Law of Obligations, Vol. II—The Law of Torts: A Comparative Introduction*   **1.G.6.**

" . . . The third point that must be made absolutely clear is that the advent of social security and private insurance has dramatically affected the function and purpose of the rules concerning compensation. This is, of course, true in all systems; but it is particularly noticeable in Germany where these days social security and insurance cover most of victims' needs and then take over the tort actions against their tortfeasors . . . In such circumstances, compensation of the victim can no longer be the prime purpose of the compensation rules. Rather, they have come to form a part of the intricate complex of rules which help allocate risks or, in some cases, seek to promote deterrence. To put it differently, the tort action, when it is taken over by the social security carrier or the insurer, helps to put the cost of accident back on the shoulders of the wrongdoer (or his insurer) . . . "

3. W.V.H. Rogers, *Winfield and Jolowicz on Tort*   **1.E.7.**

" . . . Even in those accidents which can be attributed to another's fault the role played by the law of tort should not be exaggerated . . .

Damage to property

There is little in the way of State provision for loss or damage to property, which obviously occupies a much lower position of priority than personal injury. Private insurance is, however, of very great significance in relation to property damage. Insurance takes two basic forms, 'loss' or 'first party' insurance and 'liability' or 'third party' insurance. Under the first, the owner of property has cover against loss or damage to that property from the risks described in the policy, such as fire, flood and theft, *whether or not the loss occurs through the fault of any other person.* Under the second, the assured himself is covered against legal liability which he may incur to a third party and the establishment of such liability by the third party, not merely loss suffered by the third party, is an essential prerequisite to a claim on the policy . . .

Personal injuries and death

When the Pearson Commission reported in 1978 it stated that every year in the United Kingdom perhaps 20,000 people died as a result of injury and close to three million were sufficiently seriously injured to lose four or more days' work. The vast majority of those injuries were due to accident . . . Of compensation [paid] for these injuries . . . rather more than half came from the social security system, with the balance being shared more or less equally between the tort system and other, sick pay and private insurance. Overall, therefore, the tort system accounted for no more than a quarter of all compensation paid, but the relationship would rather be different if one examined particular categories of accidents. In the field of motor accidents, tort payments considerably exceeded social security payments though the position was reversed with regard to work and other accidents."

Note
See *infra*, under **1.US.10.–11., 1.E.12.**

1.2.3. DETERRENCE OF UNDESIRABLE BEHAVIOUR

Introductory Note

While the focus of the compensatory function is on the position of the victim, the function of deterrence lays the emphasis on the position of the injurer, as it aims to deter, or prevent, socially undesirable conduct on the part of the perpetrator of harm.

Some doubt remains, however, as to whether deterrence is still a main function of tort law.[43] According to some, it might be better achieved by precise regulations enforced by administrative authorities (regulatory control), or by criminal law rules which relate the sanction to the degree of blameworthiness of the act and not to the degree of harm,[44] although, insofar as the proceeds of the tortious sanction flow into the victim's pocket, tort continues to provide a powerful incentive for the victim to sue.[45] Moreover, the deterrent edge of tort law is blunted by the fact that in practice damages are, far more often than not, paid by an insurer or social security authority rather than by the tortfeasor himself, albeit the insurer or social security authority may, depending on the insurance policy and/or applicable legislation, recover the money from the tortfeasor. Finally, deterrence is not appropriate where the injury caused, and laid at the door of the tortfeasor, is

[43] See e.g. Rogers at 30–32.
[44] Viney, *Introduction* at 64, para. 40.
[45] P. Cane, *The Anatomy of Tort Law* (Oxford: Hart Publishing, 1997) at 220; Viney, ibid.

due to unavoidable human errors against which moreover, as in traffic accidents, insurance is often compulsory. The pros and cons of the deterrent value of tort law are well summarized in the following two excerpts.

B.S. Markesinis and S.F. Deakin, *Tort Law*[46]   **1.E.8, 1.F.9.**
and
G. Viney, *Introduction à la responsabilité*[47]

1. B.S.Markesinis and S.F. Deakin, *Tort Law*   **1.E.8.**

"Deterrence is another function attributed to tort law. As traditionally understood, it plays an interesting but subsidiary part in modern tort law. This is because the deterrent or admonitory effect of money compensation is generally less than that of the corporal punishment of criminal law (e.g. imprisonment). The lighter consequence of a successful tort action, therefore, blunts its deterrent value. (This is certainly true whenever the defendant is insured . . .). Further, as already indicated, tort damages do not in principle correspond exactly to the gravity of conduct (as they tend to do in criminal law). The amount of damages is *generally* speaking the same whether the tort was committed negligently or intentionally (though some rules, e.g. those concerning 'remoteness of damage', are different); and the triviality of the fault bears little relation to the possible enormity of its financial consequences. Similarly, deterrence in the form of monetary payment is hardly effective if the tortfeasor is too poor to pay, or is not insured. The greatest objection to the deterrence theory, however, is that it is inapplicable in those numerous cases where the plaintiff's injury is the result of error rather than blameworthiness. This is particularly true of traffic accidents, the vast majority of which result from regrettable, but statistically inevitable, lapses of attention. It is interesting to note in this respect the empirical studies carried out by the US Department of Transportation in the early 1970s. These suggested that in Washington the average good driver (defined as one who had not been involved in any traffic accident during the preceding four years) commits approximately nine driving errors of four different kinds during every five minutes of driving! In such cases, how can it be said that the threat of a tort action will deter a potential tortfeasor when it appears humanly unavoidable to continue making such errors, and when it is clear that even consideration for the tortfeasor's own safety and the threat of criminal proceedings against him cannot prevent the harmful results? That such errors are actionable as 'negligence' is not because this will deter others from committing them, but most likely because, as a result of compulsory insurance, it is the easiest, if not the only, way of affording the innocent victim compensation without ruining the defendant or unduly burdening the state with the financial consequences of an accident."

2. G. Viney, *Introduction à la responsabilité*   **1.F.9.**

"It seems to us that the deterrent effect of civil liability is weak in the field of accidents caused by the use of dangerous things. Most of these are in fact imputable to chance as well as to the technical imperfection of the objects or machines used and to physical or psychological deficiencies that the ordinary man cannot always avoid because they are inherent to his nature. Therefore it is not the prospect of being found liable that can modify appreciably the behaviour of persons involved in such accidents, especially as they themselves are often exposed to the dangers they create. Furthermore, the inability of civil liability to modify individual behaviour is made worse still when

---

[46] 4th edn. (Oxford: Clarendon, 1999) at 37–38 (footnotes omitted).
[47] 2nd edn. (Paris: LGDJ, 1995) at 65–66 (footnotes omitted). Translation by A. Dumas- Eymard.

it is compulsory to take out insurance to cover the compensation that one may be ordered to pay
. . . which is often the case and is in fact desirable if victims are to be efficiently protected.

But what is true of this type of injury is not true of all others. We believe, for instance, that most
judgments finding a defendant civilly liable on the basis of professional misconduct retain a genuine deterrent effect even where the injury is compensated by the defendant's insurance. The harm
caused by such judgments to the reputation of the defendant is often felt very severely. The same
applies to legal actions intended to impose sanctions upon violations of the principles governing
trade relations, notably actions for unfair competition or counterfeiting; actions against persons
who have committed certain financial wrongs or infringements of company law or, more generally
speaking, infringements of business law; actions by salaried employees against their employers for
disregard of certain rights recognised by labour law . . .

Civil liability also plays a genuine preventive role when it provides remedies for infringement of
the rights attached to legal personality or of certain collective interests, professional or other, material or moral, which certain societies are defending nowadays with growing efficiency. Again, in this
case, a judgment finding a defendant civilly liable often has a considerable moral impact, especially
when it is published. It is sometimes more dissuasive than a financial penalty if the profit made out
of the wrong committed exceeds the amount of the penalty."

Note
See *infra*, under **1.US.10.–11., 1.E.12.**

1.2.4. AVOIDANCE OF INEFFICIENT BEHAVIOUR

Introductory Note

The idea that tort rules should provide incentives to avoid socially harmful behaviour has
been promoted by the economic analysis of the law[48]. The basic idea is that behaviour is
socially harmful if it does not lead to an optimal allocation of resources. According to
that approach, a rule of law is fair and just only when it promotes economic efficiency, in
that it leads to the maximum net aggregate social welfare (viz. social benefits as compared
with social costs). Although much criticized, in that it may seem to equate justice with efficiency (but see the first excerpt below), that approach rightly emphasizes the need to
reduce the costs of accidents and to take efficient precautions to avoid them.

---

[48] See *supra*, **1.F.1, 1.G.2, 1.E.3.**, Notes (3) and (4). See also R.A. Posner and W.M. Landes, *The Economic Structure of Tort Law* (Cambridge: Harvard University Press, 1987); A. Tunc, "Introduction" in *International Encyclopedia of Comparative Law—Vol. XI: Torts* at 88.

G. Calabresi, *The Costs of Accidents*[49]   **1.US.10.–11.,1.E.12.**
and
R.A. Posner, *Economic Analysis of Law*[50]
and
P. Cane, *The Anatomy of Tort Law*[51]

1. G. Calabresi, *The Costs of Accidents*   **1.US.10.**

"What, then, are the principal goals of any system of accident law? First, it must be just or fair, second, it must reduce the costs of accidents.

JUSTICE . . . [C]laims that particular systems are just, like those that justice is in some sense a goal concurrent with accident cost reduction, fail to ring true. They seem to suggest that a 'rather unjust' system may be worthwhile because it diminishes accident costs effectively; or, conversely, that there is one system that can be termed just to the exclusion of all others, i.e. that is supported by justice in the same sense that economic efficiency may prefer one system to all others. But the words just and unjust do not sound right to me in either of the statements. They ring true in rather different contexts, as when we say that we reject a particular system or parts of it as unjust, or that a system taken as a whole does not violate our sense of justice. This suggests that justice is a totally different order of goal from accident cost reduction. Indeed, it suggests that it is not a goal but rather a constraint that can impose a veto on systems or on the use of particular devices or structures within a given system (e.g. administrative tribunals under the fault system) even though those same structures might not be unjust in another system (e.g. administrative tribunals under workmen's compensation) . . .

All this discussion may make the concept of justice seem both negative and elusive. But it affords no excuse for ignoring justice in discussing accident law. Our reaction to accidents is not a strict dollars-and-cents one . . . An economically optimal system of reducing accident costs—whether decisions are made collectively, through the market, or through a combination of both—might be totally or partially unacceptable because it strikes us as unfair, and no amount of discussion of the efficiency of the system would do much to save it. Justice must ultimately have its due . . .

REDUCTION OF ACCIDENT COSTS. Apart from the requirements of justice, I take it as axiomatic that the principal function of accident law is to reduce the sum of the costs of accidents and the costs of avoiding accidents. This cost, or loss, reduction goal can be divided into three subgoals.

The first is reduction of the number and severity of accidents. This 'primary' reduction of accident costs can be attempted in two basic ways. We can seek to forbid specific acts or activities thought to cause accidents, or we can make activities more expensive and thereby less attractive to the extent of the accident costs they cause . . .

The second cost reduction subgoal is concerned with reducing neither the number of accidents nor their degree of severity. It concentrates instead on reducing the societal costs resulting from accidents. I shall attempt to show that the notion that one of the principal functions of accident law is the compensation of victims is really a rather misleading, though occasionally useful, way of stating this 'secondary' accident cost reduction goal. The fact that I have termed this compensation notion secondary should in no way be taken as belittling its importance. There is no doubt that the way we provide for accident victims *after* the accident is crucially important and that the real societal costs of accidents can be reduced as significantly here as by taking measures to avoid accidents

---

[49] (New Haven: Yale University Press, 1970) at 24–28 (footnotes omitted).
[50] (Boston: Little, Brown and Co., 1992) at 163–164 (footnotes omitted).
[51] (Oxford: Hart Publishing, 1997) at 222–223 (footnotes omitted).

in the first place. This cost reduction subgoal is secondary only in the sense that it does not come into play until after earlier primary measures to reduce accident costs have failed . . .

The third subgoal of accident cost reduction is rather Pickwickian but very important nonetheless. It involves reducing the costs of administering our treatment of accidents. It may be termed 'tertiary' because its aim is to reduce the costs of achieving primary and secondary cost reduction. But in a very real sense this 'efficiency' goal comes first. It tells us to question constantly whether an attempt to reduce accident costs, either by reducing accidents themselves or by reducing their secondary effects, costs more than it saves. By forcing us to ask this, it serves as a kind of general balance wheel to the cost reduction goal."

2. R.A. Posner, *Economic Analysis of Law*   1.US.11.

"Everybody takes precautions against accidents; the interesting question is how extensive the precautions taken are. If you were deciding whether to buy an auxiliary generator to make sure that a power failure didn't cut off the oxygen supply to your priceless collection of rare South American lizards, you would surely balance, at least in a rough and ready way, the benefits of the auxiliary generator in preventing the loss of the lizards against its costs. The benefits can be expressed, at least as a first approximimation, as the product of the probability of the lizards' being killed over some interval of time (say a year) by a power failure, and the dollar magnitude of the loss. Assume that the probability and the magnitude—P and L (for loss), call them—are .001 and $ 10,000 respectively. Therefore the expected accident cost, PL, will be $10 . . . Thus the expected benefit of the auxiliary generator to you is $10 a year. Suppose its annualized cost is $8. Then you will buy the generator, provided of course that no cheaper alternative precaution is available. If the generator cost more than $10, you would not buy it.

When, as in this example, the person taking precautions and the person who may be injured if they are not taken are the same, the optimal precautions will be achieved without legal intervention. But change the example; suppose the hazard is the loss not of your lizards but of your pinky finger in an automobile accident, and the cheapest way to avoid the accident is for some other driver—a complete stranger—to drive more slowly. Suppose that as before your expected accident cost is $10 (.001 × $10,000) and the cost to the other driver of driving more slowly (and thus taking longer to get to his destination) is $8. Efficiency requires that the driver drive more slowly. But because transaction costs with potential victims such as yourself are prohibitive, he will not do so unless the legal system steps in, as by holding him liable in damages (=$10,000) should an accident occur. Then he has (if we ignore legal expenses, legal error, and other frictions) an expected legal judgment cost of $10. This will induce him to invest $8 in a precaution that will drive his expected judgment cost to zero by preventing the accident.

The example illustrates the operation of the law of negligence as summarized in the negligence formula of Judge Learned Hand.[52] Defining P and L as we have, and denoting by B the cost of the precaution, Hand wrote that a potential injurer is negligent if but only if $B < PL$, which is what our example implied would be the formula for optimal accident avoidance. There is, however, an ambiguity, both in Hand's formulation and in ours. Suppose that our PL of $10 would be totally eliminated by the driver's reducing his speed by 25 m.p.h. at a cost to him of $9. But suppose further that PL could be reduced to $1 by the driver's reducing his speed by only 5 m.p.h., at a cost to him of only $2. This implies that to get PL down from $1 to zero costs the driver $7 ($9 – $2), for a net

---

[52] See *United States* v. *Carroll Towing Co.*, 159 F.2d 169 at 173 (2d Cir. 1947) and, for contemporary applications of the formula, *United States Fidelity & Guaranty Co.* v. *Jadranska Slobodna Plovidba*, 683 F.2d 1022 (7th Cir. 1982), and *McCarty* v. *Pheasant Run, Inc.*, 826 F.2d 1554 (7th Cir. 1987). For a succinct and instructive presentation of the *Learned Hand* test, see Schamps at 541–544.

social loss of $6. Clearly we want him to reduce his speed just by 5 m.p.h., which yields a net social gain of $7. This example shows that expected accident costs and accident costs must be compared at the margin, by measuring the costs and benefits of small increments in safety and stopping investing in more safety at the point where another dollar spent would yield a dollar or less in added safety . . . "

3. P. Cane, *The Anatomy of Tort Law* 1.E.12.

" . . . [S]ome economic analysts of law see deterrence as the only function of tort law. For them, the only function of tort remedies is to provide incentives for the avoidance of economically inefficient behaviour. The aim of economic efficiency is the maximization of wealth in society regardless of how that wealth is distributed amongst the members of society. For this reason, there is no place in economic analysis of tort law for protected interests. For instance, economic analysts define negligent conduct as conduct the costs of which are greater than its benefits. Conduct which produces an excess of benefits over costs increases social wealth. By contrast, negligent conduct reduces social wealth. In economic analysis, the only purpose of tort law is to ensure that the costs of inefficient behaviour are borne by the person engaging in the behaviour so as to give that person an incentive not to engage in such conduct in the future. The purpose of awarding damages to P is not to protect P's interest but to give an incentive to D not to engage in the future in inefficient conduct . . .

The economic theory of tort law (which defines tortious conduct as inefficient conduct and says that the only function of tort law is to provide incentives for the avoidance of inefficient conduct) operates at three levels. At one level it presents itself as an explanation for the structure and content of tort law; at a second level it presents itself as a tool for predicting the outcome of tort cases; and at a third level, it presents itself as a criterion for judging whether particular rules and principles of tort law are acceptable or not. I leave it to the reader to decide whether tort law ought to be aiming to maximize social wealth and whether it ought to be changed to the extent that it does not further this goal. As an explanatory theory (to which the predictive role is an adjunct), economic analysis of tort law is unattractive for two related reasons. First, it fails to account for the fact that protected interests are just as important a component of the structure of tort law as sanctioned conduct. In economic analysis, defendants are centre-stage and plaintiffs mere functionaries; whereas the rules and principles of tort law are just as concerned with plaintiffs' interests as with defendants' conduct. In tort law, for instance, an injured plaintiff is entitled to receive damages, whereas in economic theory the only reason for paying the damages to the plaintiff is a secondary one of providing an incentive for the plaintiff to sue the defendant and, in this way, to enable the legal system to create the primary incentive for the avoidance of inefficient conduct by the defendant . . .

The methodological weakness of the explanatory version of economic analysis of law is that it starts with a particular 'unitary' theory of the function of tort law and works back from that to an examination of the structure and content of tort law. In doing this, it classifies as 'mistaken' any aspect of its structure or content which is not consistent with the chosen function."

Notes

(1) Only a few remarks are to be added to the previous materials. The first remark relates to the meaning of *compensation* which, as is generally agreed, constitutes the main function of tort law. As explained by P.S. Atiyah,[53] compensation embraces at least three distinct ideas, the two main ones being compensation as an equivalent to replace (in kind

---

[53] *Supra*, **1.E.4.**

or in money) what has been lost, and compensation to enable the victim to obtain a substitute for what he has lost, alternatively, to solace him. The first of those, compensation as equivalent, has different meanings as well, depending on whether physical deprivation of property is to be compensated for, or costs incurred by the victim, or rather lost expectations. As to the second, compensation awarded as a substitute or solace, the latter, solace for pain inflicted or endured, is hardly to be understood as compensation and comes close to *appeasement*, where the award involves only nominal damages, or to *retaliation* or punishment, where large sums of money are awarded (hardly relatable to the size of damage suffered) at the expense of the tortfeasor (provided he or she cannot recover them from his insurer).

(2) As pointed out in the materials concerning loss-spreading,[54] in a vast number of cases the compensatory function of tort law has been taken over by *other compensatory systems*, mainly liability insurance and social security. That is particularly so in France, as G. Viney points out, where the development of private insurance—made compulsory in many sectors—has contributed to the rapid decline of the concept of fault. So much so, that fault is now often replaced, as a decisive liability factor, by the fact that insurance has been taken out, or should have been taken out. Of course, where the insurer of the defendant, having paid the victim, is subrogated in the victim's rights as against tortfeasors other than the defendant (and under certain circumstances also against the defendant himself or herself), fault continues to play a decisive role, albeit a subsidiary one.

(3) The development of other compensatory systems—primarily liability insurance—diminished the *deterrent* function of tort law. That is so, as explained by B.S. Markesinis and G. Viney,[55] where, as in traffic accidents, the injury is the result of human error or lapses of attention rather than blameworthiness, or where it is the result of unavoidable technical deficiencies or malfunctioning of dangerous things. In such cases actions in tort are made possible by giving a very broad interpretation to the concept of fault (if not eliminating it entirely as a liability factor) for the sake of affording compensation to the victim through compulsory insurance. However, that does not prevent tort rules from playing a substantial deterrent function in situations where professional reputation or commercial integrity is of great importance, because of the bad publicity attached to unprofessional behaviour or acts of unfair competition. In such instances, tort law may even be expected to allow *restitutionary damages* in order to take away the illicit profit which the tortfeasor may have derived from wrongful conduct.[56]

(4) In recent times, the function of deterrence has received a macro-economic dimension in the economic analysis of the law, as indicated in the short excerpt from R.A. Posner's famous book:[57] tort law is primarily seen as having a function of avoidance of inefficient behaviour. Such an approach may overemphasize tort remedies as incentives for the avoidance of inefficient behaviour to the exclusion of other roles (but see G. Calabresi's remarks in the first excerpt above) and therefore put too much emphasis on negligent conduct and too little on safeguarding the victim's protected interests (see the third excerpt, from P. Cane). Nonetheless, it has rightly underlined the necessity to

[54] *Supra*, **1.F.5.**, **1.G.6.** and **1.E.7.**
[55] *Supra*, **1.E.8** and **1.F.9.** respectively.
[56] See *infra*, Chapter VIII, 8.1.
[57] See also *supra*, **1.E.3.**, Note (3).

examine the role of tort law as part of a global analysis as to how to spend the limited means which society makes available for compensation of losses and which of those losses need to be compensated under tort law.[58]

That global analysis must concentrate not only on the wrongful or undesirable behaviour of the injurer (and the victim), but also on the protected rights and interests of both. It must be based on a comparative assessment of the effectiveness of the different kinds of compensatory systems and of their ability, where appropriate, to spread certain losses over groups of potential tortfeasors, or even large groups of the population, through private insurance, social security or pricing techniques. Such an analysis should allow the legislature to determine the role which rules of civil liability are to play within the global context of compensatory techniques.

1.3. TORT AND CONTRACT

1.3.1. CONCURRENCE

Introductory Note

a) Contract and tort are so much seen in contradistinction to one another that the exclusion of contract is often made part of the definition of tort, when it is referred to as "extracontractual liability". To understand the divide between the realms of contract and tort, it was thought useful to distinguish between two levels of rules. The primary rules provide for duties laid down in norms of behaviour and giving rise to corresponding rights. The secondary rules provide for liability when primary rules are breached, and for corresponding remedies, the most prominent one being compensation.[59]

At the level of *primary rules* and ensuing duties, tort and contract differ with respect to the scope of protection. While duties in tort are towards everyone in general (i.e. strangers until the injury actually occurs), contractual duties are directed towards the other contracting party,[60] although contracts can sometimes confer rights upon third parties.[61] Other characteristics of primary duties have obscured the divide. For instance, it was thought for some time that, while duties in tort were fixed by law, those in contract arose by voluntary agreement between the parties; this was seen as an essential difference between the two realms. This distinction lost its prominence after it was generally acknowledged that contractual duties are binding only because the law enables them to have binding force, and that many legislative provisions lay down imperative rules that are part of specific contractual relationships, first and foremost in the—Europeanized—area of consumer law.[62] It remains true however that "people are automatically subject to tor-

---

[58] P.S. Atiyah, *Accidents, Compensation and the Law* (London: Weidenfeld and Nicolson, 1978) at 479–480, notes that some of those losses are sometimes to be regarded as misfortunes which "may appear trivial by comparison with the daily life of suffering millions".

[59] For authors making this distinction see, amongst others, *Clerk & Lindsell on Torts* at 7, para. 1–07.

[60] See Markesinis and Deakin at 9; *Prosser & Keeton on Torts*, 5th edn. (St. Paul: West Publishing, 1984) at 5; *Clerk & Lindsell on Torts* at 6, para. 1–06.

[61] As now recognized under English law as well: see the Contracts (Rights of Third Parties) Act 1999, c. 31.

[62] See, amongst others, *Clerk & Lindsell on Torts* at 6, para. 1–06; Markesinis and Deakin at 8–9.

tious duties" while "no one is automatically subject to a contract without his consent".[63]
It was also held, among other controversial distinctions, that contractual duties guarantee a particular outcome, while duties in tort only bind one to take reasonable care. That
distinction would make it advantageous for a plaintiff to sue in contract rather than tort,
since then only non-performance would have to be proven. Nowadays it is well established
in all legal systems that contracts also lead frequently to duties to take care—often
implied,[64] whereas in the area of tort law liability not based on conduct—and generally
triggered by the occurrence of a given event—becomes increasingly frequent.

At the level of *secondary rules* relating to liabilities and remedies for breaches of primary duties, contract law offers a wider range of sanctions, including specific performance or rescission.[65] The most fundamental difference, however, relates to the nature of
protected interests.[66] Contract law protects the interest in having the contract performed:
different theories state that it is either morally wrong or economically inefficient to frustrate expectations engendered by a contract.[67] In case of misperformance, the plaintiff
must therefore be put in a position he or she would have been in if the contract had been
performed fully and timely, as he or she was entitled to expect. Contract law protects that
expectation interest.[68] Under tort law, however, the plaintiff must be put in as good a
position as he could have been in if no tort had been committed: tort law therefore protects the plaintiff's reliance interest.[69] Those two interests reflect two different functions:
contract law aims to enforce promises and thus to confer intended benefits, while tort law
merely aims to maintain the *status quo* and thus to repair losses.[70] In other words, contract law attempts to maximize personal wealth through exchange, while tort law tries to
preserve personal wealth as it existed. Or as T. Weir puts it:[71]

> "Human good, for which the law exists, depends on the maintenance and development of human
> goods—life, health, property and wealth, *inter alia*. To ensure their maintenance we have the law
> of tort, and to promote their development we have the law of contract. Contract is productive,
> tort law protective. In other words, tortfeasors are typically liable for making things worse, con-
> tractors for not making them better."

---

[63] *Clerk & Lindsell on Torts*, 15th edn. (London: Sweet & Maxwell, 1982) at para. 1–05.

[64] P. Cane, *The Anatomy of Tort Law*, (Oxford: Hart Publishing, 1997) at 185. See the French concepts of
obligation de moyens and *obligation de résultat* (*infra*, Chapter III, **3.F.2.**, Note (2)) the German concept of
Verhaltenspflichten and the English concept of contractual liability based on fault (G.H. Treitel, *The Law of
Contract*, 9th edn. (London: Sweet & Maxwell, 1995) at 753).

[65] Cane, ibid. at 184; T. Weir, "Complex liabilities" in *International Encyclopedia of Comparative Law—Vol.
XI/12: Torts* (Tübingen: Mohr, 1976) at 6, para. 12; *Clerk & Lindsell on Torts* at 7, para. 1–07.

[66] See *Clerk & Lindsell on Torts* at 6, para. 1–07.

[67] See the overview offered by A. Burrows, *Remedies for Torts and Breach of Contract*, 2nd edn. (London:
Butterworth, 1994) at 17–21.

[68] Different names express the same idea: performance interest—*Erfüllungsinteresse—Positives Interesse—
positief belang*.

[69] Or status quo interest—*Vertrauensinteresse—Negatives Interesse—negatief belang*; see P.A.N. Houwing,
"Positief en negatief belang bij rechtsschijn" in *Geschriften van Houwing* (Deventer: Kluwer, 1972) at 103–137
(article formerly published in WPNR 1944).

[70] Those two interests are often distinguished from still a third one: the restitution interest protected by the
law preventing unintended benefits or unjust enrichment.

[71] T. Weir, "Complex liabilities" in *International Encyclopedia of Comparative Law—Vol. XI/12: Torts*
(Tübingen: Mohr, 1976) at 5, para. 6. See also Weir at 1–2 and Markesinis and Deakin at 9–10.

b) At the level of primary duties and in the absence of exclusionary rules, the duties imposed through tort law may overlap with contractual duties (either express or implied). P. Cane gives the following example:[72]

> "Suppose you employ a solicitor to conduct a court action for damages which has a very high chance of success, but that the solicitor negligently fails to start the action in time, as a result of which you recover no damages in that claim. When you employed the solicitor, you entered a contract under which the solicitor could be liable *in contract* for damage caused by careless performance of the contract. But you could also sue the solicitor *in tort* for such negligence. In other words, in this situation you could sue the solicitor either in contract or in tort for one and the same piece of negligent conduct. In technical terms, this is somewhat confusingly described by saying that you have 'concurrent causes of action in contract and tort' against the lawyer."

Where tort law and contract law overlap, so that 'concurrent causes of action in contract and tort' may arise if the conditions for liability under each of them are fulfilled, the question is whether the law permits the plaintiff to choose, or whether it rather takes the position that the remedy in tort is excluded by the mere existence of a contract between the litigating parties. As the materials below indicate, legal systems take different positions: whilst English and German law, among others, allow the plaintiffs to choose between contractual and tortious claims, as a general rule, others systems, including French law, do not. The position of a given system is often a function of the attitude of the legal system towards the compensation of pure economic losses under tort law.[73]

Whether a plaintiff chooses to sue in contract or in tort—if the law allows him or her to do so—will of course depend on which course of action is more advantageous to him, which depends in turn on existing differences between the two realms. And indeed, in any legal system, there are many differences, some of which "can be adequately explained and justified, but some [of which] make very little sense".[74] Differences may exist, for example,[75] as regards the scope of liability, limitation or prescription periods,[76] the measure of damages,[77] the defence of contributory negligence, the burden of proof, the recoverabil-

---

[72] P. Cane, *The Anatomy of Tort Law* (Oxford: Hart Publishing, 1997) at 22–23.

[73] For an exhaustive overview, see von Bar I at 436–437, para. 418 ff., who points out that a more limited scope of protection of tort law will normally lead to the admission of concurrence since otherwise plaintiffs might not be able to obtain adequate judicial protection (at 439–440, para. 422). See also *infra*, **1.G.15.**, Note (3).

[74] P. Cane, *The Anatomy of Tort Law* (Oxford: Hart Publishing, 1997) at 23. See further A. Tunc, "Introduction" in *International Encyclopedia of Comparative Law—Vol. XI/1, Torts* (Tübingen: Mohr, 1974) at 24, para. 41 ("results of tradition, not of reason"); Asser-Hartkamp, *Verbintenissenrecht—Vol. III, De verbintenis uit de wet*, 10th edn. (Deventer: Tjeenk Willink, 1998) at 9, para. 8 ("alleen bijkomstige verschilpunten").

[75] See in general: M. Loubser, "Concurrence of contract and tort" in *Law in Motion* (Dordrecht: Kluwer Law International, 1996) at 343–356, para. 4; P. Schlechtriem, "Vertragliche und außervertragliche Haftung" in *Gutachten und Vorschläge zur Überarbeitung des Schuldrechts*, Vol. II (Bundesanzeiger, 1981) at 1603, notes 23–25; T. Weir, "Complex liabilities" in *International Encyclopedia of Comparative Law—Vol. XI/12: Torts* (Tübingen: Mohr, 1976) at 7–24; H. and L. Mazéaud, J. Mazéaud and F. Chabas, *Leçons de droit civil. Obligations. Théorie générale* (Paris: Montchrestien, 1991) at 371–372, para. 395; F. Terré, P. Simler and Y. Lequette, *Droit civil. Les obligations* (Paris: Dalloz, 1996) at 675–677, para. 828- 829; Le Tourneau and Cadiet at 129–189, para. 367–588.

[76] E.H. Hondius, "General report" in E.H. Hondius, (ed.), *Extinctive Prescription. On the Limitation of Actions* (Den Haag: Kluwer Law International, 1995) at 19, para. 15.

[77] In France, for example, the limitation of recovery to foreseeable damage applies only in the contractual realm, according to Art. 1150 C.civ.

ity of economic loss,[78] the possibility of punitive or exemplary damages,[79] the extent to which clauses limiting or excluding liability are given effect, the tests for causation or remoteness of damages,[80] the rules on jurisdiction, the rules of private international law or the regimes of liability for others.[81]

G. Viney, *Introduction à la responsabilité*[82] **1.F.13., 1.E.14., 1.G.15.**
and
House of Lords[83]
Henderson v. Merrett Syndicates Ltd.
and
BGH, 24 May 1976[84]

<small>CONCURRENCE BETWEEN CONTRACT AND TORT</small>

Under French law, a plaintiff must base his or her claim on contract in cases where a contractual relationship existed between the victim and the wrongdoer, the injury resulted from the non-performance of contractual obligations and the claim is between two parties to that contractual relationship. Under English law, there is no sound basis for a rule which automatically restricts the claimant to either a tortious or a contractual remedy. Under German law, claims in contract and in tort follow in principle their respective rules as to conditions, content and enforcement; they are also subject to their respective prescription periods, unless the delictual prescription period were to frustrate the purpose of the particularly short prescription period in contract.

1. G. Viney, *Introduction à la responsabilité*

"181. The principles.
If there is a point which appears always to have been accepted, practically without discussion, both in legal writing and case law, it is that all liability which is not specifically contractual, is necessarily delictual/tortious (*délictuelle*). The method used to define the respective domain of these two realms rests precisely upon this postulate, which has never truly been questioned to this date. The method consists in determining, starting from the criteria for the application of contract law, not only the field occupied by contract law . . . but also the domain of tort law, since the latter necessarily constitutes the "*droit commun*" and can thus cover all situations which are not contractual . . . Finally, case law has consistently denied any possible overlap between the realms of contract and tort, in fact enshrining a rule of "non-concurrence" (*non-cumul*) which, by forbidding the use of tort law principles in the realm of contract, has helped sharpen and harden the contours of the traditional distinction . . .

In the current state of French law, the application of contractual liability requires not only that a contract existed between the victim and the person who caused the injury, at the time when this

---

[78] See *infra*, Chapter II.
[79] See *infra*, Chapter VIII.
[80] See *infra*, Chapter IV.
[81] See *infra*, Chapter V.
[82] 2nd edn. (Paris: L.G.D.J., 1995) at 321, 403–5, 408, 412 and 414, para. 181, 216, 220, 223 and 224 (footnotes omitted). Translation by A. Dumas-Eymard.
[83] [1995] 2 AC 145.
[84] BGHZ 66, 315, NJW 1976, 1505.

injury occurred . . . , but also that the injury resulted from the non-performance of an obligation created by this contract or attached thereto . . . , and that the liability claim involves contracting parties or those assimilated to contracting parties . . .

216. The theories presented.
The contrast between the limited domain of contract law and the very large scope of tort law has favoured the attempts by the latter to invade the former. It should not come as a surprise that plaintiffs, who have every reason to place their claims in the realm of tort law, seek to do exactly this, either by overtly opting for the application of Articles 1382 ff. of the *Code civil*, or by simply abstaining from presenting the reasons which would lead to the application of contract law. Moreover, it is perfectly conceivable that a plaintiff would simultaneously invoke rules borrowed from one realm or the other, or that he or she would present an alternative tort claim, should his or her contractual claim fail.

Are these lines of argument admissible? . . .

In support of the theory of concurrence (*cumul*) of tort law and contract law, it has been argued that tortious liability is part of the public order (*institution d'ordre public*), so that individuals can neither derogate from it nor modify it by contract. Tort law is always present, and it underlies the relationships between contracting parties. According to this theory, tortious liability thus embodies a minimum level of protection which the contract may increase, but which it may not reduce . . .

In contrast, the majority of French legal writing has espoused the theory known as "non-concurrence" (*non-cumul*). According to it, contractual and tortious liability are distinct, albeit complementary, institutions. They are not in direct competition with one another, for they apply to different problems: contractual liability in fact imposes sanctions for the non-observance of contractual obligations, while tortious liability attaches sanctions to breaches of rules of conduct which are imposed by statute, regulation, or case law. Their relationship is not settled by proclaiming the superiority of one realm over the other, but rather by determining their respective domains. Further, proponents of "*non-cumul*" theory suggest that the public order nature of tortious liability is in no way established.

The defenders of *non-cumul* have underlined that the extension of Articles 1382 ff. of the *Code civil* into the realm of contract law risks placing the latter in check. Since contractual liability is specifically meant to impose sanctions for the non-observance of contractual obligations, so as to protect the contract itself, setting it aside in favour of tortious liability appears incompatible not only with the respect due to the law, but also with that due to contract.

This line of argument has now convinced the majority of French writers who have rallied behind a strict conception of *non-cumul*.

220. Application and Exceptions . . .
223. It is known that, according to the Criminal Chamber of the *Cour de cassation*, whenever indictable conduct takes place in connection with the non-performance of a contractual obligation and an *action civile* is brought before the criminal jurisdiction as an accessory to the action started by the public prosecutor, the case must then be decided according to the principles of tort law. Criminal courts do not take into consideration the contractual nature of the fault alleged before them . . .

However, one should note that the Criminal Chamber has always been alone in taking this position. In contrast, civil jurisdictions admit that a claim founded upon the non-observance of contractual obligations is submitted to the regime of contract law only, and thus escapes entirely the realm of Articles 1382ff. of the *Code civil*, even in the cases where the fault committed in the performance of a contract would also constitute a punishable offence under criminal law.

Moreover, it is open to question whether the Criminal Chamber itself is not willing to introduce more flexibility in its case law, since it has rendered at least two deisions by which it has admitted that the criminal judge can and must apply the rules of contractual liability.

224. Another exception to the rule of *non-cumul* concerns personal injuries arising from transportation accidents. Case law has recognized that the close relatives of the primary victim benefit from a "tacit stipulation for the benefit of another" (*stipulation pour autrui tacite*), which enables them, in case of death of the primary victim, to rely on the principles of contractual liability to obtain reparation of their "reflex injury" (*préjudice par ricochet*). In particular, such secondary victims can invoke against the transporter of passengers a breach of an obligation of result to ensure the safety of passengers (*obligation de sécurité de résultat*), which the transporter is deemed to have undertaken by virtue of the contract with the primary victim. Furthermore, courts have affirmed that the beneficiaries of this *stipulation pour autrui* can waive their right to rely on it; in such cases, they can still pursue, in their quality as affected third parties, a claim in tort against the transporter."

2. House of Lords, *Henderson* v. *Merrett Syndicates Ltd.*   1.E.14.

Direct Names at Lloyd's

Facts: Some Names at Lloyd's (the so-called Direct Names) had a direct contractual relationship (contract of agency) with the syndicates' managing agents. They suffered huge economic losses because of the alleged negligence of the agents who had taken excessive aggregate liabilities and too little reinsurance. They brought forward an action for damages in tort as well as in contract against the managing agents. The agents argued that the Direct Names could not bring forward concurrent claims in tort and in contract.

Held: The court of first instance judged in favour of the Direct Names. The court of appeal affirmed the decision of the court of first instance. The House of Lords dismissed the appeal from the decision of the court of appeal.

Judgment: LORD GOFF: "All systems of law which recognise a law of contract and a law of tort (or delict) have to solve the problem of the possibility of concurrent claims arising from breach of duty under the two rubrics of the law. Although there are variants, broadly speaking two possible solutions present themselves: either to insist that the claimant should pursue his remedy in contract alone, or to allow him to choose which remedy he prefers. As my noble and learned friend, Lord Mustill, and I have good reason to know [references omitted] France has adopted the former solution in its doctrine of non cumul, under which the concurrence of claims in contract and torts is outlawed [reference omitted]. The reasons given for this conclusion are (1) respect for the will of the legislator, and (2) respect for the will of the parties to the contract [reference omitted]. The former does not concern us; but the latter is of vital importance. It is however open to various interpretations. For such a policy does not necessarily require the total rejection of concurrence, but only so far as a concurrent remedy in tort is inconsistent with the terms of the contract. It comes therefore as no surprise to learn that the French doctrine is not followed in all civil law jurisdictions, and that concurrent remedies in tort and contract are permitted in other civil law countries, notably Germany [reference omitted]. I only pause to observe that it appears to be accepted that no perceptible harm has come to the German system from admitting concurrent claims . . .

Practical issues, which can be of great importance to the parties, are at stake. Foremost among these is perhaps the question of limitation of actions.

Other practical problems arise, for example, from the absence of a right to contribution between negligent contract-breakers; from the rules as to remoteness of damage, which are less restricted in tort than they are in contract; and from the availability of the opportunity to obtain leave to serve proceedings out of the jurisdiction. It can of course be argued that the principle established in respect of concurrent liability in contract and tort should not be tailored to mitigate the adventitious effects of rules of law such as these, and that one way of solving such problems would no doubt be to rephrase such incidental rules as have to remain in terms of the nature of the harm suffered rather than the nature of the liability asserted [reference omitted]. But this is perhaps crying for the moon: and with the law in its present form, practical considerations of this kind cannot sensibly be ignored.

At all events . . . we can see the beginning of the redirection of the common law away from the contractual solution adopted in *Groom* v. *Crocker* [1939] 1 KB 194, towards the recognition of concurrent remedies in contract and tort. First, and most important, in 1963 came the decision at your Lordships' House in *Hedley Byrne & Co. Ltd.* v. *Heller & Partners Ltd.* [1964] AC 465. I have already expressed the opinion that the fundamental importance of this case rests in the establishment of the principle upon which liability may arise in tortious negligence in respect of services (including advice) which are rendered for another, gratuitously or otherwise, but are negligently performed— viz., an assumption of responsibility coupled with reliance by the plaintiff which, in all the circumstances, makes it appropriate that a remedy in law should be available for such negligence. For immediate purposes, the relevance of the principle lies in the fact that, as a matter of logic, it is capable of application not only where the services are rendered gratuitously, but also where they are rendered under a contract . . . In this context, it is of particular relevance to refer to the opinion expressed both implicitly by Lord Morris of Borth-y-Gest (with whom Lord Hodson agreed) and expressly by Lord Devlin that the principle applies to the relationship of solicitor and client, which is nearly always contractual [reference omitted].

The decision in *Hedley Byrne*, and the statement of general principle in that case, provided the opportunity to reconsider the question of concurrent liability in contract and tort afresh, untrammelled by the ancient learning based upon a classification of defendants in terms of status which drew distinctions difficult to accept in modern conditions. At first that opportunity was not taken . . .

My own belief is that, in the present context, the common law is not antipathetic to concurrent liability, and that there is no sound basis for a rule which automatically restricts the claimant to either a tortious or a contractual remedy. The result may be untidy; but, given that the tortious duty is imposed by the general law, and the contractual duty is attributable to the will of the parties, I do not find it objectionable that the claimant may be entitled to take advantage of the remedy which is most advantageous to him, subject only to ascertaining whether the tortious duty is so inconsistent with the applicable contract that, in accordance with ordinary principle, the parties must be taken to have agreed that the tortious remedy is to be limited or excluded . . .

But, for present purposes more important, in the instant case liability can, and in my opinion should, be founded squarely on the principle established in *Hedley Byrne* itself, from which it follows that an assumption of responsibility coupled with the concomitant reliance may give rise to a tortious duty of care irrespective of whether there is a contractual relationship between the parties, and in consequence, unless his contract precludes him from doing so, the plaintiff, who has available to him concurrent remedies in contract and tort, may choose that remedy which appears to him to be the most advantageous."

3. BGH, 24 May 1976   **1.G.15.**

Frost product for lorries

Facts: A transport company purchased a product to protect its lorries against frost. Although the seller assured the purchaser that the product could protect the lorries, four of the lorries were damaged because of its ineffectiveness. The purchaser claimed for damages in tort (§ 823(1) BGB), since his claim in contract was barred by the short prescription period applicable to claims arising from latent defects in sold products (§ 477(1) BGB).[85] The question arose whether § 477(1) BGB applied as well to a claim in tort brought by the seller, or whether that claim was governed by the general three-year prescription period applicable to tort law (§ 852 BGB).[86]

Held: The court of first instance and the court of appeal dismissed the claim. The BGH reversed the decision of the court of appeal.

Judgment: "a) As the BGH repeatedly stated, in accordance with prevailing opinion, the overlap of claims for reparation arising out of breach of contract and of tort constitutes a case of genuine concurrence of claims (*echte Anspruchskonkurrenz*). If a course of conduct satisfies the conditions for liability under both contract and tort law, a claim arises under each of them. *Each claim is to be assessed on an autonomous basis, according to its respective conditions, its content and its enforcement mechanisms. Accordingly, each claim follows in principle its respective prescription period . . .* [emphasis added]. For this reason, in the case law regarding accessory warranties under the contract for services (*Werkvertrag*)—i.e. a field related to this case—the person hiring the contractor is not barred from presenting a claim in tort on account of negligent damage to his property (§ 823 BGB) within the prescription period of § 852 BGB, even though the prescription period for claims under the contract for services (§ 635 BGB) has expired . . . The same considerations apply to claims for loss or damage of the goods entrusted to a forwarding agent, warehouseman or carrier, insofar as there is concurrence between claims under contract and in tort . . .

b) *A different approach applies only if, and insofar as, the purpose of a particularly short prescription period under contract law would be frustrated—and in effect contract law would be undermined— as a result of the power given to the victim to switch over to a claim in tort* after the expiry of the prescription period for contractual claims arising from one and the same set of facts [emphasis added] . . . Along those lines, case law applied the short prescription period of § 558(1) BGB to claims of the landlord against the tenant arising from a change or a deterioration of the rented property, even though they were brought up under tort law . . . Indeed, the claim of the landlord against the tenant for change or deterioration of the rented property, to which the landlord is entitled [under the law relating to the contract of lease], generally relates to damage to property owned by the landlord [i.e. the rented property], so that in the majority of cases, the tenant could also be liable pursuant to § 823 BGB (under the prescription period of § 852 BGB). *If the landlord were able to claim in tort for a culpable infringement of his ownership [in the rented property] even after the expiry of the six-month prescription period [applicable to contractual claims, according to § 558 (1) BGB], the aim of § 558 BGB, namely the rapid settlement of the landlord-tenant relationship after the end of the lease, would be gravely undermined* [emphasis added]. In addition, § 558(1) BGB is worded in general terms. It refers to 'claims for reparation' without more—and not, more specifically, to claims arising out of the accessory contractual warranty. The wording also covers claims in tort, and the legislature obviously intended that it be so . . .

c) *The peculiarities discussed above justify that claims in tort are exceptionally made subject to a shorter contractual prescription period. They do not come to bear, however, as regards the prescription period in commercial sale contracts* [emphasis added]. In any event, the wording of § 477 BGB cannot support the inclusion of claims in tort [under the short prescription period set out therein], since

---

[85] § 477(1) BGB reads: "The claim for cancellation of the sale or reduction of the price, as well as the claim for reparation in consequence of a defect in a characteristic represented to exist, is barred, unless the seller has concealed the defect fraudulently, in six months from delivery for movables and in one year for immovable property. The limitation period can be contractually extended."

[86] § 852(1) BGB reads: "The claim for reparation in tort is barred after three years from the time at which the victim has knowledge of the harm and the identity of the person liable, and regardless of this knowledge after thirty years from the date the tortious act was committed."

it mentions only claims under accessory contractual warranties, contrary to the wording of § 558(1) BGB . . . "

Notes

(1) Concurrence of remedies in contract and in tort becomes a problem where, as a result of differences in the applicable rules, it is more advantageous for the plaintiff to sue in either contract or in tort, in view of the injury suffered. Where those differences arise not because of an inherent characteristic of the harm suffered, but rather out of historical—and now often artificial—differences relating to the contractual or delictual nature of the liability, they are cumbersome for the administration of justice. They promote inefficiency by encouraging litigants (and their counsel) to exploit artificial differences when pursuing their interests. It would, of course, be desirable to eliminate or at least reduce those artificial differences, but that may be "crying for the moon", as Lord Goff stated in his speech in the second annotated document.[87]

(2) In her *Introduction à la responsabilité*,[88] G. Viney makes a critical analysis of the differences between contract and tort in French law, in order to identify those which are justifiable and those which are not. She concludes that there is no justification, for instance, for Article 1150 C.civ., which does not allow compensation of unforeseeable damage under the law of contract (except in cases of fraud or gross fault), whereas unforeseeable damage can be recovered under the law of tort. Similarly, she sees no justification for the differential treatment of exoneration clauses, the validity of which is admitted as against contractual liability, at least in principle, but not as against tortious liability, since tortious liability is regarded, by some, to be of a public order nature (*d'ordre public*).[89] In the end, she comes to the general conclusion that, under French law, there is no decisive reason to treat the reparation of damage differently in contract than in tort.[90] As mentioned in the excerpt from her book above, litigants and their counsel already tend to ignore existing differences and to place their claims as much as possible in the realm of torts "either by overtly opting for the application of Articles 1382 ff. of the *Code civil*, or by simply abstaining from presenting the reasons which would lead to the application of contract law".[91]

(3) If and when a legal system allows differences to exist, justifiably or not, some rules of precedence are needed. As pointed out by Lord Goff in the second annotated document, there are broadly speaking two possible solutions, ie "either to insist that the claimant should pursue his remedy in contract alone, or to allow him to choose which remedy he prefers". French law chose the former solution, called *non-cumul*, or rather

---

[87] See also P. Cane, *The Anatomy of Tort Law* (Oxford: Hart Publishing, 1997) at 23.

[88] Viney, *Introduction* at 426 ff., para. 233 ff.

[89] Viney, *Introduction* at 429–31, para. 236. See Le Tourneau and Cadiet at 158–9 and 174, para. 470–2 and 532; B. Starck, H. Roland and L. Boyer, *Obligations—Vol. 2: Contrat* (Paris: Litec, 1995) at 728, para. 1764. This proposition is, however, highly criticized by other writers, who would rather recognize exoneration clauses within the boundaries applicable in the field of contract liability: see H., L. and J. Mazéaud and F. Chabas, *Leçons de droit civil—Vol. II/1: Obligations. Théorie générale,* 8th edn. (Paris: Montchrestien, 1991) at 778, para. 638.

[90] Viney, ibid. at 431, para. 236.

[91] Obviously, that holds true only for a legal system where, as in French law, the scope of protection of tort law is very extensive: see *infra*, 1.4.2.

non-option;[92] it is well established in the case law of the Cour de cassation that "Articles 1382ff. C.civ. [on tort law] do not apply where a fault has been committed in the performance of an obligation resulting from a contract".[93] The arguments in favour of this position, approved by the majority of legal writers,[94] are given in the first annotated document, an excerpt from G. Viney's book. They are based, in substance, on respect for legislative intention and the will of the contracting parties. In contradistinction, English and German law have opted for the second solution, considering that respect for the will of the contracting parties "does not necessarily require the total rejection of concurrence, but only so far as a concurrent remedy in tort is inconsistent with the terms of the contract".[95] The legislative intent is sufficiently taken into account by preventing the application of tort law where it would frustrate the meaning and purpose of a provision concerning contract law, for instance a shorter limitation period for claims arising out of the contract.[96]

According to C. von Bar,[97] a legal system would retain the second solution—ie allowing a plaintiff to choose between contract and tort—mainly because that system gives a narrow scope to protected interests under tort law, as is the case with English and German law with respect to pure economic losses (or *reiner Vermögensschaden*). If the claimant, in such a situation, were not allowed to choose, his or her rights would not be sufficiently protected. Conversely, a legal system might evolve towards "non-option", as in French law, if the law of tort begins to protect "pure" economic interests as well, since it would then wish to prevent the domain of contractual liability from being invaded entirely by tort law.

(4) In any event, "non-option", as it has been adopted in French law, suffers from many exceptions in the case law of the Cour de cassation. First, when a breach of contract also qualifies as a criminal act—e.g. because fraud, embezzlement or another criminal offense was committed in the process—the claimant may choose a tortious remedy by joining his civil claim to the penal claim before a criminal court (the so-called *action civile*[98]), an

---

[92] "Non-option" is to be preferred, as "non-cumul" gives the impression that the principle is to prohibit plaintiffs to claim compensation twice. Such prohibition follows, however, from the general principle that full compensation can be obtained but *no more*: see *infra*, Chapter VIII, 8.2. For a practical example of the workings of non-option in an area which borders on both tort and contract, see the discussion of product liability under French law, *infra*, Chapter VI, 6.3.1.B.

[93] Cass. civ., 11 January 1922, D 1922.I.16 is the leading case. It has been confirmed in many later judgments, among which Cass. civ. 2e, 9 June 1993, Bull. civ. 1993.II.204 (building contractor and employer); Cass. civ. 1re, 27 January 1993, Gaz.Pal. 1993.Jur.434, with note by F. Chabas (contrat d'assistance bénévole); Cass. civ. 1re, 4 November 1992, Bull. civ. 1992.I.276; Cass. comm., 26 February 1985, Bull. civ. 1985.IV.78 (insurance); Cass. civ. 1re, 11 May 1982, (1983) RTDciv. 145, with note by G. Durry (plumbing); Cass. civ. 2e, 9 April 1970, JCP 1970.IV.136 (free loan); Cass. civ. 1re, 23 November 1966, D 1966.313, with note by M. Cabrillac (bull fight).

[94] H. and L. Mazeaud, J. Mazéaud and F. Chabas, *Leçons de droit civil.—Vol. II/1: Obligations. Théorie générale*, 8th edn. (Paris: Montchrestien, 1991) at 385, para. 404; Le Tourneau and Cadiet at 122, para. 345–346; B. Starck, H. Roland and L. Boyer, *Obligations—Vol. 2: Contrat* (Paris: Litec, 1995) at 762, para. 1837–1838. See, however, the critical opinion of Viney, *Introduction* especially at 436–437, para. 239–1.

[95] Lord Goff in the excerpt, *supra*, **1.E.14.**

[96] As stated by the BGH in the excerpt, *supra*, **1.G.15.** In that case, the application of tort law was not excluded but instances were mentioned where that would have been the case if e.g. the short limitation period was intended, as between lessor and lessee, to avoid lengthy discussions between contracting parties at the end of the contract.

[97] von Bar I at 437 ff., para. 419 ff.

[98] For more details on the procedure, see Chapter II, 2.5.1., Introductory Note under a).

exception traditionally explained by the procedural impossibility for the claimant to plead in a criminal court on the basis of breach of contract.[99] However, if the claimant chooses to bring his or her action before a civil court, the rules on contractual liability are solely applicable. Secondly, in cases of personal injury in the performance of a transport contract, close relatives of the immediate victim who suffer "reflex" damage (*victimes par ricochet*) are sometimes regarded as third-party beneficiaries of the contract, by virtue of an implied stipulation in their favour (*stipulation pour autrui*). They can then choose to claim under contract law or tort law by either accepting or refusing the benefit of that stipulation.[100] Thirdly, where the owner of a building is liable to his or her neighbour for damage to the neighbour's property resulting from a construction defect for which the building contractor or the architect is responsible, the owner may sue the contractor or the architect to recover the sums paid to the neighbour; the recourse of the owner can be either in contract, on the basis of his or her own rights under the contract with the contractor or the architect, or in tort on the basis of rights of the neighbour under tort law, in which he or she has been subrogated.[101] Finally, some writers consider liability for fraud as between contracting parties as an instance of concurrent liability as well, but the majority view regards this instance as one of purely contractual liability.[102]

Where "non-option" is the rule, it prevents a contracting party from suing the other party not only on the basis of Articles 1382 and 1383 C.civ. (the general head of liability under French tort law), but also on the basis of the more specific heads of Article 1384(1) C.civ. (liability without fault for things) or Article 1384(5) C.civ. (vicarious liability).[103] However, the impact of non-option in this respect was lessened by the Cour de cassation, which introduced a contractual regime of liability for things used in the performance of the contract, resembling the tortious liability regime of Article 1384(1) C.civ.[104] When the implicit obligations to ensure safety (*obligations de sécurité*) in contractual relationships

---

[99] M. Espagnon, "Droit à réparation" in *Juris-Classeur Civil*, v° Art. 1146 à 1155, para. 66; H. and L. Mazeaud, J. Mazeaud and F. Chabas, *Leçons de droit civil—Vol. II/1: Obligations. Théorie générale*, 8th edn. (Paris: Montchrestien, 1991) at 386, para. 404. That proposition is criticized by Viney, *Introduction* at 412–413, para. 223 and G. Viney, Chronique, JCP 1994.I.3773; Le Tourneau and Cadiet at 122–123, para. 347; B. Starck, H. Roland and L. Boyer, *Obligations—Vol. 2: Contrat* (Paris: Litec, 1995) at 764, para. 1843.

[100] Mazeaud and Chabas, ibid. at 386, para. 404; Le Tourneau and Cadiet at 123, para. 348.

[101] G. Durry, *La distinction de la responsabilité contractuelle et de la responsabilité délictuelle* (Montréal: McGill University, 1986) at 166, para. 203; M. Espagnon, "Droit à réparation" in *Juris-Classeur Civil*, v° Art. 1146 à 1155, para. 67; Le Tourneau and Cadiet at 106, para. 348; P. Malaurie and L. Aynès, *Cours de droit civil—Vol. VI, Les obligations*, 7th edn. (Paris: Cujas, 1996), at 520–521, para. 882. See among others Cass. civ. 3e, 10 January 1984, Bull.civ. 1984.III.5.

[102] Espagnon, Ibid. at para. 64; H. and L. Mazéaud, J. Mazéaud and F. Chabas, *Leçons de droit civil—Vol. II/1: Obligations. Théorie générale*, 8th edn. (Paris: Montchestien, 1991) at 385–386, para. 404; F. Terré, P. Simler and Y. Lequette, *Droit civil. Les obligations* (Paris: Dalloz, 1996) at 440 and 682, para. 540 and 835. Contractual liability in cases of fraud is however assessed on the basis of different—and stricter—rules than other cases of contractual liability. For example, compensation will also extend to unforeseeable damage, according to Art. 1150 C.civ.

[103] Le Tourneau and Cadiet at 121, para. 343 in fine; B. Starck, H. Roland and L. Boyer, *Obligations—Vol. II: Contrat* (Paris: Litec, 1995) at 761, para. 1835. See as to Art. 1384(1) C.civ.: Cass. civ. 2e, 26 May 1992, Bull. civ. 1992.II.154 (fire damaging car in repairing a central heating system); Cass. civ. 1re, 9 March 1970, (1971) RTDciv. 139, with note by G. Durry (restaurant); Cass. civ. 1re, 30 October 1962, D 1963. Jur.57 (medical contract); Cass. civ. 1re, 7 December 1955, D 1956.Jur.136 (explosion while refilling gas cylinder). As to Art. 1384 (5) C.civ., see among others: Cass. civ. 1re, 11 January 1989, JCP 1989.II.21326, with note by C. Larroumet (insurance contract).

[104] Cass. civ. 1re, 17 January 1995, *infra*, Chapter VI, **6.F.30.**

are so broadly construed, suing under contract law becomes equally attractive for the plaintiff, and the practical impact of non-option is limited by the same token.[105]

(5) The previous paragraphs should not lead one to believe that, in contrast, no difficulties would arise in legal systems, like German or English law, which allow "option" and therefore accept as a general rule that each claim can be framed in tort or in contract, as the case may be. For instance, in the BGH decision reproduced above, the issue was whether a shorter prescription period laid down in the BGB for claims arising from a specific type of contract (commercial sale) would also apply as against a claim in tort arising from a contractual relationship of that type.[106] The answer in such situations depends on whether the application of the provision of contract law, as interpreted in accordance with its purpose and wording, would be frustrated if it did not apply to claims in tort as well. Similar questions arise where the BGB limits liability in contractual matters, as in § 521 (donor), § 599 (lender of a thing), § 680 (caretaker) or § 690 (custodian without remuneration), or where liability is limited as a result of a contractual exoneration clause. The answer depends here again on the interpretation of the rule in question; generally, the provision of the BGB or the contractual clause is held to apply to the claim in tort as well.[107]

It appears from the foregoing that, notwithstanding the general principle that claims in contract or in tort must be assessed in accordance with the rules that apply to each of them respectively, interactions (*Wechselwirkungen*) cannot be excluded.[108]

(6) In *Henderson v. Merrett Syndicates Ltd.* (second document above), the House of Lords had to decide whether the duty of care (in tort) of the agents towards the so-called Direct Names was excluded because there was a direct contractual relationship between the Names and the agents. The House of Lords answered in the negative; the duty of care would be excluded only if it appeared that "the tortious duty is so inconsistent with the applicable contract that . . . the parties must be taken to have agreed that the tortious remedy is to be limited or excluded" (per Lord Goff).

In that judgment, the House of Lords also held that the tortious duty of care was not excluded by the presence of a chain of contracts, where the relationship between the Names and the agents was not direct, but structured in two successive agreements; that issue is discussed under the following heading.

1.3.2. CONTRACTUAL CHAINS

The following cases can be found at <http://www.rechten.unimaas.nl/casebook>:
1.F.16. Cass. Ass. plén., 12 July 1991. Defective plumbing.

---

[105] For an overview of these *obligations de sécurité*, see Viney and Jourdain, *Conditions* at 398–412, para. 499–501.

[106] The reverse, i.e. tort rules which have an impact on contractual situations, does not occur according to D. Medicus, *Schuldrecht—Vol. I, Allgemeiner Teil*, 8th edn. (München: Beck, 1995) at 171, para. 359.

[107] Medicus, ibid. at 171 para. 359–60; Larenz/Canaris at 596–598.

[108] For an interesting case involving the application of § 634 BGB relating to the right of a contractor to repair defects in the work during a specified period of time (*Nachbesserungsfrist*), see BGH, 7 November 1985, NJW 1986, 922 where such interaction was accepted in order to secure the contractor's right under § 634 when a claim was brought in tort as well.

1.E.17. House of Lords, *Henderson* v. *Merrett Syndicates Ltd*. Direct names at Lloyd's.
1.G.18. BGH, 2 July 1996. Tempered steel.
1.EC.19. ECJ, 17 June 1992, *Handte* v. *TMS*. Defective metal-polishing machines.

1.4. THE APPROACH OF TORT LAWS IN GENERAL

In this section we follow a "chronological" order. Thus, we shall deal first with English law, which is still very much influenced by ancient rules. Then we shall deal with French law, where the *Code civil* of 1804 marked a reaction against the traditional piecemeal approach in laying down the general principles of Article 1382 and 1383. Thereafter we shall discuss German law, which steers a middle course. In the last two subsections, the Nordic legal systems and the more recent codifications are referred to.

1.4.1. THE ENGLISH APPROACH

1.4.1.A. SPECIFIC HEADS OF TORTIOUS LIABILITY. DUTY OF CARE UNDER THE TORT OF NEGLIGENCE. BREACH OF STATUTORY DUTY.

Introductory Note

a) English law has followed Roman law longer than the Continental legal systems by retaining *specific heads of tortious liability*, each of which was originally covered by a different "writ". Even now, after "the great reforms of 1875 . . . Anglo-American lawyers, judges and attorneys alike, still habitually and automatically tend to classify the case before them as falling within one of the traditional types of tort . . .".[109] Those traditional types of tort include various forms of trespass to the person, trespass to land, nuisance, trespass to chattels and specific economic torts, such as fraud or deceit, inducing breach of contract, passing off, malicious falsehood, conspiracy and intimidation.[110] Each of them has separate requirements which must be satisfied in order to give rise to liability. They may be relied on cumulatively, that is they are not exclusive of one another.[111]

Each of these specific torts protects a particular interest against a specified form of encroachment. As a consequence, some interests may remain unprotected; that attendant risk has been greatly reduced, however, through the evolution of the tort of negligence (developed out of the "action on the case" or "trespass on the case") into an independent ground of tortious liability in the course of the nineteenth century. Negligence has now become the most general and, in practice, also the most important tort. For a person to be liable in negligence, the following requirements must be satisfied: the defendant was under a *duty of care* owed to the *group of persons* of which the victim was one; he has been

---

[109] Zweigert and Kötz at 605.
[110] For a short description, *infra*, **1.E.19.**
[111] *Infra*, **1.E.18.**

in *breach* of that duty of care; and the *damage* was caused by the breach and was *not too remote* a consequence of it. In all of these elements the concept of foreseeability plays a part.[112]

b) Among the specific common law torts the tort of *breach of statutory duty* takes a special place because of its uneasy relationship with the tort of negligence, an issue which arose again recently in *X. v. Bedfordshire County Council*.[113] Breach of statutory duty is a specific tort which gives rise to a civil remedy in tort, *if* that is the express or implied purpose of the statutory provision in question, at the suit of a person who was intended by the statutory provision to enjoy the civil remedy and who has been injured as a result of another person—often a public authority—not complying with a duty imposed upon him or her by the statute.[114]

The question of the relationship of the tort of breach of statutory duty to the tort of negligence turns around the issue of whether it is a wholly separate tort superimposed on the tort of negligence or whether it rather "concretizes" negligence, putting it beyond controversy that non-compliance with the statutory requirement in question *per se* constitutes negligence.[115]

W.V.H. Rogers, Winfield & Jolowicz on Tort[116]   **1.E.20.–22.**
and
K. Zweigert and H. Kötz, An Introduction to Comparative Law[117]

1. W.V.H. Rogers, *Winfield & Jolowicz on Tort*   **1.E.20.**

"In the course of English legal history certain forms of tortious liability have gained specific names, such as assault, battery, libel, slander, nuisance and negligence. The fact that they acquired such names was due to mere accidents of terminology traceable probably to their frequent occurrence. In the following chapters it is proposed to deal with these particular torts. But it is important to remember that they do not exhaust the content of tortious liability. Outside these nominate torts there are wrongs which are well known to exist but which have no compendious name; beyond these again are wrongs which may possibly be torts, but of which it is impossible to say whether they are such or not. Thus, as a family group, torts may be divided into those which received names soon after birth, those which seem to be awaiting baptism in their riper years and those whose paternity is uncertain enough to make it doubtful whether they ought to be included in the family at all.

It is also important to remember that these nominate torts are not exclusive of one another and that there is no reason why a given set of facts should not contain the elements of several of them. Since the plaintiff does not, today, have to specify the particular tort on which he wishes to rely, all that is necessary for his success is that the facts of his case should include those essential to liability under one tort, without at the same time including any which are fatal to that liability. But the whole sequence of events leading up to the plaintiff's damage may include the essentials of more than one tort . . . It is not, however, in accordance with the principles of the common law to analyse

---

[112] Zweigert and Kötz at 610 and Rogers at 90 and 194.
[113] [1995] 2 AC 633, [1995] 3 WLR 152, [1995] 3 All ER 353, HL.
[114] Rogers at 247 ff.
[115] See further Rogers at 247–48.
[116] 15th edn. (London: Sweet & Maxwell, 1998) at 56–9 (under 1.), 90–1 (under 3.) (footnotes omitted).
[117] 3rd revised edn., translated by T. Weir (Oxford: Clarendon, 1998) at 605–8.

rights as something separate from the remedy given to the plaintiff, so that although we have abolished procedural restrictions of the *forms* of action, it is still necessary for the plaintiff to establish a *cause* of action. It is not therefore correct to say that a person has a basic right not to have untruths told about himself, for he is only able to restrain the publication of such untruths if the circumstances in which they are disseminated fall within a specific tort such as passing off, injurious falsehood or defamation . . .

The plaintiff may, of course, have practical reasons for not pursuing all the causes of action available. In *Joyce* v. *Sengupta* a statement published about the plaintiff was clearly defamatory on its face but the plaintiff sued only for the tort of injurious falsehood because legal aid is not available for defamation. An argument that this was an abuse of the process of the court was rejected, for

> 'when more than one cause of action is available to him, a plaintiff may choose which he will pursue. Usually, he pursues all available causes of action but he is not obliged to do so. He may pursue one to the exclusion of another . . . I have never heard it suggested before that a plaintiff is not entitled to proceed in this way . . . [or] that he must pursue the most appropriate remedy.' "

2. K. Zweigert and H. Kötz, *An Introduction to Comparative Law* 1.E.21.

"One of the oldest tort claims in the Common Law is trespass. The writ of trespass originally led to a penalty as well as to compensatory damages and was issued wherever a person forcibly and in breach of the peace—*vi et armis contra pacem domini regis*—invaded another's quiet possession of land or moveables (trespass to land or to chattels) or affected his physical integrity (trespass to the person). Just like the *actio legis Aquiliae*, trespass required a direct attack on the person or thing against the will of the plaintiff. If the harm to the plaintiff occurred only as the indirect result of the defendant's conduct or, even directly, from an omission to act, the trespass claim was unavailable; by contrast very little attention was paid in earlier times to the question whether the defendant's behaviour must have been deliberate or negligent. During the fourteenth century an action of trespass on the case, later called simply 'action on the case', was introduced to cover areas where trespass did not apply, where the plaintiff's injury was an indirect consequence of the defendant's conduct, positive or negative. The distinction was clearly drawn by Blackstone J in *Scott* v. *Shepherd* (1773) 2 WmBl 892, 96 ER 525. 'If I throw a log of timber into the highway (which is an unlawful act) and another man tumbles over it and is hurt, an action on the case only lies, it being a consequential damage; but if in throwing I hit another man, he may bring trespass because it is an immediate wrong.'

The distinction between causing harm intentionally and negligently was not clearly made in the Common Law to begin with. In the example just given, provided that the log hit the plaintiff during its flight, the trespass claim lay whether the defendant intended to cause the harm or merely acted negligently in throwing the log into the highway. As time went on, however, the trespass claim was gradually limited to cases of intentional harm, and today intentional conduct is required for those specific torts which developed out of the writ of trespass to the person, namely *assault* (the direct threat of immediate corporeal contact), *battery* (personal injury), and *false imprisonment*. The same is true for trespass to land, the unauthorized entry on premises occupied by another.

Liability in trespass is incurred by a person who enters the land of another without his consent, whether on, above or below the surface, or causes anyone else or any thing (for example rocks, refuse, water) to do so. Liability in damages only arises if the act which constitutes or causes the invasion is intentional, though the defendant need not have known that the land in question belonged to another. If a person conducts activities on his own land which unintentionally lead to damage on a neighbouring property, the modern view is that trespass only lies if he was negligent in causing the damage. For example, if bricks fall on to the plaintiff's land or harmful vibrations are caused by the defendants' explosions, the defendant is not liable in trespass if he observed the requisite precautions, though he is generally liable regardless of fault, at least in the USA, on the principle of *Rylands* v. *Fletcher*. If smoke, vapours, smells, and so on unduly affect a person's land, the person causing them is liable, again regardless of fault, in the tort of *nuisance*, whose pedigree is as long as that of trespass. The distinction between liability in trespass to land, nuisance, and *Rylands* v. *Fletcher* is extremely fine and varies from jurisdiction to jurisdiction within the common law.

Much the same is true of the tort remedies which protect a person's *moveable property* against improper invasions of his rights. Here the Common Law offers three torts which partially overlap: *trespass to chattels*, *detinue*, and *conversion*. Conversion, the most important of these in practice, is applicable when the defendant has done something in relation to the plaintiff's moveable property which is inconsistent with the plaintiff's ownership. The thief who takes the thing away from the owner is liable in conversion, but so also is a person who consumes the goods of others or destroys or alters them or who sells or pledges them with a third party . . .

The sole requirement for liability in conversion is that the defendant should consciously and intentionally have dealt with the goods. The defendant need not have been at fault: he will be liable in damages even if he believed in good faith that the thing he consumed or used was his own or reasonably thought he was entitled to consume or use it . . .

So far we have been dealing mainly with torts which generally involve an intentional interference with the integrity of person and property and which normally appear in books under the heading 'Intentional Interference with Persons or Property'. But the Common Law has a number of other torts which give protection against *economic loss* intentionally caused. These torts correspond to some of the types of case in Germany where liability is imposed under § 826 BGB for causing harm intentionally and immorally. A person who knowingly deceives another by means of a false statement of fact is liable for *fraud* or *deceit* and must pay for the consequent harm (*Derry* v. *Peek* (1889) 14 AppCas 377). A person who knowingly induces another to break a contract with the plaintiff is liable to the plaintiff for the tort of *inducing breach of contract* (see *Lumley* v. *Gye* (1853) 2 El&Bl 216, 118 ER 749). A person is liable for *passing off*, in the absence of any special statute regarding trade-marks, design patterns, and so on, if he sells goods so like those of another manufacturer in name, construction, or packaging that consumers cannot easily distinguish their origins. If a person in bad faith makes false, but not necessarily defamatory or offensive, statements about the plaintiff which cause him harm in his trade or profession, the plaintiff may recover for this economic loss by the tort of *malicious falsehood* . . . If a person threatens another with violence or other serious harm so as to cause that person to harm a third party, the third party may sue for *intimidation*, supposing he can satisfy the other requirements laid down by a series of cases.

This tort occurs most frequently in labour law, where there is an improper threat of a strike. In *Rookes* v. *Barnard* [1964] AC 1129, the defendant trade unionists threatened their employer with a strike unless he forthwith gave notice to an employee who had just left the union after repeated disputes. The employer yielded to this threat and the employee who had lost his job brought a direct claim for intimidation against the trade unionists for compensation for the loss caused to him by his dismissal. The House of Lords allowed the claim on appeal.

Other important Common Law torts are concerned with the protection of honour, professional reputation, and privacy against attack . . .

In order to complete our survey of the Anglo-American law of tort, we must now turn to the tort which is the most important in practice, namely *negligence*.

Negligence as a tort, like many other torts in the modern Common Law, developed out of the action of trespass on the case and was not recognized as an independent ground of tortious liability until the nineteenth century. The external stimulus for the development was the great growth in the use of machinery in industry and transport and the large increase in accidents which this led to. Such accidents were normally not caused intentionally, and their proliferation brought people to see that their typical feature was the reprehensible neglect of the requisite care and that *this* fact was the real ground for holding the defendant liable. This line of thought was decisively advanced by the fact that the principle of 'no liability without fault' answered the extreme liberalism of the time and served the interests of early entrepreneurial capitalism; this became the key idea of the law of tort and its appropriate legal form was the tort of negligence which now became more and more independent."

3. W.V.H. Rogers, *Winfield & Jolowicz on Tort*   **1.E.22.**

"It is not for every careless act that a man may be held responsible in law, nor even for every careless act that causes damage. He will only be liable in negligence if he is under a legal duty to take care. It may be objected that "duty" is not confined to the law of negligence and that it is an element in every tort, because there is a legal duty not to commit assault or battery, not to commit defamation, not to commit nuisance and so forth. But all that "duty" signifies in these other torts is that you must not commit them: they have their own, detailed, internal rules which define the circumstances in which they are committed and duty adds nothing to those. But in the tort of negligence, breach of "duty" is the chief ingredient of the tort; in fact there is no other except damage to the plaintiff. A general liability for carelessly causing harm to others would, at least as things are perceived by the courts, be too onerous for a practical system of law and we shall see that there are important areas of activity and important types of loss where the law of negligence does not intervene. Duty is the primary control device which allows the courts to keep liability for negligence within acceptable limits, and the controversies which have centred around the criteria for the existence of a duty reflect differences of opinion as to the proper ambit of the law of negligence.

The concept of duty has in recent years shown signs of becoming an arcane mystery but much difficulty will be avoided if it is grasped at the outset that duty is fulfilling two functions. It is true that the question in every case is 'did *this* defendant owe a duty of care to *this* plaintiff?' for the courts do not decide academic issues but disputes between parties. Nevertheless, in most of the cases in this section the courts have been concerned with broader questions which transcend the particular dispute and which are essentially concerned with whether, and if so how far, the law of negligence should operate in a situation of a certain type. Discussion is therefore couched in terms of general categories, such as 'Is there a duty of care not to cause economic loss by statements?' or 'Is there a duty to prevent a third party inflicting harm on another' and the court is essentially concerned with mapping the limits of the law of negligence and identifying those areas in which there are factors (fairness, practicability, risk of untoward consequences) which suggest that the law should not give a remedy for negligent conduct or at least should do so only to a limited extent. It was, therefore, perfectly possible for the House of Lords in *Hedley Byrne & Co. Ltd.* v. *Heller & Partners Ltd.* to decide (a) that there was a duty of care recognised by English law in respect of statements but (b) no duty was owed on the facts by the defendant to the plaintiff. In this sense the issue of duty arises comparatively rarely and tends to be the preserve of the highest courts. However, most cases of negligence arise from acts causing physical damage to person or property and there the law is much more straightforward. No one would think of opening a running-down case by citing authorities to show that a duty of care was owed by a driver to a pedestrian. Speaking of damage to property (and if anything the proposition must be even more true with regard to personal injury) the Privy Council has said that 'the question of the existence of a duty of care does not give rise to any problem because it is self-evident that such a duty exists and the contrary view is unarguable'. If, however, a duty does exist in this general sense then there may be an issue whether it is applicable to the particular facts before the court or, as it is sometimes said, whether it was owed to the particular plaintiff. For example, the House of Lords in *Donoghue* v. *Stevenson* was concerned with the general question of whether a manufacturer owed a duty of care to the ultimate user of his products and the conclusion was that he did. If, however, the product had been stolen from his factory and taken to Australia where, many years later, it caused injury to P, then it might be a difficult question to determine whether a duty was owed to P, that is to say, whether P was a foreseeable victim of the initial negligence in manufacture. This is the second sense of duty but if there is no duty in the first, general sense we never get to the second question. Unless we keep this fundamental distinction in mind we have no means of explaining those situations in which foreseeable damage goes without legal redress."

Notes

(1) The extracts reprinted above are self-explanatory. The second, taken from Zweigert and Kötz, a German textbook, has been chosen because it describes briefly and systematically various "nominate" torts and offers a general overview.[118]

(2) As Rogers emphasizes in the third excerpt, the concept of duty relates both to the question whether a duty of care should *generally* be imposed on defendants in a given set of circumstances such as those arising in the case and to the more concrete question of whether, *in the actual circumstances of the case* the defendant owed a duty of care to the particular plaintiff. As pointed out by Rogers,[119] the latter question refers to the celebrated pronouncement of the House of Lords in *Donoghue* v. *Stevenson*, where "neighbours"—those to whom the duty is owed—are defined as "persons who are so closely and directly affected by my act that I ought reasonably to have them in contemplation".[120] The test is not one of physical closeness but of foresight, that is whether the victim was a foreseeable victim. That does not mean, however, that the victim needs to be "identifiable by the defendant. It is enough that he should be one of a class within the area of foreseeable injury".[121] Thus in *Haley* v. *London Electricity Board*, it was held that the plaintiff, who was blind, could sue the defendants who, while digging a trench in the street, had failed to take appropriate precautions for blind persons, who collectively are sufficiently numerous to make it foreseeable that one of them might well walk by.[122]

(3) In the third excerpt, Rogers also points out that the existence of a duty of care is readily acknowledged in the case of *acts* causing physical damage to a person or property. The Privy Council, in a case of damage to property, said that the existence of a duty is "self-evident" and "the contrary view is unarguable".[123] However, as appears from the recent case *Marc Rich & Co AG* v. *Bishop Rock Marine Co. Ltd.*, also a case of damage to property, there are situations where the contrary view may prevail for reasons of public policy.[124] Moreover, the Privy Council pronouncement does not hold true for *omissions* causing damage to person or property, where the law is far from straightforward.[125]

---

[118] For a more extensive survey, see von Bar I at 281–97, paras. 254–73. For the specific torts of libel, malicious falsehood, trespass to the person and passing-off, see *Kaye* v. *Robertson*, *infra*, Chapter II, **2.E.32.**

[119] Rogers at 114.

[120] *Infra*, **1.E.23.**

[121] Rogers at 115.

[122] [1965] AC 778, [1964] 3 All ER 185, HL.

[123] *Mobil Oil Hong Kong Ltd.* v. *Hong Kong United Dockyards Ltd.* [1991] 1 Lloyd's Rep 309 at 328, PC, referred to by Rogers, **1.E.21.**

[124] [1996] 1 AC 211, [1995] 3 WLR 227, [1995] 3 All ER 307, HL, discussed *infra*, 1.4.1.B., Introductory Note under e).

[125] *Smith* v. *Littlewoods Organisation Ltd.*, *infra*, Chapter III, **3.E.5.**

1.4.1.B. *DONOGHUE* V. *STEVENSON* AND SUBSEQUENT DEVELOPMENTS

Introductory Note

a) As is already apparent from the foregoing, unlike French or German law, English tort law is not to be found under a civil code heading or even in a specific piece of legislation. By and large it has remained the province of the traditional case-based common law (the liability in tort of occupiers of land to lawful visitors being a notable exception). Accordingly, the general conditions for liability in negligence to arise cannot be found in any text such as Article 1382 C.civ. or § 823(1) BGB. The House of Lords decision in *Donoghue* v. *Stevenson*, however, comes close to the enunciation of a general principle.[126] In *Donoghue* v. *Stevenson*, Lord Atkin tried to find in English law "some general conception of relations giving rise to a duty of care, of which the particular cases found in the books are but instances". He found that general conception in the "neighbour principle", described in this oft-quoted passage:

> "Who then, in law, is my neighbour? The answer seems to be—persons who are so closely and directly affected by my act that I ought reasonably to have them in contemplation as being so affected when I am directing my mind to the acts or omissions which are called in question."

b) Despite the general terms in which Lord Atkin framed the "neighbour principle" in *Donoghue* v. *Stevenson*, it was not until its 1970 decision in *Home Office* v. *Dorset Yacht Co. Ltd* that the House of Lords gave effect to Lord Atkin's broad approach by holding that the "neighbour principle" is applicable in all cases, unless there is some special reason for its exclusion.[127] This trend towards a more generalized and policy-oriented analysis culminated in *Anns* v. *Merton London Borough Council*, where Lord Wilberforce introduced the so-called "two-stage test" in the following terms:[128]

> "Through the trilogy of cases in this House, *Donoghue* v. *Stevenson*, *Hedley Byrne & Co Ltd* v. *Heller & Partners Ltd*, and *Home Office* v. *Dorset Yacht Co Ltd*, the position has now been reached that in order to establish that a duty of care arises in a particular situation, it is not necessary to bring the facts of that situation within those of previous situations in which a duty of care has been held to exist. Rather the question has to be approached in two stages. First one has to ask whether, as between the alleged wrongdoer and the person who has suffered damage there is a sufficient relationship of proximity or neighbourhood such that, in the reasonable contemplation of the former, carelessness on his part may be likely to cause damage to the latter, in which case a *prima facie* duty of care arises. Secondly, if the first question is answered affirmatively, it is necessary to consider whether there are any considerations which ought to negative, or to reduce or limit the scope of the duty or the class of person to whom it is owed or the damages to which a breach of it may give rise . . ."

---

[126] *Infra*, **1.E.23.** *Donoghue* v. *Stevenson* is often seen now as enunciating a general principle, but at the time it may have been seen by many as establishing a new "tort" concerning liability to consumers on the part of negligent manufacturers of defective goods, the tort having its own rules, e.g. no opportunity for intermediate inspection.

[127] [1970] AC 1004, [1970] 2 All ER 294, HL.

[128] [1978] AC 728, HL at 751–2.

Lord Wilberforce's "elegant rationalisation"[129] was quickly taken up with enthusiasm. The high point of this period was *Junior Books Ltd* v. *Veitchi Co. Ltd*,[130] where a majority of the House of Lords, dealing with what could be viewed as economic loss, imposed liability contrary to hitherto well-established principles.[131]

Such enthusiasm did not last very long, however, and the principled approach of *Anns* was soon heftily criticized, among others by the Privy Council in *Yuen Kun Yeu* v. *Attorney-General of Hong Kong*, where Lord Keith said that the two-stage test "has been elevated to a degree of importance greater than its merits, and greater perhaps than its author intended".[132] In *Yuen Kun Yeu*, the court said that there were two possible readings of the first stage of the *Anns* formula. On the one hand, it could be that proximity means merely reasonable foreseeability of injury. On the other hand, it could be that proximity is different from reasonable foreseeability. It would then include other factors which are relevant to the assessment of the duty of care; and foreseeability would then not in and of itself imply a duty of care (always subject to the policy considerations intervening at the second stage of the *Anns* test). According to Rogers, the effect of this seems to be that proximity differs according to the type of case.[133]

c) The "renewed traditional" approach was summed up by Lord Bridge in *Caparo Industries plc.* v. *Dickman* where he wrote:[134]

> "What emerges is that, in addition to the foreseeability of damage, necessary ingredients in any situation giving rise to a duty of care are that there should exist between the party owing the duty and the party to whom it is owed a relationship characterized by the law as one of 'proximity' or 'neighbourhood' and that the situation should be one in which the court considers it fair, just and reasonable that the law should impose a duty of a given scope on the one party for the benefit of the other. But it is implicit in the passages referred to that the concepts of proximity and fairness embodied in these additional ingredients are not susceptible of any such precise definition as would be necessary to give them utility as practical tests, but amount in effect to little more than convenient labels to attach to the features of different specific situations which, on a detailed examination of all the circumstances, the law recognizes pragmatically as giving rise to a duty of care of a given scope. Whilst recognizing, of course, the importance of the underlying principles common to the whole field of negligence, I think the law has now moved in the direction of attaching greater significance to the more traditional categorization of distinct and recognizable situations as guides to the existence, the scope and the limits of the varied duties of care which the law imposes (Weir, p. 75). We must now, I think, recognize the wisdom of the words of Brennan J in the High Court of Australia in *Sutherland Shire Council* v. *Heyman* where he said:
>
>> 'It is preferable in my view, that the law should develop novel categories of negligence incrementally and by analogy with established categories, rather than by a massive extension of a *prima facie* duty of care restrained only by indefinable "considerations which ought to negative, or to reduce or limit the scope of the duty or the class of person to whom it is owed".'

One of the most important distinctions always to be observed lies in the law's essentially different approach to the different kinds of damage which one party may have suffered in consequence of the acts or omissions of another. It is one thing to owe a duty of care to avoid causing injury

---

[129] Rogers at 96.
[130] [1983] 1 AC 520, [1982] 3 All ER 201, HL.
[131] Rogers at 96.
[132] *Infra*, Chapter III, **3.E.33.**
[133] Rogers at 100.
[134] [1990] 2 AC 605 at 617–18, [1990] 1 All ER 568, HL, *infra*, Chapter 2, **2.E.47.**

to the person or property of others. It is quite another to avoid causing others to suffer purely economic loss . . .”

The motivation behind that "renewed traditional" approach was explained in the same case by Lord Oliver:[135]

"The extension of the concept of negligence since the decision of this House in *Hedley Byrne & Co Ltd* v. *Heller & Partners Ltd* to cover cases of pure economic loss not resulting from physical damage has given rise to a considerable and as yet unsolved difficulty of definition. The opportunities for the infliction of pecuniary loss from the imperfect performance of everyday tasks on the proper performance of which people rely for regulating their affairs are illimitable and the effects are far reaching. A defective bottle of ginger beer may injure a single consumer but the damage stops there. A single statement may be repeated endlessly with or without the permission of its author and may be relied on in a different way by many different people. Thus the postulate of a simple duty to avoid any harm that is, with hindsight, reasonably capable of being foreseen becomes untenable without the imposition of some intelligible limits to keep the law of negligence within the bounds of common sense and practicality. Those limits have been found by the requirement of what has been called a 'relationship of proximity' between plaintiff and defendant and by the imposition of a further requirement that the attachment of liability for harm which has occurred be 'just and reasonable'. But, although the cases in which the courts have imposed or withheld liability are capable of an approximate categorization, one looks in vain for some common denominator by which the existence of the essential relationship can be tested. Indeed, it is difficult to resist a conclusion that what have been treated as three separate requirements are, at least in most cases, in fact merely facets of the same thing, for in some cases the degree of foreseeability is such that it is from that alone that the requisite proximity can be deduced, whilst in others the absence of that essential relationship can most rationally be attributed simply to the court's view that it would not be fair and reasonable to hold the defendant responsible. 'Proximity' is, no doubt, a convenient expression so long as it is realized that it is no more than a label which embraces not a definable concept but merely a description of circumstances from which, pragmatically, the courts conclude that a duty of care exists."

This excerpt makes it plain that the return to a more traditional approach to the evolution of the law of negligence does not by any means make the law easier to ascertain.

d) In 1991, the House of Lords formally overruled *Anns* in *Murphy* v. *Brentwood District Council*.[136] There Lord Keith, one of the leading figures in the reaction to *Anns*, came to the following conclusion in his speech:

"In my opinion it is clear that *Anns* did not proceed upon any basis of established principle, but introduced a new species of liability governed by a principle indeterminate in character but having the potentiality of covering a wide range of situations . . . in which it had never hitherto been thought that the law of negligence had any proper place."

It must be pointed out that *Murphy* is by no means the final word in this debate. The judgment of the House of Lords faced much criticism from legal writers.[137]

---

[135] [1990] 2 AC 605 at 617–18, [1990] 1 All ER 568, HL, *infra*, Chapter II, **2.E.47.** at 632–3.
[136] [1991] 1 AC 398, HL.
[137] See D. Howarth, "Negligence after *Murphy*: time to re-think" (1991) 50 Camb LJ 58 and B.S. Markesinis and S. Deakin, "The Random Element of their Lordships' Infallible Judgment: An Economic and Comparative Analysis of the Tort of Negligence from *Anns* to *Murphy*" (1992) 55 Mod LR 619.

Furthermore, the other main jurisdictions in the English common law tradition have expressly refused to follow *Murphy*.[138] This came back to haunt the Law Lords in *Invercargill City Council* v. *Hamlin*, where the Privy Council was concerned with a New Zealand case whose facts were similar to *Murphy* (liability of a city council for defective buildings).[139] The Privy Council could not but acknowledge that New Zealand courts steadily refused to follow *Murphy*, like their Australian and Canadian counterparts. In view of this, the Privy Council refused to impose on New Zealand the case law of its *alter ego*, the House of Lords, and was forced to admit that "in this branch of the law more than one view is possible: there is no single answer".[140]

As a result of this criticism, some Law Lords have recently begun to make greater use of doctrinal and comparative materials in their speeches, indicating a certain willingness to re-think the law of negligence: see in particular the speeches of Lord Goff in *Smith* v. *Littlewoods*[141] and *White* v. *Jones*.[142]

e) Despite the relatively volatile state of English tort law on this point, it seems that the reaction to *Anns* has succeeded in reinstating the traditional picture of the evolution of tort law as an incremental and inductive process. In new areas, therefore, the assessment of whether a duty of care exists should proceed by analogy with established cases, and not through the application of a general overriding principle such as the one formulated by Lord Wilberforce in *Anns*.[143]

Beyond this theoretical point, there seems to be agreement among leading authors that the examination of the duty of care now involves three stages, namely (i) whether the harm was reasonably foreseeable, (ii) whether the relationship between plaintiff and defendant was sufficiently proximate and (iii) whether it is fair, just and reasonable to impose a duty of care. These three steps are however not clearly distinguished in the case law, nor are they clearly distinguishable.[144] In *Marc Rich & Co. AG* v. *Bishop Rock Marine Co. Ltd.*,[145] Lord Steyn, speaking for the majority, expressed the opinion that it is settled law that the three steps, and more particularly the last, are relevant to all cases, whatever the nature of the harm sustained by the plaintiff.

It is debatable how far the first two stages of the current understanding (foreseeability and proximity) actually differ from Lord Wilberforce's first stage in *Anns* (sufficient relationship of proximity or neighbourhood). The last stage of the current understanding (embracing fairness, justice and reasonableness) is more or less identical with the second stage of *Anns* (whether there are any policy considerations which ought to negative, or to reduce the scope of, the duty of care).

---

[138] See for instance the judgment of the Supreme Court of Canada in *Canadian National Railway Co.* v. *Norsk Pacific Steamship Co.* [1991] 1 SCR 1021.

[139] [1996] 1 AC 624, [1996] 1 All ER 756, PC.

[140] Ibid. at 766.

[141] *Infra*, Chapter III, **3.E.5.**

[142] *Infra*, Chapter II, **2.E.48.**

[143] But see the emergence of the "expanded *Hedley Byrne* principle" in the area of professional services, *infra*, Chapter II, 2.4.1., Introductory Note under d).

[144] Rogers at 96–9; Markesinis and Deakin at 83. See also the judgments of the House of Lords in *Caparo Industries plc* v. *Dickman*, *infra*, Chapter II, **2.E.47.**; *X.* v. *Bedfordshire County Council* [1995] 2 AC 633, [1995] 3 WLR 152, [1995] 3 All ER 353 and *Marc Rich & Co. AG* v. *Bishop Rock Marine Co. Ltd.* [1996] 1 AC 211, [1995] 3 WLR 227, [1995] 3 All ER 307.

[145] Ibid.

f) The main areas where the battle between a more general or principled and a more step-by-step and gradual approach has been fought are: *failure to act*,[146] *psychiatric injury*,[147] *pure economic loss*,[148] and *negligence of public authorities*.[149]

In relation to each of these categories, the controversy focuses on which conditions, if any, should be fulfilled *in addition to* reasonable foreseeability in order to find a duty of care. It is not easy to give an overview for each of them because some of the relevant cases date from the period between *Anns* and *Yuen Kun Yeu* when a more principled approach prevailed. The situation may roughly be summarized as follows:

With respect to **psychiatric injury**, the test of proximity is applied in addition to reasonable foreseeability insofar as secondary victims are concerned, whilst proximity is assumed in the case of primary victims as they are, by definition, on the scene of the wrongdoing. In the case of primary victims, therefore, reasonable foreseeability suffices to find a duty of care for both physical and psychological injury, as was decided by the House of Lords in *Page* v. *Smith*[150] whilst secondary victims must have witnessed the event or its immediate aftermath.[151]

As to **property damage and other damage consequential upon it**,[152] it suffices that harm was reasonably foreseeable to find a duty of care in principle, since it is generally assumed that proximity exists in these cases. However, that conclusion may be negatived in exceptional circumstances, if the imposition of a duty of care would not be fair, just and reasonable.[153]

As regards economic loss not consequential on harm to the plaintiff's person or on damage to property owned or possessed by the plaintiff (**pure economic loss**) and as regards **failures to act** on the part of individuals and public authorities, proximity must be found in addition to reasonable foreseeability. The degree of proximity needed differs according to the type of case. For example, in the particular case of negligent misstatements which concern liability for words and not for deeds, proximity has to be understood in terms of a "special relationship" or "relationship equivalent to contract".[154]

In addition, in the particular case of omissions on the part of **public authorities**, public policy considerations will play an important role in the overall assessment, as part of the condition that it should be fair, just and reasonable to impose a duty of care.[155]

House of Lords[156]   **1.E.23.**
Donoghue v. *Stevenson*

THE NEIGHBOUR PRINCIPLE

Snail in bottle

Despite the absence of a contractual relationship, the manufacturer of a defective product is liable under the law of negligence to a consumer injured by the product.

Facts: Mrs D went to a cafe with a friend who bought her a tumbler with ice cream, over which the shopkeeper poured a quantity of ginger beer from an opaque bottle. She drank from the tumbler and when her friend topped up the drink the remains of a decomposed snail floated out of the bottle. Mrs D became ill. The question referred to the House of Lords was whether, in the absence of any contractual relationship, the manufacturer of the ginger beer owed a duty of care to the ultimate consumer in the circumstances.

---

[146] *Infra*, Chapter III, 3.1.3.
[147] *Infra*, Chapter II, **2.E.8.–9.** and notes.
[148] *Infra*, Chapter II, 2.3.1. and 2.4.1.
[149] *Infra*, Chapter III, 3.3.1.
[150] *Infra*, Chapter II, **2.E.9.**
[151] See *Alcock* v. *Chief Constable of the South Yorkshire Police*, *infra*, **2.E.8.**
[152] Including economic loss, see *infra*, Chapter II, 2.3.1.
[153] As in *Marc Rich & Co. AG* v. *Bishop Rock Marine Co. Ltd.* [1996] 1 AC 211, [1995] 3 WLR 227, [1995] 3 All ER, 307, HL.
[154] *Infra*, Chapter II, **2.E.47.**, Notes (1) and (2).
[155] See *Hill* v. *Chief Constable of West Yorkshire* [1989] AC 53, HL and *Hughes* v. *National Union of Mineworkers* [1991] 4 All ER 278, [1991] ICR 669, QBD; see Rogers at 100–1.
[156] [1932] AC 562, [1932] All ER 1, HL.

Held: The court of first instance found that the plaintiff's ("the pursuer's")[157] statement of claim disclosed "a good cause of action" and allowed her to bring evidence that the manufacturer was at fault. The Court of Appeal reversed that judgment and rejected the plaintiff's claim, but the House of Lords, by a majority of three to two, reinstated the decision of the court of first instance.

Judgment: LORD ATKIN: "We are solely concerned with the question whether as a matter of law in the circumstances alleged the defender owed any duty to the pursuer to take care.

It is remarkable how difficult it is to find in the English authorities statements of general application defining the relations between parties that give rise to the duty. The courts are concerned with the particular relations which come before them in actual litigation, and it is sufficient to say whether the duty exists in those circumstances. The result is that the courts have been engaged upon an elaborate classification of duties as they exist in respect of property, whether real or personal, with further divisions as to ownership, occupation or control, and distinctions based on the particular relations of the one side or the other, whether manufacturer, salesman or landlord, customer, tenant, stranger, and so on. In this way it can be ascertained at any time whether the law recognizes a duty, but only where the case can be referred to some particular species which has been examined and classified. And yet the duty which is common to all the cases where liability is established must logically be based upon some element common to the cases where it is found to exist. To seek a complete logical definition of the general principle is probably to go beyond the function of the judge, for, the more general the definition, the more likely it is to omit essentials or introduce non-essentials . . .

At present I content myself with pointing out that in English law there must be and is some general conception of relations giving rise to a duty of care, of which the particular cases found in the books are but instances. The liability for negligence, whether you style it such or treat it as in other systems as a species of '*culpa*', is no doubt based upon a general public sentiment of moral wrongdoing for which the offender must pay. But acts or omissions which any moral code would censure cannot in a practical world be treated so as to give a right to every person injured by them to demand relief. In this way rules of law arise which limit the range of complainants and the extent of their remedy. The rule that you are to love you neighbour becomes in law: You must not injure your neighbour, and the lawyer's question: Who is my neighbour? receives a restricted reply. You must take reasonable care to avoid acts or omissions which you can reasonably foresee would be likely to injure your neighbour. *Who, then, in law is my neighbour? The answer seems to be persons who are so closely and directly affected by my act that I ought reasonably to have them in contemplation as being so affected when I am directing my mind to the acts or omissions which are called in question* [emphasis added]. This appears to me to be the doctrine of *Heaven* v. *Pender* as laid down by Lord Esher when it is limited by the notion of proximity introduced by Lord Esher himself and A.L. Smith LJ in *Le Lievre* v. *Gould*. Lord Esher MR says:

'That case established that, under certain circumstances, one man may owe a duty to another, even though there is no contract between them. If one man is near to another, or is near to the property of another, a duty lies upon him not to do that which may cause a personal injury to that other, or may injure his property'.

So A.L. Smith LJ says:

'The decision of *Heaven* v. *Pender* was founded upon the principle that a duty to take due care did arise when the person or property of one was in such proximity to the person or property of another that, if due care was not taken, damage might be done by the one to the other'.

I think that this sufficiently states the truth if proximity be not confined to mere physical proximity, but be used, as I think it was intended, to extend to such close and direct relations that the act complained of directly affects a person whom the person alleged to be bound to take care would know would

---

[157] In Scotland the plaintiff is called the pursuer, and the defendant is called the defender.

be directly affected by his careless act [emphasis added]. That this is the sense in which nearness or 'proximity' was intended by Lord Esher is obvious from his own illustration in *Heaven* v. *Pender* of the application of his doctrine to the sale of goods.

> 'This [i.e., the rule he has just formulated] includes the case of goods, etc., supplied to be used immediately by a particular person or persons, or one of a class of persons, where it would be obvious to the person supplying, if he thought, that the goods would in all probability be used at once by such persons before a reasonable opportunity for discovering any defect which might exist, and where the thing supplied would be of such a nature that a neglect of ordinary care or skill as to its condition or the manner of supplying it would probably cause danger to the person or property of the person for whose use it was supplied, and who was about to use it . . .'

I draw particular attention to the fact that Lord Esher emphasizes the necessity of goods having to be 'used immediately' and 'used at once before a reasonable opportunity of inspection'. This is obviously to exclude the possibility of goods having their condition altered by lapse of time, and to call attention to the proximate relationship, which may be too remote where inspection even by the person using, certainly by an intermediate person, may reasonably be interposed. With this necessary qualification of proximate relationship, as explained in *Le Lievre* v. *Gould*, I think the judgment of Lord Esher expresses the law of England. Without the qualification, I think that the majority of the court in *Heaven* v. *Pender*, was justified in thinking that the principle was expressed in too general terms. There will, no doubt, arise cases where it will be difficult to determine whether the contemplated relationship is so close that the duty arises. But in the class of case now before the court I cannot conceive any difficulty to arise."

Notes

(1) Before this landmark judgment the common law had great difficulty in making the manufacturer of defective products liable to a consumer who had not purchased the defective product him- or herself. It was thought that the manufacturer of goods was under a duty of care towards its customer but that it owed no such duty to a third person with whom it had no contract. In *Donoghue* v. *Stevenson*, such a duty of care was recognized by Lord Atkin (for the majority) in favour of third persons who were, as Lord Esher MR said in *Le Lievre* v. *Gould*, "in such proximity to the person or property of another that, if due care was not taken damage might be done by the one to the other".[158] In his speech, Lord Atkin on the one hand added that proximity should not be confined to mere physical proximity, while on the other hand emphasizing that it is necessary, for a duty of care to be found, that the goods had been "used immediately" and "used at once before a reasonable opportunity of inspection". Indeed the relationship "may be too remote where inspection even by the person using, certainly by an intermediate person, may reasonably be interposed".

(2) "Proximity", as used by Lord Atkin to acknowledge the existence of a duty of care, is not to be confused with "proximate cause", as that concept is used in the context of causation. There, the question is whether the careless behaviour is the proximate cause of the harm, i.e. whether the harm for which compensation is claimed is not too distant or too remote a consequence of the defendant's actions to be imputed to the defendant.[159] Nonetheless, both concepts cannot always easily be distinguished in practice: Zweigert

---

[158] [1893] 1 QB 491, CA.
[159] See in that connection the Privy Council's decision in *Overseas Tankship (U.K.) Ltd* v. *Morts Dock & Engineering Co. (The Wagon Mound)*: *infra*, Chapter IV, **4.E.4.**

and Kötz state that Anglo-American courts also employ the concept of "duty of care" in cases where continental courts would see only a question of causal relationship.[160]

(3) The annotated judgment still makes the outcome of an action in negligence dependent on proof of some want of care in the manufacturer. In the USA at least, the law has evolved further since the manufacturer of defective goods causing harm to the consumer is now liable even if it is not at fault at all. In order to achieve that result, the courts extended the ambit of the manufacturer's contractual guarantee so as to include the final consumer, his or her family and others close to him. At the same time, the courts also granted the final consumer a direct claim against the manufacturer as a permissible "short-cut" to save time and money.[161] Product liability in the USA has thus become strict. The United Kingdom Consumer Protection Act 1987,[162] implementing Directive 85/374,[163] has achieved the same result for personal injury and some property damage in the United Kingdom. But, beyond that, *Donoghue* v. *Stevenson* continues to apply. Furthermore, the judgment is still relevant for having laid down in *obiter dicta* a general principle of liability for unintended harm.[164]

1.4.2. THE FRENCH APPROACH

Articles 1382 and 1383 C. civ.

Article 1382. Anyone who, through his act, causes damage to another by his fault shall be obliged to compensate the damage.

Article 1383. Everyone is responsible for the damage caused not only by his act but also by his negligence or carelessness.

Introductory Note

a) In French law, there is little discussion on the scope of protection of tort law. From the point of view of French law, it is for instance incorrect to speak of **protected rights** in an exclusionary sense (whereby some other rights or interests would be left unprotected). Indeed, the general provisions of Articles 1382 and 1383 C.civ. have consistently been found not to contain any *a priori* limitations on the scope or nature of protected rights and interests. In principle, all **rights** and **interests** are protected, although, when the tort consists in the infringement of a *right*, it is easier to prove the existence of damage. The only limitation is that the right or interest which was encroached upon must be legitimate in order to be protected under tort law.[165]

Furthermore, as regards the liability regime, French law often does not make a clear distinction between contract (Article 1146 ff. C.civ.) and tort rules.[166] This holds true in

---

[160] Zweigert and Kötz at 612, referring to nervous shock cases, see *infra*, **2.E.8.–9.**

[161] See Zweigert and Kötz at 673, referring to Art. 2–318 of the Uniform Commercial Code. See also *infra*, Chapter VI, 6.3.1.C., Introductory Note under *f*.

[162] *Infra*, Chapter VI, **6.E.38.**

[163] *Infra*, Chapter VI, **6.EC.35.**

[164] Weir at 39.

[165] *Juridiquement protégé*: Viney and Jourdain, *Conditions* at 59–60, para. 271.

[166] It must be underlined that, while the scope of protection afforded by the tort and contractual liability regimes under French law may be the same, this does not mean that the two regimes are otherwise identical. As

particular for medical liability, which the Cour de cassation regards as a contractual issue.[167] For instance, the judgments reproduced in Chapter II on interference with bodily integrity all involved contractual liability. Given that the scope of protection is the same under both the contract and tortious liability regimes—to the point where the Cour de cassation sometimes does not state whether it is ruling pursuant to tort or contract law—both contract and tort law materials are used in this casebook.

b) The idea of *protected* rights or interests, if mentioned at all, relates under French law to the notion of **damage**, which is one of the three conditions (fault, damage and causation) for civil liability, whether contractual or tortious. The notion of damage itself has not been much discussed, whether in academic writings or in the case law of the Cour de cassation or Conseil d'État.[168] Frequently, only the characteristics which the damage must display in order to be recoverable are dealt with: the damage must actually exist and be certain, and it must be personal to the plaintiff.[169] French law typically regards as certain damage the loss of a chance (*perte d'une chance*) of obtaining an advantage or of preventing the deterioration of a situation, if the "chance" is real and not just hypothetical.[170] Damage is regarded not only as a condition of civil liability (as opposed to criminal liability) but also as the measure of liability, because of the principle of *réparation intégrale*.[171]

Articles 1382 and 1383 C.civ. are also widely considered not to contain any *a priori* limitation as to the **class of protected persons**. In other words, under French tort law, there is no limitation which might arise from the necessity to prove the existence, under the circumstances of the case, of a duty of care towards the plaintiff. Every plaintiff who can prove fault, damage and causation can claim compensation. French law is accordingly very different from German and English law, as it does not impose any limitations at the very outset on the kind of rights or the group of persons that are protected.

c) In this chapter as in later chapters, reference will be made not only to the general tortious (or extra-contractual) liability regime, namely Articles 1382 and 1383 C.civ. as interpreted in the last instance by the Cour de cassation, but also to the State liability regime, as it has developed, mainly in the case law of the Conseil d'État.[172] It is true that the extra-contractual liability of the State[173] is governed by an autonomous regime, as was recognized by the Tribunal des conflits in its famous *Blanco* judgment of 8 February 1873.[174] But, since that specific liability regime covers the activities of many public institutions, or

mentioned *supra*, 1.3.1., some significant differences remain between the two regimes (remedies, limitation, etc.), often giving rise to a debate as to which regime applies in a given case: see on this issue Viney, *Introduction* at 275 ff., para. 161 ff.

[167] Cass. civ., 20 May 1936, S 1937.I.321 annotated by Breton, D 1936.Jur.88; on subsisting differences in the area of medical liability, see Viney, *Introduction* at 446 ff., para. 243–4, who pleads for harmonization. See also *supra*, **1.F.13.**, and notes thereafter.

[168] See Viney and Jourdain, *Conditions* at 3–11, para. 247–8.

[169] See *infra*, Chapter IV, 4.1.3. and Chapter VIII.

[170] Viney and Jourdain, *Conditions* at 74–85, para. 280–4.

[171] Viney and Jourdain, *Conditions* at 3–7, para. 247, see *infra*, **1.F.24.–25.**, Note (2).

[172] These specific rules are sometimes also applied by the ordinary courts when dealing with liability of the administration: see C. Blumann, "État et collectivités publiques", No. 370–1 in *Juris-classeur civil—1382–1386* (Paris: Éd. du Juris-classeur) at para. 16–29.

[173] Covering both "fault" liability and "no-fault" or "risk" liability.

[174] DP 1873.III.20. See L. Neville Brown and J.S. Bell, *French Administrative Law*, 4th edn. (Oxford: Clarendon Press, 1993) at 175–6.

even of private law entities performing tasks of general or public interest, it often deals with issues which are similar to those arising under general tort law. Furthermore, this regime is not basically different from the general one based on Article 1382 ff. C.civ.:[175] existing differences tend to be reduced or even to disappear.[176]

Basically, all rights and legitimate interests which receive protection under French tort law against infringements by individuals are thus equally protected against the acts of public authorities. In the case of public authorities also, no particular duty of care need be proved. It is a particular feature of French law, that, in addition to fault-based liability, public authorities may also incur "no-fault" or "risk" liability. That latter form of liability is based on the principle of equality of all citizens before public burdens.[177]

G. Viney, Introduction à la responsabilité[178]   **1.F.24.–25.**
and
A. de Laubadère, J.C. Venezia and Y. Gaudemet, Traité de droit administratif[179]

1. G. Viney, *Introduction à la responsabilité*   **1.F.24.**

"Civil liability has often been said to be a means of sanctioning conduct which is faulty and causes harm; indeed it has even been said to be a 'private punishment'. Such a view seems to us, however, to be too narrow. *Even if the original prescriptive role of civil liability was to serve as a deterrent from socially harmful conduct, we can see nowadays that it also has a positive aspect, namely to vindicate and protect rights which have been infringed* [emphasis added] . . .

In the absence of any more specific device, civil liability constitutes . . . a method of asserting and protecting rights. For instance, it is clear that the theory of personality rights has been accepted in France largely owing to the principle of civil liability, especially Art. 1382 C.civ., which continues to be its most effective champion. The law of unfair competition, which has clearly played a prime role in laying down the rules which traders must observe in their attempts to attract custom, is likewise an application of Art. 1382 C.civ. Equally, it is through the law of tort that consumers have achieved an effective right to be properly informed both before they enter contracts and afterwards. *It is equally clear that civil liability, as developed by the courts in order to protect the victims of personal injury due to dangerous things, whether by finding* obligations de sécurité *or* obligations de garantie *in particular types of contract or by using Art. 1384(1) C.civ., has facilitated the acceptance of a genuine 'right to corporeal integrity'* . . . [emphasis added].

Thus it is that, at least when it is based on general principles such as those of Art. 1382 and 1384(1) C.civ., *the law of civil liability not only allows the courts to uphold against those who would disregard them rights already acknowledged to exist, but also contributes to the emergence and protection of rights as yet inchoate and unrecognized* [emphasis added]. It thus constitutes a method of complementing and improving the legal system, and bringing it up to date . . .

---

[175] It is interesting to note that the administrative, as compared with civil, liability rules have evolved from being more restrictive for plaintiffs, to being more generous to them: A. de Laubadère *et. al., Traité de droit administratif*, Vol. I, 13th edn. (Paris: LGDJ, 1994) at 834–5.

[176] C. Blumann, "État et collectivités publiques", No. 370–1 in *Juris-classeur civil—1382–1386* (Paris: Éd. du Juris-classeur) at para. 11.

[177] L. Neville Brown and J.S. Bell, *French Administrative Law*, 4th edn. (Oxford: Clarendon Press, 1993) at 184. These rules are further dealt with *infra*, Chapter III, 3.3.3.

[178] (Paris: LGDJ, 1995) at 63–4, 67–69 and 107–9 (footnotes omitted). Translation by T. Weir.

[179] Vol. I, 13th edn. (Paris: LGDJ, 1994) at 900–2 (references and footnotes omitted). Translation by T. Weir.

[S]tatutory and jurisprudential developments show that *the principle* [of *réparation intégrale*] *is no longer universally accepted, and that it has a potential for expansion threatening to turn into abuse* [emphasis added]. To begin with, several enactments designed to reform parts of the law of liability or to remove from it certain types of harm (accidents at work, for example) have modified this rule of *réparation intégrale* to a greater or lesser extent, either by putting a 'ceiling' on the damages recoverable or even introducing a statutory tariff for specified injuries; . . .

But what really brings into question the universal validity of the principle of réparation intégrale *is the manifest difficulties the courts are experiencing in applying it in cases of personal injury and non-material harm* [emphasis added]. Certainly the idea of making compensation match the harm as completely as possible seems not only generous but sensible, but in fact it is much too vague to serve by itself as a method of translating into money terms what is required to compensate for non-material harm. In the absence of the control which could be provided by precise rules of evaluation, the principle of *réparation intégrale* remains nothing more than a maxim of equity which barely conceals complete abdication to the discretion of the courts. In a system of law such as ours now is, this is a serious disadvantage. Since the parties are quite unable to anticipate even in broad terms what the court may hold to be the appropriate damages, the defendant is in a position to put pressure on the victim to accept an unfavourable compromise or face prolonged and expensive legal proceedings whose result is a matter of chance.

Moreover, even if the matter ever reaches a judge, the lack of rules to guide him means that he must decide on the basis of his personal feelings, which inevitably leads to a significant departure from equality before the law.

It is clear, furthermore, that the principle of réparation intégrale *has encouraged the courts to be lax not only in determining the measure of damages but also in defining the heads of recoverable damage* [emphasis added]. In cases of personal injury courts keep "discovering" novel types of harm for which special damages are awarded quite distinct from those which are designed to compensate for physical disability. Thus after damages for grief, pain and suffering and aesthetic harm we have had damages for loss of amenity, for impairment of the pleasures of childhood, for diminution of sexual prowess, for gloom due to the prospect of impending death and so on. Similarly, as to economic harm, the amount of damages has been significantly increased by taking account of losses of profit. It seems likely that, given the relaxation of the conditions of liability, this tendency is going to increase the total social cost of damages and, more specifically, to increase the cost of insurance, which may eventually become excessive or even intolerable, at any rate for burgeoning sectors of the economy where the risks are high by reason of their need to use novel techniques whose inherent dangers are *ex hypothesi* neither fully understood nor completely under control.

In the light of these considerations perhaps we should think harder about the merits and modalities of civil liability. We can no longer ignore what an author has called 'budgetary constraints'. *To put it another way, we must take account of the fact that in any country at any time there must be a limit to the sums which can be set aside as damages for the victims of accidents, or else economic development may be seriously impaired. Consequently, we must strive to effect a better distribution of that 'budget', given that it cannot be increased indefinitely* [emphasis added]. In particular we must think of a prioritisation of the different kinds of damage, giving preference to those which most seriously threaten the most important interest of individuals and groups. We can readily accept, for example, that priority should be given to compensation for personal injury and that damages for economic harm should be granted more readily than damages for harm which is purely non-material; indeed for the latter it might be better to stop awarding money damages whenever some other method of putting an end to the non-material harm suffered by the victim could be adopted."

2. A. de Laubadère, J.C. Venezia and Y. Gaudemet, *Traité de droit administratif* **1.F.25.**

"It goes without saying that when the harm is material in nature, damages are awarded. The question is—or was in the past—whether material harm alone is compensable or whether harm of a non-material nature should not also be compensated . . .

The [administrative] courts have long accepted that certain kinds of non-material harm can be compensated:

First, when the non-material damage was accompanied by a material element, as where the non-material damage could have economic consequences. Thus aesthetic damage was accepted, as was injury to reputation when the publicity was such that damage was sure to follow, and pain and suffering, provided that if the victim had died, he had himself commenced suit.

But the same is true where the damage is purely non-material, without any material aspect, such as the infringement of a purely spiritual liberty. In such cases the sum awarded by the judges may often be very small and symbolic but all the same the administration is held liable.

Although the [administrative] courts have long accepted that non-material harm may be compensated they refused to award damages for one form of it which was accepted by the regular courts, namely grief due to the loss of a dear one. It was said that 'tears do not translate into money'. Nonetheless, the administrative courts did award damages under the heading of 'compensation for disturbance of the conditions of life' which went beyond any material harm, and finally the *Conseil d'État* ended up by accepting damages for bereavement as such.

When there had been a fatal accident for which the administration was responsible, it was a question who could sue.

Here the courts long adhered to the restrictive rule that damages required a 'right infringed' and not just an 'interest invaded'.

On this principle the *Conseil d'État* dismissed the claims of cohabitants as well as persons who had no legal right to support from the primary victim.

The law has developed, however; the *Conseil d'État* has abandoned its rule that the plaintiff be an alimentary creditor and allows the cohabitant to claim."

Notes

(1) The first excerpts from Viney illustrate the fundamental differences between the French and German approach as to protected rights and interests. The German BGB starts at § 823(1) with a limitative enumeration of protected **rights** whose infringement can give rise to liability under certain conditions. In two additional general headings (§§ 823(2), and 826), it then also attaches liability, under certain conditions, to conduct which violates protective statutory provisions or *boni mores*. The French *Code civil*, on the other hand, starts with a reference to **fault** (at Articles 1382 and 1383) as a primary source of liability without limiting, or even mentioning, the rights or interests which this liability regime aims to protect. As Viney explains, French tort law was meant in the first place to discourage socially undesirable behaviour; only subsequently was it considered as a means to ensure respect for certain interests which gradually developed into subjective rights, such as the general right to privacy (*droit à la vie privée*) and the general right to bodily or physical integrity (*droit à la sécurité*).[180] At the end of the day, both those rights were eventually given protection by the legislator, either *generally* as in the case of the

---

[180] On this general right to bodily or physical integrity, see C. Radé, "Réflexions sur les fondements de la responsabilité civile" D 1999.Chron.313 and 323.

right to privacy or *partially*, that is against the most harmful interferences, as in the case of the right to physical integrity. Indeed the right to privacy is now explicitly recognized and protected at Article 9 C.civ.[181] As for the right to bodily integrity, it is protected mainly by the *Loi Badinter*, which covers compensation for the victims of road accidents,[182] and by the Act of 31 December 1991, containing provisions for the compensation of the victims of HIV following a blood transfusion.[183]

(2) The approach taken by French law, with its emphasis on protection against all kinds of harmful behaviour, regardless of who has suffered from it, allows all legitimate interests to be protected and full compensation for all injuries to such interests on the basis of the principle of *réparation intégrale* (full compensation).[184]

Réparation intégrale covers all **material** injury to the bodily integrity of a person, to his property and to his estate generally (*atteintes au patrimoine*), including material loss (for instance, loss of financial support) sustained by dependent third parties as a consequence of the death of, or physical injury to, the primary victim.

The *patrimoine* is the set of all of a particular person's "assets", i.e. all rights with an economic value, including ownership of real or personal property, money, contractual rights, etc. (*Vermögen* in German law). The *patrimoine* could roughly be rendered as "estate" in common law terms.

Réparation intégrale also covers **non-material** injury (*dommage moral*), such as:[185]

– injury resulting from direct interference with the right of personality, for instance damage to one's reputation by defamatory statements;
– injury consequential on interference with a person's bodily integrity, such as pain and suffering (*pretium doloris*), aesthetic damage or loss of amenity (*préjudice d'agrément*) by the primary victim, as well as bereavement or pain and suffering (*préjudice d'affection*) by persons suffering from the death or injury to the physical well-being of the primary victim, regardless of the proximity of their relationship;[186] as well as
– according to some, even damage inherent in the purely formal infringement (without material consequences) of one's subjective rights, including ownership.

(3) As appears from the excerpts from A. de Laubadère's treatise, the case law relating to administrative liability, in particular that of the Conseil d'État, follows by and large the case law of the Cour de cassation relating to Article 1382 ff. C.civ. concerning the scope of recoverable material and non-material damage. For some time, however, the Conseil d'État had shown some reluctance to compensate *préjudice d'affection* and, in the fatal accident cases, to accept claims from dependants who did not have a legal right to financial support from the deceased or from persons living with the deceased as an unwed couple. But, in the end, it followed the case law of the Cour de cassation.

(4) In recent times, some doubts have been voiced by authoritative legal writers as to whether the principle of *réparation intégrale* should be as literally and consistently applied as it is by the French courts, particularly with regard to non-material damage.[187]

---

[181] Added to the *Code civil* by the *Loi 70–643 tendant à renforcer la garantie des droits individuels des citoyens* of 17 July 1970, JO, 19 July 1970, 6751, D 1970.Lég.199: see *infra*, Chapter II, 2.2.2.

[182] *Infra*, Chapter VI, **6.F.18.**

[183] *Infra*, Chapter VI, **6.F.31.**

[184] Viney, *Introduction* at 107–9, para. 65, reproduced in part *supra*, **1.F.24.**

[185] See, on the various types of non-material damage, the thorough analysis of Viney and Jourdain, *Conditions* at 19–59, para. 250–70.

[186] And even regardless of the object of the affection, see the case of a person aggrieved by the death of his horse as a result of tortious conduct: Cass. civ. 1re, 16 January 1962, D 1962.Jur.199, JCP 1962.II.12552, annotated by R. Rodière.

[187] See among others Viney, *Introduction*, *supra*, **1.F.24.**; Viney and Jourdain, *Conditions* at 25–8 and 47–58, para. 254 and 266–9; M.-È. Roujou de Boubée, *Essai sur la notion de réparation* (Paris: LGDJ, 1974) and A. Tunc, *La sécurité routière* (Paris: Dalloz, 1976).

1.4.3. THE GERMAN APPROACH

§§ 823(1) and (2), 826 BGB

§ 823.   (1) Anyone who intentionally or negligently injures life, body, health, freedom, own-
             ership or any other right of another in a manner contrary to law shall be obliged to
             compensate the other for the loss arising.
             (2) The same liability is incurred by a person who infringes a law intended to protect
             another person. If such a law may be infringed without culpability, liability to com-
             pensate shall be incurred only in the event of culpability.

§ 826.   Anyone who intentionally causes harm to another in a manner *contra bonos mores* is
             liable to compensate the other for the harm thereby occasioned.

Introductory Note

a) Under § 823(1) BGB, "liability for causing injury in an unlawful and culpable manner only arises if the injury affects the victim in one of the legal interests (*Rechtsgüter*) enumerated in the text; these legal interests are life, body, health, freedom, ownership and any other right".[188] As the words "or any other right" indicate, the list of protected interests at § 823(1) BGB is not closed.[189] Interests to which the courts have accorded the status of an "other right" are those which the legal system protects *erga omnes,* such as real rights (rights *in rem*) and industrial property rights, but also, as we shall see, the *Recht am Gewerbebetrieb*,[190] some specific rights like the right to one's name or picture and finally also the general *Persönlichkeitsrecht*.[191]

In German legal writing the interests protected by § 823(1) BGB are called *Rechtsgüter*. As is shown by the terms *"oder ein sonstiges Recht"*, that is "or another right", at the end of the enumeration, the interests specifically listed in § 823(1)—life, body, health, freedom and property—are also *subjektive Rechte*, or rights. More specifically, they are "absolute rights", i.e. rights opposable to the world at large (*erga omnes*).

The concept of "subjective right" is well-known to Continental legal systems such as the German or the French (*droit subjectif*). Although numerous learned works have been written on it, the concept is still diffuse. It is generally opposed to the *objektives Recht* or *droit objectif*. Conversely, common law systems do not entertain this concept of "subjective right", possibly because there is less linguistic ambiguity in the English language. Indeed the concept of *objektives Recht* or *droit objectif* has to be translated into English as "law"(or "general law"), which in turns means that the English word "right" is more often than not used in the meaning of "subjective right" in the Continental systems.

It would not be appropriate in this casebook to devote much place and energy to defining the concepts *subjektives Recht* and *droit subjectif*. In general they refer to all kinds of legal positions which a person recognized as such by the law—thus a legal "subject"—can have (hence the name "subjective rights"). Taken in their broadest sense, *subjektive Rechte* or *droits subjectifs* comprise:

–   on the one hand, "human rights and fundamental freedoms", as they are now called in the ECHR and its
    Protocols, such as the right to life, body, and health. This category also includes certain freedoms, such as
    the freedom to have and express an opinion, to acquire, own and dispose of property or to make contracts

---

[188] Zweigert and Kötz at 599, from which the following general observations are drawn. Literally translated, *Rechtsgüter* are legal goods. In Zweigert and Kötz, the word *Rechtsgüter* is translated as "Legal interests". As for the requirements of unlawfulness and culpability, see *infra*, Chapter III.

[189] For an unsuccessful attempt at including a "right to one's employment" within the scope of § 823(1) BGB as an "other right", see BAG, 4 June 1998, NJW 1999, 164.

[190] See *infra*, Chapter II, 2.3.2.

[191] See *infra*, Chapter II, 2.2.1.

and wills. The latter freedoms are called in German legal theory *Gestaltungsrechte*, that is to say rights to shape, assign, or give up more specific rights; and

– on the other hand, more specific rights (called *Herrschaftsrechte*) whereby the holder of the right is given full or limited dominance over a specific object, such as a piece of land or a chattel, or over some form of behaviour by another person who is bound to behave in that way. Within these specific rights, a distinction is made between "real rights" and "personal rights". "Real rights" (rights *in rem*, *droits réels*, *dingliche Rechte*) give their holder dominance of some sort over tangible or intangible property. They are deemed "absolute" because they can be invoked against everyone else (who has to respect them). "Personal rights" (rights *in personam*, *droits personnels*, *Forderungsrechte*) in contrast are deemed "relative" because they can be relied on only against the person who is bound to act in accordance with them.

Whereas the fundamental rights and freedoms belong to everyone—hence their name "human rights"—the specific rights (*Herrschaftsrechte*) give a special legal position to one or more individualized persons only.

The concept of rights is not entirely unknown in the common law traditions, if only because an American professor, W.H. Hohfeld, rightly drew attention to the considerable ambiguity of the term right. In order to address this ambiguity, he developed a whole system of legal conceptions whereby, within rights, the categories of **claims, privileges, powers** and **immunities** are distinguished, and by way of correlatives, **duties, no-rights, liabilities** and **disabilities**.[192] That does not prevent common lawyers, however, from thinking still in terms of **remedies** instead of **rights**; as an English judge said: "It is not in accordance . . . with the principles of English law to analyse rights as being something separate from the remedy given to the individual . . . [In] my judgment, in the ordinary case to establish a legal or equitable right you have to show that all the necessary elements of the cause of action are either present or threatened".[193] A remedy thus relates to a cause of action, of which another English judge said that it is "simply a factual situation the existence of which entitles one person to obtain from the court a remedy against another person".[194]

Interestingly enough, the debate on the meaning of "right" may be revived albeit at another level through the evolution of European Community law in the wake of the European Court of Justice ruling, in *Brasserie du Pêcheur* and other cases, that the infringement of EC law gives rise to State liability only to the extent that the provision on which the claimant relies was intended to give "rights" to individuals in the position of the claimant.[195]

b) The *Recht am Gewerbebetrieb,* also called *Recht am eingerichteten und ausgeübten Gewerbebetrieb*, literally the "right to an established and active business", is one of the two more general rights to which the courts have accorded the status of "other right" in the sense of § 823(1) BGB. It could be described as the interest of the owner of an existing business in that business as a going concern. The existence of this right is therefore subject to two conditions relating to the business: it must be existing or established (*eingerichtet*), meaning that the business has been endowed with the requisite resources to be carried out; and it must also be active as a going concern (*ausgeübt*) and not merely dormant. Furthermore, the term *Gewerbebetrieb* refers to commercial businesses within the meaning of German law, to the exclusion of, for instance, professions or crafts. For the sake of clarity and simplicity, the shorthand German form *Recht am Gewerbebetrieb* will be used hereafter throughout the text.

[192] First laid out in W.H. Hohfeld, "Fundamental Legal Conceptions as applied in Judicial Reasoning" (1913) 23 Yale LJ 16, (1917) 26 Yale LJ 710. In Germany, Hohfeld's theory was branded a legal discovery by H. Dölle, "Aus fremden Rechten. Theoretische Jurisprudenz in Nord-Amerika" in *Gruchots Beiträge zur Erläuterung des Deutschen Rechts*, 1927, 492. In the USA, Hohfeld's system was taken over and developed further by R. Pound, *Jurisprudence* (St-Paul: West Legal Publishing, 1959) at § 117. See also W. van Gerven, *Algemeen deel* (Vol. I of R. Dillemans and W. van Gerven (eds.), *Beginselen van Belgisch Privaatrecht*), 1st edn. (Antwerpen: Standaard, 1968) at 90 ff., with many further references. The theory is still very much discussed today: see the contributions of J. De Sousa e Brito, M. Van Hoecke and M. Henket in (1996) 9 Int'l J. Semiotics of Law 173, 185 and 202 respectively. See also A. Halpin, *Rights and Law Analysis and Theory* (Oxford: Hart Publishing, 1997).

[193] *Kingdom of Spain* v. *Christie, Manson & Woods Ltd.* [1986] 1 WLR 1120, ChD at 1129, by Browne-Wilkinson VC (as he then was).

[194] Diplock J (as he then was) in *Letang* v. *Cooper* [1965] 1 QB 232, QBD at 242–3.

[195] *Infra*, Chapter IX, **9.EC.6.**

The second general right which the courts have brought under the protection of § 823(1) BGB is the *Persönlichkeitsrecht* which has been translated as the "right to one's personality" or the "right to personality". While *Persönlichkeit* or *personnalité* may be familiar concepts to German and French jurists, there is no ready equivalent in the common law. The *Persönlichkeit* is an abstraction, which comprises attributes such as amongst others, honour, integrity, image, name, privacy and autonomy.[196] Each of those attributes gives rise to a specific *Persönlichkeitsrecht*. For reasons explained below, the BGH has chosen to recognize a general (*allgemeines*) *Persönlichkeitsrecht* encompassing all of these specific rights instead of letting the law evolve incrementally through the emergence of specific rights.[197] Throughout this work, the original term *Persönlichkeitsrecht* will be used.

c) Apart from the *specific* torts provided for in § 824 (damage to another person's credit), in § 825 (unlawfully inducing a woman to engage in intercourse outside of marriage) and in § 839 (liability for breach of official duty[198]), the BGB contains two other *general* heads of tortious liability which supplement the first head in § 823(1) BGB. Thus, liability arises under § 823(2) BGB if a statute designed to protect another is culpably contravened. It also arises, pursuant to § 826 BGB, if a person "intentionally causes harm to another in a manner *contra bonos mores*". These provisions have been used by the courts to attenuate to a certain extent the limitations as to protected *Rechtsgüter* found in § 823(1). Thus, the courts have used § 826 to impose liability in a whole range of types of case where one party has caused harm to another by behaviour so improper as to be likely to incur strong disapproval from the average person in the relevant section of society,[199] whilst § 823(2) is nowadays considered a close rival to § 823(1), some writers seeing it as having "an even wider potential ambit" than § 823(1).[200] Furthermore, §§ 844–846 BGB apply in respect of actions brought by dependants of the victim.

K. Zweigert and H. Kötz, *An Introduction to Comparative Law*[201] **1.G.26–27.**
and
K. Larenz and C.-W. Canaris, *Lehrbuch des Schuldrechts*[202]

1. K. Zweigert and H. Kötz, *An Introduction to Comparative Law*   **1.G.26.**

"[Under § 823(1) BGB] it must be shown that the culpably unlawful behaviour caused harm to one of the legal interests specified in § 823(1) BGB. According to the terms of this section, these include, in particular, the integrity of the citizen's person and property . . . § 823(1) also affords protection to 'other rights'. These include all the interests which the legal order protects *erga omnes*, real rights such as servitudes and rent charges, the possessory right to acquire a thing such as enjoyed by a conditional buyer, the right to a name, patent rights, and other industrial property rights regulated in special statutes. One's estate as a whole is, however, not an 'other right' in the sense of § 823(1) BGB.

---

[196] See Zweigert and Kötz at 687 ff. and *infra*, **1.G.26.** See also Art. 49 of the Swiss Code of Obligations.
[197] *Infra*, Chapter II, **2.G.26.**
[198] See *infra*, Chapter III, 3.3.2.A.
[199] Zweigert and Kötz at 603.
[200] Markesinis at 35.
[201] 3rd revised edn., translated by T. Weir (Oxford: Clarendon, 1998) at 600.
[202] Vol. II, Pt 2, 13th edn. (München: Beck, 1994) at 354–6 (footnotes omitted). Translation by T. Weir.

Economic loss can be compensated under § 823(1) BGB only if it flows from an injury to one of the legal interests specified in that provision: a person who suffers personal injury and damage to his car in a traffic accident can claim damages for all the economic loss consequent on the personal injury, such as medical expenses, or on the property damage, such as the cost of hiring a substitute car, but if culpable behaviour causes the victim only 'pure' economic harm unconnected with any personal injury or damage to his property or the invasion of any 'other right', no claim arises under § 823(1) BGB . . .

Liability under § 823(2) BGB arises when a 'statute designed to protect another' is culpably contravened. Protective statutes in this sense include all the rules of private and public law, especially criminal law, which are substantially designed to protect a person or a group of persons rather than the public as a whole. Here too it is of some importance what form the harm takes, whether injury to health, damage to property, or merely economic harm, for harm is only compensable if it results from the very danger which it was the purpose of the protective statute to diminish or eliminate. If the protective statute is directed to the prevention of personal injury and property damage only, a claim for the compensation of pure economic loss based on § 823(2) BGB will fail. . . .

The third head of general tortious liability in the BGB is § 826. A person is liable under this section if he 'intentionally causes harm to another in a manner which offends *contra bonos mores*'. The courts have used this provision to impose liability in a whole range of types of case where one party has caused harm to another by behaviour so improper as to incur strong disapprobation from the average person in the relevant section of society. It is not necessary to show that the defendant actually intended to cause the harm; it is enough if he was conscious of the possibility that harm might occur and acquiesced in its doing so. Liability is thus incurred by a person who knowingly persuades a vendor of goods already sold but not delivered to make them over to him, or by a partner who goes behind another partner's back and indulges in private transactions of a type reserved for the partnership, or by a person who markets goods which are a 'servile imitation' of another person's unprotected wares, knowing that the public may well be deceived about their provenance, or by an employer who lures away the employee of another knowing and accepting that this will cause harm, or by a person who recklessly gives false information about the creditworthiness of another party, conscious that the person seeking information could suffer harm thereby."

2. K. Larenz and C.-W. Canaris, *Lehrbuch des Schuldrechts*   **1.G.27.**

"3. The system of the three 'minor' general headings and the decision in principle against the law of tort providing general protection of the Vermögen *and freedom of action.*

(a) In the first draft of the BGB the following provision was laid down in § 704(1): 'Where a person commits an unlawful act, whether intentionally or negligently, . . . which harms another, . . . that person shall be required to compensate the other for the damage thereby caused'. This general tortious clause, which is to some extent modelled on Art. 1382 et seq. of the French *Code civil* of 180[4] and has found its way into a series of modern codifications in one form or another, was repudiated by the second commission. Its place was taken by a far more variegated system based on the three principal heads of liability contained in §§ 823(1), 823(2) and 826 BGB and supplemented by the additional heads of liability contained in §§ 824 et seq. and 831 et seq. BGB. By adhering to flexible criteria to be applied on a case-by-case basis, the BGB avoids relapsing into the historically older system of strictly distinct heads of liability. After all, the system is one of three 'minor' general headings. § 823(1) BGB with its criterion of negligently unlawful breach, § 823(2) BGB and its concept of 'protective law' and § 826 BGB requiring an offence against morals, all require a great deal of fleshing out on a case-by-case basis.

On the other hand, by having only 'minor' general headings rather than a 'major' principle of general application, the BGB can give clearer guidelines to courts and scholars for the application of the law in individual cases and can at the same time take better into account any concerns of the potential tortfeasor which deserve protection . . . In this it is guided by fundamental ideas whose justice is immediately evident: in § 823(1) specific legal interests and individual rights (*bestimmte Rechtsgüter und subjektive Rechte*) such as life, health, ownership, etc. are afforded comprehensive protection. These interests are given pride of place in the legal system in order to show how desirable and necessary it is that they be protected . . . § 823(2) BGB enables the law of torts to make use of standards of conduct laid down legislatively in other areas, which not only ensures a textual warrant for decision-making but also makes it easier for the potential tortfeasor to identify any likely breach of the law . . . § 826 BGB, with its reference to *bonos mores*, aligns itself on those minimum standards of conduct required by legal and social ethics . . . This is in keeping with the overall structure, since the observance of those standards which everyone may be expected to observe imposes no significant fetter on a potential tortfeasor. Moreover, breach of such fundamental duties constitutes wrongdoing of a very serious nature, particularly as § 826 BGB also requires an intent to cause harm. Finally, the ancillary grounds of liability in §§ 824, 831 ff. BGB may be viewed as natural extension of one or other of the three principal bases of liability, and thus consistent with the system as a whole . . .

b) The significance of [Germany's] refusal to adopt a 'major' general clause emerges when one considers the interests which in consequence are not protected generally, but only in special circumstances; these include the *Vermögen* as such and freedom of action. This has already been seen in the case of the person who causes intentional harm to a competitor without infringing the Act on Unfair Competition (UWG). Likewise one may intentionally 'take advantage' of a contracting partner, that is, cause him economic harm, provided one abstains from duress, deceit, exploitation and so on. Nor, in the absence of other factors, is a person liable for causing economic harm who fails to take the requisite care and whose conduct, therefore, if contrary to law, would be 'negligent'. A person is not liable in delict for causing a friend to lose a lot of money by giving him poor investment advice, or for thoughtlessly misdirecting a traveller who asks the way, so that he misses an appointment to make a profitable contract. In such cases there is no interference with ownership within the meaning of § 823(1) BGB, for in the diction of the BGB ownership exists only in things, there is no breach of any protective law under § 823(2) BGB, and no liability under § 826 BGB if for no other reason than that there was no intention to cause harm . . . 'Other rights' under § 823(1) BGB should be strictly limited to rights similar to those expressly listed, such as ownership and health . . . For the same reason the idea of 'freedom' in § 823(1) BGB should be interpreted restrictively, so as to assure that freedom of action (arguably infringed in the examples given above) is no more covered than the *Vermögen* . . . Accordingly it can be seen that the law of delict in the BGB rests on the idea that different legal interests call for differentiated protection, as appears most strikingly from the differences between § 823(1) and § 826 BGB. This idea, as we shall see, is also of assistance in the application of § 823(2) BGB in individual cases."

Notes

(1) As appears from the foregoing, the German BGB tries to restrict claims in tort generally from the very outset (i) by enumerating in a limitative manner the interests protected against culpably unlawful behaviour (*Rechtsgutverletzung*, § 823(1) BGB) *and*, beyond this (ii) by allowing claims only if (a) a statute designed to protect a person or a group of persons rather than the public as a whole has been culpably contravened (*Gesetzesverletzung*, § 823(2) BGB) or (b) harm is caused intentionally in a manner which offends *boni mores* (*Sittenverstoß*, § 826 BGB). As the second excerpt shows, that restrictive attitude is still very much defended in legal writing.

Notwithstanding their restrictive purpose, each of those three heads of tortious liability has been interpreted rather broadly. Although the latter two have opened the doors to the award of damages for *reiner Vermögensschaden*, this has not led to an unrestricted admission of claims for such losses.

Vermögen corresponds to *patrimoine* in French civil law, i.e. the set of all of a particular person's rights with an economic value (including ownership of real or personal property, money, contractual rights, etc.). In common law terms, the *Vermögen* roughly corresponds to 'estate'. *Vermögensschaden* means 'damage to the *Vermögen*', i.e. damage which can be expressed in monetary terms or material damage. *Vermögensschaden* must then be contrasted with *Nichtvermögensschaden* or non-material damage, comprising all prejudice which cannot be expressed in monetary terms, such as pain and suffering, loss of amenity, prejudice to honour and reputation, etc. Within *Vermögensschaden*, a further distinction is made in German law between, on the one hand, damage flowing from a violation of one of the rights listed in § 823 BGB (life, physical integrity, health, ownership and other similar rights) and, on the other hand, damage consisting in a mere worsening of one's overall economic position (loss of profit, diminution in the value of property, etc.) that is *not* directly consequential upon injury to the person or damage to a particular piece of property. That latter type of *Vermögensschaden* is characterized as *reiner* (pure), *primarer* (direct) or *allgemeiner* (general) *Vermögensschaden* (we will use *reiner* in this book), and it is the main focus of attention in German legal writing. In this sense, *reiner Vermögensschaden* corresponds more or less to 'pure economic loss' in common law.

Harm consequential upon *nervous shock* is recoverable only if it amounts to impairment of health in the sense of § 823(1).[203]

(2) In contrast to English law, the restrictive effect of its tortious liability regime has been offset to a certain extent in German law through, amongst others, the notion of contracts with protective effects for third parties.[204] This holds true particularly in the case of *reiner Vermögensschaden* caused by negligent misstatements or legal malpractice.[205]

1.4.4. THE NORDIC APPROACH

The following materials on the law of the Nordic countries can be found at
<http://www.rechten.unimaas.nl/casebook>:
1.SW.28. *Skadeståndslag of 2 June 1972*
1.SCAN.29. C. von Bar, *Gemeineuropäisches Deliktsrecht* (excerpt)

1.4.5. RECENT CODIFICATIONS

The following legislation (relevant provisions only) can be found at
<http://www.rechten.unimaas.nl/casebook>:
1.CH.30. *Code des obligations/Obligationenrecht*
1.GR.31. *Astikos kodikas*
1.I.32. *Codice civile*
1.P.33. *Código Civil*
1.NL.34. *Burgerlijk Wetboek*

---

[203] *Infra,* **2.G.3.**
[204] See *supra,* **1.G.18.**, and *infra,* Chapter V, 5.1.1.C. under g).
[205] To the extent that damages cannot be recovered for them under § 823(2) or § 826 BGB: *infra,* Chapter II, 2.4.2.A. and 2.4.2.B.

1.5.   COMPARATIVE OVERVIEW

Meaning and functions of tort law

In all legal systems, tort law is about shifting losses from a person who sustained harm onto another person, normally the person whose wrongful course of conduct led to the harm, another person responsible for that person, or the person held responsible for creating a source of danger or risk. The decision as to whether loss should be shifted and, if so, under what conditions and to what extent, results from a balancing act: the interests of the person who suffered injury are weighed against the interests of the person onto whom the losses would be shifted; indeed, if liable, the latter will bear financial responsibility and accordingly be limited in his or her freedom of action. Tort law is therefore about (i) the protected rights and interests of both the victim and the injurer, as well as the interests of society as a whole in ensuring justice and efficiency in the compensation and distribution of losses and limiting the impact on the freedom of its citizens, (ii) the behaviour of the injurer (and also of the victim), whether wrongful or otherwise such as to justify a shifting of the loss, and (iii) remedies and defences made available to implement, or resist, such shifting of losses.[206]

All legal systems pursue the same set of objectives through tort law (although the systems differ from one another in the respective significance given to each of these objectives):

(i) **compensation** for the injury to, or deprivation of, the rights and interests, comprising the costs incurred as a result and the lost expectations;

(ii) **deterrence**, in that the application of tort law (or the threat thereof) may deter wrongdoing[207] and, as the economic analysis of the law has emphasized, inefficient behaviour;[208] and

(iii) **loss-spreading**, in conjunction with other compensatory techniques (mainly liability insurance and social security).[209]

Analysing those objectives helps to highlight the functions of tort law and to illustrate the macro-economic significance of tort law in comparison with other compensatory techniques. It then becomes clear how certain categories of injury are prioritized by making them recoverable through tort claims. On the basis of such analysis, it is for the legislature to determine, in light of global budgetary constraints, which categories of harm are eligible for full or partial compensation under tort law, or must rather be compensated through other compensatory regimes.

The divide between contract and tort

Broadly speaking, tort and contract pursue the same aim, that is to protect what makes life in society worth living. However, they look at it from a different angle: tort law aims

---

[206] *Supra*, **1.F.1**, **1.G.2.** and **1.E.3.**
[207] *Supra*, **1.E.8.** and **1.F.9.**
[208] *Supra* **1.E.3.**, Notes (4) and (5), **1.US.10.–11.**, **1.E.12.** and notes thereafter.
[209] *Supra*, **1.F.5.**, **1.G.6.** and **1.E.7.** and notes thereafter.

at preserving personal wealth and well-being as it existed before the harm was caused, while contract law aims at maximizing personal wealth and well-being through exchange and enforcement of promises.[210]

In no legal system, not even those with a recent codification,[211] are the rules governing claims in tort and in contract completely identical. Differences continue to exist: not all of them are justifiable on account of the nature of the harm or the aim of contract or tort law. Because of these differences, irrespective of whether they are justified or not, it may be advantageous for a plaintiff in a given case, if faced with the choice, to pursue compensation under either tort or contract law rather than the other. Some legal systems, like English law or German law,[212] generally allow the claimant to choose one or the other road; others, like French law,[213] do not allow contracting parties to bring forward claims in tort when the harm is the result of the non-performance of contractual obligations. Which solution will be favoured in a given system depends very much on the scope of protection of tort law under that system. If tort law protects a broad range of interests (including for instance pure economic loss or *reiner Vermögensschaden*), there will be a tendency to protect the realm of contract law from an invasion by tort law through a rule of "non-option" (or *non-cumul*). If on the other hand tort law protects a relatively narrow range of interests, the legal system will tend to permit plaintiffs to bring their claims under either contract or tort, since otherwise the rights and interests of the plaintiff might not be sufficiently protected.[214]

Irrespective of the general principle ultimately chosen, some exceptions will have to be made, so that in practice the "option" and "non-option" approaches might not differ that much. For example, under French law, where non-option is the rule, claims for reparation brought by the victim before a criminal court as an accessory to the main criminal proceedings (the so-called *action civile*), will always be decided under tort law principles, even where the proceedings concern a criminal offence that occurred in connection with the non-performance of a contractual obligation.[215] In contrast, in legal systems which allow a plaintiff to choose between the two realms, the plaintiff will not be permitted to sue in tort if this would deprive a provision of contract law (or a contract) of its substance (under German law),[216] or if this would be "so inconsistent with the applicable contract that, in accordance with ordinary principle, the parties must have taken to have agreed that the tortious remedy is to be limited or excluded" (under English law).[217]

In all legal systems examined above, there is much debate surrounding the availability of tortious or contractual remedies in cases involving contractual chains. The central issue is whether, in a chain of contracts, a party merely holds a claim in contract against its direct counterpart (i.e. the other party in contracts to which the party is privy) or can also bring a claim for compensation in tort—or even in contract—against a party to the

---

[210] *Supra*, 1.3.1, Introductory Note under a).
[211] See e.g. Articles 6:98 and 6:109 of the Dutch BW (the nature of liability can play a role in determining the quantum of damages).
[212] *Supra*, **1.E.14.** and **1.G.15.**
[213] *Supra*, **1.F.13.**
[214] *Supra*, **1.G.15.**, Note (3).
[215] *Supra*, **1.G.15.**, Note (4).
[216] *Supra*, **1.G.15.**, Note (5).
[217] Lord Goff in *Henderson* v. *Merret Syndicates Ltd.*, *supra*, **1.E.14.**

contractual chain with whom it does not stand in a direct contractual relationship. Under French law, after a number of legal writers and some case law took the position that a claim in contract could be brought by and against any party participating in the chain, the Assemblée plénière of the Cour de cassation came down against it.[218] French law nevertheless admits that a claim in contract can be brought against other parties in the chain, as regards chains of contract whereby property is transferred from one party to another (e.g. the ultimate purchaser can claim in contract against the initial seller of goods[219]), a position which was rejected by the ECJ in relation to the interpretation of Article 5(1) of the Brussels Convention on Jurisdiction and Enforcement of Judgments in Civil and Commercial Matters.[220] German law does not allow contractual claims between parties to a contractual chain who do not stand in a direct contractual relationship, such as a building owner and a sub-contractor. However, the doctrine of contracts with protective effects for third parties (*Verträge mit Schutzwirkung für Dritte*) may exceptionally support such a claim, but only where the claimant cannot bring any equivalent action in contract directly against the defendant or anyone else.[221] Under English law, a principal was allowed to pursue a tort claim against a sub-agent in *Henderson* v. *Merrett Syndicates Ltd.*, but as Lord Goff stressed, that case was "most unusual". Normally, an action against a party further up or down the contractual chain, even in tort, "may well prove to be inconsistent with an assumption of responsibility which has the effect of, so to speak, short circuiting the contractual structure so put in place by the parties."[222]

Protected interests and relationships

German and English law view the interests and relationships to be protected by tort rules differently from French law, with the former systems taking a restrictive (and coincidentally similar) approach. Under German law the protected interests and guarded relationships are enumerated in three general provisions. The first general provision presents the *Rechtsgüter* which merit protection. The *Rechtsgüter* include the rights to life, health and property. The second and third provisions aim, respectively, to guard against the breach of legal provisions protecting certain classes of persons, and against behaviour regarded as unacceptable in society. English law specifies distinct torts, including the more general tort of negligence, which guard special interests or relationships against particular forms of unacceptable conduct, each governed by its own distinct rules.

French law proceeds differently. In establishing liability the first question is not whether an interest or special relationship protected by the law is affected, as all interests and relationships warrant protection unless clearly illicit, but rather the inquiry proceeds immediately to the substance of the case, i.e. questions of fault, causation and damage. This question is also raised under German and English law, but only after the existence of an interference with a specific protected interest (under German law), or a specific relationship between tortfeasor and victim (under English law), has been proved. Accordingly, the

---

[218] *Supra,* **1.F.16.** and notes thereafter.
[219] *Supra,* **1.F.16.**, Note (2). See also *infra,* Chapter VI, 6.3.1.B., Introductory Note.
[220] *Supra,* **1.EC.19.**
[221] *Supra,* **1.G.18.** and notes thereafter.
[222] *Supra,* **1.E.17.** and notes thereafter.

introduction of tort law with a discussion of protected interests or relationships will be considered unusual, to say the least, by French jurists.

The concept of "duty of care" under English law gives expression to this restrictive stance in respect of the scope of protection of tort law. It is embodied in the famous neighbour principle laid down in Lord Atkin's speech in *Donoghue* v. *Stevenson*, with regard to the more general tort of negligence.[223] Under German law, similarly, it is understood that each of the three general clauses aims to protect a limited class of persons.[224] Accordingly, under both English and German tort laws, damages may be claimed only by those who belong to the class of persons intended to be protected by the tort provisions.

The generous approach of French law is demonstrated by the absence of any restriction as to the kind of interest, class of persons or relationship to be protected under Articles 1382 and 1383 C.civ., merely requiring the plaintiff to show that he or she has suffered loss or injury. Thus compensation can be awarded to secondary victims or the dependants of primary victims (*victimes par ricochet*), without difficulty. Only the claims of dependants whose interest in the survival of the primary victim is regarded as illicit are excluded.[225]

The restrictive attitude of German and English tort law regimes, as opposed to the generous attitude of French law, is also reflected in the heads of damage which are recoverable.

Even in the case of fatal accidents, German and English tort laws are reluctant to award damages for non-material injury other than pain and suffering.[226] By contrast, French law has no such qualms, even awarding such damages to *victimes par ricochet*, albeit that doubts are voiced as to the desirability of this approach.[227] It is challenged on grounds of distributive justice: it would be better to use the limited funds available to compensate more important kinds of damage. Moreover, the award of damages in such cases tends to serve a punitive rather than compensatory function.

It is noteworthy how the restrictive approach to compensation in respect of recoverable heads of damage in general has been developed from policy considerations by German and English courts, within the context of the general restrictive attitude of their tort laws. This is evident, for example, in decisions of the BGH[228] and the English Court of Appeal reproduced below,[229] the first concerning the infliction of worry and discomfort, and the second, pure economic loss. However, notwithstanding this restrictive stance, German courts will allow recovery where a constitutional right is infringed, in particular the general *Persönlichkeitsrecht*. That right came to be considered as an "other right" under § 823(1) BGB, following its inclusion in the *Grundgesetz*.[230] No such evolution is discernible in English law.[231]

---

[223] See *supra*, **1.E.23.**

[224] See more in particular BGH, 29 March 1971, *infra*, Chapter III, **3.G.35.**

[225] Which is no longer the case of cohabitants: see *infra*, Chapter II, **2.F.19.**

[226] See *supra*, Chapter II, **2.E.4.** and **2.E.8.**

[227] *Infra*, Chapter II, **2.F.19.**

[228] *Infra*, Chapter II, **2.G.4.**

[229] *Infra*, Chapter II, **2.E.36.**

[230] See *infra*, Chapter II, 2.2.1. and **2.G.26.**

[231] *Infra*, Chapter II, **2.E.32.** See, in contradistinction thereto, Irish law as evidenced *infra*, Chapter II, **2.IRL.33.** (in respect of injunctive relief, however).

New codifications

Confronted with these basic differences in approach, it is difficult to judge which attitude is to be preferred. As already stated, to attempt such an assessment one should have an overview not only of the various tort law regimes, but also of the respective social security and private insurance schemes.[232] The boundaries between contract and tort, and between the remedies of compensation and restitution, which differ from one jurisdiction to another, must also be ascertained. So, for example, limitations on recovery of pure economic loss may be mitigated by the broad application of the rules on contractual liability.

In the light of the differences between the three legal systems examined above, it is interesting to note how jurisdictions which have recently adopted new legislation, such as the Netherlands, are trying to tread a middle path.[233]

Unlike Articles 1382 and 1383 C.civ., where fault is the primary condition, Articles 6:162 and 6:163 BW distinguish between unlawfulness (*onrechtmatigheid*) and imputability (*toerekenbaarheid*). The German trilogy of §§ 823 (1), (2) and 826 BGB is followed, with "unlawfulness" defined as the violation of a right, or an act or omission violating a statutory duty or a rule of unwritten law pertaining to proper social conduct. An obligation to compensate arises only where the kind of damage is contemplated in the violated norm. However, unlike § 823(1) BGB, the BW does not attempt to make an exhaustive list of protected "rights".

On the other hand, in the BW the heads of damage for which compensation can be claimed *are* specified. They are enumerated in Article 6:95 ff., and defined to include, in the case of primary victims, all material harm (*vermogensschade*), covering *damnum emergens* and *lucrum cessans* (without limitation as to economic loss) and also other, i.e. non-material, harm, but only in certain circumstances, of which the most important is the infliction of bodily harm, injury to reputation and other forms of injury to the person.[234] Further limitations are found in Article 6:107 and 6:108 BW relating to injury suffered by third parties as a consequence of the primary victim's injury or death. In the latter case, only the loss of maintenance suffered by a limited group of dependants, as well as funeral expenses, may be recovered. Recovery of non-material injury suffered by third parties is excluded. Following the example of Article 44(2) of the Swiss Code of Obligations, Article 6:109 BW provides that the legal duty to compensate may be mitigated, if full compensation would lead to a manifestly unacceptable result.[235]

Common principles

It may be questioned if it is possible to bring any common principles to the fore, given the degree of diversity identified above. It is submitted that a negative answer would be wrong. There seems to be a clear tendency, as shown by the recent Dutch, Swiss, Italian, Portuguese and Greek codifications, to avoid the general and virtually unlimited scope of Articles 1382 and 1383 C.civ., as well as the overly compartmentalized model of the BGB and the

---

[232] *Supra*, General Introduction.
[233] *Supra*, **1.CH.30**, **1.GR.31.**, **1.I.32.**, **1.P.33.** and **1.NL.34.**
[234] Reparation of non-material harm takes the form of an equitable amount, pursuant to Art. 6:106 BW.
[235] See further, *infra*, Chapter II, 2.1.4., Introductory Note under c).

piecemeal approach of the English law of torts. Instead, as has been illustrated above by the BW, new codes tend to follow a middle road, taking as a starting point a general provision founded on sufficiently flexible concepts to adjust to new situations, while at the same time limiting or excluding certain heads of damage.

Secondly, if one disregards the more spectacular cases to which Articles 1382 and 1383 C.civ. can lead (keeping in mind that an award for non-material damage is often limited to a symbolic 1 FRF),[236] and if one looks instead to the core of tort law, all of the systems protect life, mental and physical health, bodily integrity, and the right to property and award compensation for economic loss consequential upon harm to person or property; and they also tend to award compensation for pure economic loss sustained as a consequence of negligent professional conduct. Moreover, the tort regimes under consideration compensate close relatives who sustain economic loss as a result of the victim's death or invalidity.

Thirdly, as has emerged from the foregoing examination, all legal systems contain a more or less explicit hierarchy of interests, with priority being given to the protection of bodily integrity and property. In Continental systems, this prioritization is achieved through the designation of such interests as subjective rights, either in the general rules or through specific legislative enactments, with a tendency even towards a right to bodily safety, in areas such as liability for traffic accidents or product liability. In the English common law, the supremacy of such interests tends to be assured by easing the fulfilment of the proximity requirement (one of the three branches of the test used to determine if there is a duty of care).

Furthermore, all of the legal systems surveyed shield specific interests by an array of statutory provisions, breach of which often leads to compensation for members of the class protected under the statute.

---

[236] Particularly in the area of invasions of privacy: see *infra*, Chapter II, 2.2.2., Introductory Note under c).

CHAPTER TWO
SCOPE OF PROTECTION

As we have seen,[1] the law of civil liability (or tort) is mainly about reparation—often through the award of damages—for the harm or *damage sustained by the victim*, as a result of the wrongful conduct of another person or of the conduct of a third party or an event for which that other person is responsible.[2]

Broadly speaking, for a claim in tort or delict to arise, the victim must be able to show that he or she has suffered damage. However, because of substantial differences between the legal systems, as is seen hereafter, the concept of damage can hardly be defined other than in the most general of terms, such as "any unwanted detriment to one's legitimate interests".[3] Even if the concept might be difficult to define, it remains nevertheless that "all the basic provisions of modern European tort laws require a plaintiff to have incurred loss for an action for damages to succeed", a condition which is "rarely fulfilled merely by a violation of the plaintiff's rights or of his person. Only if further detriment, such as financial loss or pain and suffering, is caused is damage considered to arise".[4]

As a general rule, damage, harm or injury, under whatever form, is thus a precondition to any remedy in tort. It also plays a role, as is seen in Chapter VIII, in the definition and assessment of *damages* under the principle of full reparation.[5]

In many legal systems, damage is not only a condition for a right to reparation to arise, and a yardstick for damages to be assessed, it is also part of an effort to set a certain order of priorities within tort law on an *a priori* basis, and is therefore concerned with the *hierarchization* of tort law. Such hierarchization is affected in those legal systems by limiting the legal interests which are protected by the law of tort or delict. As a result, the scope of protection of tort law is restricted *a priori*, that is from the outset and by and large independently of the facts of any individual case.[6]

---

[1] *Supra*, 1.2.

[2] "Damage" thus refers to harm sustained, "damages" to the sum awarded to compensate that harm: Markesinis and Deakin at 722.

[3] Compare with the definition which C. von Bar, "Damage without Loss" in W. Swadling and G. Jones, (eds.), *The Search for Principle. Essays in honour of Lord Goff of Chieveley* (Oxford: Oxford University Press, 2000) at 23 derives from § 1293(1) ABGB according to which damage consists in any detriment caused to another one's property, rights or person (*jeder Nachteil, welcher jemandem an Vermögen, Rechten oder seiner Person zugefügt worden ist*). However broad, that definition does not yet encompass detriment to legitimate interests which do not constitute subjective rights, which constitute a legitimate head of damage under French law: see *infra*, **2.F.19.** and notes thereafter. Markesinis and Deakin at 722 state more specifically that the common law had not concentrated—for some time at any rate—on *damnum* but on *injury*, the reason for this being that "damage awards lay, until recently, within the exclusive control of juries once the defendant's behaviour had been found to be tortious".

[4] von Bar, ibid. at 24; see also von Bar II at 8 with numerous references.

[5] See *infra*, Chapter VIII, 8.2.

[6] It goes without saying that other conditions also come into play to determine liability when the merits of the case are examined, such as wrongfulness or causation. These conditions do not usually work so as to exclude liability from the outset, however, and for the purposes of this chapter they were considered not to affect the scope of protection of tort law as such. They will accordingly be dealt with in subsequent chapters. See *infra*, Chapter III, V and VI concerning the events triggering liability (respectively one's own conduct, the conduct of others or an event not relating to conduct), Chapter IV on Causation and Chapter VIII on Remedies.

The purpose of the present Chapter is to examine those *a priori* limitations to the scope of protection of tort law, and consequently the hierarchization within tort law. In short, this Chapter seeks to answer the following basic questions:

– Does tort law protect all interests equally or are certain interests (for instance "subjective rights") worthy of more protection than others? Does it afford protection against all kind of injury (including for instance psychological disturbances or economic loss)?
– Does tort law grant the same protection to everyone or do certain persons or classes of persons enjoy a different degree of protection? Towards whom does a duty of care exist? To what extent can dependants as well as indirect or secondary victims pursue tort claims?
– Does tort law protect individual interests only, or does it also extend its protection to collective interests, at least under certain circumstances?

Not all legal systems look at damage as part of the broader issue of the scope of protection of tort law. The link between the concept of damage and that broader issue is most obvious under German law, where a list of "protected legal interests (*Rechtsgüter*)" defined as "subjective" and "absolute" rights at § 823(1) BGB is the main device used to sort out claims on an *a priori* basis, depending on the type of legal interest which was affected and gave rise to the damage for which the claimant is seeking reparation.

Neither French nor English tort law contains any comparable feature. That is particularly so under French law. Indeed, the very fact that we have included a chapter on the scope of protection of tort law may already in and of itself be incomprehensible to scholars in the French legal tradition: the *Code civil* contains little if any *a priori* limits on the scope of protection. In fact, French law does not apply any concept at all to limit claims *a priori*;[7] it seems deliberately to be aiming at the protection of plaintiffs against all kinds of socially unacceptable behaviour the injurious effects of which plaintiffs cannot be expected themselves to bear.

English common lawyers would not recognize the concept of "subjective rights" as a device to limit the scope of protection of tort law *a priori*.[8] However, as is seen from the selected cases, many of the issues and solutions dealt with in Germany in connection with the concept of "protected legal interests" resemble those dealt with under the heading "duty of care" in England. The reason for this similarity is that both the German and English legal systems put emphasis on the necessity to limit tort claims. They both try to achieve this by using restrictive concepts at the outset which, although different in name and structure, fulfil the same function and very often lead to comparable results.

The limitative enumeration of protected legal interests, as in German law, or the application of a concept of duty of care, as in English law, necessarily results in what we have called a "hierarchization", that is a certain order of priorities set within tort law. That

---

[7] None of the concepts which are common to French lawyers and might fulfil that function seems to be significant in French law: the illicit character of the relationship or of the damages claimed does not have much restrictive effect, even as regards unwed couples: see *infra*, **2.F.19.** The notion of fault, by act or omission, is construed very broadly, to the point of excluding all references to subjective fault even for minors. See *infra*, **3.7.19.**; and the notion of causation is not applied in a more restrictive way than elsewhere. Only the maxim "*nemo auditur suam turpitudinem allegans*" may have some restrictive effect, as a defence to be used by the plaintiff to defeat some damages claims: see *infra*, Chapter VII, 7.3.1.

[8] *Supra*, 1.4.3., Introductory Note under a).

does not mean, however, that legal systems where there are no *a priori* limits to the scope of protection of tort law, such as French law, do not also set priorities. As is seen below, French law has, through a combination of legislative and judicial developments, prioritized the protection against injury to the person, so much so that some speak of a "right to the safety of the person" (*droit à la sécurité*).[9] In fact, this kind of hierarchization, which all legal systems share, albeit to various degrees, transcends the boundaries of tort law altogether, not only because insurance and social security come in the picture, but also because the characteristic requirements of tort law are loosened for the protection of certain rights (mainly relating to the person).

This hierarchization can be seen in that legal systems sometimes dispense with the general requirement that the victim suffered damage, as set out above. English law, in particular, makes a distinction between torts which are actionable *per se* and those which require proof of actual damage. The former category includes torts such as trespass to land, assault, false imprisonment, and libel, where "the plaintiff need not prove damage in order to succeed. The fact that no harm was suffered will not affect liability, though it may affect the quantum of damages".[10] Similarly, under French law, the enactment of Article 9 C.civ. elevated the right to privacy to the status of an autonomous right, thereby weakening the link with the general liability regime of Articles 1382–1383 C.civ., in that both fault and damage—at least non-material—are held to be made out by the mere fact that the right to privacy was infringed.[11] More generally, various legal systems apparently tend to consider that "the violation and impairment of the psycho-physical identity of the individual constitute damage *per se*",[12] that is independently of the occurrence of concrete prejudice (be it material or non-material).

Accordingly, this Chapter will review the main categories of legal interests that are protected by the law of tort, namely life, physical integrity, health and freedom (Section 1), personality rights and privacy (Section 2), ownership and other property interests (Section 3), economic interests (Section 4) as well as collective interests (Section 5).

2.1. PROTECTION OF LIFE, BODILY INTEGRITY, HEALTH AND FREEDOM

This section starts with a discussion of German law, because at § 823(1) BGB it makes a categorization which can also be used to describe the other systems, as the subsequent discussion of English and then French law will show. The final subsection adds to the picture by surveying Belgian, Dutch, Italian and Swedish law.

---

[9] See *infra*, 2.1.3., Introductory Note.

[10] Markesinis and Deakin at 723.

[11] See *infra*, 2.2.1, Introductory Note, under b). For other types of cases where violation of a right is sufficient to engage liability, see Viney and Jourdain, *Conditions* at 6, para. 247, with reference to the case law of the Cour de cassation.

[12] C. von Bar, "Damage without loss", in W. Swadling and G. Jones, (eds.), *The Search for Principle. Essays in honour of Lord Goff of Chieveley* (Oxford: Oxford University Press, 2000) at 38–9 refers to the concept of *danno biologico* under Italian law as a forerunner in the use of so-called event-related damage (*danno evento*) instead of injury-related, or consequential, damage (*danno conseguenza*). See also *infra*, **2.P.34.**, where that type of damage is called non-material damage, however.

2.1.1. GERMAN LAW

Introductory Note

a) Among the protected rights enumerated in § 823 (1) BGB, life, body and health obviously have a special character. Infringement of the right to **life** occurs when death is caused intentionally or negligently. Liability is then incurred towards dependants of the deceased within the narrow limits laid down in §§ 844–6 BGB.[13] Infringement of someone's **bodily integrity** or **health**—those two types of infringement often but not always coincide[14]—gives rise to liability towards the primary victim or, exceptionally, his or her dependants, within the boundaries of §§ 842 and 845–7. Interference with **health** refers to causing physical or mental illness.[15] It includes medical malpractice and even, according to some, medical treatment undertaken without informed consent, but the better view is to consider the latter as an interference with the general *Persönlichkeitsrecht*.[16] Special problems arise in cases of prenatal injuries to unborn children or even those not yet conceived, which become apparent when the child is born, as well as in cases of unwanted life.[17]

Interference with **freedom** is understood to refer only to interference with freedom of physical movement (*körperliche Fortbewegungsfreiheit*), for instance by imprisonment (*Einsperrung*), and not to interference with the general freedom to act.[18] Otherwise the limited head of § 823(1) would be transformed into a general clause, contrary to the intentions of the drafters of the BGB.[19] Interference with freedom of physical movement gives rise to liability towards the primary victim or his or her dependants, within the boundaries of §§ 845–7 BGB.

b) Reference should be made here to §§ 842 and 847 BGB, which relate to loss and damage suffered by the injured person.[20] They must be read in conjunction with the general provisions of §§ 249–53 BGB regarding compensation for material and non-material damage in general.[21] The first sentence of § 249 provides that a person who is required to make compensation (a debtor) must restore the situation which would have existed if the circumstances making him or her liable had not occurred. This implies that the person receiving compensation (the creditor) need only be brought back to the same situation and is not entitled to any benefit over and above that.[22] If restitution in kind pursuant to

---

[13] See *infra*, **2.G.4.** and more explicitly 8.5.1. Note (2).

[14] See Larenz/Canaris at 378. Hitting somebody or cutting someone's hair constitutes interference with bodily integrity but not necessarily with health. Causing psychological disturbance may constitute an infringement of health, but not necessarily of bodily integrity.

[15] See *infra*, **2.G.1.–3.** and more explicitly 8.5.1.

[16] Larenz/Canaris at 383–5.

[17] Ibid.

[18] Ibid. at 385–6.

[19] See *supra*, Chapter I, **1.G.27.**

[20] §§ 844–6 BGB, which relate to damage suffered by dependants of the injured person, will be dealt with subsequently: *infra*, **2.G.4.** and Note (2).

[21] §§ 249–53 BGB are applicable to all types of obligation, contractual and non-contractual alike.

[22] In cases of personal injury or damage to property, the creditor (victim) may, pursuant to the second sentence of § 249 BGB, request that the debtor (wrongdoer) pays the amount needed for such restoration instead of the debtor him- or herself actually bringing about restitution in kind. This would enable the victim, for instance, to make his or her own arrangements for the treatment of physical injury or the repair of damaged property.

§ 249 BGB has not been brought about in due time, is impossible or insufficient, or would require disproportionate effort on the part of the debtor, §§ 250–1 BGB entitle the creditor to restitution in the form of monetary damages. § 252 specifies that the damage to be compensated also includes lost profits, as further defined in the second sentence of that provision. However, in respect of non-material damage, § 253 provides that monetary compensation may be claimed only in the instances specified by law.

The provisions of §§ 252 and 253 BGB are further implemented, in respect of tort claims, by §§ 842 and 847 BGB respectively. Thus, § 842 BGB provides that the obligation to compensate for damage on account of an unlawful act directed against the person of another extends also to the loss of income (actual or expected), whilst § 847 BGB provides that in cases of injury to body or health or deprivation of liberty, the injured person is also entitled to equitable compensation in money for his or her non-material damage.[23]

Much more could be said concerning §§ 842 and 847, but we shall restrict ourselves to a few points.[24] § 842 allows the recovery of expenses incurred to restore the injured person's health (such as medical and pharmaceutical expenses) as well as loss of income and prospects of obtaining or improving an income-earning position. By analogy with §§ 844 ff. BGB, BGH case law under § 842 also allows the victim to recover the value of healthcare services provided by close relatives of the injured person, as well as the loss of income suffered and the expenditure incurred by such relatives in the provision of such services, if such services would otherwise have been procured from third parties;[25] it is worth noting that the victim will then obtain compensation for damage which was actually suffered by the relatives.

§ 847 BGB concerns *Schmerzensgeld*. Although that term literally means money for pain and suffering, it is used in German law to designate reparation for the *whole* of non-material prejudice (*Nichtvermögensschaden*) in tort cases.[26] It thus comprises not only damages for pain and suffering, but also e.g. for reduction in well-being (*Wohlgefühl*) and happiness (*Lebensfreude*), loss of expectation of life or loss of alimony. The categorisation of heads of damage for non-material losses is more developed under French law.[27] As regards § 847, it may suffice to say that the amount of *Schmerzensgeld* will be determined taking account of all circumstances, such as the seriousness of damage and fault, the financial situation of both parties and even whether the tortfeasor is insured.[28] BGH case law shows that compensation may also be granted, under certain conditions, for interferences with the general *Persönlichkeitsrecht*.[29]

c) Apart from the general protection of life, body and health granted by § 823(1) BGB, various statutory provisions based on the concept of risk liability (*Gefährdungshaftung*) provide for liability without fault in respect of dangerous activities.[30] The most important of such provisions are to be found in §§ 7–20 of the *Straßenverkehrsgesetz* (StVG) of 19 December 1952.[31]

Other grounds of risk-based liability for dangerous activities are to be found in German law, amongst others for operators of rail transport services in § 1 of the

---

[23] No such compensation can be awarded for breach of a contract, e.g. a medical contract, in the absence of a legal provision similar to § 847 BGB in the contractual liability regime, providing for the compensation of non-material injury. As a result, persons injured as a consequence of a medical fault resort to tort law for claims based on non-material injury: see F.J. Nieper, "Schmerzensgeld bei Empfindungsunfähigkeit: Entschädigung für objektiven immateriellen Schaden" (1996) 4 Eur.R Priv.L 223 at 225.

[24] See further Larenz/Canaris at 585 ff. and 590 ff.

[25] Ibid. at 586, with references to BGH case law, including BGH, 24 October 1989, NJW 1990, 1037.

[26] Ibid. at 591.

[27] See *infra*, Chapter I, **1.F.24.–25.**, Note (2).

[28] Larenz/Canaris at 591–2.

[29] Ibid. at 494–5, 590 ff.; see also *infra*, 2.1.

[30] Risk-based liability is discussed in greater detail in Chapter VI on Liability not based on conduct.

[31] Road Traffic Act as amended, BGBl.I.837, BGBl.III.9231–1. For an English translation, see Markesinis at 813 ff. It is discussed *infra*, Chapter VI, 6.2.1.A.

Haftpflichtgesetz,[32] for holders of transport airplanes in § 33 of the *Luftverkehrsgesetz*,[33] for owners of conventional power plants in § 2 of the *Haftpflichtgesetz*, for owners of nuclear power plants in § 25 ff. of the *Atomgesetz*,[34] for those who release pollutants in the water in § 22 of the *Wasserhaushaltsgesetz*,[35] for those responsible for environmental damage in § 1 of the *Umwelthaftungsgesetz*,[36] for manufacturers in § 1 of the *Produkthaftungsgesetz*[37] and for manufacturers of medicines in § 84 of the *Arzneimittelgesetz*.[38]

BGH, 20 December 1952[39]   **2.G.1.**

Prenatal injury

Syphilitic child

The infection of a child with syphilis, as a result of a blood transfusion to the mother which occurred before the birth or even the conception of the child, constitutes an interference with the health of the child, once born.

Facts: The plaintiff's mother received a blood transfusion at the defendant hospital on 9 September 1946. Later, upon examination, it became clear that the plaintiff's mother had been infected with syphilis as a result of the transfusion and that the plaintiff, who was born on 13 October 1947, i.e. more than one year after the blood transfusion, was suffering from congenital syphilis.

Held: The plaintiff sought a declaration that the defendant hospital was liable for all present and future damage resulting from the infection of her mother with syphilis, as well as for her pain and suffering. In an earlier judgment, the same Chamber of the BGH had already stated that the situation under consideration involves not only contractual negligence towards the plaintiff's mother, who was a patient under the medical insurance scheme, but also a tort committed by the hospital workers involved in the transfusion, which can be attributed to the defendant hospital by virtue of § 31 BGB. In the present case, only the plaintiff's claim in tort for damage suffered by her was in issue. The judgments by the courts below allowing the claim were upheld.

Judgment: "1. The harmful conduct of the defendant hospital consists of its failure to take the requisite precautions when giving the plaintiff's mother a blood transfusion at a time before the plaintiff was conceived; this was a breach of a legal duty incumbent upon it. Although at first this act affected the health of the mother alone, it subsequently caused harm to the health of the plaintiff, born on 13 October 1947 . . .

2. The appellant first contends that § 823(1) BGB is by its very terms inapplicable in the present case since at the time of the harmful conduct the plaintiff had no health capable of being injured . . ., given that owing to her mother's disease she was herself already diseased at the moment of conception . . . This submission is unacceptable. It rests on a strictly objective and non-evaluative view of the rights listed in § 823(1) BGB and ignores the special nature of the vital interests at the head of that list . . .

It is a fundamental error to suppose that the distinction which the law draws between damage to *absolute subjektive Rechte* [in this context, that term refers to ownership and other property rights] and other forms of damage to the *Vermögen* can be transposed to the case where the damage is to

[32] Civil Liability Act of 4 January 1978, BGBl.I.145.
[33] Air Traffic Act of 14 January 1981, BGBl.I.61.
[34] Atomic Energy Act, version promulgated on 15 July 1985, BGBl.I.1565.
[35] Water Resources Act, version promulgated on 23 September 1986, BGBl.I.1529.
[36] Environmental Liability Act of 10 December 1990, BGBl.I.2634.
[37] Product Liability Act of 15 December 1989, BGBl.I.2198, as amended by Act of 25 October 1994, BGBl.I.3082.
[38] Drug Act of 24 August 1976, BGBl.I.2995.
[39] BGHZ 8, 243, NJW 1953, 416. Translation by T. Weir.

the *Lebensgüter* protected by § 823(1) BGB [i.e. the *Rechtsgüter* listed in § 823 (1) BGB that refer to existence: namely life, health and bodily integrity].

[These *Lebensgüter*] *are the axiomatic basis of the legal system. They reflect the nature of the individual being as a person, as a part of nature, of creation. Their content comes from the fact that they are an expression of life, of the very essence of the living person. To these* Lebensgüter *every human being has a right, a right to organic growth undisturbed and unaffected by human intervention* [emphasis added]. Any deprivation or disturbance attributable to human agency which impedes or affects natural growth and development constitutes an infringement of those *Lebensgüter*. It is therefore quite appropriate to describe "disturbance of internal biological processes" as an injury to health [reference omitted]. This is reflected in everyday speech when we refer to a child who, like the present plaintiff, is born with a significant impairment of its health, as sick, that is, as a child whose biological development has been affected and so is not in the healthy condition which creation and nature intended the living individual to enjoy . . .

. . . Conceived in the syphilitic body of the mother, the child contracted the disease and developed into a syphilitic human being. But for the harmful act or omission of the defendant this would not have occurred, that is, she would not have been a person afflicted with syphilis.

This lawsuit is not about harm to an embryo or to a child not yet conceived, but the harm suffered by the plaintiff in being born sick and syphilitic. As already indicated, the causal link between that damage and the infection of her mother is quite sufficient: the plaintiff suffered the damage on being born, and this constitutes an injury to her health. Accordingly, the preconditions for a claim under § 823(1) BGB are met."

Notes

(1) This 1952 judgment relates to injury suffered by a child which at the time of the accident was not yet conceived (*nondum conceptus*). It has to be seen in conjunction with a later BGH judgment of 1972[40] concerning brain damage suffered by a child born spastic, due to a car accident in which his mother, who was six months' pregnant at the time of the accident, was injured. In that case, the foetus was injured directly, as it was already conceived at the time of the accident, whereas in the annotated judgment the foetus was injured indirectly through interference with the health of the mother at a time when it had not yet been conceived. Both kinds of injuries are deemed to be interferences with the health of the *child*, provided that there is a causal nexus with the defendant's conduct. In both cases the claim for damages does not arise if no live birth occurs, or if the injury to the foetus has disappeared by the time of birth since, as the BGH emphasizes in both cases, the injury does not constitute an interference with the health of the *foetus* as such (which would create insurmountable difficulties in the case of a child not yet conceived at the time of the accident).

In the annotated judgment the BGH stresses the paramount value of life, thus reading into § 823(1) BGB a hierarchy of legal interests (under 2.). It therefore rejects the analogy, put forward by the defendant, with damage to property that was already defective at the time when the buyer acquired title to it.[41]

The cases referred to concern "prenatal injuries" to a child who was not "unwanted" by the parent(s). They are to be distinguished from so-called "wrongful birth" and "wrongful life" cases which concern actions brought, respectively, by the parents and the

[40] BGH, 11 January 1972, BGHZ 58, 48, NJW 1972, 1126. English translation by K. Lipstein in Markesinis at 133.
[41] See also Larenz/Canaris at 385.

child itself in situations where the child either *was* unwanted from the outset, for instance when an abortion failed, or *became* unwanted later on, because of an illness of the mother discovered during her pregnancy. Both situations are dealt with below.

(2) In the first hypothesis (child unwanted from the outset), the BGH had in a series of cases from the 1980s onwards established the principle that, if the doctor in charge of sterilization or abortion is at fault in not performing the operation correctly, he or she may be held liable for the cost of maintaining a child that would later be born. For example, in BGH, 27 November 1984, an abortion failed by reason of the doctor's fault. The mother brought a claim in damages for the cost of maintaining the child and for pain and suffering (a wrongful birth case). The BGH admitted the claim on the basis of breach by the doctor of a contract with the mother to terminate the pregnancy.[42]

In its landmark decision of 28 May 1993 on the law relating to abortion, however, the Second Chamber of the *Bundesverfassungsgericht* explicitly invited the BGH to reconsider this case law.[43] In its massive judgment, the BVerfG invalidated the provisions of the *Strafgesetzbuch* (Criminal Code) which regulated abortion. As to the legal status of abortion, the BVerfG stated that in principle abortion must be prohibited and considered contrary to law (*rechtswidrig*), except in a limited number of cases where medical, criminological, embryological or equivalent grounds exist.[44] The BVerfG drew the consequences of this position for issues of civil liability:

> "It is in principle essential that there be a civil sanction for the improper execution of the contract [of medical care to a pregnant woman] and for the tortious interference with the bodily integrity of the woman; this means . . . also compensation for losses including . . . an equitable amount for the non-material prejudice that the woman withstood in connection with a failed abortion or the birth of a handicapped child. In contrast, the *Grundgesetz* cannot allow that the *existence* of a child should be characterized as damage for [civil] law purposes (Art. 1(1) GG). All State organs are bound to respect the existence of every person in and of itself, which precludes the *obligation to maintain* a child being construed as damage. The case law of the civil courts . . . should in this respect be reviewed. The above does not affect the duty of a physician to compensate a child for the injuries which he or she has inflicted upon the child as a result of an incorrectly executed and failed abortion" [emphasis added].

The BGH duly undertook to revisit its case law. In an interesting exercise in inter-judicial dialogue, however, the BGH refused to follow the BVerfG completely. The BGH emphasized the distinction between the existence of a child and the obligation to maintain the child. While the BGH agreed with the BVerfG that the *existence* of a child cannot under any circumstances be seen as damage, the BGH could not find any constitutional reasons why, in the limited cases mentioned above where lawful grounds for abortion exist, a failed abortion could not lead to compensation for the *costs of maintaining* the child born afterwards.[45] Apart from those limited cases, the BGH followed the BVerfG and refused to allow compensation for the consequences of a failed abortion, since abortion remains

---

[42] NJW 1985, 671. English version by T. Weir in Markesinis at 166.

[43] BVerfGE 88, 203, NJW 1993, 1751.

[44] Except in the limited cases mentioned above, abortion remains contrary to law (*rechtswidrig*), according to the BVerfG, even if the Legislature can choose to leave it free of criminal sanctions (*straflos*). It therefore finds itself in a sort of legal "grey zone".

[45] BGH, 16 November 1993, BGHZ 124, 188, NJW 1994, 788.

contrary to law in principle.[46] Furthermore, in the related area of liability for the costs of maintaining a child born as a consequence of a failed *sterilization* (which is not contrary to law), the BGH refused altogether to change its case law despite the invitation of the BVerfG.[47]

(3) As for the second hypothesis (the child becomes unwanted), the BGH judgment of 18 January 1983 is in point.[48] In that case, a child was born handicapped as a consequence of her mother having suffered from rubella early on in her pregnancy. The defendant doctor failed to diagnose the condition, which would have led the mother to terminate her pregnancy. Both the child and the parents asked for a declaration that the doctor was liable to pay compensation in respect of all damage ensuing upon that failure of diagnosis. The BGH allowed the *contractual* claims of the parents, for the supplemental maintenance costs due to the handicap, and of the mother, for pain and suffering due to the complicated birth.[49] The BGH however dismissed the child's action in tort (a wrongful life claim) because there was no direct duty, enforceable by an *action in tort*, to prevent the birth of a foreseeably handicapped child on the ground that his or her life might appear "valueless". Recognizing such a duty would be inconsistent with the general protection of bodily integrity which the rules on tort have as their aim.

Here again, the BGH has refused to change its case law after the decision of the Second Chamber of the BVerfG.[50]

(4) The dialogue between the BGH and the BVerfG took on a new dimension when the first decision where the BGH refused to follow the BVerfG completely[51] was brought for review before the BVerfG.[52] This time the First Chamber of the BVerfG was hearing the case, as opposed to the Second Chamber, which had rendered the decision of 28 May 1993.[53] In its decision of 12 November 1997, the First Chamber of the BVerfG did not follow the Second Chamber; it found that the case law of the BGH, according to which a physician can be held liable for the cost of maintaining a child, did not infringe the *Grundgesetz*. What is more, the First Chamber declined to bring the matter before the full BVerfG, since it found that the statements of the Second Chamber quoted above constituted mere *obiter dicta*, from which the First Chamber could deviate without more. The Second Chamber marked its dissatisfaction by issuing a statement where it underlined its disagreement with the First Chamber.[54]

---

[46] BGH, 28 March 1995, NJW 1995, 1609.

[47] BGH, 27 June 1995, NJW 1995, 2407.

[48] BGH, 18 January 1983, BGHZ 86, 240, JZ 1983, 447. English version by K. Lipstein in Markesinis at 142.

[49] See Larenz/Canaris at 383, criticizing the decision of the BGH to grant damages to the mother for pain and suffering: "Just imagine that the child learns about the award of damages for pain and suffering!".

[50] BGH, 4 March 1997, NJW 1997, 1638.

[51] BGH, 16 November 1993, BGHZ 124, 188, NJW 1994, 788.

[52] BVerfG, 12 November 1997, BVerfGE 96, 375, NJW 1998, 519.

[53] The case came to the BVerfG by way of constitutional complaint (*Verfassungsbeschwerde*), for which the First Chamber is responsible, whereas the decision of 28 May 1993 was rendered by way of review of legislation (*Normenkontrolle*), for which the Second Chamber is responsible.

[54] BVerfG, 22 October 1997, NJW 1998, 523. For a comparative discussion of the divergence of views between the two Chambers of the BVerfG, together with the judgment of 21 February 1997 of the Hoge Raad, *supra*, **2.NL.25.**, see (1999) 2 Eur. R Priv. L 241.

BGH, 30 April 1991[55]   **2.G.2.**

Contaminated blood transfusion

Infection with HIV, following the transfusion of contaminated blood, even if it has not yet developed into full-blown AIDS, constitutes an interference with health.

Facts: The plaintiff claimed damages for the material and non-material harm resulting from his being infected with HIV following contact with his wife who had been treated with contaminated blood by the defendant, the university hospital E.

Held: The court of appeal allowed the claim on the basis of §§ 823(1) and 831 BGB. It based its reasoning on the general principles relating to product liability. The appeal for review was rejected.

Judgment: "1. The court of appeal was right in law to consider that infection by HIV constitutes an actionable injury to health within the meaning of § 823(1) BGB, for that text *includes every case where an impairment of normal bodily functioning is occasioned or exacerbated, and it is irrelevant that no pain is suffered or that no marked change is apparent* [emphasis added]. Besides, it is in line with virtually unanimous thinking to accept that contracting HIV constitutes an impairment of health even if it has not yet developed into full-blown AIDS [references omitted] . . .

3. In the result the court of appeal was right to hold that in procuring the blood which it administered to the plaintiff's wife the defendant had culpably failed in the duty of care it owed to him . . .

Fault is clearly established in this case and the defendant is liable for it. By allowing the plaintiff's wife to receive a transfusion of blood obtained in breach of best practice and so exposing the plaintiff to a life-threatening danger those responsible in the university clinic E. failed to satisfy their general duty of care.

a) In view of the fact that contamination of blood with HIV can have devastating consequences for the recipient and the persons he comes in close contact with and the further fact, as the court below correctly found, that it was known even then that the virus could be transmitted by transfusion, the university clinic E. was under an obligation to take the greatest possible care in obtaining blood and to reduce so far as currently possible the dangers from blood in which the contamination by HIV was undetected . . .

b) The University clinic E. failed to fulfil this duty . . .

c) It is no obstacle to taking such precautions as would most effectively secure the exclusion of high-risk groups that the individual donors have personality rights. Naturally such rights had to be taken into account by the university clinic in any measures it adopted to reduce the risk of HIV contamination. *If there is a stand-off between the . . . Lebensgüter of the recipients of blood and those with whom they come into close contact, on the one hand, and the privacy of donors and the possibility of their being discriminated against in public as members of groups at risk, the former must in principle be accorded priority in view of the very serious risk involved and the overriding need to protect human life* [references omitted, emphasis added]. Moreover, there is no direct invasion of the privacy of blood donors when questions are asked [in connection with the blood donation], since proper procedure allows them to decline to give blood and thus keep their condition to themselves . . .

5. Finally, the appeal also fails on the matter of damages for pain and suffering.

[55] NJW 1991, 1948. Translation by T. Weir.

a) The court of appeal was correct to regard the infection by HIV as compensable *per se* without any need to await the onset of the actual immune deficiency syndrome, AIDS. Even if the HIV infection did not apparently alter the plaintiff's physical condition, his very knowledge of the infection had a decisive effect on his psychology and his social relations. The suffering which the court of appeal found to have occurred calls for compensation for non-material harm even at the present stage of the impact on the plaintiff's health."

Notes

(1) Interference with health is *not* defined in this judgment by reference to illness and the present state of medical science.[56] Instead, in line with earlier judgments, it is defined by reference to what the general public considers to be an interference.[57] In the case under consideration, the plaintiff had been infected with HIV through the transfusion of a contaminated blood product but had not yet been affected by AIDS. The BGH emphasized that it was not necessary that the plaintiff be actually suffering or ill to hold that his health had been prejudiced within the meaning of § 823 BGB (under 1.). It suffices that the acts of the tortfeasor cause or aggravate a condition deviating adversely from normal physical functions.

(2) In its judgment, the BGH upheld the generous position taken by the court of appeal, which shifted the burden of proof onto the plaintiff as regards the cause of the HIV infection, the negligence of the defendant in the performance of its duty to avoid the use of contaminated blood (under 3.) and the imputation of the infection to the defendant's conduct. But the BGH, unlike the court of appeal, did not base its reasoning on its case law relating to product liability. It chose instead to rely on the general obligation of safety (*Verkehrspflicht*) of hospitals and their employees towards their patients. Nonetheless, the BGH reached the same conclusion as the court of appeal, in fact creating a virtually strict liability regime for blood products,[58] much as is the case now in France.[59]

(3) The impact on German private law of constitutional provisions relating to human rights and human dignity is also illustrated in the annotated judgment under 3.c), where the right to privacy and to non-discriminatory treatment of the blood donor are balanced with the right to physical integrity and health of the plaintiff and his wife, the latter ultimately outweighing the former.[60]

(4) Under 5., monetary damages are awarded for non-material loss under § 847 BGB (*Schmerzensgeld*),[61] consisting in the psychological burden for the plaintiff in knowing that he is irreversibly infected, even if the condition has not yet manifested itself.

[56] As it should be according to Larenz/Canaris at 377.
[57] BGH, 11 May 1971, BGHZ 56, 163; BGH, 4 April 1989, *infra*, **2.G.4**.
[58] E. Deutsch, "Die neue Entscheidung des BGH zur Aids-Haftung" NJW 1991, 1937.
[59] See *infra*, **2.F.18**. and Chapter VI, **6.F.30.–31.**
[60] The influence of constitutional law on private law was most explicit in the case law discussed *supra*, **2.G.1.**, Notes (3) and (4). See *infra*, 2.1.
[61] See *supra*, 1.1., Introductory Note under b).

BGH, 9 April 1991[62]   **2.G.3.**

Mᴇɴᴛᴀʟ ɪʟʟɴᴇss

Psychosomatic defects

Mental illness of the primary victim constitutes an interference with health not only when it follows from the tortious infliction of physical harm, but also when it directly follows from the wrongful act.

Facts: On 17 December 1973 the plaintiff was involved in a car accident for which the first defendant was liable. The plaintiff suffered a brain contusion, a long impact wound on the left side of the forehead, as well as various injuries to other parts of the body and contusions and abrasions. Subsequently, he began to show psycho-organic defects whose origin is disputed by the parties. They are manifested by changing character, weakness in mental performance, speech disturbances, paralysis and reduction in libido. On account of his mental debility, the plaintiff was unable to carry on the job of storekeeper which he held before the accident, nor could he take up any other gainful employment.

The plaintiff claims that the psychosomatic defects which manifested themselves are also attributable to the accident. He seeks a declaration that the defendant is liable in damages for the still uncompensated damage arising from the accident of 17 December 1973, and an order that the defendant should pay a further amount in respect of damages for pain and suffering and periodic payments under that heading.

Held: The court of first instance granted the plaintiff's claim on the basis that his psycho-organic defects were caused by the accident. The court of appeal held that the defendant was not liable for those defects. The plaintiff's appeal to the BGH succeeded.

Judgment: "[W]hen the court was assessing damages for *Schmerzensgeld* (§ 847 BGB), its refusal to take account of the plaintiff's psycho-organic defects was an error of law.

a) It was admittedly proper for the court below to take the view that the plaintiff's condition was not shown to be attributable to any organic brain injury sustained in the accident . . .

b) However, it was wrong of the court to confine itself to asking whether the plaintiff's psycho-organic defects were due to an injury to the brain itself, that is, due to a physical cause originating in the accident. *As this Chamber has held before, a tortfeasor is liable for the psychological effects of an accident for which he is responsible and is relieved of liability only in cases where the adverse psychological consequences can reasonably be said to be just part of the normal hazards of life, for then there is no connection of unlawfulness between the act and the neurosis. By contrast, it is not a precondition of the tortfeasor's liability that the psychological effects have a physical cause. It is sufficient if it is clear enough that the psychological impairment would not have occurred but for the accident* [references omitted; emphasis added].

On the basis of the expert opinions given before the court of first instance it appears possible, if not probable, that the plaintiff's defects are a psychological consequence of the accident . . .

Because of its erroneous view that there must be a physical/organic cause the court of appeal did not address . . . these expert findings . . . For this further reason the judgment under appeal must be set aside and the case remanded to the court of appeal for a finding whether the plaintiff's defects constituted psychological consequences of the accident; if so, they are to be taken into account in assessing damages for *Schmerzensgeld*."

Notes

(1) Mental illness, such as depression, neurosis and psychosis, comes within the ambit of protection of § 823(1) BGB not only when it is the result of physical injury culpably caused to the primary victim of an accident, but also in other cases where it follows imme-

---

[62] NJW 1991, 2347. Translation by T. Weir.

diately from the accident itself, as the BGH reiterates under b).[63] The BGH adds that it suffices for the plaintiff to prove that the psychological effects of which he complains would not have occurred but for the accident. Thus, if the accident merely results in the realization (*aktualisiert*) of one of life's general risks (*allgemeines Lebensrisiko*), the plaintiff is not entitled to be compensated for the illness. In such a case there is no causal link between the culpable conduct and the neurosis. The annotated judgment follows the position taken in earlier judgments.[64]

(2) For psychological disturbance to qualify for compensation under § 823(1) BGB, it must amount to what is considered an illness or disease in itself.[65] So far as entitlement to compensation is concerned, psychological disturbance must be distinguished from interferences with health which are caused by a psychological reaction (*psychisch vermittelte Gesundheitsstörungen*), as where a victim suffers a heart attack as a result of shock, fright or anger brought about by the tortious act. In such a situation problems of causation are likely to arise, especially if the tortious act as such did not cause any physical injury other than that flowing from an unforeseeable psychological reaction.[66]

(3) A victim who suffers mental illness as a consequence of tortious conduct for which the tortfeasor is liable may claim compensation for both material and non-material damage,[67] as is shown by the annotated judgment where payment of *Schmerzensgeld* was the primary issue.[68]

BGH, 4 April 1989[69]   **2.G.4.**

INFLICTION OF WORRY AND DISCOMFORT

Cancelled cruise

Natural grief and psychological disturbance on hearing of the death of a close relative do not qualify as injury to health for which compensation may be claimed from a tortfeasor.

Facts: The plaintiff and her husband had booked a cruise in the eastern Mediterranean scheduled to start on 26 April 1984 and paid the organizers the full price. On 21 April 1984 the plaintiff's son was killed in a road accident. It was not in issue between the parties that the defendant was liable in full for the damage resulting from the accident. On account of the pressures placed upon them, the plaintiff and her husband were unable to go on the cruise which began one day after the funeral. They could not claim reimbursement from the organizers. In addition to other claims, the plaintiff sought compensation for the expenditure on the lost holiday.

Held: The court of first instance awarded the plaintiff the amount paid to the organizers of the cruise, as compensation for the holiday expenses. The court of appeal upheld the decision of the court of first instance, but a further appeal to the BGH was successful.

---

[63] See further Larenz/Canaris at 378.
[64] In particular BGH, 2 October 1990, NJW 1991, 747.
[65] See also *infra*, **2.G.4.** as well as a tragic case, raising complicated issues concerning the origin of the neurosis suffered by the plaintiff, where the plaintiff was involved as a driver in an accident leading to the death of another person whose own grave fault was at the origin of the accident and therefore of the serious mental as well as material injury sustained by the plaintiff: BGH, 12 November 1985, NJW 1986, 777.
[66] Larenz/Canaris at 378 ff.
[67] *Supra*, 1.1., Introductory Note under b).
[68] See *supra*, **2.G.2.**, Note (4).
[69] NJW 1989, 2317. Translation by T. Weir.

Judgment: "1. On the facts found the court of appeal held that, as a direct consequence of the accident to their son, the plaintiff and her husband were injured in their health, an interest protected by § 823(1) BGB, and on this ground allowed their claim for compensation for the travel costs wasted as a result of having to cancel their holiday.

a) Even the very starting-point is wrong in law. True though it is, as long recognised by the case-law [references omitted], that injury to health with the meaning of § 823(1) BGB includes only physical effects to the body or health. *Feelings such as mourning and pain are intrinsically negative experiences, and may in serious cases generate physiological symptoms which may be medically relevant to one's physique, but it would run counter to the intention of the legislature if from a legal point of view they were regarded on that ground as an injury to health within the meaning of § 823(1) BGB. The legislature intended to restrict tortious liability under § 823(1) BGB to situations clearly defined both as to the interests to be protected and as to the conduct required by them* [emphasis added] and in particular (subject to the exceptions in §§ 844 and 845 BGB) to disallow claims by third parties, themselves unaffected in their own protected interests, who suffer as a result of injury to the protected interests of someone else. In cases such as the present where a person is killed, his close relatives are very likely to be upset psychologically and emotionally by the news of the death and to suffer damage both non-material and material. Nevertheless the law sets limits to the recovery of material harm by 'indirect' victims in the case of a fatal accident to the sum defined in §§ 844 and 845 BGB. This decision of the legislature to make the tortfeasor liable only for the damage suffered by the person 'directly' injured would be undermined if the psychological and emotional effects resulting from enduring such fatalities were to be compensated as injuries to health under § 823(1) BGB just because the medical profession regards them as relevant. For this reason, ever since its decision in BGH, 11 May 1971, BGHZ 56, 163, this Chamber has disallowed claims for damages for psychological harm unless it is pathological, grave and relatively long-lasting, clearly exceeding the normal effects on one's general state of health of an emotionally distressing accident, serious though they may be, harm which constitutes 'an injury to the body or health as also people generally would understand it' [references omitted]. For that reason the court of appeal was wrong to hold, at any rate in cases like the present where relatives suffer psychologically as the result of a death, that even in cases where the harm is only psychological, any disturbance of the inner person or experience of sorrow or malaise suffices, even if it cannot be held to constitute actual illness."

Notes

(1) The annotated judgment—in the case of parents suffering grief and consequential loss as a result of hearing of the fatal accident of their son—rejects the position of the court of appeal which considered any form of invasion of the plaintiff's general bodily condition, such as the infliction of worry and discomfort as damage to the plaintiff's health. Instead, the BGH follows the traditional view that for psychological injury to give rise to liability, it must be regarded by the general public and not only by medical practitioners as injury to body and health in that it amounts to a shock to the plaintiff's system. In so holding, the BGH followed its earlier decision of 11 May 1971.[70] In consequence, no claim can be made in the normal case of deeply-felt grief, even if it may have quite serious effects on a person's general well-being and even if it results in material loss.

(2) Like the earlier 1971 judgment, the annotated judgment adds that the contrary view would be inconsistent with the legislative intention manifested in § 823(1) BGB to limit tortious liability to clearly defined sets of circumstances. Persons who can show that

---

[70] BGHZ 56, 163. Translation by T. Weir in Markesinis at 109.

one or more of their *Rechtsgüter* has been infringed can recover their loss under § 823(1) BGB, even if the causal link between the tortious act and the infringement is not direct, as shown above in the prenatal injury case.[71] In that case, the child obtained damages for its own physical injury, even though it was caused indirectly through the injury which the wrongdoer inflicted on its mother.[72] Conversely, third parties whose *Rechtsgüter* have not been infringed but who have suffered loss as a result of the infringement of the *Rechtsgüter* of another cannot in principle recover under § 823(1) BGB, although the BGB makes an exception for a limited set of cases at §§ 844 and 845 BGB.[73] The coherence of this legislative scheme depends in part on the issue at stake in the annotated judgment, namely how psychological injury is understood. In cases involving tortious death, if grief and sorrow, such as that which close relatives of the victim normally experience on hearing of the death of the victim, were to be regarded as an interference with their health in the sense of § 823(1) BGB, then these close relatives could invoke § 823(1) BGB and recover their material and non-material loss pursuant to §§ 842 and 847 BGB, thereby running counter to the legislative intention behind § 823(1) BGB. Thus, in the annotated judgment, the parents tried to obtain recovery for lost expenditure on a holiday, which they could not obtain through the application of §§ 844 and 845,[74] by presenting their worry and discomfort as loss resulting from interference with their own health. The BGH rejected that argument.

(3) It follows from the preceding case law that psychological disturbance which is not regarded as an illness (because it has no *Krankheitswert* or pathological significance), i.e. disturbance such as the sorrow, pain and depression which are a normal reaction to news of death, do not benefit from the protection of § 823(1) BGB.[75]

Where the psychological disturbance is such as to constitute a direct interference with the victim's health,[76] then the victim can also recover non-material loss in accordance with § 847, but only in so far as such loss truly relates to the interference with his or her health.[77]

---

[71] *Infra*, **2.G.1**.

[72] For a similar case involving damage to property, see BGH, 4 February 1964, BGHZ 41, 123, NJW 1964, 720, also discussed *infra*, 3.2., Introductory Note: in that case, a hatchery was compensated for damage to eggs which were in the incubator when a power cut was caused by the wrongdoer cutting an electricity cable.

[73] § 844 BGB enables a third party, in cases where the wrongdoing resulted in the death of the victim, to recover from the wrongdoer funeral expenses as well as maintenance payments which were, or could have been, obtained from the victim *pursuant to a legal provision*. § 845 BGB is now for all intents and purposes obsolete: see *infra*, Chapter VIII, **8.G.42.** Note (5).

[74] In a part of the judgment which is not reproduced, the BGH rejected the plaintiff's subsidiary and hopeless argument that such lost expenditure would come within the notion of "funeral expenses" in § 844(1) BGB, on the basis that that notion included all expenditures associated with an appropriate and dignified burial.

[75] See also *supra*, **2.G.3.**, Notes (1) and (2).

[76] See also the second part of the 1971 judgment mentioned *supra*, **2.G.4.**, Note (1), as to whether the contributory fault of the plaintiff's deceased husband should offset the plaintiff's claim for injury to the plaintiff's own health. In that case, the BGH accepted an apportionment of liability, not by applying § 846 BGB but by applying by analogy § 254 BGB, which is itself an application of the more general principle contained in § 242 BGB.

[77] Larenz/Canaris at 383.

2.1.2. ENGLISH LAW

Introductory Note

a) Compensation for *intentionally* inflicted physical injury to the person can traditionally be obtained under one of the three main forms of the old "nominate" tort of trespass to the person, namely **battery** (intentional and direct application of force), **assault** (causing reasonable apprehension of the infliction of a battery), and **false imprisonment** (infliction of bodily restraint unauthorized by the law). The three have in common that the wrong must be committed by direct means, i.e. that the victim must have been struck, threatened or restrained, as the case may be, by the defendant directly.[78] If the harm is intentionally inflicted by "indirect" means, liability could arise under the *Wilkinson* v. *Downton* rule.[79] In that case the plaintiff was so violently shocked by the statement that her husband had been in a serious accident—made as a practical joke—that she fell ill. Wright J. held that a wilful act which is calculated to cause, and in fact causes, physical harm to the plaintiff—"that is to say, has infringed her legal right to safety"—is a tort, even if it does not constitute trespass to the person or any other nominate tort.

Assault and battery are crimes as well as torts. They are mostly handled by criminal courts, which in some cases have the power to make direct compensation orders against defendants.[80] The making of a compensation order often removes the need to bring a civil action.[81]

b) When physical harm to a person has been inflicted *negligently*, the present state of English law is that the only cause of action is **negligence** and not trespass.[82]

In cases of negligent *acts* causing physical damage to a person, a duty of care in the general sense[83] normally exists: for instance, the driver of a car owes a duty to all other persons on the highway to drive his or her vehicle with care so as to avoid causing them personal injury. The main issue is then whether that duty in fact exists *vis-à-vis* the particular plaintiff. In this connection the Congenital Disabilities (Civil Liability) Act 1976 should be mentioned: if a child is born disabled as a result of a wrongful act which took place before his or her birth and for which a person other than the mother is answerable, those disabilities are regarded as damage resulting from that wrongful act and are actionable at the suit of the child. The Act was passed because it was uncertain whether any duty could be owed to a person not yet born viable or even conceived.[84]

With respect to harm to the person, there are two situations in which existence of a duty of care is not necessarily acknowledged as a matter of course, namely injury due to a failure to act[85] and psychiatric injury.[86]

---

[78] See further Rogers at 60–81. For cases, see Weir at 346–61.

[79] [1897] 2 QB 57, QBD; see Rogers at 85.

[80] Powers of the Criminal Courts Act 1973 (c. 62), s. 35, as amended by the Criminal Justice Act 1988 (c. 33).

[81] Rogers at 13, 62.

[82] *Fowler* v. *Lanning* [1959] 1 QB 426, [1959] 2 WLR 241, [1959] 1 All ER 290, QBD, approved in *Letang* v. *Cooper* [1965] 1 QB 232, [1964] 3 WLR 573, [1964] 2 All ER 929, CA. On the limited practical impact of the assimilation of unintentional trespass to negligence, see Rogers at 83–5.

[83] *Supra*, Chapter I, **1.E.22.**

[84] See Weir at 117 and *infra*, **2.E.5.**

[85] Discussed *infra*, Chapter III, **3.E.5.**

[86] Discussed *infra*, **2.E.9.**

c) Unlike in Germany and France where statutes have been introduced on this issue,[87] liability for road-traffic accidents under English law is presently still governed by the principles of negligence,[88] albeit that "negligence in fact works much more strictly here than in other areas, so much so that in many instances it has become artificial to continue calling it by that name".[89]

Thus in *Roberts* v. *Ramsbottom*, a driver who suffered a heart attack and caused physical damage to persons and property in the ensuing accident was held liable.[90]

This issue of subjective versus objective standard will be further discussed in Chapter III as well as in Chapter VII in respect of the defence of contributory negligence.

d) When due to a defective product, death or personal injury as well as, to a certain extent, damage to property results, compensation by way of damages is recoverable from the person who manufactured the product (or had some other dealings with it) under the Consumer Protection Act 1987, which gave effect to Council Directive 85/374 of 25 July 1985 on liability for defective products.[91]

Congenital Disabilities (Civil Liability) Act 1976[92]   **2.E.5–6.**
and
House of Lords[93]
Macfarlane v. *Tayside Health Board (Scotland)*

CONGENITAL DISABILITIES. WRONGFUL BIRTH

A child born disabled has a cause of action against the person who committed the wrongful act from which the disability results. A physician performing a vasectomy is under a duty of care as regards the injury that might result to the parents from an unwanted pregnancy and birth of a healthy child, but not as regards the economic loss that follows from the cost of rearing the child.

1. Congenital Disabilities (Civil Liability) Act 1976   **2.E.5.**

"**1.** (1) If a child is born disabled as the result of such an occurrence before its birth as is mentioned in subsection (2) below, and a person (other than the child's own mother) is under this section answerable to the child in respect of the occurrence, the child's disabilities are to be regarded as damage resulting from the wrongful act of that person and actionable accordingly at the suit of the child.

(2) An occurrence to which this section applies is one which (a) affected either parent of the child in his or her ability to have a normal, healthy child; or (b) affected the mother during her pregnancy,

---

[87] *Infra*, Chapter VI, **6.F.18.** and **6.G.14.**

[88] Driving without due care and attention. driving whilst under the influence of alcohol or drugs, dangerous driving and causing fatal accidents are criminal offences: see Road Traffic Act 1991 (c. 40), amending the Road Traffic Act 1988 (c. 52).

[89] Markesinis and Deakin at 297.

[90] [1980] 1 WLR 823, [1980] 1 All ER 7, QBD. See also a similar case involving a driver suffering from diabetes: *Broome* v. *Perkins* [1987] RTR 321, DC. See also *Mansfield* v. *Weetabix Ltd.*, *infra*, Chapter III, **3.E.17.**

[91] See *infra*, Chapter VI, 6.3.3.C.

[92] 1976 (c. 28). The Act has been amended by the Human Fertilisation and Embryology Act 1990 (c. 37), s. 44, which inserted s. 1A, not reprinted here.

[93] 25 November 1999 (not yet reported).

or affected her or the child in the course of its birth, so that the child is born with disabilities which would not otherwise have been present.

(3) Subject to the following subsections, a person (here referred to as 'the defendant') is answerable to the child if he was liable in tort to the parent or would, if sued in due time, have been so; and it is no answer that there could not have been such liability because the parent suffered no actionable injury, if there was a breach of legal duty which, accompanied by injury, would have given rise to the liability.

(4) In the case of an occurrence preceding the time of conception, the defendant is not answerable to the child if at the time either or both of the parents knew the risk of their child being born disabled (that is to say, the particular risk created by the occurrence); but should it be the child's father who is the defendant, this subsection does not apply if he knew of the risk and the mother did not.

(5) The defendant is not answerable to the child, for anything he did or omitted to do when responsible in a professional capacity for treating or advising the parent, if he took reasonable care having due regard to then received professional opinion applicable to the particular class of case; but this does not mean that he is answerable only because he departed from received opinion.

(6) Liability to the child under this section may be treated as having been excluded or limited by contract made with the parent affected, to the same extent and subject to the same restrictions as liability in the parent's own case and a contract term which could have been set up by the defendant in an action by the parent, so as to exclude or limit his liability to him or her, operates in the defendant's favour to the same, but no greater, extent in an action under the section by the child.

(7) If in the child's action under this section it is shown that the parent affected shared the responsibility for the child being born disabled, the damages are to be reduced to such extent as the court thinks just and equitable having regard to the extent of the parent's responsibility.

2. A woman driving a motor vehicle when she knows (or ought reasonably to know) herself to be pregnant is to be regarded as being under the same duty to take care for the safety of her unborn child as the law imposes on her with respect to the safety of other people; and if in consequence of her breach of that duty her child is born with disabilities which would not otherwise have been present, those disabilities are to be regarded as damage resulting from her wrongful act and actionable accordingly at the suit of the child . . .

4. . . . (2) In this Act—

(a) 'born' means born alive (the moment of a child's birth being when it first has a life separate from its mother), and 'birth' has a corresponding meaning . . .

(5) This Act applies in respect of births after (but not before) its passing, and in respect of any such birth it replaces any law in force before its passing, whereby a person could be liable to a child in respect of disabilities with which it might be born."

2. *Macfarlane v. Tayside Health Board*   **2.E.6.**

Unsuccessful vasectomy

Facts: The Macfarlanes had four children and did not want their family to grow any larger. Accordingly, Mr. Macfarlane underwent a vasectomy operation. After the operation, fertility tests were made, in the light of which Mr. Macfarlane was told by his physician that he could have intercourse without contraceptive measures. However, some time later, Mrs. Macfarlane became pregnant. She gave birth to a fifth child, named Catherine. Mr. and Mrs. Macfarlane sued the defendant Health Board (responsible for the physician). They claimed GBP 100,000 for the cost of maintaining Catherine until majority, and Mrs. Macfarlane claimed GBP 10,000 for pain and distress arising from the pregnancy and the birth. The defendant asked for the claims to be rejected at the preliminary stage as disclosing no cause of action.

Held: The court of first instance dismissed all claims. The court of appeal reversed the decision of the court of first instance and allowed the claims to proceed to trial. The House of Lords agreed with the court of appeal as regards Mrs. Macfarlane claim for pain and distress, but it rejected the claim of both parents for the cost of maintaining the child.

Judgment:[94] LORD SLYNN OF HADLEY: "The issues raised in this case—or similar issues arising from other methods of preventing conception and birth—have arisen in cases before the courts of England and Scotland for some 20 years but have not yet been considered by your Lordships. The issues have arisen also in the courts of states of the United States, of the Commonwealth and of other European states . . . There is no single universally applied test [Lord Slynn conducted a review of cases from England, Scotland, the United States, the Commonwealth and other European countries; he referred in that connection to the judgment of the Hoge Raad of 21 February 1997 reproduced in the first edition of this casebook, now *infra*, **2.NL.25.**].

From this review it is clear that there is a wide range of opinions to consider. None is binding on your Lordships and it must be decided which of these approaches is as a matter of principle to be adopted as a rule of the law of Scotland and England.

My Lords, I do not find real difficulty in deciding the claim for damages in respect of the pregnancy and birth itself. The parents did not want another child for justifiable economic and family reasons; they already had four children. They were entitled lawfully to take steps to make sure that that did not happen, one possible such step being a vasectomy of the husband. It was plainly foreseeable that if the operation did not succeed, or recanalisation of the vas took place, but the husband was told that contraceptive measures were not necessary, the wife might become pregnant . . . It seems to me that in consequence the wife, if there was negligence, is entitled by way of . . . damages to be compensated for the pain and discomfort and inconvenience of the unwanted pregnancy and birth, and she is also entitled to . . . damages associated with both—extra medical expenses, clothes for herself and equipment on the birth of the baby. She does not claim, but in my view in principle she would have been entitled to prove, compensation for loss of earnings due to the pregnancy and birth . . .

Whether the parents should be entitled as a matter of principle to recover for the costs of maintaining the child is a much more difficult question. Logically, the position may seem to be the same. If she had not conceived because of the board's negligence there would not have been a baby and then a child and then a young person to house, to feed and to educate . . .

The question remains whether as a matter of legal principle the damages should include, for a child by then loved, loving and fully integrated into the family the cost of shoes at 14 and a dress at 17 and everything that can reasonably be described as necessary for the upbringing of the child until the end of school, university, independence, maturity?

The discussion in the American cases of the 'benefits rule' . . . persuades me that it should not be adopted here and it is significant that it has not been adopted in many American states. Of course judges have to evaluate claims which are difficult to evaluate, including assessments as to the value of the loss of a life, loss of society or consortium, loss of a limb or a function. But to do so and to get it even approximately right if little is known of the baby or its future at the time the valuation has to be made is very difficult. It may not be impossible to make a rough assessment of the possible costs of feeding, clothing and even housing a child during the likely period of the child's life up to the age of 17 or 18 or 25 or for whatever period a parent is responsible by statute for the support of a child. But even that can only be rough. To reduce the costs by anything resembling a realistic or reliable figure for the benefit to the parents is well nigh impossible unless it is assumed that the

---

[94] Lord Hope of Craighead and Lord Clyde issued concurring speeches. Lord Millett concurred as regards the costs of bringing up the claim, but dissented as regards the pain, suffering and distress related to the pregnancy and birth.

benefit of a child must always outweigh the cost which, like many judges in the cases I have referred to, I am not prepared to assume . . .

Accordingly, since I have rejected the . . . approach that nothing should be awarded at all, the choice is between awarding all costs incurred by the parents consequent upon the conception and birth of the child on the one hand and awarding damages limited to those I have already accepted, thereby excluding the cost of rearing the child.

As to this I do not accept the argument that no damages should be awarded as otherwise children will learn that their birth was not wanted and that this will have undesirable psychological consequences. An unplanned conception is hardly a rare event and it does not follow that if the conception is unwanted the baby when it is born, or the baby as it integrates into the family, will not be wanted . . .

The real question raised here is more fundamental. It is to be remembered on this part of the case that your Lordships are concerned only with liability for economic loss. It is not enough to say that the loss is foreseeable as I have accepted it is foreseeable. Indeed if foreseeability is the only test there is no reason why a claim should necessarily stop at the date when a statutory duty to maintain a child comes to an end. There is a wider issue to consider. I agree [reference omitted] . . . that the question is not simply one of the quantification of damages, it is one of liability, of the extent of the duty of care which is owed to the husband and wife.

It is to be remembered that in relation to liability the House has recognised that, in respect of economic loss, in order to create liability there may have to be a closer link between the act and the damage than foreseeability provides in order to create liability. Thus in *Caparo Industries plc* v *Dickman* [1990] 2 AC 605, [1990] 1 All ER 568 Lord Bridge said that there should be a relationship of 'neighbourhood' or 'proximity' between the person said to owe the duty and the person to whom it is said to be owed. That relationship depends on whether it is 'fair, just and reasonable' for the law to impose the duty . . . [T]he alternative test is to ask whether the doctor or the board has assumed responsibility for the economic interest of the claimant 'with concomitant reliance by the claimant'.

The doctor undertakes a duty of care in regard to the prevention of pregnancy: it does not follow that the duty includes also avoiding the costs of rearing the child if born and accepted into the family. Whereas I have no doubt that there should be compensation for the physical effects of the pregnancy and birth, including of course solatium for consequential suffering by the mother immediately following the birth, I consider that it is not fair, just or reasonable to impose on the doctor or his employer liability for the consequential responsibilities, imposed on or accepted by the parents to bring up a child. The doctor does not assume responsibility for those economic losses. If a client wants to be able to recover such costs he or she must do so by an appropriate contract.

This conclusion is not the result . . . of the application of 'public policy' to a rule which would otherwise produce a different conclusion; it comes from the inherent limitation of the liability relied on. A line is to be drawn before such losses are recoverable.

I would accordingly dismiss the board's appeal in respect of the claim for solatium by Mrs McFarlane and her claim for expenses caused directly and immediately by the pregnancy and birth, including medical expenses (if any) and the cost of the layette, but I would allow the board's appeal in respect of the claim for damages for the rearing of the child."

LORD STEYN: "*The cost of bringing up Catherine*

It will be convenient to examine first the line of English cases on which the Inner House founded its decision that the cost of bringing up Catherine is a sustainable claim . . . In *Emeh* v *Kensington and Chelsea and Westminster Area Health Authority* [1984] 3 All ER 1044, [1985] QB 1012 the Court of Appeal had to consider divergent approaches in [two previous cases before the court of first instance]. But the unwanted child in Emeh's case had been born with congenital disabilities. The defendants' contention was that the cost of upbringing should be limited to the extra costs attributable to the child's disabilities . . . Angus Stewart QC in 'Damages for the Birth of a Child' (1995) 40 JLSS 298 at 300 pointed out:

> 'The issue [in *Emeh*'s case] possibly presented as one of deceptive simplicity given that the claim was by the mother alone: it was held that the compensable loss extended to any reasonably foreseeable financial loss directly caused by the unexpected pregnancy. The formulation equates pregnancy with personal injury giving rise to *consequential* (as opposed to *pure*) economic loss which includes upbringing costs.'

. . . This decision has been considered binding on lower courts and on the Court of Appeal in regard to claims by parents for wrongful birth of a healthy child. It is the critical decision in the line of authority in England [references omitted] . . .

It is right to point out that the Court of Appeal decision in *Emeh*'s case predates the full retreat from *Anns* v. *Merton London Borough Council* [1978] AC 728, [1977] 2 All ER 118 which was announced by the decision of the House in *Murphy* v *Brentwood District Council* [1991] 1 AC 398, [1990] 2 All ER 908. Since then a judicial scepticism has prevailed about an overarching principle for the recovery of new categories of economic loss. Here the father's part of the claim for the cost of bringing up the unwanted child is undoubtedly a claim for pure economic loss. Realistically, despite the pregnancy and child birth, the mother's part of the claim is also for pure economic loss. In any event, in respect of the claim for the costs of bringing up the unwanted child, it would be absurd to distinguish between the claims of the father and mother. This feature of the claim is important. The common law has a great capacity for growth but the development of a new ground of liability, or a new head of such liability, for the recovery of economic loss must be justified by cogent reasons . . .

In the present case your Lordships have had the advantage of considering this issue in the light of . . . analytical and comprehensive arguments from both counsel . . . Claims by parents for the cost of bringing up an unwanted but healthy child as opposed to more limited claims by the mother in respect of pain, suffering and distress associated with the pregnancy have proved controversial in foreign jurisdictions [Lord Steyn reviewed the law of the United States, Canada, Australia, New Zealand, Germany and France]. From this comparative survey I deduce that claims by parents for full compensation for the financial consequences of the birth of the healthy child have sometimes been allowed. It may be that the major theme in such cases is that one is simply dealing with an ordinary tort case in which there are no factors negativing liability in delict. Considerations of corrective justice as between the negligent surgeon and the parents were dominant in such decisions. In an overview one would have to say that more often such claims are not allowed. The grounds for decision are diverse. Sometimes it is said that there was no personal injury, a lack of foreseeability of the costs of bringing up the child, no causative link between the breach of duty and the birth of a healthy child, or no loss since the joys of having a healthy child always outweigh the financial losses. Sometimes the idea that the couple could have avoided the financial cost of bringing up the unwanted child by abortion or adoption influenced decisions. Policy considerations undoubtedly played a role in decisions denying a remedy for the cost of bringing up an unwanted child. My Lords, the discipline of comparative law does not aim at a poll of the solutions adopted in different countries. It has the different and inestimable value of sharpening our focus on the weight of competing considerations. And it reminds us that the law is part of the world of competing ideas markedly influenced by cultural differences . . .

[C]ounsel argued that, if money spent on Catherine is regarded as a detriment to her parents, it is outweighed by the many and undisputed benefits which they have derived and will derive from Catherine. While this factor is relevant in an assessment of the justice of the parents' claim I do not regard such a 'set off' as the correct legal analysis of the position.

It is possible to view the case simply from the perspective of corrective justice. It requires somebody who has harmed another without justification to indemnify the other. On this approach the parents' claim for the cost of bringing up Catherine must succeed. But one may also approach the case from the vantage point of distributive justice. It requires a focus on the just distribution of burdens and losses among members of a society. If the matter is approached in this way, it may become relevant to ask of the commuters on the Underground the following question: Should the parents of an unwanted but healthy child be able to sue the doctor or hospital for compensation equivalent to the cost of bringing up the child for the years of his or her minority, ie until about 18 years? My Lords, I have not consulted my fellow travellers on the London Underground but I am firmly of the view that an overwhelming number of ordinary men and women would answer the question with an emphatic No. And the reason for such a response would be an inarticulate premise as to what is morally acceptable and what is not. [T]hey will have in mind that many couples cannot have children and others have the sorrow and burden of looking after a disabled child. The realisation that compensation for financial loss in respect of the upbringing of a child would necessarily have to discriminate between rich and poor would surely appear unseemly to them. It would also worry them that parents may be put in a position of arguing in court that the unwanted child, which they accepted and care for, is more trouble than it is worth. Instinctively, the traveller on the Underground would consider that the law of tort has no business to provide legal remedies consequent upon the birth of a healthy child, which all of us regard as a valuable and good thing.

My Lords, to explain decisions denying a remedy for the cost of bringing up an unwanted child by saying that there is no loss, no foreseeable loss, no causative link or no ground for reasonable restitution is to resort to unrealistic and formalistic propositions which mask the real reasons for the decisions. And judges ought to strive to give the real reasons for their decision. It is my firm conviction that where courts of law have denied a remedy for the cost of bringing up an unwanted child the real reasons have been grounds of distributive justice. That is, of course, a moral theory. It may be objected that the House must act like a court of law and not like a court of morals. That would only be partly right. The court must apply positive law. But judges' sense of the moral answer to a question, or the justice of the case, has been one of the great shaping forces of the common law. What may count in a situation of difficulty and uncertainty is not the subjective view of the judge but what he reasonably believes that the ordinary citizen would regard as right . . .

In my view it is legitimate in the present case to take into account considerations of distributive justice. That does not mean that I would decide the case on grounds of public policy. On the contrary, I would avoid those quick sands. Relying on principles of distributive justice I am persuaded that our tort law does not permit parents of a healthy unwanted child to claim the costs of bringing up the child from a health authority or a doctor. If it were necessary to do so, I would say that the claim does not satisfy the requirement of being fair, just and reasonable.

This conclusion is reinforced by an argument of coherence. There is no support in Scotland and England for a claim by a disadvantaged child for damage to him arising from his birth . . . Coherence and rationality demand that the claim by the parents should also be rejected . . .

The claim for pain, suffering and distress

The claim for a solatium simply alleges that Mrs McFarlane became pregnant and had to undergo a pregnancy and confinement and the pain and distress of giving birth to the child . . . The considerations of distributive justice, which militated against the claim for the cost of bringing up Catherine, do not apply to the claim for a solatium. There is nothing objectionable to allowing such a claim. And such limited recovery is supported by a great deal of authority worldwide. I would uphold it . . . "

Notes

(1) The Congenital Disabilities Act 1976 grants an action to the child only if (i) the child is born alive and disabled and (ii) the defendant was actually or potentially liable in tort (in negligence or otherwise) to either parent of the child for the act or omission which led to the disability (irrespective of whether the parent suffered actionable injury). It will be noted that the father can also be made liable under section 1 of the Act, but not the mother, with the exception of the situation referred to in section 2 (mother driving a motor vehicle and therefore insured against the liability). The defendant is not liable when he or she acted in a professional capacity for treating or advising the parent and took reasonable care as further described in section 1(5). The child's action is made subject to the same defences as those which could be raised against an action by its parents.[95] The Act does not apply to Scotland.[96]

(2) The Act does not deal with the situation where a claim is brought forward by a child born healthy, not does it deal with the situation where a claim is made for the mere fact that a child was born, healthy or disabled. In the common law systems, a distinction is usually made between "wrongful birth" and "wrongful life" cases. In the former, the parents seek compensation for the injury that they allegedly suffered because of the birth of their child, as in the annotated case. In the latter, the child himself or herself (through his or her parents) is claiming for the injury allegedly arising from his or her birth, usually because the child suffers from some disability which could have been detected on time and which would presumably have led to an abortion.

It can readily be seen that "wrongful life" cases raise very difficult questions about tort law and ethics. In England, the Court of Appeal decided in *McKay* v. *Essex Health Authority* that wrongful life claims will not be allowed on grounds of public policy:[97] physicians cannot owe a duty of care to a foetus to abort it if a disability is detected (but may owe such a duty to the mother). In addition, the assessment of damages is impossible, since it would involve a comparison between the position of a child born with a disability and a foetus that would never have been born.

(3) In the annotated case, the House of Lords was faced for the first time with a typical "wrongful birth" claim, resulting from a failed sterilisation. Such claims had already been brought before English courts, however. As explained in the speech of Lord Steyn, until the decision of the House of Lords, the leading precedent was a decision of the Court of Appeal in the *Emeh* case.[98] That case was particular in that the child was born with a disability. The Court of Appeal had allowed the claim in contract of the mother for both pain and suffering as well as the maintenance of the child.

Two speeches from the House of Lords have been excerpted above. They show how different paths led the Law Lords to the same decision. The speeches of the Law Lords in the annotated case consider numerous arguments; only the most contentious and decisive ones have been included in the excerpts above. In addition, the Law Lords relied on extensive comparative surveys, which were not reproduced.

---

[95] For a more extensive discussion of the Act, see Rogers at 828–9.
[96] Congenital Disabilities Act 1976, s. 6(2).
[97] *McKay* v. *Essex Health Authority* [1982] 2 WLR 890, CA.
[98] *Emeh* v. *Kensington, Chelsea and Westminster Area Health Authority* [1985] QB 1012, [1985] 2 WLR 233, [1985] 3 All ER 1044, CA.

(4) Both Lord Slynn and Lord Steyn have no difficulty in holding that the claim of Mrs. Macfarlane for pain, suffering and distress relating to the pregnacy and birth should proceed to trial. As they note, it is generally accepted that the physician has a duty of care in this respect.

(5) Both Law Lords also dismissed the claim of the parents for the cost of rearing their child. As a starting point, they agree on two central issues. First of all, both situate the discussion under the heading of "duty of care". As Lord Slynn noted, the problem could also be seen as one of causation or assessment of damages. However, the concept of duty of care is more suitable for the kind of general reasoning set out in the annotated case. Secondly, both Law Lords caracterize the cost of maintaining the child as pure economic loss. In the leading precedent before the annotated judgment, *Emeh*, the cost of maintenance had been characterized as economic loss consequential upon pregnancy and birth (and therefore recoverable).[99] Lord Steyn, in particular, provided a cogent explanation as to why it would be more appropriate to consider the cost of maintenance as pure economic loss.

Once it is accepted that the claim bears on pure economic loss, the general reluctance of English law to grant compensate such injury comes to bear.[100] Lord Slynn and Lord Steyn differed, however, in the reasons why they find that no duty of care arises. Lord Slynn concentrated on the issue of proximity (the second branch of the *Caparo* test[101]). He found that there was no "assumption of responsibility" such as would create a relationship of proximity between the physician and the parents as regards the costs of bringing up a child under the "extended *Hedley Byrne* principle".[102] Lord Slynn expressly avoided resting his conclusion on public policy factors. In contrast, Lord Steyn analyzed the case from the point of view of distributive justice, which is concerned with the just distribution of burdens and losses among members of a society (as opposed to corrective justice, as between the wrongdoer and the victim). He found that it would not be morally acceptable, relying on principles of justice, to grant compensation in the annotated judgment, in view of the fact that many other claims and grievances surrounding parenthood (absence of children, disabled children) do not attract compensation; in addition, from the point of view of coherence, he noted that no duty of care would arise in wrongful birth cases in England or Scotland.

---

[99] Economic loss which is consequential on injury to the person or to property (as opposed to pure economic loss) can in principle be recovered under English law: see *infra*, **2.E.36.** and notes thereafter.

[100] See *infra*, 2.3.1. and 2.4.1.

[101] The *Caparo* test is discussed *supra*, Chapter I , 1.4.1.B. Excerpts from *Caparo Industries plc* v. *Dickman* can be found *infra*, **2.E.47.**

[102] See *infra*, 2.4.1., Introductory Note under d).

House of Lords[103]   **2.E.7.**
H. West & Son v. *Shephard*

COMPENSATION FOR LOSS OF AMENITY

Victim in coma

Where the victim remains unconscious from the moment of the accident, compensation can be obtained for loss of amenity, but not for pain and suffering.

Facts: The 41-year old plaintiff was injured in an accident caused by the negligence of an employee of the defendant. She became quadriplegic as a result, and her cerebral functions were also affected. Even though she could not speak anymore, there was evidence that she could still recognize people and distinguish between foods. She required continual hospital care, without prospect of improvement, and would continue to do so for the remainder of her life (which was expected to be around five years).

Held: With reference to *Wise* v. *Kaye*,[104] where GBP 15,000 had been awarded to a permanently unconscious plaintiff, the court of first instance awarded GBP 500 for loss of expectation of life and GBP 17,500 in general damages. The defendant unsuccessfully appealed to the court of appeal. A further appeal to the House of Lords was also dismissed (Lord Reid and Lord Devlin dissenting).

Judgment: LORD MORRIS (majority opinion): "Certain particular questions have been raised. How are general damages affected if at all by the fact that the sufferer is unconscious? . . .

[This question] may be largely answered if it is remembered that damages are designed to compensate for such results as have actually been caused. If someone has been caused pain then damages to compensate for the enduring of it may be awarded. If, however, by reason of an injury someone is made unconscious either for a short or for a prolonged period with the result that he does not feel pain then he needs no monetary compensation in respect of pain because he will not have suffered it. Apart from actual physical pain it may often be that some physical injury causes distress or fear or anxiety. If, for example, injuries include the loss of a leg there may be much physical suffering, there will be the actual loss of the leg (a loss the gravity of which will depend upon the particular circumstances of the particular case) and there may be (depending upon particular circumstances) elements of consequential worry and anxiety. One part of the affliction (again depending upon particular circumstances) may be an inevitable and constant awareness of the deprivations which the loss of the leg entails. In this connection also the length of the period of life during which the deprivations will continue will be a relevant factor [reference omitted].

To the extent to which any of these last-mentioned matters depend for their existence upon an awareness in the victim it must follow that they will not exist and will not call for compensation if the victim is unconscious. An unconscious person will be spared pain and suffering and will not experience the mental anguish which may result from knowledge of what has in life been lost or from knowledge that life has been shortened. The fact of unconsciousness is therefore relevant in respect of and will eliminate those heads or elements of damage which can only exist by being felt or thought or experienced. *The fact of unconsciousness does not, however, eliminate the actuality of the deprivations of the ordinary experiences and amenities of life which may be the inevitable result of some physical injury* [emphasis added]."

---

[103] [1964] AC 326, [1963] 2 WLR 1359, [1963] 2 All ER 625.
[104] [1962] 1 QB 638, [1962] 2 WLR 96, [1962] 1 All ER 257, CA.

Notes

(1) In *Donoghue* v. *Stevenson*, the injury allegedly suffered was physical, Mrs. Donoghue having been taken ill by the thought of what she might have drunk.[105] Most physical injury cases unfortunately deal with much more personal harm. In such cases, as in the annotated judgment, various heads of damage may be at issue. Two broad categories, namely non-material and material loss, are to be distinguished. Within the first, the main heads are: pain and suffering and loss of amenity (roughly equivalent to *préjudice d'agrément*); within the second are: loss of earnings and of earning capacity (subject to deduction for benefits received[106]), reduction of life expectancy, expenses (medical or other) incurred as a result of injuries and interest.[107] The basic principle for the measure of damages in tort is *restitutio in integrum*, although it is generally acknowledged that that principle provides very limited guidance when it comes to compensation for non-material losses.[108]

In the annotated judgment, there was no disagreement between the Law Lords on whether the victim was entitled to recover for (i) her pain and suffering (nothing was awarded since the injured person was unconscious and did not suffer at all), and (ii) her financial loss (it was agreed that damages must be awarded irrespective of the plaintiff's condition). As to loss of amenity, however, the Law Lords were split three to two, the majority holding that "unconsciousness does not eliminate the actuality of the deprivations of the ordinary experiences and amenities of life which may be the inevitable result of some physical injury" (per Lord Morris). In his dissenting speech Lord Reid stated on the contrary that what principally matters is the victim's perception of daily frustrations or inconveniences, and that accordingly unconscious victims should obtain a lesser compensation for loss of amenity.

(2) According to Rogers, one of the most powerful objections that have been voiced against the majority opinion in *West* v. *Shephard* "is that one can no more compensate an unconscious person than a dead one and since there can be no award of damages for non-material loss in respect of the period after death, there may be a very great difference [as a result of *West* v. *Shephard*] between the total sum awarded to the estate of a deceased person and that awarded to an unconscious, living one, even though the latter will be unable to use the money for his benefit and the whole sum will probably at some future date pass to his relatives".[109] Yet, as he mentions, "there is a natural reluctance to treat a living plaintiff as if he were already dead".

Notwithstanding the arguments against *West* v. *Shephard*, the House of Lords has refused to overrule it in *Lim Poh Choo* v. *Camden Area Health Authority*, arguing that, if

---

[105] *Supra*, Chapter I, **1.E.23.** On the outcome of the case, which was settled for GBP 200 in 1935, see Weir at 39.

[106] As in other legal systems, the question of which deductions must be taken into account is a difficult one. For example, see *Parry* v. *Cleaver* [1970] AC 1, [1969] 2 WLR 221, [1969] 1 All ER 555, HL, on the deductibility of a disability pension from an award for lost earnings (text and comments in Weir at 643–8).

[107] For a full description see Rogers at 758–86.

[108] Ibid. at 757. In the context of pleading, a distinction is made between "general damage", which is what the law will presume to have been suffered, and "special damage", which is damage resulting from the particular circumstances of the case, and which must be strictly pleaded and proved: Rogers at 756, see *infra*, Chapter VIII, 8.2.1.

[109] Ibid. at 761.

that were to be done, it should be done by the legislature within the context of comprehensive legislation.[110]

(3) The extent of the controversy described above should not be exaggerated, since in *West* v. *Shephard* the dissenting Law Lords accepted that something must be awarded for loss of amenity even if the victim was unconscious (although the amount will be nominal), whilst the majority accepted that an award under this head would be increased if the plaintiff were conscious of his loss.[111]

House of Lords[112]   2.E.8–9.
Alcock v. *Chief Constable of the South Yorkshire Police*
and
House of Lords[113]
Page v. *Smith*

INJURY CAUSED BY PSYCHIATRIC ILLNESS

Injury caused by psychiatric illness (going beyond shock, fear or grief) is actionable in tort at the suit of (i) a primary victim, if some injury, physical or psychiatric, was reasonably foreseeable, even if no physical injury actually occurred (Page) and (ii) a secondary victim, if such psychiatric injury was reasonably foreseeable and the victim was closely and directly affected ("proximity") (Alcock).

1. *Alcock* v. *Chief Constable of the South Yorkshire Police*   2.E.8.

Crush at football stadium

Facts: The police allowed an excessive number of intending spectators to enter an already full part of a football stadium in Hillsborough. In consequence 95 spectators were crushed to death over 400 were injured. The police admitted liability in respect of those who were killed or injured but denied that they owed any duty of care to the plaintiffs, all of whom were relatives of primary victims and who had suffered nervous shock causing psychiatric illness as a result of seeing, or hearing news of, the disaster on television or the radio.

Held: The court of first instance allowed 10 of the 16 claims. The court of appeal dismissed all the claims. Ten cases were brought on appeal before the House of Lords, which dismissed them.

Judgment: LORD KEITH: "The question of liability in negligence for what is commonly, if inaccurately, described as 'nervous shock' has only twice been considered by this House, in *Hay (or Bourhill)* v. *Young* and in *McLoughlin* v. *O'Brian*. In the latter case . . . the leading speech was delivered by Lord Wilberforce. Having set out the position so far reached in the decided cases on nervous shock, he expressed the opinion that foreseeability did not of itself and automatically give rise to a duty of care owed to a person or class of persons and that considerations of policy entered into the conclusion that such a duty existed . . .

---

[110] [1980] AC 174, [1979] 3 WLR 44, [1979] 2 All ER 910, HL.
[111] Rogers at 762.
[112] [1992] 1 AC 310, [1991] 4 All ER 907, *sub nom. Jones* v. *Wright* [1991] 3 All ER 88.
[113] [1996] 1 AC 155, [1995] 2 All ER 736.

[DOES REASONABLE FORESEEABILITY OF ITSELF GIVE RISE TO A DUTY OF CARE?]
It was argued for the appellants in the present case that reasonable foreseeability of the risk of injury to them in the particular form of psychiatric illness was all that was required to bring home liability to the respondent. In the ordinary case of direct physical injury suffered in an accident at work or elsewhere, reasonable foreseeability of the risk is indeed the only test that need be applied to determine liability. But injury by psychiatric illness is more subtle, as Lord Macmillan observed in *Bourhill* v. *Young*. In the present type of case it is a *secondary sort of injury* brought about by the infliction of psychical injury, *upon another person* [emphasis added].

That [secondary sort of injury] can affect those closely connected with that person in various ways. One way is by subjecting a close relative to the stress and strain of caring for the injured person over a prolonged period, but psychiatric illness due to such stress and strain has not so far been treated as founding a claim in damages. *So I am of the opinion that in addition to reasonable foreseeability liability for injury in the particular form of psychiatric illness must depend in addition upon a requisite relationship of proximity between the claimant and the party said to owe the duty* [emphasis added] . . . The concept of a person being closely and directly affected has been conveniently labelled 'proximity', and this concept has been applied in certain categories of cases, particularly those concerned with pure economic loss, to limit and control the consequences as regards liability which would follow if reasonable foreseeability were the sole criterion.

[HOW IS THE ADDITIONAL REQUIREMENT OF PROXIMITY TO BE UNDERSTOOD?]
As regards *the class of persons* to whom a duty may be owed to take reasonable care to avoid inflicting psychiatric illness through nervous shock sustained by reason of physical injury or peril to another, I think it sufficient that *reasonable foreseeability should be the guide* [emphasis added]. I would not seek to limit the class by reference to particular relationships such as husband and wife or parent and child. The kinds of relationship which may involve close ties of love and affection are numerous, and it is the existence of such ties which leads to mental disturbance when the loved one suffers a catastrophe . . . It is common knowledge that such ties exist, and reasonably foreseeable that those bound by them may in certain circumstances be at real risk of psychiatric illness if the loved one is injured or put in peril. The closeness of the tie would, however, require to be proved by a plaintiff, though no doubt being capable of being presumed in appropriate cases. Psychiatric injury to him would not ordinarily, in my view, be within the range of reasonable foreseeability, but could not perhaps be entirely excluded from it if the circumstances of a catastrophe occurring very close to him were particularly horrific.

In the case of those within the sphere of reasonable foreseeability the proximity factors mentioned by Lord Wilberforce in McLoughlin v. O'Brian *must, however, be taken into account in judging whether a duty of care exists* [emphasis added]. The first of these is proximity of the plaintiff to the accident in *time and space.* For this purpose the accident is to be taken to include its immediate aftermath, which in *McLoughlin's* case was held to cover the scene at the hospital which was experienced by the plaintiff some two hours after the accident. In *Jaensch* v. *Coffey* the plaintiff saw her injured husband at the hospital to which he had been taken in severe pain before and between his undergoing a series of emergency operations, and the next day stayed with him in the intensive care unit and thought he was going to die. She was held entitled to recover damages for the psychiatric illness she suffered as a result . . . As regards the *means* by which the shock is suffered, Lord Wilberforce said in *McLoughlin's* case that it must come through sight or hearing of the event or of its immediate aftermath. He also said that it was surely right that the law should not compensate shock brought about by communication by a third party . . .

Of the present appellants two, Brian Harrison and Robert Alcock, were present at the ground, both of them in the West Stand, from which they witnessed the scenes in pens 3 and 4. Brian Harrison lost two brothers, while Robert Alcock lost a brother-in-law and identified the body at the mortuary at midnight. In neither of these cases was there any evidence of particularly close ties of love or affection with the brothers or brother-in-law. In my opinion the mere fact of the particular relationship was insufficient to place the plaintiff within the class of persons to whom a duty of care could be owed by the defendant as being foreseeable at risk of psychiatric illness by reason of injury or peril to the individuals concerned . . . I would, however, place in the category of members to which risk of psychiatric illness was reasonably foreseeable Mr. and Mrs. Copoc, whose son was killed, and Alexandra Penk, who lost her fiancé. In each of these cases the closest ties of love and affection fall to be presumed from the fact of the particular relationship, and there is no suggestion of anything which might tend to rebut that presumption. These three all watched scenes from Hillsborough on television, but none of these depicted suffering of recognizable individuals, such being excluded by the broadcasting code of ethics, a position known to the defendant. In my opinion the viewing of these scenes cannot be equiparated with the viewer being within 'sight or hearing of the event or of its immediate aftermath', to use the words of Lord Wilberforce in *McLoughlin* v. *O'Brian*, nor can the scenes reasonably be regarded as giving rise to shock, in the sense of a sudden assault on the nervous system. They were capable of giving rise to anxiety for the safety of relatives known or believed to be present in the area affected by the crush, and undoubtedly did so, but that is very different from seeing the fate of the relative or his condition shortly after the event. The viewing of the television scenes did not create the necessary degree of proximity."

2. *Page* v. *Smith*   2.E.9.

Chronic exhaustion

Facts: While driving along the highway the plaintiff was involved in a collision with a car driven by the defendant. The plaintiff suffered no physical injury but three hours after the accident he felt exhausted and the exhaustion had continued. For 20 years prior to the accident the plaintiff had suffered from a condition variously described as myalgic encephalomyelitis, chronic fatigue syndrome or post-viral fatigue syndrome which manifested itself from time to time with different degrees of severity. The plaintiff brought an action claiming damages for personal injuries caused by the defendant's negligence in that as a result of the accident his condition had become chronic and permanent and that it was unlikely that he would be able to take full-time employment again.

Held: The court of first instance found for the plaintiff and awarded him GBP 162,153 damages. The court of appeal allowed an appeal by the defendant on the ground that the plaintiff's injury was not reasonably foreseeable. The House of Lords reversed the court of appeal on this issue.

Judgment: LORD LLOYD (speaking for the majority of three against two): "This is the fourth occasion on which the House has been called on to consider 'nervous shock'. On the three previous occasions, *Bourhill* v. *Young* [1943] AC 92, *McLoughlin* v. *O'Brian* [1983] 1 AC 410 and *Alcock* v. *Chief Constable of South Yorkshire Police* [1992] 1 AC 310, the plaintiffs were, in each case, outside the range of foreseeable physical injury . . .

[ON THE DISTINCTION BETWEEN PRIMARY AND SECONDARY VICTIMS]
In all these cases the plaintiff was the secondary victim of the defendant's negligence. He or she was in the position of a spectator or bystander. In the present case, by contrast, the plaintiff was a participant. He was himself directly involved in the accident, and well within the range of foreseeable physical injury. He was *the primary victim*. This is thus the first occasion on which your Lordships have to decide whether, in such a case, the foreseeability of physical injury is enough to enable the plaintiff to recover damages for nervous shock.

The factual distinction between primary and secondary victims of an accident is obvious and of long-standing . . .

Although the plaintiff was, as I have said, the primary victim, the peculiarity of the present case is that, by good fortune, he suffered no broken bones and no bruising; indeed he had no external physical injury of any kind. But as a direct result of the accident he suffered a recrudescence of an illness or condition known variously as ME, CFS or PVFS, from which he had previously suffered in a mild form on sporadic occasions, but which, since the accident, has become an illness of 'chronic intensity and permanency' . . .

[ON THE NECESSITY OF FORESEEABILITY OF PSYCHIATRIC INJURY, SEPARATE FROM
FORESEEABILITY OF PHYSICAL INJURY, IN THE CASE OF A PRIMARY VICTIM]
[There follows a discussion of the conflicting views of the judge at first instance and the court of appeal as to the necessity of foreseeability in a case when the plaintiff did not suffer physical injury but only psychiatric injury].

Foreseeability of psychiatric injury remains a crucial ingredient when the plaintiff is the secondary victim, for the very reason that the secondary victim is almost always outside the area of physical impact, and therefore outside the range of foreseeable physical injury. But where the plaintiff is the primary victim of the defendant's negligence, the nervous shock cases, by which I mean the cases following on from *Bourhill* v. *Young*, are not in point. Since the defendant was admittedly under a duty of care not to cause the plaintiff foreseeable physical injury, it was unnecessary to ask whether he was under a separate duty of care not to cause foreseeable psychiatric injury . . .

As medical science advances, it is important that the law should not be seen to limp too far behind: see *Mount Isa Mines Ltd* v. *Pusey*, 125 CLR 383 at 395 per Windeyer J. As long ago as 1901 the courts were already beginning to become aware that there may be no hard and fast line between physical and psychiatric injury . . . Likewise, in more recent times, Lord Bridge of Harwich drew attention to the interrelation of physical and psychiatric injury in *McLoughlin* v. *O'Brian* [1983] 1 AC 410 at 433 . . . In an age when medical knowledge is expanding fast, and psychiatric knowledge with it, it would not be sensible to commit the law to a distinction between physical and psychiatric injury, which may already seem somewhat artificial, and may soon be altogether outmoded. Nothing will be gained by treating them as different 'kinds' of personal injury, so as to require the application of different test in law.

My noble and learned friend, Lord Keith of Kinkel, has drawn attention to an observation of Lord Wright in *Bourhill* v. *Young* [1943] AC 92 at 110, that in nervous shock cases the circumstances of the accident or event must be viewed *ex post facto*. There are similar observations by Lord Wilberforce and Lord Bridge in *McLoughlin* v. *O'Brian* [1983] 1 AC 410 at 420 and 432. This makes sense, as Lord Keith points out, where the plaintiff is a secondary victim. For if you do not know the outcome of the accident or event, it is impossible to say whether the defendant should have foreseen injury by shock. It is necessary to take account of what happened in order to apply the test of reasonable foreseeability at all. But it makes no sense in the case of a primary victim. Liability for physical injury depends on what was reasonably foreseeable by the defendant before the event. It could not be right that a negligent defendant should escape liability for psychiatric injury just because, though serious physical injury was foreseeable, it did not in fact transpire. Such a result in the case of a primary victim is neither necessary, logical nor just. To introduce hindsight into the trial of an ordinary running-down action would do the law no service.

Are there any disadvantages in taking [this] simple approach . . .? It may be said that it would open the door too wide, and encourage bogus claims. As for opening the door, this is a very important consideration in claims by secondary victims. It is for this reason that the courts have, as a matter of policy, rightly insisted on a number of control mechanisms. Otherwise, a negligent defendant might find himself being made liable to all the world. Thus in the case of secondary victims, foreseeability of injury by shock is not enough. The law also requires a degree of proximity: see *Alcock's* case [1992] 1 AC 310 per Lord Keith of Kinkel, at 396 . . .

None of these mechanisms are required in the case of a primary victim. Since liability depends on foreseeability of physical injury, there could be no question of the defendant finding himself liable to all the world. Proximity of relationship cannot arise, and proximity in time and space goes without saying . . .

Applying that test [of reasonable foreseeability] in the present case, it was enough to ask whether the defendant should have reasonably foreseen that the plaintiff might suffer physical injury as a result of the defendant's negligence, so as to bring him within the range of the defendant's duty of care. It was unnecessary to ask, as a separate question, whether the defendant should reasonably have foreseen injury by shock; and it is irrelevant that the plaintiff did not, in fact, suffer any external physical injury."

Notes

(1) As stated by Lord Keith in *Alcock* v. *Chief Constable of the South Yorkshire Police*, the issue of liability in negligence for what is commonly, if inaccurately, described as "nervous shock" had been considered only *twice* by the House of Lords before that case, namely in *Bourhill* v. *Young*[114] and *McLoughlin* v. *O'Brian*.[115]

In *Bourhill* v. *Young*, the appellant suffered a severe shock and other injuries when a motorcyclist negligently turned into the path of an oncoming car and was killed. Her view of the accident had been obscured by the tram but she heard the sound of the collision and saw blood on the road after the body had been removed. The House of Lords held that the car driver did not owe her a duty of care since he could not reasonably have foreseen that she would suffer such injuries in the circumstances. In that judgment, the issues of remoteness of damage and duty of care were hard to distinguish since both were described in terms of reasonable foreseeability. *McLoughlin* v. *O'Brian* dealt with a road accident in which the plaintiff's husband and three children were involved, some two miles from the plaintiff's home. The plaintiff was informed about an hour later by a motorist who came to her home and drove her to the hospital. There she learned of her daughter's death and found the rest of her family in pain, screaming and covered in mud, oil and blood. She suffered severe and persistent psychiatric symptoms. She succeeded in her claim despite not having been at the scene of the accident, as the House of Lords interpreted the criterion of presence at the scene of the injury to include those who came upon "the immediate aftermath".

(2) Both *Bourhill* v. *Young* and *McLoughlin* v. *O'Brian* concerned the situation of so-called *secondary victims*, that is victims who were involved in the accident not directly but only indirectly, as a spectator or bystander. In *McLoughlin*, Lord Wilberforce, after reviewing the case-law, said that in the case of secondary victims, foreseeability did not automatically give rise to a duty of care owed to a person or class of persons. He said that considerations of policy entered into the examination of the duty of care, so that recovery was confined "to those within sight and sound of an event caused by negligence or, at least, to those in close, or very close, proximity to such a situation". After weighing the policy arguments on both sides, he concluded that the admissibility of claims was conditioned on (i) the **class of persons** to which the claimant belongs (going only exceptionally beyond the closest of family ties, of parent and child, or husband and wife);[116] (ii) the **proximity** of the claimant to the accident (presence on the scene or arrival in the

---

[114] [1943] AC 92, [1942] 2 All ER 396, HL.

[115] [1983] AC 410, [1982] 2 All ER 298, HL. For an overview of the case law of the lower courts, see Weir at 109–12.

[116] The claim of a rescuer is recognized, however: *Chadwick* v. *British Transport Commission* [1967] 1 WLR 912, [1967] 2 All ER 945, QBD. Injury to rescuers is usually physical. In that case, however, the rescuer had suffered psychological injury: the plaintiff who had assisted the victims of a train accident was psychologically marked for life by the horror of what he had seen. British Rail had to pay him, on the principle that a person who negligently causes an accident may be liable to those who come to help the victims and get injured themselves: see further Weir at 111.

immediate aftermath); and (iii) the **means** by which the shock is caused (compensation for shock from seeing or hearing the event or its immediate aftermath, but not for shock caused through communication by a third party).

In *Alcock*, Lord Keith followed Lord Wilberforce's approach, saying that "in addition to reasonable foreseeability liability for injury in the particular form of psychiatric illness must depend in addition upon a requisite relationship of proximity between the claimant and the party said to owe the duty". He assimilated Lord Atkin's "neighbour principle" in *Donoghue* v. *Stevenson*[117] ("a person being closely and directly affected") with the concept of proximity. He then briefly re-examined the three limitations used by Lord Wilberforce (class of persons, proximity and means). Of these three Lord Keith in *Alcock* defined the *class of persons* somewhat differently from Lord Wilberforce in *McLoughlin*: affection can be *presumed* in some cases, and the class is not to be limited to particular relationships (the "pure" bystander could qualify: see Lord Ackner's speech, not reproduced here). As regards the *means* by which the shock is caused, Lord Keith expressly excluded plaintiffs who, although falling within the appropriate class of persons, saw the accident only on television (in *McLoughlin*, Lord Wilberforce had suggested that they could be included). Indeed television broadcasters did not, and under the Broadcasting Code of Ethics could not, depict the suffering of recognizable individuals. Lord Ackner added that in that respect a breach of that Code would constitute a *novus actus interveniens* breaking the chain of causation and relieving the defendant of liability. Weighing all those considerations, the House of Lords finally dismissed all the claims but for different reasons.

In a further case arising from the same accident, the House of Lords denied compensation to five police officers who took part in the police intervention at the stadium and suffered psychiatric injury as a result of witnessing horrible scenes.[118] According to the House of Lords, the duty of care of the police force towards its officers is similar to the duty of care of the employer towards its employees: the police force must take reasonable care to protect the officers from *physical injury*. As long as that duty was discharged (as it was in that case), there is no liability for any *psychological injury* which might occur. Furthermore, the House of Lords refined the distinction between primary and secondary victims by introducing the notion of danger: since the officers were not physically injured nor exposed to a danger of physical injury, they were secondary victims. They were thus subject to the more exacting test of *Alcock* (as opposed to *Page* v. *Smith* for primary victims) for the establishment of a duty of care. In that respect, it would be unfair if they could recover damages whereas the relatives of the victims (in *Alcock*) could not.[119]

(3) In *Page* v. *Smith*, Lord Lloyd, speaking for a majority of three to two (Lord Keith and Lord Jauncey dissenting), went to great lengths to distinguish the other nervous shock cases decided by the House of Lords (*Bourhill*, *McLoughlin* and *Alcock*) on the basis that the victim in *Page* was a primary victim involved in the accident.

For primary victims, given that direct involvement, the concept of proximity has no significance. The question arises, however, whether the foreseeability test applies exclusively to physical harm, or whether it must also be applied separately to psychological injury, particularly in a case such as *Page* where the victim suffered only psychological injury. In *Page* v. *Smith*, the House of Lords answered that it is enough "to ask whether the defendant should have reasonably foreseen that the plaintiff might suffer physical injury . . . to bring him within the range of the defendant's duty of care" in respect of both physical and psychological injury suffered by him.

In his concluding propositions in *Page* v. *Smith* (not reproduced above), Lord Lloyd emphasizes in respect of psychological injury suffered by both primary and secondary victims that "a defendant who is under a duty of care to the plaintiff . . . is not liable for damages for nervous shock unless the shock results in some recognized psychiatric illness". In other words, as he said earlier in the judgment "shock by itself is not the subject of compensation, any more than fear or grief or any other human emotion occasioned by

---

[117] *Supra*, Chapter I, **1.E.23.**

[118] *White* v. *Chief Constable of South Yorkshire Police* (sub nom *Frost* v. *Chief Constable of South Yorkshire Police*) [1998] 3 WLR 1509, HL.

[119] See a critical comment on that case by S. Todd, "Psychiatric Injury and Rescuers" (1999) 115 LQR 345.

the defendant's negligent conduct. It is only when shock is followed by recognizable psychiatric illness that the defendant may be held liable".[120] Accordingly it is better not to speak of liability for nervous shock.

(4) In *M.* v. *Newham London Borough Council*, a claim was brought for psychological injury against a local authority which had failed to respond properly to reports of sexual abuse.[121] The Court of Appeal held that the duty to diagnose and report imposed on the psychiatrist and the social worker was owed only to the local authority and not to the plaintiffs, who were involved in the inquiry of the local authority. An appeal to the House of Lords was consolidated with *X* v. *Bedfordshire County Council*.[122] The judgment of the Court of Appeal was upheld. The judgment of the House of Lords was brought before the European Commission of Human Rights, which concluded that it violated Articles 6, 8 and 13.[123] The case is now pending before the ECtHR.

Fatal Accidents Act 1976[124]   **2.E.10.**

CLAIMS FROM DEPENDANTS

When a wrongful act causes the death of the victim, the dependants of the victim, as defined by the Act, can sue the wrongdoer if the victim could have done so had death not ensued.

"**1.** (1) If death is caused by any wrongful act, neglect or default which is such as would (if death had not ensued) have entitled the person injured to maintain an action and recover damages in respect thereof, the person who would have been liable if death had not ensued shall be liable to an action for damages, notwithstanding the death of the person injured.

(2) Subject to section 1A(2) below, every such action shall be for the benefit of the dependants of the person ('the deceased') whose death has been so caused.

(3) In this Act 'dependant' means

(a) the wife or husband or former wife or husband of the deceased;

(b) any person who (i) was living with the deceased in the same household immediately before the date of the death; and (ii) had been living with the deceased in the same household for at least two years before that date; and (iii) was living during the whole of that period as the husband or wife of the deceased;

(c) any parent or other ascendant of the deceased;

(d) any person who was treated by the deceased as his parent;

(e) any child or other descendant of the deceased;

---

[120] See *Vernon* v. *Bosley (No 1)* [1997] 1 All ER 577, CA. See also *Hicks* v. *Chief Constable of the South Yorkshire Police* [1992] 1 AC 310, [1992] 2 All ER 65, HL, concerning claims brought by the estates of persons killed at Hillsborough (the accident which also lead to the *Alcock* case) on the basis of the Law Reform (Miscellaneous Provisions) Act 1934 (cf. *infra*, **2.E.10.**, Note (1)). The Court of Appeal had dismissed the claims of the estates of *primary* victims for pain and suffering and fear of impending death. The House of Lords upheld the Court of Appeal judgment: "It is perfectly clear law that fear by itself, of whatever degree, is a normal human emotion for which no damages can be awarded. Those trapped in the crush at Hillsborough who were fortunate enough to escape without injury have no claim in respect of the distress they suffered in what must have been a truly terrifying experience. It follows that fear of impending death felt by the victim of a fatal injury before that injury is inflicted cannot by itself give rise to a cause of action which survives for the benefit of the victim's estate" (Lord Bridge).

[121] [1995] AC 633, [1994] 2 WLR 554, [1994] 4 All ER 602, CA.

[122] [1995] 2 AC 633, [1995] 3 WLR 152, [1995] 3 All ER 353, HL.

[123] European Commission of Human Rights, Report of 10 September 1999, *Z* v. *UK*.

[124] (c. 30), as amended by the Administration of Justice Act 1982 (c. 53).

(f) any person (not being a child of the deceased) who, in the case of any marriage to which the deceased was at any time a party, was treated by the deceased as a child of the family in relation to that marriage;

(g) any person who is, or is the issue of, a brother, sister, uncle or aunt of the deceased . . .

(5) In deducing any relationship for the purposes of subsection (3) above:

(a) any relationship by affinity shall be treated as a relationship by consanguinity, any relationship of the half blood as a relationship of the whole blood, and the stepchild of any person as his child, and

(b) an illegitimate person shall be treated as the legitimate child of his mother and reputed father . . .

1A. (1) An action under this Act may consist of or include a claim for damages for bereavement.

(2) A claim for damages for bereavement shall only be for the benefit

(a) of the wife or husband of the deceased; and

(b) where the deceased was a minor who was never married (i) of his parents, if he was legitimate; and (ii) of his mother, if he was illegitimate.

(3) Subject to subsection (5) below, the sum to be awarded as damages under this section shall be [GBP 7,500].

(4) Where there is a claim for damages under this section for the benefit of both the parents of the deceased, the sum awarded shall be divided equally between them.

(5) The Lord Chancellor may by order made by statutory instrument, subject to annulment in pursuance of a resolution of either House of Parliament, amend this section by varying the sum for the time being specified in subsection (3) above.

2. (1) The action shall be brought by and in the name of the executor or administrator of the deceased . . .

3. (1) In the action such damages, other than damages for bereavement, may be awarded as are proportioned to the injury resulting from the death to the dependants respectively.

(2) After deducting the costs not recovered from the defendant any amount recovered otherwise than as damages for bereavement shall be divided among the dependants in such shares as may be directed.

(3) In an action under this Act where there fall to be assessed damages payable to a widow in respect of the death of her husband there shall not be taken into account the re-marriage of the widow or her prospects of re-marriage.

(4) In an action under this Act where there fall to be assessed damages payable to a person who is a dependant by virtue of section 1(3)(b) above in respect of the death of the person with whom the dependant was living as husband or wife there shall be taken into account (together with any other matter that appears to the court to be relevant to the action) the fact that the dependant had no enforceable right to financial support by the deceased as a result of their living together.

(5) If the dependants have incurred funeral expenses in respect of the deceased, damages may be awarded in respect of those expenses.

(6) Money paid into court in satisfaction of a cause of action under this Act may be in one sum without specifying any person's share.

4. In assessing damages in respect of a person's death in an action under this Act, benefits which have accrued or will or may accrue to any person from his estate or otherwise as a result of his death shall be disregarded.

5. Where any person dies as the result partly of his own fault and partly of the fault of any other person or persons, and accordingly if an action were brought for the benefit of the estate under the

Law Reform (Miscellaneous Provisions) Act 1934 the damages recoverable would be reduced under section 1(1) of the Law Reform (Contributory Negligence) Act 1945, any damages recoverable in an action under this Act shall be reduced to a proportionate extent."

Notes

(1) The Fatal Accidents Act 1976 originates in the Fatal Accidents Act 1846,[125] and it was amended in important respects by the Administration of Justice Act 1982.[126] The cause of action created by the Act for the benefit of *dependants* must be distinguished from the cause of action of the *deceased* him- or herself. The Law Reform (Miscellaneous Provisions) Act 1934 modified the common law rule that "the cause of action dies with the person" (*actio personalis moritur cum persona*), so that causes of action enjoyed by a deceased person (except for defamation) would pass on to his or her estate.[127]

(2) The English common law of tort (in the narrow sense of the law of tort that is not statutory in origin) did not allow claims by dependants. As Weir writes: "Those affected by a person's *death* had no claim at common law at all, and still have none: they may claim only under the statute".[128] The aim of the Fatal Accidents Act 1976, reprinted above, is precisely to change the common law on this point. The Act "does not lay down that any duty is owed by the tortfeasor to the survivors: it simply enables them to sue the tortfeasor if the deceased could have done so at the moment of his death (so that if the deceased had personally settled with the tortfeasor or sued him to judgment or let his claim become time-barred, the survivors have no claim)."[129]

(3) As a result of the common law rule that denied any cause of action to dependants of the victim of a tort, even where the tort caused the victim's death, and of the rule that *actio personalis moritur cum persona*, it was said that, under English law, it was cheaper to kill than to maim. In 1846, Lord Campbell's Act was passed to remedy, at least in part, that situation which, with the increasing incidence of deaths of workers in industrial accidents and of victims of raliway accidents, was becoming increasing intolerable.

(4) Only the persons listed in section 1(3) and (5) of the Fatal Accidents Act 1976 may sue: "[m]any other people may suffer loss, such as the employer, the partner or the insurance company. None of these may sue".[130] As appears from section 1(3)(b) of the Act, common law spouses, i.e. unmarried cohabitants in a stable and continuing relationship, are now allowed to claim for damages as dependants.

(5) The claim for bereavement[131] is new, and here again it constitutes a modification of the common law. It is currently fixed at a conventional cost of GBP 7,500.

(6) Dependants can also be affected by a *non-fatal* injury to the victim. Here, there is a very strong tendency to allow only the primary victim to claim but "to dress up the loss to others as being the primary victim's loss", according to Weir who cites many

---

[125] (9–10 Vict., c. 93), also known as Lord Campbell's Act.

[126] (c. 53). The amendments are consolidated in the text above.

[127] (24 & 25 Geo. 5, c. 41). See Rogers at 801–2.

[128] At 114.

[129] Ibid.

[130] Weir at 114. There was an interesting old tort in respect of a "wrongful act depriving a husband of a wife's consortium": *Kirkham* v. *Boughey* [1958] 2 QB 338, [1957] 3 WLR 626, [1957] 3 All ER 153, QBD, but a wife had no similar right: *Best* v. *Samuel Fox & Co. Ltd* [1952] AC 716, [1952] 2 All ER 394, HL. In so far as this tort may then still have existed, it was abolished by the Administration of Justice Act 1982 (c. 53): Rogers at 620.

[131] In s. 1A, as added by the Administration of Justice Act 1982; Weir at 115.

examples.[132] One of those examples has been discussed above, namely the award of large damages to a permanently unconscious person who can never use it; in fact that sum reflects the damage sustained by members of the family who cannot sue in their own names.[133]

2.1.3. FRENCH LAW

Introductory Note

a) Life, bodily integrity and health have become the most prominent objects of protection under French law, as they are under other legal systems. That is so much the case in France that G. Viney speaks of a *right*[134] to bodily security or integrity (*droit à la sécurité corporelle*), which is laid down in legislative measures imposing strict liability for injury to life, body or health caused by dangerous things as well as arising under contractual *obligations de sécurité* or *obligations de garantie* (often implied).[135] The most important of the legislative measures that impose a form of strict liability, namely the *Loi Badinter* concerning traffic accidents, had been anticipated by the case law relating to Article 1384(1) C.civ.[136]

b) The main thrust came from the famous *Jand'heur* decision of the Cour de cassation of 13 February 1930, through which the first sentence of Article 1384(1) C.civ. was transformed into a general and autonomous strict liability regime for things of all kinds.[137] That liability rests on the *gardien* (keeper) of the thing. "Things" extends to all inanimate objects, including first and foremost dangerous things such as motor vehicles, through which injury may be caused to third parties.[138] The strict liability regime created by the *Jand'heur* line of cases continues to be good law, but it has lost much of its significance due to the enactment of specific statutes, the most important being the Act 85-677 of 5 July 1985 (known as the *Loi Badinter*). The *Loi Badinter* builds on Article 211-2 of the *Code des assurances*, whereby all motor vehicles must be insured so as to cover the liability of the *gardien* and the driver to anyone injured in a traffic accident. Although the *Loi Badinter* does not change the rules governing tortious liability in substance, its effect is to enlarge their application to victims other than drivers, as regards personal injury.

The determination of French law to strengthen the legal position of the victims of injury to the person, and thus to give *special protection* to the right to bodily integrity, is also reflected in the Act 91-1406 of 31 December 1991, which created a special fund for persons infected with HIV as a result of blood transfusions.[139] The Act of 31 December 1991 was adopted in reponse to one of the most tragic events France was confronted with

---

[132] Weir at 115.
[133] *Supra*, **2.E.7.**
[134] On the notion of "subjective right", see *supra*, Chapter I, 1.4.3.
[135] *Supra*, Chapter I, **1.F.24.**
[136] See *infra*, Chapter VI, 6.1.2. (1384(1) C. civ.) and 6.2.1.B. (*Loi Badinter*).
[137] DP 1930.I.57.
[138] See *infra*, Chapter VI, **6.F.9.**
[139] See *infra*, Chapter VI, **6.F.31.**

during the med-1980s: the blood transfusion scandal. Before the Act, courts used tort liability as the main instrument to address the issue.[140]

Many years after the expiry of the implementation period, France has finally implemented Directive 85/374 on product liability, which protects the victims of defective products for injury to the person (including death) and to property used for private purposes.[141]

c) As we have seen, French law shows no reluctance to grant the same protection against harmful omissions as against harmful acts. That holds true not only for injury to the person,[142] but also for injury to reputation[143] or to property rights. In the case of injury to the person, specific provisions of French law even make it a criminal offence—and therefore, under French law, also a tort—for one to abstain from helping another person who is in serious danger, if that can be done without risk to oneself or third parties.[144]

d) The materials reprinted below show that French tort law (both the general regime of Article 1382 and ff. C.civ. and that of administrative law) is very generous towards the claims of primary and secondary tort victims. French law takes a generous approach—some consider it overly generous—because the *Code civil*, unlike the German BGB, imposes no *restrictions* on claims for non-material loss or on claims brought by dependants.[145] Nor does French law employ a notion such as the proximity concept in English law to limit the group of persons towards whom a duty of care exists, and towards whom an obligation to make good the damage sustained arises accordingly.

Compensation can even be obtained for the loss of a chance (*perte d'une chance*), for instance the chance for a child to have been born healthy if a physician had not failed to prescribe a blood test for rubella.[146]

It should however be borne in mind that damages for non-material loss will in some instances be limited to a *franc symbolique*.

Cass. civ. 1re, 16 July 1991[147]   **2.F.11.**

Gosse-Gardet v. *X.*

PRENATAL INJURY. LOSS OF A CHANCE OF BEING BORN IN GOOD HEALTH. BREACH OF DUTY OF INFORMATION.

Omitted blood test

Omitting to prescribe a blood test for rubella in the course of a pre-marital examination, as is required by law, is considered to have caused the loss of a chance for the child to be born healthy.

[140] The judgment reproduced *infra*, **2.F.18.** provides an illustration thereof.
[141] The implementation was carried out through the addition of Art. 1386–1ff. to the Code civil. See *infra*, Chapter VI, **6.F.39.**
[142] See *infra*, Chapter III, **3.F.2.**
[143] *Infra*, Chapter III, **3.F.1.**
[144] Ibid. Note (3).
[145] *Infra*, **2.F.19.**, Note (3).
[146] See *infra*, **2.F.11.**, Note (2).
[147] Bull.civ. 1991.I.248. Translation by N. Sims.

Facts: The first defendant, a doctor, had omitted to prescribe a compulsory serological test for German measles (rubella) in the course of conducting a pre-marital medical examination of Mrs. X. Four years later, on account of an allergic reaction, Mrs. X consulted the second defendant, a general practitioner, who took no further action. A few weeks later, the third defendant, a gynaecologist, ordered a test for German measles antibodies but, having seen the outcome, did not prescribe a second test. Eight months later, Mrs. X gave birth to a child who suffered from certain disabilities such as typically result from rubella contracted at the beginning of pregnancy. The *parents acting for the child* sued the three doctors.

Held: The court of first instance held the first and third defendants liable for loss of a chance and exonerated the second defendant. The court of appeal agreed that the first defendant was liable and that the second was not, but dismissed the claim against the third defendant. The Cour de cassation upheld the court of appeal judgment that the first defendant was liable, but found that the court of appeal had wrongly held that the second and third defendants were not liable.

Judgment: "[As regards the liability of the first defendant] Having regard to Art. 1147 C.civ.: . . . The appealed decision, whereby Mr. Gosse-Gardet was ordered to pay [to the child] the sum of FRF 800,000 is criticized on the grounds that: [i] a doctor is liable only if there is a direct and certain causal link between the fault of which he is found guilty and the damage for which compensation is ordered; having itself found that the culpable conduct of Mr. Gosse-Gardet had no direct relation to the damage, the court of appeal ought to have acquitted him of any liability; in deciding to the contrary, in spite of its own findings, the court of appeal failed to apply Art. 1147 C.civ. correctly; [ii] the award of damages for loss of a chance presupposes a direct and certain causal link between the fault found and the damage; therefore, in holding merely that the indirect part played by Mr. Gosse-Gardet's fault in relation to the damage suffered by the girl established the doctor's contribution to the child's loss of a chance to be born unaffected by the handicaps caused by rubella, the court of appeal did not establish the existence of a direct and certain causal link between Mr. Gosse-Gardet's fault and the clinical consequences which continue to affect the child, thus leaving its decision incapable of being supported on the basis of Art. 1147 C.civ.

But the court of appeal, having found that the doctor did not request a test for the detection of rubella on the occasion of the pre-nuptial examination, and thus committed a professional error, was then correct to infer that there was a causal link between the wrongful omission of the doctor and the child's loss of a chance to avoid the consequences of rubella contracted by the mother at the beginning of her pregnancy . . .

[The court dismissed the appeal of the first defendant and then moved on to consider the liability of the second and third defendants.] Having regard to Art. 1147 C.civ.: The court of appeal having found that Mrs. Laffereyrie did not prescribe any test to detect rubella for the purposes of a pregnancy certificate and that Mrs. Larrat did not prescribe a second examination on becoming aware of anti-rubella antibodies, then stated, in order to hold Mrs. Laffereyrie and Mrs. Larrat not liable, that it was clear from the expert report that the rubella affecting Mrs. X . . . was contracted at the beginning of her pregnancy and that, notwithstanding the failings of which they are guilty, the two doctors then treating her did not have available to them, on the dates when Mrs. X . . . consulted them, any means of preventing the malformations stemming from congenital rubella.

In thus holding Mrs. Laffereyrie and Mrs. Larrat not liable although they failed to carry out tests which would have enabled them to inform Mr. and Mrs. X . . . of the risks posed by Mrs. X's pregnancy, and therefore failed to discharge their duty to keep their patient properly informed so as to enable Mr. and Mrs. X to take a properly informed decision about the possibility of an abortion on medical grounds, the court of appeal failed to apply [Art. 1147 C.civ.] correctly . . . [The court then found that the court of appeal had wrongly exonerated the second and third defendants and remitted the case to the court of appeal on this issue.]"

Notes

(1) The above judgment concerns the contractual liability of doctors. According to Article 1147 C.civ., a person who has committed a breach of contract is bound to pay damages if, unless excused by *force majeure*, he or she has not performed his or her obligation correctly and in time.

As stated above, medical liability is in principle treated as a contractual matter since the *Mercier* judgment of the Cour de cassation of 20 May 1936.[148] The court there made the following statement, which it would confirm in many later judgments: "There is, as between the physician and his or her patient, a legally recognized contract under which the physician undertakes, if not—of course—to cure the patient, then at least to provide him or her with medical care and not just any kind of care, but diligent and heedful care which, save for exceptional circumstances, is in accordance with established medical science".[149]

Both the contractual and tortious liability regimes protect the same rights and interests, however, and in principle give rise to the same kind of awards.

The annotated judgment raises two interesting issues, namely liability for loss of a chance (*perte d'une chance*) and for not having put the plaintiff in a position to take an informed decision.

(2) Under French law, the notion of *perte d'une chance* relates to whether the damage sustained is "certain". It is generally used when an element of hazard (*aléa*) affects the very presence of damage and not just its future evolution.[150] This element of hazard may relate to obtaining an advantage or to maintaining the current state of affairs. Damage affected by that element of hazard will nonetheless be considered as direct and certain damage in so far as it represents a loss of a chance to obtain an advantage or to maintain the *status quo*. As the criminal chamber of the Cour de cassation has repeatedly stated: "the element of damage constituted by a loss of a chance is direct and certain whenever, as a result of a tort, the probability of a favourable outcome is lost, even though by definition the realization of a chance can never be certain".[151]

For compensation to be awarded in respect of loss of a chance, the chance must have been real and serious.[152] Furthermore the principle of *réparation intégrale* requires the court to assess the degree of certainty of the lost chance: a lost chance may not give rise to compensation of as much as when the chance eventuated.[153]

In the above judgment, the notion of *perte d'une chance* is used to avoid problems of causation[154]: it is plain that the fault of the first defendant (in not requesting the blood test for German measles at the time of the pre-nuptial examination) did not cause the infection of the mother as such, although if he had not committed that fault the situation of the child might have been different. Where it is difficult to establish a causal link

---

[148] S 1937.I.321, D 1936.Jur.88. *Supra*, Chapter I, 1.4.2., Introductory Note under a).

[149] See also Art. 32 of the new *Code de déontologie médicale* (Code of Medical Ethics), Decree 95-1000 of 6 September 1995, JO, 8 September 1995, D 1995.Lég.1452.

[150] See Viney and Jourdain, *Conditions* at 67–8, para. 276 ff.

[151] Since Cass. crim., 23 February 1977, Bull.crim. 1977.73. For an application of that principle, see *infra*, **2.F.43.**, and under English law, *Allied Maples*, *infra*, **2.E.49.**

[152] Viney and Jourdain, *Conditions* at 80, para. 283.

[153] Ibid. at 84–5, para. 284.

[154] For a more in depth discussion, see *infra*, Chapter IV, **4.F.14.**, Note (2) (*perte d'une chance* in the context of a failure to provide information) and 4.2.2. (*perte d'une chance* in medical liability cases).

between the actions of the defendant and the state of the plaintiff, the notion of *perte d'une chance* is used to bridge the gap. Because of the fault of the first defendant in failing to order the blood test, the mother could not take the necessary measures to be immunized against German measles before she became pregnant, and the child (not conceived at the time) therefore lost the opportunity to avoid being affected when his mother contracted German measles during her pregnancy. The concept of *perte d'une chance* as an autonomous head of damage thus enabled the court of appeal to conclude that a causal link was present between the fault of the first defendant and the lost opportunity to avoid injury, although the court of appeal could find no direct link between the omission and the actual injury suffered by the child. The *Cour de cassation* agreed.[155]

(3) The other significant issue raised in the annotated judgment concerns the failure by the second and third defendants to conduct a proper medical examination, which would have enabled them correctly to inform the parents, an issue which is also raised in the judgment annotated hereafter.[156] Although at that point in time the second and third defendants were no longer in a position to prevent the child being born disabled, they had, according to the Cour de cassation, violated their duty to give proper advice to their patient and made it impossible for the parents to take an informed decision as to whether they wanted an abortion. The court of appeal had dismissed the plaintiffs' claim on this issue.

The annotated judgment demonstrates the willingness of the Cour de cassation to award damages for violations by doctors of the general duty incumbent upon them to give all information and advice which the patient needs to make an informed decision (in that case the decision to have an abortion).[157] The fact that a doctor has not asked for a test or examination which would have enabled him or her to give full advice to his or her patient suffices to establish a violation of this general duty of information and advice.

Cass. civ. 1re, 25 June 1991[158]   **2.F.12–14.**
X. v. *Y.*
and
CÉ, 27 September 1989[159]
X. v. *CPAM de la Marne*
and
Cass. civ. 1re, 26 March 1996[160]
P. v. *Ponnoussamy*

WRONGFUL BIRTH. WRONGFUL LIFE.

Wrongful birth or wrongful life constitutes no reason for compensation when a normal healthy child is born; compensation will be awarded only under specific circumstances, such

---

[155] Compare with Cass. civ. 1re, 26 March 1996, *infra*, **2.F.14.** and Note (3) thereafter.
[156] *Infra*, **2.F.14.**
[157] On that duty, see *infra,* Chapter III, **3.F.10.** and Chapter IV, **4.F.14.** and notes thereafter as well as **4.F.17.**
[158] D 1991.Jur.566, annotated by P. le Tourneau. Translation by N. Sims.
[159] D 1991.Jur.80. Translation by N. Sims.
[160] Bull.civ. 1996.I.156. Translation by N. Sims.

as when a physician: (i) fails to conduct an abortion successfully, as a result of which a child is born with a serious physical handicap or (ii) omits to prescribe blood tests or performs them incorrectly, so that the parents cannot take a fully informed decision as to abortion, and the child develops neurological problems after birth.

1. Cass. civ. 1re, 25 June 1991   **2.F.12.**

Unsuccessful abortion. Healthy child.

Facts: On 5 June 1987, a surgeon performed an abortion on Ms. P. An echography made on 5 July 1987 showed that the pregnancy had not been terminated. Ms. P gave birth to a perfectly healthy child on 13 January 1988. On 11 February 1988 she sued the surgeon for damages in the amount of FRF 750,000.

Held: The court of appeal ruled that there was a direct and certain link between the continuation of the pregnancy and the fault of the surgeon, who had not verified that the abortion had been carried out successfully. Nonetheless, the court of appeal rejected Ms. P.'s claim, on the ground that she had not provided evidence that she had suffered any material or non-material damage as a result of the surgeon's fault. The Cour de cassation dismissed the appeal for review.

Judgment: "Ms. P criticizes the court of appeal for ruling out non-material damage on the general ground that the birth of a child, even an unwanted one, is a happy event, without inquiring whether, in the case of an unmarried woman of 22 years of age who has lost her mother and whose father is unknown, who was taken into care as a child by the social security services and who has already had one abortion, the birth did not constitute a painful event, not to say an unhappy one, which could, in particular, give rise for the mother to psychological disturbance and to be such as to prevent her from 'rebuilding' her life so that at the very least it caused damage because of the loss of a chance.

The existence of a child . . . cannot in itself constitute for the mother a legally reparable loss even if the birth occurred after an unsuccessful abortion attempt. The contested judgment points out that the child was perfectly formed and states that Ms. P did not prove that the birth definitely caused her emotional suffering and merely cited likely difficulties in her life as a young woman and her future prospects. Thus, in the absence of special damage which, in addition to the normal burdens of motherhood, would have been such as to enable the mother to claim damages, the court of appeal was . . . legally justified in reaching the decision that it did. On those grounds the appeal for review is dismissed."

2. CÉ, 27 September 1989   **2.F.13.**

Unsuccessful abortion. Injured child.

Facts: On 16 December 1980 a doctor performed an abortion on the plaintiff in the defendant public hospital. Although performed correctly, the abortion was not successful, and the doctor omitted to examine the plaintiff to verify the result of the operation. As it turned out, the failed abortion had harmed the foetus, and the plaintiff's child was born with a serious physical handicap.

Held: The defendant hospital was ordered to pay FRF 600,000 to the child and FRF 50,000 to the mother for non-material injury. It was also held liable for FRF 400,000 in medical expenses incurred by the plaintiff's health insurers on her behalf.

Judgment: "The investigation of the case and in particular the expert report commissioned by the investigating judge at the court of first instance in examining the complaint filed against Y by Mrs.

X show that, by omitting to carry out appropriate examinations in order to verify the result of the abortion carried out on 16 December 1980 on Mrs. X, although no error was committed in the prescription or performance of that abortion, the doctor who carried out the abortion at the Châlons-sur-Marne Hospital committed a serious error, notwithstanding the fact, should it be proved, that the patient's pregnancy was at a more advanced stage than the doctor had been led to believe. Furthermore, the investigation shows that the abortion carried out on Mrs. X on 16 December 1980 caused an injury to the foetus which gave rise to the deformity from which the child suffers. Thus Mrs. X is entitled to claim annulment of the judgment of 10 September 1985 whereby the court of first instance dismissed her application for an order that the Châlons-sur-Marne Hospital should pay damages on account of the injury resulting from the abortion carried out by it on 16 December 1980.

As to the damage suffered by young Alexandre X who was born with a serious disability including a total absence of the right lower limb: On a reasonable assessment of the physical suffering and aesthetic loss thereby suffered, and the interference with his quality of life, damages of FRF 600,000 are awarded to him against the Châlons-sur-Marne Hospital. To that amount there is to be added a further amount of FRF 249,449.48, representing costs of hospitalisation, transport and equipment incurred by the primary sickness fund for Châlons-sur-Marne and the further sum of FRF 178,518.65 by way of an unchallenged capital sum necessary to cover the cost of renewing prosthetic equipment. Therefore, the loss recoverable amounts to FRF 1,027,968.13.

As to the loss suffered by Mrs. X: On a reasonable assessment of the adverse effect on her quality of life, due to the disability suffered by her son, Alexandre, damages of FRF 50,000 are awarded to her against the hospital."

C. Cass. civ. 1re, 26 March 1996   **2.F.14.**

Child disabled because of rubella

Facts: Due to errors in the performance of a laboratory analysis ordered by her physician, the plaintiff, a pregnant woman, was led to believe that, in spite of external indicia, she had an immunity against German measles. She had previously indicated that she would have an abortion if she developed measles during the pregnancy. A year after birth, the plaintiff's child developed neurological disturbances, among other serious consequences linked to the mother having suffered from German measles during the pregnancy. The plaintiff sued the laboratory and her physician, both *in her own name and in the name of her child*.

Held: The laboratory admitted negligence, and the court of appeal found that the physician had failed in his duties to take care of the plaintiff and to inform and advise her. Both were held liable to make good the damage sustained by the plaintiff herself. The claim made in the name of the child was dismissed for lack of causation. This latter part of the court of appeal judgment was quashed by the Cour de cassation.

Judgment: "Having regard to Art. 1147 C.civ: . . . In dismissing the claim made by Mrs. P on behalf of her son for compensation for damage suffered by him, the contested judgment states that the fact of having to bear the consequences of the rubella because the mother decided not to terminate her pregnancy, cannot in itself constitute for the child a reparable loss. The contested judgment goes on to state that 'the very serious clinical consequences which continue to affect the child do not originate in the mistake made by the laboratory, or even in the failure of the practitioner to fulfil his contractual obligations, but solely in the rubella transmitted to him *in utero* by his mother'.

In so holding, although it was found as a fact that the parents had indicated their willingness to have the pregnancy terminated in the case of rubella, and that the errors that were made misled them into believing that the mother was immunized with the result that those errors gave rise to the damage suffered by the child owing to his mother's rubella, the court of appeal failed to apply [Art. 1147 C.civ.] correctly. On those grounds the judgment is set aside."

Notes

(1) The first judgment concerns a claim surrounding the birth of a child brought by the mother in her own name (a so-called "**wrongful birth**" claim). Dealing with a situation of a failed abortion where a normal healthy child was later born, the Cour de cassation decided that the birth of the child does not in itself give rise to recoverable injury, in the absence of specific prejudice over and above the normal burdens of motherhood. Almost 10 years earlier the Conseil d'État had taken the same position in a judgment of 2 July 1982 holding that:[161]

> "The birth of a child, even if it occurs after an abortion . . . which turned out to be unsuccessful, does not give rise to loss recoverable from the hospital where the abortion was carried out, unless, . . . there are particular circumstances or a particular situation which may be relied on by the person concerned."

In the second reproduced judgment, such a special situation was present, since the failed abortion had caused the child to be born with a serious physical handicap

(2) The third annotated judgment concerned a claim made by the mother both in her own name and in the name of her child. Following a wrongful act committed by a medical laboratory in performing a blood analysis, a child was born who later on developed serious neurological disturbances, due to rubella contracted by the mother during the pregnancy. The claim of the mother, not further specified in the judgment, was allowed by the lower court and that part of the judgment was not challenged before the Cour de cassation. However, the claim of the child was rejected by the court of appeal on grounds that the injury was due to the consequences of the mother having suffered from rubella and not to the fault of the laboratory or the doctor. The Cour de cassation overturned the court of appeal on that point: because the tests were incorrectly performed, the parents, who had expressed their decision to have an abortion if the mother suffered from German measles, had been misled into believing that the mother was immunized against this disease. Accordingly, the injury sustained by the child was caused by the wrongful acts of the laboratory and of the doctor.

(3) The third annotated judgment can be compared with the judgment of 16 July 1991.[162] In the judgment of 16 July 1991 the Cour de cassation framed its reasoning in terms of *perte d'une chance*, holding that the fault of the first doctor (who failed to have a serological test conducted as part of a pre-marital examination) had deprived the child of the chance not to have to support the consequences of rubella. It could be said then that compensation was awarded for the loss of this chance and not so much for the fact that the child was born, on the assumption that if the serological test had taken place, the mother would have taken the necessary steps to be immunized against rubella before she became pregnant. In the third annotated judgment, the Cour de cassation does not use the concept of *perte d'une chance*: it finds that the fault of the doctor gave rise to the damage suffered by the child owing to his mother's rubella. The crux of the discussion surrounding **wrongful life** claims was thus before the court: if the Cour de cassation granted compensation **to the child**, knowing that the parents would have had an abortion in the case of rubella that meant that the child was compensated for being born at all. Strangely,

[161] *R.*, D 1984.Jur.425, Gaz.Pal. 1983.Jur.193.
[162] *Supra*, **2.F.11.**

the text of the judgment makes no mention of the moral dimension of the discussion. Yet commentators have not failed to notice that the court, with the third annotated judgment, effectively allowed wrongful life claims into French tort law.[163] It can be noted that the *Conseil d'État*, in a judgment of 14 February 1997, has not followed that development and has denied a wrongful life claim.[164]

Cour d'appel de Paris, 10 November 1983[165]   **2.F.15–17.**
S. v. *Fonds de garantie automobile et CPAM des Hauts-de-Seine*
and
Cass. civ. 2e, 22 February 1995[166]
X v. *Sté Transport Agglomération Elbeuvienne*
and
Cour d'appel de Bordeaux, 18 April 1991[167]
Salabert v. *Malaganne*

RÉPARATION INTÉGRALE FOR ALL VICTIMS, EVEN IF FULLY UNCONSCIOUS

The principle of réparation intégrale *under French law remains applicable even in respect of non-material damage, such as pain and suffering and loss of amenity, for a victim that is fully unconscious or in coma.*

1. Cour d'appel de Paris, 10 November 1983   **2.F.15.**

Victim in coma

Facts (as related in the judgment): Mr. Jacques S. was involved in an accident in which he suffered an extremely serious cranio-cerebral injury leading to prolonged coma. That injury resulted in a total temporary incapacity, lasting from 27 June 1979 to 26 May 1982, the date of stabilization, and caused considerable suffering and left clinical consequences and a permanent incapacity of 100 per cent and quite serious aesthetic damage. Mr. Jacques S. who was born on 26 June 1962 was in salaried employment at the time of the accident with an average net taxable monthly income of the order of FRF 2400. Owing to the clinical consequences of his injuries, he was no longer able to take advantage of any of the recreations or engage in any of the leisure activities of persons enjoying their full physical potential.

Held: The plaintiff was awarded compensation in the amount of FRF 400,000 for infringement of his bodily integrity and in addition thereto an annual sum of FRF 121,110.78 to be increased as indicated in the judgment (all these in addition to what he received from the social security system). Moreover, the plaintiff was awarded

---

[163] See G. Viney, "Chronique" JCP 1996.I.3985; J. Roche-Dahan, Annotation, D 1997.Jur.37 at 38–9. See also M. Deguergue, "Les préjudices liés à la naissance" Resp. Ass. 1998.14 (special issue of May 1998). For another example of a successful "wrongful life" claim, see Cass. crim., 4 February 1998, JCP 1999.II.10178, with note by I. Moine-Dupuis. In that case, the Cour de cassation allowed a child who was conceived through rape to bring a claim for damages against the rapist.

[164] JCP 1997.II.22828. See G. Viney, "Chronique" JCP 1997.I.4025.

[165] D 1984.Jur.214. Translation by N. Sims.

[166] D 1996.Jur.69, annotated by Y. Chartier. Translation by N. Sims.

[167] Gaz.Pal. 1993.Jur.215, annotated by S. Piédelièvre. Translation by N. Sims.

FRF 400,000 as "personal" compensation (*indemnité à caractère personnel*). The parents of the plaintiff were each awarded FRF 30,000 for non-material damages, and his brother and sisters each received FRF 6,000.

Judgment: "On the facts as found, it is reasonable to award the plaintiff: (1) in addition to the benefits paid to him by the [sickness] fund (benefits in kind: FRF 866,788.81; daily allowances: FRF 124,507.27; periodic payments on account of an accident at work, with third party supplement, the capital sum equivalent to which as at 1 January 1983 was FRF 1,851,207.09), including the increase in periodic payments in accordance with the law as from 1 July 1983, on account of his physical injuries (medical and paramedical expenses; temporary incapacity; permanent incapacity, not including future costs of care, hospitalization and maintenance of specialized equipment, not currently assessable; assistance of third parties; dwelling-conversion costs) a capital sum of FRF 400,000 and annual payments of FRF 121,110.78, together with automatic increases as provided for by the Act of 27 December 1974 in accordance with the revalorization coefficients provided for in Art. 455 of the *Code de la sécurité sociale*, to be payable quarterly in arrears as from the date of this judgment; (2) compensation of FRF 400,000 for the heads of damage giving rise to personal compensation. As regards future costs of care, hospitalization, renewal and maintenance of specialized equipment which will be entirely, or at any rate to a great extent, funded by the [sickness] fund pursuant to the provisions of Arts. 436 and 440 of the *Code de la sécurité sociale*, the automobile guarantee fund should be ordered to reimburse those expenses, if they are proved to have been charged to and incurred by the victim. The father and mother of the victim cannot be compensated by the automobile guarantee fund, on the basis that they momentarily played the role of third parties as regards their son, since the compensation awarded to their son, to whom they should make their claim if they see fit, covers the whole of this head of damage. They may therefore successfully claim only damages for non-material injury which the Court is in a position to assess at FRF 30,000 for each of them. Likewise, it assesses damages to each of the brothers and sisters at FRF 6,000 damages for non-material injury."

2. Cass. civ. 2e, 22 February 1995   **2.F.16.**

Victim in a vegetative state

Facts: Mrs. X was hit by a car while cycling and was thereafter in a vegetative state. The victim's daughter brought an action in her own name and on behalf of her mother against, amongst others, the driver and his insurer.

Held: The Cour de cassation reversed the decision of the court of appeal in so far as the latter had denied compensation for the personal injury sustained by Mrs. X.

Judgment: "Having regard to Art. 1382 C.civ.: A tortfeasor must make full reparation for the damage he has caused. According to the judgment appealed against . . ., Mrs. X, who was travelling on a bicycle, was struck and injured by the car driven by Mr. Y . . .

In holding that Mrs. X was not entitled to compensation for [non-material injury], the judgment points out that, according to the expert, the victim, who is reduced to a vegetative state, is absolutely incapable of any feeling, whether pain or a sense of diminution arising out of a aestheticly pitiable state, or any appreciation of the loss of life's pleasures and worries. The court of appeal infers therefrom that there is no proof of a certain loss. In so deciding, the court of appeal applied [Art. 1382 C.civ.] incorrectly since the vegetative state of a human being does not exclude any head of damages and the plaintiff's loss must be made good in its entirety.

On those grounds, the judgment is quashed . . . but, solely as regards the personal loss suffered by Mrs. X, the case is remitted to the court of appeal."

3. Cour d'appel de Bordeaux, 18 April 1991   **2.F.17.**

Victim in a vegetative state

Facts: The victim, Michel Malaganne, 22 years of age at the time of the accident, was totally incapacitated for work from 12 April 1981 to 28 September 1984 and continued to suffer from 100 per cent incapacity with absence of consciousness and motor functions, life being merely vegetative, the aid of a third person and medical assistance being constantly necessary.

Held: The Cour d'appel granted full compensation, including FRF 395,000 for personal injury.

Judgment: "It is clear from the expert report of 2 July 1985 drawn up by Dr Loustanau that 'if the problem of the victim's consciousness is left out of account, the pain has been fairly considerable, aesthetic loss average and loss of amenity very major and that the only conceivable outcome can be a worsening of the victim's condition'.

The damage suffered must be compensated in full. Compensation must be based on all the needs of the victim's continuing life and the heads of [non-material injury] not covered by the social security institutions. The human dignity of someone who has suffered the gravest and greatest impairment of consciousness must be respected, and all his rights as a person observed, because otherwise, the victim would be deemed to be legally dead and henceforth a mere object in receipt of care to maintain artificial life. The victim remains a legal subject, even if, in the current state of medical science, he is to be considered as bereft of consciousness, having merely a vegetative life and being in a condition which is regarded as irreversible.

Moreover, since compensation must be proportionate to the damage suffered, its assessment is traditionally based on objective considerations (medical expenses, loss of income, occupational disqualification, permanent total or partial incapacity with at least partial retention of consciousness) and subjective considerations (pain, aesthetic detriment and loss of amenity), the latter to be assessed according to a set of values which rests on the feelings normally experienced by conscious persons.

Where the victim is apparently bereft of consciousness and, in any event, cannot give expression to it, it cannot be inferred from that fact that he cannot feel the injuries. Protection of the victim's rights dictates that they are to be assessed not by reference to the feelings of loss which that person is supposed to have but by reference to feelings commonly felt as a result of a similar injury by persons able to give expression to their will. Otherwise the person would be deprived of a part of his rights, without there being however any absolute certainty of a total absence of suffering or feeling of anything connected to pain, to aesthetic detriment or loss of amenity.

The damage suffered on account of [non-material injury] is to be made good by an award of monetary compensation, the use of which [by the victim] falls outside the discretion of the court and may not influence determination of *quantum*. Moreover, it is not proved that the amounts awarded under this heading will not make Michel Malaganne's living conditions less distressing. Like any other legal subject, a person in a vegetative state has an estate which on succession will devolve in accordance with the provisions of the law [there follows an itemized determination].

On those grounds the Court sets aside the judgment of the [court of first instance] . . . on the award of compensation to Michel Malaganne, determines his damage subject to recourse by the regional mutual agricultural insurance fund for the Adour Basin at FRF 7,993,046.16, not including third party compensation, and his personal compensation at FRF 395,000; orders Christiane Salabert and the insurance company, Via Assurance Nord et Monde, jointly and severally to pay the sum of FRF 395,000 to Mrs. Andrée Labarrère-Matot, widow of Pierre Malaganne, in her capacity as administrator under court supervision of her adult son under wardship, Michel Malaganne, together with interest . . ."

Notes

(1) The three preceding judgments illustrate the principle of *réparation intégrale* under French law, for all kinds of injury claimed by primary and secondary victims of tortious interferences with life, health and proprietary rights but also more generally with their personal well-being. In other words, all interferences amounting to a disturbance of living conditions can give rise to compensation. Primary victims will then recover not only material but also non-material losses, comprising pain and suffering, aesthetic prejudice and loss of amenity.[168] Secondary victims will also recover damages for pain and suffering, including natural grief.

The *first* judgment is included to show how self-evident it is under French law that damages are to be awarded to both the direct victim and close relatives. Compensation to close relatives is obviously awarded when the injury to the primary victim is exceptionally serious, as it was in that case, thus causing considerable grief to the close relatives who constantly see the serious state in which the primary victim finds himself. However, in a judgment of 23 May 1977, the Cour de cassation has made clear that it is not required for the compensation of non-material loss that the injury be exceptionally serious, provided that the trial judge finds that it is established with sufficient certainty (a finding of fact which is not subject to review by the Cour de cassation).[169]

The first judgment is also of interest in that it shows the interplay between social security payments and compensation under tort law. The *Loi Badinter* also contains provisions on the relationship between the wrongdoer and so-called "*tiers payeurs*" (third parties who pay some form of compensation to the victim, such as social security organizations, etc.).[170] At Articles 28–30 of the *Loi Badinter*, the *tiers payeurs* are subrogated in the rights of the victim against the wrongdoer, so as to avoid multiple procedures and ensure that the victim is not compensated for more than the loss suffered. It could be, however, that the expenses of the *tiers payeurs* "swallow up" the whole indemnity due to the victim under tort law: this is why the *Loi Badinter* sought to reserve part of the compensation to be paid by the wrongdoer for the victim directly and personally. Article 31 of the *Loi Badinter* concerns the victim's "personal compensation" (*indemnité à caractère personnel*), which comprises compensation for pain and suffering, aesthetic prejudice and loss of amenity (the main headings of non-material damage). According to this provision, the claims of *tiers payeurs* against the tortfeasor for the amounts they have paid to the victim cannot affect the "personal compensation" of the victim. The rationale behind this scheme is that the amounts paid by *tiers payeurs* are deemed to cover material damage only, and it follows that the claims for "personal compensation" must remain a matter between the victim and the tortfeasor directly.

---

[168] In the widest sense: see Y. Lambert-Faivre, "Le droit et la morale dans l'indemnisation des dommages corporels" D 1992.Chron.165. Loss of amenity, or *préjudice d'agrément*, refers to the functional deficit in the victim's living conditions or the reduction in the quality of his or her life (*perte de la qualité de la vie*) as a result of the handicap caused by the tort. However, the 2nd Civil Chamber of the Cour de cassation, 6 January 1993, Bull.civ. 1993.II.6., held that "sexual injury" is not part of "loss of amenity" and can therefore still be the subject of a claim for damages, even though compensation has already been awarded for "loss of amenity". See G. Viney, "Chronique" JCP 1993.I.3727.

[169] JCP 1977.IV.187.

[170] *Infra*, Chapter VI, **6.F.18.** The *Loi Badinter* on this point elaborated on the provisions of a previous *Loi 73-1200 relative à l'étendue de l'action récursoire des caisses de sécurité sociale en cas d'accident occasionné à un assuré social par un tiers* (Act on the recourses of social security funds in cases of injury inflicted upon the insured by third parties) of 27 December 1973, JO, 30 December 1973, D 1974.Lég.42, and accordingly the first judgment reflects in substance the provisions of the *Loi Badinter*.

(2) The open-mindedness of French tort law towards claims for non-material damage (*dommage moral*) is illustrated by the second and third judgments reproduced above. The second civil chamber of the Cour de cassation ruled, in the second judgment, that the personal compensation (comprising compensation for pain and suffering, aesthetic damage and loss of amenity, as defined in the above paragraph) does not become irrecoverable simply because the injured person is not able to feel, as "no head of damages can be excluded simply because the victim is in a vegetative state",[171] thus cutting short the disagreement among lower courts as well as between the criminal and civil chambers of the Cour de cassation.[172] The third judgment, from the Cour d'appel de Bordeaux, ranks amongst those favouring the position finally approved by the Cour de cassation, and it has been included because it contains the line of reasoning upon which the Cour de cassation has presumably based its decision.

It is interesting to see how the Cour d'appel finds that the non-material damage suffered by a now unconscious victim must be assessed "by reference to feelings commonly felt . . . by persons able to give expression to their will".

(3) Claims for non-material damage are part of the victim's *patrimoine*, and they are accordingly transmitted to the victim's heirs if the victim dies (this applies to non-material damage suffered by primary and secondary victims alike). The transmissibility of the claim for non-material damage was recognized by the Cour de cassation in two judgments of 30 April 1976.[173] That court had previously held that only when a court action had already been instituted by the deceased were these claims transmitted to the heirs. The Conseil d'État appears still to favour the latter position. However, the lower administrative courts now tend to adopt the more generous position of the Cour de cassation.[174]

Cour d'appel de Paris, 7 July 1989[175]   **2.F.18.**
Franky v. *Courtellemont*

LIABILITY FOR CONTAMINATED BLOOD PRODUCTS BEFORE THE 1991 ACT

Contaminated blood transfusion

Liability in tort was one of the main instruments first used to address the blood transfusion scandal, when the courts held that HIV infection following a blood transfusion could lead to civil liability.[176]

---

[171] The Belgian Court of Cassation has held likewise in a judgment of 4 April 1990, Pas. 1990.I.913, JT 1992.829, annotated by L. Hervé.

[172] In the second judgment reproduced here, the Cour de cassation quashed the court of appeal decision, which is seen as a strong signal from the Cour de cassation in that matter. See P. Jourdain, "Chronique de responsabilité civile" (1995) 94 RTDciv. 629 and G. Viney, Annotation at JCP 1995.I.3853.

[173] Cass. Ch. mixte, 30 April 1976, D 1977.Jur.185.

[174] See CAA Nantes, 22 February 1989, AJDA 1989.276; for a critical overview of the case law see Y. Lambert-Faivre, "Le droit et la morale dans l'indemnisation des dommages corporels" D 1992.Chron.165 at 167–8.

[175] Gaz.Pal. 1989.Jur.752, with the conclusions of Advocate General G. Pichot. Translation by N. Sims.

[176] A special compensation regime was later created by the Act 91–1406 of 31 December 1991, *infra*, Chapter VI, **6.F.31**. Even since then, the general civil liability regime has retained a role: see *infra*, Chapter VI, **6.F.32**.

Facts: The plaintiff, Mrs. Courtellemont, following injury in a road accident with the defendant, Mr. Franky, required surgical intervention and several blood transfusions. As a result of the latter, she was infected with HIV. She claimed damages for pain and suffering from the defendant, who admitted his negligence in causing the accident, but denied that there was a causal link with the HIV infection.

Held: The court of appeal awarded FRF 2,300,000, not including aesthetic damage and the *pretium doloris* for physical pain caused by the injury, damages for which were to be assessed subsequently.

Judgment: "It is common ground that Mrs. Courtellemont was involved in a road traffic accident on 15 January 1985 in which she suffered a fracture of the right collar bone and contusions to the spleen which necessitated its surgical removal on 16 January 1985 and repeated blood transfusions . . .

Infection as a result of the transfusions was established by the documents in the file, as was the full liability of Frans Franky for the collision. The latter maintains that the damage alleged by the plaintiff clearly does not directly result from the accident itself which caused only slight injuries [The court rejects this argument] . . .

Since the existence of damage and liability therefor are established it is necessary to determine the compensation to be awarded in respect thereof . . . Some preliminary observations are necessary regarding the nature and the precise reality of that damage . . . Although Mrs. Courtellemont currently appears to be a person enjoying normal health, she has nonetheless entered the stage of illness . . .

It should be borne in mind that AIDS is the most serious form of the infection brought about by the human immunodeficiency virus . . .

The social and psychological impact of AIDS which has made its brutal appearance in our time has made a profound impression on the collective consciousness, which finds itself confronted with a phenomenon which arouses reactions which are as irrational as those dictated by fear to such a point that persons suffering from the virus are marginalized or excluded from social, professional or even family life.

Mrs. Courtellemont continues to be a victim, several years after the material facts, of that exclusion originating in her own family.

Moreover, the illness triggers feelings of injustice, lassitude or frustration, often giving rise to profound psychotic conditions of anguish, depression or despair.

[The initial experts emphasize that] the suffering experienced must be considered to be major owing, on the one hand, to obligatory medical supervision with numerous repeated and often distressing examinations and, on the other hand, owing to psychological repercussions which manifest themselves in the awareness by the sufferer that she has contracted AIDS with no way of predicting the consequences.

All these sufferings, both physical and emotional, owing to medical constraints, to social reactions, uncertainty and a risk of a worsening condition, together with disturbances of emotional, marital and family life, must be taken into account by the court in assessing the award of compensation. The damage is certain, personal and present. Its cruel specificity and its exceptional gravity justify an exceptional award of compensation.

In the light of all the documents in the file, of the foregoing analysis and on the relevant grounds upheld by the court below, the judgment appealed against should be affirmed and the award of compensation for the personal damage to the victim resulting from the infection should be set at FRF 2,300,000.

The aesthetic damage resulting from the injuries on which the specialists will be called to express a definitive view, is not included in this assessment nor the *pretium doloris* stemming from the injuries."

Notes

(1) The judgment of 7 July 1989 reproduced above shows how, before the Act 91-1406 of 31 December 1991, the courts had to deal with compensation of the victims of HIV infection following blood transfusion on the basis of the traditional civil liability rules. The issue arose more often than not in the context of criminal proceedings, where the victim put a claim for compensation as *partie civile* before the criminal court, to be ruled upon at the same time as the criminal matter. In that case, the negligent car driver who had caused the accident which led to the blood transfusions was held liable in tort by applying the—sometimes overbroad—theory of *équivalence des conditions* to the causation issue, in the special context of Articles 319 and 320 of the old *Code pénal* (manslaughter and causing inability to work),[177] on which the plaintiff, as a *partie civile*, based his claim. As a result, the driver was ordered to pay damages for the physical and psychological suffering sustained by the plaintiff, taking into account the medical parameters, the social reactions, the uncertainty and risk of aggravation, the disturbance of the plaintiff's emotional, marital and family life.

However, in a part of the judgment which is not reproduced here, the court of appeal indicated that it is up to the defendant to seek (under a jurisdiction other than that of the criminal court) recovery, from others who may be primarily responsible, of the damages paid by the defendant to the plaintiff. And indeed, the doctor who ordered the blood transfusion, the hospital, above all the blood transfusion centre and even the State could also be held liable, on the basis of a range of legal rules (contract law, administrative law, *action directe*), all of which subject liability to special and far from uniform conditions.[178]

(2) Because of the immensity and complexity of the problem,[179] legislative intervention was needed, in order to co-ordinate the use of public and private funds to compensate the large number of HIV victims. This was done by Article 47 of Act 91-1406 of 31 December 1991,[180] which provides for the creation of a Fund to ensure the full compen-

---

[177] Now replaced by Art. 221–6 and 222–19 of the new *Code pénal*.

[178] Y. Lambert-Faivre, "L'indemnisation des victimes post-transfusionnelles du SIDA: hier, aujourd'hui et demain . . ." (1993) 92 RTDciv. 17.

[179] R. Errera describes the situation in "Recent Decisions of the French Conseil d'État" [1993] Pub L 537 as follows: "During the mid-1980s, around 1,200 haemophiliacs (that is, about half of those registered) have been infected with HIV following blood transfusions. Two hundred and fifty have died . . . [A]ll avenues of the law have been and are being used: a former Prime Minister and two other ministers may be indicted and tried by a special court set up under the Constitution; the former head of the National Transfusion Centre, a physician, and several other doctors and civil servants have been sentenced to imprisonment by a criminal court in Paris. Several victims have sued local transfusion centres and have obtained damages . . . Other victims have sued the state in the administrative courts, and one of these actions led to a judgment of the European Court of Human Rights finding that there had been unreasonable delay causing a breach of Art. 6(1) ECHR (*X v. France*, 23 March 1993, 14 EHRR 483, JCP 1992.II.21896, note Apostolodis; D 1992.Somm.334, note Renucci)". See also, later on, Cass. crim., 22 June 1994, JCP 1994.II.22310, English translation at [1995] ECC 346.

[180] For a thorough examination, see Y. Lambert-Faivre, "L'indemnisation des victimes post-transfusionnelles du SIDA: hier, aujourd'hui et demain . . ." (1993) 92 RTDciv. 17, as well as Y. Lambert-Faivre, "Principes d'indemnisation des victimes post-transfusionnelles du SIDA", D 1993.Chron.67, dealing with 20 decisions of the Cour d'appel de Paris of 27 November 1992, Gaz.Pal. 1992.Jur.727, concerning issues of interpretation of the Act 91-1406, such as: the rebuttable presumption of causation between the blood transfusion and the HIV contamination (Art. 47(IV)), the notion of damage specifically related to HIV infection, recovery of material losses due to the closing of the sick person's enterprise, non-splitting of the compensation payable upon the occurrence of the infection, non-material damage (chronic depression, anxiety) of close relatives and of a partner living with the sick person in a stable relationship and the kind of damage for which compensation can be obtained.

sation of all material and non-material damage sustained by the direct and indirect victims of contaminated blood transfusions made in France.[181]

Cass. Ch. mixte, 27 February 1970[182]   **2.F.19.**
Gaudras v. *Dangereux*

LEGITIMATE INTEREST

Claim by concubine

Unmarried cohabiting partners have a sufficient interest to qualify as secondary victims under French tort law.

Facts: The defendant, Mr. Dangereux, was involved in a car accident for which he was held to be fully responsible and which caused the death of Mr. Paillette. The deceased lived together with Ms. Gaudras as an unmarried couple; Ms. Gaudras brought an action for damages.

Held: The court of first instance allowed the action as the relationship appeared to be stable and was not tortious, i.e. not adulterous (adultery being, until 1975, criminal in French law). The court of appeal reversed that decision. The judgment of the court of appeal was quashed by the Cour de cassation.

Judgment: "[Article 1382 C.civ.] requires that the perpetrator of any act causing damage to another shall be bound to make reparation therefor. It does not, in the event of death, require that there be a legal tie between the deceased and the plaintiff seeking damages. Ms. Gaudras' claim was for damages for the injury caused to her by the death of her partner, Paillette, who was killed in a road traffic accident for which Dangereux was held responsible. The contested judgment sets aside the judgment at first instance which had upheld that claim on the ground that the relationship exhibited guarantees of stability and was not delictual in character, and dismissed Ms. Gaudras' claim on the sole ground that living together as an unwed couple does not create any rights as between partners or to their benefit vis-à-vis third parties. In thereby making the application of Article 1382 dependent upon a condition which the Article does not specify, the court of appeal misapplied the aforementioned provision. Its decision must therefore be quashed . . ."

Notes

(1) This 1970 judgment of the Chambre Mixte of the Cour de cassation resolved a disagreement between the civil and the criminal chambers of that court. Before the judgment, the civil chamber had followed its decision of 27 July 1937, whereby a claim by a partner in an unwed couple was rejected on the ground that, in a tort action brought pursuant to Article 1382, the plaintiff had to show not only "damage in whatever form, but the definite infringement of a legitimate—and hence legally protected—interest".[183] The criminal chamber, in contrast, admitted such claims, despite the absence of a right (or

---

[181] *Infra*, Chapter VI, **6.F.31.**

[182] D 1970.Jur.201, annotated by R. Combaldieu, JCP 1970.II.16305, with opinion of Advocate General Lindon, annotated by P. Parlange. See also *Les grands arrêts* at 475 with observations. Translation by N. Sims.

[183] DP 1938.I.5, annotated by R. Savatier, S 1938.I.321 annotated by G. Marty, also in *Les grands arrêts* at 473.

legal entitlement), provided that the relationship with the deceased had been stable and non-adulterous.[184] In its 1970 decision, the Chambre mixte opted for the latter solution, holding that the text of Article 1382 "does not require, in the event of death, that there be a legal tie between the deceased and the plaintiff seeking damages".

By emphasizing in its judgment that in the case at issue the relationship was not unlawful, i.e. not adulterous, however, the Cour de cassation showed that it was not yet ready to allow all claims whatsoever. The court has since changed its position. As early as 19 June 1975, and thus before adultery was decriminalized by the Act of 11 July 1975 (Article 17), the criminal chamber held that a defendant who was sued in tort for the harm suffered by the partner of the victim in an adulterous relationship could not "rely on the delictual character of the relationship [of the plaintiff with the victim] in order to extricate himself from the civil consequences of his own tortious liability . . . since the tortious act in question is one relating to private life and can be asserted or relied upon as a defence in legal proceedings only by the victim's spouse".[185]

The fact that a relationship is adulterous therefore no longer prevents the surviving partner from having a *legitimate* interest for the purposes of an action in tort against a tortfeasor who has caused the death of the other partner,[186] thereby allowing him or her to claim compensation for the loss of financial support received from the deceased on a voluntary basis.[187] For the claim to be admitted, the injury must however be certain, which means that the relationship of the unwed couple (whether based on adultery or not) must be sufficiently stable and continuous.[188] That does not necessarily mean that compensation may not also be payable where the couple were living separately owing to external circumstances.[189]

(2) Even if French law appears to have given considerable attention to the situation of unmarried couples, it must not be forgotten that the case law on unmarried couples, as it now stands, is but one practical application of the more fundamental principle whereby not only rights, but all legitimate interests, are protected under French tort law. That principle applies to the benefit of primary victims but also of so-called *victimes par ricochet*,

---

[184] See for instance Cass. crim., 24 February 1959, JCP 1959.II.11095, note J. Pierron.

[185] Cass. crim., 19 June 1975, D 1975.Jur.679, annotated by A. Tunc. The same reasoning was applied by the Belgian Court of Cassation in two decisions, one before and the other after the decriminalization of adultery in Belgium in 1987: Court of Cassation, 1 February 1989, RW 1989–90, 83, RGAR 1989, 11518 and Court of Cassation, 15 February 1990, AC 1989–90, 776, RGAR 1990, 11658, annotated by R.O. Dalcq.

[186] The concept of a "legitimate interest" continues to be in a state of flux, since at least one judgment to date has accepted that compensation may also be obtained by the surviving partner of a homosexual couple (whose relationship was "stable, serious and faithful") against the person responsible for the death of his partner in an accident: see the judgment of 25 July 1995 of the Belfort criminal court, JCP 1996.II.22724, annotated by C. Paulin.

[187] After this change in the case law of the Cour de cassation, one may wonder whether illegitimacy of the interest of the claimant can still be a bar to any action in tort, except perhaps in respect of damages claimed to compensate loss of illicit income (loss of earnings by a prostitute, for instance) or earnings from criminal activities: see *infra*, Chapter VII, 7.3.1.

[188] In the same vein, the termination of the relationship does not however in and of itself give rise to tortious liability as between the ex-partners, principally on the ground that the relationship is deemed to have been precarious, and the damage therefore uncertain, since the couple had either chosen not to marry or could not marry, and had therefore assumed the risk of an abrupt termination of the relationship (see for example Cass. civ. 1re, 30 June 1992, Bull.civ. 1992.I.204). Compensation may be awarded, however, if the circumstances in which the termination takes place amount to "*une faute caractérisée*" (serious fault).

[189] Cass. crim., 2 March 1982, JCP 1983.II.19972, annotated by F. le Tourneau.

i.e. secondary victims who have suffered either non-material damage (pain and suffering, psychological distress) or, if they were financially dependent upon the deceased, material damage.[190]

A telling example of this is the judgment of 16 December 1988 of the Cour d'appel de Lyon which grants without much ado, compensation for non-material injury suffered by the secondary victims, the parents and the five brothers and sisters of the deceased, none of whom was financially dependent on the deceased, as far as appears from the judgment.[191]

(3) In its earlier case law the Cour de cassation limited claims of dependants to the material and non-material damage sustained by the surviving spouse and minor or adult children provided, in the case of material damage, that loss of financial support or an expectation of it could be demonstrated. Subsequently, case law accepted that such claims might be brought by other relatives also.[192] As regards, in particular, so-called bereavement (*préjudice d'affection*), the Cour de cassation on 2 February 1931 decided that for a claim limited to non-material damage only to succeed, it was sufficient that it was "based on an affectionate *interest* arising because of a blood relationship or a relationship by marriage linking the victim of the harmful act with one of his heirs".[193] Thus, in subsequent judgments, brothers and sisters were allowed to seek damages along with sons-in-law and daughters-in-law, nephews and nieces. Finally, the Cour de cassation showed even greater liberalism by allowing actions to be brought by individuals who could prove that their affection for the victim was genuine, even if they were not related to him or her. This generous construction benefited first illegitimate children whose parentage could not be established as a matter of law, then fiancés and, finally, partners in an unwed couple.[194] The sole distinction now remaining between members of the victim's family and other persons relates to evidence: the former benefit from a rebuttable presumption of affectionate relationship to the victim, whereas the latter do not.[195]

As a result a person may under French law ask for compensation if he or she can show that the non-material damage which he or she suffered was real, i.e. certain. The damage can result from the impact on a relation of affection with the primary victim (which, as said above, is presumed in the case of close relatives), but also from psychological disturbance, for instance if the person has seen the fatal accident.[196]

[190] See further **2.F.19.**, Notes (3) and (4). French law does not distinguish between secondary victims and dependants (this distinction is made here for comparative purposes). Both categories fall under the notion of *victimes par ricochet*. See Viney and Jourdain, *Conditions* at 128, para. 304, who describes *dommage par ricochet ou réfléchi* in the following terms: "Often, among others in cases of accident causing bodily harm, the injury suffered by the victim leads to further losses for other persons, for instance those who must pay an indemnity to the victim or those who had a business or affectionate relationship with the victim and were accordingly abruptly disturbed by the accident".

[191] *Infra*, Chapter III, **3.F.2.**

[192] See Viney and Jourdain, *Conditions* at 133–4, para. 311.

[193] DP 1931.I.38.

[194] See the observations under Cass. civ., 13 February 1923, in *Les grands arrêts* at 466–7.

[195] Ibid.

[196] See further Viney and Jourdain, *Conditions* at 132 ff., para. 310 ff. Even if the psychological disturbance is brought about by the death of a horse, the Cour de cassation has approved a judgment granting damages for emotional harm to the owner of the horse (amount unspecified): "Independently of the material harm which may result from the death of an animal, that death can cause to the owner of the animal injury of a subjective and affective nature, for which compensation may be obtained" (Cass. civ. 1re, 16 January 1962, D 1962.Jur.199, annotated by R. Rodière, JCP 1962.II.12552).

It appears from the foregoing that the range of dependants who can claim compensation for damage caused by an unlawful act is no longer limited to those who can prove the existence of a "subjective right" *stricto sensu*.[197] A telling example is given in a judgment of the Belgian Court of Cassation of 4 September 1972. In that case, a religious congregation that for many years had received the teaching salary benevolently assigned to it by one of its members was allowed to bring an action against a defendant who in a car accident had caused the death of that member. The action was brought on account of a loss of income for the congregation amounting to the victim's net salary (i.e. after deduction of the expenses which the congregation paid for the maintenance of the victim). The Court allowed the claim.[198]

(4) The liberal attitude towards actions brought by *victimes par ricochet* outlined above has never been carried to its extreme. Thus as regards the prejudice suffered by persons who had an economic relationship with the deceased victim, courts have dismissed claims of, amongst others, business partners, employers or creditors.[199] Viney cites some exceptions, including Colmar, 20 April 1955, where it was held that a football club could claim damages on account of the loss that it had suffered because it had had to pay a considerable transfer fee for a replacement after one of its professional players was killed in an accident as a result of the negligence of the defendant.[200]

In respect of bereavement (*préjudice d'affection*), the French courts initially showed considerable reluctance to award compensation. By way of illustration, in earlier case law, the Cour de cassation was not willing to grant *préjudice d'affection* when the victim was merely injured.[201] The Cour de cassation had also earlier required that the suffering of the victim's relatives be "exceptionally serious".[202] Furthermore, in cases where the primary victim had only been injured but not killed, the criminal chamber of the Cour de cassation also refused to allow secondary victims to join their civil claims for non-material damage with the public prosecutor's action before the criminal court. The same chamber also held that criminal courts cannot award damages to the secondary victim in respect of mental disorders triggered by a shock.[203] However, these limitations have also been abandoned.[204]

Some academic writers have strongly criticized the proliferation of bereavement claims, arguing that they should be curtailed in order to alleviate the burdens put on insurance companies and free resources for the satisfaction of more urgent loss claims.[205] The Legislature does not seem to have heeded that call, however, judging from the *Loi*

[197] For the definition of a "subjective right" under French law, see *supra*, Chapter I, 1.4.2.

[198] *Infra*, **2.B.20.**, referred to by Viney and Jourdain, *Conditions* at 134, para. 311.

[199] Cass. civ. 2e, 21 February 1979, JCP 1979.IV.145, where the Court dismissed, for lack of a causal link, the claim of a creditor who could not recover his money when his debtor was killed in an accident as a result of the defendant's negligence, thus making the debt irrecoverable.

[200] D 1956.Jur.723, cited in Viney and Jourdain, *Conditions* at 135–6, para. 312, and in Zweigert and Kötz, *Introduction* at 658–9. The Corte di Cassazione came to the same conclusion: Cass., 26 January 1971, *infra*, **2.I.22.**

[201] Nor did it grant compensation for the material loss incurred by family members in assisting the victim: see Viney and Jourdain, *Conditions* at 141, para. 317. That position has now been abandoned by Cass. civ., 22 October 1947, JCP 1946.II.3365, annotated by A.S., D 1947.Jur.59.

[202] A requirement abandoned by Cass. civ. 2e, 23 May 1977, JCP 1977.IV.187.

[203] *Les grands arrêts* at 467. The reasoning of the court was that the right of the injured person to bring a civil claim before a criminal court as a *partie civile* is vested only in persons who have personally suffered damage that has been caused directly by the criminal act, as follows from Art. 2 of the *Code de procédure pénale*: Cass. Ass. plén., 12 January 1979, (1979) 78 RTDciv. 141; Viney and Jourdain, *Conditions* at 141–2, para. 318.

[204] By a judgment of 9 February 1989 (D 1989.Jur.614, annotated by C. Bruneau), where the criminal chamber of the Cour de cassation based its reasoning on both Arts. 2 and 3(2) of the *Code de procédure pénale*.

[205] G. Viney, *supra*, Chapter I, **1.F.24.** and A. Tunc, referred to in *Les grands arrêts* at 468.

Badinter[206] or the Act 91-1406.[207] Under both pieces of legislation, compensation for all kinds of damage can be obtained.

2.1.4. BELGIAN, ITALIAN, SWEDISH AND DUTCH LAW

Introductory Note

a) As stated above, the tort provisions of the **Italian** *Codice civile* (Articles 2043–59) start at Article 2043 with a general provision in the like of Articles 1382 and 1383 C.civ.[208] The generality of the provision is illustrated by the judgment of the Italian Corte di Cassazione of 26 January 1971.[209]

Articles 2044–6 then deal with defences and imputability of the wrongful act in a manner which, when compared with the corresponding provisions of French law, add considerable precision to the general rule, completing and updating it without changing its substance. The same holds true for Articles 2047–54 on liability for others and for things, Article 2055 on joint and several liability and Articles 2056–8 on the assessment and reparation of damage. Article 2058 of the *Codice civile* expresses a preference for reparation in kind if and to the extent possible. The most striking provision is the restrictive rule of Article 2059, whereby compensation of non-material injury is limited to instances provided by law. That is a clear departure from the prevailing situation under French law.

b) Whilst it appears from the foregoing that Italian law is closer to French than to German or English law, **Dutch** law falls more on the side of German law. Article 6:95 BW[210] states that recoverable damage means material damage (*vermogensschade*) and "other harm" (*ander nadeel*, i.e. non-material damage), the latter however only in so far as the law provides.[211] Article 6:96 BW then specifies that material damage comprises *damnum emergens* and *lucrum cessans*[212] and that the following heads of damage are also regarded as material damage: expenses to avoid or mitigate damage, expenses to assess damage and expenses to recover damage out of court. Later on, Article 6:106 NBW specifies that the primary victim is also entitled to compensation for "other harm" (i.e. non-material damage), to be assessed in equity (*naar billijkheid vast te stellen*) if: (i) the wrongdoer inflicted the injury intentionally; (ii) the victim suffered bodily harm (*lichamelijk letsel*), injury to honour or reputation, or was otherwise injured in his or her person;[213] (iii) harm to the memory of the deceased was inflicted upon one of a specified number of close relatives, such as would have entitled the deceased to compensation had he or she still been alive. Obviously, the most frequent instance of "other harm" is the one referred to under (ii), which includes pain and suffering or reduction in the enjoyment of

---

[206] *Infra*, Chapter VI, **6.F.18.**
[207] *Infra*, Chapter VI, **6.F.31.**
[208] *Supra*, *General Introduction.*
[209] *Infra*, **2.I.22.**
[210] Found in the General Part on Obligations, which is applicable to all kinds of obligations.
[211] Thus Art. 6:106 BW.
[212] See *infra*, **2.NL.25.**, for an application in a case of wrongful life; in that case contractual liability was at issue but, as said above, Art. 6:96 BW applies to all kinds of obligations.
[213] For instance his or her privacy: HR, 30 October 1987, NJ 1988, 277, mentioned in Asser-Hartkamp I, 10th edn. (Zwolle: WEJ Tjeenk Willink, 1996) at 392, para. 467.

life (*vermindering van levensvreugde*) resulting from interference with the victim's bodily integrity or mental health.

In derogation from its model, the French Code, the old BW already contained special provisions relating to injury suffered as a consequence of interference with life or bodily integrity. These provisions are now contained in Articles 6:107 and 6:108 BW. According to Article 6:107 BW, the victim itself may obtain compensation for physical or mental injury (*lichamelijk of geestelijk letsel*);[214] in addition, some expenses incurred by third parties on behalf of the injured person (unless by virtue of insurance) will be recoverable if the victim could have claimed them from the tortfeasor had he or she incurred the expenses him- or herself. That is the case for instance of expenses incurred by relatives in the course of looking after the victim, or sums paid in order to replace the victim for help in the household.[215]

As for harm sustained as a result of the death of the victim, Article 6:108 BW only allows compensation for funeral expenses (Article 6:108(2)) and loss of maintenance, but only for a limited list of persons enumerated at Article 6:108(1).

Finally, Article 6:109 BW gives courts the power to mitigate the legal duty to compensate if full compensation would lead to manifestly unacceptable consequences, taking into account all circumstances of the case.

The following cases can be found (with notes) at <http://www.rechten. unimaas.nl/casebook>:

2.B.20. Cour de cassation/Hof van Cassatie, 4 September 1972, *Association Saint-Jean Baptiste* v. *Steenhout*. Loss of income by religious community.

2.B.21. Cour de cassation/Hof van Cassatie, 3 February 1987, *De Vos* v. *Dedobbeleer*. Father sees injured son deteriorate.

Corte di Cassazione, 26 January 1971[216]   **2.I.22.**

LOSS ARISING FROM DEATH OF DEBTOR

Death of soccer player

Compensation is due under Article 2043 of the Codice civile *for the loss suffered by the creditor as a result of his debtor's death due to the defendant's tortious act if the creditor's claim is definitely and irreparably lost.*

Facts: Soccer player Luigi Meroni, under contract with the club S.P.A. Torino Calcio, was killed in a road traffic accident. Penal proceedings were brought against Attilio Romero, a minor, for involuntary manslaughter. Pending the proceedings, the club sought a judicial declaration that it was entitled to claim compensation for the damage resulting from Meroni's death.

Held: The Corte di Cassazione quashing the decision of the court of appeal admitted the claim.

---

[214] See *infra*, **2.NL.25.** at para. 3.14.

[215] See Asser-Hartkamp I, 10th edn. (Zwolle: WEJ Tjeenk Willink, 1996) at 398, para. 473.

[216] No. 174, Foro it. 1971-I-345. Translation by R. Bray.

Judgment: ". . . Now, there is no denying that the relationship entered into between the professional player and the football company which signed him up must come under the head of relationships between a creditor and a debtor, more specifically relationships of employment . . .

. . . The key issue in this case can therefore be reduced to the question of whether redress may be granted in respect of such a relationship to the person to whom the obligation is owed, where unlawful conduct of a third party affected the person of the debtor by causing him to lose his life and, even before that, to the more general question as to whether redress is available under the law of tort, namely Article 2043 of the *Codice civile*, where an obligation is impaired by a person outside the relationship between the person owing the obligation and the person to whom the obligation is due . . .

[The Court then examined Article 1372 of the *Codice civile*, which sets out the principle of relativity of contracts, as well as other provisions of the *Codice civile* which the court of appeal had invoked in support of its conclusion.] Having shown that the provisions adverted to by the court of appeal . . . do not preclude in principle the award of damages for injury caused by the third party to the right of the person to whom the obligation is owed, another more general criticism of the contested judgment put forward by Torino Calcio should now be considered: that is to say, the criticism concerning the determinative importance attached by the court below to the distinction between absolute rights and relative rights in finding, for present purposes, that redress in tort, which is universally agreed to be available in respect of absolute rights, must be denied as far as relative rights are concerned. In this connection, the court of appeal refers to the traditional concept according to which, as regards the relationship between the creditor and the debtor of an obligation, a breach of that obligation can be effected only by the debtor; the public at large is under no general duty to refrain from acting [so as to impair the right of the creditor]: it drew the conclusion that Article 2043 does not provide the person to whom the obligation is due with any immediate, direct redress against third parties who have impaired his right.

In truth, the principle that damages under Article 2043 of the *Codice civile* are to be awarded only in respect of an infringement of absolute or primary rights, such as the right to life, to physical integrity, to property or to one's honour, and cannot be claimed by a party relying on a breach of a relative right, in particular a right in respect of an obligation owed to him, is not at all unfamiliar to this court. Indeed, it has been variously affirmed and reaffirmed in different cases and from different points of view [references omitted] . . .

But this court considers that that principle whereby absolute rights and relative rights are rigidly separated and placed in contradistinction should be reconsidered in so far as it is relied on to justify different treatment of those two categories for the purposes of recovery of damages in tort . . .

Moreover, careful consideration of what is actually prescribed by the law, as expressed in Article 2043 of the *Codice civile*, leads us to the conclusion that that provision does not allow it to be assumed to be a certain, conclusive fact that there is a rigid contradistinction between absolute and relative rights as a result of which the law of tort affords protection for the former and not for the latter.

Indeed, the "wrong" which Article 2043 takes as an essential ingredient of civil liability should be understood as having the two aspects *non jure* and *contra jus*: *non jure* in the sense that the conduct which brought about the damage must not be justified under any other legal provision (*e.g.* Article 2044, 2045 of the *Codice civile*); *contra jus* in the sense that the conduct must harm an individual situation which is recognized and guaranteed by the legal system in the form of a subjective right. Whilst that interpretation leaves outside the scope of the protection of Article 2043 those interests which do not fall within the category of subjective rights [references omitted], it discloses the arbitrariness of any discrimination between categories of subjective rights for the purposes of allowing, or disallowing, the protection of the law of tort.

Acceptance of these principles, moreover, is implicit, or at least presumed, in the approach taken by this court in a number of cases, even though they have not been expressly enunciated . . .

Since this is the state of the case-law, it seems to this court that if, as the court of appeal proceeded, the protection of the law of tort were to be rigidly ruled out in the case of rights other than absolute rights, this would constitute a backward step away from positions which may now be regarded as settled and appear, moreover, more in keeping with present-day economic and social conditions, which are increasingly unconstrained by any rigid hierarchy of economic—and hence legal—values.

Having held that in principle damages may be awarded for the breach by a third party of a right under an obligation owed by the victim, the question of causation has to be considered. [In the course of its discussion of causation, the Court examines the conditions under which the extinction of a claim through the death of the debtor would constitute recoverable damage.]

It is . . . a question of establishing in what cases and under which conditions the existence of the obligation closely depends upon the debtor remaining alive, since the unlawful act of the third party, concurrently and at a stroke, deprives the person under the obligation of the benefit of his life and, the person to whom he was under the obligation of the services which the deceased was under a duty to perform.

From this angle, it is necessary, first, that the death of the debtor should bring about, *ipso facto*, the extinguishment of the obligation and, at the same time, of the right of the creditor, without there being any possibility of passing the obligation on to the successors of the debtor . . .

Secondly, the loss which the creditor has sustained as a result of the death of the debtor must be definitive and irreparable in the sense that the creditor cannot, with equal economic advantage, obtain from others the services of which he has been deprived . . .

A more delicate question is that of obligations to do something of a strictly personal nature which have been agreed *intuitu personae,* and in respect of which the binding obligation is based on a relationship of personal trust or on specific qualities of the person who entered into the obligation (professional ability, technical ability, reputation or renown acquired by him and so on). In such a case it is obvious that there can be no question of the creditor being indifferent as to whether the services in question are provided by the debtor or by another person, but nor can it be said that the death of the debtor is bound in every case to amount to a definitive and irreparable loss to the creditor.

Primary importance attaches to the criterion of the irreplaceability of the debtor, which is an essentially relative one. It would certainly be excessive to claim that someone was absolutely irreplaceable, which is virtually impossible to check, but it is equally certain that definitive and irreparable loss is not involved where, following the death of the debtor, the creditor may nevertheless obtain the same or equivalent services on terms no more onerous than those agreed with the deceased.

But, subject to these general considerations, it should be noted in addition that, in relation to the specific characteristics of each individual case, the criterion of the irreplaceability of the debtor has to be considered from many and various angles. For instance, the immanence in time of the services may sometimes be relevant in the sense that it may be impossible or extremely difficult to find an appropriate replacement given the brief interval between the deceased's death and the time when he was due to perform the services.

On the other hand, and still on the subject of immediacy, the criterion of replaceability must be seen in the context of the activity in respect of which the services to be performed by the debtor were to have been carried out . . .

Having so interpreted and defined the causal link which must exist between the damage sustained by the person to whom the obligation is owed and the act of the third party, it seems to this court that the liability of the third party is confined within sufficiently strict and certain limits and that sufficient regard is paid to the justified requirement to avoid opening the floodgates to compensation claims . . .

It follows that the contested judgment should be set aside and the case referred to another court of the same rank which . . . must comply with the following principle of law:

'A person who maliciously or culpably causes the death of a person under an obligation to another is liable in damages for the loss caused to that person where the death causes the extinction of the claim and a definitive, irreparable loss to the claimant.

The loss is definitive and irreparable in the case of obligations in terms of maintenance or alimony provided that there is no-one with like or subsequent obligations capable of defraying the relevant burden or obligations where the person subject to them cannot be replaced in the sense that equal or equivalent services cannot be acquired except on more onerous terms.'

On these grounds, the Court quashes, etc . . ."

Note

In the annotated judgment, the Italian Corte di cassazione, overruling its earlier case law, admits that liability in tort can arise when, as a result of the tortious act, the debt of a debtor (in this case, soccer player Meroni) is extinguished and the contractual claim of the plaintiff (the football club) is by the same token definitively and irreparably lost. That situation occurs for example when no one is bound to take over an obligation to provide maintenance or, as here, when the debtor is irreplaceable in the sense that it is impossible to obtain equal or equivalent performance from a person replacing him. Until then, while it was agreed that liability in tort could arise because of an interference with an "absolute" right, it was controversial in Italian law whether it could also arise because of an interference with a "relative" right (a right *in personam*), such as a contractual right. The Corte de Cassazione put this controversy to rest by holding in clear terms that interferences with both "absolute" and "relative" rights can lead to liability in tort.

The following cases can be found (with notes) at <http://www.rechten. unimaas.nl/casebook>:

2.I.23. Corte di Cassazione, 6 December 1982. Killed by a minor.
2.SW.24. HD, 4 April 1990. Woman bites police officer.

Hoge Raad, 21 February 1997[217]　　　　　　　　　　　　**2.NL.25.**

WRONGFUL BIRTH

Missing IUD

Facts: The plaintiff and her husband already had two children. They decided not to have any more children. They informed the defendant doctor of this when asking him to insert an intra-uterine device (IUD, trademark nova T). Later on, the defendant removed the IUD, but neglected to replace it with a new one and to inform the plaintiff of that fact. He and his insurer recognized this conduct to be a professional fault in the performance of the medical contract between the doctor and the plaintiff. A healthy child was born, and the plaintiff asked compensation for, amongst other heads of damage, loss of income and expenses to educate the child until the age of 18, as well as non-material injury.

---

[217] NJ 1999, 145. See for comments "Wrongful birth" (1997) 72 NJB 475; J. Hijma, "Wrongful birth (O./B.)" (1997) 46 AA 431. Translation by W. van Gerven and Y.P. Salmon.

Held: The HR quashed the interlocutory judgment of the court of appeal in which it was held that the expenses of maintaining and educating the child could only be compensated under exceptional circumstances (e.g. because the birth of the child caused the plaintiff to be in financial difficulties) and that no compensation for loss of income and for non-material damage could be obtained. The HR came to a different conclusion for the first two heads of damage.

Judgment: "3.7. At issue is the medical fault of a physician who thus failed to fulfil his contractual obligation to treat the plaintiff woman. As a result of a combined reading of Arts. 6:74, 6:94 and 6:98 BW the physician is therefore liable for all material damage which may be seen to be related to the fault, to the extent that it should be imputed to him in accordance with Art. 6:98 . . . The damage for which compensation is asked here consists of expenses which, by their very amount, must be deemed to influence in principle the financial situation of the family until the child comes of age. Such expenses are indisputably material damage . . . Contrary to what the court of appeal thought, that is not inconsistent with the legal duty of parents to take care of and educate the child; rather it follows therefrom that the expenses incurred have necessarily to be made, and therefore constitute a financial inconvenience and so material damage.

3.8. It must be examined further whether there are other objections against awarding in principle compensation for damage consisting in *the expenses incurred in the care and education of the child* [emphasis added]. Such objections have been raised in the Netherlands as in other countries. To state it briefly, it has been alleged that the award of compensation for such expenses in a case as the present one, which concerns a normal and healthy child, can only be based on the conception that the child itself must be regarded as damage or a damage factor, and that in any event such an award is contrary to the human dignity of the child, since its right to exist is thereby negated.

The Hoge Raad does not regard these objections to be convincing. The line of argument developed above within the framework of the law . . . takes as a point of departure that the parents, having accepted the child and the new situation, are asking compensation for the impact it has on the family income . . . This line of thinking does not necessarily entail the conception that the child itself is seen as damage or a damage factor. At issue is only the compensation for an additional charge which burdens the family income as a result of the physician's fault, and which arises precisely because of the parents' acceptance of the child. Nor can this line of thinking be said to be inconsistent with the human dignity of the child or to negate its right of existence. For indeed, it is also in the child's interest that the parents should not be refused the possibility of compensation on behalf of the whole family, including the new child.

3.9. As a further objection against the award of compensation of expenses for the care and education of the child, it has been alleged that such an award may result in the child being confronted later in life with the impression that it was not wanted by its parents, which may result in psychological damage to the child. The Hoge Raad does not regard this argument as convincing either. In the first place, the argument interferes with the relationship between parents and child on a point which must, in principle, be left to be decided by the parents themselves. In the second place, to prevent an enlargement of the family is a wholly different matter than the issue of the acceptance of a child once it becomes an individual. The claim for compensation relates exclusively to the first, and not to the second point. Such expenses therefore have no link with the acceptance of the child as a human being. In the third place, it may be assumed that parents are in general able to make it clear to the child that such an impression of rejection is incorrect, even apart from the fact that they themselves may contradict such an impression by raising the child with loving care.

3.10. Furthermore no arguments against granting the aforementioned claim can be derived from the idea of computation of advantages. More in particular, it cannot be accepted that the mere fact that the family is enlarged by the addition of a healthy child constitutes in itself a non-material advantage which would offset the kind of material damage discussed herein. It would be inconsistent, in the first place, with the line of thinking developed above under 3.7. to exclude the physician's liability on the basis of that fact. In the second place, that position would not be reasonable in the sense of Art. 6:100 BW, taking into account that the injury arose as a result of jeopardizing family planning which is partly based on financial considerations. It must be accepted instead that non-material advantages can only be taken into account to offset eventual non-material harm . . .

3.11 . . . As already stated in 3.7., only damage which can be imputed to the physician as a consequence of his fault is recoverable, in accordance with the criterion of Art. 6:98 BW. That criterion does not preclude the possibility of imputing responsibility to the parents rather than the physician for expenses in excess of average expenses for the care and education of a child . . . Moreover, under the law applicable as of 1 January 1992, according to Art. 6:109 BW, the possibility is given to the judge to mitigate the duty to compensate in so far as the physician's liability was not covered by insurance . . .

3.13 . . . To answer the question of whether the plaintiff is entitled to compensation for *loss of income* suffered as the consequence of her pregnancy and the child's birth, it must be determined whether her decision not to work temporarily can be deemed reasonable under the circumstances [emphasis added]. In view of this, one must attach weight, on the one hand, to the liberty of the plaintiff to organize her life, in the interests of the child, as she pleases, and keep in mind, on the other hand, that she must limit the damage she suffers as far as possible, and as much as can be reasonably expected (comp. on all this HR, 12 January 1996, NJ 1996, 335). In the assessment of whether the plaintiff's aforementioned decision is reasonable, specific family conditions may play a role, such as the number and age of other children, the employment position of the husband and the financial means of the family. . . . [T]he claim is well-founded to that extent and does not need further discussion.

3.14. With respect to the circumstances invoked in the plaintiff's claim for *compensation of non-material harm*, the court of appeal has judged that, although it is not to be excluded that those circumstances may have resulted in a degree of psychological discomfort, they have not resulted in mental harm upon which a successful claim for compensation of non-material damage could be based [emphasis added]. This judgment, involving a factual assessment does not imply an incorrect legal assessment, nor is it incomprehensible or need to be further substantiated. [That claim] is therefore unfounded.

4. Decision. The HR quashes the judgment of the court of appeal of 27 September 1995."

Notes

(1) As we have seen[218] courts hold diverging views as to whether the birth of a child which is "due" to a wrongful act of a third person, mostly a doctor or a clinic, gives rise to liability.[219] The answer may, within each legal system, depend on the general or specific circumstances of the case at issue. Circumstances of a general nature are whether the child was born healthy or with a more or less serious handicap and whether the wrongful act consisted of a fault committed by the doctor or the clinic in effecting, or following up, a surgical intervention (sterilization, vasectomy, or other) or of a failure to provide correct and complete information on the chances for the parents to have healthy children.

Whatever the divergences may be, the main questions raised and to be answered by the courts turn around the same issues: Is it against public policy as a matter of principle to consider the birth of child as a possible head of damage? In the affirmative, what are the heads of damage which may give rise to compensation: all kinds of material injury as well as non-material injury? Is there room to offset some, or all, heads of damage against each

---

[218] See *supra*, **2.G.1.**, Notes (2) to (4), **2.E.6.**, and **2.F.11.–14.**
[219] For other recent judgments see von Bar I at 602.

other, or do some heads escape comparison, so as to exclude any offsetting of claims? More specifically, is there any reason to award compensation for non-material injury—if the general laws on compensation in the specific country allow such compensation—in the case where a healthy child is born, or must such injury be deemed to be offset by the joy which a child represents for its parents? One might conclude from these divergences that we are far away from a common law of Europe, at least in this delicate area. We believe that this would be wrong, because the comparison shows how much the courts approach these questions from a very similar cultural, ethical and legal background, trying to find solutions while remaining aware that other courts may reach an opposite result starting from the same underlying principles.

(2) The Hoge Raad judgment reproduced above is dealing with many of the questions referred to under (1). The Hoge Raad is of the opinion that the award of compensation for expenses to raise the child, which in that case was born normal and healthy, is not in conflict with the human dignity of the child, or with its right to life, as it is one thing to see the child as a head of damage as such, which is unacceptable, and another thing for the parents to accept the child, once it is there, but to ask for compensation for the additional burden on the family budget which is caused by the doctor's fault, which is acceptable.[220] In line with the general laws on compensation, laid down in Article 6:95 ff. BW,[221] the judgment does not award non-material damage, as it was not proved before the trial judge that the mother suffered psychological disturbances (*psychisch onbehagen*) amounting to mental illness (*geestelijk letsel*) in the sense of Article 6:107 BW (under 3.14.). Apart from expenses for raising the child, the Hoge Raad also acknowleged the possibility of compensation for loss of income depending on whether it is reasonable for the mother under the circumstances to abandon her work *temporarily* (under 3.13.). As for the question whether economic losses can be offset by the joy which a child represents for its parents, the Hoge Raad rejects that possibility (under 3.10.).

2.1.5. COMPARATIVE OVERVIEW

Tortious liability arises to protect the individual from all harm that touches the person directly, whether it affects his or her physical well-being, psychological health, freedom or, albeit to a varying degree, personality or privacy.[222]

Interference with life and bodily integrity

As cynical as it may appear, strictly speaking, when a person dies he or she suffers no damage. Indeed, no award in damages can compensate a person who has been killed. The only assurances that private law may offer is that his or her reputation is not dragged through the mud, that his or her corpse is not treated as just another object and that he or she receives a proper burial. The truth of the matter is, that the issue of compensation for loss of life relates in fact to the rights of those who are left behind.

---

[220] Under 3.8. of the judgment; see also 3.9. Advocate-General Vranken in his opinion before the HR was of a different opinion.

[221] *Supra*, 1.4., Introductory Note under c).

[222] For the protection of personality rights and the right to privacy, see *infra*, 2.

In legal systems where life, body and health have the status of specially protected legal interests such as the *Rechtsgüter* enumerated in § 823(1) BGB, the question arises which kinds of interference with bodily integrity and health will infringe the specific legal provision and so incur tortious liability. There are instances where strictly speaking the individual suffers no injury to his or her body but where harm is nonetheless suffered in close connection with the body, as where sperm samples from a man who had subsequently become infertile were negligently destroyed by the hospital where they were being preserved.[223] In its judgment of 9 November 1993, the BGH awarded *Schmerzensgeld* on the basis of § 847 BGB, applying by analogy a broad concept of interference with physical integrity, which had been regarded as an expression of the general *Persönlichkeitsrecht* in earlier case law.[224]

Those legal systems which do not specify such rights in a limited catalogue of protected legal interests do not encounter the same difficulties in defining which interferences with bodily integrity and health are actionable in tort. The French tort law regime embodies this approach: any harm done to a legitimate interest may give rise to liability if the harm is certain and not merely hypothetical. Thus, any disturbance of living conditions suffered by primary victims and secondary victims (*victimes par ricochet*) is regarded as eligible for compensation.[225]

Liability for intentional physical injury may arise in English law under the old nominate torts of battery, assault and false imprisonment.[226] Leaving them aside, in considering which interference with physical integrity or health are actionable under the tort of negligence, the English law of torts has experienced difficulties mainly with psychological injury suffered by a primary or secondary victim of the unintentional tortious act. Liability in negligence will depend on whether a duty of care is owed by the defendant to the plaintiff on the particular facts of the case. That did not preclude courts from considering "broader questions which are essentially concerned with whether, and if so how far, the law of negligence should operate in a situation of a certain type".[227]

Interferences of a special kind

As a consequence of a tortious act, the victim may be left in a permanent vegetative state, that is in a coma without any serious chance of improvement, or even dependent upon life support equipment. Although the plaintiff is not conscious of his or her loss in enjoyment of life, nor of any damages awarded, courts in many countries will nonetheless grant damages for material and non-material injury.[228] According to the BGH, the damages should not be merely symbolic, as they express a loss of personality and human

---

[223] *Infra*, **2.G.27.**

[224] See also *infra*, 2.1.

[225] See e.g. the judgment of the Cour d'appel de Paris, *supra*, **2.F.15.**; see also for a catalogue of material and non-material injury, Chapter I, **1.F.24.–25.**, Note (2).

[226] See *supra*, 1.2., Introductory Note.

[227] See Rogers, *supra*, Chapter I, **1.E.22.**

[228] For a discussion of Austrian, Belgian, Dutch and Greek case law, see the five comments on BGH, 13 October 1992, BGHZ 120, 1, NJW 1993, 781 and Belgian Court of Cassation, 4 April 1990, Pas. 1990.I.913, JT 1992.829, at (1996) 4 Eur.R Priv.L 221 ff.

dignity.[229] Similarly, in *H. West & Son* v. *Shephard*,[230] the House of Lords decided that "unconsciousness does not eliminate the actuality of the deprivations of the ordinary experiences and merits of life . . .", and by a majority granted more than nominal damages. The French courts take a similar view.[231]

Today, it is generally acknowledged that "wrongful birth" constitutes harm to the mother, regardless of whether the child is born handicapped or healthy, albeit that the existence of the child itself, as opposed to the cost of maintaining the child, will not be regarded as recoverable damage. Under English and Scottish law, however, the cost of maintaining the child cannot be recovered.[232] In contrast, as it has no legal personality, the foetus which is injured and perishes *in utero* cannot claim damages, and has no right which could be transferred to its parents or heirs. Yet when a baby is born alive, having suffered harm *in utero*, he or she can claim damages from the moment of birth, as he or she then acquires a legal status of his or her own.[233] Liability towards the mother or child is not limited to instances of wrongful medical diagnosis or treatment, but may also arise in the case of accidents, in particular road traffic accidents.[234]

Infection of an individual with HIV through the tortious conduct of another is held to constitute bodily harm, even before the actual onset of AIDS.[235] The question whether compensation for mental pain and suffering can be awarded to a person who thought—albeit wrongly—that he or she was infected with HIV, is more contentious. The Swedish HD granted compensation for pain and suffering, including mental suffering, where a policewoman was bitten by the defendant who claimed she had AIDS.[236]

Psychological illness versus nervous shock

The Swedish case referred to above relates to purely psychological disturbances suffered by the primary, immediate, victim of the tort. Such psychological injury is recoverable, in the presence [237] or absence[238] of physical harm. It should, however, be distinguished from the so-called "nervous shock" cases, in which the question arises whether, and if so under what circumstances, a witness to *another's* suffering or death can claim damages for immediate or subsequent psychological pain and suffering. What is meant here is a sud-

---

[229] BGH, 13 October 1992, ibid., annotated by E. Deutsch and BGH, 16 February 1993, NJW 1993, 1531: these judgments recognize that non-material damages (*Schmerzensgeld*) serve a triple purpose: compensation for non-material damage (*Ausgleich für die erlittenen immateriellen Schaden*), satisfaction for the harm inflicted (*Genugtuung für das zugefügte Leid*), and compensation for the destruction of the personality (*Zerstörung der Persönlichkeit*). The latter will be awarded regardless of whether the victim can appreciate the reduction in his standard of living.

[230] *Supra*, **2.E.7.**, Note (3).

[231] See the judgments of the Cour d'appel de Bordeaux of 18 April 1991 and the French Cour de cassation of 22 February 1995, *supra*, **2.F.17.** and **2.F.16.** The Bordeaux court indicates that the damage must be assessed "by reference to feelings commonly felt . . . by persons able to give expression to their will".

[232] See *supra*, **2.E.6.** and notes thereafter.

[233] See *supra*, **2.G.1.**, relating to an accident which occurred when the child was not yet conceived, and Note (1) the Congenital Disabilities (Civil Liability) Act 1976, s. 1, *supra*, **2.E.5.**; and *supra*, **2.F.11.** and **2.F.14.**

[234] See the Congenital Disabilities (Civil Liability) Act 1976, s. 1(2), *supra*, **2.E.5.**

[235] See *supra*, **2.G.1.** as well as the French Act 91-1406, *infra*, Chapter VI, **6.F.31.**

[236] See *supra*, **2.SW.24.** But see Højesteret, 13 December 1994, UfR 1995A, 185, mentioned in von Bar I at 273, para. 247.

[237] See *supra*, **2.G.3.** and notes.

[238] See *Page* v. *Smith*, *supra*, **2.E.9.** and Note (3).

den and intense upset of the senses, on a scale somewhere between loss of happiness (*Lebensfreude*) on the one hand and hysterical and excessive reactions, neuroses and, at the extreme, even psychoses on the other hand. In adjudicating the existence of liability for this kind of suffering, many legal systems, like the German, ask the question whether the psychological pain and suffering of the plaintiff, not directly involved in the accident, is so intense that it can be considered an illness.[239]

Under other tort law regimes, such as the English common law system, even psychiatric illness due to the stress and strain of seeing the primary victim suffer is not enough to found a claim in damages: the success of such a claim is dependent upon "a requisite relationship of proximity between the claimant and the party said to owe the duty".[240]

These restrictive approaches are far removed from the position taken in legal systems following the French model, in which often generous compensation is awarded for all heads of injury, including natural grief.[241] Liability also arises for harm suffered by secondary victims, such as close relatives who are exposed to the suffering of the immediate victim.[242]

Interference with liberty

Tort law regimes accord the same prominent status to the enjoyment of liberty as to the enjoyment of good health. Some legal systems, as in Germany, achieve this by enumerating liberty as a specific legal interest to be protected.[243] This is also in line with the protection afforded by Article 5(1) ECHR, which provides that "everyone has the right to liberty and security of person" and that "no one shall be deprived of his liberty save in the following cases [enumerated in that paragraph under (a) to (f)] and in accordance with a procedure prescribed by law". The ECtHR has interpreted the "right to liberty" contained in Article 5(1) ECHR as "contemplating individual liberty in its classic sense, that is to say the physical liberty of the person. Its aim is to ensure that no one should be dispossessed of this liberty in an arbitrary fashion".[244] According to Article 5(5), "[e]veryone who has been the victim of arrest or situation in contravention of the provisions of this Article shall have an enforceable right to compensation". As a result of this provision, a person who, having been unlawfully detained in a prison or other, for example psychiatric, institution, is released in accordance with Article 5(4) ECHR but is denied compensation under domestic law, can bring a claim before the Commission of Human Rights.[245]

---

[239] See *supra*, **2.G.4.**

[240] See *Alcock* v. *Chief Constable of the South Yorkshire Police, supra*, **2.E.8.** and notes.

[241] See *supra*, **2.B.21.**

[242] See *supra*, **2.F.15.–17.**, Note (1).

[243] See further von Bar I at 591–612, para. 570–91. The protection of liberty meant here is the protection of the physical liberty to move freely, not the general ability to act as one pleases, whenever one pleases. See also Larenz/Canaris, *supra*, Chapter I, **1.G.27.**

[244] ECtHR, 8 June 1976, *Engel* v. *Netherlands* (*No. 2*), Ser. A No. 22 at para. 58. On the impact of this case law of the ECtHR on the case law of the ECJ, see ECJ, Judgment of 29 May 1997, Case C-299/95, *Kremzow* v. *Austria* [1997] ECR I-2629.

[245] European Commission of Human Rights, *Huber* v. *Austria* (1977) 6 DR 65 at para. 3.

An emerging right to bodily safety

As has been noted, German law gives prominent status to the protection of life, body, health, liberty and, as shall be seen below, personality rights.[246] The same holds true in other legal systems, in so far as bodily integrity, liberty, name, image and reputation is protected against infringement, either under special nominate torts or by special legislative provisions, over and above the general protection afforded by tort law to other rights and interests.[247] Moreover, there are legal systems, of which the French is the prime example, which protect bodily integrity by some general right to bodily security (*droit à la sécurité corporelle*) regarded as an autonomous right, much like the general right to privacy.[248] Here the mere infringement of the right constitutes proof of fault and injury, so fulfilling the necessary conditions to establish causation.[249] Such an evolution is taking place in France, through the enactment of special legislation such as the *Loi Badinter* in the area of road traffic accidents[250] and Act 91-1406 as it relates to compensation for victims of HIV infected through blood transfusions. The latter was enacted when it became clear that the classic French tort rules were not able to deal with a liability problem of such magnitude.[251] Tendencies towards an increased level of protection of bodily integrity may also be observed in other countries.

Heads and extent of compensation

Basically, primary victims are entitled under English,[252] French[253] and German[254] law to be compensated for all kinds of injury caused to them by a tortious act or omission. Under each tort law, the broad categories of material and non-material damage are distinguished. Material damage (*dommages matériels, Vermögensschaden*) comprises bodily damage (*dommages corporels, körperliche Schaden*), damage to property (*atteintes aux biens, Sachbeschädigung*), economic damage connected with damage to the person or to property, and damage independent of damage to the person or property, so-called "pure economic loss" or *reiner Vermögensschaden*. Non-material damage (*dommages moraux ou immatériels, Nichtvermögensschaden*) comprises pain and suffering and loss of amenity (*douleurs et souffrances* and *préjudice d'agrément, Schmerzensgeld*). These are neither exhaustive nor well-defined classes nor do categories used in one legal system necessarily correspond to those used in another.

Apart from the question of which heads of damage are recoverable as a matter of principle, there is the issue of whether full compensation must be awarded. This issue arises particularly in respect of non-material damage. Thus, under German law, § 847 BGB, read in conjunction with § 253 BGB, provides that in cases of injury to body or health, or

---

[246] See also *infra*, 2.1.
[247] See with reference to English law, *supra*, 1.2., Introductory Note under c).
[248] See *infra*, 2.2.
[249] *Supra*, 1.3., Introductory Note under a) and b).
[250] *Infra*, Chapter VI, **6.F.18.**; to be compared with the situation in Germany, *supra*, 1.1., Introductory Note under c).
[251] *Supra*, **2.F.18.** and *infra*, Chapter VI, **6.F.31.**, and notes.
[252] *Supra*, **2.E.7.**, Note (1).
[253] *Supra*, **2.F.15.–17.**, Note (1).
[254] *Supra*, 1.1., Introductory Note under b).

deprivation of liberty, the injured person is entitled to *equitable* monetary compensation. It should be noted that more recent codifications, such as the Swiss and Dutch, not only try to limit the heads of injury for which compensation can be claimed,[255] but also allow the court to make an equitable reduction in the amount of damages under certain circumstances.[256]

Under French law[257] and other laws which follow its model, such as Belgian law,[258] *victimes par ricochet* such as dependants, are entitled to full compensation for the harm that they suffer. That is not so under English law where, in case of fatal injury, only dependants specified in section 1(3) and (5) of the Fatal Accidents Act 1976[259] are entitled to damages, including limited damages for bereavement.[260] German law also limits claims on the part of third parties, whose *Rechtsgüter* are not directly interfered with, but who suffer loss as a result of the infringement of the *Rechtsgüter* of another, to those instances set out in §§ 844 and 845 BGB.[261]

It should be noted that under French law, *perte d'une chance* is held to meet the general conditions of directness and certainty to be recoverable damage, leading only, however, to reduced compensation, i.e. commensurate to the degree of certainty of the lost chance.[262] In *Allied Maples*, a case relating to economic loss, the English Court of Appeal distinguishes the two issues of causation and damage.[263] As regards the latter, the plaintiff must prove that he had a substantial chance, rather than a merely speculative one, of obtaining a benefit or escaping some burden. The issue of causation must then be resolved on the balance of probabilities.

2.2. PROTECTION OF PERSONALITY RIGHTS AND PRIVACY

In this section, German law is treated first, as it was the first to give straightforward protection to the general right to personality through judicial interpretation of § 823(1) BGB. In French law, special legislation has given protection to the right of privacy. As yet, in English law such general protection may not be found either in legislation or case law. Materials from Irish and Portuguese law are included thereafter.

---

[255] Art. 47 of the Swiss Code of Obligations *supra*, Chapter I, **1.CH.30.**, Art. 6:106 BW *supra*, Chapter I, **1.NL.34.**
[256] Art. 44(2) of the Swiss Code of Obligations, ibid., Art. 6:109 BW, ibid.
[257] *Supra*, **2.F.19.**, Notes (2), (3) and (4).
[258] *Supra*, **2.B.20.–21.**; and to a certain extent Italian law, *supra*, **2.I.22.–23.**
[259] *Supra*, **2.E.10.**
[260] *Supra*, Chapter I, 1.4.1.A.; see further *supra*, **2.E.10.**, Notes (1) to (6).
[261] See *supra*, **2.G.4.** and notes.
[262] See *supra*, **2.F.11.** For a case where loss of a chance is pleaded in respect of economic loss, see *infra*, **2.F.43.**
[263] *Infra*, **2.E.49.**

2.2.1. GERMAN LAW

Introductory Note

a) According to Larenz/Canaris,[264] the recognition in the 1950s of a general *Persönlichkeitsrecht* as an "other" right in the sense of § 823(1) BGB,[265] constitutes the most important change in German tort law since the enactment of the BGB.

The expression *ein sonstiges Recht* ("an other right") is rather vague. It is certainly not meant to include all kinds of rights or legitimate interests, otherwise the intention of the BGB drafters not to provide for a general tort, as in Articles 1382–1383 C. civ., would be defeated.[266] The rights referred to in § 823(1) BGB have a special public character in society (*eine sozial typische Offenkundigkeit*) in that society perceives them as legal positions that confer upon their holder a substantial degree of dominance (*Zuweisungsgehalt*), to the exclusion of third parties (*Ausschlußfunktion*).[267]

In substance the general *Persönlichkeitsrecht* does not possess the same *sozialtypische Offenkundigheit* as the rights mentioned in § 823(1) BGB or the *more specific* rights related to the *Persönlichkeit*, such as the rights to one's name and image.[268] Moreover, the general *Persönlichkeitsrecht* has another "weakness" compared with the rights referred to in § 823(1) BGB, in that it tends to conflict constantly with the rights of others.[269] It has nevertheless been brought under § 823(1) BGB in great part due to the prominent place which was attached to the protection of human dignity and the free development of one's personality, after the horrors of the Nazi regime, at Articles 1 and 2 GG.[270]

b) The recognition of the general *Persönlichkeitsrecht* as an other right within the meaning of § 823(1) BGB demonstrates the impact of constitutional provisions on matters of private law. Indeed the BVerfG wrote in its judgment of 15 January 1958:[271]

"The legal content of fundamental rights as objective norms affects private law through the rules which directly apply in this area of law. Just as new law must conform to the values embodied in the fundamental rights [guaranteed in the *Grundgesetz*], existing law must be aligned with those values. Those values impose on existing law a specific constitutional content which thereafter governs the interpretation of existing law. From a substantive and procedural point of view, a dispute between private citizens on the rights and duties that arise from rules of conduct thus influenced by fundamental rights remains a dispute of private law. It is private law which is interpreted and applied even if the interpretation must follow the public law of the constitution."

As stated in the same judgment, in regard to the application of Article 5 GG relating to freedom of expression, the opposite also holds true in relation to rules of private law, such as the rules on tort:

---

[264] At 491.

[265] See also for another "other right", the *Recht am Gewerbebetrieb*, *infra*, 3.2., Introductory Note under d).

[266] Larenz/Canaris at 392.

[267] Ibid. at 373–4.

[268] The more specific rights have readily been accepted as "other rights" in the case law of the *Reichsgericht* long before the Second World War: see *infra*, **2.G.26.**, Note (1).

[269] Larenz/Canaris at 491.

[270] Ibid. at 492.

[271] BVerfGE 7, 198 at 205–6. There is an obvious similarity between this method of interpretation of provisions of private law (new or existing) so as to conform with the Constitution, as described in this quotation, and the method of interpretation of provisions of national law so as to conform with EC law, including Directives, as propounded by the European Court of Justice: *infra*, Chapter IX, 9.4.

"rules of private law may perfectly well be ranked as 'general laws' in the sense of Art. 5(2) GG. If this has not been done by commentators hitherto [reference omitted], that is simply because basic rights have been considered good only as against the State, so that it was natural to consider as 'general laws' having a limiting effect on fundamental rights only those laws which regulated State activity *vis-à-vis* the person, that is, laws of a public law nature. But if the basic right to freedom of expression affects private law relationships as well, so as to weigh in favour of freedom of expression against another citizen, then correlatively rules of private law which aim to protect superior *Rechtsgüter* must also be taken into account as possibly limiting the basic right".

Among the permissible limitations on freedom of opinion and expression enumerated in Article 5(2) GG are "those deriving from general laws". The general rule of private law concerned in the BVerfG case referred to above was § 826 BGB,[272] which imposes liability to pay compensation for damage done to another in a manner *contra bonos mores*. The provisions of that "general law" may therefore have the effect of limiting the right of freedom of expression and opinion, since one is not entitled, simply because one is expressing an opinion, "to prejudice interests of another which deserve protection against freedom of opinion. There has to be a 'balance of interests'; the right to express an opinion must yield if its exercise infringes interests of another, being interests which have a superior claim to protection. Whether such an interest exists in a particular case depends on all the circumstances".[273]

c) In private relationships, the general *Persönlichkeitsrecht* tends constantly to conflict with the rights of others. In order to solve such conflicts, the BGH has developed in its case law a balancing test which, as we shall see, is applied in different contexts.[274]

BGH, 2 April 1957[275]   **2.G.26.**

SCOPE OF THE GENERAL PERSÖNLICHKEITSRECHT

Disclosure of medical record

In establishing an infringement of the general Persönlichkeitsrecht, *a balancing of interests is necessary. The interest of a patient in his medical files not being disclosed without his consent must give way to the interest of an insurance company engaged in investigating suspected fraudulent claims.*

Facts: The plaintiff claimed damages from the defendant, an employee of an insurance company, who had been requested by the insurance company to investigate fraud which the plaintiff had possibly committed by submitting allegedly false medical certificates to prove damage sustained by the plaintiff as a consequence of physical injury caused to him by K. In order to prove fraud, the defendant had, at the instigation of K, contacted K's attorney R and shown him the medical certificates submitted by the plaintiff to the insurance company. The plaintiff's claim for damages was based on violations of a statutory duty of confidentiality and his right to privacy in respect of his health.

Held: Both at first instance and on appeal the plaintiff's claim was rejected. The plaintiff's request for review of the court of appeal decision was dismissed.

---

[272] See *infra*, **2.G.51.–52.**
[273] BVerfG, 15 January 1958, BVerfGE 7, 198 at 210.
[274] See *infra*, **2.G.26.** and more in particular **2.G.28.**; see also in relation to the *Recht am Gewerbebetrieb*, *infra*, **2.G.38.**
[275] BGHZ 24, 72. Translation by N. Sims.

Judgment: "3. The court of appeal considered the possibility of a claim for damages under § 823(1) BGB for breach of the general *Persönlichkeitsrecht*.

(a) [RECOGNITION OF GENERAL *PERSÖNLICHKEITSRECHT*]
The court of appeal proceeded correctly on the basis that the provisions of Art. 1 and 2 GG, which establish the inviolability of human dignity and every person's right to the free development of personality, provided the rights of others are not infringed and there is no infringement of the constitutional order or offence against good morals, secure a fundamental right not only as against the State and its emanations, but also a right in private law which may be applied against any person (BGH, 25 May 1954, BGHZ 13, 334 at 338) [further references omitted; emphasis added]. That can only be understood as meaning that the second sentence of Art. 1(1) declares it to be the obligation of all State authorities to respect and protect the dignity of the human being, and that Art. 1(3) has elevated the fundamental rights laid down in the subsequent provision, including in the first instance the right to free development of personality, to directly applicable mandatory law binding on the legislature, the executive and the judiciary. On that basis the conclusion is also inescapable that the general *Persönlichkeitsrecht* is to be regarded as an "other right" (*sonstiges Recht*) within the meaning of § 823(1) BGB [references omitted].

[HORIZONTAL EFFECT]
Larenz (in 'Das "allgemeine Persönlichkeitsrecht" im Recht der unerlaubten Handlungen' (1955) 8 NJW 521) counters with the argument that, since the general *Persönlichkeitsrecht* is in the nature of a general provision, it would ride roughshod over the scheme of the law of torts as provided for in the BGB, which in § 823 laid down individual heads of tortious liability and by § 826 created a general provision only for serious infringements which are marked by intentional offences against good morals. That consideration cannot, however, prevail. Civil law must yield to the higher-ranking constitutional law and can apply, where the *Grundgesetz* differs in substance [from civil law], only subject to the necessary adjustments resulting therefrom. Even though the framers of the Constitution, as Larenz emphasizes, may have sought first and foremost to secure the individual's personality against excessive predominance of 'collective interests', and thought only secondarily of securing personality rights with the binding force of immediately applicable law towards other persons, the specific provision therefor in the *Grundgesetz* unmistakably gave expression to this more far-reaching intention of the legislature. Therefore, even legal policy considerations inspired by concerns of 'unrestrained extension' [reference omitted] cannot avail to cast doubt on the fact that *the general* Persönlichkeitsrecht *enjoys the force of law even within the civil legal order, or on the fact that it enjoys the legal protection against infringements specifically afforded by the provisions of civil law on tortious liability* [emphasis added]. Not only is it protected under § 826 BGB, but it is also afforded protection under § 823(1) BGB.

[GENERAL CHARACTER]
Admittedly, however, the notion of the general *Persönlichkeitsrecht* has the breadth of a general clause and is ill-defined. Just as the dynamic nature of personality cannot be kept within fixed limits, in the same way the substance of the general *Persönlichkeitsrecht* eludes definitive determination. The right of the person to respect for his dignity and the free development of his personality is in some way a 'generative fundamental right' (*Muttergrundrecht*) [references omitted] or a 'source right' (*Quellrecht*) [references omitted] which gives rise to the concrete shapes which it takes in relation to the manifold personality values of the individual, his vital interests, and relations with his environment. Thus, in that way the specific provisions of law hitherto protecting the life of the person, his physical integrity and health, freedom, honour, name, ownership, possession, copyright, etc. against infringements have not become meaningless, but have been broadened in the sense that

protection of personality may also be considered in addition to them. The extended protection of personality will continue to derive its support precisely from those provisions and the principles laid down in the case law for their application. In spite of the denial of a general *Persönlichkeitsrecht*, the courts have already sought a way in many cases of upholding personality rights . . .

The court of appeal rightly takes the view that the unauthorized communication of medical certificates concerning the state of health of another person. . . may constitute an interference with the domain of secrecy protected by the *Persönlichkeitsrecht* . . .

[LIMITATION]
This is not, however, an unqualified right. *The general* Persönlichkeitsrecht *does not afford the possibility of the unrestrained implementation of one's own interests. There can be no question of claims for damages or injunctions in every case where a person regards himself as having been affected in his interests and endeavours by another person* [emphasis added]. The *Persönlichkeitsrecht* is anchored in the idea that the dignity of the person and the possibility of developing individual personality must be respected and protected: therefore, the right is by its very nature based on the assumption that, in the particular area of life considered in a given case, the personality values which the *Grundgesetz* seeks to protect are significant and in the case in question have been affected. Limits are set by the twofold prohibition on infringements of the constitutional order and offences against good morals, and on infringing the rights of others. *In case of possible conflict arising from the fact that everyone has the same general* Persönlichkeitsrecht *and from the fact that the free development of personality consists of individual endeavours to excel, a dividing line is necessary in the event of conflict which must be drawn on the basis of the principle of a balancing of rights and interests* (BGH, 25 May 1954, BGHZ 13, 334 at 338) [further references omitted; emphasis added]. Depending on the configuration of circumstances, the scope of the *Persönlichkeitsrecht* may vary considerably. The question whether in an individual case the general *Persönlichkeitsrecht* has been infringed can be assessed only on the basis of a careful appraisal and balancing of all the circumstances relevant to the delineation of those rights.

b) . . . [There follows a discussion of the court of appeal's view that no interference was proved in the present case; the court of appeal had reached that conclusion on the grounds that the information related to not particularly serious physical harm and that the plaintiff himself was suspected of fraud. The BGH rejected both those reasons, since it is not the seriousness of the injury that matters but the fact that the patient's consent has not been obtained. Moreover, someone suspected of having committed a crime is nonetheless entitled to human dignity, which is protected by the general *Persönlichkeitsrecht*. The BGH nevertheless upheld the conclusion reached by the court of appeal, for the reasons that follow.]

[BALANCING OF INTERESTS IN THE PARTICULAR INSTANCE]
In truth the considerations of the court of appeal come down, then, to this: under the circumstances prevailing, the plaintiff's interest in confidentiality of the medical certificates concerning his state of health was not so great as to outweigh the interest of the defendant and of K in ascertaining whether the insurance company or K had not received undue advantage. The court of appeal thereby demonstrated the limitation of the plaintiff's *Persönlichkeitsrecht* in the preservation of confidentiality in relation to his affairs, namely a limitation based on the balancing of rights and interests on the facts of the particular case. It did not deem the scope of this right to extend so far as to enable communication of the insurance documents to lawyer R. to be considered an infringement.

That assessment is not open to legal objection."

Notes

(1) This judgment is one of many rendered in the wake of BGH, 25 May 1954, where the general *Persönlichkeitsrecht* was recognized as an "other right" within the meaning of § 823(1) BGB.[276] The 1954 judgment concerned a letter written to a newspaper by the attorney of Dr. Schacht, one of Hitler's ministers, on behalf of his client. The letter had been published as a letter to the editor, giving the impression that it represented the personal opinion of Dr. Schacht's attorney. The attorney demanded that the newspaper publish an *erratum* to indicate that the letter was written in his capacity as attorney. Before the 1954 judgment only specific rights were protected, such as the right to one's name and the right to one's picture (for example in the case concerning photographs of Bismarck's corpse). Private letters were also protected exceptionally under certain circumstances on the basis of the German Copyright Act.[277]

(2) As stated in the Introductory Note under a), the decision to grant protection to the *general Persönlichkeitsrecht* is based on the prominent place which the *Grundgesetz* of 1949 (at Articles 1 and 2), unlike any previous German constitution, gives to human dignity and personal freedom.[278] In the annotated judgment, the BGH explains why those values need to be given the same prominence in private law, that is in relations between persons, thus attaching *horizontal effect* to the provisions of the *Grundgesetz*.[279] It also explains how the general *Persönlichkeitsrecht* is limited in private law by the rights of other persons. This requires a *balancing of interests*, following which in the present case the interference with the *Persönlichkeitsrecht* was found justifiable. But see the BGH judgment of 20 May 1958 in which an interference with the general *Persönlichkeitsrecht* (a private conversation had been recorded by one of the parties) was held to be unjustified, a conclusion for which the BGH also found support in Article 8 ECHR.[280]

(3) In the BGH judgment of 25 May 1954 mentioned above, Dr. Schacht's attorney asked for a correction to remedy the prejudice which the incorrect publication of the letter had caused to his reputation, whereas in the BGH judgment of 20 May 1958 mentioned above, deletion of the recording of the conversation was sought. By contrast, in the annotated judgment the plaintiff was seeking damages by way of compensation for his financial loss (mostly legal fees).

§ 253 BGB limits the award of compensation for non-material damages to instances specified by law.[281] Until the *Herrenreiter*[282] and the *Ginseng*[283] judgments, it was uncertain whether compensation for non-material damage could be granted for an infringement of the general *Persönlichkeitsrecht*. However, in both those cases, the BGH awarded damages for pain and suffering to a person affected by the culpable infringement of his *Persönlichkeitsrecht*. In the second of the two cases, the Court referred to the fact that, at

---

[276] BGHZ 13, 334, NJW 1954, 1404, JZ 1954, 698. Translation by F. Lawson and B.S. Markesinis in Markesinis at 376.

[277] See further Zweigert and Kötz at 688–9.

[278] Ibid. at 690.

[279] See *supra*, 2.1., Introductory Note under b) and the reference to BVerfG, 15 January 1958, BVerfGE 7, 198.

[280] BGHZ 27, 284.

[281] *Supra*, 1.1., Introductory Note under b).

[282] BGH, 14 February 1958, BGHZ 26, 349.

[283] BGH, 19 September 1961, BGHZ 35, 363. Translation by F.H. Lawson and B.S. Markesinis in Markesinis at 386.

the time of the enactment of § 253 BGB, the protection of human personality had not yet received the recognition bestowed upon it by Articles 1 and 2 GG. The Court made it clear that such protection would be incomplete if adequate remedies were not available against an infringement of the *Persönlichkeitsrecht*. The BGH added, however, that only serious disturbances and not insignificant injuries call for satisfaction, and expressly referred in this connection to Article 49(1) of the Swiss Code of Obligations,[284] which restricted damages for non-material loss to serious cases.

BGH, 9 November 1993[285]   **2.G.27.**

REPRODUCTIVE RIGHTS AND *PERSÖNLICHKEITSRECHT*

Destruction of sperm

The culpable destruction of sperm constitutes an interference with bodily integrity and the autonomy of the person.

Facts: In 1987, at the age of 31, the plaintiff had to undergo surgery for cancer of the bladder. The plaintiff was aware that the operation would result in him becoming infertile, so he requested the defendant hospital to take samples of his sperm and put them into frozen storage. Later, through a mishap attributable to the hospital's negligence, the samples were destroyed without the plaintiff's consent. In the meantime the plaintiff had got married and, since he and his wife wished to have children, he requested that his wife be impregnated with a sample of his sperm. He was then informed that the samples had been destroyed. The plaintiff sued the defendant hospital for payment of *Schmerzensgeld* in the amount of DEM 25,000, basing his claim on an application, by analogy, of § 847(1) BGB (allowance of *Schmerzensgeld* in cases of interference with bodily integrity and health) to a breach of the general *Persönlichkeitsrecht*.

Held: The court of appeal upheld the rejection of the claim by the court of first instance. Reversing the lower court decisions, the BGH held the claim to be well-founded.

Judgment: "2. The plaintiff's claim for *Schmerzensgeld* is well-founded on account of the culpable (*schuldhaft*) destruction of his sperm.

a) According to the predominant though not uncontested view, a body part which is separated from the body becomes an object with the consequence that the right of the affected person to his body becomes transformed into ownership of the separated body part [references omitted]. It is maintained in some quarters that this is also applicable to preserved sperm [references omitted]. The court of appeal also takes that view. On that view the destruction of the plaintiff's sperm cannot be deemed to be a bodily injury for which § 847 BGB confers a claim sounding in damages.

This view appears, however, to this Chamber to be too narrow. *The Chamber gave a broad interpretation to the concept of bodily injury within the meaning of §§ 832(1), 847(1) BGB. It construes the right to one's own body as a legally formulated part of the general* Persönlichkeitsrecht *and views as an injury to the body, mentioned expressly in § 823(1) BGB alongside the injury to health, any unauthorized interference, not covered by the consent of the holder of the right, in that person's physical integrity. What is protected by § 823(1) BGB is not the material substance, but the existentially determined scope of personality which materializes in how one feels physically* [references omitted]. *§ 823(1) BGB protects the body as the basis of personality* [emphasis added].

---

[284] As a result of an amendment that took effect on 1 July 1985, Art. 49 of the Swiss Code of Obligations, *supra*, Chapter I, **1.CH.30.**, now allows monetary compensation having regard to the gravity of the invasion and no longer additionally requires "grave fault" on the part of the infringer: see Zweigert and Kötz at 731.

[285] NJW 1994, 127. Translation by N. Sims.

In light of present-day medical possibilities, the right of self-determination which the holder of the right derives from the *Persönlichkeitsrecht* assumes additional significance for the object of protection, namely the body. Medical advances enable components to be removed from the body and to be reincorporated in it later. That is true, for example, of skin and bone parts intended for transplantation in the person's own body, of eggs removed for fertilization and of blood donation intended for oneself. If components are removed from the body in order subsequently to be reunited with it in accordance with the intention of the holder of the right for the purpose of preserving bodily functions or of performing them, then the view taken of § 823(1) BGB as affording comprehensive protection of physical integrity whilst preserving the right of self-determination of the holder of the right, must lead to the result that those components, even when separated from the body, retain functional unity with it, from the point of view of the protective purpose of the provision. It thus appears necessary to regard damage to or destruction of such separated body parts as a bodily injury within the meaning of §§ 823(1) and 847(1) BGB.

It is otherwise where the separated body parts are not intended by the holder of the right to be reintegrated into his body. For such cases of definitive separation the position continues to be that, on separation, the separated body parts lose their attribution to the object protected, namely the body, and become things in a legal sense. This is so because here the idea whereby the body and its separated components continue to have the appearance of a functional unit, in accordance with the right to self-determination of the holder of the right, no longer holds true. That applies in particular of donated organs which, in accordance with the wishes of the donor, are intended to be implanted in another person, and of blood donations intended for third parties.

b) On the basis of these considerations, the preserved sperm intended by the holder of the right to be used for his reproduction constitutes an exceptional case. On the one hand, the sperm is definitively separated from the body of the holder of the right, on the other hand it is intended to fulfil a typical bodily function, that of the reproduction of the holder of the right. *In any event, if, as in this case, the preserved sperm is to take the place of lost reproductive capacity, it has no less weighty and substantive importance for the physical integrity of the holder of the right, and the self-determination and self-realization inherent therein, than the egg or other body parts which on the basis of the foregoing observations continue, even after removal from the body, to be covered by the protection which the body enjoys under §§ 823(1) and 847(1) BGB* [emphasis added] . . . It is this Chamber's view that, having regard to the fact, as mentioned, that sperm is analogous and equivalent to a body part which is to be returned to a person's body, and therefore that it has an analogous and equivalent need for protection under the law of tort, justice requires that the same legal consequences should be applied to it under the provisions of the law of tort. If, however, the preserved sperm is not to be treated under these legal provisions as covered by the protection of physical integrity because it is not to be returned to the donor's body, these provisions must in any event be applied by analogy, subject to the same preconditions . . .

3. . . . In determining the *quantum* of *Schmerzensgeld*, the question is not the degree of probability with which the plaintiff's wife would have had a child if she had been inseminated with his sperm. The decisive factor is the stress suffered by the plaintiff because the one chance remaining to him of having a child with his wife has been lost. This stress factor is considerable. On the other hand, it must be borne in mind that the destruction of the sperm is attributable to an oversight on the part of the defendant's employees in the course of endeavours directed specifically at maintaining the plaintiff's right of self-determination. On appraisal of these circumstances, the Chamber regards damages in the sum of DEM 25,000 as reasonable."

Notes

(1) In the annotated judgment the BGH distinguished four situations and corresponding legal solutions, namely those in which: (i) parts of the body, such as a lock of hair or

a tooth, have become permanently severed from the body, and have thus become goods subject to normal rules on personal property; (ii) separated parts, such as donated blood or organs, destined to be integrated into someone else's body, enjoy for the time being only the protection afforded to personal property unless in the circumstances of the case the general *Persönlichkeitsrecht* takes precedence; (iii) parts of a person's body, such as skin, blood or egg-cells, although removed from the body, are destined to be reintegrated into that person's body,and therefore treated as remaining part of the functional unity of the body and so continue to enjoy the same legal protection as the body; and (iv) organic matter, such as sperm, is definitively separated from the body, but is destined to be used to perform a typical bodily function—in the case of sperm, the procreation of issue. In the last situation, with which the annotated judgment is concerned, the BGH held that §§ 823(1) *and* 847(1) BGB (allowing the award of *Schmerzensgeld*) should be applied, *by analogy* with situation (ii).

(2) The judgment illustrates how courts of law can deal with new developments in medical science which may have important ethical implications. Courts very often try to draw analogies with situations for which a precedent exists. In the present instance, the destruction of samples of sperm presented the BGH with a novel problem. For the purposes of tort law, the BGH drew an analogy with the situation of egg-cells taken from a woman's body in order to be re-integrated ultimately, after *in vitro* fertilization. Somewhat surprisingly, no consideration whatsoever was given to ethical implications. In the case before the BGH, the samples of sperm were intended to be used to alleviate the consequences of a forthcoming operation which would make the plaintiff infertile. The judgment does not concern—and therefore cannot necessarily be used as a precedent for—a situation where organic matter, such as sperm or egg-cells, are destined to be used for procreation by persons other than the donor.

BGH, 12 October 1993[286]   **2.G.28.**

THE GENERAL *PERSÖNLICHKEITSRECHT* AND FREEDOM OF EXPRESSION

Greenpeace poster

Balance of interests in the particular situation of the manager of a large company claiming that his general Persönlichkeitsrecht *has been infringed by statements made on a Greenpeace poster where he, as a public figure, had himself engaged in the public discussion concerning the issue of public interest addressed on the poster.*

Facts: In 1989 talks were held between the plaintiff, the president of Hoechst AG, and the defendant, the Greenpeace organization, concerning the possibility of Hoechst ceasing to produce hydrochlorofluorocarbons (HCFCs, FCKW in German), a product known to contribute to the destruction of the ozone layer. On 25 October 1989, the plaintiff announced in the press a programme of reductions in HCFC production. The defendant issued a press release which called this programme a "swindle by misdescription" (*Etikettenschwindel*), as the products to be produced as substitutes were, in its opinion, as harmful to the ozone layer as HCFCs. The defendant also launched a poster campaign, the picture and name of plaintiff being printed on large posters with, beneath them, a sarcastic text holding the plaintiff and an executive from Kali-Chemie AG jointly responsible for the destruction of the ozone layer. The plaintiff initiated legal proceedings based on an infringement of his right to image and personality and sought an injunction to restrain the publication of the posters.

---

[286] NJW 1994, 124. Translation by N. Sims.

Held: The court of first instance dismissed the action but the court of appeal upheld it. On appeal before the BGH, the defendant successfully sought the reinstatement of the judgment of the court of first instance.

Judgment: "1. (a) In so far as the plaintiff objects to the mention made of his name, his wishes are supported by the general *Persönlichkeitsrecht* guaranteed constitutionally by Art. 2(1) in conjunction with Art. 1(1) GG, and in §§ 823(1) and 1004(1) BGB. Whether there has been a breach of that right is . . . to be determined in the individual case on the basis of a balancing of rights and interests. For, on account of the particular nature of the *Persönlichkeitsrecht* as a framework right (*Rahmenrecht*), its scope is not absolutely fixed but must in principle be determined by a balancing of rights with the interests worthy of protection of the other party [references omitted]. Thus, from both legal points of view on which the plaintiff is basing his claim for an injunction the question is whether greater weight is to be attached to the plaintiff's general *Persönlichkeitsrecht* than to the legal grounds which the defendant may invoke in support of its poster campaign.

b) In support of its poster campaign, the defendant relies first and foremost on the freedom of expression laid down in the first sentence of Art. 5(1) GG. In interpreting and applying the provisions of private law, the courts have to do justice to the meaning of this fundamental right (BVerfG, 19 May 1992, BVerfGE 86, 122 at 128, NJW 1992, 2409 with further references). The court of appeal [references omitted] acted accordingly. It proceeded on the assumption that the defendant enjoys this fundamental right and that the poster enjoys the protection afforded by the first sentence of Art. 5(1) GG. The Chamber shares that view.

aa) The text of the poster in its entirety is covered by freedom of expression. On the appeal the respondent was unsuccessful in contending that the overall textual and pictorial statement made by the poster constituted an assertion of facts which, since it was untrue, was not protected by the first sentence of Art. 5(1) GG . . . The textual analysis showed that there is here an interplay of factual assertions and evaluations. Thus the text in its entirety enjoys the protection of the first sentence of Art. 5(1) GG . . .

bb) The manner in which the rest of the poster was framed also comes under the protection of the right to freedom of expression. That is true, particularly, of the portrait of the plaintiff and the mention of his name, which form part of the poster's overall statement . . .

2. The defendant's right to freedom of expression is, as has been stated, confronted by the general *Persönlichkeitsrecht* of the plaintiff, principally in two respects. The legal positions of both parties thus have to be balanced against each other. This balancing of interests must be carried out both on the basis of a general consideration of the status of the fundamental rights affected and in the light of the intensity with which those fundamental rights are affected in the specific case [references omitted]. The appraisal which is therefore called for of the effect on the fundamental rights of both parties led the court of appeal to the conclusion that, in this dispute, the defendant's right to freedom of expression had to yield to the plaintiff's rights, where the plaintiff's general *Persönlichkeitsrecht* had been infringed by the publication of his picture and the mention of his name on the poster. The Chamber cannot agree with that view.

a) *The BVerfG and the BGH have in a number of decisions developed principles for assessing a confrontation between the general* Persönlichkeitsrecht *and freedom of expression* [emphasis added]. They may be stated as follows: since it is the purpose of any public statement contributing to the formation of opinion to attract attention, hard-hitting and even strong formulations must be accepted, in view of the current surfeit of stimulation of all kinds (BVerfG, 6 November 1968, BVerfGE 24, 278 at 286, NJW 1969, 227). That is also true of statements uttered in sharp and derogatory terms, or made in an excessively polemic manner, or couched in ironic terms (BGH, 20 May 1986, NJW 1987, 1398). The critic must in principle be permitted to express his opinion even when others consider it to be 'wrong' or 'unjust' (BGH, 20 May 1986, NJW 1987, 1398). The form of the expression is also protected by the right to self-determination of the person expressing an opinion under Art. 5(1) GG (BVerfG, 20 April 1982, BVerfGE 60, 234 at 241, NJW 1982, 2655). *Where the person expressing the opinion is not pursuing objectives of self-interest, but rather contributing to the public debate on a question of substantive concern to the public, then there is a presumption that the expression of opinion is permissible; an interpretation of the laws restricting freedom of opinion which makes excessively high demands as regards the permissibility of public criticism is not compatible with Art. 5(1) GG* (BVerfG, 11 May 1976, BVerfGE 42, 163 at 170, NJW 1976, 1680; BVerfG, 25 January 1984, BVerfGE 66, 116 at 139, NJW 1984, 1741; BVerfG, 31 October 1984, BVerfGE 68, 226 at 232, NJW 1985, 787) [emphasis added]. In determining the scope of the protection of fundamental rights under Art. 5(1) GG, a further decisive question is whether and to what extent the person affected by the statements himself took part in the process of formation of public opinion protected by Art. 5(1) GG, and thus by his own decision acquiesced in the conditions of the public debate, thereby surrendering part of his protected sphere of privacy (BVerfG, 13 May 1980, BVerfGE 54, 129 at 138, NJW 1980, 2069). *The position is different if the statement is no longer predominantly aimed towards public discussion but rather towards the humiliation of the person; then and only then, the statement, even if it concerns a question of substantive concern to the public, being in the nature of a libel, must yield to the rights of personality of the person affected* (BVerfG, 26 July 1990, BVerfGE 82, 272 at 283, NJW, 1991, 95; BVerfG, 9 October 1991, BVerfGE 85, 1 at 16, NJW 1992, 1439) [emphasis added].

(b) In accordance with these criteria of appraisal, the plaintiff must accept the publication of the poster. In its poster campaign, the defendant is not pursuing objectives of its own self-interest but rather is dealing with a topic which, owing to its fundamental importance, calls for committed expressions of opinion. The effect of HCFCs on the climate is a pressing problem of our time. Thus, the defendant's poster campaign may be seen as a contribution to public debate in a question of substantive concern to the public. There is, therefore, under the case law of the BVerfG, a presumption of legal permissibility. This is further supported by the fact that the plaintiff has also on his own initiative gone before the public on this topic . . .

The Chamber does not share the view of the court of appeal that the poster campaign is deploying an unlawful pillorying effect against the plaintiff's person or, being defamatory, must yield to his *Persönlichkeitsrecht*. [There follows an examination of the poster from this standpoint.] . . .

In the Chamber's view, it is permissible under the first sentence of Art. 5(1) GG to direct public criticism of a corporate decision involving—at any rate in the defendant's view—far-reaching consequences for society . . . against the person deemed to be responsible, as is done for public criticism of far-reaching political decisions. Because of the importance of the fundamental right of freedom of opinion to a free and open political process (cf. BVerfG, 15 January 1958, BVerfGE 7, 198 at 208, NJW 1958, 257), a person who, by virtue of his position, must bear responsibility for decisions having a scope such as that in the present case, cannot be allowed the opportunity to gag such criticism by relying on his sphere of privacy. That is particularly true where, as in the present case, the person under attack took an intensive part, on his own initiative, in the public debate on this subject."

Notes

(1) This judgment offers an excellent example of how the BGH performs a balancing of interests in cases of persons who have participated actively, in their professional capacity, in discussions of great general interest—in the case in question, the preservation of the ozone layer. With numerous references to the case law of the BVerfG and to its own case law, the BGH demonstrates how, in such a situation, there is a presumption in favour of the right to freedom of expression and opinion (see in particular under 2.a) and b)).

The German Courts have adopted a similar position in cases concerning bankers involved in the financing of international transactions and in cases concerning persons engaged in politics, who through their style may have invited their opponents to react in a personal and polemical manner.[287]

In contrast, the general *Persönlichkeitsrecht* would prevail in cases involving unknown persons who are insulted in the media out of spite.[288]

(2) Balancing of interests—in this instance balancing one person's general, or specific, *Persönlichkeitsrecht* against the exercise by someone else of a fundamental freedom—is frequently conducted by the BGH and even more by the BVerfG in their respective case law. In the area of tort law, more particularly in the application of § 823(1) BGB, balancing of interests was introduced first in connection with the *Recht am Gewerbebetrieb*[289] and later also for the general *Persönlichkeitsrecht* (two of the so-called "other" rights). In cases involving these two "other" rights, such balancing accordingly takes place in horizontal relations, that is between private persons. For instance, as in the annotated judgment, the general *Persönlichkeitsrecht* is invoked against someone else's fundamental right to freedom of expression. In another judgment reproduced above,[290] the general *Persönlichkeitsrecht* was weighed against someone else's economic interests. That judgment contains a thorough discussion of the reasons why constitutional law provisions guaranteeing fundamental rights should be applied horizontally, that is between private persons.

2.2.2. FRENCH LAW

Introductory Note

a) In France, serious interferences with some personality rights have for long been regarded as *criminal* offences: such interferences include particularly harmful interferences with physical integrity (such as murder, rape, wounding someone intentionally or negligently); infringements, if sufficiently serious, of someone's reputation (such as libel) or of his or her privacy (such as violation of someone's domicile or mail); and breach of professional secrecy.[291] Moreover, a growing number of interferences are regarded by the courts as *civil* torts falling under Article 1382 C.civ. and thus giving rise to liability for material and non-material damage, provided that the existence of fault, injury and causation is proved. Accordingly, interferences with physical integrity, honour, identity (*identité*) and privacy, whether intentional or negligent, can constitute a fault, giving rise to liability to compensate for non-material (*moral*) and material damage.[292]

---

[287] For further references, see Zweigert and Kötz at 305–6.

[288] See for example BAG, 18 February 1999, NJW 1999, 1988, where a newspaper described one of its employees, with whom it was dissatisfied, as "the laziest employee in Germany".

[289] See *infra*, **2.G.38.**

[290] *Supra*, **2.G.26.**

[291] See Goubeaux at 244–7 and 263–5, para. 273–4 and 293.

[292] Ibid. at 247; Viney and Jourdain, *Conditions* at 32–5, para. 259. See *infra*, **2.F.29.** and **2.F.30.** for two cases where this principle was applied, the first one long before the enactment of Art. 9 C.civ., discussed below, and the other only shortly before it. An interesting issue involves the interplay between freedom of expression through humour and parody, on the one hand, and the protection of the value of trade marks, on the other hand. See Cass. civ. 2e, 2 April 1997, Bull.civ. 1997.II.113, JCP 1998.II.10010, annotated by C. Bigot, D 1997.Jur.411, annotated by B. Edelman (giving precedence to the latter) and, on remittal, Reims, 9 February 1999, D 1999.Jur.449, annotated by B. Edelman, JCP 1999.II.10144, annotated by C. Bigot (giving precedence to the former).

b) Apart from these criminal or civil law provisions prohibiting particular forms of *conduct*, several legislative enactments have conferred a protected status on specific elements of the human personality.[293] To take the most prominent example, the Act of 17 July 1970 introduced a new Article 9 into the *Code civil*, according to which "Everyone is entitled to privacy".[294] By explicitly enshrining the right to privacy in the *Code civil*, the Act of 17 July 1970 has made not only a psychological impact,[295] but also a legal impact: the application of Article 1382 C.civ. is considerably simplified, to the point of becoming purely formalistic, as both fault and non-material prejudice are held to be made out by the fact that the "right" to privacy has been infringed.[296] The protection of personality has thus been strengthened by elevating privacy to the status of an autonomous right. As a direct consequence of that development, the link with the tortious liability rules of Article 1382 C.civ. was loosened, as appears also from the nature of the relief granted by the courts for violations of the intimacy of private life (*l'intimité de la vie privée*), which frequently consists of injunctions and court orders[297] rather than material compensation, otherwise the prevalent remedy under tort law.[298]

Through the Act of 4 January 1993 incorporating a new Article 9-1 in the *Code civil*, the right to be presumed innocent is also enshrined in the *Code civil*.[299] While this may appear surprising at first, the second paragraph of Article 9-1, as inserted by the Act of 24 August 1993, makes it clear that the Article does not aim so much at protecting suspects and accused against the State as at protecting, in public opinion, the reputation of suspects and accused persons.[300] That second paragraph in fact makes it possible to seek a court order compelling a publication to insert a written rectification, if it is found that, in its accounts of criminal inquiries and proceedings, this publication has given the impression that a suspect or accused person was guilty. Like Article 9 C.civ., Article 9-1 C.civ. could also lead to a loosening of the rules of Article 1382 C.civ. in cases involving the liability of the press.[301]

c) A rather unusual case fell to be decided by the Tribunal de grande instance de Paris on 1 February 1995 regarding Benetton's much publicized advertising campaign showing pictures of body parts marked "HIV positive" in a stark manner (without identifying the person(s) whose parts they were).[302] Four plaintiffs, i.e. three HIV-positive persons and an association defending AIDS victims, claimed damages for infringement of their right to privacy on the basis of Article 9 C.civ. Their claims under Article 9 C.civ. failed, but

---

[293] Goubeaux at 247–9, para. 274–5; Viney and Jourdain, *Conditions* at 29–31, para. 257.

[294] *Loi 70-643 tendant à renforcer la garantie des droits individuels des citoyens* of 17 July 1970, JO, 19 July 1970, D 1970.Lég.199. See further *infra*, **2.F.29.–30.**, Note (1).

[295] According to Goubeaux at 248, para. 275, "individuals, strengthened by the [legislative] consecration of their rights, do not baulk at requiring that they be judicially enforced".

[296] Ibid.

[297] Such as "sequestration, seizure or other measures as may be appropriate to prevent or stop the infringement . . .", as listed in Art. 9(2) C.civ.

[298] Goubeaux at 248–9, para. 275.

[299] *Loi 93-2 portant réforme de la procédure pénale* of 4 January 1993, JO, 5 January 1993, D 1993.Lég.134.

[300] *Loi 93-1013 modifiant la loi 93-2 portant réforme de la procédure pénale* of 24 August 1993, JO, 25 August 1993, D 1993.Lég.467.

[301] For further comments, see P. Auvret, "Le droit au respect de la présomption d'innocence" JCP 1994.I.3802.

[302] D 1995.Jur.569, annotated by B. Edelman.

damages of FRF 50,000 were granted to each of the three individual claimants on the basis that, by these advertisements, the defendant Benetton had abused its freedom of expression. The association was awarded a symbolic FRF 1 in damages. Benetton was also ordered to discontinue the advertising campaign and pay for the publication of the judgment in newspapers. By a judgment of 28 May 1996,[303] the Cour d'appel de Paris confirmed the holding that Benetton had used "symbols which led to stigmatization and degraded the dignity of persons who [as a result of HIV] are irremediably affected in their body and being, so as to prejudice them by creating or increasing a tendency on the part of others to shun them". However, the court of appeal reduced the amount of damages awarded to the three individual plaintiffs to a symbolic FRF 1. The court of appeal's judgment proceeds on the basis that, "by attributing to each of the individual plaintiffs, in particular, a degrading representation of their HIV-positive condition, [Benetton] has inflicted on each of them damage of a non-material nature". The other awards were confirmed. It may be noted that similar advertisements were also banned in Germany, on the ground that they infringed § 1 of the *Gesetz gegen den unlauteren Wettbewerb*,[304] without any damages being awarded.[305]

Cass. civ. 2e, 6 January 1971[306]   **2.F.29–30.**
Société Press-Office v. *Sachs*
and
Cass. civ. 1re, 28 May 1991[307]
X. v. *Y.*

S<small>COPE OF THE RIGHT TO PRIVACY</small>

The right to privacy and to one's image is infringed by the publication of a collection of previously published statements on the private life of a well-known person, as well as two pictures of him, one verging on a caricature. By contrast, there is no infringement in publishing legally obtained information on someone's financial situation, without alluding to his private life.

A. Cass. civ. 1re, 6 January 1971   **2.F.29.**

Private life of Gunther Sachs

Facts: The defendant publisher of the magazine "Lui", Société Presse-Office (SPO), published an article including particulars of the private life of the plaintiff, Gunther Sachs. The information had already been published

---

[303] D 1996.Jur.617.

[304] UWG, Unfair Competition Act of 1 June 1909, RGBl. 499, BGBl. III 43-1, as amended.

[305] BGH, 6 July 1995, NJW 1995, 2492.

[306] D 1971.Jur.263, annotated by B. Edelman, JCP 1971.II.16723, annotated by R.L.; *Les grands arrêts* at 81, with comments. Translation by R.Bray.

[307] D 1992.Jur.213, annotated by P. Kayser, JCP 1992.II.21845, annotated by F. Ringel; *Les grands arrêts* at 88. Translation by N. Sims.

in other magazines with the plaintiff's express or tacit consent. The article in "Lui" was accompanied by two pictures of the plaintiff, one very much in the nature of a caricature.

Held: By order of 2 November 1966 of the court of first instance, the plaintiff was allowed to seize the weekly magazine and compensation was also granted to him. The court of appeal ordered the defendant to pay damages to the plaintiff, but held that the extent of the prejudice was limited because the article in question merely summarized previous publications in which the facts had already been described. The Cour de cassation upheld the findings of the court of appeal.

Judgment: "According to the defendant company, the judgment could not, without being contradictory, hold, on the one hand, that the article at issue simply went back over facts previously published with Sachs' express or tacit authorization and, on the other, that it infringed his right to respect for his private life. In addition, the defendant company contends that the publication of two portraits of Sachs could not constitute an infringement of his personal rights to his image since he was a well-known person, the portraits were not taken in the course of his private life and did not depict intimate scenes and the caricature could not be penalized as an infringement of his private life. Lastly, the defendant company pleads that it was contradictory to hold, on the one hand, that the extent of damage was limited by the publication of the information prior to the article at issue, which had merely made a compilation of that previously published information, yet also, on the other hand, that the compilation constituted an infringement of his right to his private life, since there was either an infringement of that right or no infringement;

However, after finding that the article at issue gave an account solely of facts relating to Gunther Sachs' private life, the contested judgment states the following. [First,] the account caused harm to the plaintiff. [Secondly,] his past tolerance and even willingness with regard to the press did not enable it to be presumed that he had authorized, definitively and without restriction, any periodical to gather and reproduce statements which had appeared in other newspapers. [Thirdly,] his past conduct could only, if at all, limit the extent of the harm and consequently diminish the amount of damages and interest awarded. [Fourthly,] insofar as the article at issue collected and assembled morsels of information, true or false, which had appeared in various publications, and reached new categories of readers, it caused harm to the respondent, since above all the choice of the events or 'gossip' related therein cast Gunther Sach's private life in an unpleasant light. [Fifthly,] the unauthorized publication of two portraits of Sachs, one verging on a caricature, constituted an infringement of his personal rights in respect of his picture. [Finally,] the traditional tolerance in respect of persons whose profession or activity enabled tacit authorization to be presumed did not apply in this case;

Having regard to those findings and statements, the court of appeal was entitled, without incurring criticism on appeal, to hold Société Presse-Office liable both for the publication of the article and for the publication of the portraits of the person concerned; hence the ground of appeal is not founded. On those grounds, the Cour de cassation dismisses . . .".

B. Cass. civ. 1re, 28 May 1991 2.F.30.

Publication of tax returns

Facts: The defendant newspaper had published information on the financial situation of the plaintiff, including the amounts declared on his tax returns for 1984 and 1985 and excerpts from his income tax assessments for those years. That information had not been obtained through illicit means by the defendant. On the basis of the information, the defendant had alleged that the plaintiff, a rich person, did not pay taxes.

Held: The court of appeal found an infringement of the plaintiff's right to privacy, on the basis of Article 9 C.civ. The Cour de cassation quashed the decision of the court of appeal.

Judgment: "Having regard to Art. 9 C.civ.: . . . In upholding Mr. Z's claim, the court of appeal, before which it was not submitted that this information had an unlawful origin, considered that 'these particularly specific disclosures constituted an interference with [the plaintiff's] private life from the financial point of view'. It ordered the company, Editions Y, to pay to Mr Z FRF 8,000 by way of damages.

However, the respect due to the private life of every individual is not undermined by the publication of information of a purely financial kind, not including in this case any allusion to the life and personality of the person concerned. In reaching its decision, the court of appeal therefore applied [Art. 9 C.civ.] incorrectly.

On those grounds, the judgment is set aside."

Notes

(1) As explained in the Introductory Note, it follows from Article 9(1) C.civ. that the right to privacy is now generally and autonomously protected as a "right", in addition to the particular protection which specific legislation may grant to a person's name, home, image, honour and confidential facts relating to him. Moreover, Article 9(2) C.civ. provides several remedies, including actions for damages, to protect the *core of privacy*, that is the "intimacy" of private life.[308] In the *Sachs* judgment, the Cour de cassation upheld the decision of the court of appeal, which had been rendered before the Act of 17 July 1970, and allowed the seizure of all copies of the impermissible publication *as well as* compensation (albeit for a reduced amount, because of the earlier publication of the information included in the article). It appears from the court of appeal's judgment that (i) even before the Act of 17 July 1970, not only the right to one's image but also a general right to privacy was recognized and (ii) both seizure and compensation were regarded as admissible remedies, damages being awarded without it being necessary to give documented evidence of fault or damage. None of those findings was contradicted by the Cour de cassation. The second of them in particular evidences the autonomous character acquired by the general right to privacy, which thereby transcends the general limits imposed by the criteria of fault and damage in Articles 1382 and 1383 C.civ.

Since the enactment of Article 9 C.civ., the autonomous character of the right to privacy has been confirmed in two decisions of the Cour de cassation of 13 February 1985.[309] Those two decisions concerned love scenes in the movie "Mesrine" which were related to existing, identifiable persons without their consent. In the second of the decisions, the Cour de cassation held that using the names of those persons in such scenes "constitutes in itself an unlawful infringement of the intimacy of their private life . . .". Furthermore, in a recent judgment of 5 November 1996, the Cour de cassation brings this development to its logical end, holding that "pursuant to Art. 9 C.civ., the mere finding that the right to privacy has been infringed entitles [the victim] to compensation".[310]

(2) Obviously the general right to privacy is not unlimited.[311] Exceptions to the right

---

[308] See also Art. 809 of the new *Code de procédure civile*, which generally provides an even wider protection: Goubeaux at 275, para. 300.

[309] Cass. civ. 1re, 13 February 1985, JCP 1985.II.20467, annotated by Lindon.

[310] Cass. civ. 1re, 5 November 1996, JCP 1997.II.22805, annotated by J. Ravanas; discussed by G. Viney, "Chronique" JCP 1997.I.4025.

[311] Clearly, a debtor cannot rely on the general right to privacy solely in order to escape his or her legal obligations to his creditors. Thus in respect of the right to keep one's residence secret, see Cass. civ. 1re, 19 March 1991, Bull.civ. 1991.I.96.

can be based on the explicit or implicit consent of the person whose right is concerned or on the right of the public to information and the needs of historic research.[312]

Furthermore, there is no violation of the right to privacy where revelations are made about someone's public life, such as the fact that he or she participated in a public event (for instance a religious ceremony), provided that such revelations are not motivated by an intent to harm or to foster discriminatory or hostile attitudes.[313]

A remarkable exception, highlighted by the second judgment reproduced above, stems from the required transparency of financial and economic transactions. The Cour de cassation accordingly quashed the decision of the court of appeal and denied that Article 9 C.civ. is violated "by the publication of information of a purely financial kind, not including in this case any allusion to the life and personality of the person concerned", as long as the information is not obtained unlawfully. The exception is remarkable in that it echoes, for tort law, the trend apparent in many recent legislative enactments towards greater transparency in fiscal and financial matters, for instance the income of corporations and their directors and of politicians.[314]

Cour d'appel de Paris, 13 March 1996[315]   **2.F.31.**
Éd. Plon v. *Mitterrand*

ABUSE OF FREEDOM OF OPINION: INFRINGEMENT OF MEDICAL SECRECY

Le grand secret

The right of a patient and—after his death—of his close relatives to keep medical information confidential is a permissible restriction on freedom of opinion.

Facts: A few days after President Mitterrand's death, the defendant, who had been his personal doctor for more than 13 years, published as a co-author *Le grand secret*, a book in which he revealed information about the President's illness and the way the President dealt with his illness, as well as the medical treatment prescribed. In summary interim proceedings, the widow and children of the late President requested that the distribution of the book be prohibited.

Held: On 18 January 1996, the court of first instance granted the request and ordered that the book be withdrawn from distribution, under penalty of FRF 1,000 per distributed copy.[316] That order was confirmed, subject to a limitation in time, by the Cour d'appel de Paris.

Judgment: "As a matter of law, Art. 4(2) of the *Code de la déontologie médicale* (Code of Medical Ethics) concerning medical secrecy, infringements of which are subject to criminal as well as disciplinary sanctions, covers 'all matters which come to the doctor's knowledge in the exercise of his profession, that is to say not only matters confided to him but also that which he has seen, heard or understood'.

---

[312] See Goubeaux at 279 ff., para. 302 ff., with a discussion at 280–1, para. 304 of the right to reproduce information already known or divulged previously.

[313] See Paris, 11 February 1987, D 1987.Somm. 385.

[314] See Goubeaux at 279 ff., para. 302 ff. and the note under the judgment in *Les grands arrêts* at 89–92.

[315] JCP 1996.II.22632, annotated by E. Derieux. Translation by N. Sims.

[316] TGI Paris, 18 January 1996, JCP 1996.II.22589, annotated by E. Derieux.

Although the law derogates from medical secrecy in certain exceptional cases, none of those cases is relied on by the appellants . . .

The facts disclosed in the . . . book *Le grand secret* . . . came to the knowledge of Dr. Gubler in the course of the exercise of his profession as a doctor to François Mitterrand. As such those facts are manifestly covered by medical secrecy.

The arguments advanced by the appellants and the interveners to justify disclosure of those facts are without relevance. Thus, neither the alleged contribution by Dr. Gubler to the search for the solution to the problem posed by monitoring the state of health of the Head of State, nor the publication during [Mr. Mitterrand's] lifetime of bulletins relating to the state of his health can legitimize that disclosure . . .

Consequently, the disclosure by means of publication of the book *Le grand secret* of facts covered by medical secrecy by which the co-author of the book is bound is manifestly unlawful.

Mrs Mitterrand and the children of François Mitterrand have been wounded in their deepest feelings as a result of this public disclosure of matters relating to both the personality and the private life of their spouse and father and their own intimacy, by the personal physician to the deceased President of the Republic in whom the latter placed his trust under the protection of medical secrecy . . . It follows that Mrs. Mitterrand and the children of François Mitterrand have each of them individually a legitimate interest in acting to bring an end to the disturbance occasioned to them by the manifestly unlawful act constituted by the aforementioned disclosure. The Court therefore upholds as admissible their application in reliance on the provisions of Art. 809(1) of the new *Code de procédure civile* for interim injunctive relief to restrain the acts complained of.

Under that provision the court has power on an interlocutory application, even where there is a serious defence, to order the interim measures necessary to restrain such disturbance.

The appellants and the interveners cannot legitimately claim that the interlocutory measure, not for confiscation but for cessation of the distribution of the book, ordered to this end by the court below, is in breach of the constitutionally protected freedom to communicate thoughts and opinions, enshrined in Art. 11 of the Declaration of the Rights of Man and the Citizen of 26 August 1789, from which is derived the freedom of the press and publication. That same Article also lays down the principle that one is answerable for abuse of that freedom. Such an abuse is constituted by the disclosure, by means of the distribution of a printed work, of facts covered by secrecy to which the author of the work is bound on account of his status or profession, in the general interest and on public policy grounds. The interim measure adopted in order to restrain the manifestly unlawful interference stemming from that abuse therefore does not run counter to the requirements of the principles laid down by that Article . . .

It is true that a prohibition of the distribution of a book can never be other than exceptional . . .

Nonetheless, the necessarily provisional nature of such a measure requires it to be limited in time in accordance with procedures appropriate to putting the parties in a position to plead the dispute between them, within a reasonable period, before the trial court that has jurisdiction on the merits.

On those grounds: . . . The interlocutory order issued *inter partes* on 18 January 1996 by the court of first instance is upheld.

In addition, Mrs Mitterrand and the children of François Mitterrand are given a period of one month, from the date of delivery of this judgment, to apply to the court to try the merits of the matter at issue between them and Mr Gubler and the company, Editions Plon.

If the case is brought for trial on the merits within that period, the injunction prohibiting the distribution of the book *Le grand secret* shall continue to have effect, unless otherwise ordered by the court trying the merits of the case, until delivery of judgment by that court.

If the case is not brought for trial on the merits within that period, the measure shall immediately cease to have effect."

Notes

(1) The decision turns on the infringement by Dr Gubler of his obligation, as a medical practitioner, of confidentiality (*secret médical*, a species of *secret professionnel*), which finds its basis in the relationship of trust, indispensable in a medical context, between the physician and the patient. This relationship of trust continues to exist after the death of the patient. The right of privacy is not mentioned as such in the decision of the Cour d'appel. It is only said that the breach of confidence, for which no legal justification can be advanced, was wounding to the widow and children of the deceased "in their deepest feelings" by revealing aspects of "the personality and private life of their husband and father and their own intimacy". On that basis, the court found that the plaintiffs had a legitimate interest in seeking an injunction to restrain continuance of the disturbance caused by the unlawful breach of confidence.

(2) The most interesting part of the judgment deals with the legality of a prohibition on the further distribution of the book on the basis of the interim relief provisions of Article 809(1) of the new *Code de procédure civile*. At issue was whether such relief could be granted in view of the constitutional and international protection granted to freedom of opinion.[317] The Cour d'appel was of the opinion that interim relief could be granted, albeit for a limited duration, because it would be abusive to reveal information in breach of a duty of secrecy, which serves the general interest and public order, and the fundamental rights provisions concerned all allow for the prevention and termination of those types of abuse.

(3) Both courts ruled on interim relief measures only. The case on the merits went up to the Cour de cassation, which upheld the judgment of the Court of Appeal whereby the prohibition on the distribution of the book was maintained on a permanent basis and damages were awarded to Mrs. Mitterrand (FRF 100,000) and to each of Mr. Mitterrand's children (FRF 80,000 each).[318] See also, in another case relating to the unauthorized publication of photographs of Mr Mitterrand on his death-bed, the judgment of the Tribunal de grande instance de Paris of 13 January 1997 awarding FRF 1 to Mrs Mitterrand and the three children of Mr Mitterrand.[319]

2.2.3. ENGLISH LAW

Introductory Note

No better presentation of the state of English law in respect of protection of personality rights can be given than is to be found in the following judgments of Lord Justices Glidewell, Bingham and Leggatt, excerpts from which are printed below.

---

[317] Art. 11 of the Declaration of the Rights of Man and the Citizen of 26 August 1789, Art. 10-1 ECHR. See on that issue P. Kayser, "Les pouvoirs du juge des référés civil à l'égard de la liberté de communication et d'expression" D 1989.Chron.11. Because of the implications of the case for freedom of opinion and of the press, both the court of first instance and the court of appeal permitted representative press associations to intervene. See also Cass. civ. 2e, 24 January 1996, Bull.civ. 1996.II.14, discussed by G. Viney, "Chronique" JCP 1996.I.3985, in the case of a person who, according to the defendant book author, had committed suicide.

[318] Cass. civ. 1re, 14 December 1999, JCP 2000.II.10241, with the conclusions of AG Petit.

[319] JCP 1997.II.22845, annotated by E. Derieux.

Court of Appeal[320]   **2.E.32.**
Kaye v. *Robertson*

RIGHT TO PRIVACY

Interview in hospital

The tort of malicious falsehood offers a fairly limited weapon against an infringement of a person's privacy through the unauthorized publication of an interview and pictures.

Facts: Mr. Gordon Kaye, a well-known television personality, suffered severe injuries to his head and brain as a result of a car accident. Whilst he was in the hospital, visits were severely restrained, mostly to ensure his proper recovery. Even though lists on display indicated the names of allowed visitors and requested others to see the hospital staff before visiting, two journalists from a seedy, down-market Sunday newspaper gained access to his room without permission, took pictures with a flash and interviewed him. According to the tape recording of the conversation, Mr. Kaye consented to the interview on the spot. However, it later appeared that he was in no state to give his informed consent, since he had no recollection of the visit 15 minutes after the journalists left his room. Mr. Kaye sought to stop publication of the article and photographs forthwith.

Held: The court of first instance granted an injunction against the defendants. The Court of Appeal upheld the injunction but modified certain of its terms.

Judgment: GLIDEWELL LJ: "*It is well-known that in English law there is no right to privacy, and accordingly there is no right of action for breach of a person's privacy. The facts of the present case are a graphic illustration of the desirability of Parliament considering whether and in what circumstances statutory provision can be made to protect the privacy of individuals* [emphasis added].

In the absence of such a right, the plaintiff's advisers have sought to base their claim to injunctions upon other well-established rights of actions. These are:

1. Libel 2. Malicious falsehood 3. Trespass to the person 4. Passing off.

The appeal canvassed all four rights of action, and it is necessary to deal with each in turn.

1. **Libel.** The basis of the plaintiff's case under this head is that the article as originally written clearly implied that Mr. Kaye consented to give the first 'exclusive' interview to *Sunday Sport*, and to be photographed by their photographer. This was untrue: Mr. Kaye was in no fit condition to give any informed consent, and such consent as he may appear to have given was, and should have been known by *Sunday Sport*'s representative to be, of no effect. The implication in the article would have the effect of lowering Mr. Kaye in the esteem of right-thinking people, and was thus defamatory.

The plaintiff's case is based on the well-known decision in *Tolley* v. *J.S. Fry & Sons Ltd.* [1931] AC 333. Mr. Tolley was a well-known amateur golfer. Without his consent, Fry published an advertisement which consisted of a caricature of the plaintiff with a caddie, each with a packet of Fry's chocolate protruding from his pocket. The caricature was accompanied by doggerel verse which used Mr. Tolley's name and extolled the virtues of the chocolate. The plaintiff alleged that the advertisement implied that he had received payment for the advertisement, which would damage his reputation as an amateur player. The judge at the trial ruled that the advertisement was capable of being defamatory, and on appeal the House of Lords upheld this ruling.

It seems that an analogy with *Tolley* v. *Fry* was the main plank of Mr. Justice Potter's decision to grant injunctions in this case.

[The defendants submit] that, assuming that the article was capable of having the meaning alleged, this would not be a sufficient basis for interlocutory relief. In *William Coulson & Sons* v.

---

[320] [1991] FSR 62; see also Weir at 22.

James Coulson & Co. (1887) 3 TLR 846 this court held that, though the High Court has jurisdiction to grant an interim injunction before the trial of a libel action, it is a jurisdiction to be exercised only sparingly . . .

This is still the rule in actions for defamation, despite the decision of the House of Lords in *American Cyanamid Co.* v. *Ethicon Ltd.* [1975] AC 396 in relation to interim injunctions generally . . .

It is in my view certainly arguable that the intended article would be libellous, on the authority of Tolley v. Fry. *I think that a jury would probably find that Mr. Kaye had been libelled, but I cannot say that such a conclusion is inevitable* [emphasis added]. It follows that I agree with [the defendant's] submission and in this respect I disagree with the learned Judge; I therefore would not base an injunction on a right of action for libel.

2. **Malicious falsehood.** The essentials of this tort are that the defendant has published about the plaintiff words which are false, that they were published maliciously, and that special damage has followed as the direct and natural result of their publication. As to special damage, the effect of section 3 (1) of the Defamation Act 1952 is that it is sufficient if the words published in writing are calculated to cause material damage to the plaintiff. Malice will be inferred if it be proved that the words were calculated to produce damage and that the defendant knew when he published the words that they were false or was reckless as to whether they were false or not . . .

In the present case I have no doubt that any jury which did not find that the clear implication from the words contained in the defendant's draft article *were false* would be making a totally unreasonable finding [emphasis added]. Thus the test is satisfied in relation to this cause of action.

As to malice I equally have no doubt from the evidence, including the transcript of the tape-recording of the 'interview' with Mr. Kaye in his hospital room which we have read, that it was quite apparent to the reporter and photographer from *Sunday Sport* that Mr. Kaye was in no condition to give any informed consent to them interviewing or photographing him. Moreover, even if the journalists had been in any doubt about Mr. Kaye's fitness to give his consent, Mr. Robertson could not have entertained any such doubt after he read the affidavit sworn on behalf of Mr. Kaye in these proceedings. Any subsequent publication of the falsehood would therefore inevitably be *malicious* [emphasis added].

As to damage, I have already recorded that Mr. Robertson appreciated that Mr. Kaye's story was one for which other newspapers would be willing to pay 'large sums of money' [emphasis added]. If the defendants are able to publish the article they proposed, . . . Mr. Kaye's story thereafter would be worth much less to him.

I have considered whether damages would be an adequate remedy in these circumstances. They would inevitably be difficult to calculate, would also follow some time after the event, and in my view would in no way be adequate. It thus follows that in my opinion all the preconditions to the grant of an interlocutory injunction in respect of this cause of action are made out . . .

3. **Trespass to the person.** It is strictly unnecessary to consider this cause of action in the light of the view I have expressed about malicious falsehood. However I will set out my view shortly. The plaintiff's case in relation to this cause of action is the taking of the flashlight photographs may well have caused distress to Mr. Kaye and set back his recovery, and thus caused him injury. In this sense it can be said to be a battery . . . Though there must have been an obvious risk that any disturbance to Mr. Kaye would set back his recovery, there is no evidence that the taking of the photographs did in fact cause him any damage.

Moreover, the injunction sought in relation to this head of action would not be intended to prevent another anticipated battery, since none was anticipated . . .

4. **Passing off.** [The plaintiff] submits (though in this case not with any great vigour) that the essentials of the tort of passing off, as laid down by the speeches in the House of Lords in *Erven Warnink B.V.* v. *J. Townend & Sons (Hull) Ltd.* [1979] AC 731 are satisfied here. I only need say

shortly that in my view they are not. I think that the plaintiff is not in the position of a trader in relation to his interest in his story about his accident and his recovery, and thus fails from the start to have a right of action under this head."

BINGHAM LJ: "I have had the benefit of reading in draft the judgment prepared by Glidewell LJ. I agree with it, and with the order made.

Any reasonable and fair-minded person hearing the facts which Glidewell LJ has recited would in my judgment conclude that these defendants had wronged the plaintiff. I am therefore pleased to be persuaded that the plaintiff is able to establish, with sufficient strength to justify an interlocutory order, a cause of action against the defendants in malicious falsehood. Had he failed to establish any cause of action, we should of course have been powerless to act, however great our sympathy for the plaintiff and however strong our distaste for the defendants' conduct.

This case nonetheless highlights, yet again, the failure of both the common law of England and statute to protect in an effective way the personal privacy of individual citizens [emphasis added]. This has been the subject of much comment over the years, perhaps most recently by Professor Markesinis (*The German Law of Torts*, 2nd ed., 1990, at 316) . . .

The defendants' conduct towards the plaintiff here was 'a monstrous invasion of his privacy' (to adopt the language of Griffiths J in *Bernstein* v. *Skyviews Ltd.* [1978] QB 479 at 489G). *If ever a person has a right to be let alone by strangers with no public interest to pursue, it must surely be when he lies in hospital recovering from brain surgery and in no more than partial command of his faculties. It is this invasion of his privacy which underlies the plaintiff's complaint. Yet it alone, however gross, does not entitle him to relief in English law* [emphasis added].

The plaintiff's suggested cause of action in libel is in my view arguable, for reasons which Glidewell LJ has given. We could not give interlocutory relief on that ground. Battery and assault are causes of action never developed to cover acts such as these: they could apply only if the law were substantially extended and the available facts strained to unacceptable lengths. A claim in passing off is hopeless. Fortunately a cause of action in malicious falsehood exists, but even that obliges us to limit the relief we can grant in a way which would not bind us if the plaintiff's cause of action arose from the invasion of privacy of which, fundamentally, he complains. *We cannot give the plaintiff the breadth of protection which I would, for my part, wish. The problems of defining and limiting a tort of privacy are formidable, but the present case strengthens my hope that the review now in progress may prove fruitful* [emphasis added]."

LEGGATT LJ: "I agree with both judgments that have been delivered. In view of the importance of the topic I add a note about the way in which the common law has developed in the United States to meet the need which in the present case we are unable to fulfil satisfactorily.

The recognition of a right to privacy seemed to be in prospect when Lord Byron obtained an injunction to restrain the false attribution to him of a bad poem: *Byron* v. *Johnston* [1816] 2 Mer. 29, 35 ER 851 (Ch). But it was not until 1890 that in their article "The Right of Privacy", 4 Harv. L Rev. 193, Warren and Brandeis reviewed a number of English cases on defamation and breaches of rights of property, confidence and contract, and concluded that all were based on a broader common principle. They argued that recognition of the principle would enable the courts to protect the individual against the infliction by the press of mental pain and distress through invasion of his privacy. Since then the right to privacy, or 'the right to be let alone', has gained acceptance in most jurisdictions in the United States . . . [references omitted]

We do not need a First Amendment to preserve the freedom of the press, but the abuse of that freedom can be ensured only by the enforcement of a right to privacy. This right has so long been disregarded here that it can be recognized now only by the legislature. Especially since there is available in the United States a wealth of experience of the enforcement of this right both at common law and also under statute, it is to be hoped that the making good of this signal shortcoming in our law will not be long delayed [emphasis added]."

Notes

(1) The state of English law in respect of protection of personality rights, as stated in the opinions of Glidewell, Bingham and Leggatt LJJ in the case reprinted above, can be summarized as follows:

— "[I]n English law there is no right to privacy, and accordingly there is no right of action for breach of a person's privacy" (Glidewell LJ) and "this case . . . highlights, yet again, the failure of both the common law of England and statute to protect in an effective way the personal privacy of individual citizens" (Bingham LJ). Both German and French law recognize such a general right to privacy,[321] and Leggatt LJ notes that it is also well established in the USA.[322]
— There is a widespread desire amongst the judiciary (all three Lord Justices express it) for Parliament to step in and fill this gap in the common law, since the right to privacy "has so long been disregarded . . . that it can be recognized now only by the legislature" (Leggatt LJ). It has indeed been *generally* assumed that legislation is required.[323]
— In the absence of a general right to privacy, well-established causes of action may be relied upon, though with only limited effectiveness.

(2) The relevant well-established causes of action are: deceit and injurious (or malicious) falsehood;[324] defamation (libel if the defamatory statement or representation takes a permanent form; slander if it is conveyed by spoken words or gestures);[325] assault and battery;[326] and breach of confidence.[327] Furthermore, it can be added that deliberate harassment provoking injury to physical or mental health constitutes what has been described as an emergent tort of "personal injury by molestation".[328] Even though in *Kaye* v. *Robertson* the effectiveness of the relevant causes of action was further limited on account of the form of order sought (injunction), the judgments make it clear how much the established torts are inapt to protect against an invasion of privacy. Bingham LJ runs through the list: "cause of action in libel is . . . arguable", "battery and assault are causes

---

[321] *Supra*, **2.G.26.** and **2.F.29.–30.**

[322] For a discussion of some problems raised by some of the American case law on unwanted disclosure of information about a person's private life, see D. Anderson, "Fundamental Issues in Privacy Law", in B. S. Markesinis, (ed.), *The Clifford Chance Lectures—Vol. I: Bridging the Channel* (New York: Oxford University Press, 1996).

[323] For proposals to introduce a statutory tort of invasion of privacy, see *Reports of the Committee on Privacy and Related Matters*, Cm. 1102 (1990) and Cm. 2135 (1993); and *Lord Chancellor's Consultation Paper* (1993). See Markesinis and Deakin at 443 ff. for a brief and interesting discussion of the underlying difficulties.

[324] See Rogers at 353, 385, 460. See also *Spring* v. *Guardian Assurance plc* [1995] 2 AC 296, [1994] 3 All 129, where the House of Lords held that an employer who gave a reference in respect of a former employee owed that employee a duty to take reasonable care in its preparation and was liable to him in negligence if he failed to do so and in consequence the employee suffered economic loss.

[325] See Rogers at 391.

[326] *Supra*, Chapter I, **1.E.21.**

[327] Which, outside the field of contractual confidentiality, may be an independent head of tortious liability: see Rogers at 467 ff.

[328] *Clerk & Lindsell on Torts* at para. 12–16, citing *Burnett* v. *George* [1992] 1 FLR 525, CA and N. Fricker, "Personal Molestation or Harassment—Injunctions in Actions based on the law of torts" [1992] Fam Law 158.

of action never developed to cover acts such as [the ones at issue]", "a claim in passing off is hopeless", "fortunately a cause of action in malicious falsehood exists, but even that obliges us to limit the relief we can grant".

(3) Even if legislative efforts to provide for a general right to privacy have not yet succeeded, some progress towards the protection of privacy and personality rights in general has been made with the recent enactment of the Protection from Harassment Act 1997,[329] which at section 1 prohibits the intentional or negligent pursuit of a course of conduct[330] which amounts to harassment. In addition to the criminal consequences of harassment, set out at section 2, section 3(1) provides that "[a]n actual or apprehended breach of section 1 [i.e. harassment] may be the subject of a claim in civil proceedings by the person who is or may be the victim of the course of conduct in question". Section 3(2) expressly states that the claim of the victim can include damages for "any anxiety caused by the harassment and any financial loss resulting from the harassment", thus setting aside for cases of harassment the restrictive rules concerning nervous shock[331] and pure economic loss[332] under English tort law. Section 3 of the Act also enables the victim to obtain a court order restraining the wrongdoer from further harassing conduct.

(4) It will be interesting to see if the situation will change now that the Human Rights Act 1998 has entered into force.[333] The Act introduces the ECHR into English law, and allows courts to declare inapplicable legislation that would contravene the rights guaranteed by the ECHR. Furthermore, courts can grant remedies against administrative action that would infringe those rights.

2.2.4. IRISH AND PORTUGUESE LAW

The following cases can be found (with notes) at <http://www.rechten.unimaas.nl/casebook>:

2.IRL.33. High Court, *Murtagh Properties Ltd.* v. *Cleary*. No waitresses wanted.
2.P.34. Suprema Tribunal de Justiça, 28 April 1977. Noise from tunnel construction.

2.2.5. COMPARATIVE OVERVIEW

The issue of "personality rights"

The concept of a general personality right or a general right to privacy was recognized in tort only after the Second World War. Indeed, the personality right (*Persönlichkeitsrecht*) received recognition, particularly in German law, as a result of Constitutional provisions

---

[329] 1997 (c. 40). Sections 1–7 of the Act extend to England and Wales only. For Scotland (ss. 8–11) and Northern Ireland (s. 13), there are special provisions.
[330] Including speech: s. 7(4).
[331] *Supra*, **2.E.8.–9.** and notes.
[332] *Infra*, 3.1., Introductory Note, as well as **2.E.36.** and notes.
[333] Human Rights Act 1998 (c. 42). On the Human Rights Act 1998, see J. Wadham and H. Mountfield, *Blackstone's Guide to the Human Rights Act 1998* (London: Blackstone, 1999) and S. Greer, "A Guide to the Human Rights Act 1998" (1999) 24 ELRev 3.

which were enacted after the atrocities of the Nazi regime, whilst the right to privacy was awarded general protection in French law in 1970.

The distinction made in some systems between material and non-material injury may greatly affect the protection offered to personality rights. Although there may be a willing acceptance of the principle of compensation for material damage contingent upon a violation of personality interests, compensation for pure non-material harm is difficult to assess in monetary terms, and rarely adequate to redress the varied consequences of a violation.[334] That is why many of the cases reproduced above concern injunctive relief, which is often the most efficient remedy.

The concept of privacy will in all likelihood be further developed under the influence of Article 8 ECHR and the case law of the ECHR institutions.[335]

The emergence of personality rights

The protection of personality rights under French and German law is organized in a rather similar way, while English law demonstrates a pronounced individuality of approach. Both French and German law initially recognized the existence of personality rights in case law: in German law on the basis of § 823(1) BGB, and in French law on the basis of Article 1382 C.civ. In certain areas protection was then strengthened through the enactment of specific legislative provisions.

As set out in the preceding section, under German law the *Rechtsgüter* which merit a prominent place in the protection that tort rules offer are enumerated in § 823(1) BGB. Beside the rights explicitly there enumerated, § 823(1) refers to "other" rights by which is meant, *inter alia*, rights *in rem*, other than ownership,[336] as well as specific personality rights, such as the right to one's name and image.[337] The recognition of the general *Persönlichkeitsrecht*, as an "other right" protected by a claim in tort under § 823(1) BGB, was affirmed for the first time in the BGH judgment of 25 May 1954.[338] Moreover, in a later judgment of 2 April 1957, the BGH explained the need to give those values the same prominence in private law as in public law, that is in relations between persons, thus granting horizontal effect to the fundamental rights enshrined in the *Grundgesetz*.[339] In a judgment of 15 January 1958 the BVerfG confirmed that position, holding that "the legal context of fundamental rights as objective norms affects private law . . . which must conform to the values embodied in the fundamental rights [guaranteed in the *Grundgesetz*]".[340] This evolution, known as the constitutionalization of private law,[341] is also apparent in other legal systems.[342]

---

[334] See *supra*, **2.G.26.** and Note (3).
[335] *Supra*, **2.P.34.** and ECHR, Judgment of 9 December 1994, *López-Ostra* v. *Spain*, Ser. A No. 303-C.
[336] See *infra*, 3.2., Introductory Note under d).
[337] *Supra*, 2.1.1., Introductory Note under a).
[338] See *supra*, **2.G.26.**, Note (1).
[339] *Supra*, **2.G.26.**
[340] *Supra*, 2.1.1., Introductory Note under b).
[341] See Markesinis at 27–31.
[342] Such as Irish law, a legal system from the common law family, but which includes a written constitution: see *Murtagh Properties Ltd.* v. *Cleary*, *supra*, **2.IRL.33.**; see also Corte di Cassazione, 14 May 1982, *infra*, **2.I.45.**, and Suprema Tribunal de Justiça, 28 April 1977, *supra*, **2.P.34.**

An important effect of the recognition of the general *Persönlichkeitsrecht* under §823(1) BGB is acceptance of the principle that compensation is payable for non-material damage in the event of a violation, as is shown in the BGH judgments.[343] Confronted with the implied prohibition in § 253 BGB of the award of compensation for non-material damage except where specified by law, the BGH held that the protection of human dignity, derived from Articles 1 and 2 GG, would be incomplete if adequate remedies were not available for an infringement of the *Persönlichkeitsrecht*, with non-material harm a common head of damage in such a case.

In France, the general formula of Article 1382 C.civ. was used to condemn tortious attacks on private life, reputation, liberty, name, and more generally all the rights traditionally recognized as necessary in a democracy for individuals to express their personality. Until the 1940s, the notion of personality rights was assimilated to other injuries, and sanctioned by a general action in tort. The courts then started to interpret the conditions for tortious liability—in particular fault and damage—more stringently, and it is in response to this stringency that academic writers proposed the concept of personality rights. This academic systematization not only provoked an accentuation of this jurisprudential tendency, but also many legislative interventions, notably the Act of 17 July 1970,[344] inserting Article 9 into the *Code civil*, which affirms the right to privacy as a specific right, and the Act of 4 January 1993,[345] which, in the same terms, enshrines the right to the presumption of innocence in Article 9-1.[346] This evolution led to the elevation of privacy to an autonomous right, removing the duty of the plaintiff to prove fault,[347] a development which the Cour de cassation recently carried further, holding that "pursuant to Art. 9 C.civ., the mere finding that the right to privacy has been infringed entitles [the victim] to compensation".[348]

As in Germany, in France the protection of specific personality rights and of the right to privacy is clearly horizontally applicable, that is in relations between individuals. Compensation for non-material damage is also accepted under French law as a matter of principle.

The position under English law is summarized by Glidewell LJ in *Kaye* v. *Robertson*: "it is well-known that . . . there is no right to privacy".[349] In the absence of such a right, the plaintiffs sought in that case to base their claim for injunctive relief upon other well-established rights of action: the nominate torts of trespass to the person, passing off, libel and malicious falsehood. The claims under the first two torts were rejected; liability in libel was also considered, although its existence here was deemed insufficiently certain to grant interim relief. Although handicapped by the fact that the remedy of injunctive relief was sought, which is subject to more restrictive conditions than compensation, the Court of Appeal granted relief under the tort of malicious falsehood. This was a fortunate outcome,

---

[343] *Supra*, **2.G.26.**, Note (3).

[344] *Loi 70-643 tendant à renforcer la garantie des droits individuels de citoyens* of 17 July 1970, JO, 19 July 1970, D 1970.Lég.199.

[345] *Loi 93-2 portant réforme de la procédure pénale* of 4 January 1993, JO, 5 January 1993, D 1993.Lég.134.

[346] See *supra*, 2.2.2., Introductory Note under b).

[347] In contrast to German law, where the elevation of the general *Persönlichkeitsrecht* to a subjective right in the sense of § 823(1) BGB does not discharge the obligation contained in the provision to show that the infringement of the right was "unlawful" (*widerrechtlich*) and gave rise to injury (*Schaden*).

[348] See *supra*, **2.F.29.–30.**, Note (1).

[349] *Supra*, **2.E.32.**

according to Bingham LJ, since the court was otherwise "powerless to act, however great our sympathy for the plaintiff and however strong our distaste for the defendants' conduct". "The case highlights", Bingham LJ added, "the failure of both the common law of England and statute to protect in an effective way the personal privacy of individual citizens".

In the same case, Leggatt LJ states that the "right [to privacy] has so long been disregarded here [as opposed to most jurisdictions in the USA] that it can be recognized now only by the legislature". In view of the American[350] and Irish[351] experience, one may wonder whether it would be different if English courts, like their German counterparts, had the benefit of a written constitution with clearly formulated provisions. Failing those, supranational or international provisions, such as Article 8 ECHR, could be relied upon. Moreover, some relief is to be found in the recent Protection from Harassment Act 1997.[352]

Modalities in protection

Despite the relative ease with which personality rights are recognized in France and Germany, the difference in conceptualization of "personality rights" has repercussions on the mode of protection, albeit that both systems seem to recognize that certain attributes of the personality merit more rigorous protection than others.

The protection offered by French law is not uniform. As stated above, where the rights have been explicitly identified in case law, such as the right to name, and image, or identified formally by the law, such as respect for private life and the presumption of innocence, the courts today presume not only damage, but also fault, which lends the tort a clear autonomy in relation to the general law of tort.[353] That does not preclude reliance by the defendant, in certain circumstances, on one or another ground of justification,[354] such as the need for transparency of financial and economic transactions.[355] On the other hand, Article 1382 C.civ. still plays a supplementary role in the protection of personality rights, as is shown by the decisions in the *Benetton* case.[356] Although the plaintiffs' claims for damages on the basis of Article 9 C.civ. failed, damages (reduced on appeal to one symbolic FRF) were awarded on the basis of Article 1382 C.civ. because the defendant had abused his freedom of expression.

There is evidence in Germany of a similarly heterogenous approach. Those specific personality rights recognized before the judgment of 1954,[357] such as the right to name, image etc., still appear best protected, as liability for the violation of such rights falls within the scope of § 823(1) BGB. However, for the general *Persönlichkeitsrecht*, whose inclusion among the list of protected *Rechtsgüter* at § 823(1) BGB was recognized in 1954, the protection is less straightforward, since when that right is invoked by the plaintiff, the courts give effect to it only if it does not injure a right or interest considered socially more important.

---

[350] See *supra*, **2.E.32.**, the opinion of Leggatt LJ.
[351] *Supra*, **2.IRL.33.** and notes.
[352] *Supra*, **2.E.32.**, Note (3).
[353] See *supra*, 2.2.2., Introductory Note under b).
[354] See *supra*, **2.F.29.–30.**, Note (2).
[355] See *supra*, **2.F.31.** and Note (2).
[356] See *supra*, 2.2.2., Introductory Note under c).
[357] *Supra* **2.G.26.**, Note (2).

It is indeed characteristic of a right like the general *Persönlichkeitsrecht* that it should tend to conflict with the equal and opposite rights of others, for example someone else's fundamental right or freedom, or "other" subjective right. In order to solve such conflicts, the BGH has developed a balancing test in its case law, which it applies when an individual's "other right" (*sonstiges Recht*), such as the general *Persönlichkeitsrecht* or *Recht am Gewerbebetrieb* conflicts with the rights or freedoms of another.[358] A case in point is BGH, 12 October 1993, where the general *Persönlichkeitsrecht* of the manager of a large company, who had engaged in a public discussion concerning an issue of public interest (the preservation of the ozone layer), conflicted with the freedom of expression of Greenpeace.[359] The court held, that "because of the importance of the fundamental right of freedom of opinion to a free and open political process . . . a person who by virtue of his position, must bear responsibility for decisions having a scope such as that in the present case, cannot be allowed the opportunity to gag such criticism by relying on his sphere of privacy."

Injunctive relief

As may be seen from many of the German,[360] French,[361] English[362] and Irish[363] decisions reproduced in this section plaintiffs often seek injunctive relief. In the context of violations of the "intimacy" of private life,[364] Article 9(2) C.civ. thus provides for a series of measures of injunctive relief: "sequestration, seizure or other measures as may be appropriate to prevent or stop the infringement".[365] In France, actions for interim injunctive relief, now often based on Article 809(1) of the new *Code de procédure civile*, raise the interesting point of whether such relief can be granted in view of the constitutional and international protection accorded to freedom of opinion. In its judgment of 13 March 1996,[366] relating to a violation of medical confidentiality, the Cour d'appel de Paris held that, taking into account the provisional and temporary nature of the relief granted, the principle of freedom of expression was not infringed since the disclosure of facts covered by professional secrecy itself amounted to an abuse of that principle.[367] It should be noted that in this decision a balancing test is applied when freedom of expression and the right to privacy protected by a duty of confidentiality conflict, which mirrors the approach of German law noted above. The very need to weigh these issues one against the other emphasizes the potential volatility of the enforcement of personality rights, a tendency which due to the emergence of new technologies, private and public law will increasingly have to confront at an international level. In time the pursuit of solutions to shared dilemmas may further contribute to the transcontinental convergence of protection.

[358] See *infra*, 2.3.5., as well as BGH, 21 June 1966, **2.G.38.** and note.
[359] *Supra*, **2.G.28.**
[360] *Supra*, **2.G.26.**
[361] *Supra*, **2.F.29.**, **2.F.31.**
[362] *Supra*, **2.E.32.**
[363] *Supra*, **2.IRL.33.**
[364] That is the core of privacy: see *supra*, **2.F.30.**, Note (1).
[365] *Supra*, 2.2.2., Introductory Note under b).
[366] *Supra*, **2.F.31.**
[367] See also *supra*, **2.F.31.**, Note (2).

2.3. PROTECTION OF OWNERSHIP AND PROPERTY RIGHTS

In this section, English law will be discussed first: as concerns land, English law nowadays attempts to use ancient tort rules, albeit not always successfully, to regulate "emissions" between neighbours and as for chattels, it is reluctant to allow compensation for pure economic loss, that is loss which is not directly consequential upon harm to property. German law is treated thereafter: it comes to similar results albeit by different ways. French law, which is not hindered in that respect by any *a priori* limitations, is discussed in third place whereas, in the last subsection, reference is made to Italian law.

2.3.1. ENGLISH LAW

Introductory Note

English tort law provides different means of protection for the enjoyment of real and personal property, mainly under the older nominate torts. Furthermore it treats pure economic loss differently from economic loss accompanying damage to property, at least under the tort of negligence.

Among the species of real property under English law, one finds land, things attached to the land (such as buildings) and certain rights in land such as easements (nearly synonymous with Roman law servitudes). Among the species of personal property under English law, one finds chattels and "chattels real" (interests concerning realty such as a lease for a fixed period, which has the quality of immobility but lacks indeterminate duration); personal property further includes bills of exchange, bank notes and cheques, intellectual property rights, stocks and shares as well as goodwill.

a) With respect to *real property*, the torts of trespass to land, nuisance (and the rule in *Rylands* v. *Fletcher*) as well as negligence can intervene.

As seen earlier,[368] **trespass to land**, one of the oldest torts, is concerned with the unauthorized entry on premises occupied by another (on, above or below the surface). Liability in damages arises under this tort as long as the entry is voluntary (i.e. intentional or negligent): "It is no defence that the trespass was due to a mistake of law or fact, provided the physical act of entry was voluntary . . .".[369]

On the other hand, when a person conducts activities on his or her own land which lead to damage on a neighbouring property, liability may arise, even if there is no element of fault, under the tort of nuisance[370] or the rule in *Rylands* v. *Fletcher*.

Nuisance is defined as "an act or omission which is an interference with, disturbance of or annoyance to, a person in the exercise or enjoyment of (a) a right belonging to him as a member of the public, when it is a public nuisance, or (b) his ownership or occupation of land or of some easement, profit, or other right used or enjoyed in connection with land, when it is a private nuisance".[371]

---

[368] *Supra*, Chapter I, **1.E.21.**
[369] *Clerk & Lindsell on Torts* at 840, para. 17-06.
[370] Nuisance differs from trespass in that the latter "is a direct as opposed to a consequential injury, and is actionable without proof of damage. whereas damage must be proved in nuisance": ibid. at 840, para. 17-07.
[371] *Clerk & Lindsell on Torts* at 889–90, para. 18-01.

A **public nuisance** is a criminal offence, and "it is only a civil wrong and actionable as such when a private individual has suffered particular damage over and above the general inconvenience and injury suffered by the public".[372]

For the purposes of this casebook, only the tort of **private nuisance** will be dealt with (and all subsequent references to nuisance should therefore be understood as references to private nuisance). It can be described as follows:

> "Private nuisance [is the] *unlawful interference with a person's use or enjoyment of land, or some right over, or in connection with it* . . . [W]hether [such interferences] constitute an *actionable* nuisance will depend on a variety of considerations, especially the character of the defendant's conduct, and a balancing of conflicting interests [, namely] that of one occupier in using his land as he thinks fit, and that of his neighbour in the quiet enjoyment of his land. Everyone must endure some degree of noise, smell, etc. from his neighbour . . . In fact, the law repeatedly recognises that a man may use his own land so as to injure another without committing a nuisance. It is only if such use is unreasonable that it becomes unlawful".[373]

Private nuisance has traditionally been regarded as an interference with the enjoyment of land, and accordingly only the persons with rights to the land affected by the nuisance can pursue a nuisance claim before the courts. There had been some movement in England and other common law countries towards allowing mere occupiers of the land (licensees, relatives of the persons with rights to the land, etc.) to claim in nuisance as well; in England, this trend was epitomized by the Court of Appeal decision in *Khorasandjian* v. *Bush*, where the daughter of a houseowner was allowed to pursue a nuisance claim.[374] This last case was however overruled by the House of Lords (with one dissent on this point) in *Hunter* v. *Canary Wharf Ltd.*, where Lord Goff said:[375]

> "It follows that, on the authorities as they stand, an action in private nuisance will only lie at the suit of a person who has a right to the land affected. Ordinarily, such a person can only sue if he has the right to exclusive possession of the land, such as a freeholder or a tenant in possession, or even a licensee with exclusive possession. Exceptionally, however, . . . this category may include a person in actual possession who has no right to be there . . . But a mere licensee on the land has no right to sue."

Furthermore, following *Hunter* v. *Canary Wharf Ltd*, it is now questionable whether damages for personal injury can be sought in nuisance. The majority of the House of Lords in *Hunter* reaffirmed that nuisance is concerned with injury to the land and strongly suggested that claims for personal injury should be brought in negligence and not nuisance; personal injury would then be relevant only as evidence of injury to the land (e.g.

---

[372] Ibid. at 890, para. 18-02, references omitted.

[373] Rogers at 494–5. The rule is called "the principle of reasonable user—the principle of give and take between neighbouring occupiers of land . . .". See Lord Goff in *Cambridge Water Co.* v. *Eastern Counties Leather Plc, infra*, **2.E.35.** and Note (2), quoting from *Bamford* v. *Turnley* (1860) 3 B&S 62, QB, and *Miller* v. *Jackson* [1977] QB 966, [1977] 3 All ER 338, CA.

[374] [1993] QB 727, [1993] 3 WLR 476, [1993] 3 All ER 669, CA. That case related to harassment by telephone calls to the house of the mother where the defendant daughter resided. See now the Protection from Harassment Act 1997, *supra*, **2.E.39.**, Note (3).

[375] [1997] 2 WLR 684, [1997] 2 All ER 426, HL at 428. See on that case J. Wightman, "Nuisance—the Environmental Tort?: *Hunter* v. *Canary Wharf* in the House of Lords" (1998) 61 Mod LR 870.

to the extent that personal injury or the risk of it reduced the value of the land). As Lord Hoffman said:[376]

> "[I]nconvenience, annoyance or even illness suffered by persons on land as a result of smells or dust are not damage consequential upon the injury to land. It is rather the other way about: the injury to the amenity of the land consists in the fact that the persons on it are liable to suffer inconvenience, annoyance or illness."

In *Hunter* v. *Canary Wharf Ltd.*, the House of Lords also dealt with the issue whether interference with television signals can constitute a private nuisance. On that issue, a unanimous House of Lords found that no action in private nuisance lies because the mere presence of a building interferes with television reception, although each of the five Law Lords put forward separate and sometimes differing reasons to reach this conclusion; it will be noted that two Law Lords took comfort in the fact that the BGH had reached a similar result.[377]

Closely related to the tort of nuisance is the so-called "**rule in *Rylands* v. *Fletcher*"**[378] which "had its origins in nuisance but . . . has been regarded by the majority of lawyers as having developed into a distinct principle".[379] In *Rylands* v. *Fletcher* Blackburn J. used the by now classical formula:[380]

> "We think that the true rule of law is, that the person who for his own purposes brings on his land and collects and keeps there anything likely to do mischief if it escapes, must keep it in at his peril, and, if he does not do so, is *prima facie* answerable for all the damage which is the natural consequence of its escape."

Even if the rule in *Rylands* v. *Fletcher* may have developed a life of its own since it was introduced in the middle of the nineteenth century, the House of Lords drew it very close to nuisance in *Cambridge Water Co.* v. *Eastern Counties Leather Plc.*[381] Nuisance and the rule in *Rylands* v. *Fletcher* play a very important role in the area of damage to land and real property in general. As will be seen in *Cambridge Water Co.* below, however, these causes of action do not require the proof of any fault on the part of the defendant, relying on other concepts as a "filter" for meritorious cases. Indeed, fault or negligence is an element of the newer tort of negligence but not of the other torts, of a more ancient lineage, which have been imposing for many decades what would now be described as strict liability.

It is not easy to define the place of the tort of **negligence** within this overall picture, all the more since *Cambridge Water Co.* demonstrates how the conditions that must be satisfied for liability to arise under the tort of nuisance are edging closer to those applicable to the tort of negligence (with the exception of fault).

---

[376] [1997] 2 All ER 426 at 452.

[377] BGH, 21 October 1983, BGHZ 88, 344, NJW 1984, 729.

[378] While such a designation may seem odd to the lawyer foreign to the common law, it is quite common for ease of convenience to refer to the principle established in a leading case as "the rule in *X*", especially for old leading cases which have been confirmed by a long string of case law. Sometimes, subsequent case law revisits the leading case and construes it in such a way that the reader is often at a loss to find "the rule in *X*" in the original case!

[379] Rogers at 538.

[380] (1866) LR 1 Ex 265, Court of Exchequer Chamber; (1868) LR 3 HL 330, HL.

[381] *Infra*, **2.E.35.**

b) With respect to improper interference with *personal property*, the common law knows three heads of tort, as mentioned earlier: **trespass to chattels**, **detinue** and **conversion**.[382] Of the three, conversion has emerged as the most important: "(it) may be committed in so many different ways that any comprehensive definition is probably impossible but the connecting thread running through the cases seems to be that the wrong is committed by a dealing with the goods of a person which constitutes an unjustifiable denial of his rights in them or the assertion of rights inconsistent therewith".[383] The sole requirements for liability in conversion are that the defendant consciously and intentionally dealt with the goods, without the consent of the owner or possessor of them, and so as to cause loss to the latter.[384]

It should be mentioned as well that a series of common law torts, the best known of which is **passing-off**, provide protection against interferences with intellectual property.

c) *Spartan Steel & Alloys Ltd.* v. *Martin & Co. (Contractors) Ltd.* illustrates very well how the English law of negligence attaches different consequences to injury to property (real or personal), including loss of profit consequential upon it, and pure economic loss.[385] The former will be readily recovered, but there is considerable reluctance to allow compensation for the latter.

House of Lords[386]   **2.E.35.**

Cambridge Water Co v. *Eastern Counties Leather Plc*

ROLE OF FORESEEABILITY IN NUISANCE AND THE RULE IN *RYLANDS* V. *FLETCHER*

Solvent spillage

In a case of "historic pollution", foreseeability of damage of the kind that has occurred is a prerequisite to liability in nuisance as well as under the rule in Rylands v. Fletcher.

Facts: The defendant Eastern Counties Leather Plc (ECL) was a leather manufacturer which used perchloroethene (PCE), a chemical solvent, in its tanning process. In the course of the process there were regular spillages of solvent onto the concrete floor of the plant. The spilt solvent, which was not readily soluble in water, seeped through the floor into the soil below and eventually reached the strata from which, through a borehole, the plaintiffs Cambridge Water Co., extracted water for domestic use. The plaintiffs brought an action against the defendants claiming damages in negligence and nuisance and under the rule in *Rylands* v. *Fletcher* for contamination of the water extracted from the borehole. The source of the contamination was not disputed.

Held: The court of first instance dismissed the claim. The court of appeal reversed that decision, holding the defendants strictly liable for the contamination of the water and awarding damages of over GBP 1m. The House of Lords allowed the appeal.

Judgment: LORD GOFF OF CHIEVELEY: "**Nuisance and the rule in *Rylands* v. *Fletcher***

. . . [W]e are concerned with the scope of liability in nuisance and in *Rylands* v. *Fletcher* . . . [The court in *Rylands* v. *Fletcher*] was concerned in particular with the situation where the defendant collects things upon his land which are likely to do mischief if they escape, in which event the defendant will be strictly liable for damage resulting from any such escape. It follows that the essential basis of liability was the collection by the defendant of such things upon his land; and the con-

---

[382] *Supra*, Chapter I, **1.E.21.** For an historical sketch, see Rogers at 583.
[383] Rogers at 588.
[384] See for more details *supra*, Chapter I, **1.E.21.**
[385] *Infra*, **2.E.36.**
[386] [1994] 2 AC 264, [1994] 1 All ER 53.

sequence was a strict liability in the event of damage caused by their escape, even if the escape was an isolated event . . .

Of course, although liability for nuisance has generally been regarded as strict, at least in the case of a defendant who has been responsible for the creation of a nuisance, even so that liability has been kept under control by the principle of reasonable user—the principle of give and take as between neighbouring occupiers of land, under which 'those acts necessary for the common and ordinary use and occupation of land and houses may be done, if conveniently done, without subjecting those who do them to an action': see *Bamford* v. *Turnley* (1860) 3 B&S 62 at 83, [1861–73] All ER 706 at 712 per Bramwell B. The effect is that, if the user is reasonable, the defendant will not be liable for consequent harm to his neighbour's enjoyment of his land; but if the user is not reasonable, the defendant will be liable, even though he may have exercised reasonable care and skill to avoid it. Strikingly, a comparable principle has developed which limits liability under the rule in *Rylands* v. *Fletcher*. This is the principle of natural use of the land . . . The effect of this principle is that, where it applies, there will be no liability under the rule in *Rylands* v. *Fletcher*; but that where it does not apply, i.e. where there is a non-natural use, the defendant will be liable for harm caused to the plaintiff by the escape, notwithstanding that he has exercised all reasonable care and skill to prevent the escape from occurring.

Foreseeability of damage in nuisance

It is against this background that it is necessary to consider the question whether foreseeability of harm of the relevant type is an essential element of liability either in nuisance or under the rule in *Rylands* v. *Fletcher*. I shall take first the case of nuisance . . .

In the present case, we are not concerned with liability in damages in respect of a nuisance which has arisen through natural causes, or by the act of a person for whose actions the defendant is not responsible, in which cases the applicable principles in nuisance have become closely associated with those applicable in negligence: see *Sedleigh-Denfield* v. *O'Callaghan* [1940] AC 880, and *Goldman* v. *Hargrave* [1967] 1 AC 645. We are concerned with the liability of a person where a nuisance has been created by one for whose actions he is responsible. Here, as I have said, it is still the law that the fact that the defendant has taken all reasonable care will not of itself exonerate him from liability, the relevant control mechanism being found within the principle of reasonable user. But it by no means follows that the defendant should be held liable for damage of a type which he could not reasonably foresee; and the development of the law of negligence in the past 60 years points strongly towards a requirement that such foreseeability should be a prerequisite of liability in damages for nuisance, as it is of liability in negligence. For if a plaintiff is in ordinary circumstances only able to claim damages in respect of personal injuries where he can prove such foreseeability on the part of the defendant, it is difficult to see why, in common justice, he should be in a stronger position to claim damages for interference with the enjoyment of his land where the defendant was unable to foresee such damage. Moreover, this appears to have been the conclusion of the Privy Council in *Overseas Tankship (U.K.) Ltd.* v. *Miller Steamship Co. Pty. (The Wagon Mound (No 2))* [1967] 1 AC 617 . . .

It is widely accepted that this conclusion, although not essential to the decision of the particular case, has nevertheless settled the law to the effect that foreseeability of harm is indeed a prerequisite of the recovery of damages in private nuisance, as in the case of public nuisance . . .

Foreseeability of damage under the rule in *Rylands* v. *Fletcher*

It is against this background that I turn to the submission advanced by ECL before your Lordships that there is a similar prerequisite of recovery of damages under the rule in *Rylands* v. *Fletcher*.

I start with the judgment of Blackburn J in *Fletcher* v. *Rylands*, (1866) LR 1 Exch 265 itself. His celebrated statement of the law is to be found at 279–80 where he said:

'We think the true rule of law is, that the person who for his own purposes brings on his lands and collects and keeps there anything likely to do mischief if it escapes, must keep it in at his peril, and, if he does not do so, is prima facie answerable for all the damage which is the natural consequence of its escape. He can excuse himself by showing that the escape was owing to the plaintiff's default; or perhaps that the escape was the consequence of vis major, or the act of God . . . The general rule, as above stated, seems on principle just. The person whose grass or corn is eaten down by the escaping cattle of his neighbour, or whose mine is flooded by the water from his neighbour's reservoir, or whose cellar is invaded by the filth of the neighbour's privy, or whose habitation is made unhealthy by the fumes and noisome vapours of his neighbour's alkali works, is damnified without any fault of his own; and it seems but reasonable and just that the neighbour, who has brought something on his own property which was not naturally there, harmless to others so long as it is confined to his own property, but which he knows to be mischievous if it gets on his neighbour's, should be obliged to make good the damage which ensues if he does not succeed in confining it to his own property'

. . . The general tenor of his statement of principle is therefore that knowledge, or at least foreseeability of the risk, is a prerequisite of the recovery of damages under the principle; but that the principle is one of strict liability in the sense that the defendant may be held liable notwithstanding that he has exercised all due care to prevent the escape from occurring . . . [Lord Goff then distinguishes case law which might have led to the opposite conclusion and surveys legal writings on the issue.]

Even so, the question cannot be considered solely as a matter of history. It can be argued that the rule in *Rylands* v. *Fletcher* should not be regarded simply as an extension of the law of nuisance, but should rather be treated as a developing principle of strict liability from which can be derived a general rule of strict liability for damage caused by ultra-hazardous operations, on the basis of which persons conducting such operations may properly be held strictly liable for the extraordinary risk to others involved in such operations. As is pointed out in *Fleming on the Law of Torts* [8th edn. (North Ryde: Law Book Co., 1992)] at 327–328, this would lead to the practical result that the cost of damage resulting from such operations would have to be absorbed as part of the overheads of the relevant business rather than be borne (where there is no negligence) by the injured person or his insurers, or even by the community at large. Such a development appears to have been taking place in the United States, as can be seen from section 519 of the *Restatement of the Law of Torts (Second)*, vol 3, [(St-Paul: American Law Institute, 1977)] at 34–36 . . .

I have to say, however, that there are serious obstacles in the way of the development of the rule in *Rylands* v. *Fletcher* in this way . . .

I incline to the opinion that, as a general rule, it is more appropriate for strict liability in respect of operations of high risk to be imposed by Parliament, than by the courts. If such liability is imposed by statute, the relevant activities can be identified, and those concerned can know where they stand. Furthermore, statute can where appropriate lay down precise criteria establishing the incidence and scope of such liability.

It is of particular relevance that the present case is concerned with environmental pollution. The protection and preservation of the environment is now perceived as being of crucial importance to the future of mankind; and public bodies, both national and international, are taking significant steps towards the establishment of legislation which will promote the protection of the environment, and make the polluter pay for damage to the environment for which he is responsible—as can be seen from the WHO, EEC and national regulations to which I have previously referred. But it does not follow from these developments that a common law principle, such as the rule in *Rylands* v. *Fletcher*, should be developed or rendered more strict to provide for liability in respect of such pollution. On the contrary, given that so much well-informed and carefully structured legislation is now being put in place for this purpose, there is less need for the courts to develop a common law principle to achieve the same end, and indeed it may well be undesirable that they should do so.

Having regard to these considerations . . . it appears to me to be appropriate now to take the view that foreseeability of damage of the relevant type should be regarded as a prerequisite of liability in damages under the rule. Such a conclusion can, as I have already stated, be derived from Blackburn J.'s original statement of the law; and I can see no good reason why this prerequisite should not be recognised under the rule, as it has been in the case of private nuisance . . . It would moreover lead to a more coherent body of common law principles if the rule were to be regarded essentially as an extension of the law of nuisance to cases of isolated escapes from land, even though the rule as established is not limited to escapes which are in fact isolated. I wish to point out, however, that in truth the escape of the PCE from ECL's land, in the form of trace elements carried in percolating water, has not been an isolated escape, but a continuing escape resulting from a state of affairs which has come into existence at the base of the chalk aquifer underneath ECL's premises. Classically, this would have been regarded as a case of nuisance; and it would seem strange if, by characterising the case as one falling under the rule in *Rylands* v. *Fletcher*, the liability should thereby be rendered more strict in the circumstances of the present case.

[Lord Goff then proceeded to apply the above to the facts of the case, which led him to allow the appeal.]"

Notes

(1) In the annotated judgment, the House of Lords has put in jeopardy the continuing existence of the rule in *Rylands* v. *Fletcher* as an autonomous cause of action. Lord Goff has sought to re-establish this rule as but an instance of nuisance, saying that the rule in *Rylands* v. *Fletcher* should preferably "be regarded essentially as an extension of the law of nuisance to cases of isolated escapes from land, even though the rule as established is not limited to escapes which are in fact isolated".[387] In fact, Lord Goff brings the rule in *Rylands* v. *Fletcher* closer to nuisance not only by introducing in it as well the requirement of reasonable foreseeability of damage of the kind that occurred, but also in *obiter dicta* by drawing a parallel between the criterion of reasonable user in nuisance and that of natural use under the rule in *Rylands* v. *Fletcher*.

(2) Lord Goff refers to the principle of reasonable user, i.e. "the principle of give and take as between neighbouring occupiers of land". It is important to note that, because of that principle, liability in private nuisance is dependent not only on the *extent of the interference* with the plaintiff's enjoyment of his or her land, but also in some cases on the *circumstances surrounding the use* by the defendant of his or her property that gives rise to the alleged nuisance.

Thus, one has to tolerate the noise made by the crying baby of one's neighbour, even if the baby is unusually fractious. But if one's neighbour records the cries of a baby and plays the record in order to annoy one, the neighbour is liable in nuisance because of his motive or lack of legitimate interest.[388] On the other hand, certain beneficial aspects of the ownership of property are not protected by the common law: for example, one has no legal right to a view (one's right is limited to a right to adequate light reaching windows of one's house, etc.); similarly, one has no right to receive in the subsoil of one's land percolating water coming from neighbouring land (one's right is limited to a right to receive water flowing through or beside one's land in a natural, defined channel). In these latter cases, a bad motive or malice will not render the blocking of the view or the interruption and diversion of the percolating water an actionable tort.[389] Conversely, the mere fact that one is making a profitable or enjoyable use of one's land and is not motivated by a desire to annoy one's neighbour will

---

[387] See Rogers at 538–43.

[388] See *Clerk & Lindsell on Torts* at 897, para. 18-14. See also *Miller* v. *Jackson* [1977] QB 966, [1977] 3 All ER 338, CA. It would seem that in that case Lord Denning MR basically felt that playing cricket on a cricket field was an ordinary and reasonable use of property and should be treated as covered by the give and take principle. Geoffrey Lane LJ felt that the principle did not apply where the conduct complained of caused physical damage to property and threatened to cause serious physical injury.

[389] See *Clerk & Lindsell on Torts* at 928–9, 936, para. 18-75, 18-92.

generally not constitute a defence to an action for nuisance if the interference with the neighbour's enjoyment of his or her land is objectively unreasonable—motive is relevant only in what may be described as "live and let live" or "give and take" situations—i.e. situations in which, on occasions, those who live in a society have to put up with inconvenience as a normal incident of living in the society.

(3) Although nuisance was no longer an issue before the House of Lords in *Cambridge Water Co.* v. *Eastern Counties Leather Plc*, Lord Goff dealt with both the law of nuisance and the rule in *Rylands* v. *Fletcher*, in view of his position on the relationship between the two. As a consequence, he was of the opinion that for both torts "foreseeability of damage of the relevant type should be regarded as a prerequisite of liability in damages". Nonetheless, liability under both causes of action should still be regarded as strict, in the sense that the defendant may be held liable notwithstanding that he or she has exercised all due care to prevent the nuisance, or the escape, from occurring.[390] On that basis, in the instant case, applying the rule in *Rylands* v. *Fletcher*, Lord Goff was led to reject the claim of the plaintiff, since at the relevant time the defendant could not reasonably have foreseen that the damage in question might occur.

Even if he disposed of the case on the ground that damage of the kind that occurred was not reasonably foreseeable, Lord Goff briefly addressed another issue in *obiter dicta*, namely whether the *exception to liability* based on "natural use" of the land could be relied on if the rule in *Rylands* v. *Fletcher* would otherwise have been applicable. He dismissed the arguments of the defendant on this point, finding that "the storage of substantial quantities of chemicals on industrial premises should be regarded as an almost classic case of non-natural use".

(4) It is not easy—and often of little practical interest—"to define the frontiers between negligence and nuisance", as Geoffrey Lane LJ remarked in *Miller* v. *Jackson*.[391] In *Goldman* v. *Hargrave*[392] and *Sedleigh-Denfield* v. *O'Callaghan*,[393] a nuisance had arisen through natural causes or by the act of a person for whose actions the defendant was not responsible. In these cases, it was established that the occupier of the land cannot be liable in nuisance unless he or she allows the nuisance to continue once it is discovered; however, the occupier is only held to "what is reasonable to expect of him in his individual circumstances".[394] This standard is formulated in terms very similar to the standard of negligence; in fact, as stated by Lord Wilberforce, it is even more favourable to the defendant than the more objective negligence standard. In the annotated judgment Lord Goff confirmed, *obiter*, that, in such instances, "the applicable principles in nuisance have become closely associated with those applicable in negligence".

(5) In his speech, Lord Goff referred to the use of *Rylands* v. *Fletcher* in the area of environmental pollution. In his opinion, it is for Parliament rather than for the courts to provide for strict liability in that area. And, indeed, as he points out, significant steps have been taken, at national, supranational and international level to develop a specific regime of liability for environmental damage, usually based on the principle that the polluter should pay for the damage caused. In England, the common law of nuisance has thus

---

[390] See further Rogers' comments on the annotated judgment at 506 ff.
[391] [1977] QB 966, [1977] 3 All ER 338, CA.
[392] [1967] 1 AC 645, [1966] 2 All ER 989, PC.
[393] [1940] AC 880, [1940] 3 All ER 349, HL.
[394] Lord Wilberforce in *Goldman* v. *Hargrave* [1967] 1 AC 645 at 663, [1966] 2 All ER 989, PC; see further Rogers at 519 ff.

been supplemented and to a large extent replaced by an array of statutory powers designed to control environmental damage.[395] The main statute is the Environmental Protection Act 1990.[396]

Court of Appeal[397]   **2.E.36.**

Spartan Steel & Alloys Ltd. v. *Martin & Co Ltd.*

ECONOMIC LOSS

Power cable

The plaintiff can recover in negligence for damage to his or her property and other loss directly consequential thereupon, including economic loss ("parasitic" economic loss). "Pure" economic loss, not consequential on property damage, cannot be recovered because the defendant does not owe the plaintiff a duty of care with respect to such loss.

Facts: The defendants' employees were digging up a road when they negligently damaged a power cable, which the defendants knew was the direct power supply from the electricity board's power station to the plaintiff's factory. The plaintiff was without electricity until the board was able to repair the cable. Because of this power failure, it had to pour molten metal out of its furnace to prevent damage to the furnace. The plaintiff claimed compensation for: (i) the physical damage to the melt in the furnace at the time of the power cut (GBP 368); (ii) the loss of profit on that melt (GBP 400); and (iii) the loss of profit on four other melts which normally could have been carried out during the period of the power cut (GBP 1,767).

Held: The Court of Appeal held that the plaintiff was entitled to recover for the physical damage and the loss of profit on the melt in the furnace at the time of the power cut (items (i) and (ii) above), but not for the loss of profit on the four hypothetical melts (item (iii) above).

Judgment: LORD DENNING MR: "At bottom I think the question of recovering economic loss is one of policy. Whenever the courts draw a line to mark out the bounds of *duty*, they do it as matter of policy so as to limit the responsibility of the defendant. Whenever the courts set bounds to the *damages* recoverable—saying that they are, or are not, too remote—they do it as matter of policy so as to limit the liability of the defendant.

In many of the cases where economic loss has been held not to be recoverable, it has been put on the ground that the defendant was under no *duty* to the plaintiff. Thus where a person is injured in a road accident by the negligence of another, the negligent driver owes a duty to the injured man himself, but he owes no duty to the servant of the injured man [references omitted]; nor to the master of the injured man [references omitted]; nor to anyone else who suffers loss because he had a contract with the injured man [references omitted] nor indeed to anyone who only suffers economic loss on account of the accident: [references omitted]. Likewise, when property is damaged by the negligence of another, the negligent tortfeasor owes a duty to the owner or possessor of the chattel, but not to one who suffers loss only because he had a contract entitling him to use the chattel or giving him a right to receive it at some later date [references omitted].

In other cases, however, the defendant seems clearly to have been under a duty to the plaintiff, but the economic loss has not been recovered because it is *too remote*. Take the illustration given by Blackburn J. in *Cattle* v. *Stockton Waterworks Co.* (1875) LR 10 QB 453 at 457, when water escapes

---

[395] Rogers at 490; *Clerk & Lindsell on Torts* at 890–1, para. 18-03.
[396] See *infra*, 5.2.A.
[397] [1973] QB 27, [1972] 3 All ER 557.

from a reservoir and floods a coal mine where many men are working. Those who had their tools or clothes destroyed could recover: but those who only lost their wages could not. Similarly, when the defendants' ship negligently sank a ship which was being towed by a tug, the owner of the tug lost his remuneration, but he could not recover it from the negligent ship: though the same duty (of navigation with reasonable care) was owed to both tug and tow: see *Société Anonyme de Remorquage à Hélice* v. *Bennetts* [1911] 1 KB 243 at 248. In such cases if the plaintiff or his property had been physically injured, he would have recovered: but, as he only suffered economic loss, he is held not entitled to recover. This is, I should think, because the loss is regarded by the law as too remote: see *King* v. *Phillips* [1953] 1 QB 429 at 439-440.

On the other hand, in the cases where economic loss by itself has been held to be recoverable, it is plain that there was a duty to the plaintiff and the loss was not too remote. Such as when one ship negligently runs down another ship, and damages it, with the result that the cargo has to be discharged and reloaded. The negligent ship was already under a duty to the cargo owners: and they can recover the cost of discharging and reloading it, as it is not too remote: see *Morrison Steamship Co.* v. *Greystoke Castle (Cargo Owners)* [1947] AC 265. Likewise, when a banker negligently gives a reference to one who acts on it, the duty is plain and the damage is not too remote: see *Hedley Byrne & Co. Ltd.* v. *Heller & Partners Ltd.* [1964] AC 465, [1963] 2 All ER 575 (HL).

The more I think about these cases, the more difficult I find it to put each into its proper pigeon-hole. Sometimes I say: 'There was no duty'. In others I say: 'The damage was too remote'. So much so that I think the time has come to discard those tests which have proved so elusive. It seems to me better to consider the particular relationship in hand, and see whether or not, as a matter of policy, economic loss should be recoverable, or not [emphasis added] . . .

So I turn to the relationship in the present case. It is of common occurrence. The parties concerned are: the electricity board who are under a statutory duty to maintain supplies of electricity in their district; the inhabitants of the district, including this factory, who are entitled by statute to a continuous supply of electricity for their use; and the contractors who dig up the road. Similar relationships occur with other statutory bodies, such as gas and water undertakings. The cable may be damaged by the negligence of the statutory undertaker, or by the negligence of the contractor, or by accident without any negligence by anyone: and the power may have to be cut off whilst the cable is repaired. Or the power may be cut off owing to a short-circuit in the power house: and so forth. If the cutting off of the supply causes economic loss to the consumers, should it as matter of policy be recoverable? And against whom?

The first consideration is the position of the statutory undertakers. If the board do not keep up the voltage or pressure of electricity, gas or water—or, likewise, if they shut it off for repairs—and thereby cause economic loss to their consumers, they are not liable in damages, not even if the cause of it is due to their own negligence. The only remedy (which is hardly ever pursued) is to prosecute the board before the magistrates. Such is the result of many cases . . . But one thing is clear: the statutory undertakers have never been held liable for economic loss only. If such be the policy of the legislature in regard to electricity boards, it would seem right for the common law to adopt a similar policy in regard to contractors. If the electricity boards are not liable for economic loss due to negligence which results in the cutting off the supply, nor should a contractor be liable.

The second consideration is the nature of the hazard, namely, the cutting of the supply of electricity. This is a hazard which we all run. It may be due to a short circuit, to a flash of lightning, to a tree falling on the wires, to an accidental cutting of the cable, or even to the negligence of someone or other. And when it does happen, it affects a multitude of persons: not as a rule by way of physical damage to them or their property, but by putting them to inconvenience, and sometimes to economic loss. The supply is usually restored in a few hours, so the economic loss is not very large. Such a hazard is regarded by most people as a thing they must put up with—without seeking compensation from anyone. Some there are who install a stand-by system. Others seek refuge by taking out an insurance policy against breakdown in the supply. But most people are content to take the risk on themselves. When the supply is cut off, they do not go running round to their solicitor. They do not try to find out whether it was anyone's fault. They just put up with it. They try to make up the economic loss by doing more work next day. This is a healthy attitude which the law should encourage.

The third consideration is this: if claims for economic loss were permitted for this particular hazard, there would be no end of claims. Some might be genuine, but many might be inflated, or even false. A machine might not have been in use anyway, but it would be easy to put it down to the cut in supply. It would be well-nigh impossible to check the claims. If there was economic loss on one day, did the claimant do his best to mitigate it by working harder next day? And so forth. Rather than expose claimants to such temptation and defendants to such hard labour—on comparatively small claims—it is better to disallow economic loss altogether, at any rate when it stands alone, independent of any physical damage.

The fourth consideration is that, in such a hazard as this, the risk of economic loss should be suffered by the whole community who suffer the losses—usually many but comparatively small losses—rather than on the one pair of shoulders, that is on the contractor on whom the total of them, all added together, might be very heavy.

The fifth consideration is that the law provides for deserving cases. If the defendant is guilty of negligence which cuts off the electricity supply and causes actual physical damage to person or property, that physical damage can be recovered [references omitted]. Such cases will be comparatively few. They will be readily capable of proof and will be easily checked. They should be and are admitted.

These considerations lead me to the conclusion that the plaintiffs should recover for the physical damage to the one melt (GBP 368), and the loss of profit on that melt consequent thereon (GBP 400): but not for the loss of profit on the four melts (GBP 1,767), because that was economic loss independent of the physical damage. I would, therefore, allow the appeal and reduce the damages to GBP 768."

EDMUND DAVIES LJ (dissenting): "The facts giving rise to this appeal have already been set out by Lord Denning MR . . . The problem may be thus stated: Where a defendant who owes a duty of care to the plaintiff breaches that duty and, as both a direct and a reasonably foreseeable result of that injury, the plaintiff suffers only economic loss, is he entitled to recover damages for that loss?
. . .

In my respectful judgment, however it may formerly have been regarded, the law is today [in favour of the recovery of such damages]. I am conscious of the boldness involved in expressing this view, particularly after studying such learned dissertations as that of Professor Atiyah on "Negligence and Economic Loss" (1967) 83 LQR 248, where the relevant cases are cited. I recognize that proof of the necessary linkage between negligent acts and purely economic consequences may be hard to forge. *I accept, too, that if economic loss of itself confers a right of action this may spell disaster for the negligent party. But this may equally be the outcome where physical damage alone is sustained, or where physical damage leads directly to economic loss* [emphasis added]. Nevertheless, when this occurs it was accepted in *S.C.M. (United Kingdom) Ltd.* v. *W.J. Whittall & Son Ltd.* [1971] 1 QB 337 that compensation is recoverable for both types of damage. It follows that this must be regardless of whether the injury (physical or economic, or a mixture of both) is immense or puny, diffused over a wide area or narrowly localised, provided only that the requirements as to foreseeability and directness are fulfilled. I therefore find myself unable to accept as factors determinant of legal principle those considerations of policy canvassed in the concluding passages of the judgment just delivered by Lord Denning MR . . .

For my part, I cannot see why the GBP 400 loss of profit here sustained should be recoverable and not the GBP 1,767. It is common ground that both types of loss were equally foreseeable and equally direct consequences of the defendants' admitted negligence, and the only distinction drawn is that the former figure represents the profit lost as a result of the physical damage done to the material in the furnace at the time when power was cut off. But what has that purely fortuitous fact to do with legal principle? In my judgment, nothing . . .

Such good sense as I possess guides me to the conclusion that it would be wrong to draw in the present case any distinction between the first, spoilt 'melt' and the four 'melts' which, but for the defendants' negligence, would admittedly have followed it. That is simply another way of saying that I consider the plaintiffs are entitled to recover the entirety of the financial loss they sustained [emphasis added] . . ."

Notes

(1) Weir comments on the above judgment as follows:[398]

"A person's chances of obtaining the money he is claiming depend on what he is claiming it for and who he is claiming it from: in other words, both the type of injury he has suffered and the nature of his relationship with the defendant are material, perhaps vital, considerations.

Since *Donoghue* v. *Stevenson* people who act dangerously may have to pay even a complete stranger if the harm they cause is physical. So here *Spartan Steel* recovered for the physical harm they suffered (damage to the ore) but not for the purely financial harm (lost profits or undamaged ore), though both results were equally foreseeable. Plaintiff and defendant were total strangers to each other. In *Muirhead* v. *Industrial Tank Specialities* [1985] 3 All E.R. 705, C.A., the careless manufacturer of a defective recycling pump had to pay the ultimate purchaser for the damage to his property (dead lobsters) but not the purely financial harm resulting from business interruption. But while in *Spartan Steel* the parties were complete strangers, in *Muirhead* they were not: they were in the relationship of consumer and manufacturer. As *Donoghue* v. *Stevenson* laid down, that is a special relationship, but when it comes to liability for purely economic loss, is not special enough . . .

The economic loss in *Spartan Steel* occurred through the defendant's damaging an electricity cable which belonged to a third party. In cases where property has been damaged by carelessness the courts have long held that only those with a proprietary or possessory interest in that property may bring an action, not those who have merely a financial interest in the well-being of the property, whether that interest be positive, in the sense that they stand to gain if the property remains unimpaired, or negative, in the sense that they will have to pay out if it is damaged or destroyed. There are masses of cases: . . ."

Weir is of the opinion that the position adopted by the Court of Appeal in *Spartan Steel* is both right and convenient, which certainly represents the majority opinion in English law. The reasons invoked by Weir are so-called "policy considerations", discussed at length in Lord Denning's opinion. The main argument is that "if claims for economic loss were permitted for this particular hazard, there would be no end of claims". As illustrated by Edmund Davies LJ's dissenting opinion, the opposite view is not without foundation: indeed the distinction between, on the one hand, lost profits consequential upon damage to the plaintiff's own property, and on the other hand, those flowing from damage to third party property from which the plaintiff is entitled to draw benefit, appears artificial. This point of view is not challenged by Lord Denning MR, who himself admits that the more he thinks about the cases, the more difficult he finds it to put each into their proper "pigeon-hole".

[398] At 60–1.

(2) As shown by the judgment of the Court of Appeal in *Muirhead* v. *Industrial Tank Specialities*,[399] mentioned above, compensation for pure economic loss (lost profits) resulting from an interruption in the course of a business is denied regardless of whether the parties were complete strangers (as in *Spartan Steel*) or were in a relationship of consumer and manufacturer (as in *Muirhead*, which is about defective goods[400]). In all of these instances, only physical damage to property either owned by or in the possession of the plaintiff and damage directly consequential thereon, like lost profits, are recoverable in negligence. Conversely, the law of negligence does not allow recovery for lost profits on property for which the plaintiff bears the risk, without however being the owner or possessor of it; such was the case in *Leigh and Sillavan Ltd.* v. *Aliakmon Shipping Co.*[401] As a consequence, a mere financial or commercial interest in the maintenance of a piece of property or in the well-being of a person does not as a rule suffice for a valid claim at common law. Thus, as Lord Denning MR mentions, "where a person is injured in a road accident by the negligence of another, the negligent driver owes a duty to the injured man himself, but he owes no duty to the servant of the injured man who e.g. is no longer paid his salary. He does not owe a duty, *a fortiori*, to those who as a consequence of a traffic jam resulting from the accident, are affected in their business or earnings".[402]

(3) *Muirhead*, mentioned above, concerned pure economic loss in connection with defective products (a water pump). Liability for defective products has proved to be one of the most controversial issues in English tort law in the past decades. It is beyond question that the manufacturer of defective products is liable under contract law to the other contracting party according to the terms of the contract. However, the common law doctrine of privity of contract is very strict, and accordingly subsequent acquirors of the product in question have in principle no direct contractual recourse against the manufacturer. By contrast, since *Donoghue* v. *Stevenson*,[403] it is also well established that there is a recourse under tort law against the manufacturer of a product which actually causes harm to a person or to property (other than the product itself). The remaining question is whether the manufacturer can be held liable in tort for the economic loss (loss in value and/or cost of repair) that ensues from defective products which have not caused harm to a person or to property.

This question was addressed by the House of Lords in *Murphy* v. *Brentwood District Council*,[404] where the House of Lords overruled its earlier decision in *Anns* v. *Merton London Borough Council*.[405] Both cases concerned the liability of local authorities for defective buildings, given that, under English law, the local authorities had to approve building plans. In both cases, the plaintiffs had bought houses the foundations of which had turned out to be defective, although the plans had been approved by the local authority (in *Anns*, the houses had not been built according to the plans submitted to the authority, and in *Murphy*, the plans should normally not have been approved by the authority). In both cases, the plaintiffs had in consequence suffered a loss in the value of their houses

---

[399] [1986] QB 507, [1985] 3 All ER 705, CA.
[400] See Rogers at 140 ff.
[401] [1986] AC 785, HL.
[402] Compare with Cass. civ. 2e, 28 April 1965, *infra*, **2.F.40.**
[403] *Supra*, Chapter I, **1.E.23.**
[404] [1991] 1 AC 398, [1990] 2 All ER 269, HL.
[405] [1978] AC 728, HL.

and were faced with costly repairs. In *Anns*, the House of Lords characterized the loss as physical damage, and found that the local authority was under a "duty to take reasonable care . . . to secure that the builder does not cover in foundations which do not comply with byelaw requirements".[406] In *Murphy*, the House of Lords corrected the characterization made in *Anns*, and rightly found that the loss to the plaintiff was in fact pure economic loss. The House of Lords was then squarely faced with the issue of liability for economic loss arising from defective products. It unanimously rejected the idea that the manufacturer of products or the builder of a house (or the local authority approving building plans) is under any duty of care in respect of defects in products, or buildings, which cause purely economic loss. Lord Bridge formulated the relevant principles as follows:[407]

> "If a manufacturer negligently puts into circulation a chattel containing a latent defect which renders it dangerous to persons or property, the manufacturer, on the well-known principles established by *Donoghue* v. *Stevenson* [1932] AC 562, will be liable in tort for injury to persons or damage to property which the chattel causes. But if a manufacturer produces and sells a chattel which is merely defective in quality, even to the extent that it is valueless for the purpose for which it is intended, the manufacturer's liability at common law arises only under and by reference to the terms of any contract to which he is a party in relation to the chattel; the common law does not impose on him any liability in tort to persons to whom he owes no duty in contract but who, having acquired the chattel, suffer economic loss because the chattel is *defective in quality*. If a dangerous defect in a chattel is discovered before it causes any personal injury or damage to property, because the danger is now known and the chattel cannot be safely used unless the defect is repaired, the defect becomes merely a defect in quality. The chattel is either capable of repair at economic cost or it is worthless and must be scrapped. In either case the loss sustained by the owner or hirer of the chattel is purely economic. It is recoverable against any party who owes the loser a relevant contractual duty. But it is not recoverable in tort in the absence of a special relationship of proximity imposing on the tortfeasor a duty of care to safeguard the plaintiff from economic loss. There is no such special relationship between the manufacturer of a chattel and a remote owner or hirer.
>
> I believe that these principles are equally applicable to buildings. If a builder erects a structure containing a latent defect which renders it dangerous to persons or property, he will be liable in tort for injury to persons or damage to property resulting from that dangerous defect. But, if the defect becomes apparent before any injury or damage has been caused, the loss sustained by the building owner is purely economic. If the defect can be repaired at economic cost, that is the measure of the loss. If the building cannot be repaired, it may have to be abandoned as unfit for occupation and therefore valueless. These economic losses are recoverable if they flow from breach of a relevant contractual duty, but, here again, in the absence of a special relationship of proximity they are not recoverable in tort".

As was discussed above, the impact of *Anns* and *Murphy* goes beyond the issue of liability for defective products.[408] It must be noted, however, that following *Murphy*, there is in principle no duty of care on manufacturers towards subsequent acquirors of their products for defects which have not caused injury to a person or to property. This conclusion has been criticized in English legal writing.[409]

---

[406] Ibid. at 758.
[407] [1991] 1 AC 398 at 475, HL.
[408] *Supra*, Chapter I, 1.4.1.B.
[409] See, amongst others, Markesinis and Deakin at 109.

(4) *Spartan Steel* is most frequently referred to for its ruling with regard to damage for which compensation is not available and hardly ever for what it holds as regards damage for which compensation is possible, namely physical damage to the melt in the furnace at the time of the power cut *and* economic loss consisting of loss of profit *on* that melt, that is economic loss consequential upon the physical injury to property. The latter point seems to be considered so well-established in English law that it is self-evident (but see Edmund-Davies LJ's dissenting speech).

However, the recent judgment of the House of Lords in *Marc Rich & Co. AG* v. *Bishop Rock Marine Co. Ltd.* demonstrates that this is not necessarily so.[410] In the leading speech in that case Lord Steyn mentioned that it is incorrect to state, as had been argued, that in cases of physical damage to property, the only requirement for a duty of care to arise is reasonable foreseeability. Lord Steyn said that, since *Dorset Yacht*,[411] "it has been settled law that the elements of foreseeability and proximity as well as considerations of fairness, justice and reasonableness are relevant to all cases whatever the nature of the harm sustained by the plaintiff ".[412] Policy considerations, which can come into play at the stage of "fairness, justice and reasonableness" to deny the existence of a duty of care, can therefore intervene in all negligence cases, irrespective of the type of damage suffered by the victim.

2.3.2. GERMAN LAW

Introductory Note

a) After the human person and personality itself, ownership is the most significant amongst the *Rechtsgüter* deserving protection under § 823(1) BGB. The protection of § 823(1) BGB extends in the first place to culpable interferences with the *substance* of owned property, whether immoveable or moveable or whether the interference consists in damaging property (such as in a car accident), taking it away, detaining it, entering land or encroaching upon it, or even denigrating the quality of property.[413]

For instance, Mertens brings quite a wide class of actions under the concept of infringement of ownership (*Eigentumverletzung*):[414] "There is an infringement of ownership where the owner is deprived of possession of property. Since, in regard to the property, the owner's area of freedom is protected . . . , there is also an infringement of ownership in the event of any physical effect on the property which diminishes its useability in the manner intended by the owner. If for example the wall of a house is plastered against the will of the owner who wished to have it painted, § 823(1) applies. Fouling or disfigurement of a property may also be deemed to constitute an infringement of ownership, even if in the circumstances there is no substantial infringement. The removal of a property from the location designated for it by the owner may also be regarded as an infringement of ownership, as too may the writing of graffiti or the affixing of unauthorized posters, as well as the use of a right of way contrary to its dedication when it is dedicated to only a limited extent as a public thoroughfare or the occupancy of a house to the detriment of the normal use of the premises".

b) The protection afforded by § 823(1) BGB also extends to interferences with the *use and enjoyment* of property, although it is not entirely clear how far that protection reaches.

---

[410] [1996] 1 AC 211, [1995] 3 WLR 227, [1995] 3 All ER 307, HL.
[411] *Home Office* v. *Dorset Yacht Co.* [1970] AC 1004, [1970] 2 All ER 294, HL.
[412] [1996] 1 AC 211 at 235, [1995] 3 WLR 227, HL.
[413] See § 824 BGB and further Larenz/Canaris at 386 ff., Mertens at 1476–81, para. 112–22.
[414] Münchener—Mertens, § 823 at 1476–7, para. 112, footnotes omitted. Translation by N. Sims.

The waterway and oil tanker cases are in point here. Thus, in a judgment of 21 December 1970, the BGH ordered the Federal Republic of Germany to compensate the plaintiff for the *economic loss* which it suffered because its motor vessel had been immobilized for eight months at a mill without being able to leave.[415] The vessel was moored to take goods for transport under a contract with the owner of the mill. This lengthy immobilization was due to the closure of the waterway leading to the mill for repair work. The BGH refused however to grant the plaintiff damages for the loss sustained by reason of the fact that, because of the closure of the waterway, three further other vessels could not reach the mill to take goods on board, as the plaintiff was contractually bound to do.

The difference in treatment is explained by Larenz/Canaris by distinguishing between "lock-in" (*Einsperrung*) and "lock-out" (*Aussperrung*). In the first situation, the vessel cannot be put to other uses, as it is immobilized at the mill and cannot go elsewhere. In the second situation, the three other vessels are not prevented from moving but only from reaching the mill. They can be put to use to fulfil other contracts. Indeed, in the second situation ownership of the vessel does not include a claim to use property of a third person (in this case the waterway) in a certain way, whilst in the first situation ownership is affected in itself since the owner is deprived of the use of its property for a lengthy period.[416]

A similar situation arose in the oil tanker case decided by the BGH on 21 June 1977.[417] In that case, a fire broke out in the neighbourhood of the plaintiff's business premises, owing to the negligence of the defendants and of the driver of a tanker loaded with oil. Fearing that the fire might spread, the police ordered the temporary closure of the plaintiff's premises for two hours and blocked the access roads to the premises for another three hours. The BGH held that damages could be awarded only for the first two hours of evacuation, when the entitlement of the plaintiff to use its premises was directly curtailed, and not for the subsequent three hours of blockade, when the plaintiff was deprived only of the use of a public highway (albeit the only one that led to its premises).

Larenz/Canaris justify the waterway and oil tanker cases by focusing on the relationship between the damage and the purpose of protection (*Schutzzweckzusammenhang*), which leads to a distinction between interferences with the substance of property (*Substanzschaden*) and with the ability to use it for a particular purpose (*Gebrauchsschaden*). In the case of the locked-in ship and of the evacuated premises, the owner was for all intents and purposes deprived of its ownership, since the property could not be used at all and had become worthless (even if only temporarily). The core of ownership is affected, and such loss bears a relationship to the protective purposes of § 823(1) BGB. On the other hand, the owners of the locked-out ships or the blockaded premises were merely deprived of the possibility of making use of a public water or highway. They could nonetheless use their goods for another purpose.[418]

Mertens on the other hand refers in this connection to the notion of market value (*Marktwert*):"Where the use of property is typically dependent upon the guarantee of certain physically defined environmental conditions, an alteration directly affecting the relationship of the property with its environment may be regarded as an infringement of ownership if it interferes with the use of property to such an extent that its market value is thereby diminished. The protection of socially typical modes of use must in this context be advocated simply because the law of torts protects things generally not for the sake of their factual existence but rather for the sake of their socially typical function. Focusing on the requirement that the interference must be reflected in a reduction of the market value . . . ensures that only the socially typical mode of use is protected. Secondly, it also ensures a reasonable demarcation between damage to property and pure economic loss not falling under § 823(1)."[419]

Mertens concludes that, when a motor vessel or business premises, to use the above examples, are unusable for some time (locked-in ship, evacuated premises), there is an interference with property within the meaning of

---

[415] BGHZ 55, 153.
[416] Larenz/Canaris at 388–9.
[417] NJW 1977, 2264. Translation by K. Lipstein in Markesinis at 198.
[418] Larenz/Canaris at 390–1.
[419] Münchener—Mertens, § 823 at 1477–8, para. 113, references omitted. Translation by N. Sims.

§ 823(1) BGB because the market value of the property is affected. That is not so when the disturbance results from the mere unavailability of an access way, because that does not affect the market value of the property.

c) All the aforementioned authors agree that drivers who get stuck in a traffic jam as a result of an accident caused by someone's reckless driving cannot recover for *opportunities* which in consequence they have *lost*. Larenz/Canaris reach this conclusion because, even though those drivers are locked in the traffic jam, much like the owners of the ship locked by the mill, it would not be consistent with the *Verkehrspflicht* imposed on an ordinary driver to make him or her liable under § 823(1) BGB, beyond physical injury or property damage, for the prejudice to the economic interests of the other drivers blocked in the traffic jam.[420] For Mertens, the reason would rather be that the market value of the cars that were immobilized in the traffic jam was not affected.[421] In the oil tanker case referred to above, the BGH also expressed the view that users of a public highway who have suffered material loss as a result of a traffic jam following an accident cannot claim damages under § 823(2) BGB either, as indeed it is not the purpose of traffic regulations to provide that type of protection.[422]

In this context, reference should also be made to the so-called cable cases, where the claimant typically had to cease its manufacturing operations for a period of time because of a power failure caused by someone negligently cutting a power line supplying the claimant's manufacturing plant. Liability under § 823(1) BGB arises in such a case, if material damage is inflicted on property, irrespective of whether such damage was a direct consequence of the negligent act or occurred only through a causal chain. In a judgment of 4 February 1964, the BGH had to rule on a case where the defendant had cut a power cable which fed egg incubators of the plaintiff. The BGH applied the following reasoning:[423]

> "If something requires the constant supply of water, electricity or the like in order to retain its substance and keep it from spoiling, any disturbance of the supply has the effect (in the legal sense) of annihilating that thing if it destroys it by cutting off the supply . . . Such things include all products which need an electrically-maintained constant temperature (heating or cooling) in order not to spoil. If such products are spoiled as a result of electricity cables being culpably severed and this reduces or destroys the sales value of the product, the material loss simply constitutes consequential damage arising out of property damage which is to be compensated for under § 823(1) BGB."

Because of the power failure, instead of the expected 3,000 chicks, only a few birds were produced from the eggs present in the incubator, and they were unsaleable. The BGH held on the basis of the aforementioned reasoning that the loss of income flowing from this damage to the plaintiff's eggs was recoverable from the defendant under § 823(1) BGB. The BGH contrasted this case with situations where no damage to property occurred:

---

[420] Larenz/Canaris at 389–90.
[421] Münchener—Mertens, § 823 at 1478, para. 114.
[422] See Markesinis at 202.
[423] BGHZ 41, 123 at 126, NJW 1964, 720. Translation by R. Bray.

"The position is different where the power cut does not cause things to be destroyed, but merely causes the production of particular products to be temporarily interrupted. That is *reiner Vermögensschaden*."[424]

d) As already stated above, the expression "other rights" in § 823(1) BGB is not meant to include all kinds of rights or legitimate interests.[425] With respect to property rights, the expression is understood to bring within the ambit of § 823(1) BGB (in addition to ownership which is expressly mentioned at § 823(1)) *not only* rights *in rem* falling short of ownership (e.g. the rights of a mortgagee or other holder of security) and interests in incorporeal property (in particular patents, trademarks and copyright), *but also* shareholders' rights, a lessee's entitlement to possession and the like.[426] Rights *in personam* (*obligatorische Forderungen*) typically flowing from contract, are not included because of their "relative" character; nor the general right over one's overall *Vermögen* included.

Due to the exclusion of the general right over the overall *Vermögen*, there has been a tendency to include also in the "other rights" a kind of general right relating to enterpreneurial property, namely the *Recht am Gewerbebetrieb*.[427] This "other right" has been developed in the BGH case law to cover many situations, such as (i) the disclosure of correct but prejudicial information[428] or of prejudicial assessments in product tests,[429] (ii) boycotts and blockades of enterprises and even (iii) strikes.[430] As shown by the second case below it must, under certain circumstances, give way to higher ranking rights, such as one's freedom of expression.[431]

In the first judgment below,[432] the BGH however concluded that the *Recht am Gewerbebetrieb* protects only against interferences directed against the business as a whole, and not against interferences with elements of the business which can easily be conceived separately from it (personnel, equipment, stock, etc.).

e) As shown by the judgment of the BGH in the cable case referred to in c) above, German law (like English law) admits recovery of *Vermögensschaden consequential upon* property damage; and German law does so, irrespective of how close or distant the causal link is between the tortious act and the property damage.

On the other hand, as the excerpt from Larenz/Canaris reproduced above shows, German tort law, much like English law, takes a harder stance towards *reiner Vermögensschaden*, that is *Vermögensschaden* divorced from any damage to the property of the plaintiff ("pure economic loss" in common law terms).[433] *Vermögensschaden* is perceived as less worthy of protection than bodily injury or damage to property, and it is feared that it is too indeterminate for it to be shifted onto the defendant.

---

[424] The BGH added at 126–7: "Nor can compensation for such loss be claimed on the ground of impermissible interference with a *Gewerbebetrieb*, since severing the cable does not constitute—at least not as a rule—an interference with the undertaking which is direct, that is to say, intimately connected with the business (BGHZ 29, 65 [see *infra*, **2.G.37.**])."

[425] *Supra*, Chapter I, 1.4.3., Introductory Note under a) and b) and 2.2.1., Introductory Note.

[426] Larenz/Canaris at 392 ff.

[427] In addition to, and even before, the general *Persönlichkeitsrecht*: *supra*, 2.2.1., Introductory Note.

[428] BGH, 28 November 1952, BGHZ 8, 142.

[429] BGH, 21 February 1989, NJW 1989, 1923.

[430] BGH, 10 May 1957, BGHZ 24, 200; BGH, 30 May 1972, BGHZ 59, 30. See further Larenz/Canaris at 546–60, Münchener—Mertens, § 823 at 1642–3, para. 481.

[431] *Infra*, **2.G.38.**

[432] *Infra*, **2.G.37.**

[433] *Supra*, Chapter I, **1.G.27.**

Reiner Vermögensschaden is only recoverable when:

– the interference directly and specifically prejudiced a business taken as a whole, in which case it is possible that the conditions for making out an infringement of the *Recht am Gewerbebetrieb* protected under § 823(1) BGB would be satisfied (see *supra*);
– the interference can be brought within the scope of protection of §§ 823(2)[434] or 826 BGB;[435]
– the interference can be brought within the ambit of a contractual claim based on the theory of contractual third party protection;
– the interference can be brought within the scope of protection of § 839 BGB (State liability) or of Community law.[436]

f) At § 906 BGB (in the book on property law), a special provision is made to enable the owner of land under certain conditions to act to prevent emissions from neighbouring land which affect his or her own piece of land. In short, action can be taken to prevent emissions from another piece of land which affect someone's land substantially (§ 906(1)), unless they are brought about by such a use of the other land as is common at that location (*eine ortsübliche Benutzung des anderen Grundstücks*) and cannot be avoided by measures which can economically be imposed on the user of that other land (*der Benutzer wirtschaftlich zumutbar*, first sentence of § 906(2)). When emissions, although substantial, must be tolerated by virtue of the foregoing, a reasonable compensation (*angemessene Ausgleich*) may become due (second sentence of § 906(2)).

As the third case below demonstrates, the standard laid down in § 906 BGB is also applied to decide tort claims brought pursuant to § 823(1) BGB by neighbouring landowners (or persons assimilated therewith), as well as owners of moveable property (such as cars parked on a neighbouring car-park) who have sustained property damage because of disturbances in the sense of § 906 (1) emanating from the defendant's land.[437] Not only is the substantive standard of § 906 BGB used by analogy to rule on claims of the latter category, but the rules on evidence which have been developed in BGH case law are also followed in these tort actions. That is significant for environmental cases as it eases the burden of proof on the plaintiff.

BGH, 9 December 1958[438]   **2.G.37.**

SCOPE OF THE *RECHT AM GEWERBEBETRIEB*

Power cable

There is no interference with the Recht am Gewerbebetrieb *when production must be stopped because of a power failure after an electricity cable has been cut.*

---

[434] This line of argument was carefully considered in yet another cable case decided by the BGH (8 June 1976, BGHZ 66, 388, NJW 1976, 1740, translation by F.H. Lawson and B.S. Markesinis in Markesinis at 180), in which it was held that the defendant's contravening § 18(3) of the Baden-Württemberg Building Regulations did not constitute a breach of an enactment designed for the plaintiff's protection.
[435] See *infra*, 2.4.2.
[436] See *infra*, Chapter III, 3.3.2. and Chapter IX, 9.1.
[437] *Infra*, **2.G.39.**
[438] BGHZ 29, 65, NJW 1959, 479. Translation by N. Sims.

Facts: An employee of the defendant, while operating an excavator, negligently ruptured an underground power cable, which served, from the place of the break onwards, only the plaintiff's business and factory. The plaintiff contended that the power cable formed part of its business from an economic point of view and that the defendant, in cutting the cable, had interfered illegally and culpably with its business and was liable for the loss caused by the interruption of production. The defendant argued that the plaintiff's business had been only indirectly affected by the cutting of the cable and that only direct interference would have rendered him liable.

Held: The court of first instance and the court of appeal allowed the claim but, upon further appeal, the claim was dismissed by the BGH.

Judgment: "a) The *Reichsgericht* [the predecessor of the BGH], in a constant line of authorities, acknowledged the *Recht am Gewerbebetrieb* as an 'other right' (*sonstiges Recht*) within the meaning of § 823(1) BGB. [There follows a description of the *Reichsgericht*'s case law and its evolution.]

Under the case law of the BGH, the protection of § 823(1) BGB is afforded in the event of any detriment to the *Recht am eingerichteten und ausgeübten Gewerbebetrieb*, when it constitutes a direct interference with the activitites of that enterprise.

b) [There follows a discussion of how the limits of this specific right, which is not formulated in § 823(1) BGB as it was not envisaged by the legislator, have to be drawn.]

c) The position continues, however, to be that, as the court of appeal rightly recognised, direct interference with the sphere of a commercial undertaking is a prerequisite of the applicability of § 823(1) BGB. [There follows a discussion of the notion of directness.]

By virtue of . . . consistent case law . . ., any unlawful direct interference with the sphere of activity of a commercial enterprise constitutes an infringement of the *Recht am eingerichteten und ausgeübten Gewerbebetrieb* protected under § 823(1) BGB, even if the infringement is directed not at the substance itself but against one of its manifestations; legal protection has been extended beyond the mere protection, as it was initially, of the substance of the commercial enterprise. *That is not to say that, under the guise of the protection of the* Recht am eingerichteten und ausgeübten Gewerbebetrieb, *the protection of rights* in personam (Forderungsrechte) *has been introduced surreptitiously; as opposed to absolute rights, such rights are binding only on certain persons and for that reason do not fall within the concept of 'other rights' within the meaning of § 823(1) BGB* [reference omitted]; *nor has the protection been extended to protection of the* Vermögen, *which as such enjoys protection in tort only under certain conditions (e.g. by way of § 826 BGB); both would be foreign to our legal system* [emphasis added] . . . In addition, the extent and limits within which the *Recht am eingerichteten und ausgeübten Gewerbebetrieb* is to be protected must be determined by an appropriate fleshing out of the notion of the "directness" of the interference.

Direct interferences with the *Recht am Gewerbebetrieb* which are covered by § 823(1) BGB are only those that are directed in some way against the business as such, that is to say that are related to the business (*betriebsbezogen*), and not those directed against rights or interests which are entirely severable from the business. All the cases in which the highest courts have found an infringement of the *Recht am eingerichteten und ausgeübten Gewerbebetrieb* were concerned with such business-related interferences. However, the rupture by the defendant or the driver of his excavator of the electricity cable leading to the plaintiff's undertaking is not specifically linked to the plaintiff's business any more than is the injury to an employee or damage to or destruction of a firm's vehicle . . . Moreover, the supply of electricity by cable and the right to such supply do not constitute an essential attribute of an established and operating commercial enterprise but rather constitute a relationship based on the duty to supply energy on the part of the supply companies, which is of the same nature as the relationship with other consumers of electricity, e.g. households and professionals. Damage to a cable on land not belonging to the undertaking affected, and the consequential interruption in the supply of current, cannot, in the absence of circumstances not applicable in the present case, be deemed to constitute a business-related interference with the activities of that undertaking."

Notes

(1) The annotated judgment concerns the *Recht am Gewerbebetrieb*, an 'other right' (in the sense of § 823(1) BGB) which evolved from the case law first of the *Reichsgericht*[439] and thereafter of the BGH. The early case law of the *Reichsgericht* dealt with interferences, in the field of unfair competition, industrial property rights and economic boycott, going to the *existence* of the business concerned by depriving it of actual or projected profit. In later case law, first the *Reichsgericht* and then the BGH relaxed the previously narrow scope of the *Recht am Gewerbebetrieb* by extending its application beyond culpable interferences with the *existence* of the business so as to include also interferences with its *activities* within the scope of the protection afforded by § 823(1) BGB, regardless of whether such interferences occurred in the field of competition, industrial property rights or elsewhere.

In order to infringe the *Recht am Gewerbebetrieb*, however, the interference must be *direct* (*betriebsbezogen*). Case law has defined directness to include direct interference with the existence of the business or an emanation of the business. As stated in the annotated judgment, that does not include interference with rights or *Rechtsgüter* which can be severed from the business without difficulty, such as injury to an employee or damage to a lorry or a power cable, which could just as well have affected any other business in a similar situation; in these cases, the entitlement to the services of an employee or to the use of a piece of property does not characterize the substance of that particular business (*wesenseigentümliche Eigenheit*). If such rights or interests were included, then contractual rights (such as a contract for the supply of power in the judgment above) would come under the protection of § 823(1) BGB, contrary to the intention of the drafters of the BGB.

As already mentioned, the recognition of this new "other right" has not gone without criticism. For example, Larenz/Canaris continue to believe not only that this right conflicts with the basic structure of German tort law, but also that its creation was superfluous, since in most if not all its applications another legal basis could have been found to reach the same result without encroaching on the theoretical structure of German tort law.[440] Furthermore, in the absence of a legislative basis, the boundaries of the *Recht am Gewerbebetrieb* cannot easily be traced with the vague concepts of directness or *Betriebsbezogenheit.*

(2) The *Recht am Gewerbebetrieb* is closely related to § 824 BGB. Under § 824 BGB, a person who makes an untrue factual statement such as could endanger the credit of another person or prejudice his or her earning capacity or prospects is liable in damages to that other person, provided that he or she knew or ought to have known that the statement was untrue. But where the person making the statement did not know, and merely ought to have known that it was untrue, no liability is incurred if the maker or the recipient of the statement had a justifiable interest in making or receiving it. Thus, § 824 BGB concerns only liability for factually incorrect statements, whereas the *Recht am Gewerbebetrieb* offers protection against injurious value judgments. Accordingly, in the case of product tests (*Warentests*) for instance, § 824 will come into play only when the test is presented as a statement about verifiable facts;[441] otherwise § 823(1) BGB and the *Recht am Gewerbebetrieb* must be relied on.[442]

[439] Starting with RG, 27 February 1904, RGZ 58, 249.
[440] Larenz/Canaris at 560 ff.
[441] *Aussage über nachprüfbare Fakten*, in BGH, 21 February 1989, NJW 1989, 1923.
[442] BGH, 9 December 1975, BGHZ 65, 325; BGH, 10 March 1987, NJW 1987, 2222; Larenz/Canaris at 549.

BGH, 21 June 1966[443]   **2.G.38.**

CONFLICT BETWEEN THE *RECHT AM GEWERBEBETRIEB* AND FREEDOM OF EXPRESSION

Hellfire

If, following the publication of an article with strongly critical views about religious matters, a magazine is attacked by another magazine with opposite views, the Recht am Gewerbebetrieb *of the first magazine must in principle give way to the freedom of expression of the second magazine.*

Facts: The plaintiff was the publisher of the weekly news magazine *stern*. In its 14 January 1962 edition, *stern* featured an article entitled "Is hell really burning? Do any illusions about Christian unity still remain?", where the impending Vatican II council was heavily criticized. The article expressed scepticism about efforts to unite Christians, using as an example the proposals to remove any doctrinal reference to hellfire in Europe and America while keeping it in Africa and Oceania. It also suggested that the Catholic Church was seeking to exert political influence in order to bring its doctrine into the law of Germany. The defendant was the publisher of the weekly *Echo der Zeit*, which responded to the article in *stern*, alleging that the title of the article in *stern* was a "lure for idiots" ("*Dummenfang*"), that *stern* was promoting religious hatred and was recklessly distorting or ignoring the facts. The plaintiff sought an order restraining the defendant from further making the statements described above.

Held: The court of first instance dismissed the action. The court of appeal reversed the judgment of the court of first instance in part and issued a court order restraining the defendant from making certain statements about the plaintiff. On an application for review, the BGH reversed the judgment of the court of appeal and dismissed the whole of the action.

Judgment: "The crucial question in this case is whether the derogatory criticism [of the defendant] went beyond the limits set by law by infringing on the commercial activities of the plaintiff in a legally impermissible way.

[There follows a discussion of the *Konstanz* decision of the BGH (26 October 1951, BGHZ 3, 270). In that decision, the BGH had applied a balancing test to situations where the *Recht am Gewerbebetrieb* conflicted with freedom of expression. According to that test, the defendant must carefully weigh the impact of its statements on the plaintiff and choose the least damaging means to voice its opinion. The BGH then expressly reversed its *Konstanz* decision by reference to the case law of the BVerfG.]

As a starting point, the Chamber agrees with the BVerfG that there is a presumption in favour of allowing 'free speech' in cases involving contributions to the intellectual debate on an issue of significant public concern by a person who can legitimately make such a contribution. Depending on the particular circumstances of the case, the protection of personal legal interests must sometimes give way in order to secure the free discussion of important social issues. Indeed, in confrontations which transcend the interpersonal realm to address issues of broader significance to society, Art. 5 GG requires that the law guarantee a large measure of freedom to the *form* of expression as well, and that restraint be exercised in making findings of intent to defame or findings of illegal interference with commercial interests [reference omitted]. Case law has imposed a strict duty of care upon the press when it publishes information which is liable to affect the honour of an individual: it is not appropriate to impose the same duty when it voices opinions on questions of general importance, even if those opinions may be damaging to some. Considering that the *Grundgesetz* attaches immense significance to the legal guarantee of freedom of expression, this must mean that the *Grundgesetz* rests on the premise that the emancipated citizen, when called upon to decide for him-

---

[443] BGHZ 45, 296. Translation by P. Larouche.

or herself on issues of public concern, can make due allowance for ironic or vehement criticisms. Given that 'freedom is a hazardous enterprise' ('*Wagnis der Freiheit*' [reference omitted]), it must be accepted that the law does not protect against every exaggeratedly abrasive form of expression. Limitations on the protection granted by law are especially justified when the author of the criticism aims to ward off what he or she saw as an exaggerated or injurious attack on his or her own position (comp. BVerfG, 25 January 1961, BVerfGE 12, 113) . . .

[This Chamber] cannot agree with the court of appeal that an injunction must be granted against the defendant. In the assessment of the polemical position taken by *Echo der Zeit*, it must not be forgotten that Christians, in particular Roman Catholics, could see the article in *stern* as a provocation, given the 'colloquial' tone in which it was couched. [There follows an examination of the article in *stern*]. In the light of the insinuations [contained in the article], a very drastic response from the persons concerned cannot legally be prohibited. It does not matter that the author of the article believed that his insinuations were legitimate and was seriously concerned that the church and the clerics were increasingly influencing public affairs. The response to the article in *stern* is admittedly very tough . . . Yet, given the socio-political content of the dispute and the provocative effect of the article, that response—the abrasiveness of which cannot be explained otherwise than by a total divergence of opinion on the substance of the debate—cannot be considered as malicious or hateful defamation. *Accordingly, the defendant cannot be prohibited from repeating its utterances on the ground that so doing would affect the commercial activities of the plaintiff* [emphasis added]. In the overall assessment, the wide circulation of *stern*, which enables it to influence public opinion, must also be taken into account. As such, *stern* is not left without recourse against sharp criticisms from its opponents."

Note

For an interference with the *Recht am Gewerbebetrieb* to be actionable, not only must the interference be culpable; it must also be illegal in the first place. An interference is not illegal if the person infringing that right can put forward a special justification, as was the case in the annotated judgment. In that case, the question arose whether, and if so to what extent, Article 5(1) GG can provide such justification. Article 5 GG guarantees freedom of opinion and of the press, subject only to limitations provided for by general laws, laws for the protection of youth and the inviolability of personal honour (Article 5(2)). The judgment makes it clear that Article 5 GG can in principle justify interferences with the *Recht am Gewerbebetrieb*. The precise extent to which Article 5 GG can provide a justification depends on a balancing test, whereby the *Recht am Gewerbebetrieb* is weighed against the right to freedom of opinion and freedom of the press. Obviously, this is the same test as that applied in connection with the general *Persönlichkeitsrecht*.[444] The BGH judgments in both the "Greenpeace poster" and "Hellfire" cases show that when either the general *Persönlichkeitsrecht* (as in "Greenpeace poster") or the *Recht am Gewerbebetrieb* (as in "Hellfire") is balanced against freedom of expression, the balance is tipped in favour of the latter, since it is a fundamental element of the democratic order, constitutionally protected by Article 5 GG. The point at which the general *Persönlichkeitsrecht* or the *Recht am Gewerbebetrieb* outweighs freedom of expression is fairly narrowly defined: only if the expression aims primarily at, respectively, defaming the person or injuring the commercial activity in question (*Schmähkritik*) will the protection of these interests under § 823(1) BGB take precedence. In contrast, older case law had proposed a stricter

---

[444] For instance in the Greenpeace poster case, *supra*, **2.G.28.**

proportionality test, whereby the defendant had to show that the form of its statements did not disproportionately infringe on the protected interests of the plaintiff.[445]

BGH, 18 September 1984[446]   **2.G.39.**

INTERFERENCE WITH OWNERSHIP BY EMISSIONS FROM NEIGHBOURING PLANT

Dusty car

The substantive standards of § 906 BGB and the rules of evidence developed in BGH case law under § 906 BGB are applied by analogy to a claim pursuant to § 823(1) BGB for interference with property rights as a consequence of emissions from a neighbouring plant.

Facts: The car of the plaintiff, which was parked on the premises of his employer during working hours, was damaged by dust emanating from a neighbouring plant.

Held: Both in first instance and in appeal the claim of the plaintiff was rejected. The BGH quashed the judgment of the court of appeal and remitted the case to it for further determination.

Judgment: "a) . . . [A]s the court of appeal correctly explains, the claim of the plaintiff does not come within the scope of the second sentence of § 906(2) BGB. That provision guarantees reparation in cases of interference with the use or the exploitation of a piece of land, and [its application] is determined and limited by the relationship with the piece of land that is affected by the emissions. Claims under that provision derive from the ownership of the piece of land [reference omitted]. They also extend to consequential losses, if and insofar as they follow from the interference with the substance or use of the piece of land in question.

The present claim does not concern damage which would have been inflicted to the vehicles of the plaintiff through the piece of land of company O and the use thereof, but rather damage which is alleged to have been caused directly by the emissions of the defendant . . .

2. The court of appeal was accordingly correct in envisaging the law of tort as the only possible ground for the claim of the plaintiff. This Chamber cannot however follow the reasons of the court of appeal as concerns the burden of allegation and proof in tort law claims. Contrary to the opinion of the court of appeal, the plaintiff does not carry alone the burden of alleging and proving that the defendant is liable, on account of a breach of a duty of care, for the damage which it caused to the vehicles. Rather, the defendant must also contribute to the establishment of the facts . . .

b) The general principles regarding the burden of proof in claims based on tort law do not come into play as regards unlawfulness (*Rechtswidrigkeit*) and culpability (*Verschulden*) in the present case. In reliance upon the evidentiary principles of the BGH case law under § 906 BGB and in continuation of the principles developed by this Chamber regarding the reversal of the burden of proof in product liability cases, this Chamber finds that it is up to the defendant to allege and prove that the emissions from his piece of land remained within the limits of the common use of land at that location (*ortsübliche Benutzung ihres Grundstücks*) and that it had taken all precautions which could economically be expected of him (*wirtschaftlich zumutbar*) in order to prevent damage to the vehicles of the plaintiff by emissions of dust from his cupola-furnace.

aa) The person responsible for the emissions is not obliged under all circumstances to avoid any interference to the other landowners who are affected by those emissions. According to the first sentence of § 906(2) BGB, the landowners in question cannot oppose the emissions if the person

---

[445] See the *Konstanz* judgment, BGH, 26 October 1951, BGHZ 3, 270, NJW 1952, 660, Translation by F.H. Lawson and B.S. Markesinis in Markesinis at 342, overruled in the annotated judgment.
[446] NJW 1985, 47. Translation by P. Larouche.

responsible for them remains within the limits of the common use of land at that location (*ort-sübliche Benutzung seines Grundstücks*). Even in that case, he must still take such measures to prevent the inconvenience to others as are technically possible and can be economically expected (*wirtschaftlich zumutbar*) from the average holder of such a source of emissions. When the interference cannot be prevented even when that obligation is discharged, then the [person responsible for the emissions] is not forced to stop using his land in a way which results in emissions; the landowners who are affected must be content with reparation pursuant to the second sentence of § 906(2) BGB. The law imposes on the defendant the burden of alleging and proving that the damaging emissions relate to a use of land which is common at that location (*ortsübliche Benutzung*) and that they could not be prevented through measures which were possible and could be economically expected (*wirtschaftlich zumutbar*) from him [reference omitted].

bb) In the opinion of this Chamber, the same [principles] must also apply to the tort claims at issue here, concerning damage to the vehicles of the plaintiff from emissions of dust by the defendant. It is true that the present case does not involve the right of landowners to obtain the termination of emissions, for which § 906 BGB is designed, but rather a claim for damages put forward by a property owner who does not stand in a neighbour relationship with the defendant and who alleges that the defendant breached a *Verkehrssicherungspflicht* incumbent upon him. However, this Chamber considers that the first sentence of § 902(2) BGB consitutes a legislative statement of the obligations of the person responsible for emissions, which must also be taken into account in such relationships, as regards both the need to accept injurious emissions which remain within what is common at that location and the burden of allegation and proof imposed on the defendant, as was discussed above. Since the provisions relating to the relationship between neighbouring landowners are, within their scope, dispositive of the issue whether conduct is unlawful (*widerrechtlich*) within the meaning of § 823(1) BGB, the person responsible for emissions is not liable in tort towards landowners affected by those emissions where such landowners cannot obtain the termination of those emissions pursuant to the first sentence of § 906(2) BGB, because those emissions follow from a use of land which is common at that location (*ortsübliche Benutzung*) and no measures which can economically be expected (*wirtschaftlich zumutbar*) of the person responsible for the emissions can prevent them [references omitted]. The scope of the protection granted by tort law to other property owners [i.e. besides neighbouring landowners] cannot go any further; in that sense [§ 906 BGB] draws the outer limits of the legal interest (*Schutzgut*) which it protects. Indeed, the interests of landowners are no doubt the most affected by the emissions; when the law is such that those landowners cannot prevent the person responsible for the emissions from using his or her land in a way which produces such emissions, then neither can third parties [i.e. other property owners besides neighbouring landowners]. Moreover, the fact that third parties cannot request reparation, pursuant to the second sentence of § 906(2) BGB, cannot justify that the permissibility of such a use of land would be assessed differently in relation to them.

By the same token it appears appropriate, in cases relating to third parties as well, for the defendant to bear the burden of alleging and proving that the emissions remained within the realm of a use of land which is common at that location (*ortsüblichen Benutzung*) and that he took the measures which could economically be expected (*wirtschaftlich zumutbar*) of him in order to restrict their environmental impact. Yet the rules of § 906 BGB, which cover conflicts between the interests of landowners, cannot be applied to the legal relationships involved in the present case without further elaboration . . .

In the present case, in view of the conclusions of the court of appeal on the scope of the damage to the vehicles, a considerable interference is present. In that case, when it comes to decide whether [the owner of the vehicles] must accept such interference, in view of the scope granted under the first sentence of § 906(2) BGB to the right of the person responsible for the emissions to use his land, it appears appropriate to lay the burden of proof upon the party which must carry it according to the provisions relating to the relationship between neighbouring landowners. Ultimately, it is for the [owner of the vehicles] also a matter of whether the person responsible for the emissions can benefit from what remains a legal exception.

cc) In any event injurious emissions will not always lead to compensation under tort law for affected property owners who do not stand in a neighbourhood relationship [with the defendant] on the mere ground that they exceed what a landowner would have to bear, pursuant to the first sentence of § 906(2) BGB. As was mentioned, that provision draws but the outer limits of the interests (*Schutzgut*) which it protects; when the defendant complies with the conditions contained in that provision, tort claims by property owners [who do not stand in a neighbourhood relationship with the defendant] are in any event excluded. That does not mean that these claims will always be successful when the landowner did not take adequate measures to prevent emissions . . .

In such a case, however, where it is established that emissions for which the defendant is responsible cause considerable interference (such as damage to property in the present case), the defendant must allege and prove that he has taken the preventive measures which were required under the circumstances. In that respect, the approach which underpins the reasoning of this Chamber as regards the reversal of the burden of proof in product liability cases [references omitted] is also relevant."

Notes

(1) The interference with property at issue in the annotated judgment (intrusion of dust from the defendant's plant in the paint, glass and plated parts of the plaintiffs' cars) is most certainly a violation of ownership (*Eigentumverletzung*) within the meaning of § 823(1) BGB,[447] and therefore fulfills the *Tatbestand* requirement of § 823(1) BGB.[448] To determine whether the interference also fulfils the requirements of unlawfulness and fault, earlier BGH case law established that, as between neighbouring lawful possessors of land (see under a)), § 906(2), first sentence BGB provides the decisive criterion not only for disputes under § 906 BGB (duty to tolerate emissions, subject eventually to compensation), but also for tort claims under § 823(1) BGB.[449] In the annotated judgment, the BGH goes one step further and applies the substantive and procedural standards of § 906 BGB to tort claims lying "outside of the relationship between owners of neighbouring lands" (*außerhalb eines nachbarschaftlichen Gemeinschaftsverhältnisses stehender Sacheigentümer*). It would indeed be incomprehensible if the protection afforded against emissions from neighbouring land properties under § 823(1) BGB would differ according to whether damage is caused to a neighbouring land or to moveable property.

The foregoing only means that no action in tort under § 823(1) BGB for emissions from a neighbouring land will lie when the conditions of the first sentence of § 906(2) BGB are fulfilled, i.e. the supposedly substantial interference complies with a use of the other land that is common at that location (*eine ortsübliche Benutzung des anderen Grundstücks*) and could not be prevented by measures which can economically be imposed on the user of that other land (*der Benutzer wirtschaftlich zumutbar*), so that the owner of the affected property is bound to tolerate the emission in question. Yet that does not mean that, when the conditions of § 906(2) BGB are not fulfilled, tortious liability will automatically follow. Whether that is so depends on the concrete circumstances of the case (see under cc)).

---

[447] See, *supra*, 3.2., Introductory Note under a).

[448] See, *supra*, Chapter III, 3.2.1., under b) for a discussion of the three elements of *Tatbestand*, *Rechtswidrigkeit* (unlawfulness) and *Verschulden* (fault).

[449] BGH, 2 March 1984, NJW 1984, 2207 referred to in the judgment under bb).

(2) § 906 BGB covers the subjection to gas, vapours, odours, smoke, soot, heat, noises, vibrations and other similar interferences coming from another piece of land (*Zuführung von Gasen, Dämpfen, Gerüchen, Rauch, Russ, Wärme, Geräusch, Erschütterungen und ähnliche von einem anderen Grundstück ausgehender Einwirkungen*). This non-exhaustive enumeration shows how important § 906 BGB can be for the protection of the environment, at least in neighbourly relationships between individual owners, occupiers or possessors, especially now that it also applies by analogy to property rights in moveable property. However, it must be emphasized that on the other hand § 906 BGB puts the victim of an interference under a rather considerable duty to tolerate that interference. § 906(2) now also provides a defence against tort claims under § 823(1) BGB, yet the second sentence of § 906(2) does not apply to tort actions so as to counterbalance the effects of the first sentence of § 906(2) BGB (see under bb)). In view of that, the significance of the annotated judgment for environmental protection lies primarily in the BGH findings regarding the burden of proof, in conformity with earlier case law. According to the Court, it is for the defendant to prove that the conditions of the first sentence of § 906(2) are fulfilled such as to be exonerated from liability under § 823(1) BGB.

In parts of the judgment which are not reproduced here, the BGH adds some interesting points, relating namely to (i) the burden of proof resting on the plaintiff as regards causation; (ii) the extent to which the burden of proof on the issue of substantial impact on the plaintiff's property, as defined in § 906(1), may have to be understood differently in the case of interference with moveable property (in the annotated judgment there was no doubt, however, that the impact was substantial); (iii) the relationship to BGH case law on product liability (where the onus of proof is also partly put on the defendant), which can be applied here by analogy, since the defendant releasing emissions on someone else's property was under a *Verkehrssicherungspflicht* to install controls to check whether the disturbances remain within permissible limits (see under cc)).

2.3.3. FRENCH LAW

Introductory Note

a) Property rights in the widest sense of the word are all protected by French tort law against interferences of any kind. Viney describes the breadth of protection of property rights as follows:[450]

"Every loss resulting from the destruction, deterioration or depreciation of property (*d'un bien existant*) is in principle recoverable. There is no reason to draw from the outset a distinction between losses in use value and in market value."

Similarly, the loss of profit, the need to incur certain expenses, the obligation to contract on less favourable conditions than was foreseen or the impossibility of obtaining or benefiting from a right with an economic value are all heads of damage on which an action in tort can be based.[451]

---

[450] Viney and Jourdain, *Conditions* at 19, paras. 251–1, references omitted.
[451] Ibid. at 19–22, para. 251 to 251–3.

b) As discussed above, it is also typical for French law that the *loss of a chance* to obtain an advantage or maintain a favourable position can lead to compensation if that loss is caused by tortious behaviour.[452] Parts of the case law go even further in awarding compensation for a mere expectation that was tortiously defeated. Moreover, as in other areas, omissions leading to interferences with property rights or interests can give rise to civil liability in the same way as do positive acts.[453]

c) As in other legal systems, a special liability regime was developed very early in French law for inconveniences in excess of normal limits as between neighbours (*troubles de voisinage anormaux*). In a judgment of 27 November 1844, the Cour de cassation quashed a court of appeal judgment in a case of noise caused by operations of a neighbouring factory in the following terms:[454]

> "Having regard to Arts. 544 and 1382 C.civ.; On the one hand, it cannot be denied that the noise from a factory, when it becomes intolerable for neighbouring properties, can be a legitimate ground for compensation. On the other hand, it is not the law that any type of noise whatsoever caused by industrial operations amounts to the kind of damage which can be recovered [in an action in tort]".

The factory concerned was also emitting smoke, which caused harm to the plaintiff; the court of appeal had found against the defendant for failing to take steps to avoid that harm and had awarded damages in respect of it. That part of the judgment was upheld, as the court of appeal had, according to the Cour de cassation, rightly considered that 'it was possible, without infringing the legitimate rights [of the defendant factory owner], to avoid this type of damage through appropriate measures'.

It follows from that judgment that in the early days liability for *troubles de voisinage* was founded on Articles 544[455] and 1382 C.civ. and, in view of that latter reference, accordingly fault-based in principle. Subsequently, the Cour de cassation abandoned the reference to Article 1382 C.civ., transforming liability for *troubles de voisinage* into a kind of no-fault liability, on the basis of a general principle of law according to which "one shall not interfere with the enjoyment of neighbouring property in a manner going beyond the normal".[456]

In an overview of the case law, V. Gaillot-Mercier shows that the abnormal character of the inconvenience (*l'anormalité du trouble*) is the decisive element, that the inconvenience may take so many forms that it is impossible to give an exhaustive enumeration, that the liability is imposed on any neighbour regardless the type of right by virtue of which he/she occupies the premises and that the defence of "first occupancy" can only be raised by the defendant in situations where special statutory provisions make allowance for it.[457] The most important of those provisions is Article L 112-16 of the *Code de la construction*

---

[452] *Supra*, **2.F.11.**

[453] *Infra*, Chapter III, 3.31.1.

[454] DP 1845.I.13.

[455] "Ownership is the right to use and dispose of things in the most absolute manner . . .".

[456] Cass. civ. 2e, 13 November 1986, Bull.civ. 1986.II.172; Cass. civ. 2e, 19 February 1992, Bull.civ. 1992.II.60; see also, in respect of a lessee who causes harm to a neighbour, Paris, 15 January 1993, D 1993.IR.117: "The liability of the owner or lessee is engaged through the mere fact that there was excessive inconvenience, without there being any need to show fault (*faute*)". See also Cass. civ. 2e, 11 February 1998, D 1999.Jur.529, reaffirming the separate existence of liability for *troubles de voisinage* and liability under Articles 1382–1383 C.civ.

[457] "Troubles de voisinage", in *Repértoire de droit civil* (Paris: Dalloz).

et de l'habitation, which reads: "Damage caused to the occupiers of a building by inconvenience resulting from agricultural, industrial or commercial activity cannot be recovered if the building permit for the building affected by the inconvenience was requested, or the sale or lease [for such building] was notarized, at a time when the activities causing the inconvenience were already being conducted, provided that those activities complied with applicable legal and regulatory provisions and have continued to do so".

Cass. civ. 2e, 28 April 1965[458]   **2.F.40.–42.**
Régie autonome des transports de la ville de Marseille (RATVM) v. *Marcailloux*
and
Cass. civ. 2e, 8 May 1970[459]
Lafarge v. *SARL des Papeteries Allamigeon Frères*
and
CÉ, 2 June 1972[460]
Compagnie Générale de Travaux Hydrauliques (SADE) v. *Société Thomson-Houston-Hotchkiss-Brandt (STHHB)*

ECONOMIC LOSS

Liability to pay damages can arise in respect of not only loss of income consequential on property damage, such as loss of profit on property damaged as a consequence of a tortious act, but also "pure economic loss" not directly consequential on damage to property or personal injury.

1. Cass. civ. 2e, 28 April 1965   **2.F.40.**

City buses

Facts: Due to a traffic accident caused by the defendant, the buses of the plaintiff company were delayed, leading to loss of passenger fares.

Held: The Cour de cassation upheld the judgment of the court of first instance granting damages.

Judgment: "According to the judgment of the lower court, certain vehicles of the [plaintiff] RATVM were delayed as a result of the congestion of the city street along which they were passing. RATVM alleged that Marcailloux was responsible for that congestion which caused it a loss of revenue, and sought . . . damages accordingly. The contested judgment is criticized for upholding that claim on the ground that in Marseille users did not wait long for the buses, without any explanation being given of the duration of the congestion or the calculation of the loss which is said [by the defendant] to be merely hypothetical and indirect. But it was found in the judgment that, following a collision of vehicles for which Marcailloux was responsible, the road was congested for a

---

[458] D 1965.Jur.777. Translation by N. Sims.
[459] Bull.civ. 1970.II.122. Translation by N. Sims.
[460] AJDA 1972.356. Translation by R. Bray.

certain period of time and RATVM's vehicles were delayed as a result. The judgment goes on to state that that delay occasioned a loss of revenue constituting for RATVM certain damage. In upholding RATVM's claim on the basis of these findings and statements, by which it was established that the immobilization of RATVM's vehicles, for which Marcailloux was responsible, had caused a loss of revenue, constituting for RATVM a loss which was neither hypothetical nor indirect, the lower court was legally entitled to hold as it did."

2. Cass. civ. 2e, 8 May 1970   **2.F.41.**

Gas main

Facts: While conducting public works, Lafarge's bulldozer ruptured a gas main that supplied natural gas to the plaintiff's factory and thereby caused production to cease. The plaintiff sued the defendant for compensation on the basis of Articles 1382 and 1384 C.civ.

Held: The Cour de cassation upheld the decision of the court of appeal that the injury suffered by the plaintiff was the direct consequence of the cutting of the gas main and that the damage was recoverable.

Judgment: "[A]ccording to the contested judgment, which set aside the judgment rendered in first instance, a gas pipeline of the Compagnie française du méthane supplying the factory of the company, Allamigeon Frères et Lacroix, was ruptured by a bulldozer in the course of works carried out by the Lafarge undertaking. The plaintiff suffered loss therefrom, as it was compelled to suspend its operations. It therefore sued Lafarge for damages.

The court of appeal, which held Lafarge liable, is criticized for not drawing the necessary legal consequences from its findings, which showed an indirect loss not capable of sounding in damages.

But, after finding that the facts were undisputed and that the action was founded on Art. 1382 and 1384 C.civ., the judgment states that the damage suffered by Allamigeon Frères et Lacroix appeared to be a direct consequence of the rupture of the pipeline since that [rupture] led to a suspension of the factory's operation, and that the damage was therefore in direct relation to the conduct of the defendant.

In so deciding, the court of appeal based its decision on a correct legal basis which gives rise to no criticism on review."

3. CÉ, 2 June 1972   **2.F.42.**

Power cable

Facts: In the course of execution by SADE of public works on the highway at Maisons-Laffite on behalf of the Compagnie Générale des Eaux, one of SADE's employees cut a high-tension cable belonging to Electricité de France (EDF). As a result of the ensuing power cut, work at the factory of Société Thomson (STHHB) had to be stopped for one hour and 10 minutes. STHHB claimed damages in tort from SADE and not in contract from EDF, its supplier of electricity, as there was a clause in the supply contract between EDF and STHHB that restricted damages to a minimal amount.

Held: The court of first instance granted the claim up to the amount of the salaries paid to the employees for the one hour and 10 minutes during which they had had to remain idle. The Conseil d'État upheld the decision, adding interest, as requested, to the award.

Judgment: "The loss sustained by [STHHB] was the *direct consequence* of the public works carried out by [SADE], which is therefore liable to [STHHB]. Having regard to the duration and the consequences of the stoppage imposed on [STHHB's] factory by the temporary interruption in the supply of electricity, the court of first instance made a correct assessment of the total loss suffered by that company by setting at FRF 14,267 the damages which it ordered [SADE] to pay . . . The payment of the damages due from [SADE] to [STHHB] should be made conditional on [STHHB's] subrogating [SADE] to any claims that [SADE] may assert against [EDF] for compensation for the loss caused to it by the interruption in the supply of electricity."

Notes

(1) The preceding judgments, two of the Cour de cassation and one of the Conseil d'État, show that under French law the application of tort law in cases of "pure economic loss" is not restricted by means of some concept of protected interests, as under German law, or some concept of a duty of care existing only against some persons, or remoteness of damage, as under English law. In the first of the annotated judgments, the transport company was prevented from transporting customers and collecting fares, because of delay due to a traffic accident. The ensuing loss of revenue was held to be recoverable damage since it was a certain and direct (and not merely hypothetical or indirect) consequence of the tortious act, even if it was not consequential on damage to property (the buses themselves had not been damaged). The other two cases are gas or power line cases, comparable to the German and English cases discussed above.[461] The plaintiffs in all those cases had to stop their industrial activities and thereby incurred losses. Even though in the French cases the losses were not consequential upon damage to property (damage to the machinery of the plaintiffs, for instance), the losses were held, both by the Cour de cassation and the Conseil d'État, to be the direct consequence of the tortious act and therefore recoverable.

(2) In the case decided by the Conseil d'État, the *Commissaire du gouvernement*[462] had voiced doubts in his opinion as to whether it is proper for tort law to shift liability for economic loss resulting from an accident which affects many persons onto the shoulders of one single person, namely the wrongdoer. Such a shift is particularly questionable, in the eyes of the *Commissaire*, when the loss does not consist in damage to property as such and moreover cannot be recovered from the utility, typically because the contract for the supply of gas or power between the utility and the plaintiff contains an exemption clause (as is often the case in gas or power line cases). As the *Commissaire* states, if recovery for economic loss is allowed in principle, the only scope for limiting liability is then through application of the criterion of causation, for instance if a break in the causation chain can be proved.[463] However, that could be a difficult task, as illustrated by the many examples, mentioned by the *Commissaire* in his opinion, drawn from both the Cour de cassation and the Conseil d'État.[464] The *Commissaire*'s own—rather unconvincing—theory, was that

---

[461] *Supra*, **2.G.37.** and **2.E.36.**

[462] The *Commissaire du gouvernement*, created in 1831, has a similar function to the Advocate General at the ECJ. L. Neville Brown and J.S. Bell, *French Administrative Law*, 4th edn. (Oxford: Clarendon Press, 1993) write at 46: "Intended originally to present the viewpoint of the government, this officer rapidly arrogated to himself an independent function and began to represent the public interest rather than the policy of the administration".

[463] See *infra*, Chapter IV, 4.3.3.

[464] One of these, CÉ, 14 October 1966, *Marais*, D 1966.Jur.636, illustrates the circumstances in which the need to establish causation could operate so as to limit liability. The *Commissaire du gouvernement* in that case, Mr Galmot, recalled in his opinion that the administrative courts had always refused to apply the doctrine of *équivalence des conditions* (see *infra*, Chapter IV, 4.1.3.), which had, for a long time, been applied by the Cour

the contract with the utility might be seen as a "screen" between the tortious act committed by the defendant and the harm sustained by the plaintiff.[465] The Conseil d'État flatly rejected that theory.

Cass. crim., 6 June 1990[466]   **2.F.43.**
Micheneau

LOSS OF A CHANCE

Race horses

When a horse-breeder was incapable of working due to a tortious act and could not train a mare for a race, the ensuing loss of a chance constitutes "certain damage" for which the wrongdoer is accordingly liable.

Facts: The plaintiff, a horse-breeder, who earned his income from races in which the horses that he trained participated, was temporarily unable to work due to an accident for which the defendant was responsible. As a result, one of his mares could not participate in two races.

Held: The court of appeal decided that the plaintiff could recover only for personal and direct injury, and that, for the purposes of calculating injury, no account should be taken of possible receipts from races in which the mare could not participate. The Cour de cassation quashed the judgment of the court of appeal.

Judgment: "The court of appeal ruled on a claim by Alfred Galerneau, a breeder of race horses, as *partie civile* for compensation of the loss resulting from the injuries involuntarily inflicted by Yann Micheneau and for which the latter was found liable. The claim extended to the loss of a chance to make profit because of the fact that, as a result of his incapacity for work, Alfred Galerneau was unable to train a mare from his stable for two races in which the mare was to have taken part.

In dismissing that claim, the lower court held that, in regard to the period of incapacity for work, only the victim's personal and direct loss could be compensated, and that the calculation of that loss 'cannot be made on the basis of race earnings which are subject to chance and even to the physical development' of the mare.

However, the element of damage constituted by a loss of a chance is direct and certain whenever, as a result of a tort, the probability of a favourable outcome is lost, even though by definition the realization of a chance can never be certain; in its judgment the court of appeal disregarded that principle . . .

de cassation. He had proposed to use the concept of "normal consequence", and therefore to retain as the cause of the damage "only the event which, at the time when it took place, normally and objectively entailed the harm".

[465] Among the hypothetical situations which the *Commissaire* mentioned to illustrate the extreme consequences of holding a third party wrongdoer liable against a large group of injured persons, there is the case of a power cut caused by the crash of an aircraft. Such a case was decided under Dutch law in HR, 14 May 1958, "*Stroomafnemers*", NJ 1961, 570. In that case an aircraft of the Dutch Air Force, flown by a pilot in the service of the State, flew into a high-tension line of the provincial power utility in the neighbourhood of Winterswijk, thereby interrupting the supply of power. The plaintiff, who drew power from the line in question, suffered damage to its business amounting to NLG 1,001. The plaintiff was not entitled to recover from the electricity company, since the contract with that company contained an exemption clause. The State admitted liability for the unlawful act, but denied liability for damages as regards the injury suffered by the plaintiff. The HR upheld the court of appeal's award of damages on the ground that it was foreseeable that, in the event of damage to the cable, users of electricity would suffer loss and that accordingly those responsible should have avoided the special hazard of allowing low-level flying in the proximity of a high-tension cable.

[466] Bull.crim. 1990.224. Translation by N. Sims.

On those grounds, the judgment is quashed."

Note

The above judgment is a good example of the application of the notion of *perte d'une chance* (loss of a chance) in a case dealing with damage to property.[467]

Cass. civ. 2e, 3 March 1988[468]   **2.F.44.**
S. A. France direct service v. *Gustin*

LOSS OF UNLAWFULLY RAISED EXPECTATION

Fake jackpot

A wrongfully raised expectation leading someone to believe, on the basis of a personalized document, that he had won a substantial sum of money in a lottery gives rise to liability to pay compensation.

Facts: The Société France direct service (FDS) had sent to the plaintiffs fictitious documents made out in the plaintiffs' own names, more specifically a newspaper heading, a cheque and a letter of congratulations, leading them to believe that they had won FRF 250,000. The plaintiffs sued FDS for compensatory and punitive damages.

Held: The judgment of the trial judge finding fault and damage was upheld.

Judgment: "The court of first instance . . . found that the document at issue, sent in a partially transparent envelope, began by stating that the addressee had won FRF 250,000 and went on to explain that there would be a ceremony at which a cheque for that amount would be handed over by the director of FDS. The court inferred therefrom that, by holding out the definite prospect of a hypothetical event, FDS had been guilty of a mistake of such a nature as to render it liable since it was shown that Messrs Gustin and Nicolet had suffered loss from the personalization of the document sent to them and the vain belief that they were to receive a considerable sum of money. In so deciding, the court brought its decision within the terms of Art. 1382 C.civ.

On those grounds, the appeal is dismissed."

Note

This judgment illustrates how far French law is prepared to go in awarding damages for injury of whatever nature. The injury found here to be sufficiently certain was that the plaintiffs did not obtain the money which the defendant company had led them to believe that they had won. The damage sustained was not the loss of a chance, but rather the loss of an illusionary certainty that the chance of winning in a lottery had materialized and that they were going to receive a substantial sum. The quantum of damages does not appear from the judgment. If it were the amount of money which the plaintiffs were promised, then they would have been better off than if they had been compensated for the mere loss of a chance (in this case to win in a lottery), since compensation for loss of

---

[467] See *supra*, **2.F.11.** and Note (3), as well as **2.E.49.**
[468] JCP 1989.II.21313. Translation by N. Sims.

a chance is affected by the degree of uncertainty.[469] And indeed in a later case, the Cour de cassation upheld a decision fixing the quantum of damage at the amount of money promised.[470] That did not prevent the Cour de cassation from asserting in other types of cases that the mere creation of a risk that damage may occur, however without evidence that any damage actually occurred, does not give rise to a right to compensation.[471]

2.3.4. ITALIAN LAW

Introductory Note

As stated above in the General Introduction, Article 2043 of the *Codice civile*, the general tortious liability provision, was first interpreted to cover only culpable interference with absolute rights and only later on to cover all interferences with legally relevant interests. This evolution is illustrated by two judgments of the Corte di Cassazione.[472] As von Bar points out, the starting point for this evolution was to be found, as in English law, in cases regarding the professional liability of banks and other suppliers of services.[473] The evolution of Italian case law is not unlike that which took place in France more than a century earlier, when the interpretation of Articles 1382–1383 C.civ. evolved along the same lines: from interference with absolute rights (and violation of specific legal provisions) to interference with any legitimate interest.[474]

Corte di Cassazione, 4 May 1982[475]   **2.I.45.**

PURE ECONOMIC LOSS DUE TO UNFAVOURABLE CONTRACT TERMS. INTERFERENCE WITH THE RIGHT OF PATRIMONIAL INTEGRITY.

Forged de Chirico

Compensation falls due under Article 2043 C.civ. because of economic loss resulting from paying too high a price for a forged painting culpably certified as authentic.

Facts: The plaintiff had bought a de Chirico painting from a third party (not the painter) believing it to be authentic because of the painter's signature on the back. When the painting was proved to be a forgery and it appeared that the painter put his signature on it without duly verifying the authenticity of the painting, the purchaser brought an action in tort against the painter, claiming compensation for the damage caused by the false declaration of authenticity.

Held: The judgment of the court of appeal rejecting the claim was quashed by the Corte di Cassazione.

---

[469] *Supra*, **2.F.11.**, Note (2).
[470] Cass. civ. 2e, 28 June 1995, D 1996.Jur.180, with note by J.L. Mouralis. See Viney and Jourdain, *Conditions* at 5, para. 247 who regard this as the imposition of a private sentence (*peine privée*) using tort law.
[471] See Cass. civ. 1re, 16 June 1998, JCP(E) 1999.2077.
[472] *Supra*, **2.I.22.** and *infra*, **2.I.45.**
[473] von Bar I at 31–2, para. 21.
[474] Ibid. at 32–3, para. 21.
[475] No. 2765 (*De Chirico*), Giur. it. 1983-I-1-786. Further references in von Bar I at 31, para. 21. Translation by Y.P. Salmon and P. Larouche.

Judgment: "The view that 'unjust injury' (*danno ingiusto*) within the meaning of Article 2043 of the *Codice civile* . . . is to be equated with injury to an 'absolute or primary subjective right' (*diritto soggettivo o primario*) was abandoned some time ago in the case-law of this Court which [reference omitted] admits that injury caused to a right *in personam* (*diritto di credito*), which is certainly neither absolute nor primary, can lead to tortious liability.

Moreover, the subsequent enlargement of the scope of protection of tort law cannot be ignored, given that it has sometimes been held that an interference with an expectation (as opposed to a 'subjective right') is 'unjust', provided that the expectation is legitimate [references omitted].

In the present case . . . the [plaintiff] has always maintained that the decision to acquire the painting at the requested price was based on the existence of a second signature by de Chirico on the back of the painting, and on the declaration of provenance which that signature obviously implied. It seems clear, therefore, that . . . the harm the [plaintiff] has suffered is an injury to the right to patrimonial integrity (*diritto all'integrità del proprio patrimonio*)*, and more specifically the right to freely determine transactions concerning the *patrimonio* (guaranteed within the bounds of Art. 41 of the Constitution), as it is reasonable for him to rely on the truthfulness of any relevant statements, whoever makes them, and not be harmed by false statements, whether made fraudulently or negligently (in violation of the fundamental duty of social solidarity provided in Art. 2 of the Constitution).

The Court has no doubt that an infringement of such a right is—in principle—recoverable and thus that the infringement can be characterized as 'unjust injury' within the meaning of Art. 2043 of the *Codice civile*. The tort claim does not of course exclude the contractual claim of the buyer towards the vendor, that issue goes however beyond the scope of this case, and the tort claim is not affected by the success or failure of any contractual claim which may be brought.

The judgment of the court of appeal must accordingly be quashed insofar as it excluded the recovery of the injury alleged by the [plaintiff] on the basis of an erroneous and restrictive conception of 'unjust injury' . . .

In conclusion, the judgment of the court of appeal was wrong in law, as regards the notion of 'unjust injury' recoverable under Art. 2043 of the *Codice civile*. It must accordingly be quashed and the case remitted . . . to be determined according to the following legal proposition: 'The buyer of a painting whose decision to purchase was based on a reasonable faith in the authenticity of the work, derived from the fact that the painter had placed his own signature on the back of the painting, can bring a tort claim against the painter to obtain compensation for the injury suffered if it is established that the painting was forged and that the signature was given without prior diligent verification as to its authenticity.' . . ."

Note

The above judgment provides a good illustration of how the term *danno ingiusto* in Article 2043 of the *Codice civile* has been interpreted expansively over time to cover what would be a case of pure economic loss under English law or *reiner Vermögensschaden* under German law.

2.3.5. COMPARATIVE OVERVIEW

The general regime of tort protection for ownership and property rights

In all the systems examined, the general tort regime affords protection against interference with ownership or other property rights, in the form of damage to property.

Under English law, for instance, even if a series of older torts afford protection in certain specific instances of interference with property, the more general and comparatively more recent tort of negligence can also apply. As *Spartan Steel* shows,[476] it is well established that a duty of care generally exists between a tortfeasor and a plaintiff whose property has been damaged through the negligence of the tortfeasor. In these situations, the plaintiff is a "neighbour" within the meaning of *Donoghue* v. *Stevenson*,[477] the relationship between the plaintiff and the defendant is sufficiently proximate and it is fair, just and reasonable to impose a duty of care, although as the House of Lords reiterated in *Marc Rich & Co. AG* v. *Bishop Rock Marine Co. Ltd.*, the application of these categories to any situation can never be taken for granted.[478]

Under German law, ownership is included, with life, body, health and liberty amongst the *Rechtsgüter* explicitly designated in § 823(1) BGB as deserving special protection under the law of torts. Other types of property rights qualify as "other rights" within the meaning of § 823(1). Hence there is no doubt in principle that culpable and wrongful conduct causing damage to property leads to liability under § 823(1) towards the owner of the property or the holder of another property right over it.

Similarly, under French law, it is beyond question that any interference with "existing property" (*un bien existant*) can lead to civil liability, provided that all conditions for liability under Articles 1382–1383 C.civ. (fault, causation and damage) are fulfilled.[479]

Yet the general tortious liability regimes described above constitute only the backdrop against which more specific regimes are set.

Disputes involving land

In the systems studied in this section, a more specific liability regime exists for disputes involving land.[480] As can be seen from the materials, this regime usually involves some form of strict liability, where some standard of reasonable, common or normal use replaces fault.[481]

Under German law, § 906 BGB provides a legal foundation for this regime, since it enables landowners to seek an end to damaging emissions from neighbouring land.[482] Under that article, the normal standard of *Verschulden* laid out in § 276 BGB is replaced by commonness of use (*ortsübliche Benutzung*). If the defendant cannot show that the land is put to a common use, the use must then be stopped unless this requirement cannot economically be imposed on the defendant (*wirtschaftliche Unzumutbarkeit*), in which case reasonable compensation is payable. The regime of § 906 BGB (standard for liability, burden of proof, defences) has seeped through case law to apply under § 823(1) BGB as well, whenever a tort claim is based on emissions from land. As shown by BGH, 18

---

[476] *Supra*, **2.E.36.**
[477] *Supra*, Chapter I, **1.E.23.**
[478] *Supra*, **2.E.36.**, Note (4).
[479] As appears from the excerpt from Viney and Jourdain, *Conditions*, *supra*, 2.3.3., Introductory Note.
[480] See J. Gordley, "Immissionsschutz, Nuisance and Troubles de Voisinage in Comparative and Historical Perspective" [1998] ZEuP 13.
[481] Compare with *supra*, **2.E.35.**, Note (2), **2.G.39.**, Note (1) and 2.3.3., Introductory note under c).
[482] *Supra*, 2.3.2., Introductory Note under f).

September 1984, the regime of § 906 BGB is even applied to tort claims involving damage to moveable property caused by emissions from a neighbouring land.[483]

Under French law, liability for *troubles de voisinage* (interferences from neighbouring property) appears somewhat more subdued, being a creature of case law, but it nonetheless strays from the general fault-based liability regime. The Cour de cassation now considers that, regardless of fault on the part of the defendant, liability can be imposed for interferences with neighbouring property going beyond the normal.[484]

It is under English law that the most developed of these regimes can be found, consisting in the tort of nuisance and the rule in *Rylands* v. *Fletcher*, the relationship of which with one another and with the tort of negligence is only now being authoritatively settled through cases such as *Cambridge Water Co.*[485] and *Hunter* v. *Canary Wharf*.[486] Private nuisance and the rule in *Rylands* v. *Fletcher* give a particular form of protection to landowners and other persons with a right to the land in question (and not to mere occupiers of the land, as held in *Hunter* v. *Canary Wharf*). Accordingly, a case such as BGH, 18 September 1984, where the regime for disputes between landowners was applied to a claim by the owner of moveable property (a car that was parked near the land of the defendant), could probably not arise in English law under the tort of nuisance or the rule in *Rylands* v. *Fletcher*, in the wake of *Hunter* v. *Canary Wharf*; it would have to be dealt with under negligence. Nuisance applies to losses and inconveniences arising from the use of the defendant's land, while the rule in *Rylands* v. *Fletcher* covers interferences caused by the escape of things brought by the defendant upon his or her land. In both cases, "the principle is one of strict liability in the sense that the defendant may be held liable notwithstanding that he has exercised all due care . . .",[487] a major difference with the tort of negligence, where the standard of reasonable care applies. Nuisance and the rule in *Rylands* v. *Fletcher* were drawn closer to one another in *Cambridge Water Co.*, where the House of Lords made a parallel between the standards of "reasonable user" under the former and "natural use" under the latter; in both cases, it must be shown that the damage caused to the plaintiff's land is of a kind that is a reasonably foreseeable consequence of the occurrence in question. In *Hunter* v. *Canary Wharf*, the House of Lords was also of the opinion that, unlike under the tort of negligence, only property damage (and not personal injury) can be recovered in nuisance (and probably also under the rule in *Rylands* v. *Fletcher*).

Even if the contours of the respective regimes may differ, all systems studied here therefore afford a form of strict liability protection in disputes between neighbouring landowners.

Interferences not resulting in any material damage to property (Pure economic loss or Vermögensschaden)

Some interferences do not result in material damage to a piece of property, for instance when the actions of the defendant cause a loss in the value of the plaintiff's property

---

[483] *Supra,* **2.G.39.**
[484] *Supra,* 2.3.3., Introductory Note under c).
[485] *Supra,* **2.E.35.**
[486] *Supra,* 2.3.1., Introductory Note under a).
[487] *Cambridge Water Co., supra,* **2.E.35.**

without any damage to it, or prevent the plaintiff from putting his property to use in order to derive economic value from it.

Both German and English law share a fundamental reluctance to allow tort claims based on such interferences, out of moral/ethical grounds (plaintiffs should be encouraged to bear their losses and move on while defendants should not be overburdened with claims), economic considerations (it is inefficient to shift these losses onto defendants) or on practical grounds (the courts would be overwhelmed with claims).[488]

Under English law, such *economic loss* is recoverable only to the extent that it is consequential upon physical injury to the plaintiff or damage to his or her property, as shown in *Spartan Steel*, where the Court of Appeal confined compensation to the damage caused to the one batch of steel that was in the furnace at the time of the power cut, including the profits which could have been made from it. Otherwise, as comes out from the judgments of the Court of Appeal in that case, such loss constitutes *pure economic loss*, for which English law in general does not allow recovery; hence the ruling that the plaintiff could not recover the profits it would have made from the four batches of steel that it could have processed during the power cut. Of course, it is always open to the plaintiff to try to bring his or her case within one of the limited categories of cases where English tort law allows compensation for pure economic loss, on the basis that the elements of foreseeability, proximity and fairness that create a duty of care are present.[489]

German tort law has developed in a rather similar way. Indeed, the kinds of loss described above do not involve the infringement of any of the protected *Rechtsgüter* listed in § 823(1) BGB, i.e. life, health, the body and freedom: the overall *Vermögen* was purposely not mentioned as a *Rechtsgut* deserving protection under § 823(1) BGB.[490] These kinds of loss are thus *reiner Vermögensschaden* and cannot be recovered under § 823(1) BGB.

German tort law treats *reiner Vermögensschaden* in the same way as English law approaches pure economic loss, with compensation allowed under certain circumstances, with liability arising under §§ 823(2), 826 or 839 BGB.[491]

However, as German law has evolved, the rules of § 823(1) BGB have been "bent" so as to mitigate the basic reluctance to compensate *reiner Vermögensschaden*, in a way that is not present under English law. First, it has been acknowledged that the protection of ownership under § 823(1) BGB encompasses not only the material integrity of the property that is owned, but also to a certain extent its use and enjoyment.[492] As the waterway and oil tanker cases decided by the BGH show, to the extent that, due to a tortious act, the owner is deprived of any use of his property, the ensuing loss of profit is recoverable;

---

[488] See *Spartan Steel, supra*, **2.E.36.**

[489] Some of them are surveyed *infra*, 2.4.1.

[490] See the excerpt from Larenz/Canaris, *supra*, Chapter I, **1.G.27.** and note (1), and compare with French and Italian law, where all interferences with the *patrimoine* may lead to tortious liability: *supra*, 2.3.3., Introductory Note and 2.3.4., Introductory Note.

[491] Those cases are surveyed *infra*, 2.4.2. and Chapter III, 3.3.2.

[492] Under German law, protection attaches not to the piece of property itself, but rather to the right therein, i.e. ownership (or other rights in real property, considered as "other rights" within the meaning of § 823(1) BGB). In German law as in other civil law systems, ownership comprises the right to use propery (*usus*) and the right to derive benefits from it (*fructus*), cf § 903 BGB, Art. 544 C.civ. It is therefore not inconsistent to extend the protection granted to ownership, as a *Rechtsgut* listed under § 823(1) BGB, to the use and enjoyment of property.

that is not the case, however, when the tortious act merely prevents the property from being used in a certain way.[493] There is no agreed doctrinal explanation for this line of case law.

Secondly, the BGH has recognized as an "other right" within the meaning of § 823(1) BGB some sort of a general right that relates to the running of a business, namely the *Recht am Gewerbebetrieb*.[494] This "other right" affords protection against interferences which would otherwise typically be characterized as *reiner Vermögensschaden*. The BGH judgment of 9 December 1958, a cable case, demonstrates that only direct interferences with the existence of the business or (pursuant to the criterion of *Betriebsbezogenheit*) an emanation of it are covered by the *Recht am Gewerbebetrieb*. In contrast, interferences with rights or interests which can be severed from the business without difficulty, for instance injury to an employee or losses following from the temporary shutdown of a plant, are not covered (or otherwise the restrictive approach of § 823(1) BGB would be altogether defeated). The scope of the *Recht am Gewerbebetrieb* is however limited by other rights which may conflict with it; in BGH, 21 June 1966, the plaintiff's *Recht am Gewerbebetrieb* had to give way to the constitutionally guaranteed freedom of expression of the defendant.[495] Through the *Recht am Gewerbebetrieb*, German tort law recognizes that when tortious conduct gives rise to such consequences that a business is affected in its very existence, the reluctance to grant compensation for *reiner Vermögensschaden* must be tempered. There appears to be no equivalent trend in English law.

In contrast to both German and English law, French tort law does not differentiate between material damage to property and material loss which is not accompanied by injury to the person or property damage. All types of loss are equally protected, as appears from the excerpt from Viney above,[496] where she refers to interferences with property of any kind, including interference with a contractual right[497] or even more broadly, as the title of the excerpt indicates, interferences with one's *patrimoine* (*atteintes au patrimoine*, the conceptual equivalent to *reiner Vermögensschaden* under French law).[498] French law thus allows for the recovery of pure economic loss or *reiner Vermögensschaden*, as is shown by the *RATVM*, *Allamigeon* and *SADE* cases.[499]

In *RATVM*, the unfortunate defendant was condemned to pay to the *RATVM* all the passenger fares lost while traffic was affected because of an accident caused by the defendant; this is precisely the type of situation which Lord Denning MR in *Spartan Steel* (on the basis of authorities) and Larenz/Canaris[500] present as a clear example of claims which should not be allowed under their respective legal systems. By the same token, cable cases from each system have been included in order to show how, on the basis of almost identical facts, the three legal systems studied above come to different conclusions.[501]

---

[493] *Supra*, 2.3.2., Introductory Note under b).

[494] See *supra*, Chapter I, 1.4.3., Introductory Note under b), 2.3.2., Introductory Note under d) and BGH, 9 December 1958, **2.G.37.**

[495] *Supra*, **2.G.38.** See also *supra*, 2.2.5. and **2.G.28.**

[496] *Supra*, 2.3.3., Introductory Note under a),

[497] Compare with the Corte di Cassazione, *supra*, **2.I.22.**

[498] Compare with the Corte di Cassazione, *supra*, **2.I.45.**

[499] *Supra*, **2.F.40.–42.**

[500] At 389–90.

[501] *Spartan Steel*, *supra*, **2.E.36.**; BGH, 9 December 1958, *supra*, **2.G.37.**; *Allamigeon*, *supra*, **2.F.41.** and *SADE*, *supra*, **2.F.42.**

Contrary to what one might expect on the basis of a rough distinction between common law and civil law, on this matter German law sides with English law, not only on the applicable rule, but also more deeply on the underlying rationale.

Probabilities and expectations

Under French law, the notion of *atteintes au patrimoine* is so broad that it extends to interferences with any and all legitimate economic interests, thus making it rather superfluous to provide for a separate section on interference with economic interests under French law in the next section. It also covers interferences with mere probabilities or expectations of gain or avoidance of loss.

Through the device of *perte d'une chance* French tort law has the theoretical framework for recovery of loss of mere opportunities, which would otherwise be dismissed as uncertain damage.[502] Indeed the loss of the opportunity to make a gain or avoid a loss is viewed as an autonomous head of actual damage. The judgment of Cass. crim., 6 June 1990, shows how *perte d'une chance* is used to justify the award of compensation for the revenues which a horse-breeder could have made had he not been injured.[503] On the basis of the Court of Appeal judgment in *Allied Maples Group Ltd.* v. *Simmonds & Simmonds*, it seems that English law is following the path of French law in recognizing loss of a chance as an autonomous head of damage.[504]

French tort law goes further in protecting mere expectations of gain if they were raised through the fault of the defendant, as in *France Direct Service*.[505] The plaintiffs there were allowed to recover from the defendants what could be characterized as no more than an illusion that they had won a substantial amount.

2.4. PROTECTION OF ECONOMIC INTERESTS

As in the previous section, English law is discussed first, in order to illustrate its limited approach towards the protection of purely economic interests, at least under the tort of negligence. Here again German law resembles English law; both those legal systems are to be contrasted with French law, which evidences generosity towards the plaintiffs in protecting all kinds of legitimate interests, economic or not. In the last subsection, the laws of the Nordic countries are referred to.

---

[502] That concept was examined *supra*, **2.F.11.**, as it relates to medical liability.
[503] *Supra*, **2.F.43.**
[504] *Infra*, **2.E.49.**
[505] *Supra*, **2.F.44.**

2.4.1. ENGLISH LAW

Introductory Note

a) As seen in the previous section, more particularly in the case law discussed in connection with *Spartan Steel*, the English law of negligence shows a clear reluctance to protect economic interests.[506] That reluctance comes to the fore in the discussions surrounding so-called "pure economic loss", i.e. loss which is not accompanied by harm to the person or damage to property. Nevertheless there are several other torts that protect economic interests against interference, including interference with a subsisting contract, malicious falsehood, conspiracy, intimidation, interference with trade by unlawful means as well as passing-off.[507] The common thread among these torts might be that liability arises if one causes intentional harm to another by wrongful means.[508] In addition, EC law adds a new dimension to economic torts.[509]

We shall not here go further into these specific torts, with the exception of one, interference with a subsisting contract, which is dealt with in one of the judgments reproduced below. A commits a tort if, without lawful justification, he or she intentionally interferes with a contract between B and C, *either* by persuading B to break that contract with C, *or*, using unlawful means, by directly or indirectly preventing B from performing that contract with C.[510]

b) Prejudice to economic interests, including pure economic loss, may also be recoverable if it flows from a breach of a statutory duty, that is a duty imposed by a specific Act of Parliament. It must however be Parliament's intent to grant such a remedy in tort and to do so to a person in the position of the plaintiff, as illustrated in *Merlin* v. *British Nuclear Fuels PLC*.[511] That case turned around the Nuclear Installations Act 1965, which at section 12 explicitly obliged the defendant (owner and occupier of the Sellafield nuclear fuel reprocessing plant) to compensate third parties for any injury or damage that had been caused in breach of a duty imposed by the Act.[512] Under section 7(1) of the Act, a duty was imposed upon the defendant not to cause injury to any person or damage to any property. The issue was whether the duty to compensate arising out of sections 12 and 7(1) included pure economic loss, in that case the diminution in the value of the neighbouring property of the plaintiffs. The court found against the plaintiffs on this point. It also held that the increased risk of the plaintiffs developing cancer, even if it was admitted by the defendant, did not amount to physical injury for the purpose of section 7(1).

The question whether a breach of statutory duty may give rise to tortious liability is even more delicate when the statute in question does not principally aim at the imposition of tortious liability, but rather pursues primarily regulatory or criminal objectives.[513]

---

[506] *Supra*, **2.E.36.**

[507] See for an overview Zweigert and Kötz, *supra*, Chapter I, **1.E.21.** and further Rogers at 618, 621–77 and Weir at 565.

[508] Weir at 568.

[509] *Infra*, Chapter IX, 9.1. For a thorough discussion of some of the aforementioned economic torts in relation to EC law, see J. Steiner, "How to Make the Action Suit the Case" (1987) 12 ELRev 102 at 110–13.

[510] Rogers at 621.

[511] [1990] 2 QB 557, [1990] 3 WLR 383, [1990] 3 All ER 711, QB.

[512] 1965 (c. 57).

[513] See Rogers at 247 for a detailed treatment of this problem.

Among statutory provisions with a mainly regulatory or criminal purpose, one finds provisions of primary or secondary EC law. Even before the ECJ judgment in *Francovich*,[514] English courts were faced with the question whether an action in tort to recover pure economic loss could be founded on a breach of a duty imposed by a provision of the EC Treaty which does not explicitly allow for such an action. In *Bourgoin*, now superseded by case law of the ECJ, the Court of Appeal had to rule on a duty imposed on a *public authority*.[515] In *Garden Cottage Foods Ltd* v. *Milk Marketing Board*, a duty imposed on all *persons* (whether private or public) was at issue before the House of Lords.[516] Lord Diplock there said that:[517]

> "[a] breach of the duty imposed by Article 86 [EC Treaty] not to abuse a dominant position in the Common Market or in a substantial part of it, can . . . be categorised in English law as a breach of a statutory duty that is imposed not only for the purpose of promoting the general economic prosperity of the Common Market but also for the benefit of private individuals to whom loss or damage is caused by a breach of that duty.
>
> If this categorisation be correct, and I can see none other that would be capable of giving rise to a *civil cause* of action in English private law on the part of a private individual who sustained loss or damage by reason of a breach of a directly applicable provision of the Treaty of Rome, the nature of the cause of action cannot, in my view, be affected by the fact that the legislative provision by which the duty is imposed takes the negative form of a prohibition of particular kinds of conduct rather than the positive form of an obligation to do particular acts."

c) Apart from specific torts and breach of statutory duty, some measure of protection for economic interests is also offered under the tort of negligence. At a certain point in time, it looked as if negligence was going to develop, with the help of the "neighbour principle" laid down in *Donoghue* v. *Stevenson*, into a broad instrument allowing defendants to obtain compensation for economic losses in a wide range of situations. However, as described earlier, that development was recently reversed abruptly in favour of a more gradual step-by-step approach, with the law now being in a state of flux.[518] The judgment of the House of Lords in *Caparo Industries plc* v. *Dickman* was rendered as this reversal was almost accomplished.[519] It revisits the issue of liability for false statements, which had been dealt with in a momentous case of the "expansive" period, *Hedley Byrne & Co.* v. *Heller & Partners Ltd.*[520] In *White* v. *Jones*, the House of Lords proceeded to apply the current step-by-step approach to a case of professional liability, filling, in the words of Lord Goff, "a lacuna in the law and so prevent[ing] . . . injustice".[521]

---

[514] ECJ, Judgment of 19 November 1991, Joined Cases C-6/90 and 9/90, *Francovich* v. *Italy* [1991] ECR I-5357, and in later cases: *infra*, Chapter IX, 9.1., Introductory Note and **9.EC.6.–7.**

[515] *Bourgoin S.A.* v. *Minister of Agriculture, Fisheries and Food* [1986] QB 716, [1985] 3 WLR 1027, [1985] 3 All ER 585, CA.

[516] [1984] AC 130, [1983] 2 All ER 770, [1983] 3 CMLR 43, HL.

[517] Both *Bourgoin* and *Garden Cottage* are discussed in detail by J. Steiner, "How to Make the Action Suit the Case." (1987) 12 ELRev 102 at 108–9. That article was however written before the ECJ judgments in *Francovich* and in *Brasserie du Pêcheur*, discussed *infra*, Chapter IX, 9.1.

[518] *Supra*, Chapter I, 1.4.1.B. and *Murphy* v. *Brentwood District Council* [1991] 1 AC 398, [1990] 2 All ER 269, HL.

[519] *Infra*, **2.E.47.**

[520] [1964] AC 465, [1963] 2 All ER 575, HL.

[521] *Infra*, **2.E.48.**

d) In *Henderson* v. *Merrett Syndicates Ltd.*,[522] *Hedley Byrne* was reformulated, in the light of the developments in the second and third cases annotated below, into a more general principle that would be applicable to liability for the provision of services. The "extended *Hedley Byrne* principle", as it is now known, was explained as follows by Lord Steyn for a unanimous House of Lords in *Williams* v. *Natural Life Health Foods Ltd.*:[523]

> "First, in *Henderson's* case it was settled that the assumption of responsibility principle enunciated in the *Hedley Byrne* case is not confined to statements but may apply to any assumption of responsibility for the provision of services. The extended *Hedley Byrne* principle is the rationalisation or technique adopted by English law to provide a remedy for the recovery of damages in respect of economic loss caused by the negligent performance of services. Secondly, it was established that once a case is identified as falling within the extended *Hedley Byrne* principle, there is no need to embark on any further inquiry whether it is 'fair, just and reasonable' to impose liability for economic loss [reference omitted]. Thirdly, and applying *Hedley Byrne*, it was made clear that 'reliance upon [the assumption of responsibility] by the other party will be necessary to establish a cause of action (because otherwise the negligence will have no causative effect) . . . ' [reference omitted]. Fourthly, it was held that the existence of a contractual duty of care between the parties does not preclude the concurrence of a tort duty in the same respect."

The key elements are therefore an *assumption of responsibility* by the defendant and *reliance* upon it by the plaintiff. If, as seems to be the case,[524] the extended *Hedley Byrne* principle becomes established as the criterion to judge whether there was a duty of care with respect to pure economic loss in cases of professional services, the general reluctance to grant compensation for pure economic loss under the tort of negligence will suffer from a significant exception. Furthermore, a significant step would be taken away from the model of incremental evolution of the law of tort which was put forward in *Murphy* v. *Brentwood District Council*, back to an approach that relies more on the application of general principles to the facts of each case.[525]

Court of Appeal[526]   2.E.46.
Rickless v. *United Artists Corporation*

THIRD PARTY INTERFERENCE WITH A CONTRACTUAL RELATIONSHIP

The Pink Panther returns

A defendant is liable in tort for inducing a breach of a negative covenant surviving a contract which has otherwise been fully performed between the parties.

Facts: The well-known actor Peter Sellers starred in a series of five *Pink Panther* films. Except for one movie, Peter Sellers did not himself contract to provide his services but did so through "loan-out" companies, which contracted with production companies created by the producer of the *Pink Panther* series, Blake Edwards. After

---

[522] *Supra*, Chapter I, **1.E.14.** and **1.E.17.**

[523] *Williams* v. *Natural Life Health Foods Ltd.* [1998] 2 All ER 577, [1998] 1 WLR 830.

[524] The extended *Hedley Byrne* test was already applied at least twice by the House of Lords, in *Williams*, ibid., and in the speech of Lord Slynn in *Macfarlane* v. *Tayside Health Board*, *supra*, **2.E.6.**

[525] See *supra*, Chapter I, 1.4.1.B., Introductory Note.

[526] [1988] QB 40.

Peter Sellers' death, and without having obtained permission from his personal representatives, *another* production company, also created by Blake Edwards, made a sixth *Pink Panther* movie (*The Trail of the Pink Panther*), using previously unreleased material left over from the earlier films. Such use gave rise to breaches of the contracts between the "loan-out" companies and the *original* production companies. The personal representatives of Peter Sellers and the "loan-out" companies sued (i) the production company responsible for *The Trail of the Pink Panther* and (ii) the distributor of that film. Since it was not possible to claim under contract given the strict privity rules of English law, the plaintiffs sought damages in tort for wrongful interference with contractual relations (i.e. those between the "loan-out" companies and the original production companies). A separate issue raised by the plaintiffs relates to a breach of performer's rights under the Dramatic and Musical Performers' Protection Act 1958.[527]

Held: The court of first instance gave judgment for the plaintiffs. The Court of Appeal dismissed the appeal, holding (i) that the defendants had breached performer's rights and were liable for those breaches (not reproduced below) and (ii) that, under the terms of agreements concluded for each of the five films, the defendants were obliged to use the actor's performances only for the film to which each agreement related; since the making of the "sixth" film constituted a breach of that negative covenant, the defendants were liable in tort for procuring such breach.

Judgment: BINGHAM LJ: "On this part of the case the issues to be decided are these: (a) On the true construction of each of the agreements, did the production company expressly or impliedly undertake that Peter Sellers' performance would be used only for the purposes of the film to which such contract related? (b) Should such term be limited so as to prohibit the use of such performances for other purposes only during the lifetime of Peter Sellers? (c) Can the defendants be held liable for inducing a breach of a purely negative obligation under a loan-out agreement which in other respects has long since been performed? . . .

[Upon consideration of the agreements, Bingham LJ agreed with the conclusions of the court of first instance that question (a) should be answered in the affirmative and question (b) in the negative. He then moved to question (c).] . . . Where those negative covenants were all that survived of the agreements, which had otherwise been fully performed, could the defendants be held liable (if other ingredients of the tort were present) for inducing a breach of those negative covenants?

The defendants argued that they could not. I found that contention startling, and a familiar example will show why. Take the case of an employment contract containing a valid covenant against competition for 12 months after termination. The contract comes lawfully to an end. The employee has performed all the service required of him and has received all the pay to which he is entitled. The only contractual term remaining in force is the employee's negative covenant not to compete. A third party, knowing of the covenant, induces the employee to work for him during the period of the covenant and in obvious breach of it. It is accepted that an action would lie (and an injunction in all probability be granted) against the employee. But if the defendants are right, no action would lie against the third party. They contend that it would not. I can find no basis in principle for such an anomalous result, which conflicts with both the law and the practice as I have long believed them to be.

I hope I shall not be thought discourteous if I do not discuss the authorities cited by the defendants in support of their submission. It is, I think, enough to say that in my judgment there is no authority which does support it. By contrast, the plaintiffs do gain support from the decision of Roxburgh J in *British Motor Trade Association* v. *Salvadori* [1949] Ch. 556. The plaintiff complained, among other things, that the defendants had wrongfully induced or procured breaches of a negative covenant given by buyers of new cars. They succeeded. Roxburgh J said, at p. 565:

'But, in my judgment, any active step taken by a defendant having knowledge of the covenant by which he facilitates a breach of that covenant is enough. If this be so, a defendant by agreeing to buy, paying for and taking delivery of a motor car known by him to be on offer in breach of covenant, takes active steps by which he facilitates a breach of covenant and it is not seriously contended that in any of the cases with which I am

---

[527] c. 44.

concerned the defendant did not know of the existence of the covenant or thought that the covenantor had obtained a release.'

This authority was referred to without disapproval by Jenkins LJ in the leading case of *D.C. Thomson & Co. Ltd.* v. *Deakin* [1952] Ch. 646 at 694, and has never to my knowledge been doubted. I regard it as good law. If, therefore, authority to counter the defendants' arguments is needed, it exists . . .

For these reasons . . . I would dismiss this appeal."

Notes

(1) The tort of interference with a subsisting contract has expanded into many variants, which are surveyed in the following paragraphs, namely direct persuasion, direct inducement, some other forms of direct interference ("other direct intervention"), and indirect intervention.

A person who, with knowledge of a contract made between others and with an intention to interfere with performance of that contract, induces a party to the contract to commit a substantial breach of it has undoubtedly been liable in tort in English law since the decision of a majority of the Court of Queen's Bench in *Lumley* v. *Gye*.[528] In that case of **direct persuasion**, the defendant, owner of a rival theatre, wished to attract a famous opera singer, Johanna Wagner (niece of Richard) and persuaded her to refuse to perform at the Queen's Theatre with which she had a contract to perform exclusively for a certain time.[529]

(2) **Direct inducement** of breach of contract includes cases where a third party, with knowledge of a contract, "has dealings with the contract-breaker which the third party knows to be inconsistent with the contract",[530] as was the case in *British Motor Trade Association* v. *Salvadori*.[531] There, during the post-war period of shortages, including a shortage of new motorcars, the plaintiff Association, of which all British motorcar manufacturers and authorized dealers were members, required that all purchasers of new cars should sign a deed of covenant (a contract under seal) with the Association, whereby the purchaser undertook not to resell the car for a period of a year. The defendant, by purchasing cars known to him to be on offer in breach of contract, was held to have tortiously "interfered" with the car-owner's contract with the Association. The annotated case was held to fall within the category of direct inducement of breach of contract.[532]

---

[528] (1853) 2 El&Bl 216, 118 ER 749.

[529] As to the special position of trade unions as defendants in proceedings for "economic torts" generally, see now the Trade Union and Labour Relations (Consolidation) Act 1992 (c. 52) and note, in particular, that s. 219(1) of that Act provides that: "An act done by a person in contemplation or furtherance of a trade dispute shall not be actionable in tort on the ground only: (a) that it induces another person to break a contract or interferes or induces another person to interfere with its performance . . .".

[530] Per Jenkins LJ in *D.C. Thomson & Co. Ltd.* v. *Deakin* [1952] Ch 646, CA at 651.

[531] [1949] Ch 556, ChD. Commenting on that case, Rogers writes at 623: "In the case of land, statutory provisions may give priority to a later contract registered as a land charge even if entered into with knowledge of an earlier, unregistered transaction, but it seems that this affects only proprietary rights and does not bar an action in tort based on interference with the earlier contract" (references omitted).

[532] An interesting feature of the annotated case is that, in recognizing the right of Peter Sellers' personal representatives as well as his loan-out companies to sue for inducement of breach of contracts made by the loan-out companies, the Court of Appeal effectively "pierced the corporate veil" of the latter, although Bingham LJ's judgment makes no reference to that aspect of the case.

(3) Where there is neither direct persuasion nor direct inducement of the sort just considered, the mere fact that a person *causes* a breach of contract between others will in English law only give rise to tortious liability under certain "other" circumstances (sometimes called "**other direct intervention**").

G.W.K. Ltd. v. *Dunlop Rubber Co. Ltd.* provides a good example of such other circumstances.[533] There, car manufacturer A, a competitor of C, unlawfully substituted its own tyres on cars manufactured and exhibited by B, thereby preventing B from exhibiting tyres manufactured by C on its cars, as B had contractually agreed with C. A was held liable to C for unlawful interference with his contract with B.[534]

In such cases, the means employed by the defendant are of crucial importance, as shown by the following example:[535]

> "To illustrate this, let us suppose that a photographer, A, contracts with a newspaper proprietor, X, that he will supply the latter with the first aerial photograph of Luneville, for publication in X's journal. X thereupon incurs certain preparatory expenses. Y, knowing of the contract, succeeds in securing, before A does so, an aerial photograph of Luneville, which he presents to a rival of X's for publication. It is quite clear from *Thomson* v. *Deakin* itself that Y would not here be liable in tort to X. Yet he has 'procured' a breach of contract by A to as great an extent as Dunlop procured a breach of contract by G.W.K. in *G.W.K.* v. *Dunlop.* The element which is missing in our example is the use of unlawful means. This will be clearly seen if we alter the facts of the illustration by supposing that A succeeds in taking the first aerial photograph of Luneville, but that he is deliberately prevented from delivering it to X, owing to its theft by Y who then gives it to X's rival. Harm having been deliberately inflicted on X, there can be no doubt that the addition of the use of unlawful means by Y against the photographer, A, gives X a good cause of action against Y."

The precise limits of what constitute "unlawful means" for this purpose are not yet entirely clear: threats to commit torts, as well as their actual commission, and threats to commit breaches of contract undoubtedly constitute unlawful means. Yet, so far as actual breaches of contract are concerned, it would seem that the English law doctrine of privity of contract precludes A from suing B because B's breach of contract with C has caused loss to A, even if that was B's intention.[536]

(4) Finally, in the area of tortious procurement of breach of contract, there are cases of so-called "**indirect intervention**", which can occur for instance when a third party would intentionally hire employees away from a firm, so that that firm would become unable to perform a contract of which the third party was aware.[537]

(5) In addition to the variants of interference with a subsisting contract, mention should briefly be made of the tort of **intimidation**, which is committed where the defen-

---

[533] (1926) 42 TLR 376.

[534] For further references, see Rogers at 624.

[535] Taken from J. Lever, "Means, Motives and Interests in the Law of Torts" in A.G. Guest, (ed.), *Oxford Essays in Jurisprudence*, 1st series (Oxford: Clarendon, 1961).

[536] *Rookes* v. *Barnard* [1964] AC 1129 at 1187, [1964] 2 WLR 269, [1964] 1 All ER 367, HL. Although the annotated case was treated as one of direct inducement of breach of contract, it could perhaps equally well have been treated as a case of direct interference through use of unlawful means (i.e. "other direct intervention"), the unlawful means being the defendants' civilly actionable breaches of the performer's rights under the Dramatic and Musical Performers' Protection Act 1958 (c. 44).

[537] See *Clerk & Lindsell on Torts* at para. 23-32, citing *D.C. Thomson & Co. Ltd.* v. *Deakin*, [1952] Ch 646, CA.

dant, with the intention of injuring the plaintiff, utters a threat to someone (whether the plaintiff or a third party) that he, the defendant, will do something unlawful as against the person threatened and, as a result, the latter does or refrains from doing something that he or she was entitled to do, thereby causing loss to him- or herself (if he or she is the plaintiff) or to a third party (if the plaintiff is a third party).

Intimidation, like "other direct intervention" that unlawfully causes a breach of contract, may be merely species of the wider "relatively underdeveloped tort" of unlawful interference with economic and other interests: the deliberate causing of harm to the plaintiff by means of the commission of an actionable wrong against another person.[538] The contours of that broader principle are not yet clearly established, which is why the two other narrower torts of procurement of breach of contract (in its many variants) and intimidation are still relied on. That broader principle was recognized by Lord Reid in *J. T. Stratford & Son Ltd.* v. *Lindley,* where he wrote: "The defendant's action made it practically impossible for the appellants to do any new business . . . It was not disputed that such interference with business is tortious if any unlawful means are used".[539]

House of Lords[540]   **2.E.47.**
Caparo Industries plc v. *Dickman*

LIABILITY IN TORT FOR FALSE STATEMENTS

Inaccurate audit

Auditors, having made inaccurate statements in their audit of a company's accounts are under no duty of care towards potential investors or existing shareholders who have suffered financial losses as a consequence thereof.

Facts: The plaintiff bought, with a take-over in view, 100,000 shares in Fidelity Plc, a company which had some weeks earlier announced unexpectedly poor results, leading to a fall in share price from 143p to 64p. When the accounts and the audit report prepared by the defendants were issued to the shareholders four days after the plaintiff's initial purchase of shares, the plaintiff bought a further 50,000 shares and finally bought the rest of the shares at 125p. The take-over proved to be a very bad bargain, since, far from making a profit of GBP 1.3 million as indicated in the accounts, Fidelity made a loss of GBP 400,000. In addition to claims in deceit against Fidelity's directors, Caparo sued the auditors for negligence.

Held: The court of appeal held that the accountants owed a duty to existing shareholders but not to prospective investors. A unanimous House of Lords was of the opinion that no duty was owed to either group.

Judgment: LORD BRIDGE:[541] "The damage which may be caused by the negligently spoken or written word will normally be confined to economic loss sustained by those who rely on the accuracy of the information or advice they receive as a basis for action. The question what, if any, duty is owed by the maker of a statement to exercise due care to ensure its accuracy arises typically in relation to statements made by a person in the exercise of his calling or profession. In advising the client

---

[538] See generally J. Steiner, "How to Make the Action Suit the Case" (1987) 12 ELRev 102 at 111–12.
[539] [1965] AC 269, [1964] 3 All ER 102, HL. See for other references and discussion, Rogers at 649.
[540] [1990] 2 AC 605, [1990] 1 All ER 568.
[541] Some passages from Lord Bridge's speech, preceding the one reproduced here, were included *supra*, Chapter I, 1.4.1.B, Introductory Note, together with some passages from Lord Oliver's concurring speech.

who employs him the professional man owes a duty to exercise that standard of skill and care appropriate to his professional status and will be liable both in contract and in tort for all losses which his client may suffer by reason of any breach of that duty. But the possibility of any duty of care being owed to third parties with whom the professional man was in no contractual relationship was for long denied . . . until the decision of this House in *Hedley Byrne & Co. Ltd.* v. *Heller & Partners Ltd* [1964] AC 465, [1963] 2 All ER 575 . . . [I]t is to [this and other] authorities . . . that we should look to determine the essential characteristics of a situation giving rise, independently of any contractual or fiduciary relationship, to a duty of care owed by one party to another to ensure that the accuracy of any statement which the one party makes and on which the other party may foreseeably rely to his economic detriment . . .

[THE PROXIMITY TEST]

The most recent decision of the House, which is very much in point, is that of the two appeals heard together of *Smith* v. *Eric S. Bush* and *Harris* v. *Wyre Forest District Council* [[1990] 1 AC 831]. The plaintiffs in both cases were house purchasers who purchased in reliance on valuations of the properties made by surveyors acting for and on the instructions of the mortgagees proposing to advance money to the plaintiffs to enable them to effect their purchases. In both cases the surveyors' fees were paid by the plaintiffs and in both cases it turned out that the inspections and valuations had been negligently carried out and that the property was seriously defective so that the plaintiffs suffered financial loss . . . The House held that in both cases the surveyor making the inspection and valuation owed a duty of care to the plaintiff house purchaser . . .

The salient feature of all these cases is that the defendant giving advice or information was fully aware of the nature of the transaction which the plaintiff had in contemplation, knew that the advice or information would be communicated to him directly or indirectly and knew that it was very likely that the plaintiff would rely on that advice or information in deciding whether or not to engage in the transaction in contemplation [emphasis added]. In these circumstances the defendant could clearly be expected, subject always to the effect of any disclaimer of responsibility, specifically to anticipate that the plaintiff would rely on the advice or information given by the defendant for the very purpose for which he did in the event rely on it. So also the plaintiff, subject again to the effect of any disclaimer, would in that situation reasonably suppose that he was entitled to rely on the advice or information communicated to him for the very purpose for which he required it. *The situation is entirely different where a statement is put into more or less general circulation and may foreseeably be relied on by strangers to the maker of the statement for any one of a variety of different purposes which the maker of the statement has no specific reason to anticipate* [emphasis added]. To hold the maker of the statement to be under a duty of care in respect of the accuracy of the statement to all and sundry for any purpose for which they may choose to rely on it is not only to subject him, in the classic words of Cardozo CJ, to 'liability in an indeterminate amount for an indeterminate time to an indeterminate class': see *Ultramares Corporation* v. *Touche* (1931), 174 NE 441 at 444; it is also to confer on the world at large a quite unwarranted entitlement to appropriate for their own purposes the benefit of the expert knowledge or professional expertise attributed to the maker of the statement. Hence . . . I should expect to find . . . in this category of the tort of negligence, as an essential ingredient of the 'proximity' between the plaintiff and the defendant, that the defendant knew that his statement would be communicated to the plaintiff, either as an individual or as a member of an identifiable class, specifically in connection with a particular transaction or transactions of a particular kind (e.g. in a prospectus inviting investment) and that the plaintiff would be very likely to rely on it for the purpose of deciding whether or not to enter on that transaction or on a transaction of that kind . . .

[TEST APPLIED TO POTENTIAL BUYERS OF SHARES AND TO EXISTING SHAREHOLDERS]
These considerations amply justify the conclusion that auditors of a public company's accounts owe no duty of care to members of the public at large who rely on the accounts in deciding to buy shares in the company. If a duty of care were owed so widely, it is difficult to see any reason why it should not equally extend to all who rely on the accounts in relation to other dealings with a company as lenders or merchants extending credit to the company. A claim that such a duty was owed by auditors to a bank lending to a company was emphatically and convincingly rejected by Millett J in *Al Saudi Banque* v. *Clark Pixley* [1990] Ch 313, [1989] 3 All ER 361 . . .

I should . . . be extremely reluctant to hold that the question whether or not an auditor owes a duty of care to an investor buying shares in a public company depends on the degree of probability that the shares will prove attractive either en bloc to a take-over bidder or piecemeal to individual investors . . .

The position of auditors in relation to the shareholders of a public limited liability company arising from the relevant provisions of the Companies Act 1985 is accurately summarised in the judgment of Bingham LJ in the Court of Appeal [1989] QB 653 at 680–681 . . . No doubt these provisions establish a relationship between the auditors and the shareholders of a company on which the shareholder is entitled to rely for the protection of his interest . . . But in practice no problem arises in this regard since the interest of the shareholders in the proper management of the company's affairs is indistinguishable from the interest of the company itself and any loss suffered by the shareholders, e.g. by the negligent failure of the auditor to discover and expose a misappropriation of funds by a director of the company, will be recouped by a claim against the auditor in the name of the company, not by individual shareholders . . ."

Notes

(1) The annotated judgment puts the earlier judgment of the House of Lords in *Hedley Byrne & Co. Ltd.* v. *Heller & Partners Ltd.* in perspective.[542] In that case the defendant bank had made an innocent but negligent misrepresentation concerning a company's financial strength. In *obiter dicta*, the bank was held to owe the plaintiff a duty of care under the special circumstances of the case.[543] That judgment is one of the three mentioned by Lord Wilberforce in *Anns* to illustrate his two-stage test.[544] It introduced into the law of tort the concept of liability for losses caused by negligent mispresentations and made it clear that there is no blanket rule forbidding recovery of economic loss in negligence[545] at a point in time when *Spartan Steel* had not yet been decided by the Court of Appeal.[546] The judgment in *Caparo*, however, was rendered at a time when the initial enthusiasm for Lord Wilberforce's attempt in *Anns* to turn the "neighbour principle" of *Donoghue* v. *Stevenson* into a general rule had ebbed away with *Yuen Kun Yeu*. In spite of that, *Hedley Byrne* and *Caparo* are based on the same concept, that of *proximity*, which in *Hedley Byrne* was understood to refer precisely to a relationship "equivalent to contract". In *Hedley Byrne*, Lord Devlin wrote of such a relationship that:[547]

---

[542] [1964] AC 465, [1963] 2 All ER 575, HL.

[543] In fact, a disclaimer of liability ultimately led to the dismissal of plaintiff's claim. In *Smith* v. *Eric S. Bush* [1990] 1 AC 831, the purported exclusions of liability were struck down pursuant to s. 2(2) and 11(3) of the Unfair Contract Terms Act 1977 (c. 50), ss. 2(2), 11(3).

[544] *Supra*, 4.1., Introductory Note under c).

[545] Rogers at 124.

[546] *Supra*, **2.E.36.**

[547] *Hedley Byrne & Co. Ltd.* v. *Heller & Partners Ltd.* [1964] AC 465, [1963] 2 All ER 575, HL at 530.

"[It] may be either general or particular. Examples of a general relationship are those of solicitor and client and of banker and customer . . . Where there is a general relationship of this sort it is unnecessary to do more than prove its existence and the duty follows. Where, as in the present case, what is relied on is a particular relationship created ad hoc, it will be necessary to examine the particular facts to see whether there is an express or implied undertaking of responsibility . . ."

In the annotated judgment, Lord Oliver then formulated a list of criteria from which a sufficient relationship of proximity might be established, based on his analysis of *Hedley Byrne*. These criteria are:

"(1) [The] advice is required for a purpose, whether particularly specified or generally described, which is made known, either actually or inferentially, to the adviser at the time when the advice is given; (2) the adviser knows, either actually or inferentially, that his advice will be communicated to the advisee, either specifically or as a member of an ascertainable class, in order that it should be used by the advisee for that purpose; (3) it is known, either actually or inferentially, that the advice so communicated is likely to be acted on by the advisee for that purpose without independent inquiry, and (4) it is so acted on by the advisee to his detriment."

On the basis of this list, which as Lord Oliver wrote should not be regarded as "either conclusive or exclusive", Lord Oliver agreed with Lord Bridge to deny the existence of a duty on the part of the auditors against both investors and shareholders.[548]

(2) *Hedley Byrne* and *Caparo* both deal with whether liability for pure economic loss can arise in respect of negligent misstatements *outside the realm of contract*. Tortious liability for negligent misstatements is a species of liability for negligent *words*, spoken or written, which give rise to liability only when they are uttered in a general or particular relationship of proximity. In *Hedley Byrne*, Lord Reid described the reasons why, in his view, English law must treat negligent words differently from negligent acts:[549]

"The appellants' first argument was based on *Donoghue* v. *Stevenson*. That is a very important decision, but I do not think that it has any direct bearing on this case. That decision may encourage us to develop existing lines of authority, but it cannot entitle us to disregard them. Apart altogether from authority, I would think that the law must treat negligent words differently from negligent acts. The law ought so far as possible to reflect the standards of the reasonable man, and that is what *Donoghue* v. *Stevenson* sets out to do. The most obvious difference between negligent words and negligent acts is this. Quite careful people often express definite opinions on social or informal occasions even when they see that others are likely to be influenced by them; and they often do that without taking that care which they would take if asked for their opinion professionally or in a business connection. The appellant agrees that there can be no duty of care on such occasions . . . But it is at least unusual casually to put into circulation negligently made articles which are dangerous . . .

Another obvious difference is that a negligently made article will only cause one accident, and so it is not very difficult to find the necessary degree of proximity or neighbourhood between the negligent manufacturer and the person injured. But words can be broadcast with or without the consent or the foresight of the speaker or writer. It would be one thing to say that the speaker

---

[548] For an extended list of relevant features, see *James McNaughton Paper Group Ltd.* v. *Hicks Anderson & Co.* [1991] 2 QB 113, [1991] 1 All ER 134, CA, a judgment also rendered in connection with a takeover of a rival company. For an extensive overview of the case law in various sectors or relationships (insurance, securities, solicitors, employers, banking, sale), see Weir at 72–4.

[549] *Hedley Byrne & Co. Ltd.* v. *Heller & Partners Ltd.* [1964] AC 465, HL at 482–3.

owes a duty to a limited class, but it would be going very far to say that he owes a duty to every ultimate 'consumer' who acts on those words to his detriment . . .

So it seems to me that there is good sense behind our present law that in general an innocent but negligent misrepresentation gives no cause of action. There must be something more than the mere misstatement . . ."

The "something more" in addition to reasonable foreseeability to which Lord Reid refers is "proximity", as discussed above, a concept whose content may vary from one type of situation to another.[550]

Lord Reid rightly distinguishes between acts and words if the latter are pronounced, as he says, on social or informal occasions and without the speaker taking the same care if asked for a professional or business opinion. In a professional or business context, however, words are more often written (in audit reports, accounts, legal opinions or documents) than spoken or, if spoken, then on the basis of notes prepared in writing. Professional or business utterances therefore come closer to acts and, if they are false or incomplete, to failures to act correctly. The real difference is, as Lord Reid also mentions, that the written or spoken word, even in a professional or business context, is more apt to harm an unlimited class of people, including people who were not contemplated at all by the speaker or writer in connection with the words pronounced. In such a situation, the relationship of proximity needed for a duty of care to arise is less likely to be present than in the case of acts or failures to act, for example, in the manufacture of a product or the provision of medical care.

House of Lords[551]   **2.E.48.**
White v. *Jones*

SOLICITOR'S DUTY OF CARE

Will comes too late

A solicitor who prepares a will is under a duty of care towards the intended beneficiary of the will, where it is foreseeable that the beneficiary could be deprived of the benefit of the will if the solicitor is negligent, without the testator or the estate having any remedy against the solicitor.

Facts: A man quarrelled with his two daughters had his will altered to deprive his daughters of inheritance. Afterwards the testator made up with his daughters and instructed his solicitor the defendant, to prepare a new will leaving GBP 9,000 to each daughter. The defendant received a letter from the testator informing the defendant of his intention to have a new will drawn. The defendant did nothing for a month, missing three appointments with the testator, and went on holiday for two weeks, intending to visit the testator later. Unfortunately, the testator died three days before a meeting was to be held. The daughters sued the defendant, alleging negligence in the preparation of the new will and claiming GBP 9,000 each in damages.

Held: The court of first instance was of the opinion that the defendants owed no duty of care to the plaintiffs and dismissed the action. The court of appeal held on the contrary that under the circumstances liability arose because it was foreseeable that the intended beneficiaries would suffer financial loss, there was a sufficient degree

---

[550] See *supra*, Chapter I, 1.4.1.B., Introductory Note under c) and f).
[551] [1995] 2 AC 207. The Court of Appeal decision is reported at [1993] 3 All ER 481.

of proximity between the solicitor and the beneficiaries and it was fair, just and reasonable that liability should be imposed in negligence. The House of Lords dismissed the appeal from the court of appeal's decision, Lords Keith and Mustill dissenting.

Judgment: LORD GOFF [for the majority]: "My Lords, in this appeal, your Lordships' House has to consider for the first time the much discussed question whether an intended beneficiary under a will is entitled to recover damages from the testator's solicitors by reason of whose negligence the testator's intention to benefit him under the will has failed to be carried into effect. In *Ross* v. *Caunters* [1980] Ch 297, a case in which the will failed because, through the negligence of the testator's solicitors, the will was not duly attested, Sir Robert Megarry VC held that the disappointed beneficiary under the ineffective will was entitled to recover damages from the solicitors in negligence . . .

Experience in other countries
I turn to the principal issue which arises on the appeal, which is whether in the circumstances of cases such as *Ross* v. *Caunters* [1980] Ch 297 and the present case the testator's solicitors are liable to the disappointed beneficiary . . . [T]he question is one which has been much discussed, not only in this country and other common law countries, but also in some civil law countries, notably Germany. There can be no doubt that *Ross* v. *Caunters* has been generally welcomed by academic writers [references omitted]. Furthermore, it does not appear to have been the subject of adverse comment in the higher courts in this country, though it has not been approved except by the Court of Appeal in the present case. Indeed, as far as I am aware, *Ross* v. *Caunters* has created no serious problems in practice since it was decided nearly 15 years ago. A similar conclusion has been reached in the courts of New Zealand [references omitted] and the law appears to be developing in the same direction in Canada [references omitted]. The position in Australia . . . is at present less clear. In the United States . . . the trend now appears to be moving strongly in favour of liability [references omitted]. In Germany, a disappointed beneficiary may be entitled to claim damages from the testator's negligent auditor under the principle known as contract with protective effect for third parties (*Vertrag mit Schutzwirkung für Dritte*) . . . It also appears that a similar conclusion would be reached in France [references omitted], which appears to be based on the broad principle that a notary is responsible, even as against third parties, for all fault causing damage committed by him in the exercise of his functions. On facts very similar to those of the present case, the Court of Appeal of Amsterdam has held a notary liable in negligence to the intended beneficiary [see 31 January 1985, NJ 1985, 740] . . .

The conceptual difficulties
Even so, it has been recognised on all hands that *Ross* v. *Caunters* raises difficulties of a conceptual nature. . . .
   (1) First, the general rule is well established that a solicitor acting on behalf of a client owes a duty of care only to his client. The relationship between a solicitor and his client is nearly always contractual, and the scope of the solicitor's duties will be set by the terms of his retainer; but a duty of care owed by a solicitor to his client will arise concurrently in contract and in tort: see *Midland Bank Trust Co. Ltd.* v. *Hett, Stubbs & Kemp* [1979] Ch 384, recently approved by your Lordships' House in *Henderson* v. *Merrett Syndicates Ltd.* [1995] 2 AC 145, [1994] 3 All ER 506. But, when a solicitor is performing his duties to his client, he will generally owe no duty of care to third parties . . .

   In these circumstances, it is said, there can be no liability of the solicitor to a beneficiary under a will who has been disappointed by reason of negligent failure by the solicitor to give effect to the testator's intention . . . There can be no liability in contract, because there is no contract between the solicitor and the disappointed beneficiary . . . Nor could there be liability in tort, because in the performance of his duties to his client a solicitor owes no duty of care in tort to a third party such as a disappointed beneficiary under his client's will.

(2) A further reason is given which is said to reinforce the conclusion that no duty of care is owed by the solicitor to the beneficiary in tort. Here, it is suggested, is one of those situations in which a plaintiff is entitled to damages if, and only if, he can establish a breach of contract by the defendant. First, the plaintiff's claim is one for purely financial loss; and as a general rule, apart from cases of assumption of responsibility arising under the principle in *Hedley Byrne & Co. Ltd.* v. *Heller & Partners Ltd.* [1964] AC 465, [1963] 2 All ER 575, no action will lie in respect of such loss in the tort of negligence. Furthermore, in particular, no claim will lie in tort for damages in respect of a mere loss of expectation, as opposed to damages in respect of damage to an existing right or interest of the plaintiff. Such a claim falls within the exclusive zone of contractual liability; and it is contrary to principle that the law of tort should be allowed to invade that zone . . . [Items 3 and 4 are omitted] . . .

(5) There is however another objection of a conceptual nature, which was not adumbrated in argument before the Appellate Committee. In the present case, unlike *Ross v. Caunters* itself, there was no act of the defendant solicitor which could be characterised as negligent. All that happened was that the solicitor did nothing at all for a period of time . . . As a general rule . . . there is no liability in tortious negligence for an omission, unless the defendant is under some pre-existing duty. Once again, therefore, the question arises how liability can arise in the present case in the absence of a contract . . .

The impulse to do practical justice

Before addressing the legal questions which lie at the heart of the present case, it is, I consider, desirable to identify the reasons of justice which prompt judges and academic writers to conclude . . . that a duty should be owed . . . to a disappointed beneficiary . . .

(1) In the forefront stands the extraordinary fact that, if such a duty is not recognised, the only persons who might have a valid claim (i.e. the testator and his estate) have suffered no loss, and the only person who has suffered a loss (i.e. the disappointed beneficiary) has no claim . . . It can therefore be said that, if the solicitor owes no duty to the intended beneficiaries, there is a lacuna in the law which needs to be filled. This I regard as being a point of cardinal importance in the present case. [Lord Goff provided three further reasons which have been omitted here] . . .

The German experience

. . . I have already referred to problems created in the English law of contract by the doctrines of consideration and of privity of contract. These, of course, encourage us to seek a solution to problems of this kind within our law of tortious negligence. In German law, on the other hand, in which the law of delict does not allow for the recovery of damages for pure economic loss in negligence, it is natural that the judges should extend the law of contract to meet the justice of the case. In a case such as the present, which is concerned with a breach of duty owed by a professional man, A, to his client, B, in circumstances in which practical justice requires that a third party, C, should have a remedy against the professional man, A, in respect of damage which he has suffered by reason of the breach, German law may have recourse to a doctrine called *Vertrag mit Schutzwirkung für Dritte* (contract with protective effect for third parties), the scope of which extends beyond that of an ordinary contract for the benefit of a third party . . . In these cases, it appears that the court will examine 'whether the contracting parties intended to create a duty of care in favour of' the third person . . ., or whether there is to be inferred 'a protective obligation based on good faith' . . . But any such inference of intention would, in English law, be beyond the scope of our doctrine of implied terms; and it is legitimate to infer that the German judges, in creating this special doctrine, were extending the law of contract beyond orthodox contractual principles.

I wish next to refer to another German doctrine known as *Drittschadensliquidation*, which is available in cases of transferred loss (*Schadensverlagerung*) . . .

Under this doctrine, to take one example, the defendant, A, typically a carrier, may be held liable to the seller of goods, B, for the loss suffered by the buyer, C, to whom the risk but not the property in the goods has passed. In such circumstances the seller is held to have a contractual claim against the carrier in respect of the damage suffered by the buyer. This claim can be pursued by the seller against the carrier; but it can also be assigned by him to the buyer. If, exceptionally, the seller refuses either to exercise his right for the benefit of the buyer or to assign his claim to him, the seller can be compelled to make the assignment . . . [Both] doctrines have the effect of extending to the plaintiff the benefit of what is, in substance, a contractual cause of action; though, at least as seen through English eyes, this result is achieved not by orthodox contractual reasoning, but by the contractual remedy being made available by law in order to achieve practical justice . . .

I turn next to English law in relation to cases such as the present. Here there is a lacuna in the law, in the sense that practical justice requires that the disappointed beneficiary should have a remedy against the testator's solicitor in circumstances in which neither the testator nor his estate has in law suffered a loss . . .

A contractual approach

It may be suggested that, in cases such as the present, the simplest course would be to solve the problem by making available to the disappointed beneficiary, by some means or another, the benefit of the contractual rights (such as they are) of the testator or his estate against the negligent solicitor, as is for example done under the German principle of *Vertrag mit Schutzwirkung für Dritte*. Indeed that course has been urged upon us by Professor Markesinis [in 'An Expanding Tort Law— The Price of a Rigid Contract Law' (1987)] 103 LQR 354 at 396–397, echoing a view expressed by Professor Fleming [in 'Comparative Law of Torts'] (1984) 4 OJLS 235 at 241. Attractive though this solution is, there is unfortunately a serious difficulty in its way. The doctrine of consideration still forms part of our law of contract, as does the doctrine of privity of contract which is considered to exclude the recognition of a *jus quaesitum tertio*.[552] To proceed as Professor Markesinis has suggested may be acceptable in German law, but in this country could be open to criticism as an illegitimate circumvention of these long-established doctrines . . . Furthermore, I myself do not consider that the present case provides a suitable occasion for reconsideration of doctrines so fundamental as these . . .

The tortious solution

I therefore return to the law of tort for a solution to the problem . . . [F]or the reasons I have previously given, the *Hedley Byrne* . . . principle cannot, in the absence of special circumstances, give rise on ordinary principles to an assumption of responsibility by the testator's solicitor towards an intended beneficiary. Even so, it seems to me that it is open to your Lordships' House . . . to fashion a remedy to fill a lacuna in the law and so prevent the injustice which would otherwise occur on the facts of cases such as the present . . . [where] the nature of the transaction was such that, if the solicitors were negligent and their negligence did not come to light until after the death of the testator, there would be no remedy for the ensuing loss unless the intended beneficiary could claim. In my opinion, therefore, your Lordships' House should in cases such as these extend to the intended beneficiary a remedy under the *Hedley Byrne* principle by holding that the assumption of responsibility by the solicitors towards his client should be held in law to extend to the intended beneficiary who (as the solicitor can reasonably foresee) may, as a result of the solicitor's negligence, be

---

[552] Note of the authors: Lord Goff here refers to the principles of English law that a contract not under seal must be supported by consideration which must be given by the person who is seeking to enforce the contractual promise and that only a party to a contract can enforce the contract so as to take advantage of it.

deprived of his intended legacy in circumstances in which neither the testator nor his estate will have a remedy against the solicitor . . .

As I see it, not only does this conclusion produce practical justice as far as all parties are concerned, but it also has the following beneficial consequences.

(1) There is no unacceptable circumvention of established principles of the law of contract.

(2) No problem arises by reason of the loss being of a purely economic character.

(3) Such assumption of responsibility will of course be subject to any term of the contract between the solicitor and the testator which may exclude or restrict the solicitor's liability to the testator under the principle in *Hedley Byrne* . . .

(4) Since the *Hedley Byrne* principle is founded upon an assumption of responsibility, the solicitor may be liable for negligent omissions as well as negligent acts of commission . . .

(5) I do not consider that damages for loss of an expectation are excluded in cases of negligence arising under the principle in the *Hedley Byrne* case . . . simply because the cause of action is classified as tortious . . .

Conclusion
For these reasons I would dismiss the appeal with costs."

Notes

(1) The annotated judgment is about a failure of a solicitor, in his professional capacity, to draft a will, causing pure economic loss to the intended beneficiaries of the will (who obviously had not themselves retained him). It is not the first case on the tortious liability of members of the legal profession. After *Hedley Byrne*, it could indeed no longer be argued that such liability could not arise in respect of pure economic loss due to negligent acts or failures to act in the professional field.[553] Of course, those participating in legal proceedings "must be given a degree of immunity to ensure that priority is given to the independence and proper functioning of those proceedings".[554] However, that immunity from negligence suits does not cover advice unconnected with litigation, as was discovered by a solicitor who carelessly allowed the husband of a named beneficiary to witness a will, thereby causing the will to be invalid, in *Ross* v. *Caunters*.[555] In that case, the Chancery Division held that there was sufficient proximity for a duty of care to exist between the solicitor and an identified beneficiary under the will (who was not his client).

As Lord Goff pointed out, *Ross* v. *Caunters* had not been the subject of adverse comment and in the 15 years since it was decided, had not created any serious problem in practice. However, before the present case, it had not yet been approved by either the Court of Appeal or the House of Lords. Even so, Lord Goff added, it has been recognized that the judgment raised difficulties of a conceptual nature that are enumerated in the reprinted part of the judgment. Furthermore, the annotated case did not concern negligence committed in the drafting of a will, as *Ross* v. *Caunters* did, but rather a failure to act. Lord Goff wrote: "All that happened was that the solicitor did nothing at all for a period of time", adding that as a general rule, in the absence of a contract, "there is no liability in

---

[553] Under English law duties in contract and in tort can co-exist: see *Midland Bank Trust Co.* v. *Hett, Stubbs and Kemp* [1979] Ch 384, [1978] 3 WLR 167, [1978] 3 All ER 571, ChD, approved by *Henderson* v. *Merrett Syndicates Ltd.* [1995] 2 AC 145, [1994] 3 WLR 761, [1994] 3 All ER 506, HL.

[554] *Clerk & Lindsell on Torts* at 329, para. 7-111, where the scope and the limits of that immunity are discussed.

[555] [1980] Ch 297, [1979] 3 WLR 605, [1979] 3 All ER 580, ChD.

tortious negligence for an omission, unless the defendant is under some pre-existing duty".[556]

(2) The annotated judgment is remarkable for its blunt recognition that there was a lacuna in the law in the case at issue, which had to be filled as a matter of "practical justice". The lacuna consisted in the fact that the only persons who might have a valid claim (the testator and his estate) had suffered no loss, and that the only person who had suffered a loss (the disappointed beneficiary) had no claim. It is equally remarkable that the House of Lords, per Lord Goff, uses comparative law, namely "the German experience" with doctrines like *Vertrag mit Schutzwirkung für Dritte* (contract with protective effect for third parties) and *Drittschadensliquidation* in order to find a solution under English law (he also referred to French and Dutch law).

When he could not find a way to make use of the German "contractual approach", Lord Goff turned to the law of tort to fill the lacuna. He recommended that the law should "extend to the intended beneficiary a remedy under the *Hedley Byrne* principle by holding that the assumption of responsibility by the solicitors towards his client should be held in law to extend to the intended beneficiary . . .". At the end of his speech he enumerated the beneficial consequences of that recommendation, noting amongst other points that no problem arises even if the loss is purely economic and even though the solicitor is made liable for negligent omissions as well as acts.

Court of Appeal[557]   **2.E.49.**
Allied Maples Group Ltd v. *Simmons & Simmons*

Loss of a chance

Bad advice for take-over

Where the negligence of the defendant results in a loss to the plaintiff, the extent of which depends on the behaviour of a third party, the matter properly belongs to the assessment of the quantum of damages, which will then depend on the likelihood that the third party would have taken the action that would have avoided the loss to the plaintiff.

Facts: The defendant solicitors were negligent in advising the plaintiff on the take-over of a going business from G. As a result, the plaintiff inherited liabilities which it could not recover from the seller and against which it would have sought a guarantee from the seller had it known of their existence (failing which the sale would not have taken place). The plaintiff sought to recover from the defendant solicitors as damages the substantial losses suffered as a result of these liabilities.

Held: On the preliminary issue of whether liability could arise in view of the fact that the outcome of the transaction but for the negligent advice cannot be determined with certainty, the court of first instance found in favour of the plaintiffs. The Court of Appeal upheld the judgment of the court of first instance by a majority (2:1). Leave to appeal to the House of Lords was denied.

Judgement: Stuart-Smith LJ: ". . . where the plaintiff's loss depends upon the actions of an independent third party, it is necessary to consider as a matter of law what is necessary to establish as a matter of causation, and where causation ends and quantification of damage begins.

---

[556] See also his speech in *Smith* v. *Littlewood Organisation Ltd.*, *infra*, **3.E.5.**
[557] [1995] 1 WLR 1602, [1995] 4 All ER 907.

(1) What has to be proved to establish a causal link between the negligence of the defendants and the loss sustained by the plaintiffs depends in the first instance on whether the negligence consists in some positive act or misfeasance, or an omission or non-feasance. In the former case, the question of causation is one of historical fact. The court has to determine on the balance of probability whether the defendant's act, for example the careless driving, caused the plaintiff's loss consisting of his broken leg. Once established on the balance of probability, that fact is taken as true and the plaintiff recovers his damage in full. There is no discount because the judge considers that the balance is only just tipped in favour of the plaintiff; and the plaintiff gets nothing if he fails to establish that it is more likely than not that the accident resulted in the injury.

Questions of quantification of the plaintiff's loss, however, may depend upon future uncertain events. For example, whether and to what extent he will suffer osteoarthritis; whether he will continue to earn at the same rate until retirement; whether, but for the accident, he might have been promoted. It is trite law that these questions are not decided on a balance of probability, but rather on the court's assessment, often expressed in percentage terms, of the risk eventuating or the prospect of promotion, which, it should be noted, depends in part at least on the hypothetical acts of a third party, namely the plaintiff's employer.

(2) If the defendant's negligence consists of an omission, for example to provide proper equipment, or to give proper instructions or advice, causation depends, not upon a question of historical fact, but on the answer to the hypothetical question, what would the plaintiff have done if the equipment had been provided or the instruction or advice given. This can only be a matter of inference to be determined from all the circumstances . . .

Although the question is a hypothetical one, it is well established that the plaintiff must prove on the balance of probability that he would have taken action to obtain the benefit or avoid the risk. But again, if he does establish that, there is no discount because the balance is only just tipped in his favour. In the present case the plaintiffs had to prove that, if they had been given the right advice, they would have sought to negotiate with G to obtain protection . . .

(3) In many cases the plaintiff's loss depends on the hypothetical action of a third party, either in addition to action by the plaintiff, as in this case, or independently of it. In such a case does the plaintiff have to prove on the balance of probability . . . that the third party would have acted so as to confer the benefit or avoid the risk to the plaintiff, or can the plaintiff succeed provided he shows that he had a substantial chance rather than a speculative one, the evaluation of the substantial chance being a question of quantification of damages? . . .

Although there is not a great deal of authority . . . I have no doubt that the second alternative is correct . . .

[Stuart-Smith then reviews the case law]

[I]n my judgment, the plaintiff must prove as a matter of causation that he has a real or substantial chance as opposed to a speculative one. If he succeeds in doing so, the evaluation of the chance is part of the assessment of the quantum of damage, the range lying somewhere between something that just qualifies as real or substantial on the one hand and near certainty on the other. I do not think that it is helpful to seek to lay down in percentage terms what the lower and upper ends of the bracket should be.

All that the plaintiffs had to show on causation on this aspect of the case is that there was a substantial chance that they would have been successful in negotiating total or partial (by means of a capped liability) protection . . .

[Stuart-Smith then reviews the evidence and agrees with the trial judge that the plaintiffs had provided sufficient evidence in this respect]

[Counsel for the defendant] submits that the plaintiffs do not even establish that they had a substantial chance of successful negotiation with Gillow. First, he submits that they cannot prove anything beyond a speculative chance in the absence of evidence of Gillow's and Theodore Goddard's reaction. I wholly reject this submission. The prospect of success depends on all the circumstances of the case and the third party's attitude must be a matter of inference. In many cases direct evidence from the third party will not be available, . . . Secondly, [he] submits that the finding of substantial chance is against the weight of the evidence. He relies on the following findings of fact of the judge to lay the ground for this submission . . .

[I]n my judgment, there was ample evidence to support the conclusion that the plaintiffs did have a substantial chance, in the sense I have already defined, of successfully negotiating . . ."

Notes

(1) Compensation for loss of chance, a well-known concept under French law, is also possible under English law, as the annotated judgment illustrates. Actually, the first precedent which Stuart-Smith LJ reviews, namely *Chaplin* v. *Hicks*,[558] concerns the loss of a chance in a situation where the defendant prevented the plaintiff from taking part in a beauty contest and so deprived her of the chance of winning one of the prizes (compare with Cass. crim, 6 June 1990).

(2) It is interesting to see how the Court of Appeal distinguishes the two issues of causation and assessment of damages. Causation must be resolved on a balance of probabilities; it must be established that the negligence of the defendant was causally linked with the loss sustained by the plaintiff. If the negligent conduct consists in some positive act or misfeasance, the question of causation boils down to whether the defendant's act caused the plaintiff's loss. Once that is established on a balance of probabilities, causation is then taken as given and the plaintiff recovers the *full amount* of his or her loss. The same holds true if the negligent conduct of the defendant consisted in an omission or non-feasance, although causation then depends not upon historical facts, but on the hypothetical question of what the plaintiff would have done (or what would have happened to him or her) without the omission, if the defendant had acted as he should have.

The issue of causation becomes more obscure where the extent of the damage to the plaintiff (or even the very occurrence of such damage) depends on the conduct of a third party, i.e. where the conduct of the defendant deprived the plaintiff of the chance that some benefit might accrue to him or her or that some burden would escape him or her (in the case at issue that the plaintiff, if he had received the proper advice from the defendant would have sought, and eventually depending on the outcome of his negotiations with the third party, would have obtained a favourable settlement as to the issue of liabilities incumbent upon him). Stuart-Smith LJ formulates the key question that French courts also had to grapple with: is that uncertainty to be factored in at the level of causation, meaning that the plaintiff will not be able to recover unless he or she can prove on a balance of probabilities that the chance would have materialized? Or is it rather to be taken into account in the assessment of the quantum of damage, on the assumption that a loss which has occurred is worth more than a loss whose occurrence is uncertain?

As French courts have done, Stuart-Smith LJ opted for the second hypothesis. He concludes that, as far as causation is concerned, the plaintiff must show that he or she had a substantial chance rather than a merely speculative one, so that the plaintiff can be said to have lost at least a concrete chance. If the plaintiff succeeds in proving that, the element of uncertainty surrounding the loss will then be reflected in the quantum of dam-

---

[558] [1911] 2 KB 786, [1911-13] All ER 224, CA. *Supra*, **2.F.43.**

ages: the court will have to evaluate the prospects for the plaintiff to obtain the benefit, or to avoid the loss, which means that the quantum of damage will be assessed in terms of a percentage of the eventual loss that could have occurred, depending on the greater or lesser likelihood that the chance would have materialized unfavourably to the plaintiff (in that case, that no settlement would have been reached with the third party).

2.4.2. GERMAN LAW

2.4.2.A. INFRINGEMENTS OF PROTECTIVE ENACTMENTS (§ 823(2) BGB)

Introductory Note

a) According to § 823(2) BGB, liability arises when an "enactment designed to protect someone else" (a "protective enactment") is culpably contravened. Any legal norm may qualify as a protective enactment in the sense of § 823(2), including ordinances, municipal regulations and even unwritten norms derived from customary law or other legal sources.[559] Legal rules that have as their object the protection of the general interest qualify as protective enactments under § 823(2) if they also have as their object the protection of private interests, and provided that the injured person belongs to the class of persons whom the enactment intended to protect and that the *Rechtsgut* which has been prejudiced falls within the ambit of protection of the enactment.[560]

b) Within the general framework of the tort provisions of the BGB, the purpose of § 823(2) is in the first place to clarify and implement the protection offered under § 823(1), either by "concretization", i.e. making an existing *Verkehrspflicht* more concrete or by "abstraction", i.e. extending it in the abstract,[561] without affecting the range of *Rechtsgüter* protected by § 823(1) BGB.

Beyond that, however, the second broad purpose of §823(2) BGB is to enable compensation for *reiner Vermögensschaden*.[562] As will be recalled, a clear policy choice has been made by the drafters of the BGB to leave that head of damage as such outside the list of interests protected by § 823(1) BGB. Only under §§ 823(2) or 826 BGB can compensation for *reiner Vermögensschaden* be sought. Yet, as will be seen below, in order to obtain compensation pursuant to § 826 BGB, the tortious act must have been done intentionally. § 823(2) BGB is the sole provision enabling a plaintiff to recover damages for *reiner Vermögensschaden* resulting from "merely" negligent acts, provided of course that the protective enactment in question can be contravened through such negligent behaviour.

c) The protection afforded by § 823(2) BGB must not be extended so far as to upset the general system of tort law laid down in the BGB by turning § 823(2) into a general

---

[559] Larenz/Canaris at 433.

[560] Ibid. at 433–4, 443.

[561] Taking, by way of example, the duty to drive safely, an example of the first situation (concretization) is a statutory provision that requires a driver to adapt the speed of his or her car to special circumstances of the road, weather conditions, etc. Such a provision can be seen as a special instance of the duty to drive safely. An example of the second situation (abstraction) is a statutory provision prohibiting speeds in excess of 50 km/h within municipalities. Such a provision goes beyond the duty to drive safely by laying down a general and abstract speed limit: Larenz/Canaris at 431 and 402–3.

[562] Ibid. at 431–2.

provision that affords protection against *reiner Vermögensschaden*. Therefore, the protection under § 823(2) must be brought into line with the *Rechtsgüter* doctrine underlying § 823(1) which, as a matter of principle, grants protection against negligent behaviour in German tort law only to the *Rechtsgüter* mentioned in § 823(1) BGB. It will be recalled that the combination of a low fault threshold (mere negligence instead of intention) with a broad scope of liability (without a limitative list of protected interests) was rejected by the drafters of the BGB.[563] Accordingly, there must be a special legitimating element in a protective enactment for § 823(2) to operate so as to afford protection for *reiner Vermögensschaden* against negligent behaviour.[564]

The main legitimating element for a protective enactment to lead to liability for *reiner Vermögensschaden* pursuant to § 823(2) BGB is provided by the "criminal" character of the provision in question. German law distinguishes between *Straftaten* (*mala in se*) and *Ordnungswidrigkeiten* (*mala prohibita*). *Straftaten* comprise basically acts that are inherently wrong (violations of a minimal set of legal-ethical principles, *rechtsethische Minimum*), while *Ordnungswidrigkeiten* typically have no intrinsic moral quality but are prohibited by the law (competition law being a prime example). This allows Larenz/Canaris to write that "in fact, as far as *Vermögensschaden* and infringements of the general freedom to act (*Handlungsfreiheit*) are concerned, the criminal enactment is the paradigm of the protective enactment within the meaning of § 823(2) BGB".[565]

By contrast, enactments relating to *Ordnungswidrigkeiten* will qualify as protective enactments with respect to *reiner Vermögensschaden* only when the *Vermögen* is the primary and immediate interest which the enactment concerned seeks to protect.[566] Even then, the BGH has formulated in relation to *Ordnungswidrigkeiten* the so-called "subsidiarity" doctrine, which requires that, before § 823(2) BGB can be applied, it must be shown that the interests of the injured person cannot be sufficiently protected through other means.[567]

BGH, 6 June 1994[568]   **2.G.50.**

Requirement to file bankruptcy petition

New creditors

A statutory provision that requires the manager of a GmbH to file a bankruptcy petition if the GmbH is unable to pay its debts constitutes a protective law in the sense of § 823(2) BGB in favour of creditors in respect of damage that they suffer because of credit that they have granted to the GmbH after the point of time when the bankruptcy petition should have been filed.

Facts: The defendant was the manager and since 1985 had been the sole shareholder of the company, S. Handels-GmbH ("GmbH") incorporated in May 1981 with an authorized share capital of DEM 50,000. In December 1985 and January 1986 he ordered on behalf of the GmbH from the plaintiff goods to the total value of DEM 98,236.22. The plaintiff delivered the goods subject to reservation of title in January and February 1986. Upon application by the defendant, bankruptcy proceedings over the assets of the GmbH were opened on 25 April 1986. The plaintiff, receiving no payment for delivery of the goods, identified and recovered goods to the value of DEM 7,960.11.

In respect of the remainder of the claim for the amount which it alleged it would lose in the bankruptcy, the plaintiff sought damages from the defendant. It alleged that already in 1985 the GmbH's liabilities exceeded its

---

[563] See *supra*, Chapter I, **1.G.27.**

[564] Larenz/Canaris at 436–7.

[565] Ibid. at 436.

[566] Ibid. at 442. By way of example, that is not the case of *Land* regulations (*landesrechtliche Vorschriften*) concerning public utility installations, such as electricity cables. These regulations aim to protect the ownership of the cable but not the *Vermögen* of the electricity users: ibid. at 437. See also *supra*, 3.2., Introductory Note under e).

[567] Larenz/Canaris at 435 and 439.

[568] BGHZ 126, 181. Translation by N. Sims.

assets and that the GmbH was unable to make payments. That, it said, was known to the defendant when it ordered the goods.

Held: The court of first instance dismissed the action. The court of appeal reversed and allowed it. On appeal by the defendant, the judgment of the court of appeal was set aside and the case was referred back to the lower court.

Judgment: "1. Under § 64(1) GmbHG (Act on Limited Liability Companies) the manager must, in the case of inability to pay [debts when they fall due] or of an excess of liabilities over assets, file a petition for bankruptcy immediately ("without culpable delay"). As has long been acknowledged, that provision is a protective law within the meaning of § 823(2) BGB in favour of creditors of the company. With respect to those creditors who acquired their claims prior to the time when the bankruptcy petition should have been filed, the resulting liability of the manager is limited to the amount of the reduction of the dividend in the bankruptcy proceedings that they would have received if the bankruptcy petition had been filed in due time (the so-called *Quotenschaden*) [The BGH then held that such liability also extended to 'new' creditors, i.e. those who gave credit after the point in time when a petition for bankruptcy should have been filed. There follows a discussion of the judicial and doctrinal controversy as to the extent of liability towards 'new' creditors. The BGH decided to overrule previous case law.]

2. With the approval of the civil chambers of the BGH concerned . . . as well as the third chamber of the *Bundesarbeitsgericht*, the present chamber regards a manager who is guilty of a breach of the duty to file a bankruptcy petition in accordance with § 64(1) GmbHG to be liable in damages for the full loss (even beyond the *Quotenschaden*) suffered by [new] creditors who entered into business relations with the GmbH and granted credit to it as a result of that breach.

a) As already observed, by virtue of the duty to petition for bankruptcy imposed on the manager of a GmbH, protection is enjoyed not only by creditors of the company at the time when the bankruptcy petition should have been filed ('old creditors'), but also by those who come on the scene subsequently ('new creditors'). *If the manager had fulfilled his duty, the latter would not have become creditors: they would no longer have entered into contractual relations with the company, would not have granted it credit and thus would not have suffered loss at all. That loss is occasioned by the breach of the protective provision contained in § 64(1) GmbHG. Consequently, under the general rules governing damages, the damage thus caused to the contractual partner contrary to law and culpably must be made good in full* [references omitted; emphasis added]. The fact that, contrary thereto, an old creditor is compensated only in the amount of the reduction of the dividend that he would have received if the bankruptcy petition had been filed in time, is no reason for treating new creditors in the same way . . .

b) The statutory purpose of the legal duty to petition for bankruptcy is to take out of circulation insolvent companies with limited funds to meet liabilities, so that creditors are not harmed or put at risk by the eventuation of such phenomena [reference omitted] . . .

c) . . . *As an instrument for the protection of creditors, the requirement to petition for bankruptcy in due time must be sanctioned in such a way to render the protection effective, not only in criminal law, but in tort law as well. If the liability of managers were limited to the* Quotenschaden, *and there were no liability for individual damage going beyond that, the statutory purpose of the protection could not be attained* [emphasis added] . . . Calculation of that *Quotenschaden* poses "worrisome problems of assessment of damages" [reference omitted] which are further accentuated in the case of creditors appearing after the time when a bankruptcy petition should have been filed [reference omitted]. The efforts associated with this task are so considerable that in practice it is not regarded as worthwhile . . ."

Notes

(1) According to earlier BGH case law, "new creditors" (and not only "old creditors") are entitled to obtain compensation directly from the managers of a bankrupt company on the basis of § 823(2) BGB.[569] "New creditors" of a GmbH (a limited liability company) are creditors who entered into an agreement with the GmbH *after* the point in time when the GmbH managers should have filed a bankruptcy petition pursuant to § 64(1) of the German Act on Limited Liability Companies (GmbH-Gesetz, GmbHG). In other words, § 64(1) GmbHG was regarded as a protective enactment (*Schutznorm*), in the sense of § 823(2) BGB, towards not only old but also new creditors, both categories of creditors being held to fall within its *personal* scope of application.

However, in accordance with the *objective* scope of § 64(1) GmbHG, for old and new creditors alike, the amount of compensation was previously limited to the so-called *Quotenschaden*. The *Quotenschaden* is the reduction in the value of the claims against the bankrupt estate that was attributable to the culpable omission of the managers to request the opening of the proceedings in due time: for instance, if the creditors would have recovered 10 per cent of the value of their claims had the managers filed for bankruptcy in due time but are now faced with 8 per cent recovery, the *Quotenschaden* would amount to 2 per cent of the claims. Accordingly, new creditors (like old ones) could not obtain compensation for the full amount of the loss (i.e. the difference between the original value of their claims and their current value against the bankrupt estate) that they suffered because they extended credit to the company under an agreement entered into after the point in time when managers should have filed for bankruptcy as specified in § 64(1) GmbHG.

(2) The annotated judgment overrules the earlier case law in that it holds that the interests of the new creditors fall within the *objective* protective scope of § 64(1) GmbHG for the full amount of their loss and not just for the *Quotenschaden*.[570]

The argument used by the BGH under 2.c) is noteworthy: "As an instrument for the protection of creditors, the requirement to petition for bankruptcy in due time must be sanctioned in such a way to render the protection effective, not only in criminal law, but in tort law as well". The relevance of this *effet utile* argument is further illustrated by the BGH's reference to the insignificant monetary value of the *Quotenschaden* in practice. The BGH also indicates that the bases suggested in the earlier case law and legal writings somehow to provide protection to the new creditors were "doctrinally untenable" (*dogmatisch nicht haltbar*).

(3) From a procedural point of view it is interesting to note that, before giving judgment and thereby reversing earlier case law, the 2nd Civil Chamber of the BGH consulted other civil chambers of the same court as well as a chamber of the *Bundesarbeitsgericht* (Federal Labour Court). The *Gerichtsverfassungsgesetz* (GVG) provides at § 132 that a plenary session of all the civil and/or criminal law senates of the BGH must be convened when one chamber envisages deviating from the case law of another.[571] That other chamber must however first be asked whether it still maintains the position expressed in its case law (§ 132(3)

---

[569] BGH, 16 December 1958, BGHZ 29, 100.

[570] See further, in particular, the reasoning under 2.b. and 2.c. of the judgment (not reproduced here) reversing the position taken earlier in BGH, 16 December 1958, BGHZ 29, 100.

[571] (Courts of Justice Act), Version promulgated on 9 May 1975, BGBl.I.1077.

GVG). A similar procedure applies between the various German Supreme Courts to ensure the consistency of the case law.[572]

2.4.2.B. ACTS *CONTRA BONOS MORES* (§ 826 BGB)

Introductory Note

a) § 826 BGB provides that a person is liable if he or she intentionally causes harm to another in a manner that is *contra bonos mores*. The practical significance of this third general heading of German tort law lies in the absence of any reference to protected *Rechtsgüter* (contrary to § 823(1) BGB) or to an underlying protective enactment (contrary to § 823(2) BGB). Instead, § 826 BGB protects all legal interests, including *reiner Vermögensschäden* in general, against interferences, *provided* that they are *contra bonos mores* and intended to cause harm. The practical significance of § 826 BGB becomes clear when one looks at the kinds of factual situations to which it has mainly been applied, such as: participating as a third person in a breach of contract committed by a contracting party; delaying someone's bankruptcy to draw personal benefit at the expense of other creditors; giving false information or omitting to give information in circumstances where there is a duty to give it; abusing one's right or position.[573]

Rechtsmißbrauch or *abus de droit* are familiar notions to lawyers trained in civil law jurisdictions. These notions are here translated as "abuse of right". Put briefly, an abuse of right occurs when the exercise of a right by its holder, even if lawful, results in harm to a third party, in circumstances, such as where that exercise was not useful to the holder of the right, where the holder of the right could have chosen a less harmful way of exercising his or her right or where the advantages brought to the holder of the right by the exercise of that right are outweighed by the harm done to the third party. The abuse of right doctrine evolved out of the field of disputes between neighbours and is now used throughout the civil law of the Continental countries.

b) § 826 lays down, as a first condition for its application, the requirement that the conduct must be *contra bonos mores* (*sittenwidrig*). *Boni mores* is a flexible and changing notion, which refers to a minimal set of legal-ethical principles (*rechtsethische Minimum*) seen as a set of legal value assessments (*rechtliche Wertungen*).[574] Conduct *contra bonos mores* consists in behaviour that significantly offends the "fundamental concepts of morally acceptable conduct towards persons with whom one is in a legal relationship".[575] The second condition of the application of § 826 is *Schädigungsvorsatz*, which can perhaps best be translated as "will to harm". *Schädingungsvorsatz* comprises intention and recklessness. It is therefore not necessary "that the defendant actually intended to cause the harm; it is enough if he was conscious of the possibility that harm might occur and acquiesced in its doing so".[576] It is thus sufficient to be aware of the consequences of one's conduct and to accept them as inevitable even without desiring them.[577] Deception

---

[572] See §§ 2 and 14 of the *Gesetz zur Wahrung der Einheitlichkeit der Rechtsprechung der obersten Gerichtshöfe des Bundes* (Act to ensure the consistency of the case law of the federal supreme courts) of 19 June 1968, BGBl.I.661.

[573] Larenz/Canaris at 455–62.

[574] Ibid. at 450–1.

[575] *Grundanschauungen loyalen Umgangs unter Rechtsgenossen*: BGH, 2 June 1981, NJW 1981, 2184 at 2185, quoted by Larenz/Canaris at 451.

[576] Zweigert and Kötz at 603.

[577] *Dolus eventualis*, see Markesinis at 895.

(*Tauschung*) and recklessness (*Leichtfertigkeit*) are qualifications often used in this context.[578] It must be noted that gross negligence (i.e. an objectively gross deviation from reasonably careful conduct) does not in itself qualify as wilfulness for the purposes of § 826 BGB, although in practice "lesser" forms of wilfulness such as recklessness may very well cover gross negligence cases.[579]

BGH, 19 October 1993[580]   **2.G.51.**

INTERFERENCE WITH CONTRACTUAL RELATIONSHIPS

Conspiring wife

Participating as a third party in a breach of contractual duty (here a bank taking part in a scheme whereby a wife defrauded her husband) does not as such constitute an act contra bonos mores *within the meaning of § 826 BGB.*

Facts: The plaintiff bought a house in 1973. In 1974, after marriage, he conveyed the house to his wife, and the conveyance was duly recorded in the *Landregister*. The couple subsequently entered into a notarized contract whereby they agreed that the wife had put up one-sixth of the value of the house and the plaintiff five-sixths and that, in case of divorce, the wife accepted the obligation to return the property to the plaintiff on payment by him of one-sixth of the value of the house. After the plaintiff and his wife had separated in June 1979, the wife, without the knowledge of her husband, granted three liens (*Grundschulden*), each of DEM 100,000, over the property. Particulars of the liens were entered in the *Landregister* in August 1979 and the liens were transferred to the wife's brother-in-law, Dr S, in 1980.

In October 1981 the plaintiff petitioned for divorce and in December 1981 he requested a priority notice of conveyance (*Auflassungsvormerkung*) to be entered in the *Landregister*. Earlier, in January 1981, the wife had, through her lawyer K, asked for a credit of DEM 300,000, which the wife obtained from the defendant bank in February 1982. The earlier liens on the property were given to the bank as collateral security for the loan. In addition to the liens, part of the credit granted by the bank, in an amount of DEM 150,000 DM, was pledged to the bank as security. The wife failed to make any repayments to the bank, and instalments of interest fell due. In February 1984, the divorce was pronounced and the court ordered the wife to return the property to the plaintiff. The defendant bank thereupon terminated the credit to the wife and initiated proceedings for the compulsory sale of the property by public auction (*Zwangversteigerung*).

The plaintiff sued the bank, claiming that his ex-wife had wished to cause him harm by issuing liens on the property which she was obliged to return in the event of divorce, that the defendant bank was aware of that fact and that it colluded with the wife's brother-in-law, Dr S, and with her lawyer, K, to cause injury to the plaintiff. The plaintiff relied on § 826 BGB against the defendant bank to seek a declaration that the compulsory sale of the property was unlawful.

Held: The claim was rejected by the court of first instance but upheld by the court of appeal. The BGH allowed the appeal from the judgment of the court of appeal.

Judgment: "2. The defendant acquired the real estate securities from the person formally holding title at the request of the owner registered in the Land Register. Unknown to the defendant when he made the acquisition, the priority notice of conveyance in favour of the plaintiff did not preclude assignment of the real estate securities already effected [references omitted]. The defendant was not required to inquire as to whether the plaintiff's former wife or her brother-in-law incurred tortious liability to third parties by effecting and assigning liens (*Grundschulden*) by way of security. *Contractual claims are not amongst the rights infringement of which in itself gives rise to claims in tort. Nor does the moral order oblige an independent third party in a case of conflict to subordinate its own interests to those of the contracting parties* [references omitted]. *Thus, there is no claim under § 826*

---

[578] Larenz/Canaris at 452–3.
[579] Ibid. at 454–5.
[580] NJW 1994, 128. Translation by N. Sims.

BGB for damages against a third party simply on the ground of his cooperation in the violation by the debtor of his creditor's rights under the contract [reference omitted, emphasis added]. In accordance with settled BGH case-law, involvement by a third party in a breach of contract is *contra bonos mores* only if his interference with the contractual relations is marked by a particular lack of consideration for the person concerned. Such a lack of consideration may above all be constituted by collusion with the debtor under the contract in order specifically to frustrate the claims of the creditor concerned [reference omitted]. *The allegation of conduct* contra bonos mores *is well-founded only in cases of serious offences to feelings of decency, where the course of conduct of a third party is incompatible with the basic requirements of a proper view of the law (Grundbedürfnissen loyaler Rechtsgesinnung)* [references omitted, emphasis added].

3. The court of appeal found that the conduct of the defendant did not satisfy these requirements.

a) In particular, the court does not proceed on the assumption that the defendant was aware of the intention of the plaintiff's former wife of whittling away at her obligation to reconvey. It is not even established that the defendant was aware that she had incurred that obligation. The court of appeal considers it sufficient that the defendant carelessly closed its mind to the knowledge that the conduct of the plaintiff's wife could result in some kind of injury to an unspecified third party . . . *An ethical obligation on the part of banks to investigate the possible adverse consequences of their loan decisions on third parties cannot be derived from the basic requirements of a proper view of the law within the meaning of § 826 BGB* [emphasis added].

b) Moreover, contrary to the view of the court of appeal, the borrower's conduct was not at all suspicious. To take up a loan and secure half of the borrowing by a credit on time deposit is not manifestly unreasonable and so is not an unmistakable expression of an intention to cause injury to a third party. 'Sham transactions' of that kind are not infrequently entered into for tax reasons . . ."

Note

The question whether, and under what conditions, a third party participating in a breach of contract committed by one of the contracting parties is liable in tort is much debated in many legal systems. German tort law, taking a restrictive view, does not regard interference with someone else's contractual rights as tortious conduct in and of itself. As the BGH writes, good morals do not in general require third parties to give rights arising from contracts to which they are not party precedence over their own rights and interests. Tortious liability can arise only when interference with contracts made between others amounts to conduct *contra bonos mores*, that is when it is inconsistent with the fundamental requirements of *loyaler Rechtsgesinnung*.[581]

The key sentence in the annotated judgment is the reference to the well-established case law of the BGH, whereby a third party's interference with a contractual relationship existing between others is *contra bonos mores* (*sittenwidrig*) only when the third party shows a special degree of wanton or reckless behaviour (*Rücksichtslosigkeit*) towards the contracting party who is prejudiced by the breach of contract that occurs. That is the case in particular when the third party colludes with a debtor to jeopardize the contractual rights of the creditor. The BGH found that such conduct had not been established in the present case, since the bank could not be held to have acted *contra bonos mores* merely because

---

[581] This is another way of describing the "legal-ethical principles" mentioned *supra*, 4.2., Introductory Note.

it failed to investigate whether its decision to extend credit to the wife might have unfavourable consequences for the husband.

BGH, 26 November 1986[582]   **2.G.52.**

NOTION OF SCHÄDIGUNGSVORSATZ. "PROTECTIVE AMBIT OF CONTRACT" THEORY

Inaccurate audit

An auditor supplying incorrect financial statements is acting contra bonos mores *vis-à-vis a bank which used these statements, even if the statements were not prepared for the bank.*

Facts: The plaintiff, a bank, had allowed credit, in the amount of DEM 500,000, to its client to finance his purchase of shares in V-GmbH. The credit was granted on the basis of interim financial statements of V-GmbH. Those statements had been prepared and certified by the defendant, who was V-GmbH's tax adviser and who had been engaged by V-GmbH's sole shareholder and manager, M, to prepare and certify the statements. One copy of the statements was supplied to M and two other copies were supplied to the plaintiff bank's client, who used the statements to obtain the credit from the plaintiff.

One year after the purchase V-GmbH was declared bankrupt. The plaintiff who as a creditor of the bankrupt company remained unpaid, sought compensation from the defendant, claiming that the certified statements were false. The firm of the defendant was also sued as a second defendant, on the basis of a contractual relationship with the plaintiff.

Held: The court of first instance dismissed the action. The court of appeal upheld that judgment. The BGH allowed the appeal and remitted the matter to the court of appeal.

Judgment: "I. The court *a quo* is of the opinion that the plaintiff has no right to claim damages in contract or in tort. Its reasoning on both counts is, however, not free from error.

1. The question whether the action may be founded in tort is examined by the court *a quo* under § 826 BGB. It proceeds on the correct assumption that a careless and unconscionable (*gewissenlos*) conduct can also be *contra bonos mores* within the meaning of the abovementioned provision. However, the court *a quo* held that no action for damages lay, on the ground that the plaintiff was unable to prove that the defendant had acted intentionally . . . *The question whether, in drawing up the interim statement and issuing the certificate, the defendant acted carelessly and intentionally caused injury to a third party, can be answered appropriately only by first clarifying whether and on what points the interim statement contains objective errors* [reference omitted, emphasis added]. On this point the following observations should be made:

a) . . . The state of the GmbH's books of account was of decisive importance for the person having to take a decision on the basis of the certified interim statement. The lack of properly kept books of account did not merely cast doubt on the balance sheet items; it was rather this factor which in itself was capable of giving rise to well-founded doubts as to the proper management of the company . . .

b) Subjective consequences also flow from this. If the defendants were aware that the books of account of the V-GmbH disclosed serious irregularities, and for that reason considered that it was not possible to draw up a reliable interim balance sheet, then it was careless conduct to certify the interim statement of 31 May 1981 . . . However, the court of appeal agreed with the lower court that an intention to cause injury was not proved and took the view that such could only be assumed if the defendants could at least expect that their careless and incorrect interim statement would reach the plaintiff or at least another bank to be used as a basis for a loan decision . . .

---

[582] NJW 1987, 1758. Translation by N. Sims.

[However,] for there to be intent it is sufficient if it was conceivable on the part of the defendants that the statement could be used in negotiations with a provider of finance and could lead that person into taking a decision disadvantageous to him [emphasis added]. [The BGH then concluded that the defendant, on the basis of its professional experience as tax adviser, had to take into account that the purchaser of V-GmbH would have recourse to bank financing for his purchase. It noted furthermore that only the defendant tax adviser, and not his firm, had the requisite *Schädigungsvorsatz* for the application of § 826 BGB.]

2. [The BGH then examines if and on what basis the defendant's firm could also be held liable.] The court of appeal correctly assumed that there was a contract to draw up an interim statement, the contract being between the partnership of the defendants and V-GmbH (or its manager and sole shareholder M). It took the view, however, that the plaintiff was not included within the scope of protection of the contract, and that such could be the case only if the party who was in a contractual relationship with the defendant owed a duty of protection toward the injured third party. According to the court of appeal, however, no such relationship subsists between V-GmbH (or its shareholder M) and the plaintiff. *That legal assessment is, however, not in conformity with the case law of the BGH . . . whereby the contracting parties may create a duty of protection also in favour of persons who are not entrusted to their welfare. Whether there was such intent is for the court trying the merits of the case to determine on the basis of general principles of interpretation* [emphasis added]. In the present case there is evidence to suggest that the contracting parties did wish to include third parties within the protective scope of the contract . . . In so far as the second defendant infringed a contractual duty of protection, the plaintiff may also proceed against the first defendant on a claim for damages. As partners the defendants are jointly and severally liable for any breach of contract by one of them . . ."

Notes

(1) The first part of the judgment illustrates how broadly the notions of unethical conduct (*Sittenwidrigkeit*) and will to harm (*Schädigungsvorsatz*) have been interpreted. Both the court of appeal and the BGH found that the defendant, in too readily and superficially preparing and certifying interim financial statements, had acted in a way which could be regarded as being *contra bonos mores*. Unlike the court of appeal, the BGH believed that the defendant had acted wilfully. In order to reach that conclusion, the BGH based itself on the lack of regular corporate accounts on which the defendant could have founded his certificate (the objective element), and on the fact that the defendant must have known from general experience that his report might be used to obtain credit from the plaintiff bank.[583]

(2) In the annotated judgment, tortious liability fell on the defendant, who prepared the interim accounts and issued the statement himself. The defendant operated in a partnership with another business adviser, and the contract for the preparation of the accounts and the statement was between V-GmbH (the company whose interim financial accounts had to be prepared and certified) and the partnership. His partner in the firm was not liable in tort, since he had not prepared and signed the accounts and the statement. The only way for the plaintiff bank to obtain compensation from that partner as well, was to argue that there was also a breach of the contract between V-GmbH and the

---

[583] See also *supra*, 4.2.B., Introductory Note under b).

partnership. The question then arose whether the plaintiff bank could benefit from that contract.[584]

The BGH recognized that a third party may indeed rely on the terms of a contract concluded between others. That is the case, as the BGH states in a part of the judgment not reproduced here, when the third party's interests for good or ill (*Wohl und Wehe*) are entrusted to one of the contracting parties who (like V-GmbH) has a contractual right against the other. But it is also the case when, in the particular circumstances of the case, elements can be found in what the contracting parties have declared, or in their behaviour, pointing to the existence of a tacit agreement between them to extend the protective scope of the contract to a specific class of third parties (*eine überschaubare, klar abgrenzbare Personengruppe*), such as money-lenders or purchasers. In the present case, V-GmbH was not acting objectively as a custodian of the interests of the plaintiff bank, but could be held to have indicated in its dealings with the consultancy firm that the plaintiff was to be able to rely on the contract. Of course, even then it must be established that the contracting party against whom a claim is brought has failed to perform the contract properly (see under 2).

2.4.3. FRENCH LAW

Introductory Note

Under French tort law, the right to life, physical and moral integrity, specific and general rights of personality and privacy, as well as property rights are all fully protected against interference and damage of any kind, including pure economic loss and *perte d'une chance* (loss of a chance), irrespective of whether the damage is suffered by the primary victim or by secondary victims or dependants. As stated above, the concept of subjective right,[585] and the general right to privacy in particular, have made it easier for persons who have suffered damage to claim in tort under Articles 1382–1383 C.civ.[586] Unlike in German law, however, the concept of subjective right is not used in French law to limit the class of protected interests. French tort law offers full protection, as a matter of principle, to all kinds of legitimate interests. If subjective rights have played any role, it was more to ease the burden on claimants by making claims for violation of the right to privacy, for example, largely autonomous: as mentioned above, the mere infringement of the right suffices to satisfy the conditions of fault and damage for the purposes of liability under Article 1382 C.civ.

As a consequence of that general unrestrictive approach, French law, unlike German or English law, does not actually need an additional body of rules to deal with "protec-

---

[584] See generally on the theory of contracts that give legal protection to third parties, W. Lorenz, "Contracts and Third Party Rights in German and English law" and, more particularly in relation to incorrect or false statements, C. von Bar, "Liability for information and opinions causing pure economic loss to third parties: a comparison of English and German case law" both in B. Markesinis, (ed.), *The Gradual Convergence*, (Oxford: Clarendon Press, 1994) 65 and 98 respectively. See also *supra*, Chapter I, 1.3.

[585] On the concept of subjective right, a concept unknown to English law, see *supra*, Chapter I, 1.4.3., Introductory Note.

[586] *Supra*, Chapter I, **1.F.24.–25.**, Note (1).

tion against professional negligence". We nevertheless provide for such a heading in order to ensure greater ease of comparison with English and German law. It is then possible to see, from a functional (not conceptual) point of view, how the same tortious conduct, namely unprofessional behaviour, is dealt with in a comparable manner under each of the three legal systems.

Cass. civ. 3e, 8 July 1975[587]   **2.F.53.**
Société de copropriété et réalisation immobilières v. *Servim*

DISREGARDING SOMEONE ELSE'S CONTRACT AMOUNTS TO A FAULT

Promised land

A purchaser of real estate commits a fault within the meaning of Article 1382 C.civ. against a third person to whom the seller had previously promised to sell, if and when the purchaser knew of the existence of that promise.

Facts: On 19 June 1969 Mrs Sabatier, by a unilateral promise contained in an *acte sous seing privé* (a private, unnotarized agreement), granted the Pravat Company an option over certain real property that she owned; the option was exercisable up to 30 September 1969. On 11 July 1969, by *acte sous seing privé*, Pravat assigned the benefit of that option to the plaintiff. However, on 21 September 1969, by a further *acte sous seing privé*, Pravat again assigned the benefit of the option, on this occasion to the defendant, the Servim company. On 26 September 1969, Servim learnt of the earlier assignment of the option to the plaintiff. On 3 October 1969, Mrs Sabatier formally conveyed the property (*acte authentique*) to Servim. As a consequence of that formal conveyance, which secured priority to the defendant, the plaintiff lost the benefit of the option that Pravat had, with the defendant's knowledge, assigned to it.

Held: The court of appeal held that the defendant had not committed a fault in the sense of Article 1382 C.civ., because it had been assured by Pravat that the latter was no longer bound *vis-à-vis* the plaintiff, and could thus not be regarded as having acted fraudulently. The Cour de cassation quashed that decision.

Judgment: "Having regard to Art. 1382 C.civ: The beneficiary of a promise of sale is entitled to invoke against a person who is not a party to that promise either the fraud with which that person is associated or merely the fault of which that person was guilty in agreeing to acquire a building which it knew to be subject to the promise.

In dismissing the claim by the Société de copropriété et réalisations immobilières (SCRI) against Servim for the loss suffered in consequence of the sale which was completed on 3 October 1969 and was effective as against SCRI, the court of appeal stated that 'if Servim had really been informed of the promise of sale entered into between SCRI and Pravat, the latter company had assured Servim that it was freed of any obligation with regard to SCRI and had stated in the document of 22 September 1969 that it was making it its own personal matter'; and that 'since proof of fraudulent collusion between Pravat and Servim has not been adduced, Servim cannot be held liable'.

Nevertheless, it is clear from the court of appeal's own findings that, after learning of the promise of sale binding Pravat to SCRI under the document of 22 September 1969, Servim was informed by a letter from Thabaut [the notary] dated 26 September 1969 of the difficulties that might arise owing to the existence of that promise, and that Servim itself indicated to the notary, in a letter of 3 October 1969, that it relieved him of all liability. Having thus established all the elements constituting fault (*faute*), the court of appeal, in deciding as it did, applied [Article 1382 C.civ.] incorrectly."

[587] Bull.civ. 1975.III.249, D 1975.IR.200. Translation by N. Sims.

237

Notes

(1) It is no longer controversial under French law that a third party who participates knowingly in a contractual breach committed by a contracting party can itself incur non-contractual liability towards the other contractual party on the basis of a fault under Article 1382 C.civ. The third party would then be held liable to pay damages, generally jointly and severally (*in solidum*) with the contracting party who has broken the contract.[588] That principle is now known as "liability of a third-party accomplice to a contractual breach".[589] In applying the principle, no distinction is drawn between contracts concerning rights *in rem* (*droits réels*) and contracts concerning rights *in personam* (*droits personnels*), even though the former can be enforced *erga omnes* whereas the latter bind only the debtor. That is irrelevant in the present context since rights *in personam* "while they 'bind' the debtor only, are nevertheless also there for third-parties who must respect them".[590] In other words, the existence of a right *in personam* emanating from a contract (such as, in the judgment above, an option granted by a unilateral promise to sell) is a legal fact which third parties are under a duty to take into account, even if they are not parties to the contract and, as such, not bound to perform its terms.

Under French law certain contracts, e.g. conveyances of real property and mortgages, must be publicized through their entry in a public register.[591] For the purposes of liability under Article 1382 C.civ., third parties will be deemed to have knowledge of such contracts if they have been registered as required by law. However, even without registration, a third party may be liable for wrongful interference with the contract if he or she had actual knowledge of it, as was the case here.[592]

(2) Sole purchase and distributorship agreements, contracts granting options as well as rights of first refusal over real estate or company shares seem to be the types of contract most frequently interfered with. In these cases, instead of, or in combination with, an action for breach of contract against the other party to the contract, the beneficiary of the contractual rights in question usually also sues the third party whose dealings with the other contracting party have deprived it of the benefit to which it was entitled.[593]

When considering the case law regarding sole purchase and sole distributorship agreements, one should however keep in mind the impact of EC competition rules on the validity of those agreements. Article 81(1) EC prohibits agreements that have the object or effect of prevention, restriction or distortion of competition and which may affect trade between Member States. Article 81(2) renders such prohibited agreements automatically void. Article 81(3) creates a possibility of exemption from the prohibition of Article 81(1). In the absence of such an exemption, which can be a group exemption, interference with an agreement prohibited by Article 81(1)—and therefore void under Article 81(2)—should not give rise to tortious liability any more than a breach of the agreement would give rise to contractual liability.

(3) Whilst the principle of liability for third party interference with a contractual relationship is uncontroversial, the same cannot be said of the conditions of liability. A key

[588] See Viney, *Introduction* at 367–8, para. 202.

[589] First coined by P. Hugueney, *De la responsabilité du tiers complice de la violation d'une obligation contractuelle* (Dijon: 1910).

[590] Viney, *Introduction* at 369, para. 203.

[591] Registration is not a condition of validity or enforceability *as between the parties to the contract*, but it affects the ability of the beneficiary to oppose his/her rights under the contract to third parties who would also claim an interest in the property in question. For example, the owner of a piece of land mortgages it first to A and subsequently to B; if A has failed to register its mortgage or does so only after B has registered its own mortgage, B will be able to claim priority over A.

[592] Viney, *Introduction* at 371–2, para. 204.

[593] For a study of the case law in both areas, see J. Schmidt-Szalewski, *Droit des contrats—Jurisprudence française*, vol. 5 (Paris: Litec, 1989) at 470–84.

question here is whether there must be collusion or fraudulent concertation between the third party defendant and the contracting party who is acting in breach of contract, or whether it suffices that the third party knew of the contract and acted in disregard of it. Whereas the first view is more in line with privity of contract under Article 1165 C.civ. and with the general freedom of third parties to act and to compete, the second view is more in line with the general concept of fault under Article 1382 C.civ. The second view seems to prevail (in the annotated judgment as well), although the distinction between the two views is not always discernible, as appears from the following statement of G. Viney: "most case-law as well as almost all writers agree that, in order to ground liability, the third party must be proven in bad faith, i.e. the third party effectively knew of the contract whose violation it has contributed to".[594]

Tribunal de grande instance de Paris, 19 November 1980[595]   **2.F.54.**
Sté Kléber Colombes v. *Union fédérale des consommateurs*

HARMING ONE'S BUSINESS. RIGHT TO INFORM CONSUMERS.

Defective tyres

A consumer organization may criticize commercial products and eventually take steps with the competent authorities to prohibit those products, provided that the organization has properly verified the facts on which it is basing its actions.

Facts: In its periodical *Que choisir?* a consumer organization, the Union fédérale des consommateurs (UFC) published a letter from a subscriber who reported the blow-out of a Kléber V10 tyre, and wished to receive information on the frequency of such accidents. In a later issue of the periodical, two other similar accidents were mentioned. In an article in the periodical Kléber was blamed not having withdrawn the series of tyres in question from the market. The consumer organization informed the Ministries of Economy and of Industry and requested them to order the withdrawal of tyres of the series in question. Kléber brought an action against the organization, seeking FRF 900,000 for defamation and publication of the requested judgment. The defendant organization continued its campaign despite a warning from the court at the interim stage to be more cautious, whereupon Kléber increased its claim to FRF 20,000,000.

Held: Compensation in the amount of FRF 250,000 was granted and publication of the judgment ordered.

Judgment: "**On the merits**: The contested article was published in Issue 144 for the month of October 1979 of the periodical *Que choisir* at page 28. Regarding the placing on the market by Kléber of V10 and V12 tyres, it states: 'The matter in issue is very serious—safety—after the investigation that we have conducted it seems to us today that it would be a culpable fault, not to say criminal, for the manufacturer not to withdraw this category of tyre immediately'.

Such an allegation accusing the manufacturer of neglecting the safety of users of its tyres and of not immediately withdrawing them, in spite of the certain risks established by an investigation, constitutes defamation injurious to the integrity and reputation of Kléber. In order to prove its good faith, UFC must support its assertions on the basis of specific and prior verifications and technical results which justify it in assuring readers that 'it would be culpable, not to say criminal' not to withdraw immediately the incriminated category of tyre. In actual fact, it merely refers to assertions of

---

[594] Viney, *Introduction* at 382, para. 207-2, see also J. Schmidt-Szalewski, ibid.
[595] Gaz.Pal. 1981.Jur.273. Translation by N. Sims.

three readers, which were neither explicit nor specific, without, to this day, giving details of the other cases said to have been notified to it, or of the result of the investigation which the author of the study claims to have conducted.

Thus, proof of good faith has not been adduced by the defendants.

The claim for damages . . .: A consumer association may legitimately reveal to users defects in or dangers associated with products that have been put on the market and may, in an emergency, bring such matters to the attention of the authorities responsible for those products. The corollary of this right is the obligation to carry out serious and objective prior studies in order to provide the public with impartial information which respects the rights of third parties.

In the present case, UFC, in the light of certain circumstances and on the basis of hypotheses that required further investigation, did not hesitate to conduct a very lively press campaign without observing its duty to its readers to provide them with objective information. It thus failed to fulfil its obligation of prudence and exceeded by a wide margin the limits of the criticism in which it may indulge, pursuant to its objectives. Thus, proof is adduced of the fault committed to the detriment of the plaintiff.

Compensation for the loss: Kléber seeks the appointment of an expert to assess the definitive loss that it suffered and payment of provisional compensation in the sum of FRF 20,000,000.

In support of that claim, Kléber produced before the court, on the one hand, an impact study carried out by an advertising agency and, on the other hand, statistics . . . Although the impact study shows that articles in the periodical *Que choisir*, pamphlets and notices, were able to reach and influence a large number of possible buyers, it provides no information enabling a direct assessment of loss.

On the other hand, although the statistics showed an appreciable fall in sales on the replacement market, Kléber has not established that, in a period of recession, that fall was entirely attributable to the actions of UFC . . .

However, the documents before the court enable the amount of damages payable to Kléber to be set at FRF 250,000, for all heads of damage together.

In order to make full amends for the damage done, UFC must be ordered to publish this judgment in the periodical *Que choisir* and Kléber must be allowed to have this judgment published in three newspapers of its choice at UFC's expense . . ."

Notes

(1) This judgment may be seen as a counterpart to the BGH case on protection against interferences with the *Recht am Gewerbebetrieb* originating from persons or organizations exercising their freedom of opinion to inform the public.[596] This judgment can also be read with *Branly* v. *Turpain*, the 1951 judgment of the Cour de Cassation in which an inventor's heirs successfully vindicated his scientific reputation which had been prejudiced by omissions from an historical study.[597] The omissions were held to constitute a breach of the general obligation of objectivity incumbent upon an historian. In the present case also, the defendant organization was found to be in breach of its general obligation of objectivity which it owed to its readers in respect of the information that it provided to them.

Earlier in the judgment the court had stated that the allegations made by the defendant were defamatory of the plaintiff company. It is indeed widely accepted in French law that

[596] *Supra*, **2.G.38**. See also *supra*, **2.G.28**.
[597] *Infra*, Chapter III, **3.F.1**.

legal persons enjoy certain personality rights, so that they are capable of bringing proceedings for defamation.[598]

(2) It is interesting to note that the court awarded FRF 250,000 in damages "for all heads of damage together", whereas the plaintiff had claimed FRF 20 million.

Cass. comm., 17 October 1984[599]   **2.F.55.**
S. A. T. et H. v. *T.*

FAULT TOWARDS A NEW SHAREHOLDER

Inaccurate corporate documents

An accountant and a corporate auditor who had negligently certified incorrect corporate accounts are liable in damages to a shareholder who subscribed to an increase in capital on the basis of the documents.

Facts: The plaintiff, a company called T and H, had subscribed to an increase in the share capital of the N company. It did so on the basis of financial accounts drawn up by N's accountant, the first defendant T, and purportedly verified by N's statutory auditor, the second defendant C. Over and above the nominal value of the new shares of FRF 710,000, the plaintiff paid a premium of a further FRF 540,000. It subsequently emerged that, at the time of the increase in capital, contrary to what the financial accounts led one to believe, the N company suffered from shortfall in assets, which was subsequently assessed at over FRF 3,000,000.

Held: The court of appeal, having found that the financial statements were inaccurate, had, according to the Cour de cassation, incorrectly dismissed the plaintiff's action in tort.

Judgment: "Having regard to Art. 1382 C.civ.: In dismissing the claims by T and H, the court of appeal stated that T had not been guilty of fault because it had not been proved that he had been in a position to verify the 'state of execution' of certain transactions and that there was no causal link connecting C to the alleged loss.

In so holding, although it found that the accounts drawn up by T, an accountant, and verified by C, statutory auditor, were factually inaccurate, the court of appeal did not draw the appropriate legal consequences from its findings. It thus applied the provisions of [Article 1382 C.civ.] incorrectly."

Notes

(1) This judgment is to be compared with the English and German cases dealing with compensation for economic loss resulting from incorrect financial statements.[600] Whereas under English tort law, pure economic loss will be recovered only in exceptional cases if sufficient proximity is shown between plaintiff and defendant, under German law supplying a false statement will lead to liability if it amounts to an act *contra bonos mores*. Conversely under French law it suffices to prove fault, damage and causation. In the annotated judgment the Cour de Cassation quashed the decision of the appeal court for contradictory reasons because the latter had denied the existence of fault and causation

---

[598] Viney and Jourdain, *Conditions* at 35–6, para. 260.
[599] JCP 1985.II.20458, annotated by A. Viandier. Translation by N. Sims.
[600] *Supra*, **2.E.47.** and **2.G.52.**

in spite of having acknowledged earlier that the financial statements "were factually inaccurate".

It would, of course, be possible for accountants, without committing a fault within the meaning of Article 1382 C.civ., to certify accounts that were factually incorrect, since the obligation of accountants in such circumstance is an *obligation de moyens*, and not an *obligation de résultat*. It appears from the case, however, that once the plaintiff had shown that the accounts were factually inaccurate, the defendants were not able to demonstrate that they had taken all reasonable care to avoid such an inaccuracy.

(2) As noted by A. Viandier, the plaintiff company could have sought to recover its loss by attacking directly the capital increase, on the basis of *either* fraud as regards the excessive premium paid on the share issue (in view of the shortfall in assets) *or* absence of true consent to the transaction.[601] Perhaps because the N company lacked the funds to meet any judgment against it, the plaintiff instead brought an action against the accountant who had drafted the inaccurate financial statements and the statutory auditor who had purportedly verified them.

Cass. civ. 1re, 21 February 1995[602]   **2.F.56.**
Broux v. *T.*

OBLIGATION OF A NOTARY TO GIVE PROPER ADVICE TO HIS OR HER CLIENT

Advice on security for payment

A notary is liable for failure to advise his clients, the sellers of a house, on how most efficiently to secure the payment of the unpaid part of the purchase price, even though the clients had also been advised by a third party and the notary had acted in accordance with his clients' instructions.

Facts: The plaintiffs, Mr and Mrs Broux, sold their house to Mr and Mrs Bangratz. The deed was drawn up by the defendant notary fully in accordance with the plaintiffs' instructions. The purchasers failed to pay the unpaid part of the agreed purchase price, and the house was sold in the course of insolvency proceedings against Mrs Bangratz. However, the whole of the sale proceeds were paid to another creditor who had a first lien on the house. The plaintiffs sued the notary for not having advised them as to how to secure priority for their claim in such circumstances.

Held: The defendant was liable in tort and the decision of the court of appeal to the contrary was quashed.

Judgment: "Having regard to Art. 1382 C.civ.: In dismissing the plaintiffs' claim, the contested judgment states first that the duty of the notary T was merely to draw up the deed in accordance with the information provided by Mr Broux and that it did not extend to any further investigation beyond ensuring the effectiveness of the deed in itself, and secondly it notes that the terms of the letter of 5 October showed that the Broux were advised by a third party, which led to the finding that they had not sought the notary's advice and that they were able themselves to seek the guarantees which they criticize him for not having recommended.

The notary as the draftsman of the deed is required to take all steps in order to ensure its effectiveness. Notwithstanding that the Broux were being advised by a 'third party', T was not relieved

---

[601] In his annotation of the judgment at JCP 1985.II.20458.
[602] Bull.civ. 1995.I.95. Translation by N. Sims.

of his duty to warn them of the risks of accepting payment eight months after the sale without any guarantee other than the rights of a vendor. In holding as it did, the court of appeal did not apply [Art. 1382 C.civ.] correctly."

Notes

(1) Here again when the annotated judgment is compared with similar cases under English and German law, it becomes clear that French law has no difficulty whatsoever in granting protection against wrongful acts or omissions on the part of professionals. The case was decided in tort and not in contract, because the notary, in his capacity as *officier ministériel* (public officer), is bound by tort rules towards all parties to the transaction concluded before him.[603] French tort law protects all third parties who have sustained damage through the fault of the notary.[604]

(2) As A. Tunc and G. Viney observe, the weight of professional duties to investigate and advise is growing at a spectacular rate, and so does the ensuing liability in case of breach.[605] That is particularly true for notaries. The judgment in the *Broux* case shows that it is not enough for a notary scrupulously to follow the instructions of the client; even if the client has taken other advice, the notary is not exonerated from his or her obligation to advise the client on effective steps to ensure full payment of the purchase price.

2.4.4. THE LAW OF THE NORDIC COUNTRIES

The following cases can be found at <http://www.rechen.unimaas.nl/casebook>:
2.DK.57. Vestre Landrets Dom, 4 September 1948. *Pedersen* v. *Pedersen*. House on marshlands.
2.SW.58. HD, 14 October 1987. Inaccurate valuation.
2.FIN.59. KKO, 18 April 1989. Immigration to Canada.

2.4.5. COMPARATIVE OVERVIEW

The aim of this section is to concentrate on the situations where English and German tort law allow the grant of compensation for injury to mere economic interests, despite the general reluctance to protect pure economic loss and *Vermögensschaden*, respectively.[606] French law, which shows no such reluctance, is surveyed in order to provide a point of comparison with the other two legal systems. Some materials from Danish, Swedish and Finnish law are also reproduced.

---

[603] For further references, see A. Tunc and G. Viney, "L'évolution du droit français de la responsabilité civile" (1992) 14 Jour. Soc. lég. comp. 123 at 133.

[604] Compare with *White* v. *Jones, supra,* **2.E.48.**

[605] A. Tunc and G. Viney, "L'évolution du droit Français de la responsabilité civile" (1992) 14 J. soc. lég. comp. 123.

[606] See also C.J.H. Jansen and A.J. van der Lely, "Haftung für Auskünfte; ein Vergleich zwischen englischem, deutschem und niederländischem Recht" [1999] ZEuP 229.

Protection against interference with economic interests in general

In English law, some specific economic interests are protected against interference under several "nominate" torts, among which interference with a subsisting contract, which is dealt with below.[607] Moreover, a number of specific enactments impose a duty of care; compensation may then be awarded for the loss resulting from a breach of that statutory duty, including pure economic loss, if such was the legislative intention.[608] As for the more general tort of negligence, the scope of protection afforded to the economic interests of the plaintiff depends on whether, in the particular circumstances of the case, the defendant owed a duty of care to the plaintiff. It is generally agreed that, as the law now stands, the following elements must be present for such a duty of care to exist: injury to the plaintiff must have been foreseeable; there must be a relationship of proximity between plaintiff and defendant; and it must be fair, just and reasonable to impose a duty of care upon the defendant.[609]

The workings of the proximity criterion can very well be observed in cases involving economic interests, where the loss typically is purely economic. In this respect, it should be recalled that in the course of a contractual relationship, it is for the parties to explicitly or implicitly agree on how their economic interests are to be protected as between themselves. Similarly, when it comes to the protection of economic interests under the tort of negligence, in which the parties involved are typically strangers to one another, the search for a relationship of proximity could be seen, by analogy, as a search for elements which make the relationship between plaintiff and defendant "equivalent to contract".[610] Reliance or trust often count among those elements.[611]

As always, English law nonetheless proceeds cautiously. For instance, the ambit of negligent misrepresentation within the meaning of *Hedley Byrne & Co. Ltd.* v. *Heller & Partners* remains limited: in *Caparo Industries plc.* v. *Dickman*, the House of Lords held that, in the absence of any contractual or fiduciary relationship, auditors are under no duty of care towards potential investors or existing shareholders who have suffered financial losses as a consequence of inaccurate statements in the audit of the accounts of a company.[612] Even if German tort law is as reticent towards *Vermögensschaden* as English law towards pure economic losses, the BGH, when faced with a broadly similar case, found that the auditor had to know that potential investors would rely on the company accounts (and that the negligence of the auditor in that situation was such as to constitute conduct *contra bonos mores*!).[613] And of course, it will come as no surprise that on a similar fact-pattern, an accountant and an auditor were held liable under French law.[614]

While *Caparo Industries plc* v. *Dickman* confirmed the persistence of the *Hedley Byrne* case law on negligent misstatements, the three-stage test remains a barrier to the imposition of a duty of care in other types of case involving pure economic loss, as illustrated

---

[607] *Supra*, 4.1., Introductory Note under a).

[608] *Supra*, 4.1., Introductory Note under b).

[609] *Supra*, Chapter I, 1.4.1.B.

[610] In *Hedley Byrne & Co. Ltd.* v. *Heller & Partners Ltd.*, *supra*, **2.E.47.**, Notes (1) and (2).

[611] For a list of criteria from which a sufficient relationship of proximity may be established, see Lord Oliver's speech in *Caparo Industries plc.* v. *Dickman,* quoted *supra*, **2.E.47.**, Note (1).

[612] *Supra*, **2.E.47.**

[613] BGH, 26 November 1986, *supra*, **2.G.52.**

[614] Cass. comm., 17 October 1984, *supra*, **2.F.55.**

by the House of Lords decision in *White* v. *Jones*, where a solicitor had clearly been negligent in failing to draw a will in due time and in consequence, the solicitor's client having died, the intended beneficiaries suffered loss.[615] The speech of Lord Goff in that case is certainly remarkable for the thoroughness of its comparative analysis,[616] and it must be hailed as an example of how the common law of Europe is progressively emerging through comparative dialogue between judges, practitioners and academics. In the result, Lord Goff concluded that "an ordinary action in tortious negligence . . . must . . . be regarded as inappropriate because it does not meet any of the given conceptual problems which have been raised" but that it was open to the House of Lords "to fashion a remedy to fill a lacuna in the law which would otherwise occur on the facts of cases such as the present". In the light of the "extended *Hedley Byrne* principle" which is taking hold in English case law, it seems that it will generally be possible to recover pure economic loss from professional service providers where they have assumed responsibility and the plaintiff has relied on that assumption.[617]

As shown by the Court of Appeal in *Allied Maples* v. *Simmonds*, in assessing the damage suffered as a result of professional negligence, English courts will take into account the loss of a chance (assuming that the conditions for liability, including the existence of a duty of care, are otherwise fulfilled).[618] In that case, the plaintiff, buyer of a going business, was ill-advised and as a result failed to seek a guarantee—which it might have obtained— from the seller for certain liabilities which it had now inherited. *Allied Maples* illustrates that, once the general rule against recovery of pure economic loss has been set aside by showing that the case fits one of the situations where a duty of care arises, English law seems to show the same willingness as French law to extend compensation even for loss affected by an element of probability foreign to the defendant. The Court of Appeal carefully distinguished the two issues of causation and *quantum* of damages: the fact that the loss was affected by an element of probability does not negate the causal link between the wrongdoing and the loss, as long as it can be shown that, on a balance of probabilities, the wrongdoing did impact adversely on the chance to make a gain or avoid a loss. The element of probability affecting the loss is reflected in the *quantum* of damages, which is correspondingly reduced by a certain percentage. French courts would proceed in the same way.[619]

German law has taken a somewhat different approach to the problem of protection against interference with economic interests, focusing more on the quality of the conduct than the relationship between the plaintiff and the defendant. The limitative list of protected *Rechtsgüter* at § 823(1) BGB works much like the general rule against recovery of pure economic loss in negligence, in that the *Vermögen* with its expansive scope is not included in the list and thus *reiner Vermögensschaden* is in principle not recoverable.[620] The restrictive effect of § 823(1) BGB is, however, partially offset by §§ 823(2) and 826 BGB.[621] Moreover, it appears from those provisions that, in contrast to English law, in German law the emphasis lies more on the inappropriateness of precluding recovery of

---

[615] *Supra*, **2.E.48.**

[616] In his speech Lord Goff cites a number of decisions rendered by courts from other countries in similar cases. To cite only those from EU Member States: BGH, 6 July 1965, NJW 1965, 1955; Cass. civ. 1re, 23 November 1977, JCP 1979.II.19243 and Cass. civ. 1re, 14 January 1981, JCP 1982.II.19728; Hof van Beroep Amsterdam, 31 January 1985, NJ 1985, 740.

[617] See *supra*, 2.4.1, Introductory Note under d).

[618] *Supra*, **2.E.49.**

[619] See *supra*, **2.F.11.** and **2.F.43.**

[620] It must not be forgotten, however, as was seen *supra*, 3.2., that the exclusion of the *Vermögen* from the list of § 823(1) BGB has been moderated by the case law on the notion of ownership and on the *Recht am Gewerbebetrieb*.

[621] To be complete, one must also add § 839 BGB (to be compared with the English tort of misfeasance in public office) dealt with *infra*, Chapter III, 3.3.2., as well as §§ 824 and 825 BGB, whose scope is very specific.

Vermögensschaden when the conduct of the defendant is especially reprehensible, in that specific legal prohibitions or basic moral precepts are infringed. On the other hand, it must be recalled, as the House of Lords acknowledges in *White* v. *Jones*, that the German rules on the relativity of contract are less strict than the corresponding English rules. Hence, with devices such as *Vertrag mit Schutzwirkung für Dritte*, many cases are brought into the realm of contract law.[622] Against that background, it is less crucial for German tort law to search for contract-like relationships, since these will often be dealt with under contract law. Given the foregoing, the practical outcome of cases concerning the protection of economic interests may differ from German to English law.[623]

As said above, §§ 823(2) and 826 BGB make the restrictive effect of § 823(1) BGB less acute. Indeed, § 823(2) BGB allows recovery of *Vermögensschaden* when a *Schutznorm* (protective enactment) has been infringed, provided that the *Schutznorm* concerned a "true crime", a *malum in se* (*Straftat*) or, if not, that it was expressly aimed to protect the *Vermögen* in its entirety.[624] *Schutznormen* can be found in all areas of law, as shown in BGH, 6 June 1994, where § 64(1) GmbHG, the statutory provision requiring the manager of a GmbH to file a bankruptcy petition in case of insolvency, was regarded as a *Schutznorm* for the protection of "old" and "new" creditors alike.[625] However, § 64(1) GmbHG is not concerned with a *Straftat*. Therefore, before the BGH could rule on the plaintiff's claim for *reiner Vermögensschaden*, it had to conduct a careful and thorough analysis of the purpose of § 64(1) GmbHG.[626]

§ 826 BGB can also lead to compensation of *reiner Vermögensschaden* in cases where the defendant (1) has committed an act *contra bonos mores* (*sittenwidrig*) with (2) the requisite *Schädigungsvorsatz* (involving the wilful infliction of harm).[627] Two BGH judgments reproduced above illustrate the workings of those two conditions.[628] As mentioned above, in the latter of those two cases, the BGH dealt with the tortious liability of an auditor towards a bank which relied on the accuracy of his audits, although they had not been prepared at the bank's request. The judgment shows that the conditions of § 826 BGB may not be so difficult to fulfil as might appear at first sight: the BGH found that the auditor was acting *contra bonos mores*, in too readily and superficially preparing and certifying interim financial statements, and thereby wilfully (*vorsätzlich*) inflicted harm.

By now, it may appear redundant to state that French tort law offers full protection, as a matter of principle, to all kinds of legitimate interests, including economic interests, and that it awards compensation for all kinds of damage, including what would correspond to pure economic loss or *reiner Vermögensschaden*.[629] That explains why, in the judgments reproduced above—selected because of their factual resemblance with the English and

---

[622] See *supra*, **2.G.52.**, Note (2); see also, *supra*, 1.2., Introductory Note under c).

[623] As seen with *Caparo Industries plc* v. *Dickman*, *supra*, **2.E.47.** and BGH, 26 November 1986, *supra*, **2.G.52.**

[624] *Supra*, 4.2.A., Introductory Note under c).

[625] *Supra*, **2.G.50.**

[626] See further *supra*, **2.G.50.**, Notes (1) and (2).

[627] For a list of situations where the provision is applied, see *supra*, 4.2.B., Introductory Note under a) and b).

[628] BGH, 19 October 1993, *supra*, **2.G.51.** and BGH, 26 November 1986, *supra*, **2.G.52.**

[629] *Supra*, 4.3., Introductory Note under a).

German cases included in this section—French courts had no difficulty in finding tortious liability under Articles 1382–1383 C.civ.[630]

In this respect, it is interesting to compare TGI Paris, 19 November 1980, where the defendant consumer union was found liable for statements that it had made about the safety of the products of the plaintiff, a tyre manufacturer, with the *Greenpeace*[631] and *Hellfire*[632] cases. While the French consumer union certainly exaggerated when it branded the tyre manufacturer a criminal, the allegations in the German cases were no less grievous: Greenpeace had accused the president of Hoechst of destroying the ozone layer and the parties in *Hellfire* had engaged in a war of devastating articles. It appears that the direct impact of Article 5 GG (freedom of expression) in civil law, which tipped the balance in favour of the defendants in Germany, has no parallel in French law.[633]

The judgments of the Danish Vestre Landrets[634], the Swedish Högstra Domstolen[635] and the Finnish Korkein Oikeus[636] included above seem to indicate that liability for incorrect professional information or statements is treated in the same fashion in the Nordic legal systems as in England, Germany and France, whatever considerable differences in legal reasoning there may be.

Interference with a contractual relationship

In many legal systems, the issue of whether, and under what conditions, a third party involved in a breach of contract committed by one of the contracting parties is liable in tort is much debated. A key question is whether there must be collusion or fraudulent concertation between the third party (the defendant in the tort action) and the contracting party who is in breach of the contract, or whether it suffices that the third party knew of the contract and acted in disregard of it. Whereas the first view is more in line with the principle of privity/relativity of contract, the second is based on a broad interpretation of the notion of wrongfulness, considering that the existence of a contract—even when it grants rights *in personam, a fortiori* when it grants rights *in rem*[637]—is a legal fact which third parties cannot totally ignore in their dealings with one of the contracting parties.

Not unexpectedly, the latter view seems to underpin French law, as is illustrated by Cass.civ. 3e, 8 July 1975, where the Cour de cassation quashed a judgment of the court of appeal which had held that, for liability to arise, the third party needed to have acted fraudulently (*collusion frauduleuse*).[638] The Cour de cassation disagreed: it sufficed that the third party committed a "fault of which that person was guilty in agreeing to acquire a building which it knew to be subject to the promise".

German law, as evidenced by BGH, 6 June 1994, seems less inclined to impose tort liability for interference in contractual relationships, since under § 826 BGB,[639] liability of

---

[630] TGI Paris, 19 November 1980, *supra*, **2.F.54.** (slight harm to the plaintiff's business); Cass. comm., 17 October 1984, *supra*, **2.F.55.** (negligent certification of accounts) and Cass. civ. 1re, 21 February 1995, *supra*, **2.F.56.** (failure by a notary to give proper advice).

[631] BGH, 12 October 1993, *supra*, **2.G.28.**

[632] BGH, 21 June 1966, *supra*, **2.G.38.**

[633] See *supra*, 2.1., Introductory Note under b).

[634] *Supra*, **2.DK.57.**

[635] *Supra*, **2.SW.58.**

[636] *Supra*, **2.FIN.59.**

[637] Contracts granting rights to real property are in many legal systems generally required to be registered in a public registry.

[638] *Supra*, **2.F.53.** and notes.

[639] § 826 BGB requires wilful infliction of harm by behaviour *contra bonos mores*.

the third party will arise only when "[the interference of that party] with the contractual relations is marked by a particular lack of consideration for the person concerned", and not "simply on the ground of his cooperation in the violation by the debtor of his creditor's rights under the contract".[640] "Collusion with the debtor under the contract in order specifically to frustrate the claims of the creditor concerned" is needed.

As described above, the English tort of interference with a subsisting contract has expanded into many variants, namely direct persuasion, direct inducement, other direct intervention and indirect intervention.[641] It would seem that English law remains somewhere between the two approaches named above: mere knowledge that a contract exists is not enough to hold a third party liable in tort; there must be at least "dealings with the contract-breaker which the third party knows to be inconsistent with the contract"[642] or other circumstances characterized by unlawful means. Direct persuasion and knowingly doing something to prevent the contracting party from performing (such as hiring away employees) also engage the third party's liability.

2.5. PROTECTION OF COLLECTIVE INTERESTS

The previous sections in this chapter have dealt with interests which properly belong to the person, namely life, health, bodily integrity, personality, property and economic interests. Natural persons enjoy all of these interests, and legal persons many of them. More often than not, these interests are specific to a single person. For instance, if A is injured in an accident, only A's bodily integrity has been infringed (which does not exclude the possibility that other persons may also be able to claim for damage suffered as a result of the accident, to the extent that their own interests have been infringed).

Some interests, however, are shared by many persons. For instance, those who live in the neighbourhood of a large factory which releases polluting emissions in the air all share an interest in clean air. Obviously, it could be said that that interest is none other than their respective individual interests in health and bodily integrity. Yet such a description would fail to grasp this phenomenon fully, for there is an obvious link between all of those neighbours in that they are all affected in their shared quality as persons living in the neighbourhood of the plant. They have a **collective interest** in clean air.

Boré attempts to place collective interests in relation to individual interests and the general (or public) interest. Collective interests, he writes, "differ from individual interests in that they are the interests of many individuals; in that sense, they are an aggregation of individual interests, not so much in the way they are defined but rather in their purpose".[643] As for the distinction between collective interests and the general interest, he rejects the idea that collective interests are a subset of the general interest, either because they are shared by less than the whole society or because they are more "specialized" than

---

[640] *Supra,* **2.G.51.**
[641] *Rickless* v. *United Artists Corporation, supra,* **2.E.46.**, Notes (1) to (4).
[642] *Per* Jenkins LJ in *D.C. Thomson & Co. Ltd.* v. *Deakin, supra,* **2.E.46.**, Note (2).
[643] Boré at 9, para. 11.

the general interest (which would then be a synthesis of all collective interests in the environment, employment, product safety, consumer protection, etc.); in his view, these distinctions are not supported in practice. The only distinction which he can put forward at the end is that collective interests are pursued by private persons (or groups of private persons), while the general interest is pursued by public bodies—an admittedly unsatisfactory distinction, which does, however, possess some practical significance. He concludes that "a collective interest is the interest of a group of persons represented by a private person".[644] Even if Boré conducted his definitional exercise within the French context, his reasoning and conclusions appear appropriate in a comparative context as well.

This section is concerned with the protection of collective interests under tort law. As will have become apparent from the foregoing sections, tort law has historically been concerned and is still now mostly concerned with relationships involving few persons: generally a plaintiff and a defendant, sometimes a small number of plaintiffs or defendants, rarely both at once. The idea of a large group of persons using tort law to seek protection of a collective interest[645] is at best difficult to reconcile with the historical framework of tort law in most systems. It raises the following questions, among others:

- Which, if any, collective interests are protected by tort law?
- How can a collective interest properly be articulated? How does the group in question speak? How is it represented?
- Can a group of persons as such suffer any harm distinct from that of its individual members? What form of relief can be granted for a violation of a collective interest: injunctive relief only or monetary compensation as well?

Despite those problems, this section shows that legal systems have risen to the challenge of protecting collective interests under tort law with a range of solutions.

In this section, we will first deal with French tort law, where the protection of collective interests has been tackled without major changes in the legal framework, by broadening the requirements of qualification to sue (*qualité pour agir*) to enable private associations to act on collective interests. That has been done both legislatively and judicially. The situation of English law and common law systems is surveyed next. In English law, the protection of collective interests in general has always been linked to special procedural devices, which have been developed over centuries. At this point in time, those devices show serious limitations, especially as regards the protection of collective interests under tort law, and various reforms are under consideration. Since English law is in a transitory state, attention will briefly be drawn to North American legal systems, where the procedural devices of the common law have been brought one logical step further with the introduction of class actions. German law will then be briefly examined. Finally, Dutch and Swedish law materials are reproduced relating to the protection of the environment by private and public legal entities.

---

[644] Boré at 14, para. 14.

[645] This chapter deals with plaintiffs seeking redress for breaches of collective interests. While the legal developments in most systems also allow for actions to be brought against groups of defendants, the protection of collective interests is usually not at stake when relief is sought against a group of defendants, and that situation is accordingly not dealt with here.

2.5.1. FRENCH LAW

Introductory Note

a) In France, more and more attention has recently been devoted to the issue of compensation for damage suffered by groups of persons. To the extent that the prejudice affecting the group is felt personally by some individuals, *each of them* may claim compensation for the specific damage which he or she has sustained, but not for the damage which the others have suffered.[646] For instance when the persons living in a neighbourhood suffer damage because zoning laws are infringed, only the immediate neighbours will be in a position to claim damage individually.

Those claims, however, have often been conceived as infringements of collective interests, and the usual procedure that has been adopted to seek redress for such infringements under French law has tended to be for a legal entity to bring such infringement before the courts on behalf of its members. This explains why the debate has centred on whether such legal entities are qualified to act for their members or not. Furthermore, this debate has taken place within the particular framework of French procedural law, whereby many distinctive procedures are available to those who wish to obtain compensation for a violation of their rights (a factor which blurs the situation but must be taken into account in order to gain a proper understanding). Thus:

– An action can be brought within the framework of the *Code de procédure civile*. Article 31 of the new *Code de procédure civile* states that "Anyone who has a legitimate interest in the success or failure of a claim can launch an action, except in cases where the law reserves the right to launch an action to those persons who are by law qualified to put forward or oppose a claim or to defend a given interest". A legitimate interest is broadly construed to include a purely "moral" interest and the right to bring an action exists unless it has been reserved to someone else.[647] Such an action is then ruled upon by the civil courts, subject to the jurisdiction of the civil chambers of the Cour de cassation.

– When the alleged tort is also punishable under criminal law, a party can join a criminal procedure as a civil party (*partie civile*) in order to have his or her tort claims adjudicated at the same time as the court rules in the criminal matter. This so-called "civil action" (*action civile*) is governed by Article 2 of the *Code pénal* (Criminal Code), which reads "The civil action, whereby compensation is sought for damage caused by the [commission of a criminal offence], is open to anyone who has personally suffered injury as a direct result of the offence". The civil action thus requires that the plaintiff show direct and personal injury. This requirement represents a serious bar to civil actions.[648] The civil action comes under the jurisdiction of the criminal courts and ultimately of the criminal chamber of the Cour de cassation.

– Tort actions against public authorities and public bodies are brought before the administrative courts, under the control of the Conseil d'État.

---

[646] Viney and Jourdain, *Conditions* at 96–7, para. 291.
[647] See *infra*, **2.F.61.**, Note (1).
[648] See *infra*, **2.F.61.**, Note (2).

The following paragraphs explain the direction in which French law has evolved.[649]

b) Since **trade unions** and **professional associations** (the Bar, the College of Physicians, etc.) are frequently authorized by law or decree to defend the interests of their members as well as the broader collective interests of the profession,[650] it is now generally recognized that they are qualified to join criminal proceedings as *partie civile* to defend the collective interests of their members or even of the profession as a whole, as long as damage has occurred as a consequence of an infringement of these interests.[651] Similarly, even if there is no explicit statutory text on the point, civil courts also tend to admit actions brought by trade unions or professional associations for prejudice to the collective interests of their members or the profession as a whole, especially in unfair competition matters. Administrative courts will, however, treat trade unions and professional associations in the same way as other associations.

c) As to such **other associations**, such as consumer, neighbour, social associations, etc., the situation is not so rosy, with the exception of those associations which benefit from a legal authorization to act before the courts. Here French law makes a distinction according to the aims of the association. Some associations are "**self-interested**" (*égoïstes*), in that they are established for the purpose of vindicating the rights of a group of persons, whether co-owners, neighbours, etc. (typically also called *associations de défense*). When bringing a tort claim before the courts, a self-interested association will then be seeking compensation for injurious conduct which has affected the individual rights of its members. In contrast, "**disinterested**" associations (*altruistes*) have as an associative purpose the defence of interests going beyond the individual rights of their members, the pursuit of causes (also called *grandes causes* or broad causes). For instance, an association for the protection of animals could initiate tort proceedings against persons alleged to have mistreated or illegally killed animals. The collective interests then relied upon are common to a more or less diffuse class of persons, such as public service users, consumers, users of ground water or pure air, or even to society as a whole, such as the remembrance of the victims of nazi crimes, etc.

In the case of self-interested associations, criminal courts will declare tort actions inadmissible.[652] The same is true of administrative courts, unless the association has received an express mandate from its members to act for them.[653] The long-standing case law to this effect has not been subject to any significant exception.[654] In contrast, civil courts have in principle admitted tort actions by self-interested associations, essentially on the

---

[649] See J. Vincent and S. Guimard, *Procédure civile*, 24th edn. (Paris, Dalloz, 1996) at 110–19, paras. 122–3, 125–9 and P. Maistre du Chambon, "Action en réparation—Parties à l'instance" No. 220 in *Juris-classeur civil—1382–1386* (Paris: Éd. du Juris-classeur) at 14–20, paras. 68–103.

[650] By way of example, in the judgment reproduced *supra*, **2.F.31.**, relating to the distribution of *Le grand secret*, professional associations of newspaper and periodical publishers were allowed to intervene in the court proceedings.

[651] Cass. Ch. réun., 5 April 1913, DP 1914.I.65, legislatively recognized in 1920, now at Art. L.411-11 of the *Code du travail*. See also *infra*, **2.F.63.–64.**, Note (1).

[652] In line with Cass. crim., 16 December 1954, D 1955.Jur.287; see also Cass. crim., 23 June 1986, Bull.crim. 1986.218 and Cass. crim., 16 January 1990, Bull.crim. 1990.24.

[653] In line with CÉ, 10 March 1893, *Matière*, S 1895.III.8 and CÉ, 27 November 1896, *Ville de Limoges*, S 1898.III.134.

[654] Boré at 84–7, para. 101–2.

basis that the members can do collectively, through the association, what they would have been able to accomplish individually.[655]

In the case of disinterested associations, the position of the administrative courts is not clear-cut.[656] Both civil and criminal chambers of the Cour de cassation have steadfastly refused to entertain tort claims by disinterested associations, following the landmark decision of the joined chambers (*Chambres réunies*) of the Cour de cassation of 15 June 1923; according to this line of case law, it is not for private persons to replace public authorities in defending objectives of general interest.[657] There is, however, a minority line of case law in both civil and criminal courts cases going in the other direction,[658] including the *Le Pen*[659] and the *Aide à toute détresse*[660] cases.[661]

d) Moreover, if a self-interested association has been established to defend the rights of the members of a group—for instance a committee of apartment co-owners—the members of that group who wish to present individual claims must then prove not only that they have sustained specific injury to themselves, but also that they are not interfering with the prerogatives of the association.[662] However, the possibility that actions brought by associations and their members run in parallel is not excluded,[663] potentially leading to double compensation.[664]

Exceptionally, when the whole group or association is not in a position, or because of a conflict of interest is unlikely, to claim compensation, individual members may seek compensation not only for personal injury but also for injury suffered by the group or the association.[665]

e) Given the relative reluctance of the courts to admit actions by disinterested and even self-interested associations, the legislature has increasingly intervened to allow such actions explicitly in certain areas.[666] If an association has been statutorily authorized to act, courts will bow to the will of the legislature and admit the actions it brings; in some cases, courts will also admit a tort action brought by an association which enjoys explicit statutory recognition but no explicit power to act before the courts in pursuit of collective interests.[667]

---

[655] In line with Cass. civ., 25 November 1929, Gaz.Pal. 1930.I.29; for an apparent broadening of that basis, see Cass. civ. 1re, 27 May 1975, *infra*, **2.F.60.**, and Note (1).

[656] Boré at 335–40, para. 333–6.

[657] S 1924.I.49, DP 1924.I.153; see further *infra*, **2.F.61.**, Note (1) and also **2.F.60.**, Note (1).

[658] Boré at 99–102, para. 118–19.

[659] Cass. crim, 14 January 1971, *infra*, **2.F.61.**

[660] Colmar, 10 February 1977, *infra*, **2.F.62.**

[661] See also the *Benetton* case referred to *supra*, 2.2.2., Introductory Note under c), where the association *Aides fédération nationale* was allowed to claim compensation for injury to the collective interests which it represented, namely giving assistance to seropositive persons and defence of their image, dignity and rights. The association was recognized by special decree to be in the public interest (*utilité publique*). It requested and was awarded one symbolic FRF in damages.

[662] Viney and Jourdain, *Conditions* at 98–101, para. 293.

[663] Cass. civ., 25 November 1929, Gaz.Pal. 1930.I.29; Cass. civ. 1re, 14 May 1992, Bull.civ. 1992.I.138, commented by G. Viney, JCP 1992.I.3625.

[664] A solution criticized by G. Viney, JCP 1992.I.3625 and Boré at 91–7, para. 109–14.

[665] Viney and Jourdain, *Conditions* at 101–3, paras. 294–6.

[666] Boré counts some 38 such interventions at 43–54, para. 44–58.

[667] See further *infra*, **2.F.63.–64.** and notes.

Important recent examples of such legislative intervention include: the Act 88-14 of 5 January 1988[668] and the Act 92-60 of 18 January 1992,[669] allowing consumer organizations, under certain circumstances, to obtain injunctions and to bring proceedings on behalf of consumers who have individually suffered damage from a common cause as a result of the conduct of one and the same professional person,[670] and the Act 95-101 of 2 February 1995[671] enacting general provisions for the protection of the environment at the initiative of authorized interest groups.[672]

Cass. civ. 1re, 27 May 1975[673]   **2.F.60.**
SA Général Foods France Café Legal v. *Comité de défense contre la pollution atmosphérique des quartiers de Drancy, Blanc-Mesnil et Le Bourget*

QUALITY TO ACT FOR A SELF-INTERESTED (*ÉGOÏSTE*) ASSOCIATION BEFORE THE CIVIL COURTS

Coffee roasting plant

An association legally constituted for the defence of the collective interests of its members, who have suffered and continue to suffer injury because of emissions from the defendant's plant, is allowed to bring a claim for compensation of the injury suffered by its members.

Facts: Following many years of complaints by its neighbours about disturbances by smoke, dust and unpleasant odours, the defendant, which operates a coffee roasting plant, was summoned by the authorities to comply with the regulations applicable to the category of enterprises to which it belonged. In September 1971, the defendant's neighbours formed an "Action Committee" (*comité de défense*) having as a purpose protection from atmospheric pollution. That association claimed damages for the injury caused to its members, including that suffered before the date of its establishment.

Held: The court of appeal allowed the claim and gave instructions to assess the injury. The Cour de cassation affirmed the decision.

Judgment: "On 2 September 1971, the *Comité de défense contre la pollution atmosphérique des quartiers de Drancy, Blanc-Mesnil et Le Bourget* (Action committee against air pollution in the Drancy, Blanc-Mesnil and Le Bourget sectors) was created, the purpose of which was 'defence against air pollution'. It sued General Foods France for damages to compensate the prejudice which is allegedly caused by the plant of that company since September 1966. The judgment of the court of appeal, whereby the action was found admissible and certain measures were ordered in order to assess the injury withstood since September 1966, is criticized on the following grounds: firstly, the association is a legal person distinct from its members and could not on that account have suffered injury before its creation; secondly, the statutes of the association, where it is stated that its purpose is the 'defence against air pollution', were misconstrued in that the court of appeal read other purposes into them and gave them retroactive effect.

---

[668] *Loi 88-14 relative aux actions en justice des associations agréées de consommateurs et à l'information des consommateurs* of 5 January 1988, JO, 6 January 1988, D 1988.Lég.93.

[669] *Loi 92-60 renforçant la protection des consommateurs* of 18 January 1992, JO, 21 January 1992, D 1992.Lég.129.

[670] Art. L.421-2 to L.421-6, L.422-1 of the *Code de la consommation*. See *infra*, **2.F.63.**

[671] *Loi 95-101 relative au renforcement de la protection de l'environnement* of 2 February 1995, JO, 3 February 1995, D 1995.Lég.123.

[672] Art. 252-3 and Art. 252-5 of the *Code rural*. See *infra*, **2.F.64.**

[673] D 1976.Jur.318, with annotation by G. Viney. Translation by P. Larouche.

A legally formed association, however, may claim compensation for the injury to the collective interests of its members. Such a claim is admissible if it falls within the purposes for which the association was formed, even if the injury on which the claim is based predates the creation of the association. In the case at bar, the court of appeal found that since 1966, a certain number of persons had been trying, individually or through petitions, to obtain the termination or the reduction of the nuisances caused by the presence of the plant of General Foods France. It fell within the exclusive purview of the court of appeal to interpret the statement of associative purposes in the statutes of the association, given the ambiguity thereof. The court of appeal found as a fact that the persons in question did not intend 'to break with the past' in creating a *comité de défense*, but 'quite to the contrary to continue with the actions undertaken so far by entrusting the association with the task of supporting the interests of each [member], as they already exist and as they may subsequently arise'. The court of appeal could accordingly derive from those findings the conclusion that the claims were admissible for the period prior to 16 September 1971. The ground for appeal is not founded, and hence the appeal is dismissed."

Notes

(1) The above judgment concerns the admissibility of a claim in damages brought by a legally established association formed to defend the collective interests of its members (a "self-interested" association, as the expression goes).

In a judgment of 15 June 1923, the joined chambers (*chambres réunies*) of the Cour de cassation[674] decided that a legally established professional association, which unlike a trade union does not automatically (*de plein droit*) cover the whole profession—in that case civil service staff employed within the State education sector—is not qualified to bring an action in damages on behalf of its members for an infringement of their collective interest, since its membership does not extend to the whole profession and accordingly it cannot claim to act for the profession as a whole.[675] That case arose under special circumstances, which nevertheless did not prevent it from becoming a landmark decision.[676] The right of associations to bring actions to defend collective interests was thus severely curtailed, even if it was not excluded altogether; the reluctance on the part of the judiciary was inspired initially by traditional suspicion of private legal entities with political ambitions, and subsequently by the reluctance of the criminal courts, in particular, to see private parties compete with the public prosecutor in the prosecution of criminal offences.[677]

Nonetheless, the *civil* chambers of the Cour de cassation, whose position was "defeated" in the joined chambers judgment of 1923, did not take very long to return to a more favourable attitude towards actions brought by associations in pursuit of the collective interests of their members. The judgment of 25 November 1929 established the admissibility of such actions, at least so far as "self-interested" associations were concerned, on the basis of an explicit or implied mandate *ad litem* (i.e. the association can do what its members individually could also do).[678] The annotated judgment is the first to

---

[674] The joined chambers of the Cour de cassation (in 1967 the designation *Chambres réunies* was replaced by *Assemblée plénière*) regroup all the chambers of the Cour de cassation for rulings of prime importance for the overall evolution of the law.

[675] S 1924.I.49, annotation by E. Chevegrin, DP 1924.I.153.

[676] G. Viney, Annotation, D 1976.Jur.318 at 319.

[677] Ibid.

[678] Gaz.Pal. 1930.I.29, mentioned *supra*, 2.5.1., Introductory Note under c).

break away from that rationale, in that the entitlement of the association to bring proceedings in the interests of its members appears to flow from the mere fact that the associative purpose of the association encompasses those interests, without the need to imply a mandate *ad litem*. This represents a substantial strengthening of the position of "self-interested" associations (the same has not happened for "disinterested" associations), since the right of associations to bring proceedings is no longer presented as an exception to the rule that an association cannot claim damages for its members, but emerges, rather, as a general rule of its own.[679]

(2) The requirement that the association must show personal injury in order to be able to sue[680] has also been interpreted broadly by civil courts, to the point where, for instance, in a judgment of 15 May 1990, the Cour de cassation held that, if an association's claim is based on injury suffered by its members, then by the same token a collective injury is at stake, which is personal to the association and for which it can accordingly seek compensation.[681] Still the association must show that its action falls within its associative purpose.[682]

Cass. crim., 14 January 1971[683]   **2.F.61.**
Le Pen

QUALITY TO ACT FOR A DISINTERESTED ASSOCIATION BEFORE THE CRIMINAL COURTS

Nazi phonograph record

An association legally established for the purpose of remembering the victims of nazi camps is allowed to bring an action before a criminal court as a partie civile *for compensation for injury suffered by it directly and personally.*

Facts: The defendant, Jean-Marie Le Pen, was accused of certain criminal offences pursuant to Article 24(3) of the Act of 29 July 1881 (which prohibits arguments that war crimes were justified, *apologie des crimes de guerre*),[684] on the grounds that he had published and distributed a phonograph record with an accompanying sleeve, on which a photo of Hitler as well as several of his speeches and nazi songs were reproduced. Two associations, the Comité d'action de la Résistance and the Réseau du souvenir joined in the prosecution before the criminal courts as *parties civiles*, asking for compensation.

Held: The court of appeal upheld the conviction of the accused, but only for the publication of the texts printed on the sleeve; it annulled his conviction for the distribution of the phonograph records, because this form of reproduction did not come within Article 23 of the Act of 29 July 1881. The actions brought by the *parties civiles* were dismissed. The criminal chamber of the Cour de cassation confirmed the judgment of the court of appeal as regards the printed texts but quashed that judgment as regards the phonograph recordings.[685] As regards the

---

[679] G. Viney, Annotation, D 1976.Jur.318 at 319.

[680] See also *infra*, **2.F.61.**, Note (1).

[681] Cass. civ. 1re, Bull.civ. 1990.I.102.

[682] Cass. soc., 11 October 1994, Bull.civ. 1994.IV.266, annotated by G. Viney, JCP 1995.I.3853.

[683] D 1971.Jur.101, JCP 1971.II.17022, annotated by H. Blin. Translation by P. Larouche.

[684] *Loi sur la liberté de la presse* (Freedom of the Press Act) of 29 July 1881, D 1881.IV.65, as amended by the *Loi 51-18 portant amnistie, instituant un régime de libération anticipée, limitant les effets de la dégradation nationale et réprimandant les activités antinationales* of 5 January 1951, JO, 6 January 1951, D 1951.Lég.24.

[685] The Act of 29 July 1881, ibid. was amended in the wake of this judgment by the *Loi 72-546 relative à la lutte contre le racisme* of 1 July 1972, JO, 2 July 1972, D 1972.Lég.328 so as to cover distribution of recordings, etc.

actions brought by the *parties civiles*, the Cour de cassation reversed the court of appeal on the admissibility of the action brought by the Réseau du Souvenir; finding that the action was admissible, it remitted the claim to the court of appeal for further determination. The Cour de cassation confirmed the inadmissibility of the action brought by the Comité d'action de la Résistance on purely procedural grounds.[686]

Judgment: "The court of appeal correctly found that, in the absence of any mention of the crimes which marked Hitler's rise to power and the climate of terror which surrounded it, the disputed writings (and accompanying illustrations) were combined so as to give the impression that Hitler legally seized power and that the judgment of the Nuremberg International Tribunal on the activities of the German National-Socialist movement should be questioned. The selection and the combination of the song titles were bound to give rise to an exhilarating effect and thereby present as an explosion of popular strength what was in fact the orchestration of a vast criminal enterprise. Accordingly, that publication taken as a whole was such as to lead the reader to make a favourable moral judgment on the leaders of the German National-Socialist party, who were condemned as war criminals; it thus constituted at least a partial attempt to justify their crimes. It is immaterial that the writings bear on a period preceding the Second World War, since to [attempt to] justify [the actions of] a criminal, without any reservation, is to [attempt to] justify his crimes globally. The publication of the writings in question therefore constituted an attempt to justify war crimes (*apologie des crimes de guerre*) within the meaning of Art. 24 of the Act of 29 July 1881. Furthermore, the court of appeal concluded that Le Pen, who purports to work as an historian, could not consequently fail to know that in publishing such writings it would constitute an attempt to justify war crimes. The intentional character of the infraction was thereby established. It follows from the foregoing that the court of appeal, far from misconstruing Art. 24 of the Act of 29 July 1881, in fact duly applied it . . .

As regards the appeal of the association Le Réseau du Souvenir, arguing that the court of appeal did not apply Arts. 2 and 3 of the *Code de procédure pénale* (Code of criminal procedure): Art. 2 of the *Code de procédure pénale* states that the *action civile*, whereby compensation is sought for damage caused by the [commission of a criminal offence], is open to anyone who has personally suffered injury as a direct result of the offence. After having found that the association Le Réseau du Souvenir was recognized to be in the public interest (*reconnue d'utilité publique*) and aimed to 'awaken and perpetuate the remembrance of deported persons who died for liberty in Nazi concentration camps', [the court of appeal] held its claim as a *partie civile* inadmissible on the ground that 'since the association as a legal person is distinct from its individual members and in the absence of any provision entrusting it with a specific mission in respect [of the above purpose], the association had not suffered direct and personal injury as a result of the [offence] in question in the criminal proceedings'. With that ruling, the court of appeal wrongly applied Art. 2 of the *Code de procédure pénale*. Indeed, the Réseau du Souvenir does not purport to defend the interests of its members. It brings together, along with persons who were deported, the families of victims of deportation as well as those who wish to perpetuate the remembrance of their sacrifice and the ideal for which they fell. The purpose of that association is to ensure the safeguard of fundamental moral values attached to human dignity. Given that that association was created specifically to preserve the remembrance of those who died in concentration camps and that in light of that purpose it was recognized to be in the public interest, it suffers direct and personal injury from the attempt to justify war crimes, deportation being one of those crimes. It flows from the specificity of its purpose and mission that its claim is admissible. The grounds for appeal are founded accordingly.

For the foregoing reasons . . ., [the judgment of the court of appeal] is quashed . . ., but only as regards the *action civile* of the association Le Réseau du Souvenir . . . and it is remitted to the court of appeal."

---

[686] The time period for appealing against the judgment at first instance had expired. For the same reasons, the appeal of the *Procureur général* was declared inadmissible.

Notes

(1) As mentioned above, Article 31 of the new *Code de procédure civile* governs the admissibility of an action brought before civil courts. Pursuant to it, an action can be brought by all those who have a legitimate interest in the outcome of a claim (*prétention*), provided that they are qualified to act (*qualité pour agir*). As such, because courts construe the notion of legitimate interest broadly to include also a purely "moral" interest and because the only constraint in the text of Article 31 on *qualité d'agir* is a negative one (it must not have been reserved to someone else: see the wording of Article 31), one might have thought that Article 31 would not present a serious impediment to disinterested associations bringing a tort action before civil courts.[687] Yet, as seen above, as a consequence of the line of Cour de cassation case law flowing from the landmark decision of 15 June 1923, disinterested associations have been held to be more or less barred from presenting tort claims before civil courts.[688] According to the 1923 judgment, an association is only qualified to act when it either is statutorily authorized to protect a collective interest in court, or has suffered a *personal* injury to its own rights.[689] However, as mentioned above, there is minority current within the case law which would allow these actions. For instance, in a judgment of 16 November 1982, the first *civil* chamber of the Cour de cassation has recognized that an association the object of which was the study and protection of migrating birds had suffered moral damage directly and personally, in relationship to its purpose and activities, because of the killing of a bird of prey.[690] Similarly, an association to fight alcoholism was allowed to bring a claim against illegal advertising for alcoholic beverages.[691]

(2) The purpose of the 1923 judgment, since it was rendered by the joined chambers of the Cour de cassation, was to ensure uniformity in the case law of the civil and criminal chambers. Accordingly, claims brought by a disinterested association as *partie civile* before the *criminal* courts on the basis of Article 2 of the *Code de procédure pénale* will also be declared inadmissible in the light of Article 2, usually because the collective interest pursued by the association overlaps with the public interest, the defence of which is entrusted to the State alone.[692]

The annotated judgment is a rare example of a disinterested association successfully bringing a claim before a criminal court as a *partie civile*. It shows how the requirement of direct and personal injury (mentioned in Article 2) to the association itself can be construed flexibly, the Cour de cassation holding that the association concerned "does not purport to defend the interests of its members . . . The purpose of that association is to ensure the safeguard of fundamental moral values attached to human dignity . . . [T]hat association . . . suffers direct and personal injury from the attempt to justify war crimes . . .".[693] Boré lists only two other cases where the *criminal* chamber of the Cour de

[687] G. Viney, Annotation, JCP 1992.II.21954.
[688] See also *supra*, **2.F.60.**, Note (1).
[689] G. Viney, Annotation, JCP 1992.II.21954.
[690] Bull.civ. 1982.I.331.
[691] Cass. civ. 2e, 25 June 1998, JCP 1998.II.10204, annotated by L. Boré.
[692] *Supra*, 2.5.1., Introductory Note under a). See Cass. crim., 6 March 1990, Bull.crim. 1990.104, and G. Viney, Annotation, JCP 1992.II.21954.
[693] The decision has resulted, as G. Viney, ibid. points out, in the enactment of Arts. 2–4 of the *Code de procédure pénale*, authorizing the associations of members of the Resistance to act as *partie civile* in proceedings relating to war crimes and crimes against humanity.

cassation has allowed a disinterested association to join as a *partie civile*,[694] namely two judgments of 7 February 1984 and 29 April 1986, where an association specifically created to fight smoking was allowed to claim compensation as a *partie civile* for "a direct and personal injury resulting from hidden advertising for tobacco products".[695]

(3) A key theoretical issue concerning tort actions by disinterested associations is the nature of the damages which are awarded. Indeed, since the association is acting for disinterested purposes, it is not seeking redress for injury to the interests of its members. Furthermore, the association as such will rarely have suffered a pecuniary loss of any form. If there is any loss to be compensated, it must be a form of non-material loss which the association has suffered because the conduct of the defendant has had an adverse effect on its associative purpose. Yet it is widely agreed that legal persons such as associations cannot really suffer non-material loss; this may explain why the quantum of damages is sometimes assessed at one symbolic franc.[696] As Boré points out, the award of damages to a disinterested association casts doubt on the official doctrine that damages in tort fulfil a compensatory function (*conception indemnitaire*) and reveals how a tort law sanction sometimes works as a private sentence (*peine privée*).[697]

A judgment of the second civil chamber of the Cour de cassation of 18 December 1995 provides an illustration of the above.[698] In that case, disinterested associations had brought an action in tort before civil courts in connection with public statements made by a politician. The court noted that the statements were not caught by the provisions of the Act of 29 July 1881 which prohibit statements that are calculated to provoke discrimination, hatred and racial violence.[699] Nonetheless, the statements still constituted a fault (*une faute*) within the meaning of Article 1382 C.civ. The Cour de cassation accordingly upheld the judgment of the court of appeal, which found that each of the associations, having regard to its aims and object, had suffered a distinctive prejudice and proceeded to grant an unstated amount of compensation to each of them. In this case, since the associations could not really be said to have suffered a non-material loss, the awards were really in the nature of fines, for conduct which the court found could not have been prosecuted by the State.

Cour d'appel de Colmar, 10 February 1977[700]　　　　　　　　**2.F.62.**
Association "Aide à toute détresse" v. Arlen

DISINTERESTED ASSOCIATION ACTING AS *PARTIE CIVILE* WHERE THE DIRECT VICTIMS ARE
UNABLE TO SUE

Expulsion of needy family

The mayor of a village, in unlawfully expelling a needy family from its lodgings, inflicted personal and direct injury on a disinterested association which aimed to protect the poor. Since the direct victims were unable to bring proceedings for the wrong, the association was entitled to sue.

---

[694] Boré at 304, para. 310.
[695] Cass. crim., 7 February 1984, Bull.crim. 1984.41; Cass. crim., 29 April 1986, Bull. crim. 1986.146. See *infra*, **2.F.62.** and further **2.F.63.–64.**, Note (1).
[696] See e.g. the *Benetton* case, *supra*, 2.2.2., Introductory Note under c).
[697] Boré at 310–16, para. 315–18. See on this subject, S. Carval, *La responsabilité civile dans sa fonction de peine privée*, Bibliothèque de droit privé, Vol. 250 (Paris: LGDJ, 1995).
[698] Cass. civ. 2e, 18 December 1995, Bull.civ. 1995.II.314, annotated by G. Viney in JCP 1996.I.3985.
[699] *Loi sur la liberté de la presse* (Freedom of the Press Act) of 29 July 1881, D.1881.IV.65, as amended.
[700] D 1977.Jur.471, annotated by D. Mayer. Translation by P. Larouche.

Facts: Aide à toute détresse, a legally-constituted association whose object was to protect the lowest classes of society (the so-called *sous-prolétariat* or *quart-monde*) joined as *partie civile* in criminal proceedings, which it had set in motion by filing a complaint, against the mayor of Hoerdt (a village near Strasbourg) who had ordered municipal workers to expel a gipsy couple with their 10 children from their lodgings. Since then, the family had not been able to find a place to live.

Held: The Court of appeal allowed the association to join as *partie civile*.

Judgment: "Case law has tended to refuse to associations the right to set in motion [criminal proceedings] through a complaint coupled with a claim as *partie civile*, on the grounds that they would not personally have suffered the alleged injury and that their complaint would duplicate the work of the public prosecutor (*ministère public*), who is in charge of protecting the public interest. Exceptions have been made to this principle, however, in the case of the remembrance of the victims [of concentration camps], where an association created specifically to ensure the remembrance of deported persons who died in Nazi concentration camps was allowed to act against an attempt to justify war crimes, and in the case of mistreatment of animals, where associations for the protection of animals are often permitted to act as *partie civile*. If criminal courts have allowed associations with a disinterested purpose to proceed with *actions civiles* in these two sets of cases, it is because the victims of those offences could obviously not defend themselves. By analogy—and *a fortiori* in the light of the interest at stake here—the same result must obtain for the claim of Aide à toute détresse, since by definition that association only takes care of persons without any means, who are rejected by society and incapable of safeguarding their rights and interests, and whom the judiciary and the administration fail to support, as in the case at bar. The public prosecutor advocates the opposite, yet that would amount to cutting off access to justice for these 'outcasts' to whom the activities of the complainant are directed and which the complainant alone is willing and able to defend. In the light of the purpose and the role of the [complainant] association, and taking into account the expenses it undertakes to assist and protect the disadvantaged, the offences allegedly committed against the Weiss family have a personal and direct impact upon it and result in injury, for which it is entitled to request compensation by putting forward a claim as *partie civile* . . .

On the basis of the foregoing, the complaint, coupled with a claim as *partie civile* . . . is admissible."

Notes

(1) The above judgment is included as another illustration of how French courts progressively tend towards greater leniency in respect of actions brought by disinterested associations.[701] In a judgment reprinted earlier, the criminal chamber of the Cour de cassation had adopted a broad interpretation of direct and personal injury which the association was deemed to have suffered,[702] and the Colmar court of appeal followed suit in the present judgment (also in respect of a claim as *partie civile* in a criminal case), by holding that the action of an association is admissible when its aim and object are to protect "persons without any means, who are rejected by society and incapable of safeguarding their rights and interests". Taking into acount the objective pursued and the role played by the association concerned "the offences allegedly committed against the Weiss family have a personal and direct impact upon it and result in injury, for which it is entitled to request compensation by putting forward a claim as *partie civile*".

[701] G. Viney, "Chronique" JCP 1992.II.21954.
[702] *Supra*, **2.F.61.**

(2) It is interesting to note how the Colmar court tries to formulate its reasoning so as to bring it within the case law of the Cour de cassation. The Colmar court regards that case law as an expression of a general principle that associations must be able to bring actions on behalf of those who are not able to defend themselves (by which not only dead persons and protected species of animals are meant but also, according to the Colmar court, needy persons). In fact, the court of appeal is trying to read a generalized exception into what remain exceptional decisions of the criminal chamber of the Cour de cassation (on the association for the remembrance of the victims of nazi camps)[703] and lower criminal courts (on associations for the protection of animals).

Code de la consommation[704]   **2.F.63.–64.**
and
Code rural[705]

1. Code de la consommation   **2.F.63.**

"Art. L.421-1.   Legally constituted associations whose explicit associative purpose is the defence of consumer interests and which have been authorized for that purpose may exercise the rights granted to the *partie civile* as regards conduct which directly or indirectly injures the collective interests of consumers . . .

Art. L.422-1.   Whenever many identified natural persons, in their quality as consumers, have each suffered individual injury and where those individual injuries result from the conduct of one and the same person acting in a professional capacity and share a common origin, any association which has been authorized and recognized as representative at the national level . . . may, if it has received a mandate from at least two of the consumers in question, claim compensation before any court in the name of those consumers.

The mandate cannot be solicited through a call to the public on television or radio or through signs, flyers or personalized letters. It must be given in writing by each consumer.

Art. L.422-2.   Any consumer who consented under the conditions provided in Art. L.422-1. to the pursuit of a claim before a criminal court is then considered to be exercising the rights granted to the *partie civile* under the *Code de procédure pénale*. Nevertheless, any form of service or notification concerning the consumer is made to the association.

Art. L.422-3.   When bringing an action pursuant to Art. L-422.1 and L-422.2, an association may file its claim as *partie civile* before the [court] of the place where the head office of the defendant company is located, or in the absence thereof, of the place where the first offence occurred."

---

[703] Ibid.
[704] Translation by P. Larouche.
[705] Translation by P. Larouche.

2. Code rural   **2.F.64.**

"Art. L.252-3.   Associations which have been authorized pursuant to Art. L.252-2 may exercise the
rights granted to the *partie civile* as regards conduct which directly or indirectly
injures the collective interests which they aim to defend and which violates provisions relating to:
  –   the protection of nature and the environment;
  –   the improvement of the surroundings;
  –   the protection of water, air, ground, sites and countryside;
  –   land and country planning;
or aiming to combat pollution and inconveniences, as well as any implementing
provisions . . .

Art. L.252-5.   Whenever many identified natural persons have each suffered individual injury and
where those individual injuries result from the conduct of one and the same person
and share a common origin, any association which has been authorized pursuant
to Art. L.252-1 may, if it has received a mandate from at least two of the persons in
question, claim compensation before any court in the name of those persons.

The mandate cannot be solicited. It must be given in writing by each natural person.

Any person who consented to the pursuit of a claim before a criminal court is
then considered to be exercising the rights granted to the *partie civile* under the
Code de procédure pénale. Nevertheless, any form of service or notification is made
to the association.

When bringing an action pursuant to the previous paragraphs, an association
may file its claim as *partie civile* before the [court] of the place where the head office
of the defendant company is located, or in the absence thereof, of the place where
the first offence occurred."

Notes

(1) Because of the relative reluctance of French courts to allow tort actions brought
by associations on the basis of collective interests, as seen above, the legislature has frequently intervened, mainly in specific matters, to grant express authorization to associations—or public authorities—to institute such actions before civil courts or before
criminal courts as *partie civile*.[706]

One of the broadest legal authorizations was given to consumer organizations by the
Act 88-14 of 5 January 1988 and the Act 92-60 of 18 January 1992, which have been cod-
ified at Articles L.421-1 to L.422-3 of the *Code de la consommation*.[707]

According to Article L.421-1 of the *Code de la consommation*, "[l]egally constituted
associations whose explicit associative purpose is the defence of consumer interests and
which have been authorized for that purpose may exercise the rights granted to the *partie
civile* as regards conduct which directly or indirectly injures the collective interests of consumers". Subsequent provisions (Article L.421-2 and 421-6) relate primarily to the power

---

[706] As mentioned above, Boré counted 38 such authorizations. For some examples, see G. Viney,
"Chronique" JCP 1992.II.21954. On the action of public authorities, see D. Guital, Annotation, D 1996.Jur.96.
[707] *Loi 88-14 relative aux actions en justice des associations agréées de consommateurs et à l'information des
consommateurs* of 5 January 1988, JO, 6 January 1988, D 1988.Lég.93 and *Loi 92-60 renforçant la protection des
consommateurs* of 18 January 1992, JO, 21 January 1992, D 1992.Lég.129.

to seek injunctions to stop unlawful practices and to request the deletion of unlawful contractual clauses in consumer contracts.

Since the enactment of the Act 88-14 of 5 January 1988, consumer associations have become active in bringing cases before the courts. One example is the *Hermitte* case decided by the criminal chamber of the Cour de cassation on 6 July 1994.[708] In that judgment the Cour accepted, on the basis of the very general character of the authorization contained in the Act 88-14 of 5 January 1988, that consumer associations, as partie civile, could also join with a claim for damages a prosecution against a surgeon for extortion against his patients, on the basis of an interference with "the collective interest of consumers of medical care". In the same case, the Ordre national des médecins (French College of Physicians) was also admitted as partie civile, not on the basis of a specific legal authorization but because of its general objective, which, as specified in Article L.382 of the Code de la santé, was "to ensure that the principles of morality, integrity and dedication, which are indispensable to the practice of medicine, are upheld and to defend the honour of the medical profession".[709] The criminal chamber held that the Ordre could bring an action "in conjunction with a prosecution against one of its members for offences committed in the exercise of his functions, such as could harm the reputation of the whole profession".[710]

The right of recognized (*agréées*) consumer associations to bring an action as *partie civile* in respect of criminal offences causing direct or indirect injury to the collective interest of consumers, as provided for in Article L.421-1 of the *Code de la consommation*, is enlarged and extended by Article L.422-1 ff., pursuant to which such associations may bring an action before any jurisdiction (and not only as *partie civile* before a criminal court) to claim compensation for *personal* injury suffered by *individual* consumers if that injury has a common source and has been caused by one and the same professional, provided that the association is mandated by at least two consumers who have suffered personal damage (Article L.422-1(1)). Those individual consumers are then also deemed to consent to act as *partie civile* in criminal procedures (Article L.422-2).

(2) The articles of the *Code de la consommation* discussed in the above paragraph paved the way for the introduction of an enlarged right for associations to bring legal proceedings, whereby they could seek compensation not only for injury to collective interests, but also for the personal injury suffered by several individual consumers from the same source and inflicted by the same person. It has been followed within the area of environmental protection by Article L. 252-5 of the *Code rural*.[711] The wording of Article L.252-5 of the *Code rural* is substantially the same as that of Articles L.422-1 to L.422-3 of the *Code de la consommation*.

Here also the right of the association to sue before any jurisdiction to seek compensation for personal injury suffered by several individual persons is combined with the right

---

[708] JCP 1994.IV.2376, discussed by G. Viney, "Chronique" JCP 1994.I.3809.

[709] See *supra*, 2.5.1., Introductory Note under b).

[710] G. Viney, "Chronique" JCP 1994.I.3809, refers to other decisions of the criminal and civil chambers of the Cour de cassation which allow hunter associations (*fédérations départementales de chasseurs*) to bring an action in damages for having suffered "direct and personal injury as a result of breaches of hunting regulations", by virtue again of the general authorization conferred upon such *fédérations* to pursue the aims of "fighting poaching, creating hunting reservations, protecting and ensuring the reproduction of game" (Art. L. 221-2 of the *Code rural*): see Cass. civ. 2e, 2 February 1994, Bull.civ. 1994.II.43. But see Cass. crim., 8 February 1995, D 1996.Jur.96, which allows an action brought as a *partie civile* by Parc national des Cévennes in relation to a violation of hunting regulations, and yet rejects in the same context the action brought by the Fédération départementale des chasseurs de la Lozère for lack of any injury which would be distinct from the one suffered by the general public.

[711] Introduced in the *Code rural* by the *Loi 95-101 relative au renforcement de la protection de l'environnement* of 2 February 1995, JO, 3 February 1995, D 1995.Lég.123.

to act as *partie civile* in criminal proceedings for injury caused to the association.[712] Pursuant to Article L.253-1 of the *Code rural*, the same right to act as *partie civile* in criminal proceedings is also given to several public law entities.[713]

(3) It must be pointed out that both Article L.422-1 of the *Code de la consommation* and Article L.253-5 of the *Code rural* require that the associations receive a mandate from the individual members whom it purports to represent before the courts. This seems to be a consequence of a decision of the Conseil constitutionnel whereby it was held that it is a constitutional principle that individual actions cannot be introduced against the will of the individual in question.[714] Unlike the class action procedures which will be examined later, these procedures do not therefore really provide an efficient way to adjudicate on the claims of a whole class of persons, since a mandate *ad litem* has to be obtained from each member of the class.

2.5.2. ENGLISH AND NORTH AMERICAN LAWS

2.5.2.A. PROCEDURAL DEVICES UNDER ENGLISH LAW

a) English law has not dealt with collective interests in the same way as French law; in fact, the term "collective interest" itself is not used. In English tort law, there is no history of associations, whether self-interested or disinterested, having brought claims before the courts to defend the interests of a group of persons.

Yet English courts have developed pragmatic rules for litigation where there is "a multiplicity of plaintiffs between whom there is sufficient common ground to justify them all being joined in one action", as happens in a variety of situations, such as consumer claims for defective goods (including medicines), claims by investors in a collapsed investment fund, disaster claims arising out of a common cause, such as a train disaster, claims by a number of tenants against a common landlord or claims arising out of environmental pollution.[715] Many devices have been developed under English law to deal with such large numbers of claims. They are essentially procedural in nature, however, in that they allow for the efficient bundling of what remain individual claims with "sufficient common ground"; contrary to French law, the courts do not have to discern the substantive interests of a whole profession or of consumers as a whole and determine whether they have been affected. The *Guide for use in Group Actions* lists four such devices:

–   the simultaneous trial of separate actions by individual plaintiffs;
–   the test case or lead action;

---

[712] Art. L. 252-3 of the *Code rural*, similar on this point to Art. 421-1 of the *Code de la consommation* discussed above.

[713] In a judgment of 8 February 1995, the criminal chamber of the Cour de cassation has recognized a national park as the possessor of such right. Strangely enough, as pointed out by D. Guital in his note at D 1996.Jur.96, national parks are not mentioned at Art. L.253-5 of the *Code rural*, and were even struck off the draft list during the parliamentary debates held not long before the Cour de cassation issued its judgment.

[714] 89-257 DC, 25 July 1989, AJDA 1989.796. See J. Vincent and S. Guimard, *Procédure civile*, 24th edn., (Paris: Dalloz, 1996) at 115, para. 127.

[715] Supreme Court Practice Committee, *Guide for use in Group Actions* (May 1991) at 5.

- the joinder of parties in one action; and
- the representative action.

The first three are known in some form or another to most legal systems, and they will only briefly be discussed below.

b) The simultaneous trial of **separate actions** and the **test case** are governed by Order 4, Rule 9 of the Rules of the Supreme Court,[716] which provides that:

> "Where two or more causes or matters are pending in the same division[717] and it appears to the Court—
> (a) that some common question of law or fact arises in both or all of them, or
> (b) that the rights to relief claimed therein are in respect or arise out of the same transaction or series of transactions . . .
> the Court may order those causes or matters to be consolidated on such terms as it thinks just or may order them to be tried at the same time or one immediately after the other or may order any of them to be stayed until after the determination of any other of them."

This rule allows the court to bring together separate actions by individual plaintiffs in order to try them all at once (even if they will ultimately be determined separately). The court can also stay all actions but one (or a few), which then becomes (or become) test cases; it is assumed that the actions that have been stayed will thereafter be solved in the same fashion as the test case, if possible through a settlement between the parties. These two devices represent technical means of managing a large number of individual actions.

c) The **joinder of parties** is the most rudimentary means of bringing out a collective interest in the course of a tort action. It is based on Order 15, Rule 4 of the Rules of the Supreme Court, which reads:

> "[T]wo or more persons may be joined together in one action as plaintiffs or as defendants with the leave of the Court or where—
> (a) if separate actions are brought by or against each of them, as the case may be, some common questions of law or fact would arise in all the actions, and
> (b) all rights to relief claimed in the action . . . are in respect of or arise out of the same transaction or series of transactions."

It should be noted here that since all of those whose rights have been affected must be joined as plaintiffs, this procedural device imposes a relatively heavy burden on those who wish to launch a multi-plaintiff action.

The *Hunter* v. *Canary Wharf Ltd.* cases decided by the House of Lords in 1997 involved two multi-plaintiff actions (690 plaintiffs in one, 513 in the other), where issues of private nuisance and negligence, as well as public nuisance,[718] were raised; before the House of Lords, only *private* nuisance was

---

[716] The Supreme Court of England and Wales comprises the High Court of Justice (superior civil court of first instance) and the Court of Appeal.

[717] The High Court of Justice comprises the following "divisions": the Queen's Bench Division, the Chancery Division and the Family Division.

[718] Under English law, an interference that affects the comfort and convenience of a class of citizens may amount to a *public* nuisance. That term covers a wide category of activities, such as "carrying on an offensive trade, keeping a disorderly house, selling food unfit for human consumption, obstructing public highways, throwing fireworks about in the street and holding an ill-organised pop festival" (Rogers at 492, see also *supra*, 2.3.1., Introductory Note). Given that a public nuisance has a widespread effect on the public at large, it would not be reasonable to expect one individual person to take proceedings to put a stop to it (Rogers at 492). It is a crime prosecuted by the Attorney-General. So long as only the public, or some section of it, is injured no civil action can be brought by a private individual, although civil actions may be brought, with the consent, and in

invoked.[719] In the first action, the plaintiffs sued Canary Wharf Ltd. for damages, because a large tower in the Canary Wharf development interfered with the proper reception of TV signals in their neighbourhood (until a new transmitter was built to solve the problem). In the second action, the plaintiffs brought proceedings against the London Docklands Development Corporation (LDDC), the city authority responsible for planning, claiming damages on account of the accumulation of dust on their properties in the course of construction works in the Docklands area. The House of Lords ruled against the plaintiffs in both actions.[720]

In addition to its significance for the law of nuisance, the *Hunter* v. *Canary Wharf Ltd.* proceedings show that the joinder of parties, while creating a hurdle for the plaintiffs in having to join every concerned person in the action, on the other hand enables the court to manage a large case very flexibly. Indeed, while the issue of television reception affected all plaintiffs, the issue of the kind of interest in land required for a claim in nuisance concerned only those plaintiffs who did not have a proprietary interest. Nonetheless, the court ruled on those issues without making any distinction between the plaintiffs for procedural purposes, since they were all joined in one action.

d) The most remarkable device for handling multi-party claims is the **representative action**, which has evolved over centuries from medieval group litigation.[721] Its modern expression is found in the Rules of the Supreme Court, Order 15, Rule 12:

> "Where numerous parties have the same interest in proceedings . . . the proceedings may be begun and, unless the Court otherwise orders, continued, by or against any one or more of them as representing all or as representing all except one or more of them."

The representative action involves a class of persons who have *the same interest* in proceedings, i.e. whose legal position is similar. As the House of Lords held, "[g]iven a common interest and a common grievance, a representative suit is in order if the relief sought is in its nature beneficial to all whom the plaintiffs propose to represent".[722] The class is thus defined not by membership of an association, as in French law, but by the commonality of interest. Whereas French law thus preserves at least the appearance of consent of all those concerned in the proceedings, since membership of the association can be taken to imply at least tacit consent to the association embarking in litigation to defend the collective interests of its members, English law moves away from consent as a defining requirement for the class to be represented before the court. Indeed, as long as the plaintiff and the class of persons he or she seeks to represent fulfill the criteria laid down in Rule 12 and the House of Lords case law, it is not required that all members of the class should have expressed their consent to be represented by the plaintiff. They will be bound by the judgment, irrespective of whether it is favourable or not, although they can object to being represented by the plaintiff and thereby join the litigation to ensure their views are taken into account.[723]

The representative action already contains many of the elements of the class action as it has been developed in North America. Yet it has been applied with reserve and restrictively by English courts, and as a result it has not fully reached its potential as a device for

---

the name, of the Attorney-General, by private citizens who, as a result of the public nuisance, have suffered special damage beyond that suffered by the public at large; such actions are called "relator actions" since they are brought nominally by the Attorney-General "on the relation of" the substantive claimant (see Rogers at 492–4, Markesinis and Deakin at 450–4).

[719] *Hunter* v. *Canary Wharf Ltd.* [1997] 3 AC 655, [1997] 2 WLR 684, [1997] 2 All ER 426, HL.

[720] See *supra*, 3.1., Introductory Note.

[721] See S.C. Yeazell, *From medieval group litigation to the modern class action* (New Haven: Yale University Press, 1987).

[722] *Duke of Bedford* v. *Ellis* [1901] AC 1, HL.

[723] D. Barnard and M. Houghton, *The New Civil Court in Action* (London: Butterworths, 1993) at 53.

the protection of collective interests.[724] With respect to tort law, in particular, English courts have long held that a representative action cannot be used to seek damages on behalf of a class of plaintiffs, since damages are peculiar to each plaintiff and must be proved individually;[725] this line of case law has only recently been called in question,[726] and it seems now that the use of representative actions in tort claims is likely to become more frequent. As will be seen below, the rules relating to class actions in North America are more flexible and have been applied less restrictively, and as a result they have become a powerful instrument for the enforcement of collective interests.

e) In general, the procedural devices described above, while pragmatic, have been criticized for failing to provide sufficient protection for collective interests. For instance, in some product liability cases relating to pharmaceutical products, the legal system has failed, according to commentators.[727] Following the Final Report of Lord Woolf MR on Civil Justice,[728] proposals for a new "multi-party situation" (MPS) framework have now been put forward by the United Kingdom government in a consultation paper.[729] The proposed MPS would be a new procedural device, which would bear some resemblance to the class action mechanisms used in North America and studied further below.

f) In the area of *environmental pollution*, given the inadequacies of the common law as described above, Parliament has sought to supplement the common law through the creation of an array of statutory powers. For example, Part II of the Environmental Protection Act 1990 contains a large and complex body of regulatory and criminal provisions to control the deposit of waste. Infringement of those provisions may give rise to civil liability for any damage caused as a result.[730] Part III of the Act institutes various "statutory nuisances" and imposes upon a local authority which is satisfied that such a nuisance exists a duty to serve an abatement notice requiring the nuisance to be terminated. However, statutory nuisances do not, as such, give rise to civil liability. The principal remedy for a victim of a statutory nuisance is to complain about it to the local authority, which then has a duty to take such steps as are reasonably practicable to investigate the complaint.

g) Similarly, in the area of *consumer protection*, English law shows a preference for public action rather than private enforcement through, for instance, group actions. The Director General of Fair Trading enjoys an "enforcement monopoly" over the Fair Trading Act 1973, to the exclusion of consumers associations.[731] Since Directive 93/13 on unfair terms in consumer contracts provides for the granting of a right of action to consumer associations in order to seek a court decision on alleged unfair contractual terms,

---

[724] *Halsbury's Laws of England*, Vol. 37 "Practice and Procedure", 4th edn. (London: Butterworths, 1982) at 177, para. 233.

[725] *Markt & Co. v. Knight Steamship Co. Ltd.* [1910] 2 KB 1021, CA.

[726] *Irish Shipping Ltd. v. Commercial Union Assurance Co. Plc* [1991] 2 QB 206, [1990] 2 WLR 117, [1989] 3 All ER 853, CA.

[727] J. Burnett-Hitchcock et al., "Class Action" (1995) 92:42 Law Society Gazette 16.

[728] *Final Report to the Lord Chancellor on the civil justice system in England and Wales* (July 1996).

[729] *Proposed New Procedures for Multi-Party Situations—A Lord Chancellor's Department Consultation Paper.* See J. Seymour, "Representative Procedures and the Future of Multi-Party Actions" (1999) 62 Mod LR 564.

[730] c. 43, as amended by the Noise and Statutory Nuisance Act 1993 (c. 40) and the Environment Act 1995 (c. 25). See further Rogers at 498–504.

[731] See G.G. Howells and S. Weatherill, *Consumer protection law* (Aldershot: Dartmouth, 1995) at 548–50.

some form of associative action or *Verbandsklage* is likely to be introduced in English law, at least for the limited purposes of Directive 93/13.[732]

2.5.2.B. CLASS ACTIONS IN NORTH AMERICA

Introductory Note

a) The procedural means for a large number of parties to pursue tort claims efficiently were developed further in North America with the advent of the class action, which has blossomed since the 1960s. There are now special rules of procedure for class actions in the USA at the federal level and in almost all states, and in Canada in three provinces. Although this casebook is not primarily concerned with the law of North American jurisdictions, an exception will be made for class actions, since there appears to be no equivalent mechanism in any European jurisdiction and class actions represent an interesting development as regards the protection of collective interests.

Class actions are an outgrowth of representative actions. In a class action, a single plaintiff is allowed to present a claim against the defendant(s) on behalf of a whole *class* of persons.[733] The *members* of the class are then represented by that plaintiff (who is then accordingly termed the *representative*). The main distinctive feature of a class action, when compared to a representative action, is that no express consent is given by the members of the class for the representative to act for them.[734] The members of the class do not even need to be identified individually, as long as the class itself is defined. They will probably not appear at all in the court proceedings (so-called *absent members*). Yet members of the class will be bound by the judgment rendered in the class action, whether it is favourable to them or not.

Newberg on Class Actions summarizes the main objectives of class actions as follows:[735]
– judicial economy and efficiency;
– protection of defendants from inconsistent obligations;
– protection of the interests of absentees;
– access to judicial relief for small claimants;
– enhanced means for private suits to enforce laws and to deter wrongdoing.
It must be underlined that class actions have not been conceived as a new substantive remedy, but rather as an innovative procedural means for plaintiffs to bring before the courts claims which could otherwise also have been pursued individually (at least in theory). The legal provisions on class actions are not therefore meant to create any substantive rights.[736]

b) Rule 23 of the US Federal Rules of Civil Procedure, adopted in 1966, is widely seen as the most influential provision concerning class actions. It has served as a model for most of the class action legislation in North America. The following excerpt shows the main

---

[732] [1993] OJ L 95/29, Art. 7(2). The UK has not implemented this provision so as to give a right to action to consumer associations. The correctness of this implementation is being questioned in a request for preliminary ruling pending before the ECJ: Case C-82/96, *R. v. Secretary of State for Trade and Industry*, ex p. *Consumers' Association and Which (?) Ltd.* [1996] OJ C 145/3. That case may not come to a decision, given that the UK government has now announced that it intends to give a right of action to consumer associations along the lines of Art. 7(2) of Directive 93/13.

[733] As mentioned above, only class actions involving a multiplicity of plaintiffs are dealt with here.

[734] *Newburg on Class Actions*, 3rd edn. (Colorado Springs: Shepard's/McGraw-Hill) at 1-5, § 1.02.

[735] Ibid. at 1-20, § 1.06.

[736] Ibid. at 1-7, § 1.02.

features of the class action procedure. Amongst the conditions for class actions to be admissible, there are the conditions of commonality and preponderance of common issues. The conditions laid down in Rule 23 are found as well in other legal systems that have introduced class actions, such as Quebec; a judgment of the Quebec Court of Appeal is reproduced where the conditions of commonality and preponderance are dealt with.[737]

The following materials can be found (with notes) at <http://www.rechen. unimaas.nl/casebook>:

2.US.65. *US Federal Rules of Civil Procedure* (excerpts).

2.QC.66. Quebec Court of Appeal, *Comité d'environnement de la Baie Inc*. v. *Alcan Ltée*. Pollution by dust.

2.5.3. GERMAN LAW

a) Unlike French or English law (or the North American legal systems), German tort law has so far remained true to the liberal and individualist perspective which underlies its law of tort (and its civil procedure). Indeed the main head of tortious liability, § 823(1) BGB, focuses specifically on the individual, since the *Rechtsgüter* listed therein are all individual rights. German tort law thus does not in principle afford protection to collective interests, even if they are linked to the own interests of the members of a group (in so-called *egoistische Verbandsklagen*, self-interested claims by associations). It appears that German civil courts allow associations to bring *egoistische Verbandsklagen* in the interest of their members but under their own name, as long as the statutes of the association can be construed to imply that the members have authorized the association to act in their name; no assignment of claims is then necessary.[738] That does not seem to have had a major influence on tort law. Tort law is *a fortiori* reluctant towards claims going beyond the individual interests of the group members towards the general interest (so-called *altruistische Verbandsklagen*, disinterested claims by associations).

b) Certain associations have been legislatively authorized to bring *Verbandsklagen* in specific situations. For instance, pursuant to § 13(2) of the *Gesetz gegen den unlauteren Wettbewerb*, associations whose purpose is the advancement of commercial or consumer interests, as well as *Industrie- und Handelskammer* (Chambers of Industry and Commerce) and *Handwerkskammer* (Chambers of Crafts), can bring claims for injunctions against certain unfair trading practices (misleading advertising, etc.).[739] The standing of commercial and consumer associations is, however, subject to certain conditions designed to ensure that their claims concern situations where the interests of their members are truly affected. Claims for damages are not foreseen. Similarly, § 13(2) of the *Gesetz zur Regelung des Rechts des Allgemeinen Geschäftsbedingungen* allows those same

---

[737] *Infra*, **2.QC.66.**

[738] H. Koch, "Group and Representative Actions in West German Procedure" in E. Jayme, (ed.), *German national reports in civil law matters for the XIIIth Congress of Comparative Law in Montreal 1990* (Heidelberg: Müller, 1990) 27 at 32; Boré at 186.

[739] UWG, Unfair Competition Act of 1 June 1909, RGBl. 499, BGBl. III 43-1, as amended.

associations to request that standard contract terms which violate the Act be prohibited and withdrawn.[740]

On the other hand, in the area of environmental law, there is no provision for group actions, at least in federal legislation. Environmental associations can participate in administrative proceedings pursuant to the *Bundesnaturschutzgesetz*,[741] but the laws relating to environmental liability do not provide for those associations to bring forward tort claims. The general *Umwelthaftungsgesetz* creates a regime that imposes liability in respect of the environmental impact of emissions caused by "facilities" (*Anlagen*, as defined in Annex to the Act);[742] yet, although the UHG creates a far stricter liability than the general tort regime for the protection of life, body, health and ownership, it does not contain any kind of group action. The same is true of the earlier *asserhaushaltsgesetz*,[743] even though § 22 WHG establishes a special civil liability in respect of "water quality".[744] In other words, victims of harmful environmental effects must individually prove the damage caused to them. The situation does not appear to have been changed by the inclusion in 1994 of the protection of the environment as one of the aims of the German State (*Staatszielbestimmung*) at Article 20a GG.[745]

c) Besides the limited instances of claims by associations outlined above, however, German law does not recognize group or class actions, which "are considered incompatible with German procedural concepts and not necessary for efficient law enforcement".[746] This has not prevented certain groups from trying to act collectively, through test cases, for instance.[747]

H. Koch identifies the following explanations for the lack of development of tort law mechanisms to protect collective interests in Germany:

– collective systems, like social security, liability insurance and public funds, intervene to provide compensation for the type of widespread losses (affecting a large number of individuals in a similar fashion) generally associated with infringements of collective interests;

---

[740] AGBG, Act on Standard Contract Terms of 9 December 1976, BGBl.I.3317.
[741] BNatSchG, Federal Act on Nature Protection of 20 December 1976, BGBl.I.374, as amended, § 29.
[742] UHG, Environmental Liability Act of 10 December 1990, BGBl.I.2634.
[743] WHG, Water Resources Act of 23 September 1986, BGBl.I.1529.
[744] *Beschaffenheit des Wassers*. See further H. Schlemminger and H. Wissel, (eds.), *German Environmental Law for Practitioners* (The Hague: Kluwer International Law, 1996) and W.C. Hoffman, "Germany's new Environmental Act: Strict liability for facilities causing pollution" (1991) 38 NILR 27. In the former work at 187 ff., an overview of the existing civil law instruments for the protection of environmental interests can be found. Apart from the special Acts mentioned above, victims must fall back on general provisions of the law of torts and the law of property. As for the first, § 823(1) BGB gives protection against harmful effects on the environment which materialize in damage to the objects of protectionmentioned therein (primarily health and ownership). Notwithstanding case law which has alleviated the burden of proof (see *supra*, **2.G.39.**) claims for compensation often fail because the plaintiff cannot prove which particular noxious substances caused the damage. As for § 823(2) BGB, only very few environmental law provisions have the quality of a protective statute in the sense of that legal provision. As for the law of property, see §§ 906 (discussed *supra*, 2.3.2.) and 1004 BGB.
[745] See R. Steinberg, "Verfassungsrechtlicher Umweltschutz durch Grundrechte und Staatszielbestimmung" (1996) 49 NJW 1985.
[746] That is how H. Koch, "Group and Representative Actions in West German Procedure" in E. Jayme, (ed.), *German national reports in civil law matters for the XIIIth Congress of Comparative Law in Montreal 1990* (Heidelberg: Müller, 1990) 27 at 31–2, describes the reaction to proposals in the 1980s to introduce class actions for damages in unfair competition law.
[747] Ibid. at 32–4.

– as a consequence of that, German procedural law is underdeveloped as regards complex claims involving collective interests, since it has not had to deal with them very often so far;

– more speculatively, the German public has not yet become as assertive of its right to be compensated for infringement of collective interests as the American public, for instance.[748]

As far as the protection of collective interests under tort law is concerned, therefore, German law offers little material for discussion.[749] The topic has been discussed again lately, from the perspective of liability for mass torts. Various suggestions for reform have been made, but no concrete proposal has emerged yet.[750]

2.5.4. DUTCH AND SWEDISH LAW

The following materials can be found (with notes) at <http://www.rechen.unimaas.nl/casebook>:

2.NL.67. HR, 27 June 1986, *De Nieuwe Meer*. Dumping sludge.

2.NL.68. Rechtbank Rotterdam, 15 March 1991, *Borcea*. Oil spill.

2.NL.69. *Burgerlijk Wetboek* (excerpts).

A judgment of the Swedish Högstra Domstolen of 19 April 1995 is reproduced below, relating to an action brought by the State to recover expenses incurred for the protection of animals of a particular species.[751]

Högstra Domstolen, 19 April 1995[752]   **2.SW.70.**

ACTION IN TORT BROUGHT BY STATE FOR INJURY TO PROTECTED ANIMAL SPECIES

Gluttons killed

A defendant who had killed two gluttons, a protected animal species in northern Sweden, was required to pay damages to the State on the ground that the State incurred considerable costs in protecting that species.

Facts: Lars S was indicted for violations of the hunting laws and regulations, on ground that he in December 1987 unlawfully hunted gluttons on land belonging to the State, and that in doing so he killed two gluttons. The

---

[748] H. Koch, "Mass Torts in German Law" in E. Jayme, (ed.), *German national reports in civil law matters for the XIVth Congress of comparative law in Athens 1994* (Heidelberg: C.F. Müller, 1994) 67 at 84–5.

[749] H. Koch, ibid., mentioned in his report at 67 that the very fact of attempting to track the treatment of mass torts in Germany was innovative.

[750] See C. von Bar, "Empfehlen sich gesetzgeberische Maßnahmen zur rechtlichen Bewältigung der Haftung für Massenschäden?" NJW 1998, Annex to issue 23 at 5; H. Koch, "Haftung für Massenschäden—Recht, Abwicklungspraxis, rechtspolitischer Handlungsbedarf" JZ 1998, 801; J. Braun, "Haftung für Massenschäden" NJW 1998, 2318.

[751] *Infra*, **2.SW.70.**

[752] NJA 1995, 249. Translation by M. Tranålv.

270

State, represented by the *länsstyrelsen* (County Administration) claimed damages of SEK 50,000 against Lars S for each of the two gluttons.

Held: The HD confirmed the lower court decisions as regards damages.

Judgment: "In international treaties, Sweden has undertaken to protect endangered animals, among them the glutton. The glutton is protected by law in Sweden and can only be hunted for so-called *skyddsjakt* [protective hunting] and in principle the glutton must be forfeited to the State, no matter who holds the hunting rights.

In cases of unlawful hunting, the holder of the hunting rights is entitled to compensation according to the general principles of tort law. In principle, damages are then supposed to compensate the loss of the chance to avail oneself of the game in the particular area through hunting, or the loss of the value of the hunting right that the holder of the hunting right has suffered.

When it comes to gluttons, the State has to protect and preserve the glutton stock, on grounds of public policy; compare the role of the State according to the Act 1988:950 on Cultural Monuments etc (NJA 1993, 753). Damage of the kind that is here at issue can be considered to fall in the borderline area between non-material and material damage. In a case of unlawful hunting of gluttons, as well as in a case of unlawful hunting of elk, it is however quite natural that one pays attention to the damage inflicted upon the stock of the specific type of game in question. Since the glutton is protected by law it must, however, be considered that it does not have any economic value [since it cannot be hunted]. At the same time, it is established that the State incurs great expenses for the preservation of this species of animal and that those expenses can be said to have become to some extent without purpose, because two gluttons have been killed . . . and the species' breeding capacity has diminished. Compensation in cases of unlawful hunting of gluttons shall therefore be paid for, and amount to, the animal's breeding value. The amount of the damages is to be decided through an estimation based on *skälighetsbedömning* [fairness test], using the costs to the State for the preservation of the protected species as a starting point. There is no reason to lower the amount of damages below the amount reached by the [lower courts]."

Note

This case is of interest, since it revolves around the assessment of the *quantum* of compensation for a tortious act impinging on a collective interest, namely the protection of the natural environment, more specifically of endangered species. Since the plaintiff is a part of the Swedish State, it appears not to be at issue that it is entitled to seek compensation for the infringement of that collective interest. Then the next hurdle in the tortious protection of collective interests comes to the fore here: how is the amount of monetary compensation to be assessed, since here, as is often the case with collective interests, the interest has no readily ascertainable monetary value? The HD finds that, since the collective interest lies in the preservation of the gluttons, the loss should amount to the two gluttons' breeding value, which is also difficult to assess. Ultimately, the HD concludes that that breeding value can be estimated by taking the costs to the State for the preservation of gluttons as a starting point.

2.5.5. COMPARATIVE OVERVIEW

At the beginning of this section the following questions were put forward:

– Which, if any, collective interests are protected by tort law?

- How can a collective interest properly be articulated? How does the group in question speak? How is it represented?
- Can a group of persons as such suffer any harm distinct from that of its individual members? What form of relief can be granted for a violation of a collective interest: injunctive relief only or monetary compensation as well?

This overview seeks to answer those questions in the light of the materials reviewed in this section.

Collective interests protected by tort law

In French law, the judiciary first allowed actions to be brought by trade unions and professional associations, either before civil courts or as *partie civile* before criminal courts (administrative courts did not follow suit). That development took place at the beginning of this century, at a time when such associations were already well-established and their activities in the furtherance of the interests of their members were recognized. Legislative authorization of such associations to act as a *partie civile* came in parallel.[753]

From then on, it is worth noting that the French judiciary and legislature went their different ways. The judiciary framed its case law in *general terms*, with the result that the conditions for associations to bring forward claims for infringement of collective interests are quite strict, as shown by the cases reproduced above. In general, courts have been reluctant to allow such claims, except for civil courts in the case of actions brought by "self-interested" associations. For instance, in Cass. civ. 1re, 27 May 1975, the *Comité de défense* formed by the neighbours of the coffee-roasting plant was allowed to bring a claim on behalf of its members, since it came within the associative purpose of the association to act for its members.[754] In the case of "disinterested" associations seeking redress before the courts for the infringement of interests going beyond those of their members individually (quality of the environment, conservation of fauna and flora, remembrance of war victims), civil, criminal and administrative courts alike have adopted a fairly restrictive attitude. Civil courts have allowed the actions of disinterested associations to proceed in a limited number of cases,[755] and only in a few exceptional cases has the criminal chamber of the Cour de cassation allowed a disinterested association to act as *partie civile* in a criminal proceeding: one of these cases, Cass. crim., 14 January 1971, was included above.[756] Lower criminal courts seem to be more open towards disinterested associations, as shown by Colmar, 10 February 1977.[757]

Against the background of the modest progress achieved by associations in the case law, the legislature has continued to grant capacity to act for the protection of *specific collective interests* to a considerable number of associations, particularly consumer and environmental associations, as seen in the excerpts from the *Code de la consommation* and the *Code rural*.[758]

---

[753] Boré at 44–54, para. 46–58.
[754] *Supra*, **2.F.60.**
[755] Boré at 101–2, para. 119.
[756] *Supra*, **2.F.61.**
[757] *Supra*, **2.F.62.**
[758] *Supra*, **2.F.63.–64.**

In the result, a series of collective interests are protected under French tort law because of specific legislative enactments (labour, professional, consumer and environmental interests, to name but the main ones). Apart from those enactments, tort law does not grant complete protection to other collective interests, since only civil courts—but not criminal courts deciding on claims brought by a *partie civile*—will take a relatively favourable attitude towards associations acting for the protection of collective interests, and even then only when they are acting out of "self interest".

In English law,[759] it seems that the medieval group litigation which was at the source of the modern representative action was not a *general* mechanism and was not necessarily conceived as such.[760] Rather, a series of *specific* groups were allowed to pursue claims before courts through a representative. By the nineteenth century, group litigation was used mostly in disputes surrounding companies and non-profit associations; as Acts of Parliament granted such organizations capacity to sue by in the second half of the century, the need for group litigation vanished. A general mechanism for representation remained in the Rules of Procedure, but it has not been used extensively in tort law to this day, for reasons explained above.[761] In sum, under English law, all sorts of collective interests can be protected in theory through the device of the representative action, but in practice it is not used. Similarly, although the class action provisions in North America, of which Rule 23 of the Federal Rules of Civil Procedure has been included above as an example,[762] could be used to seek tort protection for any collective interest, class actions in tort are in practice the purview of consumer, environmental and labour organizations, as is discussed further below.

In Germany, there appears to be no mechanism for the protection of collective interests under tort law. *Verbandsklagen* are allowed in limited areas only, such as the law relating to unfair competition or standard contractual terms.

The representation of collective interests

From the moment it is admitted that tort law can protect at least some collective interests, key issues of representation arise. At first sight, it appears that two very different mechanisms are used to ensure that collective interests are properly identified and adequately represented before the courts in tort actions: through an action by an association having as its purpose the protection of a given collective interest, or through an action by an individual on behalf of a group or a class of persons.

Under French and Dutch law, for example, collective interests, *when* they receive protection under tort law, are represented *through associations*, such as a neighbours' association,[763] an association for the remembrance of the victims of Nazi concentration camps,[764] an association for the protection of the poor and needy,[765] environmental

---

[759] See S.C. Yeazell, *From medieval group litigation to the modern class action* (New Haven: Yale University Press, 1987) at 210–12.

[760] Ibid. at 277.

[761] Now in Order 15, Rule 12 of the Rules of the Supreme Court: see *supra*, 5.2.A., Introductory Note under d).

[762] *Supra*, **2.US.65.**

[763] As in Cass. civ. 1re, 27 May 1975, *supra*, **2.F.60.**

[764] As in Cass. crim., 14 January 1971, *supra*, **2.F.61.**

[765] As in Colmar, 10 February 1977, *supra*, **2.F.63.**

groups[766] or a Bird Protection Society.[767] The rationale for allowing associations to act for the protection of collective interests is as follows.[768] As long as the defence of a given collective interest comes within the associative purpose of the association, it can be said that the individuals who have joined the association as members agree with that purpose; membership in the association thus identifies a class of persons sharing a collective interest. As for representativeness, it can be assumed from the statutes of the association that the members of the association upon joining have at least given it a mandate to act on their behalf.[769] Furthermore, since the functioning of the association is governed by its statute, it can also be taken for granted that, when the association acts before the courts, it has the support of its members in taking steps to represent their collective interest adequately. With larger associations whose aims may not be very precisely defined, those assumptions no longer hold good.

In contrast, the North American class action (and the English representative action) does not apparently rely on associations. Rather, representation of collective interests is ensured *by an individual acting on behalf of a class of persons*. Whereas under French law the association is deemed to guarantee the identification of the collective interest and the representativeness of the party appearing before the court, in North American systems these elements are assessed by the court itself in the course of the proceedings, as described above.[770] The judgment of the Quebec Court of Appeal in *Comité d'environnement de la Baie inc.* v. *Alcan Ltée* shows how this assessment is conducted as regards one of the central issues, i.e. whether there is a sufficient commonality of interest between the members of the class to allow for a class action to proceed.[771] Other core issues include the representativeness of the plaintiff and his or her adequacy, as well as the appropriateness of a class action as opposed to other methods of adjudication.

Even if in theory the class action system does not rely on the presence of an association to ensure the identification of the collective interest and its adequate representation, it must be said that, in practice, it is very likely that a well-organized association—in tort cases, typically a consumer or environmental association or a trade union—will be found behind the plaintiff in a class action, given the high costs involved.[772] Only when public funding is available to support the launch of a class action, as in Quebec, can a prospective plaintiff truly escape from the practical necessity of seeking the backing of a powerful association.

In the end, therefore, even if French and Dutch law on the one hand, and English and North American law on the other, may have chosen seemingly different procedural

---

[766] As in *Nieuwe Meer, supra,* **2.NL.67.**

[767] As in *Borcea, supra,* **2.NL.68.** With the inclusion of Article 3:305a and 3:305b in the new BW, *supra,* **2.NL.69.**, the Dutch legislature has sought to establish a general legislative framework for the protection of all collective interests. However, as mentioned further below, those provisions do not allow claims for damages, although such claims may still be brought on the basis of earlier case law.

[768] See the discussion in Boré at 91–7, 102–6, para. 109–14, 120–2.

[769] French courts have even been willing to derive representativeness from the mere mention of the collective interest in the statutes of the association, as seen in Cass. civ. 1re, 27 May 1975, *supra,* **2.F.60.**

[770] *Supra,* **2.US.65.** and notes.

[771] *Supra,* **2.QC.66.**

[772] See S.C. Yeazell, *From medieval group litigation to the modern class action* (New Haven: Yale University Press, 1987) at 262–6.

avenues to enable collective interests to be represented before the courts, they are not so far from another when seen from a broader perspective.

As a result of Directive 98/27 on injunctions for the protection of consumers' interests,[773] the legal systems of the EU Member States might be brought closer to the French or Dutch model. At Article 4, that Directive binds Member States to allow "qualified entities" from other Member States to bring claims for injunctions before their national courts in order to protect the collective interests of consumers, as they are laid out in a number of Directives dealing with consumer protection. Pursuant to Article 3, "qualified entities" can be either public bodies responsible for consumer protection or private organizations whose purpose is the protection of consumers. Accordingly, Directive 98/27, while it does not force Member States to allow claims on the French or Dutch model from associations within their own jurisdictions, will see such claims made available to associations from other Member States. With time, it may be that Member States would decide to follow suit and adopt the French or Dutch model for associations within their own jurisdiction.

Remedies available for infringements of collective interests

In all legal systems, it is possible to obtain an injunction or court order restraining the defendant from infringing the collective interests of the plaintiff (or from continuing to do so). While that is certainly a most useful and powerful remedy, it does not raise the same issues as the award of damages, where the legal systems studied here differ in approach.

Dutch law, for instance, has established with Article 3:305a and 3:305b BW a general legislative framework in which the capacity of associations to act in furtherance of any collective interest (defined as a commonality of interest) is recognized.[774] Claims from monetary damages are, however, specifically excluded. Nonetheless, means of obtaining damages may still exist, on the basis of case law mostly concerned with collective interests in the environment.[775]

In French law, irrespective of whether the associations act in a "self-interested" or "disinterested" fashion, any compensation that the association may obtain will be for its own personal damage, since the rules on standing in French procedural law do not allow the association to claim for the harm suffered by its members.[776] The precise nature of the damage withstood by the association is uncertain: the association generally does not suffer any material loss from the conduct of the wrongdoer, but it is "hurt" in that the

---

[773] Directive 98/27 of 19 May 1998 on injunctions for the protection of consumers' interests [1998] OJ L 166/51.

[774] *Supra*, **2.NL.69**.

[775] As discussed *supra*, **2.NL.67.–69.**, Note (4). In *Nieuwe Meer*, *supra*, **2.NL.67.**, the HR found that the interest in the protection of the environment fell within the protective scope of the general provisions of Dutch tort law.

[776] See *supra*, 2.5.1., Introductory Note under a). Only at Art. L.422-1 of the *Code de la consommation* and Art. L.252-5 of the *Code rural*, *supra*, **2.F.63.–64.** does French law provide for associations to present claims for the damages suffered by individuals. It is noteworthy that these provisions require an express mandate from the individuals concerned (who may or may not be members of those associations), since then the assumptions made above regarding the representativeness of associations cannot hold any longer.

wrongdoer infringes the very collective interests which the association seeks to promote. For instance, in Cass.crim., 14 January 1971, the defendant Le Pen had distributed a record containing speeches of Hitler, which obviously morally "injured" the plaintiff association, whose aim was the remembrance of the victims of Nazi concentration camps.[777] The Cour de cassation found that the association itself had suffered non-material harm. As mentioned, doctrinal writers consider that these awards serve a punitive rather than a truly compensatory function.[778]

French law accordingly allows individuals to pursue their claims in parallel to the association, since the claims relate to different damage. It is interesting to note that Dutch law, on the other hand, will not allow an association to act in pursuance of a collective interest on the basis of its articles of association alone, unless it is shown that individual actions cannot provide adequate judicial protection to the interests involved.[779]

The use of the representative action for tort cases in England has been impeded precisely by the belief—only recently dispelled—that certain precedents excluded the possibility of claiming damages in representative actions.[780]

The class action in North American legal systems, in contrast to French law, usually leads to an elaborate judgment whereby a system is put in place to ensure that the sums awarded against the defendant are distributed to all the members of the class which the plaintiff represented.[781] Of all the legal systems surveyed in this section, the North American legal systems which provide for a class action on the model of Rule 23 of the Federal Rules of Civil Procedure are the only ones which really enable "self-interested" claims to be handled effectively: the representative plaintiff recovers not for the non-material harm of the class as a separate whole, but for the harm which each of the members of the class has suffered *qua* member.

The North American class action model does not allow "disinterested" claims, however. Since the class action is only a procedural vehicle, the members of the class, and especially the representative plaintiff, must themselves have a claim which could theoretically be pursued on an individual basis. The "disinterested" association seems particular to the French legal tradition, among the legal systems surveyed here. Although it cannot be denied that "disinterested" claims fulfil a useful purpose within the French legal system, the award of damages in such claims becomes even more difficult to rationalize than in "self-interested" claims, since the association does not represent the victims of the tortious conduct; it can hardly be argued then that the damages would benefit the victims indirectly through redistribution to the membership of the plaintiff association. This is why the *quantum* of damages is often symbolic.[782]

In fact, the difficulty seems to lie not so much with the collective nature of the interest, but rather with the compensatory function traditionally attached to tort law:[783] the award of damages for non-material harm to "disinterested" associations under French law has a definite punitive overtone, turning "disinterested" associations into a form of private

---

[777] *Supra*, **2.F.61.**
[778] Ibid., Note (3).
[779] *Supra*, **2.NL.67.–69.**, Note (1).
[780] See *supra*, 5.2.A., under d).
[781] See *supra*, **2.QC.66.**, Note (3).
[782] See *supra*, **2.F.61.**, Note (3).
[783] See *supra*, Chapter I, 1.2., as well as *infra*, Chapter VIII, 8.1.3.

prosecutor. If the award of damages in a claim by a "disinterested" association is to have a compensatory function only, then it would be limited to a small number of cases, including for example cases where the association had incurred some expense in promoting or safeguarding the collective interest in question. Thus, the Rechtbank Rotterdam in *Borcea* did not see any difficulty in concluding that the Bird Protection Society could recover the sums it had spent on cleaning birds soiled by the oil leak allegedly caused by the defendant.[784] Yet associations are rarely entrusted with such financial obligations; the State usually undertakes the expenses linked to those collective interests. Accordingly, in the HD decision of 19 April 1995, it was possible to award compensatory damages for a violation of the collective interest in the preservation of endangered species, since the Swedish State, which brought the claim, was entrusted with that task and spent considerable sums to that end.[785]

---

[784] *Supra*, **2.NL.68.**
[785] *Supra*, **2.SW.70.**

CHAPTER THREE
LIABILITY FOR ONE'S OWN CONDUCT

The central theme of this Chapter is liability for one's own conduct, i.e. the conditions under which one's conduct gives rise to liability to make good the injury that was caused to a legally protected interest of another person. Whilst the previous Chapter dealt with the victim's protected interests, this Chapter focuses on the harmful conduct of the tortfeasor. In the first section two types of harmful conduct are examined, namely acts and omissions; not all legal systems treat them in the same fashion. Section 2 then analyses the notion of wrongfulness (or fault in the broad sense of the word) and its two elements: the objective element of unlawfulness, and the subjective element of culpability (or fault in the narrow sense of the word). The concept of unlawfulness includes the standard of care used to establish the unlawfulness of a person's conduct. The concept of culpability refers to both the capacity of a person to be responsible and to blameworthiness (or what is left of it). Section 2 also discusses grounds of justification, that is to say, the exceptional instances where liability is not imposed, even though the conditions for wrongfulness are fulfilled. Section 3 examines the standards applicable to the conduct of public authorities. Such authorities constitute a special category of defendants, who may be liable not only for wrongful conduct but also, under certain circumstances and in certain legal systems, for lawful conduct.

It is symptomatic of the evolution of tort law in the Western legal systems during the 20th century that fault no longer constitutes a straightforward concept.[1] Starting from a purely subjective meaning—conduct for which one can be personally blamed—it has acquired a broader objective meaning: fault is now generally seen as conduct which is unacceptable in society, regardless of whether the tortfeasor can be blamed for it. Indeed, throughout the 20th Century, Western legal systems evidenced a strong tendency toward the "objectivization" of civil liability. And also beyond that, such "objective" fault has been replaced in many areas (usually through specific legislation) by a system of liability where it is irrelevant whether or not the conduct of the defendant amounted to fault — objective or subjective, e.g. in the fields of product liability, liability for accidents and to some extent also in environmental liability. As will be discussed further in Chapter VI, there are various explanations for that phenomenon: the need for particular protection of the victims, the need for a particularly stringent liability regime for certain risks, the difficulty of proving fault or, the relative ease of insuring against certain risks.[2]

As already mentioned in Chapter I,[3] the decline of fault in modern tort law was to a large extent influenced by insurance. Thus, it has been noted that, largely because of insurance, "the theoretical distinction [in German law] between fault and risk-based liability is often very blurred in practice, especially where it is aided by a statutory (e.g.

---

[1] In *Brasserie du Pêcheur, infra*, Chapter IX, **9.EC.6.** at para. 76, the ECJ noted the ambiguity of the concept of fault and refused to apply it as a condition for liability for breaches of Community law.

[2] See, together with a discussion of the emergence of strict liability regimes in Germany, France, Italy and the United Kingdom, Zweigert and Kötz at 647–684, especially at 671.

[3] *Supra*, Chapter I, 1.2.2.

§§ 836 and 833(2) BGB) or case-law-created (e.g. § 823 (2) BGB) reversal of the onus of proof, or the notion of *prima facie* proof . . .".[4] In English law, an illustration of the same phenomenon is found in the strict application of the tort of negligence in the context of road accidents.[5]

The following excerpt illustrates that development particularly well, in the context of French law, and shows how much fault is on the retreat, although it is still presented in French legal writing as one of the foundations of the law of civil liability[6]:

"Perhaps one ought to mention, before undertaking any further research, a hundred-year old controversy within French legal literature, in order to notice that fault has retained all its prestige as the basis for civil liability.

The commonly held opinion would probably be not only that all fault entails liability, but also that there is no liability without fault. One readily concedes that liability for fault has a moral value.

This is a phenomenon which may seem slightly odd if one notes that: a) compulsory insurance, the realm of which is constantly expanding, is gradually obliterating civil liability; b) accidents in the workplace and, to a large extent, traffic accidents, which are the main causes of personal injuries, escape, in whole or in part, the realm of liability for fault; c) EC directives or proposals for directives base liability upon risk or at least upon presumptions of fault; d) disturbances caused by neighbours have, for a long time, been compensated without regard for fault and on account of the mere fact that they caused abnormal or excessive inconvenience; e) a number of laws have, in the course of the 20th Century, created instances of liability without fault; f) risk-based liability is inspired by a spirit of solidarity and thus it would be paradoxical to consider it immoral; g) that, moreover, fault is a purely social notion, not a moral one, since a fault can be committed by a mentally ill person or by a child devoid of discernment.

Furthermore, the place of solidarity within the law is constantly growing, even beyond the form it has taken in social security. The legislature, over the past few years, has recognised its necessity in specific fields, notably in the field of personal injuries. . . [There follows a long list of legislative acts, especially in the medical sector]. . .

One should note that all these laws . . . afford the victim a particularly attractive regime where he or she is only required to prove a material fact, not that someone is responsible for it. . ."

The regimes of liability without fault mentioned above will be examined in Chapter VI. Here we are concerned with the notion of fault, or rather wrongfulness, as we call it, in order to emphasize its primarily objective content.

3.1. ACTS AND OMISSIONS

In this section, French law will be discussed first since it has had no difficulty in dealing with omissions, because of the generality of Articles 1382 and 1383 C.civ. Then the

---

[4] Markesinis at 74.

[5] Markesinis and Deakin at 158 and 162–163, referring to among others *Nettleship* v. *Weston*, *infra*, **7.E.16.** and *Roberts* v. *Ramsbottom* [1980] 1 WLR 823, [1980] 1 All ER 7 (QBD). But see *Mansfield* v. *Weetabix Ltd.*, *infra*, **3.E.17.**, and Notes thereafter.

[6] A. Tunc and G. Viney, "L'évolution du droit français de la responsabilité civile" (1992) 14 Jour. Soc. lég. comp. 123. References omitted. See also *supra*, Chapter I, **1.F.1.** and **1.F.5.**

sophisticated German system of *Verkehrspflichten,* whereby failures to act are turned into violations of a pre-existing duty, is dealt with. The description of the English system which follows illustrates its reluctance, as a matter of principle, to recognize liability for pure omissions. Finally reference is made to Greek and Danish legal materials.

3.1.1. FRENCH LAW

Introductory Note

a) Article 1383 C.civ. provides explicitly that a tortfeasor is liable for damage resulting not only from his or her actions but also "from his or her negligence or carelessness" (*par sa négligence ou par son imprudence*). There is therefore no objection in principle to attaching liability to omissions in French law. Nonetheless, the question arises whether only a failure to act in compliance with a legislative or regulatory prescription can give rise to liability or whether a failure to act in accordance with a non-legally-binding rule of proper social conduct can also entail liability. The first decision reproduced below is a well-known Cour de cassation decision which made it clear that omissions in the professional field are included in the scope of Articles 1382 and 1383 C.civ.; that interpretation was confirmed and broadened in subsequent case law and applied in various other fields.[7] The second judgment shows that courts are also expanding the application of Articles 1146 and 1147 C.civ. on contractual liability, by construing contractual relationships as including a so-called *obligation de sécurité*.[8]

An *obligation de sécurité* (a duty to ensure safety) is very commonly read into contractual relationships as a form of ancillary obligation on a contracting party to ensure the safety of the other party in the course of performing the primary contractual obligations (sometimes even before or after performance). It originates from transport law, but has now been extended to all sorts of contractual relationships. The *obligation de sécurité* first protected the life and physical integrity of the other contracting party, but its scope has since been extended to property as well.

The same tendency can be observed in respect of Articles 1382 and 1383 C. civ. on tortious liability.[9]

b) One type of omission is especially disapproved of under French law, so much in fact that it was made a criminal offence by the Decree of 25 June 1945 amending Article 63 of the *Code pénal*, which punishes (and consequently subjects to tortious liability) "anyone who, through immediate action and without risk to himself or to third parties, could prevent a criminal, or delictual violation of bodily integrity and wilfully refrains from doing so" as well as "anyone who wilfully refrains from helping and assisting a person in danger, when he could have done so or caused others to do so without risk to himself or third parties".[10]

---

[7] *Infra,* **3.F.1.** and Note (2).
[8] *Infra,* **3.F.2.**
[9] See Viney and Jourdain, *Conditions* at 337–41, para. 456–56–1.
[10] Now Art. 223-6 of the new *Code pénal*.

INFRINGEMENT OF ART. 1382 C.CIV. BY OMISSION

The imprudent historian

An historian who omits to render a truthful account of a discovery made by another infringes his duty of objectivity, which is actionable in tort.

Facts: In 1931 Professor Turpain challenged the value and place of the scientific work of E. Branly in articles which provoked lively controversies. In 1939 he wrote a new article in which he gave an account of the work of Herz and of other scientists, including himself, who had, according to him, played a role in the development of wireless telegraphy. On this occasion he neither mentioned Professor Branly by name nor made the slightest reference to his work. The successors in title of Professor Branly, deceased, criticized Turpain for failing in the abovementioned article in his duty to give his readers accurate information and alleged that he committed in this regard a fault of such a nature as to incur liability.

Held: The court of first instance and the court of appeal rejected the claim on the ground that only an omission made in bad faith could found an action in tort. The Cour de cassation disagreed: negligence sufficed to allow the claim. The judgment of the court of appeal was quashed and the case remitted to the court of appeal for further determination.

Judgment: "Having regard to Art. 1382 and 1383 C.civ.: The fault provided for in those Articles may consist in an omission or a positive act. Omission to act, even if it is not dictated by malice or an intention to cause harm, renders the person refraining from action liable when the act ought to have been performed in pursuance of either a legal, a regulatory or a contractual obligation or, at a professional level, in the case of a historian, in accordance with the requirements of providing objective information . . . The contested judgment setting aside the decision of the court below, whilst accepting from the 'elements of the case' that Edouard Branly is acknowledged as the author of decisive experiments by leading scientific personalities and by Marconi himself, nonetheless considered that Turpain did not act in bad faith in deciding to omit to mention the work and name of Branly in connection with the origins of wireless telegraphy, nor that he acted out of malice and with the intention to harm. But without it being necessary to take into consideration the findings that Turpain's attitude was not dictated by malice or a desire to harm, that finding was inoperative in regard to the quasi-delict relied on by the applicants, which does not require any element of intention. It is nonetheless the case that the contested judgment could not legally exempt Turpain, *qua* historian, from the obligation to make good the damage resulting from the alleged omission on the sole ground that that was 'his opinion, perhaps wrong but apparently sincere'. In fact, in order correctly to assess the liability to be attributed under this head to the person occasioning the damage, the court ought not to have limited itself solely to mentioning Turpain's opinion, since the contested judgment itself adds that it is 'possible that he gave way to this opinion out of ambition motivated by a desire—wrongly held by the Poitiers court to be excusable—to overestimate his own experiments'. The court had to ascertain whether, in writing a history of wireless telegraphy in which the work and name of Edouard Branly was deliberately omitted, Turpain had conducted himself as a prudent informed writer or historian sensibly aware of the duties of objectivity incumbent on him. By failing to do so, the court of appeal gave a decision which is without legal foundation. On those grounds . . . the judgment is set aside and the case is referred back to the court of appeal."

[11] D 1951.Jur.329. Translation by T. Weir.

Notes

(1) In the annotated judgment, the Cour de cassation interprets Articles 1382 and 1383 C.civ. expansively by bringing within the scope of tortious conduct omissions in the professional scientific field, whether committed intentionally or merely negligently. Moreover, the judgment makes it clear that not only omissions consisting in a failure to abide by legal or contractual obligations, but also those residing in failures to comply with an—unwritten—general duty of care, are actionable. The latter situation arises when the defendant's behaviour is not in accordance with what the law expects of a cautious and thoughtful person (*une personne prudente et avisée*) under similar circumstances—in the case of an historian writing a scientific article, when he fails to live up to the standard of objectivity which, under the circumstances, may be expected of a normally cautious and thoughtful historian.

(2) The judgment is typical of the manner in which French law deals with liability for omissions, even though the judgment does not contain any discussion of that issue at the level of principle. According to H. Desbois in his comment on the decision,[12] liability can arise as a result of omissions occurring both in a course of action (*omissions dans l'action*) and outside any specific course of action (*omissions pures et simples*).[13] Furthermore, H. Desbois infers from the judgment a general liability rule applying to omissions occurring not only in the professional but also in the non-professional sphere. In general, for liability to arise, the defendant must be in a position to act without serious risk of harm to him- or herself.

The broad scope given in the annotated judgment to liability for omissions has been confirmed in later case law in respect of both categories of omissions mentioned above (*omission dans l'action* and *omission pure et simple*) and, for each category, in respect of two kinds of omission: those consisting in failing to fulfil a specific legal obligation to act, and those consisting in violating the general duty of care through a failure to act. According to P. Le Tourneau and L. Cadiet,[14] the annotated judgment is an example of an *omission pure et simple* occurring in violation of the general duty of care.

(3) The annotated judgment can also be seen as a contribution to the protection of personality rights in a broader sense (i.e. including scientific reputation and respectability), long before Article 9 had been incorporated in the *Code civil* through the Act of 17 July 1970.[15] Even after the introduction of Article 9, this judgment remains of interest, since it is far from clear whether professional reputation forms part of the right to privacy. The judgment illustrates how Articles 1382 and 1383 C.civ. can continue to play a role after the Act of 17 July 1970 as regards the protection of personality rights in general, insofar as those rights go beyond the right of privacy.

---

[12] D 1951.Jur.329.

[13] See *Smith* v. *Littlewoods Organisation Ltd.*, *infra*, **3.E.5.**, where the same distinction is made under English law.

[14] Le Tourneau and Cadiet at 822–5, with many references to case law on both accounts.

[15] See *infra*, Chapter II, 2.2.2., Introductory Note under a).

Cour d'appel de Lyon, 16 December 1988[16]   **3.F.2.**
L'Olympique Lyonnais v. *Fuster*

INFRINGEMENT OF DUTY OF CARE. FATAL ACCIDENT

Hooligans harming spectators

The organizer of a football match is under a duty to take adequate security measures. It must pay compensation in respect of injury suffered by spectators as a result of hooliganism as well as in respect of non-material injury suffered by close relatives.

Facts: On 7 April 1984, the 21-year old Serge Fuster, while watching a football game between Lyon and Marseille in the Lyon stadium, was seriously injured by the explosion of a flare thrown by an unidentified spectator. He died of his wounds on 18 April 1984. His parents, brothers and sisters brought an action in tort against the Lyon football club, organizer of the game, to recover both non-material and material loss.

Held: The court of appeal, essentially confirming the court of first instance, held that the football club was liable on the ground that it had infringed its duty of diligence and care *vis-à-vis* the spectators. Each of the parents was held to be entitled to damages of FRF 40,000 and each of the five brothers and sisters, to damages of FRF 10,000, on account of their grief. Damages for material loss were also awarded. The appeal for review was denied by the Cour de cassation.[17]

Judgment: "It is not in dispute that Olympique Lyonnais was the organizer of the match following which Serge Fuster was killed after being injured by a flare set off by an unidentified spectator. The organizer of a sporting event is bound, as far as the safety of the spectators is concerned, only to comply with an *obligation de moyens*. It is for Mr and Mrs Fuster to prove that the organizers failed to fulfil their *obligation de moyens*; in this case the testimony given during the police inquiry shows that, as from the beginning of the match, various acts of violence were committed by spectators . . . Mr Faccioli, the manager of Olympique Lyonnais, explained that, in view of the number of spectators (33,000 had paid for their seats), all the supervisory and security services had been stepped up . . . It was stated that the police intervened during the match on account of flares being thrown . . . The trial court held, as was relevant, that the managers of Olympique Lyonnais were not unaware that the match was liable to be marked by incidents, notably in view of what was at stake, the number of spectators and the climate of violence prevailing during the first-leg match. It must be held that the said association disregarded Art. 20 of the Rules of the National Football League, to which it does not claim that it is not subject and which provides that persons in possession of articles liable to cause injury to spectators (including fireworks, such as bangers, rockets or bengal lights) must be debarred from entering the stadium. In order to comply with that obligation, supervision or inspections must be effected, even if only of a visual nature, in order to identify persons carrying such articles, without it being necessary to carry out body searches. In this case it is common ground that such an inspection was not effectively carried out . . . The court of first instance correctly considered that the organizers of the match had not placed the supporters of the Lyon and Marseille teams at such a distance apart as to afford every guarantee of safety . . . The court of first instance held, rightly in law, that the organizers of the sporting event failed to fulfil their duty of diligence and care, and declared that Association Olympique Lyonnais was bound to make full reparation for the harmful consequences of the incident. The victim, whose parents are Mr Fuster, born in 1922, and Mrs Fuster, born in 1933, was 21 years of age, and he had five brothers and sis-

---

[16] JCP 1990.II.21510, with observations by P. Collomb. Translation by R. Bray.
[17] Cass. civ. 1re, 12 June 1990, Bull.civ. 1990.I.167, Gaz. Pal. 1990.Jur.191.

ters. The court has sufficient information to evaluate the non-material harm as follows: each of the parents FRF 40,000, each of the brothers and sisters FRF 10,000. The sum of FRF 50,760 paid by Olympique Lyonnais will be charged against the above sums awarded to the victim's relatives. The physical damage, which, moreover, is not contested and is borne out by the documents produced, amounts to FRF 17,347.87."

Notes

(1) As appears from this case, French law comes quite readily to the conclusion that a defendant, in this case the organizing club, is liable for an omission in respect of deliberate wrongdoing on the part of a third party, in this case an unknown spectator. That may seem different from English law, for instance, where it is stated in *Smith* v. *Littlewoods*, in respect of damage to property, that there is no general principle holding someone responsible for a third party's wrongdoing "founded simply upon foreseeability that the [plaintiff] will suffer loss or damage".[18] But in *Cunningham* v. *Reading FC*, the club was held liable to pay compensation to policemen injured by fans who threw at them pieces of the underfoot concrete which could easily be taken up, as had been shown in the last riot four months previously.[19] The club's liability was based by Drake J on "negligence and breach of statutory duty under the Occupiers' Liability Act 1957 since, given the appallingly dilapidated state of the ground, the conduct of the spectators was easily foreseeable by the defendants and was a strong probability." Both the policemen on duty and the spectators were regarded as visitors.

(2) Under French law, as exemplified by the judgment in the *Olympique Lyonnais* case, in order to come to that result an obligation to ensure the safety of spectators is read into the contractual relationship between organizers of sporting events and the spectators (to whom they have sold entry tickets). That is an *obligation de moyens*[20] and not an *obligation de résultat*, imposing upon the organizers a duty to assess the risks involved and to choose, and duly implement, the measures which are appropriate in order to prevent the risks from materializing.[21]

One of the key doctrinal distinctions in the French law of contract relates to the intensity of the obligation: contractual obligations can be "obligations of means" (*obligation de moyens*) or "obligations of result" (*obligation de résultat*). As a general rule, contractual obligations are of the latter type: the contracting party is bound to reach a particular result and cannot excuse himself or herself simply by showing that, despite all reasonable care, the result could not be reached. Only an extraneous cause (*cause étrangère*)[22] can lead to the exoneration of the defaulting party, but the contributory fault of the other party can be invoked to reduce liability. Some contractual obligations, however, are obligations of means, whereby the contracting party is bound only to use his or her best efforts to achieve a certain goal. If the party has indeed done all it could, the obligation has been fulfilled and no liability will arise if the goal has not been reached. For instance, the main obligation of a

[18] *Infra*, **3.E.5.**, per Lord Goff.
[19] [1991] TLR 153, QBD, also in Weir at 158.
[20] As explicitly noted in the judgment of the court of first instance of 25 June 1984 in this case.
[21] After the Heysel accident in Brussels on 29 May 1985, a European Convention On Spectator Violence and Misbehaviour at Sports Events and in particular at Football Matches, ETS No. 120, was adopted on 19 August 1985, providing for a number of safety measures to be put into effect by the Contracting States: see J.C. Taylor, "The war on soccer hooliganism: the European convention on spectator violence and misbehaviour at sports events" (1987) 27 Va J. Int'l L. 603.
[22] An extraneous cause (*cause étrangère*) presents the following characteristics: it was beyond the control of the defendant (hence it is extraneous), and it was unforeseeable and unavoidable by the defendant. It can consist in a natural event (*force majeure*), the conduct of a third party or the conduct of the victim. For more details, see *infra*, 3.2.3. as well as Chapter IV, **4.F.38.–39.** and notes thereafter.

physician under a contract for medical care is generally seen as an obligation of means to cure the patient.[23] The implied obligations read into contracts by case law are often obligations of means.[24] An obligation of means can also be compared with the general duty of care imposed under the law of delict at Article 1382 C.civ.: if all reasonable care has been taken, then there is no fault under that Article (although the standard of Article 1382 has been upgraded in many cases to be almost equivalent to an *obligation de résultat*).

In a comment on the judgment reproduced above,[25] Collomb points out that the court of appeal held the organizing club liable without clearly stating whether it did so (i) because of the club's own fault (as the trial judge had done), in so far as it acted through its *management* or (ii) vicariously, because of the fault of other persons for whom it was responsible, such as the employees of the club and private security staff, or even, P. Collomb ventures to say, the other spectators. The question of any possible negligence on the part of the police force would have to be decided by the administrative courts in accordance with the rules of administrative law.

3.1.2. GERMAN LAW

Introductory Note

a) Much like French law, German law sees no reason in principle to treat omissions differently from actions. As Larenz writes "the omission to act in a way that would have prevented a result repugnant to the legal order is equivalent to a positive action to produce this result, as long as the person alleged to be liable was under an obligation to avoid this result and to act in consequence."[26] The crucial question under German law is therefore whether there was an underlying obligation to act which would warrant the conclusion that the omission leads to liability. Within the context of the three general clauses of German tort law (§§ 823(1), 823(2) or 826 BGB), an omission may well constitute a breach of a specific protective statute and therefore be actionable under § 823(2) BGB or a violation of *boni mores*, and therefore actionable under § 826 BGB. It is less easy, however, to see in § 823(1) BGB a general obligation to act positively simply in order to protect the *Rechtsgüter* listed therein, such that liability would follow from the mere fact that an omission of the defendant had resulted in an infringement of a *Rechtsgut*.

In order to make § 823(1) BGB more concrete in the case of omissions, German case law has developed the concept of *Verkehrssicherungspflicht*, or more shortly *Verkehrspflicht*, which may be freely translated as a duty of safety to be observed in various situations of social interaction. That duty arises in the various instances where one creates or perpetuates a source of danger for others, and it essentially requires the taking of the appropriate steps to ensure the safety of others.[27]

b) The impact of the *Verkehrspflicht* must be seen in connection with the concepts that German tort law uses to define a tort. Those concepts are: *Tatbestand*, *Rechtswidrigkeit* and *Verschulden*. Whereas the latter two are quite easy to translate as, respectively, unlawfulness and culpability, that is not true of the first of the notions, which refers to the kind of behaviour (as an actual set of facts, irrespective of unlawfulness *and* fault), against

---

[23] See *supra*, Chapter II, **2.F.11.**

[24] On this point, see *infra*, Chapter VI, 6.3.1.B.

[25] JCP 1990.II.21510.

[26] K. Larenz, *Lehrbuch des Schuldrechts*, Vol. I, 14th edn. (München: Beck, 1987) at 457.

[27] Larenz/Canaris at 400. For concrete illustrations of the workings of *Verkehrspflichten*, see *infra*, Chapter V, 5.1.1.C. (liability for employees) and Chapter VI, 6.3.1.A. (liability for defective products).

which German tort law, either under a general or specific head, aims to provide protection. For instance, the *Tatbestand* of § 823(1) BGB is an interference with life, body, health, etc.[28] As will be explained later, there is much theoretical discussion on whether the concept of unlawfulness (*Rechtswidrigkeit*) is more closely linked to *Tatbestand* or to *Verschulden*.[29]

However controversial the Result and Conduct Theories may be in German doctrine, the practical significance of the discussion is limited.[30] It is generally acknowledged, however, that the Conduct Theory provides a useful contribution in areas where the Result Theory appears weak, such as liability for omissions (as mentioned above, it is difficult to conceive that an omission to act would be unlawful just because it resulted in an interference with a legally protected interest within the meaning of § 823(1)).[31]

c) The concept of a duty of safety (*Verkehrspflicht*) plays a central role in defining the essence of unlawfulness under the Conduct Theory, particularly in the case of liability for omissions. That role is defined as follows by Markesinis:[32]

"From Roman times to today, it has been well known that liability for an omission could be imposed if a previous duty to act could be discovered. In early times, statute and contract were the main progenitors for duties of affirmative action. Later, the area of liability for omission was widened . . . [O]ne of the most fertile sources of the development of liability for omissions and, indeed, of the whole law of tort, was the development of the idea that a preceding dangerous (or potentially dangerous) activity or state of affairs should give rise to a duty of care. From this idea, the courts slowly but steadily developed the famous *Verkehrssicherungspflichten*."

What the concept of *Verkehrspflicht*[33] tries to do is to delineate where, and to what extent, a duty of care should be recognized in situations referred to in the preceding quotation, where a person has, in any situation of social interaction, created a source of potential risk for the rights or interests of others, so that this person is obliged to take positive action to protect them against the risk.

In the first judgment below, the Reichsgericht (the German Supreme Court until 1945) laid the theoretical foundations for the *Verkehrspflicht* doctrine. The second judgment shows how this doctrine is applied to an everyday situation.

---

[28] The roughly corresponding concepts of *actus reus* and *élément matériel* are familiar to the English and French lawyers respectively in the context of criminal law but not civil law, whereas in German law the notion of *Tatbestand* is found in both civil and criminal law.

[29] See *infra*, Chapter III, 3.2.1. under b).

[30] See Zweigert and Kötz at 599–600. See also *infra*, Chapter III.

[31] Ibid., at 600.

[32] Markesinis at 74–5.

[33] The leading monograph is that of C. von Bar, *Verkehrspflichten: richterliche Gefahrsteuerungsgebote im deutschen Deliktsrecht* (Köln: Heymanns, 1980).

RG, 23 February 1903[34]   **3.G.3.–4.**
and
OLG Hamm, 26 October 1981[35]

OMISSIONS AND VERKEHRSPFLICHT

1. RG, 23 February 1903   **3.G.3.**

Snow-covered steps

The owner of a piece of land which is dedicated to public use must comply with the require-ments of Verkehrssicherheit.

Facts: On the evening of 19 February 1901 the plaintiff fell on steps open to public traffic which connected two local streets, and suffered injuries. He sued the municipal authorities as being responsible for the accident on the basis that, as owners of the steps, they ought to have ensured that they were cleared and gritted in the snowy conditions then prevailing, especially as the steps were in a very neglected state and unlit.

Held: The court of first instance allowed the action. The court of appeal reversed the decision. The RG allowed the appeal from the court of appeal and remitted the matter to the court of appeal for determination.

Judgment: "Ownership is relevant to the question of liability under § 823 BGB in that the power of disposition which the owner enjoys over his property enables him to impinge on the legal sphere of others, and its exercise can impose on him a duty to have regard to their interests. It is not the right of ownership as such which is crucial, for the power of disposition attaches to rights other than ownership and may give rise to an analogous duty of care. The question is whether, in the light of a person's factual and legal relationship to property, he owes a duty of care to third parties in the exercise of his power of disposition over it or in the way he manages or uses it. If so, and he falls short of the socially requisite standard of care, he acts negligently (first sentence of § 276(1) BGB) and if anyone suffers injury thereby, he is . . . liable for such unlawful injury under § 823(1) BGB . . .

Here, then, the main focus of attention is not on ownership but rather on the responsibility attaching to the use to which the property is put; and though in this case the duty of maintenance was rooted in public law, it was accepted that its breach could give rise to liability in private law . . .

The general principle inferable from the provisions of the BGB which render the owner of land liable for damage flowing from it (particularly § 836 BGB) is that, contrary to the position in principle adopted by Roman law, a person is now liable for damage caused by his property if, paying due regard to the interests of others, he ought to have guarded against it [reference to RG, 30 October 1902, RGZ 52, 373].

It may be going too far to hold that simply by 'tolerating public passage over his land' the owner is bound to see to it that passage is free from danger. Nonetheless, it may be said that a person who makes his land available for use by the public is obliged to do so in a manner which accords with public safety, and that he remains under a duty of care in this connection; accordingly, a person who has created and maintained a right of way is liable for damage due to defective maintenance or failure to eliminate hazards on it."

---

[34] RGZ 54, 53. Translation by T. Weir.
[35] VersR 1983, 43. Translation by T. Weir.

2. OLG Hamm, 26 October 1981   **3.G.4.**

Lettuce leaf

A shopkeeper's failure to keep the floor clean and safe for customers amounts to a breach of a Verkehrssicherungspflicht *incumbent on him in the circumstances.*

Facts: While on the defendant's premises the plaintiff slipped on a lettuce leaf and fell.

Held: The court of first instance accepted the plaintiff's claim both in contract and in tort, the latter on the basis of § 823(1) BGB because of the breach of a *Verkehrssicherungspflicht*. It also accepted, however, that the plaintiff had been guilty of contributory negligence. The court of appeal upheld the decision fixing the reduction of liability because of contributory negligence at one-third.

Judgment: "The court below was correct to impose liability both for positive breach of contract and in tort under § 823(1) BGB for breach of the duty of safety . . .

It is common ground that while on the defendant's premises the plaintiff slipped on a lettuce leaf and fell to the ground. Objectively, therefore, a breach of the duty of care is established. The defendant was bound to take care of the plaintiff, its customer, both under an ancillary obligation arising out of the contract of sale and under the general duty of safety. He failed to do so. In any event the defendant has neither adduced evidence to the contrary nor rebutted the *prima facie* proof of breach of its duty to ensure safe passage. That means that the plaintiff may in principle claim compensation not only for her actual loss but also for her non-material harm . . .

The only way the defendant could avoid liability or rebut the *prima facie* proof would be to show that the lettuce leaf had been on the floor for only a short time. He failed to do so, and indeed could not do so, by invoking the freshness of the lettuce leaf. At the very least, the defendant would have had to prove that shortly before the accident the area had been checked and nothing found on the floor . . .

The plaintiff herself was, however, partly at fault, but the assessment of her contribution by the court below was excessive: she was at most one-third to blame.

Since absolute safety cannot be attained, it cannot reasonably be expected. It is true that the plaintiff was only going to make out a cheque and had only a few metres to walk to reach the counter. That does not, however, relieve her of her own duty of care. The customer's own duty of care admittedly varies depending on the part of the supermarket in question, especially the fruit and vegetable department. However, one must be on the look-out for fallen lettuce leaves at the check-out point, since that is where customers pack up the goods they have bought. Furthermore, as the plaintiff must have realized, it was Friday afternoon and very busy.

In view of the fact that the plaintiff's fault was momentary inattention, whereas the defendant could and should have made better long-term arrangements, and the fact that this was not the only lettuce leaf lying dangerously on the floor, it seems right to make the defendant liable as to two-thirds."

Notes

(1) In the first case, the defendant city had based its argument on the classical notion of ownership as an absolute and unfettered right, arguing that nowhere in the provisions of the BGB concerning ownership could an obligation to maintain one's property in a safe condition for third parties be found. According to the city, the application of § 823 BGB was therefore excluded. The court of appeal accepted the argument of the city on this point.

The RG took a different approach to ownership. It emphasized the power over a thing which comes with ownership or perhaps also with other rights. Such power over a thing grounds liability for a failure to take the necessary care towards third parties in the use and disposal of that thing. The RG added that even under the classical view of ownership, liability attaches to damage positively caused by the crumbling of buildings and works. For the RG, this is but an instance of the more general principle that the owner must compensate others for the damage caused by his or her property which could have been prevented by reasonable care. The RG accordingly found that the defendant was in breach of a *Verkehrspflicht* (although it was not yet so called).

In later case law, the reasoning of the RG has been carried far beyond cases of damage due to a failure to keep property in a safe condition. The early focus on safety of things used in traffic and movement has been abandoned and *Verkehrspflichten* now also arise in situations where a person exercises certain duties, mostly of a professional nature. For instance, a veterinarian is under a *Verkehrspflicht* to ensure that he or she carries out the treatment of animal diseases without endangering the health of humans.[36] Moreover, *Verkehrspflichten* can also arise as a consequence of previous actions: the person who created a source of danger is bound to take reasonable care to ensure that no harm later ensues.

(2) The second judgment concerns a simple case, yet it illustrates how normal the concept of *Verkehrspflicht* has become and how courts readily use it in dealing with all sorts of cases, here where the owner or occupier of commercial premises had created a risk for customers.[37]

It is chosen from numerous others because of its "ordinary life" character. In it, the court holds the defendant liable on the same basis, both in contract and in tort, namely that in the specific situation—and subject to contributory negligence of the plaintiff[38]— the defendant had infringed a duty imposed upon him and was therefore liable for the injury sustained by the plaintiff. As a matter of contract law, the shopkeeper had infringed an implied safety requirement and as a matter of tort law he had infringed a *Verkehrspflicht* that arose in that particular situation of social interaction. It is interesting to note that both approaches led in substance to shifting the burden of proof onto the defendant shopkeeper, who then had to prove that he had taken all reasonable steps to avoid harm to potential purchasers.

3.1.3. ENGLISH LAW

Introductory Note

Liability in negligence for failure to act (so-called "omissions") is one of the battlefields mentioned above where the general evolution of the English tort of negligence has been

---

[36] RG, 19 September 1921, RGZ 102, 372.

[37] For an overview of numerous other instances of risk-creation in normal social interaction, and corresponding obligations on the part of the creator of the risk to undertake positive action, see Palandt-Thomas, *BGB-Kommentar, § 823*, 55th edn. (München: Beck, 1996) at 953–67, para. 58–139.

[38] See *infra*, Chapter VII, 7.1.2.

described.[39] As a general rule, English law does not impose tortious liability for failure to act, regardless of whether the ensuing injury is to person or to property. A leading case is *Smith* v. *Littlewoods Organisation Ltd.*, where property damage was at issue.[40] An interesting case involving personal injury is *Topp* v. *London Country Bus (South West) Ltd.*, where the defendant's minibus had been left unlocked and unattended near a pub, when it was stolen by a third party who knocked down the plaintiff's wife: the reasoning of the Court of Appeal is in line with *Smith* v. *Littlewoods Organisation Ltd.*[41]

The rationale behind the general refusal of English law to impose tortious liability for omissions, harsh as it may be,[42] is "that I must not *harm* my neighbour (misfeasance), not that I am required to save him (nonfeasance)".[43] In *Smith* v. *Littlewoods Organisation Ltd.*, Lord Goff quotes a passage from Lord Diplock's speech in *Home Office* v. *Dorset Yacht Co. Ltd*,which has become the standard restatement of English law on this issue.[44] Or, to use T. Weir's example: "Even where physical harm is in view, silence, the omission to warn, does not of itself give rise to liability: thus you need not tell a complete stranger that he is about to fall over a cliff—unless it is your cliff. If it is your cliff, you as occupier will be in a special relationship with the visitor, which generates liability for unreasonable failure to inform".[45]

House of Lords[46]   3.E.5.
Smith v. *Littlewoods Organisation Ltd*

No liability in principle for omissions

Vandals setting fire

In the absence of special circumstances, a failure by the owner of land to act to prevent deliberate wrongdoing by a third party who has come onto the land does not expose the owner to liability in negligence.

Facts: The defendants had bought an old movie theatre with the intention of demolishing it to make way for a supermarket. While the premises were empty, vandals gained access and attempted to start a fire, though neither the defendants nor the police knew of this. A fire was eventually set; it spread to cause damage to the adjacent property belonging to the plaintiffs.

Held: The plaintiffs' claim was unanimously rejected as there is no general duty of care to prevent a third party from causing damage to the plaintiff by deliberate wrongdoing, however foreseeable such harm may be, because the common law does not normally impose liability for pure omissions.

Judgment: Lord Griffiths (expressing the majority view): "The fire in this case was caused by the criminal activity of third parties upon Littlewoods' premises. I do not say that there will never be

---

[39] *Supra*, Chapter I, 1.4.1.B., Introductory Note under f).

[40] *Infra*, **3.E.5.**

[41] [1993] 3 All ER 448, CA.

[42] Even "repugnant to modern thinking" if carried to its extreme, as acknowledged by Lord Goff in *Smith* v. *Littlewoods Organisation Ltd.*, *infra*, **3.E.5.**

[43] Rogers at 117.

[44] [1970] AC 1004, HL at 1060.

[45] Weir at 82. See also *infra*, **3.E.5.**, Note (4), as well as Lord Nicholls' speech in *Stovin* v. *Wise* [1996] 1 AC 923, [1996] 3 All ER 801, HL, referred to *infra*, **3.E.5.**, Note (2) and 3.1.5.

[46] [1987] 5 AC 241, [1987] 2 WLR 480, [1987] 1 All ER 710.

circumstances in which the law will require an occupier of premises to take special precautions against such a contingency but they would surely have to be extreme indeed. It is common ground that only a 24-hour guard on these premises would have been likely to prevent this fire, and even that cannot be certain, such is the determination and ingenuity of young vandals . . .

I doubt myself if any search will reveal a touchstone that can be applied as a universal test to decide when an occupier is to be held liable for a danger created on his property by the act of a trespasser for whom he is not responsible. I agree that mere foreseeability of damage is certainly not a sufficient basis to found liability. But with this warning I doubt that more can be done than to leave it to the good sense of the judges to apply realistic standards in conformity with generally accepted patterns of behaviour to determine whether in the particular circumstances of a given case there has been a breach of duty sounding in negligence."

LORD GOFF (expressing a minority view on this point): "My Lords, the Lord President founded his judgment on the proposition that the [defendants], who were both owners and occupiers of the cinema, were under a general duty to take reasonable care for the safety of premises in the neighbourhood.

[NO GENERAL DUTY TO PREVENT THIRD PARTIES FROM CAUSING HARM]
Now if this proposition is understood as relating to a general duty to take reasonable care *not to cause damage* [emphasis in original] to premises in the neighbourhood (as I believe that the Lord President intended it to be understood) then it is unexceptionable. But it must not be overlooked that a problem arises when the [plaintiff] is seeking to hold the [defendant] responsible for having failed to *prevent* a third party from causing damage to the [plaintiff] or his property by the third party's own deliberate wrongdoing [emphasis in original]. In such a case, it is not possible to invoke a general duty of care; for it is well recognized that there is no general duty of care to prevent third parties from causing such damage . . . I wish to add that no such general duty exists even between those who are neighbours in the sense of being occupiers of adjoining premises . . .

There is no general duty on a householder that he should act as a watchdog or that his house should act as a bastion, to protect his neighbour's house. Why does the law not recognize a general duty of care to prevent others from suffering loss or damage caused by the deliberate wrongdoing of third parties? The fundamental reason is that the common law does not impose liability for what are called pure omissions. If authority is needed for this proposition, it is to be found in the speech of Lord Diplock in *Dorset Yacht Co Ltd.* v. *Home Office* [1970] AC 1004, where he said, at 1060:

> The very parable of the good Samaritan (Luke 10, 30) which was evoked by Lord Atkin in *Donoghue* v. *Stevenson* [1932] AC 562 illustrates, in the conduct of the priest and of the Levite who passed by on the other side, an omission which was likely to have as its reasonable and probable consequence damage to the health of the victim of the thieves, but for which the priest and Levite would have incurred no civil liability in English law.

Lord Diplock then proceeded to give examples which show that, carried to extremes, this proposition may be repugnant to modern thinking. It may therefore require one day to be reconsidered, especially as it is said to provoke an invidious comparison with affirmative duties of good-neighbourliness in most countries outside the Common Law orbit (see Fleming, *The Law of Torts*, 6th ed., Sydney: Law Book Co., 1983 at 138). But it is of interest to observe that, even if we do follow the example of those countries, in all probability we will, like them, impose strict limits upon any such affirmative duty as may be recognized . . .

[CIRCUMSTANCES IN WHICH LIABILITY MAY ARISE]
That there are special circumstances in which a [defendant] may be held responsible in law for injuries suffered by the [plaintiff] through a third party's deliberate wrongdoing is not in doubt.

[Lord Goff then reviews cases involving contractual relationships, licensee/visitor relationships with the occupier of land, control and care relationships, and the creation of nuisances].

These are all special cases. But there is a more general circumstance in which a [defendant] may be held liable in negligence to the [plaintiff], although the immediate cause of the damage suffered by the [plaintiff] is the deliberate wrongdoing of another. This may occur where the [defendant] negligently causes or permits to be created a source of danger, and it is reasonably foreseeable that third parties may interfere with it and, sparking off the danger, thereby cause damage to persons in the position of the [plaintiff] [emphasis added]. The classic example of such a case is, perhaps, *Haynes* v. *Harwood* [1935] 1 KB 146, where the defendant's carter left a horse-drawn van unattended in a crowded street, and the horses bolted when a boy threw a stone at them. A police officer who suffered injury in stopping the horses before they injured a woman and children was held to be entitled to recover damages from the defendant. There, of course, the defendant's servant had created a source of danger by leaving his horses unattended in a busy street. Many different things might have caused them to bolt—a sudden noise or movement, for example, or, as happened, the deliberate action of a mischievous boy. But all such events were examples of the very sort of thing which the defendant's servant ought reasonably to have foreseen and to have guarded against by taking appropriate precautions . . .

Haynes v. *Harwood* was a case concerned with the creation of a source of danger in a public place. We are concerned in the present case with an allegation that the [defendants] should be held liable for the consequences of deliberate wrongdoing by others who were trespassers on the [defendants'] property . . . It is well established that an occupier of land may be liable to a trespasser who has suffered injury on his land . . . It is, in my opinion, consistent with the existence of such liability that an occupier who negligently causes or permits a source of danger to be created on his land, and can reasonably foresee that third parties may trespass on his land and, interfering with the source of danger, may spark it off, thereby causing damage to the person or property of those in the vicinity, should be held liable to such a person for damage so caused to him. It is useful to take the example of a fire hazard, not only because that is the relevant hazard which is alleged to have existed in the present case, but also because of the intrinsically dangerous nature of fire hazards as regards neighbouring property. Let me give an example of circumstances in which an occupier of land might be held liable for damage so caused. Suppose that a person is deputed to buy a substantial quantity of fireworks for a village fireworks display on Guy Fawkes night. He stores them, as usual, in an unlocked garden shed abutting onto a neighbouring house. It is well known that he does this. Mischievous boys from the village enter as trespassers and, playing with the fireworks, cause a serious fire which spreads to and burns down the neighbouring house. Liability might well be imposed in such a case; for, having regard to the dangerous and tempting nature of fireworks, interference by naughty children was the very thing which, in the circumstances, the purchaser of the fireworks ought to have guarded against.

But liability should only be imposed under this principle in cases where the [defendant] has negligently caused or permitted the creation of a source of danger on his land, and where it is foreseeable that third parties may trespass on his land and spark it off, thereby damaging the [plaintiff] or his property. Moreover, it is not to be forgotten that, in ordinary households in this country, there are nowadays many things which might be described as possible sources of fire if interfered with by third parties, ranging from matches and firelighters to electric irons and gas cookers and even oil-fired central heating systems. These are commonplaces of modern life; and it would be quite wrong if householders were to be held liable in negligence for acting in a socially acceptable manner [emphasis added]. No doubt the question whether liability should be imposed on [defendants] in a case where a source of danger on his land has been sparked off by the deliberate wrongdoing of a third party is a question to be decided on the facts of each case, and it would, I think, be wrong for your Lordships' House to anticipate the manner in which the law may develop: but I cannot help thinking that cases where liability will be so imposed are likely to be very rare.

There is another basis upon which a [defendant] may be held liable for damage to neighbouring property caused by a fire started on his (the [defendant's]) property by the deliberate wrongdoing of a third party. This arises where he has knowledge or means of knowledge that a third party has created or is creating a risk of fire, or indeed has started a fire, on his premises, and then fails to take such steps as are reasonably open to him (in the limited sense explained by Lord Wilberforce in *Goldman* v. *Hargrave* [1967] 1 AC 645 at 663–664) to prevent any such fire from damaging neighbouring property . . .

[NO LIABILITY FOR HARM CAUSED BY VANDALS]
The present case is, of course, concerned with entry not by thieves but by vandals. Here the point can be made that, whereas an occupier of property can take precautions against thieves, he cannot (apart from insuring his property and its contents) take effective precautions against physical damage caused to his property by a vandal who has gained access to adjacent property and has there created a source of danger which has resulted in damage to his property by, for example, fire or escaping water. Even so, the same difficulty arises. Suppose, taking the example I have given of the family going away on holiday and leaving their front door unlocked, it was not a thief but a vandal who took advantage of that fact; and that the vandal, in wrecking the flat, caused damage to the plumbing which resulted in a water leak and consequent damage to the shop below. Are the occupiers of the flat to be held liable in negligence for such damage? I do not think so, even though it may be well known that vandalism is prevalent in the neighbourhood. The reason is the same, that there is no general duty to *prevent* third parties from causing damage to others, even though there is a high degree of foresight that this may occur [emphasis in original]. In the example I have given, it cannot be said that the occupiers of the flat have caused or permitted the creation of a source of danger (as in *Haynes* v. *Harwood* [1935] 1 KB 146, or in the example of the fireworks I gave earlier) which they ought to have guarded against; nor of course were there any special circumstances giving rise to a duty of care . . .

I remain of the opinion that to impose a general duty on occupiers to take reasonable care to prevent others from entering their property would impose an unreasonable burden on ordinary householders and an unreasonable curb upon the ordinary enjoyment of their property; and I am also of the opinion that to do so would be contrary to principle [emphasis added]. It is very tempting to try to solve all problems of negligence by reference to an all-embracing criterion of foreseeability, thereby effectively reducing all decisions in this field to questions of fact. But this comfortable solutions is, alas, not open to us. The law has to accommodate all the untidy complexity of life; and there are circumstances where considerations of practical justice impel us to reject a general imposition of liability for foreseeable damage . . .

For these reasons I would dismiss these appeals."

Notes

(1) As explained in the introductory note, English law is reluctant to impose liability for omissions; this applies however only to "true" omissions, not to "apparent" omissions which are simply an item in a chain of active negligent conduct, such as the failure of a driver to brake at crossroads, or the failure of a doctor to inform his or her patient of the nature and risks of treatment.[47] Moreover, even in the event of true omissions, the law may impose a duty to act, and it does so not infrequently.[48] Thus, it appears from case law that a duty to act exists when "the plaintiff is under the care or control of the defendant and is incapable of protecting himself. Thus claims have succeeded against schools for

---

[47] Rogers at 117.
[48] Rogers at 120.

failing to safeguard pupils against injury and against health care providers and the police for failing to prevent harm (even self-inflicted harm) to persons in their care or custody",[49] but the question of parental liability in tort for failing to protect a child against danger has not been much explored in England.[50]

The situation of rescuers is also special: one is not required to rescue somebody who is in danger; one is not required to do so even when the potential rescuer can do so without risk for his or her own life. But if one has chosen to come to someone else's rescue and then bungles the job, actually injuring that other person who might otherwise have escaped unharmed, liability in negligence may arise.[51]

(2) As appears from the annotated case, the rule against liability for failure to act applies with equal force when the injury is brought about by the act (criminal or not) of a third party, so that the defendant's omission consists in insufficient care to prevent or avoid that act. There are however many ways to come to this result, as shown by the speeches in that case by the members of the House of Lords. At issue is the liability of the occupier of land for having failed to prevent deliberate acts by third parties that led to damage to adjoining property, one of the many typical fact patterns of liability for failure to act involving the acts of third parties.

One approach, espoused by Lord Goff, is that the occupier is in principle under no duty to guard against risks of injuries to others through the wrongdoing of a third party; there may, however, be special as well as more general circumstances where liability arises even if the deliberate wrongdoing of a third party was the immediate cause of damage. *Special* circumstances are enumerated by Lord Goff in the course of a survey of case law. The first of the *general* circumstances is where the defendant "negligently causes or permits to be created a source of danger, and it is reasonably foreseeable that third parties may interfere with it and, sparking off the danger, thereby cause damage to persons in the position of the plaintiff". A second general circumstance is "where (the defendant) has knowledge or means of knowledge that a third party has created or is creating a risk of fire . . . on his premises, and then fails to take such steps as are reasonably open to him . . .". According to Lord Goff, to impose a general duty outside the special and more general circumstances named by him, would indeed place an unreasonable burden on the landowner and his family.

Three other members of the House were, on the contrary, of the opinion that there is a general duty upon the occupier to ensure that his or her property does not become a source of danger to others.[52] Those Law Lords thought, however, that wilful human conduct (deliberate wrongdoing on the part of a third party) does not present a sufficient degree of likelihood for the occupier to contemplate it as a reasonable probability rather than a more remote possibility. Accordingly, they also came to the conclusion that the claim of the plaintiff had to be dismissed.

[49] Rogers at 121.

[50] *Van Oppen* v. *Clerk to the Bedford Charity Trustees* [1990] 1 WLR 235, [1989] 3 All ER 389, CA, is cited, among other cases, for its holding that while a *school* is under a duty to prevent a pupil from suffering injury, it is under no duty to take out personal accident insurance for the child nor to advise the parents to do so. But as to Australia, see Dixon J. in *Smith* v. *Leurs*, as quoted in *Yuen Kun Yeu, infra,* **3.E.33.**

[51] See Deane J in *Jaensch* v. *Coffey* (1984) 54 ALR 417 at 440, mentioned by Lord Keith in *Alcock* v. *Chief Constable of the South Yorkshire Police, infra,* Chapter II, **2.E.8.** See further on the situation of rescuers, Weir at 89–90, and on the issue of assumption of risk or contributory negligence, *infra,* Chapter VII, 7.2.1. and 7.1.3.

[52] Lords Brandon, Griffiths and Mackay. Lord Keith expressed agreement with both sides on this issue.

The position of Lord Goff seems to be strengthened by the subsequent decision of the House of Lords in *Stovin* v. *Wise*,[53] where it was alleged that a public authority had been negligent in omitting to carry out works on adjoining land to improve the visibility at a particular street crossing. Lord Hoffmann spoke for the majority (including Lord Goff) in the following terms (without any reference either to a general duty on the occupier to avoid that his or her property becomes a source of danger or even to *Smith* v. *Littlewoods Organisation Ltd.*):

"There may be a duty to act if one has undertaken to do so or induced a person to rely upon one doing so. Or the ownership or occupation of land may give rise to a duty to take positive steps for the benefit of those who come upon the land and sometimes for the benefit of neighbours. In *Hargrave* v. *Goldman* the High Court of Australia held that the owner and occupier of a . . . property . . . had a duty to take reasonable steps to extinguish a fire, which had been started by lightning striking a tree on his land, so as to prevent it from spreading to his neighbour's land. This is a case in which the limited class of persons who owe the duty (neighbours) is easily identified and the political, moral and economic arguments . . . [against imposing liability for omissions] are countered by the fact that the duties are mutual. [Lord Hoffmann discusses the decision of the Privy Council upholding the judgment of the High Court in that case] . . . This is quite different from the duty owed by a person who undertakes a positive activity which carries the risk of causing damage to others. If he does not have the resources to take such steps as are objectively reasonable to prevent such damage, he should not undertake that activity at all."

(3) Among the *special* circumstances enumerated by Lord Goff in which liability may arise for failure to prevent third parties from harming the plaintiff, one finds the presence of a relationship between the defendant and the third party in question by virtue of which the defendant has control over the third party. Such was the case in *Home Office* v. *Dorset Yacht Co Ltd.*, to which Lord Goff referred.[54] In that case, seven young offenders ran away from a penal reform institution on an island one night when the three officers in charge of them were all in bed, contrary to their instructions. The offenders took one of the many vessels found in a nearby harbour and brought it into collision with the plaintiff's yacht, which they then boarded and damaged further. The House of Lords concluded that a duty of care was owed by the defendant Home Office to the plaintiff.

The decision in *Dorset Yacht* is one of the three cases to which Lord Wilberforce referred in *Anns* v. *Merton London Borough Council* (the others being *Donoghue* v. *Stevenson* and *Hedley Byrne & Co. Ltd.* v. *Heller and Partners Ltd.*) to construct his general two-stage approach to determine whether there is a duty of care in particular cases.[55] As has already been mentioned there, *Anns* came under heavy criticism in later decisions, including *Yuen Kun Yeu* v. *Attorney General of Hong Kong*,[56] before it was ultimately overturned in *Murphy* v. *Brentwood District Council*.[57] In *Yuen Kun Yeu*, *Dorset Yacht* was itself explained on the basis that "[h]aving regard to [the] circumstances, it was not difficult to arrive, as a matter of judgment, at the conclusion that a close and direct relationship of proximity existed between the officers and the owners of the yachts, sufficient to

---

[53] [1996] 1 AC 923, [1996] 3 All ER 801, HL. See also *infra*, 3.1.5.
[54] [1970] AC 1004, [1970] 2 All ER 294, HL.
[55] See *supra*, Chapter I, 1.4.1.B., Introductory Note under b).
[56] *Infra*, **3.E.33.**
[57] [1991] 1 AC 398, [1990] 2 All ER 269, HL.

require the former, as a matter of law, to take reasonable care to prevent the boys from interfering with the yachts and damaging them".

(4) Since the Occupiers' Liability Acts 1957 and 1984 the duty of occupiers towards visitors and trespassers is governed by special statutory provisions in respect of dangers due to the state of the premises or to acts or *omissions* of the occupier.[58]

3.1.4. GREEK AND DANISH LAW

The following cases can be found (with notes) at <http://www.rechten. unimaas.nl/casebook>:

3.GR.6. Areios Pagos 1891/1984. Incubator without power.

3.GR.7. Areios Pagos 81/1991. Pesticide.

3.DK.8. Høgesteretsdom, 27 October 1989, *Dansk Eternit Fabrik* v. *Möller.* Asbestos in the workplace.

3.1.5. COMPARATIVE OVERVIEW

Civil liability may arise due to an omission as well as a positive act, under the French and German civil codes and many other tort laws. Under some other legal systems, and particularly in the English common law, there is a general reluctance to accept unrestricted liability for "mere omissions", as opposed to "omissions in action". Whilst the latter occur in the course of positive conduct, and are treated as an integral part of such conduct, the former do not occur in the course of positive conduct. The basis of this distinction is that, while it is logical that I should be held responsible for the consequences of events that I have initiated, the same cannot be said of harm which results from a chain of events I have not, unless special circumstances arise. The reluctance of English law to impose liability for mere omissions extends to failures to prevent another from causing harm.

Liability for mere omissions

The following excerpt from Lord Hoffmann's speech in *Stovin* v. *Wise* is a good illustration of the rationale behind this attitude towards *mere* omissions under English common law:[59]

"There are sound reasons why omissions require different treatment from positive conduct. It is one thing for the law to say that a person who undertakes some activity shall take reasonable care not to cause damage to others. It is another thing for the law to require that a person who is doing nothing in particular shall take steps to prevent another from suffering harm from the acts of third parties . . . or natural causes. One can put the matter in political, moral or economic terms. In political terms it is less of an invasion of an individual's freedom for the law to require him to consider the safety of others in his actions than to impose upon him a duty to rescue or protect.

---

[58] 5&6 Eliz. 2, c. 31 and c. 3 respectively.
[59] [1996] 1 AC 923 at 943–4, [1996] 3 All ER 801 at 406–7.

A moral version of this point may be called the 'why pick on me?' argument. A duty to prevent harm to others or to render assistance to a person in danger or distress may apply to a large and indeterminate class of people who happen to be able to do something. Why should one be held liable rather than another? In economic terms, the efficient allocation of resources usually requires an activity should bear its own costs . . . So liability to pay compensation for loss caused by negligent conduct acts as a deterrent . . . But there is no similar justification for requiring a person who is not doing anything to spend money on behalf of someone else . . . So there must be some special reason why he should have to put his hand in his pocket."

What are these political, moral and economic considerations which impose a duty to act in order to preserve another's safety? Under German and French law where liability for omissions, including mere omissions, is readily accepted, such a duty is derived from the existence, under the circumstances, of a *Verkehrspflicht*[60] or an *obligation de sécurité*, that is a duty to safeguard another's interests. It can be noted that, in contrast to German law, French law does not emphasize a need for a positive duty to act in cases involving omissions, although it is not oblivious to the issue: that inquiry appears to be subsumed in the consideration of fault. Circumstances under which such a duty is held to exist under many legal systems such as German and French law and are not unknown in English law are as follows.

(i) *The existence of a special relationship with the plaintiff.* The duty of parents to prevent their children from harming themselves is widely accepted.[61] Similar positive duties arise, where an individual or institution voluntarily assumes responsibility for others, even though the obligation has no contractual basis.[62] So even when taking an offender into custody, the police must ensure that nothing befalls him due to the stress of the situation.[63] Likewise, much emphasis is placed on the obligation of employers to ensure the safety of their employees.[64]

(ii) *The creation, to one's own, often economic, benefit, of a source of danger.* The special duty imposed upon keepers of licensed premises, not only to ensure the safety of the premises, but also the safety of guests who get drunk, is one example.[65]

The notion of a duty to prevent harm resulting from a source of danger that the person on whom the duty is imposed has created to his or her own benefit, can be seen as an extension under German and French law, of the notion of control over things underlying the liability arising for animals, real property and chattels, from which the various categories of *gardien* liability have evolved. Thus, while the concept of a duty of care arising from a prior danger-increasing act (*Ingerenz*) was originally considered in German law to be an independent source of duty, it is almost impossible today to distinguish it from liability for things, or liability for dangerous acts. It encompasses situations such as where a

---

[60] *Supra*, 3.1.2., Introductory Note and **2.G.3.–4.**

[61] See *inter alia*: BGH, 20 September 1994, NJW 1994, 3348 and BGH, 23 May 1995, VersR 1995, 973.

[62] Corte di Cassazione, 20 April 1991, No. 4290, Giur. It. 1992-I-1-1350; Brussels, 7 December 1993, RGAR [1995] 12416; HR, 13 January 1995, RvdW 1995, 31.

[63] Østre Landsret, 17 November 1995, UfR 1996A, 353.

[64] Many of these affirmative duties are imposed by specific legislative provisions, others have become part of social law.

[65] See for example, OGH, 28 June 1990, JBl 1991, 387.

tree is felled in a populated area,[66] or when a vehicle is abandoned.[67] Moreover, in justifying the existence of such a duty, it is hardly necessary to refer to the concept of creation
of danger as, of course, I should not only guard against dangers which I create myself,
but also dangers which arise from things which I acquire in a dangerous condition, where
the danger should be apparent to me.

(iii) *The imposition of duties by law, contract, ethical rules (particularly of a professional
nature), or a general principle of good faith in society.* An illustration of a duty imposed
by *law*, is offered by French law and many other legal systems,[68] where liability arises as
a matter of criminal law, in the case of a failure to help a person in danger, or to prevent
a crime or a wrongful violation of bodily integrity, where such action would not put the
would-be rescuer, or third parties, at risk.[69] However, under German and English law
(and in some other jurisdictions),[70] liability would arise only when the law imposing the
duty aimed to protect the victim from the kind of harm concerned.[71]

Assuming that concurrent delictual and contractual liability is not excluded by the
principle of *non-cumul des responsabilités*, tortious liability may also arise because of a
failure to comply with an obligation imposed by *contract*, but only when the plaintiff is a
party to it, or is protected by it as a third party.[72] This was the case when a claim against
a shopkeeper was accepted both in contract and tort for failure to ensure a customer's
safety.[73]

Under French law, unwritten *ethical rules* may impose a duty to act. Thus, an historian
who failed to give a truthful account of a discovery made by another, was held liable for
failing to live up to the standard of objectivity which could be expected of him.[74] And the
judgments of the Areios Pagos reproduced above[75] demonstrate how under Greek law,
the concept of good morals or good faith to be observed in society[76] may impose a duty
to avoid causing damage to third parties, particularly when the defendant creates the
harmful situation for his own benefit. In the first case, the duty was violated by a failure
to give prior notice of an interruption in the electricity supply, even though the user, a lessee, had no contractual relationship with the supplier,[77] and in the second case, by the failure of the manufacturer to put a safe product on the market. Within the European Union,
the latter situation should now be covered by national law implementing Directive
85/374.[78]

---

[66] Compare *Goldman* v. *Hargrave* [1967] AC 645, [1966] 2 All ER 989, PC.
[67] Paris, 29 April 1985, Gaz.Pal. 1985.Somm.421; *Campbell* v. *Gillespie* [1996] SLT Rep. 503 (Outer House).
[68] See von Bar I at 624, para. 601.
[69] *Supra*, 3.1.1., Introductory Note under b).
[70] See von Bar I at 623–5, para. 601.
[71] See for example *Gorris* v. *Scott* (1874) LR 9 Exch 125, see further von Bar I at 600–1.
[72] As set out *supra*, Chapter II, 2.4., a third party may also incur tortious liability for disregarding a contract
concluded between other persons. However, for such liability to arise some kind of positive conduct is required.
[73] See *supra*, **3.G.4.**
[74] *Supra*, **3.F.1**.
[75] *Supra*, **3.GR.6.–7.**
[76] To be compared with the liability arising under § 826 BGB, see *supra*, Chapter II, 2.4.2.B., Introductory
Note under a) and *infra*, **2.G.51.–52.**
[77] To the extent that a clause in the supply contract with the lessor, exonerating the supplier from liability to
the lessee using the premises, would be invalid.
[78] *Infra*, Chapter VI, **6.EC.35.**

Failure to prevent the deliberate wrongdoing of a third party

Thus far, liability arising from a failure to prevent damage resulting from one's own conduct has been considered. The judgment of the House of Lords in *Smith* v. *Littlewoods Organisation Ltd.*[79] examines, on the other hand, liability arising from a failure to prevent the deliberate wrongdoing of a third party, an issue also considered in a judgment of the Cour d'appel de Lyon,[80] where a football club was held liable in contract against injured spectators, and their close relatives, for having failed to take all appropriate measures that may be expected of a cautious and diligent person to prevent potential dangers from materializing, including the deliberate wrongdoing of other spectators.

There is no such general obligation in English law, but there are many circumstances under which such a duty is imposed, as discussed in Lord Goff's judgment in *Smith* v. *Littlewoods Organisation Ltd.* A duty to act may arise as a consequence of a relationship of care and control, between the occupier of land and licensee or visitor,[81] under contract, or through the creation of a nuisance. More generally, a duty may be imposed where the defendant negligently causes or allows a hazard to arise, and it is reasonably foreseeable that third parties may interfere and cause damage by activating the danger.[82]

In his speech, Lord Goff asks whether the English law is not "repugnant to modern thinking" in denying liability for mere omissions, to the extent that, as Weir writes, "you need not tell a complete stranger that he is about to fall over a cliff unless it is your cliff ".[83] Or, to put it in Lord Hoffmann's words quoted at the outset of this overview, is it too great an invasion of the freedom of the individual to oblige him to open his mouth? Is it morally sound to exonerate him from a duty to call out on the basis of the "why pick on me?" argument? Is it imposing too much of an economic burden to require him to warn, when any harm incurred could be made recoverable from the person rescued, if not from the person who is responsible for the situation?

The answer to each of these questions may depend on the kind of effort required to act: if it imposes too great a burden on the rescuer, for example putting himself or third parties in peril, liability should not arise.

The first section of the Chapter is made up of Section 2 of *Scope of Protection* (pp. 56–82), with the following modifications.

3.2. WRONGFULNESS

As stated in the introduction to the present Chapter, wrongfulness contains two elements: unlawfulness (the objective element) and culpability (the subjective element). Unlawfulness will be examined first. Culpability is then discussed with emphasis on the

---

[79] *Supra*, **3.E.5.**

[80] *Supra*, **3.F.2.**

[81] For a case similar to the one decided by the Cour d'appel de Lyon, see *Cunningham* v. *Reading FC, supra,* **3.F.2.**, Note (1).

[82] The classic example cited by Lord Goff is *Haynes* v. *Harwood* [1935] 1 KB 146, CA. It is to be compared with the circumstances of creating a source of danger under German law mentioned above.

[83] *Supra*, 3.1.3., Introductory Note.

different attitude which French law, as compared with English and German law, seems to take with regard to *discernment* on the part of minors and mentally disturbed persons. Finally, the grounds of justification will be reviewed. Before going into those subjects, some basic notions will be compared.

3.2.1. BASIC NOTIONS

Even elementary notions like *faute*, "breach of duty" or *Verschulden* and *Rechtswidrigkeit*, as they exist in French, English and German tort law respectively, are not easily compared.

a) At first sight French law applies a unitary notion of *faute*, seen as an act or omission that is both unlawful and imputable to the tortfeasor. However, a closer look shows that the apparently unitary notion of *faute* comprises two elements: (i) an "objective" element, called unlawfulness (*illicéité*) which consists in the violation of a legal duty or obligation, i.e. an inconsistency between the conduct required by the duty or obligation concerned and the actual conduct of the tortfeasor; and (ii) a "subjective" element, called by some imputability (*imputabilité*), by others culpability (*culpabilité*), which points to the psychological capacity of the wrongdoer to understand and accept the consequences of his or her conduct.[84]

Both elements continue to be controversial. The debate concerning "unlawfulness" is mainly about terminology. Indeed, all authors recognize that the failure to abide by a legal duty or obligation, or to comply with a general duty of care, is a prerequisite for *faute*.[85] It is also generally recognized, as seen in Section 1, that actions as well as omissions, whether intentional or negligent, may qualify as faute.[86] Of greater significance is the debate about whether *faute* requires that "culpability" is proved as well, in other words whether the unlawful behaviour must be "imputable" to the wrongdoer, in the sense that he or she can be personally blamed for it. That debate was fostered by the enactment of Article 489–2 C. civ.[87] according to which "someone who has caused injury to another under the influence of a mental disturbance (*sous l'empire d'un trouble mental*) is nonetheless liable to make good the injury", a rule which was subsequently extended by the Cour de cassation to harm caused by minors regardless of their age, as discussed further below.[88]

It is worthwhile to reproduce here the statement which the Minister of Justice (*Garde des Sceaux*) made in Parliament when the bill which was to become the Act 68–5 of 3 January 1968 was discussed:[89]

---

[84] Viney and Jourdain, *Conditions* at 320, para. 442.
[85] Depending on the author, it is described as "illicit" or "deviant" behaviour (*écart de conduite*). The first term was introduced by Planiol and followed by many, whereas the second was preferred by H. and L. Mazeaud and G. Marty: see the references in Viney and Jourdain, *Conditions* at 321–323, para. 443.
[86] *Supra*, **3.F.1.**
[87] Through the Act 68–5 of 3 January 1968, JO, 4 January 1968, 114.
[88] That was done through a series of judgments of 9 May 1984, one of which is discussed *infra*, Chapter VII, **7.F.3.** That reasoning was applied in a judgment of 12 December 1984, *infra*, **3.F.18.**
[89] JO, Déb. Ass. Nat. 1966, 5712.

"Here, we are in the presence of a small revolution . . .

[It was said] that we have abandoned the *notion of fault* with regard to the liability of the mentally ill. In this respect I do not agree . . .

Within the *concept of fault*, there are indeed two elements that must be distinguished from one another:

First, an objective element whereby what qualifies as a fault is conduct which is not in conformity with a rule. Secondly, a subjective element whereby conduct which is not in conformity with a certain rule or a certain pattern of behaviour can be imputed to the person who carried it out and give rise to an obligation on his part to provide compensation only if he was aware of what he was doing and had the will to do it—this is what was accepted by case law.

What we propose to remove, through Article 489–2 C.civ., is the subjective element, not the objective element.

Consequently it is clear that, if a person who lacked capacity to understand the consequences of his conduct causes damage to another through a course of conduct which is objectively and intrinsically innocent, he does not incur any liability."

As a result the prevailing opinion is now that *faute* no longer necessarily means—subjectively—morally reprehensible or blameworthy conduct but that it refers in substance to conduct which is regarded—objectively—as unacceptable behaviour in society.[90] That does not mean, however, that the subjective element is no longer important. It continues to play a role in criminal law and, thus also in civil law, insofar as the same facts constitute both a criminal offence and a civil tort, given the identity between penal and civil fault.[91] It also continues to play in role in tort law in cases where the seriousness of the fault is taken into account; there the blameworthiness of the tortfeasor's conduct may be a relevant factor.[92] Finally, the subjective element may lead to the application of a ground of justification.[93]

b) Unlike French law, German law uses not one concept but three, all of which must be present for liability to arise on account of one's own conduct. They are: *Tatbestand*, *Rechtswidrigkeit* and *Verschulden*. As previously explained,[94] *Tatbestand* refers to the kind of behaviour (as an actual set of facts, irrespective of unlawfulness and fault), against which German tort law aims to provide protection (for instance, under § 823(1) BGB, an interference with life, body, health, freedom, ownership and any "other right"). By contrast, the notion of unlawfulness (*Rechtswidrigkeit*) indicates the violation of a legal norm in the absence of a legally recognized excuse. Culpability (*Verschulden*) is then understood as the state of mind of a person who intentionally or negligently causes damage to another.[95] The core provision of § 823(1) BGB is built around these three notions:

"Anyone who intentionally or negligently injures life, body, health, freedom, ownership or any other right of another in a manner contrary to law shall be obliged to compensate the other for the loss arising."

There is considerable controversy in German legal writing as to how far the concepts of unlawfulness and culpability can be kept apart. Broadly speaking, a distinction can be

[90] Le Tourneau and Cadiet at 753–4, para. 3064; Viney and Jourdain, *Conditions* at 323–6, para. 444 to 444–1.

[91] As acknowledged in case law since Cass. civ., 18 December 1912, D 1915.I.17: see Le Tourneau and Cadiet at 754, para. 3064 and 65–66, para. 180.

[92] Viney and Jourdain, *Conditions* at 565–9, para. 611 to 611–1; blameworthiness also plays a role in a series of specific regimes relating to work accidents and traffic accidents, in connection with the concept of *faute inexcusable*, even though here also fault becomes more and more objective: see Viney and Jourdain at 571, para. 613 ff. The meaning of *faute inexcusable* under the *Loi Badinter*, relating to road traffic accidents, is surveyed *infra*, Chapter VI, **6.F.16.** and **6.F.20.**

[93] *Infra*, 3.2.4.

[94] *Supra*, 3.1.2., Introductory Note under b).

[95] Markesinis at 68.

drawn between the more traditional "Result Theory" (*Erfolgstheorie*), and the more recent "Conduct Theory" (*Handlungstheorie*). The Result Theory links unlawfulness (*Rechtswidrigkeit*) more closely to the factual basis of the infringement (*Tatbestand*) and deems it to be present as soon as the *Tatbestand* (eg under § 823(1) BGB, interference with life, body, health, etc.) is made out, subject to any ground of justification which may be invoked to negative unlawfulness.[96] Unlawfulness here flows from, and almost coincides with, the result of the behaviour, i.e. the infringement of a lawfully protected right or interest. Issues of culpability are discussed at the further stage of *Verschulden*.

In the Conduct Theory, on the other hand, the concept of unlawfulness plays an additional or autonomous role in relation to *Tatbestand* and is, instead, more closely linked to culpability. The starting point for the Conduct Theory is that, in modern life, there are many courses of conduct which may indeed infringe someone else's protected interests (e.g. driving a car which is involved in an accident) while not being unlawful as such (driving is generally allowed). Under the Conduct Theory unlawfulness flows from the *wrongful* character of the tortious conduct, and not merely from its result (i.e. interference with someone else's legal interest), i.e. for unlawfulness to be made out, the conduct at issue must be *objectively* blameworthy. This means that, under that theory, unlawfulness already encompasses a large portion of fault (its objective element) and that culpability (*Verschulden*) is understood to refer only to the more subjective element, that of imputability of the conduct to the particular defendant. Zweigert and Kötz give the following overview of this ongoing debate:[97]

"The requirement of *unlawfulness*, according to most writers, is satisfied by any invasion of one of the legal interests specified in § 823 par. 1 BGB which is not justified by any of the few special privileges such as self-defence, necessity, and so on. The requirement of *culpability* or fault is satisfied if the harmful conduct is either intentional, that is, accompanied by the intention of invading the protected legal interest, or negligent. Negligence connotes a want of that degree of care which is generally regarded as necessary in society (§ 276 BGB); for this purpose one must consider how a conscientious and considerate man would have behaved in the same situation. If the harm was caused in the course of some specialist activity, the courts ask whether the defendant showed the degree of care to be looked for in the average member of the specialist group in question, professional or not.

In the last few years there has been some dispute among German lawyers concerning the meaning and scope of the concepts of 'unlawfulness' and 'culpability'. According to one modern view, harmful behaviour should only be qualified as 'unlawful' if it is discountenanced by law as contravening some legal prohibition or command addressed to the citizen. On this view, behaviour does not become unlawful under § 823 par. 1 BGB simply because it causes an infringement of one of the legal interests there specified; it is unlawful only if the person causing the harm behaved either deliberately or without the care generally required in society. This leaves the further question when behaviour which is unlawful in this sense is also *culpable*. Here the new doctrine simply asks whether the defendant, on the ground of his minority (§§827, 828 BGB), was unable to realize that his conduct was unlawful and that he might have to answer for the resulting damages, or whether the defendant's culpability was excluded by such individual factors as his inability to appreciate the objective circumstances which rendered the situation dangerous. There are still many points of dissension between the adherents of this new doctrine, but in fact these borderline disputes are not of much practical significance; given that a person who causes harm despite observing all the requisite precautions is not liable, it is normally quite immaterial whether his non-liability is attributed to want of *unlawfulness* or want of *culpability*."

---

[96] The Result Theory recognizes as a ground of justification in medical treatment cases, for instance, the informed consent of the patient, in order to avoid the conclusion that interference with a patient's physical integrity (which inevitably occurs in the course of treatment) is unlawful per se. Other possible grounds of justification include self-defence, necessity and duress: see *infra*, 3.2.4.

[97] Zweigert and Kötz at 599–600. See also Markesinis at 68 ff., who explains the reasons for the greater popularity of the new approach.

While the debate concerning the Result and Conduct Theories might not have much of a practical impact, it does make clear that under the more modern Conduct Theory there is little room left for culpability, since, under the theory, the only question asked in that respect, is whether the defendant's culpability was excluded by his or her unawareness that the conduct concerned was unlawful, or by his or her inability to appreciate the objective circumstances which rendered the situation dangerous. Under the Conduct Theory, culpability is therefore about imputability (*Vorwerfbarkeit*) only. Moreover, as is also the case in France, it seems to leave little space for a requirement that the conduct of the wrong-doer was reprehensible or blameworthy. That is particularly so where the defendant has acted negligently (*fahrlässig*), as opposed to intentionally (*vorsätzlich*), since, as is stated in § 276 (1) BGB,[98] the emphasis is then clearly on behaviour that is not in conformity with what is required in society (*Sozialadäquanz*).[99]

c) It has been mentioned earlier that the English law of torts is characterized by the lack of a general head of tortious liability, relying instead on a series of specific heads of tortious liability. Nevertheless, we have seen that, over the course of time, negligence has become the most general tort and, in practice, also the most important.[100]

An essential component of the tort of negligence is that the defendant owed a duty of care to persons such as the victim and that he or she committed a breach of that duty of care.[101] This chapter will focus on the element of "breach of duty". The test for deciding whether there has been such a breach is crystallized in the following definition by Alderson B. in *Blyth* v. *Birmingham Waterworks Co:*[102] "Negligence is the omission to do something which a reasonable man, guided upon those considerations which ordinarily regulate the conduct of human affairs, would do, or doing something which a prudent and reasonable man would not do."

It seems to be characteristic of English law that it makes no distinction between what French and German law call the "objective" and "subjective" elements of wrongfulness. The conduct of a "reasonable man" constitutes "an essential ingredient in the law of negligence, whether that word be used to indicate an independent tort or a mental element in the commission of certain other torts". It "might be described as the behaviour of the ordinary person in any particular event or transaction, including in such behaviour obedience to the special directions (if any) which the law gives him for his guidance in that connection".[103] That standard is "objective and impersonal in the sense that it eliminates the personal equation and is independent of the idiosyncrasies of the particular person whose conduct is in question . . .".[104] And, indeed, as a general rule "if conduct is presumptively unlawful, a good motive will not exonerate the defendant" except for the application of "defences like necessity and private defence . . . (which) depend to a cer-

---

[98] According to § 276(1) BGB, which relates to all kinds of obligations (contractual and delictual), "a person who does not exercise the care required in ordinary intercourse acts negligently".

[99] Markesinis at 69.

[100] *Supra*, Chapter I, **1.E.21.**

[101] For the duty of care, see *supra* Chapter II; for the requirement that the damage was not too remote a consequence of the breach of the duty of care, see *infra*, Chapter IV.

[102] (1856) 11 Ex 781 at 784. Compare the dictum of Pearson J in *Hazell* v. *British Transport Commission* [1958] 1 WLR 169 at 171.

[103] Rogers at 52–53. See further *infra*, 3.2.2.C.

[104] Ibid. at 171.

tain extent on a good motive on the part of the defendant".[105] Nor will a bad motive make the defendant liable.[106] In applying the standard of reasonable care, an English court will, instead, try to strike a balance between on the one hand the magnitude of the risk, that is the likelihood injury will be incurred and the seriousness of that injury, and on the other hand the burden to the defendant in doing (or not doing) what it is alleged he should (or should not) have done.[107]

3.2.2. UNLAWFULNESS

It is remarkable to see how, beneath such divergent notions as *faute, Rechtswidrigkeit/ Verschulden* and breach of duty, French, German and English law use quite similar criteria to assess the unlawfulness of the conduct of the defendant. Indeed, each legal system has developed similar general criteria to recognize reasonable, prudent and/or careful conduct, such as is required in a modern society, and has defined the standard of assessment in objective terms, meaning that the defendant's conduct is assessed *in abstracto* rather than *in concreto* (which does not exclude many concrete circumstances being incorporated in the abstract standard, as seen below).[108]

In all legal systems, failure to observe legal norms which regulate generally and imperatively the behaviour of persons in well-defined circumstances constitutes unlawful behaviour in and of itself, in the absence of excuse or justification.[109] That proposition is included in the general standard of conduct under tort law, since a reasonable and prudent person does not infringe legal norms. In that way statutory provisions, which are numerous in contemporary society, not only help to give substance to the notion of fault, but also to lower the threshold for the proof of fault.[110] In *France,* that proposition is rigorously applied in that, in the absence of justification, any violation of an explicit mandatory rule is as such illicit, and amounts to fault; the plaintiff does not need to prove that the tortfeasor acted negligently, imprudently or carelessly.[111] That applies more particularly to rules of conduct which the legislature itself has chosen to condemn by imposing punishment under criminal law, to the extent that in such instances there is even a complete assimilation of crime and tort.[112]

---

[105] Ibid. at 55.

[106] Ibid.

[107] See further Rogers at 179–180 and Markesinis and Deakin at 166 ff., where this approach is discussed in relation with the "Learned Hand formula" and the economic analysis of the law: see *supra*, Chapter I, **1.US.11.**

[108] See the comparative overview in H. and L. Mazeaud and A. Tunc, *Traité théorique et pratique de la responsabilité civile délictuelle et contractuelle*, Vol. I, 6th ed. (Paris: Montchrestien, 1965) at 507–11, para. 441–4.

[109] See *infra*, 3.2.4.

[110] See von Bar I at 45, para. 31.

[111] Viney and Jourdain, *Conditions* at 328, para. 448; Le Tourneau and Cadiet at 757, para. 3074 ff.

[112] See *supra*, 3.2.1. under a). Le Tourneau and Cadiet at 754, para. 3064 find that the identity between criminal and civil fault runs "against nature" (*un état contre nature*) and should be abandoned as soon as possible. Under Belgian law, the identity is very much criticized, to the point that a bill was introduced in Parliament to change the situation (Parl. St. Kamer, 1997–98, no. 1574/1). See also J. Limpens, R.M. Kruithof and A. Meinertzhagen-Limpens, "Liability for One's Own Act" in *International Encyclopedia of Comparative Law— Vol. XI/2: Torts* (Tübingen: Mohr, 1979) at 74–75, para. 152–153, with further references.

At first sight, *German* law does not seem to take as a starting point that non-compliance with a legal norm constitutes wrongfulness in and of itself. And indeed § 823(2) BGB, which makes it a tort not to observe a protective norm (a so-called *Schutzgesetz*[113]), provides in its second sentence that "if such a norm may be infringed without culpability, liability to compensate shall be incurred only in the event of culpability." However, as von Bar notes,[114]

> "the French and German positions are not as far apart as may at first glance appear. The German legislator sought from the outset to clarify that 'culpability' in the second sentence of § 823(2) BGB concerns only the protective law; and neither an infringement of a right or legally protected interest, nor the actual loss sustained. In addition, the German courts . . . promptly added a further provision: where the violation of a law has been established, fault is rebuttably presumed whenever a statute prescribes a specific standard of conduct."

Due to this change in the onus of proof, § 823(2) BGB is even more favourable to the plaintiff than § 823(1).[115] It should be added that, because of the *Normzwecktheorie*, whether a criminal offence amounts to a civil fault depends entirely on whether or not the provision in question is designed to protect the individual, in the sense of the first sentence of § 823(2) BGB.[116]

Matters are quite different in *English* law where, as seen above,[117] breach of statutory duty is a specific tort which gives rise to a civil remedy in tort, but only under the following conditions: (i) the duty must be owed to persons in the position of the plaintiff, (ii) the injury must be of the kind which the legal norm is intended to prevent; (iii) the defendant must be guilty of a breach of his statutory obligation; and (iv) the breach of duty must have caused the damage.[118] Culpability has no autonomous role to play in this context: what matters is that the conduct of the tortfeasor constitutes a violation of the statutory obligation which implies that the measure of the duty (i.e. its relative or absolute nature) must be found in the statute itself, and only in the statute.[119] Whether a statutory duty, to which a criminal penalty or some other sanction is attached, does give rise to a civil action in tort as well, is a much debated question. The answer depends again on the wording of the statute, and in particular on the question whether the legislature intended to create the claimed civil liability.[120]

---

[113] *Supra*, Chapter I, **1.G.26.** For an example of a protective norm, see *supra*, Chapter II, **2.G.50.**

[114] von Bar I at 46, para. 31 (footnotes omitted).

[115] Markesinis at 891, who adds that § 823(2) BGB is also more favourable to the plaintiff in another respect, "notably in its recognition of the compensability of purely economic loss". This explains why the plaintiffs in the cable case discussed earlier (*supra*, Chapter II, **2.G.37.**) tried to base their claims on § 823(2) BGB.

[116] See, with examples of provisions of the *Strafgesetzbuch* (StGB, Penal Code) which at that time were considered to be protective enactments, J. Limpens, R.M. Kruithof and A. Meinertzhagen-Limpens, "Liability for One's Own Act" in *International Encyclopedia of Comparative Law—Vol. XI/2: Torts* (Tübingen: Mohr, 1979) at 76, para. 155.

[117] *Supra*, Chapter I, 1.4.1.A., Introductory Note under c).

[118] See Rogers at 260–264; Markesinis and Deakin at 336–353.

[119] Rogers at 261–262, with illustrations. In that sense, it can be said that breach of statutory duty is sometimes a strict liability tort: see *infra*, Chapter VI, **6.E.11.**

[120] See, with numerous references to case law, Rogers at 255–9, who concludes that the state of the law is not very satisfactory. This was also the opinion of Lord Denning MR, who commented that the legislature "has left the courts with a guess-work puzzle. The dividing line between the pro-cases and the contra-cases is so blurred and so ill-defined that you might as well toss a coin to decide it": *Ex parte Islands Records* [1978] Ch 122 at 134–5. Moreover, that state of the law may be affected by European Community law if the violation concerned constitutes a breach of Community law: see *infra*, Chapter IX, **9.EC.6.**, Note (5).

It may be noted that in some legal systems, as under Article 6:162 (1) BW, interference with someone else's right (*rechtsinbreuk*) is deemed to be an autonomous ground of unlawfulness (in addition to infringement of a statutory duty or breach of the general duty of care) which implies that, subject to grounds of justification, such infringement or interference in itself constitutes unlawful behaviour,[121] i.e. without further proof of carelessness.[122]

3.2.2.A. FRENCH LAW

Introductory Note

In France, the formulation of Articles 1382 and 1383 C.civ. was deliberately made open-ended, unlike the system of specific torts under the *ancien régime*. The authors of the *Code Napoléon* preferred, by attaching sanctions to imprudent and negligent behaviour, to refer indirectly to a general norm of civilized social conduct. By the same token, it was made clear that the mere observation of all legal and regulatory requirements would not suffice to shelter a person from civil liability.[123] It is generally accepted that, in the absence of legislative guidance, the court, in order to assess the conduct of the defendant, should refer to an abstract "reasonable and circumspect person" (*l'homme raisonnable et avisé*) or, to use the ancient Roman formula, a *bonus pater familias* (*bon père de famille*). Various reasons are advanced nowadays to justify using an abstract criterion. In the first place, from a moral and philosophical perspective a person is free to choose between good and bad (*le libre arbitre de l'homme*), so that it is appropriate to measure conduct against the abstract person who chooses to behave well. Secondly, an abstract assessment is to be preferred because of the impossibility for the court to bear judgment on fellow human beings otherwise than from the outside, i.e. on the basis of their conduct. Thirdly, the abstract criterion is said to guarantee a minimum of certainty by entitling everyone to expect that others respect rules of normal social conduct. Finally, the criterion plays an important preventive role by dissuading clumsy, inept or incompetent persons to engage in activities which go beyond their abilities.[124]

Use of an abstract criterion however, does not preclude courts from taking into account the concrete circumstances of the case which have influenced the behaviour of the defendant. The standard of the "reasonable person" (*l'homme raisonnable*), is not unique but varies depending on the characteristics of the activity in question. Accordingly, the abstract standard actually becomes stricter when it comes to assessing the duties incumbent upon a professional. Beyond that, it remains open to discussion, as in any legal system, to what extent the personal circumstances of the defendant, be they physical (age, sex, health), psychological (intelligence, emotional state, etc.), cultural

---

[121] In addition to unlawfulness, Article 6:162(3) of the Dutch BW requires also that the conduct can be imputed to the wrongdoer on the basis of a personal fault, or according to law or common opinion. For the text of Article 6:162 BW, see *supra*, Chapter I, **1.NL.15.**

[122] For an extensive examination, see C. Sieburgh, *Toerekening van een onrechtmatige daad* (Groningen: Groningen University, 2000), where the concept of *rechtsinbreuk* is further analysed and limited to the interference with the right as such, and not extended to bodily or material damage resulting from such interference.

[123] Viney and Jourdain, *Conditions* at 331–2, para. 450. See *infra*, **3.F.9.**

[124] See, with references, Viney and Jourdain, *Conditions* at 351–2, para. 463.

(level of education) or social, are to be taken into account. In France the "objectiviza-tion" of the standard of care seems to be carried to its extreme, as shown by the legislation concerning mentally disturbed persons and the case law of the Cour de cassation in respect of young children.[125]

Assessing typical behaviour (ordinary or professional)

Cass. civ. 2e, 14 June 1972[126]   **3.F.9.**
Coopérative agricole de Limours v. *Volinetz*

ABIDING BY THE RULES NOT SUFFICIENT

Uninformed beekeeper

Having acted in accordance with applicable regulations is not sufficient to establish that the defendant acted with due care, if he omitted to warn those in his neighbourhood of the harmful effect that his conduct could have.

Facts: A farmer applied an insecticide to protect a field of rape (colza). Aware of the toxic effect of the product, he nonetheless omitted to warn his neighbour, whom he knew to keep bees. Bees gathered honey from the flowers on the field and died.

Held: The court of first instance and the court of appeal granted damages. The Cour de cassation confirmed the judgment of the court of appeal.

Judgment: "The defendant alleges that the judgment is inconsistent in finding, on the one hand, that the regulations were complied with and, on the other, that the [defendant] did not take any precaution. However, the fact that an action is authorized by statute or regulation, under certain conditions in the general interest, does not have the effect of relieving those who take such action from their general obligation of caution and diligence, as laid down in Article 1382 C.civ. Whilst the court of appeal found that the [defendant] did not breach the applicable legal provisions, it also stated that the [defendant] knew of the toxic nature of the product used, that he was aware of the fact that the flowers would fully blossom within 48 hours, that he did not inform the bee-keepers in the neighbourhood before starting the harmful treatment and that he could not be unaware of the presence of the beehives. In drawing from these findings the conclusion that the mere fact that the [defendant] observed the legislation in effect could not exonerate him from the harmful consequences of his fault, the judgment cannot be criticized."

Notes

(1) The judgment makes it clear that, although non-compliance with applicable regulations is, under French law, sufficient in itself to prove the unlawful character of one's behaviour,[127] the opposite is not true. For indeed, compliance with applicable regulations, in the present case by respecting the conditions under which a course of action is author-

---

[125] See *infra*, **3.F.19.** and notes thereafter; but see also *infra*, **3.F.20.** and notes thereafter.
[126] 1973.Jur.423, with annotation by E. Lepointe. Translation by the authors.
[127] *Supra*, 3.2.1.A., Introductory Note.

ized by regulation, does not exclude the possibility that the defendant acted in violation of the general duty to act cautiously and diligently (*obligation générale de prudence et de diligence*). In other words, complying with applicable norms constitutes a necessary but not a sufficient condition to avoid being at fault.[128] Whether one acted carelessly in the application of a legal norm depends on whether one took the necessary precautions under the circumstances. In this respect, the wording of the regulation may be of importance: the more precise and explicit the legal norm, the less likely it is that the person acting in accordance with it omitted to take the necessary precautions.[129]

(2) In the annotated judgment the defendant breached his general duty of care when he failed to warn the plaintiffs, his neighbours, that the product used was harmful for their bees, although he knew that the flowers from which the bees gather honey would blossom within the next 48 hours. A breach of the duty of care consisting in not giving appropriate information is also at issue in the following case.

Cass. civ. 1re, 7 October 1998[130]   **3.F.10.**
C. v. Clinique du Parc

DUTY TO INFORM PATIENT

From the vertebra to the eye

Except for cases of emergency, impossibility or refusal by the patient, a physician is under a duty to give the patient faithful, clear and appropriate information on the serious risks relating to the proposed examination and treatment; the sole fact that these risks materialize only exceptionally does not relieve the physician of this obligation.

Facts: Following a surgical operation on a vertebra, the plaintiff began having troubles with her left eye. As soon as the surgeon heard of this, he came to her assistance, changed the prescribed treatment and organised an urgent eye examination. A thrombosis of the cavernous sinus was diagnosed, which led to the permanent loss of use of the eye. The plaintiff argued, among others, that the surgeon had breached his duty to give information by not warning the plaintiff of the risk involved in the operation to the vertebra.

Held: The court of appeal rejected the claim. That judgment was quashed by the Cour de cassation.

Judgment: "Having regard to Article 1147 C.civ.;

Save in cases of emergency, impossibility to inform the patient or refusal by the patient to be informed, a physician is bound to give the patient faithful, clear and appropriate information about any serious risks associated with the proposed course of examination and treatment. He is not relieved from this obligation by the mere fact that those risks materialise only exceptionally.

In order to dismiss the claim, the contested decision states that the physician is only required to provide information on normally foreseeable risks. In the case at hand, thrombosis of the cavernous sinus is a known complication, although a very rare occurrence. The court of appeal inferred from this that the physician did not have to warn [the plaintiff] against it.

In so holding, the court of appeal applied [Article 1147 C.civ.] incorrectly . . ."

---

[128] See the annotation of E. Lepointe, D 1973.Jur.425, who discusses in that connection the distinction to be made between "legislative" and "administrative" norms. See also *infra*, 3.2.4.A. (grounds of justification).
[129] Ibid. at 426–7.
[130] JCP 1998.II.10179. Translation by A. Dumas-Eymard.

Notes

(1) As mentioned above,[131] the general abstract criterion of the reasonable person (*l'homme raisonnable*) does not exclude concrete circumstances being taken into account, so as to ensure that a defendant's behaviour is compared with that of a person who is placed in the same circumstances of time, place and action (*placé dans les mêmes circonstances de temps, de lieu et d'action*).[132] In this regard French law makes a distinction between external and internal circumstances. External circumstances (*circonstances externes*) relate to the nature of the activity concerned, and to time and place. The professional character of the activity counts amongst those external circumstances. On the other hand, internal circumstances (*circonstances internes*) affect the personality of the person whose behaviour is to be assessed. They comprise physical characteristics (age, sex, health condition, etc.), psychological characteristics (intelligence, qualities, abilities, etc.), and cultural and social characteristics (level of education, background, etc.).[133]

Theoretically only the external circumstances must be factored in, thus allowing an assessment *in abstracto* of the tortfeasor's conduct; when internal circumstances are also brought into the measure of assessment, the assessment becomes more *in concreto*.[134] That may lead to either a less rigorous test, where those internal circumstances point to an inferiority of the defendant, or to a more rigorous test in the opposite case.[135] In the first case, the victim's chances of succeeding are less, whereas in the second case they are obviously greater. From an analysis of French case law, it would appear that certain internal circumstances of inferiority (such as physical inabilities) or of superiority (such as professional experience or specialized education) are taken into account in determining the degree of caution or diligence required; other circumstances (such as shortcomings of a mental or psychological nature, or a person's character) are however disregarded.[136]

(2) The annotated judgment concerns the standard to be applied to the conduct of medical professionals, i.e. an activity requiring special skills. Since the nature of the activity concerned is seen as an external circumstance, as stated above, that element will be incorporated into the standard to be applied.[137] The reasonable person is thus considered to have the same profession as the defendant.[138] By the same token, in a judgment of 27 February 1951 relating to the liability of an historian, reproduced in the preceding section,[139] the Cour de cassation held that an historian writing a scientific article is expected

---

[131] *Supra*, 3.2.1.A., Introductory Note.

[132] Le Tourneau and Cadiet at 765, para. 3105.

[133] Viney and Jourdain, *Conditions* at 353, para. 465.

[134] On this distinction, see N. Dejean de la Bâtie, *Appréciation in abstracto et appréciation in concreto en droit civil français* (Paris: LGDJ, 1965).

[135] For a further analysis, see Viney and Jourdain, *Conditions* at 352–61, para. 464–72.

[136] Ibid. at 360–1, para. 472.

[137] The annotated case was decided on the basis of Article 1147 C.civ., relating to contractual performance. However, that does not matter since, under French law, the same principles of civil liability apply to both contract and torts. See *supra*, Chapter II, **2.F.11.**, Note (1) and *supra*, Chapter I, 1.4.2., Introductory Note under a).

[138] For another case relating to the medical professions, see Cass. civ. 1re, 10 June 1980, D 1981.IR.11, where different standards were used to assess the liability of a surgeon and of a nurse.

[139] *Supra*, **3.F.1.**

to live up to the standard of objectivity of a normally cautious and thoughtful historian under the circumstances.[140]

(3) The annotated judgment concerns a specific issue, namely the extent to which a doctor is bound to inform his or her patient. Together with two other judgments, one of the same day[141] and the other of 27 May 1998,[142] it confirms the evolution of the case law of the Cour de cassation which, since 1977, has obliged physicians to inform patients of any grave risks (*risques graves*) associated with a proposed medical intervention,[143] regardless of whether these risks are exceptional or normally foreseeable.[144] The judgment provides for three exceptions: emergencies, impossibility and the refusal by the patient to be informed.[145] In the wake of that case law, the question arose whether the duty to provide information also extends to other risks of a minor nature. Clearly this is not the case if the risks are merely exceptional.[146] However, minor risks can be exceptional but foreseeable. In a judgment of 17 February 1998,[147] where the Cour de cassation distinguished grave risks from minor risks (mere "inconveniences"), the court found that the duty to inform extends to minor risks only in the case of cosmetic surgery.[148]

(4) The obligation of a doctor or physician to inform his or her patients must be seen in the broader context of increasing civil liability for medical acts. Under French law, a physician is in principle under an obligation of means (*obligation de moyens*) as regards the treatment of his or her patient.[149] Accordingly, in order to obtain compensation, the plaintiff must prove that the physician failed to fulfill that obligation, i.e. committed a fault. A number of recent developments have contributed to reduce the significance of that general principle.

First of all, following the enactment of Article 16–3 C.civ.,[150] according to which "the consent of the [patient] must be obtained in advance, unless the condition [of the patient] requires a medical intervention to which he is not in a position to consent", French case law, as seen above, has become very severe as regards the duty of the physician to inform the patient of the risks associated with the intervention. It is up to the physician to prove that he or she properly discharged the duty.[151] Moreover, as was decided by the annotated judgment and the other judgments referred to above, the scope of the duty to inform depends not only on the statistical risk, but also on the severity of the consequences: the patient must be informed of the risk of grave injury, even if it is infrequent.[152]

---

[140] Ibid., Note (1).

[141] Cass. civ. 1re, 7 October 1998, JCP 1998.II.10179.

[142] Cass. civ. 1re, 27 May 1998, Bull.civ. 1998.I.187, D 1998.Jur.530 with observations by F. Laroche-Gisserot.

[143] "Grave" risks comprise risks which may have fatal, invalidating or even serious aesthetic consequences, in the light of their psychological and social repercussions: see the report of P. Sargos in Cass. civ. 1re, 14 October 1997, JCP 1997.II.22942.

[144] In the previous case law, only normally foreseeable risks were subject to the duty to inform: see e.g. Cass. civ. 1re, 12 May 1978, Bull.civ. 1978.I.132; Lyon, 8 January 1981, JCP 1981.II.19699, annotated by F. Chabas.

[145] The physician bears the burden of showing that the case fell within one of these exceptions.

[146] P. Jourdain, Chronique, RTDciv. 1999, 111 at 112.

[147] Cass. civ. 1re, 17 February 1998, Bull.civ. 1998.I.45.

[148] See also the Opinion of AG J. Sainte-Rose in the annotated case, at JCP 1998.II.10179.

[149] On the concept of *obligation de moyens*, see *supra*, 3.F.2., Note (2).

[150] Through the Act 94–653 of 29 July 1994, JO, 30 July 1994, 11056.

[151] Cass. civ. 1re, 25 February 1997, Gaz.Pal. 1997.Jur.274, with the report of P. Sargos, JCP 1997.I.4025, annotated by G. Viney.

[152] The Conseil d'Etat has followed the Cour de cassation on this point: CÉ, 5 January 2000 (not yet reported).

Accordingly, it becomes possible to invoke a breach of the duty to inform—which by its nature is an obligation of result (*obligation de résultat*)—in an increasing number of cases where medical intervention has proved not to be successful.[153] *Secondly*, physicians (as well as hospitals) are put under an obligation of result to ensure the safety of their patients with respect to infectious diseases contracted during medical treatment or during a stay in a hospital or clinic.[154] Both the Conseil d'Etat and the Cour de cassation have thus imposed what is in fact a regime of liability without fault for such diseases. *Thirdly*, the Cour de cassation has read into the contract for medical care an obligation of result on the part of the physician as regards the equipment and material used in the provision of care.[155]

In the light of the above, it is fair to ask what exactly remains within the realm of the general regime of liability based on the fault of the physician. Essentially, that regime applies only in cases where either the injury results from the actual conduct of the physician (manipulation, operation, prescription of drugs, etc.) or the precise cause of the injury cannot be identified, as the Cour de cassation reaffirmed in a judgment of 27 May 1998.[156] Nevertheless, a number of writers (as well as interest groups) are calling for a further segmentation of that remainder. According to them, a specific regime should be established for injury which occurs in the course of medical treatment and the cause of which cannot be precisely identified (the so-called "therapeutic risk" or *aléa thérapeutique*, i.e. the statistical complication rate of a given treatment). That risk would then be assumed by the State or by an insurance fund.[157] As regards public hospitals and the physicians for whom they are responsible, the Conseil d'Etat has introduced a regime of liability not based on fault for the *aléa thérapeutique*, under relatively strict conditions, starting with *Bianchi* in 1991.[158] As regards private physicians, in a few cases lower courts have held physicians liable for therapeutic risk, on the basis of an accessory obligation to ensure the safety of the patient throughout the medical treatment;[159] the matter is now before the Cour de cassation.[160]

---

[153] See C. Benayoun, "Réflexions sur le devoir d'information en matière de risques thérapeutiques" Resp. civ. ass. 1999.Chron.9 and S. Porchy, "Lien causal, préjudices réparables et non-respect de la volonté du patient" D 1998.Chron.379.

[154] So-called "nosocomial infections", i.e. infections that were not present when the patient began the treatment or was admitted in the hospital.

[155] Cass. civ. 1re, 9 November 1999, JCP 2000.II.10251, annotated by P. Brun, D 2 000.Jur.117, annotated by P. Jourdain.

[156] Cass. civ. 1re, 27 May 1998, D 1998.Jur.21, with annotation by S. Porchy.

[157] See on this discussion C. Larroumet, "L'indemnisation de l'aléa thérapeutique" D 1999.Chron.33.

[158] *Infra*, **3.F.43.**

[159] For instance Paris, 15 January 1999, JCP 1999.II.10068, with annotation by L. Boy.

[160] See P. Sargos, "L'aléa thérapeutique devant le juge judiciaire" JCP 2000.I.202.

Assessing atypical behaviour

Cass. civ. 2e, 15 December 1965[161]   **3.F.11.**
Buguel v. *Morin*

MENTALLY SICK BUT SUFFICIENTLY CONSCIOUS

Drunken patient

A person who is mentally deficient but is not completely deprived of awareness and free will is liable in tort for the injury which he or she caused if he or she has failed to take care of himself or herself.

Facts: The defendant, who had been drinking heavily for two days, shot the plaintiff and injured him seriously. The penal proceedings against him were terminated on the ground of insanity.

Held: The court of appeal granted compensation to the plaintiff. The Cour de cassation confirmed the judgment of the court of appeal.

Judgment: "The judgment states . . . that if was clear from the conduct of [the defendant] that his mental deficiency (*anomalies mentales*) left him with sufficient awareness and free will. It was up to [the defendant], who had just been released from a psychiatric institution, without however having fully recovered, to take care of himself. By omitting to take all necessary precautions and continuing to drink heavily instead, [the defendant] certainly committed a fault for which he was to be held liable. This reasoning shows that the [defendant's] mental deficiency, which continued to exist, did not deprive him of all awareness and free will. The court of appeal therefore correctly decided."

Notes

(1) In the annotated judgment the Cour de cassation had to decide whether a mentally deficient person, who had been released from a psychiatric institution and against whom penal proceedings could not be brought because of his condition, could nonetheless be held liable in civil proceedings to pay compensation. The court of appeal found, within its *pouvoir souverain* to make findings of fact, that the mentally deficient person was left with enough awareness and free will to be responsible to take care of himself (i.e. to take all necessary precautions to avoid causing injury). Instead, he chose to continue to drink heavily, which constituted a fault. As Viney and Jourdain remark in connection with the judgment and other similar cases, French courts will take into account a condition of illness or infirmity in order to assess the conduct of a person *in concreto*. However, as the annotated judgment shows, that does not necessarily operate to the advantage of the defendant, as it may lead a court to impose a duty upon the defendant moderate his conduct in proportion to his ability to engage in it (*mesurer ses entreprises à ses capacités*),[162] or to take the precautions needed including, as in the annotated case, taking good care of himself.[163] That does not, however, preclude a court from comparing the conduct of an

---

[161] D 1966.Jur.397. Translation by the authors.
[162] German courts take the same attitude: see *infra*, **3.G.12.**
[163] Viney and Jourdain, *Conditions* at 357 with further references.

313

ill person with that of a circumspect ill person rather than with that of a normal person.[164] That means actually that internal circumstances, in this case the defendant's psychological state, are sometimes taken into account in order to effect an assessment that is more *in concreto* than usual.[165]

(2) The annotated judgment was rendered before Article 489–2 was incorporated in the Code civil in 1968.[166] Article 489–2 provides that someone who has caused injury to another under the influence of a mental disturbance is nonetheless liable to make good the injury. The scope of application of the Article will be discussed more fully later.[167] If it had been in force at the date of the annotated case, the court could have come to the same conclusion but through a different reasoning, relying on Article 489–2 C.civ. to hold the drunken defendant liable even if he acted under the influence of a mental disturbance.[168] Still the principle laid down in the annotated judgment remains valid; indeed, the duty of an ill person to take the precautions which his or her condition requires applies to all kinds of illness.[169]

3.2.2.B. GERMAN LAW

Introductory Note

Under German law the core question will be whether a person has caused harm because of his or her negligence (*Fahrlässigkeit*).[170] Unlike other legal systems, the second sentence of § 276(1) BGB provides a legal definition of "negligence": a person who does not apply the level of care required by society (*wer die im Verkehr erforderliche Sorgfalt außer acht läßt*) acts negligently. Like French and English law, the standard of assessment is essentially an objective one. What matters is what can on the average be required from a member of the relevant social group (*durchschnittlich*) placed in the same circumstances, regardless of the personal characteristics of the person acting, i.e. his or her individual capacities, knowledge and experience.[171] There is no uniform description of the standard of reference: typical formulations include the *bonus pater familias*, the average, normal, orderly, intelligent person, and the circumspect and conscientious member of the relevant social group.[172]

---

[164] Ibid., with reference to N. Dejean de la Bâtie, *Appréciation in abstracto et appréciation in concreto en droit civil français* (Paris: LGDJ, 1965).

[165] See *supra*, **3.F.10.**, Note (1).

[166] *Supra*, 3.2.1. under a).

[167] *Infra*, 3.2.3.A.

[168] As seen *infra*, **3.F.18.**, case law held that Article 489–2 C.civ. does not create an autonomous liability regime, but rather allows persons who fall within its scope of application to be held liable under Article 1382ff. C.civ. even if they were probably not subjectively culpable.

[169] Ibid. at 537.

[170] On intentional wrongdoing, see *infra*, 3.2.3.B.

[171] See *infra*, **3.G.12.** and for further references to case law, Münchener-Hanau, § 276 at 834, para. 78. The author specifies at para. 79 that, in the notion of "what is on average required" (*durchschnittliche Anforderungen*) what is factually customary and what is legally required are equally important.

[172] Ibid. at para. 79. See also Markesinis at 470–2 with comparative references.

Assessing typical behaviour (ordinary or professional)

BGH, 20 October 1987[173]   **3.G.12.**
Critical self-examination

Fatigued father-in-law

Before taking the wheel, a driver should critically assess whether his or her physical and mental condition allows him or her safely to meet the demands of road traffic.

Facts: The plaintiff was a front-seat passenger in a car driven by his 71-year old father-in-law. He suffered severe injuries in a traffic accident when the car wandered off the motorway without external cause. The father-in-law was unconscious when the accident happened. The plaintiff claimed that his father-in-law, as a result of fatigue, had fallen asleep; he had already shown symptoms of fatigue before the day of the accident. Moreover, on the day of the accident, he was suffering from the after-effects of an earlier bout of flu, yet despite warnings had insisted on driving the car. The father-in-law maintained that he had lost consciousness not because he fell asleep but as a result of an unforeseeable faint.

Held: The court of first instance and the court of appeal dismissed the claim. The BGH quashed the judgment of the court of appeal and remanded the case for further consideration.

Judgment: "The arguments of the court of appeal do not support the conclusion that [the father-in-law] did not act negligently within the meaning of §§ 823(1) and 276(1) BGB. Rather he acted culpably in that he absolutely insisted on driving his vehicle.

The court of appeal appropriately starts from the point of view that under § 276(1) BGB, which refers to the requisite care in social intercourse, an objective standard of assessment applies for the examination of whether an action or omission is to be held negligent. It therefore boils down to whether the care which was required in the actual situation was in fact observed. Personal characteristics of the tortfeasor, his capacities, knowledge and experience are in principle irrelevant for the assessment on the basis of the standardised yardstick of § 276(1) BGB. At the same time, on account of the expectations of society, it is necessary to refer to the situation of the relevant professional group, or where relevant, of the relevant sphere of social intercourse, and to focus in consequence on the degree of circumspection and care which can and must be expected of a person in the role in which the person concerned entered into social intercourse . . .

High demands are to be made regarding the duties of care of the driver, on account of the special dangers associated with driving motor vehicles. The ensuing requirements are not confined to driving the vehicle itself. The dangers of road traffic require in the first place that care must be exercised before starting out on the journey. In particular, the driver, before sitting at the wheel, must always make sure that he is (still) able, according to his physical and mental condition, to meet the demands of the traffic. . . A duty to meet the risk of a decline in performance during the journey in advance through corresponding safety measures—by deciding not to drive the vehicle—does not arise only when the driver knows or can know the precise reason for a possible collapse. It suffices in this respect that he registers failings which, in dutiful self-critical examination, give rise to doubts as to whether he is still physically and mentally up to the demands of driving a vehicle. Equally, the driver may be held responsible for a sudden collapse without prior warning if particular deficiencies in his physical or mental health, of which he knew or should have known, may lead to such a breakdown . . ."

---

[173] NJW 1988, 909. Translation by M. Jelbert.

315

Notes

(1) § 276(1) BGB requires a person not to act negligently, or in other words to exercise the care requisite in social intercourse (*die im Verkehr erforderliche Sorgfalt*):[174] the degree of care there to be applied "is normally to be gauged by reference to a view of a certain limited circle of persons and by the typical qualities of the group of persons who represent a specific range of human relations".[175] In the annotated judgment the BGH explicitly confirms the objective nature of the standard of assessment under § 276(1) BGB: the personal characteristics, skills, knowledge and experience of the tortfeasor are essentially irrelevant in this respect. At the same time, the judgment illustrates that one should apply this standard in the light of the circumstances of the case at hand, that is taking into account the nature of the activity. The BGH attaches great importance to the dangers inherent in driving a car. Those dangers result in a duty for the driver not only to drive carefully, but also to verify *before* starting to drive whether he or she is still able, physically and mentally, to cope with the requirements of traffic.

(2) The BGH emphasises that the self-examination to which a driver must submit himself or herself is not to be undertaken lightly: it must be carried out in a self-critical (*selbstkritisch*) and dutiful (*pflichtmäßig*) manner. According to the BGH, in a further part of the judgment not excerpted above, that implies that, if need be, the driver should consult a doctor to find out whether he or she can compensate a possible reduction in driving ability (e.g. because of old age) through experience acquired as a driver. The duty to conduct a self-examination is even stricter when the driver's condition is affected by special circumstances, such as having had the flu, unfavourable weather conditions, or having already driven a long way, and so on.

BGH, 29 January 1991[176]   **3.G.13.**

OBJECTIVE STANDARD FOR PROFESSIONALS

Deadly ozone-injection

Although a health therapist (Heilpraktiker) *should not generally be subject to the same professional standards as a specialist physician, a health therapist practicing an invasive treatment is under the same requirements of care, in terms of knowledge and training, as a general physician who would apply the same treatment.*

Facts: Since January 1981, Mrs. T had been treated by the defendant, a health therapist (*Heilpraktiker*, i.e. someone who practises alternative medicine). The treatment involved ear acupuncture, ozone injections and ionic radiation. On 4 February 1982, the defendant injected Mrs. T, over 5 to 7 minutes, with 10 cm² of an ozone-oxygen mixture in a superficial vein in the area of the knee joint of the right leg. During that time, Mrs. T was lying down and the flow of blood in her right upper thigh was stemmed by means of a bandage. Some 20 minutes later the bandage was removed. When Mrs. T arose, she collapsed. Supply of oxygen and heart massage could not prevent death. Mrs. T's husband and her two children sued the health therapist for damages.

Held: The court of first instance rejected the claim. The court of appeal reversed the judgment of the court of first instance and allowed the claim. The BGH reversed the judgment of the court of appeal.

[174] See also *supra* **3.G.3.–4.** and Notes (1) and (2) thereafter.
[175] See RG, 14 January 1928, RGZ 119, 397 (English translation by K. Lipstein in Markesinis at 447–50).
[176] BGHZ 113, 297, NJW 1991, 1535. Translation by M. Jelbert.

Judgment: "The court of appeal was right in not holding the defendant liable on account of an error of treatment, solely because he applied the ozone-oxygen therapy, even though at the time it was largely unrecognized by so-called traditional medicine, but undertaken only by unconventional medical and health therapists . . .

The use of unconventional forms of therapy and even alternative treatment is in principle allowed by law . . . The decisive factor is that each patient who undergoes a treatment which is not or not yet recognised by traditional medicine must be able to decide, under his or her own responsibility and within the limits set by § 138 BGB and § 226a StGB, which forms of treatment he or she wishes to undergo . . .

The prerequisites to specialised treatment must be known and observed not only by a physician, but also by a health therapist. No particular prior medical training is required to become a health therapist, however, . . . the only condition for access to the profession being that his knowledge and abilities are examined by the competent public health office . . . *Such a health therapist is therefore under an obligation to acquire sufficient competence with regard to the treatment methods used by him (including their risks) and especially the correct techniques for using those methods without danger. Accordingly, in the same way as a physician, he fails to exercise the required care if he chooses a therapy without being familiar in advance to the necessary extent, with its use, specific characteristics and risks* [emphasis added]. Beyond the forms of treatment expressly prohibited by specific laws, the health therapist may not apply methods which, in view of the risk involved, require training in medical science and the experience of a qualified physician, as long as the health therapist has not acquired the corresponding technical knowledge and ability. *Observing the requisite care also implies that the health therapist—in just the same way as a newly qualified doctor—examines self-critically in individual cases whether his skills or knowledge are sufficient to draw up an adequate diagnosis and to start a proper treatment and, in the event of an invasive intervention for diagnostic or therapeutic purposes, to be able to observe all necessary safety measures* [emphasis added]. In the absence of such knowledge and skills, he must refrain from the intervention [references omitted]. Moreover, he must obviously also keep abreast of progress in medical science and also of knowledge obtained otherwise about the indications and risks of the therapies that he uses.

The court of appeal, however, carries the duty of care to be imposed on a health therapist too far.

The degree and scope of the care to be required of him is determined, as in civil law generally, according to the magnitude of any attendant risk. It largely dependent upon social expectations. In this respect, even if there were a homogenous 'profession of health therapist', *it is not. . . a matter of focussing on their view of the adequate conduct. The decisive factor is rather the expectations of an average patient who consults a health therapist. . .* [emphasis added] Those expectations will be influenced by *inter alia* the general impression among laypeople (albeit not always justified) that the methods of the health therapist are as a rule risk-free and involve little stress, especially where they have their origin in natural or popular therapies. The health therapist must focus on this in his procedure and in particular when explaining to a patient the potential risks associated with a course of treatment.

On the other hand, when assessing whether the defendant acted negligently, one should not apply the standards against which the fault of a specialist physician, for example a heart specialist, would be measured in a comparable situation. *It is true that an objective concept of negligence applies in civil law* [references omitted] *but in its interpretation, differences must be observed according to the relevant group. . . and on the basis of social expectations. Hence a specialist physician owes a different measure of care and ability from that required of a general physician. . . As the[defendant] rightly asserts, a health therapist cannot be required to have the same level of general education and training as a specialist physician* [emphasis added]. If and insofar as he uses invasive treatment methods, however, the same requirements of care must be imposed on him, with regard to his knowledge and training, as on a general physician who also uses such methods.

As long as it is not established that the defendant should have been aware that specific risks were associated with the ozone-oxygen treatment, even when all safety measures are observed, he cannot be charged with any omission as regards the information provided to the patient. A health therapist's duty to inform his patient is admittedly in principle comparable with that of a physician. . . From that it does not follow, however, that when applying the ozone-oxygen therapy, he had in any event to inform his patients—solely because at the time the [proposed] therapy was not generally recognised—that the therapy could possibly entail dangers which had not yet been researched and were also unknown to him. In such types of treatment, physicians and health therapists only have to explain the dangers which for them lie in the realm of the possible."

Notes

(1) The annotated judgment makes it clear that the professional nature of the activity is an important element to be factored into the standard of assessment of due care under § 276 (1) BGB. As seen above,[177] it is an objective standard under which attention is paid not to the personal characteristics of the tortfeasor but, on the contrary, to what in French law would be called the external circumstances, such as the nature, time and place of the activity concerned.[178] As a result, as is well illustrated by the annotated judgment, the duty of care varies not only with regard to the professional activity as a whole but also, within each profession, with regard to specific sub-groups, eg specialist physicians, surgeons, general physicians, trainee physicians and more broadly health therapists, even though they are not physicians.[179] It is typical of German law that, in measuring the duty of care to be applied by each of these groups, emphasis is laid not on the conceptions of the members of the group, but on the expectations of an average patient.[180]

(2) Irrespective of such differentiation, the duty of care referred to in § 276(1) BGB implies that the defendant must have taken all requisite precautions, particularly in assessing whether his or her abilities, in the particular circumstances of the case, are adequate for the kind of activity concerned as well as the dangers and risks inherent in them. In both the annotated judgment, relating to a professional activity, and the preceding one, relating to a general activity (driving), the BGH pointed out that the defendant should have carried out a critical self-examination of his or her abilities. As we have seen, a similar duty may apply also under French law.[181]

(3) As illustrated by the annotated judgment, the same approach is followed when it comes to the duty to inform patients of the risks involved in medical treatment: the standard of care is objective but varies with the nature of the activity (and the expectations of the patients).[182] Like French law,[183] German law expects the doctor to prove that the patient consented.[184] As to how much information must be disclosed, German law emphasizes very much the patient's right to self-determination: "to respect the patient's

---

[177] *Supra*, **3.G.11.**, Note (1).
[178] *Supra*, **3.F.10.** and notes thereafter.
[179] To be compared with Cass. civ. 1re, 10 June 1980, D 1981.IR.11, mentioned *supra*, **3.F.10.**, Note (2).
[180] See *infra*, Note (3). Compare with *supra*, Chapter II, **2.G.4.**, Note (1).
[181] *Supra*, **3.F.11.** and notes thereafter.
[182] To be compared with *supra*, **3.F.10.**
[183] Ibid., Note (3).
[184] See Markesinis at 473 with reference, for German law, to E. Deutsch, *Artzrecht und Arzneimittelrecht*, 2nd edn. (Berlin: Springer-Verlag, 1991) at 39. In the case of an infant or a young child, consent must be given by those responsible for his or her care, usually the parents: Markesinis, ibid.

own will is to respect his freedom and dignity as a human being".[185] Thus, the principle of full disclosure is repeatedly stressed, albeit with differences in emphasis according to whether the treatment is for diagnostic, therapeutic or cosmetic purposes.[186] In the last case, the doctor "must inform the patient especially carefully and thoroughly of the odds that the operation may fail to produce the desired results".[187]

Once it has been found that the patient did not receive adequate information, it must still be shown that the patient would not have consented to treatment if properly informed, in order to establish a causal link between the breach and the injury.[188]

Assessing atypical behaviour

BGH, 9 June 1967[189]   **3.G.14.**

VISUAL IMPAIRMENT IS NO EXCUSE

Blinded motorist

In assessing negligence in a case where a visual impairment led to an accident, it is irrelevant which circumstances led to the impairment. Rather, the question is whether the defendant ought to have known about the effects of the impairment and therefore the limits of his or her individual capacity to see.

Facts: On an early morning, while it was still dark and raining slightly, R was cycling to his place of work on an illuminated road. The defendant's car ran into him from behind, catapulting him onto the other side of the road where he was hit and killed by an oncoming car. R's widow and children sued the defendant under § 823(1) BGB on the ground that he alone was responsible for the accident, because he drove without due care (and with a dirty windscreen). The defendant denied any responsibility, stating that he had been blinded by an oncoming car owing to a visual impairment of which he was previously unaware.

Held: The court of first instance dismissed the claim. The court of appeal reversed that judgment and held the defendant liable. The BGH upheld the judgment of the court of appeal.

Judgment: "1. The court of appeal starts from the fact that the fault lies *prima facie* with the defendant. The defendant drove with dimmed headlights into the cyclist R, who was riding in front of him, because he had not seen him. In such a course of events, according to practical experience, culpable conduct on the part of the defendant is evident, in the sense that the defendant was either inattentive or was driving at a speed not in keeping with his range of vision.

2. The existence of such *prima facie* finding is not called into doubt by the defendant . . .

a) The court of appeal assumes, in favour of the defendant, that in the particular light conditions at the time of the accident he was blinded as a result of a visual impairment of which he was unaware. Nevertheless, it does not exonerate the defendant. It rightly focuses on whether the defendant could at least recognise the limits of his ability to see. The court of appeal is convinced that he was.

---

[185] BGH, 9 December 1958, BGHZ 29, 46 at 53–56, as quoted by Markesinis at 476.
[186] See the many references in Markesinis at 476.
[187] Ibid.
[188] See *infra*, Chapter IV, **4.F.14.**, Note (4).
[189] JZ 1968, 103, VersR 1967, 808. Translation by M. Jelbert.

... [The] defendant, like any driver, must at least be aware of how good his eyesight is. ... Accordingly, from the point of view of determining negligence, it does not matter why a person's eyesight deviates from normal vision. Hence a driver [with impaired vision] is not treated differently from a driver without sight problems. The latter too is expected to know the limits of his ability to see, of which he is aware, like the driver with sight problems, not through precise figures, but through his own experience. When determining the defendant's negligence the question which then arises is ... whether he should have known about ... the limits of his visual ability. This was answered in the affirmative by the court of appeal without error in law. This judgment is all the more valid since the defendant's sight problem, according to the comments of the expert, existed since birth and he had been driving a motor vehicle in traffic since 1956.

If, however, the defendant was able to recognise that his ability to see was less than normal, then he could and should have regulated his driving and especially his speed accordingly in order to meet the traffic requirements and to stop in time when necessary [emphasis added]. The court of appeal held correctly that the defendant failed to show that he met this requirement."

Note

Unlike French law, it would seem,[190] German law, in assessing negligence in a case of impaired vision while driving, does not compare the defendant with a standard person having the same deficiency, but uses the normal person having normal eyesight as the yardstick. That does not mean, however, that the courts of France and Germany come to a different conclusion. For indeed, in both legal systems, the reasonable person, whether having normal or deficient eyesight, will be required to verify in advance whether his or her visual ability was adequate for the kind of activity in which he or she was going to engage.[191] The German approach seems to be more logical, however since a visual impairment will be considered as an "internal circumstance" (specific to the person of the tortfeasor) which under French law would not normally be incorporated in the yardstick to be applied.[192]

3.2.2.C. ENGLISH LAW

Introductory Note

Under English law, the standard of care, as described by courts in the most general of terms,[193] is objective and impersonal, in that it is not dependent on the idiosyncrasies of the person whose conduct is at issue.[194] The standard of assessment is not that of the defendant but that of a "man of ordinary prudence",[195] a man using "ordinary care and skill"[196] (therefore susceptible to the occasional error of judgments, particularly in emergencies[197]), a "hypothetical man".[198] But what is this hypothetical reasonable man like?

[190] *Supra*, **3.F.11.**, Note (1).
[191] For French law, see ibid.
[192] *Supra*, **3.F.10.**, Note (1).
[193] *Supra*, 3.2.1. under c).
[194] Rogers at 171.
[195] *Vaughan v. Menlove* (1837) 3 Bing NC 468 at 475, CA (per Tindal CJ).
[196] *Heaven v. Pender* (1883) 11 QBD 503 at 507, CA (per Brett MR).
[197] As quoted by Markesinis at 471.
[198] *King v. Phillips* [1953] 1 QB 429 at 441, [1953] All ER 617, CA per Denning LJ.

He has been pictured as "the man on the Clapham omnibus", even as "the man who takes the magazines at home, and in the evening pushes the lawn-mower in his shirt sleeves".[199] "He has not the courage of Achilles, the wisdom of Ulysses or the strength of Hercules. . . . He is a reasonable man but he is neither a perfect citizen nor a paragon of circumspection."[200] Colourful as these comparisons may be, they provide little guidance for assessing a person's behaviour in a particular set of circumstances. It has been rightly observed that the definition of a reasonable man is not complete unless the words "in the circumstances" are added to it.[201] It is indeed generally accepted that "reasonable" varies with the circumstances and that particular circumstances can even modify the objective standard, which raises the question how far the standard of the "reasonable man" remains an objective one. We will turn back to that question when dealing with the standard of care for persons with reduced abilities.[202]

Assessing typical behaviour (ordinary or professional)

House of Lords[203]   **3.E.15.**
Glasgow Corporation v. *Muir*

REASONABLE MAN OF ORDINARY INTELLIGENCE

Scalded by hot tea

No liability is incurred for the consequences of acts which a reasonable person of ordinary intelligence and experience would not have had in contemplation.

Facts: Mrs. Alexander managed a public tea room. A group of 30–40 people asked her if they could take shelter and eat their food there. Mrs. Alexander agreed. A heavy tea urn was carried in by Mr. McDonald and a boy. As they entered the tea room, to which access was obtained by way of a small shop, Mr. McDonald inexplicably dropped his side of the urn and six children were scalded by hot tea. The corridor was 1,5 m wide, narrowing to 1 m, and a number of children were in there buying sweets. The plaintiffs alleged that Mrs. Alexander was negligent in allowing the urn to be carried into the tea room through a narrow passage where the children were congregated.

Held: The court of appeal allowed the claim. The House of Lords reversed that judgment.

Judgment: LORD MACMILLAN: "My Lords, the degree of care for the safety of others which the law requires human beings to observe in the conduct of their affairs varies according to the circumstances. *There is no absolute standard, but it may be said generally that the degree of care required varies directly with the risk involved. Those who engage in operations inherently dangerous must take precautions which are not required of persons engaged in the ordinary routine of daily life* [emphasis added]. It is, no doubt, true that in every act which an individual performs there is present a potentiality of injury to others. All things are possible, and, indeed, it has become proverbial that the unexpected always happens, but, while the precept alterum non laedere requires us to abstain from intentionally injuring others, it does not impose liability for every injury which our conduct may

---

[199] Markesinis at 471.
[200] Rogers at 53.
[201] M. Brazier and J. Murphy, *Street on Torts*, 10th edn. (London: Butterworths, 1999) at 237.
[202] *Infra*, 3.2.3.C.
[203] [1943] AC 448, [1943] 2 All ER 44.

occasion. In Scotland, at any rate, it has never been a maxim of the law that a man acts at his peril. Legal liability is limited to those consequences of our acts which a reasonable man of ordinary intelligence and experience so acting would have in contemplation. "The duty to take care", as I essayed to formulate it in *Bourhill* v. *Young* ([1943] AC 92 at 104), "is the duty to avoid doing or omitting to do anything which may have as its reasonable and probable consequence injury to others, and the duty is owed to those to whom injury may reasonably and probably be anticipated if the duty is not observed." This, in my opinion, expresses the law of Scotland and I apprehend that it is also the law of England. The standard of foresight of the reasonable man is, in one sense, an impersonal test. It eliminates the personal equation and is independent of the idiosyncrasies of the particular person whose conduct is in question. Some persons are by nature unduly timorous and imagine every path beset with lions. Others, of more robust temperament, fail to foresee or nonchalantly disregard even the most obvious dangers. The reasonable man is presumed to be free both from over-apprehension and from over-confidence, but there is a sense in which the standard of care of the reasonable man involves in its application a subjective element. It is still left to the judge to decide what, in the circumstances of the particular case, the reasonable man would have had in contemplation, and what, accordingly, the party sought to be made liable ought to have foreseen. Here there is room for diversity of view, as, indeed, is well illustrated in the present case. What to one judge may seem far-fetched may seem to another both natural and probable.

With these considerations in mind I turn to the facts of the occurrence on which your Lordships have to adjudicate. . . The question, as I see it, is whether Mrs. Alexander, when she was asked to allow a tea urn to be brought into the premises under her charge, ought to have had in mind that it would require to be carried through a narrow passage in which there were a number of children and that there would be a risk of the contents of the urn being spilt and scalding some of the children. If, as a reasonable person, she ought to have had these considerations in mind, was it her duty to require that she should be informed of the arrival of the urn, and, before allowing it to be carried through the narrow passage, to clear all the children out of it in case they might be splashed with scalding water?. . .

In my opinion, Mrs. Alexander had no reason to anticipate that such an event would happen as a consequence of granting permission for a tea urn to be carried through the passage way where the children were congregated, and, consequently, there was no duty incumbent on her to take precautions against the occurrence of such an event. I think that she was entitled to assume that the urn would be in charge of responsible persons (as it was) who would have regard for the safety of the children in the passage (as they did have regard), and that the urn would be carried with ordinary care, in which case its transit would occasion no danger to bystanders. The [plaintiffs] have left quite unexplained the actual cause of the accident. The immediate cause was not the carrying of the urn through the passage, but McDonald's losing grip of his handle. How he came to do so is entirely a matter of speculation. He may have stumbled or he may have suffered a temporary muscular failure. We do not know. . . Yet it is argued that Mrs. Alexander ought to have foreseen the. . . reasonable probability of an occurrence the nature of which is unascertained. Suppose that McDonald let go his handle through carelessness. Was Mrs. Alexander bound to foresee this as reasonably probable and to take precautions against the possible consequences? I do not think so."

Notes

(1) The annotated judgment provides some welcome guidance as to what a "reasonable" person is expected to do in a given set of circumstances. Although Lord MacMillan stresses the objective and impersonal nature of the test, he has to admit that judges may come to divergent views in this respect. It has been said, nevertheless, that "in most cases the courts can apply the standard of care of the reasonable man with some confidence for

it is to be assumed that the judges who staff them have the qualities of the hypothetical creature well in mind".[204]

(2) The annotated judgment illustrates the central importance of the question of *foreseeability* when it comes to *apply* the "reasonable person" test. The question then is "what, in the circumstances of the particular case, the reasonable man would have had in contemplation, and what, accordingly the [defendant] ought to have foreseen". In the case at issue, what should Mrs. Alexander have had in contemplation? Could she foresee that Mr. McDonald would have stumbled and that, accordingly, she needed to get the children out of the way? Obviously, that is a question of subjective appreciation as it will be incumbent upon the court to decide whether or not a particular item of knowledge is to be imputed to the reasonable person. In order to find out what is reasonably foreseeable, it must therefore first be decided what knowledge and experience is to be attributed to the reasonable person in the circumstances of the case.[205]

(3) That subjective element in the application of the standard of reasonable care may help a judge to assess the defendant's conduct in a particular case. However, for the system "not to collapse under the weight of accumulated precedent"[206] a more general proposition is needed. It could well be that in each case a balance must be struck between the magnitude of the risk (i.e. the *probability* that injury will be incurred *and* the *seriousness* of that injury) and the consequences of not taking the risk, to be examined in light of the object to be attained,[207] and the cost of prevention (that is the cost of practical measures that could have been taken to eliminate, or reduce the risk).[208] Case law contains many examples to illustrate that these elements play a role in fleshing out the objective standard of reasonable care.

Queen's Bench Division[209]　　　　　**3.E.16.**
Bolam v. *Friern Hospital Management Committee*

ACCEPTED PRACTICES

The fractured pelvis

A physician who acted in accordance with a practice accepted as proper by a responsible body of physicians skilled in that particular art was not negligent merely because there is a body of opinion that takes a contrary view.

Facts: The plaintiff consented to and underwent electroconvulsive therapy as treatment for his mental illness. While undergoing the therapy, he suffered a fracture of the pelvis. He sued the defendants in negligence, claiming (i) that he should have been warned of the risk of fracture, and either (ii) that relaxant drugs should have been administered to eliminate the risk or (iii) that he should have been restrained during the treatment. At the time, medical opinion on those issues was divided.

---

204 Rogers at 173.
205 Rogers at 173–4. Foreseeability also plays a role in establishing negligence in the case of the exercise of professional (medical) activities: see *Roe* v. *Minister of Health* [1954] 2 QB 66, [1954] 2 WLR 915, [1954] 2 All ER 131, CA.
206 Rogers at 179.
207 For instance, if all trains were restricted to a speed of 5 miles an hour, there would be fewer accidents, but life would be intolerably slowed down: Rogers at 181–2.
208 Rogers at 182. See further Markesinis and Deakin at 166–71.
209 [1957] 1 WLR 582, [1957] 2 All ER 118.

Held: The claim was rejected.

Judgment: McNair J: "In the ordinary case which does not involve any special skill, negligence in law means a failure to do some act which a reasonable man in the circumstances would do, or the doing of some act which a reasonable man in the circumstances would not do; and if that failure or the doing of that act results in injury, then there is a cause of action. How [does one] test whether this act or failure is negligent? In an ordinary case it is generally said [one judges] it by the action of the man in the street. He is the ordinary man . . . *But [in] a situation which involves the use of some special skill or competence, then the test as to whether there has been negligence or not is not the test of the man on the top of a Clapham omnibus, because he has not got this special skill. The test is the standard of the ordinary skilled man exercising and professing to have that special skill. A man need not possess the highest expert skill; it is well established law that it is sufficient if he exercises the ordinary skill of an ordinary competent man exercising that particular art* [emphasis added] . . . [The plaintiff] put it in this way, that in the case of a medical man, negligence means failure to act in accordance with the standards of reasonably competent medical men at the time. That is a perfectly accurate statement, as long as it is remembered that there may be one or more perfectly proper standards; and if he conforms with one of those proper standards, then he is not negligent. [The plaintiff] was also quite right, in my judgment, in saying that a mere personal belief that a particular technique is best is no defence unless that belief is based on reasonable grounds. That again is unexceptionable. But the emphasis which is laid by the defence is on this aspect of negligence, that the real question . . . on each of the three major topics [listed above in the statement of facts] is whether the defendants, in acting in the way they did, were acting in accordance with a practice of competent respected professional opinion. [The defendants] submitted that if . . . they were acting in accordance with a practice of a competent body of professional opinion, then it would be wrong . . . to hold that negligence was established . . .

. . . I myself would prefer to put it this way, that *he is not guilty of negligence if he has acted in accordance with a practice accepted as proper by a responsible body of medical men skilled in that particular art.* I do not think there is much difference in sense. It is just a different way of expressing the same thought. *Putting it the other way round, a man is not negligent, if he is acting in accordance with such a practice, merely because there is a body of opinion who would take a contrary view* [emphases added]. At the same time, that does not mean that a medical man can obstinately and pig-headedly carry on with some old technique if it has been proved to be contrary to what is really substantially the whole of informed medical opinion . . . That clearly would be wrong.

Before I get to the details of the case, it is right to say this, that it is not essential . . . to decide which of two practices is the better practice, as long as . . . what the defendants did was in accordance with a practice accepted by responsible persons; if the result of the evidence is that . . . this practice is better than the practice spoken of on the other side, then it is really a stronger case."

Notes

(1) The annotated judgment is quite famous and has given rise to "the *Bolam* test", which is of particular application to doctors. With regard to the three questions before the court (failure to use relaxant drugs, alternatively failure to use manual restraint; and failure to inform the patient of the risk), the court was of the opinion that the test to be applied to establish negligence in a situation which involves the use of some special skill or competence, is not the test of the man on the top of a Clapham omnibus (because he has not got this special skill or competence), but the test of "the ordinary skilled man exercising and professing to have that special skill", which does not mean that he or she needs to possess the highest expert skill. However, as the judge stated, that does not

exclude the possibility that there may be one or more perfectly proper standards and "if he conforms with one of those proper standards, then he is not negligent". As to what a proper standard is, at the time of the facts, the judge was ready to look at the opinion of "a responsible body of medical men skilled in that particular art", and accepted that there might be more than one. The *Bolam* test has been confirmed by legislation, such as the Congenital Disabilities (Civil Liability) Act 1976,[210] which states at section 1(5) that a defendant is "not answerable to the child, for anything he did or omitted to do when responsible in a professional capacity for treating or advising the parent, if he took reasonable care having due regard to then received professional opinion applicable to the particular class of case; but this does not mean that he is answerable only because he departed from received opinion".

(2) The *Bolam* test is regarded by some as "paternalistic in nature", insofar as it relates to the duty of doctors to warn their patients of risks involved in a proposed medical treatment, since it refers more specifically to the opinion of a responsible body of professional persons, without regard to the patient's interests.[211] It is rejected by most common law jurisdictions "which adopt the so-called doctrine of 'informed consent' taking the view that the doctor must disclose as much information as a reasonable patient would require to make an informed choice . . .".[212]

The *Bolam* test was considered and broadly confirmed by the House of Lords in *Sidaway* v. *Bethlem Royal Hospital*,[213] which concerned precisely the question of 'informed consent' and the extent of the physician's obligation to inform the patient of significant risks attached to a particular course of treatment. In that case, the risk was small (put by the trial judge at 1–2 percent), but it materialized, although the operation was performed with full care and skill. The plaintiff was paralysed as a result of interference with the spinal cord. The House of Lords noted that expert witnesses agreed that, for a responsible body of neuro-surgical opinion, it was proper practice not to disclose the risk in question; for the House of Lords, the defendant physician had therefore a complete defence against the claim in negligence. Lord Bridge, who gave the leading speech, did not accept however that the *Bolam* test would apply in every instance. He acknowledged that, notwithstanding agreement among expert witnesses, a judge "might in certain circumstances come to the conclusion that disclosure of a particular risk was so obviously necessary to an informed choice on the part of the patient that no reasonably prudent medical man would fail to make it".[214]

Interestingly enough, the *Bolam* test was subsequently adopted in relation to other professions, e.g. accountants[215] and lawyers.[216] It is striking, though, that outside the medical sphere courts have been more readily disposed to find negligence, notwithstanding

---

[210] See *supra*, Chapter II, **2.E.5.**
[211] Markesinis at 475.
[212] Ibid.
[213] *Sidaway* v. *Bethlem Royal Hospital* [1985] AC 871, HL. See also *Whitehouse* v. *Jordan* [1981] 1 WLR 246, HL, where a mere error of judgment was held not to amount to carelessness, despite the potentially grave consequences of such an error: Markesinis and Deakin at 164.
[214] Markesinis and Deakin at 164, with further references and comments.
[215] *Mutual Life Citizens' Assurance Co. Ltd.* v. *Evatt* [1971] AC 793, HL.
[216] *Saif Ali* v. *Sydney Mitchell & Co.* [1980] AC 198, HL.

that the impugned professional conduct was accepted by expert opinion. In conformity with general principles in relation to negligence, they have not treated such opinion as conclusive of reasonable conduct.[217]

(3) Whereas for some three decades after *Bolam*, judges generally tended to "rest upon well- worn formulae rather than to puzzle out the real reason why one case is different from another",[218] the last ten years have witnessed a pronounced shift in the case law on medical negligence towards a more interventionist stance. By the mid-1990s, lower court decisions displayed clear signs that the judicial appreciation of reasonableness and permissible risk-taking is relevant in determining the requisite standard[219] and that it is appropriate to ask what information the reasonable patient would have expected to receive.[220] This development found an echo before the House of Lords in *Bolitho* v. *City and Hackney Health Authority*.[221] That tragic case involved a two-year old boy who, after having been discharged from hospital after treatment for croup, was re-admitted with further respiratory difficulties. The boy's breathing deteriorated twice within a few days, in both cases without the doctor on duty responding to the call of the hospital personnel. The first time the boy recovered; but on the second occasion he suffered total respiratory collapse and cardiac arrest, sustained severe brain damage and subsequently died. The House of Lords upheld the lower court decisions that, despite the doctor's negligence in not attending or arranging for a suitable deputy to attend, the claim failed for want of causation. Five expert witnesses had maintained that an appropriate treatment (intubation) should have been ordered by any competent doctor after the second episode; however, the doctor in charge argued that she would not have intubated if present and three other expert witnesses testified that intubation would not have been appropriate on the symptoms as described.

Lord Browne-Wilkinson, noted that McNair J in *Bolam* made reference to a "*responsible* body of medical men" and that the practice should be regarded as proper by a "*reasonable* body of opinion"; similarly, in *Maynard* v. *West Midlands Regional Health Authority*[222] Lord Scarman had referred to a "respectable" body of professional opinion. Lord Browne-Wilkinson observed that[223]

"The use of these adjectives . . . shows that the court has to be satisfied that the exponents of the body of opinion relied upon can demonstrate that such opinion has a logical basis. In particular in cases involving, as they so often do, the weighing of risks against benefits, the judge before accepting a body of opinion as being responsible, reasonable or respectable, will need to be satisfied that, in forming their views, the experts have directed their minds to the question of comparative risks and benefits and have reached a defensible conclusion on the matter . . . I emphasise that in my view

---

[217] H. Teff, "The Standard of Care in Medical Negligence—Moving on from *Bolam?*" [1998] OJLS 473 at 476.

[218] Lord Justice Hoffman, "The Reasonableness of Lawyers' Lapses" (1994) 10 Professional Negligence 6 at 9.

[219] See the cases discussed by H. Teff, "The Standard of Case in Medical Negligence—Moving on from *Bolam?*" [1998] OJLS 473 at 478.

[220] See the speech of Lord Scarman in *Sidaway* v. *Bethlem Royal Hospital* [1985] AC 871, HL as noted in Markesinis and Deakin at 165.

[221] *Bolitho* v. *City and Hackney Health Authority* [1998] AC 232, [1997] 4 All ER 771, [1997] 3 WLR 1151, HL.

[222] [1984] 1 WLR 634, HL at 639.

[223] Ibid. at 241–2 and 243.

it will very seldom be right for a judge to reach the conclusion that views genuinely held by a competent medical expert are unreasonable . . . It is only where a judge can be satisfied that the body of expert opinion cannot be logically supported at all that such opinion will not provide the benchmark by reference to which the defendant's conduct falls to be assessed."

(4) Even if English courts were to jettison *Bolam* and were to more actively question expert evidence in medical cases, the outcome of the cases might not be affected substantially. As H. Teff observes: "Causation would continue to play a decisive role in many cases, and the various considerations which have prompted judicial reluctance to set standards for doctors could still be accomodated within the open-textured and elusive nature of current negligence criteria".[224]

(5) The standard of a reasonable medical person was recently applied to a physician's treatment of a patient without consent in a situation of necessity.[225]

Assessing atypical behaviour

Court of Appeal[226]   **3.E.17.**

Mansfield v. Weetabix Ltd.

No STRICT LIABILITY IMPOSED

Lorry crashing into a shop

In the case of a driver who was involved in an accident caused by a disabling event of which he or she was not aware, the standard of care to be applied is that of a reasonably competent driver unaware that he or she might be suffering from a condition that impaired his or her ability to drive.

Facts: Mr. Tarleton, a lorry-driver employed by the defendant, was unaware that he suffered from malignant insulinoma, a condition that resulted in hypoglycaemia, as a result of which the brain is unable to function properly. In the course of a 40-mile journey he was involved in two incidents of erratic driving and in a minor accident with another vehicle. Subsequently he failed to negotiate a bend and crashed into the plaintiff's shop, causing extensive damage.

Held: The court of first instance allowed the claim. The court of appeal reversed the decision of the court of first instance.

Judgment: LEGGATT LJ: "There is no reason in principle why a driver should not escape liability where the disabling event is not sudden, but gradual, provided that the driver is unaware of it. A person with Mr. Tarleton's very rare condition commonly does not appreciate that his ability is impaired, and he was no exception. Although by the time of trial Mr. Tarleton was dead, and there was no direct evidence of his actual state of awareness, the judge held that 'he would not have continued to drive if he had appreciated and was conscious that his ability was impaired'. Of course, if he had known that it was, he would have been negligent in continuing to drive despite his

---

[224] H. Teff, "The Standard of Case in Medical Negligence—Moving on from *Bolam*?" [1998] OJLS 473 at 483–484. See *infra*, Chapter IV, **4.E.18.** and **4.E.23.** for a discussion of causation in medical liability cases under English law.

[225] See *In re F* [1990] 2 AC 1, [1989] 2 WLR 1025, [1989] 2 All ER 545, HL.

[226] [1998] 1 WLR 823.

327

knowledge of his disability. So also if he ought to have known that he was subject to a condition that rendered him unfit to drive. . .

In my judgment, the standard of care that Mr. Tarleton was obliged to show in these circumstances was that which is to be expected of a reasonably competent driver unaware that he is or may be suffering from a condition that impairs his ability to drive. To apply an objective standard in a way that did not take account of Mr. Tarleton's condition would be to impose strict liability. But that is not the law. As Lord Wilberforce said in *Snelling* v. *Whitehead*, The Times, 31 July 1975, a transcript of the speeches in which is before the court:

> The case is one which is severely distressing to all who have been concerned with it and one which should attract automatic compensation regardless of any question of fault. But no such system has yet been introduced in this country and the courts, including this House, have no power to depart from the law as it stands. This requires that compensation may only be obtained in an action for damages and further requires, as a condition of the award of damages against the [driver], a finding of fault, or negligence, on his part . . . [I]t is . . . not disputed that any degree of fault on the part of the [driver], if established, is sufficient for the [plaintiff] to recover. On the other hand, if no blame can be imputed to the [driver], the action, based on negligence, must inevitably fail.

In the present case the plaintiffs may well have been insured. Others in their position may be less fortunate. A change in the law is, however, a matter for Parliament. Meanwhile, since in my judgment Mr. Tarleton was in no way to blame, he was not negligent. I would therefore allow the appeal."

Notes

(1) In *Nettleship* v. *Weston*,[227] the Court of Appeal, referring to the objective standard of care laid down in *Glasgow Corporation* v. *Muir*,[228] held that the standard of care for an apprentice driver does not differ from the one required from a driver of skill and experience: the apprentice "must drive in as good a manner as a driver of skill, experience and care, who is sound in mind and limb, who makes no errors of judgment, has good eyesight and hearing, and is free from any infirmity". Lord Denning MR commented as follows on the high standard imposed by the judges:[229]

> "The high standard thus imposed by the judges is, I believe, largely the result of the policy of the Road Traffic Acts. Parliament requires every driver to be insured against third-party risks. The reason is that a person injured by a motor-car should not be left to bear the loss on his own, but should be compensated out of the insurance fund. The fund is better able to bear it than he can. But the injured person is only able to recover if the driver is liable in law. So the judges see to it that he is liable, unless he can prove care and skill of high standard [references omitted]. Thus we are, in this branch of the law, moving away from the concept: 'No liability without fault'. We are beginning to apply the test: 'On whom should the risk fall?' Morally the learner-driver is not at fault; but legally she is liable to be because she is insured and the risk should fall on her . . ."

It is striking to see in the annotated judgment, how, in sharp contradistinction to the high standard imposed in *Nettleship v. Weston*, the Court of Appeal was prepared to take into account the personal circumstances of the driver. Leggatt LJ distinguished

---

[227] *Nettleship* v. *Weston, infra*, Chapter VII, **7.E.16.**
[228] *Glasgow Corporation* v. *Muir, supra*, **3.E.15.**
[229] [1971] 2 QB 691 at 699–700.

Nettleship v. *Weston* from the present case by holding that it "does not refer to cases in which a driver is unaware that he is subject to a disability".

(2) The annotated judgment must also be contrasted with *Roberts* v. *Ramsbottom*.[230] In that case, a driver suffered a heart attack and caused physical damage to persons and property in the ensuing accident. Neill J. held him liable, finding that[231]

> "the driver will be able to escape liability if his actions at the relevant time were wholly beyond his control. But if he retained some control, albeit imperfect control, and his driving, judged objectively was below the required standard, he remains liable. His position is the same as a driver who is old or infirm."

It appeared from *Roberts* v. *Ramsbottom* and from *Nettleship* v. *Weston* that, in road traffic cases at least, the courts apply an "objective" test, under which no account is taken of individual frailty or inexperience. The test is that of a normal average driver, whose judgment is not impaired because of reduced consciousness or lack of experience. The result is that the law of traffic accidents, although stil nominally based on negligence, in practice comes very close to strict liability.[232]

(3) The annotated judgment was about a driver who was unaware of his inability to drive, which was the result not of a sudden but a gradual disabling event. The ensuing conduct, ie driving erratically, was not that different, it would seem, from that in *Roberts* v. *Ramsbottom*. The Court of Appeal nonetheless came to a different conclusion, stating that if an objective standard were to be applied without taking into account the disabling condition of the defendant, strict liability would in fact be imposed, which "is not the law".[233]

In the words of Leggatt LJ, since the driver "was in no way to blame, he was not negligent".[234] Of course, as Leggatt LJ had said just before, "if [the driver] had known that [his ability was impaired] he would have been negligent in continuing to drive despite his knowledge of his disability. So also if he ought to have known that he was subject to a condition that rendered him unfit to drive".[235]

The latter statement indicates that English law reaches the same result as French and German law,[236] however not because it considers that a driver is under a duty to verify in advance whether he or she is up to the dangerous activity he or she is on the point of

---

[230] *Roberts* v. *Ramsbottom* [1980] 1 WLR 823, [1980] 1 All ER 7, QBD. See also a similar case involving a driver suffering from diabetes: *Broome* v. *Perkins* [1987] RTR 321, DC.

[231] [1980] 1 WLR 823 at 832.

[232] See Markesinis and Deakin at 298. See also *Henderson* v. *Henry E. Jenkins & Sons* [1970] AC 282, HL, where the appellant's husband had been run over and killed by a lorry, the brakes of which had failed because of a hole in a pipe in the hydraulic brake system caused by corrosion. The House of Lords held that the respondents could not rely on the defence of a latent defect not discoverable by the exercise of reasonable care unless they showed that there were no special circumstances in the past use of the vehicle to indicate that the lorry might have been subjected to a corrosive agent resulting in the corrosion of the pipe. Accordingly, since the respondents had not adduced evidence of the past history of the vehicle, they could not rely on the defence of a latent defect and therefore, they had not discharged the inference that they had been negligent.

[233] On the relationship between liability based on fault (or negligence) and strict liability under English law, see *infra*, Chapter VI, 6.1.3.

[234] To be compared with *Waugh* v. *James K. Allen* (1964) SLT 269, HL, where (according to the description made by Weir at 135) "the man at the wheel could not be said to be driving at all, as he had suffered a total blackout, and he was not liable for remaining at the wheel since there was no premonition of the heart-attack".

[235] That seems also to be the approach in several American states, as exemplified by *Breunig* v. *American Family Insurance Co.* (1970) 173 NW 2d 619, mentioned in Markesinis and Deakin at 162–3.

[236] *Supra*, **3.F.11.**, Note (1), **3.G.14.**, Note.

engaging in; but simply because it considers that the driver conducted himself in a way in which the reasonable man would not have done. However, when a driver, prior to taking the wheel, is wholly unaware of the disability, he or she cannot be held to have acted negligently in driving. That means that, at the end of the day, the individual situation of the driver is taken into account as part of the circumstances in which the standard of care is applied.

3.2.3. CULPABILITY

Culpability, understood as personal responsibility for reprehensible behaviour, was for a long time seen as the essence of fault. However, that has changed in the course of the twentieth Century. Fault is now essentially understood "objectively" as acting wrongfully; in all of the legal systems examined, it is defined as a course of conduct, whether acting or failing to act, in a way that was in breach of what society expects from an average citizen carrying out the same activity under the same circumstances as the person whose conduct is assessed. That hypothetical "average citizen" or "reasonable person" provides an objective standard.

The remaining question is whether, apart from wrongfulness as outlined above, culpability is still also a condition for fault to be established; in other words, whether something remains of the old conception that a person causing harm must be personally responsible for it in one way or another before that person will be found liable to make good the harm. Culpability is still required in penal law, where, as a general rule, for a penal sanction to be imposed, a person must not only have acted in violation of a written penal law (*nulla poena sine lege*) but must also be personally to blame for it (*nulla poena sine culpa*). As long as the essence of civil fault was personal responsibility, civil and penal responsibility therefore coincided in every case where a penal sanction was attached to unlawful conduct.[237] Now that fault has, as explained above, a different connotation, the identity between penal and civil liability is far from evident.[238]

Legal systems do not offer a uniform picture as regards the remaining role of personal culpability. In this context, it is worth noting that being personally culpable may have a double meaning.

It can mean that one is not responsible for the harm which results from the unlawful behaviour if one could not help the harmful event occurring, in other words that it was not one's conduct which led the event to happen. That, however, is as much a question of causation as one of fault: if the injury was unforeseeable or unavoidable, then the defendant's conduct did not cause, or contribute to cause, the harm. The harm was then caused by an event beyond the control of the defendant, i.e. by *force majeure*. All the systems studied have recognized that *force majeure*[239] negates any liability on the part of the

---

[237] Indeed, in many legal systems, it was, and still is, possible for the victim to join his or her civil liability claim with any penal proceedings which might have been instituted against the wrongdoer in relation to the wrongdoing. See for instance the *action civile* under French law, explained *supra*, Chapter II, 2.5.1., Introductory Note under a).

[238] In English law, if only because actions in tort have provided proprietary remedies, fault was never universally a necessary element in tortious causes of action and one can even find cases, albeit rare, of criminal acts, e.g. perjury, committed in the knowledge that they will or may injure someone, without that person having in consequence a cause of action in tort against the wrongdoer.

[239] The term is also used in English law. German law uses the term *Höhere Gewalt*.

defendant. It appears that the concept of *force majeure* has been developed most fully under French law, where it has been integrated within the broader theory of extraneous causes (*causes étrangères*).[240] An "extraneous cause" is a cause of the injury[241] which presents three characteristics:

(i) It was *outside the control* of the defendant, in the sense that it did not lie within the realm controlled by the defendant. An extraneous cause can therefore consist in a natural phenomenon (storm, lightning, etc., often called "acts of God"), the conduct of a third party over whom the defendant had no influence (excluding thus employees, children, etc.) or even the conduct of the victim himself or herself;

(ii) It was *not foreseeable* by the defendant;

(iii) It was also *unavoidable* (*irrésistible*), meaning that the defendant could not have done anything to prevent it happening.

It is apparent that the last two conditions (unforeseeability and unavoidability) not only negate any causal link between the conduct of the defendant and the injury,[2420] but also imply that the defendant was not at fault.[243] One of the most remarkable features of the theory of extraneous causes under French law is that it applies across the whole spectrum of civil liability, i.e. in contractual liability regimes,[244] under the general regime of delictual liability based on fault (Art. 1382–3 C.civ.)[245] as well as under the various regimes of liability without fault.[246]

Culpability, such as we are concerned with here, has also another meaning which refers to whether conduct that caused harm, or contributed to it, and amounted to unlawful conduct in the objective sense of the word (because it should have been avoided by a reasonable person) also constituted culpable conduct, in that, by reason of his or her conduct, the defendant was at fault personally, i.e. subjectively.

French law gives a straightforward answer: unlawful conduct is enough, even where conduct of mentally disturbed persons or very young children is concerned (which does not exclude age affecting the standard of the "reasonable person"[247]). Most of the other legal systems do not wish to go that far. Notably in the case of disturbed persons and young children, liability will not arise in the absence of capacity "to realize that [one's]

[240] See Viney and Jourdain at 217, para. 383 and Le Tourneau and Cadiet at 293, para. 895. See also von Bar II at 352, para. 322 who recommends adopting the French approach as the best developed and most coherent treatment of the problem.

[241] Within the meaning of the applicable theory of causation, as outlined *infra*, Chapter VI, 6.1.

[242] Since the injury will have resulted from a course of events that was unforeseeable and unavoidable. The theory of extraneous cause is seen as one of the major manifestations of probabilistic causation (adequacy theory) under French law: see *infra*, Chapter IV, 4.1.3., Introductory Note under h).

[243] On the relationship between *force majeure*, causation and fault under French law, see Viney and Jourdain, *Conditions* at 247–50, para. 403–4.

[244] A showing by the defendant of extraneous cause will free him or her of contractual liability, irrespective of whether the contractual obligation was one of means or result (as to the distinction between the two, see *supra*, 3.F.2., Note (2). See *infra*, Chapter IV, 4.F.21.

[245] The defendant can always escape liability by showing that an extraneous cause intervened in the occurrence of injury, even though it suffices to prove absence of fault, without actually pointing to an extraneous cause.

[246] See *infra*, Chapter V, 5.1.1. under c) and 5.F.24.–25., and Chapter VI, 6.F.5. and Note (2) thereafter. In the realm of road traffic accidents, however, the *Loi Badinter* has restricted the availability of extraneous cause as a means of avoiding liability: see *infra*, Chapter VI, 6.F.16. and notes thereafter.

[247] *Supra*, 3.F.10., Note (1).

conduct was unlawful and that [one] might have to answer for the resulting damages".[248] Such an approach may be put into effect either through a legislative provision, or by leaving it to the courts to decide whether a disturbed person or a little child is capable of committing fault and being held liable for the harm caused. Regardless of which of those two ways is chosen, the legal system in question may also provide for the possibility of awarding the injured person an equitable amount of money nonetheless, depending upon the circumstances of the case and the financial position of the parties involved. Such a possibility can prove particularly useful where harm is caused by a mentally disturbed person for whom no other person such as a parent or custodian can be made liable.

Apart from the special case of mentally disturbed persons and little children, where the absence of culpability is obvious and, so to speak, structural, there remains the question of whether culpability is a pre-condition for liability for all other persons.[249] As we shall see, the answer to that question appears to be, in all legal systems, that culpability is only exceptionally seen as a condition of liability or, alternatively, that the absence of culpability will only in exceptional cases provide the defendant with a defence against liability for unlawful conduct (leaving aside conduct which constitutes a criminal offence at the same time as a civil tort).

For the purposes of the present casebook, the important thing is to see how, notwithstanding those theoretical differences, the practical outcome is often not that different. And, indeed, to take liability of young children as an example, it is interesting to see that such liability will be limited under every legal system, irrespective of whether that occurs either through some condition of culpability or through the assessment *in concreto* of the conduct of children under a modified "reasonable person" standard, or by statutory enactment.

3.2.3.A. FRENCH LAW

Introductory Note

Under French law, culpability (or imputability, as it is also called) is no longer a condition for civil liability to arise, or rather it is no longer part of the general concept of *faute*. That means that it operates, alongside *faute* (understood as socially unacceptable behaviour), as a condition which *may* be required in certain types of case but then not always with the same intensity, depending on the type of case.[250] The last obvious trace of subjective culpability is found in cases where intentional or fraudulent fault (*faute intentionnelle ou dolosive*) plays a role, often to increase the burden of liability for the harmful consequences of the wrongful conduct[251] or to deprive exemption clauses of their

---

[248] Zweigert and Kötz, in the excerpt reproduced *supra*, 3.2.1. under b).

[249] Including legal persons, in which case the question is asked with regard to the organ, mainly the manager of the legal entity, who is responsible for the action under scrutiny: for comparative references, see von Bar II at 209–17, para. 188–93. Liability of legal persons for the conduct of their organs is discussed *infra*, Chapter V, 5.1.1.A. under g), 5.1.1.B. under g) and 5.1.1.C. under h). It is clear that the decline of subjective culpability and the rise of objective unlawfulness as the benchmark for assessing wrongfulness in tort law was encouraged not only by the growth of insurance, but also by the fact that many claims were brought against legal entities: ibid. at 211–2, para. 189.

[250] See Viney and Jourdain, *Conditions* at 326, para. 444–1.

[251] See for instance in the area of insurance or labor accidents. Ibid. at 553 ff., para. 601–4.

effect.[252] In those cases, the prevailing opinion seems to define intentional or fraudulent fault as the intention not only to pusue the course of conduct but also to bring about the harmful consequences,[253] which clearly implies a subjective element on the part of the tortfeasor. Other serious faults, such as grave fault (*faute grave*) which is neither intentional nor fraudulent, or inexcusable fault (*faute inexcusable*), may also contain a subjective element as well, where they refer to a certain degree of wilful blindness to injury.[254] However, even then, such wilful blindness extends not only to actual but also to constructive knowledge of the risk of injury, which leads again to an assessment *in abstracto*.

The abandonment of culpability as a requirement for liability is felt most acutely in the case of minors and mentally disturbed persons. That does not prevent courts, though, from resorting to devices to limit liability in such cases, particularly in respect of very young children (infants).

Capacity of mentally disturbed persons and young children to act culpably

Cass. civ. 2e, 4 May 1977[255]   **3.F.18.**
Cie d'assur. La Foncière C.P. v. *Pecquigney*

No LIABILITY SUI GENERIS

Mentally disturbed pedestrian

Article 489–2 C. civ. does not provide for a specific liability regime and applies to all regimes of liability laid down in Articles 1382 ff. C.civ.

Facts: The first defendant, a mentally disturbed person, threw himself before a bus. The plaintiff was sitting in the bus and was hurt when the driver manoeuvred to avoid the pedestrian. She claimed damages from the first defendant and the second defendant (his liability insurance company). The insurance company argued that it was not liable for the conduct of the first defendant, on the ground that any liability that he had to the plaintiff arose under Article 489–2 C.civ., which constitutes a head of liability separate from Article 1382 and 1383 C.civ.

Held: The court of appeal dismissed the argument of the second defendant. The Cour de cassation upheld the judgment of the court of appeal.

Judgment: "The decision of the court of appeal is criticised for upholding [the plaintiff's] claim whereas, as was alleged by the [insurance] company . . ., the *sui generis* nature of the responsibility ascribed to mentally disturbed persons by the new . . . Article 489–2 C.civ . . . precluded the court of appeal from denying the particular nature of this head of liability and from conflating it . . . with that under Articles 1382 and 1383 C.civ., to which the insurance policy referred specifically in order to define the type of risk which it covered.

However, the court of appeal correctly held that Article 489–2 C.civ. does not provide for any form of liability of a particular nature; it applies to all forms of liability provided for in Articles

---

[252] See Cass. Ass. Plén., 30 June 1998, JCP 1998.II.10146, with annotation by P. Delbecque, where it was held that the exemption clause laid down in Article 13 of the *Code des postes et télécommunications* (Post and Telecommunications Code) did not apply where the Post Office, or the carrier operating on its behalf, had committed a grave fault (*faute lourde*).

[253] Viney and Jourdain, *Conditions* at 589, para. 624–5.

[254] Ibid. at 567 and 573, para. 611–1 and 616.

[255] D 1978.Jur.393, with annotation by R. Legeais. Translation by A. Dumas-Eymard.

1382ff. C.civ. By these statements, the court of appeal provided a legal basis for its decision. . . It follows that the ground of appeal is not well founded."

Notes

(1) Early case law had excluded the liability of mentally disturbed persons, on the ground that they lacked capacity to commit a fault. The Act 68–5 of 3 January 1968[256] inserted a new Article 489–2 in the *Code civil*:

> "A person who causes damage to another when suffering from mental disturbance is nevertheless bound to repair the damage caused".

In the annotated case, the Cour de cassation found that Article 489–2 C.civ. does not create an autonomous liability regime for mentally disturbed persons; instead, it subjects those persons to the general liability regime of Articles 1382–1383 C.civ.[257] As a result, the liability of the mentally disturbed person will arise, under the general regime, if the conduct of that person is unlawful (i.e. constitutes a fault in the objective sense of the word). On that basis, in the annotated case, the insurance policy (which dated from before the introduction of Article 489–2 C.civ.) was held to be applicable insofar as it covered liability under Articles 1382–1383 C.civ. in general. For the Cour de cassation, by enacting Article 489–2 C.civ., the French legislature wanted to remove subjective imputability altogether as a prerequisite for civil liability[258] on the part of the persons who have acted "when suffering from mental disturbance" and, in so doing, wanted to submit those persons to the same liability regime as normal persons placed in the same circumstances.[259] So far, it is not yet clear whether Article 489–2 also subjects mentally disturbed persons to liability in the special types of cases where a certain level of culpability is required by law. The prevailing opinion seems to reject that view, since, in those type of cases, the higher level of culpability implies that liability becomes a kind of "private sanction" (peine privée) which would require "moral responsibility (imputabilité)".[260]

(2) As regards the types of mental disorder which fall within its scope, the Cour de cassation has interpreted Article 489–2 C.civ. narrowly. Only conduct that occurs under the influence of mental disturbance in the strict sense is covered, and not the results of a brief lapse of consciousness due to, for instance, a heart attack.[261] *A fortiori* Article 489–2 does not apply to the consequences of physical disabilities without mental implications (e.g., sickness, paralysis precluding one to act etc.).[262]

---

[256] Act 68–5 of 3 January 1968, JO, 4 January 1968, 114: see *supra*, 3.2.1. under a).

[257] The annotated case was followed in later judgments: see Cass. civ. 1re, 17 May 1982, Gaz.Pal. 1983.Jur.185, annotated by P. Jourdain; Cass. civ. 2e, 24 June 1987, Bull.civ. 1987.II.78.

[258] See the reference to the statement of the Minister of Justice, supra 3.2.1. under a).

[259] Viney and Jourdain, *Conditions* at 533–4, para. 589.

[260] Ibid. at 535–6, para. 590.

[261] Cass. civ. 2e, 4 February 1981, Bull.civ. 1981.II.15, D 1983.Jur.1, annotated by P. Gaudrat, JCP 1981.II.19656. See also *supra* **3.F.11.**, Note (2).

[262] Viney and Jourdain, *Conditions* at 537, para. 591.

Cass. civ. 2e, 12 December 1984 [263]   **3.F.19.**
SAMDA v. *Molina*

<small>DISCERNMENT NOT RELEVANT</small>

A violent schoolmate

A 7-year old boy who injures a schoolmate by pushing him violently commits a fault for which he is liable, without any need to prove that he was able to appreciate the consequences of his actions.

Facts: While playing tag in a schoolyard Jean-Claude Sabatier, a 7-year old boy, pushed a schoolmate, Nicolas Desprats, who fell and struck a bench, causing a bursting of his spleen and a haemorrhage.

Held: The court of first instance dismissed the claim against the minor. The court of appeal held the minor liable. The Cour de cassation upheld the judgment of the court of appeal.

Judgment: "The judgment of the court of appeal is attacked on the following grounds: . . . in failing to try to determine whether Jean-Claude Sabatier had the ability to appreciate the consequences of his act, . . . the court of appeal applied Article 1382 C.civ. incorrectly;

However, the court of appeal found that Jean-Claude Sabatier pushed Nicolas Desprats against a bench in the schoolyard, with such violence that this caused a bursting of the spleen and internal bleeding.

Having regard to those statements, the court of appeal, which was not required to verify whether Jean-Claude Sabatier was capable of appreciating the consequences of his actions, established the fault committed by him."

Notes

(1) The annotated judgment came in the aftermath of five judgments rendered on 9 May 1984, in which the Cour de cassation made it clear that the notion of fault has an objective meaning only. In other words, [264] fault is a purely social concept and not a moral one. In one of the judgments of May 1984, reproduced below, [265] the Cour de cassation held, in connection with the *contributory fault* of a child of five years who was fatally injured in an accident, that the child had committed a fault in spite of his lack of discernment (*manque de discernement*). The question remained whether the same solution applied where a minor allegedly committed a fault, not as a victim but as the wrongdoer. The Court gave an affirmative answer in the annotated judgment: when the wrongdoer is a minor, discernment is not needed for liability to arise under Articles 1382–1383 C.civ.

(2) Despite the foregoing interpretation, liability under Articles 1382–1383 C.civ. requires that the *fault* of the child is established, i.e. an act which is objectively unlawful (*illicite*). [266] And, indeed, in the annotated judgment, the Cour de cassation emphasizes that the child had pushed his schoolmate in a particularly violent way. The

---

[263] Bull.civ. 1984.II.137. Translation by A. Dumas-Eymard.
[264] See A. Tunc and G. Viney, "L'évolution du droit français de la responsabilité civile" (1992) 14 Jour. Soc. lég. comp. 123.
[265] *Infra*, **7.F.3.**
[266] J. Huet, Chronique, (1986) RTDciv. 120.

judgments referred to above confirm that, subject to special statutory provisions,[267] the concept of fault, whether in the context of "principal" negligence or contributory negligence, is *objective,* consisting in the mere existence of socially unacceptable behaviour (*un comportement socialement défectueux*)[268] As a consequence, in order to find that a minor was at fault, even when he or she is an infant, it suffices to show that he or she did not act as "a prudent and circumspect individual placed in the same circumstances" (*un individu prudent et avisé placé dans les mêmes circonstances*) would have done.[269] An infant is a child of very young age who has not reached the age of reason, normally 7 years of age.[270] French law has thus moved from the complete irresponsibility (or immunity) of children of young age to their complete responsibility.[271] In quite a number of cases however, it remains difficult to assess whether a young child acted in an objectively illicit, that is an "abnormal" way. As seen in the next annotated case, age is not fully disregarded in the assessment of the unlawfulness of a child's conduct.

(3) The 1984 judgments of the Cour de cassation did not come as a surprise, as they were fully in line with a development set in motion by the enactment of Art. 489–2 C.civ. in 1968, dealt with in the preceding case. And indeed, after the introduction of Article 489–2 in the Code civil, many argued that the same rule should be applied by analogy to minor children, especially once the Cour de cassation decided, on 20 July 1976,[272] that Article 489–2 applied to all mentally ill persons, whether adults or minors. Accordingly, the 1984 judgments, by eliminating discernment (*discernement*) as an element in the assessment of fault on the part of minors, could be seen as a logical step towards the further objectivization of fault. However, discernment remains a requirement for fault under the criminal law.[273]

(4) The 1984 judgments of the Cour de cassation have been criticized in legal writing, particularly insofar as they removed responsibility (*imputabilité*) from the assessment of the contributory negligence of young children. Viney and Jourdain write:[274]

"Is this reasonable solution, intended by the legislature in 1968 for damages caused by mentally ill persons (and other persons suffering from "mental disturbance"), equally justified for damages caused by very young children not yet endowed with sufficient discernment to understand the consequences of their actions? One may seriously doubt it in view of the role of the requirement of responsibility (*imputabilité*). That requirement in fact conveys the feelings of comprehension for the individual held to be responsible for the damage. Although this requirement must logically disappear whenever the interests of the victim prevail—which is certainly the case for acts committed under the influence of insanity—it is not at all certain that, in the conflict

[267] Such as Article 3 of the *Loi Badinter* in respect of contributory negligence on the part of children of less than 16 years. See *infra*, Chapter VI, 6.2.1.B. and Chapter VII, 7.1.1.

[268] Cf. H. Mazeaud, "La faute objective et la responsabilité sans faute" D 1985.Chron.13.

[269] *Les grands arrêts* at 498. See also the excerpt from a statement by the Minister of Justice, quoted *supra*, 3.2.1.

[270] Viney and Jourdain, *Conditions* at 537–8, para. 592–1; Le Tourneau and Cadiet at 199- 200, para. 622. In one of the judgments of 9 May 1984, the contributory fault of a 3-year old child was involved: see *infra*, **7.F.3.**

[271] In the words of G. Viney, Chronique, JCP 1985.I.3138.

[272] Cass. civ. 1re, 20 July 1976, Bull.civ. 1976.I.218.

[273] See Article L. 122–1 of new *Code pénal* (Penal Code). See also G. Viney, Chronique JCP 1993.I.3727, referring to case law confirming the principle that "the criminal decision binds the civil law" (*l'autorité de la chose jugée au criminel sur le civil*).

[274] Viney and Jourdain, *Conditions* at 542–3, para. 593–1. The judgment of 19 February 1997 referred to in the quotation is reproduced *infra*, Chapter V, **5.F.24.**

between concern that victims should be compensated and the desire to preserve infants from the consequences of a civil judgment against them, the balance will still tilt the victims' way. This is all the more true since these victims can turn to the natural guarantors of minors, their parents, whose liability has in fact been considerably reinforced by a judgment of 19 February 1997. If one adds to these considerations the fact that a judgment finding a young child personally liable, which is of little use to the victims since they will generally be faced by insolvent persons, may have effects that are psychologically damaging to the children and that are in any event contrary to the protective spirit of our laws concerning incapable minors, one easily understands the reservations of predominant legal thinking towards the principle of liability of the infant."

As the authors point out, the liability of minors must be viewed in relation to the liability of their parents as guardians under Article 1384(4) C.civ.[275]

Cass. civ. 2e, 4 July 1990[276]   **3.F.20.**
Lacouture v. *Société Pyrotechnique Industrielle et agricole*

NO FAULT BECAUSE OF LACK OF DISCERNMENT

Child wounded by explosion

A child of nine years, who was not warned of the risk of injury involved in a course of action and could normally have believed that no injurious event would occur, was not at fault.

Facts: A nine-year old child was wounded by a plastic object, part of a firework, left on the beach which exploded when the child picked it up. The parents of the child sued the person with whom the child was at the time. That person argued in defence that the child himself was also at fault.

Held: The court of appeal dismissed the allegation that the child had committed a fault and held the person accompanying the child fully liable. The Cour de cassation upheld the judgment.

Judgment: "The contested judgment is criticized [for having denied the contributory fault of the child] . . . on the basis that he did not commit a fault, having regard to the fact that he did not have the discernment needed to appreciate the danger. Yet, [the appellant contends that] the court of appeal had found that the [child] had handled the device which he had picked up in the area where [the fireworks] had been launched and had brought it close to glowing embers. The court of appeal made an incorrect application of Article 1382 C.civ. by not drawing from those findings the conclusion that the victim had committed a fault by negligence.

However, the contested judgment found that the child, having collected a plastic object in the form of a small bottle without a wick, had not been warned by [the accompanying person] of the dangerous nature of pyrotechnic devices, and that he would not normally have understood that an explosion would follow since the fuses had already been used.

On the basis of those arguments alone, the court of appeal made no error in law in coming to the conclusion that the victim had not committed a fault."

Notes

(1) Although age is in principle considered to be an internal circumstance, which is therefore not taken into account when comparing the conduct of an individual tortfeasor with

[275] *Infra*, **5.F.24.** and notes thereafter.
[276] Bull.civ. 1990.II.84. Translation by the authors.

the standard of a reasonable person acting under the same circumstances,[277] the case law of the Cour de cassation is not always consistent in that respect. Since the 1970s, and thus before the judgments of 1984 referred to above,[278] there was already a tendency to accept age, in case of both the young and the old, as an "element of inferiority" (*facteur d'infériorité*) which the courts would factor into the assessment in order to make the standard more concrete; courts would thus compare the conduct of the defendant child against that of a reasonable person of the same age rather than an average adult.[279] The annotated judgment is an example of such case law. Moreover, it was rendered after the 1984 judgments, where lack of *discernment* was held not to prevent young children from being found at fault within the meaning of Articles 1382–1383 C.civ.[280]

In the annotated judgment the child was older than seven years (and had therefore attained the age of reason), but in another judgment (prior to 1984 however) the Cour de cassation upheld a decision which followed the same approach as the annotated judgment and applied an *in concreto* standard of assessment to the conduct of a 3-year old child.[281]

(2) The fact that the age of infants and of adolescents—and also of elderly persons[282]—is sometimes taken into account in the standard of the "reasonable person acting in the same circumstances" does not mean, of course, that culpability as such is or remains a condition of fault. However, incorporating age into the objective standard often leads to the same result as including culpability as a condition of liability: in both cases, the child is not liable, under the former approach since the child had not acted "unlawfully", and under the latter since the child had not acted "culpably".

In any event, the case law of the Cour de cassation lacks clarity. Le Tourneau and Cadiet, who regret this state of affairs, observe with references to recent case law and legal writing:[283]

"The real significance of this case law is far from clear. Whilst certain later judgments [that is after 1984] seem to go on referring to discernment in order *to qualify the fault of the child* . . . or to *exculpate adults* accompanying the child . . . other judgments confirm that lack of discernment is irrelevant . . . With hindsight we must regret that this case law distorts the notion of fault so much".

---

[277] *Supra*, **3.F.10.**, Note (1).
[278] *Supra*, **3.F.19.**, Note (1).
[279] Viney and Jourdain, *Conditions* at 355–7, para. 467. The same trend is present as regards disability and illness, but not as concerns psychological or pathological deficiencies: ibid. at 357–9, para. 468–9. See also *supra*, **3.F.11,** Note (1).
[280] One of these judgments, relating to contributory fault, is found *infra*, **7.F.3.**
[281] Cass. civ. 2e, 29 April 1976, JCP 1978.II.18793, note by N. Dejean de la Bâtie.
[282] See the judgments quoted by Viney and Jourdain, *Conditions* at 356–7, para. 467.
[283] Le Tourneau and Cadiet at 199, para. 621.

Involuntary acts

Cass. civ. 2e, 3 July 1991[284]   **3.F.21.**
Lignon v. Avril

INVOLUNTARY ACT

Inexperienced player

An involuntary gesture causing injury to another does not, in and of itself, constitute fault within the meaning of Articles 1382–1383 C.civ.

Facts: In the course of an improvised volleyball match, the defendant fell and accidentally injured the plaintiff.

Held: The court of appeal allowed the claim for damages. The Cour de cassation quashed the judgment of the court of appeal

Judgment: "The judgment [of the court of appeal] found that, while falling down in the course of a volleyball game, [the defendant] incidentally kicked and injured [the plaintiff], who claimed reparation for the injury sustained. In order to hold [the defendant] liable, the judgment merely stated that he had recognized that he was 'unable to perceive distances' and that, taking account of the informal nature of the game, he should have told the other players of his inability. He had been negligent in failing to do so.

In so holding the court of appeal did not provide a legal basis for its decision. Even though it accepted that [the defendant's] action was involuntary, it failed to establish that [the defendant's] behaviour was wrongful [or] that it was in breach of the rules of the game."

Note

The annotated judgment is not the only decision where an involuntary and unfortunate movement that causes harm to another is found not to be negligent within the meaning of Articles 1382–1383 C.civ.[285] That does not necessarily mean that culpability is a condition of fault, since the outcome can also be explained on the basis of the objective notion of unlawfulness, in that a reasonable person may very well act clumsily or awkwardly.[286] Nonetheless, it comes very close to a finding of lack of culpability, in the sense of lack of free will or absence of awareness of the risk of harm.

---

[284] Bull.civ. 1991.II.111. Translation by the authors.
[285] See, another sports case, Cass. civ. 2e, 4 May 1988, Bull.civ. 1988.II.56, where the Cour de cassation held that the fact that the victim had been kicked in the heat of the action did not amount to fault, since it had not been proved that the kick was a voluntary movement or that the conduct was in breach of the rules of the game.
[286] See Grenoble, 22 January 1979, D 1979.IR.346, with note by C. Larroumet where a mountain-climber was held not to have committed a blunder (*une maladresse*) under the difficult circumstances of the situation.

339

3.2.3.B. GERMAN LAW

Introductory Note

As explained earlier,[287] in German law three notions—*Tatbestand, Rechtswidrigkeit* and *Verschulden*—play a role in determining liability for one's own conduct. It has also been pointed out that, under the modern Conduct Theory, the concept of unlawfulness (*Rechtswidrigkeit*)[288] encompasses much of the objective element of fault[289] and that culpability (*Verschulden*) is understood to refer only to the more subjective element of responsibility (*Zurechenbarkeit* or *Vorwerfbarkeit*, also *subjektive* or *innere Fahrlässigkeit*).[290]

Under the Conduct Theory,[291] in the case of children culpability comes down to "whether the defendant, on the ground of his minority (§§ 827, 828 BGB), was unable to realize that his conduct was unlawful and that he might have to answer for the resulting damages, or whether the defendant's culpability was excluded by such individual factors as his inability to appreciate the objective circumstances which rendered the situation dangerous". The first limb of this statement (referring to §§ 827 and 828 BGB) relates to the capacity to be culpable (*Verschuldensfähigkeit*), drawing a distinction between full incapacity (first sentence of § 827 and § 828(1)) and limited incapacity (mainly § 828(2)).

Like French law, German law distinguishes between intentional and negligent behaviour. In contradistinction to French law, however, German law knows many forms of intentional behaviour. Moreover, the significance of intentional behaviour depends on the statutory provision concerned. Liability for conduct *contra bonos mores*, at § 826 BGB, thus requires that the *harm* be *caused* intentionally. It is not sufficient that the conduct of the wrongdoer was intentional: the harm must have been intended as well, although the infliction of harm need not have been the sole purpose of the conduct and the wrongdoer need not have had a precise idea of the scope of the harm, the chain of causation or even the identity of the victim.[292] Conversely, under § 823(1) and § 839(1) BGB, liability will be incurred for both intentional (*vorsätzlich*) and negligent (*fahrlässig*) conduct. Under these provisions, conduct is intentional if the interference with a protected interest was deliberate; intention to cause harm is not required. Furthermore, under § 823(2) BGB, it depends upon the protective norm (*Schutzgesetz*) in question whether intention is required and, if so, in what form. Since many protective norms are found in criminal law, which usually prohibits intentional conduct only, § 823(2) BGB will not often result in liability for negligent fault.[293]

The question then becomes what "intention" (*Vorsatz*) precisely entails. It is commonly accepted that it comprises an element of knowledge (*das Wissen*) and an element of will

---

[287] *Supra*, 3.2.1. under b).

[288] *Supra*, 3.2.2.B.

[289] I.e. behaving either deliberately (*vorsätzlich*) or without the care generally required in society (*fahrlässig*).

[290] P. Schlechtriem, *Schuldrecht, Besonderer Teil*, 4th edn. (Tübingen: Mohr, 1995) at 355, para. 781.

[291] See the excerpt from Zweigert and Kötz, *supra*, 3.2.1. under b).

[292] Larenz/Canaris at 454; J. Limpens, R.M. Kruithof and A. Meinertzhagen-Limpens, "Liability for One's Own Act" in *International Encyclopedia of Comparative Law—Vol. XI/2: Torts* (Tübingen: Mohr, 1979) at 30, para. 60.

[293] Larenz/Canaris at 376 and 445–6.

(*das Wollen*).[294] As regards the latter, a distinction is commonly drawn between *dolus directus* (*direkter Vorsatz*) and *dolus eventualis* (*bedingter Vorsatz*).[295] Markesinis describes these notions as follows:[296]

> "*(a) Dolus directus.* It can come in two forms, e.g. I aim at a child standing behind a house window and I kill it. *Alternatively,* I set fire to a house in order to burn it *knowing* that a young child is inside and knowing (and accepting) that the inevitable result of my burning the house will be the death of the child.
>
> *(b) Dolus eventualis.* For instance, I hit a man on the head with the intention of injuring him; but I also realise that he *may* die as a result of the blow. Despite this knowledge, I persist with my action."

The borderline between intentional and negligent behaviour (including gross, ordinary and slight negligence)[297] is not easy to draw; in particular, it is often difficult to distinguish *dolus eventualis* from gross negligence (*grobe Fahrlässigkeit*). Thus, for the purposes of § 826 BGB, it is accepted that *dolus eventualis* is present when the tortfeasor acts recklessly or at random.[298] Moreover, wilful blindness[299] on the part of the wrongdoer is, as a general rule, equated to *Vorsatz*.[300] Furthermore, certain legislative provisions equate *dolus* and gross negligence.[301] Contractual exclusion of liability for gross negligence (*grobe Fahrlässigkeit*) is generally prohibited.[302] The notion of gross negligence is defined in well-established BGH case law.[303]

Capacity of mentally disturbed persons and young children to act culpably

The BGB provides explicitly at § 827 that persons cannot incur liability for having caused harm to another if they were "in a condition of unconsciousness or mental illness (*krankhafter Störung der Geistestätigkeit*) that excludes the exercise of free will." In the second sentence of § 827 BGB, however, it is added that where a person has brought himself or herself temporarily into such a condition through his or her own fault, for instance by consuming alcohol, he or she is responsible for any damage unlawfully caused while in that condition, in the same way as if negligence were directly imputable to him or her.

§ 827 BGB has a broad scope, since it applies not only to the mentally ill, but also to persons who are in an inconscious state. On the basis of a comparative

---

[294] See Münchener-Hanau, § 276 at 825–30, para. 49–65, for a detailed analysis of both elements.

[295] See also Münchener-Hanau, § 276 at 830, para. 62–5, for references to legislative provisions requiring plan (*Absicht*) or deceit (*Arglist*).

[296] Markesinis at 72.

[297] Ibid.

[298] "*ins Blaue hinein*": see BGH, 17 September 1985, NJW 1986, 180.

[299] I.e. simply closing his or her eyes (*geradezu die Augen verschließen*).

[300] Larenz/Canaris at 454.

[301] See e.g. Art. 34 GG which stipulates, with regard to the breach of duty by a person in the exercise of public office, that the right of recourse against the official is preserved in the event of intention or gross negligence; § 61 of the *Gesetz über den Versicherungsvertrag* (Law on Insurance Contracts), pursuant to which an insurer is relieved of its obligations if the insured person has caused the damage for which he or she is ensured either intentionally or by gross negligence.

[302] See § 11(7) of the *Gesetz zur Regelung des Rechts der Allgemeinen Geschäftsbedingungen* (AGBG, Law on General Terms).

[303] See e.g. BGH, 8 October 1991, NJW 1992, 316 (with regard to a credit institution not examining, when acquiring a bill of exchange from a casino, whether the underlying claim is not in breach of public morality).

analysis of the laws of EU Member States, von Bar summarizes the legal situation as follows:[304]

> "In practice the most important example of the liability of 'unconscious' persons is found in road accident law, where a motorist suffers an epileptic fit, falls asleep due either to fatigue or medicine, or suddenly loses control of the vehicle as a result of a heart attack or stroke. Where the driver knew of the risk, or would have known had he exercised the care expected of a driver, he is liable for fault."

Accordingly, § 827 BGB applies only to a condition of unconsiousness that arises in circumstances which could not be anticipated.

Furthermore, at § 828, the BGB also deals with the capacity of minors to incur liability, an issue that is explored in the case reproduced below. § 828 BGB makes a distinction between a young child (infant) who is less than seven years old (at § 828(1) BGB) and a minor who is seven years or older (at § 828(2) BGB). While the fomer is not responsible for any injury inflicted upon another, the latter may be held liable unless "when he engaged in the course of conduct that led to injury, he did not have the requisite understanding to be aware of his responsibility".[305]

In cases where no liability arises because the person who caused the injury is not capable of incurring liability, for one of the reasons mentioned in §§ 827, 828(1) or 828(2) BGB (see above), that person may still be under a duty to make good the harm, on grounds of equity (*aus Billigkeitsgrunden*), pursuant to § 829 BGB. However, that Article provides that compensation will be ordered only where reparation cannot be obtained from a third party charged with the duty of supervision and where, "insofar as, according to the circumstances, in particular according to the relative positions of the parties, equity requires indemnification, and [the person to whom §§ 827 or 828 BGB applies] is not thereby deprived of the means which he needs for his own maintenance . . . and for the fulfilment of his statutory duties to furnish maintenance to others." It should be noted that, since in the case of minors reparation will often be available from the parents or another person exercising authority (pursuant to § 832 BGB[306]), § 829 BGB will therefore more easily find application in the case of unconscious or mentally ill persons.[307] Finally, as seen in greater detail in Chapter VII, § 829 BGB can also apply, in cases of contributory negligence, to reduce compensation where the victim fell within the classes of persons mentioned in §§ 827–828 BGB.[308]

---

[304] von Bar I at 116, para 94 (references omitted). See *supra*, for German law, **3.G.12.**
[305] § 828(2) BGB is also applicable to deaf mute persons.
[306] See *infra*, Chapter V, 5.2., Introductory Note under b).
[307] von Bar I at 113, para. 89.
[308] See *infra*, Chapter VII, **7.G.7.** In that case, the victim was a 5-year old child, who was and therefore fully incapable of being liable, pursuant to § 828(1) BGB.

BGH, 28 February 1984[309]   **3.G.22.**

Insight of children

Children with candles

*Minors who have a general understanding (*Einsichtsfähigkeit*) that their conduct may cause danger may be held fully liable even though they were unable to moderate their conduct according to their understanding (*Steuerungsfähigkeit*).*

Facts: The defendants, two 10-year old boys, were playing in a hay-loft. In order to illuminate the room, they had bought candles, and had been offered matches by another boy. They tried to use molten wax from the candle to fix a lighted candle on a rafter. They did not succeed; the candle fell down several times and set fire to hay on the floor. The children failed in their efforts to put out the fire, and the whole shed burnt down, including agricultural tools that were stored there. The farmer to whom the shed and the tools belonged sued the two boys, who were both covered by compulsory insurance. According to the plaintiff, the boys had the insight required to be aware of their responsibility for their conduct.

Held: The court of first instance and the court of appeal rejected the claim. The BGH reversed the decision of the lower courts and found that the defendants were liable.

Judgment: "According to established case law, a general understanding that a course of conduct may create some danger is sufficient; the law does not further require that the minor had the capacity to envisage the legal and economic consequences of his conduct in practice [references omitted]. In contradistinction to the position in criminal law—where the ability to control [one's conduct] is taken into account, in addition to discernment, when examining responsibility—the BGH, in matters of civil liability, is guided in particular by the fact that, according to the wording of § 828(2) BGB, only the discernment of the minor can be examined (ie his intellectual ability to recognize the danger created by his conduct and to be aware of his responsibility for the consequences of such conduct) and not the individual capacity of the minor to behave in accordance with such insight. Liability under civil law to compensate for injury is subject to criteria other than those applicable under criminal law . . . If, according to his individual intellectual development, a minor possesses the ability to discern the wrongful nature of his conduct—presumed by the law in the case of children as from their seventh birthday—then he is fully liable, insofar as he also acted culpably within the meaning of § 276 BGB. On the other hand, if he demonstrates that he lacked discernment, then for that reason alone he is not liable to answer for the consequences of his conduct. Civil law—unlike criminal law—does not provide for reduced responsibility. Under civil law, the minor is therefore made liable for the damage he has caused to a far greater extent than he is made answerable for his conduct under criminal law. Under the law of civil liability, the need for an all-inclusive assessment is stronger, lest the standard of care necessary in society—as required by § 276 BGB—breaks down. *For this reason, personal shortcomings can be taken into account to only a limited extent in assessing a person's capacity to incur civil liability for wrongful (and culpable) conduct. Liability should not depend on whether the individual tortfeasor is sufficiently mature to live up to the average expectations of suitable behaviour.* In this respect, having regard to the purpose of the law, the victim cannot be held responsible for the risk of damage."

---

[309] NJW 1984, 1958.

Notes

(1) The annotated judgment confirms an earlier BGH judgment of 10 March 1970.[310] Both judgments show a tendency to readily accept that a minor (aged seven years or older) is capable of insight: it is sufficient for the minor to have a general understanding of the fact that his or her conduct may cause danger. Discernment is enough, that is the intellectual capacity to recognize that a course of conduct may create danger and to be aware of one's responsibility for the consequences of such conduct (*Einsichtsfähigkeit*). It is not required, in addition to discernment, that the minor should also be able to conduct himself or herself in accordance with that insight (*Steuerungsfähigkeit*).

(2) Consequently, as the BGH explained in the annotated judgment, minors are subject to a heavier liability under civil law than under criminal law. This discrepancy has given rise to criticism and has led to constitutional challenges.[311] In a judgment of 13 August 1998, the *Bundesverfassungsgericht* rejected those claims.[312]

Involuntary acts

BGH, 12 February 1963[313]   **3.G.23.**

INVOLUNTARY INTERFERENCE

Hostile bowlers

The plaintiff must prove that the defendant committed a tortious act, that is conduct which the defendant was able to control and direct. Accordingly, it is for the plaintiff to show that the conduct of the defendant did not result from physical constraint or occur as a reflex response to external force.

Facts: Whilst playing bowls, the plaintiff's brother struck the defendant who had made an offensive remark following a discussion about who should play first. As he was struck, the defendant released the ball that was in his hand. The ball hit the plaintiff in the face. According to the defendant, the ball was released because of a reflex movement upon being hit.

Held: The court of first instance dismissed the claim of the plaintiff. The court of appeal reversed the judgment of the court of first instance. The BGH reinstated the decision of the court of first instance.

Judgment: "The court of appeal accepted that [the plaintiff's brother] struck the defendant in the region of the stomach and that the ball was put in motion as a result, which led to the plaintiff being injured. However, the court could not establish whether the defendant threw the ball voluntarily or whether he did so in an involuntary reflex movement . . .

The court of appeal found it problematic to ascertain upon whom the duty rests to prove whether a harmful act was voluntary or involuntary. In its unanimous view, it is for the plaintiff to prove

---

[310] BGH, 10 March 1970, NJW 1970, 1038, VersR 1970, 467.

[311] See e.g. OLG Celle, 26 May 1989, JZ 1990, 294. See also LG Dessau, 25 September 1996, VersR 1997, 242 and, concerning the latter decision, H.-J. Ahrens, "Existenzvernichtung Jugendlicher durch Deliktshaftung?— Zu einer Fehlentscheidung des LG Dessau" VersR 1997, 1064.

[312] NJW 1998, 3557. See on this problem further K. Goecke, *Die unbegrenzte Haftung Minderjähriger im Deliktsrecht* (Berlin: Duncker & Humblot, 1997) at 26 ff.

[313] BGHZ 39, 103.

that the conditions for his claim are made out. However, several counter-examples can be found . . . to show that that principle is not without exceptions. For one, it is up to the tortfeasor to establish the existence of a ground of justification or to prove that he did not have the capacity to commit a culpable act (*schuldunfähig*) or to have liability imputed to him (*unzurechnungsfähig*); indeed, the law considers that a person is normally capable of committing a culpable act and incurring liability for it. The general principle of the law of evidence comes to bear in these instances: it is for the person who seeks to rely on a state of fact which deviates from what is normal to prove that that state of fact actually occurred . . .

Accordingly, the court of appeal came to the conclusion that, in the present case, the defendant had to prove that he acted merely involuntarily. As he was unable to do so, the presumption must be that he acted voluntarily . . .

The [defendant] is right in attacking this assessment . . .

The first condition for a claim in tort to succeed . . . is the occurrence of conduct within the meaning of § 823 BGB, that is human action which is undertaken consciously and determined by free will (*ein menschliches Tun, das der Bewußtseinskontrolle und Willenslenkung underliegt*) and which is therefore controllable [reference omitted]. It follows that movements occurring under physical constraint or as a result of an involuntary reflex response to an external force do not amount to such conduct.

The court of appeal misjudged the allocation of the burden of proof when it based its judgment on what the normal situation is and what deviates from it. Surely, life experience may be significant where . . . it points to what would normally have happened. However, inferences from life experience constitute only one of the means of proof to convince the judge of what really happened. They do not count as legal presumptions or rules of law resulting in a shifting of the burden of proof [reference omitted]."

Notes

(1) The judgment is reproduced here for two reasons. First, it emphasizes that, in order for an act to be culpable within the meaning of § 823 BGB, it must have been committed voluntarily and not, as was alleged by the defendant in the annotated case, as a result of an involuntary reflex movement. Secondly, the judgment reviews the basic principles regarding the burden of proof. As a basic principle (in tort law as elsewhere), it is for the plaintiff to prove that the factual conditions for the defendant to be liable are met, including the fact that the defendant was at fault in causing the harm. In many cases, however, that basic principle suffers from exceptions in that the burden of proof of certain facts is shifted onto the defendant, e.g. by presuming that the defendant was at fault in certain types of accidents.[314] Even where the onus of proof remains on the victim, German law has other means to make the task of the victim easier, including *prima facie* proof (*Anscheinsbeweis*). Thus a victim who cannot establish facts which constitute direct evidence of the defendant's fault may still succeed if he or she proves other facts which, in the light of general experience as to how events unfold, justify the conclusion that the

[314] Zweigert and Kötz at 650 with references to German, French and other legal systems. More specifically on German law, see H. Kötz, *Deliktsrecht*, 7th edn. (Neuwied: Luchterhand, 1996) at 103–105, para. 253–259. For an example of how the rules of evidence under German law can be used to shift the burden of proof onto the defendant and thereby increase the chances that the defendant will be found liable, see the discussion of product liability under § 823 BGB, *infra*, Chapter VI, **6.G.24.** and notes (4) and (6) thereafter. The rules of evidence concerning causation are discussed *infra*, Chapter IV, **4.G.19.** and notes thereafter. Furthermore, specific rules concerning the burden of proof also apply under § 831 BGB (liability for injury caused by employees), *infra*, Chapter V, 5.1.3. under and under § 830 BGB (multiple tortfeasors and multiple causes), *infra*, Chapter IV, 4.4.1. under a) and **4.G.43.**

defendant failed to exercise due care under the circumstances.[315] Nevertheless, the burden of proof is not reversed, since the defendant does not have to bring positive evidence that he behaved carefully to defeat a *prima facie* proof by the victim; it is sufficient if he shows that there was something atypical and extraordinary in the circumstances of the case, so as to suggest an alternative explanation for the accident.[316]

(2) In the annotated judgment, the BGH reversed the decision of the court of appeal as regards the allocation of the burden of proof. The court of appeal had started by noting that, although as a rule the victim bears the onus of proving that the conditions of liability are fulfilled, the law of tort contains many exceptions to that rule. There is a common thread, to those exceptions, namely that the person who seek to rely on a state of fact that deviates from the normal situation must establish that state of fact. For instance, it is up to the defendant to establish: (i) the existence of a ground of justification, (ii) the impossibility to impute a *culpa* to him or her, (iii) the impossibility of holding him or her responsible for his or her conduct (since the absence of justification, *culpa* and responsibility, are the norm). According to the court of appeal, the annotated case fits within that common thread, since the defendant alleged that he acted under the influence of an unavoidable compulsion (a reflex response) and therefore involuntarily. The BGH disagreed, not with the underlying reasoning of the court of appeal, but with its application in the specific case of involuntary conduct. According to the BGH, it is incumbent upon the plaintiff to show that the conduct of the defendant came within the ambit of the definition of "tortious conduct" under § 823 BGB, namely human action which is undertaken consciously and determined by free will, and therefore controllable. If the plaintiff does not succeed in convincing the court that the defendant behaved voluntarily, then the plaintiff fails to discharge the applicable burden of proof and the claim must therefore fail.

3.2.3.C. ENGLISH LAW

Introductory Note

(1) As explained earlier, under the English tort of negligence (or other torts where an element of negligence is involved), the applicable standard for assessing whether a particular defendant has acted negligently is "objective and impersonal in the sense that it eliminates the personal equation and is independent of the idiosyncrasies of the particular person whose conduct is in question".[317] The standard of care refers to a person of ordinary prudence, acting in circumstances similar to those under which the defendant was acting. It follows that the judge must strike a balance between the magnitude of the risk of injury—that is the likelihood that injury will result—and the burden upon the defendant to prevent injury from occurring.[318]

Beyond that, the question remains whether a defendant must also have acted culpably. The answer to that question will depend on the tort in question, and more specifically on

---

[315] See also *supra*, **3.G.14.** for an example where the plaintiff relied on *prima facie* proof.

[316] Zweigert and Kötz at 651–2. The authors point out that this kind of proof is similar to the doctrine of *res ipsa loquitur* in English law and refer to the leading case of *Scott* v. *London & St. Katherine Docks Co.* (1865) 3 H&C 596 (on appeal to the Exchequer Chamber). *Anscheinsbeweis* may also be used to establish causation: see *infra*, Chapter IV, **4.G.19.** and notes thereafter.

[317] Rogers as quoted *supra*, 3.2.1. under c).

[318] Ibid. and also *supra*, **3.E.15.** and notes thereafter.

whether the tort requires negligence or a mental state, such as an intention to deceive or to injure. As in other legal systems, culpability is discussed particularly with regard to persons of unsound mind and young children; the two judgments reproduced below deal with those two classes of persons. As appears from the first case,[319] even where the tort at issue—there trespass to the person—does not require culpability, it must nevertheless be established that the allegedly tortious act was voluntary.[320] The second case concerns 15-year old schoolgirls, and it shows that age is not regarded as a characteristic that is personal to the defendant but rather as a "characteristic of humanity at [the young person's] stage of development and in that sense normal", and therefore as a factor to be taken into account in the objective "standard of ordinariness".[321]

(2) When it comes to the seriousness of fault under English law, it must be emphasized that notions used in German or French law such as *Vorsatz* or *faute intentionnelle* cannot simply be equated with "intention" or "intentional fault" under English law.[322] "Intention" in English law refers to conscious and deliberate behaviour: intention within that meaning is a condition of certain specific torts (eg trespass to land, trespass to goods, defamation), but those torts do not require any intention to cause harm to a person or to property.[323] The common law notion of "malice" comes closest to *Vorsatz* or *faute intentionnelle*. But malice is also a rather variable notion, the content of which may again differ depending on the type of tort involved:[324]

"What constitutes malice is entirely dependent on the context in which the word is used. Malice may be synonymous with intention; 'a wrongful act done intentionally without just cause or excuse.' A pleading of malice may be a mere formality as in libel where it is common to plead that the publication is 'malicious' albeit no proof of malice is required of the plaintiff and a defendant 'may be the publisher of a libel without a particle of malice or improper motive.' Malice in the popular sense imports some evil motive. A person acts maliciously when he acts out of spite, revenge and/or desire to cause hurt. Malice in that sense may be relevant in tort. In libel, the defences of fair comment and qualified privilege can be defeated by evidence of spite, of intent to abuse the privilege solely to harm the plaintiff, and not for its proper purpose. Conduct on the part of a neighbour may constitute unreasonable interference and thus nuisance because it is motivated by spite . . .

Where proof of malice is required in tort, in many instances it is defined more broadly than spite or overtly evil intent. Proof of any dishonest, irrelevant or improper motive will suffice. In malicious prosecution, for example, it is not necessary to show that the defendant acted out of hatred or dislike for the plaintiff, but simply that he instituted the proceedings for purposes other than the pursuit of justice."

[319] *Infra*, **3.E.24.**

[320] That is not the case where a person inflicted grievous injury in a condition of complete automatism. See *supra*, **3.E.17.**, where Leggatt LJ comes to the conclusion that a driver who was unaware of the disabling event which impaired his ability to drive "was in no way to blame, he was not negligent".

[321] *Infra*, **3.E.25.**

[322] von Bar II at 266, para. 24.

[323] The mental state of the defendant (in so far as it goes beyond that of one who is conscious of what he is doing and acts of his own free will) is relevant in a number of torts, whether as an element in the plaintiff's cause of action or as something that deprives a defendant of a defence that would otherwise be open to him. The position varies from tort to tort (thus e.g. under the tort of deceit, see *Derry v. Peck* (1889) 14 App. Cass. 337, HL, or under the tort of passing off, see *Spalding & Bros. v. A. W. Gamage Ltd.* (1915) 84 L.J. Ch. 449, under the tort of defamation, see *Clerk & Lindsell on Torts* at 1047–1056, para. 21–59 to 21–73 and at 1014–1016, para. 21–08 to 21–10). It is here that on e sees particularly clearly that English law still has a law of *torts* rather than a law of *tort*.

[324] *Clerk & Lindsell on Torts* at 28, para. 1–41 (references omitted).

Under English law, it is clear, however, that an evil motive alone cannot lead to liability in tort, save perhaps in one exceptional case, the anomalous tort of conspiracy;[325] likewise, if conduct is presumptively unlawful, a good motive will not exonerate the defendant.[326] This general rule was set out by the House of Lords in *Bradford Corporation* v. *Pickles* in relation to nuisance.[327] Likewise, save in a few exceptions, the English law of tort is not concerned with degrees of negligence, such as gross negligence. However, recklessness—indifference to the potentially injurious consequences of one's conduct or willingness to run the risk of those consequences—will generally be sufficient to establish liability in intentional torts, since remaining indifferent to a result is as culpable as deliberately seeking to achieve it.[328]

Queen's Bench Division[329]   **3.E.24.**
Morriss v. *Marsden*

UNSOUNDNESS OF MIND AND TRESPASS

Aggressive schizophrenic

A person who suffers from a mental disease but is aware the nature and quality of his or her actions is liable in trespass even though he or she did not know that what he or she was doing was wrong.

Facts: The defendant suffered from schizophrenia. He violently attacked the plaintiff, a hotel manager. After the defendant was found unfit to stand criminal trial, the plaintiff claimed damages. It was found that, although the defendant was aware of the nature and quality of his actions, his mental illness was such that he did not know that he was doing wrong.

Held: The defendant is liable.

Judgment: STABLE J: "The chief problem which this case raises can be compendiously, though not very accurately, formulated as: What degree of mental illness, if any, can constitute a defence to an action in tort, and in what circumstances? . . . So far as I know, it has never been decided . . .

Counsel for the plaintiff says in effect that where the action is an action of trespass in the highly technical sense, no averment either of negligence or intention is essential to support it. Counsel for the defendant, on the contrary, argues that, whatever the position may have been 150 or two hundred years ago, the whole trend of modern decisions is that in an action, whether it be founded on trespass or on case, negligence or intention must be averred. I cannot think that, if a person of unsound mind converts my property under a delusion that he is entitled to do it or that it was not property at all, that affords a defence. . . On the whole, I accept the view that an intention—i.e., a voluntary act, the mind prompting and directing the act which is relied on, as in this case, as the tortious act—must be averred and proved. For example, I think that, if a person in a condition of com-

---

[325] *Clerk & Lindsell on Torts* at 29, para. 1–42.
[326] Rogers at 55.
[327] *Bradford Corporation* v. *Pickles* [1895] AC 587, HL. In that case Lord Macnaghten said: "If the act, apart from motive, gives rise merely to damage without legal injury, the motive, however reprehensible it may be, will not supply that element" (at 601). The rule remains the general rule today "for better or worse", thus Rogers at 55 with a reference to H.C. Gutteridge, "Abuse of Rights" (1946) 5 Camb LJ 22.
[328] *Clerk & Lindsell on Torts* at 31, para. 1–45.
[329] [1952] 1 All ER 925.

plete automatism inflicted grievous injury, that would not be actionable. In the same way, if a sleep-walker inadvertently, without intention or without carelessness, broke a valuable vase, that would not be actionable . . .

The next matter to consider is whether, granted that the defendant knew the nature and quality of his act, it is a defence in this action that, owing to mental infirmity, he was incapable of knowing that his act was wrong. If the basis of liability be that it depends, not on the injury to the victim, but on the culpability of the wrongdoer, there is considerable force in the argument that it is, but I have come to the conclusion that knowledge of wrongdoing is an immaterial averment, and that, where there is the capacity to know the nature and quality of the act, that is sufficient although the mind directing the hand that did the wrong was diseased."

Notes

(1) There is little English authority as to the liability of persons of unsound mind for torts committed by them.[330] In any event, mental illness or disturbance certainly does not in and of itself provide immunity from liability in tort; it depends in each case on whether the defendant possessed the requisite state of mind for liability under the particular tort that he is alleged to have committed.[331] The annotated case concerned an action in trespass.[332] The court had to choose between the position of the plaintiff, according to whom negligence or intention is not essential to support an action in trespass, and the position of the defendant, according to whom the overall trend of modern decisions points in the other direction. The judge steered a middle course: in his view, a person of unsound mind cannot raise as a defence to conversion that he or she was operating under a delusion that he or she was entitled to deal with the converted property; yet on the whole, intention must be proved, that is "a voluntary act, the mind prompting and directing the act".[333] As a telling example of an involuntary act, he refers to a sleepwalker who broke a valuable vase; that would not be actionable.

(2) When it comes to the tort of negligence, the precise impact of unsoundness of mind will depend on how it is factored into the standard of care: on the one hand, unsoundness of mind could be seen as an individual characteristic which must be disregarded, but on the other hand, it could be seen as a relevant characteristic, so that the conduct of a schizophrenic defendant would be measured against that of an average person having the same condition. In the latter case, negligence will probably not be found, unless the defendant was or ought to have been aware of that condition.[334] The same conclusion would result *a fortiori* if the defendant concerned retained no control whatsoever over his or her conduct, ie if the illness turned him or her into an automaton.[335]

[330] See Rogers at 839.
[331] Ibid. at 840.
[332] See, *supra*, Chapter I, **1.E.21.** The reference in the judgment to a person converting another person's property is to the tort of conversion—a species of action on the case, which arises where the defendant has appropriated the plaintiff's goods to his use or has otherwise wrongfully deprived the plaintiff of their use and possession.
[333] Compare with the similar German definition, *supra*, **3.G.23.** and Note (2) thereafter.
[334] See *supra*, **3.E.17.**, where it was said by Leggatt LJ that, in the absence of a legislative provision imposing strict liability, the defendant was in no way to blame for his action.
[335] Rogers at 841.

Court of Appeal[336]   **3.E.25.**
Mullin v. *Richards*

ORDINARILY PRUDENT SCHOOLGIRL

Fencing with rulers

Children will be held to the degree of care and foresight that can reasonably be expected of a child of the age of the defendant.

Facts: The plaintiff and the defendant were both 15-year old schoolgirls. While sitting at their desks during a mathematics lesson, they engaged in a mock sword fight using plastic rulers. One of the rulers snapped and a fragment of plastic entered the plaintiff's right eye, ultimately causing her to lose sight in that eye.

Held: The court of first instance allowed the claim. The Court of Appeal reversed the decision of the court of first instance and dismissed the claim.

Judgment: HUTCHISON LJ: "I would summarise the principles that govern liability in negligence in a case such as the present as follows. In order to succeed the plaintiff must show that the defendant did an act which it was reasonably foreseeable would cause injury to the plaintiff, that the relationship between the plaintiff and the defendant was such as to give rise to a duty of care, and that the act was one which caused injury to the plaintiff. In the present case, it seems to me, no difficulty arose as to the second and third requirements because Teresa and Heidi were plainly in a sufficiently proximate relationship to give rise to a duty of care and the causation of the injury is not in issue. The argument centres on foreseeability. The test of foreseeability is an objective one; but the fact that the first defendant was at the time a 15-year-old schoolgirl is not irrelevant. *The question for the judge is not whether the actions of the defendant were such as an ordinarily prudent and reasonable adult in the defendant's situation would have realised gave rise to a risk of injury, it is whether an ordinarily prudent and reasonable 15-year-old schoolgirl in the defendant's situation would have realised as much* [emphasis added]. In that connection both counsel referred us to, and relied upon, the Australian decision in *McHale* v. *Watson* (1966) 115 CLR 199 especially at 213–214 in the judgment of Kitto J. I cite a portion of the passage I have referred to . . .:

> The standard of care being objective, it is no answer for him [that is a child], any more than it is for an adult, to say that the harm he caused was due to his being abnormally slow-witted, quick-tempered, absent-minded or inexperienced. But it does not follow that he cannot rely in his defence upon a limitation upon the capacity for foresight or prudence, not as being personal to himself, but as being characteristic of humanity at his stage of development and in that sense normal. By doing so he appeals to a standard of ordinariness, to an objective and not a subjective standard.

. . . It is perhaps also material to have in mind the words of Salmon LJ in *Gough* v. *Thorne* [1966] 3 All ER 398 at 400, [1966] 1 WLR 1387 at 1391, which is cited also by [counsel for the defendant], where he said:

> The question as to whether the plaintiff can be said to have been guilty of contributory negligence depends on whether any ordinary child of 13 _ can be expected to have done any more than this child did. I say "any ordinary child". I do not mean a paragon of prudence; nor do I mean a scatter-brained child; but the ordinary girl of 13½.

. . . Applying those principles to the facts of the present case the central question to which this appeal gives rise is whether on the facts found by the judge and in the light of the evidence before

---

[336] [1998] 1 All ER 920, [1998] 1 WLR 1304.

him he was entitled to conclude that an ordinary, reasonable 15-year-old schoolgirl in the first defendant's position would have appreciated that by participating to the extent that she did in a play fight, involving the use of plastic rulers as though they were swords, gave rise to a risk of injury to the plaintiff of the same general kind as she sustained . . .

. . . First, there certainly was no evidence as to the propensity or otherwise of such rulers to break or any history of their having done so. There was evidence . . . that ruler fencing was commonplace . . . There was no evidence at all that the practice was banned or even frowned on. There was no evidence that it was discouraged in any way. The question of foreseeability therefore has to be judged against that background, the prevalence of the practice, the absence of prohibition, the absence of warning against it or of its dangers and the absence of any evidence of there having been any previous injury as a result of it . . ."

Notes

(1) In the law of tort, young age as such is no defence. And indeed, depending on their maturity, minors may be held to the same standard of care as an adult engaged in the same kind of activity, such as driving or shooting. Thus in *Gorely* v. *Codd*,[337] Nield J held that a 16½-year old boy was negligent when he accidentally shot the plaintiff with an air-rifle in the course of "larking about".[338] However, age is relevant for very young children because the standard of conduct that is reasonably to be expected of persons of such a tender age may effectively exclude liability or because such children may be incapable of the necessary state of mind for torts involving negligence or malice.[339] As the annotated judgment shows, in the case of older children (15 years), their age precludes the application to them of the test of how the "reasonable person" (i.e. adult) would have behaved, which would be applied if the defendant was older.[340] In the annotated judgment, the court finds support for its position in *McHale* v. *Watson* (an Australian decision),[341] where Kitto J held that the capacity of a child for foresight or prudence cannot be considered as a personal characteristic of the child, but rather must be seen as a "characteristic of humanity at his stage of development".[342] Beyond that, however, as further stated in *McHale* v. *Watson*, "it is no answer for [the child] any more than it is for an adult, to say that the harm was due to his being abnormally slow-witted, quick-tempered, absent-minded or inexperienced".

In the annotated judgment, the Court of Appeal endorsed that view by holding that "the question for the judge is . . . whether an ordinarily prudent and reasonable 15-year old shoolgirl in the defendant's position would have realised [that her action gave rise to a risk of injury]".

(2) The more vulnerable a child is, the less the chance that an action in negligence will succeed. At the same time, however, a higher standard will be imposed on those responsible for the care of the child.[343] Parents are therefore responsible to ensure the safety of

[337] *Gorely* v. *Codd* [1967] 1 WLR 19.
[338] Quoted by Rogers at 832 who adds: "and it is obvious that a motorist of 17 1/2 is as responsible for negligent driving as one six months older" (18 being the age of majority).
[339] Ibid.
[340] Markesinis and Deakin at 160–1.
[341] *McHale* v. *Watson* (1966) 115 CLR 199.
[342] That is an "external circumstance" (as opposed to internal) in the terminology used in French law: *supra*, **3.F.10.**, Note (1).

their children at home by keeping dangerous household items out of their reach or, at an appropriate age, by instructing them on how to use them.[344]

3.2.4. GROUNDS OF JUSTIFICATION

3.2.4.A. STATUTORY DUTY, AUTHORITY OR PERMISSION

The following cases can be found (with notes) at <http://www.rechten. unimaas.nl/casebook>:

3.F.26. Cass. civ. 2e, 10 June 1970, *Caisse régionale d'assurance mutuelle agricole contre les accidents des Alpes-Maritimes* v. *Follis.* Hot pursuit.

3.E.27. House of Lords, *Allen* v. *Gulf Oil Refining Co. Ltd.* Nuisance caused by oil refinery.

3.G.28. BGH, 24 June 1953. Denouncing enemies of the State.

3.2.4.B. SELF DEFENCE

The following cases can be found (with notes) at <http://www.rechten. unimaas.nl/casebook>:

3.F.29. Cass. civ. 2e, 22 April 1992, *Baumberger* v. *Wadoux.* Three men in the night.

3.E.30. Court of Appeal, *Lane* v.*Holloway.* A savage blow.

3.G.31. BGH, 23 September 1975. Shot after a spring party.

3.2.4.C. NECESSITY

This heading can be found at <http://www.rechten.unimaas.nl/casebook>.

3.2.5. COMPARATIVE OVERVIEW

In general, liability for one's own conduct is still based on the idea of wrongfulness.[345] On the Continent, wrongfulness comprises two elements: the "objective" element of unlawfulness (*illiceité, Rechtswidrigkeit*) and the "subjective" element of culpability (*culpabilité,*

---

[343] The liability of parents under English law for injury caused by their child is discussed *infra*, Chapter V, 5.2., Introductory Note under a).

[344] Markesinis and Deakin at 161, with a reference to *Kite* v. *Nolan* [1983] RTR 253, CA.

[345] In every legal system, a number of specific liability regimes do not relate to the actual conduct of the defendant in a given case, attaching liability instead to other factors. Under those regimes, accordingly, the quality of the defendant's conduct is generally irrelevant. These regimes are discussed *infra*, Chapter V (liability for the conduct of others) and Chapter VI (liability not based on conduct, regrouped under various headings such as *responsabilité de plein droit, Gefährdungshaftung* or strict liability). Furthermore, certain regimes of State liability are not based on fault: see *infra*, 3.3.2.B. (German law) and 3.3.3.B. (French law).

Verschulden), whether intention or negligence. Under English law, the tort of negligence does not seem to distinguish between these two elements, since wrongfulness (breach of duty) is assessed under an essentially objective standard; nevertheless, subjective factors such as bad or evil motive may play a role under certain torts. However, even in a legal system such as German law, where culpability is still expressly mentioned as an autonomous element in addition to the condition of unlawfulness (at § 823(1) and (2) BGB), culpability retains only limited significance, at least according to the prevailing "Conduct Theory".[346] As a result, in all of the legal systems examined here, unlawfulness is defined in such a way that it leaves little room for a consideration of culpability.

Unlawfulness

In all three legal systems studied here, a similar standard of care is used to assess whether the conduct of the defendant was unlawful. That standard refers to the abstract model of a normally "reasonable and circumspect person" placed in the same circumstances as those prevailing for the person whose conduct is to be judged. Of course, it is influenced by statutory and regulatory provisions, but in a complex fashion. On the one hand, it is not consistent with the standard of care to infringe provisions which prohibit certain behaviour, or allow it only under certain conditions. However, acting contrary to such provisions is not in and of itself evidence of unlawful conduct—that depends on the kind of conduct which the norm is intended to prevent.[347] Moreover, compliance with such provisions is not in and of itself evidence that one acted with the requisite care.[348]

The abstract model of the "reasonable person" implies that no account should be taken of the idiosyncrasies of the person whose conduct is at issue, or to put it more precisely, no account should be taken of *internal circumstances* which relate to the personality of the person concerned and are peculiar to him or her.[349]

Conversely, *external circumstances* relating to the time, place or nature of the conduct in question tend to have an impact on the application of the abstract model. As a result, the standard of care is not the same for "ordinary behaviour" and for behaviour which requires special skills. For instance, in all legal systems, the conduct of a medical professional will be assessed against that of an ordinary person exercising and professing that specific medical skill.[350] Therefore, the general standard will apply subject to such differentiations as are required from the point of view of the relevant group or sub-group (or even, under German law, from the perspective of the higher expectations which an average patient may have).[351] That "upgraded" standard is also used to measure the scope of the obligation, incumbent upon medical professionals, to inform the patient of the risks involved in a proposed treatment or intervention. Nonetheless, the emphasis differs somewhat, in that English law tends to refer to received professional opinion as the standard, that is the opinion of "a responsible body of medical men skilled in that particular art"

---

[346] *Supra*, 3.2.1. under b).
[347] *Supra*, 3.2.2.
[348] See, for French law, *supra*, **3.F.9.**
[349] *Supra*, **3.F.10.**, Note (1), **3.G.12.**, Note (1) and 3.2.2.C.
[350] *Supra*, **3.F.10.**, Notes (1) and (2) and **3.E.16.**, Note (1).
[351] *Supra*, **3.G.13.** and Note (1) thereafter.

(the *Bolam* test),[352] whilst German law definitely favours a standard which is fundamentally based on the patient's right to self-determination.[353] French law tends to construe the obligation to give information broadly by limiting exceptions, as regards grave risks, to situations of emergency, impossibility to inform the patient or refusal by the patient to be informed.[354]

In the end, the standard of care referring to the average ordinary person or, in the case of activities which require a certain skill, the average skilled person, remains an abstract model which is not easily defined. It would seem that English law has gone the furthest in giving substance to the standard by emphasizing that in each case a balance must be struck between (i) the magnitude of the foreseeable risk, ie the probability that injury will occur and the seriousness of the injury, (ii) the consequences of not incurring the risk and (iii) the cost of prevention, that is the cost of practical measures that could have been taken to eliminate, or reduce the risk.[355]

Further difficulties arise when atypical conduct must be assessed, namely the conduct of inexperienced persons or persons with reduced abilities, because of age (young or old), physical illness or mental handicap. Apart from young children and mentally disturbed persons, who as a class are subject to a special regime, the legal systems examined here tend to agree that the applicable standard is whether the person concerned was aware of his or her disabling condition, or could have been aware of it if he or she had submitted himself or herself to a critical self-examination, taking into account the risks of the activity concerned.[356]

Culpability

Culpability or responsibility (*imputabilité*) is understood to refer not to unlawfulness, as defined above, but to an additional element of blameworthiness, in the sense that the wrongdoer realized that his or her conduct was wrongful and that it could have harmful consequences. Blameworthiness is undoubtedly a pre-requisite for *criminal* liability, but it is far less certain whether the conduct of the wrongdoer must be blameworthy as a general condition for *civil* liability to arise (except in the case of special provisions requiring intentional fault or serious fault understood as subjective fault).[357]

In that respect, the legal systems examined here seem to agree that involuntary acts and *a fortiori* acts which occurred in a state of *full* unconsciousness or without any free will do not give rise to liability.[358] However, in order to reduce the unfavourable impact on the victim, many systems nonetheless impose on the wrongdoer a duty to compensate under certain circumstances. In France, that is the case for damage caused by someone suffering from mental disorder[359] and in Germany, for all cases where §§ 827 or 828 BGB exclude liability for lack of capacity.[360]

---

[352] *Supra*, **3.E.16.** and notes thereafter.
[353] *Supra*, **3.G.13.**, Note (3).
[354] *Supra*, **3.F.10.**, Note (3).
[355] *Supra*, **3.E.15.**, Notes (2) and (3).
[356] *Supra*, **3.F.11.** and Note (1), **3.G.14** and Note, **3.E.17** and Note (3).
[357] On the impact of gravity of fault, see *supra*, 3.2.3.A., 3.2.3.B and 3.2.3.C.
[358] *Supra*, **3.F.21.**, **3.G.23.**, **3.E.17.** and **3.E.24.** See also § 827 BGB, referred to *supra*, 3.2.3.A.
[359] Article 489–2 C.civ. applies to all forms of liability laid down in Articles 1382ff. C.civ., but only with regard to a state of unconsciousness due to mental disturbance: *supra*, **3.F.18.** It does not apply, in principle, to a situation where the mentally disturbed person is the victim: ibid., Note (1).

In the same fashion, very young children (infants of less than seven years of age[361]) lack the capacity to commit a culpable act, which as a general rule is regarded as an impediment to holding them liable in tort. In Germany, for instance, § 828(1) BGB expressly excludes their liability, with the proviso, however, that reparation can be ordered on grounds of fairness under the conditions spelled out in § 829 BGB.[362] In England, a young child will probably escape liability for negligence unless he or she acted in a way other than that in which an "ordinary" child of the same age might be expected to act and will probably be incapable of forming the necessary state of mind for liability in torts involving negligence or malice;[363] yet contrary to German law, in the absence of tortious liability, there is no possibility of compensation for the victim where it would be equitable to require compensation. Since the milestone judgments of the Cour de cassation on 9 May 1984, however, French law has broken this consensus. It is now firmly established that a child can be liable under Articles 1382–1383 C.civ. even in the absence of any discernment on his or her part, and that the same solution will be applied *mutatis mutandis* where the child is the victim, to reduce compensation on account of contributory fault.[364] Nevertheless, as seen below, young age may still be regarded under French law as an element which influences the standard of care applied to assess unlawfulness.

Beyond the instances surveyed in the previous paragraphs (full unconsciousness, total absence of free will or lack of discernment because of very young age), there is a grey area, where the judgment of the defendant was affected because of impairments or young age, without fully preventing him or her from realizing that his or her conduct was wrongful and that it might have harmful consequences for others. Under English law, the liability of the defendant in those instances will depend on whether he or she was possessed of the state of mind required for liability under the particular tort which is pleaded.[365] Thus, in a case involving trespass to the person of the victim, it was held that "where there is the capacity to know the nature and quality of the act, that is sufficient although the mind directing the hand that did the wrong was diseased".[366] It is questionable whether the same proposition applies to liability in negligence, however.[367]

In the case of minor children (except for very young children, discussed previously), blameworthiness may be reduced on account of the inability to perceive the legal and economic consequences of a course of conduct (even though the children were able to understand that their conduct created danger). In a German case involving 10-year old children, the BGH nonetheless held the children fully liable.[368] It follows from § 828 (2)

---

[360] According to § 829 BGB, reparation can be ordered on grounds of fairness, taking account of the circumstances and in particular the financial condition of the parties: see *supra*, 3.2.3.A. and *infra*, Chapter VII, **7.G.7.**, where § 829 was applied by analogy to the conduct of the victim, in that case a minor who had contributed to the occurrence of the damage.

[361] See § 828 BGB; see also *supra*, **3.F.20**, Note (1).

[362] See also *infra*, Chapter VII, **7.G.7.**

[363] Rogers at 832.

[364] See *supra*, **3.F.19** and notes thereafter, where the victim was already seven years old. In one of the decisions of May 1984 referred to in the notes, the contributory conduct of a five year old boy was in issue: see *infra*, Chapter VII, **7.F.3.**

[365] Rogers, as quoted *supra*, **3.E.24.**, Note (1).

[366] *Morriss* v. *Marsden*, *supra*, **3.E.24.**

[367] Ibid., Note (2).

[368] *Supra*, **3.G.22.**

BGB that in such a case, the care expected from minors is based on "the understanding necessary to be aware of his responsibility" present in a minor of the same age.

The same result was reached by the Court of Appeal in *Mullin* v. *Richards*:[369] the conduct of a 15-year old schoolgirl must be compared with that of an ordinarily prudent and reasonable 15-year old schoolgirl. It is interesting to see how the Court, in reaching that conclusion, refers with approval to a case where it was said that a "defence [based] upon a limitation upon the capacity for foresight or prudence" can be accepted because it is not "personal to [the child itself] but. . . characteristic of humanity at his stage of development. . ."; it is therefore in line with the objective standard of the ordinary reasonable person.[370] It would seem that, under French law as well, quite a few decisions go in the same direction,[371] even if age is regarded there as a purely internal circumstance.[372]

Grounds of justification

Apart from defences based on the plaintiff's conduct, or on conduct for which he or she is responsible,[373][1] a number of grounds of justification, which are alien to the parties involved, nonetheless remove the wrongful character of the defendant's conduct. The most important are discussed in this chapter: (i) statutory duty, authority or permission, (ii) self-defence and (iii) necessity.

It is practically impossible to bring these defences within a conceptual framework which is valid for the three systems under examination. In common law countries, the defences are part of a very wide field, including not only grounds of justification *stricto sensu*, but also personal immunity and various excuses resulting from extraneous causes such as contributory negligence of the injured party, act of a third party and act of God. In French law, justifications (*faits justificatifs*)—which, in the absence of any provision on this subject-matter in the *Code civil*, find their roots in criminal law—have in common that they affect directly the event triggering civil liability by removing illegality. These justifications operate *in rem*, i.e. unlike subjective grounds for non-responsibility, they benefit all co-authors and accomplices. They include, in particular, statutory duty or statutory authority (*ordre/permission de la loi*), order from a legitimate authority (*commandement de l'autorité légitime*), self-defence (*légitime défense*) and necessity (*état de nécessité*).[374] Of the three legal systems examined, German law is probably the most systematic in distinguishing grounds of justification (*Rechtfertigungsgründe*) from grounds of exculpation (*Entschuldigungsgründe*), a distinction closely connected to that between objective unlawfulness (*Rechtswidrigkeit*) and subjective culpability (*Verschulden*). Grounds of justification remove the unlawfulness of the harmful conduct: they include self-defence (*Notwehr*), necessity (*Notstand*), self-help (*Selbsthilfe*), the safeguarding of justified interests (*Wahrnehmung berechtigter Interessen*), consent of the victim (*Einwilligung des Verletzten*) and the exercise of statutory authority (*gesetzliche Ermächtigung*). Grounds of exculpation exculpate the tortfeasor in the sense that they take away the subjective element of culpability (*Verschulden*): they include exculpating necessity (*entschuldigender*

---

[369] *Supra*, **3.E.25.**
[370] Ibid.
[371] *Supra*, **3.F.20.**
[372] Ibid., Note (1).
[373] Such as contributory fault, assumption of risk, and illegality, discussed *infra*, Chapter VII.
[374] Sometimes assumption of risk and consent of the victim are also included.

Notstand) and unavoidable misunderstanding of a legal prohibition (*unvermeidlicher Verbotsirrtum*).

In all three legal systems, a duty imposed by law or an authority or permission given by law constitutes a defence. Statutory duty or authority is most often invoked to justify the acts of public authorities when they interfere with a person's property or personal rights.[375] Article 73 of the French *Code pénal* (Penal Code) is an example of statutory permission: it entitles any person to arrest a person openly committing a criminal offence and to take him or her to the nearest police station.[376] Under some varying conditions, individuals can also rely on superior orders to escape liability for harm caused to another person. Under French law, for example, Article 122–4(2) of the *Code pénal* frees a person from criminal liability if he or she acts pursuant to an order from a legitimate authority, unless if it is manifestly illegal. By contrast, English law does not recognize a general defence of obedience: if a person orders another to commit a tort, they are both answerable as joint tortfeasors. Under German law, persons who carry out orders (eg soldiers, enforcement officers) will escape liability, unless obedience would amount to a crime or an insult to human dignity. More generally, a person will be at fault if he or she stuck rigidly to an order or a statutory duty which is in conflict with a more fundamental rule or interest.[377]

Self-defence (private defence, *défense légitime*, *Notwehr*) is accepted in all three legal systems as a general defence against the person who rendered it necessary.[378] The following conditions must be fulfilled however: (i) there was aggression (to the person himself or herself, to another person, or to their legally protected goods or interests) by another person;[379] (ii) the aggression was actual or at least imminent (it cannot be merely imagined); (iii) the aggression was unlawful; and (iv) the action of the person relying on the defence was necessary to repel the attack and remained proportionate. In English law, these requirements form a standard of reasonableness;[380] in German law, they are interpreted as leaving considerable leeway to the person defending himself or herself: in principle he or she may choose the means of defence which, immediately and decisively, fends off the danger with certainty, and does not need to choose a less dangerous means of defence if its efficacy is doubtful.[381]

Necessity (*état de nécessité*, *Notstand*) is accepted as a ground of justification in all three systems (although with some hesitation and uncertainty in France). It is firmly anchored in the BGB, which knows both defensive necessity (*defensiver/passiver Notstand* at § 228 BGB) and aggressive necessity (*aggressiver Notstand* or *Notstandsangriff* at § 904 BGB). It has also for a long time been recognized in English common law. It is important to note, however, that, even if necessity is accepted as a defence, French and German courts may still hold the tortfeasor liable on grounds of equity.

---

[375] *Supra*, **3.E.27.**, relating to nuisance in the public interest.
[376] *Supra*, **3.F.26.**
[377] *Supra*, **3.G.28.**
[378] *Supra*, **3.F.29.**, **3.E.30.** and **3.G.31.**
[379] And not by an animal or a thing, for instance: this would rather be a case of necessity.
[380] *Supra*, **3.E.30.**
[381] *Supra*, **3.G.31.**, but see Note (2) thereafter.

3.3. CONDUCT OF PUBLIC AUTHORITIES

This section begins with an examination of English law, which, in principle, subjects the conduct of public authorities to the same tort rules as those that are applicable to individuals. German law regulates the conduct of civil servants in the BGB, the liability of public authorities in the GG. In both legal systems (and apart from European Union law), liability for wrongful legislative or judicial acts is but an exceptional occurrence. French law, on the contrary, is characterized by a sharp distinction between private and public law, not least because of the existence of a well-developed administrative court system, which has resulted in the development of a special form of liability without fault (in addition to fault-based liability). The section ends with Belgian case law on State liability for judicial acts.

3.3.1. ENGLISH LAW

Introductory Note

a) As already pointed out in the General Introduction, English tort rules generally apply equally to tortious conduct by individuals or public authorities.[382] The only noteworthy exception is the tort of misfeasance in public office. The elements of that tort have recently been defined by the House of Lords in *Three Rivers District Council* v. *Bank of England*[383] as follows: (1) The defendant must be a public officer, in a relatively wide sense: thus, a local authority exercising private-law functions as a landlord is potentially capable of being sued.[384] (2) The act complained of must consist of the exercise of power as a public officer; the principles of vicarious liability apply as much here as to other torts involving malice, knowledge or intention. (3) The public officer must either have intended to injure the plaintiff or persons of which the plaintiff was one or have acted knowing that he had no power to do the act complained of (or with reckless indifference to the illegality of that act) and knowing that the act would probably injure the plaintiff. (4) The plaintiff must have a sufficient interest to found a legal standing to sue.[385]

b) The two torts of negligence and breach of statutory duty are the usual grounds on which tortious liability of public authorities is based. The relationship between them is not wholly clear, as mentioned above.[386] The central issue is whether breach of statutory duty is a wholly separate tort or rather a concretization of the concept of duty under the

---

[382] On the civil liability of public authorities, see S. Arrowsmith, *Civil Liability and Public Authorities* (Winteringham: Earlsgate Press, 1992).

[383] [2000] 2 WLR 1220, HL, affirming in part the decision of the Court of Appeal [2000] 2 WLR 15 and the "impressive and careful judgments" of Clarke J. at first instance [1996] 3 All ER 558 and 634.

[384] *Jones* v. *Swansea City Council* [1990] 1 WLR 54, 85F, CA, reversed on the facts but not on the law [1990] 1 WLR 1453, 1458.

[385] As to elements (1)–(4), see especially [2000] 2 WLR at 1230–1236, *per* Lord Steyn.

[386] *Supra*, Chapter I, 1.4.1.A., Introductory Note under c).

tort of negligence.[387] The matter has been clarified to a certain extent by the judgment of the House of Lords in *X.* v. *Bedfordshire County Council*, particularly in Lord Browne-Wilkinson's speech.[388] There his Lordship examined the range of tort claims for damages caused by authorities which acted in breach of their statutory duties. He distinguished four different categories: (A) actions for breach of statutory duty *simpliciter*, in which the cause of action depends neither on proof of any breach of the plaintiff's common law rights nor on any allegation of carelessness; (B) actions based solely on the careless performance of a statutory duty; (C) actions based on a common law duty of care; and (D) misfeasance in public office (the latter tort was not at issue in that case).

Under (A) a private law cause of action may only exceptionally arise, "if it can be shown, as a matter of construction of the statute, that the statutory duty [of a limited and specific nature] was imposed for the protection of a limited class of the public and that Parliament intended to confer on members of that class a private right of action for breach of the duty".

As for (B), according to Lord Browne-Wilkinson, the correct view is that, in the absence of a statutory right of action (category (A)), the "mere assertion of the careless exercise of a statutory power or duty is not sufficient" if it cannot be shown "that the circumstances are such as to raise a duty of care at common law" (category (C)). Category (B) is therefore a misnomer, since it does not exist as an independent cause of action.

When it comes to the application of the common law of torts under (C), English law finds itself in a state of flux following the decision of the ECtHR in *Osman* v. *UK*[389] and the recent decision of the House of Lords in *Barrett* v. *Enfield London Borough Council*, excerpted below, which went back on *X.* v. *Bedfordshire County Council*[390] without however ever expressly abandoning it.

The central difficulty in that area is how to translate into operational criteria the common sense impression that some of the actions of public authorities should not be able to give rise to liability. Indeed, to take an extreme case, an administrative decision fixing the basic level of social security benefits, in the light of the applicable legislation, involves complex policy considerations, and it is difficult to see how a court of law could possibly entertain a claim that the State was liable for having failed to provide for a sufficient level of benefits. At the other extreme, there is little doubt that public authorities could be liable, under the same conditions as any private party in the same position, for injury that had arisen from the carrying out of works on public land or in a public building.

An additional difficulty arises from the need to ensure consistency with administrative law. It is generally seen as desirable that the range of cases where public authorities can be made liable is broadly in line with the range of cases where, on substantive grounds (unreasonableness, etc.), judicial review offers administrative remedies (annulment, etc.) against the actions of public authorities.

---

[387] Rogers at 247.
[388] [1995] 2 AC 633, [1995] 3 WLR 152, [1995] 3 All ER 353, HL.
[389] *Infra*, Chapter IX, **9.ECHR.10.**
[390] *X.* v. *Bedfordshire County Council* [1995] 2 AC 633, [1995] 3 WLR 152, [1995] 3 All ER 353, HL.

A classical approach to the difficulty was to distinguish between "policy" and "operational" activities of public authorities, but that distinction cannot suffice in the large "grey area" where the actions of public authorities comprise both policy and operational elements,[391] as is often the case for education, social security or the maintenance of public order through the police force.

The issue is therefore to ascertain under what circumstance public authorities have a duty of care towards the plaintiff. In *X. v. Bedfordshire County Council*, the House of Lords put forward the following test, which seeks to integrate administrative law and tort law into one set of criteria:[392]

- Where the public authority is acting within the ambit of discretion conferred upon it by statute, courts will not second-guess the actions of the authority and accordingly, no duty of care can arise at common law.
- A duty of care can arise if the plaintiff can prove that the authority exercised its discretion so carelessly or unreasonably that it cannot be held to have acted within its discretion. However, if the action of the authority involved policy considerations, it is not justiciable and courts will not look at whether it might have been unreasonable, so that no duty of care can arise in such cases.
- If the authority acted outside its statutory discretion, then the now-standard three-branch approach outlined in *Caparo Industries* v. *Dickman* will be used to determine whether a duty of care indeed arises.[393] Accordingly, the plaintiff must establish that (i) the harm was reasonably foreseeable, (ii) there was a relationship of proximity between the defendant and the plaintiff, and (iii) it is "fair, just and reasonable" to impose a duty of care. In the case of liability of public authorities, the third condition traditionally played a more important role than elsewhere in the law of negligence, as discussed below in connection with the first annotated case, *Barrett*.

Subsequently, in *Stovin v. Wise*, the House of Lords elaborated on that issue, in particular as it may apply to acts or omissions of the public bodies.[394] There the House of Lords, by a majority of three to two, found that the local authority was not liable for omitting to conduct remedial work to improve visibility at an intersection; road-users must take the highways network as they find it. For the majority, Lord Hoffman said in his speech:[395]

"Since *Mersey Docks and Harbour Board Trustees* v. *Gibbs* (1866) LR 1 HL 93 it has been clear that in the absence of express statutory authority, a public body is in principle liable for torts in the same way as a private person. But its statutory powers or duties may restrict its liability. For example, it may be authorised to do something which necessarily involves committing what would otherwise be a tort. In such a case it will not be liable [references omitted]. Or it may have discretionary powers which enable it to do things to achieve a statutory purpose notwithstand-

---

[391] As pointed out by Lord Slynn in his opinion in *Barrett* v. *Enfield London Borough Council*.

[392] As summarized by P. Craig and D. Fairgrieve, "*Barrett*, Negligence and Discretionary Powers" (1999) Public Law 626 at 627.

[393] See *supra*, Chapter I, 1.4.1.B., Introductory Note under c). *Caparo Industries* v. *Dickman* is excerpted *supra*, Chapter II, **2.E.47.**

[394] [1996] 1 AC 923, [1996] 3 All ER 801.

[395] Ibid. at 408–40, 415.

ing that they involve a foreseeable risk of damage to others. In such a case, a bona fide exercise of the discretion will not attract liability [references omitted].

In the case of positive acts, therefore, the liability of a public authority in tort is in principle the same as that of a private person but may be *restricted* by its statutory powers and duties [emphasis added] . . .

[. . . In the case of an omission] I think that the minimum preconditions for basing a duty of care upon existence of a statutory power, if it can be done at all, are, first, that it would in the circumstances have been irrational not to have exercised the power, so that there was in effect a public law duty to act, and secondly, that there are exceptional grounds for holding that the policy of the statute requires compensation to be paid to persons who suffer loss because the power was not exercised."

In *X.* v. *Bedfordshire County Council* and *Stovin* v. *Wise*, the House of Lords showed itself to be averse, in the context of the law of tort, to finding that decisions of public authorities fell outside the ambit of their discretion, so as to render them potentially liable in part. Alternatively, when no statutory discretion is involved and thus the standard three-stage approach is applied in order to determine whether a duty of care arises, courts have often concluded that no duty of care arose, either—as in the second annotated case, *Yuen Kun Yeu*—because there was no proximity (second stage)[396] or—as in the first annotated case, *Barrett* v. *Enfield London Borough Council*—because it was not fair, just and reasonable to impose a duty of care (third stage).[397] In *X.* v. *Bedfordshire City Council* itself, the House of Lords set out at length a series of factors why it would not be fair, just and reasonable to impose a duty of care on child protection or educational services. Under the approach set out in *X.* v. *Bedfordshire City Council*, accordingly, it would appear that public authorities will not often be liable in negligence.

Following the decision of the ECtHR in *Osman* v. *UK*[398] but also after a re-examination of the issue,[399] the House of Lords adopted a different approach in *Barrett*. There it tried to reduce the differences between cases involving public authorities and other cases (involving private parties) when it comes to assessing whether a defendant owes a duty of care to the plaintiff. That case is excerpted and discussed below.

The impact of *Barrett* still has to be felt in the case law, but the Court of Appeal has already followed its more liberal approach in a first case.[400]

c) *X* v. *Bedfordshire County Council*, *Stovin* v. *Wise* and *Barrett* v. *Enfield London Borough Council* were concerned specifically with statutory duties imposed on local authorities. The same principles seem to apply, however, to duties imposed on other authorities. Because of Community law, Parliamentary Acts which are in conflict with directly applicable Community law provisions, may now also give rise to liability under

---

[396] Among other recent cases where it was found that no relationship of proximity arose between the plaintiff and the defendant public authority, see *Capital and Counties plc* v. *Hampshire County Council* [1997] QB 1004, CA (fire emergency service), *W.* v. *Home Office* [1997] Imm AR 302, CA (immigration services), *Phelps* v. *Hillingdon London Borough Council* [1999] 1 All ER 421, CA (psychology service in schools) and *Palmer* v. *Tees Health Authority* [1999] Lloyd's Rep Med 351, CA (psychiatric service in hospital).

[397] Among other recent cases where it was found that it would not be fair, just and reasonable to impose a common law duty of care on the public authority, see *Harris* v. *Evans* [1998] 1 WLR 1285, CA (health and safety inspector).

[398] *Infra*, Chapter IX, **9.ECHR.10.**

[399] As P. Craig and D. Fairgrieve, "*Barrett*, Negligence and Discretionary Powers" (1999) Public Law 626 point out at 640.

the conditions discussed below.[401] Liability for judicial actions may arise under English law only under exceptional circumstances.[402] It is assumed that judicial officers should benefit from a particularly wide immunity, in order to bolster their independence.[403] As Lord Denning MR observed in *Sirros* v. *Moore*: "but, whatever it is, the immunity of the judges, and each of them, should rest on the same principle. Not liable for acts done by them in a judicial capacity. Only liable for acting in bad faith, knowing they have no jurisdiction to do it".[404]

d) Since, under English law, the liability of public authorities is governed by the same law as that of private persons, it follows that public authorities can be vicariously liable for the torts committed by their employees (including civil servants), much like any other employer.[405] The plaintiff must then establish that the conditions for liability are fulfilled as regards the employee in question; in particular, it must be shown that the employee owed a duty of care to the plaintiff.

Given that English courts, at least until *Barrett*, were somewhat reluctant to impose a duty of care on public authorities *directly*, vicarious liability offered a possibility to "circumvent" that restrictive attitude by claiming that the authority was liable on account of the conduct of the employee. In *X* v. *Bedfordshire County Council*, a number of the claims before the House of Lords relied in whole or in part on vicarious liability. The House of Lords held, as regards the claims against social workers and psychiatrists working for social services, that those professionals "were retained by the local authority to advise the local authority, not the plaintiffs . . . [They] did not . . . assume any general professional duty of care to the plaintiff children."[406] In contrast, in the claims brought against employees of educational authorities (educational psychologists, staff members of education authorities, head teachers and advisory teachers), the House of Lords found that "[t]here is no potential conflict of duty between the professional's duties to the plaintiff and his duty to the educational authority. Nor is there any obvious conflict between the professional being under a duty of care to the plaintiff and the discharge by the authority of its statutory duties".[407] Accordingly, in those cases, the local authority could be vicariously liable, even though it could not incur any direct liability, given the absence of any duty of care on the authority itself.

In the wake of *X* v. *Bedforshire County Council*, a number of plaintiffs filed claims alleging that local education authorities were vicariously liable, which led the Court of Appeal to find that it would not be just, fair and reasonable for employees of educational author-

---

[400] See *Gower* v. *London Borough of Bromley*, The Times, 28 October 1999, CA.

[401] See *infra*, Chapter IX, **9.EC.6.**

[402] S. Arrowsmith, *Civil Liability and Public Authorities* (Winteringham: Earlsgate Press, 1992) at 104 ff.

[403] See Sir W. Wade and C. Forsyth, *Administrative Law*, 7th edn. (Oxford: Clarendon Press, 1994) at 796.

[404] [1975] QB 118, [1974] 3 WLR 459, [1974] 3 All ER 776, CA. For a further discussion, see Rogers at 824–6 and S. Arrowsmith, *Civil Liability and Public Authorities* (Winteringham: Earlsgate Press, 1992).

[405] The regime of vicarious liability under English law is discussed *infra*, Chapter V (in particular under 5.1.1.B., Note h). The vicarious liability of the Crown (as opposed to other public authorities) is subject to certain limits set out in the Crown Proceedings Act 1947, c. 44.

[406] *X.* v. *Bedfordshire County Council* [1995] 2 AC 633 at 752 and 753, [1995] 3 WLR 152 at 185 and 186, [1995] 3 All ER 353 at 383 and 384, HL.

[407] [1995] 2 AC at 764, [1995] 3 WLR at 196, [1995] 3 All ER at 393.

ities to have a duty of care towards pupils.[408] Following *Barrett*, it appears that the Court of Appeal will take a more liberal attitude towards such claims.[409]

e) The first annotated case, *Barrett*, also discusses the factors coming into play in assessing whether it is fair, just and reasonable to impose a duty of care upon public authorities (the third branch of the *Caparo* test[410]). In addition to *Barrett*, a second annotated case, *Yuen Kun Yeu*, has been included, which provides a good illustration of how proximity (the second branch of the *Caparo* test) is dealt with in cases involving public authorities.

House of Lords[411]   **3.E.32.**
Barrett v. *Enfield London Borough Council*

DUTY OF CARE OF PUBLIC AUTHORITIES

Child in care of local authority

Public authorities may be under a duty of care towards individuals, but that is to be decided in every case, in the light of the justiciability of the issue and of the general criteria for assessing whether a duty of care arises.

Facts: When he was 10 months old, the plaintiff was taken away from his mother by court order and put under the care of the local childcare authority. During his childhood, he went from one placement to another and his case was handled by a succession of social workers. He developed, among others, behavioural and alcohol problems. When he reached majority, he sued the authority for negligence in the discharge of its duty of care towards him.

Held: The court of first instance and the court of appeal held, as a preliminary matter, that the local authority was under no duty of care towards the plaintiff. The House of Lords allowed the appeal from the judgment of the court of appeal and ordered the case to proceed to trial.

Judgment: LORD SLYNN OF HADLEY:[412] "It is obvious from previous cases and indeed is self-evident that there is a real conflict between on the one hand the need to allow social welfare services exercising statutory powers to do their work in what they as experts consider is the best way in the interests first of the child, but also of the parents and of society, without an unduly inhibiting fear of litigation if something goes wrong, and on the other hand the desirability of providing a remedy in appropriate cases for harm done to a child through the acts or failure to act of such services.

It is no doubt right for the courts to restrain within reasonable bounds claims against public authorities exercising statutory powers in this social welfare context. It is equally important to set reasonable bounds to the immunity such public authorities can assert . . .

The position is in some respects clear; in others it is far from clear. Thus it is clear that where a statutory scheme *requires* a public authority to take action in a particular area and injury is caused, the authority taking such action in accordance with the statute will not be liable in damages unless

---

[408] *Phelps* v. *Hillingdon London Borough Council* [1999] 1 All ER 421, CA. That case was decided before *Barrett*.

[409] See *Gower* v. *London Borough of Bromley*, The Times, 28 October 1999, CA.

[410] See *supra*, Chapter I, 1.4.1.A., Introductory note under c). *Caparo Industries* v. *Dickman* is excerpted *supra*, Chapter II, **2.E.47.**

[411] [1999] 3 WLR 79, [1999] 3 All ER 193, HL.

[412] Lord Nolan and Lord Steyn concurred with Lord Slynn of Hadley.

the statute expressly or impliedly so provides. Nor will the authority be liable in damages at common law if its acts fall squarely within the statutory duty. Where a statute *empowers* an authority to take action in its discretion, then if it remains within its powers, the authority will not normally be liable under the statute, unless the statute so provides, or at common law. This, however, is subject to the proviso that if it purports to exercise its discretion to use, or it uses, its power in a wholly unreasonable way, it may be regarded as having gone outside its discretion so that it is not properly exercising its power, then liability in damages at common law may arise. It can no longer rely on the statutory power or discretion as a defence because it has gone outside the power. . .

On this basis, if an authority acts wholly within its discretion—i.e. it is doing what Parliament has said it can do, even if it has to choose between several alternatives open to it, then there can be no liability in negligence. It is only if a plaintiff can show that what has been done is outside the discretion and the power, then he can go on to show the authority was negligent . . .

This, however, does not in my view mean that if an element of discretion is involved in an act being done subject to the exercise of the overriding statutory power, common law negligence is necessarily ruled out. Acts may be done pursuant and subsequent to the exercise of a discretion where a duty of care may exist—as has often been said even knocking a nail into a piece of wood involves the exercise of some choice or discretion and yet there may be a duty of care in the way it is done. Whether there is an element of discretion to do the act is thus not a complete test leading to the result that, if there is, a claim against an authority for what it actually does or fails to do must necessarily be ruled out.

Another distinction which is sometimes drawn between decisions as to 'policy' and as to 'operational acts' sounds more promising. A pure policy decision where Parliament has entrusted the decision to a public authority is not something which a court would normally be expected to review in a claim in negligence. But again this is not an absolute test. Policy and operational acts are closely linked and the decision to do an operational act may easily involve and flow from a policy decision. Conversely, the policy is affected by the result of the operational act [reference omitted].

Where a statutory power is given to a local authority and damage is caused by what it does pursuant to that power, the ultimate question is whether the particular issue is justiciable or whether the court should accept that it has no role to play [emphasis added]. The two tests (discretion and policy/operational) to which I have referred are guides in deciding that question. The greater the element of policy involved, the wider the area of discretion accorded, the more likely it is that the matter is not justiciable so that no action in negligence can be brought . . . A claim of negligence in the taking of a decision to exercise a statutory discretion is likely to be barred, unless it is wholly unreasonable so as not to be a real exercise of the discretion, or if it involves the making of a policy decision involving the balancing of different public interests; acts done pursuant to the lawful exercise of the discretion can, however, in my view be subject to a duty of care, even if some element of discretion is involved. Thus accepting that a decision to take a child into care pursuant to a statutory power is not justiciable, it does not in my view follow that, having taken a child into care, an authority cannot be liable for what it or its employees do in relation to the child without it being shown that they have acted in excess of power. It may amount to an excess of power, but that is not in my opinion the test to be adopted: the test is whether the conditions in *Caparo Industries plc* v. *Dickman* [1990] 1 All ER 568, [1990] 2 AC 605 have been satisfied. . .

Both in deciding whether particular issues are justiciable and whether if a duty of care is owed, it has been broken, the court must have regard to the statutory context and to the nature of the tasks involved. The mere fact that something has gone wrong or that a mistake has been made, or that someone has been inefficient does not mean that there was a duty to be careful or that such duty has been broken. Much of what has to be done in this area involves the balancing of delicate and difficult factors and courts should not be too ready to find in these situations that there has been negligence by staff who largely are skilled and dedicated . . .

This means I accept that each case has to be looked at on its own facts and in the light of the statu-tory context [emphasis added]. But this is so in many areas of the law and it is not in itself a reason for refusing to recognise a liability in negligence.

In the present case, the allegations which I have summarised are largely directed to the way in which the powers of the local authority were *exercised*. It is arguable (and that is all we are con-cerned with in this case at this stage) that if some of the allegations are made out, a duty of care was owed and was broken. Others involve the exercise of a discretion which the court may consider to be not justiciable—e.g. whether it was right to arrange adoption at all, though the question of whether adoption was ever considered and if not, why not, may be a matter for investigation in a claim of negligence. I do not think it right in this case to go through each allegation in detail to assess the chances of it being justiciable. The claim is of an on-going failure of duty and must be seen as a whole. I do not think that it is the right approach to look only at each detailed allegation and to ask whether that in itself could have caused the injury. That must be done but it is appro-priate also to consider whether the cumulative effect of the allegations, if true, could have caused the injury. . .

On the basis that *X* v. *Bedfordshire County Council* does not conclude the present case in my view it is arguable that at least in respect of some matters alleged both individually and cumulatively a duty of care was owed and was broken."

LORD HUTTON:[413] "In *X* v. *Bedfordshire County Council* [1995] 3 All ER 353 at 380, [1995] 2 AC 633 at 749 Lord Browne-Wilkinson said that 'the public policy consideration which has first claim on the loyalty of the law is that wrongs should be remedied', but he held that in that case there were very potent counter-considerations to override that consideration. In the present case the circum-stances are different in a number of important respects. Unlike *X* v. *Bedfordshire County Council* this is not a case where the child was in the care of his natural parent or parents when the negligence by the local authority is alleged to have occurred. And this is not a case, unlike *X* v. *Bedfordshire County Council*, where the local authority is alleged to have been negligent in respect of investigat-ing or acting upon an allegation or suspicion of sexual abuse. Whilst I recognise that the arguments are closely balanced I have come to the view that the arguments on behalf of the local authority are not sufficiently powerful to outweigh the argument that if the plaintiff has suffered personal injury by reason of its negligence he should be compensated by the courts.

In *X* v. *Bedfordshire County Council* the counter-considerations which this House considered should prevail are those enumerated by Lord Browne-Wilkinson (see [1995] 3 All ER 353 at 380–381, [1995] 2 AC 633 at 749–751). In my opinion, by reason of the differences in the circum-stances to which I have referred, these considerations become less powerful and are of insufficient weight to prevail. The first consideration was that a common law duty of care would *cut across the whole inter-disciplinary system set up by statute* for the protection of children at risk, which involved the participation of the police, educational bodies, doctors and others [emphasis added]. But in the present case it appears that other disciplines were not involved, or were not closely involved. The second consideration was that the *task of a local authority* and its servants in deciding whether to remove a child from his parents because of the fear of sexual abuse *was an extraordinarily delicate one* [emphasis added]. But in the present case, where the plaintiff was already removed from his nat-ural mother, the duties of the defendant were not so delicate, although questions did arise as to whether the plaintiff should remain with particular foster parents. The third consideration was that if liability and damages were to be imposed it might well be that *local authorities would adopt a more cautious and defensive approach* to their duties [emphasis added]. In the circumstances of this case I would not give this consideration great weight and I am in agreement with the opinion of Evans LJ in this case that

---

[413] Lord Nolan and Lord Steyn concurred with Lord Hutton.

'If the conduct in question is of a kind which can be measured against the standards of the reasonable man, placed as the defendant was, then I do not see why the law in the public interest should not require those standards to be observed.' (See [1997] 3 All ER 171 at 181, [1998] QB 367 at 380.)

The next consideration was that the relationship between a social worker and a child's parents is frequently one of conflict, particularly in a case of child abuse, and a fertile ground in which to breed *hopeless and costly litigation* [emphasis added]. But again, in the circumstances of the present case, this consideration is of less weight.

A further consideration was that there was a *statutory procedure for complaint* and for the investigation of grievances, and that the local authority ombudsman would have power to investigate the cases [emphasis added]. Again this consideration applies here, but if the plaintiff suffered psychiatric injury by reason of carelessness amounting to negligence at common law, I consider that the jurisdiction of the court should not be excluded because of the existence of other avenues of complaint. The final consideration in *X* v. *Bedfordshire County Council* was that there was *no analogous category of cases* to justify the imposition of liability on the local authority, and that the nearest analogy was cases where the courts had declined to impose common law liability on bodies, such as the police or statutory regulators of financial dealings, seeking to protect members of society from injury by criminals or from financial loss by the dishonesty of others [emphasis added]. But in the present case the plaintiff was not a member of a wide class of society which the defendant was obliged to seek to protect, but was an individual person who had been placed in the care of the defendant by statute, and I consider that it would not constitute a novel category of negligence to hold that the defendant owed him a common law duty of care."

Notes

(1) In his speech, Lord Slynn revisited the issue of when and under what conditions public authorities can be under a duty of care towards citizens, four years after *X* v. *Bedfordshire County Council*.[414]

A first notable feature of Lord Slynn's speech is how he limited the ambit of the so-called "public law hurdle", namely the first two of the three elements of the test set out in *X.* v. *Bedfordshire County Council*.[415] Lord Slynn reviewed at length the discussion of discretion in *X* and also alluded to the policy/operational distinction which used to be a leading criterion. He concluded, however, that both concepts ("discretion" and "policy/operational") are only guidelines, the central issue being *justiciability*, i.e. whether the matter is such that a court should not entertain a negligence claim (because it involves policy considerations, discretion or both). Neither discretion (which is found everywhere, as noted by Lord Slynn) nor policy are sufficient to exclude *a priori* the existence of a duty of care. In the end, Lord Slynn made the "public law hurdle" very fluid, since matters become "more or less likely" to be justiciable. Thus Lord Slynn is willing to accept that the decision as to whether a child should be taken from his or her parents and put into the care of the local authority can be non-justiciable. The subsequent conduct of the authority towards the child would be justiciable, however, in which case any consideration relating to the public interest in allowing the authority to be sued would have to take place under the standard *Caparo* test for the duty of care, presumably under its third branch ("fair, just and reasonable").

[414] *X.* v. *Bedfordshire County Council* [1995] 2 AC 633, [1995] 3 WLR 152, [1995] 3 All ER 353, HL.

[415] As set out *supra*, 3.3.1., Introductory Note under b). The term "public law hurdle" is borrowed from P. Craig and D. Fairgrieve, "*Barrett*, Negligence and Discretionary Powers" (1999) Public Law 626.

(2) For a better understanding of the evolution of the case law, it is necessary to mention briefly the procedural background. Most of the cases discussed in this section, including leading cases such as *Hill* v. *Chief Constable of West Yorkshire*,[416] *X.* v. *Bedfordshire County Council*,[417] *Osman* v. *Ferguson*[418] and the annotated case (*Barrett*), were decided not on the merits, but rather at a preliminary stage, on the basis of an application by the defendant to strike out the plaintiff's claim. Pursuant to the applicable rules of procedure, defendants can request the court to strike out, i.e. reject at the outset, claims where "the statement of case discloses no reasonable grounds for bringing or defending the claim" even if all the facts are as pleaded by the plaintiff.[419] In cases where the plaintiff alleges that a public authority is liable, the defendant authority will typically argue that it was under no duty of care to the plaintiff (so that the authority could not be made liable to the plaintiff in negligence) and ask for the claim to be struck out. As a consequence, the debate will then centre upon general elements such as the "public law hurdle" resulting from *X.* v. *Bedfordshire County Council* (including concepts such as discretion, policy and justiciability) as well as the proximity and "fair, just and reasonable" branches of the *Caparo* test. More often than not, before *Barrett*, the plaintiff's claim was thus rejected without any in- depth examination of the substance of the individual case.

This widespread use of the strike-out power to dismiss liability claims against public authorities in England was at the heart of the criticism of the ECtHR in *Osman* v. *UK*.[420] In the annotated case, the House of Lords also sought to reduce the scope for use of that power.[421] As Lord Slynn concluded, "each case has to be looked at on its own facts and in the light of the statutory context"; and indeed, in the annotated case, the House of Lords rejected the application of the defendants to strike out the claim. That does not mean that the public authority will necessarily be liable; the decision of the House of Lords simply opened the door for the claim to be tried on the merits.

(3) The annotated case not only reduced the significance of the "public law hurdle" that resulted from *X* v. *Bedfordshire County Council*, but it also cast a different light on how the third branch of the *Caparo* test ("fair, just and reasonable") would be applied in cases involving the liability of public authorities. Indeed, in the leading cases mentioned above (*Hill* v. *Chief Constable of West Yorkshire*, *X.* v. *Bedfordshire County Council*), the House of Lords had put forward a set of general reasons why it would not be fair, just and reasonable to impose a duty of care upon public authorities. The reasoning of the House of Lords had been very influential in the case law, as shown in a number of cases where the

---

[416] *Hill* v. *Chief Constable of West Yorkshire* [1989] AC 53, HL.

[417] *X.* v. *Bedfordshire County Council* [1995] 2 AC 633, [1995] 3 WLR 152, [1995] 3 All ER 353, HL.

[418] *Osman* v. *Ferguson* [1993] 4 All ER 344, brought before the ECtHR: see *infra*, Chapter IX, **9.ECHR.10.**

[419] Following the 1999 reform, the power of the court to strike out a case is now found at Rule 3.4 of the Civil Procedure Rules.

[420] Discussed *infra*, Chapter IX, **9.ECHR.10.**

[421] It can be debated whether the House of Lords did so by way of reaction to the judgment of the ECtHR in *Osman* v. *UK* or on its own motion. Lord Slynn did not make any reference to *Osman* in his speech, and Lord Hutton expressly refused to address *Osman* in his speech, despite the fact that both speeches went in the same direction as *Osman*. Only Lord Browne-Wilkinson, in a separate concurring speech, discussed *Osman*, which he found "extremely difficult to understand".

Court of Appeal found that it was generally applicable to the activities of public author-ities.[422]

In the annotated case, as reflected in the excerpts from the speech of Lord Hutton, the House of Lords looked at each of the main considerations put forward in *X* v. *Bedfordshire County Council* to sustain a finding that it would not be fair, just or reason-able to impose a duty of care upon public authorities, and for each of them presented a counter-argument as to why, in the circumstances of the annotated case, they should not apply. It is worth noting, in particular that:

– the argument that authorities would be overly cautious and defensive if put under a common law duty of care is answered by referring to the public interest in seeing the observance of standards of conduct, where they can be applied;
– the availability of alternative procedures is given less weight, on the ground that the court should not abdicate jurisdiction in cases involving negligence;
– the lack of an analogous category of cases is not seen as a bar to the claim, since the plaintiff was not merely a member of a broad class of society, but an individual in the care of the local authority.

The annotated case thus shows that many factors must be balanced in determining whether it would be fair, just and reasonable to impose a duty of care upon a public authority, and accordingly that it is difficult to make a general determination at the out-set, without looking at the circumstances of the particular case. Here as well, the position taken by the House of Lords is consistent with the judgment of the ECtHR in *Osman* v. *UK*.[423]

(4) Although it is too early to see how the annotated case will change English law, it can already be ventured, as some commentators have noted, that it will mark a shift from duty to breach as the central issue in cases concerning the liability of public authorities.[424] If the "public law hurdle" becomes less significant, and if the general considerations that play a role in the third branch of the *Caparo* test ("fair, just and reasonable") must be examined on a case-by-case basis, the chances are that a duty of care will more often be imposed upon public authorities. If that is the case, then all the arguments surveyed above, concerning discretion, policy, etc. could well surface again when it comes to assess-ing whether, in the circumstances of the case, the public authority (or its employee, in vicarious liability cases) actually committed a breach of its duty of care.

---

[422] The reasoning in *Hill*, relating to the liability of the police, was even seen as creating some form of immu-nity: see *Alexandrou* v. *Oxford* [1993] 4 All ER 328, CA and *Osman* v. *Ferguson* [1993] 4 All ER 344, CA. In *Swinney* v *Chief Constable of Northumbria Police* [1997] QB 464, [1996] 3 All ER 449, [1996] 3 WLR 968, how-ever, the Court of Appeal found that there were countervailing considerations under the "fair, just and reason-able" branch, so that a duty of care could not be excluded at the outset. The reasoning in *X* was influential in *Phelps* v. *Hillingdon London Borough Council* [1999] 1 All ER 421, CA, among other cases.

[423] *Infra*, Chapter IX, **9.ECHR.10.**

[424] P. Craig and D. Fairgrieve, "*Barrett*, Negligence and Discretionary Powers" (1999) Public Law 626 at 638–640. See also R. Mullender, "Negligence, Public Authorities and Policy-Level Decisions" (2000) 116 LQR 40.

Judicial Committee of the Privy Council[425]   **3.E.33.**
Yuen Kun Yeu v. *Attorney-General of Hong Kong*

DUTY OF CARE OF THE SUPERVISORY AUTHORITY AGAINST DEPOSITORS IN A BANK

Depositors losing money

Between the Commissioner in charge of supervising banks and the banks themselves or the general public, there is no sufficiently close and direct relationship as would give rise to a duty of care when the Commissioner exercises its statutory powers of supervision.

Facts: The appellants lost money when a registered deposit-taking company went into liquidation. They claimed compensation from the Hong Kong government on the ground that the Commissioner of Deposit-Taking Companies, who was charged, under the Deposit-Taking Ordinance 1976, with various regulatory functions, knew or ought to have known that the company was not a fit and proper body, that he owed depositors and potential depositors a duty to ensure that the company complied with the Ordinance and that he ought not to have registered the company or that he should have revoked its registration.

Held: The relations between the Commissioner and the plaintiffs were insufficiently close and direct for him to owe them any duty such as that alleged by the plaintiffs.

Judgment: LORD KEITH: "The foremost question of principle is whether in the present case the commissioner owed to members of the public who might be minded to deposit their money with deposit-taking companies in Hong Kong a duty, in the discharge of his supervisory powers under the Ordinance, to exercise reasonable care to see that such members of the public did not suffer loss through the affairs of such companies being carried on by their managers in fraudulent or improvident fashion . . .

The argument for the plaintiffs in favour of an affirmative answer to the question started from the familiar passage in the speech of Lord Wilberforce in *Anns* v. *Merton London Borough Council*, [1978] AC 728 at 751–752 [There follows a discussion of Lord Wilberforce's so-called two-stage test in *Anns*. As explained earlier, the *Anns* test was treated with much reservation in the opinion of the Privy Council delivered by Lord Keith]

The primary and all-important matter for consideration, then, is whether in all the circumstances of this case there existed between the commissioner and would-be depositors with the company such close and direct relations as to place the commissioner, in the exercise of his functions under the Ordinance, under a duty of care towards would-be depositors . . . No doubt it was reasonably foreseeable by the commissioner that if an uncreditworthy company were placed on or allowed to remain on the register, persons who might in the future deposit money with it would be at risk of losing that money. But mere foreseeability of harm does not create a duty, and future would-be depositors cannot be regarded as the only persons whom the commissioner should properly have in contemplation. In considering the question of removal from the register, the immediate and probably disastrous effect on existing depositors would be a very relevant factor. It might be a very delicate choice whether the best course was to deregister a company forthwith or to allow it to continue in business with some hope that, after appropriate measures by the management, its financial position would improve . . .

That raises the question whether there existed between the commissioner and company and its managers a special relationship of the nature described by Dixon J in [the Australian case of] *Smith* v. *Leurs*, 70 CLR 256 at 261–262, and such as was held to exist between the prison officers and the Borstal boys in *Dorset Yacht Co.* v. *Home Office* [1970] AC 1004, [1970] 2 All ER 294, so as to give

[425] [1988] AC 175, [1987] 3 WLR 776, [1987] 2 All ER 705.

rise to a duty on the commissioner to take reasonable care to prevent the company and its managers from causing financial loss to persons who might subsequently deposit with it.

In contradistinction to the position in the *Dorset Yacht* case, the commissioner had no power to control the day-to-day activities of those who caused the loss and damage. As has been mentioned, the commissioner had power only to stop the company carrying on business, and the decision whether or not to do so was clearly well within the discretionary sphere of his functions. In their Lordships' opinion the circumstance that the commissioner had, on the appellants' averments, cogent reason to suspect that the company's business was being carried on fraudulently and improvidently did not create a special relationship between the commissioner and the company of the nature described in the authorities. They are also of opinion that no special relationship existed between the commissioner and those unascertained members of the public who might in future become exposed to the risk of financial loss through depositing money with the company. Accordingly their Lordships do not consider that the commissioner owed to the appellants any duty of care on the principle which formed the *ratio* of the *Dorset Yacht* case. To hark back to Lord Atkin's words in *Donoghue* v. *Stevenson* [1932] AC 562 at 581, there were not such close and direct relations between the commissioner and appellants as to give rise to the duty of care desiderated . . .

The final matter for consideration is the argument for the Attorney-General of Hong Kong that it would be contrary to public policy to admit the appellants' claim . . . It was maintained that, if the commissioner were to be held to owe actual or potential depositors a duty of care in negligence, there would be reason to apprehend that the prospect of claims would have a seriously inhibiting effect on the work of his department. A sound judgment would be less likely to be exercised if the commissioner were to be constantly looking over his shoulder at the prospect of claims against him, and his activities would be likely to be conducted in a detrimentally defensive frame of mind. In the result, the effectiveness of his functions would be at risk of diminution . . .

Their Lordships are of opinion that there is much force in these arguments, but as they are satisfied that the appellants' statement of claim does not disclose a cause of action against the commissioner in negligence they prefer to rest their decision on that rather than on the public policy argument."

Note

In the case above decided by the Judicial Committee of the Privy Council,[426] the plaintiff brought an action in negligence for the recovery of economic loss. It sought to base it on a common law duty of care, in the case of careless performance by a public authority (here the Commissioner of Deposit-Taking Companies) of its statutory duty. The Privy Council found that there was no common law duty of care, because no such close and direct relations existed so as to give rise to a relationship of proximity between the Commissioner and depositors who in the future might become exposed to the risk of financial loss. Given that conclusion, the Privy Council preferred not to rest its decision

---

[426] The Judicial Committee of the Privy Council hears appeals from UK colonies (such as Hong Kong until July 1997) and from a number of British Commonwealth countries (New Zealand being the main one). On any particular appeal, the Judicial Committee of the Privy Council comprises Law Lords and, on occasions, other members of the Privy Council who hold or have held high judicial office in the UK or elsewhere in the British Commonwealth. The Committee's conclusions are embodied in "opinions", not judgments, since the Committee formally "advises" the Queen as to the appropriate outcome of an appeal. Dissenting opinions are now possible. Whereas the decisions of the House of Lords are binding on all lower courts and tribunals in the UK, the opinions of the Privy Council are not binding but enjoy great persuasive authority and are usually followed.

on public policy arguments invoked by the defendant to deny the existence of a duty of care.

In *Davis* v. *Radcliffe*, the Privy Council (per Lord Goff) again held that there was neither a statutory duty nor a common law duty of care owed to depositors by the Treasurer and Finance Board of the Isle of Man.[427] Plaintiffs had sued the defendant in respect of alleged failures in the discharge of its duties under the Banking Act 1975 to supervise a bank.[428]

3.3.2. GERMAN LAW

3.3.2.A. STATE LIABILITY BASED ON FAULT

Introductory Note

a) The first sentence of § 839(1) BGB provides that a public official who intentionally or negligently commits a breach of official duty that he or she owes to a third party shall be liable to compensate the third party for any damage arising therefrom. In the second sentence of § 839(1) as well as in § 839(2) and (3), liability of public officials is made subject to important limitations. Those limitations have the effect of rendering officials liable for negligent conduct only when the victim cannot obtain redress from another source (§ 839(1)), and denying liability when the victim has either intentionally or negligently failed to avoid the damage by making use of some other available legal remedy (§ 839(3)). As for judicial acts, dealt with in § 839(2), liability arises only if the judicial officer, when infringing his or her official duty, also committed a criminal offence.

b) § 839 BGB does not make the State or other public bodies liable for breaches of official duty committed by their officials. However, such liability arises under the first sentence of Article 34 GG which provides that "[i]f any person, in the exercise of a public office entrusted to him, violates his official obligations to a third party, liability shall rest in principle on the State or the public body which employs him". It appears from the whole of Article 34 first that liability towards third parties rests on the State or the public body employing the official, rather than on the official, who as a corollary is him- or herself not liable in principle[429] and secondly that even the right of recourse against the civil servant is limited to the case of intentional or *grossly* negligent (*culpa lata*) conduct. Article 34 GG therefore shifts liability for breaches of official duty from the official to the State or public body, but does not otherwise change the conditions for liability laid out in § 839 BGB.

---

[427] [1990] 1 WLR 821, PC, [1990] 2 All ER 536.

[428] *Davies* v. *Radcliffe* is discussed together with the annotated judgment, in the light of Directive 77/780 on the taking up and pursuit of the business of credit institutions (First Banking Directive) [1977] OJ L 322/20, in *Three Rivers District Council* v. *Bank of England* [2000] 2 WLR 1220, HL.

[429] BGH, 15 May 1951, BGHZ 4, 10 at 45–6.

c) The scope of application of § 839 BGB in combination with Article 34 GG is severely limited:

- the breach must be committed by a "public official", an expression which is interpreted as covering all persons including private enterprises or persons, who perform acts falling within the reach of sovereign activities of the State;[430]
- the act complained of must have been committed in the exercise of a public office entrusted to the official, and in breach of a duty owed to the plaintiff individually or as a member of an identifiable class of persons—a requirement which normally excludes liability for wrongs committed by the legislature;[431]
- the alleged injury must fall within the protective ambit of the infringed norm; and
- the breach must have been committed intentionally or negligently.

As we shall see later, some of those limitations may have to be set aside in respect of breaches committed in violation of provisions of Community law that grant rights to persons.[432]

d) It follows from the foregoing that, depending on the protective ambit of the rule infringed by public officials in the exercise of a duty entrusted to them, § 839(1) BGB in combination with Article 34 GG may lead to compensation of *reiner Vermögensschäden* as well.[433] See the judgment following below on this point.

BGH, 16 June 1977[434]   **3.G.34.**

ACTION BY FLIGHT CONTROLLERS IN BREACH OF OFFICIAL DUTY

Go-sick, go-slow

"Go sick" and "go slow" action by flight controllers constitutes a breach of an official duty owed to an enterprise and gives rise to liability on the part of the State to pay compensation even for reiner Vermögensschaden *suffered in consequence.*

Facts: The plaintiff runs a travel company. The defendant (the Federal Republic of Germany) provides air-traffic control services at all inland airports. The employees of the control services (air-traffic controllers) for the most part enjoy the status of civil servants. In the early part of 1973, because of dissatisfaction with working conditions, the air-traffic controllers decided to take militant action. In the period from 31 May to 23 November 1973 a significant number of air-traffic controllers reported sick on certain specific days ("go sick"). Others reduced their work performance over a longer period ("go slow"). Civil aviation was considerably disrupted as a result of these measures. By the end of June 1973 the disruption was such that the defendant was compelled temporarily to close individual airports, including Hanover airport, to all air traffic. The plaintiff was affected by the disruption to air traffic. On account thereof, it sought damages from the defendant.

Held: The court of first instance dismissed the action. The court of appeal reversed and allowed the action. The appeal to the BGH was unsuccessful.

---

[430] Markesinis at 903–4. For breaches of official duties in pursuit of private law interests (that is outside the reach of sovereign activities) of the State, the State may be liable under § 31 or § 831 BGB: Markesinis at 904.

[431] *Infra*, **8.G.100.** See, in respect of the issue of building permits requiring conformity with building regulations, BGH, 27 May 1963, BGHZ 39, 358, Translation in Markesinis at 581.

[432] *Infra*, Chapter IX, **9.EC.6.**

[433] For a case where breach of official duty was found to exist on the part of a public authority entrusted with the supervision of foundations (*Stiftungen*), as against the *Stiftung* itself, see BGH, 3 March 1977, BGHZ 68, 142.

[434] BGHZ 69, 128. Translation by N. Sims.

Judgment: "I. The court *a quo* proceeded on the assumption that the air-traffic controllers had acted in the exercise of a public office entrusted to them (Art. 34 GG) in impeding air traffic by repeatedly reporting sick and reducing their work performance.

The pleas on appeal directed against that finding are to no avail.

1. *In accordance with the Chamber's settled case law, the question whether specific conduct of a person is to be regarded as being in the exercise of a public office is to be determined according to whether the actual objective pursuant to which that person was acting is deemed to be State activity and, if so, whether as between that objective and the injurious act there is such a close external and internal connection that the action must also be deemed to belong to the area of State activity* [references omitted; emphasis added]. The court of appeal was correct in its approach on these issues.

2. . . . As employees of the Bundesanstalt für Flugsicherung (Federal Institute for Air-Traffic Control), air-traffic controllers perform . . . tasks connected with the monitoring of air space (§§ 29, first sentence of 31(1) and 31(2)(18) LuftVG (Air-Traffic Control Act)) . . . It is the duty of the Bundesanstalt für Flugsicherung, together with its agencies [references omitted], to operate the air-traffic control services of which air-traffic control including air-space movements and ground movements, form a part . . . All these operations constitute the exercise of public powers [references omitted].

3. Furthermore, the court *a quo* rightly concluded that there was not only an external but also an internal link between this activity and the actions of the air-traffic controllers challenged by the plaintiff . . .

II. 1. *For the defendant to be liable for the damage in respect of which the plaintiff claims, the air-traffic controllers must have been culpably in breach of an official duty owed to the plaintiff as a 'third party'* (Art. 34 GG and first sentence of § 839(1) BGB) [emphasis added] . . .

2 (a) The content and extent of the official duties of an official are determined by the provisions (whether imposed by law or regulation, administrative provision or service instruction) governing his tasks and sphere of duties, and also by the nature of the tasks to be performed [reference omitted].

Whether the person injured (here the plaintiff) is a "third party" *within the meaning of § 839 BGB* is determined according to whether the official duty is intended specifically, though not necessarily exclusively, to serve his interests. Only if it is clear from the provisions underpinning and defining the official duty, and from the special nature of the official business, that the person injured is amongst the persons whose interests are to be protected and promoted, in accordance with the purpose and objective of the official business, is liability in damages incurred to that person in the event of a culpable breach of duty . . .

Moreover, a person in whose favour an official duty is to be fulfilled need not be a 'third party' as regards all his interests. Rather it must be verified in each case whether the purpose and legal objective of the official activity is such that the interest in question in that case should be protected [references omitted]. The matter therefore turns on the protective purpose of the official duty infringed.

b) . . . The controllers engaged in the air-traffic control service have . . . a threefold task: first, to prevent collisions between aircraft in the air and on airport runways; secondly, to prevent collisions between aircraft and other vehicles, as well as other obstacles on airport runways; finally, to deal with air traffic as quickly and smoothly as possible . . .

3. There is much evidence in the present case in favour of a finding that the *Vermögen* of the plaintiff falls within the protective area of the official duties incumbent on air-traffic controllers . . . This question does not need to be discussed further because the applicant's claim is justified on another ground not mentioned by the court *a quo*.

4. a) *Every official may use the means associated with the exercise of public power only within the limits of the office. By virtue of his office, he is under an obligation to take care that in the exercise of*

his office he does not interfere in any way in the sphere pertaining to others [reference omitted]. *Accordingly, the official exercising his official power is obliged to refrain in the exercise of his office from any interferences in the rights of others which would be tortious within the meaning of the civil law, and thus also under § 823(1) BGB* [emphasis added]. An official who, in the exercise of his public office, commits a tort in this manner, thereby at the same time commits a breach of an official duty toward the holder of the right or *Rechtsgut* [references omitted].

b) *As the Bundesgerichtshof has held, the 'other rights' protected by § 823(1) BGB include the* Recht am Gewerbetrieb [references omitted; emphasis added] . . .

Protection of *Recht am Gewerbebetrieb* under § 823(1) BGB is, however, limited to interferences which are business-related (BGH, 9 December 1958, BGHZ 29, 65 at 74). The relationship to the business operation may arise out of, *inter alia,* the objective of the interference, if it is for example the intention of the tortfeasor to affect the business by taking specific measures [references omitted].

c) By disrupting air traffic, which led to the temporary closure of Hanover airport, the air-traffic controllers responsible for that airport were in breach of their official duties toward the plaintiff and thereby unlawfully infringed its *Recht am eingerichteten und ausgeübten Gewerbebetrieb* . . .

Such an intentional disruption of the commercial activity of a travel company which, for the smooth operation of its planned and organized flights, is dependent on the orderly conduct of air-traffic control constitutes a business-related interference with the protected sphere of that business.

d) The interference was also unlawful because the injurious conduct was, in its purpose and execution, reprehensible [references omitted] . . .

In this context, it is above all reprehensible that the air-traffic controllers systematically neglected their policing duties and used the means that had been made available to them for public administration in order to harm innocent undertakings which were dependent on the due performance of official activities and which were defenceless against this campaign, as a means of bringing indirect pressure to bear on the State, their real opponent . . .

Travel companies which, like the plaintiff, operate the charter flight business on the basis of forward planning, count on the undisrupted functioning of air-traffic control. That expectation is worthy of protection because the operation of air-traffic control by the public sector denies them the possibility of themselves carrying on that activity [i.e. air-traffic control], *so as to limit or eliminate the risk that provision of that service which is essential to air travel would not be ensured* [emphasis added] . . .

5. Through this unlawful interference with the plaintiff's business operation, the air-traffic controllers were at the same time in breach of their official duties to the plaintiff *qua* third party (first sentence of § 839(1) BGB)."

Notes

(1) This judgment illustrates some of the limitations on State liability flowing from the strict conditions of § 839(1) BGB and Article 34 GG, as mentioned above in the Introductory Note. The first limitation, discussed under I.1. of the judgment, is that the civil servant must have acted in the exercise of a public office, falling in the realm of sovereign activities of the State (Article 34 GG). The judgment shows that that condition is fulfilled when the real objective of the official duty performed by the official involved falls within the area of sovereign activity and there is an intimate connection between that sovereign activity and the tortious conduct. The BGH found that in the case in issue both elements (the sovereign character of the activity and a sufficiently close connection) were present.

The second limitation, discussed under II.2. of the judgment, relates to the protective scope of the duty, in that case the duty to ensure safety and prevent collisions in the air-space and on the ground at the airport as well as to ensure the quick and efficient flow of air traffic.[435] In that respect, the BGH concluded that the scope of the official duty concerned did encompass *ratione personae* the plaintiff and *ratione materiae* the kind of loss suffered by the plaintiff as a result of the "go sick" and "go slow" action of the flight controllers.

(2) On this last issue, although the BGH found under II.3. of the judgment that the plaintiff's *reiner Vermögensschaden* could very well fall within the protective scope of the duty, it did not make any determination on the issue, since it ultimately established a link between the injury and the duty through another approach. Thus in the next section (under II.4.a), the BGH drew a link between the official duties within the meaning of § 839(1) BGB and the *Rechtsgüter* protected in § 823(1) BGB.[436] As the BGH explained, if a civil servant wrongfully interferes with a protected interest in the sense of § 823(1) BGB in the exercise of any official duty incumbent upon him or her, a violation of the official duty imposed on all officials towards the holders of protected interests within the meaning of § 823(1) BGB will be made out. In short, the infringement of one of the protected interests under § 823(1) BGB in the exercise of an official duty will by the same token constitute a breach of official duty within the meaning of § 839(1) BGB. In such cases, the link between the official duty and the prejudice is thus readily established.

Having stated that principle, the BGH finally examined whether, in the present case, there was an unlawful interference with the "other" *Recht am Gewerbebetrieb*, and more specifically whether the interference was directed against the plaintiff's business (*betriebsbezogen*) in the sense that it was one of the defendants' purposes (*Willensrichtung*) that their action should have an impact on that business. The Court answered that question also in the affirmative (see under II.4.b-d, and 5 of the judgment).

(3) The judgment also discusses § 826 BGB (under II.5.b, not reproduced here) and its relationship with § 823(1) BGB. In the present instance, the BGH chose to apply the latter provision (in conjunction with § 839 BGB).

In a later judgment in respect of the same "go sick" and "go slow" action of the flight controllers, the BGH held that the conduct of the *flight controllers* was *contra bonos mores* in the sense of § 826 BGB because the rules relating to fair labour disputes (*faire Arbeitskampf*) had not been observed.[437] At the same time the Court found that the flight controllers *union* was a joint tortfeasor (*Mittäter*) in the sense of § 830 BGB, notwithstanding the fundamental freedom of association guaranteed at Article 9(3) GG. The BGH found that that freedom did not permit the flight controllers union to act *contra bonos mores*.[438]

---

[435] See *supra*, 3.3.2., Introductory Note under c).
[436] In this case more specifically the *Recht am Gewerbebetrieb*: on that right see *supra*, **2.G.37.**
[437] BGH, 31 January 1978, BGHZ 70, 277.
[438] See also *supra*, **2.G.51.–52.**

LEGISLATIVE WRONG

Rent controls

A "legislative wrong" (here failure to abrogate regulations concerning rent caps for apartments) does not give rise to liability under § 839 BGB unless there is a special relationship between the infringed official duty and the injured third party.

Facts: The plaintiffs were the owners of a block of flats to let in Düsseldorf which in 1966, as an old building, was subject to residential property management and fixed rentals. The plaintiffs maintained that, because as at 31 December 1965 the housing shortage was less than 3 per cent, the defendant regional authority (the *Land*) should have discontinued residential property management in Düsseldorf. If on 1 July 1966 the defendant had done so, the plaintiffs would have been able, by way of notice of review or by agreement, to introduce a reasonable increase of 25 per cent in the rents on the 14 flats let by them. The plaintiffs sought damages for the loss of rent incurred by them as a result of the failure to take the flats out of the fixed rentals scheme.

Held: The action for recovery of loss of rent for July and August 1966 failed before all courts.

Judgment: "**2. Claims based on breach of official duty:**

. . . *In so far as torts, including under our legal system also breaches of official duty within the meaning of § 839 BGB, confer a cause of action, the present-day law of torts is governed by the principle that not every person who has in some way, even if only indirectly, been placed at a disadvantage by the commission of such a tort is entitled to seek damages* [emphasis added]. Thus, only the person suffering direct injury as a result of a tort within the meaning of § 823(1) BGB (that is the holder of the *Rechtsgüter* listed in that provision) is entitled to sue. In the case of § 823(2) BGB the only person entitled to damages is the person afforded protection by the law infringed. In the case of §§ 824 to 826 BGB the persons mentioned in the law as being entitled to damages are only those who are the immediate victims of the tort. This restriction in the number of persons entitled to damages to those directly injured is reflected in § 839 BGB for the purposes of which the person directly injured is the third party in regard to whom there was an official duty which was infringed [references omitted]. *Whether in a given case the person injured is among the third parties as defined above must be determined according to whether the official duty is intended specifically, though not necessarily exclusively, to serve the interest of this injured party. Only if it is clear from the provisions underpinning and defining the official duty, and from the special nature of the official activity, that the person injured is amongst those whose interests are to be protected and promoted in accordance with the purpose and legal objective of the official activity, does liability in damages toward him arise. On the other hand, there is no such liability towards other persons, even if the breach of official duty has had more or less disadvantageous consequences for them* [references omitted; emphasis added]. There must therefore be a special relationship between the official duty of which a breach has occurred and the injured third party.

All official duties of public office-holders primarily serve the public interest in maintaining an ordered community. Where the official duties are confined to the service of the general interest, and no special relationship subsists between those official duties and specified persons or groups of persons as defined above, a breach of the duties cannot give rise to claims for damages by unrelated third parties. *We are concerned in particular with that kind of official duty in the case of the duties of persons with responsibility for legislative tasks. Legislative acts and regulations contain entirely general and abstract rules and accordingly, as a rule, the legislature, in acting and omitting to act, performs*

---

[439]   BGHZ 56, 40. Translation by N. Sims.

exclusively tasks in the general interest which are not directed to specific persons or groups of persons [references omitted; emphasis added]. Only exceptionally, for example in the case of so-called *Maßnahmegesetze* (acts adopting specific measures) or *Einzelfallgesetze* (acts concerned with a specific case), may it be otherwise in the sense that the interests of specific individuals are affected in such a way as to enable them to be deemed to be third parties within the meaning of § 839 BGB [references omitted]. But that is not so in the present case."

Notes

Wrongs committed by public bodies entrusted with legislative tasks (*Gesetzgebungsaufgabe*) can give rise to liability under § 839 BGB only if the members of the body in question (in the annotated case the members of the government of the *Land* of Nordrhine-Westphalia) are to be treated as public officials and, when the allegedly tortious conduct amounts to an omission (in the annotated case an omission to repeal certain secondary legislation), if that omission constitutes culpable (i.e. wilful or negligent) behaviour. The BGH in the annotated judgment mentioned, but did not rule on, those issues.[440]

The BGH instead focused on directness. Indeed, under 2 of its judgment, the BGH points out that, in line with the other tort provisions of the BGB (§§ 823(1) and (2), 824–826) claims are admissible under § 839 BGB only if the plaintiff has been directly injured by the breach, which means that the official duty at issue must have been owed to the plaintiff individually or as a member of an identifiable class of persons. This point is discussed at length in the judgment, which states that, more particularly in the case of the enactment by legislators of primary or secondary legislation containing general-abstract rules, there is normally no special relationship between a specific person or class of persons and the infringed official duty.

3.3.2.B. STATE LIABILITY NOT BASED ON FAULT

The following cases can be found (with notes) at <http://www.rechten.unimaas.nl/casebook>:

3.G.36. BGH, 26 January 1984. Sand pit.

3.G.37. BGH, 26 September 1957. Treatment for syphilis.

3.3.3. FRENCH LAW

3.3.3.A. STATE LIABILITY NOT BASED ON FAULT

Introductory Note

a) As already stated, there are two extra-contractual liability regimes for public authorities under French administrative law. The first is fault-based and in substance very similar to the general regime of tortious liability contained in Article 1382 ff. C.civ. Under this

---

[440] Members of a municipal council are considered to be civil servants: BGH, 24 June 1982, BGHZ 84, 292 at 299.

regime, liability applies whenever any administrative action is found by the Conseil d'État to be unlawful.[441] The second is a no-fault regime applicable in certain circumstances, and is based on the fundamental principle of equality before public burdens (*égalité devant les charges publiques*). The no-fault liability of the State under French law is discussed at greater length in the next heading.[442]

b) Apart from the circumstances where no-fault liability is admitted, an Act of Parliament does not normally entail liability, even if enacted in breach of international treaty law—or Community law, at least until the Conseil d'État decision in *Nicolo*.[443] After *Nicolo*, the Conseil d'État remained reluctant to declare Acts of Parliament in breach of superior rules of law in respect of EC directives. That explains why, in *Société Arizona Tobacco Products*, *Commissaire du gouvernement* Laroque, although she acknowledged that an Act of Parliament can be reviewed for its *compatibility* with a Community directive, nonetheless recommended to the Conseil d'État that it should hold liable not the legislature proper, but instead the competent Minister, on the ground that he misused the discretionary power which the Act had conferred upon him in violation of Community law.[444] Only in exceptional cases, when an Act itself is the source of the harm, or when the Minister has no discretion whatsoever in applying an Act (*compétence liée*), is it possible to envisage holding the legislature as such liable, according to *Commissaire* Laroque.[445] The Conseil d'État followed her Opinion.

As set out below, national courts should no longer refuse to hold the legislature proper liable for breaches of Community law. Indeed, in its *Brasserie du Pêcheur* judgment of 5 March 1996, the ECJ explicitly stated that the principle of State liability for violations of Community law arises by virtue of Community law and applies irrespective of the State organ (legislature, judiciary or executive) which is accountable for the breach of Community law.[446]

c) The decisions reproduced below show that in French administrative law, as well as in private law, there is no restriction on the scope of protection of tort law along the lines of protected rights or interests or protected persons (with the exception, in the no-fault liability regime, of the requirement that the burden falling on the claimant must be special in comparison to the burden falling on other citizens).

French law, however, steadfastly holds to the principle that Acts of Parliament cannot lead to fault-based liability (except, after years of slow evolution, for breaches of Community law). Underpinning this position is the belief that such an Act constitutes "the highest manifestation of public power . . . inspired by considerations of the general interest",[447] and that the courts should not interfere with it. Notwithstanding these reser-

---

[441] See the Opinion of *Commissaire du gouvernement* Laroque in *Societé Arizona Tobacco Products*, AJDA 1992.210 at 217 (reproduced in part *infra*, **8.F.39.**).

[442] *Infra*, 3.3.3.B.

[443] CÉ, 20 October 1989, *Nicolo*, Leb 1989.190. In that case, the Conseil d'État finally accepted that it could review the compatibility of Acts of Parliament with Community treaty law and set them aside if they proved incompatible. The Cour de cassation had much earlier accepted that such review was possible: Cass. Ch. mixte, 24 May 1975, D 1975.Jur.497, concerning whether an Act is consistent with the EC Treaty.

[444] *Infra*, **8.F.39.**

[445] See the decisions cited in *Commissaire* Laroque's Opinion, AJDA 1992, 210 at 219–20.

[446] *Infra*, Chapter IX, **9.EC.6.**

[447] Opinion of *Commissaire* Laroque, *infra*, **8.F.39.**

vations in principle, in concrete instances of "legislative wrongs" no limitation relating to the group of persons protected has been used under French law, unlike under German law.[448]

French law is also reluctant to recognize liability of the State for judicial acts. The conditions for such liability to arise are laid down in Article L. 781-1 of the *Code de l'organisation judiciaire*.[449]

CÉ, 26 January 1973[450]   **3.F.38.**
Ville de Paris v. *Driancourt*

COMPENSATION FOR AN ILLEGAL ADMINISTRATIVE ACT

Gaming machines

An administrative act which has been annulled gives rise to fault-based liability on the part of the public authority. An individual can recover loss of income and non-material damage, even when the illegality of the action is due to a mere error in exercising a discretion (simple erreur d'appréciation).

Facts: The City of Paris seeks annulment of the judgment of 22 June 1971 whereby the court of first instance ordered it to pay compensation of FRF 85,745 to Mr Driancourt for the loss occasioned to him by a police order of 7 December 1962 enjoining him to cease operating games installed on his premises.

Held: The Conseil d'État upheld the decision of the administrative court whereby the plaintiff was compensated for damage sustained because of an illegal administrative action.

Judgment: "By a police order dated 7 December 1962 . . . Mr Driancourt was enjoined to cease operation of various gaming machines installed in the premises of which Mr Driancourt was the owner . . . That decision was held to be *ultra vires* and set aside upon application by Mr Driancourt by a judgment of the Paris Administrative Court of 27 October 1964 against which no appeal was lodged. In a second judgment of 22 June 1971 the same court ordered the City of Paris to pay Mr Driancourt compensation of FRF 85,745. The City of Paris appeals against that judgment.

The principle of liability: The police order of 7 December 1962 was found to be unlawful by a judgment which has acquired the status of *res judicata*. Even if it is supposed that the illegality was attributable to a mere error in exercising discretion, it constituted a fault such as to render the public authorities liable. Mr Driancourt was entitled to obtain compensation for the direct and certain loss stemming from application of that unlawful decision.

The amount of the loss: By awarding Mr Driancourt [i] FRF 50,000 for loss of the profit which would have accrued from the operation of the gaming machines which were subject to the prohibition order, [ii] FRF 25,745 in respect of the loss from the resale of those machines and [iii] FRF 10,000 for disruption of Mr Driancourt's life, the court of first instance correctly assessed all the circumstances of the case. The City of Paris is not, therefore, entitled to seek revision of the judgment appealed against."

---

[448] *Supra*, **8.G.35.**
[449] *Infra*, **8.F.40.**
[450] Leb 1973.78. Translation by N. Sims.

Note

When administrative action has been found illegal, compensation can be obtained for both loss of income and non-material injury, even when the illegality occurred in the exercise of a power subject to limited judicial review. In the annotated judgment, the Conseil d'État finds non-material damage in the disruption of plaintiff's life (*troubles dans les conditions d'existence*), whose business had suffered because of the illegal decision whereby he was prohibited from exploiting gaming machines on his premises.

The *Legoff* case illustrates how far compensation for illegal administrative actions can go.[451] In that case, a student failed his examinations for a degree in business management at the University of Paris. The decision to fail that student was annulled, on the ground that the examination committee had based its decision on the final examination marks, without taking into account the marks on previous work during the year.[452] Given the delays caused by that review procedure, that student graduated in March 1982 instead of December 1978, and he sought to recover the chance he had lost of earning considerable income due to his management degree. The Conseil d'État granted him FRF 100,000 by way of compensation.[453]

CÉ (plén.), 28 February 1992[454]   **3.F.39.**
Société Arizona Tobacco Products

LIABILITY FOR BREACH OF COMMUNITY LAW

Price controls on tobacco

The State is liable when the administration wrongly applies an Act of Parliament in breach of a Community directive.

Facts: The French Ministry of Economy and Finances decided not to grant price increases for some of the tobacco products of the plaintiffs. The plaintiffs sued for some FRF 6 million in damages, claiming that that decision had been taken in breach of a Community directive.

Held: The court of first instance refused to order the State to compensate the plaintiffs. The Conseil d'État annulled the decision of the court of first instance and ordered the State to pay FRF 230,000 in compensation.

Judgment: "The aforementioned provisions of Art. 6 of the Act of 24 May 1976 confer on the Government a specific power to fix the price of tobacco imported from the Member States of the European Community, independently of the application of national legislation on price control. Those provisions thus permit the Government to fix the sales price of imported tobacco under conditions not provided for in Art. 5(1) of the Directive of 19 December 1972 and are incompatible with the objectives laid down in that directive. It follows that Art. 10 of the Decree of 31 December 1976, which was made on the basis of Art. 6 of the Act of 24 May 1976, which must be disapplied, is itself without legal foundation. It follows from the foregoing that, contrary to the judgment of the court of first instance, the ministerial decisions adopted in pursuance of the Decree of

---

[451] CÉ, 27 May 1987, *Legoff*, Leb 1987.286.

[452] The examination committee is a public authority under French law.

[453] On loss of a chance (*perte d'une chance*) as a head of recoverable damage in French law, see also *supra*, Chapter II, **2.F.11.** and **2.F.43.**

[454] AJDA 1992. 210. Translation by N. Sims.

31 December 1976 refusing, in respect of the period from 1 November 1982 to 31 December 1983, to fix prices for the applicants' manufactured tobacco, are unlawful, and that the illegality is such as to render the State liable.

The loss: The loss in respect of which the companies are claiming compensation is equal to the difference between the revenue which they received on the basis of the retail prices fixed in pursuance of the decisions which have been found to be unlawful and the revenue which they would have received on the basis of prices lawfully fixed. It is clear from the investigation that, if the price of tobacco during the period in question had been fixed in accordance with national legislation on price control under the Order of 30 June 1945 and its implementing Decrees, the price rise could have been limited to 7% without constituting a measure having equivalent effect to a quantitative restriction on imports. A decision of 14 June 1982 imposed a general price freeze and a timetable was established which limited price rises for comparable products to 3.5% with effect from 1 November 1982, rising to 7 % with effect from 1 July 1983. Material in the file establishes that in the same period the Minister allowed price rises for tobacco products of 5.5 % with effect from 24 January 1983, rising to 6.1 % with effect from 1 July 1983, leaving aside increases resulting from the application of the relevant fiscal and social legislation. In these circumstances, the loss suffered by the plaintiff companies will be fairly assessed if the damages to which they are entitled are set at FRF 230,000."

Opinion of *Commissaire du gouvernement* LAROQUE:
"3. There is certainly a strong temptation in the present case to blame the legislature for the illegality to which the applicants attribute their loss. Indeed you take the view that, where the defect apparently vitiating the administrative decision is in reality merely the consequence of a strict application of a legislative provision, it is that Act of Parliament and only it which is in issue . . .

However, even if, on the one hand, notwithstanding the very small number of decisions awarding compensation, it is not possible to speak in terms of 'immunity of the legislature from liability' (the title of the article by Professor Morange, D 1962.Chron.163) and even if, on the other hand, the legislature is today no longer beyond challenge, by virtue of its status, the Act of the legislature remains, even under the present Constitution, the highest manifestation of public power. 'It must on this account continually arbitrate within the framework of the State, between opposing groups of interests', thus characterizing the effort on the part of the legislature to re-establish an equilibrium that has been upset by economic developments (Morange, ibid.).

And the Act of the legislature is in such a case on principle inspired by considerations of the general interest so that, if its direct application entails loss capable of giving rise to compensation, that can only be because of the burden which, in the public interest, it has imposed, rightly or wrongly, and possibly in disregard of the international obligations of the State, on certain categories of its citizens.

If you were to take the view that the illegality of the contested regulatory decisions is a direct consequence of the Act of Parliament and is such as in the present case to render the State liable, you would be creating, but that is part of your judicial function, a new head of no-fault State liability for legislation . . .

I therefore tend to favour another option . . .

In deciding to leave inoperative an Act of Parliament that is inconsistent with an international treaty and, where necessary today, with secondary Community law, you create an obligation not only binding on a court determining a case but also on the executive power, that is the administrative authority.

Contrary to appearances, it is not a case of that authority disobeying the legislature, but on the contrary—in the name of the principle of legality—it is a case of duty to respect the constitutional order of rules of law. *The governmental or administrative authority on which, as in the present case, the legislature has conferred a regulatory power which is inconsistent with a provision of international law and which, moreover, it is not obliged to apply in a manner contrary to that provision, may not lawfully avail itself of the power since it must of its own motion give primacy to the provision of international law over its own national law. The illegality of the injurious administrative decision does not therefore flow directly from the Act of the legislature, but from the conduct of the administrative authority* [emphasis added].

The illegality of the regulatory decisions fixing the prices of tobacco products, certain of which will be annulled if you adopt my proposals, is due to the fact that the Minister for the Economy and Finance erroneously believed he was able to avail himself of a power conferred on him (but without laying down the conditions in which it was to be used) by the legislature, whereas the Minister ought to have kept clear of the Act of 24 May 1976 which was inconsistent with the Community Directive of 19 December 1972.

It is therefore the unlawful regulatory act itself, which interposed itself between the Act of Parliament and the person submitted to the administrative action, that gives rise directly to the latter's loss."

Notes

(1) In *Arizona Tobacco Products*, both the decision of the Conseil d'État of 28 February 1992 and the Opinion of *Commissaire du gouvernement* Laroque are remarkable for their ambiguity. On the one hand, they mark the end of the virtual refusal of French administrative courts to examine the compatibility of national law, including provisions of an Act of Parliament, with Community directives. On the other hand, they remain cautious as to the consequences to be drawn from any incompatibility for individuals seeking compensation for the loss suffered as a result. Instead of basing its decision to declare the conduct of the administration illegal on the illegality of the underlying Act, the Conseil d'État, following the advice of the *Commissaire*, chose to attach liability to the faulty conduct of the administration, as it could and should have used the discretionary power conferred by the Act to leave unimplemented the provisions of the Act to the extent of their incompatibility with the Community directive.[455] Indeed, as *Commissaire* Laroque said, the non-application by the administration of statutory provisions that are in breach of Community law does not constitute disobedience of the legislature, but is to be viewed as restoring, in accordance with the rule of law, the constitutional hierarchy of rules which provides for the primacy of Community law.

The Conseil d'État followed a similar line of reasoning in a case concerning French legislation on the hunting season.[456] There an Act adopted by the French National Assembly purported to fix the beginning and end dates of the hunting season directly, whereas this was otherwise done by a ministerial order. The dates fixed in the Act were not in line with Community law, as interpreted by the ECJ.[457] According to the Conseil d'État, the Act was thus inapplicable and could therefore not *of itself* legally justify the conduct of the administration. It followed that, when wildlife protection associations petitioned him to do so, the competent minister should have issued a ministerial order on the beginning and end of the hunting season, setting dates that were in line with Community law.

[455] See also J.F. Flauss, "Rapport français" in J. Schwarze, (ed.), *Das Verwaltungsrecht unter europäischen Einfluss* (Baden-Baden: Nomos, 1996) 31 at 89–90.
[456] CÉ, 3 December 1999, D 2000.Jur.17.
[457] ECJ, Judgment of 19 January 1994, C-435/92, *Association pour la protection des animaux sauvages* v. *Préfet de Maine-et Loire et Préfet de la Loire-Atlantique* [1994] ECR I–67.

(2) In a judgment of 1 July 1992 in the *Dangeville* case, the Cour administrative d'appel de Paris adopted a more straightforward approach.[458] The court ordered the State to compensate the plaintiff because it was subjected to VAT on the basis of an Act of the French legislature at a time when subjection to VAT under the circumstances of the case was inconsistent with a Community directive. The decision to require VAT from the plaintiff had been taken by the administration and upheld by the tax court.

The Cour administrative d'appel "found the State as a whole liable, without identifying the State organ to which the breach of Community law could be attributed".[459] That seems, indeed, to be the correct approach from a Community law perspective, especially now that the ECJ, in its *Brasserie du Pêcheur* judgment of 5 March 1996, has firmly recognized the liability of Member States for breaches of Community law committed by the Legislature proper.[460] For indeed, as Advocate-General Léger stated, "any distinction between State liability for breach of Community law attributable to legislative action and State liability for breach of Community law attributable to administrative action or action by some other State body would be *alien* to Community law. The requirements of Community law are identical in any event: it sees only one liable party (the State), just as, in proceedings for failure to fulfil Treaty obligations, it sees only one defendant (the State)".[461]

The *Dangeville* decision of the Paris Cour administrative d'appel has not been upheld by the Conseil d'État in its judgment of 30 October 1996,[462] for reasons unrelated to the liability issue, however. According to the Conseil d'État, Dangeville's claim was *res judicata*, having the same object as an earlier claim which had already been rejected by the Conseil d'État in a judgment of 19 March 1986.

(3) In another case, the Cour de cassation has held that the Ministry of Justice committed gross negligence (*faute lourde*) in adopting a set of administrative guidelines (*circulaire*) in violation of the EC Treaty.[463]

Code de l'organisation judiciaire[464] **3.F.40.**

STATE LIABILITY FOR JUDICIAL ACTS

The State is liable for gross negligence by the judicial power or denial of justice by the civil courts.

---

[458] *Société Jacques Dangeville*, AJDA 1992.768, annotated by X. Prétot, discussed by R. Errera, "Recent Decisions of the French Conseil d'État" [1993] Pub L 535.

[459] See Opinion of Advocate-General Léger in Case 5/94, *R. v. Ministry of Agriculture*, ex p. *Hedley Lomas* [1996] ECR I-2553 at para. 123.

[460] *Infra*, Chapter IX, **9.EC.6.** at para. 32 of the judgment.

[461] Opinion of Advocate-General Léger in Case 5/94, *R. v. Ministry of Agriculture, ex p. Hedley Lomas (Ireland) Ltd.* [1996] ECR I-2553 at para. 126. See also the dicta of Lord Goff in *Kirklees Metropolitan Borough Council* v. *Wickes Building Supplies Ltd.* [1993] AC 227, [1992] 3 WLR 170, [1992] 3 All ER 717, HL to the effect that, where a local authority applies a provision of national law that is incompatible with EC law, the damages will fall to be paid by central government and not by the local authority.

[462] CÉ, 30 October 1996, RFDA 1997. 1056, concl. G. Gaulard, AJDA 1996. 1045.

[463] Cass. comm., 21 February 1995, D 1995.IR.100.

[464] Translation by P. Larouche.

"**Book Seven** [of the *Code de l'organisation judiciaire*]
Title VIII. Liability for defects in the functioning of the judicial power
Article L.781-1.   The State shall be liable for the damage caused by defects in the functioning of the judicial power. Such liability is engaged only upon gross negligence or a denial of justice . . .

  The State shall assume the burden of liability towards the victims of injury caused by the personal fault of judges and other magistrates, without prejudice to its recourses against them."

Notes

(1) The first paragraph of Article L.781-1 of the *Code de l'organisation judiciaire* (Courts of Justice Act) sets out the general regime of State liability for acts of the civil judiciary under French law. Certain specific liability regimes are provided for in French criminal law as regards *erreur judiciaire* (erroneous criminal convictions, at Article 626 of the *Code de procédure pénale*) and unjust *détention provisoire* (pre-trial custody, at Articles 149–150 of the *Code de procédure pénale*).

(2) The general regime of Article L.781-1, first paragraph, extends to all cases where the civil judicial power[465] (as opposed to administrative courts) would have *malfunctioned* (*faute d'organisation*) so as to cause injury to the plaintiff. Article L.781-1 applies only to State liability towards the users of the justice system (i.e. the citizens), and not to State liability towards the professionals who work within with the justice system.[466] The standard of fault required to engage the liability of the State, however, is very high, namely either gross negligence or denial of justice. In the judicial context, case law has interpreted "gross negligence" so as to mean "such a fundamental error that no conscientious judge could have made it".[467] Denial of justice covers cases where a judge would refuse to rule on a case before him or her or would fail to proceed with cases ready for judgment.[468]

(3) The third paragraph of Article L.781-1 above provides that the State will assume any liability which judges might incur as a result of a *personal* fault on their part. The conditions under which judges would commit a fault in the exercise of their functions are not defined in the *Code de l'organisation judiciaire*. It seems that the mere fact that a judge may have decided erroneously in a given case does not suffice, or otherwise the judicial function could not be exercised independently. In order for a judge to be at fault, the same kind of conduct as would constitute a malfunction of justice within the meaning of the first paragraph of Article L.781-1 would have to be present. Accordingly, the third paragraph of Article L.781-1 does not add much to the first paragraph, and constitutes essentially a guarantee that judges will not personally be targeted by claims in tort resulting from the exercise of their functions.[469]

(4) Article L.781-1 does not concern administrative jurisdictions. There is no legal text governing State liability for the acts of administrative jurisdictions in France. The case

---

[465] Including not only the judges themselves, but the civil servants working for the civil courts, such as clerks, etc. See for instance Cass. civ.1re, 9 March 1999, JCP 1999.I.867, where Art. L.781–1 was applied to the conduct of police investigators acting under the supervision of an investigating judge.

[466] For instance trustees in bankruptcy, Cass. civ. 1re, 30 January 1996, D 1997.Jur.83.

[467] Cass. civ. lre, 16 October 1968, D 1969.Somm.44.

[468] R. Perrot, *Institutions judiciaires*, 7th edn. (Paris: Montchrestien, 1995) at 90, para. 88.

[469] Ibid. at 89, 91, paras. 86, 88.

law of the Conseil d'État has however acknowledged that the State can be liable under conditions similar to those applicable to civil courts, namely when the administrative judge would commit "a grave fault in the exercise of the judicial function".[470]

3.3.3.B. STATE LIABILITY NOT BASED ON FAULT

The following materials can be found (with notes) at <http://www.rechten. unimaàs.nl/casebook>:

3.F.41. A. de Laubadère, J.C. Venezia and Y. Gaudemet, *Traité de droit administratif.*

3.F.42. CÉ, 1 July 1977, *Commune de Coggia.* Volunteer lifeguard.

3.F.43. CÉ (plén.), 9 April 1993, *Bianchi.* Vertebral arteriography.

3.F.44. CÉ, 13 May 1987, *Aldebert.* Roadside lay-by.

3.3.4. BELGIAN LAW

Cour de cassation/Hof van Cassatie 19 December 1991[471]   **3.B.45.**
De Keyser v. *Belgian State*

STATE LIABILITY FOR WRONGFUL JUDICIAL DECISION

Wrong judicial declaration of bankruptcy

A judicial finding that a company is bankrupt can engage the liability of the State if it is found to be wrong on appeal.

Facts: Anca, a small company, was declared bankrupt by the Brussels Commercial Court in February 1982. The Brussels Court of Appeal invalidated that judgment in May 1982, on the ground that bankruptcy had been declared in violation of Anca's rights of defence. Even though the Court of Appeal quashed the declaration of bankruptcy, this proved too late for the company, as the trustees in bankruptcy had already sold the company's going business. The company instituted proceedings to obtain damages from the State.

Held: The court of first instance dismissed the claim by judgment of 24 December 1987. Its decision was confirmed by the court of appeal on 21 November 1989. The Court of cassation quashed the judgment.

Judgment: "By conferring exclusive jurisdiction upon the courts and tribunals to determine issues of litigation concerning civil rights, Art. 92 of the Constitution grants judicial protection to all civil rights. To effect such protection the Constitution takes into account neither the capacity of the litigating parties nor the nature of the acts which may have infringed someone's right, but takes into account only the nature of the right at issue.

---

[470] CÉ, 29 December 1978, D 1979.Jur.278, annotated by M. Vasseur; see ibid. at 91–2, para. 89–90.

[471] AC 1991–92, 364, Pas. 1992.I.316, with the opinion of first Advocate-General J. Velu, RW 1992–93, 377, annotated by A. Van Oevelen. Translation by the authors.

The State, like its citizens, is subject to the law and more particularly to rules concerning reparation of damage resulting from the infringement of rights and legitimate interests caused by someone's fault.

As a general rule an act committed by an organ of the State which causes damage to another, will
give rise to State liability in tort, on the basis of Arts. 1382 and 1383 of the Civil Code, where the
organ has acted in a manner which a reasonable and cautious person would regard to be within the
limits of its legal powers.

The principles of separation of powers, independence of the judiciary, and its members, and *res
judicata* do not imply that the State is exonerated from the liability it incurs, as provided in the aforementioned provisions, for the reparation of damage which it has caused by its fault or that of its
organs in the administration of justice, more particularly in actions which are of the essence of the
judicial function . . .

The liability of the State is . . . not necessarily excluded when the organ concerned cannot be held
liable, itself, for the tortious act which it has committed, whether because the organ is unidentifiable, or because the organ itself may rely upon a ground of exoneration such as that of unavoidable
error, or because the act constitutes a fault giving rise to liability for which the organ itself is exempt.

In the present legislation the State may, as a rule, be held liable on the basis of Arts. 1382 and
1383 of the Civil Code for damage caused by the fault of a judge or a public prosecutor if he or she
has acted within the limits of his or her legal powers or would be regarded by a reasonable and cautious person as having so acted. However, where the act pertains to the essence of the judicial function, as a general rule the claim for compensation can only be entertained if the act under review
has been withdrawn, amended, annulled or retracted by a final decision on the ground of a breach
of a well established legal norm, whereby the decision is no longer *res judicata*.

Within these limits, the liability of the State for the tortious acts of the judiciary is not contrary
to constitutional or legal provisions, nor is it incompatible with the principle of the independence
of the judiciary . . . such independence appearing to be sufficiently secured by the immunity from
personal liability of members of the judiciary unless they are convicted for a criminal offence or, in
exceptional cases, when they are subject to an action for miscarriage of justice ['*prise à partie*'],
under Art. 1140 of the Judicial Code [Code judiciaire/Gerechtelijk Wetboek].

The judgment of the court of appeal is quashed."

Notes

(1) The annotated judgment is significant in several respects. First, it shows how
Belgian tort law is keen to provide protection against all wrongful infringements of subjective rights or legitimate interests.[472] Secondly, under Belgian law the protection granted
to rights and legitimate interests is in principle just as broad when the infringement
emanates from the State or its emanations as when it does from other private persons.
Thirdly, the liability of the State can be engaged by any of its organs, including also the
judiciary acting in its judicial function, according to the present judgment. Only the second and third points will be further explored here, the first having already been covered
earlier.[473]

(2) The judgment must be seen in the context of the Court's earlier case law on State
liability.[474] As early as 5 November 1920 the Court of Cassation declared that, on the

---

[472] See *supra*, Chapter II, **2.B.20.** and Note.

[473] *Supra*, Chapter II, **2.B.20.** and **2.B.21.**

[474] This case law also led to the ECtHR judgment of 20 November 1995, *Pressos Compania Naviera S.A.*,
infra, Chapter IX, **9.ECHR.9.**, in which Belgian legislation was held to violate Art. 1 of the First Protocol to the
ECHR in so far as it attempted to set aside case law of the Court of cassation with retrospective effect.

basis of Article 144 of the Constitution (then Article 92), public authorities (even when acting in their official capacity) are not immune from tort actions brought by individuals whose rights have been infringed.[475] Subsequent judgments gradually extended the principle. In a landmark judgment of 26 April 1963, the Court found that State liability could also be triggered by the wrongful exercise of rule-making competences on the part of the executive.[476] That case related to a Royal Decree ordering the compulsory vaccination of babies against smallpox; in that particular case, vaccination had led to harmful side-effects. In its judgment, the Court ruled that "although judges are not empowered to assess whether administrative measures were appropriate . . ., they may review the legality of such measures". Accordingly, it held that the health protection law authorizing the King to take general preventive measures against contagious diseases "did not exempt the administration from the duty of care which Articles 1382 and 1383 of the Civil Code impose upon it". In other words, the Court made it clear that the administration is bound by tort law (as found in the Civil Code) in the same way as individuals and private law entities, even in the exercise of its rule-making function. Subsequently, in a judgment of 23 April 1971, the Court added that the principles outlined in its judgment of 26 April 1963 also apply to the failure of the administration to execute Acts of Parliament within the period of time provided therein and, in the absence of such provision, within a reasonable period of time.[477] Failure to execute may give rise to tortious liability towards those individuals who through the delay in implementation did not obtain rights or claims which they would otherwise have obtained.[478]

The above shows that Belgian law, unlike French law, does not subject State liability to a special administrative liability regime and, unlike German law, does not even have special rules in the Civil Code concerning that topic. Not unlike English law, Belgian law submits the conduct of public bodies to the same rules as individuals and also confers jurisdiction on tort claims against public bodies upon ordinary courts.

(3) Until the judgment excerpted above, it was controversial whether the case law of the Court of cassation would also apply to wrongful conduct on the part of the judiciary.[479] While acknowledging in the annotated judgment that the principles outlined in its case law concerning State liability also apply to judiciary actions, the Court at the same time provided for some important restrictions, however. For one, a tort action against a judicial act will only be successful if the "act under review has been withdrawn, amended, annulled or retracted by a final decision on the ground of a breach of a well-established legal norm, whereby the act is no longer *res judicata*". Furthermore, only the State, of which the judiciary is an organ,[480] and not the individual judge(s), can be held liable

---

[475] Pas. 1920.I.193.

[476] Pas. 1963.I.306, RW 1963–64, 287.

[477] Leaving aside the question of enforcing a judgment against the State for which an absolute immunity existed, until the Act of 30 June 1994, Art. 1, inserted Art. 1412bis in the Judicial Code (*Gerechtelijk Wetboek/Code Judiciaire*), allowing enforcement against certain property under certain conditions.

[478] The subject has been thoroughly discussed by A. Van Oevelen, *De overheidsaansprakelijkheid voor het optreden van de rechterlijke macht* (Antwerpen: Maklu, 1987).

[479] Pas. 1971.I.351, RW 1970–71, 1793.

[480] Organs of the State are all officials which exercise the sovereign powers of the State, even in minute part. In addition, the State may also be vicariously liable for the conduct of civil servants that it employs under contract.

(apart from exceptional situations based on express statutory provisions). Yet, on the other hand, the Court of cassation does not limit the potential liability of the State for judicial actions through some requirement of grave fault, contrary to French,[481] Italian or Dutch law[482] but in agreement with Spanish law.[483]

The foregoing does not mean that the Belgian State was liable in the annotated case. The Court of cassation remitted the case to the Court of appeal of Liège. Upon reconsideration in the light of the annotated judgment, the court of appeal held that the fact that the initial judgment declaring bankruptcy was found to be wrongly decided was a necessary but insufficient condition for the liability of the State to arise. Before the State can be held liable, the conduct of the court that rendered the initial judgment had to be assessed *in concreto*, in order to determine if it fulfilled the standard of a "normally careful and circumspect judge placed in the same circumstances at the relevant point in time". For the court of appeal, that meant that the rule of law that was infringed in the initial judgment was sufficiently established and known at the time of the decision, and that the court in arriving at the wrong decision made a manifestly inexcusable error, taking into account the information which was available to it. In the light of the foregoing, the court of appeal found that there was no fault on the part of the judge who rendered the initial judgment,[484] and the Court of cassation upheld the judgment of the court of appeal in a new judgment of 8 December 1994.[485]

(4) The annotated judgment came one month after *Francovich*, where the ECJ found that the principle of State liability for breaches of Community is a principle of Community law inherent in the system put in place by the EC Treaty. As was put beyond doubt in the subsequent ECJ judgment in *Brasserie du Pêcheur*, this principle of Community law applies regardless of "whether the breach which gave rise to the damage is attributable to the legislature, the judiciary or the executive . . . since all State authorities . . . are bound in performing their tasks to comply with the rules laid down by Community law directly governing the situation of individuals".[486]

3.4. COMPARATIVE OVERVIEW

At first sight the differences between the French, German and English legal systems, as well as the systems that follow one or other of these models, seem considerable.[487] French law, and in particular French tort law, is characterized by a sharp distinction between pri-

---

[481] *Supra*, **8.F.40.**

[482] See HR, 3 December 1971, NJ 1971, 137 and 17 March 1978, NJ 1979, 204 confirmed by many more recent ones, which accept liability of the State for judicial acts only when the judicial act constitutes an infringement of a fundamental principle, in a way that one cannot speak of a fair trial in the sense of Art. 6 ECHR. It should be recalled that the annotated judgment related also to a case where the rights of defence of the plaintiff had been infringed by the judgment for which the State was held liable.

[483] See Art. 221 of the *Constitución española* and Arts. 292–297 of the *Ley organica del poder judicial* of 1 July 1985. Judicial error and abnormal functioning of the administration of justice are the two grounds for liability. See E. Bribosia, "Le droit espagnol" in Vandersanden and Dony 183 at 190–3.

[484] Liège, 28 January 1993, TBBR 1995, 106, annotated by D. Deli.

[485] Cass., 8 December 1995, RW 1995–96, 180, annotated by A. Van Oevelen.

[486] *Infra*, Chapter IX, **9.EC.6.** at para. 34 of the judgment.

[487] See also J. S. Bell and A. W. Bradley (eds.), *Governmental Liability: A Comparative Study* (London: British Institute of International and Comparative Law, 1991).

vate and public law. The division is primarily apparent in the existence of separate and well-developed civil and administrative court systems. It can also be seen in the existence of two distinct bodies of liability rules, one applying to relations between individuals, the other applying mainly to claims against, or between, public authorities (or private law entities performing tasks of general or public interest), albeit that differences between the two are tending to disappear.[488]

When compared with the French model, German law does manifest certain similarities, in that separate liability rules for civil servants (including members of the judiciary) are laid down in § 839 BGB, whilst the liability of the State and other public bodies for breaches of official duty committed by their officials arises under Article 34(1) GG.[489] However, while the German court system is at least as specialized if not more so than the French one, tort claims against public authorities are heard before civil courts.[490]

These divisions are not present in English law. There is no separate administrative court system for public authorities or bodies, not even for matters of judicial review and, apart from the seldom seen tort of misfeasance in public office, there are no separate tort rules.[491] The other torts, including the tort of negligence, are equally applicable to unlawful conduct by private persons and by public authorities. This also holds true for the tort of breach of statutory duty, although the duty in question is often incumbent upon a public authority.[492]

Exercise of wide discretion

Despite these differences, it is unavoidable that the same issues should arise in each of these legal systems. One such issue is the question of whether tort liability can arise in relation to a decision taken by the public authority in the exercise, under statutory duty, of a wide discretion. In English law, that issue was at the heart of a series of very important decisions throughout the 1990s. Decisions of the House of Lords in cases such as *X.* v. *Bedfordshire County Council*[493] and *Stovin* v. *Wise*[494] seemed to suggest that decisions of public authorities will not readily be held to fall outside the ambit of their discretion, so that the law of negligence would rarely apply to them.[495] Because of the generality of their reasoning, those decisions worked as a bar to most claims in negligence against public authorities. That trend was reversed in *Barrett* v. *Enfield London Borough Council*.[496] There the House of Lords in effect limited the scope of the "public law hurdle" which— because the authority enjoyed discretion—makes a case non-justiciable under the law of negligence.[497] The practical impact of *Barrett* could very well be that arguments relating

---

[488] See *supra*, Chapter I, **1.F.25.** and Note (3).

[489] *Supra*, 3.3.2.A, Introductory Note under a) to d).

[490] See further Markesinis at 1–7.

[491] *Supra*, 3.3.1., Introductory Note under a). In practice, certain members of the courts are specialized in administrative law matters.

[492] See *supra*, Chapter II, 2.4.1., Introductory Note under b).

[493] [1995] 2 AC 633, [1995] 3 WLR 152, [1995] 3 All ER 353, HL.

[494] [1996] 1 AC 923, [1996] 3 WLR 388, [1996] 3 All ER 801, HL.

[495] *Supra*, 3.3.1., Introductory Note under.

[496] *Supra*, **3.E.32.**

[497] The decision of the House of Lords was motivated in part by the criticism of *X* v. *Bedfordshire County Council* and in part as well as by the condemnation of the UK in *Osman* v. *UK*, discussed *infra*, **9.ECHR.10.**

to the specific position of the public authority—presence of discretion, need to work within budgetary constraints, need to ensure efficient operations, etc.—will now be considered on a case-by-case basis, when it comes to establishing whether the authority committed a breach of duty of care.[498]

The general three-branch test for determining whether there is a duty of care is thus likely to be applied more and more often to public authorities as well. In this respect, in addition to the third branch ("fair, just and reasonable"), which remains significant after *Barrett*, the second branch of the test (proximity) is likely to play a larger role. For instance, in *Yuen Kun Yeu* v. *Attorney- General of Hong Kong*, it was held that no duty arose between the Commission in charge of supervising banks and the banks themselves or the general public.[499]

In French law, the issue of whether a tort can be committed in the exercise of wide discretion seems not to have been raised as explicitly as in English law (at least not in public law liability cases as opposed to judicial review cases). In *Driancourt*, compensation was awarded on the basis of fault liability for an administrative decision which had already been declared illegal, even when the illegality was due to a mere fault in judgment (*erreur d'appréciation*).[500] It would seem, however, that this is no more than the exercise of "operational" as opposed to "policy" discretion. Such an exercise of "policy" discretion was at issue in *Société Arizona Tobacco Products*, but under special circumstances: in that case a government minister had a discretionary power in the implementation of certain national legislation; the Conseil d'État held that to exercise that discretion in breach of Community law was unlawful.[501] In following that line of reasoning the Conseil d'État was able to avoid the issue of liability of the legislature proper, "the Act of the legislature remain[ing] . . . the highest manifestation of public power", as the *Commissaire du gouvernement* said. The reluctance of the French judiciary with regard to tort claims, to enter into the ambit of discretion is most clearly discernible in the standard of care which is used by the administrative courts to gauge the liability of public authorities based on fault. In many areas where policy decisions are involved, that standard is one of gross negligence or grave fault (*faute lourde*).[502] Gross negligence is held to be necessary when the task of the public service is particularly *difficult* or sensitive, for instance in the area of medical treatment[503] or in the case of police activities.[504] Another field where the "gross negligence" standard is used, is in the area of banking supervision.[505]

German law, that is § 839(1) BGB, takes a similar approach to English law (in respect of decisions not taken within the ambit of discretion), in that it makes a public official[506]

---

[498] See *supra*, **3.E.32.**, Note (4).

[499] *Supra*, **3.E.33.** See also *Davis* v. *Radcliffe* [1990] 1 WLR 821, [1990] 2 All ER 536, PC, referred to in the note.

[500] *Supra*, **3.F.38.** Before that judgment the administrative courts denied the existence of liability in case of exercise of discretion: M. Dony, "Le droit français", in Vandersanden and Dony 235 at 240.

[501] *Supra*, **3.F.39.**

[502] See M. Dony, "Le droit français", in Vandersanden and Dony 235 at 242–4, who notes that the test of *faute lourde* tends to disappear.

[503] See *supra*, **3.F.13.** But see *infra*, Chapter VI, **6.F.31.–32.**, Note (4), where recent CÉ decisions concerning the liability of hospitals and blood transfusion centres are discussed.

[504] See L.N. Brown and J.S. Bell, *French Administrative Law*, 4th edn. (Oxford: Clarendon, 1993) at 182–3.

[505] See CÉ, 24 January 1964, Leb 1964.43, where the State was held liable for *faute lourde* by the Commission de contrôle des banques. Compare with *Yuen Kun Yeu* v. *Attorney-General of Hong Kong*, *supra*, **3.E.33.**

[506] And as a consequence the State, through Art. 34(1) GG.

who commits a breach of official duty liable only if he or she owes that duty to a third party. From BGH, 16 June 1977, it follows that, for liability to arise, the scope of official duty must encompass the plaintiff, and the kind of loss suffered by the plaintiff.[507] In that case the issue was whether *reiner Vermögensschaden* would fall within the protective scope of the duty, which was the duty of flight controllers to ensure the safety and flow of air traffic.[508] Although the court accepted that such could very well be the case, it followed another line of reasoning to determine the issue of compensation for *reiner Vermögensschaden*. It held that, whenever a civil servant, in the exercise of an official duty, interferes with one of the *Rechtsgüter* protected in § 823(1) BGB, in this case the *Recht am Gewerbebetrieb*, a duty towards the holders of such protected interests is violated.[509] The 1977 judgment related to liability for operational activities.

Legislative and judicial wrongs

English law has generally been reluctant to allow public authorities to be sued in negligence for decisions taken in the exercise of a statutory duty. Recent developments, with *Barrett* v. *Enfield London Borough Council*,[510] essentially mean that such reluctance will not be allowed to go as far as to work as a bar to claims in negligence from the outset; however each case will receive consideration in the light of its own particular facts. *A fortiori* Acts of Parliament enacted within the sovereign power of Parliament cannot give rise to liability.[511] In contradistinction to English law, German law does not automatically exclude the liability of the legislature. Thus, in its judgment of 29 March 1971, the BGH applied the criteria laid down in § 839(1) BGB to a "legislative wrong" whereby it focused more particularly on the question of duty towards a third party.[512] The BGH held that an enactment of primary or secondary legislation containing general abstract rules (*generelle und abstrakte Regeln*) will not give rise to liability, even though the other conditions of § 839(1) BGB are fulfilled, *unless* there is a special relationship between a specific person or class of persons and the infringed official duty.[513] As has been noted above, apart from the application of no-fault liability in exceptional circumstances,[514] French law does not recognize liability for legislative acts either.[515]

Given the reluctance of national legal systems to recognize State liability for legislative acts or omissions, the ECJ judgment in *Brasserie du Pêcheur*, where it was held that "the principle that Member States are obliged to make good damage caused to individuals by breaches of Community law is applicable where the national legislature was responsible for the breach in question",[516] has wide implications. It may spur a new examination of

---

[507] *Supra*, **3.G.34.**

[508] Ibid., Note (1).

[509] Ibid., Note (2).

[510] *Supra*, **3.E.32.**

[511] C. Smits and A. Vallery, "Le droit anglais" in Vandersanden and Dony 95 at 98–9, with reference to Sir W. Wade and C. Forsyth, *Administrative Law*, 7th edn. (Oxford: Clarendon Press, 1994) at 766.

[512] *Supra*, **3.G.35.**

[513] Ibid., Note (1).

[514] *Supra*, 3.3.3., Introductory Note under b).

[515] As for Belgian, Spanish and Italian law, see the reports in Vandersanden and Dony. Spanish law seems to be the most favourable to the principle of liability of the legislature: see E. Bribosia, "Le droit espagnol" in Vandersanden and Dony 183 at 193–208.

[516] *Infra*, Chapter IX, **9.EC.6.**, para. 36 of the judgment.

the issue of legislative liability in general, not only in relation to breaches of Community law, but also in the context of breaches of superior national rules, such as constitutional provisions or fundamental principles of law.[517]

Liability for judicial acts presents a special problem. Liability for judicial officers arises under English law only where they have acted in bad faith, knowing that they have no jurisdiction,[518] and under German law only when the breach of duty committed by the judicial officer consists in a criminal offence (§ 839(2) BGB; to be read in conjunction with Article 34 GG). In France, State liability for the exercise of judicial power occurs when there is gross negligence or a denial of justice. The personal liability of judicial officers (for which the State is then liable subject to its right to recourse) arises under the same conditions.[519] The judgment of the Belgian Court of cassation of 19 December 1991 is an example of how that Court applies to the judiciary its general doctrine on State liability without resorting to a concept of gross negligence such as is used in French law, while making allowance for the principle of independence in that judicial officers can only be personally liable if they have committed a criminal offence or in the exceptional cases provided for in Article 1140 of the Judicial Code.[520]

As in the case of liability for legislative acts, Community law will also have an impact on liability for judicial acts when those acts infringe Community law. In *Brasserie du Pêcheur*, the ECJ held that "in international law a State whose liability for breach of an international commitment is in issue will be viewed as a single entity, irrespective of whether the breach which gave rise to the damage is attributable to the legislature, the judiciary or the executive. This must apply *a fortiori* in the Community legal order".[521]

State liability not based on fault

This section also surveyed State liability not based on fault under French and German law; it should be emphasized at the outset that there is no comparable regime under English law. Nevertheless, despite its absence in one of the major legal traditions of the EU, State liability not based on fault has already been argued a number of times before the ECJ and the CFI, on the grounds that it would form a general principle common to the laws of the Member States. So far the ECJ and the CFI have refused to introduce a regime of Community liability for lawful acts, but it was indicated that, were it to exist, then it would resemble the French and German regimes discussed in this section, in particular insofar as those regimes require the plaintiff to prove that he or she suffered a special injury going above and beyond what other persons might have suffered.[522]

The French and German laws of State liability not based on fault may appear fragmented, since they each concern a number of specific situations, without any general regime. Indeed, under both French and German law, State liability remains in principle

---

[517] See *infra*, Chapter IX, 9.1.
[518] *Infra*, 3.3.1., Introductory Note under c).
[519] *Supra*, **3.F.40.** and note.
[520] *Supra*, **3.B.45.** and notes.
[521] See *infra*, Chapter IX, **9.EC.6.**, para. 34 of the judgment.
[522] See CFI, Judgment of 28 April 1998, Case T–184/95, *Dorsch Consult Ingenieurgesellschaft mbH* v. *Council* [1998] ECR II–667.

based on fault.[523] Nevertheless, under both French and German law, it is acknowledged in case law and legal writing that the disparate instances of State liability not based on fault rely on a single general principle. What is more, the general principles put forward under French and German law are very similar.

Under French law, State liability without fault rests on the principle of equality before public burdens (*égalité devant les charges publiques*): public burdens, including the impact of the actions of public authorities, must be spread equally over all citizens.[524] Consequently, when a citizen is called upon to bear more than an equal share of that burden, he or she is entitled to compensation from the State. As the Conseil d'État has held, lawful measures taken by public authorities, in the general interest, may give rise to a duty to compensate persons who suffer *abnormal and special injury* as a result of the measures.[525] In a number of specific situations, case law has already defined the "exceptional or abnormal state of fact"[526] more precisely: it can consist in the exceptional impact of public works,[527] exceptional participation in the public service,[528] or exposure to an exceptional danger or risk.[529]

Similarly, under German law, State liability not based on fault is based on the principle of "sacrifice" (*Aufopferung*), according to which the State should compensate individuals when their legal interests are sacrificed for a greater good.[530] As under French law, however, not every sacrifice—i.e. not every burden imposed by the State—will give rise to a right to compensation. Rather, the plaintiff must show a "*special burden*" (*Sonderopfer*), going above and beyond the burden imposed on others. In the context of interference with property, the victim must thus demonstrate that the interference went beyond the general limits imposed on ownership and property rights within the social context (*Sozialbindung*).[531] In the context of interference with life, health or bodily integrity, the victim must show that the interference exceeded what everyone had to bear according to the legislative intent.[532]

That general principle is not completely unrelated to the other foundations for liability which are commonly advanced in private law regimes, such as fault or risk. For instance, it can be argued that a wrongful course of conduct on the part of the State will as such impose a special burden on any individual who may suffer injury as a result, so that State liability for wrongful conduct could be seen as a specific application of the general principle of equality before public burdens or compensation for sacrifice, as the case may

[523] As mentioned *supra*, 3.3.2.B., Introductory Note, liability regimes for expropriatory measures (*enteignender Eingriff*) or quasi-expropriations (*enteignungsgleicher Engriff*) are meant to compensate for gaps in the general regime of liability for fault (*Amtshaftung*) of § 839 BGB in conjunction with Art. 34 GG, or to establish a parallel with private law regimes such as that of § 906 BGB.

[524] See *supra*, **3.F.41.**

[525] See *supra*, **3.F.44.**

[526] To use the words of Laubadère, de Venezia and Gaudemet, *supra*, **3.F.41.**

[527] See for instance liability for damage caused by public works, as in *supra*, **3.F.44** and Note (1) thereafter.

[528] As in *supra*, **3.F.42.**

[529] For instance the risk arising from certain installations or activities (police interventions, etc.) or the therapeutic risk (*aléa thérapeutique*) in public hospitals, as in *supra*, **3.F.43.**

[530] See *supra*, 3.3.2.B., Introductory Note. In its decision of 26 January 1984, *supra*, **3.G.36.**, the BGH expressly rested the regime of compensation for quasi-expropriation on the general principle of *Aufopferung*.

[531] See *supra*, **3.G.36.** and Note (2) thereafter.

[532] See *supra*, **3.G.37.** and Note (2) thereafter.

be.[533] Furthermore, while the liability of public hospitals for therapeutic risk under French law[534] can be derived from the principle of equality before public burdens (citizens should generally not suffer from grievous injury as a result of the operation of a public service), it could also be seen as a species of risk-based liability.[535]

Beyond that common principle, the French and German regimes follow the general organization of their respective laws of civil liability. For instance, under German law, compensation is linked to the violation of a protected legal interest (*Rechtsgut*), be it life, health or bodily integrity (in the case of the *Aufopferung* regime[536]) or property rights (in the case of the regimes concerning expropriatory measures (*enteignender Eingriff*) or quasi-expropriations (*enteignungsgleicher Eingriff*)[537]). It will be noted that, in line with the French and German regimes of State liability for unlawful conduct, it is difficult to engage the liability of the State for lawful legislative action. French case law has traditionally been very reluctant to find the State liable for such action.[538] Under German law, since the judgment of the BVerfG of 15 July 1981,[539] unless legislative measures which affect property rights and constitute expropriations within the meaning of Article 14 GG provide for compensation, they are void; accordingly, the German constitution forbids courts would "reading" compensation "into" such measures where it is not provided for.[540] Measures that affect property rights without constituting expropriations do not need to provide for compensation and will not give rise to it.[541] Legislative measures that affect protected interests other than property rights are not "protected" in the same fashion, however.[542]

---

[533] See for instance *supra*, **3.G.36.**, where the BGH underlines that injury caused by unlawful State action constitutes a "special burden" (*Sonderopfer*).

[534] Established in *Bianchi*, *supra*, **3.F.43.**

[535] Indeed, if *private hospitals* are to be made liable for therapeutic risk (*aléa thérapeutique*), as is currently discussed in France (see *supra*, **3.F.10.**, Note (4)), that regime will most likely constitute another instance of risk-based liability imposed by legislation (see the list drawn up *infra*, Chapter VI, **6.F.4.**).

[536] See *supra*, **3.G.37.**

[537] See *supra*, **3.G.36.**

[538] The plaintiff must show that a number of supplementary conditions are met, for instance that compensation was not explicitly excluded by the legislative measure in question and that it is not excluded either by the objective of the legislation and the nature of the activities which are affected by it: see *supra*, **3.F.44.**, Notes (3) and (4).

[539] BVerfG, 15 July 1981, BVerfGE 58, 300.

[540] See *supra*, 3.3.2.B., Introductory Note, as well as **3.G.36.** and notes thereafter.

[541] See *supra*, **3.G.36.** and Notes (2) and (4) thereafter.

[542] See *supra*, **3.G.37.**, where the State was liable for what was at the time a lawful legislative measure (compulsory treatment of victims of syphilis).

CHAPTER FOUR
CAUSATION

It is sometimes thought that causation is a factual question which does not involve truly legal issues. Once it has been shown that the victim suffered some damage which comes within the scope of protection of tort law[1] and that an event occurred which can trigger the liability of the alleged tortfeasor[2] or the liability of another person who must answer for him or her,[3] establishing causation should then be no more than a matter of examining how events unfolded.

The present chapter aims to demonstrate that such a conclusion is ill-founded. Despite its innocuous appearance, the question of causation is infused with legal considerations.[4] Indeed, if one considers for a moment the phrase "causal *link*", which is often used as an alternative label for "causation",[5] the true nature of the problem comes to the fore. Causation is about *linking* the event triggering the liability of the defendant with the damage suffered by the victim, in other words answering the question: under the circumstances of the case and assuming other conditions for liability are met, ought *this* defendant to be held liable for *this* damage?[6] That is a value-laden question, to which the legal systems surveyed in this Chapter frequently apply concepts of fairness and justice in addition to, or instead of, reconstructions of facts or events.[7]

This Chapter is divided into four main sections. The first presents the general approach to causation in the main legal systems. The second deals with specific difficult issues which have arisen in almost every system, such as causation in cases of omissions, loss of a chance, etc. The third covers situations where a series of possible causes play a role in the sequence of events leading up to the damage, when one may be confronted with a phenomenon often—if sometimes inaccurately—referred to as "breaking", "intervening in" or "interfering with" the so-called "chain of causation". The last section concerns more complex cases involving multiple causes (often because of multiple tortfeasors). The Chapter ends with a comparative overview.

4.1. THE GENERAL APPROACH

In this section, German law is presented first, since of all the legal systems under study, it is the one where causation problems have drawn the most attention from courts and legal writers. English law, where the criterion of remoteness of damage supplements cause-in-

---

[1] See Chapter II.

[2] Whether because of wrongful conduct (see Chapter III) or on another basis (see Chapter VI).

[3] See Chapter V.

[4] See von Bar II at 439–40, 462–3, para. 414, 438–9.

[5] Under German law, causation is usually dealt with under the heading of "*Kausalzusammenhang*". Under French law, the discussion takes place under the heading of "*lien de causalité*".

[6] See also von Bar II at 463, para. 440.

[7] See von Bar II at 438, para. 413.

fact in a two-stage process, is then examined. The avowedly empirical approach of French law is studied last.

4.1.1. GERMAN LAW

Introductory Note

a) Some sixty years ago, a leading French civil law professor, G. Marty, commented that "the causal problem in tort law could not but appeal to German legal minds".[8] Indeed in no other legal system have legal writers undertaken so many efforts to tie together the results of the case law into a coherent theory of causation. Many such theories have been put forward, and their respective proponents regularly attempt to show that one or the other provides the best explanatory and normative construct.

Under the BGB, the requirement of causation can generally be derived from the text of the main provisions creating liability, such as §§ 823(1), 823(2), 826 or 839 BGB.[9] Nonetheless, in accordance with the general structure of the BGB, in which the general comes before the specific,[10] causation is considered not within the specific framework of tort law, but rather within the general part of the law of obligations, more precisely within the general theory of *Schadensersatz* (reparation of damage), which applies to contract, tort and other forms of obligations.[11]

German legal writers generally consider causation (*Kausalzusammenhang, Ursächlichkeit*) under the broader heading of *Schadenszurechnung*, i.e. imputability of damage, thus highlighting the normative nature of the issue.[12] Irrespective of the causation theory that they espouse, legal writers generally agree on the distinction between two aspects of causation, *haftungsbegründende* and *haftungsausfüllende Kausalität*;[13] the distinction is relevant mostly in the context of § 823(1) BGB:

– *Haftungsbegründende Kausalität* can be translated as "causation as a foundation for liability". It is the causal link between the conduct of the defendant and the result which leads to liability. Under § 823(1) BGB, liability attaches to violations of one of a number of protected *Rechtsgüter* (life, health, bodily integrity, ownership, "other rights").[14] If the plaintiff seeks damages for a violation of bodily integrity, for instance in the form of a broken leg, *haftungsbegründende Kausalität* exists if the conduct of the defendant caused the broken leg. In fact, it is essential in establishing

---

[8] "*Le problème causal en matière de responsabilité civile était fait pour séduire l'esprit des juristes d'Allemagne*", from G. Marty, "La relation de cause à effet comme condition de la responsabilité civile" (1939) 38 RTDciv. 685 at 689, as mentioned in Markesinis and Lawson, *Tortious liability for unintentional harm in the Common law and the Civil law* (Cambridge: Cambridge University Press, 1982) at 106.

[9] See *supra*, Chapter I, 1.4.3. for the text of § 823 and 826 BGB.

[10] See *supra*, General Introduction.

[11] Since causation is not expressly mentioned in the provisions of the BGB dealing with *Schadensersatz* in general (§§ 249–255), commentaries generally treat it in their introduction to § 249 BGB.

[12] See the outlines of Staudinger-Medicus, § 249, Münchener-Grunsky, § 249 and Soergel- Mertens, § 249.

[13] Staudinger-Medicus, § 249 at 40, para. 47; Soergel-Mertens, § 249 at 247, 116; Münchener-Grunsky, § 249 at 364–5, para. 37–9, is skeptical about the usefulness of the distinction.

[14] See *supra*, Chapter I, 1.4.3.

unlawfulness, since it links the conduct of the defendant and the unlawful result (infringement of a protected interest);

— *Haftungsausfüllende Kausalität* can be rendered as "causation as a determinant of the scope of liability". It is the causal link between the conduct of the defendant and the items of damage alleged by plaintiff, the operative principle being that the defendant is liable only for the damage which is causally connected with his or her conduct. To use the example given above, if the plaintiff is claiming the medical expenses required to treat the broken leg as well as a subsequent fall while walking with crutches, *haftungsausfüllende Kausalität* requires that the conduct of the defendant be the cause of each of these items of expense.

In practice, the distinction is relevant since different standards of proof apply to each aspect.[15]

b) The starting point for causation under German law is the *Äquivalenztheorie*, translated as the theory of the equivalence of conditions or equivalence theory.[16] Under the equivalence theory, every condition without which the damage would not have occurred (*conditio sine qua non*) is a cause of the damage;[17] this is the familiar "but for" test, the application of which is not always simple.[18] Some authors argue that the equivalence theory provides a sufficient basis for the *haftungsbegründende Kausalität*,[19] but all agree that it cannot be conclusive for the *haftungsausfüllende Kausalität*, since the scope of liability could be extended almost *ad infinitum*. The following theories have accordingly been put forward to correct or complement the equivalency theory.

c) At the turn of the century, German authors put forward what was to become the *Adäquanztheorie*,[20] translated as the "adequacy theory" or the "adequate cause theory".[21] The theory is formulated in two ways: under the positive formulation, the conduct of the defendant is the adequate cause of the damage if it is in general apt to cause a result such as happened, or at least "if it significantly increased the probability of that result happening"; under the negative formulation, the conduct of the defendant is not the adequate cause of the damage "if it could produce the result in question only under particularly unique and quite improbable circumstances to which no attention would be paid if events had followed a normal course".[22] As Honoré notes, the adequacy theory is essentially based on probabilities.[23]

---

[15] *Haftungsbegründende Kausalität* must be proved by the plaintiff, while *haftungsausfüllende Kausalität* can be assessed by the court on the basis of available evidence: see *infra*, **4.G.19.**, Note (4).

[16] Honoré at 33, para. 60.

[17] Ibid.; Staudinger-Medicus, § 249 at 33, para. 29; Münchener-Grunsky, § 249 at 364, para. 36; Soergel-Mertens, § 249 at 247–8, para. 117.

[18] See *infra*, 4.2.1.

[19] Soergel-Mertens, § 249 at 247–8, para. 117; Münchener-Grunsky, § 249 at 364, para. 38. Staudinger-Medicus, § 249 at 41, para. 48, would see a role for the adequacy and "scope of rule" theories at the *haftungsbegründende Kausalität* stage as well.

[20] Among the authors closely associated with the *Adäquanztheorie* are A. von Kries, "Über den Begriff der objektiven Möglichkeit und einige Anwendugen desselben" (1888) 12 Vierteljahrschrift für wissenschaftliche Philosophie 179, 287, 393, L. Traeger, *Der Kausalbegriff im Straf- und Zivilrecht* (Marburg, 1904) and G. Rümelin, "Die Verwendung der Causalbegriffe im Straf- und Civilrecht" (1900) 90 AcP 171.

[21] Honoré at 49, para. 80.

[22] Münchener-Grunsky, § 249 at 365–6, para. 40; Staudinger-Medicus, § 249 at 36–7, para. 34–6.

[23] Honoré at 49, para. 80.

d) A generation later, other German authors developed the theory of the *Schutzzweck der Norm*,[24] translated as the "scope of rule theory".[25] According to this theory, damage can be recovered only when it is within the scope of protection of the norm which has been infringed.[26] The *Schutzzweck der Norm* theory takes the assessment of causation away from the actual circumstances of the case towards the analysis of the norm that was infringed, and Honoré can rightly term it a "legal policy theory".[27]

e) More recent writing has put forward a new line of reasoning based on the concept of *Risikobereich*, which could be translated as "sphere of risk".[28] The *Risikobereich* analysis is not yet a full-fledged theory, and some authors claim that it adds nothing to the discussion.[29] According to this analysis, every person has to bear a certain amount of risk; some risks come within his or her *Risikobereich*. The best-known of these is the *allgemeines Lebensrisiko*, the "general risk associated with existence",[30] which everyone has to bear. It follows that when the occurrence of damage represents no more than the realization of a risk which was within the *Risikobereich* of the plaintiff, the damage cannot be imputed to the defendant.[31] The *Risikobereich* analysis is one step further removed from the actual circumstances of the case, and it implies a value judgment—which may be present, but not so transparent in the preceding theories—on the risks which one should or should not be expected to bear.[32]

f) There is no consensus amongst German writers as to which theory is to be preferred. Some favour the adequate cause[33] or the scope of rule[34] theory to the exclusion of other theories: others would use them both in a complementary fashion.[35] As might be expected, case law does not clearly follow any one theory, but tends to use them side by side. The following cases have been selected to convey some impression of how German courts, in particular the BGH, handle the theories. The first case dates from 1951, and it still remains the leading case on causation and the adequacy theory. The second one was decided 20 years later in 1972, and it shows how the scope of rule theory is present in the reasoning of the BGH. Another 20 years later, in 1991, the BGH rendered another leading judgment on causation, where the *Risikobereich* analysis can be discerned.

---

[24] Among the authors closely associated with the theory of *Schutzzweck der Norm* are E. Rabel, *Recht des Warenkaufs* (Berlin: de Gruyter, 1958), W. Wilburg, *Elemente des Schadensrechts* (Marburg: Elwert, 1941) and E. von Caemmerer, *Das Problem des Kausalzusammenhangs* (Freiburg: Schulz, 1956).

[25] Honoré at 60, para. 97.

[26] Staudinger-Medicus, § 249 at 38, para. 40; Münchener-Grunsky, § 249 at 369, para. 44. A variant of the *Schutzzweck der Norm* theory is the *Rechtswidrigkeitszusammenhang* theory (literally "coherent relationship with unlawfulness"), under which the damage must be related to the unlawful element in the conduct of the tortfeasor. Authors generally subsume this theory under the *Schutzzweck der Norm* theory: Staudinger-Medicus, § 249 at 39, para. 42; Münchener- Grunsky, § 249 at 369, para. 44; Larenz at 446–7.

[27] Honoré at 60, para. 97.

[28] The leading publication appears to be M. Mädrich, *Das allgemeine Lebensrisiko. Ein Beitrag zur Lehre von der Haftungsbegrenzung im Schadensersatzrecht* (Berlin: Duncker und Humbolt, 1980).

[29] Larenz at 447.

[30] Discussed *supra*, Chapter II, **2.G.4.**

[31] Staundiger-Schäfer, § 823 at 62, para. 90.

[32] Ibid.

[33] Soergel-Mertens, § 249 at 251–2, para. 123.

[34] Münchener-Grunsky, § 249 at 367–8, para. 42.

[35] Staudinger-Medicus, § 249 at 39, para. 43; Larenz at 455–7.

BGH, 23 October 1951[36]   **4.G.1.**

ADEQUATE CAUSATION. EQUITY CONSIDERATIONS

Vessel sunk in lock

In order to assess whether an event was the adequate cause of another event, regard must be had to the normal course of events, from the perspective of an "optimal observer" knowing all the circumstances existing at the time of the event and those which the alleged tortfeasor actually knew and armed with the general experience of mankind at the time of judgment.

Facts: Two ships, the "Edelweiß" and the "Heinrich Hirdes 9" (HH9) were moored side by side in a lock. The construction of the lock was such that its width at water level decreased as the water level was reduced. The vessels' respective operators were asked to specify the width of their vessels before the water level was lowered, in order to ensure that the operation could proceed safely. The operator of the HH9 mistakenly understated the width of the HH9. As the water level was lowered, the Edelweiß and the HH9 became stuck in the lock. The lock personnel proceeded to refill the lock in order to free the vessels; that manoeuvre was improperly executed, and in the course of it the Edelweiß was submerged and sank. The insurer of the Edelweiß sued the insurer of the HH9; by way of defence, the latter pleaded that the mistakes of the lock personnel, and not the inaccurate answer of the operator of the HH9, were the cause of the accident.

Held: The court of first instance gave judgment for the plaintiff, and the court of appeal confirmed that judgment. The BGH reversed the judgment of the court of appeal and remitted the case for further examination.

Judgment: ". . . The appellant rightly states that the court of appeal was mistaken in its discussion of causation as a condition for the liability of the defendant. For one, the assumption that the fault of the operator [of the HH9] directly caused the injury is not correct. [The BGH found that the inaccurate answer as regards the width of the ship was a *conditio sine qua non* for the events which followed.]

This finding, however, does not allow any conclusion to be reached yet as regards the *haftungsbegründende Kausalität* between the [conduct of the] operator and the injury. It is well-established in case law and legal writing that the range of such "logical" causes [i.e. "causes-in-fact"] is generally far too large to justify imposing the full burden of the consequences of each such cause on the person who initiated it. The notion of "adequate causation" was thus created in academic writing; according to the decision of the Reichsgericht of 18 November 1932 (reference omitted):

> '[Adequate causation] is meant to allow individual events that are conditions for a result—in the logical sense that the result would not have happened but for them—to be eliminated from causation in the legal sense. Those conditions that are logically the furthest removed from the result in question must be eliminated, since one would be led to unfair results if these conditions were to be taken into account for legal purposes . . .'

Adequate causation was formulated foremost by Von Kries, Rümelin and Traeger [reference omitted]. The formulations [of those three authors] have in common that they assess a given event—which already constitutes a *conditio sine qua non* [a logical cause or cause-in-fact]—according to its influence on the result [eg the injury], in the light of general criteria. They differ as regards the point of view from which this assessment is carried out. For Von Kries, who created the notion of adequate causation, the influence of such an event on the result should be assessed on the basis of all the circumstances that were known to, or could be known by, the person who brought about the occurrence of that event at the time of such occurrence (ex ante); the general [human]

---

[36] BGHZ, 3, 261. Translation by A. Hoffmann and Y.P. Salmon.

399

experience available at the time of the assessment (ex post) should also be taken into account. In contrast, Rümelin supports the theory of the "objective subsequent prognosis". In order to assess the probability [that the event influenced the result], he proposes that consideration should be given to the entire spectrum of human experience and to all circumstances that were somehow present at the time the event occurred, regardless of whether they could be known to the person who brought about the occurrence of the event (even with the utmost cognition) or whether they only became known afterwards through the chain of events that followed the event in question.

The approach of Von Kries, based on subjective foreseeability at the time of the event, proved to be too restrictive in cases of risk-based liability (*Gefährdungshaftung*) or contractual liability. The approach of Rümelin, based on objective foreseeability with hindsight, proved to be insufficient to guarantee that the unfair results of the equivalence theory [as explained at the beginning of the excerpt] would be avoided . . . Traeger avoids the shortcomings of both theories [reference omitted] with the following formulation: *An event is the adequate condition for a result if such event generally increases, in a significant way, the objective probability of a result of the kind which occurred* [emphasis added]. The assessment must extend to, but no further than:

a) all circumstances that an optimal observer could know at the time of the occurrence of the event; and
b) any additional circumstances which were indeed known to the person responsible for the occurrence of the event.

Traeger proposes to examine the event in question in light of those circumstances, taking into account the whole of human experience available at the time of assessment, to see whether it had a significant influence on the occurrence of the injury.

Since the judgment of 22 June 1931, RGZ 133, 126 at 127 the case law of the Reichsgericht essentially followed Traeger's formulation [of the adequate causation theory], which it restated as follows: adequate causation is established "*if an event was generally suitable to lead to the occurrence of the result, and not only under particularly unique and quite improbable circumstances to which no attention would be paid if events had followed a normal course*" [emphasis added].

This chamber adheres to the above statement [of the adequate causation theory]—which essentially remained unchanged in numerous decisions until now [references omitted]—while retaining the basis for assessment as it was set out by Traeger. Admittedly [reference omitted], the starting point for the inquiry must not be forgotten, that is to say the search for a corrective device which reduces the range of logical consequences to those consequences that can reasonably be imputed [upon the tortfeasor]. The formulation [of the adequate causation theory] set out above can become overly schematized, thus jeopardizing the attainment of fair results; this danger can only be avoided if the courts keep in mind that the inquiry does not actually concern causation, but rather the determination of the limits up to which a person who brought about an event can, in all fairness and reasonableness, be made liable for the consequences of such a event; this is in truth an autonomous condition for liability in its own right [references omitted].

[The BGH then found that the inaccurate answer was the adequate cause of the two ships becoming stuck as the water level was lowered, but that this did not mean that it was also the adequate cause of the subsequent sinking of the Edelweiß as the lock was refilled.] The Reichsgericht repeatedly stated in its case law that everyone who causes an accident is also liable for the consequential injury that arises only later, through a mistake in the course of a [remedial] intervention that is made unavoidable by the accident. According to common experience, it must be expected that [remedial] interventions will not always be performed in an absolutely proper manner, so as to result in the desired outcome [references omitted]. However, this principle does not apply without exception and cannot have as a result that the person responsible for initiating the events leading to the accident is burdened indiscriminately with all the consequences that arise independently of his conduct by the completely unusual and improper intervention of a third party who was not [necessarily] habilitated to intervene [references omitted].

[The BGH then found that the court of appeal had omitted to assess whether "an optimal observer would have expected the lock personnel to behave as they did once the *haftungsbegründende* event—the understated width of the HH9—had taken place", and remitted the case for further inquiry.]"

Notes

(1) The annotated case set the direction for the examination of causation in the post-War era. In it, the BGH took a position on many key points relating to causation in general and to the adequacy theory in particular, each of which were going to give rise to much discussion amongst legal writers. Despite variations in wording, it seems that in subsequent case law the BGH has not intended to move away from the explanation of the adequacy theory which it gave in the annotated case.[37]

(2) First, the BGH recalled that the starting point of the inquiry is the *conditio sine qua non* formula (or "but for" test), which however leads to unacceptable results because it is too broad. The aim of the adequacy theory is therefore to *reduce* the potential scope of liability of the defendant.

(3) Secondly, the BGH adopted both the positive and the negative formulation of the adequacy theory (both are emphasized in the above excerpt), as they have been outlined previously,[38] viz. that "an event is the adequate condition for a result if such event generally increases, in a significant way, the objective probability of a result of the kind which occurred", and that it is not the adequate cause of another event if the other event occurred "under quite improbable circumstances". In any case, adequacy thus involves an assessment of probabilities, and the next question naturally is on what basis or from whose perspective that assessment is to be made. It is no coincidence that the BGH discussed that issue at length in the annotated case.[39]

The original proponent of the adequacy theory, von Kries, thought that probability was to be assessed from the perspective of the alleged tortfeasor, *i.e.* the question for him was whether, on the basis of the circumstances that the tortfeasor knew or could have known at the time of the allegedly injurious conduct (and taking into account general experience), the sequence of events leading to the damage was probable. As the BGH notes, von Kries' position is too favourable to the alleged tortfeasor, especially in cases of risk-based liability (*Gefährdungshaftung*), since the very idea of risk-based liability implies that liability does not depend on elements relating to the situation of the alleged tortfeasor. Another author, Rümelin, frames the test quite differently: probability is to be assessed on the basis of all circumstances that existed at the time of the event, whether they were known to the alleged tortfeasor or not (including those circumstances which became known only after the event), again taking into account general experience. Here, contrary to von Kries, Rümelin's position is too favourable to the plaintiff. The BGH chose to side with a third author, Traeger, who came up with the idea of the "optimal

---

[37] Staudinger-Medicus, § 249 at 37, para. 37.

[38] Introductory Note under c).

[39] See Honoré at 50–2, para. 82 for a complete and critical description of the three theories mentioned by the BGH and described in the main text.

observer": probability is to be assessed from the perspective of all circumstances which would have been known to the "optimal observer" at the time of the event as well as all circumstances which the alleged tortfeasor himself knew, taking into account general experience.

As may be expected, the "optimal observer" is difficult to pin down: the more he or she is deemed to know about the circumstances which surrounded the sequence of events, the more that sequence will be seen as a probable consequence of the alleged tortfeasor's conduct.[40] If the "optimal observer" is given great perspicacity and perceptiveness, with almost perfect knowledge of all the circumstances which could be known at the time of the events, then the only difference between Traeger and Rümelin is that Traeger's "optimal observer" is not aware of circumstances which became known only after the events; even then, as Medicus observes, a court looking at the facts with hindsight will tend to endow the "optimal observer" also with knowledge of those circumstances.[41] If that is so, then very few consequences would appear not to be the probable consequence of the conduct of the alleged tortfeasor, and accordingly the adequacy theory would not significantly curtail the perceived excesses of the *conditio sine qua non* test. Indeed there are few cases where claims were rejected on the ground that the conduct of the defendant was not the adequate cause of the injury to the victim. That is the main criticism that is levelled at the current understanding of the adequacy theory as set out in the annotated judgment and the case law deriving from it.[42] Authors who still would leave a place for the adequacy theory generally advocate either that the observer should be made less optimal[43] or that some teleological element in addition to probability should be included in the adequacy theory.[44]

(4) Thirdly, building on the RG case-law,[45] the BGH took the adequacy theory somewhat beyond the issue of causation as such when it stated that "the inquiry does not actually concern causation, but rather the determination of the limits up to which a person who brought about an event can, in all fairness and reasonableness, be made liable for the consequences of such an event; this is in truth an autonomous condition for liability in its own right". The reference to fairness was criticized as foreign to the regime of *Schadensersatz* of the BGB;[46] Grunsky notes perhaps more accurately that, from the moment when it is recognized that an element of fairness—divorced from "natural" causation—must come into play to correct the excesses of the *conditio sine qua non* test, it can be called into question whether the adequacy theory, with its emphasis on probability, is best suited to achieve such fairness.[47] As will be seen in the judgments reproduced below,

---

[40] Larenz at 437.

[41] Staudinger-Medicus, § 249 at 38, para. 39.

[42] Münchener-Grunsky, § 249 at 367–8, para. 42, would do away with the adequacy theory on that basis. See also Staudinger-Medicus, § 249, ibid.; Soergel-Mertens, § 249 at 250–1, para. 121; Staudinger-Schäfer, § 823 at 57–8, para. 85.

[43] Larenz at 439–40. Staudinger-Medicus, § 249 at 39–40, para. 44–6, agrees with Larenz on this point, but sees a danger that the adequacy theory would then come too close to the requirement of *Verschulden* (which is discussed *supra*, Chapter III, 3.2.1 and 3.2.2.B.).

[44] Soergel-Mertens, § 249 at 250–1, para. 121.

[45] The excerpt from the RG case law quoted in the annotated case already made reference to equity.

[46] See a summary of those criticisms in Staudinger-Schäfer, § 823 at 57–8, para. 85. Staudinger Medicus, § 249 at 37, para. 36, finds that criticism misplaced.

[47] Münchener-Grunsky, § 249 at 367–8, para. 42.

considerations of fairness have subsequently been infused with new doctrines such as the *Schutzzweck der Norm* theory, which brought the inquiry into causation even further away from a mere examination of the sequence of events.

BGH, 16 February 1972[48]　　　　　　**4.G.2.**
Bremen v. Federal Republic of Germany

THE "SCOPE OF RULE" THEORY

Drivers on the pavement

Damage caused by impatient drivers driving on the pavement to avoid the scene of an accident cannot be imputed to the person responsible for the accident.

Facts: A military lorry collided with a car and thereby blocked a street in Bremen. Impatient car drivers went round the scene of the accident by driving on the adjacent bicycle and pedestrian paths, thereby damaging them. The drivers were not sued for that damage. Instead the City of Bremen sued the Federal Republic, which was legally responsible for damage caused by the military.

Held: The court of first instance rejected the claim. The court of appeal reversed the judgment of the court of first instance. The BGH reinstated the judgment of the court of first instance.

Judgment: "II. 1. It is true, as the court of appeal found, that the conduct of the lorry driver, which led to the accident, was the adequate cause of the damage to the bicycle path and the pavement . . . Experience shows that in accidents of the kind at issue here, there are always drivers who . . . cannot wait until it is possible to drive through the scene of accident again or until the police allows drivers to drive round it. It is well known that such behaviour on the part of drivers occurs again and again, so that it can even be assumed that the driver of a motor vehicle must expect that, if he causes an accident at a location where traffic is considerable, drivers who are forced to wait behind the accident scene could well react in such a way, thereby causing damage to public highways, private grounds, fences, etc . . .

2. If adequate causation cannot thus . . . be disputed, the outcome of the litigation depends on whether the consequences of "free" initiatives taken by third parties can also be imputed to the wrongdoer . . .

[The BGH found that the conduct of the impatient drivers was an act of free will for which the accident was not a *Herausforderung*,[49] and which accordingly could not be imputed to the driver who was responsible for the accident. It then added an analysis based on the "scope of rule" theory.] From a normative point of view, the connection between the conduct of the lorry driver and the damage to property is not sufficient to warrant making the driver liable. According to the applicable law, in particular road traffic regulations, the spheres of responsibility were clearly divided. The driver and the keeper (*Halter*) of the lorry were responsible for the collision and its consequences, both for other road-users who, for instance, would have become involved in the accident and for things that would have been detrimentally affected by the collision. But according to the course of events in the present case, only the drivers who drove over the bicycle paths and the pavement are responsible for the damage inflicted to them. The obligations and prohibitions which the law imposes upon the lorry driver protect the interests of those whose property lies close to the

---

[48]　BGHZ 58, 162. Translation by A. Hoffmann and Y. P. Salmon.
[49]　Strictly speaking, a "challenge" to the impatient drivers: see *infra*, **4.G.35.** and notes thereafter on the doctrine of *Herausforderung* under German law.

highway only inasmuch as the driver should not drive his lorry on the pavement and should not force other vehicles to drive on the properties that adjoin the highway in order to avoid a collision with him. On the other hand, his obligations, in fact and in law, do not extend as far as to compel him to prevent that, once the accident had occurred, drivers who were behind him and who had already managed to stop [before the scene of the accident] would drive across the bicycle path and the pavement in order to move ahead more quickly. The consequences of the actions of those drivers do not fall within his sphere of responsibility . . .

III. For the damage which was inflicted by those drivers, the plaintiff can only claim against them. Since these drivers can no longer be identified, the plaintiff runs the risk of ultimately having to bear the damage alone. But this is a general risk which falls upon every owner of property which adjoins a public highway; it cannot be shifted onto the defendant [reference omitted]."

Notes

(1) The annotated judgment illustrates well the articulation between the adequacy theory and the "scope of rule" (*Schutzzweck der Norm*) theory. The BGH explains (under II.1. of the judgment) how the car accident must be seen as the adequate cause of the damage to the pavement, since it normally follows from an accident that impatient drivers will try to drive round the scene of the accident and thereby cause damage.

Yet this does not complete the examination: the BGH adds (under II.2.) that the case must also be subjected to a *wertender Betrachtung* (normative assessment). The BGH thus makes it explicit that considerations of fairness come into play, quite separately from considerations relating to causation as such but, contrary to its pronouncement in the previous annotated judgment,[50] the BGH seems to consider that adequacy does not involve considerations of fairness. Accordingly, the annotated judgment has been hailed by some as marking a definitive break, away from causation and to imputability (*Zurechnung*);[51] in truth the BGH leaves room for consideration of both adequacy and fairness.

(2) The normative assessment of the BGH relies on an examination of the scope of the road traffic rules.[52] The BGH concludes that these rules protect the owners of property near public highways only to the extent that they prohibit drivers from driving on that property or forcing other drivers to do so in order to avoid an accident.

While writers may agree on the foundations of the "scope of rule" (*Schutzzweck der Norm*) theory, they certainly disagree on its application in the annotated judgment. While many authors support the BGH decision,[53] others think that the purpose of the road traffic regulations is also to protect property adjoining the highway, and that, contrary to what the BGH found, the type of damage in the annotated case would come within the scope of those regulations.[54] In fact, the annotated judgment and the ensuing discussion show that the "scope of rule" theory does not necessarily give more definite results than

---

[50] See *supra*, **4.G.1.**, Note (4).

[51] E. Deutsch, JZ 1971, 244, as mentioned in Staudinger-Schäfer, § 823 at 73, para. 102.

[52] Including the rule at § 7 StVG that the driver and keeper (*Halter*) of a motor vehicle are liable for accidents and their consequences. On § 7 StVG, see *infra*, Chapter VI, 6.2.1.A.

[53] E. Deutsch, "Regreßverbot und Unterbrechung des Haftungszusammenhangs im Zivilrecht" JZ 1972, 551; U. Huber, "Verschulden, Gefährdungshaftung und Adäquanz" in *Festschrift Eduard Wahl* (Heidelberg: Winter, 1973), 301; E.A. Kramer, "Schutzgesetze und adäquate Kausalität" JZ 1976, 338. Soergel-Mertens, § 249 at 262, para. 140, also agrees with the BGH on the result, but would have based the reasoning on his vision of the adequacy theory.

[54] Münchener-Grunsky, § 249 at 377, para. 58. Staudinger-Medicus, § 249 at 46–7, para. 68, also doubts whether the BGH came to the correct conclusion.

the adequacy theory. As Schäfer notes, one of the central weaknesses of the scope of rule theory is that it offers little by way of general guidance; it gains substance only through the development of case-law relating to specific norms and types of cases.[55] It is generally acknowledged, however, that it tends to lead to a denial of liability in cases where an analysis based on the adequacy theory alone would impute the damage to the conduct of the alleged tortfeasor.[56]

The usefulness of the scope of rule theory for cases brought under § 823(2) or § 839 BGB has generally been recognized:[57] in these cases, the liability of the defendant is alleged to originate in a violation of a specific protective norm (*Schutznorm*) or official duty (*Amtspflicht*) which led to damage to the plaintiff.[58] It then appears logical to inquire into the scope of protection of the specific protective norm or official duty to see if it covers the plaintiff's case. Similarly, the scope of rule theory can contribute to the inquiry in contractual liability cases, where a violation of a specific contractual provision is alleged. Many writers cast doubt on the usefulness of the theory when liability arises pursuant to § 823(1) BGB, since there the rule the scope of which is to be assessed is § 823(1) BGB itself, and the aim of § 823(1) BGB is precisely to provide a comprehensive protection to the *Rechtsgüter* listed in it.[59]

Furthermore, the "scope of rule" theory plays a central role in the assessment of causation under most of the risk-based liability regimes (*Gefährdungshaftung*), where the central issue is whether the injury to the plaintiff constituted a specific manifestation of the exceptional risk which underpins the liability regime.[60]

(3) Under III. of the annotated judgment, the BGH concludes by stating that the City of Bremen must bear the general risk that damage may be done to property which adjoins a highway. Considerations based on the division of risks ("sphere of risks" or *Risikobereich*) amongst members of society were to play an increasing role in the reasoning of German courts as regards imputability, as seen in the next judgment.

BGH, 2 July 1991[61]   **4.G.3.**

THE "SCOPE OF RULE" THEORY. SPHERE OF RISK

Panic in the piggery

The defendant cannot be held responsible for risks which properly fell within a sphere of risk that the plaintiff had himself created.

Facts: The plaintiff operated a pig farm where intensive farming was practiced (ie a relatively large number of pigs were kept together in relatively small areas within the piggery). The defendant was responsible for a car

[55] Staudinger-Schäfer, § 823 at 63–4, para. 91.
[56] Staudinger-Schäfer, § 823 at 58, para. 86.
[57] On the usefulness of the scope of rule theory for the various possible heads of liability, see Staudinger-Medicus, § 249 at 38, para. 41; Münchener-Grunsky, § 249 at 369–70, para. 45; Larenz at 441–7.
[58] See *supra*, Chapter II, 2.4.2.B.
[59] See *supra*, Chapter I, 1.4.3.
[60] See *infra*, **4.G.3.** as well as *infra*, Chapter VI, **6.G.2.** and Notes (4) to (6) thereafter, and **6.G.3.** and notes thereafter.
[61] BGHZ 115, 84. Translation by A. Hoffmann and Y.P. Salmon.

405

accident which occurred on the street corner some 50m away from the plaintiff's piggery. The accident produced a bang, and shortly afterwards the pigs were heard squeaking and shrieking. As it subsequently emerged, the pigs had panicked, and many died or were injured. The plaintiff sought damages from the defendant for his resulting loss.

Held: The court of first instance rejected the claim. The court of appeal reversed the judgment of the court of first instance. The BGH reversed the decision of the court of appeal and rejected the claim.

Judgment: "1. . . . There are limits to a liability under § 7 StVG which . . . result from the scope of that provision [reference omitted] . . . Liability only arises . . . if the injury can be imputed to the operation of a motor vehicle, according to the scope of protection of that risk-based liability regime. The injury cannot be imputed [to the defendant] if it is no longer a specific realization of the risks from which the liability regime aims to provide indemnity [references omitted]. This is all the more so if it represents the realization of a sphere of risk independent from the risk resulting from the operation [of a motor vehicle].

2. . . . The damage suffered by the plaintiff resulted from a reaction of the animals which was indeed triggered by the bang produced by the accident. The injury would thus be causally connected with the operation of the motor vehicle driven by the defendant. It can also be said, as the court of appeal remarks, that the noise caused by a traffic accident represents the realization of a risk related to motor vehicle traffic.

Nevertheless, if the limits of the liability of the keeper (*Halter*) of a motor vehicle are determined using the scope of rule [theory], the defendant should not be held liable for the damage which occurred in the plaintiff's piggery as a consequence of the noise generated by the accident. The injury is in the first place the realization of a risk which had been created by the plaintiff himself when he kept his pigs in an environment which makes them particularly susceptible to noises that can arise through road traffic. Such an environment can lead to panic amongst the animals, which can result in damage of the kind at issue here.

The panic reaction of the pigs to the noise generated by the accident . . . is to be attributed to an unusual sensitivity of the animals, which is caused by contemporary farming conditions. Modern intensive farming, where large numbers of animals are kept in small stalls, makes pigs in particular very prone to react to unusual noises with fright and aggression, to the point where they end up killing each other.

If the injured party nevertheless freely decides to keep pigs in such an environment, he himself creates the decisive cause for the injury. Keeping pigs in such an environment is not compatible with the kind of noises which road traffic occasionally produces. The farmer must therefore take distur-bances and adverse consequences into account; from a normative perspective, they are the price which the farmer must pay for the farming method that he chose. They cannot be seen as a disad-vantage arising from the fact that the operation of motor vehicle is permitted, from which § 7 StVG aims to relieve the victim. Accordingly, the plaintiff created for his business an autonomous sphere of risk, which he must himself bear; that sphere is to be distinguished from that which relates to the operation of a motor vehicle. The keeper (*Halter*) of a motor vehicle cannot in all fairness be bur-dened with [the reparation of] injury which represents the realization of a risk created by the plain-tiff himself. Injury of that kind is no longer covered by the scope of protection of § 7 StVG . . .

The above reasoning is not affected by the fact that [intensive pig farming] is no longer excep-tional nowadays; it is a normal phenomenon of life, and must therefore be taken into account by everybody, including drivers of motor vehicles. As regards the law of liability, the decisive criterion remains that the operator of such a farming installation takes a particular risk upon himself, the consequences of which he must accept as his own loss, without burdening the keeper (*Halter*) of a motor vehicle with it."

Notes

(1) In this case, which was decided some two decades after the previous annotated judgment, it can be seen that the "scope of rule" (*Schutzzweck der Norm*) theory had established itself more firmly in the reasoning of the BGH.[62] In fact, with respect to risk-based liability (*Gefährdungshaftung*) such as is created by § 7 StVG, the adequacy theory plays no role and the "scope of rule" theory lies at the core of the assessment of causation.[63]

Whereas in the previous annotated judgment the BGH based its examination of the scope of the road traffic regulations on the duties imposed on drivers and raised issues relating to risk in its conclusion only, here § 7 StVG imposes liability without regard to the fault of the driver; the duties imposed on drivers were thus less relevant and the division of risks played the central role. Essentially, according to the BGH, § 7 StVG is intended to protect third parties against the dangers created by the operation of motor vehicles.[64] If some damage represents the realization of a risk which was not related to the dangers of operating a motor vehicle, then there will be no liability under § 7 StVG, even if the operation of a motor vehicle was a cause of the damage. The annotated judgment represents a milestone in the case law, in that the BGH opposed, on the one hand, the risk created by the defendant through the use of a motor vehicle and, on the other hand, an equally well-defined sphere of risk for which the plaintiff is deemed to be responsible. The issue then becomes in whose sphere of risk the injury is found to fall.

In the annotated judgment, the BGH took a relatively unsympathetic attitude towards operators of intensive farming installations (injury is "the price which the farmer must pay for the farming method that he chose"), by finding that the plaintiff is responsible for the risks related to his choice of farming method, which made the pigs particularly sensitive to disturbances of their environment. That risk was not related to the risks arising from the operation of motor vehicles. Since the damage suffered by the plaintiff represented no more than the realization of that risk, the plaintiff had to bear it.

(2) As mentioned above, legal writing is still discussing whether the use of *Risikobereich* or "sphere of risk" reasoning represents no more than a refinement of the "scope of rule" theory[65] or a new theory in its own right.[66] In any event, the increasing consideration of risk in the assessment of imputability under German law also reflects an increasing concern for the economic implications of tort law.

---

[62] The annotated case has been discussed from a comparative viewpoint by J. Shaw (UK), M. van Quickenborne (Belgium) and T.E. Abeltshauser (Germany) in (1993) 1 Eur. R Priv. L 241 ff.

[63] *Infra*, Chapter VI, **6.G.3.** and notes thereafter.

[64] It will be recalled that the "operation" of motor vehicles is the key element defining the scope of protection of § 7 StVG: see *infra*, Chapter VI, 6.2.1.A.

[65] Münchener-Grunsky, § 249 at 384–5, para. 72. Staudinger-Schäfer, § 823, at 30, para. 86, presents it as a "terminological variant".

[66] U. Huber, "Normzwecktheorie und Adäquanztheorie" JZ 1969, 677. Larenz at 447–9 presents it as an autonomous theory.

4.1.2. ENGLISH LAW

Introductory Note

a) Legal writers in England generally divide the assessment of causation into two stages, usually called "cause-in-fact" and "legal cause". "Cause-in-fact" is presented as the assessment of whether the conduct of the alleged tortfeasor is a *conditio sine qua non* of the harm suffered by the plaintiff, *i.e.* whether the harm would have occurred "but for" the conduct in question. At the stage of "legal cause", the focus of the inquiry then moves away from the historical reconstruction of events to issues of policy, the issue becoming whether the alleged tortfeasor (assuming other conditions for liability in tort are fulfilled) ought to be liable for the harm which the plaintiff suffered.[67] This second stage tends to be labelled "remoteness of damage" under English law or "proximate cause" under US law, but that does not necessarily mean that some form of temporal or physical distance test is involved. The matter is more complex, as will be seen from the cases excerpted below.

b) The two-stage test is by no means universally accepted. Markesinis and Deakin point out that it creates the illusion that the first stage is purely technical, involving no "policy issues".[68] In their acclaimed work *Causation and the Law*, H.L.A. Hart and A. Honoré take issue more fundamentally with the idea that once one finds that the *conditio sine qua non* is satisfied, *everything* else not only should be, but in practice is, purely a question of policy.[69] They set out a more elaborate view of causation, whereby many conclusions which are elsewhere presented as being dictated by policy considerations over and above the "but for" test can in fact be explained by a broader, "common sense" vision of causation which does not involve policy at all. It is beyond the scope of this casebook to present and comment Hart and Honoré's views on causation. Unlike German courts, English courts do not usually discuss abstract theories in their judgments, and accordingly the influence of Hart and Honoré's views on English law, while undeniable, is difficult to assess.[70]

c) In a series of cases in the 1960s, the House of Lords and the Privy Council reshaped the law concerning the second stage of the inquiry, "remoteness of damage". The two most relevant cases for the law of negligence, *The Wagon Mound (No. 1)* and *Hughes* v. *Lord Advocate*, are excerpted below. Furthermore, even if causation is often reviewed in connection with negligence, it is an element of many other torts as well. The impact of the negligence cases on other torts is reviewed in the notes under these two cases.

d) The reasoning behind the "scope of rule" (*Schutzzweck der Norm*) theory under German law is not foreign to English law, although it has not yet been turned into a general feature of tort law. As regards the tort of breach of statutory duty, however, it is acknowledged that the court must examine whether the harm suffered by the plaintiff came within the scope of protection of the statute whose breach is invoked, as shown by *Donaghey* v. *Boulton & Paul Ltd.*, the third case excerpted below.

---

[67] Markesinis and Deakin at 174; *Clerk & Lindsell on Torts* at 40, para. 2–02; Rogers at 195ff.

[68] Markesinis and Deakin at 175–6.

[69] Hart and Honoré, in particular at 3–4.

[70] See Markesinis and Deakin at 175. Compare with *supra*, **4.G.1.**, where the BGH "settles" the debate between von Kries, Rümelin and Traeger.

More generally, as noted by Hart and Honoré,[71] "[w]here a legal rule has been violated and harm has occurred which may be regarded as 'within the risk' in the sense that the harm is of a kind which the rule was designed to prevent, the courts may consider it enough that the defendant, by his breach of the rule, has done something without which the harm would not have occurred and so provided an occasion for it. They then hold him responsible for the harm, wherever the way in which it has eventuated from the occasion which he has provided, even if it was by a most unusual intervention or coincidence."

Privy Council[72]   **4.E.4.–5.**

Overseas Tankship (UK) Ltd. v. *Morts Dock & Engineering Co. Ltd.*
The Wagon Mound (No. 1)
and
House of Lords[73]
Hughes v. *Lord Advocate*

REMOTENESS OF DAMAGE. REASONABLE FORESEEABILITY TEST.

A. Privy Council, *The Wagon Mound (No. 1)*   **4.E.4.**

Oil spill in Sydney harbour

Facts: The defendant Overseas Tankship was the charterer of "The Wagon Mound". While the Wagon Mound was moored in Sydney harbour, bunkering oil was carelessly discharged from the ship into the waters. The oil was carried by the wind and the tide to the wharf of the plaintiff, Morts Dock & Engineering, some 200 yards away. The plaintiff used the wharf in the course of its shipbuilding and repair operations, which involve the use of welding equipment, among others. Some two-and-a-half days after the Wagon Mound had left the harbour, the plaintiff's employees resumed welding work, having received advice that it was safe for them to do so, despite the continued presence of floating oil around the wharf. At some point, molten metal fell from the wharf and set fire to some cotton waste which was floating on the surface. As a direct or indirect result thereof, the bunkering oil was set on fire. The flames engulfed the wharf, causing considerable damage to it and to the equipment stored on it. The plaintiff sought damages from the defendant.

Held: The court of first instance and the court of appeal allowed the claim. The Privy Council advised that the judgments of the courts below be reversed and the action dismissed.

Judgment: VISCOUNT SIMONDS: ". . . It is inevitable that first consideration should be given to *Re Polemis and Furness, Withy & Co Ltd* [1921] 3 KB 560, [1921] All ER 40, which will henceforward be referred to as *Polemis*. For it was avowedly in deference to that decision and to decisions of the [English] Court of Appeal that followed it that the [court of appeal] was constrained to decide the present case in favour of the respondents . . .

There can be no doubt that the decision of the Court of Appeal in *Polemis* plainly asserts that, if the defendant is guilty of negligence, he is responsible for all the consequences, whether reasonably foreseeable or not. The generality of the proposition is, perhaps, qualified by the fact that each of the Lords Justices refers to the outbreak of fire as the direct result of the negligent act. There is thus introduced the conception that the negligent actor is not responsible for consequences which

---

[71] Hart and Honoré at 6.
[72] [1961] AC 388. It is customary under English law to refer to shipping and maritime cases by the name of the ship involved, here "The Wagon Mound".
[73] [1963] AC 837.

are not 'direct', whatever that may mean. It has to be asked, then, why this conclusion should have been reached. [Viscount Simonds then proceeded to review the authorities which were considered in *Re Polemis*, as well as other authorities both before and after *Re Polemis*.]

Enough has been said to show that the authority of *Polemis* has been severely shaken, though lip-service has from time to time been paid to it. In their Lordships' opinion, it should no longer be regarded as good law. It is not probable that many cases will for that reason have a different result, though it is hoped that the law will be thereby simplified, and that, in some cases at least, palpable injustice will be avoided. For it does not seem consonant with current ideas of justice or morality that, for an act of negligence, however slight or venial, which results in some trivial foreseeable damage the actor should be liable for all consequences, however unforeseeable and however grave, so long as they can be said to be 'direct'. It is a principle of civil liability . . . that a man must be considered to be responsible for the probable consequences of his act. To demand more of him is too harsh a rule, to demand less is to ignore that civilised order requires the observance of a minimum standard of behaviour.

. . . For, if it is asked why a man should be responsible for the natural or necessary or probable consequences of his act (or any other similar description of them), the answer is that it is not because they are natural or necessary or probable, but because, since they have this quality, it is judged, by the standard of the reasonable man, that he ought to have foreseen them. Thus it is that over and over again it has happened that in different judgments in the same case, and sometimes in a single judgment, liability for a consequence has been imposed on the ground that it was reasonably foreseeable or, alternatively, on the ground that it was natural or necessary or probable. The two grounds have been treated as coterminous, and so they largely are. But, where they are not, the question arises to which the wrong answer was given in *Polemis*. For, if some limitation must be imposed on the consequences for which the negligent actor is to be held responsible—and all are agreed that some limitation there must be—why should that test (reasonable foreseeability) be rejected which, since he is judged by what the reasonable man ought to foresee, corresponds with the common conscience of mankind, and a test (the 'direct' consequence) be substituted which leads to nowhere but the never-ending and insoluble problems of causation . . .

. At an early stage in this judgment, their Lordships intimated that they would deal with the proposition which can best be stated by reference to the well-known dictum of Lord Sumner[74]: 'This, however, goes to culpability, not to compensation.' It is with the greatest respect to that very learned judge and to those who have echoed his words that their Lordships find themselves bound to state their view that this proposition is fundamentally false.

It is, no doubt, proper when considering tortious liability for negligence to analyse its elements and to say that the plaintiff must prove a duty owed to him by the defendant, a breach of that duty by the defendant, and consequent damage. But there can be no liability until the damage has been done. It is not the act but the consequences on which tortious liability is founded. Just as (as it has been said) there is no such thing as negligence in the air, so there is no such thing as liability in the air . . . If, as admittedly it is, [the defendant's] liability (culpability) depends on the reasonable foreseeability of the consequent damage, how is that to be determined except by the foreseeability of the damage which in fact happened . . . ? And, if that damage is unforeseeable so as to displace liability at large, how can the liability be restored so as to make compensation payable?

But, it is said, a different position arises if [the defendant's] careless act has been shown to be negligent and has caused some foreseeable damage to [the plaintiff]. Their Lordships have already observed that to hold [the defendant] liable for consequences however unforeseeable of a careless act, if, but only if, he is at the same time liable for some other damage however trivial appears to be

---

[74] [1920] AC 956 at 984. Author's Note: The preceding words in Lord Sumner's speech were: "What a defendant ought to have anticipated as a reasonable man is material when the question is whether or not he was guilty of negligence, that is, of want of due care according to the circumstances."

neither logical nor just. This becomes more clear if it is supposed that similar unforeseeable damage is suffered by A and C, but other foreseeable damage, for which B is liable, by A only. A system of law which would hold B liable to A but not to C for the similar damage suffered by each of them could not easily be defended. Fortunately, the attempt is not necessary. For the same fallacy is at the root of the proposition. It is irrelevant to the question whether B is liable for unforeseeable damage that he is liable for foreseeable damage, as irrelevant as would the fact that he had trespassed on Whiteacre be to the question whether he had trespassed on Blackacre . . . Each of them rests on its own bottom, and will fail if it can be established that the damage could not reasonably be foreseen . . . As Denning LJ said in *King v. Phillips* [1953] 1 QB 429 at 441, [1953] 1 All ER 617 at 623: 'there can be no doubt since *Bourhill* v. *Young* [[1943] AC 92, [1942] 2 All ER 396] that the test of *liability for shock* is foreseeability of *injury by shock*' [emphasis in original]. Their Lordships substitute the word 'fire' for 'shock' and endorse this statement of the law.

Their Lordships conclude this part of the case with some general observations. They have been concerned primarily to displace the proposition that unforeseeability is irrelevant if damage is 'direct'. In doing so they have inevitably insisted that the essential factor in determining liability is whether the damage is of such a kind as the reasonable man should have foreseen . . . Who knows or can be assumed to know all the processes of nature? But if it would be wrong that a man should be held liable for damage unpredictable by a reasonable man because it was 'direct' or 'natural', equally it would be wrong that he should escape liability, however 'indirect' the damage, if he foresaw or could reasonably foresee the intervening events which led to its being done . . . Thus foreseeability becomes the effective test . . ."

B. House of Lords, *Hughes* v. *Lord Advocate*

Explosion in manhole

Facts: Workers were maintaining underground telephone equipment in Edinburgh and for that purpose had put up a tent over the manhole where they were working. When they left the site at the end of the day, they did not put the cover back over the manhole. They left the tent unguarded, with red warning paraffin lamps besides it. An eight-year-old boy took one of the lamps and went into the tent. He lowered or accidentally knocked over one of the lamps into the hole, as a result of which an explosion occurred. The explosion drew the boy into the hole and he suffered severe injuries. The employer of the workers was sued for damages.

Held: Both the court of first instance and the court of appeal rejected the claim. The House of Lords reversed those judgments and allowed the claim.

Judgment: LORD GUEST:[75] ". . . In dismissing the appellant's claim the [court of first instance] and the majority of the [court of appeal] reached the conclusion that the accident which happened was not reasonably foreseeable. In order to establish a coherent chain of causation it is not necessary that the precise details leading up to the accident should have been reasonably foreseeable: it is sufficient if the accident which occurred is of a type which should have been foreseeable by a reasonably careful person [references omitted] . . . [T]he precise concatenation of circumstances need not be envisaged. Concentration has been placed in the courts below on the explosion which, it was said, could not have been foreseen because it was caused in a unique fashion by the paraffin forming into vapour and being ignited by the naked flame of the wick. But this, in my opinion, is to concentrate on what is really a non-essential element in the dangerous situation created by the allurement. The test might better be put thus: Was the igniting of paraffin outside the lamp by the

---

[75] All five Law Lords (Lords Reid, Jenkins, Morris, Guest and Pearce) delivered speeches, but Lord Guest gave the leading speech.

flame a foreseeable consequence of the breach of duty? In the circumstances there was a combination of potentially dangerous circumstances against which the [defendant] had to protect the [plain-
tiff]. If these formed an allurement to children it might have been foreseen that they would play with
the lamp, that it might tip over, that it might be broken, and that when broken the paraffin might
spill and be ignited by the flame. All these steps in the chain of causation seem to have been accepted
by all the judges in the courts below as foreseeable. But because the explosion was the agent which
caused the burning and was unforeseeable, therefore the accident, according to them, was not reasonably foreseeable. In my opinion this reasoning is fallacious. An explosion is only one way in
which burning can be caused. Burning can also be caused by the contact between liquid paraffin
and a naked flame. In the one case paraffin vapour and in the other case liquid paraffin is ignited
by fire. I cannot see that these are two different types of accident. They are both burning accidents
and in both cases the injuries would be burning injuries. On this view the explosion was an immaterial event in the chain of causation. It was simply one way in which burning might be caused by
the potentially dangerous paraffin lamp . . ."

Notes

(1) In *The Wagon Mound (No. 1)*, the Privy Council overruled the decision of the
Court of Appeal in the earlier case of *Re Polemis*.[76] At stake were two different conceptions of the test for remoteness of damage under the tort of negligence. It must be underlined that the debate concerns the extent to which a tortfeasor will be held liable for the
consequences of his or her conduct, and not the test for liability as such. In any case, all
agree that liability can occur only if the defendant has been negligent,[77] *i.e.* if under the
circumstances of the case,[78] the foreseeable harm was such that a reasonable person
would not have behaved as the defendant. An element of foreseeability thus undeniably
comes to bear when assessing whether there was negligence.[79] Once it has been established
that there was a *duty of care*, that the defendant was *negligent*, and that the negligence of
the defendant *in fact caused harm* to the plaintiff (under the "but for" test), the issue is to
what extent the defendant must be held liable for all the consequences of that negligence;
that is what is meant by "remoteness of damage".[80] Under both the conception defended
in *Re Polemis* and that retained in *The Wagon Mound (No. 1)*, there is agreement that
some limit must be set to the extent of the defendant's liability, as Viscount Simonds notes
in his speech. *Re Polemis* stood for the proposition that the defendant will be held liable
for all the "direct consequences" of his or her conduct; that criterion does set some limit
on liability, yet it is plain that it can in some cases cast a wide "net".[81] In the annotated
judgment, the Privy Council rejected the test of directness of damage and held instead
that the extent of liability should be determined by a criterion of reasonable foreseeability, namely whether the damage which actually occurred could be foreseen by a reasonable person.

---

[76] [1921] KB 560, CA.

[77] See *supra*, Chapter III, 3.2.1 and 3.2.2.C.

[78] Including the severity of the harm which could occur and the means required to prevent it.

[79] Foreseeability of harm also comes into play in determining whether there is a duty of care: see *supra*, Chapter I, 1.4.1.B.

[80] A certain parallel can be established between the issue of remoteness of damage under English law and the *haftungsausfüllende Kausalität* under German law.

[81] See *infra*, **4.F.7.** for an examination of the application of the directness criterion under French law.

(2) Even if, as Viscount Simonds suggested, moving to a criterion of reasonable fore-seeability is not likely to affect the outcome of many cases, the annotated judgment provides a practical example of where the two criteria lead to differing conclusions. As a preliminary matter, the other elements of negligence (not discussed by the Privy Council) are not affected by the choice of criterion for remoteness. First, the defendant was under a *duty of care* not to cause physical damage to nearby property in its operations. Secondly, the defendant was indeed *negligent* in allowing the bunkering oil to spill in the waters of the Sydney harbour, since a reasonable person would not have done that, in view of the harm which could foreseeably occur as a result (if only because of damage by pollution). Thirdly, the plaintiff certainly suffered *harm*, which, fourthly, had in fact been *caused* by the oil spill (but for the spill, there would have been no fire). When it comes to *remoteness of damage*, however, if one follows *Re Polemis*, the assessment must be made according to whether the harm was a direct consequence of the oil spill; the Australian courts found that that was the case and held for the plaintiff.[82] If one follows *The Wagon Mound (No. 1)*, however, remoteness of damage is to be assessed according to whether the harm was reasonably foreseeable; the Privy Council found that it was not (it was a freak occurrence) and held for the defendant. In his speech, Viscount Simonds mentions also that the reverse case is possible, namely that the test of reasonable foreseeability could lead to a finding of liability where damage was *not* a direct consequence of the conduct of the defendant.

(3) Viscount Simonds' reasoning rests on the assumption that it is only fair that the criterion for remoteness of damage should somehow incorporate an element of probability, since "a man must be considered to be responsible for the probable consequences of his act", no more, no less. Secondly, the criterion for remoteness of damage must be consistent with that for liability, which rests on reasonable foreseeability. Both those assumptions have been severely criticized.[83] The first assumption views the situation exclusively from the point of view of the defendant: to the extent the plaintiff is not himself or herself at fault, why should it be fair to leave him or her without redress because the harm was not a foreseeable consequence of the defendant's conduct? The second assumption confuses two different kinds of foreseeability. For the purposes of establishing negligence, it must be shown that a reasonable person would have behaved differently in view of the harm which could foreseeably result. As Hart and Honoré point out, negligence cannot be assessed as regards ulterior or consequential harm: it is pointless to ask whether the reasonable person would also have behaved differently in view of the ulterior harm, which by definition occurred only after the initial harm, which the reasonable person should not have caused in any event.[84] Yet it is often precisely with respect to that ulterior harm that the issue of remoteness of damage arises most acutely. In the context of remoteness of damage, foreseeability thus involves an examination of whether the sequence of events as such was foreseeable in the abstract. It cannot thus be said that the inquiry is simplified by using the same foreseeability criterion for both negligence and remoteness of damage.

---

[82] Apparently the actions of the welders of the plaintiff, which caused molten metal to fall on the water surface, did not "break the chain of causation", according to the lower courts.

[83] See Rogers at 216–7; Markesinis and Deakin at 196–7; Hart and Honoré at 254–84.

[84] Hart and Honoré at 264.

(4) Authors generally agree that in practice the impact of the *The Wagon Mound (No. 1)* has been relatively limited.[85] Indeed, as will be seen below,[86] in some instances, in particular where the plaintiff is exceptionally vulnerable (the "thin-skull rule"), the law has remained unchanged after *The Wagon Mound (No. 1)*, even if it is difficult to reconcile these instances with the opinion of the Privy Council.

Furthermore, as shown by the second annotated case, *Hughes* v. *Lord Advocate*, the effect of *The Wagon Mound (No. 1)* has been lessened by "structuring" the application of the reasonable foreseeability criterion. It was apparent in *The Wagon Mound (No. 1)* already that the reasonable foreseeability test required for its application that the harm suffered by the plaintiff be characterized: harm by pollution, which was foreseeable in that case, is different from harm from fire, which was not foreseeable, according to Viscount Simonds. In *Hughes*, the House of Lords added that once the kind of harm suffered by the plaintiff was reasonably foreseeable, the extent of the harm of that kind as well as the events leading up to it need not have been foreseeable. In that case, the House of Lords found that it was foreseeable that leaving paraffin lamps around an unguarded site could allure children and cause them injury *by burns*; that the burn occurred quite unforeseeably as a result of an explosion of paraffin vapour, resulting in considerable injury, did not matter. However, if the explosion had caused damage to neighbouring property, absence of foreseeability of an *explosion* would have precluded the owner of the property successfully suing the employer of the careless workmen. As can be seen, therefore, the key issue becomes the characterization of the injury, since a broadly characterized injury will more easily have been foreseeable. On this point, no clear guidance has yet emerged from English case-law.[87]

It is interesting to note that German law knows of a similar principle. In a BGH decision of 21 February 1961,[88] the plaintiff had been hit by a metal splinter which flew off the tip of a pick-axe used to break a pavement. The BGH found that the workers were liable, since even if it was highly improbable that the axe itself would splinter, splinters of concrete could fly off the pavement, and no adequate precautions had been taken to protect passers-by from splinters.

(5) The reasonable foreseeability test has been extended to other torts as well, even torts of strict liability where, in the absence of an element of negligence (or fault) in the definition of the tort, the rationale of *The Wagon Mound (No. 1)*, as explained above, does not really hold.

For instance, the Privy Council held in *The Wagon Mound (No. 2)*[89] that the test of reasonable foreseeability also applied to nuisance, even if nuisance does not necessarily involve fault:

[85]   Rogers at 216; Hart and Honoré at 273–5.

[86]   *Infra*, 4.3.1.

[87]   See Markesinis and Deakin at 196–200; Rogers at 212–5. For a recent application of *Hughes* v. *Lord Advocate*, where the injury was found to be of a kind that could not reasonably be foreseen, see *Jolley* v. *Sutton London Borough Council* [1998] 1 WLR 1546.

[88]   VersR 1961, 465, *Spitzhackenfall*.

[89]   *Overseas Tankship (UK) Ltd* v. *The Miller Steamship Co. Pty. (The Wagon Mound (No. 2))* [1967] AC 617, PC. This case arose from the same facts as *The Wagon Mound (No. 1)*, except that the plaintiff was not the owner of the wharf which was engulfed by the fire, but was the owner of a ship which was moored at that wharf and was also damaged by the same fire. In *The Wagon Mound (No. 2)*, claims were made both in nuisance and negligence, and the findings of fact made by the court of first instance were not the same as in *The Wagon Mound (No. 1)*. On the facts, as thus found, the Privy Council held that damage by fire being reasonably foreseeable, the plaintiff's claim should be allowed.

[T]he similarities between nuisance and other forms of tort to which *The Wagon Mound (No. 1)* applies far outweigh any differences . . . It is not sufficient that the injury suffered by the respondents' vessels was the direct result of the nuisance if that injury was in the relevant sense unforeseeable.

Similarly, in *Cambridge Water Co.* v. *Eastern Countries Leather plc*,[90] the House of Lords extended the test of reasonable foreseeability to the rule in *Rylands* v. *Fletcher* as well.

House of Lords[91]   **4.E.6.**
Donaghey v. *Boulton & Paul Ltd.*

"SCOPE OF RULE" ANALYSIS FOR BREACH OF STATUTORY DUTY

Fall from the roof

In an action for breach of statutory duty, it is enough if the plaintiff suffered harm of the kind which the statute aimed to prevent, even if it did not occur exactly as the statute foresaw.

Facts: The plaintiff Donaghey was laying asbestos sheets on the roof of an aircraft hangar, and the defendant Boulton & Paul Ltd. was the contractor responsible for ensuring the safety of workers on that site. In the course of work, the plaintiff was asked by the foreman to adjust a sheet of asbestos. In so doing, he lost his balance and fell through a hole in the sheeting. He sued the defendant for damages, alleging a breach of *inter alia* Regulation 31(3) of the Building (Safety, Health and Welfare) Regulations, 1948,[92] which read:

> (3) Where work is being done on or near roofs . . . covered with fragile materials through which a person liable to fall a distance of more than 10 feet—
> (a) where workmen have to pass over or work above such fragile materials, suitable and sufficient ladders, duck ladders or crawling boards, which shall be securely supported, shall be provided and used . . .

Held: The court of first instance allowed the claim. The court of appeal reversed that decision and rejected the claim. The House of Lords reversed the judgment of the court of appeal and allowed the claim.

Judgment: LORD REID: ". . . [T]he respondents rely on *Gorris* v. *Scott* (1874), LR 9 Ex 125. There a regulation required that pens should be provided in any vessel in which animals were imported. Sheep were carried in a vessel without there being such pens, and it was alleged that as a result the sheep were swept overboard by the sea. But it was clear that the purpose of the regulation was to prevent the spread of disease: it had nothing to do with the safety of animals . . .

I entirely agree with that decision: but it was dealing with something very different from the present case. Here one of the main objects of the [Factories Act 1937] was to promote safety: and the sole purpose of the regulations was to prevent men working on a roof from falling to the ground. It is one thing to say that if the damage suffered is of a kind totally different from that which it is the object of the regulation to prevent, there is no civil liability. But it is quite a different thing to say that civil liability is excluded because the damage, though precisely of the kind which the regulation was designed to prevent, happened in a way not contemplated by the maker of the regulation. The difference is comparable with that which caused the decision in *Overseas Tankship (UK) Ltd* v. *Morts Dock & Engineering Co. Ltd. (The Wagon Mound [No. 1])* to go one way and the decision in *Hughes* v. *Lord Advocate* to go the other way.

---

[90] *Supra*, Chapter II, **2.E.35.**
[91] [1968] AC 1.
[92] SI 1948 No. 1145.

In deciding against the appellant on Regulation 31(3) [the court of appeal] said . . .:

> 'But I think it is plain that the mischief against which the regulation is directed is the risk of a collapse of the fragile materials causing the workman to fall through it.'

I do not think that that is quite right. The mischief against which the whole regulation is directed is the risk of injury from a fall from the roof, not the risk of collapse of the material . . .

That a person is to be entitled to recover damages for injury caused by a breach of this kind of regulation is an inference which the courts have drawn from various Acts of Parliament. They were passed for the benefit of employees and it is inferred that Parliament intended that a person injured by reason of a breach of their provisions or of provisions in regulations made under them should have a civil remedy. But it would seem odd to go on to infer that Parliament intended to withhold this benefit from every person who, though his injury was caused by a breach, did not suffer that injury in precisely the way contemplated in the statute or regulation. I am not prepared to attribute any such intention to Parliament."

Notes

(1) The annotated judgment builds on *Gorris* v. *Scott*,[93] a leading case which is often cited to show that the "scope of rule" theory is present in English law.[94] The facts of *Gorris* v. *Scott* are set out in the annotated judgment. That case was perhaps too clear an example of a claim based on injury which is not within the purview of the statutory provision in question: the statute required sheep to be kept in pens, in order to avoid the spread of disease during sea transport. If the absence of pens had resulted in sheep being infected, the harm would have been within the scope of protection of the statute. While the absence of pens may be a *conditio sine qua non* of the sheep being swept overboard, that kind of damage was not of the sort which the statute sought to avoid.

(2) In the annotated judgment, the situation is less clear-cut, which brings the House of Lords to distinguish *Gorris* v. *Scott*. Lord Reid achieves this by using the same reasoning as in *The Wagon Mound (No. 1)* and *Hughes* v. *Lord Advocate*, which draws on a distinction between the *kind* of damage and the *occurrence* thereof: as long as the harm is of the kind which the statutory provision seeks to ward off, it does not matter if it did not occur precisely like the statute contemplated. As commentators have noted, modern case-law, including the annotated judgment, has softened the impact of *Gorris* v. *Scott* through such constructions.[95] While that brings the law in line with the reasonable foreseeability test under the tort of negligence, the problems surrounding the characterization of harm, as outlined above,[96] are introduced into the tort of breach of statutory duty as well.

(3) In order to determine the scope of protection of Regulation 31(3), Lord Reid looks at the purpose of the provision, according to the so-called "mischief rule", one of the main principles of statutory interpretation under English law, whereby statutes are presumed to have been enacted to correct a given injustice (the "mischief") and must be interpreted in light thereof.[97] In so doing, Lord Reid takes a broad view of the statutory

---

[93] LR 9 Ex 125.

[94] Honoré at 60, para. 97. *Gorris* v. *Scott* is even used by H. Kötz, *Deliktsrecht*, 7th edn. (Neuwied: Luchterhand, 1996) at 64, para. 157 as an example to illustrate the *Schutzzweck der Norm* theory in German law!

[95] Rogers at 261.

[96] *Supra*, **4.E.4.–5.**, Note (2).

[97] See F.A.R. Bennion, *Statutory Interpretation: A Code*, 3rd edn. (London: Butterworths, 1997) at 731ff.

provision in question, looking at Regulation 31(3) not in isolation but in light of the whole statutory and regulatory scheme of which it is part, in order to come to the conclusion that the mischief which Regulation 31(3) aims to remedy is "the risk of injury from a fall from the roof". Lord Reid's interpretation is certainly fair and just, but it construes the aim of the statute relatively broadly: on its face, Regulation 31(3) was directed at the risk of falling through fragile roofing materials.

(4) There is no indication that such a "scope of rule" approach has been applied to other torts than breach of statutory duty. As Hart and Honoré observe: "Is there any case for presenting such limitations in causal language . . . ? Obviously there is none."[98] Yet it seems that reasoning similar to the "scope of rule" theory finds a place in the discussion of the scope of the duty of care, as appears from *Banque Bruxelles Lambert SA* v. *Eagle Star Insurance Co.*[99] That case concerned inaccurate property valuations, which lenders took into account in their decisions to lend money against a mortgage on the properties in question. The borrowers defaulted, and the lenders were able to recover, through the sale of the mortgaged properties, only part of what they were due. The lenders sought compensation from the valuers for their losses (eg the difference between the amount that was lent and the net amount that was recovered), arguing that they would not have lent money if the valuations had been accurate. The Court of Appeal had found in favour of the defendants. A unanimous House of Lords reversed the decision of the Court of Appeal and held that the valuers were only liable for the difference between their inaccurate valuation and a correct valuation at the time of the transaction. Lord Hoffmann wrote:[100]

> The real question in this case is the kind of loss in respect of which the duty was owed.
>
> How is the scope of the duty determined? In the case of a statutory duty, the question is answered by deducing the purpose of the duty from the language and context of the statute: *Gorris* v *Scott* (1874) LR 9 Ex 125. In the case of tort, it will similarly depend upon the purpose of the rule imposing the duty . . . In the case of an implied contractual duty, the nature and extent of the liability is defined by the term which the law implies . . .
>
> There is no reason in principle why the law should not penalise wrongful conduct by shifting on to the wrongdoer the whole risk of consequences which would not have happened but for the wrongful act . . . But that is not the normal rule.
>
> Rules which make the wrongdoer liable for all the consequences of his wrongful conduct are exceptional and need to be justified by some special policy. Normally the law limits liability to those consequences which are attributable to that which made the act wrongful. In the case of liability in negligence for providing inaccurate information, this would mean liability for the consequences of the information being inaccurate.

Lord Hoffmann expressed his reasoning by reference to the concept of duty of care, but it is apparent from the above excerpt that it could also be seen as a causation issue. In a subsequent passage, he writes that "the Court of Appeal's principle offends common sense because it makes the doctor responsible for consequences which, though in general

[98] Hart and Honoré at 306.

[99] Decided by the House of Lords as *South Australia Asset Management Corporation* v. *York Montague Ltd.* [1997] AC 191, [1996] 3 All ER 365, HL.

[100] Ibid. at 212–3.

terms foreseeable, do not appear to have a sufficient causal connection with the subject matter of the duty".[101]

4.1.3. FRENCH LAW

Introductory Note

a) In contrast to German or English law, French tort law takes a decidedly empirical approach to causation. Many writers express some reluctance to venture into the subject-matter, for example Starck:[102]

> Causation is one of the most obscure issues in the law of torts. Masses of cases shed no further light on the subject-matter, dominated as they are by the individual circumstances of the case and the intuition of the court.

While it is true that there are no doctrinal controversies of the type found in Germany or outright reversals of case law as took place in England, it would not do justice to French law to abstain from any further inquiry into its general approach. For indeed, as other writers note, it is possible to draw some inferences from the case law, so as to be able to discern the outlines of the French approach to causation problems.[103]

b) The starting point for causation is the *Code civil*, which mentions causation expressly not only in the main provision creating tortious liability for one's own conduct, at Articles 1382 ("anyone who . . . *causes* damage to another . . .") and 1383 ("Everyone is responsible for the damage *caused* . . ."), but also in the provisions concerning liability for others or for things, at Articles 1384 to 1386. As with the provisions of the BGB dealing with tortious liability, those provisions of the *Code civil* do not give any further indication as to how causation is to be approached.

c) Causation is sometimes viewed in the light of two requirements concerning damage, namely directness and certainty. The former requirement is derived from Article 1151 of the *Code civil*, which reads: ". . . Damages extend . . . only to the direct and immediate consequences of the breach of contract." Even if this article only concerns liability for breach of contract, it is generally seen as the expression of a general principle which applies to tort law as well.[104] The requirement of certainty has long been recognized by the Cour de cassation.[105] The first two cases reproduced below show that neither of these two requirements is very firmly established, and as such they cannot provide an accurate picture of causation in French law.

d) At the theoretical level, French law has been influenced by German writers. Most doctrinal works refer to the *théorie de l'équivalence des conditions* (*Äquivalenztheorie*, equivalence theory) and the *théorie de la causalité adéquate* (*Adäquanztheorie*, adequacy

---

[101] *South Australia Asset Management Corporation* v. *York Montague Ltd.* [1997] AC 191, [1996] 3 All ER 365, HL at 214.

[102] Starck, Roland and Boyer at 438, para. 1066. See the overview of doctrinal opinions made by Viney and Jourdain, *Conditions* at 156, para. 335.

[103] Jourdain at 160/6, para. 20; Le Tourneau and Cadiet at 270, para. 825.

[104] Viney and Jourdain, *Conditions* at 166, para. 348; Le Tourneau and Cadiet at 287, para. 877; Starck, Roland and Boyer at 438, para. 1063.

[105] Le Tourneau and Cadiet at 271, para. 828.

theory).[106] It must be noted that, whereas German writers consider that the two theories are complementary (adequacy comes "on top" of *conditio sine qua non*), French writers tend to see them as alternatives or opposites.[107] In general, French academic literature tends to consider that while equivalence leads to "excesses", adequacy is too vague and is less logical than equivalence.[108]

e) In order to give a proper overview of the general approach to causation under French law, it is necessary to take into account not only what is presented under "causation" as such, but also matters often discussed under the "defences" heading, such as *force majeure*.

It should be stressed that, as a starting point, French law remains true to *équivalence des conditions* (the "but for" test).[109] As a consequence, French law tends to be generous in finding a causal link between events and injury, which very often leads French courts to hold that many events have caused injury.[110]

f) Nevertheless, the full impact of equivalence is moderated by a series of developments.

First, even if it is not often acknowledged as such,[111] French case-law often complements equivalence with an explanatory theory: it is then not enough that the injury would not have happened without the conduct of the tortfeasor, rather the conduct must *explain* the injury. In the words of N. Dejean de la Bâtie:[112]

> Any event which occasioned damage does not necessarily deserve to be characterized as its cause, as shown by the cases where liability is denied when, in view of a chain of consequences flowing from the conduct of the defendant, one feels that the injury suffered by the victim does not quite find its root in the wrongfulness of that initial conduct . . .
>
> [Instead of using the adequacy theory,] it is preferable . . . to stick to the idea that the inquiry is about the progression of the wrong that ultimately reaches the victim. It does not matter whether that progression was short or long, normal or exceptional, so long as it is continuous. It must be made up of a series of deficiencies which lead up to one another without gaps. When a series of intermediate steps intervened between the initial conduct and the damage, continuity presupposes not only that each of these steps somehow suffers from a deficiency, but also that such deficiency can be at least partially explained by the deficiency which affected the previous step, all the way down to the initial conduct that was itself wrong . . . When the wrong thus followed a continuous path that can be traced back from the injury to the . . . fault of the defendant, a true causal link . . . can be said to exist.

[106] Viney and Jourdain, *Conditions* at 159–61, para. 338–40; Starck, Roland and Boyer at 444–6, para. 1077–81; Le Tourneau and Cadiet at 268–70, para. 821–4; Jourdain at 160/5, para. 13–5. Subsequent developments in the German theories of causation, such as the *Schutzzweck der Norm* theory and the rise of reasoning based on *Risikobereich*, do not seem to have affected French law yet.

[107] As noted by Viney and Jourdain, *Conditions* at 159, para. 338, who would rather see them as complementary at 162 ff., para. 341 ff.

[108] Viney and Jourdain, *Conditions* at 162–3, para. 342–4; Jourdain at 160/5–6, para. 16–9; Starck, Roland and Boyer at 446–7, para. 1082; Le Tourneau and Cadiet at 269–70, para. 824.

[109] Viney and Jourdain, *Conditions* at 163–4, 168–70, para. 346, 352–3.

[110] Viney and Jourdain, *Conditions* at 169–72, para. 353–1 to 355. Accordingly, French law has a fairly well-developed regime for sorting out multiple causes: see *infra*, **4.F.38.–39.** and notes thereafter.

[111] Besides its proponent N. Dejean de la Bâtie, in Aubry & Rau, *Droit civil français*, Vol. VI–2, 8th edn. (Paris: Librairies techniques, 1989) at 121–40, § 444*ter*, this theory has also been endorsed by Viney and Jourdain, *Conditions* at 164, para. 346–1.

[112] Ibid. at 131, 139–40, § 444*ter*, references omitted.

One can argue whether that explanatory theory differs from adequacy. On the one hand, Dejean de la Bâtie makes a distinction between the two, his theory being factual while adequacy (at least as it has been developed in Germany) is *probabilistic*.[113] He is of the opinion that a probability-based adequacy theory cannot be derived from French case-law. On the other hand, Viney and Jourdain consider that Dejean de la Bâtie's explana-tory theory concerns some instances of a more general trend whereby French courts would require adequate causation between fault and damage. The conduct of the defen-dant would then need to be the "efficient" or "generating" cause of the injury to the plain-tiff.[114]

It appears that this explanatory/adequacy theory has been used among others in the following situations:[115]

- as regards liability for things, in the requirement that the thing played an "active role" in the injury;[116]
- when it appears that a cause which is nearer in time to the occurrence of the harm has played a greater role in it;
- when many faults of differing gravity have contributed to the injury, so that the gravest one "absorbs" the others.

The third case reproduced below is a prominent example of the application of this theory.

Certain authors link the prevailing theory to the liability regime: whereas the equiva-lency theory should be applied to causation issues under the fault-based liability regimes, in no-fault regimes the absence of fault should be "compensated for" by using the more exacting explanatory/adequacy theory for causation.[117] Starck, Roland and Boyer would draw the line elsewhere: the equivalency theory would be appropriate for intentional fault, while the explanatory/adequacy theory should be used for non-intentional fault and *a for-tiori* for no-fault liability.[118]

g) Secondly, Viney and Jourdain consider that the adequacy theory is helpful to solve problems relating to the evidence of the causal link in practice. Thus, while the court would be looking in substance to determine if the harm would have occurred but for the conduct of the alleged tortfeasor (taking into account the moderating effect of the explanatory/adequacy theory mentioned above), in practice it will be basing its assess-ment on probabilistic evidence.[119]

h) Thirdly, the adequacy theory, in the probabilistic sense under which it is understood in Germany, comes to play a major role in situations where, as a result of the application of *équivalence des conditions*, many events qualify as causes of the injury to the victim. Indeed, here also, even if it is often not acknowledged as such, the "defence" of *cause*

---

[113] This is also the position of Honoré at 38–40, para. 67–70.

[114] Viney and Jourdain, *Conditions* at 164, para. 346–1; Jourdain at 160/10, para. 40. It must be noted that such terminology does not really refer to probabilities, and as such does not truly reflect the adequacy theory as it has been developed in Germany. See Honoré, ibid.

[115] Jourdain at 160/10–13, para. 41–59; Viney and Jourdain, *Conditions* at 172–7, para. 356 to 358–2.

[116] *Infra*, Chapter VI, **6.F.6.–7.** and notes thereafter.

[117] Le Tourneau and Cadiet at 270, para. 825; Jourdain at 160/6, para. 19.

[118] Starck, Roland and Boyer at 447–8, para. 1084–5.

[119] Viney and Jourdain, *Conditions* at 165, para. 347.

étrangère constitutes a straightforward instance of probabilistic assessment of causation.[120]

In short, an event can qualify as *cause étrangère* if it was (i) external to the alleged tortfeasor (i.e. not within his or her control), (ii) unforeseeable *and* (iii) unavoidable.[121] Once a *cause étrangère* is established, any liability of the alleged tortfeasor is denied,[122] even if his or her conduct was a necessary condition to the injury of the plaintiff under the "but for" test. In other terms, because an unforeseeable and unavoidable event intervened in the sequence of events leading to injury, the consequences of the conduct of the alleged tortfeasor were brought beyond what was foreseeable. Given a *cause étrangère*, the injury to the victim was no longer the foreseeable consequence of the conduct of the alleged tortfeasor.

i) In the end, it is difficult to draw any conclusion as to the presence in French tort law of theories other than *équivalence des conditions*. It is possible to argue that French courts use an explanatory/adequacy theory as outlined above, as many authors do, yet the Cour de cassation continues to render judgments which cannot be squared with any theory other than *équivalence des conditions*.[123] The Conseil d'État seems to be more open in admitting that it is applying an explanatory/adequacy theory.[124] Only the doctrine of *cause étrangère* constitutes a clear and well-established inroad made by adequacy into French law.

The apparent lack of a clear direction as regards causation should not disguise the fact that French law is very rich, at the level of both academic literature and case law, with regard to particular problems, such as *perte d'une chance* and the interplay of multiple causes.

Yet it is difficult to select cases that offer a general picture. The following cases are intended to illustrate key issues: the first two cases illustrate the two main requirements of directness and certainty which have traditionally been associated with causation; the third case is, in the opinion of commentators, an example of the Cour de cassation using the adequacy theory; the fourth case offers a rare instance where it could be argued that the Cour de cassation applied, in effect, the "scope of rule" theory, which, in French law, is known as *relativité aquilienne*.

---

[120] Viney and Jourdain, *Conditions* at 247–9, para. 403.

[121] *Force majeure* is discussed also in Chapter III, 3.2.3.

[122] See *infra*, **4.F.38.–39.**, Note (2).

[123] See for instance Cass. civ. 2e, 28 April 1965, reproduced *supra*, Chapter II, **2.F.40.**, where the driver who was responsible for an accident was held liable for the loss of revenue of the public transport company whose buses were delayed because the road was blocked by the accident.

[124] See Laubadère, Venezia et Gaudemet at 817, para. 1307; Gour at 35–6, para. 383–8. See also *supra*, Chapter II, **2.F.42.** and Note (2) thereafter.

Cass. civ. 2e, 3 October 1990[125]   **4.F.7.**
X. v. *GAN*

DIRECT CAUSAL LINK

Back to France

The causal link between the conduct of the alleged tortfeasor and the harm to the plaintiff must be direct.

Facts: The mother of a young child was killed in a car accident for which the defendant was responsible. The child then left France to live with his father, the plaintiff, who was working in Saudi Arabia. The child could not adapt to life in Saudi Arabia, and as a consequence, the plaintiff had to give up his well-paid position in order to return to France with his son. He sued the defendant for the damage flowing from the loss of his employment.

Held: The court of first instance allowed the claim. The court of appeal reversed the judgment of the court of first instance and found against the plaintiff. The Cour de cassation upheld the judgment of the court of appeal.

Judgment: ". . . [The plaintiff claims that] in deciding that the harm resulting from his having resigned from his employment was not caused directly by the traffic accident in which the child's mother . . . was killed, the court of appeal would have breached Art. 1384(1) C.civ. Furthermore, in omitting to inquire, as it had been invited to do by the plaintiff, whether the interest of the child did not justify that the father abandon his well-paid expatriate position, the court of appeal would have failed to give a legal basis to its decision . . .

However, the judgment [of the court of appeal] rightly states that no direct causal link exists between the harm resulting from the plaintiff's voluntary resignation from his employment and the traffic accident of which [the child's mother] was the victim.

These grounds alone were sufficient for the court of appeal to justify its decision."

Notes

(1) In this case as in many others dealing with causation, the Cour de cassation ruling is very brief and does not really give one an insight into the reasoning of the court. The Cour de cassation only mentions that the court of appeal was correct in finding that there was no direct causal link between the fault of the defendant in causing the accident and the harm to the plaintiff from having to give up his position.[126]

As can be seen from the summary of the arguments of the appellant, the case revolved around the issue of whether the plaintiff was for all intents and purposes bound to give up his position to come back to France with his son, or whether that decision was made on a voluntary basis. In the first case, it could have been said that the harm to the plaintiff resulted directly from the car accident (albeit not immediately). The Cour de cassation agreed with the findings of the court of appeal that the harm suffered by the plaintiff arose from his own decision to come back to France and that it was unnecessary to inquire into whether that decision was voluntary or "forced".

---

[125] Bull. civ. 1990.II.184. Translation by Y.P. Salmon.
[126] The annotated judgment is listed among the leading examples of cases where no direct causal link was present by Starck, Roland and Boyer at 253, para. 878 and Le Tourneau and Cadiet at 288, para. 878.

(2) The above judgment might thus be thought to be authority for the proposition that in French law loss which is a direct result of voluntary conduct of the victim (or of a third party or of a cause foreign to the defendant) cannot be said to have been caused directly by the defendant's wrongful act. Yet, among others, two cases reviewed earlier appear to support the conclusion that causation is not necessarily negatived by subsequent intervention. In *L'Olympique Lyonnais* v. *Fuster*,[127] the football club was found liable to spectators who had been injured by hooligans, on the ground that it had not taken proper measures to ensure the safety of spectators. In that case, a direct causal link was found, since the omissions of the football club had put the hooligans in a position to injure spectators. In *Franky* v. *Courtellemont*,[128] the plaintiff had been infected with HIV as a result of blood transfusions following an accident for which the defendant was responsible. The *Cour d'appel de Paris* found that there was a direct causal link between the two, on the basis of the equivalence theory. In a similar case, the Cour de cassation agreed that there was a direct causal link.[129]

(3) In consequence, while the annotated judgment took a relatively strict view of directness, it must be seen in the light of other cases where the French courts have found that a direct causal link was present even if the harm was but an ulterior consequence of the conduct of the defendant.

Writers do not agree on the conclusions to be derived from the case-law on directness. Starck, Roland and Boyer point out that there is conflicting case-law on materially the same facts in cases where the victim committed suicide after the alleged faulty conduct of the defendant took place or where a further accident occurred after the first accident for which the defendant is responsible (*dommages en cascade*).[130] According to Le Tourneau and Cadiet, an intervening act "breaks the chain of causation" only if it constitutes a fault of at least equal importance to that of the defendant; otherwise, the defendant is to be held responsible for the ulterior consequences of his or her conduct.[131] For Jourdain, there is so much case law where causation is not denied despite the fact that the harm is an ulterior consequence of the defendant's conduct that it can no longer be said that directness is relevant to causation; cases where causation is denied because of indirectness should rather be construed as cases of uncertain causation or absence of fault, *inter alia*.[132]

(4) Even if there are no general conclusions to be derived from the case law of the French courts relating to the directness of the causal link, as will be seen in the coming section, the courts have developed specific solutions for a series of situations, including third-party intervention in the sequence of events, predispositions of the victim, etc.[133]

---

[127] *Supra*, Chapter III, **3.F.2.**
[128] *Supra*, Chapter II, **2.F.18.**
[129] Cass. civ. 1re, 17 February 1993, JCP 1994.II.22226.
[130] Starck, Roland and Boyer at 441–4, para. 1070–6.
[131] Le Tourneau and Cadiet at 287–9, para. 877–9. Starck, Roland and Boyer, ibid., also give a role to fault in the assessment of directness, but not as affirmatively as Le Tourneau and Cadiet.
[132] Jourdain at 160/10, para. 39.
[133] See Viney and Jourdain, *Conditions* at 177–81, para. 359.

Cass. civ. 2e, 20 June 1985[134]   **4.F.8.**
Ghigo v. *Surdin*

CERTAIN CAUSAL LINK

Sent home barefoot

The causal link between the conduct of the alleged tortfeasor and the harm to the plaintiff must be certain.

Facts: The plaintiff, a teenager, was caught committing theft in the defendant's store. As a form of punishment, the defendant sent her home barefoot. The plaintiff was so psychologically disturbed by the events that, upon arriving at her home, she jumped out of a window, inflicting grave injury upon herself. She and her parents sued the defendant for the resulting damage.

Held: The court of first instance rejected the action. The court of appeal reversed and allowed the action. The Cour de cassation quashed the decision of the court of appeal and remitted the case to a lower court.

Judgment: ". . . [The court of appeal] held the defendant—at least partly—liable under Art. 1382 C.civ., after it found that he was at a fault in seeking to bring the theft to the attention of the parents through a course of action which humiliated [the plaintiff] and was inappropriate under the circumstances. It found that the fault of the defendant had contributed, together with the age of the plaintiff and her strict family environment, to affect her seriously enough to cause her to act as she did.

In relying on such a reasoning, from which it is not clear that the fault of the defendant had contributed with certainty to the realization of the injury for which compensation was claimed, the court of appeal failed to give a legal basis to its decision."

Notes

(1) In the annotated judgment, the Cour de cassation quashed the judgment of the court of appeal on the basis that it had not been shown with certainty that the fault of the shopkeeper in imposing a humiliating punishment on the plaintiff was the cause of the plaintiff's actions. Here as well, the judgment is fairly terse and does not give much insight into the reasoning which may have led the court to its conclusion.

It appears that the court of appeal had identified as causes of the plaintiff's actions, together with the acts of the shopkeeper, her strict family environment and her age, and had not gone further into which of these causes had really contributed to the damage. In other words, the Cour de cassation was not satisfied that the punishment inflicted by the shopkeeper was really a *conditio sine qua non* of the plaintiff's conduct ("but for" test).

(2) In affirming that the causal link between the harm and the allegedly faulty conduct must be certain, the annotated judgment actually reaffirms the applicability of the equivalence theory under French law: the alleged fault must be such that the harm would not have occurred but for it.[135] However, as will be seen in the next sections, under French law,

---

[134] Bull. civ. 1985.II.125. Translation by Y. P. Salmon.
[135] French doctrine generally agrees with this position: Viney and Jourdain, *Conditions* at 169, para. 353; Jourdain at 160/6, para. 22; Starck, Roland and Boyer at 449, para. 1089; Le Tourneau and Cadiet at 271, para. 828.

the impact of the requirement that causation must be certain is softened by a series of exceptions:

– first, evidentiary rules allow plaintiffs to overcome difficulties in establishing the certainty of causation;[136]
– secondly, even where there is uncertainty as to the causal link, the concept of *perte d'une chance* can be used in a number of cases to characterize the harm in such a way that such uncertainty is overcome;[137]
– thirdly, in cases where the actual identity of the wrongdoer is uncertain, a number of means have been devised to avoid that liability would be denied because of that uncertainty.[138]

Cass. civ. 2e, 20 December 1972[139]   **4.F.9.**
Pagani v. Zucchelli

EXPLANATORY/ADEQUACY THEORY

Explosives in the shack

The conduct of the alleged tortfeasor must be at the origin of the harm for there to be a causal link between the two.

Facts: The plaintiff, a child, stole explosives from a shack belonging to the defendants, and injured himself while playing with them. The shack was not locked and was left in a state of disrepair such that it was possible to enter it at will. It had not been established how and by whom the explosives were placed in the shack. The plaintiff sued the defendants for the resulting damage, on the basis that they were at fault in failing to keep a proper watch over their shack and its contents and ensure that it was not freely accessible.

Held: The court of first instance rejected the claim. The court of appeal reversed the judgment of the court of first instance and allowed the claim. The Cour de cassation quashed the judgment of the court of appeal and remitted the case to a lower court.

Judgment:"In holding the defendants partly liable under Art. 1382 C.civ., the [court of appeal] took note of the state of disrepair of the shutter of the shack window and did not overlook that the detonators might have been left in the shack without the knowledge of the defendants. It [went on to] state that it did not matter that the origin of the explosives could not be established, since the defendants failed to watch over their shack and the things which may have been within it and failed to preclude access by third parties *efficiently and under normal conditions*. [For the court of appeal,] those failures constituted a fault and made the defendants liable; the plaintiff also contributed to the realization of the injury through his fault in manipulating the explosives.

However, there is no causal relationship between the injury which forms the basis of the claim and the alleged cause, that is to say the opportunity given [through the fault of the defendants] for a third party to leave the explosives [in the shack] and for the plaintiff to remove them.

It follows from the above that in holding as it did, the court of appeal contravened Article 1382 C.civ."

---

[136] See *infra*, **4.F.20.–22.** and notes thereafter.
[137] See *infra*, **4.F.15.–17.** and notes thereafter.
[138] See *infra*, **4.F.42.** and notes thereafter.
[139] JCP 1973.II.17541. Translation by Y. P. Salmon.

Notes

(1) In the annotated judgment, it was alleged that the defendants were at fault in not keeping a proper watch over their shack and in not keeping it locked and inaccessible. The harm consisted in injuries suffered by a trespassing child while playing with explosives stolen from the shack. According to the theory of *équivalence des conditions*, the harm would not have occurred but for the lack of precautions taken by the defendants, since, if proper precautions had been taken, the explosives would not have been placed in the shack or, if they were, children would not have been able to steal them. Yet the Cour de cassation held that there was no causal link between the fault and the harm. The Cour de cassation must therefore have relied on a theory of causation other than *équivalence des conditions*.

(2) N. Dejean de la Bâtie, in his comment on the annotated judgment, analyses the case as follows: since causation involves an inquiry into the "source of the mischief", it must be shown that the harm occurred in the wake of an uninterrupted series of mishaps which flow one from the other, so that the fault *explains* the harm.[140] In the annotated judgment, the failure to watch and secure the shack did not in and of itself explain the harm to the plaintiff. The annotated judgment would therefore constitute a good example of the application of the explanatory/adequacy theory.

Cass. civ. 3e, 2 July 1974[141]   **4.F.10.**
Biscarrat v. *André*

RELATIVITÉ AQUILIENNE

Shadow from non-adjoining property

A landowner cannot recover on the basis of a breach by a third party of a city planning regulation which was not intended to confer rights upon the landowner.

Facts: The plaintiff owned a house, the view from which was restricted by the top floors of a building owned by the defendant. That building was located across the street from the plaintiff's house, some 50m away from it. The top floors of the defendant's building had been constructed in breach of city planning regulations, which limited the permitted height of buildings in the area relative to adjoining buildings. The plaintiff claimed damages and an order that the defendant remove the top floors of its building.

Held: The court of first instance allowed the action. The court of appeal reversed and rejected the action. The Cour de cassation upheld the decision of the court of appeal.

Judgment: "[The court of appeal] found that the house acquired by the plaintiffs on 5 February 1964 is situated some 50m from the defendant's house, with, between them, first the Avenue Lympia and then another property . . . It correctly held that the plaintiffs, whose property is not bordering that of the defendant, 'cannot hold against the defendant that he failed to respect a right of prospect [*servitude de prospect*] because the height of the building diminished their view. Moreover, the town-planning rights which they invoke in their favour do not aim to guarantee the views of the neighbour, which is evident from the fact that . . . the height [of a building] could be double if the

---

[140] JCP 1973.II.17541. See also *supra*, Introductory Note under f).
[141] D 1975.Jur.61. Translation by Y. P. Salmon.

wall was blind and that height would not be at issue according to the distance to the borderline, if the owners of adjacent properties had decided to abut their building upon one another'.

The court of appeal, relying on the lack of a causal relationship between the possible violation of town-planning regulations invoked and the injury to the views, rightly found 'that the plaintiffs could not evidence direct and personal harm', from which it follows that the decision . . . was legally justified."

Note

In the annotated case, the Cour de cassation rejected the plaintiff's claim[142] on the ground that the damage suffered by the plaintiff was not direct. In fact, however, the court applied the "scope of rule" theory or theory of *relativité aquilienne*, as it is known in French law.[143] The court examined the city planning regulation; in a part of the judgment not reproduced above, it found that it did not aim at providing views to the adjoining buildings, but rather at ensuring that these buildings received proper sunlight. Moreover, the plaintiff's house did not even adjoin the defendant's building. The Cour de cassation accordingly approved the reasoning of the court of appeal.

The Cour de cassation has confirmed its holding in subsequent cases dealing with similar city planning issues,[144] but it has not yet been applied in other situations, so that the theory of *relativité aquilienne* has not really become part of French law.[145]

4.2. ESTABLISHMENT OF CAUSAL LINK

This section will be concerned with problems which commonly arise in the establishment of the causal link. Firstly, the general operation of the *causa sine qua non* ("but for") test is surveyed, focussing specifically on cases involving omissions or breaches of a duty to inform, as well as the issue of "alternative causation". Secondly, the issue of loss of a chance or *perte d'une chance* in the context of causation is examined. The third part concerns the burden of proof, which plays a very significant role as regards causation.

4.2.1. OPERATION OF THE *CONDITIO SINE QUA NON* ("BUT FOR") TEST

The following cases can be found at <http://www.rechten.unimaas.nl/casebook>:
4.G.11. BGH, 2 July 1957. Diverticulum.
4.E.12. House of Lords, *The Empire Jamaica.*Uncertificated officer at the helm.
4.G.13. BGH, 24 October 1985. Early payment.
4.F.14. Cass. civ. 1re, 3 November 1983. *SA Agence Waastels* v. *Gombert.* No insurance against fire in hotel.

---

[142] Including a claim for an injunction: this topic is discussed *infra*, Chapter VIII, 8.6.

[143] Viney and Jourdain, *Conditions* at 157–8, para. 336; Jourdain at 160/11, para. 45. See also the comment of E. Frank after the annotated judgment at D 1975.Jur.61.

[144] Cass. civ. 3e, 17 March 1976, JCP 1976.IV.163; Cass. civ. 3e, 23 November 1977, JCP 1978.IV at 30; Cass. civ. 3e, 29 January 1992, Bull.civ. 1992.III.34; Cass. civ. 3e, 19 February 92, JCP 1992.IV.1189.

[145] Viney and Jourdain, *Conditions* at 158, para. 336.

4.2.2. LOSS OF A CHANCE AND PROPORTIONAL LIABILITY

The following cases can be found at <http://www.rechten.unimaas.nl/casebook>:

4.F.15. Cass. civ. 1re, 17 November 1982. *Goddé* v. *Debrune*. Mishap in sinus operation.

4.F.16. Cass. civ. 1re, 12 November 1985. *Konstantinow* v. *Manrique*. Thrombosis.

4.F.17. Cass. civ. 1re, 7 February 1990. *Jugnet* v. *Hérard*. Damage to the eye.

4.E.18. House of Lords, *Hotson* v. *East Berkshire Area Health Authority*. Schoolboy falls from a tree.

4.2.3. BURDEN OF PROOF

The following cases can be found at <http://www.rechten.unimaas.nl/casebook>:

4.G.19. BGH, 4 October 1983. Icy pavement.

4.F.20. Cass. civ. 2e, 15 November 1989. *Hirou* v. *Audinet*. Shed burns down.

4.F.21. Cass. civ. 1re, 16 February 1988. *Anquetil-Lelièvre* v. *Houivet*. Bad car repair.

4.F.22. Cass. civ. 2e, 13 October 1971. *Agent judiciaire du Trésor* v. *Pozin*. Supersonic bang.

4.E.23. House of Lords, *Wilsher* v. *Essex Area Health Authority*. Excess oxygen.

4.3. ISSUES RELATING TO THE SEQUENCE OF EVENTS

a) In this section, a series of issues relating to the sequence of events are surveyed. The first sub-section deals with the predisposition of the plaintiff, namely those factors which make the plaintiff more vulnerable to damage at the time when the conduct of the alleged tortfeasor intervenes. The second sub-section covers the general issue of subsequent events, i.e. events which occur once the plaintiff has suffered injury from the alleged tortfeasor and which either render that injury irrelevant or cause additional consequential damage. Finally, the third sub-section addresses a specific subset of subsequent events, namely the intervention of a third party (or the victim him- or herself) in the sequence of events, with specific emphasis on pursuit and rescue cases.

b) It should be mentioned at the outset that all legal systems under study here acknowledge that the rules concerning the sequence of events are relaxed when an intentional tort has been committed. As a matter of principle, it would be unfair for a defendant who has intended to cause harm to benefit from rules or theories which are designed to limit the burden put on the defendant.

Under English law, it is settled that "the intention to injure the plaintiff disposes of any question of remoteness".[146] The leading case for that statement remains *Scott* v. *Shepherd*, where the defendant intentionally threw a lighted firework into a marketplace, with the result that the plaintiff was injured by its explosion; the plaintiff's claim suc-

---

[146] *Quinn* v. *Leathem* [1901] AC 495 at 537, cited by *Clerk & Lindsell on Torts* at 52, para. 2–20; Rogers at 219.

ceeded even though the firework had been thrown in alarm by others from stall to stall before it reached the plaintiff.[147]

Under German law, it is also generally agreed that, when the defendant's conduct is intentional, he or she is liable for all consequences, and the principles of adequate causation are not applied to limit the ambit of liability.[148]

Similarly, under French law, the tortfeasor will be liable for all consequences of intentional conduct, however remote they may be.[149]

4.3.1. PREDISPOSITIONS OF THE PLAINTIFF

The following cases can be found at <http://www.rechten.unimaas.nl/casebook>:

4.E.24. Queen's Bench Division. *Smith* v. *Leech Brain & Co. Ltd.* Cancer from burn by molten metal.

4.G.25. OLG Karlsruhe, 25 January 1966. Amputation due to step on the foot.

4.F.26. Cass. civ. 2e, 19 July 1966. *Leven* v. *Thépaut*. Loss of only eye.

4.E.27. House of Lords, *Liesbosch Dredger* v. *Edison Steamship (The Liesbosch)*. Replacement dredger.

4.G.28. BGH, 5 July 1963. Damage to sole lorry.

4.3.2. SUBSEQUENT EVENTS

The following cases can be found at <http://www.rechten.unimaas.nl/casebook>:

4.E.29. House of Lords, *Baker* v. *Willoughby*. Shot in the injured leg.

4.E.30. House of Lords, *Jobling* v. *Associated Dairies Ltd.* Injury followed by illness.

4.G.31. BGH, 24 April 1952. Artillery fire.

4.F.32. Cass. civ. 2e, 8 February 1989. *Chardin* v. *Garnier*. Caught by fire.

4.3.3. VOLUNTARY INTERVENTION OF THIRD PARTY—PURSUIT AND RESCUE CASES

The following cases can be found at <http://www.rechten.unimaas.nl/casebook>:

4.F.33. Cass. civ. 2e, 17 March 1977. *Sarl Les transports héandais* v. *SA Les grands travaux du Forez*. Vandalism with stolen excavator.

4.G.34. BGH, 10 December 1996. Theft from damaged armoured vehicle.

4.G.35. BGH, 13 July 1971. Pursuit in train station.

4.E.36. Court of Appeal, *Knightley* v. *Johns*. Riding wrong way through tunnel.

4.G.37. BGH, 30 June 1987. Kidney donation.

---

[147] *Scott* v. *Shepherd* (1773) 2 W.Bl. 892.

[148] BGH, 27 January 1981, *infra*, Chapter VI, **6.G.3.**; see also Staudinger-Medicus, § 249 at 41, para. 49. Münchener-Grunsky, § 249 at 366, para. 41a, is not so positive and leaves room for adequacy to apply even in cases of intentional harm; he is however in the minority on this point.

[149] Starck, Roland and Boyer at 447, para. 1084. See also Le Tourneau and Cadiet at 265, para. 815.

4.4. MULTIPLE TORTFEASORS AND MULTIPLE CAUSES

This section is concerned with cases involving many alleged tortfeasors or many possible causes. The first subsection deals with cases where two or more persons have inflicted injury upon another through a joint or common course of conduct. Because these cases raise relatively few problems, no materials are excerpted in the subsection. The second subsection addresses cases where two or more causes have combined to cause injury to the victim. The third subsection touches upon those cases where causality appears well-established, but for one difficulty: one of a class of persons accounts for the cause of the injury, but it is not possible to ascertain which one.

4.4.1. JOINT TORTFEASORS

a) Under German law, a specific provision, § 830 BGB, has been enacted to cover cases involving multiple tortfeasors or multiple causes. Its relevant parts read as follows:

1. If many persons have caused injury through an unlawful act which they committed jointly, each of them shall be responsible for the injury. The same shall apply if it cannot be ascertained which of many participants caused the injury through his conduct.[150]
2. Instigators and accomplices shall be assimilated to co-authors.

The persons referred to in the first sentence of § 830(1) are usually called co-authors (*Mittäter*). The applicable definitions of co-author, instigator (*Anstifter*) and accomplice (*Gehilfe*) are to be found in German criminal law.[151]

The rationale behind this provision is that, since co-authors, instigators and accomplices all willed the injurious result, it is fair to relieve the plaintiff of evidentiary difficulties (*Beweisnot*) related to causation in respect of all of them.[152] In such cases, the plaintiff will usually be able to show injury, wrongful and faulty conduct of the main author, and a causal link between the two. Problems arise when it comes to establishing that co-authors, instigators and accomplices also caused the injury, since these are cases of "psychological causation" (*psychisch vermittelte Kausalität*).[153]

The operation of the first sentence of § 830(1) BGB remains somewhat disputed.[154] According to the orthodox position (BGH case-law and most writers), that provision requires that **co-authors** knowingly and intentionally combined to bring about the injurious result (*bewußtes und gewolltes Zusammenwirken zur Herbeiführung des Verletzungserfolges*), irrespective of whether (and to what extent) each of the co-authors

---

[150] The second sentence of § 830(1) BGB is discussed *infra*, **4.G.43.** and notes thereafter.

[151] At § 25(2), 26 and 27 of the *Strafgesetzbuch* (StGB, Criminal Code) respectively. Staudinger-Belling/Eberl-Borges, § 830 at 7–8, para. 21 are of the opinion that, at least as regards co-authorship under the first sentence of § 830(1) BGB, civil courts have not kept up with developments in the criminal law.

[152] Staudinger-Belling/Eberl-Borges, § 830 at 4, para. 7–8; Münchener-Stein, § 830 at 1768, para. 4.

[153] See *supra*, 4.3.1., Introductory Note under c).

[154] For an example where § 830(1) BGB was applied, see *supra*, Chapter III, **3.G.34.**, Note (3). See also, in relation to the same events, BGH, 31 January 1978, BGHZ 70, 277.

actually caused it. The co-authors must thus have shared a common intention (*gemein-schaftlicher Entschluß*). Given that the requirement of causation is more or less obviated, § 830(1) BGB would then constitute an autonomous ground for liability, since it cannot be assumed that the co-authors would otherwise have been liable under another provision.[155] In the early decades of the BGB, the RG took a broad view (revived in recent writing), whereby a combination of a series of negligent courses of conduct leading to the plaintiff's injury was sufficient to trigger the application of the first sentence of § 830(1) BGB, even in the absence of any common intention on the part of the co-authors.[156] At the opposite extreme, some other writers would rather restrict the scope of application of the provision, by finding that it merely relieves the plaintiff of the burden of proving the extent to which each co-author contributed to the injury or shifts the burden of proof onto the defendants, who can then attempt to prove that their conduct did not result in the injury.[157] Finally, it must be mentioned that the BGH has given § 830 BGB a more restrictive interpretation in cases where participants in large protest actions were sued for the physical and property damage caused in the course of the action; even though the freedom of assembly guaranteed at Art. 8 GG does not extend to the infliction of damage on others, the mere fact of taking part in a protest action should not suffice to lead to liability under § 830 BGB in the absence of more concrete evidence linking the person to the damage.[158]

As for § 830(2) BGB, **instigators** are those who "intentionally induce someone else to intentional wrongful conduct",[159] while **accomplices** are those who "intentionally help another in his intentional wrongful conduct".[160]

Co-authors, instigators and accomplices are liable jointly and severally with the main author and with one another, pursuant to § 840(1) BGB.[161]

According to BGH case law, the scope of application of the first sentence of § 830(1) as well as § 830(2) BGB is therefore limited to intentional wrongs. In other cases where mere negligence (*Fahrlässigkeit*) is alleged on the part of the tortfeasor, the plaintiff cannot benefit from the relief conferred by these provisions as regards causation.[162]

b) Under English law, "joint tortfeasors" are those whose "respective shares in the commission of a tort are done in furtherance of a common design",[163] as opposed to "several tortfeasors", whose negligent courses of conduct also combine to cause injury to the plaintiff, but without such common design. Unlike German law, however, English law does not afford the plaintiff any form of relief from evidentiary burdens in the case of

---

[155] Staudinger-Belling/Eberl-Borges, § 830 at 5–6, para. 11–4. That is the position of Münchener-Stein, § 830 at 1767, para. 1.

[156] Staudinger-Belling/Eberl-Borges, § 830 at 6–7, para. 16–8.

[157] Ibid. at 7, para. 19–20, and adopting that position at 8, para. 22. See also Larenz/Canaris at 572.

[158] See BGH, 24 January 1984, BGHZ 89, 383 and BGH, 4 November 1997, NJW 1998, 377.

[159] See Staudinger-Belling/Eberl-Borges, § 830 at 9–11, para. 26–36; Münchener-Stein, § 830 at 1772–3, para. 14–6.

[160] See Staudinger-Belling/Eberl-Borges, § 830 at 11–4, para. 37–47; Münchener-Stein, § 830 at 1773, para. 17–8.

[161] BGH, 19 February 1953, BGHZ 9, 65. See *infra*, **4.F.38.–39.**, Note (4) for a more detailed discussion of the workings of these provisions.

[162] These cases are then to be dealt with like cases where there is a plurality of established causes, *infra*, **4.F.38.–39.**, Note (4).

[163] *The Koursk* [1924] P 140, CA.

joint tortfeasors. In fact, but for one slight distinction between the two categories,[164] the treatment of joint tortfeasors is the same as that of several tortfeasors (when the injury to the victim cannot be divided).[165]

c) There seems to be no specific rule in French law for joint tortfeasors over and above the general regime applicable when there is a plurality of established causes, as seen below.

4.4.2. PLURALITY OF ESTABLISHED CAUSES

Introductory Note

a) Throughout this Chapter, attention has focused on how the various legal systems will or will not recognize that there is a causal link between the course of conduct of one alleged tortfeasor and the injury to the victim. As human experience teaches, however, it happens sometimes that many events contribute to a given result, or in legal terms, that many events will satisfy the rules relating to causation and thereby qualify as causes for the purposes of tort law. For example, two companies whose respective chemical plants simultaneously release pollutants in a river: assuming that other conditions for liability are satisfied, both companies will be liable because each discharge has caused the pollution of the river under any of the legal systems studied here.

b) This subsection is concerned with how the legal systems under study deal with situations where two or more causes combine to cause a single, indivisible injury to the victim, as in the pollution example above. These situations must be distinguished from occurrences where it is possible to identify how each cause contributed to the damage:[166] under those circumstances, French,[167] German[168] and English[169] law will simply hold each tortfeasor for that part of the final injury for which he or she was responsible.

c) The first two cases annotated below are key French cases which contributed to putting an end to the debate on the regime applicable to cases where an injury has many causes. The last two cases are fairly similar English and German cases which introduce one further level of complexity in the problem by adding some contributory negligence or *Mitverschulden* on the part of the victim.[170]

---

[164] Rogers at 731–3: the release from liability of one joint tortfeasor operates to the benefit of the others, which is not the case for several tortfeasors.

[165] Several tortfeasors are dealt with in the next subsection: see *infra*, **4.F.38.–39.**, Note (5).

[166] For instance, when the plaintiff sustains injury to both legs from separate shots in a hunting accident, and it can be determined which hunter was responsible for each shot: Cass. civ. 2e, 19 April 1956, JCP 1956.II.9381.

[167] Le Tourneau and Cadiet at 276, para. 846.

[168] Münchener-Grunsky, § 249 at 372, para. 50; Larenz/Canaris at 580–1.

[169] Rogers at 729–31.

[170] Contributory negligence and *Mitverschulden* in general are dealt with *infra*, Chapter VII, 7.1.

Cass. civ. 2e, 4 March 1970[171]   **4.F.38.–39.**
Séguier v. Sfolcini
and
Cass. civ. 2e, 17 March 1971[172]
Scaglia v. Ferricelli

PLURALITY OF CAUSES
OBLIGATION IN SOLIDUM

The defendant remains liable for the whole of the injury sustained by the plaintiff even where there is a concurring external cause or third-party fault. When the faults of two defendants combined to cause the injury, they are liable in solidum.

A. Cass. civ. 2e, 4 March 1970   **4.F.38.**

Motorcycle passenger

Facts: The plaintiff Sfolcini was riding as a passenger with the defendant Cavelier on his motorcycle. A car in front of them was driven by the defendant Séguier. As Séguier manoeuvred to avoid a parked car, he collided with it, and Cavelier's motorcycle then ran into Séguier's car. Sfolcini was injured in the collision. She sued both Cavelier and Séguier for the damage which she suffered.

Held: The court of first instance and the court of appeal held the two defendants liable *in solidum* for the whole of the injury suffered by Sfolcini. Séguier argued before the Cour de cassation that he should have been held liable only for his share of the whole injury after it had been divided between him and Cavelier. On that issue, the Cour de cassation confirmed the decisions of the courts below.

Judgment: "The [defendant Séguier] argues that the court of appeal erred in holding him, as keeper (*gardien*) of his vehicle, liable to compensate Ms. Sfolcini for the full extent of her injury, whereas he should only be liable towards the victim within the bounds of the apportionment of liability between him and Cavelier.

However, the keeper (*gardien*) of the thing that was instrumental in causing the harm is liable towards the victim for full compensation (*réparation intégrale*), except where he establishes that an event qualifying as *force majeure* [caused the injury and thus] exonerated him completely. The foregoing is without prejudice to any recourse against a third party who would have contributed to the injury."

B. Cass. civ. 2e, 17 March 1971   **4.F.39.**

Car passenger

Facts: The plaintiff Scaglia was riding with the defendant Ferricelli in Ferricelli's car, when it collided with Sellier's car. Scaglia suffered injury and sued Ferricelli, but not Sellier, for damages. At issue was whether Ferricelli's liability should be reduced to take into account Sellier's contribution to Scaglia's injury.

Held: The court of first instance found that Ferricelli was liable for the whole of Scaglia's injury. The court of appeal reduced Ferricelli's liability to half of Scaglia's injury. The Cour de cassation quashed the decision of the court of appeal and remitted the case for further consideration.

[171] Bull.civ. 1970.II.76, JCP 1971.II.16585. Translation by Y. P. Salmon.
[172] D 1971.Jur.494. Translation by Y.P. Salmon.

Judgment: "In the cases of concurrent liability, where each of those liable for the injury contributed to causing the whole injury, each of them must be liable towards the victim for full compensation [of the injury], regardless of any recourse against another co-author . . .

The court of appeal agreed with the court of first instance that each driver was at fault, that the respective faults contributed to the occurrence of the accident, and an apportionment [of the full amount of damages] in two halves reflected the respective seriousness of the faults of the two drivers. The court of appeal then noted that Scaglia had brought his action against Ferricelli only, and concluded that Ferricelli should accordingly be liable only for half of the injury sustained by the victim. In so doing, the court of appeal contravened [Article 1382 C.civ.]."

Notes

(1) As a preliminary remark, it should be noted that the provisions of the Act of 5 July 1985 would apply to both annotated cases if they arose today, so as to prevent the drivers from arguing that their liability should be reduced on account of the fault of a third party.[173] In any event, the Cour de cassation reached the same result in the annotated cases on the basis of the general provisions of the *Code civil*.

(2) In the two annotated cases, the Cour de cassation brought to an end some doctrinal controversies which had arisen in the 1950s and 1960s[174] and chose to return to the traditional position as regards the split of liability in cases where a plurality of causes are involved. In essence, the Cour de cassation confirmed the following propositions:

– A defendant can be fully exonerated from liability only if the other cause involved in the occurrence of the injury qualifies as *cause étrangère* (extraneous cause) (first annotated case), i.e. if the other cause was extraneous (or foreign) to the defendant (*cause étrangère au défendeur*), unforeseeable (*imprévisible*) and unavoidable (*irrésistible*).[175] *Cause étrangère* is generally conceived of as a natural event (lightning, etc. then called *force majeure*), but it is also acknowledged that, as long as it meets those three conditions, the conduct of a third party or of the victim will be assimilated to *cause étrangère* and will thus also lead to a complete exoneration of the defendant.[176]

– If the other cause does not qualify as *cause étrangère* (it was foreseeable or avoidable), then the defendant is liable towards the plaintiff for the whole of the injury which the plaintiff suffered (first annotated case).[177] If the other cause is attributable to a person, the victim can choose to sue the defendant or that other person or both.

---

[173] See *supra*, Chapter VI, **6.F.16.**, Art. 2 and Note (3) thereafter.

[174] On these controversies, see Viney and Jourdain, *Conditions* at 260 and 263–6, para. 414 and 417–9; Jourdain at 162/4 and 162/6–8, para. 15 and 24–27; Le Tourneau and Cadiet at 275–6, para. 844. See also J. Boré, "La causalité partielle en noir et blanc ou les deux visages de l'obligation 'in solidum'" JCP 1971.I.2369; F. Chabas, "Bilan de quelques années de jurisprudence en matière de rôle causal" D 1970.Chron.26 and B. Starck, "La pluralité des causes de dommage et la responsabilité civile (La vie brève d'une fausse équation: causalité partielle = responsabilité partielle)" JCP 1970.I.2339.

[175] *Cause étrangère* is also discussed *supra*, Chapter III, 3.2.3.

[176] Viney and Jourdain, *Conditions* at 246–7, para. 402; Le Tourneau and Cadiet at 309–10 and 311–12, para. 950–3 and 958–60; Starck, Roland and Boyer at 462 and 470, para. 1121 and 1143. On exoneration on account of the victim's conduct, see *infra*, Chapter VII, 7.1.1.

[177] See Viney and Jourdain, *Conditions* at 259–61, para. 414; Jourdain at 162/4–5, para. 16. See, for instance, a case where the defendant requested a reduction in his liability for a car accident on account that ice on the road (foreseeable and avoidable under the circumstances) also contributed to causing the accident: Cass. civ. 2e, 30 June 1971, D 1971.Somm.135.

- A defendant who is held liable towards the plaintiff for the whole of the injury can subsequently look to any other person who was also responsible for the injury and can require contribution from that other person (first annotated case). *However*, when that other person is also a party to the litigation,[178] the court must keep the relationship of each of the defendants to the plaintiff separate from that of the defendants amongst themselves: the defendants must all be found liable to the plaintiff for the whole of the injury (second annotated case).[179] Apportionment only takes place for the purpose of contributory recourse between the defendants.
- The above proposition is subject to one exception in cases where the victim also caused his or her own injury and the conduct of the victim was such as to constitute a fault. In such cases the two stages will generally be collapsed into one and the award of damages will be reduced to reflect the part of the injury which the victim himself or herself caused,[180] and that is so irrespective of whether the claim is brought by the primary victim or by secondary victims.[181]

In sum, under French law, beside cases where a defendant is totally exonerated by establishing *cause étrangère*, a defendant cannot be partly relieved from liability on account of an external cause which—partly—contributed to the injury of the plaintiff, unless that external cause consists in conduct of the victim such as would constitute a fault.

(3) Accordingly, under French law, each co-defendant will be bound to compensate the plaintiff for the full amount of the injury, under what is called "obligation *in solidum*". Since the *Code civil* (Art. 1202) did not provide for *solidarité* (joint and several liability) in these cases, case-law has developed the *in solidum* regime, which is by and large similar to *solidarité*, in order to sidestep the *Code civil*.[182] When two defendants are bound *in solidum*, the plaintiff can essentially execute judgment against any defendant up to the full amount of damages (as long as the plaintiff does not recover more than the full amount from all defendants combined), and it is then up to the co-defendants to settle their accounts amongst themselves in contribution proceedings.

Two main reasons are invoked in order to justify the imposition of an obligation *in solidum* on co-defendants: first, the injury to the victim cannot be divided (it is not possible to weigh causes against one another) and secondly—this appears to be the most widespread opinion today—the victim must be protected against the risk that one of the

---

[178] Either as a defendant or as a *mis en cause*. For the sake of simplicity, it will be assumed here that the other person is a co-defendant.

[179] The annotated case followed upon Cass. civ. 2e, 2 July 1969, JCP 1971.II.16582 and has been followed ever since, for instance in Cass. civ. 2e, 31 May 1972, JCP 1972.IV.184; Cass. civ. 2e, 14 December 1972, JCP 1973.IV.37; Cass. civ. 2e, 5 March 1975, JCP 1975.IV.138 and Cass. civ. 2e, 11 July 1977, JCP 1977.IV at 239.

[180] See Viney and Jourdain, *Conditions* at 285–99, para. 426–33; Jourdain at 162/12–17, para. 56–80; Le Tourneau and Cadiet at 312–17, para. 963–83; Starck, Roland and Boyer at 470–80, para. 1144–73. For a discussion at greater length, see *infra*, Chapter VII, 7.1.1.

[181] After extensive controversy in the case law and amongst writers, the Assemblée plénière of the Cour de cassation held on 19 June 1981, *infra*, **7.F.5.**, that the fault of the primary victim could also be opposed to secondary victims.

[182] Contrary to the regime of *solidarité*, co-defendants under an obligation *in solidum* cannot be seen as mutual representatives of one another for procedural purposes. Accordingly, they are not automatically affected when one of them is sued (e.g. interruption of prescription period), held liable by a court decision (e.g. *res judicata*) or brings an appeal from a judgment given in first instance: see Le Tourneau and Cadiet at 274–5, para. 842, who note that the distinctions between the two regimes tend to vanish.

co-defendants may not be able to pay compensation (otherwise the victim would be in a worse position than if only one—solvent—defendant had been brought before the court).[183]

(4) Under German law, given that the general approach to causation is less likely to result in a plurality of causes than under French law,[184] a defendant is less likely to seek a reduction of liability because the damage has been caused in part by a natural cause. It is not infrequent, however, that more than one defendant will be found to have caused injury to the victim. It may be that these defendants are co-authors, or that one is an instigator or accomplice, in which case the plaintiff will usually avail himself or herself of the specific rules of § 830(1) or § 830(2) BGB.[185] It may also be that the defendants did not share any common purpose and that the injury resulted from the "coincidental" combination or superimposition of their wrongful conducts, in which case they are usually termed *Nebentäter* (several concurrent tortfeasors).[186] *Nebentäter* are not covered by any specific provision of the BGB, so that the plaintiff must show that the conditions of liability are fulfilled for each of them. Once that it done, it is agreed in the case law and among authors that *Nebentäter* are liable jointly and severally (*Gesamtschuld*) towards the victim, according to § 840 BGB.[187]

§ 840 BGB refers to the general regime of joint and several liability as set out at §§ 421ff. BGB. § 421 BGB allows the plaintiff to pursue any of the *Nebentäter* up to the full amount of the award of damages, provided that he or she does not recover more than that amount from all of them combined. The co-defendants can then settle their respective contributions amongst themselves in a subsequent stage of proceedings (*Regreß*).

(5) Under English law, similarly, tortfeasors whose actions contributed to a single injury to the victim (so-called "several" or "several concurrent" tortfeasors) will be found jointly and severally liable towards the victim, which enables the victim to recover from any of them up to the full amount of the award of damages (provided, here again, that the total recovery from all tortfeasors does not exceed that amount).[188] At common law it was impossible for one co-defendant to turn around and instigate contributory proceedings against the other(s), however the Civil Liability (Contribution) Act 1978 opened that possibility.[189]

(6) It is beyond the scope of this book to review the often complex rules regarding contribution amongst tortfeasors in the legal systems under study. In short, French law relies principally on the gravity of the respective faults of the co-defendants (or the absence thereof when a co-defendant is liable pursuant to a no-fault regime), and in the last resort will admit an equal sharing amongst co-defendants.[190] Under German law, the basic prin-

---

[183] Viney and Jourdain, *Conditions* at 254–9, para. 406–12; Jourdain at 162/7, para. 28.

[184] See *supra*, 4.1.1. In any event, as discussed *infra*, **4.G.43.**, Note (1), if some uncertainty remains as to whether the injury was caused by the defendant or by a natural cause, the plaintiff will not be able to invoke the second sentence of § 830(1) BGB to overcome that uncertainty and the claim may well fail for lack of proof of causation.

[185] See *supra*, 4.4.1. under a).

[186] See for instance the two defendants in BGH, 16 June 1959, *infra*, **4.G.41.**

[187] Staudinger-Medicus, § 249 at 56–7, para. 96; Münchener-Stein, § 830 at 1769, para. 5–6; Larenz/Canaris at 580; Staudinger-Schäfer, § 840 at 1231–2, para. 9–11.

[188] Rogers at 730; Markesinis and Deakin at 785–6. See also *infra*, **4.E.40.**

[189] c. 47, Art. 1(1). Rogers at 733ff.; Markesinis and Deakin at 786 ff.

[190] Viney and Jourdain, *Conditions* at 280–5, para. 424 to 424–2; Jourdain at 162/11–2, para. 52–5.

ciple is equal sharing (§ 426 BGB), although in tort law other formulae taking into account the gravity of the respective faults are often used.[191] Under English law, the Civil Liability (Contribution) Act 1978 provides that contribution is assessed on a "just and equitable" basis,[192] and courts have interpreted that provision to mean that contribution is to be determined by taking into account causation and culpability.[193] The apportionment of liability between the plaintiff and the defendant, in cases of contributory fault or negligence on the part of the plaintiff, is a closely related issue; it is discussed at greater length in Chapter VII.[194]

House of Lords[195]   **4.E.40., 4.G.41.**
Fitzgerald v. *Lane*
and
BGH, 16 June 1959[196]

SHARING OF LIABILITY BETWEEN PLAINTIFF AND TWO DEFENDANTS

Under English law, the contributory negligence of the plaintiff must be assessed against the defendants taken as a whole, the apportionment between the defendants being determined in a second stage. Under German law, the Mitverschulden *of the plaintiff must be weighed against each defendant separately (*Einzelabwägung*); the liability of both defendants is however limited at a global level (*Gesamtabwägung*).*

A. House of Lords, *Fitzgerald* v. *Lane*   **4.E.40.**

Double hit

Facts: The plaintiff Fitzgerald negligently started to cross a street at a crossing while the traffic lights were red against him. He was hit by the car of the defendant Lane and, following the impact, he was thrown into the path of another lane of traffic. He was then hit by the car of the defendant Patel, who was coming in the opposite direction in that lane. The plaintiff suffered severe injury. Before the House of Lords, it was admitted that the plaintiff and both defendants were negligent, and the sole issue was the split of liability between them.

Held: The court of first instance allowed the plaintiff's claim against both defendants, subject to a reduction of one-third on account of the plaintiff's contributory negligence. As between them, each defendant was liable for an equal share of one-third of the plaintiff's claim. The court of appeal modified the award; it reduced the plaintiff's damages against both defendants by one-half on account of his contributory negligence; as between them, each defendant was again liable for an equal share of one-quarter of the plaintiff's claim. The House of Lords confirmed the judgment of the court of appeal.

Judgment: LORD ACKNER:[197] "It is axiomatic that whether the plaintiff is suing one or more defendants, for damages for personal injuries, the first question which the judge has to determine is

---

[191] Larenz at 642 ff.; Staudinger-Schäfer, § 840 at 1253–5, para. 68–74. See also the cases covered by § 840(2) and (3) BGB.

[192] c. 47, Art. 2(1).

[193] Rogers at 734; Markesinis and Deakin at 788–9.

[194] See *infra*, Chapter VII, 7.1.

[195] [1989] 1 AC 328.

[196] BGHZ 30, 203. Translation by A. Hoffmann and Y. P. Salmon.

[197] Lord Bridge, Lord Brandon, Lord Templeman and Lord Oliver concurring.

whether the plaintiff has established liability against one or other or all the defendants, i.e. that they, or one or more of them, were negligent (or in breach of statutory duty) and that that negligence (or breach of statutory duty) caused or materially contributed to his injuries. The next step, of course, once liability has been established, is to assess what is the total of the damage that the plaintiff has sustained as a result of the established negligence. It is only after these two decisions have been made that the next question arises, namely, whether the defendant or defendants have established (for the onus is upon them) that the plaintiff, by his own negligence, contributed to the damage which he suffered. If, and only if, contributory negligence is established does the court then have to decide, pursuant to section 1 of the Law Reform (Contributory Negligence) Act 1945, to what extent it is just and equitable to reduce the damages which would otherwise be recoverable by the plaintiff, having regard to his 'share in the responsibility for the damage.'

All the decisions referred to above are made in the main action. Apportionment of liability in a case of contributory negligence between plaintiff and defendants must be kept separate from apportionment of *contribution between the defendants inter se*. Although the defendants are each liable to the plaintiff for the whole amount for which he has obtained judgment, the proportions in which, as between themselves the defendants must meet the plaintiff's claim, do not have any direct relationship to the extent to which the total damages have been reduced by the contributory negligence, although the facts of any given case may justify the proportions being the same.

Once the questions referred to above in the main action have been determined in favour of the plaintiff to the extent that he has obtained a judgment against two or more defendants, then and only then should the court focus its attention on the claims which may be made between those defendants for contribution pursuant to the Civil Liability (Contribution) Act 1978 . . . In the contribution proceedings, whether or not they are heard during the trial of the main action or by separate proceedings, the court is concerned to discover what contribution is just and equitable, having regard to the responsibility between the tortfeasors inter se, for the damage which the plaintiff has been adjudged entitled to recover. That damage may, of course, have been subject to a reduction as a result of the decision in the main action that the plaintiff, by his own negligence, contributed to the damage which he sustained.

Thus, where the plaintiff successfully sues more than one defendant for damages for personal injuries, and there is a claim between co-defendants for contribution, there are two distinct and different stages in the decision-making process—the one in the main action and the other in the contribution proceedings . . . .

In the instant case the plaintiff's conduct set in motion the chain of events that led to the accident. If the plaintiff had not ignored or failed to observe that the lights were against him and in favour of the traffic, when he decided to cross the pelican crossing, then the accident would never have happened. It was the negligent response of each of the defendants to the dangerous situation thus created by the plaintiff which established their joint and several liability . . .

[T]he exercise of assessing the plaintiff's share in the responsibility for the damage which he has sustained [does not] necessitate the determination of the extent of the individual culpability of each of the defendants, once the judge is satisfied that the defendants each caused or materially contributed to the plaintiff's damage. While the plaintiff's conduct has to be contrasted with that of the defendants in order to decide to what extent it is just and equitable to reduce the damages, which would be awarded to him if the defendants were solely liable, it does not involve an assessment of the extent to which the fault of each of the defendants contributed to that damage. What is being contrasted is the plaintiff's conduct on the one hand, with the totality of the tortious conduct of the defendants on the other. As previously stated, the determination of the extent of each of the defendants' responsibility for the damage is not made in the main action but in the contribution proceedings between the defendants, inter se, and this does not concern the plaintiff."

B. BGH, 16 June 1959   **4.G.41.**

Motorcycle accident

Facts: The plaintiff was riding his motorcycle, when the first defendant came out of a petrol station and drove onto the street in front of him. The plaintiff went towards the middle of the street to overtake the first defendant, but in so doing he found himself riding between tram rails, which allegedly slowed him down. Before he could complete the overtaking manoeuvre, he collided with the car of the second defendant and was severely injured. At issue before the BGH was the split of liability between the plaintiff and the two defendants.

Held: The court of first instance found that the first defendant was not liable and that the second defendant was liable for one-fifth of the plaintiff's injury. The court of appeal modified that decision, finding that each defendant was responsible for one-fifth of the plaintiff's injury and found the two defendants jointly and severally liable for two-fifths of the injury. The BGH allowed the appeal against the decision of the court of appeal, finding that each defendant was responsible for one-fifth of the plaintiff's injury, but that their joint and several liability was not to exceed one-third of the injury.

Judgment: "1. The court of appeal was correct in starting from the assumption that the contribution (*Mitverantwortung*) of the plaintiff is to be assessed as against each defendant separately. Hence the Court rightly applied . . . § 254 BGB first of all to the relationship between the plaintiff and the [first] defendant, and examined afterwards how the damage . . . is to be apportioned under § 254 BGB as between the plaintiff and the [second] defendant. Such a separate assessment is required because the plaintiff's claims for damages against each defendant are autonomous. Each defendant is responsible for a cause that generated the damage and that [independently] fulfils the legal requirements for delictual liability . . . .

The spheres of responsibility of several tortfeasors can be . . . cumulated, with the result that each one will be responsible to the victim for the contribution of the other to the accident; but such a solution can only be justified where the requirements of the first sentence of § 830(1) BGB are met, namely where the damage was caused by *an unlawful act committed by the tortfeasors in common*. That is not the case here . . . While the injury was not caused through a common course of conduct, it was nevertheless caused by both [defendants] together, through autonomous individual courses of action. The present case is one of so-called "several concurrent negligence" (*fahrlässige Nebentäterschaft*) to which the first sentence of § 830(1) BGB is not applicable . . .

2. The court of appeal believes that it can find support in § 840 BGB for its conclusion that the respective shares of liability of the defendants (1/5 each) should be added. The court fails to see that, pursuant to that provision, joint and several liability can only arise with respect to 1/5 of the plaintiff's injury, since § 840(1) BGB provides for joint and several liability only insofar as the obligations of the defendants coincide. In contrast with § 830(1) BGB, [§ 840(1) BGB] provides no legal basis to assume that both defendants together made a single contribution [to the injury, for which they are liable], and to oppose that contribution to that of the plaintiff . . . The [solution of the court of appeal] is unfair, since, in case where several persons contributed to the injury, each *defendant* must bear the risk that the other tortfeasors would be insolvent (when it comes to apportioning liability as between the defendants), whereas the *plaintiff*, who might be responsible to the same extent or even predominantly, is completely exempted from this risk . . . .

6. A satisfactory result can only be reached if one reconciles the principle of joint and several liability [under § 840(1) BGB] and the principle of apportionment (*Abwägung*) under § 254 BGB . . . by combining the individual apportionment (*Einzelabwägung*) with a general apportionment (*Gesamtabwägung*) made from the overall perspective . . .

7. . . . [In the case at bar, the overall perspective] dictates that liability be apportioned in such a way that, on the one hand, the respective shares of liability of the two defendants remain identical

while, on the other hand, the ratio of 4:1 is retained in the relationship of the plaintiff [to the first defendant] as well as [to the second defendant]. The general apportionment therefore results in a ratio of 4:1:1. This means that the plaintiff is responsible for 4/6 (2/3) and the two defendants, for 1/6 each so that, in the end, the plaintiff has to bear 2/3 of the damage himself and receives compensation for 1/3 of the [damage] from the defendants, but cannot however . . . recover compensation for more than 1/5 of the damage from a single defendant."

Notes

(1) The facts of the two annotated cases are similar; both involved two defendants whose faults combined to cause injury to the victim, with contributory negligence or *Mitverschulden* on the part of the victim. Yet the House of Lords and the BGH came to two rather different solutions.

In the first annotated case, the House of Lords essentially had to decide on the application of two statutes in relation to each other. It decided that the apportionment of liability between the plaintiff and the defendant—pursuant to the Law Reform (Contributory Negligence) Act 1945[198]—had to take place before the apportionment of contribution between the defendants—pursuant to the Civil Liability (Contribution) Act 1978.[199] For the purposes of the first apportionment, therefore, the two defendants had to be put together as one. The assessment of the respective contributions would come at a later stage.

In the first annotated case, accordingly, on the basis of a finding that the contributory negligence of the plaintiff was such that the damages to which he was entitled should be reduced by half, the defendants were found jointly and severally liable for the other half of the damages. The plaintiff could accordingly recover the half from either defendant or partly from one and partly from the other. As to contribution between the two defendants, it was to be settled on an equal basis (half each), so that in the end each defendant would have been liable, as between each other, to pay the plaintiff an amount equal to one-fourth of the total amount that the plaintiff would have recovered but for his contributory negligence.

(2) The approach of the BGH in the second annotated case is somewhat more complex. In that case, the two defendants did not act with a common purpose, so that they were *Nebentäter*.[200] Therefore, according to the BGH, there was no reason to put their liability together when assessing the *Mitverschulden* of the plaintiff, as the court of appeal had done. Rather, that *Mitverschulden* had to be assessed against each defendant separately (*Einzelabwägung*, under 1. of the second annotated judgment).[201] The separate apportionment established the upper limit to the liability that each defendant could ultimately be called upon to bear if, for instance, the other defendant was insolvent (in the annotated case, 1/5 of the full amount of damages that would have been recovered in the absence of *Mitverschulden*). That is why the court of appeal was wrong in simply adding the shares of each defendant and giving judgment for the plaintiff against each defendant jointly

---

[198] c. 28.
[199] c. 47.
[200] See *supra*, **4.F.39.–40.**, Note (4).
[201] It is in fact conceivable that the degree of *Mitverschulden* of the plaintiff might not be the same against each defendant.

and severally for 2/5s of the full amount of damages (under 2. of the annotated judgment).

As the BGH added under 6. of the second annotated judgment, in order to assess the amount which the plaintiff can recover from the two defendants jointly and severally (i.e. the amount of the *Gesamtschuld*), a global apportionment (*Gesamtabwägung*) must be made, which results in a slight variant of the normal *Gesamtschuld* regime. For the global apportionment, all the shares of the parties must be considered together. In the separate assessment, the apportionment of liability between the plaintiff and the first defendant was 4:1, and between the plaintiff and the second defendant, 4:1 as well. Since, as the BGH mentioned, the respective contributions of each defendant were to be given equal weight, the overall relationship was 4:1:1, or when the shares of the two defendants were put together, 4:2 (or 2:1). The plaintiff could therefore recover, as a result of the global apportionment, one-third of the full amount of damages from the two defendants together, jointly and severally (as *Gesamtschuldner*), but not more than one-fifth of the full amount of damages from either one of the two defendants, as a result of the separate apportionment. The BGH was thus more generous to the plaintiff in its approach than the House of Lords, while avoiding that any defendant would be liable to pay more than if he had been the sole defendant (so that a defendant does not have to bear the risk that another defendant may be unable to pay compensation to the plaintiff).

(3) For the sake of comparison, had the House of Lords approach been used in the second annotated case, the plaintiff would have been entitled to recover, from the defendants jointly and severally, no more than one-fifth of the full amount of damages.

Had the BGH approach been used in the first case, the separate apportionment would probably have been 1:1 as regards each defendant, so that the global apportionment would have been 1:1:1, or 1:2 when the shares of the defendants were combined. Accordingly, the plaintiff would have been entitled to recover two-thirds of the full amount of damages from both defendants jointly and severally, but not more than half of it from either defendant alone.

4.4.3. UNCERTAINTY CONCERNING THE ACTUAL TORTFEASOR

Introductory Note

a) In many cases, it will be possible for the victim to show that he or she has suffered injury, that it has been caused by someone who must have been at fault, but the author of that fault will not be identifiable. The best that the victim will be able to achieve is to define a class of persons of which the actual tortfeasor must be a member. Strictly speaking, however, the basic *conditio sine qua non* test will not be met, since it cannot be said of any member of the class that the injury would not have happened "but for" his or her conduct, given that in fact any other member could have caused the injury. Nonetheless, all the legal systems studied here have acknowledged that it would be patently unfair to deny recovery to the victim for that reason. This subsection reviews the mechanisms used to overcome that causation problem.

b) It may be that the tortfeasor is a member of a closed class of persons, as in the typical hunting accident case where someone is hit by a shot coming from a group of hunters.

One such case, which arose in France, is included below as an example of how imaginative French case law has been in escaping from the causation conundrum. English law is also reviewed in connection with that case.

The second annotated case illustrates the application of the second sentence of § 830(1) BGB, which is specifically designed to cover such cases.

c) The actual tortfeasor may also be a member of a more open class of persons, or even worse, one or more members of that open class. That situation would typically arise in "mass tort" cases, for instance product liability litigation where a generic product has been put on the market by a large number of manufacturers and distributors and caused injury to a considerable number of persons, as happened with diethylstilbestrol (DES). The solutions adopted for "traditional" cases (e.g. hunting accidents) may not be appropriate in these situations, and a number of new constructs have been put forward to deal with uncertainty about the tortfeasor in "mass torts" cases. They are reviewed by the Dutch Hoge Raad in the third annotated case.

Cass. civ. 2e, 5 June 1957[202]   **4.F.42.**

Litzinger v. *Kintzler*

LIABILITY FOR COLLECTIVE ACTION

Hunting accident

A group of hunters may be held liable for concerted action in which they were collectively engaged and which resulted in injury, even if the actual author of the injury is not known.

Facts: The plaintiff and the seven defendants went deer hunting together. At 16:00, as the hunt came to an end, the plaintiff left the other defendants to return to his home. The seven defendants decided to fire a salvo to mark the end of the hunt. The plaintiff was hit by a shot from the salvo and almost lost an eye as a consequence. It was not possible to determine from which of the defendants the shot came. The plaintiff sued all seven defendants for damages.

Held: The court of first instance and the court of appeal allowed the claim. The Cour de cassation upheld the judgment of the court of appeal.

Judgment: "In order to condemn [the defendants] jointly and severally (*solidairement*), the court of appeal finds . . . that 'the real cause of the accident lies in the concerted action of the seven defendants who participated in the firing of a salvo that did not qualify as a normal act of hunting, with a level of imprudence and carelessness that is imputable to all of them.'

The joint and several liability of the defendants was thus sufficiently made out and correctly found. It was not necessary to go further and identify which one, among them, had fired the shot that caused the injury. Indeed, several individuals may, in a concerted action or even spontaneously as a consequence of shared exhilaration, indulge in a course of action for which, if harmful consequences ensue, each of them must bear responsibility. Indeed such consequences will result either from a single course of action in which all participated, or from a series of connected courses of action which cannot be separated given that their conception and execution are so closely related."

---

[202] D 1957.Jur.493. Translation by Y.P. Salmon.

Notes

(1) The French case law on hunting accidents shows how French courts have striven to overcome problems of uncertainty regarding the actual tortfeasor. In principle, when the victim cannot identify who amongst the group of hunters fired the shot which wounded him, causation cannot be established for lack of a tortfeasor, and the claim should be rejected.[203]

(2) Since the 1950s, French courts have sought to avoid that result, essentially by shifting the basis for liability away from the conduct which immediately led to the injury (e.g. firing the shot) towards some conduct which could be imputed to the whole class of persons of which the actual tortfeasor must have been one.[204] The annotated case provides a good example of that process. Although the victim could not identify the hunter who fired the shot that wounded him, the Cour de cassation agreed with the courts below that the whole group of hunters was at fault for firing a salvo for no purpose after the hunt had ended. The whole group created a risk through its negligent conduct, and the injury to the plaintiff constituted a realization of that risk. That reasoning has been reaffirmed in subsequent cases,[205] and it has been extended to cases where children took part in a dangerous game[206] or where a group of young people committed acts of violence.[207] A second strand of French cases relies on the regime of liability for things under Art. 1384(1) C.civ., finding that the members of the group were collectively the keepers (*garde collective*) of the thing that caused the damage.[208]

(3) As a corollary of the reasoning expounded in the above paragraph, all members of the class of persons in question will be found liable, and will be put under an obligation *in solidum*, towards the plaintiff.[209] Writers have tried to go beyond the artificiality of the judicial solutions in order to explain why those solutions appear fair and just: the most adequate explanation seems to be that the victim is in all fairness relieved of the burden of identifying the actual tortfeasor, once he or she has shown injury, fault by an unidentified member of an identifiable group and causation (between that fault and the injury). A presumption of causation will then arise, and it will be up to each of the defendants to try to demonstrate that his or her conduct was not the cause of the injury.[210] For that

---

[203] As happened in many cases: see for instance Cass. civ. 2e, 4 January 1957, D 1957.Jur.264.

[204] See Viney and Jourdain, *Conditions* at 204–10, para. 375–9; Jourdain at 160/19–20, para. 93–9; Le Tourneau and Cadiet at 271–4, para. 832–7; Starck, Roland and Boyer at 453–5, para. 1100–2. Some parallel could be drawn between the situations where French courts followed that line of reasoning and the type of situations where the first sentence of § 830(1) as well as § 832 BGB would come to the aid of the victim by relieving him or her from some of the burden of proving causation.

[205] See Cass. civ. 2e, 19 May 1976, Bull. civ. 1976.II.129, JCP 1978.II.18773.

[206] Cass. civ. 2e, 12 July 1971, D 1972.Jur.227; Cass. civ. 2e, 6 March 1975, JCP 1975.IV.138, Bull.civ. 1975.II.67; Cass. civ. 2e, 29 November 1978, D 1979.IR.345; Cass. civ. 2e, 16 January 1991, Bull.civ. 1991.II.22.

[207] Cass. civ. 2e, 6 March 1968, Bull.civ. 1968.II.76; Cass. civ. 2e, 2 April 1997, JCP 1997.IV.1156.

[208] See Viney and Jourdain, *Conditions* at 209–10, para. 379; Jourdain at 160/20, para. 96–9; Le Tourneau and Cadiet at 273, para. 835–7; Starck, Roland and Boyer at 454–5, para. 1102. On the notion of *garde* under Article 1384(1) C.civ., see *infra*, Chapter VI, **6.F.8.** and notes thereafter. See also *infra*, Chapter VII, **7.F.24.**, for an example of *garde collective.*

[209] In the annotated case, the court of appeal found that the defendants were jointly and severally (*solidairement*) liable, whereas the appropriate conclusion should have been an obligation *in solidum* (see *supra*, **4.F.39.**, Note (3)). Such a mistake will not warrant the intervention of the Cour de cassation, however: Jourdain at 162/5, para. 20.

[210] See Viney and Jourdain, *Conditions* at 210–3, para. 380; Jourdain at 160/20–1, para. 100–2; Le Tourneau and Cadiet at 274, para. 839.

rationale to hold, however, writers insist that the plaintiff must bring before the court all the persons who may have caused the damage, i.e. all the members of the identifiable group.[211]

(4) It would seem that hunting accidents occur less frequently in England, for the leading British Commonwealth case on that problem comes from the Supreme Court of Canada. In *Cook* v. *Lewis*, the court found that where a plaintiff cannot prove which one of two hunters fired the shot that wounded him, the onus of proof should be shifted onto the hunters to exonerate themselves, failing which they would both be liable.[212] That solution is generally accepted by writers.[213]

BGH, 1 October 1957[214]   **4.G.43.**

PARTIES (*BETEILIGTE*) TO A DELICT

Fall on rough track

The second paragraph of § 830(1) BGB may also apply in cases where the liability lies in the failure to maintain a track properly.

Facts: On 16 January 1953, the plaintiff went out to buy some milk. She had to go by way of a street that had not yet been completed. Because heavy machinery was blocking the way for pedestrians, people had taken the habit of walking on a narrow strip of land belonging to the defendant and adjacent to the street. The resulting track was not in a proper state and was icy at the time when the plaintiff passed by. The plaintiff fell and injured herself. She claimed that she fell on the track, which had not been correctly maintained by the defendant; in reply the defendant alleged that the plaintiff fell while walking on the street, for which the city was responsible. It was not possible to ascertain precisely where the plaintiff fell.

Held: The court of first instance and the court of appeal dismissed the claim. The BGH allowed the appeal from the decision of the court of appeal and remitted the case for further consideration.

Judgment: "If it is not possible to discover which one of several parties to a delict actually caused the damage by his unlawful act, each of them will be responsible for the damage (second sentence of § 830(1) BGB). This provision aims to overcome an evidentiary problem faced by the victim in a situation where it remains uncertain, inter alia, which of several persons, each of whom could have been the author of the harm, actually caused it [reference omitted]. It is based on the idea that the claim of someone who was injured by one of several parties to a delict should not fail just because the identity of the actual tortfeasor cannot be discovered with certainty [reference omitted]. The only conditions [for the application of the second sentence of § 830(1) BGB] are that *one* of the several parties actually caused the injury, that the injury could possibly have been caused by each and everyone of them and that fault could be established for each of them, if he were the actual tortfeasor.

The notion of 'participation' in the second sentence of § 830(1) BGB means . . . that several persons—between whom there is no legal connection since each acted independently of the others [reference omitted]—have committed an unlawful act that could have caused the injury; that one of

---

[211] See Viney and Jourdain, *Conditions* at 210–3, para. 380; Jourdain at 160/20–1, para. 100–2; Le Tourneau and Cadiet at 272, para. 833.

[212] *Cook* v. *Lewis* [1951] SCR 830, (1952) 1 DLR 1, SCC.

[213] *Clerk & Lindsell on Torts* at 48, para. 2–13; Markesinis and Deakin at 185. Rogers at 186–7, however, expresses some reservations about the applicability of the Canadian decision in England.

[214] BGHZ 25, 271. Translation by A. Hoffmann and Y. P. Salmon.

these acts, that is the unlawful act of one of these persons, actually caused the injury; that the conduct of each of these persons could have caused the injury and that the actual author of the course of conduct that led to the injury cannot be ascertained [references omitted]. The only prerequisite is thus a course of events [i] which is made up of several independent unlawful acts, [ii] which constitutes a single transaction and is coherent as regards time and place, and [iii] during which the event that led to injury took place [references omitted] . . .

In light of the above, the defendant also 'participated'—in addition to the municipality—in the general condition of the track at the place of the accident, and thereby in the physical injury of the plaintiff. There can be no doubt that the course of events was coherent as regards time and place and constituted a single transaction. Uncertainty remains only as to whether, within the narrowly defined place of the accident, the event which led to the physical injury of the plaintiff arose on the property of the municipality or on the adjacent property of the defendant. The second sentence of § 830(1) BGB aims to relieve the claimant of this very inability to produce conclusive evidence, because it is fairer to let liability fall on all of those who culpably participated in the joint creation of the risk and who could each have caused the damage, rather than leave the victim without compensation [reference omitted]."

Notes

(1) The annotated case is one of the leading precedents on the second sentence of § 830(1) BGB, which reads: "[Joint and several liability] shall apply if it cannot be ascertained which of many participants (*Beteiligte*) caused the injury through his conduct". Since that provision constitutes an exception to the principle that the plaintiff must prove that the conduct of the alleged tortfeasor caused the injury, it had been interpreted relatively strictly.

As the BGH explained, the purpose of that provision is to relieve the victim of the burden of proof in situations where it would be unfair to deprive him or her of compensation because of uncertainty regarding the identity of the tortfeasor. The conditions for the provision to apply, as set out in the annotated case and developed further in case law and writing, are as follows:[215]

- Many persons (the *Beteiligte* or participants) have acted (or omitted to act) in such a way as to endanger the victim, and have done so independently of each other (otherwise the case would fall under the *first* sentence of § 830(1), or under § 830(2) BGB). Accordingly, the conduct of each person must have been such as to meet *all the conditions required to establish liability*, except for causation (e.g. under § 823(1) BGB, *Tatbestand*, *Rechtswidrigkeit* and *Verschulden* must be present).[216] It does not matter whether the participants would have been liable under fault-based regimes, risk-based regimes (*Gefährdungshaftung*) or a combination of both.
- The conduct of each participant could theoretically have brought about the whole of the injury to the plaintiff; in other words, there must be some minimal threshold of potential causation. Participants can then exonerate themselves by proving that their conduct could not possibly have led to the injury of the victim. In contrast, if it is clear

---

[215] The following explanations are based on Staudinger-Belling/Eberl-Borges, § 830 at 20–29, para. 66–98; Münchener-Stein, § 830 at 1774–7, para. 21–30; Larenz/Canaris at 572–8.

[216] For instance, in BGH, 24 January 1984, BGHZ 89, 383, it was not certain that some of the defendants were present at the time when the injury was inflicted, and the BGH held that the second sentence of § 830(1) BGB was not applicable (at 399–400).

that each defendant caused only part of the injury, but the respective parts cannot be separately ascertained, then it is a matter for § 287 of the *Zivilprozeßordnung* (ZPO, Ordinance on Civil Procedure): the court will have to estimate the part of the injury caused by each defendant.[217]

– The conduct of one of the participants caused the injury to the victim (so-called *alternative Kausalität* or alternative causation, as in the annotated case) or the conduct of many participants combined to cause the injury to the victim (so-called *kumulative Kausalität* or cumulative causation). The second sentence of § 830(1) BGB is not applicable if the injury could also have been caused by a natural event, or by the conduct of a person not party to the proceedings or by the conduct of the victim.[218]

– The identity of the actual tortfeasor cannot be determined (*Urheberzweifel*, in cases of alternative causation) or the respective shares of the actual tortfeasors cannot be ascertained (*Anteilszweifel*, in cases of cumulative causation). If one of the defendants is certainly liable for the whole injury and the other(s) could also be liable for part of it, then the second sentence of § 830(1) BGB is not applicable, since its purpose is not to enable the plaintiff to add potential tortfeasors as defendants when one defendant is liable in any event. Such a situation typically arises when a pedestrian is hit first by one driver and then by another before he or she could be rescued and taken into safety. After some debate and a series of key cases, the BGH found that since the first driver is responsible for the whole of the injury in any event,[219] the second driver cannot be added as a *Gesamtschuldner* (i.e. one who is jointly and severally liable for the whole) on the basis of the second sentence of § 830(1) BGB.[220]

The annotated case mentions another condition, namely that the respective courses of conduct of the participants should be related in time and space and constitute a single transaction (*tatsächlich einheitlicher, örtlich und zeitlich zusammenhängender Vorgang*). The BGH has restated this condition throughout its case-law, although it has never played a decisive role and has been criticized by almost all commentators as being inconsistent with the rationale behind the second sentence of § 830(1) BGB.[221] In more recent cases, the BGH has left it open whether this is still a condition for the application of that provision.[222]

---

[217] See *supra*, **4.G.19.**, Note (4). It is also possible that the full injury was caused by the combined conduct of the defendants so that their respective shares cannot be identified, but that the conduct of each of the defendants alone could have led to only part of the damage. In that case, the defendants would be liable as *Gesamtschuldner* pursuant to the second sentence of § 830(1) BGB for that part of the damage which could have been caused by either of them alone (estimated pursuant to § 287 ZPO): see BGH, 11 January 1994 (Children's tea—*Kindertee*), NJW 1994, 932.

[218] On this point, many authors think that it would be better to reduce the damages that are awarded to reflect the possibility that a natural cause, a third-party or the victim could have been responsible for the injury and apply the second sentence of § 830(1) BGB to that reduced amount: Staudinger-Belling/Eberl-Borges, § 830 at 24, para. 83; Larenz/Canaris at 577–9. Such an approach is followed when contributory fault (*Mitverschulden*) could have been invoked by one or more of the defendants against the victim; on contributory fault, see *infra*, Chapter VII, 7.1.2.

[219] See *supra*, **4.G.34.** and notes thereafter.

[220] See BGH, 15 November 1960, BGHZ 33, 286; BGH, 15 December 1970, BGHZ 55, 86; BGH, 22 June 1976, BGHZ 67, 14 and BGH, 7 November 1978, BGHZ 72, 355.

[221] Staudinger-Belling/Eberl-Borges, § 830 at 29–31, para. 99–104; Münchener-Stein, § 830 at 1777–8, para. 31–2; Larenz/Canaris at 573–4.

[222] BGH, 27 May 1987, BGHZ 101, 106.

(2) The participants are liable jointly and severally (as *Gesamtschuldner*), as in the case of co-authors, instigators, accomplices or *Nebentäter*.[223]

Hoge Raad, 9 October 1992[224]   **4.NL.44.**
B. v. Bayer Nederland BV

MARKET SHARE LIABILITY

DES daughters

Art. 6:99 BW[225] *may apply to situations where a large number of manufacturers (or distributors) may have caused injury to the plaintiff by putting their product on the market, even if the injury could have been caused by a manufacturer which is not at fault or not even brought before the court as a defendant.*

Facts: The six plaintiffs were exposed to Diethylstilbestrol (DES) before their birth, since their respective mothers took DES during pregnancy. As a typical result, they developed a specific form of cervical/vaginal cancer. The ten defendants were pharmaceutical companies who, according to research done by the plaintiffs, had put DES on the Dutch market during the time of the pregnancy of the plaintiffs' mothers, although it was not possible to prove that the DES taken by the mothers of the plaintiffs did not come from some company other than one of the ten defendants.

Held: The court of first instance and the court of appeal dismissed the claims of the plaintiffs. The Hoge Raad quashed the judgment of the court of appeal and remitted the case back for further consideration.

Judgment: "[APPLICABILITY OF ARTICLE 6:99 BW]
3.7.1. . . . The court of appeal erroneously held that Article 6:99 BW would not be applicable in the present case . . .

The facts of the present case fall under that provision, on the assumption that it can be proved that [i] each of the firms which put DES in circulation in the relevant period was at fault (*fout*) in so doing and could thus be held liable, [ii] the total injury of each victim could have been caused by any of these "events"—i.e. putting DES in circulation—and [iii] the injury occurred because of at least one of these "events" . . .

[Article 6:99 BW] aims to remove the unfairness arising from the fact that the victim must bear his or her own damage because he or she cannot prove whose action caused his or her harm. The victims in the present are faced with such an evidentiary difficulty . . .

3.7.2. Furthermore, it is worth keeping in mind that the view taken by the court of appeal leads to an unacceptable result.

Although we have to start from the presumption that the pharmaceutical companies have each committed a fault by putting DES in circulation and that the DES daughters suffered severe injury because their mothers used DES, the DES daughters would still remain without any compensation, under the view [of the court of appeal], simply because they cannot prove which company marketed the DES tablets used by their respective mothers.

In this respect, it must be noted that the regime of 'market share liability' . . . also enables the DES daughters to recover compensation. However, this regime . . . cannot be accepted [for reasons stated further below].

---

[223] See *supra*, **4.F.38.–39.**, Note (4).
[224] NJ 1994, 535. Translation by Y.P. Salmon.
[225] The text of Article 6:99 BW is found at Note (1) after the case.

3.7.3. When seen against all the foregoing, one is not swayed by the . . . argument that Article 6:99 BW is not suitable for cases such as the present one, where injury was inflicted upon a great number of victims and each producer merely caused a—statistically measurable—proportion of the total injury of all victims.

In the present case, each DES daughter claims damages from each of the pharmaceutical companies. From a legal perspective, [the DES daughters] do not act as a group, and moreover they could not do so. Hence it is unfair, just because there are many victims, to put them in a position, as regards evidence, that is less favourable than that provided for in Article 6:99 BW. In addition, the producers, while liable to compensate the victims for the whole injury, can seek contribution from each other, so that in principle they ultimately do not have to bear more than their share of the total damages.

Furthermore, as contribution is not at issue in this case, it need not be decided what share each producer must bear in relation to the others.

3.7.4. As already . . . indicated, the court of appeal . . . considered that Article 6:99 BW was not applicable because the DES daughters did not—and cannot—prove who belonged to the class of persons who put DES in circulation. In so ruling, the court of appeal made an error of law . . .

[It cannot] be demanded that the victim introduces evidence as to who belongs to the circle of responsible persons . . . Such a demand would lead to an unfair result already in the typical cases falling under the scope of Article 6:99 BW, ie cases in which many persons fire shots or throw stones in the same direction: where all those persons cannot be identified, the victim would then have to bear the damage himself or herself. *A fortiori*, in a case such as the present one, that demand would lead to an unfair result: the victim would have to bear her own damage if she could not identify all the producers who put DES in circulation in the relevant period, even if such an identification is in fact almost impossible . . .

3.7.5. . . . It is sufficient for each DES daughter to establish . . . in relation to each of the pharmaceutical companies:

(i) that the pharmaceutical company in question put DES in circulation during the relevant period and can therefore be found liable because it committed a fault;

(ii) that another or several other producers—regardless of whether they are parties to the proceedings or not—also put DES in circulation during the relevant period and can therefore also be found liable because it (they) committed a fault; and

(iii) that she suffered injury that resulted from the use of DES, but that it is no longer possible to determine from which producer the DES originated.

In principle the burden of proof on these issues rests on the DES daughter concerned.

Conversely, the final words of Article 6:99 BW imply that [each pharmaceutical company] can put up a defence as against any DES daughter by alleging, and if necessary establishing, that the injury suffered by the DES daughter was not caused by DES which it put in circulation.

3.7.6. Finally, it is conceivable that it will be established that, during the relevant period, DES was also put in circulation by one or more producer(s) which is (are) not liable because it was (they were) not at fault, so that the injury of a given DES daughter could also have been caused by DES coming from that (those) producer(s). However, this does not relieve the other producers from their liability to compensate the whole injury, unless that liability would, in all reasonableness and fairness, become unconscionable under the circumstances, including the probability that the damage suffered by the DES daughter in question was caused by DES from a producer which was not responsible . . .

3.8. [The plaintiffs claim] that each pharmaceutical company 'is liable to compensate the injury suffered by each individual victim in proportion to its share in the total injury caused when the drug was put in circulation; that proportion can (or in principle may) be equated with the share of the company in the total amount of the drug marketed for that particular use by the companies'.

... [S]uch a regime of 'market-share liability' ... cannot be accepted.

Indeed this regime is not satisfactory, since it leaves the victim, and not the producers, with the risk that a producer is insolvent, no longer exists or can no longer be traced. Another questionable aspect is that the victims must bring as many producers as possible in their proceedings, and that the market share of each of the producers must [then] be determined in the course of the proceedings between victim and producer. Furthermore, in a case such as the present one, there is no need for market-share liability in order to protect victims because each producer is ... in principle liable to compensate the whole injury.

At present it can be left open whether the market share of each producer can be relevant in determining their respective contributions between one another.

[LIABILITY OF THE DEFENDANTS FOR A COLLECTIVE ACTION]

3.10. [The plaintiffs claim] that 'a collective unlawful act was committed against the victims taken as a whole', so that each firm is bound to make complete (or partial) reparation of the injury suffered by each individual victim; or at least each must establish, with the other firms, a common fund for the benefit of the victims. To the extent that claim goes beyond what has been accepted in the previous paragraphs, it finds no support in the law."

Notes

(1) The annotated case turns round the interpretation of Art. 6:99 BW, which reads:[226]

Where the damage may have resulted from two or more events for each of which a different person is liable, and where it has been determined that the damage has arisen from at least one of these events, the obligation to repair the damage rests upon each of these persons, unless he proves that the damage is not the result of the event for which he himself is liable.

The Hoge Raad judgment has received much attention from Dutch legal writers.[227]

The essential problem in the annotated case was whether and, if so, how Art. 6:99 BW, a provision which is not unlike the second sentence of § 830(1) BGB, could be applied to "modern" situations. In the previous annotated cases (hunting accident, fall on rough track), the number of possible tortfeasors was small and the sequence of events relatively clear. By contrast, in the annotated case, a large number of companies were marketing the product in question, and it was by no means clear how the action of the actual tortfeasor

---

[226] Translation from P.P.C. Haanappel and E. Mackaay, *New Netherlands Civil Code: Patrimonial Law: Property, Obligations and Special Contracts* (Deventer: Kluwer, 1990).

[227] T. Hartlief, "Alternatieve causaliteit" (1992) TVVS 308; J. Hijma, "DES-dochters" (1993) 42 AA 2/123; E. Hondius, "A Dutch DES Case: Pharmaceutical Producers Jointly and Severally Liable" [1994] Cons LJ 40; P. Ingelse, "Hoge Raad in Des-arrest: ruim baan voor artikel 6:99 BW" NJB 1992, 1403; C.J.M. Klaassen and A.A. van Rossum, "DES-tijd(s), en hoe nu verder?" (1994) RM Themis 1; P. Kottenhagen-Edzes, Note (1992:12) M en R 137 at 668; G.J. Rijken and J.G.J. Rinkes, Note (1992) TvC 5/325; J. Spier, "De Des-dochters" (1992) NTBR 193. See as well the comparative comments of J.J. Phillips and J. Bridgeman at [1994] Cons LJ 43 ff. and of E. Hondius, M.A. Parra, G. Häger, I. Geers, O. Guillod and A. Leuba, D. Tzouganatos, J. Calvão da Silva at (1994) 2 Eur. R Priv. L 409 ff.

was linked to the injury: the mothers of the DES daughters may have taken DES made by several manufacturers; and beyond the fact that exposure to DES was likely to have led to the condition of the DES daughters, it was not possible really to know at what point in time or how that happened.

The DES daughters thus found themselves in precisely the kind of evidentiary quagmire at which Art. 6:99 BW is directed, as the Hoge Raad recalled under 3.7.1. and 3.7.2. of the annotated case: they had suffered injury, which had been caused by negligent and wrongful conduct, but they could not identify whose conduct it was.

(2) The Hoge Raad then reviewed the main objections which had been voiced against the application of Art. 6:99 BW in the annotated case.[228] For one, it was argued that Art. 6:99 could not be applied to "mass torts" since, on a statistical basis, each manufacturer (or distributor) could not have caused the whole injury but, at most, only part of it. To reverse the burden of proof and hold all manufacturers before the court liable jointly and severally (*hoofdelijk*) would mean that, at least in a group action, those manufacturers would end up paying for more than the injury that they might have caused, since they would have to pay the shares of the manufacturers who are untraceable, insolvent or out of the business. If that argument holds true for group actions, then there is no reason why it should not also be valid in an action brought by an individual, as in the annotated case.

The Hoge Raad (under 3.7.3. of the annotated judgment) turned that argument on its head: the plaintiffs in the annotated case were acting not as a group, but as individual claimants. They should not be deprived of the benefit of Art. 6:99 BW merely because they were numerous. Moreover, a manufacturer who has paid damages for the whole of the injury suffered by a plaintiff can seek contribution from the others.

(3) Another objection, which has been the focus of much debate amongst Dutch writers,[229] is that Art. 6:99 BW should apply only if the plaintiff can bring before the court all the potential tortfeasors. Otherwise, there is a risk that the actual tortfeasor may not be amongst the defendants, in which case the underlying rationale for Art. 6:99 BW will no longer hold.[230] Under 3.7.4. of the annotated case, the Hoge Raad answered that even in "classical" cases such as hunting accidents, it would be unfair to require the plaintiff to bring all the potential tortfeasors before the court; the same holds for the annotated case, where in fact it was impossible to identify all the manufacturers and distributors of DES during the relevant period.

(4) Under 3.7.5. of the annotated case, the Hoge Raad concluded by setting out how Art. 6:99 BW applies in the circumstances of the annotated case. Once the plaintiffs had shown that more than one manufacturer or distributor was at fault in putting DES onto the market in the relevant period and that they could not point to the one whose DES caused their injury, the burden of proof then shifted on to the DES manufacturers and distributors to exonerate themselves by proving that they could not have caused the injury. The Hoge Raad made only one concession to the peculiarities of "mass torts" cases under 3.7.6.: given that it was also possible that the injury might have been caused

---

[228] A good exposition of these objections can be found in the opinion of AG Hartkamp, who concluded that Art. 6:99 BW should not be applied in the annotated case: see NJ 1994, 535 at 2489–91.

[229] See the references listed in the opinion of AG Hartkamp, ibid. at 2488.

[230] It will be recalled that, under both French (*supra*, **4.F.42.**, Note (3)) and German (*supra*, **4.G.43.**, Note (2)) law, the plaintiff has to bring all possible tortfeasors before the court.

by a manufacturer or distributor who was not at fault (e.g. because that manufacturer took appropriate precautions to avoid its DES being given to pregnant women), the defendants could be relieved from liability *for the whole* of the injury, but only where equity and fairness so required under the circumstances, in particular if there was a high degree of probability that the injury had been caused by the "innocent" manufacturer or distributor.

(5) Having concluded that Art. 6:99 BW was applicable, the Hoge Raad nevertheless examined alternative arguments brought forward by the plaintiffs, which reflect the solutions reached in other jurisdictions.

The plaintiffs argued for liability based on market shares, on the model of *Sindell* v. *Abbott Laboratories*, a California case also involving DES daughters.[231] In *Sindell*, the court had concluded that the defendant manufacturers were liable to compensate the plaintiffs for their injuries, in proportion to their share of the market for DES at the relevant time. That solution was very controversial, since it clashed with many well-established principles of the common law of torts.[232] The Californian decision received considerable attention in the Netherlands also, and in fact Advocate-General Hartkamp argued for it at length in his Opinion before the Hoge Raad.[233] However, the Hoge Raad found that market-share liability was not acceptable under Dutch law, since it burdened the plaintiffs with the task of bringing as many manufacturers as possible before the court and left them to bear the part of the damages awarded corresponding to the market share which could not be accounted for. Furthermore, the parties and the court would have to go through the difficult process of market definition and analysis. The application of Art. 6:99 BW was in fact more advantageous for the plaintiffs, who would then recover the full amount of their injury; market shares could still be used at the contribution stage for the purposes of apportionment among the defendants.

(6) The Hoge Raad (under 3.10.) also briefly dismissed the argument that the defendants should be held liable for a "collective wrongful act" against the plaintiffs, a solution that French courts have used to overcome causation difficulties.[234]

(7) In the annotated judgment, the Hoge Raad insisted that it was dealing with a series of actions brought by individuals against a class of defendants, and not with a group action, a fact which certainly comforted it in its finding that Art. 6:99 BW was applicable. Nonetheless, as Advocate-General Hartkamp underlined in his Opinion, it must not be forgotten that in a "mass tort" situation such as that in the annotated case, there are many individuals in the same position, whether they choose to proceed before the courts individually or as a group.[235] If one considers that, on the strength of the Hoge Raad decision, each plaintiff DES daughter was entitled to judgment jointly and severally against all the manufacturers which she could join as defendants, but that no provision was made to coordinate the execution of this large number of individual judgments and that victims who were not before the court in the annotated case were not relieved from the need to obtain a judgment, it would appear that the mechanism of Art. 6:99 BW may be too crude to ensure proper and efficient compensation for all victims.

[231] *Sindell* v. *Abbott Laboratories* (1980) 607 P 2d 924, Supreme Court of California.
[232] See for instance the dissent of Richardson J. in *Sindell*, ibid.
[233] See NJ 1994, 535 at 2491–4.
[234] See *supra*, **4.F.42.** and Note (2) thereunder.
[235] This is also the core of the criticism made by Akkermans at 355ff. See also Larenz/Canaris at 579–80.

Class action mechanisms of the kind introduced in the laws of most North American jurisdictions were already studied earlier in the section dealing with the protection of collective interests.[236] It was seen there that they offer an attractive means of dealing with cases where a large class of victims want to hold a defendant liable for a violation of a collective interest shared by them. If, in addition to a large class of victims, there is also a large class of defendants, the class action mechanism may become even more attractive, in that it gives greater discretion to the court to fashion a form of relief—such as a lump-sum payment to set up a fund from which victims will be compensated—which enables victims to obtain compensation expeditiously and defendants to settle their liabilities in a quick and orderly fashion. Moreover, the evidentiary difficulties surrounding causation—which have proved a stumbling block in all systems studied in this subsection—are alleviated to some extent, since the main adjudication is done *in abstracto*, on the basis of the "average" plaintiff and the "average" defendant, where causation cannot really be denied. Once the main adjudication is completed, the defendants can hardly argue on causation in each and every case at the subsequent stage at which each plaintiff receives compensation.[237] The main disadvantage of class actions may be that, since the form of relief will necessarily be conceived on the basis of statistics, certain victims may receive less than they would have obtained in an individual action.

4.5. COMPARATIVE OVERVIEW

One of the aims of this Chapter, as set out at the beginning, was to demonstrate that the question of causation was more than a factual question and was indeed infused with legal considerations. In the light of the materials reviewed above and the notes and comments accompanying them, it is to be hoped that the reader does not feel that the law relating to causation is totally heterogeneous.

Causation as an inquiry into the sequence of events

In the section dealing with the general approach, it was seen that all systems under study take as a starting point the notion of *conditio sine qua non*, or "but for" test, as crisply expressed in the common law: in order for an event or a circumstance to be considered at all as a cause of the injury to the victim, it must be demonstrated that the injury would not have occurred *but for* that event. Under German law, the notion of *conditio sine qua non* is decisive in establishing causation in the natural or logical sense (*Kausalität im natürlichen Sinne*), the first stage of the causation inquiry: according to the *Hinwegdenken* process, the conduct of the plaintiff must be "assumed away" from the remaining course of events in order to see whether the same result (with the same legal significance) would then have occurred.[238] Under English law, the "but for" test forms the first stage of the

---

[236] Class actions are discussed at greater length *supra*, Chapter II, 2.5.2.B.

[237] See *supra*, Chapter II, **2.QC.66.**, Note (4).

[238] BGH, 2 July 1957, *supra*, **4.G.11.**, provides a good example of the application of the *Hinwegdenken* process.

causation inquiry, called "cause-in-fact".[239] Under French law, the theory of *équivalence des conditions*, which relies essentially on the "but for" test, still underpins causation.[240]

The "but for" test reflects a fairly rudimentary understanding of causation, since it assumes that an event either caused or did not cause a certain result (all-or-nothing approach). The role of causation is then simply to establish a factual link between the event triggering the liability of the alleged tortfeasor and the injury to the plaintiff. Furthermore, the "but for" test is applied strictly, at least in German and English law, without there being any possibility to argue that an event may have been merely an occasion for injury to happen.[241] Such a strict application of the "but for" test, whereby a single event could potentially have far-reaching legal consequences, appears to run contrary to common sense. As C. von Bar underlines, the key weakness of the "but for" test is that it cannot suffice to distinguish between causes and mere circumstances.[242]

The introduction of probabilistic elements and the normative approach to causation

Accordingly, all the systems studied here have sought to limit the potential scope of a strict "but for" test.[243] Under German law, a distinction is made between logical or natural causation (*Kausalität im natürlichen Sinne*), which is assessed according to the *conditio sine qua non* test, and a further step in the inquiry, called causation in the legal sense (*Kausalität im rechtlichen Sinne*). The adequacy theory (*Adäquanztheorie*) was the first to be put forward as a criterion for causation in the legal sense. It is in essence a probabilistic theory, whereby an event is the adequate cause of a particular result "if [it] generally increases, in a significant way, the objective probability of a result of the kind which occurred" or, seen from the other side, "if [it] was generally suitable to lead to the occurrence of the result, and not only under particularly unique and quite improbable circumstances to which no attention would be paid if events had followed a normal course".[244] These probabilities must be assessed from the point of view of an "optimal observer" who knows all the circumstances surrounding the injurious event which could be known at the time of that event and is furthermore equipped with the general experience of mankind.[245]

A similar development has taken place under English law, where a second stage of inquiry, called causation-in-law or remoteness of damage, takes place following causation-in-fact. In the 1960s, "reasonable foreseeability" was adopted as the test for remoteness of damage, as opposed to "directness", which appears to have been the prevailing criterion until then.[246] Here as well, the test is based on probabilities: damage becomes too remote when it is of such

---

[239] *Supra*, 4.1.2., Introductory Note under a) and b). As mentioned there, both the division in two stages and the use of the "but for" test for the first stage are challenged by leading authors.

[240] This is expressed in the requirement that the causal link be certain: see for instance Cass. civ. 2e, 20 June 1985, *supra*, **4.F.8.** On the other hand, the requirement of directness which appears to flow from the text of Art. 1151 C.civ. has been rendered largely devoid of meaning by subsequent case law: see *supra*, **4.F.7.** and notes thereafter.

[241] *Supra*, **4.G.11.** and Note (1) thereunder.

[242] von Bar II at 461, para. 437.

[243] This is openly admitted under German law, see BGH, 23 October 1951, *supra*, **4.G.1.**

[244] Both these formulations have been endorsed by the BGH, ibid.

[245] See BGH, ibid. and Note (3) thereafter.

[246] See *The Wagon Mound (No. 1)*, *supra*, **4.E.4.** and notes thereafter.

a kind as the reasonable person could not have foreseen.[247] Characterization of the damage plays a central role under English law: once it is established that the kind of damage was reasonably foreseeable, the liability of the defendant will extend to the whole extent of that damage, irrespective of how it was actually brought about.[248]

Even if French law remains more attached to the theory of *équivalence des conditions* and thus often relies on the "but for" test alone for the assessment of causation, probabilistic considerations play a significant role at two levels. First, even if the conduct of the alleged tortfeasor is a *conditio sine qua non* of the injury to the plaintiff, it may be that another event external to the defendant (a natural event, conduct of a third party or conduct of the plaintiff) also intervened in the causation of the injury. If that other event was unforeseeable (*imprévisible*) and unavoidable (*irrésistible*) for the alleged tortfeasor, it constitutes a *cause étrangère* and results in the complete exoneration of the defendant.[249] As Viney points out, exoneration on the ground of *cause étrangère* is but a manifestation of the adequacy theory.[250] Secondly, irrespective of whether other causes were present, in a number of cases, for reasons reflecting an explanatory/adequacy theory, French courts have denied that the conduct of the alleged tortfeasor caused the injury to the plaintiff;[251] it cannot be said, however, that such explanatory/adequacy theory governs causation under French law, since a number of cases continue to rely solely on *équivalence des conditions*.[252] Accordingly, as in German and English law, the defendant can thus also present arguments based on unforeseeability to attempt to deny causation under French law.

Even if a probabilistic element is introduced into the assessment of causation under all three major legal systems,[253] the precise tests and criteria used under each system vary sufficiently that diverging solutions are reached in some cases. For instance, when it comes to the pre-existing condition of the plaintiff, while the maxim "the tortfeasor takes his victim as he finds him" is seen as an exception to the test of "reasonable foreseeability" under English law,[254] the equivalent principle under German law is thought to fit within the adequacy theory.[255]

As probabilistic reasoning is introduced in the assessment of causation, the role of causation undergoes some changes. As the BGH expressed it, the issue becomes not causation, "but rather the determination of the limits up to which a person who brought about an event can, *in all fairness and reasonableness*, be made liable for the consequences of such an event; this is in truth an autonomous condition for liability in its own right" [emphasis added].[256] Similarly, the reasoning of the House of Lords in *The Wagon Mound (No. 1)* very much centres on the unfairness of making a defendant liable for consequences which could not be foreseen.[257] The purpose of the inquiry into causation is then to ensure not only that the conduct of the alleged tortfeasor did in fact contribute to the

---

[247] Ibid.
[248] See *Hughes* v. *Lord Advocate*, *supra*, **4.E.5.**
[249] *Cause étrangère* is dealt with *supra*, Chapter III, 3.2.3.
[250] Viney and Jourdain, *Conditions* at 247–9, para. 403.
[251] See *supra*, 4.1.3., Introductory Note under f), and for examples *supra*, **4.F.9.** and **4.F.32.**
[252] *Supra*, 4.1.3., Introductory Note under i).
[253] For a survey including other European legal systems, see von Bar II at 473–80, para. 449–56.
[254] See *Smith* v. *Leech Brain*, *supra*, **4.E.24.** and notes thereafter.
[255] See OLG Karlsruhe, 25 January 1966, *supra*, **4.G.25.** and notes thereafter.
[256] BGH, 23 October 1951, *supra*, **4.G.1.** and Note (4) thereafter.
[257] *Supra*, **4.E.4.** and Note (3) thereafter.

injury of the victim, but also that under the circumstances the alleged tortfeasor *ought to* be held liable for that injury. A normative aspect (or *wertende Betrachtung*, as it is called under German law) is thus added to the assessment of causation.[258]

In all legal systems studied here, the introduction of a probabilistic element into the assessment of causation echoes the standard used for fault or negligence. For instance, under German law, the generally accepted justification for adequacy is that inadequate consequences lie outside the sphere of influence of the defendant, and thus are not connected with the defendant's free will (and his or her resulting liability for injury to others).[259] Accordingly, authors generally agree that adequacy has little independent role to play at the *Haftungsbegründung* stage[260]—at least for fault-based liability under § 823(1) BGB—, since the requirement of fault (*Verschulden*) addresses the same issues as adequacy.[261] Similarly, in *The Wagon Mound (No. 1)*, the House of Lords based its reasoning on the need to streamline the tests of negligence and remoteness of damage, so that the extent of liability (reasonably foreseeable damage) corresponds to the standard of care expected from the defendant (prevention of reasonably foreseeable damage).[262] Finally, under French law, authors consider that complete exoneration in cases of *cause étrangère* can be justified either on the ground of lack of causation (lack of adequacy) or on the ground of lack of fault (absence of fault).[263] Furthermore, in cases where adequacy is used to deny causation, the conduct of the defendant is in fact often "masked" by a graver fault by someone else, so that the conduct of the defendant appears not to be an adequate cause of the harm.[264]

While it appears that all the legal systems under study have added a normative dimension to the basic test of causation by introducing probabilistic elements in the assessment of causation, some divergences appear thereafter. Indeed German law has gone further by adding another major theoretical dimension to the assessment of causation, namely the "scope of rule" (*Schutzzweck der Norm*) theory, whereby the liability of the defendant can be engaged only if the injury of the plaintiff comes within the scope of protection of the norm which has been infringed.[265] The BGH has adopted that theory and now applies it alongside adequacy.[266] In comparison,[267] in English law, "scope of rule" analysis is

---

[258] Under both German and English law, there is discussion as to whether this normative aspect should still be considered under the heading "causation", together with the "first stage" inquiry (*conditio sine qua non*, "but for" test), rather than as a separate condition for liability. For the purposes of this casebook, in any event, both are discussed in this Chapter.

[259] Lange at 87; Larenz at 439.

[260] *Haftungsbegründung* refers to the link between the conduct of the alleged tortfeasor and the event which leads to liability (injury, etc.), in contrast with *Haftungsausfüllung*, which relates to the link with subsequent injurious consequences (loss of income following injury, etc.): see *supra*, 4.1.1. under a).

[261] Lange at 96–7; Staudinger-Medicus, § 249 at 41, para. 48.

[262] *Supra*, **4.E.4.** and Note (3) thereunder, where it is pointed out that many commentators have criticized the position of the House of Lords in this respect.

[263] See Viney and Jourdain, *Conditions* at 247–9, para. 403.

[264] See **4.F.9.**, where the unidentified person who was responsible for the presence of the explosives in the shack committed a graver fault than the defendants who had failed to supervise their shack, as well as **4.F.33.**, where the fault of the defendant in leaving its excavator unguarded was overshadowed by the thief's wanton vandalism. See Viney and Jourdain, *Conditions* at 173–4, para. 357.

[265] See *supra*, 4.1.1., Introductory Note under d) as well as **4.G.2.** and notes thereafter.

[266] See for instance BGH, 16 February 1972, *supra*, **4.G.2.** and BGH, 2 July 1991, *supra*, **4.G.3.**

[267] For a comparative discussion of the "scope of rule" theory covering all European legal systems, see von Bar II at 495–501, para. 475–80.

limited to the tort of breach of statutory duty[268] and only traces of it are found in French law.[269]

Moreover, more recent German legal writing and case law evidences the emergence of a further approach to the assessment of causation, based on the respective "spheres of risk" of the parties: the defendant is not liable for injury which represents no more than the realization of a risk which came within the plaintiff's sphere of risk (comprising among others the general risk associated with existence or *allgemeines Lebensrisiko*).[270] German courts have already included sphere of risk considerations in their reasoning,[271] but it is still not clear whether these considerations truly constitute a new theoretical approach or merely a refinement of existing theories.[272] While similar lines of reasoning are present in Community law,[273] there appears to be no equivalent development under English or French law.

One may wonder why the general approach to causation under German law appears to be more complex than under the other legal systems. Without claiming to constitute a complete answer, the following considerations may provide some explanation. When the role of causation evolves from an inquiry into the sequence of events to a normative assessment of the objective imputability of the plaintiff's injury to the defendant, it is only natural that the normative elements of causation should reflect the overall normative structure of the respective tort law systems.

It was seen earlier that the German law of civil liability relies on a number of general headings of liability,[274] each of which provides protection within defined limits.[275] The *Schutzzweck der Norm* theory is perfectly consistent with that approach, inasmuch as it ensures that only injury which comes within the scope of protection of each of these headings will be imputed to the defendant. That is most obvious in cases involving liability for breach of a protective statute (§ 823(2) BGB) or of an official duty (§ 839 BGB)— and for contractual liability —, but the *Schutzzweck* theory also supports the general approach of German tort law in the case of other bases for liability.[276] Under § 823(1) BGB, for instance, limits can be set using the *Schutzzweck der Norm* theory in cases where the limitative structure of § 823(1) BGB is put under the most strain, namely where judicial creations such as *Verkehrssicherungspflichten*[277] or the complementary *Rechtsgüter* (*Recht am Gewerbebetrieb*[278] or general *Persönlichkeitsrecht*[279]) are involved.[280] That

[268] See *supra*, **4.E.6.** and notes thereafter.

[269] See *supra*, **4.F.10.** and note thereafter.

[270] See *supra*, 4.1.1., Introductory Note under e) as well as **4.G.3.** and notes thereafter.

[271] See for instance BGH, 2 July 1991, *supra*, **4.G.3.** and OLG Karlsruhe, 25 January 1966, *supra*, **4.G.25.**

[272] *Supra*, **4.G.3.**, Note (2).

[273] See the requirement that the injury suffered by the plaintiff, to be recoverable, "must go beyond the bounds of the normal economic risks inherent in the activities in the sector concerned": *infra*, Chapter IX, **9.EC.3.** and Note (4) thereafter.

[274] As they are called by Larenz/Canaris, *supra*, Chapter II, **1.G.8.**

[275] *Supra*, Chapter I, 1.4.3.

[276] See Münchener-Grunsky, § 249 at 367 ff., para. 42 ff., who would reject adequacy altogether in favour of the *Schutzzweck der Norm* theory. At the other end of the spectrum, Soergel-Mertens, § 249 at 249 ff., para. 120 ff., would dismiss *Schutzzweck der Norm* and rely exclusively on adequacy in order to assess legal causation.

[277] See *supra*, Chapter III, 3.1.2. as well as, for practical examples where *Verkehrspflichten* are used, the case of liability for employees, *infra*, Chapter V, 5.1.1.C. and product liability, *infra*, Chapter VI, 6.3.1.A.

[278] See *supra*, Chapter II, 2.3.2.

[279] See *supra*, Chapter II, 2.2.1.

[280] See Lange at 116–20.

theory can thus be seen as an echo of the general headings approach of German law in the area of causation, infusing a normative assessment (*wertende Betrachtung*) in the concept of causation.

Under English law, in particular as regards the law of negligence, the general approach relies on the concept of duty of care as the central limitative element.[281] "Policy" or normative factors are dealt with in the course of establishing whether there is duty of care. Indeed for a duty of care to arise, the current law requires not only (i) that the harm was foreseeable, but also (ii) that the plaintiff and the defendant stood in a relationship of proximity and (iii) that it be fair, just and reasonable to impose a duty of care.[282] Once it has been established that the defendant was under a duty of care to the plaintiff, it would appear pointless to conduct the same inquiry over again within the context of causation: this could explain why remoteness of damage depends solely on the reasonable foreseeability test, without any further normative considerations. On the other hand, a "scope of rule" inquiry takes place in cases involving the tort of breach of statutory duty, where the issue of duty of care does not arise in the same way as under the tort of negligence.[283] There are some indications that in other torts, considerations pertaining to the "scope of rule" would rather arise in relation to the duty of care.[284]

In contrast with German and English law, the general approach of French law is based on one single heading of civil liability. It is not characterized by a concern to provide *a priori* limits or boundaries to the potential liability of the defendant. In accordance with that approach, French law rather appears to seek to provide as wide-ranging a protection as possible to the victims of injury.[285] Accordingly, beyond a probabilistic element which ties in with the main requirement of fault on behalf of the defendant, no need is felt under French law for the kind of complex normative assessment which characterizes causation under German law.

The "but for" test and its application

Despite differences in the general approach to causation, the legal systems under study here show a fair degree of convergence—in the underlying policy concerns, the instruments used and the results reached—when it comes to specific problem areas.

As recalled above, the *conditio sine qua non* or "but for" test is applied relatively mechanically under English, German and French law: no difference is made between "real" causes and mere occasional factors.[286] In principle, any limitation or sorting process occurs at a later stage (*Kausalität im rechtlichen Sinne* under German law, remoteness of damage under English law or when *cause étrangère* is invoked or the equivalency/adequacy theory is applied under French law).

Even then, the application of the "but for" test runs into a number of difficulties. It may be relatively straightforward when an act of the defendant is alleged to have led to the

---

[281] *Supra*, Chapter I, 1.4.1.A.

[282] *Supra*, Chapter I, 1.4.1.B.

[283] *Supra*, **4.E.6.** and notes thereafter.

[284] See *South Australia Asset Management Corporation* v. *York Montague Ltd.* (sub. nom. *Banque Bruxelles Lambert SA* v. *Eagle Star Insurance Co.*) [1997] AC 191, [1996] 3 All ER 365, HL, discussed *supra*, **4.E.6.**, Note (4).

[285] See *supra*, Chapter I, 1.4.2.

[286] See *supra*, **4.G.11.** and Note (2) thereafter.

injury, since it is a matter of seeing how things would have evolved if the act of the defendant is "assumed away" (*Hinwegdenken* process under German law) from the course of events.[287] Nonetheless, the result of the "but for" test may depend on further assumptions being made as to the conduct of third parties (e.g. if the defendant had not negligently hit the plaintiff with his car, would another person have hit the plaintiff in any event?), a problem which becomes even more acute in cases of omissions (e.g. if the defendant had not omitted to throw a lifebuoy to the victim, would she have been saved from drowning in any event?).[288] Under German law, no further assumptions are to be made in the course of the "but for" test; further assumptions can be taken into account only at the later stage of normative assessment described above,[289] a result which may be too strict.[290]

In some instances, the defendant will argue under the "but for" test that he or she could have inflicted the same injury on the plaintiff even if he or she had behaved lawfully (i.e. if the unlawful act or omission is assumed away), a specific issue called *rechtmäßiges Alternativverhalten* under German law. All legal systems studied here allow the defendant to put forward such an argument, within certain limits. Under English law, it is a matter to be dealt with in the course of the "but for" test.[291] Under French law, the matter rather falls to be considered as an application of the adequacy theory.[292] Under German law, the success of the argument will depend on the scope of the rule which the defendant contravened: as a general matter, if that rule did not aim at preventing the occurrence of damage altogether, but rather the occurrence of damage in a certain way, the defendant should be able to argue that he or she could have caused the same damage lawfully.[293]

The "but for" test generally lacks relevance in cases where the sequence of events leading to the damage involves the free and voluntary conduct of the victim or a third party:

– It may be that the victim or the third party intervenes *following* the conduct of the defendant, in which case French[294] and English[295] law replace the "but for" test with a probabilistic test (necessary and foreseeable consequence) and German law uses the *Herausforderung* criterion as the key factor for imputability;[296]

– It may be that the defendant was under a *duty to inform* the plaintiff, where it cannot be known how the plaintiff would have decided with proper information. Under French law, causation will sometimes be denied, but often the defendant is found liable for a *perte d'une chance*; in a number of cases, courts have even assumed that the plaintiff would have decided otherwise than as he or she did.[297] English and German

---

[287] Ibid., Note (1) thereafter.
[288] It will be noted that all legal systems accept that omissions be seen as "causes" (see on acts and omissions in general *supra*, Chapter III, 3.1.).
[289] See *supra*, **4.G.13.**, Note (6).
[290] See Honoré at 74–6, para. 117, who shows that it is appropriate to make further assumptions in certain cases.
[291] *Supra*, **4.E.12.** and Note (2) thereafter.
[292] *Supra*, **4.E.12.**, **4.G.13.**, Note (4).
[293] *Supra*, **4.G.13.** and Notes (2) and (3) thereafter.
[294] *Supra*, **4.F.33.**, **4.F.38.**, and notes thereafter.
[295] *Supra*, **4.G.34.**, Note (4) as well as **4.E.36.** and notes thereafter.
[296] *Supra*, **4.G.35.**, **4.G.37.** and notes thereafter.
[297] *Supra*, **4.F.14.** and Note (2) thereafter.

law are stricter on this point, and they require the plaintiff to prove that he or she would indeed have decided otherwise but for the failure to inform.[298]

– Finally, it may be that the defendant is alleged to have *influenced or helped* another party to engage in conduct injurious to the plaintiff.[299] Here, English law replaces the "but for" test with the notion of providing someone with the opportunity to cause harm.[300] A specific provision, § 830(2) BGB, governs these cases in German law.[301]

The application of the "but for" test is also set aside in cases where the conduct of many tortfeasors has resulted in a single, indivisible injury to the plaintiff. In those cases, all legal systems recognize that it would be unfair to allow the defendants to invoke the "but for" test in their favour by arguing that the injury would have occured in any event as a result of the conduct of the other tortfeasor(s). Under French law, the defendants would be held liable *in solidum*.[302] Under German law, the defendants would be held liable as *Gesamtschuldner* pursuant to § 840 BGB, either through the operation of § 830(1) BGB[303] or because they are *Nebentäter*.[304] Under English law, the defendants would be held liable jointly and severally, either as joint[305] or several concurrent[306] tortfeasors.

The above paragraphs show that, in all the legal systems studied, the practical workings of the "but for" or *conditio sine qua non* test are far less simple than they may appear to be.

Complex cases: perte d'une chance *and relaxation of the burden of proof*

The classical causation analysis sometimes fails to produce satisfactory results. Indeed, the "but for" or *conditio sine qua non* test results in the conduct of the defendant being either a cause of the injury or not; further stages and refinements in the analysis (*Kausalität im rechtlichen Sinne*, remoteness, etc.) will reverse the result of that test, usually by denying causation altogether even if the "but for" test is met, more rarely the other way round. In any event, causation remains an all-or-nothing matter. In an increasing number of cases (often dealing with medical liability), however, the truth lies somewhere in between: the conduct of the defendant has affected the realm of possible outcomes to the disadvantage of the plaintiff, even if the actual outcome might have been the same (i.e. the plaintiff could have suffered harm) but for the impugned conduct of the defendant. The conduct of the defendant is then one of many possible causes of the outcome, but as often happens, the precise sequence of events cannot be reconstructed. At best the causal impact of the defendant's conduct can be expressed in probabilistic terms.[307] The legal systems under study here have addressed this problem in differing ways.

---

[298] *Supra*, **4.F.14.**, Notes (3) and (4). An exception is made under German law as concerns the duty to inform in medical liability cases, where the burden of proof on the plaintiff is lessened.

[299] See von Bar II at 443–4, para. 417–8.

[300] See *supra*, 4.2.1., Introductory Note under c) and Hart and Honoré at 186–204.

[301] *Supra*, 4.4.1., Introductory Note under a).

[302] *Supra*, **4.F.38.–39.** and Notes (1) to (3) thereafter.

[303] *Supra*, 4.4.1., Introductory Note under a).

[304] *Supra*, **4.F.38.–39.**, Note (4).

[305] *Supra*, 4.4.1., Introductory Note under b).

[306] *Supra*, **4.F.38.–39.**, Note (5).

[307] See *supra*, 4.2.2., Introductory Note under b).

French law stands out with its widespread use of "loss of a chance" (*perte d'une chance*).[308] That concept has been fairly controversial within both case law and legal writing, but by now it seems settled that, even if the plaintiff has actually suffered injury the cause of which cannot be determined, it is possible to obtain compensation for the loss of a chance of avoiding that injury, as long as there was a fault and its causal link to the loss of chance is clear.[309] Typical instances where loss of a chance is used are failures to provide medical treatment[310] or breaches of the duty to inform the patient of the risks associated with medical treatment.[311] The value of the lost chance will then be expressed as a proportion of the actual injury suffered by the plaintiff.[312]

The French concept of *perte d'une chance* offers perhaps the best example of proportional liability amongst the legal systems studied here. Proportional liability is a response to causal uncertainty, whereby the all-or-nothing approach is set aside and the defendant is made liable for the "amount" of causation which his or her conduct accounts for, in order to avoid the perceived unfairness of either leaving the plaintiff completely without compensation or making the defendant liable for the full amount of the damage.[313] As a consequence, the main drawback of proportional liability from the plaintiff's perspective is that it leaves the actual injury uncompensated in part. The proponents of proportional liability would also see room for it in cases of uncertainty regarding the tortfeasor[314] as well as in mass torts (multiple tortfeasors and multiple victims).[315] It is interesting to note that in French law, while some form of proportional liability has been introduced in *perte d'une chance* cases, the application of proportional liability in the other cases has never been envisaged; instead, solutions have been found to ensure full compensation for the victim.[316]

German law has followed a different path from French law, relying on procedural rules concerning the burden of proof instead of substantive concepts such as *perte d'une chance*. The underlying rationale is that when the conduct of the defendant put the plaintiff in a position where causation cannot be proved, then the plaintiff should be relieved of the burden of proof, up to the point where the burden could be shifted upon the defendant (*Beweiserleichterung bis zum Beweislastumkehr*). However, the plaintiff can benefit from that relief only in medical liability cases, and then only if the conduct of the defendant constituted gross fault.[317] When compared to French law, the German approach, in addition to its limited scope of application, may put a greater hurdle on the plaintiff, since gross fault must be proved; on the other hand, unless the defendant can somehow discharge the burden of proof, the plaintiff will then receive full compensation.

It should be mentioned that German law also enables the plaintiff to rely on a *prima facie* case (*Anscheinsbeweis*) or on the lower standard of proof regarding consequential

---

[308] For a survey of the use of *perte d'une chance* in other European systems, see von Bar II at 467–70, para. 444–5.

[309] *Supra*, **4.F.15.–17.** and notes thereafter.

[310] See Cass. civ. 1re, 12 November 1985, *supra*, **4.F.16.**

[311] See Cass. civ. 1re, 7 February 1990, *supra*, **4.F.17.**

[312] *Supra*, **4.F.15.–17.**, Note (5).

[313] For a thorough discussion of proportional liability in a comparative context, see Akkermans.

[314] See *supra*, 4.4.3.

[315] See *supra*, **4.NL.44.** and notes thereafter.

[316] See *supra*, **4.F.42.** and Notes (1) to (3) thereafter.

[317] See *supra*, **4.G.19.** and Note (2) thereunder.

damage at § 287 ZPO.[318] Similarly, in addition to *perte d'une chance*, French law also offers the plaintiff some relief from the burden of proof as regards causation, comprising presumptions of causation under certain circumstances as well as reliance on presumptions of fact.[319]

Compared with French or German law, English law appears to have remained closer to the traditional approach to causation by refusing to follow either the French or German route. First, in *Hotson* v. *East Berkshire Area Health Authority*, the House of Lords left little room for loss of a chance in medical liability cases.[320] Secondly, in *Wilsher* v. *Essex Area Health Authority*,[321] the House of Lords made clear that its previous decision in *McGhee* v. *National Coal Board*[322] did not support a reversal of the burden of proof of causation. In fact, *McGhee* was controversial because of a proposition put forward in Lord Wilberforce's minority speech, namely that when the defendant negligently creates a risk and injury occurs within the scope of that risk, the defendant should be liable unless he or she can show that the injury was caused by some event other than his or her negligence.[323] *McGhee* had put English law on the same path as German law, albeit with a different and arguably stronger rationale (negligent creation of risk instead of impossibility for the plaintiff to prove causation). Furthermore, it must be noted that some French legal writers are advocating that French law moves away from *perte d'une chance* towards a reversal of the burden of proof on the basis of the negligent creation of risk.[324] It is unfortunate that the House of Lords retreated from *McGhee* at a time when laws were converging. In the end, the sole relief for the plaintiff under English law is that it suffices for the purposes of causation to show that the conduct of the defendant made a material contribution to the injury, even if it was not its sole cause.[325]

By way of summary, therefore, the legal systems under study have addressed the problems of causation in medical liability and other complex cases either by adopting some form of proportional liability through *perte d'une chance* (French law) or by introducing specific rules concerning the burden of proof (German law). English law has not specifically adressed these problems.

The chain of events

The third section of this Chapter was devoted to a series of issues that arise when it is alleged that the causal impact of the conduct of the defendant was influenced by another event in the chain of causation, either coming before (predisposition) or after (subsequent events). The legal systems surveyed here show a fair amount of convergence on these issues.

As regards the predisposition of the plaintiff to injury, none of English, German or French law permits the defendant to argue that the liability *for physical injury* should be

---

[318] See ibid., Notes (3) and (4).
[319] See *supra*, **4.F.20.–22.** and Notes (1), (2) and (4) thereafter.
[320] *Supra*, **4.E.18.**
[321] *Supra*, **4.E.23.**
[322] [1973] 1 WLR 1, [1972] 3 All ER 1008, HL.
[323] *Supra*, **4.E.23.**, Note (1).
[324] Including Viney and Jourdain, *Conditions* at 192–4 and 202–4, para. 369 and 373. See *supra*, **4.F.20.–22.**, Note (3).
[325] *Supra*, **4.E.23.**, Note (4).

reduced on account of oversensitivity of the plaintiff.[326] As is most succinctly put in England, "a tortfeasor takes his victim as he finds him".[327] That maxim is subject to some minor limitations, however. Under English law, liability for psychological harm will not arise if it was not foreseeable that a person of reasonable fortitude would suffer some psychological harm; once that is shown, however, the defendant cannot invoke the psychological oversensitivity of the plaintiff.[328] Under German law, the defendant will not be liable if his or her conduct was not an adequate cause of the injury. In OLG Karlsruhe, 25 January 1966, for instance, a step on the foot resulted in amputation because the plaintiff suffered from circulatory problems; this was held to constitute too extraordinary a consequence of what remains an everyday occurrence for liability to ensue.[329] Under French law, the additional injury flowing from a "stable and consolidated pathological condition", as opposed to a "predisposition without any external injurious manifestation", is not imputed to the defendant;[330] nonetheless, if the defendant's conduct changes the nature of the injury (a person loses his or her only good eye), the defendant will be liable to the full extent of the injury.[331]

As regards predisposition to suffer *economic loss*, the leading precedent under English law frees the defendant from liability for the additional injury due to the plaintiff's impecuniosity.[332] That precedent has been much criticized, however, and it seems that if the issue arose again today, English law might go in the same direction as German law. There the defendant is also liable for the additional injury which ensues from the impecuniosity of the plaintiff, but liability can be reduced if the plaintiff was not sufficiently diligent in mitigating losses.[333]

Amongst subsequent events, specific issues arise with *supervening events*, i.e. events which would have caused the same injury as the conduct of the defendant.[334] The key point is whether the defendant can invoke the supervening event to be exonerated from liability as of the moment when that event took place. Under English law, the House of Lords has dealt with supervening events in two decisions which are not completely consistent with one another, namely *Baker* v. *Willoughby*[335] and *Jobling* v. *Associated Dairies*.[336] The two decisions are to be reconciled only if the scope of the former is limited: the outcome appears to be that the defendant can invoke supervening events in his or her favour, except when the supervening event is a tort committed by a third party.[337] Much energy has been devoted to the treatment of supervening events under German law (under the keywords *Reserveursache*, *hypothetische Kausalität* or *überholende Kausalität*).[338] It seems well-established that the defendant can invoke supervening events

---

[326] See *supra*, **4.E.24.**, **4.G.25.**, **4.F.26.** and notes thereafter. Materials from other legal systems as well are reviewed in von Bar II at 489–92, para. 466–9.

[327] *Smith* v. *Leech Brain & Co. Ltd.*, *supra*, **4.E.24.**

[328] Ibid., Note (4).

[329] *Supra*, **4.G.25.**

[330] *Supra*, **4.F.26.**, Note (3).

[331] Ibid. and Note (4) thereafter.

[332] *Liesbosch Dredger* v. *Edison Steamship (The Liesbosch)*, *supra*, **4.E.27.**

[333] See BGH, 5 July 1963, *supra*, **4.G.28.**

[334] For an overview of different types of supervening events, see *supra*, 4.3.2., Introductory Note under b).

[335] *Supra*, **4.E.29.**

[336] *Supra*, **4.E.30.**

[337] See *supra*, **4.E.29.–30.**, Notes (1) and (2).

[338] See Ibid., Notes (3) and (4).

in his or her favour if they consist in a pre-existing condition which would in time have caused the same injury, but not if they consist in conduct which would have led to the liability of a third party.[339] Beyond that, the majority opinion is that supervening events exonerate the defendant of liability as regards consequential damage (*Vermögensfolgeschaden*) but not as concerns the primary injury to a *Rechtsgut* or protected interest (*Objektschaden*). Although no comparable debate has taken place under French law, there is reason to believe that it would reach the same solutions as English and German law, at least as concerns cases such as *Baker* v. *Willoughby* and *Jobling* v. *Associated Dairies Ltd*.[340]

Another difficulty arises when subsequent events aggravate the situation of the victim some *time* after the conduct of the defendant caused the injury, but yet in a way which would not have happened but for the original injury caused by the defendant. In controversial decisions, both the BGH[341] and the Cour de cassation[342] have found that the conduct of the defendant could not be seen as the adequate cause of the aggravation caused by the subsequent event. In fact, in both those cases, the defendant had already been found liable and had paid compensation for the original injury. It seems that the courts may have wanted to avoid burdening the defendant with the further consequences of his conduct once the initial injury had been "liquidated".

Finally, another large group of difficult cases involves subsequent events, namely those where it is alleged that the *voluntary intervention of the victim or a third party* "broke the chain of causation" between the conduct of the defendant and the injury to the plaintiff.[343] These cases very often arise in a pursuit or rescue context. On this point, French and English law follow very similar principles: the defendant will be responsible for the consequences of the wilful intervention of the victim or a third party if that intervention was "normally foreseeable", "came within the risk created by the defendant's conduct" or was "a natural and probable consequence" of it.[344] These principles are also found in German law,[345] but a further criterion, "invitation" (*Herausforderung*), has been developed as the main test for imputability in cases of wilful intervention of the victim or a third party. The BGH first relied on the "invitation" criterion in a decision of 13 July 1971 concerning a pursuit case,[346] and later extended the use of that criterion to rescue cases as well.[347] In essence, the injury caused by the intervention of the victim or a third party will be imputed to the defendant if that intervention was "invited" (*herausgefordert*) by the conduct of the defendant, and if the person who intervened was justified in feeling "invited" to intervene. The risks associated with the intervention must be proportional to the purpose of the intervention, and the defendant is only liable for damage resulting

---

[339] On that basis, it can be concluded that *Baker* v. *Willoughby*, *supra*, **4.E.29.** and *Jobling* v. *Associated Dairies*, *supra*, **4.E.30.** would have been decided the same way in Germany.

[340] See *supra*, **4.E.29.–30.**, Note (5).

[341] BGH, 24 April 1952, *supra*, **4.G.31.**

[342] Cass. civ. 2e, 8 February 1989, *supra*, **4.F.32.**

[343] See also von Bar II at 444–8, para. 419–22.

[344] For French law, see *supra*, **4.F.33.** and Notes (1) and (2) thereafter. For English law, see *supra*, **4.F.33.**, Note (3) and **4.E.36.**

[345] See *supra*, **4.G.34.** and notes thereafter.

[346] *Supra*, **4.G.35.**

[347] See BGH, 30 June 1987, *supra*, **4.G.37.**

from the supplementary risks taken by the person who intervened.[348] The "invitation" criterion is construed generously in rescue cases, so that even the decision to give a kidney to a relative, freely taken some time after the accident which caused the relative to need a kidney transplant, was held to constitute a rescue act, thus making the defendant liable for the damage suffered by the donor.[349] Even without a specific construct such as *Herausforderung*, it appears that French and English law have reached results broadly similar to those of German law in rescue cases.[350]

Multiple tortfeasors and multiple causes

The fourth section dealt with cases involving a plurality of defendants, either because a number of causes are found to account for the damage or because there is uncertainty as to who the actual tortfeasor was.

Under German law, specific provisions govern the liability of joint tortfeasors (first sentence of § 830(1) BGB) as well as instigators and accomplices (§ 830(2) BGB).[351] These provisions relieve the plaintiff from the burden of proving causation with respect to such persons, who are held liable to the plaintiff jointly and severally (as *Gesamtschuldner*). The scope of the provisions is limited, since they apply only to intentional wrongs. No equivalent provisions are found in the other legal systems.[352]

It happens more frequently that a number of independent causes produce (separately or together) a single indivisible injury to the plaintiff. The relationship between these causes then becomes a key issue, in particular when these causes consist in human conduct (several concurrent tortfeasors under English law, *Nebentäter* under German law). Since French law relies more extensively on the theory of *équivalence des conditions*, it tends to produce many such cases; French case law accordingly developed the following principles. First, a defendant can be exonerated fully from liability only if the other cause is external and constitutes *force majeure* (i.e. it is unforeseeable and unavoidable); otherwise, each defendant is liable for the whole of the damages arising from injury.[353] Secondly, in subsequent proceedings defendants can have the total liability apportioned amongst themselves, but the relationship between the defendants is conceptually separate from the relationship between each defendant and the plaintiff, so that the right of the plaintiff to seek reparation for the full amount of damages against any defendant is not thereby affected.[354] Thirdly, the relationship between the defendants and the plaintiff is called an obligation *in solidum*; it bears the essential characteristics of joint and several liability under French law (*solidarité*).[355] Fourthly, the sole exception to these principles occurs when the plaintiff was also at fault, in which case the liability of the defendant will

---

[348] See *supra*, **4.G.35.**, Notes (4) and (5).

[349] See BGH, 30 June 1987, *supra*, **4.G.37.**

[350] See *Knightley* v. *Johns*, *supra*, **4.E.36.** for English law and Cass. crim., 25 June 1969, *infra*, Chapter VII, **7.F.22.** for French law.

[351] See *supra*, 4.4.1. under a). The terms are defined by reference to the criminal law.

[352] English law makes a distinction between joint tortfeasors, on the one hand, and several concurrent tortfeasors, on the other, but it does not result in a significant difference in the applicable legal regime: *supra*, 4.4.1. under b).

[353] See *supra*, **4.F.38.** and Note (2) thereunder.

[354] See *supra*, **4.F.39.** and Note (2) thereunder.

[355] See *supra*, **4.F.38.–39.**, Note (3).

be directly reduced to take into account the fault of the plaintiff.[356] By and large, German[357] and English[358] law follow similar principles.

A particularly complex situation occurs when injury is caused by the fault of two or more defendants and the plaintiff was also at fault (*Mitverschulden*, contributory negligence) in bringing about his or her own injury. On this point, English and German law follow different routes. Under English law, the assessment of contributory negligence on the part of the plaintiff and of contribution as between the defendants are kept separate. First, the conduct of the plaintiff is set against that of the defendants taken as a whole in order to determine the part of the injury attributable to contributory negligence. The full amount of damages which could be recovered by the plaintiff will be reduced accordingly, and the defendants will be jointly and severally liable for the reduced amount; afterwards liability is apportioned as between them in a second stage.[359] In contrast, under German law, the *Mitverschulden* of the plaintiff is assessed as against each defendant separately (*Einzelabwägung*) in order to fix the maximum amount for which each defendant can be liable. Thereafter, the complete picture is considered (*Gesamtabwägung*) in order to determine the total amount that the plaintiff can recover against the defendants taken together.[360]

In certain cases, the plaintiff can show that he or she suffered injury, that it was caused by some person and that the other conditions of liability are otherwise fulfilled but for the fact that the actual tortfeasor cannot be identified among the members of a class of persons. In these cases, the strict application of the "but for" test would result in the claim of the plaintiff being dismissed, but all systems under study here make an exception to the rules of causation to provide the plaintiff with compensation.

In traditional cases of uncertainty concerning the actual tortfeasor, there is a small and closed class of potential tortfeasors, for instance in a hunting accident where it cannot be determined who fired the shot which harmed the plaintiff. French law has imaginatively avoided the difficulty by finding another basis for liability: the whole class of persons is made liable *in solidum*, for instance for a collective fault or on account of the collective keeping (*garde collective*, pursuant to Article 1384(1) C.civ.) of the thing which caused the injury.[361] English law has reached similar results by shifting the burden of proof of causation onto the defendants.[362] Under German law, a specific provision, the second sentence of § 830(1) BGB, makes an exception to the general rules concerning causation, whereby the defendants can be held liable jointly and severally (as *Gesamtschuldner*) when the identity of the actual tortfeasor cannot be determined (*Urheberzweifel*) or the shares of the tortfeasors in the injury cannot be apportioned (*Anteilszweifel*).[363]

A more modern variant of uncertainty concerning the actual tortfeasor occurs in "mass tort" cases, where a large and often open class of potential tortfeasors has caused injury to a large number of victims, so that while in each individual case the injury has definitely been caused by one (or more) member(s) of that class, it is not possible to identify which one has

---

[356] Ibid., Note (2). See at greater length *infra*, Chapter VII, 7.1.
[357] Ibid., Note (4).
[358] Ibid., Note (5).
[359] See *Fitzgerald* v. *Lane*, *supra*, **4.E.40.** and Note (1) thereafter.
[360] See BGH, 16 June 1959, *supra*, **4.G.41.** and Note (2) thereafter.
[361] See *supra*, **4.F.42.** and Notes (1) to (3) thereafter.
[362] *Supra*, **4.F.42.**, Note (4).
[363] See *supra*, **4.G.43.** and notes thereafter.

caused injury to which victim. The leading case on this point in Europe is *B.* v. *Bayer Nederland BV*, a Hoge Raad decision on a case involving victims of an injurious pharmaceutical product ("DES daughters").[364] At issue was the applicability of Article 6:99 BW, a provision which, in cases of uncertainty concerning the actual tortfeasor, shifts the burden of proof onto the defendants to show that they did not cause the harm. The Hoge Raad decided that Article 6:99 BW was applicable in a "mass tort" context, so that the defendants were liable jointly and severally (*hoofdelijk*) to each victim for the whole of the injury; the Hoge Raad rejected market-share liability, a solution which had been adopted in a famous US decision[365] and had been proposed by Dutch legal writers.

The appropriateness of causation theories

At the end of this overview, the reader may have noticed that, even if the legal systems under study take different general approaches to causation, they tend to converge when it comes to the treatment of specific problems, such as predisposition, subsequent events, plurality of causes, etc.

The main areas where the legal systems under study go in different directions relate to cases where the traditional all-or-nothing approach is put into question, in particular medical liability cases. The law is not settled yet, and many solutions have been put forward; legal systems often hesitate between them:

– moving towards proportional liability, as is done under French law with *perte d'une chance*;

– changing the basis for liability by introducing some notion of risk within it, for instance by making the defendant who negligently creates a risk liable for injury which is a realization of that risk; that solution is applied in all systems for cases involving the voluntary intervention of a third party, but it has been rejected under English law in medical liability cases; or

– keeping the traditional approach intact by shifting the burden of proof onto the defendant, a solution which is used in German law (medical liability), but also in French and English law (for uncertainty concerning the actual tortfeasor).

In the end, given that in all legal systems studied here the role of causation has been expanded to include a normative assessment, one may legitimately wonder whether it is still relevant to try to formulate general theories of causation, as opposed to concentrating on certain types of problems. As authors have noted, general theories of causation which attempt to include a normative assessment tend to become far removed from the circumstances of individual cases, since a normative assessment will necessarily branch into the other conditions of liability (especially fault and wrongfulness).[366] The general theory of causation will then tend to merge with the general approach to tort law, as was noted before, and it will have little practical relevance unless it is accompanied by a survey of typical cases (*Fallgruppen*). Once one moves away from general theories towards these typical cases, the large extent of commonality between the various legal systems studied here becomes more apparent.

[364] *Supra,* **4.NL.44.**
[365] *Sindell* v. *Abbott Laboratories* (1980) 607 P 2d 924, Supreme Court of California.
[366] See von Bar II at 463 ff., para. 440 ff.

CHAPTER FIVE
LIABILITY FOR THE CONDUCT OF OTHERS

Chapter III concerned the traditional rationale for imposing liability on a person, namely a *wrongful* and *faulty* course of conduct *of that person*, which leads to injury. This Chapter and the next cover alternative rationales for imposing liability. The present Chapter deals with situations where someone is made liable for the conduct *of other persons*, irrespective—or independently—of any liability which he or she may have personally incurred. The rationale for imposing liability in these cases usually revolves around the particular characteristics of the relationship between the person whose conduct caused injury and the person whose liability is in issue. The next Chapter concerns other cases where a person incurs liability irrespective of any wrongful conduct on his or her part or on the part of others.

A brief survey of liability for others in the various legal systems under study reveals a fairly diverse range of regimes. At the one end is French law which, since the beginning of the 1990s, comprises a general regime of tort liability for others in addition to the general regime governing contractual liability for others, as well as specific regimes concerning the liability of, amongst others, parents for their children, employers for their employees and teachers for their students. At the other end is English law, where a regime of vicarious liability for employees exists, along roughly similar lines as the French regime, but where no other specific regime, much less a general regime of liability for others, has been developed to the same extent.[1] German law is difficult to place: it includes a few instances of liability for others (including contractual liability for others), but no general regime of liability for others. In particular, delictual liability for employees does not truly count as a regime of liability for others, since it is still based on the presumed fault of the employer (from a functional perspective, it should nonetheless be dealt with in this Chapter).

In view of this diversity, it may be more appropriate to concentrate in the first section on the one area where French, English and German law are equally well-developed, namely the liability of the employer for the harm caused by employees (including related areas such as contractual liability for others or liability for corporate organs). The second section will then review the other regimes of liability for others as they exist, with specific focus on the general regime which has recently emerged in French law.

5.1. LIABILITY FOR HARM CAUSED BY EMPLOYEES

In this section, after an overview of the respective regimes of liability for harm caused by employees, two subsections are devoted to the two key elements of these regimes, namely the concept of employee and the limitations relating to the scope of employment.

---

[1] See Markesinis and Deakin at 142–4.

5.1.1. GENERAL APPROACH

5.1.1.A. FRENCH LAW

a) Under French law, liability for harm caused by employees is based on Article 1384(5) C.civ., which must be read in conjunction with Article 1384(1) C.civ.:

[1] Everyone is liable for the damage caused not only by one's own conduct, but also by the conduct of persons for whom one is responsible or things in one's keeping (*garde*) . . .

[5] Principals [*maîtres*] and "employers" [*commettants*] [are liable] for the damage caused by their servants [*domestiques*] and "employees" [*préposés*] in the course of the functions for which they are employed;

The first paragraph of Article 1384 C.civ. creates a general regime of liability for others[2] and for things.[3] Given the fairly recent emergence of a general regime of delictual liability for others, the liability of employers for harm caused by their employees in the course of the performance of their functions has traditionally been seen as a self-contained regime.

"*Commettants*" and "*préposés*" could be roughly translated as "employers" and "employees" respectively, although for the purposes of Article 1384(5) C.civ., as will be seen in the next subsection, these terms extend beyond the employer-employee relationship as it is usally conceived.[4] It is generally agreed that "*commettants*" includes principals ("*maîtres*"), and "*préposés*" includes servants ("*domestiques*"), so that in the end Article 1384(5) C.civ. creates but one regime of liability of "*commettants*" for "*préposés*".[5]

b) The conditions for Article 1384(5) C.civ. to apply are relatively straightforward:

– The *préposé* him- or herself must be liable: the conditions of Article 1382–3 C.civ. must be met, namely injury suffered by the victim,[6] fault of the *préposé*[7] and causation.[8] There is some discussion as to whether it is truly necessary to prove fault on the part of the *préposé*. It is agreed that pursuant to Article 489–2 C.civ., the *préposé* can be liable if he or she was mentally impaired (*sous l'empire d'un trouble mental*); the liability of the *commettant* will then be engaged as well, according to Article 1384(5) C.civ.[9] Beyond that, given the evolution of the regime of parental liability for children and the emergence of a general regime of liability for others,[10] it is not impossible that case law will evolve so as to remove the requirement that the *préposé* be at fault, as leading authors have been advocating.[11]

---

[2] See *infra*, 5.2.

[3] See *infra*, Chapter VI, 6.1.2.

[4] See *infra*, 5.1.2., in particular **5.F.1.** and the notes thereafter.

[5] Overstake at 143/4, para. 2.

[6] On the various types of injury for which reparation may be sought under French law, see in general *supra*, Chapter II.

[7] See on fault in general, *supra*, Chapter III.

[8] See on causation in general, *supra*, Chapter IV.

[9] Cass. civ. 2e, 3 March 1977, D 1977.Jur.501. See Overstake at 143/23–4, para. 133–4; Viney and Jourdain, *Conditions* at 892–4, para. 807; Bénac-Schmidt/Larroumet at 34, para. 361–2.

[10] See *infra*, **5.F.24.–25.**, Note (2).

[11] See Viney and Jourdain, *Conditions* at 892–4, para. 807 and Bénac-Schmidt/Larroumet at 34, para. 359–67. Contra: Overstake at 143/24, para. 125–35, Dejean de la Bâtie at 239–40, para. 103 and J.-C. Saint-Pau,

- There must be a *lien de préposition* between the *commettant* and the *préposé*. *Lien de préposition* could be spontaneously translated as "employment relationship", but that translation would fail to account properly for the fact that the *lien de préposition*, for the purposes of Article 1384(5) C.civ., can extend beyond employment relationships, for instance to situations where someone renders a friendly and gratuitous service to another.[12]

- The conduct of the *préposé* which led to injury must fall "within the functions" (*dans les fonctions*) of the *préposé*. The interpretation of that short phrase has given rise to one of the greatest debates in the French law of civil liability, with which the Cour de cassation has occupied itself over the past forty years.[13]

Once the plaintiff proves that these conditions are fulfilled, Article 1384(5) C.civ. is applicable and the liability of the *commettant* is engaged.

c) The true nature of the French regime of liability for harm caused by employees becomes apparent once the means of exoneration of the *commettant* are considered. Article 1384(5) C.civ. creates a form of *responsabilité de plein droit*, a irrebuttable presumption of liability, which the *commettant* **cannot** defeat (i) by showing that it was not personally at fault (e.g. in selecting, instructing or supervising the *préposé*) and thus could not prevent the occurrence of damage, or even (ii) by going further and actually producing evidence that the damage was due to an event qualifying as *cause étrangère* towards the *commettant* (i.e. an event which the *commettant* could neither foresee nor avoid).[14] Once the conditions for the application of Article 1384(5) C.civ., as laid out in the above paragraph, are met, then the only possible escape for the *commettant* is to show that the injury was caused by an event qualifying as *cause étrangère* towards the *préposé* (i.e. an event which the *préposé* could neither foresee nor avoid) or that some other defence operated to exonerate the *préposé* (i.e. contributory fault, assumption of risk, etc.).[15]

d) The victim can thus seek reparation from the *commettant* for any injury caused by the *préposé* for which the *préposé* would be legally liable. From a procedural point of view, the victim can proceed directly against the *commettant*; before civil courts, the victim does not need to sue the *préposé*.[16]

"La responsabilité du fait d'autrui est-elle devenue une responsabilité personnelle et directe?" Rep.Ass. 1998.Chron.22.

[12] *Infra*, **5.F.1.** and notes thereafter.

[13] *Infra*, **5.F.10–11.** and notes thereafter.

[14] This can be deduced *a contrario* from Article 1384(7) C.civ., where *commettants* are not mentioned. According to Dejean de la Bâtie at 239–40, para. 103, case law has consistently held that Article 1384(5) C.civ. created a *responsabilité de plein droit* since the beginning of the nineteenth-century, the last restatement of the principle taking place in Cass. crim., 3 May 1979, Bull.crim. 1979.157, JCP 1979.IV.219. See also Viney and Jourdain, *Conditions* at 895–6, para. 809; Overstake at 143/34–5, para. 208–18; Le Tourneau and Cadiet at 845, and 855–6, para. 3441 and 3486. On *cause étrangère*, see *supra*, Chapter III, 3.2.3. and Chapter IV, 4.1.3., Introductory Note under h).

[15] Ibid. On defences, see also *infra*, Chapter VII, 7.1.1. (contributory fault) and 7.1.2. (assumption of risk).

[16] Cass. civ. 2e, 17 June 1970, Bull.civ. 1970.II.212, D 1970.Somm.195; Cass. civ. 2e, 11 March 1971, Bull.civ. 1971.II.113, D 1971.Somm.211, JCP 1971.IV.108. Before criminal courts, the *préposé* must be joined, since he or she will bear penal liability; in the accompanying *action civile*, criminal courts will then find that the *commettant* must bear civil liability for the injury caused by the *préposé*: Cass. crim., 17 December 1970, JCP 1971.IV.23; Cass. crim., 17 May 1976, D 1977.Jur.650; Cass. crim., 26 October 1982, JCP 1983.IV.17. See Viney and Jourdain, *Conditions* at 891–2, para. 806; Le Tourneau and Cadiet at 855, para. 3485; Bénac-Schmidt/Larroumet at 40, para. 428–31 and Overstake at 143/33, para. 205.

Traditionally, the rights of action of the victim against the *commettant* and the *préposé* have been thought of as distinct and independent from one another. The former is based on Article 1384(5) C.civ.,[17] while the latter is based on Article 1382 C.civ. The victim can therefore seek reparation from one, the other or both of them.[18] If both the *commettant* and the *préposé* are found liable, they will be placed under an obligation *in solidum* to compensate the victim.[19]

As between the *commettant* and the *préposé*, the traditional view is that the *commettant* can recover from the *préposé* the sums paid by way of compensation to the victim pursuant to Article 1384(5) C.civ. for injury caused by the conduct of the *préposé*.[20] In practice, however, such a recourse is fairly infrequent.[21] Should the victim choose to sue the *préposé* only, the latter has no recourse against the *commettant*. In other words the irrebuttable presumption of liability at Article 1384(5) C.civ. is not directed against the *commettant*, but rather in favour of the third-party victim.[22] Many authors have expressed doubts as to the fairness of these solutions, which in the end potentially leave the *préposé* with the whole burden of paying compensation for the injurious consequences of actions which were accomplished within the framework of a *lien de préposition*.[23]

The traditional view expounded above was shaken by the Cour de cassation on 12 October 1993.[24] In that case, a perfume company was seeking damages from a competitor for unfair trade practices and trademark violations, and it had also sued, in their personal capacity, the two employees of the competitor whose actions were material in causing the injury. The court of appeal had found that the competitor was liable under Article 1384(5) C.civ. for the conduct of its employees, but that the employees themselves were not personally liable under Article 1382 C.civ. The Cour de cassation upheld the judgment of the court of appeal in those terms:

> Having noted that it was not challenged that [the two individuals] were employees of [the competitor of the plaintiff], the court of appeal found that they had acted within the framework of the task which their employer had entrusted to them and that it had not been demonstrated that

[17] That does not exclude that the *commettant* could also be liable for a fault he or she personally committed in connection with the injurious event (pursuant to Article 1382 C.civ.), or because he or she was the *gardien* of the thing which caused the injury (pursuant to Article 1384(1) C.civ.): the victim could then sue the *commettant* on all these bases in parallel.

[18] Bénac-Schmidt/Larroumet at 40, para. 425; Le Tourneau and Cadiet at 855, para. 3484; Dejean de la Bâtie at 253–4, para. 107; Overstake at 143/22, para. 119.

[19] Bénac-Schmidt/Larroumet at 40, para. 435; Le Tourneau and Cadiet, ibid.; Dejean de la Bâtie, ibid.; Overstake at 143/33, para. 206. On obligations *in solidum*, see *infra*, Chapter IV, **4.F.38.–39.**, Note (3).

[20] If the *commettant* was also at fault, then liability will be apportioned between the *commettant* and the *préposé*. See Overstake at 143/35–6, para. 220–3; Dejean de la Bâtie at 254–5, para. 107; Le Tourneau and Cadiet at 857, para. 3492; Bénac-Schmidt/Larroumet at 40–1, para. 436–9.

[21] Not only does such a recourse undermine sound industrial relations, but in addition, to the extent that the liability of the *commettant* is shifted upon its liability insurer, Article L.–121–12 of the *Code des assurances* prohibits the insurer from exercising a right of recourse against the *préposé* personally. See G. Viney, Comment, Cass. comm., 12 October 1993, D 1994.Jur.124; Overstake at 143/36, para. 226–7; Le Tourneau and Cadiet, ibid.; Bénac- Schmidt/Larroumet at 41, para. 446–7.

[22] Unless the *commettant* was also at fault, in which case, as mentioned previously, liability will be apportioned between the two. See Overstake at 143/36, para. 229; Dejean de la Bâtie, at 254–5, para. 107; Le Tourneau and Cadiet at 857, para. 3546; Bénac-Schmidt/Larroumet at 40, para. 426–7.

[23] See Viney and Jourdain, *Conditions* at 898–900, para. 811–1 as well as M.-T. Rives-Lange, "Contribution à l'étude de la responsabilité des maîtres et commettants" JCP 1970.I.2309, both echoed in Bénac-Schmidt/Larroumet at 41, para. 443–4.

[24] Cass. comm., 12 October 1993, D 1994.Jur.124, with comment by G. Viney.

they had gone beyond that framework. It could accordingly conclude that no *personal fault* in the injurious course of action had been made out against the employees, such as would engage their liability [emphasis added].

That judgment, if followed,[25] implies, first that the *préposé* is no longer automatically liable to the victim for every fault which is committed in the functions for which he or she is employed, within the meaning of Article 1384(5) C.civ. Rather, the *préposé* will incur liability only if he or she committed "*faute personnelle*" (personal fault). The Cour de cassation did not define *faute personnelle* any further.[26]

A second implication of the judgment would seem to be that the *commettant* who is found liable to the victim pursuant to Article 1384(5) C.civ. cannot recover from the *préposé* the amount paid to the victim unless the *préposé* committed *faute personnelle*. There would thus be three categories of cases:

– the *préposé* acted "within his or her functions" within the meaning of Article 1384(5) C.civ. but did not commit *faute personnelle*: following the decision of 12 October 1993, the *commettant* alone is liable to the victim and cannot recover from the *préposé*;
– the *préposé* acted "within his or her functions" and also committed *faute personnelle*: the traditional view will continue to apply, namely both the *commettant* and the *préposé* are liable to the victim, and the *commettant* can recover from the *préposé* anything which it has been required to pay to the victim;[27]
– the *préposé* did not act "within his or her functions" and by the same token inevitably committed *faute personnelle*: as has always been the case, the *préposé* alone is liable to the victim.

Authors generally agree that in its decision of 12 October 1993, the Cour de cassation sought to alleviate the burden put on the *préposé*, in response to the criticism mentioned above, and bring the regime of Article 1384(5) C.civ. closer to the regime of State liability for the conduct of civil servants.[28] Whether the Cour de cassation in its decision of 12 October 1993 understood the term *faute personnelle* to bear the same meaning as it has in administrative law remains to be seen.

e) The judgment of 12 October 1993 also has consequences for the theoretical rationale underlying Article 1384(5) C.civ.[29] Many rationales have been put forward in legal writing.[30] Some authors have argued that the regime of liability for *préposés* was based on the notion that the *commettant* is assumed to have been at fault, whether in choosing, instructing or monitoring the *préposé*. That rationale appears difficult to reconcile with

[25] See for instance Cass. civ. 1re, 30 October 1995, Bull.civ. 1995.I.383, JCP 1995.IV.2696, which appears to reject the position of the commercial chamber in its judgment of 12 October 1993, but which in fact seems to leave the door open for it, according to G. Viney, Chronique, JCP 1996.I.3944. See also Cass. civ. 2e, 19 February 1997, Bull.civ. 1997.II.53; Cass. comm., 27 January 1998, Bull.civ. 1998.IV.48, D 1998.Jur.605 and Cass. comm., 28 April 1998, Bull.civ. 1998.IV.139, JCP 1998.II.10177, where the reasoning of the decision of 12 October 1993 is followed in the context of liability for corporate organs.

[26] See Viney and Jourdain, *Conditions* at 901–5, para. 811–2.

[27] See the comment of G. Viney, D 1994.Jur.124 and B. Puill, "Les fautes du préposé: s'inspirer de certaines solutions du droit administratif?" JCP 1996.I.3939.

[28] See *infra* under h), as well as B. Puill, ibid.

[29] See G. Viney, Comment, D 1994.Jur.124.

[30] The following exposition has been derived from Overstake at 143/37–40, para. 234–52 and Bénac-Schmidt/Larroumet at 27–30, para. 272–304.

the fact that the *commettant* cannot be exonerated for lack of fault. The two rationales most currently advanced in legal writing, however, rely on risk and warranty respectively.

The traditional view of the relationships between the *commettant*, the *préposé* and the victim expounded in the preceding paragraph is most consistent with **warranty** as a rationale for Article 1384(5) C.civ.:[31] the *commettant* acts towards the victim as a guarantor of its *préposés*; the victim can seek redress from the *commettant* for the injury caused by the *préposé*, and the *commettant* can subsequently recover from the *préposé*.

In the wake of the changes heralded by Cass. comm., 12 October 1993, the rationale of Article 1384(5) C.civ. may move from warranty to **risk**.[32] If the *préposé* is not personally liable for injury caused while he or she was "in his or her functions" (except in cases of *faute personnelle*), then the *commettant* is in fact charged with the risks associated with the activity which it is undertaking. Indeed at least overall, the *commettant* profits (or benefits) from the conduct of its *préposés* in the performance of their functions and should therefore accept liability for that conduct; moreover, the *commettant* rather than the *préposé* can reasonably be expected to take out third-party liability insurance in respect of conduct undertaken by the *préposé* for the *commettant*. Such an explanation is especially cogent in the case of *préposés* working for large business organizations.

f) Some other liability regimes overlap with Article 1384(5) C.civ. to some extent; they are surveyed hereunder.

Even if there is no provision in the *Code civil* dealing specifically with this point,[33] a general regime of *contractual* liability for others has developed in French case law and legal writing.[34] According to that regime, the person subject to a contractual obligation of any kind (a debtor) towards another (the creditor) is responsible for the persons whom he or she calls upon to execute the contractual obligation in whole or in part.[35] Essentially, the conduct of those persons is imputed to the debtor, since in principle under contract law the debtor is not allowed to assign his or her obligation without the consent of the creditor. Therefore, entrusting the performance of a contractual obligation to another person does not relieve the debtor of his or her obligation towards the creditor.[36]

A typical example would be the transport company which relies on its employees or on third-party agents to undertake the actual transport of the goods of the creditor, or the building contractor which gives to a sub-contractor part of the construction work which it is bound to do for the creditor. The range of persons for whom the debtor is responsible towards the creditor is thus much larger than the class of persons for whom the *commettant* can be held liable under Article 1384(5) C.civ.: whereas the liability of the *commettant* is limited to harm caused by a *préposé*, i.e. a person under a *lien de préposition* with him or her, the contractual debtor is responsible for the harm caused to the cred-

---

[31] This is the view of Bénac-Schmidt/Larroumet, ibid., among others.

[32] A position advocated, among others, by Viney and Jourdain, *Conditions* at 905, para. 812.

[33] Some provisions of the *Code civil* cover contractual liability for others within the context of specific contractual relationships: see among others Articles 1245, 1735 (lease), 1797 (construction), 1782 (surface transport), 1953 (hotels) and 1994 (agency).

[34] See Viney and Jourdain, *Conditions* at 913–7, para. 818–9; Le Tourneau and Cadiet at 473, para. 1595; Légier at 17–8, para. 146–7.

[35] Viney and Jourdain, *Conditions* at 919, para. 823; Le Tourneau and Cadiet at 473–4, para. 1596.

[36] Viney and Jourdain, *Conditions* at 914–5, para. 818.

itor not only by its *préposés*, but also by partners, sub-contractors and any other persons whom he or she may have called upon in executing the contractual obligation.[37]

Since the debtor answers for the conduct of the persons whom he or she has entrusted with the performance of his or her contractual obligations, the creditor needs only to prove a breach of contract. If the contractual obligation was one of result (as is often the case), then the mere failure to attain the promised result (irrespective of fault) is sufficient for a breach to be made out. In cases of *obligations de moyens*, then the creditor will have to show that the person actually in charge of executing the obligation did not exercise the requisite degree of care.[38]

Where *préposés* are used to execute contractual obligations, the differences between the delictual regime of Article 1384 C.civ. and the contractual regime of liability for others are slight. Just as the *préposé* must have been acting "within his or her functions" under Article 1384(5) C.civ., the *préposé* must have been acting in the course of executing the debtor's contractual obligations for the debtor to be liable under the contractual regime.[39] Furthermore, the breach of contractual obligations will often be coterminous with a fault of the *préposé* (particularly in cases involving contractual *obligations de moyens*). In view of these similarities, courts sometimes even rule pursuant to Article 1384(5) C.civ. in cases where contractual liability for others is at stake.[40]

g) Legal persons of all kinds (corporations, etc.) can be liable not only for the harm caused by their *préposés* (pursuant to Article 1384(5) C.civ.)—where the victim is not under any contractual relationship with the legal person—or by the persons whom they call upon to perform their contractual obligations—where the victim is under a contractual relationship with the legal person; they can also be liable for the damage caused by their corporate organs, that is to say the natural persons who are in charge of representing the legal person vis-à-vis the outside world (e.g. board members, executive officers, trustees in bankruptcy, etc.).[41] Under French law, in order for such liability to be triggered, the corporate organ in question must have acted *qua* corporate organ, i.e. within its powers to represent the corporation,[42] and an obligation binding upon the legal person (through law or contract) must have been breached by the conduct of the corporate organ.[43] Furthermore, in certain cases, the natural person acting as a corporate organ will also be personally liable for the consequences of the injurious conduct.[44]

---

[37] Ibid. at 919–25, para. 824–7; Le Tourneau and Cadiet at 474, para. 1597–8; Légier at 18, para. 149–51. The debtor may even be liable for harm caused by third parties which he or she has put in a position to prevent the execution of the contractual obligation.

[38] Viney and Jourdain, *Conditions* at 928–31, para. 830–1; Le Tourneau and Cadiet at 474, para. 1599; Légier at 18, para. 148.

[39] See for instance Cass. civ. 1re, 19 December 1995, Bull.civ. 1995.I.485, JCP 1996.IV.382, where the Cour de cassation found that a carpet shop which recommended carpet fitters was not responsible for an assault committed by the carpet fitter chosen by the carpet buyer from the list of recommended carpet fitters. Indeed, the contractual obligations of the carpet shop did not extend to the laying of the carpet. See the comment by G. Viney in her Chronique, JCP 1996.I.3944.

[40] See Viney and Jourdain, *Conditions* at 909–10, para. 813–4; Le Tourneau and Cadiet at 475, para. 1601.

[41] See Viney and Jourdain, *Conditions* at 943–6, para. 848–50.

[42] Taking into account the possibility that the corporation will be bound if it appears to third parties that the organ was acting within its powers (*mandat apparent*): Viney and Jourdain, *Conditions* at 947–8, para. 851.

[43] See Viney and Jourdain, *Conditions* at 948–50, para. 852 and 852–1.

[44] Viney and Jourdain, *Conditions* at 953–73, para. 855 to 867–1.

Despite the theoretical distinction between the liability of the legal person for its *préposés* (liability for the harm caused by another pursuant to Article 1384(5) C.civ.) and its corporate organs (liability for the harm caused by itself acting through a natural person), the conditions of the two regimes are relatively similar, so that in practice it does not make much of a difference whether the person who caused the harm was lower (*préposé*) or higher (organ) in the corporate hierarchy.[45] Indeed, in both cases the liability of the legal person will ultimately be engaged, unless the injurious conduct was not "within the functions" of the *préposé* or exceeded the powers of the natural person acting as corporate organs; those respective limitations on the liability of the legal person are considered to produce similar effects in practice.[46]

h) Finally, as mentioned above, there appears to be a tendency for the regime of liability for *préposés* pursuant to Article 1384(5) C.civ. to converge with the regime of State liability for civil servants, as it has been developed through administrative case law.[47] Pursuant to that regime, the State is liable for injury caused to third parties when civil servants commit "fault in their service" (*faute en service*), but not when civil servants commit "fault without relation to their service" (*faute sans rapport avec le service*).[48] As for the personal liability of the civil servant to the victim, it remains if the fault of the civil servant was such as to constitute "personal fault" (*faute personnelle*); in all other cases, the fault will be characterized as "official fault" (*faute de service*) and the civil servant will be relieved of personal liability towards the victim.[49] There is no sharp definition of *faute personnelle*, but it seems that, in general, malicious conduct and gross fault are typical instances thereof.[50] The superimposition of these two principles gives the following picture:[51]

- A *faute de service* by definition is always committed "in the service" and thereby also constitutes a *faute en service*, for which the State alone is liable towards the victim;
- A *faute personnelle* can nonetheless be linked to the service of the civil servant, for instance if it is committed during working time or using means which are put at the disposal of the civil servant in the course of his or her service. It is then a "personal fault not devoid of any relationship with the service" (*faute personnelle non dépourvue de lien avec le service*), and as such falls within the class of "fault in the service" (*faute en service*). As a result, both the State and the civil servant personally are liable to the victim;
- Finally, a *faute personnelle* can be devoid of any relationship to the service and thus qualify as a *faute sans rapport avec le service*, in which case the civil servant alone will be liable towards the victim.

---

[45] Viney and Jourdain, *Conditions* at 944–5, para. 848.

[46] Viney and Jourdain, *Conditions* at 947, para. 851.

[47] On State liability in general under French law, see *supra*, Chapter III, 3.3.3.

[48] Laubadère, Venezia and Gaudemet at 780–1, para. 1252–4; Gour at 12–3, para. 108–20.

[49] Laubadère, Venezia and Gaudemet at 769–70, para. 1237. For applications of the concepts of *faute de service* and *faute personnelle*, see *supra*, Chapter III, 3.3.3.A. and *infra*, Chapter IX, **9.EC.2.**, Note (1).

[50] Gour at 5, para. 20–1.

[51] See Gour at 6–7, para. 25–47; B. Puill, "Les fautes du préposé: s'inspirer de certaines solutions du droit administratif?" JCP 1996.I.3939.

In the end, since an objective link between the fault and the service suffices to result in a *faute en service*,[52] the State is liable in most cases where civil servants as such cause injury through their fault.[53]

Furthermore, the State can generally recover from the civil servant where it paid damages to the victim but the injury was caused by a *faute personnelle* of the civil servant.[54] The picture is made more complex by rules governing the respective jurisdictions of the administrative and civil courts.[55]

5.1.1.B. ENGLISH LAW

a) Under English law, the liability of employers for their employees[56] evolved over the centuries and stabilized in its current form at the beginning of the twentieth century.[57] It is the main species of liability for others, or "vicarious liability" as it is known in the common law.[58] In truth, legal writing has not put forward any theoretical construct to justify or underpin liability for employees; there is general agreement, however, that that regime pursues valuable public policy objectives. As Lord Pearce put it in *Imperial Chemical Industries Ltd.* v. *Shatwell*:[59]

> "The doctrine of vicarious liability has not grown from any very clear, logical or legal principle but from social convenience and rough justice. The master having (presumably for his own benefit) employed the servant, and being (presumably) better able to make good the damage which may occasionally result from the arrangement, is answerable to the world at large for all the torts committed by his servant within the scope of it. The doctrine maintains that liability even in respect of acts which the employers had expressly prohibited [reference omitted] and even when the employers are guilty of no fault themselves [reference omitted] . . ."

Similarly, Scarman LJ wrote in *Rose* v. *Plenty*:[60]

> "I think it is important to realise that the principle of vicarious liability is one of public policy. It is not a principle which derives from a critical or refined consideration of other concepts in the common law, for example the concept of trespass or indeed the concept of agency. No doubt in particular cases it may be relevant to consider whether a particular plaintiff was or was not a trespasser. Similarly, when . . . it is important that one should determine the course of employment of the servant, the law of agency may have some marginal relevance. But basically . . . the employer is made vicariously liable for the tort of his employee not because the plaintiff is an invitee, nor because of the authority possessed by the servant, but because it is a case in which

---

[52] In this respect, there are obvious parallels with the discussion surrounding the limitations relating to the scope of employment (i.e. the phrase "in the functions for which they are employed") under Article 1384(5) C.civ.: see *infra*, **5.F.10.–11.** and notes thereafter.

[53] See Laubadère, Venezia and Gaudemet at 781, para. 1254.

[54] Ibid. at 783–5, para. 1259.

[55] See ibid. at 774–5, para. 1243–7 and, in general, Gour.

[56] The terms "master" and "servant" were previously used instead of "employer" and "employee" respectively.

[57] See Rogers at 694–5; Salmond and Heuston at 430.

[58] On possible other instances of vicarious liability, see *infra*, **5.E.2.**, Note (3).

[59] [1965] AC 656 at 685–6, HL, per Lord Pearce.

[60] [1976] 1 WLR 141 at 147, CA.

the employer, having put matters into motion, should be liable if the motion that he has originated leads to damage to another."

Accordingly, it seems that the prime rationale for the vicarious liability of employers
under English law is that employers must support the liabilities arising from courses of
activity from which they otherwise derive profit.[61] As shown in the excerpt from Lord
Pearce's speech above, English courts are also aware that the employer almost invariably
has a "deeper pocket" than the employee and is thus more likely to be able to pay compensation to the injured victim or, alternatively, that the employer can more reasonably
be expected to be insured against such liability than the employee. Furthermore, it seems
that vicarious liability also contributes to ensuring that employers devote the requisite
care to prevent that their employees cause injury.[62]

b) The conditions for vicarious liability under English law are fairly similar to those of
Article 1384(5) C.civ.:

– The employee must have committed a *tort*, irrespective of its nature (e.g. negligence,
   trespass, conversion, etc.).[63] Under English law, therefore, it is beyond question that
   the victim must prove that the employee committed a tort for vicarious liability to
   arise. In *Staveley Iron & Chemical Co. Ltd.* v. *Jones*, Lord Morton said:[64]

   > "My Lords, what the court has to decide in the present case is: Was the [servant] negligent?
   > If the answer is 'Yes,' the employer is liable vicariously for the negligence of his servant. If
   > the answer is 'No,' the employer is surely under no liability at all. Cases such as this, where
   > an employer's liability is vicarious, are wholly distinct from cases where an employer is under
   > a personal liability to carry out a duty imposed upon him as an employer by common law or
   > statute."

   Lord Reid said in the same case:[65]

   > "[I]f this means that the [employer] could be held liable even if it were held that the
   > [employee] was not herself guilty of negligence, then I cannot accept that view. Of course, an
   > employer may be himself in fault by engaging an incompetent servant or not having a proper
   > system of work or in some other way. But there is nothing of that kind in this case. . . It is a
   > rule of law that an employer, though guilty of no fault himself, is liable for damage done by
   > the fault or negligence of his servant acting in the course of his employment. The maxims
   > respondeat superior and qui facit per alium facit per se are often used, but I do not think that
   > they add anything or that they lead to any different results. The former merely states the rule
   > baldly in two words, and the latter merely gives a fictional explanation of it."

Under the regime of vicarious liability for employees, the employer is made liable for
the consequences of a tort committed by the employee as if that tort were the
employer's own.[66] As appears from the above excerpts, vicarious liability co-exists

---

[61] Although, as will be seen below, for vicarious liability to arise it is not necessary that the injurious conduct
of the employee was for the benefit of the employer: *infra*, **5.E.21.** and Note (2) thereafter.
[62] Salmond and Heuston at 430–1.
[63] See Markesinis and Deakin at 542–3.
[64] [1956] AC 627 at 639, HL.
[65] Ibid. at 643.
[66] See *Bartonshill Coal Co.* v. *McGuire* (1853) 3 Macq. 300 at 306, HL, per Lord Chelmsford LC, cited with
approval in *Staveley Iron & Chemical Co. Ltd.* v. *Jones*, ibid.

with the liability of the employer for any tort which may be imputed to him or her personally.

- The person who committed the tort must indeed be an *employee* of the employer in question (and not e.g. an independent contractor).[67]
- The tort must have been committed *in the course of employment*. The precise delineation of the course of employment has given rise to many difficulties in English law, just as in French law.[68]

c) Once these conditions are met, the employer will be liable for the injurious consequences of the tort committed by the employee. The only possibility for the employer to escape vicarious liability is to argue that the three conditions mentioned above are not met; in particular it may be argued that some defence can be made out which would exonerate the employee from liability in whole or in part (e.g. contributory negligence, assumption of risks, etc.). Such was the case for example in *Imperial Chemical Industries Ltd.* v. *Shatwell*, mentioned above, where the employer successfully argued that it should not be vicariously liable for the injury caused by its employee, since—in breach of express instructions from the employer—the victim (another employee) had deliberately assumed the risks associated with the injurious course of action.[69]

d) Vicarious liability of the employer does not negate the liability of the employee towards the victim. Accordingly, the victim can seek compensation from the employee whose allegedly tortious conduct led to injury, from the employer or from both. In the last of those cases, the employer and the employee will be joint tortfeasors, and thus jointly and severally liable to the victim for the whole of the injury suffered.[70]

The right of the employer to subsequent contribution from the employee (i.e. recovery of the amounts paid to the victim by way of vicarious liability for the tort of the employee) has given rise to some controversy in English law. At common law, the general rule was that there was no contribution between joint tortfeasors, except when one of the joint tortfeasors was innocent.[71] But that rule was abrogated by the Law Reform (Married Women and Joint Tortfeasors) Act 1935, which introduced a statutory right of contribution as between joint tortfeasors.[72] In addition, in *Lister* v. *Romford Ice and Cold Storage Co.*,[73] the House of Lords held (3:2) that an employer was contractually entitled to full indemnity by an employee for whose negligence the employer had been held to be vicariously—and only vicariously—liable, even though the employer was insured against the liability in question and the action against the employee, though brought in the name

---

[67] *Infra*, **5.E.2.** and notes thereafter.

[68] *Infra*, **5.E.12.** and notes thereafter.

[69] [1965] AC 656, HL.

[70] *Clerk & Lindsell on Torts* at 160, para. 4–66; Markesinis and Deakin at 553; Rogers at 714. On the regime applicable to joint tortfeasors, see *supra*, Chapter IV, 4.4.1. under b) and **4.F.38.–39.**, Note (5).

[71] *Merryweather* v. *Nixan* (1799) 8 TR 186. The rule was subsequently criticized as lacking in principle and was not adopted in Scotland: see per Lord Shaw of Dumfermeline in *The Drumlanrig* [1911] AC 16 at 27, HL.

[72] Law Reform (Married Women and Joint Tortfeasors) Act 1935, c. 30, s. 6(1)(c). That provision was replaced by the Civil Liability (Contribution) Act 1978, c. 47, which extended the basic rules established by the 1935 Act in respect of joint tortfeasors so as to cover not only joint tortfeasors but also others who are jointly and severally liable to the plaintiff. The 1978 Act also regulates successive actions brought by a victim against a number of persons in respect of the same damage. The 1978 Act did not affect *Lister* v. *Romford Ice and Cold Storage Co.*, discussed in the main text.

[73] [1957] AC 555, HL.

of the employer, was actually brought by its insurers.[74] The dissatisfaction with *Lister* was such that, following a committee of inquiry, insurers entered into a gentlemen's agreement not to seek contribution from employees personally (save in cases of collusion or wilful misconduct).[75] In any event, *Lister* has been narrowly interpreted[76] or even ignored[77] by subsequent case law, so that in practice it will be rare for the employer to seek contribution from the employee.[78]

e) As under French law, a number of other liability regimes bear some relationship with vicarious liability for torts committed by employees.

For one, it is a well-established principle in English law that a person is liable for the breaches of *contract* committed by other persons who were brought in to execute the contractual obligations of the first person.[79] As Lord Diplock said in *Photo Production Ltd. v. Securicor Transport Ltd.*:[80]

> [I]t is characteristic of commercial contracts, nearly all of which today are entered into not by natural . . . persons, but by fictitious ones, i.e. companies, that the parties promise to one another that some thing will be done; for instance, that property and possession of goods will be transferred, that goods will be carried by ship from one port to another, that a building will be constructed in accordance with agreed plans, that services of a particular kind will be provided. Such a contract is the source of primary legal obligations upon each party to it to procure that whatever he has promised will be done is done . . .
>
> Where what is promised will be done involves the doing of a physical act, performance of the promise necessitates procuring a natural person to do it; but the legal relationship between the promisor and the natural person by whom the act is done, whether it is that of master and servant, or principal and agent, or of parties to an independent sub-contract, is generally irrelevant. If that person fails to do it in the manner in which the promisor has promised to procure it to be done, as, for instance, with reasonable skill and care, the promisor has failed to fulfil his own primary obligation. This is to be distinguished from "vicarious liability"—a legal concept which does depend upon the existence of a particular legal relationship between the natural person by whom a tortious act was done and the person sought to be made vicariously liable for it. In the interests of clarity the expression should . . . be confined to liability for tort.

It is clear from the above passage that liability for persons called upon in the execution of a contractual obligation under the English law of contract is to be distinguished from vicarious liability under the law of tort. Furthermore, the scope of persons for which one can be liable is much broader under the contractual regime; as Lord Diplock mentions, it includes not only employees, but also agents and independent sub-contractors.

f) Furthermore, under English law, the primary (or personal) liability of the employer continues to play a large role alongside vicarious liability.[81] In particular, under *tort* law,

---

[74] The fact that in *Lister* the victim was the employee's father may have contributed to the insurers' action.

[75] That agreement is reproduced in *Morris* v. *Ford Motor Co. Ltd.* [1973] QB 792, CA.

[76] See *Harvey* v. *O'Dell Ltd.* [1958] 2 QB 78, QBD, where it was held that the employer could not seek contribution from the employee where the employee committed the tort while in the course of employment, but not in carrying out the duties for which he was actually employed.

[77] See *Morris* v. *Ford Motor Co. Ltd.* [1973] QB 792, CA.

[78] See *Clerk & Lindsell on Torts* at 160–1, para. 4–66; Markesinis and Deakin at 553–4; Rogers at 715–6.

[79] See A.G. Guest (ed.) *Chitty on Contracts*, Vol. I., 27th edn. (London: Sweet & Maxwell, 1994) at 987 ff., para. 19–046 ff.

[80] [1980] 2 AC 827 at 848, [1980] 1 All ER 556, HL.

[81] See for instance *R.* v. *Associated Octel Co. Ltd.* [1996] 1 WLR 1543, [1996] 4 All ER 846, HL. The distinction between primary and vicarious liability is sometimes blurred, as in the case of the liability of hospitals for the negligence of doctors: see *infra*, **5.E.5.** and notes thereafter.

a person may under certain circumstances be liable towards a third party for the injury caused by independent contractors working for him or her.[82] While the general rule remains that one is not vicariously liable for the torts of his or her independent contractors, since by definition these are not employees,[83] the person using an independent contractor will be liable for the injury caused to a third party through the tortious conduct of the independent contractor if the duty of care, of which the independent contractor committed a breach, was one of a number of "non-delegable duties" which have been recognized by case law. As the expression indicates, these duties remain with the person using an independent contractor, even if the independent contractor is in fact carrying out the activities where that duty should be observed. The class of non-delegable duties comprises duties imposed by statute upon a person as well as a number of common law duties.[84] The list of non-delegable duties is not exhaustive, and it tends to expand.[85] However, the person using an independent contractor will not be liable for the "casual" or "collateral" negligence of that contractor, i.e. negligence unrelated to the very matter which was entrusted to the contractor.[86]

g) Under English law, as under French law, corporations are liable for the acts of their corporate organs.[87] As was said in the House of Lords in *Lennard's Carrying Company Ltd.* v. *Asiatic Petroleum Company Ltd.*:[88]

> [A] corporation is an abstraction. It has no mind of its own any more than it has a body of its own; its active and directing will must consequently be sought in the person of somebody who . . . is really the directing mind and will of the corporation, the very ego and centre of the personality of the corporation . . . [The fault of that person] is the fault . . . of somebody who is not merely a servant or agent for whom the company is liable upon the footing respondeat superior, but somebody for whom the company is liable because his action is the very action of the company itself.

The class of persons for whom the company will be so liable is fairly limited, essentially comprising persons who are entrusted with the exercise of the powers of the company (pursuant to the memorandum and articles of association or to action taken by the directors or by the general meeting of the company); a branch manager, for instance, should not qualify as "the mind and will of the corporation".[89]

h) Finally, as was mentioned in Chapter III, the English law of torts—including vicarious liability—generally applies to public authorities as well as to private persons.[90]

---

[82] A person using independent contractors can also be directly liable if he or she is in breach of some duty of care, for instance to select competent contractors: *Clerk & Lindsell on Torts* at 192–3, para. 5–46; Rogers at 718; Markesinis and Deakin at 554–5.

[83] Ibid.

[84] Including: liability for interference with support for neighbouring land; for creation of danger on the highway; under the rule in *Rylands* v. *Fletcher*; for escape of fire; for nuisance; for harm caused by extra-hazardous operations in general; and the duties of the bailee and the occupier, as well as those of the employer for the safety of employees.

[85] See *Clerk & Lindsell on Torts* at 194–202, para. 5–48 to 5–62; Rogers at 720–2; Markesinis and Deakin at 554–7.

[86] Rogers at 723–4; *Clerk & Lindsell on Torts* at 202–3, para. 5–63 and 5–64.

[87] See Rogers at 836–7; *Clerk & Lindsell on Torts* at 140–3, para. 4–44 to 4–49, as well as R.R. Pennington, *Company Law*, 7th edn. (London: Butterworths, 1995) at 132–5.

[88] [1915] AC 705 at 713–4, HL per Viscount Haldane LC.

[89] *Tesco Supermarkets Ltd.* v. *Nattrass* [1972] AC 153 at 199–200, HL per Lord Diplock.

[90] *Supra*, Chapter III, 3.3.1.

Accordingly, the Crown[91] and other public authorities[92] are vicariously liable for the torts committed by their servants within the scope of their employment.[93] Some specific restrictions nonetheless apply to Crown liability: the Crown is liable only for public officers paid out of funds provided by Parliament;[94] it is not liable if the servant in question would not also be personally liable in tort (thus giving the Crown the benefit of defences open to the individual servant, such as act of state or the exercise of statutory or prerogative powers)[95] and it is not liable either for acts of the judiciary.[96]

5.1.1.C. GERMAN LAW

a) The primary provision dealing with the liability for harm caused by employees under German law is § 831(1) BGB, which reads:[97]

> Anyone who employs another person for a task is liable for the injury unlawfully caused to a third party by that other person in the accomplishment of the task. No liability shall arise if (i) the employer (*Geschäftsherr*) exercised reasonable care in the selection of the employee and—when the employer himself procures tools or directs the accomplishment of the task—in the procurement of tools and the direction [of the employee] or (ii) the injury would also have been caused if the employer had taken such reasonable care.

A cursory reading of that provision itself reveals that the regime of liability for harm caused by employees under German law is fundamentally different from the corresponding regimes under French and English law, in that the liability of the employer (*Geschäftsherr*) is not triggered automatically once the conditions of the first sentence of § 831(1) BGB are met. Instead, the employer is presumed to be liable, but the second sentence of § 831(1) BGB enables the employer to rebut that presumption by showing either the absence of fault or the lack of causation. § 831(1) BGB does not therefore create a true regime of liability for others, but rather a regime of liability for presumed fault.[98]

b) For § 831(1) BGB to apply, the victim must prove the following:

– the victim suffered damage which was caused wrongfully by the employee (*Verrichtungsgehilfe*, literally "work assistant"). Going back to the three-stage con-

---

[91] By virtue of the Crown Proceedings Act 1947, c. 44, s. 2(1)(a), reversing in this respect the common law rule that "the King can do no wrong".

[92] By virtue of the common law.

[93] See *Clerk & Lindsell on Torts* at 112–3, para. 4–04; Rogers at 819–21; Markesinis and Deakin at 354–5, 380–1.

[94] Crown Proceedings Act 1947, c. 44, s. 2(6). Accordingly, the Crown is not liable for police officers, who are paid by local authorities, or for public corporations that derive their income from their activities: *Clerk & Lindsell on Torts* at 113, para. 4–04; Rogers at 820–1. In the case of police officers, it should be pointed out that, pursuant to the Police Act 1964, c. 48, s. 48(1), the chief police officer is liable for the torts committed by police agents (constables) under his or her control.

[95] Crown Proceedings Act 1947, ibid., s. 2, *proviso*. *Clerk & Lindsell on Torts* at 112–3, para 4–04; Rogers at 821.

[96] Crown Proceedings Act 1947, ibid., s. 2(5). *Clerk & Lindsell on Torts* at 116, para. 4–11; Rogers, ibid.

[97] There is second paragraph to § 831 BGB, which imposes the same liability on persons who undertake for the employer one of the tasks mentioned in the second sentence of § 831(1) BGB. It is of minor importance and will not be dealt with here.

[98] See Staudinger-Belling/Eberl-Borges, § 831 at 71, para. 55.

struction of torts under German law (*Tatbestand, Rechtswidrigkeit, Verschulden*),[99] the victim must prove the relevant facts (*Tatbestand*) and the wrongfulness (*Rechtswidrigkeit*) of the impugned conduct. § 831(1) BGB does not require the victim to prove that the employee was at fault (*Verschulden*) in causing the damage; indeed, as mentioned above, § 831(1) BGB does not make the employer answer for the fault of the employee, but rather makes the employer liable for his or her own presumed fault. Accordingly, if the employee's conduct was such as to breach a *Schutznorm* protecting the *Vermögen* in general (under § 823(2) BGB) or to be *contra bonos mores* within the meaning of § 826 BGB, then § 831(1) BGB allows the imposition of liability for *reiner Vermögensschaden* where the fault of the employer is of a lesser degree, such as negligence (*Fahrlässigkeit*);[100] such an outcome is exceptional for German law.[101]

– the author of the damage was indeed an employee (*Verrichtungsgehilfe*) of the employer.[102]
– the injury was caused by the employee in accomplishing his or her tasks (*in Ausführung der Verrichtung*).[103]

Once the victim has demonstrated that the three conditions set out above are met, it is presumed that the injury was caused because of the fault (*Verschulden*) of the employer and that a causal link exists between the fault of the employer and the conduct of the employee which itself caused the injury, and it is for the employer to attempt to exonerate itself pursuant to the second sentence of § 831(1) BGB.

c) If, in addition to the case against the employer based on § 831 BGB, the victim can also show that the employee is personally liable pursuant to one of the headings of § 823 ff. BGB, then both the employer and the employee will be held liable as *Gesamtschuldner* (jointly and severally) pursuant to § 840 BGB.[104] Subsequently, the employee or the employer can seek contribution (*Regreß*) from the other. However, when the employee is bound to the employer by a work contract (i.e. the employee is an *Arbeitnehmer*), labour case law has brought significant modifications to the rules of joint and several liability as they apply between employer and employee. That case law has created a so-called *Freistellungsanspruch*, or right to be exempt from liability, for the benefit of the *Arbeitnehmer*.[105] Indeed, the Federal Labour Court (Bundesarbeitsgericht) has held that it would be unfair and disproportionate for the employee to be personally liable for injury caused while undertaking a task assigned by the employer.[106] The quantum of damages often vastly exceeds the means of the employee, and after all the employee was acting within the organization and under the control of the employer. The Court also relied on

[99] See *supra*, Chapter III, 3.1.2., Introductory Note under b) and 3.2.1. under b).
[100] Larenz/Canaris at 476–7.
[101] *Supra*, Chapter I, **1.G.26.** and Chapter II., 2.4.2.A., Introductory Note under b) and c).
[102] *Infra*, **5.G.3.** and notes thereafter.
[103] *Infra*, **5.G.13.** and notes thereafter.
[104] The rules applicable in this case are surveyed *supra*, Chapter IV, **4.F.38.–39.**, Note (4).
[105] See Staudinger-Belling/Eberl-Borges, § 831 at 49–50, para. 13–5; Münchener-Glöge, § 611 at 274–5, para. 476–9; von Bar I at 204–5, para. 188.
[106] The reasoning of the Federal Labour Court was set out in recent times in BAG (Joined Chambers), 27 September 1994, ZIP 1994, 1712. In that case, the BAG—following a consultation with the BGH—decided to abandon the condition that the work in question be prone to danger (*gefahrgeneigt*) before the employee can seek indemnity from the employer.

the principles of § 254 BGB: the risk created by the activity of the employee is part of the operational risk of the employer's firm, and that operational risk has a causal impact, so that apportionment with the fault of the employee must take place.[107]

Accordingly, the employer will have to indemnify the employee from liability to a third party arising from activities connected to the operation of the firm. The apportionment between the employer and the employee depends to a great extent on the degree of fault of the employee: in cases of gross negligence or intentional conduct, the employee will usually bear most of the burden of liability, whereas in cases of "slight negligence" (*leichtester Fahrlässigkeit*), the employer will bear the whole burden.[108] The employee can assign its claim for indemnity to the victim (even if the employee did not actually have to pay damages to the victim), so that in practice the disadvantages of § 831 BGB for the victim can be avoided.[109]

d) According to the second sentence of § 831(1) BGB, the employer can exonerate itself in either of two ways:

– *Absence of fault*: the employer was not at fault (i.e. met the required standard of care) as regards the selection (*Auswahl*) of the employee and, to the extent required in the particular case, the direction (*Leitung*) of the employee or the provision of equipment to the employee. The only duty applicable in all cases is the duty to select employees properly. As case law evolved, it has been recognized that that duty comprised not only the proper selection, but also the instruction (*Übertragung*, *Einweisung*) and supervision (*Überwachung*) of the employee;[110]

– *Absence of causation*: even if the employer had not been at fault, the same injury would have been caused.[111]

In a contemporary context, where the employer is usually a large business with numerous employees and a number of levels of hierarchy, it is of course illusory to expect the employer to discharge personally the duties to select, instruct and supervise employees, so that in fact it would be practically impossible for the employer to rebut the presumption of § 831(1) BGB. The RG therefore introduced the concept of *dezentralizierter Entlastungsbeweis* (decentralized exoneration), which was confirmed by the BGH in a leading decision of 25 October 1951.[112] In that case, the employer was the owner of a large agricultural facility, who had appointed a manager to take care of the day-to-day running of the facility. An employee had caused damage, and the employer argued that he had satisfied his duties of selection, instruction and supervision as regards the manager, and that he should therefore be exonerated. The BGH held:[113]

---

[107] BAG, 27 September 1994, ibid. The principles applicable to apportionment between a fault and a source of risk under German law are reviewed *infra*, Chapter VII, **7.G.9.** and notes thereafter.

[108] BAG, 27 September 1994, ibid.

[109] See BGH, 24 November 1975, BGHZ 66, 1, as well as von Bar I at 205, para. 188 and Münchener-Glöge, § 611 at 274–5, para. 477.

[110] See Staudinger-Belling/Eberl-Borges, § 831 at 96–108, para. 92–104; Münchener-Stein, § 831 at 1784–8, para. 9–19; Larenz/Canaris at 481. For a case involving the duty to monitor employees, see BGH, 4 November 1953, *infra*, **5.G.16.**

[111] See Staudinger-Belling/Eberl-Borges, § 831 at 112–4, para. 111–4; Larenz/Canaris at 482.

[112] BGH, 25 October 1951, BGHZ 4, 1.

[113] Ibid. at 2–3.

In the present case, the manager appointed and supervised [the employee], thereby acting as an intermediary between the employee . . . and the defendant employer . . . [I]n large businesses, the employer cannot be expected to select and supervise the whole personnel. When a large number of persons is employed in such a way that one is subordinated to another, the duty of the employer is directed at the selection and supervision of the superior employee which he himself chose, namely the manager [references omitted].

The RG allowed such a reduction in the evidentiary burden under § 831 BGB for reasons of proportionality and fairness. The employer must however exert a sufficient degree of control, so that the business is adequately conducted and supervised. Even if the immediate personal supervision of the agricultural employee was left to the manager, the employer remains under a duty to issue general instructions which offer guarantees for the proper conduct of the business. If the organization is inadequate, the employer is liable under § 823(1) BGB for having neglected his general duty to supervise [the organization] [references omitted].

Decentralized exoneration obviously offers a major relief to the employer, and introduces some imbalance between larger and smaller employers (to whom it is not available) in the application of § 831 BGB. Accordingly, legal writers have been critical of the decision.[114] In subsequent cases, the BGH has not relied on decentralized exoneration again, and it left open the question whether it should still be available to employers.[115]

e) Liability for employees under § 831(1) BGB is one of the few areas in the German law of civil liability where the academic debate between the Result Theory (*Erfolgstheorie*) and the Conduct Theory (*Handlungstheorie*) actually has practical significance.[116]

It will be recalled that, under the Result Theory, the mere fact that the *result* of a certain course of conduct (*Tatbestand*) is capable of giving rise to civil liability[117] automatically entails unlawfulness (*Rechtswidrigkeit*), subject to any defences which the *defendant* may put forward to justify the course of conduct (necessity, etc.). The plaintiff then has only to prove fault (*Verschulden*) for liability to arise. In the context of § 831(1) BGB, the Result Theory would mean that, once the plaintiff had proven the relevant facts (*Tatbestand*) on the part of the employee,[118] unlawfulness is made out. Since § 831(1) BGB gives rise to a presumption of fault (*Verschulden*) on behalf of the employer, the onus is then on the employer to disprove fault.

Under the Conduct Theory, on the other hand, the mere fact that a given course of conduct has resulted in, for instance, the violation of a *Rechtsgut* within the meaning of § 823(1) BGB does not suffice to establish unlawfulness. Since many forms of potentially injurious conduct are generally permitted (e.g. driving a car), it must also be shown that a norm of conduct was infringed. Only then is the conduct wrongful (*Rechtswidrig*); fault (*Verschulden*) will usually flow unless the injurious conduct cannot be imputed to the defendant (because of insanity, young age, etc.). Applied to § 831 BGB, the Conduct

---

[114] See Staudinger-Belling/Eberl-Borges, § 831 at 115–9, para. 118–20; Münchener-Stein, § 831 at 1803–5, para. 66–7; Larenz/Canaris at 481–2.

[115] See BGH, 17 October 1967, NJW 1968, 247 at 248. The issue has not been raised before the BGH since then, and it is generally assumed that "decentralized exoneration" is now obsolete.

[116] See *supra*, Chapter III, 3.1.2., Introductory Note under b) and 3.2.1. under b). The following discussion follows the thorough exposition in Staudinger-Belling/Eberl-Borges, § 831 at 81–89, para. 68–76. See also Münchener-Stein, § 831 at 1080–1, para. 57–8 and Larenz/Canaris at 479–80.

[117] E.g. the conduct resulted in the violation of a protected *Rechtsgut* according to § 823(1) BGB.

[118] Ibid.

Theory requires that the victim proves not only that the conduct of the employee for instance injured a protected *Rechtsgut* within the meaning of § 823(1) BGB, but also that a norm of conduct was thereby infringed, so as to establish wrongfulness. Under § 831 BGB, the plaintiff is thus required to prove more under the Conduct Theory than under the Result Theory.

In substance, the difference between the two theories as applied to § 831(1) BGB can be seen in a hypothetical case where an employee would have respected all applicable norms of conduct but nonetheless caused injury to a protected *Rechtsgut* within the meaning of § 823(1) BGB. Under the Result Theory, the employer would be liable (unless it can rebut the presumption of fault), since wrongfulness would result from the mere fact that a *Rechtsgut* has been injured. In contrast, under the Conduct Theory the employer would not be liable, for lack of a wrongful conduct.

The controversy made its way to the BGH. In a first judgment of 14 January 1954, the BGH laid out the basic principle that the employer should not be liable for the employee in cases where the employer would not have been liable had he or she personally inflicted the injury.[119] In a subsequent judgment of 4 March 1957, the Joined Civil Chambers (*Großer Zivilsenat*) of the BGH were called upon to decide the issue, in a case where a person had been injured while trying to board a tram. The question was whether the tram operator should be held liable even if its employees had respected all the applicable norms.[120] In its judgment, the BGH first acknowledged that the Result Theory could not satisfactorily account for cases where dangerous conduct is nonetheless allowed in principle,[121] but then explained the placing of the burden of proof under § 823(1) BGB along the lines of the Result Theory.[122] It then ruled as follows:[123]

> The placing of the burden of proof is different under § 831 BGB. Here the Legislature deliberately chose to make the liability of the employer depend only upon a wrongful infliction of injury by the employee, and not to require also proof of intention or negligence [on the part of the employee]. As far as the conduct of the employee is concerned, then, only the rules on the burden of proof as regards wrongfulness come to bear. Accordingly, the victim must prove that the conduct of the employee was the adequate cause of an infringement of one of the protected *Rechtsgüter* of § 823(1) BGB. The employer must then bear the burden of proving that the conduct of the employee was in accordance with the law (*rechtsmäßig*) because it met the legal requirements surrounding road and rail traffic (*verkehrsrichtig*). Any doubts in that respect count against the employer. . .
>
> It must be acknowledged that, in cases of traffic accidents, the occurrence of which is not fully explained, the rules relating to the burden of proof as laid out above put the victim in a better position . . . than if the employer had personally caused the accident . . . Yet it can be seen that this is what the Legislature wanted to achieve in setting less severe conditions for the victim to satisfy in order to establish a claim in cases involving the conduct of an employee. This compensates in a way for the otherwise unfavourable position of the victim in such cases, given that it is possible for the employer to bring forward—usually with success—exonerating evidence [pursuant to the second sentence of § 831(1) BGB].

[119] BGH, 14 January 1954, BGHZ 12, 94 at 96.
[120] BGHZ 24, 21.
[121] Ibid. at 25–6.
[122] Ibid. at 28–9.
[123] BGHZ 24, 21 at 29–30.

In that case, the BGH therefore combined elements from the two opposing theories. It took from the Conduct Theory the principle that wrongfulness can be denied if a course of conduct complies with applicable norms (*verkehrsrichtiges Verhalten*). Yet in accordance with the Result Theory it turned that idea into a justification (*Rechtsfertigungsgrund*) which the defendant bears the burden of establishing. As a result, wrongfulness remains presumed as soon as the victim proves that the *Tatbestand* (e.g. infringement of a *Rechtsgut* pursuant to § 823(1) BGB) is made out. As might be expected, such a compromise was not well received by commentators,[124] and although it had been thought that the BGH would abandon it, it surfaced again in a recent decision.[125]

f) In the end, the regime of liability for employees under § 831(1) BGB puts the employer in a fairly favourable position, since the doctrine of decentralized exoneration facilitates reliance by employers on the two means of exoneration provided for in the second sentence of § 831(1) BGB (absence of fault and absence of causation), and case law has added an additional justification, namely that the conduct of the employee complied with applicable norms (*verkehrsrichtiges Verhalten*). Many writers find that § 831(1) BGB is no longer appropriate and should be modified;[126] however, no such modification has been made or is in sight. It will come as no surprise that, in consequence, German case law and legal writing have sought to find other ways, mostly through the extension of related liability regimes (which are discussed in the following paragraphs), to circumvent the perceived weaknesses of § 831(1) BGB, in particular the possibility of exoneration.[127]

g) A first way of circumventing § 831 BGB was to extend the scope of contractual liability for others pursuant to § 278 BGB, which reads in the relevant part:

> The debtor [of a contractual obligation] shall answer for the negligence of the persons that he uses for the fulfilment of his obligation under the same conditions as for his own negligence.

The rationale behind that provision is that the "debtor" should answer for those who are brought in to perform his or her obligations as if the debtor had performed them personally, or in other words, that the debtor guarantees the proper conduct of those persons.[128] In contrast with § 831(1) BGB, § 278 BGB is not a stand-alone basis for liability (*Anspruchgrundlage*), but rather a provision which imputes the conduct of one person to another (*Zurechnungsnorm*). The conditions that must be satisfied for § 278 BGB to apply are:

– An **obligation already existed** between the plaintiff (the "creditor") and the defendant (the "debtor") at the moment when injury was caused. The most common situation is

---

[124] See, for instance, Larenz/Canaris at 479–80 ("The decision . . . should not be followed") or B. Kupisch, "Die Haftung für Verrichtungsgehilfen" [1984] JuS 250 at 253–4 ("a feeble decision in many respects"). In general, the BGH was criticized most of all for putting the burden of proving compliance with applicable norms of conduct (*verkehrsrichtiges Verhalten*) upon the defendant, instead of requiring the victim to prove wrongfulness (*Rechtswidrigkeit*). A summary of the main criticisms is to be found in G. Erdsiek, "Die Problematik des § 831 BGB und seine Einwirkung auf unsere Vertrags- und Amtshaftung" (1967–68) 8 Juristen-Jahrbuch 36 at 42–4.

[125] See a recent confirmation in BGH, 12 July 1996, NJW 1996, 3205 at 3207.

[126] Larenz/Canaris at 484, for instance, would favour eliminating any possibility of exoneration for large businesses. Staudinger-Belling/Eberl-Borges, § 831 at 124–7, para. 127, would support moving to a system of liability imposed by law, as in French law, in the interest of harmonization. Münchener-Stein, § 831 at 1793–4, para. 8, would favour a similar solution, through removing the requirement of a contractual obligation in § 278 BGB. See also G. Brüggemeier, "Organisationshaftung" (1991) 191 AcP 33.

[127] See von Bar I at 202–7, para. 185–90.

[128] Staudinger-Löwisch, § 278 at 261, para. 1; Münchener-Hanau, § 278 at 890, para. 1; Larenz at 297–8.

undoubtedly that the defendant is bound by contract to the plaintiff, but § 278 BGB also applies to certain property relationships (e.g. servitudes or easements (*Dienstbarkeit*)) and to certain public law relationships (including civil service, treatment in public hospitals, use of public facilities, etc.).[129]

- The debtor **voluntarily used an *Erfüllungsgehilfe*** (literally an "assistant in execution") to discharge that obligation.[130] The concept of *Erfüllungsgehilfe* under § 278 BGB is broader than that of employee (*Verrichtungsgehilfe*) under § 831(1) BGB: *Erfüllungsgehilfe* extends not only to employees, but also to independent contractors, for instance.[131]

- The *Erfüllungsgehilfe* was **used to execute an obligation**, and not for instance to bring about a pre-condition for the execution. In a contract of sale between a reseller and a buyer, for example, the manufacturer of the goods to be sold is not an *Erfüllungsgehilfe* of the reseller, since the manufacture of the goods is merely a necessary pre-condition for the sale.[132]

- The injurious conduct of the *Erfüllungsgehilfe* took place **in the execution of the task**, and not merely coincidentally. This criterion is, by and large, coterminous with that of "accomplishment of the task" (*in Ausführung der Verrichtung*) under § 831(1) BGB.[133]

- The *Erfüllungsgehilfe* was at **fault** (*Verschulden*), and injury was thereby caused to the victim. In contrast to § 831(1) BGB, the victim must prove the fault of the *Erfüllungsgehilfe* under § 278 BGB. The level of care to be expected from the latter is to be determined by reference to the level of care to be expected from the debtor. The limitations of liability applicable to the debtor personally also apply to the conduct of the *Erfüllungsgehilfe*,[134] with the extra proviso that the debtor can stipulate that he or she shall not be liable for intentional conduct of the *Erfüllungsgehilfe* (which he or she cannot do for his or her own personal conduct).[135]

Even though damages for non-material injury cannot be obtained pursuant to § 278 BGB, the provision does not allow any exoneration, which makes it attractive in comparison to § 831(1) BGB.[136]

The scope of application of § 278 BGB has been extended through case law, essentially by broadening the scope of contractual obligations through the following devices:

- Liability for breach of accessory contractual obligations (subsumed under the heading "*positive Forderungsverletzung*" in German law). The scope of these obligations has been broadened constantly, so as to include, for instance, obligations of safety or information.[137]

---

[129] See Staudinger-Löwisch, § 278 at 262–4, para. 5–12; Münchener-Hanau, § 278 at 891- 4, para. 5–9.

[130] See BGH, 21 April 1954, BGHZ 13, 111.

[131] See Staudinger-Löwisch, § 278 at 264–8, para. 13–30; Münchener-Hanau, § 278 at 894- 6, para. 12–4; Larenz at 299–300.

[132] For further examples drawn from case law, see Münchener-Hanau, § 278 at 897–903, para. 17–30 and Staudinger-Löwisch, § 278 at 268–71 and 275–83, para. 31–40 and 54–96.

[133] See *infra*, **5.G.13.** and notes thereafter and, for a case where that condition is discussed, BGH, 12 July 1977, *infra*, **5.G.22.**

[134] Staudinger-Löwisch, § 278 at 273–5, para. 47–53; Münchener-Hanau, § 278 at 905, para. 35.

[135] Second sentence of § 278 BGB, making an exception to the rule in § 276(2) BGB.

[136] There is no equivalent provision to § 847 BGB for § 278 BGB: Staudinger-Belling/Eberl-Borges, § 831 at 53, para. 24.

[137] See Staudinger-Belling/Eberl-Borges, § 831 at 54–5, para. 27–30.

- Liability for pre-contractual dealings (known as *culpa in contrahendo* in German law), which has been extended so far as to apply to accidents occurring while a prospective customer is going through a department store, for instance.[138]
- Contracts with protective effects for third parties (*Vertrag mit Schutzwirkung zugunsten Dritter*), a construction under which the protective scope of the contractual obligation is extended to identifiable third parties who have a close relationship with the execution of the contract and with the creditor and who require protection against the consequences of contractual breaches.[139] Such third parties can then rely on contract law, including § 278 BGB, to support claims against the "debtor".
- Recovery of sums on account of damage sustained by third parties (*Drittschadensliquidation*), in certain cases where the creditor is allowed to claim for the damage suffered by a third party as a result of a contractual breach by the debtor, for instance when the property of a third party is entrusted to the creditor to be used in the performance of the contract with the debtor and is then damaged by the debtor.[140]

In all these cases, the extensive interpretation of the substantial and personal scope of the contract enables § 278 BGB to be used in cases where injury is caused by an *Erfüllungsgehilfe*, so that the limitations of § 831(1) BGB are overcome.

h) Liability for corporate organs under § 31 BGB offers a second way to circumvent § 831 BGB:

> The association is liable for the damage caused to a third party by the board of directors, a member of the board or another representative appointed in accordance with the articles of association, through a course of conduct that was taken in execution of the tasks entrusted to it or him and that was such as to give rise to liability.

That provision is generally applicable to all forms of legal persons under German law, whether they are governed by private law[141] or public law,[142] and it is also applied by analogy to partnerships such as the general partnership[143] or the limited partnership[144]; whether it applies also to partnerships under the BGB is still open.[145] It is not truly a case of liability for others, since the organs of the legal person act for that person, and their conduct is thus the conduct of that legal person itself.[146] Furthermore, § 31 BGB does not of itself create liability; it presupposes that the conduct of the natural person acting as an organ of the legal person fulfils all the conditions for liability, whether under a contract

---

[138] See Staudinger-Belling/Eberl-Borges, § 831 at 54, para. 26 as well as (in great detail) G. Erdsiek, "Die Problematik des § 831 BGB und seine Einwirkung auf unsere Vertrags- und Amtshaftung" (1967–68) 8 Juristen-Jahrbuch 36 at 45–51.

[139] See Staudinger-Belling/Eberl-Borges, § 831 at 55–7, para. 31–3 as well as Erdsiek, ibid. at 54–9. See also *supra*, Chapter II, **2.E.48.**, **2.G.52.** and notes thereafter.

[140] See Erdsiek, ibid. at 51–4.

[141] Including forms such as the public limited company (*Aktiengesellschaft* or AG), the private limited company (*Gesellschaft mit beschränkter Haftung* or GmbH), the registered association (*eingetragener Verein* or eV), the foundation (*Stiftung*, pursuant to § 86 BGB).

[142] Pursuant to § 89 BGB.

[143] *Offene Handelsgesellschaft* or OHG.

[144] *Kommanditgesellschaft* or KG.

[145] See Staudinger-Weick, § 31 at 156–7, para. 42–8. For the application of § 31 BGB to partnerships under the BGB, see *infra*, **5.G.3.** and Note (1) thereafter.

[146] The natural person acting as organ remains personally liable towards the victim, jointly and severally (*Gesamtschuldner*) with the legal person which is liable pursuant to § 31 BGB: ibid. at 157, para. 49.

or under one of the heads of tort liability created by § 823 ff. BGB, or under one of the forms of risk-based liability (*Gefährdungshaftung*) or otherwise.[147] For the purposes of establishing liability, it does not matter that the corporate organ in question did not act within the precise terms of its powers (e.g. alone instead of jointly with another corporate officer), as long as it was acting within the general scope of business which was entrusted to it (a restriction similar to the "accomplishment of the task" under § 831(1) BGB).[148]

§ 31 BGB has been used to circumvent the weaknesses of § 831(1) BGB essentially by enlarging the class of "organs" within the meaning of that provision.[149] § 31 is expressed to apply to the board of directors (*Vorstand*) and its members, and to other representatives "appointed in accordance with the articles of association [of the legal person]". Case law has interpreted that expression to cover not only those other representatives who are specified in the articles of association (chief executive, etc.), but also other persons exercising management functions within large organizations, such as branch directors, department heads, etc. As the BGH held:[150]

> It is enough that the representative is charged, through the general operational guidelines and practices of the business in question, with the autonomous execution of significant and essential functions of the legal person.

In that way, the legal person is made directly liable for the tortious consequences of the conduct of these persons, so that some have characterized the regime of § 31 BGB, as broadened by case law, as "liability for representatives".[151] Moreover, case law has even gone so far as to hold that, when a natural person should be a representative, as that expression has been construed, but has not in fact been appointed as a representative— so that the liability of the legal person cannot be engaged under § 31 BGB but would fall to be considered under the less advantageous regime of § 831 BGB—then the legal person is liable under § 823 BGB for an organizational fault (*Organisationsverschulden*).[152] In that latter case, it is almost impossible for the legal person to escape liability.

i) Thirdly, § 823 BGB has been used more broadly to alleviate the perceived weaknesses of § 831(1) BGB.[153] In the course of the 20th century, case law and legal writing have developed the theory of *Verkehrspflichten* to underpin certain aspects of German tort law.[154] The duties of selection, instruction and monitoring incumbent upon the employer under § 831(1) BGB have come to be seen as specific instances of *Verkehrspflicht*, expressly

---

[147] Ibid. at 146–7, para. 4–12.

[148] See BGH, 8 July 1986, BGHZ 98, 148 at 157–8, as well as BGH, 12 July 1977, *infra*, **5.G.22.** See also ibid. at 147–9, para. 13–21.

[149] See Staudinger-Weick, § 31 at 149–54, para. 23–36; Staudinger-Belling/Eberl-Borges, § 831 at 64–6, para. 42. The definition of "corporate organs" under § 31 BGB is accordingly broader than under comparable provisions in other legal systems: von Bar I at 193, para. 173.

[150] BGH, 30 October 1967, BGHZ 49, 19 at 21.

[151] See Staudinger-Weick, § 31 at 152, para. 33.

[152] That type of *Organisationsverschulden* —failure to appoint a representative within the meaning of § 31 BGB—is called "*körperschaftliches Organisationsverschulden*" (fault in structural organization), in order to differentiate it from the other type of organizational fault —relating to the general supervisory duty— discussed in the next paragraph. See ibid. at 151–2, para. 29, and for more details G. Hassold, "Die Lehre vom Organisationsverschulden" [1982] JuS 583 at 586–7.

[153] See von Bar I at 193–4, para. 173–4.

[154] Including, for instance, liability for omissions to act: see *supra*, Chapter III, 3.1.2., Introductory Note under a) and c).

governed by a distinct provision.[155] Other *Verkehrspflichten* also apply in the context of business operations: in the excerpt from the decision of 25 October 1951 given above (in paragraph d), the BGH alluded to the general duty to organize the business properly (*Organisationspflicht*) which lies upon the employer personally. In a subsequent decision the BGH found that that *Organisationspflicht* could not be delegated, so that if the employer left it entirely in the hands of managers or other subordinates, then the employer committed an organizational fault (*Organisationsverschulden*) from which no exoneration was possible.[156] § 823(1) BGB provides the remedy for a violation of that *Organisationspflicht*; since the victim can rely on *prima facie* evidence (*Anscheinsbeweis*) to make out his or her case, it is often fairly difficult for a business to escape liability.[157] These developments have been criticized in legal writing.[158]

j) Finally, as regards State liability, § 831(1) BGB applies to all non-sovereign activities of the State.[159] The various means of avoiding the limitations § 831 BGB described in the preceding paragraphs are available as against the State as well. In the realm of sovereign activities, however, § 839 BGB takes precedence over § 831(1) BGB, and it puts the victim in a more favourable position. Since German courts have tended to construe the realm of sovereign activities broadly, the regime of § 839 BGB has thus, to a certain degree, also been used to circumvent § 831(1) BGB.[160]

5.1.2. THE CONCEPT OF EMPLOYEE

Introductory Note

a) As was seen in the above subsection, the French, English and German regimes of liability for harm caused by employees all require that the claimant establish that the person whose conduct led to the damage was indeed a *préposé*, an employee or a *Verrichtungsgehilfe*, as the case may be, of the *commettant*, employer or *Geschäftsherr*, respectively. In this section, greater attention is devoted to how these regimes define what constitutes the relationship between the employer and the employee. The first three cases reproduced below have been selected for their representativeness in their respective system.

b) In all three systems, the regime of liability for harm caused by employees was established in the 19th century. As the organization of production and delivery of goods and services both in the private and public sector underwent massive changes throughout the 20th century, the concept of employee has had to evolve accordingly.

---

[155] See Staudinger-Belling/Eberl-Borges, § 831 at 45–6, para. 10–11.
[156] BGH, 9 February 1960, BGHZ 32, 53 at 59. That type of *Organisationsverschulden* is then called "*betriebliches Organisationsverschulden*" (fault in operational organization).
[157] See Staudinger-Belling/Eberl-Borges, § 831 at 52, para. 21 and G. Hassold, "Die Lehre vom Organisationsverschulden" [1982] JuS 583 at 585.
[158] Staudinger-Belling/Eberl-Borges, § 831 at 46–8, para 11–2; Hassold, ibid.; Larenz/Canaris at 483.
[159] See *supra*, Chapter III, 3.3.2.A., Introductory Note under c) and d).
[160] See Staudinger-Belling/Eberl-Borges, § 831 at 63, para. 41 and G. Erdsiek, "Die Problematik des § 831 BGB und seine Einwirkung auf unsere Vertrags- und Amtshaftung" (1967–68) 8 Juristen-Jahrbuch 36 at 59–61. For an example, see BGH, 16 July 1977, *supra*, Chapter III, **3.G.34.** and notes thereafter.

One of the problem areas concerned the organization of the professions into larger economic units. While the traditional status of professionals emphasized their individual independence as a corollary of their specialized knowledge and specific duties, in reality, doctors in large public or private hospitals or lawyers or accountants in large firms were becoming parts of a larger whole, without necessarily losing their command of specialized knowledge or being relieved of their individual professional duties. The medical profession may provide the best example of this development, and accordingly cases concerning whether and under what conditions physicians can qualify as *préposés*, employees or *Verrichtungsgehilfe* are included below.

c) Another difficult issue arises when workers are temporarily "lent" to another business, for example in connection with the lease of specialized equipment which only they can operate or because they are provided to the business by a temporary work agency. It could then be that the workers become employees of the host business, remain employees of the original business or are employees of both. Cases have been included on this issue.

Cass. crim., 15 February 1972[161]   **5.F.1.**
Geoffroy

LIEN DE PRÉPOSITION AND APPEARANCE

Crook apparently working for someone

A lien de préposition *arises when one person has the power to give instructions to another as to how the functions of that other person are to be fulfilled; however, that power must really exist and not merely be apparent.*

Facts: The plaintiff was defrauded by a crook named Buckzkowski, who gave the impression that he was an employee of the defendant, Mounie. The plaintiff joined to the criminal case against the crook an *action civile* against the defendant. At issue was whether it sufficed that the crook appeared to be the employee of the defendant—even if he was not in reality—for the defendant to be liable.

Held: The court of appeal found that the defendant was not liable. The Cour de cassation upheld the judgment of the court of appeal.

Judgment: "The [judgment] cannot . . . be quashed . . . If one admits . . . that Mounie willingly allowed the appearance of a subordination relationship between him and Buckzkowski to arise, that might make him liable under Article 1382 C.civ. by reason of a fault of his own. However, liability for that personal fault . . . should not be confused with the liability of the *commettant* provided for at Article 1384(5) C.civ. Indeed, subordination cannot exist without the right for the *commettant* to give orders and instructions to the *préposé* regarding how the functions for which he or she is employed are to be fulfilled. Authority and subordination are correlatives, without which there are truly no *commettants* and *préposés* within the meaning of [Article 1384(5) C.civ.]. Such authority and subordination must be real and cannot result from a situation of pure appearance."

Notes

(1) The annotated case restates the classical test under French law for the existence of a *lien de préposition* within the meaning of Article 1384(5) C.civ.: the *commettant* has "the

[161] D 1972.Jur.368, JCP 1972.II.17159. Translation by Y.P. Salmon.

right to give orders and instructions to the *prépose* regarding how his or her functions are to be fulfilled". This test is applied fairly broadly, however. It is well-established under French law that the power of the *commettant* does not need to rest on a legal or contractual right; it may also arise from factual circumstances.[162] Furthermore, it does not need to be effectively exercised, as long as it exists,[163] nor does the *commettant* need to have the requisite level of technical knowledge to deal competently with the work of the *prépose*.[164]

Whilst that power over the *prépose* is assessed quite liberally, the annotated case makes it clear, however, that it must be real: the mere fact that one person may *appear* to have the power to give instructions to another does not suffice to make the latter a *prépose* of the former. Yet as the Cour de cassation mentions, the would-be *commettant* may incur personal liability pursuant to Art. 1382 C.civ. for having been at fault in letting or making it appear as if the other was in fact a *prépose*.[165]

(2) French authors have in the past suggested that the power to instruct should be replaced by socio-economic dependency as the operational criterion.[166] According to them, anyone whose activity makes him or her dependent on another should be treated as the *prépose* of that other. However that criterion has been rejected by the majority of writers and by case law as too broad and vague.[167] As a consequence, the independent contractor does not become the *prépose* of the person (*maître d'ouvrage*) who engages it, even though some measure of economic dependency may be present;[168] in a few cases, however, the opposite conclusion was reached.[169]

(3) On the other hand, more recently, some academic writers have been moving away from exclusive reliance on the power to give instructions.[170] Indeed, given that, as mentioned above, that power does not need to be effectively exercised or backed up with the technical knowledge required to exercise it competently, one may wonder whether it is still a meaningful criterion. Viney and Jourdain have suggested that the most important feature of the *lien de préposition* is not the fact that the *prépose* works *for* the *commettant* (rather than in the pursuit of his or her own interests).[171] Indeed, according to Le Tourneau and Cadiet, there is a *lien de préposition* when "the *prépose* takes part in the

---

[162] Bénac-Schmidt/Larroumet at 30, para. 306; Overstake at 143/5, para. 16–17.

[163] Overstake at 143/5–6, para. 18; Le Tourneau and Cadiet at 847, para. 3453.

[164] Overstake at 143/6, para. 19; Bénac-Schmidt/Larroumet at 30, para. 315; Le Tourneau and Cadiet, ibid.

[165] See also Overstake at 143/7, para. 28; Bénac-Schmidt/Larroumet at 30, para. 312–4; Le Tourneau and Cadiet at 847, para. 3454.

[166] The leading proponent of that approach was R. Savatier; see his *Traité de la responsabilité civile*, vol. I, 2nd edn. (Paris: LGDJ, 1951) at 369, para. 289.

[167] See Bénac-Schmidt/Larroumet at 30, para. 307–8 and Overstake at 143/6, para. 21. At 143/6–7, para. 25–7, Overstake suggests that the "dependency" criterion, understood as the lack of complete freedom to act in the accomplishment of one's task, be revived.

[168] See for instance Cass. civ. 3e, 17 December 1997, Bull.civ. 1997.III.227.

[169] See Viney and Jourdain, *Conditions* at 873, para. 795–2; Overstake at 143/13–4, para. 59–65; Bénac-Schmidt/Larroumet at 33, para. 340–1. Indeed, as pointed out by Viney, Chronique, JCP 1998.I.187, now that the Cour de cassation has set out the bases for a general regime of liability for others (see *infra*, **5.F.23.**), there is no reason why that regime could not also support an extension of liability for others, in the economic sphere, beyond the *commettant-prépose* relationship.

[170] According to Bénac-Schmidt/Larroumet at 32, para. 332, the power to give instructions still remains the orthodox test for the existence of a *lien de préposition*.

[171] See Viney and Jourdain, *Conditions* at 864–7, para. 792. Cf the "composite" test used in English law: *infra*, **5.E.2.**

activities of the *commettant* and the latter remains in command of those activities".[172] So far case law has not openly followed these writers.

(4) Irrespective of how it is defined, the *lien de préposition* is peculiar to the liability regime of Article 1384(5) C.civ., and it does not necessarily coincide with categories found in other fields of law. As might be expected, the classical case of *lien de préposition* occurs in the employment relationship (*contrat de travail*).[173] As appears from what is said below, some debate has arisen under French law as to whether professionals (physicians, lawyers, etc.) can be *préposés* of some other person.[174] It is accepted that a *lien de préposition* can also arise under certain limited circumstances between, amongst others, principal and agent.[175] Outside any contractual relationship, it is possible that a momentary *lien de préposition* could arise between relatives.[176] Furthermore, French law is generally liberal in recognizing that a *lien de préposition* can arise out of casual relationships, for instance when a person does a favour for a friend.[177] In a judgment of 25 May 1971, the Cour de cassation found that a *lien de préposition* had arisen when a nurse who was in charge of a first aid station requested a volunteer helper to use her vehicle for an errand.[178]

Privy Council[179]   **5.E.2.**
Lee v. *Chung*

THE "COMPOSITE APPROACH"

Mason

In order to determine whether a person is the employee of another, the whole economic relationship should be examined, as reflected in a series of factors, including control, ownership of tools, level of responsibility and assignment of risks and profit.

Facts: The plaintiff, a mason, was in charge of chiselling concrete for the defendant, a sub-contractor at a construction site. He received instructions from and used tools supplied by the defendant, whilst the main contractor inspected his work periodically. The defendant paid him either at a daily or piece-work rate. He also worked for other contractors from time to time, but he gave priority to his work for the defendant. He was injured during a time when he was working for the defendant. At issue was whether he was an employee of the defendant for the purposes of Hong Kong workers compensation legislation.

---

[172] Le Tourneau and Cadiet at 846–7, para. 3451. Cf the "organization" test proposed for use in English law: *infra*, **5.E.2.**, Note (1).

[173] Viney and Jourdain, *Conditions* at 867, para. 793; Overstake at 143/9, para. 39; Bénac-Schmidt/Larroumet at 32, para. 336.

[174] *Infra*, **5.F.4.** and notes thereafter.

[175] See Viney and Jourdain, *Conditions* at 871–4, para. 795 ff.; Overstake at 143/12, para. 54–6; Bénac-Schmidt/Larroumet at 32–3, para. 337–9.

[176] See Viney and Jourdain, *Conditions* at 874–6, para. 796; Bénac-Schmidt/Larroumet at 32, para. 331; Overstake at 143/15–6, para. 80–2.

[177] See Viney and Jourdain, *Conditions*, ibid.; Bénac-Schmidt/Larroumet at 32, para. 330; Overstake at 143/16–7, para. 83–90.

[178] Cass. crim., 25 May 1971, D 1971.Somm.168. Nonetheless, the mere fact of offering to help does not suffice to make the helper a *préposé*: Cass. soc., 21 July 1986, Bull.civ. 1986.V.421; see also Bénac-Schmidt/Larroumet at 30, para. 316; Overstake at 143/16–7, para. 86.

[179] [1990] 2 AC 374.

Held: The court of first instance found that the plaintiff was not an employee but an independent contractor and dismissed his claim. The court of appeal dismissed the appeal of the plaintiff. The Privy Council reversed the judgment of the court of appeal and remitted the case back for further determination.

Judgment: LORD GRIFFITHS:[180] "The question is to be answered by applying English common law standards to determine whether the workman was working as an employee or as an independent contractor.

What then is the standard to apply? This has proved to be a most elusive question and despite a plethora of authorities the courts have not been able to devise a single test that will conclusively point to the distinction in all cases. Their Lordships agree with the Court of Appeal when they said that the matter had never been better put than by Cooke J. in *Market Investigations Ltd.* v. *Minister of Social Security* [1969] 2 QB 173 at 184–185:

> 'The fundamental test to be applied is this: "Is the person who has engaged himself to perform these services performing them as a person in business on his own account?" If the answer to that question is "yes", then the contract is a contract for services. If the answer is "no", then the contract is a contract of service. No exhaustive list has been compiled and perhaps no exhaustive list can be compiled of the considerations which are relevant in determining that question, nor can strict rules be laid down as to the relative weight which the various considerations should carry in particular cases. The most that can be said is that control will no doubt always have to be considered, although it can no longer be regarded as the sole determining factor; and that factors which may be of importance are such matters as whether the man performing the services provides his own equipment, whether he hires his own helpers, what degree of financial risk he takes, what degree of responsibility for investment and management he has, and whether and how far he has an opportunity of profiting from sound management in the performance of his task.'

With this test in mind it is now necessary to turn to the facts of the present case [Lord Griffiths then reviewed the facts.] . . .

Upon these findings of fact their Lordships would have had no hesitation, if sitting as a court of first instance, in concluding that the [plaintiff] was working for the [defendant] as an employee and not as an independent contractor. All the tests, or perhaps it is better to call them indicia, mentioned by Cooke J. in *Market Investigations Ltd.* v. *Minister of Social Security* [1969] 2 QB 173, 184–185 point towards the status of an employee rather than an independent contractor. The [plaintiff] did not provide his own equipment, the equipment was provided by his employer. He did not hire his own helpers; this emerged with clarity in his evidence when he explained that he gave priority to the [defendant]'s work and if asked by the [defendant] to do an urgent job he would tell those he was working for that they would have to employ someone else: if he was an independent contractor in business on his own account, one would expect that he would attempt to keep both contracts by hiring others to fulfil the contract he had to leave. He had no responsibility for investment in, or management of, the work on the construction site, he simply turned up for work and chipped off concrete to the required depth upon the beams indicated to him on a plan by the [defendant]. There is no suggestion in the evidence that he priced the job which is normally a feature of the business approach of a subcontractor; he was paid either a piece-work rate or a daily rate according to the nature of the work he was doing. It is true that he was not supervised in his work, but this is not surprising, he was a skilled man and he had been told the beams upon which he was to work and the depth to which they were to be cut and his work was measured to see that he achieved that result. There was no question of his being called upon to exercise any skill or judgment as to which beams required chipping or as to the depths that they were to be cut. He was simply told what to do and left to get on with it as, for example, would a skilled turner on a lathe who was required to cut a piece of metal to certain dimensions.

Taking all the foregoing considerations into account the picture emerges of a skilled artisan earning his living by working for more than one employer as an employee and not as a small

---

[180] Lord Bridge, Lord Templeman, Lord Goff and Lord Lowry concurring.

businessman venturing into business on his own account as an independent contractor with all its attendant risks. The [plaintiff] ran no risk whatever save that of being unable to find employment which is, of course, a risk faced by casual employees who move from one job to another . . ."

Notes

(1) The annotated case is the latest authoritative pronouncement under English law on the test to determine whether someone is an employee or not. As can be seen from the opinion given by Lord Griffiths, there is no hard and fast rule under English law, but the courts will look at a series of factors in what authors have called the "composite approach"[181] or the "multiple test".[182]

Under English law, that issue has traditionally been said to boil down to the distinction between a "contract of service", which would correspond to an employer-employee relationship, and a "contract for services", as would arise when an independent contractor is used. However, it is now settled that this is but a restatement of the problem.[183]

The first operational criterion put forward in the case law was **control**. As Hilbery J wrote in *Collins* v. *Hertfordshire County Council*:[184]

"[T]he distinction between the contract for services and the contract of service can be summarized in this way: In the one case the master can order or require what is to be done, while in the other case he can not only order or require what is to be done but how it shall be done."

According to that criterion, an employment relationship would be characterized by a high level of control by the employer, extending for instance to the manner in which the work is done (tools or technique used, time to be devoted, materials, etc.). As appears from the excerpt from *Market Investigations Ltd.* v. *Minister of Social Security*[185] quoted with approval by Lord Griffiths in the annotated case, the control test still retains some relevance as a starting point. However, in view of the realities of the labour market, it is no longer appropriate as the sole determinant, since most employees possess some area of discretion as to how they accomplish their tasks and most employers—especially large businesses—do not exercise a very detailed control over their employees.[186]

In *Stevenson, Jordan and Harrison Ltd.* v. *Macdonald*, Denning LJ proposed an alternative test based on the organization of the employer's business:[187]

"One feature which seems to run through the instances is that, under a contract of service, a man is employed as part of the business, and his work is done as an integral part of the business; whereas under a contract for services, his work, although done for the business, is not integrated into it but is only accessory to it."

While it avoids some of the pitfalls of the control test when applied to large businesses, that criterion is not very precise.[188]

---

[181] Rogers at 698.
[182] *Clerk & Lindsell on Torts* at 168, para. 5–09.
[183] *Clerk & Lindsell on Torts* at 164, para. 5–03; Markesinis and Deakin at 533.
[184] [1947] 1 KB 598 at 615, KBD.
[185] [1969] 2 QB 173, QBD.
[186] *Clerk & Lindsell on Torts* at 166–7, para. 5–05 to 5–07; Rogers at 697–8; Markesinis and Deakin at 535–7; Salmond and Heuston at 436–7.
[187] [1952] 1 TLR 101 at 111, CA.
[188] See *Clerk & Lindsell on Torts* at 167–8, para. 5–08; Rogers at 699.

Nowadays, it seems that English courts have abandoned the search for a crisp operational criterion and instead rely on an analysis of the **economic relationship** taken as a whole. As the annotated case shows, the following factors are relevant:

- control;
- ownership of tools;
- hiring of helpers (assistants, etc.);
- allocation of financial risks (i.e. who shall bear the burden if the work turns out to be more expensive to accomplish than had been thought?) and profits (i.e. who shall benefit if the work is executed more efficiently than foreseen?);
- management of work (working hours, timetable, etc.);
- pricing (i.e. who determines it?, is it based on a certain result or on time?).

The reasoning of the Privy Council appears to centre around the notion of risk: only if the worker bears the overall risks relating to the task will he or she be an independent contractor. If the risks lie with the employer and the worker is faced with no risks beyond those faced by every employee (e.g. risk of unemployment), then the worker is an employee. In the annotated case, the Privy Council carefully reviewed all of the above factors and came to the conclusion that the plaintiff was an employee of the defendant and not an independent contractor, even if he worked for many employers.

In addition to the criteria mentioned above, English courts will also give some weight to the will of the parties: while the nature of the relationship cannot be determined by the parties alone, in borderline cases the will of the parties can tip the balance in favour of one characterization over the other.[189]

(2) The annotated case does not concern vicarious liability as such, but rather the liability of the employer towards employees for work accidents pursuant to Hong Kong worker compensation legislation. However, contrary to French or German law, it is generally recognised under English law that the concept of "employee" is the same for the purposes of vicarious liability and the various fields of labour law (including determining eligibility to workers' compensation and the liability of the employer for various forms of social security charges).[190]

Furthermore, the English concept of employee is very much centred upon the distinction between employees and independent contractors: a person is either one or the other.

That distinction has been criticized, in view of the growing number of self-employed persons, who are sufficiently autonomous not to qualify as employees (under the "composite" approach outlined in the previous paragraph), without enjoying the financial strength of independent contractors. Treating such self-employed persons as independent contractors may impose too heavy a burden on them and at the same time leave victims without full compensation. Possible responses to this concern include expanding the primary liability of the employer,[191] extending vicarious liability to independent contractors or more simply recognizing that it may not be sustainable to maintain a single concept of "employee" across the various fields of law.[192]

---

[189] Markesinis and Deakin at 539–40; *Clerk & Lindsell on Torts* at 164–5, para. 5–03; Rogers at 696–7.
[190] Markesinis and Deakin at 534; Rogers at 696.
[191] See *supra*, 5.1.1.B. under f).
[192] See E. McKendrick, "Vicarious Liability and Independent Contractors—A Re-examination" (1990) 53 Mod LR 770.

(3) The concept of "employee" under the English regime of vicarious liability for harm caused by employees should thus be understood essentially to apply to persons in an employment relationship in the business or economic sense. There are very few examples of vicarious liability for persons who have become "casual employees", for instance by doing a favour to a friend.[193] Some mention should be made, however, of a series of cases concerning motor vehicle owners who requested relatives or friends to drive for them. In the leading case on this matter, the House of Lords held that when the owner of a vehicle expressly or impliedly requests someone else to drive it for purposes in which the owner has a specific and identifiable interest (and thus delegates a task or duty), then the owner is vicariously liable for the damage which that other person may cause while driving.[194] Legal writers have been at a loss to rationalize this extension of vicarious liability, picturing it as a *sui generis* liability regime[195] or as a doctrine motivated by equity concerns which does not fit into any existing legal category.[196]

BGH, 30 June 1966[197]   **5.G.3.**

CONCEPT OF *VERRICHTUNGSGEHILFE*

Brake fluid leak

A person qualifies as Verrichtungsgehilfe *when he or she is dependent on the instructions of the* Geschäftsherr.

Facts: The first and second defendants operated a garage under a civil law partnership (without legal personality) pursuant to §§ 705 ff. BGB. The plaintiff left his car with them for repair, which was undertaken by the first defendant. The repair was improperly completed (a brake valve was not tightened, and the brake fluid eventually leaked out), leading to an accident. The plaintiff sued the first defendant under § 823(1) BGB and sought to make the second defendant also liable pursuant to § 31 or § 831 BGB.

Held: The court of appeal gave judgment for the plaintiff against both defendants. The BGH upheld the judgment of the court of appeal as against the first defendant, but reversed it as against the second.

Judgment: "The facts of the case do not support a finding that the [second defendant] is liable in tort . . .

It is generally agreed that § 31 BGB is not applicable to a [basic civil law partnership under the BGB]. Unlike the general commercial partnership (*offene Handelsgesellschaft*) or the limited partnership (*Kommanditgesellschaft*) [references omitted], the civil law partnership is not sufficiently organized as a corporate entity for those partners who are acting on its behalf to be qualified as its organs. It is thus not possible to derive from § 31 BGB that the [second defendant] should be liable for the tortious conduct of his partner.

Accordingly, only liability under § 831 BGB would come into question . . .

---

[193] See Salmond and Heuston at 438–9.
[194] *Morgans* v. *Launchbury* [1973] AC 127, [1972] 2 All ER 605, HL; *Norwood* v. *Navan* [1981] RTR 457, CA. But it is not enough that the driver was merely authorized, directly or indirectly, by the owner to drive the car if the owner had no interest in the purposes for which the car was driven: *Morgans* v. *Launchbury*, ibid. at 135, 139–40, 142 and 151.
[195] *Clerk & Lindsell on Torts* at 203–5, para. 5–65 to 5–68.
[196] Rogers at 716–8. See also Markesinis and Deakin at 542 and Salmond and Heuston at 439–40.
[197] BGHZ 45, 311. Translation by A. Hoffmann and Y. P. Salmon.

A person only qualifies as Verrichtungsgehilfe *in the sense of § 831 BGB when he or she is dependent on the instructions of the employer* (Geschäftsherr) [emphasis added]. The employer need not have a detailed right of control (*Weisungsrecht*); it is sufficient that the employer can at any time determine the scope and duration of the tasks of the employee, restrict them or terminate them. There is no sign of such authority in the present case, as regards the work which [the first defendant] undertook to conduct on the plaintiff's car. 'Dependence', within the meaning explained above, cannot follow merely from the fact that both defendants are mutually bound through a partnership agreement, in pursuit of the objective of their business (*Gesellschaftszweck*), which is to carry out the repair work which may be entrusted to them [reference omitted]. As a rule, liability under § 831 BGB cannot arise in such cases for lack of a *conditio sine qua non*, namely the possibility to have avoided liability through the exercise of the right of control [over the employee] or the termination of employment."

Notes

(1) In the annotated case, the plaintiff sought to recover damages from not only the first defendant, whose defective repair work was responsible for the accident in which the plaintiff was injured, but also from the first defendant's business partner, who was joined as second defendant to the action. Since the plaintiff wanted to obtain compensation for non-material injury, he had to sue in delict (where § 847 BGB allows for that injury to be recovered), as opposed to contract.[198] The plaintiff accordingly contended that either the first defendant had acted as a organ of the partnership, for whom the whole partnership would be liable pursuant to § 31 BGB, or the first defendant was a *Verrichtungsgehilfe* of his partner the second defendant, in which case the latter could be liable pursuant to § 831 BGB.

With regard to the argument based on § 31 BGB, the BGH found that the partnership pursuant to §§ 705 ff. BGB (the basic civil law partnership in German law, which does not possess legal personality[199]) did not reach a sufficient level of corporate organization for the partners to be treated as "organs" of the partnership. The analysis of the BGH on this point has been criticized in legal writing, where authors generally agree that § 31 BGB should apply to partnerships under the BGB at least under certain circumstances.[200]

(2) The sole remaining possibility was to find the second defendant liable on the ground that the first defendant was his *Verrichtungsgehilfe*. The BGH recited the basic test used for that purpose: a *Verrichtungsgehilfe* is "dependent on the instructions of the employer (*Geschäftsherr*)". The right of the employer to give instructions (*Weisungsrecht*) is thus the determining feature of the concept of employee for the purposes of § 831 BGB.[201] As the BGH stated in the annotated case, the right to give instructions does not need to extend to the details of how the employee is to accomplish the task. The essence of the right to give instructions is rather the possibility for the employer of determining the scope and duration of the task of the employee, and of limiting it or terminating it. In the annotated case, the BGH referred to a previous judgment of 15 February 1957, where that point is well illustrated: there the BGH found that a lawyer was to be treated as the

---

[198] On § 847 BGB, see *supra*, Chapter II, 2.1.1, Introductory Note under b).

[199] See on this point the recent study of J. Berndt and K.T. Boin, "Zur Rechtsnatur der Gesellschaft bürgerlichen Rechts" (1998) 51 NJW 2854.

[200] See Staudinger-Weick, § 31 at 156, para. 45.

[201] See Münchener-Stein, § 831 at 1701, para. 31; Larenz/Canaris at 478.

Verrichtungsgehilfe of his client, since while, for lack of specialist knowledge, the client could not control in detail the legal steps which the lawyer was to take on his behalf, he nevertheless retained the general right to give instructions.[202]

Under German law, the right to give instructions can also arise from the facts, independently of any legal relationship (it is then more of a power to control), and it does not need to be effectively exercised as long as it exists.[203]

In the annotated case, the second defendant had no such right to give instructions to the first defendant: their mutual obligations as partners did not give one control over the other.[204] The annotated case is thus a rare occurrence where a gap arises between §§ 31 and 831 BGB: as seen before, persons acting for a business are generally either lower-ranking employees for whom the business is liable under § 831 BGB or higher-ranking personnel for whom, as "organs", corporate liability arises under § 31 BGB.[205]

(3) It is interesting to see how the BGH then relates the right to give instructions to causation: the right must be such that if the employer had exercised it appropriately, the injury would not have happened. Such a view is consistent with § 831 BGB as a liability regime based on a presumption of fault and causation (between the fault of the employer and the injurious conduct). By contrast, under English law for instance, to the extent that the liability of the employer is engaged on a risk or guarantee basis, the existence of a right to give instructions, such as could have been exercised to prevent the injury, is less relevant.

(4) According to some authors, the right to give instructions cannot suffice to determine whether a person is a *Verrichtungsgehilfe*:[206] attention should also be paid to whether the person in question works on his or her own account or in the interests of another. That criterion was present in the early case law of the RG on § 831 BGB.[207] Only then is it possible to reach satisfactory results in the case of specialists who work relatively free of control from the persons who entrust them with certain tasks.[208]

(5) Furthermore, the characterization of a person as *Verrichtungsgehilfe* for the purposes of § 831 BGB is not necessarily consistent with other fields of law, including contract law and labour law. On the one hand, workers (*Arbeitnehmer*) under an employment contract within the meaning of §§ 611 ff. BGB are generally subject to the direction of their employer (*Arbeitgeber*) and as such would qualify as *Verrichtungsgehilfe*; yet commercial representatives (*Handelsvertreter*), who are also bound to their principal by an employment contract, will as a rule not be *Verrichtungsgehilfe* given their autonomy. On

---

[202] BGH, 15 February 1957, LM § 823 BGB (Hb) 5.

[203] Staudinger-Belling/Eberl-Borges, § 831 at 72, para. 57–8; Münchener-Stein, § 831 at 1701, para. 31.

[204] Similarly, under French law, partners are not each others' *préposés*: Overstake at 143–14, para. 69; Viney and Jourdain, *Conditions* at 873, para. 795–3.

[205] See *supra*, 5.1.3. under h). See also *infra*, **5.G.6.**, Note (3).

[206] Staudinger-Belling/Eberl-Borges, § 831 at 71, para. 56, consider that the right to give instructions (and the distinction between *Verrichtungsgehilfe* and independent contractors) is put too much in the foreground now, whereas the rationale of § 831 BGB is to make the *Geschäftsherr* liable for those which are wilfully brought into his or her sphere of responsibility (*Verantwortungsbereich*).

[207] See RG, 17 April 1902, RGZ 17, 199 at 200. For the RG, the employee worked in furtherance of the employer's interest *and* under the instructions of the employer.

[208] Staudinger-Belling/Eberl-Borges, § 831 at 71–2, para. 57.

the other hand, independent contractors, craftspersons and traders can be *Verrichtungs-gehilfe* depending on circumstances under which they work.[209]

It is conceivable that the current fragmentation of the labour market (part-time work, self-employed, etc.) may not have much of an impact upon the scope of application of § 831 BGB, to the extent that the definition of *Verrichtungsgehilfe* appears to be relatively independent of particular contractual settings for labour or tax law purposes, although there is little evidence on that point yet.

(6) Even though the application of § 831 BGB to casual relationships, such as those arising out of a friendly request, is not expressly excluded, there are few instances where it has been invoked in that context.

The following cases can be found at <http://www.rechten.unimaas.nl/casebook>:

5.F.4. Cass. crim., 5 March 1992, *Groupe des assurances nationales (GAN)*. Fault by anaesthetist.

5.E.5. Court of Appeal, *Gold* v. *Essex County Council*. Grenz rays.

5.G.6. BGH, 14 February 1995. Eclamptic cramps.

5.F.7. Cass. crim., 20 October 1987, *Suteau*. Trailer stuck at railway crossing.

5.E.8. House of Lords, *Mersey Docks and Harbour Board* v. *Coggins & Griffith Ltd.* Crushed by crane.

5.G.9. BGH, 26 January 1995. Stadium roof collapses.

5.1.3. LIMITATIONS RELATING TO THE SCOPE OF EMPLOYMENT

Introductory Note

a) As was seen above in the subsection dealing with the general approach to liability for harm caused by employees,[210] the legal systems studied here all require, as a condition for liability of the *commettant*, employer or *Geschäftsherr*, that the conduct of the *préposé*, employee or *Verrichtungsgehilfe* should have been within the scope of his or her employment. Each system uses its own phrase: under French law the *préposé* must have been acting "within his or her functions" (*dans ses fonctions*: Article 1384(5) C.civ.), English law requires that the employee caused the injury "in the course of employment" and German law, that the *Verrichtungsgehilfe* was acting "in the accomplishment of his or her tasks" (*in Ausführung der Verrichtung*: § 831(1) BGB). Those phrases are not identical, nor is their interpretation in their respective systems.

Nonetheless, common to all these systems is the idea that some limits must be set to the scope of liability for harm caused by employees. It is not enough that the person who caused the harm was an employee of the person whose liability is sought: otherwise the liability of the employer would be triggered if the employee, for instance, inadvertently

---

[209] See Staudinger-Belling/Eberl-Borges, § 831 at 72–2, para. 59; Münchener-Stein, § 831 at 1699–700, para. 27.

[210] *Supra*, 5.1.1. under b), 5.1.2. under b), 5.1.3. under b).

damaged a precious object while eating at a friend's house. Some link must be shown between the harm which was caused and the fact of employment.[211]

This subsection begins by surveying the general developments in French, English and German law as regards limitations relating to the scope of employment, with the help of four leading cases, two from France and one each from England and Germany. Since this issue has been the subject of considerable debate in France, the French cases are analyzed at greater length.

b) The subsection then focuses on certain problem areas. First, two cases relating to car (or airplane) accidents have been selected, since such cases often fall on the borderline and appear to account for a significant part of litigation on the issues covered in this subsection.

A second difficult point occurs when the employee commits a crime, most commonly theft. In principle, it can never be part of the employee's tasks to commit crimes, yet on the other hand it seems somewhat unfair that the employer should be liable for damage caused unintentionally but exonerated from any liability in the more outrageous cases where the employee commits a crime. A series of three cases explores how each system has sought to solve that conundrum.

Thirdly, specific problems occur in fraud cases, where the employee represents to the victim that he or she is acting in the course of his or her employment whereas that is not the case in reality. Here it must be decided whether appearances and the victim's expectations are to be allowed to prevail over the objective state of facts. Four cases have been included on that issue.

Cass. Ass. plén., 17 June 1983[212]   **5.F.10.–11.**
Communes de Chignin et Saint Jeoire-Prieuré
and
Cass. Ass. plén., 19 May 1988[213]
Société d'assurances "La Cité" v. Héro

Abuse of functions

The commettant *can be exonerated only if the* préposé *acted "outside the functions" for which he or she is employed, without authorization and for purposes foreign to the tasks entrusted to him or her.*

---

[211] Even though it may appear obvious, the application of that proposition can give rise to practical problems, for instance when the course of conduct which would lead to liability is in fact made up of the joint action of an employee (for which the employer would be liable) and of a third party: see *Crédit Lyonnais Bank Nederland NV* v. *Exports Credits Guarantee Department* [1999] 2 WLR 540, HL.

[212] D 1984.Jur.134, with note by D. Denis, JCP 1983.II.20120, with conclusions of Advocate General P.-A. Sadon and note by F. Chabas. Translation by Y. P. Salmon.

[213] Bull.civ. 1988. Ass. plén. 5, D 1988.Jur.513, with note by C. Larroumet, Gaz.Pal. 1988.Jur.640, with conclusions of Advocate General M. Dorwling-Carter. Translation by Y. P. Salmon.

A. Cass. Ass. plén., 17 June 1983   **5.F.10.**

Oil spilt in quarry

Facts: A driver employed by the defendant transport company did not deliver the full quantity of oil ordered by a customer, keeping some 1500l aside for himself, which he was going to unload into a tank at his father's home. On his way there, he noticed he was being followed. He escaped his pursuers and drove into a quarry where he discharged the remaining oil, which eventually seeped into the water reservoirs of the two plaintiff municipalities. At issue was whether the acts of the driver were performed within his functions ("*dans les fonctions*"), so that the transport company would be liable for the damage which he caused, pursuant to Article 1384(5) C.civ.

Held: On 1 June 1978, the court of appeal found that the driver was not acting within his functions. On 3 May 1979, the criminal chamber of the Cour de cassation quashed that decision and remitted the case for further determination.[214] On 20 December 1979, a second court of appeal found again that the driver was not acting within his functions. On 16 December 1980, the criminal chamber of the Cour de cassation again quashed the decision of the court of appeal and remitted the case once more for further determination. On 26 March 1982, a third court of appeal found yet again that the driver was not acting within his functions. The case was referred to the full Cour de cassation (Assemblée plénière), which on this occasion upheld the decision of the court of appeal.

Judgment: "Against the decision of the court of appeal that the [defendant transport company] was not liable for the damage caused by [the driver], its *préposé*, the two municipalities argue that since a *commettant* is liable for damage caused by its *préposé* 'within the functions' for which he is employed, criminal acts committed by the *préposé* on the occasion of and during his working time and in the discharge of his functions lead to the liability of the *commettant*.

However, Article 1384(5) C.civ. does not apply to the *commettant* in cases for injury caused by a *préposé* who, *acting without authorization, for purposes foreign to the tasks entrusted to him, put himself outside the functions for which he was employed* [emphasis added].

Accordingly, having established that the injury resulted from a deliberate act which was foreign to the functions [of the préposé] and was done [by him] in furtherance of his own purposes, the court of appeal rightly found that the [defendant transport company] was not liable."

B. Cass. Ass. plén., 19 May 1988   **5.F.11.**

Embezzlement by insurance salesman

Facts: Héro was a travelling insurance salesman working for the insurance company La Cité. He was empowered to solicit prospective clients at their home, sell financial products to them and receive payments from them for those products. He came into contact with the plaintiff, an elderly woman, to whom he sold financial products. He received two payments of FRF 60 000 each, of which he fraudulently kept more than half for himself. On learning what had happened, the plaintiff sued Héro and impleaded the insurance company as his employer. At issue was whether the insurance company was liable under Article 1384(5) C.civ. on the ground that Héro was acting within his functions (*dans les fonctions*).

Held: On 19 October 1983, the court of appeal found that Héro had acted within his functions. On 15 May 1986, the criminal chamber of the Cour de cassation quashed that decision and remitted the case for further consideration. On 24 March 1987, a second court of appeal found again that Héro had acted within his functions. The case was referred to the full Cour de cassation (Assemblée plénière), which upheld the decision of the court of appeal.

---

[214] Cass. crim., 3 May 1979, Bull.crim. 1979.157.

Judgment: "Against the judgment [of the court of appeal] which held it . . . liable for its *préposé* Héro, La Cité brings forth the [following] grounds of appeal. On the one hand, the court of appeal found only that La Cité benefitted from the payments [made by the plaintiff], which does not suffice to explain why [La Cité] should answer for the embezzlement committed by its *préposé* . . . On the other hand, Mr. Héro did not act on behalf and in the interests of La Cité, but used his position for purposes that are foreign to those which his employer assigned to him . . .

However, the *commettant* can be exonerated only if the *préposé* acted *outside the functions for which he was employed, without authorization, and for purposes foreign to the tasks entrusted to him* [emphasis added].

Moreover, the [court of appeal] found that in making [the plaintiff] sign investment contracts, Mr. Héro was discharging his functions and had acted under authorization, in accordance with his tasks. [The plaintiff] was convinced that he was acting for the benefit of La Cité, which had, moreover, regularly accepted the investments and derived profit from them.

In the light of these findings, it follows that Mr. Héro, in embezzling funds with which he had been entrusted in the discharge of his functions, did not act outside those functions. The court of appeal rightly held that La Cité was not exonerated from liability."

Notes

(1) Judging from the attention which it has received from the Cour de cassation, the interpretation of the phrase "in the functions for which he is employed" at Article 1384(5) C.civ. must rank among the most debated issues in French civil law. Indeed the two annotated cases are part of a string of five decisions taken by the highest formation of the Cour de cassation in the past 30 years, including four decisions between 1977 and 1988.

(2) In French law, the discussion turns around the relevant factors (*points de rattachement*) which link the conduct of the *préposé* with the *lien de préposition*,[215] which are generally agreed to include **objective** factors such as:

- **time**, i.e. did the injurious conduct occur during working time?
- **place**, i.e. did the injurious conduct take place on work premises? and
- **means**, i.e. did the *préposé* use tools or other means put at the disposal of the *préposé* by the *commettant* to cause the injury?

as well as **subjective** factors such as:

- **consent** of the *commettant*, i.e. was the injurious conduct ordered, or authorized, or at least tolerated by the *commettant*? and
- **benefit** of the *commettant*, i.e. did the injurious conduct advance the purposes or serve the interests of the *commettant*, or was it self-serving on the part of the *préposé*?

As a rule of thumb, the more one insists on subjective factors being present, the **narrower** the range of conduct falling "in the functions" of the *préposé* within the meaning of Article 1384(5) C.civ. becomes. If only objective factors are required, then the range of conduct becomes **broader**.

As an illustration of how these relevant factors work, let us take the example of the driver in the first annotated case. If he had inadvertently injured a customer or passer-by while operating the oil discharge equipment or if he had damaged property by spilling oil

---

[215] See Bénac-Schmidt/Larroumet at 35, para. 372; Viney and Jourdain, *Conditions* at 876–9, para. 797–9; Overstake at 143/24–5, para. 140–5.

while delivering it to a customer, all possible relevant factors would point towards his having caused injury while going about his tasks. The *commettant* (the transport company) would therefore be liable. On the other hand, if he were to harm someone in a brawl at the local pub in the evening, no relevant factor could link his action to his employment, and the transport company would not be liable for it. Problems arise when the relevant factors do not all go in the same direction, for instance if, as in the first annotated case, the driver causes environmental damage by discharging oil which he had intentionally failed to deliver and instead wanted to put into a tank at his father's house. While that action was certainly not part of his tasks for the transport company and was certainly not authorized by it, the driver discharged the oil in the course of returning from a delivery, when he was driving a lorry of the transport company, and thus some form of physical and temporal link with the *lien de préposition* was present.

French writers tend to characterize these in-between situations as *"abus de fonctions"* (abuse of functions), although that term does not necessarily improve the understanding of the problem and in any event has not been used in the leading cases of the Cour de cassation.[216] The real problem lies in whether the link to be established between the conduct of the *préposé* and the *lien de préposition* is construed broadly and generously (hereinfter the **broader approach**, whereby a conjunction of objective relevant factors such as time and place would suffice) or narrowly and strictly (hereinafter the **narrower approach**, whereby subjective relevant factors, such as authorization and the purpose of the employee, must also be present).

(3) A certain parallel could be drawn between the two approaches and the competing mainstream theories of causation under French law, namely *équivalence des conditions* and *causalité adéquate*.[217] The broader approach would echo the former theory (i.e. the *préposé* was acting within his or her functions if the injury would not have occurred but for the *lien de préposition*), whereas the narrower approach would correspond to the latter (i.e. the *préposé* was so acting if the fact that he or she was the *préposé* of the *commettant* significantly increased the probability that the injurious course of conduct would take place).[218]

(4) The *Code civil* itself provides no guidance. Article 1384(5) C.civ., in using the phrase *"dans les fonctions auxquelles ils les ont employés"* ("in the functions for which they are employed") is framed in relatively imprecise terms, in comparison with other provisions, in particular in the *Code pénal* (Penal Code), where the wording typically runs *"dans l'exercice ou à l'occasion des fonctions"* ("in the course or on the occasion of performance of the functions"), denoting a relatively broad approach.

(5) During the first century and a half of application of the *Code civil*, it appears that French courts tended to follow the broader approach and thus readily found the *commettant* liable for the injury caused by the *préposé* as long as objective relevant factors were present.[219] In 1954, however, the second civil chamber of the Cour de cassation broke ranks and espoused a narrower approach, requiring that subjective relevant factors

---

[216] See Bénac-Schmidt/Larroumet at 36, para. 388.

[217] See *supra*, Chapter IV, 4.1.3.

[218] See Overstake at 143/25, para. 147.

[219] The historical information given in the text is largely drawn from the Opinion delivered by Advocate General M. Dorwling-Carter in the second annotated case, to be found at Gaz.Pal. 1988.Jur.640.

also be established.[220] The criminal chamber of the Cour de cassation —the other chamber which often had to rule upon Article 1384(5) C.civ.—refused to follow the reasoning of the second civil chamber and remained with the traditional broader approach. In view of the open disagreement between those two chambers of the court, the whole Cour de cassation was brought together to settle the issue in a case decided on 9 March 1960.[221] The compromise solution tended to favour the narrower approach of the second civil chamber but was not worded very strongly, so that the disagreement did not subside. The issue went back before the Assemblée plénière[222] for a decision on 10 June 1977.[223] That decision also tended to favour the narrower position of the second civil chamber, but it was afterwards confined to its facts (unauthorized use of a company vehicle) by the criminal chamber.

(6) It is thus against that background that the issue came back to the Assemblée plénière anew in the first annotated case, after the courts of appeal had twice refused to follow the criminal chamber of the Cour de cassation.

For the first time, in the first annotated case, the Assemblée plénière issued a generally applicable statement of principle on the issue: "Article 1384(5) C.civ. does not apply to the *commettant* for injury caused by a *préposé* who, acting without authorization, for purposes foreign to the tasks entrusted to him, put himself outside of the functions for which he was employed." On that basis, the court found that the transport company was not liable under Article 1384(5) C.civ., since the driver acted deliberately, in a manner that was alien to his functions and served his personal purposes.

It is difficult to assess the real significance of the first annotated case in view of the conflicting interpretations put upon it by different writers. The key issue is the relationship between the phrases of the sentence quoted above.

For some authors, the Cour de cassation has stated two conditions for conduct to fall "outside the functions": the absence of authorization and, most importantly, the pursuit of foreign purposes (i.e. acting out of self-interest and not in the interest of the *commettant*).[224] The phrase ". . . put himself outside the functions for which he was employed" would then be no more than the logical conclusion to be derived from the absence of authorization *and* the pursuit of foreign purposes.

For other authors, the Cour de cassation stated three *alternative* conditions for the *commettant* to be exonerated, namely (i) the absence of authorization, (ii) the pursuit of foreign purposes and (iii) the objective overstepping by the employee of his or her functions.

---

[220] Cass. civ. 2e, 1 July 1954, JCP 1954.II.8352 (2 cases).

[221] Cass. Ch. réun., 9 March 1960, D 1960.Jur.329, with note by R. Savatier, JCP 1960.II.11559, with note by R. Rodière.

[222] Pursuant to Art. L.121–6 of the *Code de l'organisation judiciaire* (Courts of Justice Act), the Assemblée plénière (Plenary Assembly) of the Cour de cassation is made up of the Premier président (Head of the court) with the presidents of each chamber of the court, together with the most senior judge as well as a second judge from each chamber (in total 19 persons). It is called upon to rule on cases which raise issues of principle, in particular where a disagreement arose between the courts of appeal or between them and the Cour de cassation, and in any event when the court of appeal to which a case is remitted after a chamber of the Cour de cassation quashed a judgment refuses to follow the decision of the Cour de cassation (*Code de l'organisation judiciaire*, Art. L.131–2).

[223] Cass. Ass. plén., 10 June 1977, D 1977.Jur.465, with note by C. Larroumet, JCP 1977.II.18730, with the conclusions of Advocate General Gulphe.

[224] See the note of F. Chabas at JCP 1983.II.20120.

If one of those conditions is met, then the *préposé* was not acting within his or her functions and the *commettant* would escape liability.[225]

Both these readings of the first annotated case have in common the emphasis put on the subjective relevant factors (authorization, purpose), and thus evidence a narrow approach to the issue, in line with the second civil chamber of the Cour de cassation. A third possible reading would be to see the three conditions just mentioned not alternatively, but *cumulatively*, in the sense that only the lack of **both** an objective (condition (iii)) and subjective (conditions (i) and (ii)) connection between the injurious conduct and the *lien de préposition* could exonerate the *commettant* under Article 1384(5) C.civ.[226] That third reading would come closer to the broader approach advocated by the criminal chamber.

(7) In a further decision of 15 November 1985, the Assemblée plénière seemed to opt for the second of the three readings above.[227] In that case, a security guard deliberately set fire to the plant he was in charge of protecting, in order to draw the attention of his employer to the lack of resources dedicated to the protection of that plant. The Cour de cassation upheld the judgment of the court of appeal to the effect that the mere fact that the employee had deliberately acted to bring a result opposite to that which he was employed to achieve sufficed to exonerate the employer from liability under Article 1384(5) C.civ. The decision was severely criticized by legal writers for its narrow approach which left victims in an unfavourable position.[228]

(8) In view of continuing disagreements amongst French courts, the matter came back once again before the Assemblée plénière in 1988. In the second annotated case, the Cour de cassation put to rest any doubts concerning the reading of the 1983 judgment, while at the same time making almost an about-turn from its 1985 judgment by adopting a broader approach, more favourable to the victim.

Thus, in the second annotated case, the Cour de cassation turned its 1983 formula on its head: "the *commettant* can be exonerated only if the *préposé* acted outside the functions for which he was employed, without authorization, *and* for purposes foreign to the tasks entrusted to him [emphasis added]". The use of "and" leaves no doubt that there are three cumulative conditions for the conduct of the *préposé* not to fall "in the functions" within the meaning of Article 1384(5) C.civ. Furthermore, the objective condition relating to the scope of the functions is brought to the fore, and the whole formula is framed so as to emphasize that the exoneration of the *commettant* is meant to be the exception rather than the rule.

The court proceeded to apply its statement to the facts of the annotated case by finding that, since it was part of Héro's functions to receive money and payments from clients, he did not place himself outside of his functions (first condition) by embezzling the sums paid by the plaintiff.

---

[225] See C. Larroumet, Comment, D 1984.Jur.170 and D. Denis, Comment, D 1984.Jur.134.

[226] See G. Durry at (1983) 82 RTDciv. 749. See also G. Viney at JCP 1986.II.20568.

[227] Cass. Ass. plén., 15 November 1985, Bull.civ. 1985. Ass.Plén.9, D 1986.Jur.81, with note by J.-L. Aubert, JCP 1986.II.20568, with note by G. Viney.

[228] See, in addition to the notes mentioned ibid., Y. Lambert-Faivre, "L'abus de fonction" D 1986.Chron.143. et J. Huet, Chronique (1986) 85 RTDciv. 128.

(9) The decision of the Cour de cassation in the second annotated case has subsequently been followed by both the second civil[229] and the criminal[230] chambers. In general, it has been positively, albeit prudently, welcomed in legal writing.[231] In the ten years which have since elapsed, the issue has not made its way back to the Assemblée plénière, although it is far from being completely settled, as the French judgments excerpted further in this sub-section show.

The three conditions set out in the second annotated case have been developed as follows:

–   *Overstepping of the* préposé's *functions*: following the second annotated case, this condition now assumes the main role. It is generally agreed that it refers to the objective scope of the functions entrusted to the *préposé*. For liability under Article 1384(5) C.civ. to arise, the injurious conduct seen objectively must not fall outside the realm of the *préposé*'s functions:[232] in the second annotated case, for instance, it was part of Héro's functions to receive payments as he did. In practice, that condition has been construed to mean that as long as the conduct of the *préposé* presents some objective link with the *lien de préposition* (i.e. one of the objective relevant factors identified above, such as time, place or means), the *préposé* will have been acting "within his or her functions" for the purposes of Article 1384(5) C.civ.[233]

–   *Absence of authorization*: if the conduct of the *préposé* fell outside his or her functions, then it must in addition be proved that that conduct was in fact not authorized.[234]

–   *Pursuit of foreign purposes*: moreover, it must be shown that the *préposé* did not act for the purposes or in the interest of the *commettant*.[235]

It has been pointed out that, once it is established that the conduct of the *préposé* fell outside the objective realm of his or her functions, then it will usually follow that the conduct was not authorized and was in pursuance of foreign purposes, so that the first condition is in practice decisive.[236] In the end, therefore, the second annotated case has led French law for all intents and purposes back to the traditional broader approach which prevailed before the second civil chamber broke away with a narrower approach in 1954.[237]

---

[229] See Cass. civ. 2e, 3 July 1991, JCP 1991.IV.346.

[230] See Cass. crim., 23 June 1988 (Cases 1 to 6), Bull.crim. 1988.289 (case 4 is reproduced *infra*, **5.F.16.**). Three other cases from the same day seemed to be at variance with the second annotated case, but in Cass. crim., 16 February 1999, Bull crim. 1999.23, however, the Criminal Chamber removed any doubt as to its agreement with the solution reached in the second annotated case.

[231] See the comments of P. Jourdain in (1989) 88 RTDciv. 89 and J.-L. Aubert in [1988] Rep. Not. Defr. 1097, as well as *Les grands arrêts* at 589–91. C. Larroumet, in his note at D 1988.Jur.513, however, finds that the Cour de cassation took an impracticable compromise position, whereas it should have held that *abus de fonction* fell either entirely in or out of the functions of the *préposé* for the purposes of Art. 1384(5) C.civ.

[232] Le Tourneau and Cadiet at 853–4, para. 3478–9; P. Jourdain, Comment at (1989) 88 RTDciv. 89 at 92–3.

[233] See, for the criminal chamber, the decisions of 23 June 1988 (Cases 1 to 6), Bull.crim. 1988.289, and for the second civil chamber, cases such as Cass. civ. 2e, 3 July 1991, Bull.civ. 1991.II.209; Cass. civ. 2e, 13 November 1991, Bull.civ. 1991.II.304.; Cass. civ. 2e, 8 November 1993, Bull.civ. 1993.II.321; Cass. civ. 2e, 19 January 1994, Bull.civ. 1994.II.34 and Cass. civ. 2e, 22 May 1995, JCP 1995.IV.1740, D 1995.IR.172. See further *infra*, **5.F.16.**

[234] Le Tourneau and Cadiet at 854, para. 3481.

[235] Le Tourneau and Cadiet at 854–5, para. 3482.

[236] J.-L. Aubert, Comment at [1988] Rep. Not. Def. 1097 at 1098.

[237] See Viney and Jourdain, *Conditions* at 889–91, para. 805.

House of Lords[238]   **5.E.12.**
Century Insurance Co. Ltd. v. *Northern Ireland Road Transport Board*

IN THE COURSE OF EMPLOYMENT

Driver of petrol tanker

In order to assess whether the conduct of the employee was in the course of employment, that conduct must be examined in the light of surrounding circumstances and must not be taken in isolation.

Facts: Davison was driving a petrol tanker for the Transport Board. While petrol was being pumped from his truck into the underground tank of a petrol station, he lit a cigarette and threw the match on the ground. The match ignited some material left on the ground, and soon the fire reached the point where the nozzle of the hose from the tanker entered the petrol station's tank. The owner of the garage attempted to extinguish the fire and told Davison to shut off the valve on the tanker. Instead, Davison tried to drive the tanker away. The fire caught up with the tanker, and the ensuing explosion caused significant damage to property. At issue was whether Davison acted in the course of his employment in lighting his cigarette, so that the Transport Board was vicariously liable for his conduct, with the result that Century Insurance Co. Ltd., the Board's insurer, was liable to indemnify the Board.

Held: The court of first instance and the court of appeal found that the driver was acting in the course of his employment. The House of Lords upheld the judgment of the court of appeal.

Judgment: VISCOUNT SIMON LC:[239] "[E]very judge who has had to consider the matter . . . agrees . . . in holding that Davison's careless act which caused the conflagration and explosion was an act done in the course of his employment. Admittedly, he was serving his master when he put the nozzle into the tank and turned on the tap. Admittedly, he would be serving his master when he turned off the tap and withdrew the nozzle from the tank. In the interval, spirit was flowing from the tanker to the tank, and this was the very delivery which [the Transport Board was] required under [its] contract to effect. Davison's duty was to watch over the delivery of the spirit into the tank, to see that it did not overflow, and to turn off the tap when the proper quantity had passed from the tanker. In circumstances like these, 'they also serve who only stand and wait.' He was presumably close to the apparatus, and his negligence in starting smoking and in throwing away a lighted match at that moment is plainly negligence in the discharge of the duties on which he was employed by the [Transport Board]."

LORD WRIGHT:[240] "On the . . . question . . . whether Davison's negligence was in the course of his employment, all the decisions below have been against the appellants. I agree with them and need add little. The act of a workman in lighting his pipe or cigarette is an act done for his own comfort and convenience . . . [It is not] prima facie negligent. It is in itself both innocent and harmless. The negligence is to be found by considering the time when and the circumstances in which the match is struck and thrown down. The duty of the workman to his employer is so to conduct himself in doing his work as not negligently to cause damage either to the employer himself or his property or to third persons or their property, and thus to impose the same liability on the employer as if he had been doing the work himself and committed the negligent act. This may seem too obvious as a matter of common sense to require either argument or authority. I think what plausibility the contrary argument might seem to possess results from treating the act of lighting the cigarette in abstraction from the circumstances as a separate act."

---

[238] [1942] AC 509.
[239] Lord Romer and Lord Porter concurring.
[240] Lord Porter concurring here as well.

Notes

(1) Even if it has not given rise to the same controversies as under French law, the limitation of vicarious liability according to the scope of employment has proved to be a difficult issue under English law as well. To the extent that any general statement can be made, case law has repeatedly cited with approval the following passage from Salmond and Heuston:[241]

> A master is not responsible for a wrongful act done by his servant unless it is done in the course of employment. It is deemed to be so done if it is either (1) a wrongful act authorised by the master, or (2) a wrongful and unauthorised mode of doing some act authorised by the master . . . [I]t is clear that the master is responsible for acts actually authorised by him . . . But a master . . . is liable even for acts which he has not authorised, provided they are so connected with acts which he has authorised that they may rightly be regarded as modes—although improper modes—of doing them. In other words, a master is responsible not merely for what he authorises his servant to do, but also for the way in which he does it. If a servant does negligently that which he was authorised to do carefully, or if he does fraudulently that which he was authorised to do honestly, or if he does mistakenly that which he was authorised to do correctly, his master will answer for that negligence, fraud or mistake. On the other hand, if the unauthorised and wrongful act of the servant is not so connected with the authorised act as to be a mode of doing it, but is an independent act, the master is not responsible: for in such a case the servant is not acting in the course of his employment, but has gone outside it.

From Salmond and Heuston's statements, three groups of cases can be distinguished, namely:

- where the employer authorized the very conduct which caused injury to the victim, and the liability of the employer will be engaged; these cases are relatively simple and are not discussed further;[242]
- where the conduct of the employee remains in the course of employment, although it was not a correct mode of discharging the tasks entrusted to the employee; and
- where the conduct of the employee lacks connection with the course of employment, so that it can be seen as an independent conduct for which the employer cannot be vicariously liable; English courts often say in such cases that the employee was "on a frolic of his own".[243]

As appears from the above excerpt from Salmond and Heuston, English law thus seems to take an objective view of the scope of employment as a point of departure. Furthermore, English law favours a broad construction of the scope of employment to ensure a better protection for third parties;[244] in borderline cases, courts will tend to find in favour of victims rather than employers.[245] Beyond that, it is widely acknowledged that

---

[241] At 443, footnotes omitted.

[242] As Markesinis and Deakin note at 544, these cases can be solved without even using vicarious liability, since the fact of authorizing the conduct also makes the employer personally (i.e. primarily) liable.

[243] That expression was coined in *Joel* v. *Morison* (1834) 6 C&P 501 at 503, Parke B.

[244] *Clerk & Lindsell on Torts* at 176, para. 5–22.

[245] This was already so as long ago as the eighteenth-century, as evidenced by the classic passage of Sir John Holt CJ in *Hern* v. *Nichols* (1701) 1 Salk. 289: "[F]or seeing [that] somebody must be a loser by this deceit, it is more reason that he that employs and puts a trust and confidence in the deceiver should be a loser than a stranger". That passage is still referred today, for instance by Diplock LJ in an unreproduced part of his opinion in *Morris* v. *CW Martin & Sons Ltd.*, *infra*, **5.E.17.**

whether a course of conduct falls in the course of employment or constitutes "a frolic of [the employee's] own" boils down to a question of fact, so that no hard-and-fast rules can be put forward.[246]

(2) The annotated case provides a good example of the English approach to the issue. The speeches of Viscount Simon and Lord Wright are not very far apart. On the one hand, Viscount Simon found that waiting and watching was part of the duties of Denison and thus that, in lighting a cigarette and throwing away the match, he "negligently waited". On the other hand, Lord Wright was of the opinion that the act of lighting up and throwing away the match, while innocent and unconnected with employment in the abstract, could not be divorced from the surrounding circumstances, so that the course of employment broadly comprised all acts done concomitantly to the accomplishment of the tasks which were entrusted to the employee.

In any event, both of their Lordships took a fairly broad view of the scope of employment, whereby it is not necessary to show that the injurious conduct as such was part of the tasks of the employee. Nonetheless, *how* Denison conducted himself while doing the things that he was employed to do constituted conduct in the course of his employment. Similarly, in *Kay* v. *ITW Ltd.*,[247] the driver of a fork-lift truck, upon seeing that a five-ton lorry from another company blocked his way into the warehouse, took it upon himself to move the lorry (even though the lorry driver was nearby) and thereby caused injury to another employee. The Court of Appeal found that the driver was still acting in the course of his employment when he attempted to move the lorry to gain access to the warehouse, since his task was to move goods with the fork-lift truck in and out of the warehouse.

On the other hand, mere temporal or physical coincidence between the injurious conduct and the course of employment will not suffice.[248] For instance, in the following cases, the English courts have found that employees had engaged in "frolics" outside of the course of their employment:

- firemen who failed to show up in due time at a fire site because of a "go-slow" action directed at their employer;[249]
- employees of a telephone cleaning company who had used telephones on clients' premises to make long-distance calls.[250]

(3) Under English law the mere breach of a prohibition by the employer does not take the conduct of the employee outside the course of his or her employment, unless the prohibition delineated the scope of employment.[251] Here again each case will fall to be decided mainly on its own facts.[252] For instance, in the 1945 case of *Twine* v. *Bean's*

---

[246] *Clerk & Lindsell on Torts* at 176, para. 5–22; Rogers at 703; Markesinis and Deakin at 546.

[247] [1968] 1 QB 140, CA.

[248] Salmond and Heuston at 444; Markesinis and Deakin at 545.

[249] *General Engineering Services Ltd.* v. *Kingston & St. Andrew Corporation* [1989] 1 WLR 69, CA. It is interesting to note that in a similar case of "go-slow" action, the BGH found that the employees had remained within the accomplishment of their tasks: BGH, 16 June 1977, *supra*, Chapter III, **3.G.34.**

[250] *Heasmans* v. *Clarity Cleaning Co.* [1987] ICR 949, CA.

[251] *Clerk & Lindsell on Torts* at 177, para. 5–23 to 5–25; Salmond and Heuston at 446–7; Rogers at 707–9; Markesinis and Deakin at 547–9.

[252] In addition to the cases discussed hereafter, see also *Limpus* v. *London General Omnibus Co.* (1862) 1 H&C 526, Exch. Ch; *Conway* v. *George Wimpey & Co. Ltd.* [1951] 2 KB 266, CA; *LCC* v. *Cattermoles (Garages) Ltd.* [1953] 1 WLR 997, CA and *Ilkiw* v. *Samuels* [1963] 1 WLR 991, CA.

Express Ltd., a van driver had given a lift to a passenger, even though his employer had expressly prohibited him from giving lifts to anyone, and the passenger was killed in an accident; the court found that the driver had acted outside the scope of his employment.[253] Thirty years later, in *Rose* v. *Plenty*, the Court of Appeal faced a similar case, in which a milkman had taken a 13-year old boy on board his vehicle to help him with his round, contrary to express instructions from his employer, and the boy was injured due to the negligent driving of the milkman. There the court distinguished *Twine* on the basis that the boy was not just given a lift, but was meant to help the milkman with his run. Accordingly, in taking the boy on board, the milkman was discharging his task improperly, but remained in the course of his employment.[254]

(4) Furthermore, the employee may still be acting in the course of employment if he or she takes an initiative that is not *per se* part of his or her tasks, but can be seen to fall within his or her discretion. A common example is the defence of the employer's property or economic interests. It is generally considered that the employee can take reasonable action in an emergency to protect the employer's property and will remain in the course of employment in so doing.[255] In *Poland* v. *John Parr & Sons*,[256] for instance, an employee thought that a little boy was going to steal sugar from the cart that he was attending; he hit the boy on the back of the head, whereupon the boy fell and suffered injury. The Court of Appeal found that the employee was acting in the course of his employment. In *Keppel Bus Co Ltd* v. *Sa'ad bin Ahmad*,[257] on the other hand, a bus driver assaulted a passenger who had complained that the driver had used abusive language towards another passenger; in the absence of any emergency which would have called for such action, the Privy Council found that the assault fell outside of the course of employment.

(5) Recently, a discussion has arisen as to whether the words "in the course of employment" as found in similar provisions of the Race Relations Act 1976[258] and the Sex Discrimination Act 1975[259] should be interpreted in the same fashion as for the purposes of vicarious liability at common law. While these provisions aim at ensuring that employers are liable for the injurious consequences of racial or sexual discrimination committed by their employees and as such are clearly modelled on the principles of vicarious liability at common law, English courts have found that the words "in the course of employment" have to be interpreted more broadly under these two statutes, so that racially-motivated abuse by co-workers, for instance, would fall "in the course of employment" for the purposes of the Race Relations Act.[260]

---

[253] *Twine* v. *Bean's Express Ltd.* (1946) 62 TLR 458, CA.

[254] *Rose* v. *Plenty* [1976] 1 WLR 141, CA.

[255] See *Clerk & Lindsell on Torts* at 182–4, para. 5–31 to 5–33; Markesinis and Deakin at 544–5; Rogers at 706.

[256] [1927] 1 KB 236, CA.

[257] [1974] 1 WLR 1082, [1974] 2 All ER 700, PC.

[258] Race Relations Act 1976, c. 74, s. 32(1); and see s. 78(1) (definition of "employment").

[259] Sex Discrimination Act 1975, c. 65, s. 41; and see s. 82(1) (definition of "employment").

[260] See *Jones* v. *Tower Boot Co. Ltd.* [1997] 2 All ER 406, [1997] ICR 254, CA, concerning the Race Relations Act 1976. That case was mentioned in *obiter* in the context of the Sex Discrimination Act 1975 in *Waters* v. *Commissioner of the Metropolitan Police* [1997] ICR 1073, CA.

BGH, 20 September 1966[261]   **5.G.13.**

IN ACCOMPLISHING THE TASK
"*IN AUSFÜHRUNG DER VERRICHTUNG*"

Excavator on the highway

The conduct of the Verrichtungsgehilfe *takes place "in accomplishing the task" within the meaning of § 831(1) BGB if it is substantively connected to the task and thus falls within the range of activities which the task entails.*

Facts: The defendant instructed his employee, an excavator operator, to bring an excavator from his yard to the repair workshop for a check-up and then to take it back to the yard. The excavator was self-propelled, but it was not licensed to be driven on public highways, and accordingly the employee was told to use a low-loading trailer to carry the excavator. However, the employee simply drove the excavator on the highway. On his way back from the workshop, he collided with, and injured, the plaintiff. The plaintiff sued the defendant pursuant to § 831 BGB. At issue was whether the employee was accomplishing his task (*in Ausführung der Verrichtung*) at the time.

Held: The court of first instance and the court of appeal found that the employee was accomplishing his task and allowed the claim against the defendant. The judgment of the court of appeal was upheld by the BGH.

Judgment: "1. The [defendant] argues that [the employee] did not act in the accomplishment of the tasks assigned to him when he drove [the excavator] and caused the accident, since the instructions given to [the employee] were to take the excavator to the repair workshop and return it only in the prescribed manner, i.e. by using a low-loading trailer. Thus [the employee] was not entrusted, within the meaning of § 831 BGB, with the actual course of conduct which led to the accident . . . In driving [the excavator on the highway], [the employee] acted arbitrarily and outside his remit, in a way similar to a *Schwarzfahrt* [use of a vehicle without the knowledge and without the authorization of its keeper (*Halter*)]. It is irrelevant in this respect that, in so doing, [the employee] intended to serve the interests of the defendant . . .

This reasoning cannot be accepted. An act is done "in the accomplishment" of an assigned task if it falls within the range of conduct which the accomplishment of the task entails. In this respect, a substantive connection between the conduct leading to injury and the entrusted task is necessary and sufficient [reference omitted]. Where there is such a substantive connection, the *Gehilfe* acts in principle in the accomplishment of the task with which he was entrusted, even if he overstepped his powers arbitrarily or mistakenly in a given situation [reference omitted]. That was precisely the situation in the present case. [The employee] was an excavator driver, and . . . his employer . . . requested him to take the excavator to the repair workshop. It thus cannot be denied that driving [the excavator on the highway], which led to the accident, was substantively connected with the instructions given to the [employee]. This connection was not set aside because of [the employee's] failure to use a low-loading trailer, as the defendant . . . had instructed him to do. [The employee] deviated from the instructions of the employer only as regards the manner in which the task was to be accomplished, which did not mean that driving the excavator as such fell outside the tasks assigned to him.

Furthermore, the [defendant] cannot argue that the liability of the keeper (*Halter*) [of the vehicle], as it arises through § 831 BGB, is generally excluded in cases of *Schwarzfahrt*, because [the employee] would not be acting within the scope of the tasks entrusted to him [reference omitted]. This principle cannot be applied here, since [the employee] used the vehicle with the knowledge and

[261] VersR 1966, 1074. Translation by A. Hoffmann and Y. P. Salmon.

authorization of the keeper. Therefore, this case cannot be characterized as one of *Schwarzfahrt* or one of arbitrary deviation that would amount to a *Schwarzfahrt*."

Notes

(1) Much like French and English law, German law has experienced difficulties with the determination of the limits to liability under § 831(1) BGB based on the scope of employment—the German keywords being "in accomplishing the task" (*in Ausführung der Verrichtung*).[262] At the outset, it must be recalled that similar limits are found in the provision dealing with liability for corporate organs (§ 31 BGB)[263] and have been read into the regime of contractual liability for others (§ 278 BGB);[264] the case law pertaining to each of these provisions is relevant for the others.[265]

(2) In the annotated case, the BGH set out the general principles of its case law on the meaning of "in accomplishing the task": the injurious conduct must fall "within the range of conduct which the accomplishment of the task... entails", whereby it is a necessary and sufficient condition that a substantive connection (*innerer, sachlicher Zusammenhang*) objectively exists between the conduct and the task.[266] A substantive connection is to be distinguished from a mere extraneous connection (*äußerer Zusammenhang*), such as coincidence in time or place. It is often said in German law that injurious conduct which presents merely an extraneous connection to the task is done "on the occasion of the task" (*bei Gelegenheit der Ausführung*) and not in its accomplishment.

(3) Beyond that, the issue becomes a matter of fact; in the end, the distinction between substantive and extraneous connection may not be so clear and it may come down to how much the *Verrichtungsgehilfe* actually deviated from his or her assigned tasks.[267] Here, as under English law,[268] the distinction is between badly or faultily accomplishing a task and exceeding the bounds of the entrusted task.[269] As in English law as well, the fact that the *Verrichtungsgehilfe* may have disobeyed a prohibition by the *Geschäftsherr* is not conclusive.[270]

By way of example, in the annotated case, the BGH found that the action of the driver in taking the excavator on the highway was substantively connected with his task, which was to take the excavator to and from the repair workshop. The BGH added that the driver, in not using a low-loading trailer contrary to the instructions of the defendant, simply chose a wrongful method of discharging his task, which did not take him outside the accomplishment of the task for the purposes of § 831(1) BGB.

[262] Münchener-Stein, § 831 at 1798, para. 48, and Larenz/Canaris at 480 point out that no meaningful criterion has yet emerged in that respect.

[263] For a leading case on that aspect of § 31 BGB, see BGH, 30 October 1967, BGHZ 49, 19. See also Staudinger-Weick, § 31 at 154–5, para. 39–40.

[264] For an example, see *infra*, **5.G.22.** See Staudinger-Löwisch, § 278 at 271–3, para. 41–6; Münchener-Hanau, § 278 at 903–5, para. 31–4.

[265] Münchener-Stein, § 831 at 1800, para. 54. § 839 BGB, concerning State liability for civil servants, also contains a similar limit.

[266] See also Münchener-Stein, § 831 at 1798, para. 48; Staudinger-Belling/Eberl-Borges, § 831 at 89–90, para. 77–9 and the case law referred at 1799, para. 53 and 92–3, para. 84–5, respectively.

[267] See e.g. BGH, 29 April 1964, VersR 1964, 754, as well as Staudinger-Belling/Eberl-Borges, § 831 at 90, para. 80.

[268] *Supra*, **5.E.12.**, Note (1).

[269] See the terminology used by Staudinger-Belling/Eberl-Borges, § 831 at 89–90, para. 77–9.

[270] In addition to the examples given below, see also BGH, 15 December 1959, BGHZ 31, 358 and BGH, 6 October 1970, NJW 1971, 31.

By contrast, in its decision of 14 February 1989, the BGH found that a pilot, who took it upon himself to fly guest passengers despite express instructions to stay with the guests and wait for another pilot (who was late), was no longer acting in the accomplishment of his task, for lack of substantive connection between flying guest passengers himself and the task of informing passengers that the pilot for whom they were waiting was late.[271]

(4) Some authors would frame the matter in terms of adequate causation:[272] the aim of the limitation introduced with the phrase "in the accomplishment of the task" (*in Ausführung der Verrichtung*) would be to restrict liability under § 831(1) BGB to cases where the assignment of certain tasks to a *Verrichtungsgehilfe* (as opposed to action by the *Geschäftsherr* personally) increased the risk of injury.[273] A good example of that can be found in the BGH decision of 24 June 1958, where an employer had asked an employee to drop off some mail and deliver an order form for him when the employee drove home at the end of the day (without urgency and without need to change course). On the way home, the employee was killed in an accident.[274] The BGH found that the journey back home was not in the accomplishment of a task (and thus that the employer was not liable to the relatives of the employee pursuant to § 831(1) BGB), since the errands were not such as to require the employee to hurry or change course, and thereby did not increase the probability of an accident on the way back home, which the employee would in any event have followed when he finished his day's work.

The following cases can be found at <http://www.rechten.unimaas.nl/casebook>:

5.G.14. BGH, 14 February 1989. Flight without autorisation.

5.E.15. House of Lords, *Smith* v. *Stages*. Accident on way back from work.

5.F.16. Cass. crim., 23 June 1988, *Jaux*. Theft by security guard.

5.E.17. Court of Appeal, *Morris* v. *CW Martin & Sons Ltd*. Theft by fur cleaner.

5.G.18. BGH, 4 November 1953. Theft by construction workers.

5.F.19. Cass. civ. 2e, 23 June 1993, *Caisse régionale du Crédit agricole de Toulouse* v. *Devic*. Gems, coins and stamps.

5.F.20. Cass. civ. 2e, 7 July 1993, *Société Manufacturers Hanover Bank France* v. *Pouteaux*. Shady operations.

5.E.21. House of Lords, *Lloyd* v. *Grace, Smith & Co.* Fraud by conveyancing clerk.

5.G.22. BGH, 12 July 1977. Fraud by bank manager.

---

[271] *Infra*, **5.G.14.**
[272] See *infra*, Chapter IV, **4.G.1.** and notes thereafter.
[273] See Münchener-Stein, § 831 at 1798, para. 48; Larenz/Canaris at 480.
[274] BGH, 24 June 1958, MDR 1958, 680.

5.2. OTHER REGIMES OF LIABILITY FOR OTHERS

Introductory Note

a) While the legal systems under study here all have a fairly well-developed regime of liability for harm caused by employees, they have little in common as regards other regimes of liability for others.[275]

Under English law, liability for employees is by and large the only vicarious liability regime, where one is made liable for the injury caused by another, irrespective of whether one was at fault.[276] There are other instances where one can incur liability for the injurious conduct of another, but then that liability is based on one's own fault.[277] Examples include liability for persons under one's custody,[278] liability for persons who find themselves on one's property,[279] as well as the liability of parents and educational institutions for children.[280] As regards the latter, the House of Lords framed the nature of the liability in the following terms in *Carmarthenshire County Council* v. *Lewis*,[281] a case where it was alleged that a school was liable for an accident which had been caused by a four-year old child wandering on the street:

> There is no absolute duty; there is only a duty not to be negligent, and a mother is not negligent unless she fails to do something which a prudent or reasonable mother in her position would have been able to do and would have done . . . I think that all but the most careless mothers do take many precautions for their children's safety and the same precautions serve to protect others. I cannot see how any person in charge of a child could be held to have been negligent in a question with a third party injured in a road accident unless he or she had failed to take reasonable and practicable precaution for the safety of the child.

b) It was seen in the preceding section that the German regime of delictual liability for harm caused by employees, at § 831(1) BGB, is not a regime of liability for others, but rather a regime of presumed fault and causation.[282] However, a number of related regimes are true regimes of liability for others, such as § 278 BGB (contractual liability for others) and the more specific regimes of § 702(2) BGB (liability of innkeeper for personnel), § 431 HGB[283] (liability of transport company for personnel), §§ 454 and 456 HGB

---

[275] For a discussion of the other areas of liability for others, see von Bar I at 155 ff., para. 131 ff. (liability for children), 182 ff., para. 160 ff. (liability for pupils and apprentices), 187–9, para. 166–7 (liability for other persons under supervision) and 346–9, para. 330–4 (same topics in Nordic law and English common law).

[276] Rogers at 716–8 mentions that the principal is also vicariously liable for the agent, but that such liability is widely coterminous with vicarious liability for employees. The only area where some case law has arisen as to vicarious liability for agents other than employees concerns vehicle drivers, but that area is still rather confused. See also *supra*, **5.E.2.**, Note (3).

[277] See Markesinis and Deakin at 142–5.

[278] See *Home Office* v. *Dorset Yacht Co. Ltd.* [1970] AC 1004, HL.

[279] See *Smith* v. *Littlewoods Organization Ltd.*, *supra*, Chapter III, **3.E.5.**

[280] See Rogers at 833–4; Markesinis and Deakin at 142–3.

[281] *Carmarthenshire County Council* v. *Lewis* [1955] AC 549 at 566, HL, per Lord Reid.

[282] See among others *supra*, 5.1.1.C. under a).

[283] *Handelsgesetzbuch* (Commercial Code) of 10 May 1897, BGBl.III.41000–1.

(liability of railway company for personal and property damage to passengers caused by personnel) and § 607 HGB (liability of charterer for personnel).[284]

Indeed, the provisions of the BGB concerning *delictual* liability (§§ 823–53 BGB) contain no true regime of liability for others. Nevertheless, mention should be made of § 832 BGB, which reads:

> (1) Anyone who is bound by law to exert authority over another person, because that person requires supervision on account of minority or of his physical or mental condition, is liable for the injury wrongfully inflicted by that person upon a third party. No liability arises when the duty to exert supervisory authority has been satisfied or when the injury would also have occurred even if that duty had been satisfied.
> (2) Anyone who undertakes by contract to exert the supervisory authority referred to in paragraph (1) is also liable under the terms of that paragraph.

It is apparent from the structure and wording of this provision that it is closely related to § 831(1) BGB. Indeed, it also creates a regime of presumed fault and causation, concerning parents and other persons who exert a right of supervision over minors or over adults who require supervision (because of a mental or physical handicap).[285]

The conditions for § 832 BGB to apply are as follows:

– The child or adult under supervision must have inflicted injury upon a third party. As is the case with the conduct of the *Verrichtungsgehilfe* under § 831(1) BGB, the victim must prove the *Tatbestand* and the unlawfulness (*Rechtswidrigkeit*), but not the fault (*Verschulden*) of the minor or adult under supervision.[286]
– The defendant was under a duty to supervise the minor or adult in question. The range of persons covered by § 832(1) BGB comprises among others parents, tutors, instructors (pursuant to the German system of workplace instruction or *Berufsbildung*); as for teachers and reform institutions, they are covered by § 839 BGB instead.[287] § 832(2) BGB extends the scope of § 832(1) BGB to persons who undertake the duty to supervise through contract (express or implied), including among others foster parents, health, educational and psychiatric institutions, nannies and nurses as well as relatives whom a child visits for a long period of time.[288]

Once these conditions are met, the defendant is presumed to have failed to discharge the duty to supervise and to have thereby caused the injury. It is up to that person to exonerate himself or herself by showing that the duty to supervise was complied with or that the injury would still have occurred even if that duty had been complied with. There is a considerable body of case law pertaining to the duty to supervise,[289] which is summed in this passage from a decision of the BGH from 10 July 1984:[290]

---

[284] On these regimes, see Staudinger-Belling/Eberl-Borges, § 831 at 66–8, para. 43–6.

[285] See on the regime of § 832 BGB in general Larenz/Canaris at 485–7.

[286] See Münchener-Stein, § 832 at 1809–10, para. 16–7. For the *Verrichtungsgehilfe*, see *supra*, 1.1.C. under b).

[287] See Münchener-Stein, § 832 at 1807–8, para. 5–12.

[288] Ibid. at 1808–9, para. 13.

[289] See ibid. at 1810–4, para. 18–28.

[290] BGH, 10 July 1984, NJW 1984, 2574 at 2575 (references omitted). See also the following leading cases, each concerning the scope of the duty to supervise for children at different ages: BGH, 29 May 1990, BGHZ 111, 282 (7-year old child); BGH, 6 April 1976, NJW 1976, 1684 (12-year old child) and BGH, 27 November 1979, NJW 1980, 1044 (17-year old child).

The scope of the duty to supervise minor children varies according to age, personality and character. The range of measures which are required and must be expected is to be determined by reference to the reasonable demands put on sensible parents, in the actual set of circumstances, to do something to prevent their child from inflicting upon a third party the kind of injury which actually occurred. In particular, depending on the personality of the child and his or her level of upbringing, it may be that general explanations and prohibitions alone would suffice or, on the other hand, that compliance with them should also be monitored. In that respect, it must not be forgotten that the degree of success in bringing up the child stands in correlation to the degree of supervision which must be exercised: the less effective the upbringing has been, the closer the supervision must be.

German law therefore leaves adequate room for persons in charge of supervising a child or adult in need of supervision to exonerate themselves.

c) The regime of liability for the harm caused by *préposés* pursuant to Article 1384(5) C.civ. is only one of the liability regimes contained in that provision, the relevant parts of which read:

[1] Everyone is liable for the damage caused not only by one's own conduct, but also by the conduct of persons for whom one is responsible or things in one's care (*garde*) . . .

[4] The father and the mother, if they have custody of the child, are jointly and severally liable for the damage caused by their minor child living with them;

[5] Principals [*maîtres*] and "employers" [*commettants*] [are liable] for the damage caused by their servants [*domestiques*] and "employees" [*préposés*] in the course of the functions for which they are employed;

[6] School teachers and craftsmen [are liable] for the damage caused by their pupils and apprentices while under their supervision;

[7] The aforementioned liability does not arise if the father and the mother, or the craftsmen, can establish that they could not prevent the injurious course of conduct;

[8] Any mistake, carelessness or negligence on the part of school teachers, which is alleged to have caused the injurious course of conduct, shall be established by the plaintiff . . .

That provision thus creates at least four distinctive liability regimes, namely:

1. liability of **parents** for damage caused by their minor children, at Article 1384(4) and (7). That regime is surveyed further below;[291]
2. liability of *commettants* for damage caused by their *préposés*, at Article 1384(5), as discussed in the previous sub-section;[292]
3. liability of **school teachers** for damage caused by pupils under their supervision, at Article 1384(6) and (8). The addition of Article 1384(8) in 1937[293] has turned it into a fault-based regime where the victim must prove fault, as under the general regime of Article 1382 C.civ. That regime will not be discussed further;[294]

---

[291] See *infra*, **5.F.24.** and Note (1) thereafter.

[292] As mentioned *supra*, 5.1.1.A. under a), the class of *commettants* and *préposés* include *maîtres* and *domestiques* respectively, so that but one regime applies to them.

[293] Added by the Act of 5 April 1937, DP 1938.Lég.41, which also provided for the State to assume any liability which may fall upon public school teachers pursuant to Article 1384(6) C.civ.

[294] See among others Le Tourneau and Cadiet at 859–64, para. 353–68 for further details.

4. liability of **craftsmen** for damage caused by their apprentices, at Article 1384(6) and (7). That regime follows the same lines as that of parents, and since it has lost much importance today, it will not be discussed further.[295]

In addition, there has been a long-standing debate among French legal writers as to whether Article 1384(1) C.civ. fulfilled merely an introductory function or, rather, gave rise to a general regime of liability for others, of which the four specific regimes mentioned in the subsequent paragraphs might be but illustrations.[296] The first interpretation dominated until 1991, when the Assemblée plénière of the Cour de cassation made an about-turn in the first case reproduced below.

Furthermore, within a few weeks in 1997, the Cour de cassation handed down two very significant decisions which are reproduced below, whereby fault (with a presumption against the defendant) was definitely displaced as the basis for the liability of parents for their children (second case), and the objective nature of the general regime of liability for others was recognized (third case).

Cass. Ass. plén., 29 March 1991[297]   **5.F.23.**
Association des centres éducatifs du Limousin v. *Blieck*

GENERAL REGIME OF LIABILITY FOR OTHERS

Fire lit by mentally handicapped person

A body which takes charge of the organization and control of the activities of a mentally handicapped person is liable pursuant to Article 1384(1) C.civ. for the damage caused by that person.

Facts: X suffered from a mental handicap. He was placed in a centre operated by the defendant association, where a relatively open form of caretaking was practised, which involved the mentally handicapped person being entrusted with some work outside the centre during the day. While working outside the centre one day, X set fire to a forest belonging to the plaintiff Blieck. Since the defendant association did not fall within any of the specific categories of persons who are liable for others in Articles 1384(2) to (8) C.civ., the plaintiffs sued the association on the basis of Article 1384(1) C.civ.

Held: The court of first instance and the court of appeal found that the defendant association was liable. The Cour de cassation upheld the decision of the court of appeal.

Judgment: "Against the judgment of the court of appeal finding [the defendant] liable for damages under Article 1384(1) C.civ., [the defendant argues] that liability for others only arises in those cases provided for by law, and that the court of appeal did not state on which legal basis the association should be responsible for people that are entrusted to its care.

However, the [court of appeal] found that the centre operated by the association was intended to receive mentally handicapped people supervised in a protected environment, and that X . . . was under a programme involving total freedom of movement during the day.

---

[295] See among others Le Tourneau and Cadiet at 843–4, para. 3431–9 for further details.

[296] With respect to liability for things, the same debate took place earlier: see Chapter VI, 6.1.2.

[297] Bull.civ. 1991.Ass.plén.1, D 1991.Jur.324, with note by C. Larroumet, JCP 1991.II.21673, with conclusions of Advocate General D.H. Dontenwille and note by J. Ghestin, Gaz.Pal. 1991.Jur.513, with note by F. Chabas. Translation by Y. P. Salmon.

In the light of these findings, from which it is clear that the association had accepted the task of organizing and controlling the life of this handicapped person on a permanent basis, the court of appeal rightly decided that the association should answer for him under Article 1384(1) C.civ. and was liable to provide reparation for the damage which he had caused. It follows that the plea is not founded."

Notes

(1) At the time the annotated case came before the Assemblée plénière of the Cour de cassation, in spite of sporadic resistance by courts and legal writers, it was received wisdom under French law that Article 1384(1) C.civ. did *not* create a general regime of liability for others. Even though it had been established since the turn of the century that the same provision created a general regime of liability for things,[298] the wording of Article 1384(1) C.civ. as it relates to persons ("Everyone is liable for the damage caused . . . by the conduct of persons for whom one is responsible") was thought to be tautological, so that the following paragraphs of Article 1384 C.civ. contained an exhaustive enumeration of the persons for whom one is answerable.[299] Moreover, liability for others was perceived as a derogation from the individualistic approach of the *Code civil*, so that it should be confined to the specific cases listed in Article 1384 C.civ.

(2) Nonetheless, the Assemblée plénière in the annotated case chose to turn received wisdom on its head and to recognize the existence of a general regime of liability for others. In his conclusions, Advocate General Dontenwille mentions a series of reasons that may have led the court to decide as it did:[300]

– It is difficult to argue that Article 1384(1) C.civ. gives rise to a general regime of liability for things but not for others. The general regime of liability for things was developed out of "social need", in view of the increasing risk created through the mechanization of production, transport, etc. A similar need has arisen in view of the "social risk" created by the use of improved methods to take care of the mentally handicapped, whereby they experience greater integration into the social fabric.
– In Germany, under § 832 BGB, liability for others is extended beyond parents to those in charge of the mentally handicapped.[301]
– Under administrative law, public institutions in charge of mentally handicapped persons that used the same method of care as the private association at issue in the annotated case would engage the liability of the State on a no-fault basis for injury caused by their patients, given that the methods in question expose the general public to a special risk of injury.[302]

(3) The opinion of the Advocate General was thus very much centred on the facts of the annotated case and did not request the court to make a broad statement of principle

---

[298] That regime is discussed *infra*, Chapter VI, 6.1.2.
[299] That argument is developed in the note of F. Chabas on the annotated case at Gaz.Pal. 1991.Jur.513.
[300] These conclusions are reproduced at JCP 1991.II.21673.
[301] On § 832 BGB, see *supra*, Introductory Note under b).
[302] On the no-fault State liability regime, see *supra*, Chapter III, 3.3.3.B. For a more complete analysis of the annotated case in the light of administrative law, see the note of P. Bon, "La responsabilité du fait des personnes dont on a la garde: sur un rapprochement des jurisprudences administrative et judiciaire" (1991) 7 RFDA 991.

on the general regime of liability for others as it may apply under different circumstances. The Cour de cassation followed suit and ruled narrowly on the facts of the case, finding that Article 1384(1) had rightly been applied by the court of appeal. The reasoning of the court appeared to be based on the fact that the defendant association had accepted permanent responsibility for organizing and controlling the activities of the person who caused injury.[303]

Despite the narrowness of the holding of the Cour de cassation, authors who commented upon the annotated case, while generally positive in their assessment, did not fail to underline that it opened the door to the progressive development of a general regime of liability for others.[304]

(4) It is still too early to give a precise picture of the scope of application of that general regime. In subsequent cases, it was found to apply to an association to which the custody (*garde*) of a child had been transferred pursuant to a court order under Article 375 C.civ., along the same lines as the annotated case.[305] But the general regime was also extended to amateur sport clubs whose mission is to organize, lead and control the activities of their members in sporting events in which they take part, but not on a permanent basis as in the annotated case,[306] and possibly also to a municipality for the damage caused to adjacent properties by persons who squatted in one of its buildings, although the municipality was not in charge of controlling the activities of the squatters.[307] The general regime has thus been extended beyond the rationale of the annotated case.

On the other hand, the Cour de cassation has refused to extend the general regime of liability for others under Article 1384(1) C.civ. to school teachers (who are covered by the specific regime of Article 1384(6) C.civ.),[308] to a grandparent and an aunt,[309] or to the tutor and legal administrator of a mentally handicapped adult.[310] The conclusions of the Advocate General in the latter case make it clear that the Cour de cassation is reluctant to make natural persons liable pursuant to Article 1384(1) C.civ.[311]

---

[303] As noted by C. Larroumet in his case comment on the annotated case at D 1991.Jur.324.

[304] See the notes of J. Ghestin, JCP 1991.II.21673; F. Chabas, Gaz.Pal. 1992.Jur.613; C. Larroumet, ibid. as well as P. Jourdain, Chronique at (1991) 90 RTDciv. 541 and G. Viney, "Vers un élargissement de la catégorie des 'personnes dont on doit répondre': la porte entrouverte sur une nouvelle interprétation de l'article 1384, alinéa 1er du code civil" D 1991.Chron.157.

[305] Cass. crim., 10 October 1996, Bull.crim. 1996.357, D 1997.Jur.309, JCP 1997.II.22833, with note by F. Chabas. See also *infra*, **5.F.25.**

[306] Cass. civ. 2e, 22 May 1995 (2 cases), Bull.civ. 1995.II.155, D 1996.Somm.29, JCP 1995.II.22550.

[307] Cass. civ. 2e, 22 May 1995, Bull.civ. 1995.II.149. See the comments of G. Viney, JCP 1995.I.3893; P. Jourdain (1995) 94 RTDciv. 902 and T. Le Bars and K. Buhler, D 1996.Jur.453.

[308] Cass. civ. 2e, 16 March 1994, Bull.civ. 1994.II.92.

[309] Cass. civ. 2e, 18 September 1996, Bull.civ. 1996.II.217, D 1998.Jur.118, with note by M. Rebourg. See also the comments of P. Jourdain (1997) 96 RTDciv. 436 and G. Blanc, "À propos de la responsabilité des grands-parents . . . (brève contribution à la réflexion sur la responsabilité du fait d'autrui)" D 1997.Chron.327.

[310] Cass. civ. 2e, 25 February 1998, D 1998.Jur.315, JCP 1998.II.10149.

[311] Conclusions of Advocate General R. Kessous, at D 1998.Jur.315. See also the comments of G. Viney, JCP 1998.I.144 and A.-M. Galliou-Scanvion, "L'article 1384, alinéa 1er, et la responsabilité du fait d'autrui: un fardeau non transférable sur les épaules du tuteur" D 1998.Chron.240.

Cass. civ. 2e, 19 February 1997[312]   **5.F.24.–25.**
Bertrand v. *Domingues*
and
Cass. crim., 26 March 1997[313]
Foyer Notre-Dame des Flots

Objective liability regimes

The general liability for others pursuant to Article 1384(1) C.civ. and parental liability for children pursuant to Article 1384(4) C.civ. are objective liability regimes.

A. Cass. civ. 2e, 19 February 1997   **5.F.24.**

Child cyclist on highway

Facts: As he was riding his bicycle, the 12-year old S. Bertrand made a sudden dash across a main road, cutting across the path of the plaintiff Domingues on his motorcycle. The plaintiff was injured in the resulting collision, and he sued the boy's father, J.-C. Bertrand, pursuant to Article 1384(4) C.civ.

Held: The court of appeal held that the defendant was liable. The Cour de cassation upheld the decision of the court of appeal.

Judgment: "Against the judgment [of the court of appeal] which held J.-C. Bertrand liable, [the defendant] argues that the presumption that the parents are liable for their minor child, under Article 1384(4) C.civ., can be set aside not only in case of *force majeure* or contributory negligence by the victim, but also when the parents prove that they did not commit a fault in the supervision or upbringing of the child. [Accordingly,] the court of appeal did not apply Article 1384(4) C.civ. correctly when it refused to examine whether J.-C. Bertrand could prove that he committed no fault in the supervision [of his child], on the ground that only *force majeure* or contributory negligence could exclude his objective liability.

However, having correctly held that only *force majeure* or contributory negligence could relieve J.-C. Bertrand from the objective liability resulting from the damage caused by his minor son which lived with him, the court of appeal did not need to examine whether there was a lack of supervision on the part of the father."

B. Cass. crim., 26 March 1997   **5.F.25.**

Car stolen by teenager gang

Facts: Three teenage girls, Z, D and C, had been placed in the defendant care centre, Foyer Notre-Dame des Flots, pursuant to a court order under Article 375 C.civ. While under the care of the centre, they committed a series of thefts, including that of E's car. E alleged that the Foyer was liable under the general regime of liability for others created by Article 1384(1) C.civ.

---

[312] Bull.civ. 1997.II.56, JCP 1997.II.22848, with conclusions of Advocate General R. Kessous and note by G. Viney, D 1997.Jur.496, with note by P. Jourdain, Gaz.Pal. 1997.Jur.572, with note by F. Chabas. Translation by Y. P. Salmon.
[313] Bull.crim. 1997.124, No. 2, JCP 1997.II.22868, with report of F. Desportes, D 1997.Jur.496, with note by P. Jourdain. Translation by Y. P. Salmon.

Held: The court of first instance and the court of appeal found that the defendant was liable. The Cour de cassation upheld the decision of the court of appeal.

Judgment: "The [court of appeal] found that, since it was entrusted with the custody and care [of Z, C and D], the [Foyer Notre-Dame des Flots] was in charge of controlling and organizing their life on a permanent basis. It held 'that [the Foyer] is thus liable in the sense of Article 1384(1) C.civ. without the need to prove fault' on its part.

In so holding, the court of appeal correctly applied the law.

Indeed the persons who are liable for others pursuant to Art. 1384(1) C.civ. cannot escape the objective liability resulting from that provision by demonstrating that they committed no fault."

Notes

(1) The French regime of parental liability for harm caused by their children has undergone profound change in the last fifteen years, ending with the first annotated case.

The conditions for parental liability pursuant to Article 1384(4) C.civ. to apply are as follows:

— A minor child has caused injury to the victim. Since a decision of the Assemblée plénière of 9 May 1984, it seems that it would even no longer be necessary to prove even that the conduct of the child, viewed objectively, constituted a fault; only causation is relevant.[314]
— The defendant is the child's father or mother [315] and has the custody of the child.[316]
— The child was living with him or her.[317] Authors generally agree that the case law relating to this condition will have to be revisited in light of the first annotated case.[318]

Up until the first annotated case, the application of Article 1384(4) C.civ. led to a presumption of fault. The parents could escape liability if they could show that the injurious conduct of the child was due to no fault on their part in the upbringing and supervision of the child. That defence had already became somewhat incongruous as a result of the decision of 9 May 1984 mentioned above, which appeared to make parents potentially liable for any conduct of their child which led to injury, irrespective of whether that conduct would objectively constitute a fault.

In the first annotated case, the Cour de cassation decided to return to a literal reading of Article 1384(7) C.civ., whereby parents can escape liability "if [they] can establish that they could not prevent the injurious course of conduct".[319] That provision makes no reference to fault or its absence, and accordingly the parents should be liable unless they can show *cause étrangère* (including *force majeure*)[320] or the fault of the victim.

---

[314] Cass. Ass. plén., 9 May 1984, *Fullenwarth*, Bull.civ. 1984.Ass.plén.4, D 1984.Jur.525, JCP 1984.II.20255. See also *supra*, Chapter III, **3.F.19**.
[315] No other relative can be made liable for harm caused by a child pursuant to Article 1384(4) C.civ., as recalled in Cass. civ. 2e, 25 January 1995, Bull.civ. 1995.II.29.
[316] See F. Alt-Maes, "La garde, fondement de la responsabilité du fait du mineur" JCP 1998.I.154.
[317] On that condition, see Le Tourneau and Cadiet at 839–40, para. 3396–401.
[318] See the comments of P. Jourdain, D 1997.Jur.265 and G. Viney, JCP 1997.II.22848.
[319] See the conclusions of Advocate General R. Kessous in the first annotated case, JCP 1997.II.22848.
[320] The Cour de cassation does not mention from whose perspective *cause étrangère* is to be appreciated, but it should logically be from that of the parents, i.e. the parents will be exonerated if the cause of injury was unforeseeable and irresistible by *them*: see the comments of P. Jourdain, D 1997.Jur.265; F. Chabas, Gaz.Pal. 1997.Jur. 572 and G. Viney, JCP 1997.II.22848. On the difficulties in applying the concept of *cause étrangère* to the conduct of a child, see Cass. crim., 25 March 1998, JCP 1998.II.10162, with note by M. Huyette.

(2) The decision of 29 March 1991 of the Cour of cassation, discussed previously, did not specify the nature of the general regime of liability for others.[321] Most commentators, however, thought that the Cour de cassation implicitly acknowledged that it was an objective liability regime, or that such a conclusion was unavoidable.[322] Their opinion was strengthened by the first annotated case, where the regimes of liability for presumed fault at Article 1384 C.civ. were turned into objective liability regimes.[323]

Accordingly, the Cour de cassation in the second annotated case expressly stated that the general regime of liability for others pursuant to Article 1384(1) C.civ. is an objective liability regime, whereby the defendant cannot avoid liability by showing that he or she was not at fault. Thus, it would seem that in such cases, only proof that the injury was caused by a *force majeure* or through the victim's fault will afford a good defence.[324]

(3) As a result of the first and second annotated cases, the various regimes of liability for others at Article 1384 C.civ. have been brought in line: the general regime, liability for children and apprentices as well as liability for employees are all objective regimes. Only the liability of school teachers for injury caused by pupils remains under a fault-based regime, but that is expressly mandated by Article 1384(8) C.civ.

The stage is therefore set for the elaboration of a general theory of liability for others under French law, which would bring all those regimes together. As a consequence, it is likely that remaining differences will be questioned and perhaps removed. Among them, one of the most significant is the requirement that the *préposé* be shown to be at fault for the *commettant* to be liable under Article 1384(5) C.civ.[325] Although the issue is not settled, it is arguable that under the other liability regimes, the child or person under control and supervision, as the case may be, need only have caused injury to the victim for liability to be triggered. Accordingly, some authors have already begun to argue that the requirement of fault on the part of the *préposé* should be removed.[326]

5.3. COMPARATIVE OVERVIEW

The first section has shown that the legal systems under study all have fairly well-developed regimes of liability for harm caused by employees, which share much in common but differ on certain significant aspects. Beyond those regimes, however, only French law offers significant developments as regards liability for others.

---

[321] See *supra*, **5.F.23.**

[322] See J. Ghestin, JCP 1991.II.21673; P. Jourdain, (1991) 90 RTDciv. 541; F. Chabas, Gaz.Pal. 1992.Jur.513.

[323] The effect of the first annotated case must logically extend to the regime of liability for apprentices, which is structured along the same lines as liability for children: see G. Viney, JCP 1997.II.22848.

[324] See the comment of P. Jourdain, D 1997.Jur.496.

[325] *Supra*, 5.1.1.A. under b).

[326] See Viney and Jourdain, *Conditions* at 892–4, para. 807 and Bénac-Schmidt/Larroumet at 34, para. 359–67. Contra: Overstake at 143/24, para. 125–35, Dejean de la Bâtie at 239–40, para. 103 and J.-C. Saint-Pau, "La responsabilité du fait d'autrui est-elle devenue une responsabilité personnelle et directe?" Rep. Ass. 1998.Chron.22.

The two approaches to liability for employees

Irrespective of any specific regime in that respect, a person who entrusts certain tasks to another person can always incur direct personal liability for injury which was the immediate result of the conduct of that other person, provided that the conditions for liability under the general regime in French law (Articles 1382–1383 C.civ.), under one of the general clauses in German law (§§ 823(1), 823(2) or 826 BGB) or under one of the causes of action in tort in English law, as the case may be, are met. Such liability may be incurred if, for instance, the first person carelessly chose the other person and gave that other person the requisite means (tools, etc.) to cause damage. In all the legal systems studied here, however, the organization of the economy into larger units of production in the course of the 19th century made it obvious that such a solution was, by itself, totally inappropriate, since it imposed a very heavy evidentiary burden on the victim.

Broadly speaking, once it is decided to create a specific regime covering liability for harm caused by employees, two approaches are possible. On the one hand, the basic idea that the employer is personally liable for its own fault can be preserved, but the burden of proof can be shifted onto the employer in certain respects in relation to which it is deemed that the employer is in a better position than the victim to present the relevant evidence. On the other hand, the very rationale for imposing liability upon the employer can be questioned, and fault-based liability can be replaced with objective liability. In the modern context, it makes sense simply to make the employer liable whenever liability is incurred by an employee, that is to say, it makes better sense to do so from a moral perspective (the employer is the one who deploys the workforce and derives the benefit from its activities) and an economic perspective (the employer is arguably better placed to take efficient precautionary measures, to insure the liability arising from the conduct of its employees and to shoulder the risk by spreading the costs, as it does for other risks related to the firm). Liability can then be imposed on the basis either that the employer must bear the risks associated with its activities or that it should act as a guarantor towards third parties as regards injury caused by its employees.

The three systems reviewed here have taken different paths:

- the framers of the German BGB have chosen to retain a liability regime based on the fault of the *Geschäftsherr* at § 831(1) BGB, with a presumption of fault (*Verschulden*) and a presumption of causation between that fault and the injurious conduct of the *Verrichtungsgehilfe*;[327]
- under French law, it became established in the course of the 19th century that Article 1384(5) C.civ. created a objective liability regime whereby the *commettant* had to shoulder the burden of compensating third parties injured by its *préposé*, irrespective of any fault on the part of the *commettant*; to this day debate still continues as to whether the rationale for this regime lies in risk or guarantee;[328]
- vicarious liability of employers for their employees under English law also results in the employer being bound to assume liability for harm caused by its employees, regardless of its own primary liability; it appears that this objective liability regime

---

[327] *Supra*, 5.1.1.C. under a).
[328] *Supra*, 5.1.1.A. under c) and e).

rests on the proposition that the employer should bear the risks associated with its operations.[329]

German law has therefore followed a different path from French and English law. Nonetheless, the contrast between German law, on the one hand, and French and English law, on the other, is not so sharp as their differing theoretical foundations would make it appear. For one thing, German legal writers widely acknowledge that the regime of § 831(1) BGB is deficient,[330] so that it has been "displaced" in part by an expansive construction of neighbouring liability regimes that do not depend on the fault of the *Geschäftsherr*—including contractual liability for others (§ 278 BGB), liability for corporate organs (§ 31 BGB) and primary liability for organizational deficiencies (*Organisationsverschulden* under § 823(1) BGB) as well as State liability (§ 839 BGB).[331] Where those neighbouring regimes come to bear, then German law operates under objective liability. Furthermore, even if the French and English liability regimes generally do not depend on the primary liability of the *commettant* or employer, in certain areas their approach shows traces of a fault-based regime. For instance, under French law, the existence of a *lien de préposition* is still primarily determined by reference to the power to give instructions (which would mean that the *commettant* should be liable only for those persons whose behaviour it could have influenced),[332] as opposed to English law, where the overall economic relationship is taken into account.[333] Similarly, English case-law relating to certain areas (liability for doctors working in a hospital, liability for theft committed by employees) is very much focussed on the primary liability of the employer.[334]

General conditions

The general conditions of the French, English and German regimes of liability for employees are broadly similar.[335] Under all three regimes, the victim must show that:

– he or she suffered injury that was unlawfully caused by someone ('X'), so that in principle X would also be liable in tort or delict.[336] Under German law, it suffices to show that X's conduct fulfilled the *Tatbestand* of a head of liability and was wrongful (*rechtswidrig*); it is not necessary to show that X was at fault (*Verschulden*);[337]

– X stood—broadly speaking—in an employment relationship to the person whom the victim is seeking to make liable. Under French law, the former is called *préposé*, the latter *commettant* and the relationship *lien de préposition*. Under English law, the terms employee and employer are now commonly used. Under German law, the first person is called *Verrichtungsgehilfe* and the second, *Geschäftsherr*;

---

[329] *Supra*, 5.1.1.B. under a) and c).
[330] *Supra*, 5.1.1.C. under f).
[331] *Supra*, 5.1.1.C. under g) to j).
[332] *Supra*, **5.F.1.** and notes thereafter.
[333] *Supra*, **5.E.2.** and notes thereafter.
[334] *Supra*, **5.E.5.**, **5.E.17.** and notes thereafter.
[335] *Supra*, 5.1.1.A. under b), 5.1.1.B. under b), 5.1.1.C. under b). See also von Bar I at 198 ff., 351 ff., para. 179 ff. and 337 ff.
[336] See on this, from a broader perspective, von Bar I at 213–6, para. 196–9.
[337] See *supra*, 5.1.1.C. under e) for a discussion of how the debate between the Result and Conduct Theories may affect what the victim has to show with respect to the person who caused the injury.

– the conduct which caused the injury came within the scope of employment: Article 1384(5) C.civ. refers to "the functions for which [the *préposé*] is employed" (and case law thus requires that the conduct should have taken place "within such functions"), the common law refers to the course of employment and § 831(1) BGB refers to "the accomplishment of the task".

Beyond that, the differences between the regimes come to the fore. Under the French and English regimes, once the victim has demonstrated that the three conditions set out above are fulfilled, the liability of the *commettant* or employer is engaged, unless for some reason the liability of the *préposé* or employee is negated (force majeure affecting the *préposé*, assumption of risk by the victim, etc.).[338] In contrast, under § 831(1) BGB, as interpreted in German case law, the following means of exoneration are available to the *Geschäftsherr*: absence of fault on its part (assessed on a decentralized basis), absence of causation between any fault of the *Geschäftsherr* and the injury, as well as compliance of the *Verrichtungsgehilfe* with all applicable norms of conduct (*verkehrsrichtiges Verhalten*); on balance, the case law under § 831(1) BGB has put the *Geschäftsherr* in a relatively favourable position.[339]

The position of the employee, préposé *or* Verrichtungsgehilfe

It might be thought that, besides its main purpose of improving the position of victims, the liability regime for harm caused by employees would also seek to channel liability away from the employee towards the employer.

Under French law, the position of the *préposé* is undergoing a change, in the wake of a decision of the Cour de cassation of 12 October 1993.[340] Traditionally the *préposé* remained liable to the victim and could be called upon to indemnify the *commettant* against the sums paid to the victim pursuant to Article 1384(5) C.civ. Now a new concept of "personal fault" has been introduced, so that the *préposé* will not be directly liable to the victim or liable to indemnify the *commettant* unless he or she committed a "personal fault". These new developments owe much to the desire to bring the liability regime of Article 1384(5) C.civ. into line with the regime prevailing for civil servants in administrative law. Yet the precise meaning of "personal fault" in the context of Article 1384(5) C.civ. still remains to be developed. Under English law, the employee remains liable to the victim but, as between the employer and the employee, although the employer has a right to contribution from the employee, in practice the employer virtually never seeks it.[341] Similarly, under German law, the *Verrichtungsgehilfe* remains liable to the victim directly if his or her personal liability is engaged,[342] but if the *Verrichtungsgehilfe* is a worker (as is most often the case), the contributory recourse of the employer against the employee is limited.[343]

It therefore appears that in all three systems, the employee receives some protection, whether through law or practice, from recourses against him or her by the employer, but

[338] *Supra,* 5.1.1.A. under c), 5.1.1.B. under c).
[339] *Supra,* 5.1.1.C. under d) to f).
[340] See *supra.* 5.1.1.A. under d).
[341] See *supra,* 5.1.1.B. under d).
[342] I.e. if the victim can also prove *Verschulden* as regards the *Verrichtungsgehilfe*.
[343] *Supra,* 5.1.1.C. under c).

that with the apparent exception of French law under certain circumstances, the employee remains exposed to personal liability towards the victim, should the victim decide to pursue a claim against the employee directly. In this respect, a number of other European legal systems seem to have gone further than the three systems under study here.[344]

Relationship with other liability regimes

In the legal systems studied here, the regime of tort liability for harm caused by employees interacts with other liability regimes.

Firstly, **contractual liability for others** is present in varying degrees of development in French, English and German law. Unlike tort liability for harm caused by employees, it runs along fairly similar lines in all three systems: a person who is under a contractual obligation towards another (the "debtor") will be liable for any breach that may be committed by other persons whom the debtor has brought in to discharge his or her contractual obligations.[345] Contractual liability for others can be more advantageous for the plaintiff than tort liability for employees, in that no particular relationship needs to be shown between the person who was the immediate cause of the damage and the defendant.[346] On the other hand, it must be shown that the defendant was under a contractual obligation to the plaintiff, whereas tort liability for employees will also apply between strangers.[347] Under French and English law, contractual liability for others leads to the same result as tort liability for employees, namely the objective liability of the employer/debtor, so that in the end it may not matter much which one is used.[348] Under German law, contractual liability for others under § 278 BGB has been given a wide scope of application in order to overcome the deficiencies of § 831(1) BGB.[349]

Secondly, **liability for corporate organs** is equally known to French, English and German law.[350] All these systems operate a similar regime: once it is established that a person (or a group of persons) was acting as a corporate organ, any civil liability incurred by the persons or group in that capacity will automatically be imputed to the corporation.[351] Liability for corporate organs does not per se constitute a form of liability for others, since the conduct of the corporate organs is in fact deemed to be the conduct of the

---

[344] See von Bar I at 210–2, para. 193, giving as an example Belgian law, where the employee is not liable to third parties for accidental injury.

[345] See *supra*, 5.1.1.A. under f), 5.1.1.B. under e), 5.1.1.C. under g).

[346] Contractual liability for others reaches beyond the class of *préposés*, employees or *Verrichtungsgehilfe*, as the case may be, to include all persons who execute the obligations of the debtor, including independent contractors, among others.

[347] In addition, under German law, damages for non-material injury (e.g. pain and suffering) cannot be claimed under § 278 BGB since, in relation to contractual liability, there is no provision similar to § 847 BGB.

[348] Under French law, Article 1384(5) C.civ. is frequently used as a legal basis in situations where the principles of contractual liability for others should have been applied: see *supra*, 5.1.1.A. under f). Under English law, the cases concerning the negligence of physicians operating in hospitals have been solved by reference to contractual liability for others, which has enabled courts to avoid having to go into the issue whether a physician can be an employee: see *supra*, **5.E.5.** and Note (2) thereafter.

[349] See *supra*, 5.1.1.C. under g) and, for a concrete example where § 278 BGB can provide relief to the plaintiff whereas the *Geschäftsherr* would not be liable under § 831(1) BGB, see *supra*, **5.G.22.**

[350] Liability for corporate organs is discussed from a broader perspective in von Bar I at 189 ff., 349–51, para. 168 ff. and 335–6.

[351] See *supra*, 5.1.1.A. under g), 5.1.1.B. under g), 5.1.1.C. under h).

corporation itself.[352] Liability for corporate organs offers a structure comparable to that of liability for employees: instead of establishing that the person who caused the injury was an employee, *préposé* or *Verrichtungsgehilfe*, as the case may be, it must be shown that that person qualified as a corporate organ. Under French and English law, liability for corporate organs complements liability for employees, in that it ensures "seamless coverage": in practice, a person working within a large corporation should either be one of its employees or *préposés*, or be acting as one of its organs. Under German law, liability for corporate organs pursuant to § 31 BGB does not offer any means of exoneration to the corporation, in contrast to the regime of § 831(1) BGB: § 31 BGB has therefore been given a wide scope in order to compensate for the weaknesses of § 831(1) BGB, by adopting a wider conception of the corporate organ than under French or English law. Accordingly, under German law, there might be some overlap between liability under §§ 31 and 831(1) BGB:[353] for instance, the branch manager of a bank, while a *Verrichtungsgehilfe* for the purposes of § 831(1) BGB, would likely also qualify as a corporate organ,[354] so that the bank should assume civil liability for his or her conduct pursuant to § 31 BGB.[355]

Thirdly, **State liability** also exerts an influence on the regime of liability for harm caused by employees. Under English law, the State is liable, under the general rules of vicarious and corporate liability, for torts committed in the course of their office or employment by State employees (civil servants and members of the armed forces) and by Government ministers.[356] Under German law, the specific regime of State liability for officials (*Beamte*) pursuant to § 839 BGB applies to all the sovereign activities of the State; § 831(1) BGB remains applicable to non-sovereign activities.[357] § 839 BGB does not provide the State with means of defence such as that afforded in other cases by § 831(1) BGB; accordingly the realm of sovereign activities has been construed generously in order to circumvent the weaknesses of § 831(1) BGB. French administrative law contains a liability regime for damage caused by State employees, which runs in parallel to Article 1384(5) C.civ.[358] In recent times, there has been a growing tendency for the two systems to converge. A concern for equality of treatment under Article 1384(5) C.civ. and under administrative law has been behind many of the recent breakthroughs concerning that provision,[359] including the introduction of the concept of "personal fault" to limit the range of cases where the *préposé* remains liable to the victim personally and liable to indemnify the

---

[352] Even if the end-result is the same (the corporation pays for the damage caused by a person), it is therefore inappropriate to speak of "objective" or "vicarious" liability in the case of liability for corporate organs.

[353] It is also possible that a gap would arise, in the case of less structured forms of business organization which generally do not enjoy legal personality, like civil law partnerships (i.e. pursuant to C.civ. or BGB provisions) or general partnerships (at common law) partnership. In such cases, the partners will generally not qualify as employees, nor will they be corporate organs: see for example *supra*, **5.G.3.**

[354] See *supra*, **5.G.22.** and Note (6) thereafter.

[355] Failure to appoint as an organ a person who qualifies as one according to the criterion put forward under German case law constitutes an organizational fault which gives rise to liability under § 823(1) BGB: *supra*, 5.1.1.C. under h).

[356] *Supra*, 5.1.1.B. under h).

[357] *Supra*, 5.1.1.C. under j).

[358] *Supra*, 5.1.1.A. under h).

[359] In addition, the same concern has played a significant role in the "discovery" of a general regime of liability for others under Article 1384(1) C.civ.: see *supra*, **5.F.23.**, Note (2).

commettant[360] and the recognition that, under certain circumstances, a doctor can be the *préposé* of a private hospital.[361]

Last but not least, a subtle balance exists between liability for harm caused by employees and the **direct and personal liability** of the employer. Indeed, one of the main advantages of the liability regime for harm caused by employees is that it can be invoked by any and all third parties with whom employees may come in contact and to whom they may cause injury, irrespective of whether there was any pre-existing relationship between the employer and the third party. Yet, as more and more general duties are imposed by law or through case law upon the employer, the likelihood increases that the employer may be in breach of one of those duties when a third party (passer-by, etc.) suffers injury through a purely random encounter with an employee, and, in some cases, it may then be more advantageous for the victim to go down the direct liability route against the employer.[362] Under German law, § 831(1) BGB is now seen as a specific provision concerning some of the *Verkehrspflichten* resting upon the *Geschäftsherr*:[363] since § 831(1) BGB allows the *Geschäftsherr* generous means of exoneration, it may be that the *Geschäftsherr* would be in a more difficult position under § 823(1) BGB in having to deny the violation of another *Verkehrspflicht*, such as a duty to provide for the performance of certain functions (surveillance, etc.) within its organization.[364] In English and French law, since the liability regime for harm caused by employees is more favourable to the victim than under German law, direct liability of the employer plays a complementary role. Under English law, the employer is under a growing number of non-delegable duties, a breach of which entails the employer's direct liability, even if committed by an independent contractor for whom the employer is not vicariously liable.[365] Similarly, under French law, liability under Article 1382 C.civ. may be engaged for fault in allowing a third party to believe that a person was a *préposé* when that was not so.[366]

The concept of employee

As seen above, the liability regimes for harm caused by employees studied here all require that the victim show that the person whose conduct led to injury was an employee of the person whose liability is sought. However, the test for determining whether that was the case varies slightly from one system to the other; French and German law (like the other codification systems) focus on control, whereas English law takes a broader view.[367]

In line with its risk-based rationale for vicarious liability, English law has moved away from exclusive reliance on control over the work as the criterion for employment, towards

---

[360] See *supra*, 5.1.1.A. under d).

[361] *Supra*, **5.F.4.** and notes thereafter.

[362] As, for instance, when the individual employee who caused the injury was not himself or herself negligent or at fault, but when the organization of the business was deficient, e.g. because too few people were assigned to a task or the employees were not given the requisite equipment.

[363] *Supra*, 5.1.1.C. under i).

[364] For an example, see the organizational duty (*Organisationspflicht*) to appoint persons to watch over employees working on third-party property at BGH, 4 November 1953, *supra*, **5.G.18.** and Note (3) thereafter.

[365] *Supra*, 5.1.1.B. under f).

[366] See *supra*, **5.F.1.** and Note (1) thereafter.

[367] See von Bar I at 207 ff., para. 191 ff. (codification systems) and 354 ff., para. 340 ff. (Nordic and common law systems).

a so-called "composite approach".[368] Pursuant to that approach, a series of factors are examined in order to see who bears the various risks related to the task in question. Normally the employee bears little risk beyond that of unemployment; the employer bears the other risks (e.g. risk that the work would not be ready on time, etc.), and it is only logical that it should also bear the risk that the employee causes damage to a third party.

Under French law, on the other hand, the hallmark of the *lien de préposition* remains the power of the *commettant* to give instructions to the *préposé*.[369] To the extent that the foundation of the regime of Article 1384(5) C.civ. is shifting away from guarantee towards risk, however, it is possible that French law may also evolve an approach similar to that of English law: the fact that the *préposé* was working for the *commettant* and not for himself or herself would then play the decisive role.[370]

German law also relies essentially on the right to give instructions (*Weisungsrecht*) as the criterion to assess whether a person is a *Verrichtungsgehilfe* for another: since § 831(1) BGB creates a regime of presumed fault and causation, it is logical that the *Geschäftsherr* should be liable only for those persons whose injurious conduct it could have prevented through the proper use of its right to give instructions.[371]

It is also noteworthy that English law uses a single concept of employee for the purposes of vicarious liability, social security, labour law and other fields of law. Vicarious liability in English law therefore applies only to employees.[372] By contrast, both *préposé* and *Verrichtungsgehilfe* are concepts specifically used for the purposes of the liability regimes of Article 1384(5) C.civ. and § 831(1) BGB, respectively. Even if the *préposé* is more often than not an employee within the meaning of labour law, Article 1384(5) C.civ. has also been applied to agents, contractors, relatives or even persons who did a friendly favour.[373] Similarly, the concept of *Verrichtungsgehilfe* can extend beyond workers (*Arbeitnehmer*) in the sense of labour law, so as to cover contractors, craftsmen or traders, depending on the circumstances.[374]

All three systems studied here have faced a challenge in resolving the position of professionals, especially physicians, who possess specialist knowledge which they apply under their own control, and who are usually bound by professional rules to remain independent. Nevertheless, today professionals are often part of larger organizations (e.g. physicians in hospitals) and work much like specialized employees; accordingly, plaintiffs have sought to make the large organizations in question liable for the professionals working within them. In the case of the liability of hospitals for harm caused by physicians, the legal systems studied here have taken different starting points, but they have all reached the same conclusion, namely that physicians can under certain circumstances be *préposés*, employees or *Verrichtungsgehilfe*, as the case may be. French law appears to have been the most reluctant to reach that conclusion, although the issue does not arise all that

---

[368] See *supra*, **5.E.2.** and notes thereafter.
[369] See *supra*, **5.F.1.** and Note (1) thereafter.
[370] Ibid., Note (3).
[371] See *supra*, **5.G.3.** and Notes (2) and (3) thereafter.
[372] See *supra*, **5.E.2.**, Notes (2) and (3): there are few cases where vicarious liability has been applied outside of the employment context.
[373] See *supra*, **5.F.1.**, Note (4).
[374] See *supra*, **5.G.3.**, Notes (5) and (6).

often, since decisions are frequently taken on the basis of contractual or administrative liability regimes, where the issue is irrelevant.[375] With respect to delictual liability under Article 1384(5) C.civ., the starting point was the physician and his or her duty of independence under professional rules, which was thought to be incompatible with the right—which characterizes the *lien de préposition*—of anyone else (such as an hospital) to give him or her instructions; it was only in 1992 that the Cour de cassation concluded that physicians who held salaried positions at private hospitals could be *préposés* of the hospital despite their professional duty of independence.[376] Under English tort law, the starting point was the duty of care of the hospital. In a series of cases starting with *Gold* v. *Essex County Council*, English courts have come to focus more on the primary liability of the hospital than on the issue whether physicians are employees or not. As a result, hospitals will in principle be liable for harm negligently caused by all physicians working in the hospital, except in the limited class of cases where the patient expressly selected and hired the physician who treated him.[377] Under German law, the starting point is the contract between the patient and the hospital. In every case, one of a limited number of—regulated—contracts arises. In the end the hospital will generally be liable for the fault of the physician both under § 278 BGB and § 831 (or § 31) BGB, except where the patient is treated by an outside physician who uses the hospital facilities (*Belegarzt*), under a so-called split physician/hospital contract (*gespaltener Arzt-Krankenhausvertrag*).[378]

In the case of temporary workers who are dispatched by their general employer to a temporary employer (either in connection with a lease of equipment or not), the main difficulty is to determine whether the worker becomes an employee of the temporary employer. Under French law it is a matter of ascertaining which firm retained the right to give instructions to the *préposé*.[379] There is a presumption, in German and English law, that the employee or *Verrichtungsgehilfe* remains with the general employer.[380] The situation is somewhat different in the case of workers sent by a firm specializing in the hire of temporary workers (*Leiharbeit*, *intérim*), who are then, albeit only temporarily, fully integrated into the temporary employer's organization; there it is generally recognized that the temporary employee becomes a *préposé*, employee or *Verrichtungsgehilfe* of the temporary employer, as the case may be.[381]

In the legal systems under study here, the distinction between *préposés*, employees or *Verrichtungsgehilfe*, on the one hand, and *entrepreneurs*, independent contractors or *Werkunternehmer*, on the other, is always put forward to illustrate the concept of employee.[382] The current labour market, however, shows a clear trend away from the traditional long-term employment relationship towards less "stable" forms of employment (limited duration contracts, etc.) as well as contractual arrangements which aim to avoid

---

[375] See *supra*, **5.F.4.**, Note (2).

[376] Cass. crim., 5 March 1992, *supra*, **5.F.4.** and note (3) thereafter.

[377] *Supra*, **5.E.5.** and notes thereafter.

[378] See BGH, 14 February 1995, *supra*, **5.G.6.** and notes thereafter.

[379] It is even possible to break down the activities of the *préposé* between the general and temporary employer, as in Cass. crim., 20 October 1987, *supra*, **5.F.7.** and Note (2) thereafter.

[380] See *supra*, **5.G.8.**, **5.E.9.** and Notes (3) to (5) thereafter.

[381] Ibid., Note (6).

[382] By way of example, see for French law, Le Tourneau and Cadiet at 850, para. 3466; for English law, Rogers at 696 and for German law, Staudinger-Belling/Eberl-Borges, § 831 who, at 73, para. 60, recall that the distinction is no more than a rule of thumb. See also von Bar I at 216–8 and 361–3, para. 200–1 and 350–3.

creating an employment relationship (the so-called "self-employed"). Under these new forms of employment, workers may well not qualify as employees, yet they do not have the same "strength", whether financial or otherwise, as traditional independent contractors generally have. One of the main challenges for the legal systems studied here will certainly be to fit these new forms of employment within the regime of liability for harm caused by employees. Since they rely on the power to give instructions, French and German law may find it difficult to include them among *préposés* or *Verrichtungsgehilfe*, even if those concepts are *prima facie* open. The broader economic analysis of English law may lead to different results, but then the unitary definition of employee across all fields of law might have to be abandoned, given that for social or taxation purposes the "self-employed" are usually expressly and deliberately not given employee status.[383] In any event, if the regimes of Article 1384(5) C.civ., vicarious liability under English law or § 831(1) BGB are not flexible enough to be extended to these new forms of employment, a resurgence of direct, personal liability of the employer or an expansion of contractual liability for others could occur, if victims are not to be left with a recourse only against the "self-employed" wrongdoer.

Limitations relating to the scope of employment

The liability regimes for harm caused by employees studied in this section all have in common that the liability is limited to conduct by the employee falling within the scope of his or her employment.[384] Here again, each system has its own expression, be it *"dans les fonctions auxquelles ils les ont employés"* at 1384(5) C.civ., "in the course of employment" as used in English law or *"in Ausführung der Verrichtung"* at § 831(1) BGB. Furthermore, the regimes of contractual liability for others as well as liability for corporate organs contain similar limitations, which are interpreted in the same fashion.[385] These limitations are therefore central to the topic of this section.

The crux of the problem is the kind or the intensity of the link that is required between the injurious conduct which caused damage and the fact of employment. In this respect, many options exist, and the systems studied here have moved closer to one or the another at various times in their respective history.

First, the **strictest approach** is to require that the employer has **authorized** (or not **prohibited**) the injurious conduct *and* that the conduct be for the employer's **benefit** or **purposes**. Under that approach, as soon as the employee does something which goes against the interests of the employer or has been prohibited by the employer, that conduct falls outside the scope of his or her employment. All systems studied here toyed with this approach but have moved away from it. Under French law, the strict approach was adopted by the second civil chamber of the Cour de cassation in 1954, and it was arguably adopted by the Assemblée plénière of the Cour de cassation of 17 June 1983, especially in light of the subsequent decision of 15 November 1985.[386] It has been definitively

---

[383] See E. McKendrick, "Vicarious Liability and Independent Contractors—A Re-examination" (1990) 53 Mod LR 770.

[384] See von Bar I at 218–22, 359–61, para. 202–5, 347–9.

[385] The German regime of State liability for officials, pursuant to § 839 BGB, also contains such a limitation. As for State liability for officials under French administrative law, certain parallels can be drawn as well: see *supra*, 5.1.1.A. under h).

[386] See *supra*, **5.F.10.** and Notes (6) and (7) thereafter.

repudiated, however, by another decision of the Assemblée plénière of 19 May 1988.[387] Under English law, it is established that the mere fact that an employee acted without authorization or against a prohibition from the employer does not take that conduct outside of the course of employment.[388] Moreover, since *Lloyd* v. *Grace, Smith & Co.*, it is also recognized that the conduct of the employee does not need to have been in the interest of the employer for it to remain in the course of employment.[389] Similarly, under German law, injurious conduct can still be *in Ausführung der Verrichtung* even if it was against a prohibition by,[390] or not in the interest of,[391] the *Geschäftsherr*. Furthermore, in all three systems it is possible under certain circumstances that a criminal act such as theft would remain within the scope of employment, even if it is obviously not in the interest of the employer.[392]

Secondly, a **middle approach** would require that the conduct of the employee come within the **"objective" scope** of his or her functions. The key difficulty then becomes how that objective scope is defined. It cannot refer (as under the first approach mentioned above) only to the tasks that the employer may have expressly entrusted to the employee or to the tasks that the employee executes in the interest of the employer. There is therefore a broader range of conduct that is sufficiently close to the entrusted task to remain linked to it, and it would need to be defined in the light of general human experience.

English law follows this approach when it seeks to draw a distinction between "wrongful modes of doing some authorised act" and "frolics of the employee's own".[393] It is recognized that there is a range of conduct which comes in the course of employment even if not explicitly part of the tasks entrusted to the employee: for instance, in *Century Insurance Company Ltd.* v. *Northern Ireland Transport Board*, the House of Lords found that the course of employment of a petrol tanker driver also included acts such as lighting up a cigarette whilst discharging the cargo of petrol.[394]

German law also espouses this approach when it requires, as recalled by the BGH in its judgment of 20 September 1966, that the injurious conduct bear a substantive connection (*innerer, sachlicher Zusammenhang*) with the tasks entrusted to the *Verrichtungsgehilfe*, as opposed to a mere extraneous connection (*äußerer Zusammenhang*). In other words, the injurious conduct must come within the range of conduct that the accomplishment of the task entrusted to the *Gehilfe* entails.[395] Otherwise, the assigned tasks merely provided the opportunity for the injurious conduct (*bei Gelegenheit der Ausführung*).

Under both English and German law, it is acknowledged that this approach is fairly imprecise, and that in the end it is an issue of how far the employee strayed from the task with which he or she had been entrusted.[396] Two cases concerning driving (or piloting) accidents have been included as an illustration. As regards accidents involving the use of

---

[387] *Supra*, **5.F.11.** and Note (8) thereafter.
[388] See *supra*, **5.E.12.**, Note (3).
[389] *Supra*, **5.E.21.** and Note (2) thereafter.
[390] See *supra*, **5.G.13.**, Note (3).
[391] See BGH, 12 July 1977, *supra*, **5.G.22.** and Note (5) thereafter.
[392] See *supra*, **5.F.16.**, **5.E.17.**, **5.G.18.** and notes thereafter.
[393] See *supra*, **5.E.12.** and Notes (1) and (2) thereafter.
[394] *Supra*, **5.E.12.** and Note (2) thereafter. See also the line of cases concerning acts done to protect the employer's property or economic interests, ibid., Note (4).
[395] *Supra*, **5.G.13.** and Notes (2) and (3) thereafter.
[396] *Supra*, **5.E.12.**, Note (1) and **5.G.13.**, Note (3).

vehicles belonging to the employer, it is accepted by both German and English law that minor deviations from the task or the journey assigned will not mean that the employee was driving outside the scope of his or her employment.[397] Furthermore, as shown by *Smith* v. *Stages* for English law, it is equally difficult to determine whether the use of a private vehicle to go to or come back from a work location comes within the scope of employment.[398]

Thirdly, a **broader** approach would require that some **objective factors**, such as time, place, means used, etc. connect the injurious conduct with the scope of employment. As long as some of these factors are present, then it should not be necessary to show that the injurious conduct actually came within the substantive scope of employment, which makes this approach easier to apply. On the other end, this approach marks a substantial enlargement of the "scope of employment".

Under French law, this broader approach was followed by all courts until 1954, when the second chamber of the Cour de cassation broke ranks.[399] In its decision of 19 May 1988, the Assemblée plénière of the Cour de cassation seemed to espouse the middle approach described above, but in practice that decision has heralded a return to the pre-1954 approach, under which it suffices that the injurious conduct be linked with the *lien de préposition* through objective relevant factors.[400]

The middle and the broader approach can also be viewed in terms of causation.[401] The middle approach corresponds to the adequacy theory of causation, under which one event is the cause of another if it substantially increased the possibility of the other happening. Indeed, when an employee is engaged to accomplish certain tasks, a range of potentially injurious conduct substantially connected with that task become more likely to happen. The broader approach comes closer to the equivalency theory of causation, under which one event is the cause of another if that other event would not have happened "but for" the first one. As long as the injurious conduct occurred during work, at work or due to means provided by work, then it can be said that it would not have occurred but for work.

The distinction between the middle approach of German and English law and the broader approach of French law is well illustrated by the cases relating to crimes committed by employees. Under French law, as shown by the decision of 23 June 1988 of the Cour de cassation, it suffices that theft was committed at the workplace, during working hours and using the possibilities offered by the employee's position for it to fall within the scope of employment for the purposes of Article 1384(5) C.civ.[402] By comparison, under both English and German law, it is considered that crimes committed by employees do not *prima facie* fall within the scope of employment. Under English law, as shown in *Morris* v. *CW Martin & Sons Ltd.*, in order for theft to remain in the course of employment, the employee must have been specifically entrusted with the keeping of the stolen

---

[397] For German law, see *supra*, **5.G.13.** as well as **5.G.14.** and Note (1) thereafter. For English law, see *supra*, **5.G.14.**, **5.E.15.**, Note (2).

[398] *Supra*, **5.E.15.** and Note (2) thereafter.

[399] See *supra*, **5.F.10.–11.**, Note (5).

[400] *Supra*, **5.F.11.** and Notes (8) and (9) thereafter.

[401] See *supra*, **5.F.10.–11.**, Note (3) and **5.G.13.**, Note (4). On the various theories of causation, see *supra*, Chapter IV, 4.1.

[402] *Supra*, **5.F.16.** and Note (1) thereafter.

property, so that a specific relationship can be shown to exist between the theft and the course of employment: the mere fact that employment would have afforded an opportunity to commit a crime does not imply that the crime was committed in the course of employment.[403] Similarly, under German law, as recalled by the BGH in its decision of 4 November 1953, criminal acts will remain in the accomplishment of the task if the *Verrichtungsgehilfe* was specifically instructed to do the opposite or to prevent the occurrence of the crime in question.[404]

Finally, in cases involving fraud by the employee, all the systems studied here take into account the perspective of the victim in assessing whether the fraud was perpetrated within the scope of the fraudster's employment. Under French law, the *préposé* will be found to have acted "within his or her functions" if the victim could entertain the legitimate belief that in performing the fraudulent operation the *préposé* was discharging his or her functions.[405] Under English law, the fraudulent employee will have been acting in the course of employment if the employer explicitly or implicitly held the employee out to the victim as acting within the limits of his or her authority.[406] Similarly, in fraud cases under German law, the objective scope of employment will be appreciated from the point of view of an outsider: conduct which an outsider would not consider foreign to the position of the *Verrichtungsgehilfe* will be "in the accomplishment of the task" for the purposes of § 831(1) BGB.[407]

Other regimes of liability for others

In the second section, it was seen that English law contains no significant regime of vicarious liability besides liability for employees (and agents).[408] Under German law, it was seen in the first section that liability for employees pursuant to § 831(1) BGB does not truly qualify as a regime of liability for others, since it rests on the fault of the employer (*Geschäftsherr*), even if it is presumed; the main other comparable regime, liability for children, is equally based on the presumed fault of the parents.[409]

In contrast, in the 1990s, French case law has embarked on an expansion and consolidation course as regards liability for others. Indeed Article 1384 C.civ. sets out a number of regimes of liability for others, in addition to that of Article 1384(5) (liability of *commettants* for their *préposés*), namely liability of parents for their minor children (Article 1384(4) and (7))[410] and liability of schoolteachers for their pupils (Article 1384(6) and (8)). The latter is expressly based on fault, without any presumption, as set out at Article 1384(8). The former used to be based on presumed fault.

In 1991, the Cour de cassation went further and turned the introductory clause of Article 1384(1) C.civ. ("Everyone is liable for the damage caused . . . by the conduct of

---

[403] *Supra*, **5.E.17.** and Note (2) therafter.
[404] *Supra*, **5.G.18.** and Note (3) thereafter.
[405] See *supra*, **5.F.19.–20.** and Note (1) thereafter.
[406] See *supra*, **5.E.21.** and Note (3) thereafter.
[407] See *supra*, **5.G.22.** and Note (5) thereafter.
[408] *Supra*, 5.2., Introductory Note under a).
[409] *Supra*, 5.2., Introductory Note under b).
[410] Art. 1384(6) and (7) also create a regime of liability of craftsmen for their apprentices, but it is very similar to the regime of parental liability and in any event it has lost in significance.

persons for whom one is responsible") into a general regime of liability for others,[411] as it had done in respect of things some 60 years before.[412] Although it is still to early to tell with any certainty, it appears that the concept of control over another person (be it a child or a person under care) will play a large role in defining the range of persons that could be made liable under that regime.[413] Subsequently, the Cour de cassation determined that such liability was not based on fault or presumed fault, so that the defendant can only avoid liability by showing that the injury was caused by a *cause étrangère* or the fault of the victim.[414]

At the same time, the Cour de cassation also turned the regime of parental liability into an objective regime, without reference to fault,[415] so that by now the general liability for others, the liability of *commettants* for their *préposés* and the liability of parents for their children are broadly in line.

---

[411] See *supra*, **5.F.23.** and notes thereunder.
[412] See *infra*, Chapter VI, 6.1.2.
[413] See *supra*, **5.F.23.**, Note (4).
[414] See *supra*, **5.F.25.**
[415] See *supra*, **5.F.24.**

CHAPTER SIX
LIABILITY NOT BASED ON CONDUCT

As mentioned in the opening of the preceding chapter, this chapter is concerned with the instances where the various legal systems impose liability without regard to the actual conduct of the defendant in the instant case, in particular regardless of whether the conduct of the defendant, or of some other person for whom the defendant is responsible, was wrongful.[1]

The basic elements for a liability regime to qualify as such are the requirement that the victim should have suffered damage,[2] together with criteria to impose on another person the obligation to compensate the victim that damage. As mentioned in Chapter I,[3] a central issue in tort law is to discern those criteria for the imposition of liability, whereby some balance must be found between the interests of the victim and of the person whose liability is sought. The most rudimentary criterion that is consonant with basic concepts of—corrective—justice is the basic causal equivalence test (the "but for" test, *Äquivalenz, équivalence des conditions*) taken alone.[4] However, a liability system based strictly on causal equivalence alone (*Kausalhaftung* in German legal terminology), under which a person would essentially be bound to compensate for the injury that he or she causes, while arguable, has generally been, and continues generally to be, viewed as excessively favourable to the plaintiff.

Starting from the 19th century, all the major systems studied here refined the criteria for liability by focussing on the conduct of the defendant. As a consequence, wrongfulness was introduced and firmly established as a necessary condition for liability in most cases. The evolution of the concept of wrongfulness, including its progressive objectivization, has been explored in a preceding chapter.[5] The assessment of causation also evolved to include elements of foreseeability, as set out in the chapter on causation.[6] Moreover, the analysis of injury to the victim was also refined, and in certain systems a certain hierarchy among types of damage has been established.[7] Even though the legal systems studied here show substantial differences, they have all generally followed this path. When procedural rules are considered, under which the victim, as plaintiff, generally bears the burden of proof, it can be seen that the resulting systems have become increasingly favourable to the defendant as the factual context surrounding the injury to the victim has become increasingly complex, so that the victim may often simply not be in a position to show that all the criteria relating to wrongfulness and causation are met.

---

[1] Liability for one's own conduct is discussed *supra*, Chapter III, whereas liability for the conduct of others is surveyed *supra*, Chapter V.

[2] On the various types of injury against which tort law grants protection, see *supra*, Chapter II.

[3] See *supra*, Chapter I, 1.1.

[4] On the various theories of causation and their use in the legal systems under study here, see *supra*, Chapter IV, 4.1.

[5] See *supra*, Chapter III, 3.2.

[6] See *supra*, Chapter IV, 4.1.

[7] That is the case for English and German law: see *supra*, Chapter I, 1.4.1. and 1.4.3. Under French law, on the other hand, no such hierarchy between the types of injury has emerged, although some are better protected than others: see *supra*, Chapter I, 1.4.2.

It is important to remember that liability based on the wrongful conduct of the defendant is thus only one of the options in the design of a liability regime, even if it may remain the most widespread and established option.[8] The aim of the present chapter is to survey the use of criteria other than wrongful conduct to impose liability in the various legal systems under study. In terms of balance between the interests of the victim and the person whose liability is sought, these criteria generally range between liability based on causal equivalency alone (more favourable to the plaintiff) and liability based on wrongful conduct (more favourable to the defendant).

As will be seen throughout this Chapter, the creation of risk or danger by the defendant is the most widespread rationale invoked to impose liability, besides wrongful conduct.[9] It could be described at a very general level as follows: the defendant is made liable because he or she is responsible for a source of danger that led to the injury. From that basic proposition, a fairly diverse range of liability regimes have emerged, as this Chapter will show.

Under that basic proposition, the conduct of the defendant in a given case is not as such relevant to establish liability: the defendant is "responsible" for having created a source of danger and not because of any course of conduct, wrongful or not, that would have led to the injury. Nevertheless, the line between liability based on wrongful conduct and liability not based on conduct is sometimes difficult to draw, and some elements of the regimes studied in this Chapter—among others the concept of keeper (*gardien*, *Halter*)—are inspired or influenced by considerations relating to the conduct of the defendant.

This chapter is not primarily concerned with liability regimes which are still based on wrongful conduct but where the burden of proof has been put in whole or in part on the shoulders of the defendant (for instance, the regime of § 831 BGB, reviewed in the preceding chapter).[10] Those regimes are reviewed only to the extent necessary for proper comparison between legal systems (for instance, UK law relating to traffic accidents or the German regime of product liability under § 823(1) BGB[11]). Nor does this Chapter deal in depth with regimes which no longer qualify as liability regimes, since they rest on compulsory "first-party insurance"[12] and the injury is thus not shifted onto another person. Such is the case generally for work accidents, where employees (directly or through the employer or both) contribute to their own insurance.

At the beginning of the present chapter, the general approach of the legal systems under study is surveyed, in order to see how far they include liability not based on conduct and whether they have developed a general theory for such liability.

The three subsequent sections are devoted to three great areas, which together cover most of the instances of liability not based on conduct, namely liability for road and other transport accidents, liability for defective products and finally liability between neighbours and environmental liability. It is no coincidence that those three areas have in common that the injury to the victim generally results not from the direct intervention of

---

[8] See *supra*, Chapter I, 1.1.
[9] See in this respect the in-depth comparative study conducted by Schamps.
[10] See *supra*, Chapter V, 5.1.1.C.
[11] See *infra*, 6.3.1.B.
[12] "First-party insurance", or loss insurance, covers one's own injury. "Third-party insurance", or liability insurance, covers liability towards others (i.e. the injury to a third party which one is liable to compensate).

the person whose liability is sought, but rather from a complex process involving things, be it cars, manufactured products or various types of installations running on a piece of property. As mentioned above, in these complex situations, the traditional criterion for liability, based on the wrongful conduct of the defendant which the plaintiff must prove, becomes too favourable to the defendant, and it has generally been recognized that it would be appropriate to use an alternative criterion.

The introduction and development of regimes of liability not based on conduct throughout the 20th century cannot be fully accounted for unless one also examines the progress of insurance. As was mentioned in the excerpts included in Chapter I,[13] the rise of insurance changed the loss-shifting function of tort law to loss-spreading: as soon as it is clear that insurance coverage can be obtained against liability arising from a certain activity or installation (e.g. a car, a plant, etc), it appears less crucial to ensure that the defendant did indeed engage in wrongful conduct so as to justify the imposition of liability. Rather, the prime concern is to channel liability upon the person best able to ensure against the risk of injury. Accordingly, it is no coincidence that, in areas such as liability for accidents or environmental liability, the imposition of liability not based on conduct generally goes hand-in-hand with an obligation to take out insurance cover for such liability.[14]

6.1. GENERAL APPROACH

In this section, German law will be surveyed first, since it offers the most developed theoretical approach in relation to what is there called risk-based liability (*Gefährdungshaftung*). Next, French law is considered; it shows perhaps less of an overall theoretical framework than German law, but it arguably leaves greater scope in practice to what is there called "liability without fault" or "liability by virtue of the law" (*responsabilité sans faute* or *responsabilité de plein droit*). In particular, the French regime of liability for things pursuant to Article 1384(1) C.civ. constitutes one of the great distinguishing features of French tort law, and it is studied here in greater detail. English law, where a number of torts entail "strict liability", comes next.

6.1.1. GERMAN LAW

Introductory Note

As mentioned above, German legal writers have developed a fairly sophisticated theoretical framework to try to make sense of the various instances of liability not based on conduct under German law and, if possible, to give them some overall consistency. The work of these writers has to some extent been reflected in the case law.

---

[13] See *supra*, Chapter I, **1.F.5.**, **1.G.6.** and **1.E.7.**
[14] In the case of road traffic accidents, the obligation to hold liability insurance was even the prime focus of the harmonization efforts at the EC level: see *infra*, 6.2.1.D.

The first case reproduced below has been selected as an introduction to the topic because in it the BGH was forced by the arguments of the parties to explore the foundations of liability not based on conduct under German law. It confirmed that in the post-War era the relationship between liability regimes based on wrongful conduct and risk-based liability (*Gefährdungshaftung*) was still based on the *Enumerationsprinzip* (exhaustive list principle).

The second document, an excerpt from an article by E. Deutsch, provides a survey of the risk-based liability regimes currently in place under German law, and tries to group them, so far as possible, into more general categories.

The third case below shows how, in a regime of risk-based liability, the other conditions of liability, especially causation, are also framed somewhat differently than under fault-based liability.

BGH, 15 October 1970[15]   **6.G.1.**

THE FAULT PRINCIPLE IN GERMAN TORT LAW

No red light

*There is no risk-based liability (*Gefährdungshaftung*) under German law except in those cases where the legislature has expressly provided for it.*

Facts: The defendant was a municipality responsible for the traffic lights at an intersection where the plaintiff was involved in a collision with another car. At the time of the accident, the lights at the intersection were green in favour of the plaintiff and were not working in the direction in which the other car was travelling. Since the other car came from the right of the plaintiff's car, the driver of the other car assumed that, in the absence of any signal coming from the traffic light, he had priority (as is the rule in Germany). The plaintiff was not able to recover his damage from the driver of the other car. The plaintiff sued the defendant municipality on the ground that it was liable either because it had been negligent in relation to the operation of the traffic lights or, alternatively, because it had to bear the risk of malfunction of the traffic lights.

Held: The court of first instance and the court of appeal rejected the plaintiff's claim. The BGH upheld the judgment of the court of appeal.

Judgment: "[In the first part of the reasons, the BGH found that there was no fault that could trigger liability under § 823(1) or § 839 BGB, and then moved on to the claim under risk-based liability.] Our legal order attaches liability to the wrongful conduct of the tortfeasor. The legislature has expressly provided for risk-based liability (*Gefährdungshaftung*) only in a few exceptional situations, which it has outlined in more detail [references omitted], because it found it necessary to make an exception to the fault principle. However, in other areas in which risk-based liability could have been introduced or has for years been proposed [reference omitted], in particular in the limited area of the malfunction of traffic lights, the legislature has not chosen to establish risk-based liability, although the concerns which have arisen in connection with those areas cannot have gone unnoticed by the legislature. In such a case, the judiciary cannot pre-empt the legislative power if the latter knowingly refrains from intervening, all the more since it is not at all possible—or only possible over a long period time with the ensuing legal uncertainty—for case law to delineate the extent to which risk-based liability should exceptionally be applicable, by way of deviation from the fault principle enshrined in the law.

[15] BGHZ 54, 332. Translation by Y.P. Salmon.

The [plaintiff] raised the principle of fairness (§ 242 BGB) in his argument. He also referred to the basic idea underlying § 836 BGB, namely that everyone is to be held liable for damage caused by his things to the extent that he should have prevented that damage if he had paid reasonable attention to the interests of others. These considerations are not sufficient to justify a departure from the fault principle laid down in the law for cases such as the one at hand. Moreover, it should be noted that § 836 BGB does not constitute an exception to the fault principle; rather, liability is imposed under that provision on the basis of a—rebuttable—presumption of fault."

Notes

(1) The facts of the annotated case were simple: at an intersection with traffic lights, for some reason the traffic light in one direction was not working. As one might have expected, an accident happened when a car coming across the intersection through a green traffic light was hit from the right by another car for which the light was not working. For an unexplained reason, the driver of the first car could not recover his damage from the other driver. He thus sued the city as the public authority that was responsible for the traffic lights on the basis of either § 823 or § 839 BGB.[16] However, it was not possible to establish that the malfunctioning of the lights was attributable to a fault on the part of the city or any of its servants.[17] The only alternative basis on which the plaintiff could formulate his claim for compensation from the city was to argue that the city was liable despite the absence of fault on its part.

(2) First, the plaintiff argued that the city was liable because of the risk created for the users of the streets by the malfunctioning of the traffic lights, which would be a form of risk-based liability (*Gefährdungshaftung*). Here the BGH was very firm: there is no legal basis for such liability. As the BGH stated, the fault principle is firmly anchored in German law; accordingly, exceptions to that principle, such as risk-based liability, can be made only through legislative intervention. The courts cannot venture beyond the cases of risk-based liability introduced by the legislature to create new regimes. The BGH noted that the problem of malfunctioning traffic lights had been raised for some time past in legal writing, and that risk-based liability had been advocated as a solution. Yet the legislature has not acted upon those suggestions, which according to the BGH showed that the intention of the legislature was to leave the problem to be dealt with under existing fault-based liability regimes. By way of substantive arguments against the judicial creation of new risk-based liability regimes, the BGH essentially put forward legal certainty: while the legislature can enact a "clean" exception to the fault principle, it would take more time to create a coherent regime through case law, and would create years of uncertainty. As is seen below in the study of French law, while it is true that uncertainty is bound to result from the judicial development of liability regimes not based on fault, such uncertainty can remain within manageable limits.[18]

(3) The view expressed by the BGH[19] that risk-based liability is confined to those

---

[16] Under § 823 BGB, the city would have been liable for its own fault. Under § 839 BGB, the city would be liable for a breach of official duty committed by a civil servant: see *supra*, Chapter III, 3.3.2.A. and Chapter V, 5.1.1.C. under j).

[17] That point is discussed in detail by the BGH in a part of the judgment not reproduced here, where it agreed with the court of appeal that no fault had been proved against the city or one of its servants.

[18] See *infra*, 6.1.2.

[19] And confirmed in subsequent cases: see BGH, 7 November 1974, BGHZ 63, 234 at 237.

regimes that have been expressly introduced by legislation (the exhaustive list principle or *Enumerationsprinzip*), remains the dominant view in German legal writing to this day.[20] For some leading writers, however, the *Enumerationsprinzip* no longer corresponds to reality, in view of the significance that the various regimes of liability not based on fault have assumed. In the words of H. Kötz:[21]

"The view that fault-based liability pursuant to §§ 823 ff. BGB and risk-based liability are two different but equal principles of liability now prevails. Risk-based liability is based on the idea that the person who operates for his or her own purposes a particularly dangerous installation or otherwise creates a source of particular risk must assume liability for the damage that results from the realization of that risk, whether there was fault or not on his or her part. The rationale for fault-based liability is rather that the damage is a consequence of the violation of a standard of behaviour imposed by the legal order under the concrete circumstances in order to avoid an unreasonably large risk of damage to others. It follows therefrom that risk-based liability is not an 'exception' from the 'principle' of fault-based liability, but rather relies on a rationale of its own for imposing liability. Both forms of liability make the person causing damage 'responsible' for that damage in a similar fashion, since fault-based liability—when seen as liability for conduct which objectively violates a duty—is no less a 'mode of imputing risk' (Stoll) than risk-based liability. Indeed both forms of liability are based on risk, and impose liability on the person who caused damage irrespective of the actual blameworthiness of the damaging conduct, because that person either failed to respect certain standards of behaviour generally required in society and thereby caused injury (fault-based liability) or created a particular risk of injury which materialized (risk-based liability). Obviously, the reasons for which a person is held responsible are not the same for both forms of liability. Yet risk-based liability is no less worthy because it does not rely on the fault of the defendant being proven."

Furthermore, it must be added that the BGH, while adopting a restrictive approach to the creation of new liability regimes not based on fault, tends to take a rather generous view of the scope of those regimes that the legislature has introduced. For instance, the BGH found that the liability of rail operators for accidents occuring "in the operation of rail transport" also extended to damage caused by barriers at railway crossings.[22]

Moreover, in accordance with the general principles relating to the relationship between causes of action (*Anspruchkonkurrenz*) under German law,[23] plaintiffs can plead in the same action claims under both fault-based and risk-based liability regimes, and each will be treated independently of the other, a position which tends to support the point of view of H. Kötz whereby the two forms of liability are really co-existing as equals.[24]

(4) In the annotated case, the plaintiff went so far as to advance an argument that, in line with the general concepts of equity and good faith enunciated in § 242 BGB, the principle that a person is liable for damage caused by his or her property, which underlies liability pursuant to § 836 BGB,[25] should be extended to cover the facts in issue. In so doing, the plaintiff was advocating the judicial creation under German law of a general liability regime for things, not unlike that which was developed by French courts under Art. 1384(1) C.civ. The BGH flatly rejected the argument, recalling that § 836 BGB itself was fault-based.

---

[20] See Larenz/Canaris at 601–2 and 608–9. See also Münchener-Mertens, Vor §§ 823–53 at 1408, para. 20; RGRK-Steffen, § 823 at 13, para. 15 and E. Deutsch, *infra*, **6.G.2.**

[21] H. Kötz, "Gefährdungshaftung" in Federal Ministry of Justice, *Gutachten und Vorschläge zur Überarbeitung des Schuldrechts*, Vol. II (Köln: Bundesanzeiger Verlag, 1981) 1779 at 1792.

[22] BGH, NJW 1963, 1107, VersR 1963, 583. See, with respect to the liability of motor vehicle keepers under § 7 StVG, *infra*, **6.G.13.** and *supra*, Chapter IV, **4.G.3.**

[23] See *supra*, Chapter I, 1.3.1.

[24] RGRK-Steffen, § 823 at 14, para. 17.

[25] See *infra*, 6.4.2. under b).

(5) In a part of the case not reproduced above, the plaintiff also argued (without success) that the city was liable pursuant to regimes of liability without fault applicable to public authorities, namely quasi-expropriation (*enteignungsgleicher Eingriff*) and the sacrifice of a legal position (*Aufopferung*). Both those regimes were considered in greater detail before.[26]

E. Deutsch, *"Das neue System der Gefährdungshaftungen:*   **6.G.2.**
Gefährdungshaftung, erweiterte Gefährdungshaftung und Kausal-Vermutungshaftung"[27]

"II. Origins and foundations of risk-based liability (*Gefährdungshaftung*)

1. Liability based on fault and liability based on risk

Fault-based and risk-based liability are clearly distinct from one another, yet they often are both applied to the same case, like two overlapping circles . . . According to the majority point of view, risk-based liability is an exception to fault-based liability. It would be better to present risk-based liability as a complement to fault-based liability. Since, in the industrial age, the meaning of negligence has changed, it became necessary to complement the law of civil liability with risk-based liability. Whereas previously proper care consisted in behaving so as to avoid danger, the concept of care has evolved through the 20th century, so that now proper care consists in dealing appropriately with danger . . .

The real distinction between fault-based and risk-based liability appears in relation to unlawfulness (*Rechtswidrigkeit*). In short, one can say that fault-based liability prohibits, while risk-based liability permits . . .

2. Compensation for the retreat of fault-based liability within the framework of fault-based liability

At the same time as proper care was redefined from risk-avoidance to risk-management, the number of specific protective duties (*Schutzpflichten*) increased. These duties were either introduced by the legislature in protective enactments (*Schutzgesetze*) . . . and then included in civil [liability] law through § 823(2) BGB, or developed in the case law as duties to take care (*Verkehrspflichten*). A breach of these duties leads to liability on the basis of fault. Protective enactments and duties to take care frequently contain behavioural norms, which require a [specific] behaviour . . . These behavioural norms constitute the first line of defence of the law . . .

3. Compensation for the retreat of fault-based liability through risk-based liability

With the redefinition of the concept of proper care, dangerous behaviour became permissible. Accordingly, it became necessary to put particularly dangerous endeavours under an objective liability regime. It is called *risk-based liability* (*Gefährdungshaftung*). Often, risk-based liability was introduced only after a considerable time period where dangerous behaviour was permissible. Risk-based liability therefore provides a remarkably limited compensation: seen against a real retreat of fault-based liability, the compensation [through risk-based liability] was usually limited to material damage, often denied in cases of *force majeure* (*höhere Gewalt*) and also frequently put under a ceiling as regards damages.

[26] See *supra*, Chapter III, 3.3.2.B.
[27] NJW 1992, 73. Emphasis in original unless otherwise indicated. Footnotes omitted. Translation by P. Larouche.

4. Foundations of risk-based liability

Risk-based liability rests on the idea of excessive danger. When a person creates such a danger for others, maintains it or exploits it, he or she is bound to assume the injury that results from the realization of the [risk of] injury. In principle, risk-based liability thus aims to reduce injury by transferring risks. The basic justifications for imposing risk-based liability are: the victims cannot be expected to bear the loss themselves; costs should be assigned to the persons who derive benefits; the risk is managed at the micro-economic level by allocating the costs [to one person]. . . When a risk is considerable—i.e. unusual, difficult to control or unavoidable—so that the victim cannot be expected to bear the consequences of its realization, that risk is transferred to the operator or other person creating the risk. The assignment of costs upon a large class of persons is usually carried out through compulsory liability insurance. Finally. . ., it is known that risk-based liability fulfils a *micro-economic prevention* function: if the costs of the risk for third parties [i.e. the compensation to be paid for injury] cannot be assumed economically, then the firm will cease operations.

III. . . . Narrow risk-based liability (*enge Gefährdungshaftung*)

The classical risk-based liability regimes, namely those covering the deployment of speed, the accumulation and transport of energy and the keeping of animals, follow the model of narrow risk-based liability. The starting point is a precisely defined risk, namely that associated with railways, motor vehicles, aircraft, animals, electricity networks, networks of pipes and canalizations, etc. (§ 1ff. HaftpflG, § 7 StVG, §§ 44 ff. LuftVG, § 833(1) BGB) . . .

The hallmark of narrow risk-based liability is that the scope of liability coincides with the basis for liability. Because of that, it is not necessary to use the adequacy theory to define the scope of liability; rather, the infringement [of a protected interest] and the injury must represent a realization of the risk that was the basis for the introduction of a risk-based liability regime . . .

IV. Broader risk-based liability (*erweiterte Gefährdungshaftung*)

In recent times, a few regimes of objective liability have appeared where the risk does not underpin the regime, but only provides a justification for its introduction. I am thinking here of the product liability regimes of § 84 AMG (Drug Act) and of the *Produkthaftungsgesetz* (Product Liability Act) . . .

It follows that, in broader risk-based liability regimes, the scope of liability does not really coincide [with the risk which justified the regime]. Liability is conditional on a causal link, but not on the realization of the specific risk that led to the introduction of the regime. Under the *Produkthaftungsgesetz*, liability can also arise with respect to products that were not manufactured industrially and were sold directly [to the end-user]. Similarly, if a pharmacist prepares a medication himself or herself and that preparation produces an unacceptable side-effect, liability will arise under the AMG . . .

V. Liability with a presumption of causation (*Kausal-Vermutungshaftung*)

So far, liability with a presumption of causation has been introduced for precisely-defined risks, namely the specific risks associated with mining, genetic engineering and intervention on the environment. The basis for liability is carried through in the scope of liability . . .

Causation as it relates to the scope of liability (*haftungsausfüllende Kausalität*) is assessed according to the normal rules. It follows that there must be a causal link between the activity or operation, on the one hand, and the infringement of a protected interest and the injury, on the other hand.

Adaquate causation is not necessary here either, but the injury must represent a realization of the specific risk which justified the imposition of risk-based liability ...

The distinctive feature of liability with a presumption of causation is that the hurdle [for the victim] to establish liability, namely the proof of causation, is made easier to overcome . . ."

Notes

(1) This article from E. Deutsch has been selected because it provides a good and crisp overview of risk-based liability (*Gefährdungshaftung*) under German law.

E. Deutsch first deals with the general theory of risk-based liability. He draws an interesting parallel between the rise of the *Verkehrspflichten* and of risk-based liability.[28] In the course of the 20th century, the meaning of care—a central concept for the determination of fault—has shifted from the avoidance of danger to the dealing with it properly. Accordingly, a fair range of conduct that does not avoid danger yet constitutes a proper way of dealing with it (e.g. driving a car prudently) can be engaged in without leading to liability if it results in injury to someone. What may then seem as a retreat of tort law was in fact counter-balanced by two phenomena. First, the doctrine of *Verkehrspflichten* was developed, under which the concept of proper conduct in the light of danger was made more precise and concrete, so that within the traditional realm of fault-based liability, it becomes easier to establish that someone has acted wrongfully. The *Verkehrspflichten* remain firmly anchored within fault-based liability, since they serve to concretize unlawfulness (*Rechtswidrigkeit*, the objective component of wrongfulness).[29]

Secondly, there still remains a range of potentially dangerous conduct that will not be wrongful, even with a well-developed doctrine of *Verkehrspflichten*. This is where risk-based liability comes in: as E. Deutsch underlines, the cardinal difference between fault-based and risk-based liability under German law is the absence of unlawfulness (*Rechtswidrigkeit*) requirement in the latter. Risk-based liability therefore covers conduct which is in principle allowable.

(2) The core concept behind risk-based liability, as E. Deutsch states, is the concept of *exceptional danger*, because of either the high risk of injury or the gravity of potential injury, or both.[30] The basic principle is that the *risk of loss resulting from the creation of an exceptional danger to others must be transferred from the persons subjected to that danger to the person creating it*. He lists three main reasons which justify such a transfer of risk: (i) it cannot be expected from victims that they would support the loss, (ii) it is sensible to leave the costs related to resulting loss with the person who otherwise benefits from the source of danger in question and (iii) the risk of loss is better controlled (or better insured against) when it is borne by the person responsible for the creation of the danger. Other authors generally put forward a similar rationale for risk-based liability.[31]

---

[28] Münchener-Mertens, Vor §§ 823–53 at 1408–9, para. 21–22, also points out that fault-based liability infused with *Verkehrspflichten* and risk-based liability come close to one another, the main difference being in the area of risks which cannot be controlled even with the greatest care, where fault-based liability tends to lead to exoneration, while risk-based liability tends to lead to liability.

[29] This discussion ties into the debate between the two theoretical conceptions of fault-based liability under German law, namely the Result Theory (*Erfolgstheorie*) and the Conduct Theory (*Handlungtheorie*): see *supra*, Chapter III, 3.1.2., Introductory Note under b) and 3.2.1. under b).

[30] See also Larenz/Canaris at 607.

[31] See Larenz/Canaris at 604–6; RGRK-Steffen, § 823 at 13, para. 25; Münchener-Mertens, Vor §§ 823–53 at 1408, para. 19.

(3) Under German law, risk-based liability therefore does away with the concepts of culpability (*Verschulden*) and unlawfulness (*Rechtswidrigkeit*) and, as is shown in the next annotated case, it uses a concept of causation that differs from that used under fault-based liability. However, in one respect, namely the scope of protection, risk-based liability builds on the same theoretical construct as fault-based liability, that is to say the limitative list of protected interests (*Rechtsgüter*). With one exception,[32] the various risk-based liability regimes protect only life, health, bodily integrity and ownership,[33] i.e. the *Rechtsgüter* expressly listed at § 823(1) BGB. The *Recht am Gewerbebetrieb* is therefore not covered by the risk-based liability regimes.[34]

Furthermore, in the absence of a specific enabling provision such as § 847 BGB (for fault-based liability) in most risk-based liability regimes, the rule of § 253 BGB generally applies to deny compensation for non-material injury (*Schmerzensgeld*).[35] Many authors consider that the extension of risk-based liability regimes to cover non-material injury is one of the most needed changes in German tort law.[36]

A distinctive feature of risk-based liability regimes as regards the scope of protection, however, is the general limitation of liability to a maximum sum. Some of the regimes do not comprise such a limitation, however,[37] and furthermore the rationale for such limitations—making the risk more easily insurable—is questioned.[38]

(4) After having set out the general theory of risk-based liability under German law, E. Deutsch outlines how the existing regimes differ in certain aspects relating mostly to the scope of liability and causation. He regroups the existing risk-based liability regimes into three broad categories, namely a narrow risk-based liability (*enge Gefährdungshaftung*), a broader one (*erweiterte Gefährdungshaftung*) and liability with a presumption of causation (*Kausal-Vermutungshaftung*).

Narrow risk-based liability comprises the "older" regimes where liability was imposed on the keeper (*Halter*) of a source of exceptional danger or the operator of an installation (*Anlage*) which presented an exceptional danger, namely:

– the liability of keepers of so-called "luxury animals" (*Luxustiere*) for damage caused by the animals, under § 833 BGB;

---

[32] § 22 of the *Wasserhaushaltsgesetz* (WHG), in the version promulgated on 23 September 1986, BGBl.I.1529, discussed *infra*, 6.4.3., Introductory Note under d).

[33] Ownership is generally held to include other real rights and possession. The range of property which is actually protected is often restricted. For instance, product liability generally does not extend to damage to the defective product itself: see for German law *infra*, **6.G.24.**, Note (7) where the BGH case law on "creeping damage" (*Weiterfresserschaden*) is discussed. See Larenz/Canaris at 602–3; RGRK-Steffen, § 823 at 20–1, para. 26.

[34] Ibid. On the *Recht am Gewerbebetrieb*, see *supra*, Chapter I, 1.4.3., Introductory Note under b) and Chapter II, 2.3.2., Introductory Note under d), **2.G.37.** and notes thereafter.

[35] The only exceptions are liability for animals (§ 833 BGB, which is covered by § 847 BGB, see *infra*, 6.2.2.), liability for nuclear installations (§ 29(3) of the *Atomgesetz* (AtomG), in the version promulgated on 15 July 1985, BGBl.I.1565, see *infra*, 6.4.2. under e)) and liability for military airplanes (§ 53(3) of the *Luftverkehrsgesetz* (LuftVG) in the version promulgated on 14 January 1981, BGBl.I.61, see *infra*, 6.2.2.).

[36] See Münchener-Mertens, Vor §§ 823–53 at 1410, para. 25; H. Kötz, "Gefährdungshaftung" in Federal Ministry of Justice, *Gutachten und Vorschläge zur Überarbeitung des Schuldrechts*, Vol. II (Köln: Bundesanzeiger Verlag, 1981) 1779 at 1824–5.

[37] Liability for animals under § 833 BGB, *infra*, 6.2.2. and liability for water pollution under § 22 WHG, *infra*, 6.4.3., Introductory Note under d).

[38] Larenz/Canaris at 604.

– the liability of the keeper of a car for damage caused in its operation, under § 7 of the *Straßenverkehrsgesetz* (StVG);[39]

– the liability of railway, tram and suspension railway operators for damage in the operation of these transportation means, under § 1 of the *Haftpflichtgesetz* (HaftpflG);[40]

– the liability of operators of cables, conduits, pipes, etc. for the transmission and delivery of electricity, gas, vapours or fluids for damage resulting from the "effect" of these substances, under § 2 HaftpflG;

– the liability of aircraft keepers for damage caused to persons other than passengers on the aircraft by accidents in the operation of the aircraft, under §§ 33 of the *Luftverkehrsgesetz* (LuftVG);[41]

– the liability of operators of nuclear power plants for damage caused by a "nuclear event" (*nukleares Ereignis*), under § 25 of the *Atomgesetz* (AtomG);[42]

– the liability of those in possession of materials used for nuclear reactions, materials emitting radiation or particle accelerators for damage caused by the "effect" thereof, under § 26 AtomG;

– the liability of those who bring or discharge into water substances which alter its properties for the damage resulting therefrom, under § 22(1) of *Wasserhaushaltsgesetz* (WHG)[43]; and

– the liability of the owners of installations from which substances leak into water for the damage resulting from the leakage, under § 22(2) WHG.

All these risk-based liability regimes have in common not only that fault (*Verschulden*) and wrongfulness (*Rechtswidrigkeit*) are displaced by the exceptional risk in question as the basis for liability (*Haftungsgrund*), but also that such risk becomes the standard for the scope of liability (*Haftungsumfang*), thereby also displacing the adequacy test for causation that is used under fault-based liability.[44] As the next annotated case shows, the injury must be a manifestation of the exceptional risk that forms the basis for the liability regime. The *Schutzzweck der Norm* theory of causation—adapted in the context of risk-based liability—therefore plays a central role for these regimes.

(5) The situation is somewhat different in the two more recent regimes that E. Deutsch characterizes as "enlarged risk-based liability" regimes, namely:

– the liability of persons who put a drug into circulation, where the injurious effects of the drug are disproportionate or where no appropriate information was given, for injury caused by the use of the drug, under § 84 of the *Arzneimittelgesetz* (AMG);[45] and

– the liability of the manufacturer of defective products (as well as of certain other persons) for resulting damage, under § 1 of the *Produkthaftungsgesetz* (ProdHaftG).[46]

---

[39] Road Traffic Act of 19 December 1952 as amended, BGBl.I.837, BGBl.III.9231–1. See also *infra*, **6.G.12.**

[40] Civil Liability Act in the version promulgated on 4 January 1978, BGBl.I.145. See also *infra*, 6.4.2. under d).

[41] Air Traffic Act, in the version promulgated on 14 January 1981, BGBl.I.61. See also *infra*, 6.2.2.

[42] Atomic Energy Act, in the version promulgated on 15 July 1985, BGBl.I.1565. See also *infra*, 6.4.2. under e).

[43] Water Resources Act, in the version promulgated on 23 September 1986, BGBL.I.1529. See also *infra*, 6.4.3. under d).

[44] See *supra*, Chapter IV, 4.1.1., in particular **4.G.1.**

[45] Drug Act of 24 August 1976, BGBl.I.2445. See *infra*, **6.G.34.**, Note (4).

[46] Product Liability Act of 15 December 1989, *infra*, **6.G.34.**

Under these regimes, the basis for liability (*Haftungsgrund*) remains—as with all risk-based liability regimes —the exceptional risk in question, i.e. the risk for consumers of exposure (i) to a drug that has disproportionate effects or in respect of which inadequate information was given or (ii) to a defective product, respectively. The scope of liability (*Haftungsumfang*), however, is not as much influenced by the basis of liability as in the case of the "narrow" regimes. As E. Deutsch points out, product liability also extends to non-industrial products, and liability for drugs also extends to preparations made up by a pharmacist. Given that these two liability regimes are framed in broad terms that go beyond the exceptional risk that prompted the introduction of such regime, the assessment of causation is less determined by the *Schutzzweck der Norm* (scope of the norm)— i.e. whether the injury is a manifestation of the exceptional risk underpinning the liability regime—and relies more on the less restrictive adequacy (*Adequanz*) test, hence their characterization as "enlarged risk-liability regimes". Considerations relating to *Schutzzweck* remain nonetheless relevant: as Larenz/Canaris point out, to the extent that the exceptional risk is made more concrete by requiring evidence that the product was defective, it is less open to question whether the exceptional risk manifested itself in the injury;[47] nevertheless, the injury must still come within the range of injuries against which the liability regime aims to provide protection.[48]

(6) In the third category of "liability with a presumption of causation", E. Deutsch puts:

– the liability of mining operators for damage caused by mining operations and installations, under § 114 of the *Bundesbergbaugesetz* (BBergG);[49]
– the liability of persons undertaking genetic work (*gentechnische Arbeit*) for injury caused by the properties of an organism that result from the work, under § 32 of the *Gentechnikgesetz* (GenTG);[50] and
– the liability of the operators of certain installations for damage flowing from the environmental impact of such installations, under § 1 of the *Umwelthaftungsgesetz* (UHG).[51]

As far as causation is concerned, these regimes are in substance close to the narrow regimes listed above, in that considerations relating to the scope of the rule or *Schutzzweck der Norm* (i.e. whether the injury represents the materialization of the exceptional risk) are determinative. In these regimes, however, the task of the plaintiff is made easier through presumptions relating to causation, which vary from one regime to the other. As E. Deutsch points out, once presumptions of causation come into play, risk-based liability can become very strict for the defendant, since in cases where the presumption cannot be rebutted liability follows from a fairly limited set of conditions to be

---

[47] Larenz/Canaris at 648.
[48] So that "nervous shock" (*Schockschäden*, see *supra*, Chapter II, **2.G.3**, **2.G.4**. and notes thereafter) and "rent neurosis" (*Rentenneurose*, see *supra*, Chapter IV, **4.G.25.**, Note (3)) will not be compensated under these regimes anymore than under fault-based liability: Münchener-Cahn, § 1 ProdHaftG at 2156, para. 70; Staudinger-Oechsler, § 1 ProdHaftG at 300, para. 33.
[49] Federal Mining Act of 13 August 1980, BGBl.I.1310.
[50] Genetic Engineering Act of 20 June 1990, BGBl.I.1080. See *infra*, 6.4.3., Introductory Note under e).
[51] Environmental Liability Act of 10 December 1990, BGBl.I.2634. See *infra*, **6.G.40.**

proved by the plaintiff, namely injury and the events which trigger the presumption, which may be no more than the undertaking of an activity.

BGH, 27 January 1981[52]   **6.G.3.**

Roof collapses when helicopter flies by

Under risk-based liability regimes, the adequacy theory does not apply; liability will be excluded only if the injury does not represent a specific manifestation of the exceptional risk that underpins the liability regime.

Facts: The roof of the plaintiff's building collapsed as a German military helicopter flew over it at a low altitude. The plaintiff sued the German State under § 33 LuftVG.

Held: The court of first instance and the court of appeal dismissed the plaintiff's claim. The BGH allowed the appeal and remitted the case for further consideration.

Judgment: "Today, the 'filter' of adequacy . . . is generally recognized as a means to exclude the chains of events for which the defendant cannot in all fairness be made liable . . .

However, the court of appeal failed to appreciate . . . that the meaning and purpose of that exclusionary 'filter' differs according to whether it is used in the context of a liability for a breach of a duty to take care . . . or in the context of . . . risk-based liability, as . . . is the case . . . here.

a) When it comes to liability for negligence (the consequences of a deliberate act are always 'adequate' [reference omitted]), the defendant will not be held liable for a quite unusual or unexpected course of events; that proposition is inseparably . . . linked with the content of the concrete duty to take care . . .

b) . . . Risk-based liability does not rest on a duty to take care; rather, it serves to offset the manifestations of a concrete danger, the creation of which is usually not prohibited. In this respect, it does not matter whether the actual course of events which lead to the injury should have been foreseen on the basis of past experience [reference omitted]. The key issue is whether the injury represented a specific manifestation of the danger against which the general public was meant to be indemnified, according to the liability regime [references omitted]. In this regard, it cannot reasonably be doubted . . . that [the regime of § 33 LuftVG] extends to the risk that a building be damaged through the air pressure created by a helicopter . . .

However, the above cannot be interpreted to mean that in the field of risk-based liability, no limits are set to liability for injurious consequences beyond the basic test of causation [the "but for" test]. Indeed, the limits of liability are reached where the injury no longer represents a specific manifestation of the risk against which the liability regime is meant to provide protection. In the present case, the 'adequacy limit' would have been exceeded if, for instance, the vibration which led to the collapse could just as well have been caused by a road vehicle driving past in conformity with road traffic regulations [reference omitted]."

Notes

(1) In this key case, the BGH set out how the assessment of causation is to proceed under risk-based liability regimes (*Gefährdungshaftung*). As a starting point, the BGH

---

[52] BGHZ 79, 259. Translation by Y.P. Salmon.

goes back to its decision of 23 October 1951,[53] recalling that "adequacy" was "generally recognized as a means to exclude the chains of events for which the defendant cannot in all fairness be made liable".[54] With respect to causation, fault-based and risk-based liability thus share as a common starting point a concern for keeping the liability of the defendant within reasonable limits. Nevertheless, as the BGH explained, that common concern leads to significantly different approaches to causation.

(2) Under fault-based regimes, the focus is on the breach of a norm of conduct. Accordingly, the adequacy theory is meant to exclude liability for consequences which were "quite unusual or unexpected", since no norm of conduct goes so far as to oblige someone to avoid such consequences.[55] As explained in the chapter concerning causation, the assessment of causation is complemented with a normative examination (*wertende Betrachtung*) revolving around the scope of the norm giving rise to liability (*Schutzzweck der Norm*).[56]

(3) As the BGH found in the annotated case, the situation is different in the case of risk-based liability (*Gefährdungshaftung*)—at least for the narrow risk-based regimes and those comprising a presumption of causation, according to the classification made by E. Deutsch.[57] Since no norm of conduct underlies these regimes, it serves no purpose to try to exclude liability for extraordinary or unexpected consequences. The adequacy theory therefore plays no role there, and the assessment of causation therefore centres on the *Schutzzweck der Norm* theory, more precisely on its restatement in the context of risk-based liability. The exceptional danger or risk, which underpins risk-based liability, also becomes the defining factor in the assessment of causation: liability will not extend to injury which does not represent a specific manifestation of the risk against which the liability regime is meant to protect the general public.

The annotated case illustrates well the reasoning set out by the BGH: the collapse of the roof would probably qualify as a "quite unusual or unexpected course of events" such as to exclude liability under the adequacy theory (that was indeed the position taken by the court of appeal in that case). Under the test put forward by the BGH, however, foreseeability is not a concern, and the issue becomes whether the collapse of a roof is a manifestation of the risk created by the operation of helicopters. According to the BGH, in order to show that the injury was outside the scope of the risk, it should be demonstrated that under comparable circumstances, the same injury could equally have been caused otherwise (e.g. if a vehicle driving by could have caused the same damage). In such circumstances, the intervention of the source of exceptional danger for which the defendant must respond would not have increased the risk of injury, or in other words, the injury would represent the manifestation of a risk to which the plaintiff was exposed in any event.

[53] See *supra*, Chapter IV, **4.G.1.**

[54] It should be pointed out that, in the annotated case, the BGH appears to use "adequacy" inconsistently: when discussing fault-based liability under a), the expression refers to the adequacy test for causation as such; elsewhere it refers to the more general idea that some limits must be put on the basic equivalency test on grounds of equity and reasonableness (these limits then comprise both the adequacy and the *Schutzzweck der Norm* theories).

[55] The adequacy theory as it is applied in the fault-based regimes is discussed *supra*, Chapter IV, **4.G.1.** and notes thereafter.

[56] See, *supra*, Chapter IV, 4.1.1., Introductory Note under d) as well as **4.G.2.** and notes thereafter.

[57] See *supra*, **6.G.2.**

(4) This line of thought was developed further in a judgment of 2 July 1991, reproduced in the chapter concerning causation.[58] In its reasoning there, the BGH expressly outlined a "sphere of risk" for which the plaintiff must be held responsible, whether that is the general risk encountered in life (*allgemeines Lebensrisiko*) or a more specific risk, such as, in that case, the risk created by the choice of intensive farming methods. The sphere of risk borne by the plaintiff is then opposed to the sphere of exceptional risk for which the defendant is liable under the risk-based liability (*Gefährdungshaftung*) regime in question. The analysis accordingly shifts from assessing whether the injury fell within or outside the range of specific realizations of the risk created by the defendant to determining in whose sphere of risk the injury should fall.

6.1.2. FRENCH LAW

Introductory Note

a) When compared to German law, French law shows perhaps less theoretical development by way of a general theory of liability not based on fault or, as it is called under French law, liability without fault (*responsabilité sans faute*) or liability by virtue of the law (*responsabilité de plein droit*). Yet it more than compensates by the willingness of French courts to introduce regimes not based on fault in French tort law, and by the significance which such regimes have come to take.

The first document below, an excerpt from G. Viney, provides a good survey of the evolution of liability without fault in French case law and legislation.

b) The most remarkable development in French case law regarding civil liability, and certainly one of the distinctive features of French civil law in that respect, was the creation, by the end of the 19th century, of an autonomous regime of liability without fault for damage caused by things under one's *garde*, on the basis of Article 1384(1) C.civ. The main features of that regime cristallized in the first half of the 20th century. Broadly speaking, it can apply to almost all "accidents", as that term is commonly understood, since an object usually intervenes in causing accidental damage. Accordingly it provided a welcome alternative to Article 1382 C.civ. to many a victim of the new forms of injury typical of industrialized societies (accidents involving motor vehicles, machinery, tools, equipment, applicances, etc.). At some point in time, the regime of Article 1384(1) C.civ. probably played a more significant role than the general fault-based regime of Article 1382 C.civ. in the practical workings of French tort law. In recent times, however, its field of application has been progressively curtailed by the enactment of specific statutes which created particular regimes for certain categories of accidents,[59] the main one being the *Loi Badinter*, which removed traffic accidents from the realm of Article 1384(1) C.civ.[60] Nevertheless, these statutory regimes all build on the developments that took place in the case law concerning Article 1384(1) C.civ.

---

[58] BGH, 2 July 1991, *supra*, Chapter IV, **4.G.3.**
[59] See Viney and Jourdain, *Conditions* at 602–3, para. 628.
[60] Act of 5 July 1985, *infra*, **6.F.16.**

Accordingly, and given that the subject-matter of the general regime of liability for things neither fits under the broad themes covered in the next sections nor has any equivalent in the other legal systems under study, four cases are included below in order to discuss the main aspects of that regime. The first case (the well-known *Jand'heur* decision) concerns the nature of the regime. The others deal with the main conditions for liability under Article 1384(1) C.civ., namely the *fait de la chose* (intervention of the thing in the occurrence of the injury) as well as the notion of *garde*.

G. Viney, Introduction à la responsabilité[61]   6.F.4.

"Every author who tried to describe the evolution of civil liability during the 20th century was struck first and foremost by the declining significance of subjective fault as a condition for civil liability . . .

First of all, since 1896, the courts have given a specific interpretation to Article 1384(1) C.civ., turning it into a regime of 'liability by virtue of the law' (*responsabilité de plein droit*) applicable to every injury caused by the 'behaviour of a thing' (*fait d'une chose*). Today, the practical impact of that regime is considerable, since it can govern virtually every instance of accidental injury that does not fall under a specific regime.

But the courts did not stop there. They continued to create new instances of liability without fault (*responsabilité sans faute*). For example, as of the end of the 19th century, a regime of liability by virtue of the law (where absence of fault is no defence) was in fact invented for the benefit of the victims of inconveniences as between neighbours. Moreover, courts interpreted Article 1384(5) C.civ., concerning the liability of the employer (*commettant*) for his employees (*préposés*), in such a way that that provision can no longer be seen as a sanction for fault in choosing or supervising employees, but rather as a mechanism whereby third parties are indemnified against certain risks created by the firm.

In the realm of contractual liability, the distinction between 'obligations of result' (*obligations de résultat*) and 'obligations of means' (*obligations de moyens*), which had been put forward in legal writing, was taken over in the case law. What is more, courts were generous in characterizing as 'obligations of result' the duties which they themselves had read into contractual relationships, so that in the end a number of instances of liability by virtue of the law were created, including the liability of the carrier for the injury to passengers during transport or the damage caused to transported goods, the liability of the manufacturer and the seller of defective products towards the victims of the defect, the liability of the building contractor towards the other party in cases of construction defects, etc . . .

[G. Viney then reviews the specific instances of no-fault liability created by legislation, namely:

– loss or injury suffered as a result of an accident at work;[62]
– damage caused by dangerous installations;[63]
– harm caused by the defence industry;[64]
– damage suffered on the ground as a result of the operation of aircraft;[65]

---

[61] 2nd edn. (Paris: LGDJ, 1995) at 28–9, 93, 95–6 and 98, para. 22–3, 56, 58 and 59. Translation by P. Larouche.

[62] Act of 9 April 1898.

[63] Act of 10 December 1917.

[64] Act of 3 May 1921, JO, 5 May 1921, D 1923.IV.181, Art. 1, superseded by the Act 46–2389 of 28 October 1946, JO, 29 October 1946, D 1946.Lég.431.

[65] Act of 31 May 1924, JO, 26 July 1924, D 1925.IV.41, Art. 53, now Art. L.141–2 of the *Code de l'aviation civile*: see *infra*, 6.2.2.

- injury caused by cable-cars;[66]
- damage caused to aircraft passengers as a result of the operation of the aircraft;[67]
- harm from the use of atomic energy;[68]
- marine pollution;[69]
- construction defects in buildings;[70]
- loss or injury suffered as a result of a traffic accident;[71]
- injury to subjects of medical experiments with no immediate therapeutical purpose;[72]
- injury to blood donors;[73]

to which the Act of 19 May 1998 on product liability (adding Articles 1386–1 to 1386–18 to the *Code civil*)[74] should be added.]

. . .The presence of a number of instances of objective liability (*responsabilité objective*) is by now well established and accepted. Furthermore, many authors would even agree with the extension of such liability to most dangerous activities. Nevertheless, they generally continue to express a true endearment to the concept of fault, which they would like to keep not only as part of the law of civil liability, but even as its foundation . . .

Must we reform the law of civil liability on a piecemeal basis, with specific statutes concerning activities for which the 'common law of civil liability' seem no longer appropriate? Or should we rather reconstruct that 'common law', so that the unity of civil liability can be maintained as much as possible? . . .

[French law] is in fact torn between those two options. If legislative intervention remained exceptional until the 1970s and 1980s, that was because the legislature preferred to leave the judiciary, as much as possible, with the task of adapting the law of civil liability to the requirements of society. As a result of that approach, the 'common law of civil liability' was enriched with new principles of a very general nature, such as the well-known regime of liability by virtue of the law for the keeper (*gardien*) of a thing, on the basis of Article 1384(1) C.civ., or the distinction between obligations of means and obligations of result . . . The legislature was not totally absent, however. The evolution of industrial technology brought about new fields of endeavour, which soon became commonplace; the dangerous nature of those activities touched public opinion sometimes so much that the legislature felt the need to adopt specific rules. The enactment of those rules can be seen as a sign that

---

[66] Act of 8 July 1941, JO, 27 August 1941, DA 1941.436, Art. 6: see *infra*, 6.2.2.

[67] Act 57–259 of 2 March 1957, JO, 3 March 1957, D 1957.Lég.83, Art. 1, now Art. L.321–3 and L.322–3 of the *Code de l'aviation civile*, extending the application of the Warsaw Convention of 12 October 1929 to all air transport to, from and within France: see *infra*, 6.2.2.

[68] France has ratified the main conventions applicable in this field, namely the Paris Convention on Third-Party Liability in the Field of Nuclear Energy of 29 July 1960, JO, 11 February 1969, the Brussels Convention supplementing the Paris Convention of 31 January 1963 (1963) 2 ILM 685, the Brussels Convention relating to Civil Liability in the Field of Maritime Carriage of Nuclear Material of 17 December 1971, JO, 3 August 1975, and subsequent protocols applicable to these conventions. In addition, some legislation has been enacted to implement or complement these conventions: see the Act 65–956 of 12 November 1965, JO, 13 November 1965, D 1965.Lég.261, the Act 68–943 of 30 October 1968, JO, 31 October 1968, D 1968.Lég.303 and the Act 90–488 of 16 June 1990, JO, 17 June 1990, D 1990.Lég.260.

[69] Act 77–530 of 26 May 1977, JO, 27 May 1977, D 1977.Lég.208, Art. 1. This Act implements in France the Brussels Convention on Civil Liability for Oil Pollution Damage of 29 November 1969, (1970) 9 ILM 45.

[70] Act 78–12 of 4 January 1978, JO, 5 January 1978, D 1978.Lég.74, Art. 1, replacing Art. 1792 C.civ.

[71] Act of 5 July 1985 (*Loi Badinter*), *infra*, **6.F.16.**

[72] Act 88–1138 of 20 December 1988, JO, 22 December 1988, D 1989.Lég.12, Art. 1, introducing Art. L. 209–7 in the *Code de la santé publique*.

[73] Act 93–5 of 4 January 1993, JO, 5 January 1993, D 1993.Lég.154, introducing Art. L.668–10 in the *Code de la santé publique*.

[74] Act 98–389 of 19 May 1998, *infra*, **6.F.37.**

the 'common law of civil liability' is receding in favour of a new approach which puts more emphasis on the peculiarities of each activity than on the overall consistency of the law of civil liability.

A look at the substance of these specific regimes, however, reveals striking similarities between them. Furthermore, they follow the very same ideas that inspired courts in their interpretation of the general rules. Among others . . . most of those regimes are remarkably remote from any requirement that the person who caused the injury be personally 'at fault', and they all strive to link the imposition of liability with the ability to obtain insurance coverage . . .

The outlines of the area where it would be desirable to set aside the traditional principles of civil liability are still fairly uncertain. Nevertheless, it seems that the concept of 'danger for the safety of persons and property' is best suited to describe the set of activities that should be removed from the fault-based liability regime."

Notes

(1) In France, the appropriate basis for imposing liability has been the focus of much discussion in academic circles. By the end of the 19th century, many authors had expressed their doubts on the adequacy of fault as a basis for imposing liability, in view of the increasing number of accidents caused by the use of machines, where fault and causation were difficult to establish and more often than not the victim of a grave injury ended up without compensation. They argued that the basis for imposing liability should be moved away from fault towards risk (the risk theory or *théorie du risque*). Accordingly, persons should be made liable not because their conduct was blameworthy, but rather— depending on the formulation of the theory —because they derive profit from an activity which exposes others to a risk of injury («*risque-profit*») or because they control a source of risk for others («*risque-maîtrise*»).[75]

These doctrinal developments have had considerable impact on French law. As G. Viney points out at the beginning of the excerpt, fault as the basis for liability has been in constant decline throughout the 20th century.

(2) Indeed, contrary to the situation in Germany, where the principle of fault was firmly anchored in the BGB, it was possible for case law to find some bases within the system of the Code civil itself to support a move away from fault. The key provision in this respect remains Article 1384(1) C.civ., which reads:

> "Everyone is liable for the damage caused not only by one's own conduct, but also by the conduct of persons for whom one is responsible or things in one's care (*garde*)"

There is some historical evidence that that provision was intended to be no more than a reminder that fault could be derived not only from one's conduct, but also from the failure to prevent other persons or things from causing damage.[76] Nevertheless, the prevailing view soon became that Article 1384(1) constitutes an explicit acknowledgement that liability could be justified on a basis other than fault.[77]

In practice, the main development remains without doubt the creation of a regime of liability without fault for things under one's *garde*, on the basis of Article 1384(1) C.civ. That regime is studied in greater detail in the next four cases below.

---

[75] The two main proponents of the risk theory at the time were R. Saleilles and L. Josserand. See Viney, *Introduction* at 82–4, para. 49 and Schamps at 605–10.

[76] See Schamps at 595–7.

[77] See Viney and Jourdain, *Conditions* at 313, para. 438.

G. Viney notes three other developments in French case law which have undermined the position of fault as the basis for civil liability:

– An autonomous regime of liability was created for inconveniences in excess of normal limits as between neighbours (*troubles de voisinage anormaux*), which now operates without reference to fault.[78] In a similar fashion, liability for a breach of privacy (protected at Article 9 C.civ.) will arise by the mere fact that the right was breached, which suffices to establish fault for the purposes of Article 1382 C.civ.[79]
– Article 1384(5) C.civ., concerning liability for injury caused by employees (*préposés*), was interpreted so as to deny the employer (*commettant*) any possibility of exoneration on grounds of absence of fault on his or her part.[80] It should be added that in 1997, the Cour de cassation held that, under the regime of parental liability for injury caused by children (Article 1384(4) C.civ.) and the general regime of liability for others (Article 1384(1) C.civ.) as well, absence of fault on the part of the parent or custodian could not defeat liability;[81]
– In the realm of contractual liability, the case law followed the ideas put forward in legal writing, whereby, on the basis of Article 1147 C.civ., a large number of contractual obligations should be characterized as obligations of result (*obligations de résultat*),[82] thus depriving the person under the obligation of the defence that, despite his or her best efforts (i.e. despite the absence of fault), the result stipulated in the contract could not be attained.

(3) G. Viney then reviews the numerous instances where specific regimes of liability without fault have been introduced by legislation.[83] As she remarks, most of these regimes, especially the more recent ones, are based on the rationale that the party who is in the best position to insure against the risk of injury in question should be made liable without fault.[84]

(4) Even if no all-encompassing theory has yet been developed under French law to tie together all the regimes of liability without fault that arose from the case law or through legislation, there is nonetheless a fair degree of similarity between all of them, as G. Viney notes. They all follow more or less the following path. As seen before, the three conditions for fault-based liability under French law are fault, damage and causation. In order to integrate liability without fault into a coherent general model for liability, these three conditions are usually restated as "triggering factor" (*fait générateur de responsabilité*), damage and causation. In the standard presentation of French tort law under Art. 1382–6 C.civ., the triggering factor can then be a fault, the conduct of another person (*fait d'autrui*), for instance the conduct of an employee (*préposé*) under Article 1384(5) C.civ.

---

[78] See *supra*, Chapter II, 2.3.3., Introductory Note under c) and *infra*, 6.4.1. under b).

[79] See *supra*, Chapter II, **2.F.29.–30.**, Note (1).

[80] See *supra*, Chapter V, 5.1.1. under c).

[81] In Cass. civ. 2e, 19 February 1997, *supra*, Chapter V, **5.F.24.** and Cass. crim., 26 March 1997, *supra*, Chapter V, **5.F.25.**, respectively.

[82] The distinction between obligations of means and of result is explained *supra*, Chapter III, **3.F.2.**, Note (2).

[83] These regimes have not received the same kind of attention from academics in France as in Germany, and accordingly they will not be studied here in the same detail.

[84] These regimes often bind the party on whom liability is imposed to obtain insurance against such liability.

or the "conduct" of a thing (*fait de la chose*).[85] Statutory regimes of liability without fault simply attach liability to another "triggering factor".

Consequently, the conditions of causation and damage generally remain the same as under fault-based liability pursuant to Article 1382–3 C.civ., with some exceptions. First of all, the assessment of causation is subject to certain modifications in the case of liability for things under Article 1384(1) C.civ.,[86] as well as the *Loi Badinter* concerning motor vehicle accidents,[87] which builds on it. Secondly, with respect to damage, liability regimes relying on international conventions or EC directives generally incorporate some limitations on recoverable damage.[88]

(5) Under French law, the various regimes of liability without fault are also called "*responsabilité de plein droit*" (liability by virtue of the law). That term is opposed to the general fault-based liability (*responsabilité pour faute*) regime and to the regimes where fault is presumed (*responsabilité pour faute présumée*). That terminology shows that the regimes of liability without fault are conceived as regimes in which an element of fault is missing (i.e. liability flows by virtue of the law as soon as damage and causation are established) and not as regimes where a concept other than fault is at the root. In other words, the various elements making up the *fait générateur* (triggering factor) instead of fault constitute not so much an alternative rationale for imposing liability, but simply a condition for liability to arise. That point will be developed in greater detail below in relation to liability for things pursuant to Article 1384(1) C.civ.[89] Accordingly, even if the *théorie du risque* developed at the turn of the century had an impact on French legal minds, it did not become the recognized basis for the various regimes of liability without fault. As a consequence, French law does not exhibit the close relationship observed in *Gefährdungshaftung* under German law between the rationale for imposing liability (*Haftungsgrund*)—usually the creation of an exceptional danger—and the scope of liability (*Haftungsumfang*), as evidenced in the German rule that the injury must represent a materialization of the risk in question.[90] This is consistent with the general insignificance of anything analogous to the "scope of rule" theory (*Schutzzweck der Norm*) in French tort law.

(6) As G. Viney notes, even if the significance of fault as a basis for liability under French law has been notably reduced, it is still generally agreed that fault should not be removed from the law of delict altogether. The general progress of liability without fault

---

[85] See Viney and Jourdain, *Conditions* at 313, para. 438.

[86] See *infra*, **6.F.6.–7.**

[87] See *infra*, **6.F.16.**

[88] See for instance the liability regimes pertaining to air transport, *infra*, 6.2.2. (based on the Warsaw Convention for the Unification of Certain Rules relating to International Carriage by Air of 12 October 1929, 137 LNTS 11, which provides for a maximum limit on damages to be paid), nuclear accidents, *infra*, 6.4.2. under e) (based on the Paris Convention on Third-Party Liability in the Field of Nuclear Energy of 29 July 1960, JO, 11 February 1969, which excludes certain property from its coverage), as well as the new product liability regime, *infra*, **6.F.37.**, which takes over some limitations found in Directive 85/374, *infra*, **6.EC.33.** (exclusion of damage to defective product).

[89] See *infra*, **6.F.6.–7.**

[90] See *supra*, **6.G.3.** and notes thereafter, as well as **6.G.2.** and Note (4) thereafter. As mentioned by E. Deutsch, *supra*, **6.G.2.** and Note (5) thereafter, however, the "broader risk-based liability" (*erweiterte Gefährdungshaftung*) regimes concerning defective products (§ 1 ProdHaftG) and drugs (§ 84 AMG) do not evidence such a close relationship between *Haftungsgrund* and *Haftungsumfang*: they are then closer to the French model.

has been left to the hazards of the evolution of case law, which has not gone as far as to change the very foundation of delictual liability. The activity of the legislature has been limited to the introduction of specific regimes.

The creation of a general regime of liability without fault which would stand besides the general fault-based liability regime would require, as G. Viney points out, agreement upon the underlying rationale for such regime. As mentioned in the previous note, the *théorie du risque* has not emerged as the explicit basis for the various regimes of liability without fault, which seem to be applied for their own sake. G. Viney, together with other authors,[91] would favour the concept of "danger to the safety of persons and property" as the basis for a general regime of liability without fault.

Cass. Ch. réun., 13 February 1930[92]   **6.F.5.**
Jand'heur v. Les galeries belfortaises

LIABILITY WITHOUT FAULT FOR THINGS

Pedestrian run over

The regime of Article 1384(1) C.civ. applies to all things, irrespective of whether they are (i) immoveable or moveable, (ii) directed by a human being or "autonomous", (iii) defective or not or (iv) dangerous or not.

Facts: On 22 April 1925, the plaintiff was gravely injured when she was struck by a truck of the defendant company as she was crossing the street. She sued the company in its quality as *gardien* of the truck pursuant to Article 1384(1) C.civ. The company pleaded by way of defence that no fault had been committed, and that the regime of Article 1384(1) C.civ. was not applicable, since the truck was driven by human hand and did not otherwise suffer from any defect which could have caused the damage.

Held: On 7 July 1925, the court of first instance allowed the claim. On 29 December 1925, the court of appeal reversed the judgment of the court of first instance and dismissed the claim. On 21 February 1927, in a first decision in the case, the civil chamber of the Cour de cassation quashed the decision of the court of appeal and remitted the case back for further consideration.[93] On 7 July 1927, the second court of appeal refused to follow the Cour de cassation and dismissed the plaintiff's claim.[94] The case was then put before the joined chambers of the Cour de cassation, where the judgment of the court of appeal was quashed and the case remitted for further determination.

Judgment: "The presumption of liability found at Art. 1384(1) C.civ. runs against the one who had under his *garde* an inanimate object which caused harm to another. It can only be rebutted by proof of an unforeseeable event (*cas fortuit*), *force majeure* or an extraneous cause that cannot be imputed to him. It does not suffice to adduce evidence that he committed no fault or that the cause of the injurious event is unknown.

The [court of appeal] refused to apply the aforementioned provision on the ground that, in the absence of any evidence that the vehicle was defective, the accident caused by a car in motion which was driven by someone would not qualify as the behaviour of a thing which is under one's *garde*, within the meaning of Article 1384(1). Accordingly, in order to obtain compensation for the harm, the victim would have had to establish that a fault was imputable to the driver.

91   See also Le Tourneau and Cadiet at 20, para. 56 and the thorough comparative study of Schamps.
92   DP 1930.I.57, S 1930.I.121. Translation by Y.P. Salmon.
93   Cass. civ., 21 February 1927, DP 1927.I.97, S 1927.I.137.
94   Lyon, 7 July 1927, DH 1927.423.

However, when it comes to the application of the presumption [of Article 1384(1) C.civ.], the law makes no distinction according to whether the thing which caused the damage was operated by a person or not. It is not necessary that the thing suffered from a defect which was inherent to its nature and liable to cause damage, since Article 1384 imposes liability on account of the *garde* of the thing, and not on account of the thing itself.

It follows that, in ruling as it did, the [court of appeal] wrongly decided that the burden of proof fell on the plaintiff and infringed [Article 1384(1) C.civ.]."

Notes

(1) As mentioned above, case law construed the regime of liability without fault for things under one's *garde* on the basis of Article 1384(1) C.civ., the relevant part of which reads: "Everyone is liable for the damage caused . . . by the conduct of . . . things in one's care (*garde*)" Irrespective of the issue of the basis for liability,[95] the received wisdom for most of the 19th century was that this clause merely introduced the specific regimes of liability for animals and buildings which followed at Articles 1385 and 1386 C.civ. respectively. Similarly, the mention of "the conduct of persons for whom one is responsible" in the same provision was thought of as a header for the various cases of liability for others which followed in the other paragraphs of Article 1384 C.civ., an interpretation that remained valid until 1991.[96]

As regards things, however, the proponents of a more adequate, risk-based approach to accidents caused by mechanical devices (*théorie du risque*)[97] soon turned to Article 1384(1) C.civ. as a possible legal basis for their views to find application in French law.[98] The Cour de cassation heeded their suggestions in a celebrated judgment of 1896, where it "discovered" that Article 1384(1) C.civ. was not just an introductory clause, but rather contained an autonomous regime of liability for injury caused by things.[99]

In the wake of that decision, much debate arose within case law and legal writing as to the basis and the conditions of liability pursuant to Article 1384(1) C.civ. That debate was to a great extent brought to an end in the annotated case, where the Cour de cassation settled many controversies. Accordingly, the annotated case is as noteworthy for the position taken by the Cour de cassation as for the alternative positions which it chose *not* to take.

(2) In the annotated case, the Cour de cassation first held that Article 1384(1) C.civ. created a "presumption of liability" (*présomption de responsabilité*) from which the defendant could escape only by showing that the injury resulted from *cause étrangère*, a cause foreign to the defendant, which he or she could neither foresee nor resist (a natural event or the conduct of a third party or the victim).[100] In particular, evidence of absence of fault or causal uncertainty did not suffice to exonerate the defendant. Some doubt remained after the judgment in the annotated case, since the court had spoken of a "pre-

---

[95] See *supra*, **6.F.4.**, Note (2).
[96] See *supra*, Chapter V, **5.F.23.** and notes thereafter.
[97] See *supra*, **6.F.4.**, Note (1).
[98] See Viney and Jourdain, *Conditions* at 604–7, para. 629.
[99] Cass. civ., 18 June 1896, *Teffaine*, S 1897.I.17, D 1897.I.433.
[100] The Cour de cassation used the terms "fortuitous event or . . . *force majeure* or . . . extraneous cause that cannot be imputed to [the defendant]" (*cas fortuit ou . . . force majeure ou . . . cause étrangère qui ne lui soit pas imputable*). Since the time when the annotated case was decided, the various exonerating causes have been regrouped under a unified theory of "extraneous causes" comprising natural events (the classical cases of *cas fortuit* and *force majeure*) and the conduct of third parties: see *supra*, Chapter III, 3.2.3.

sumption", implying that it could somehow be rebutted. Since the 1950s, however, the Cour de cassation uses the phrase "liability by virtue of the law" (*responsabilité de plein droit*) to describe liability for things pursuant to Article 1384(1) C.civ., leaving no doubt that it is a case of liability without fault.[101]

(3) Given that Article 1384(1) C.civ. leads to liability without fault, the definition of the *fait générateur* (triggering factor) for liability to arise (in place of fault) becomes crucial. On this point, the text of Article 1384(1) C.civ. provides little help, and it was left more or less to legal writers and judges to develop a definition. In the annotated case, the Cour de cassation dealt with many points regarding the concept of "thing" under Article 1384(1) C.civ.

First, the Cour de cassation worded its decision broadly enough to dispel doubts that the regime of Article 1384(1) C.civ. applied to immoveable as well as moveable property.[102] Nonetheless, Article 1384(1) C.civ. will not apply in the cases falling under the more specific regime of liability for injury caused by the collapse of buildings.[103]

(4) Secondly, since the decision of 1896, some authors and some case law (including the court of appeal in the annotated case) had been trying to "contain" the potentially vast scope of liability under Article 1384(1) C.civ. by putting forward a distinction between the "autonomous" intervention of the thing in the causation of damage and the intervention of a thing as a result of the conduct of a person (*fait de l'homme*). Only the former would come under Article 1384(1) C.civ., while the latter would be left to the general fault-based liability regime of Article 1382–3 C.civ. (i.e. liability would arise only upon proof that the person "driving" the thing did not exercise due care). Typically, traffic accidents would thus have been excluded from the scope of Article 1384(1) C.civ. In the annotated case, the Cour de cassation repudiated that distinction and held that liability under Article 1384(1) C.civ. applies as soon as a thing causes the injury in question, irrespective of whether the thing behaved "autonomously" or not.[104]

(5) Thirdly, another restrictive construction of Article 1384(1) C.civ. would have limited its application to *defective* things, i.e. those which present a *vice* (defect). The victim would then have had to show that the thing which brought about the injury had some defect, and consequently that the injury could be traced back to that defect. Imposing that burden on the victim would, to a considerable extent, have defeated the purpose of the regime of liability without fault under Article 1384(1) C.civ., bearing in mind that evidentiary problems relating to fault and causation—which often left victims without compensation—were one of the main reasons why that regime was introduced. In addition, a great number of things involved in accidents are not defective, so that the scope of the regime would have been severely curtailed: in those cases, the victim would have been left with no recourse other than the general fault-based regime of Article 1382 C.civ.. In the annotated case, the Cour de cassation, following on a previous decision,[105] rejected that construction.[106] As the court stated, liability attaches to the defendant not because of the

---

[101] Viney and Jourdain, *Conditions* at 607, para. 629; *Les grands arrêts* at 524.

[102] See Viney and Jourdain, *Conditions* at 610, para. 633.

[103] Bénac-Schmidt/Larroumet at 5, para. 37; Viney and Jourdain, *Conditions* at 693–5, para. 735 to 739–1.

[104] See Viney and Jourdain, *Conditions* at 608–9, 631–2, para. 632 and 659.

[105] Cass. civ., 16 November 1920, S 1922.I.97, DP 1920.I.169.

[106] See Viney and Jourdain, *Conditions* at 630–1, para. 658.

thing as such, but because he or she was the keeper (*guardien*) of the thing, so that it does not matter whether the thing in question was defective or not.

It should be noted that in Belgium, where courts also "discovered" a regime of liability for things in Article 1384(1) of the Belgian Civil Code, case law has gone the other way, requiring that the victim prove that the thing was defective.[107]

(6) Fourthly, some authors, whose point of view had been to some extent echoed in case law, had maintained that Article 1384(1) C.civ. should apply only to *dangerous* things. Here as well, the aim was to restrict the potential scope of application of that article, on the basis that only in the case of things presenting a specific danger of injury would it be justifiable to impose liability without fault upon the keeper of the thing. In other cases, since non-dangerous things do not affect the general risk of injury to which one is exposed, the general fault-based regime should apply. In a previous decision in the annotated case, the civil chamber of the Cour de cassation had seemed to espouse that view.[108]

In the decision reproduced above, the joined chambers (*Chambres réunies*) of the court did not expressly dismiss such a limitation, but the wording of the decision is broad enough to be construed as an implicit rejection.[109] In any event, the distinction between dangerous and non-dangerous things did not surface again in the case law under Article 1384(1) C.civ., and it was explicitly rejected by the Cour de cassation in 1984.[110]

(7) In broad terms, the restrictive interpretations of Article 1384(1) C.civ.—proposing to limit its scope to moveable, "autonomous", defective or dangerous things, respectively—which the Cour de cassation rejected in the annotated case all aimed to introduce limitations into the practical workings of Article 1384(1) C.civ., in order to reflect somehow the scope of the risk against which Article 1384(1) C.civ. might be intended to provide relief, namely the increased risk of injury caused by the use of machines. In a sense, they would all have brought into the regime of Article 1384(1) C.civ. the same type of limitation based on the scope of the norm (*Schutzzweck der Norm*) as is found in most risk-based liability (*Gefährdungshaftung*) regimes under German law.[111] Through the rejection of such attempts to limit the scope of application of liability for things pursuant to Article 1384(1) C.civ., the Cour de cassation in the annotated case also demonstrated that Article 1384(1) C.civ. could not be explained through the risk theory, or at least that its scope of application would not reflect that theory.[112]

As F. Bénac-Schmidt and C. Larroumet write:[113]

"However, it must be understood that, as soon as the increase in the use of machines enabled the discovery of a new principle of civil liability, it would have been absurd and arbitrary to limit its application to damage that resulted from such use. In truth, it cannot be denied that the use of machines gave the impetus . . . for the introduction of a regime of liability for things, but logic dictated that such regime be applied extensively, since its introduction evidenced a fundamental change in the law of civil liability. Indeed, the mere fact that a specific need, namely the need to provide protection against the consequences of the increased use of machines, may have played a role in the creation of a [legal] regime does not mean that such regime cannot be applied in other fields, as long as the extension of its scope of application remained in tune with the evolution of ideas, which tends to put the victim of injury in a privileged position."

[107] See Schamps at 659 ff.
[108] Cass. civ., 21 February 1927, D 1929.I.129, DP 1930.I.57.
[109] Viney and Jourdain, *Conditions* at 611, para. 634.
[110] Cass. civ. 2e, 15 November 1984, D 1985.Jur.20.
[111] See *supra*, **6.G.2.** and Note (4) thereafter, as well as **6.G.3.** and notes thereafter.
[112] Schamps at 600.
[113] Bénac-Schmidt/Larroumet at 5, para. 36.

Accordingly, the scope of application of Article 1384(1) C.civ., in all its generality, was dictated not so much by the willingness to keep some consistency with an underlying theory that would justify the imposition of liability, but rather by the concern that the victim of injury should not be "arbitrarily" denied the benefit of a favourable regime. As many authors also point out, the development of liability insurance in the course of the 20th century did not provide courts with any incentive to restrict the scope of application of Article 1384(1) C.civ. in order to avoid putting an undue burden on the defendants.[114]

In the end, therefore, any thing can potentially lead to the liability of its keeper under Article 1384(1) C.civ. The only condition which must be satisfied in order for liability to be imposed is that the thing *intervened* in the causation of injury, or in other words that the "behaviour of the thing" (*fait de la chose*) caused the injury. That condition is explored in greater detail in the following two cases.

Cass. civ. 2e, 19 March 1980[115]   **6.F.6.–7.**
SA Shell Française v. *SA L'Union maritime de Dragage*
and
Cass. civ. 2e, 8 July 1992[116]
Tallut v. *Société Adam*

Fait de la chose
Behaviour of the thing

When the thing was not in motion or did not collide with either the body or the property of the victim, the victim must show that the thing behaved abnormally, was abnormally positioned or suffered from an internal defect.

A. Cass. civ. 2e, 19 March 1980   **6.F.6.**

Part of dredger lost in harbour

Facts: The plaintiff suffered loss because its ship was prevented from mooring safely, because of the hazard created by a part of the defendant's dredger (a sling), which had been lost in the waters of the harbour. The location of the part was not known at the time, so passage through the entrance to the harbour was restricted; when the part was later found, it turned out that it did not create any danger for ships using the harbour. The plaintiff sued the defendant as keeper (*gardien*) of the part in question under Article 1384(1) C.civ.

Held: The court of first instance and the court of appeal dismissed the claim. The Cour de cassation quashed the decision of the court of appeal and remitted the case for further consideration.

Judgment: "In order to reject the claim based on Article 1384(1) C.civ., the [court of appeal] found that, taking into account the draught of the [plaintiff's] ship and the depth at which the dredger sling had ultimately been found, the sling was not in a position where it could have prevented the passage of the ship, so that it played no part in the occurrence of the harm.

---

[114] Ibid.
[115] Bull.civ. 1980.II.65. Translation by Y.P. Salmon.
[116] Bull.civ. 1992.II.201. Translation by Y.P. Salmon.

However, the [defendant] had the *garde* of the sling, and it was unaware of the position and the depth at which it lay. It had thus made an area unsafe for ships of a certain draught, which resulted in the prohibition to enter the harbour. Accordingly, in ruling as it did, the court of appeal did not give a legal basis to its decision."

B. Cass. civ. 2e, 8 July 1992   6.F.7.

Car runs into concrete pillars

Facts: The victim drove his car into concrete pillars left by the defendant construction company on the side of a highway. He and his wife sued the defendant as keeper (*gardien*) of the pillars, on the basis of Article 1384(1) C.civ.

Held: The court of first instance and the court of appeal dismissed the claim. The Cour de cassation upheld the judgment of the court of appeal.

Judgment: "The court of appeal is criticized on the following grounds for having dismissed the claims of the [plaintiffs]. First of all, it infringed Article 1384(1) C.civ. in requiring from the [plaintiffs] that they prove that the pillars were abnormal or dangerous. Secondly, it failed to draw from the appropriate legal consequences from its findings when it concluded that the pillars were sufficiently well indicated and had not been the instrument of damage. Finally, it did not give a proper legal basis to its decision, in view of Article 1384(1) C.civ., when it denied altogether the liability of the [defendant], the keeper (*gardien*) of the pillars, without explaining how the conduct of the victim would have been unforeseeable and unavoidable.

However, the court of appeal found that the concrete pillars were placed on a central embankment, 1,7 m away from the continuous white line separating the two lanes of traffic and the said embankment. The side of the pillars were shielded with a bundle of straw marked out by a fluorescent band, and two road signs placed in front of the pillars indicated to road users that they must keep to the right hand lane. In the light thereof, the court of appeal held that the pillars appeared neither to be in an abnormal 'position' nor to create a danger because of an encroachment on the highway or an insufficient indication. From these findings and statements, the court of appeal could validly conclude that the pillars had not been instrumental in the occurrence of the harm, and that the accident was due to the victim's lack of control [over his vehicle].

Consequently, the court of appeal did not have to establish whether the conduct of the victim had been unforeseeable and unavoidable for the holder of the pillars."

Notes

(1) It was seen above in connection with the *Jand'heur* case that Article 1384(1) C.civ. applies to all "things" in general.[117] For liability to arise, however, it must be shown that the damage arises from the "behaviour of the thing" (*fait de la chose*), that is to say, that the thing *intervened in the causation of injury* or, as the Cour de cassation expressed it in the second annotated case, that the thing was the instrument of damage. Accordingly, the requirement of *fait de la chose* has a double impact: it is on the one hand the triggering factor (*fait générateur*) which justifies the imposition of liability—together with the position of the defendant as *gardien* of the thing in question—and it is on the other hand

---

[117] *Supra*, **6.F.5.** and notes thereafter.

clearly related to causation as well.[118] It is for the victim to show that the thing in question had intervened in the causation of injury, but once that is done, a rebuttable presumption of causation arises.[119] How useful for the victim that presumption really is depends on how easy or difficult it is for the victim to discharge the threshold of causal intervention (*fait de la chose*). Through the decades, French case law has developed a complex set of propositions on that point, which the two annotated cases illustrate.

The key factors to be taken into account are whether the thing was moving and whether it came in contact with body or property of the victim.

(2) The easiest situation occurs where the thing both was in motion at the time when the injury was inflicted and came in contact with the body or property of the victim. For all intents and purposes, the *fait de la chose* is thereby established so that liability is triggered, and at the same time causation is accordingly presumed.[120]

(3) In the first annotated case, no contact had taken place between the thing and the body or property of the victim: the plaintiff's vessel was prevented from entering the harbour because of the hazard created as a result of the defendant's dredger having lost a part in the harbour; but she never hit it.

However, according to French case law, actual contact is not necessary for liability under Article 1384(1) C.civ. to arise.[121] But causal intervention cannot be so easily assumed in the absence of contact, and hence the victim must show that the thing played an "active role" in the infliction of injury.[122] To that end, the victim must show "abnormal behaviour" (*comportement anormal*) by the thing, an "abnormal position" (*position anormale*) of the thing or an "internal defect" (*vice interne*) of the thing.[123]

In the first annotated case, for instance, the dredger part (a sling) was lost in the harbour; its precise position was unknown so that it was thought that it might create a danger for ships such as the plaintiff's, which could have collided with it (in fact, there was no danger, as was discovered later). In the result, as the Cour de cassation held, the part was in an abnormal position (it was not with the dredger), and thus it played an active role in the infliction of injury, even though there was no contact with the plaintiff's ship. The court mentioned that the defendant had "made an area unsafe", thus explicitly referring to the creation of risk as a rationale for its decision.

---

[118] Whether the *fait de la chose* is presented as part of the triggering factor (*fait générateur*) for liability or as part of the assessment of causation does not seem to make much practical difference. Most authors follow the former approach, while emphasizing that the behaviour of the thing is related to causation: Viney and Jourdain, *Conditions* at 633, para. 661; Le Tourneau and Cadiet at 874, para. 3637; Bénac-Schmidt/Larroumet at 31–2, para. 322–3.

[119] Viney and Jourdain, *Conditions* at 635, para. 665; Le Tourneau and Cadiet at 875–6, para. 3639, 3643; Bénac-Schmidt/Larroumet at 34, para. 349–50. The only way to rebut that presumption is to show that the injury was in fact caused by a extraneous cause (*cause étrangère*, an event foreign to the defendant which could be neither foreseen nor resisted). On extraneous cause, see *supra*, Chapter III, 3.2.3.

[120] The defendant could always attempt to show that the thing did not play an active role in the causation of damage (as in the cases where the thing did not move or did not make contact with the victim), but authors agree that this possibility has little relevance in practice: Viney and Jourdain, *Conditions* at 637–8, para. 668; Le Tourneau and Cadiet at 876–7, para. 3647–9; Bénac- Schmidt/Larroumet at 35, para. 358–9.

[121] See Le Tourneau and Cadiet at 874–5, para. 3638; Viney and Jourdain, *Conditions* at 638–9, para. 669.

[122] It could also be, for instance, that the thing in question intervened in the causation of injury through another object, as in the case of a car that is damaged when another car causes pebbles to fly into the air: see Le Tourneau and Cadiet at 874, para. 3638; Bénac-Schmidt/Larroumet at 35, para. 353–4.

[123] Viney and Jourdain, *Conditions* at 640, para. 671; Le Tourneau and Cadiet at 874–5, para. 3638–9; Bénac-Schmidt/Larroumet at 34–5, para. 351–2.

(4) In the second annotated case, the thing (concrete pillars) was stationary, even though there was contact with it. Here as well, the application of Article 1384(1) C.civ. is not a priori excluded merely because the thing was not in motion when the victim's car collided with it.[124] Nevertheless, it cannot be presumed that a motionless thing intervened in the causation of injury merely because of contact. As in cases where no contact has taken place, it is up to the victim to show that the thing in question played an active role in the infliction of injury, because it behaved abnormally, was abnormally located or had an internal defect.[125]

In the second annotated case, the victim was not able to show that the concrete pillars had played an "active role" in the accident, since there was no evidence that it had been placed abnormally. It is worth noting that the Cour de cassation also mentioned that the pillars were not "dangerously" placed, even though in theory the dangerous nature of the thing is not relevant.[126]

(5) In sum, the victim is put in a relatively favourable position when the thing in question was in motion *and* collided with the body or the property of the victim. The *fait de la chose*, i.e. the intervention in the causation of injury, will then be assumed, thus triggering liability and leading to a presumption that the thing was the actual cause of the damage. In contrast, if the thing either did not move or did not collide with the body or property of the victim (or both), the victim must then show that the thing played an active role in the causation of injury.[127]

Such active role requires an anomaly in the behaviour, the position or the condition of the thing. As a first remark, these concepts have certain overtones of wrongfulness: the anomaly will usually result from someone having failed to take the appropriate care in relation to the thing.[128] Secondly, by showing that there is an anomaly, the victim is establishing that the injury can be *explained* by the presence of the thing in question (because of the anomaly) or, in probabilistic terms, that the *probability of injury was significantly increased* by the presence of the thing (because of the anomaly). The concept of "active role" is thus a manifestation of the explanatory/adequacy theory of causation which is present in various areas of French tort law.[129] In other words, once the victim has demonstrated that the behaviour, position or condition of the thing was abnormal, not only has the *fait de la chose* been made out, but causation has by the same token also been shown. Accordingly, in those cases, the presumption of causation which follows from the *fait de la chose* does not actually add much.

(6) It should also be mentioned that in the first annotated case, compensation was awarded under Article 1384(1) C.civ. for injury which would qualify as pure economic loss under English law or *reiner Vermögensschaden* under German law and as such would not in principle fall within the scope of protection of tort law.[130] The plaintiff (a transport company) had been forced to pay contractual penalties to its clients because its ship

---

[124] Viney and Jourdain, *Conditions* at 641, para. 673; Bénac-Schmidt/Larroumet at 33, para. 337–9.

[125] See Viney and Jourdain, *Conditions* at 641–3, para. 673–4; Le Tourneau and Cadiet at 876, para. 3644–6; Bénac-Schmidt/Larroumet at 35–6, para. 360–5.

[126] See *supra*, **6.F.5.**, Note (6).

[127] See Viney and Jourdain, *Conditions* at 643, para. 674; Bénac-Schmidt/Larroumet at 34, para. 347.

[128] See von Bar II at 338–9 and 345–6, para. 311 and 316.

[129] Viney and Jourdain at 176–7, para. 358–1. See *supra*, Chapter IV, 4.1.3., Introductory Note under f).

[130] See *supra*, Chapter II, 2.3.1. (English law) and 2.3.2. (German law).

had been delayed, but the ship itself had not been damaged. The plaintiff had merely lost money in the incident. As mentioned before, the general fault-based liability regime under Article 1382–3 C.civ. also protects economic positions, and the same is true of Article 1384(1) C.civ.[131]

Cass. Ch. réun., 2 December 1941[132] **6.F.8.**
Connot v. Franck

CONCEPT OF *GARDIEN*

Car thief causes accident

*The keeper (*gardien*) is the person who in fact holds the power to use, direct and control the thing.*

Facts: The defendant's car was stolen by an unknown person, who, while driving the car, later killed the plaintiff's husband in an accident. The plaintiff sued the defendant, arguing that he had remained the *gardien* of the car even though it had been stolen.

Held: The court of appeal rejected the claim. In a first decision of 3 March 1936,[133] the civil chamber of the Cour de cassation quashed the decision of the court of appeal and remitted the case for further consideration. On 27 February 1937, the second court of appeal refused to follow the Cour de cassation and rejected the claim once more.[134] The case was brought before the joined chambers of the Cour de cassation, which then upheld the judgment of the second court of appeal, rejecting the claim.

Judgment: "In order to reject the claim of the [plaintiff], the court of appeal stated that, at the time of the accident, [the defendant], who had been dispossessed of his car when it was stolen, was unable to exercise any supervision over the said car. It results from that finding that [the defendant], who was deprived of the use, direction and control of his car, no longer had the *garde* over it. From that moment on, he was no longer presumed to be liable under Article 1384(1) C.civ. In holding as it did, the court of appeal did not infringe [Article 1384(1) C.civ.]."

Notes

(1) Under Article 1384(1) C.civ., liability is imposed on the keeper (*gardien*) of the thing. The concept of *garde* is therefore central to that liability regime, and much like *fait de la chose*, it has been developed by case law in the light of legal writing, since Article 1384(1) C.civ. itself does not provide any further guidance. The annotated case still remains the central case on the definition of *garde* and *gardien* for the purposes of Article 1384(1) C.civ.

The same concepts of *garde* and *gardien* also play a role in determining who is liable under the regime of liability for animals pursuant to Article 1385 C.civ. and, most importantly, under the *Loi Badinter* concerning liability for traffic accidents.[135]

---

[131] For Art. 1382–3 C.civ., see *supra*, Chapter II, 2.3.3., Introductory Note under a) as well as **2.F.40.–42.** and notes thereafter.
[132] DC 1942.25, S 1941.I.217, JCP 1942.II.1766. Translation by Y.P. Salmon.
[133] Cass. civ., 3 March 1936, DP 1936.I.81.
[134] Besançon, 27 February 1937, DH 1937.182.
[135] *Infra*, **6.F.16.**

(2) Essentially, *garde* implies a power over the thing in question.[136] Among others, the annotated case is notable for having laid down the terms of that power, namely the power to "use, direct and control" the thing in question. As P. Le Tourneau and L. Cadiet write:[137]

> Use is the *factual use* of the thing, for one's own *purposes* . . . and in the course of one's activities . . . Making contact with or resting upon a thing does not constitute use. Control means that the keeper (*gardien*) can watch the thing and even . . . has *the ability to prevent it from causing damages*. Finally, direction evidences the *effective power* of the *gardien* over the thing: he or she can use it at will, have it moved where he or she desires . . ., without interference. *Garde* therefore implies that the keeper enjoys an *autonomous* power.

It follows that the *préposé* (employee) for the purposes of Article 1384(5) C.civ. will usually not be the keeper of the things which he or she uses for his or her work, since he or she may have the use of the thing, but not its direction and control: by definition, the *préposé* is subject to the power of the *commettant* (employer) to give instructions,[138] which includes the power to give instructions with respect to the things used by the *préposé*. Accordingly, French case law has consistently held that a *préposé* cannot be the keeper of the things used for work.[139]

(3) In the earlier part of the 20th century, before the judgment of the joined chambers (*Chambres réunies*) of the Cour de cassation in the annotated case, two competing approaches were put forward as to the nature of the power over the thing. On the one hand, certain authors maintained that a legal power, such as results from ownership, was sufficient, irrespective of whether it was exercised or could be exercised in fact (so-called *garde juridique*). On the other hand, other authors argued that the real situation was decisive, and that the person who in fact exercised power over the thing in question, even without a legal entitlement to do so, should be considered as the *gardien* (so-called *garde matérielle*).[140]

In its first decision of 3 March 1936 in the annotated case, the civil chamber of the Cour de cassation had followed the first approach. When the case came back before the joined chambers following the refusal of the court of appeal to follow the decision of 3 March 1936, the Cour de cassation espoused the second approach, finding that, since the defendant had been deprived of the factual power over the car following its theft, he was not the *gardien* of the car at the time of the accident (the thief had become the *gardien*) and therefore could not be held liable under Article 1384(1) C.civ.

(4) Most authors agree that the above decision of the Cour de cassation made a dent in the hope, shared by many, that Article 1384(1) C.civ. might evolve into a self-contained, coherent regime of liability without fault.[141] By opting for a factual assessment of *garde*,

---

[136] Bénac-Schmidt/Larroumet at 18, para. 183; Viney and Jourdain, *Conditions* at 644–5, para. 675.

[137] Le Tourneau and Cadiet at 877, para. 3650 (references omitted, emphasis in original). See also Bénac-Schmidt/Larroumet at 19, para. 192–9.

[138] See *supra*, Chapter V, **5.F.1.** and notes thereafter.

[139] Viney and Jourdain, *Conditions* at 653–4, para. 684; Le Tourneau and Cadiet at 856–7, para. 3490; Bénac-Schmidt/Larroumet at 19, para. 197. Only in a case where the employee was using work-related things while not acting "in his functions" within the meaning of Article 1384(5) C.civ., could he or she have acquired the requisite power over the thing to qualify as *gardien* for the purposes of Article 1384(1) C.civ. Such cases are rare, given that French case law now gives quite a broad interpretation to the phrase "in his functions": see *supra*, Chapter V, **5.F.10–11.** and notes thereafter.

[140] See Viney and Jourdain, *Conditions* at 645–6, para. 675; Bénac-Schmidt/Larroumet at 18, para. 183.

[141] See Viney and Jourdain, *Conditions* at 647, para. 675.

the Cour de cassation implies that only someone who in fact exerts power over the thing can incur liability under Article 1384(1) C.civ.; conversely, liability will not result if someone has in fact lost the ability to exert power over the thing, even if he or she legally holds such power. One could be forgiven for thinking that liability is thus imposed on the person who *should* have prevented the injury from occurring, i.e. that liability is imposed on the person who is presumably at fault; nevertheless, the influence of the above decision on the overall regime of Article 1384(1) C.civ. has not been so great as to reverse the direction taken in the *Jand'heur* case in 1930.[142]

Indeed it is interesting to note that, in the annotated case, the solution reached on the basis of Article 1384(1) C.civ. comes very close to the solution which would have been reached under Article 1382–3 C.civ.: while in the annotated case the theft of the car deprived the defendant of the *garde* and thus precluded liability under Article 1384(1) C.civ., the theft would have "broken the chain of causation" and thus freed the defendant from liability under Article 1382–3 C.civ., unless the defendant had committed such a gross fault that theft became foreseeable.[143]

(5) In order to ease the task of the plaintiff, French case law has established that there is a presumption that the owner is the keeper of the thing which intervened in the causation of damage.[144] The owner cannot rebut that presumption by arguing that he or she did not have the requisite discernment to incur liability.[145] The only way for the owner to rebut the presumption is by showing that someone else was in fact exercising the "power to use, direct and control" the thing. That power may have been lost against the owner's will, as in the annotated case, but it can also be transferred, through the grant of a *droit réel* over the thing to a third party or through a contractual dealing involving the transfer of the thing (and of the power over it) to the other party. There is a considerable amount of case law on whether specific dealings actually lead to a transfer of the *garde* over a thing, which cannot easily be summarized.[146]

(6) In principle, only one person can be the keeper of a given thing at any given moment (as often stated, *garde* is alternative, not cumulative).[147] A few exceptions are made in certain cases where many persons exert the "power to use, direct and control" the thing in the same capacity (e.g. co-owners, sports players, etc.); in these cases, French courts will find that *garde* is collectively exerted by all these persons (*garde collective*).[148]

---

[142] *Supra*, **6.F.5.** See Bénac-Schmidt/Larroumet at 19, para. 190.

[143] See Cass. civ. 2e, 17 March 1977, *supra*, Chapter IV, **4.F.33.** and notes thereafter.

[144] See Viney and Jourdain, *Conditions* at 650–3, para. 677–81; Le Tourneau and Cadiet at 878–9, para. 3655; Bénac-Schmidt/Larroumet at 19–20, para. 201–8.

[145] This is one of the consequences of the series of decisions handed down by the Assemblée plénière on 9 May 1984, which effectively removed the requirement of subjective imputability from French tort law. In one of these decisions, *Gabillet*, the court found that a young child could nevertheless qualify as *gardien* if he had an autonomous power over a thing: Cass. Ass. plén., 9 May 1984, Bull.civ 1984.Ass.plén.1, D 1984.Jur.525, JCP 1984.II.20255. These decisions are discussed *supra*, Chapter III, **3.F.19.** and notes thereafter and *infra*, Chapter VII, **7.F.3.** and notes thereafter. See Viney and Jourdain, *Conditions* at 655–6, para. 685.

[146] See Viney and Jourdain, *Conditions* at 657–63, para. 688–90; Le Tourneau and Cadiet at 879–81, para. 3659 to 3665–1; Bénac-Schmidt/Larroumet at 21–25, para. 219–55.

[147] Viney and Jourdain, *Conditions* at 647–9, para. 676; Le Tourneau and Cadiet at 881, para. 3667; Bénac-Schmidt/Larroumet at 26, para. 266–9.

[148] Viney and Jourdain, *Conditions*, ibid.; Le Tourneau and Cadiet at 881–2, para. 3668–9; Bénac-Schmidt/Larroumet at 29–30, para. 293–304. The device of *garde collective* can be used to circumvent uncertainty regarding causation, as when for instance the victim was hit by a bullet coming from an unidentifiable member of a group of hunters: see *infra*, Chapter IV, **4.F.43.** and notes thereafter.

A more controversial development involved splitting the *garde* in two, namely structure (*garde de structure*) and behaviour (*garde de comportement*).[149] The keeper of the structure would remain liable for injury resulting from a hidden defect in the thing, while the keeper of the behaviour would be liable for injury resulting from the use of the thing. The latter would be determined by using the criteria set out in the annotated case, while the former could be the owner, the manufacturer or the distributor. The obvious advantage of such a solution is to enable the victim to have a recourse against a "deeper pocket" for injury resulting from hidden defects. However, this distinction adds a further layer of complexity to the identification of the *gardien*, and it marks a further step towards a reintroduction of fault in the regime of Article 1384(1) C.civ. Accordingly, the distinction between *garde de structure* and *garde de comportement* has been criticized by writers, and it has found only limited echo in case law.[150]

6.1.3. ENGLISH LAW

Introductory Note

a) Liability not based on wrongful conduct occupies less space under English than French or German law, both in legal thinking and in tort law as such, even though a number of relatively ancient torts not requiring an element of fault have survived the onslaught of the tort of negligence up to now. Furthermore, the distinction between the realms of fault-based liability (i.e. torts which require an element of fault) and so-called "strict liability" is not so clearly made as in French or German law.[151] It may be more correct to say that there is a continuum between a fault-based model and "strict liability" where fault plays no role. The first excerpt below, from *Clerk & Lindsell on Torts*, explores these theoretical issues and surveys the cases of liability not based on fault in the English law of torts.

b) The tort of negligence of course remains the paradigm of fault-based liability under English tort law. Its rise to pre-eminence in the 19th century could not but have an influence on the law of tort in general, leading to the emergence of a general principle whereby tort liability should rest on an element of fault. In the 1947 case annotated below, the House of Lords refused to follow the evolution of US law towards the creation of new torts (or the extension of existing ones) not based on fault.

c) Finally, one tort may be either fault-based or strict, namely the tort of breach of statutory duty. Whether some fault requirement is present or not will depend on the content of the statute the breach of which is alleged to lead to liability. This marks a crucial difference with the equivalent provision under German law, § 823(2) BGB, the second sentence of which reads a fault requirement into any protective statute that does not contain one.[152] A case from the House of Lords has been included on this point.

---

[149] That approach was put forward in a thesis by B. Goldman, *La détermination du gardien responsable du fait des choses inanimées* (Paris: Sirey, 1947).

[150] See Viney and Jourdain, *Conditions* at 663–70, para. 691–701; Le Tourneau and Cadiet at 882–4, para. 3671–8; Bénac-Schmidt/Larroumet at 26–9, para. 271–92.

[151] Markesinis and Deakin, for instance, deal with the main regimes of liability not based on fault under the heading "Stricter Forms of Liability".

[152] See *supra*, Chapter III, 3.2.3.B., Introductory Note.

M.R. Brazier (gen. ed.), Clerk & Lindsell on Torts[153]   6.E.9.

"**Strict liability.** Within the law of torts today, on a number of occasions the defendant may be found liable for injury or damage in respect of conduct which is not, or cannot be proved to be, either intentional or negligent. The producer of an unsafe product is liable for injuries ensuing to the unlucky consumer under the Consumer Protection Act 1987. The landowner from whose property a dangerous substance escapes causing damage to neighbouring property is liable under *Rylands* v. *Fletcher*. In neither case need the plaintiff prove that the event which caused his injury was either calculated by the defendant or the result of any lack of care or prudence on his part. Such liability is generally styled strict liability and sometimes referred to as 'absolute liability'. The latter term is misleading as it suggests erroneously that where strict liability is engaged the defendant's liability is unchallengeable and that is rarely the case. Strict liability must also be sharply distinguished from 'no fault' compensation. Within a 'no fault' scheme . . ., all the plaintiff . . . need prove is the occurrence of a prescribed injury. Within strict liability torts the plaintiff must establish that his injury results from the kind of conduct proscribed within the relevant tort. So in a products liability action under the Consumer Protection Act 1987 the consumer must prove that the product was defective, *i.e.* failed to meet the standard of safety 'persons are generally entitled to expect'. In *Rylands* v. *Fletcher* the plaintiff must establish that the damage of which he complains results from the escape from the defendant's property of something 'not naturally' accumulating on land. In both torts a number of defences are available to the defendant in effect allowing him to plead that the injury was 'not his fault'. Strict liability is often not much more than a modified form of fault, albeit the relevant fault is far removed from real moral culpability. Both at common law and where strict liability arises by virtue of statute, the underlying policy discernible may be seen to be founded on judgment that prima facie the risk of harm inherent in particular kinds of conduct should rest primarily on the defendant who created that risk. It is in a sense his 'fault' for creating the risk.

Strict liability at common law. The development of strict liability at common law has been haphazard and can be understood properly only within the context of each particular tort . . . It is within the torts protecting interests in land that strict liability at common law appears most prevalent. The interpretation of 'intention' in trespass to land as requiring no more than a deliberate and voluntary act, so that liability arises even where the defendant has no idea he had intruded on another's property and remains liable even if he was subject to duress in his intrusion, means that, semantics apart, liability for trespass to land is strict in substance. Liability in nuisance, particularly where the nuisance related to the highway, can arise without proof of any intent or carelessness. The classic example of strict liability at common law is of course *Rylands* v. *Fletcher* . . .

The primacy afforded to protection of property interests is further illustrated by the tort of conversion where any dealing with another's goods in a manner constituting a denial of the latter's rights is tortious even through the defendant acted in good faith. Defamation is often cited as a further example of strict liability at common law. The defendant may be found liable for a defamatory statement albeit he neither intended to defame the plaintiff nor was negligent in so doing. However there must be a deliberate intent to publish and the risk of publication is thus found to rest with the publisher. The apparent harshness of the rule in defamation is mitigated by the provision, in section 4 of the Defamation Act 1952, of a statutory defence of 'unintentional defamation'.

Where some form of strict liability exists at common law it is likely to be long established and rooted in the importance attached by the common law to the interest violated by the defendant . . .

Strict liability: statute. Strict liability derives from statute in three main instances. (1) Legislation such as the Animals Act 1971 has been enacted to clarify, or on occasion modify, strict liability as developed by the common law . . . (2) A novel form of strict liability may derive from legislation.

---

[153] (London: Sweet & Maxwell, 1995) at 33–5, para. 1–50 to 1–52. Footnotes omitted.

The implementation of the European Community Directive on Product Liability in the Consumer Protection Act 1987 creating strict liability for personal injury, and within limits damage to private property, caused by defective products is of crucial importance. (3) Liability may arise in the tort of breach of statutory duty when the plaintiff suffers injury as a consequence of a breach of a statutory obligation imposed on the defendant . . ."

Notes

(1) In the above excerpt, M.R. Brazier outlines the main liability models of liability under English law.[154] The dominant model at this point in time is based on fault (either negligence or intent). Nonetheless, many torts do not require that the defendant be at fault for liability to arise; the name "strict liability" is used for that liability model.[155]

(2) It is worth noting that the author does not draw a clear line between fault-based liability and strict liability. In her words, "strict liability is often not much more than a modified form of fault". Similarly, Rogers notes that "the strictness of the liability varies considerably along a spectrum from near-absolute liability to little more than a reversed burden of proof . . .".[156] Under English law, therefore, there is no established theoretical model for liability not based on fault, which could compare to the *Gefährdungshaftung* theory under German law[157] or the *théorie du risque* under French law.[158] As M.R. Brazier and other authors note, strict liability regimes are generally justified by the perceived need to shift the risk of harm arising from certain endeavours onto the person undertaking those endeavours.[159] With the rise of the economic analysis of law, for which tort law has always been a favourite topic, the economic foundations for and against fault-based or strict liability have been explored in greater detail.[160] It suffices to say here that, despite what one might think at first sight, these studies do not necessarily lead to the conclusion that strict liability is more efficient than fault-based liability: eliminating the requirement to prove fault, while it may simplify the law and reduce the costs related to the administration of tort law, may under some circumstances provide incentives for defendants to behave inefficiently.[161] The economic analysis of tort law, while influential in the USA, does not seem to have had a major impact on English law.[162]

(3) Accordingly, English common law comprises a few strict liability torts, whose development took place before the rise of the tort of negligence (and of the general idea that fault should be an ingredient of each tort), at a time when the conditions for liability to

---

[154] Rogers discerns the same models at 37–43.

[155] M.R. Brazier notes in this respect that the term "absolute liability", which is sometimes used, may be too strong, in that it gives the impression that the defendant cannot escape liability.

[156] Rogers at 37.

[157] See *supra*, **6.G.2.** and notes thereafter.

[158] Even if such theory may not actually be reflected in the operation of the regime of liability without fault, such as liability for things under Article 1384(1) C.civ.: see *supra*, **6.F.4.** and Note (1) thereafter.

[159] See Rogers at 37: "It is unlikely that any consistent policy has been followed in the creation of those areas of strict liability, though it is perhaps possible to discern behind them some very hazy idea of unusual or increased risk".

[160] See e.g. P. Newman, (ed.), *The New Palgrave Dictionary of Economics and the Law* (London: Macmillan, 1998), under "Causation and Tort Liability", "Customary Practices and the Law of Torts" and "Products Liability".

[161] For a relatively accessible review of the economic implications of various models of tort liability, see A.M. Feldman and J.M. Frost, "A Simple Model of Efficient Tort Liability Rules" (1998) 18 Int'l Rev. L. Econ. 201.

[162] Markesinis and Deakin at 23–4.

arise could differ widely from one tort to the other, and there was no particular reason to include fault as an ingredient of the tort.[163] They are enumerated in the excerpt above:

- trespass to land, where liability ensues as long as the act of the defendant was voluntary;[164]
- nuisance, in some cases;[165]
- the rule in *Rylands* v. *Fletcher*, usually considered as the classical instance of strict liability under English common law;[166]
- conversion, which occurs even if the defendant acted in good faith;[167]
- defamation, where liability can be engaged even if the defendant had no intention to defame and was not negligent.[168]

As the case below demonstrates, the tort of negligence has had such an impact on the overall tort law that it is now difficult to conceive that new torts would be recognized (or existing torts expanded) without some element of fault.

(4) Alongside strict liability at common law, the Parliament has introduced certain strict liability regimes in English law in a few cases. The Animals Act 1971 has complemented the common law as regards liability for animals.[169] More importantly, the Consumer Protection Act 1987, in implementing Directive 85/374,[170] created a new regime of strict liability for defective products, which is studied in greater detail further below.[171] A final, indirect source of strict liability by statute is the tort of breach of statutory duty, which can result in strict liability if the underlying statute does not require fault in order to be breached; that aspect of breach of statutory duty is studied in the second next document below.

House of Lords[172]   **6.E.10.**
Read v. *J. Lyons & Co. Ltd.*

THE FAULT PRINCIPLE

Explosion in ammunition factory

It is for Parliament to enact liability regimes not based on fault, at least as regards liability for personal injury.

Facts: The plaintiff, a government inspector, was injured in an explosion in the ammunition factory of the defendant, where she was conducting an inspection. She sued the defendant for damages, yet she did not allege negligence against the defendant, but rather framed her claim in strict liability for "ultra-hazardous activities".

---

[163] See Rogers at 29.
[164] See *supra*, Chapter I, **1.E.21.** and Chapter II, 2.3.1., Introductory Note under a).
[165] Ibid.
[166] Ibid. Nuisance and the rule in *Rylands* v. *Fletcher* were brought closer to one another by the House of Lords in *Cambridge Water Co.* v. *Eastern Counties Leather Plc.*, *supra*, Chapter II, **2.E.35.** and notes thereafter.
[167] See *supra*, Chapter I, **1.E.21.** and Chapter II, 2.3.1., Introductory Note under b).
[168] On libel, a subset of defamation, see *supra*, Chapter II, **2.E.32.** and notes thereafter.
[169] See *infra*, 6.2.2.
[170] For Directive 85/374, see *infra*, **6.EC.33.**
[171] *Infra*, 6.3.3.C.
[172] [1947] AC 156.

571

Held: The court of first instance allowed the claim. The court of appeal reversed the decision of the court of first instance and dismissed the claim. The House of Lords upheld the decision of the court of appeal.

Judgment: LORD MACMILLAN:[173] "The action is one of damages for personal injuries. Whatever may have been the law of England in early times I am of the opinion that as the law now stands an allegation of negligence is in general essential to the relevancy of an action of reparation for personal injuries . . . Suffice it to say that the process of evolution has been from the principle that every man acts at his peril and is liable for all the consequences of his acts to the principle that a man's freedom of action is subject only to the obligation not to infringe any duty of care which he owes to others . . .

The appellant . . . thus poses the question to be determined: 'Whether the manufacturer of high-explosive shells is under strict liability to prevent such shells from exploding and causing harm to persons on the premises where such manufacture is carried on as well as to persons outside such premises' . . .

[T]he appellant sought to convince your Lordships that there is category of things and operations dangerous in themselves and that those who harbour such things or carry on such operations in their premises are liable apart from negligence for any personal injuries occasioned by these dangerous things or operations. I think that [the appellant] succeeded in showing that in the case of dangerous things and operations the law has recognized that a special responsibility exists to take care. But I do not think that it has ever been laid down that there is . . . liability apart from negligence where persons are injured in consequence of the use of such things or the conduct of such operations. In truth it is a matter of degree. Every activity in which man engages is fraught with some possible element of danger to others . . . The more dangerous the act the greater is the care that must be taken in performing it. This relates itself to the principle in the modern law of torts that liability exists only for consequences which a reasonable man would have foreseen. One who engages in obviously dangerous operations must be taken to know that if he does not take special precautions injury to others may very well result. In my opinion it would be impracticable to frame a legal classification of things as things dangerous and things not dangerous . . . Accordingly I am unable to accept the proposition that in law the manufacture of high-explosive shells is a dangerous operation which imposes on the manufacturer an absolute liability for any personal injuries which may be sustained in consequence of his operations . . . The sound view, in my opinion, is that the law in all cases exacts a degree of care commensurate with the risk created. It was suggested that some operations are so intrinsically dangerous that no degree of care however scrupulous can prevent the occurrence of accidents and that those who choose for their own ends to carry on such operations ought to be held to do so at their peril . . . Should it be thought that this is a reasonable liability to impose in the public interest it is for Parliament so to enact . . .

The mainstay of [the appellant's] argument was [her] invocation of the doctrine of *Rylands* v. *Fletcher* . . . [That doctrine], as I understand it, derives from a conception of mutual duties of adjoining or neighbouring landowners and its congeners are trespass and nuisance. If its foundation is to be found in the injunction sic utere tuo ut alienum non laedas, then it is manifest that it has nothing to do with personal injuries . . . The two prerequisites of the doctrine are that there must be the escape of something from one man's close to another man's close and that that which escapes must have been brought upon the land from which it escapes in consequence of some non-natural use of that land . . . Neither of these features exists in the present case . . .

Your Lordships' task in this House is to decide particular cases between litigants and your Lordships are not called upon to rationalize the law of England. That attractive if perilous field may well be left to other hands to cultivate. It has been necessary in the present instance to exam-

---

[173] Viscount Simon, Lord Porter, Lord Simonds and Lord Uthwatt all delivered separate concurring speeches.

ine certain general principles advanced on behalf of the appellant because it was said that consistency required that these principles should be applied to the case in hand. Arguments based on legal consistency are apt to mislead for the common law is a practical code adapted to deal with the manifold diversities of human life . . ."

Notes

(1) The annotated case provides an excellent glimpse into the changes in the attitude of the common law towards strict liability in the 20th century. There the plaintiff was in a difficult position, since she probably could not prove that anyone was negligent in relation to the explosion that injured her, as typically happens in cases of accidents in a mechanized context. She was not an employee of the defendant, so she could not benefit from legislation concerning accidents at the workplace. Her only chance was to try to convince the court to hold the defendant liable, even without evidence of negligence, on the basis that the defendant was conducting dangerous activities which created a risk of injury that it should bear. In fact, she was trying to import into English law the principle of strict liability for "ultra-hazardous activities" which had been developed in many jurisdictions in the United States.[174]

(2) The House of Lords was unwilling to modify or develop the common law in the direction suggested by the plaintiff. As Lord Macmillan made clear at the beginning of his speech, by the mid-20th century, the requirement of fault[175] had become essential in order to succeed in claims for personal injuries, irrespective of the tort relied on. The common law has evolved from a position relatively favourable to the victim to a position where the requirement of fault is intended to ensure that a person's freedom of action remains unimpeded as much as possible.

Accordingly, the House of Lords refused to create a new separate category in tort law for dangerous things, which would be subject to strict liability.[176] Instead, the House stated that a high level of risk or danger would simply make the duty of care more exacting, but cannot justify dispensing with the fault requirement. In the end, Lord Macmillan stated that it was up to Parliament to create new regimes of strict liability—at least as far as personal injuries are concerned—under English law. Through the annotated case, therefore, the House of Lords elevated the requirement of fault to the rank of a general rule of tort law, thereby confining strict liability to exceptional cases.

(3) The plaintiff's argument relied on the existing cases of strict liability in the common law of England, especially on the rule in *Rylands* v. *Fletcher*, which she sought to have extended to her case by analogy. The House of Lords confined *Rylands* v. *Fletcher* to its narrow facts, namely damage to property caused in the context of relations between neighbouring property owners; it will be recalled that the House of Lords confirmed that position, albeit in part implicitly, in its 1997 opinion in *Hunter* v. *Canary Wharf Ltd.*[177]

---

[174] See Markesinis and Deakin at 504 ff. and Schamps at 553 ff.

[175] Lord Macmillan spoke of "negligence" in the sense not of the tort of negligence as such, but of the requirement that the plaintiff be proved negligent, i.e. at fault.

[176] Lord Macmillan uses the term "absolute liability", but as mentioned *supra*, **6.E.9.**, in the context of tort law it is equivalent to "strict liability" and the latter terms should preferably be used.

[177] [1997] 2 WLR 684, [1997] 2 All ER 426, HL. See *supra*, Chapter II, 2.3.1., Introductory Note under a).

By the same token, the House of Lords in the annotated case refused to follow developments in the United States, where strict liability for "ultra-hazardous activities" was derived from *Rylands* v. *Fletcher*.[178]

(4) Lord Macmillan concluded his speech by warning against the temptation of changing the foundations of the law of England for the sake of consistency, given that the common law must remain oriented towards the practical problems raised by individual cases. That attitude towards the evolution of the common law bears a close resemblance to the attitude currently prevailing, following the opinion in *Murphy* v. *Brentwood District Council*.[179] As a result, English law finds itself in quite a similar situation to German law, where *Gefährdungshaftung* is limited to the instances where it has been introduced by specific statutory provisions (*Enumerationsprinzip*).[180]

House of Lords[181]   **6.E.11.**
London Passenger Transport Board v. *Upson*

STRICT LIABILITY AND BREACH OF STATUTORY DUTY

Pedestrian crossing

The tort of breach of statutory duty is a strict liability tort, unless the underlying statutory duty contains an element of negligence (e.g. a duty to take care).

Facts: The plaintiff was crossing the street at a pedestrian crossing, with the traffic lights showing red for pedestrians. She walked in front of a taxicab which had stopped to pick someone up. The taxicab hid her from oncoming traffic. As she got past the taxicab and went further on the pedestrian crossing across the next lane of traffic, she was knocked down by a bus driven by a driver of the defendant Transport Board. Evidence showed that the bus (for which the traffic light was green) was approximately 2,7 m (9 feet) away from the plaintiff when she walked out of the "shadow" of the taxicab, and that the bus was going at about 25 km/h (15 miles an hour). Even if the driver had braked immediately and hard once he saw the plaintiff, the bus nonetheless could not have come to a stop before it was well into the area of the pedestrian crossing. The plaintiff invoked the vicarious liability of the defendant for negligence and breach of statutory duty on the part of its driver.

Regulation 3 of the Pedestrian Crossing Places (Traffic) Regulations 1941, at issue in the case, read at the relevant time: "The driver of every vehicle approaching a crossing shall, unless he can see that there is no passenger thereon, proceed at such a speed as to be able if necessary to stop before reaching such crossing."[182]

Held: The court of first instance found that the driver had been negligent and held the defendant vicariously liable.[183] The court of appeal found that the driver had not been negligent but had committed a breach of statutory duty, for which it held the defendant vicariously liable. The House of Lords upheld the decision of the court of appeal.

Judgment: LORD WRIGHT:[184] "I think the authorities . . . show clearly that a claim for damages for breach of statutory duty intended to protect a person in the position of the particular plaintiff is a specific common law right which is not to be confused in essence with a claim for negligence. The

---

[178] See Markesinis and Deakin at 504 ff. and Schamps at 553 ff.

[179] [1991] 1 AC 398, HL. On the impact of *Murphy* on tort law in general, see *supra*, Chapter I, 1.4.1.B.

[180] See *supra*, **6.G.1.** and Note (3) thereafter.

[181] [1949] AC 155.

[182] St R&O 1941, No. 397. The same duty would now be found in the "Zebra" Pedestrian Crossing Regulations 1971, SI 1971, No. 1524.

[183] Before all courts, the plaintiff's compensation was reduced on account of contributory negligence.

[184] Lords Porter, Uthwatt, du Parcq and Morton of Henryton all delivered separate concurring speeches.

statutory right has its origin in the statute, but the particular remedy of an action for damages is given by the common law in order to make more effective, for the benefit of the injured plaintiff, his right to the performance by the defendant of the defendant's statutory duty. It is an effective sanction. It is not a claim in negligence in the strict or ordinary sense; as I said in *Caswell* v. *Powell Duffeyn Associated Collieries Ltd.* [1940] AC 152 at 177:

> 'I do not think that an action for breach of a statutory duty such as that in question is completely or accurately described as an action in negligence. It is a common law action based on the purpose of the statute to protect the workman, and belongs to the category often described as that of cases of strict or absolute liability. At the same time it resembles actions in negligence in that the claim is based on a breach of statutory duty to take care for the safety of the workman.'

But, whatever the resemblances, it is essential to keep in mind the fundamental differences of the two classes of claim . . . One duty does not in truth enhance the other, though the same damage may be caused by action which might equally be characterized as ordinary negligence at common law or as breach of the statutory duty. On the other hand the damage may be due either to negligence or to breach of statutory duty. There is . . . a logical distinction which accords with . . . the correct view that the causes of action are different."

Notes

(1) It was seen earlier that one of the main conceptual problems arising in tort law in common law jurisdictions is the relationship between the torts of negligence and breach of statutory duty.[185] The annotated case is one of the key cases on this point in English law. In his speech, Lord Wright restated the position of English law on this point, according to which the torts of negligence and breach of statutory duty are independent causes of action which must be kept separate from one another.[186] Other common law jurisdictions, including most North American jurisdictions, have taken the opposite view, treating breach of statutory duty as a sub-species of negligence, the breach of statute then being used as evidence that a duty of care was breached.[187]

(2) As a result of the position taken by English law, it is possible for a case to lead to liability in negligence but not for breach of statutory duty, or vice versa. In the annotated case, for instance, the court of appeal and the House of Lords found that the driver of the defendant was not negligent. He was driving at a very moderate speed as he approached the pedestrian crossing, and in any event he could not have seen the plaintiff, who was hidden from his view by the taxicab.

As far as breach of statutory duty was concerned, however, the applicable regulation, excerpted above, provided that drivers approaching a pedestrian crossing must drive at a speed which would enable them to stop before the crossing. The court of appeal and the House of Lords both held that the driver was in breach of that duty, since the bus could not be stopped before entering the area marked as a pedestrian crossing.

The annotated case provides a good illustration of how the tort of breach of statutory duty can operate as a strict liability tort. As Lord Wright had himself noted in a previous

---

[185] See *supra*, Chapter I, 1.4.1.A., Introductory Note under c), Chapter II, 2.4.1., Introductory Note under b).

[186] This position was reconfirmed in recent times: see for instance *X.* v. *Bedfordshire County Council* [1995] 2 AC 633, [1995] 3 WLR 152, [1995] 3 All ER 353, HL, discussed *supra*, Chapter III, 3.3.1., Introductory Note under b).

[187] See Rogers at 248; Markesinis and Deakin at 338.

speech in *Caswell* v. *Powell Duffryn Associated Collieries Ltd.*, breach of statutory duty may give rise to strict liability,[188] since as long as that the other conditions are met (injury, causation[189]), liability will follow from the mere fact that the statute was breached. If the statute itself is worded so as not to require an element of fault, then the defendant is put under a form of strict liability. In the annotated case, for instance, despite the absence of fault on the part of the driver (the claim in negligence failed), the defendant was liable for a breach of a statutory duty.[190]

(3) In view of the above, breach of statutory duty could represent a significant source of strict liability under English tort law. The key question then becomes whether and under what conditions statutes will qualify to give plaintiffs causes of actions in tort for breach of statutory duty. Some statutes specifically mention that civil remedies are (or shall not be) available in case of breach, but many do not deal with the issue. In the case of "silent statutes", the House of Lords has taken a relatively restrictive stance. In 1992, it was held in *R.* v. *Deputy Governor of Parkhurst Prison*, ex p. *Hague* that[191]

"it must always be a matter for consideration whether the legislature intended that private law rights of action should be conferred upon individuals in respect of breaches of the relevant statutory provision. The fact that a particular provision was intended to protect certain individuals is not of itself sufficient to confer private law rights of action upon them, something more is required to show that the legislature intended such conferment."

What that "something more" could be is still not settled (it could be the intent to create a civil remedy), and authors generally remark that this area of tort law is not in a very satisfactory state.[192] Moreover, it will be recalled that, as regards State liability for breaches of Community law, following the *Brasserie du Pêcheur* and *Dillenkofer* judgments of the ECJ, liability on the part of Member States for breaches of Community law can arise when "the rule of law infringed [was] intended to confer rights on individuals".[193]

6.1.4. COMPARATIVE OVERVIEW

The present section sought to provide an overview of liability not based on conduct in the legal systems under study, with emphasis on the significance of such liability and on any general theory which might underlie it.

---

[188] [1940] AC 152 at 177.

[189] For the tort of breach of statutory duty, English law follows a "scope of the norm" approach to causation: the injury must thus be of a kind which the statute was intended to prevent: see *Donaghey* v. *Boulton & Paul Ltd.*, *supra*, Chapter IV, **4.E.6.** and notes thereafter.

[190] However, such liability is not absolute, since there is no breach of the Regulation where the driver fails to accord precedence to a predestrian on a pedestrian crossing solely because his control of the vehicle was taken from him by the occurrence of an event outside his possible and reasonable control and in respect of which he was in no way at fault, e.g. a latent defect in the vehicle's braking system in relation to which the defendant was not to blame: *Burns* v. *Bidder* [1967] 2 QB 227, DC.

[191] [1992] 1 AC 58 at 170–1, HL.

[192] See Rogers at 249–60; Markesinis and Deakin at 342–7; *Clerk & Lindsell on Torts* at 566–76, para. 11–12 to 11–24. In *Lonrho Ltd.* v. *Shell Petroleum Co. Ltd. (No. 2)* [1982] AC 173 at 182, HL, Lord Diplock also alluded to a second possibility for a cause of action to arise, namely when the statute creates a public right and the plaintiff suffers damage different from that suffered by the rest of the public. That statement finds few applications in English tort law other than public nuisance (see *supra*, Chapter II, 2.3.1., Introductory Note under a)).

[193] See *Brasserie du Pêcheur*, *infra*, Chapter IX, **9.EC.6.** at para. 51 and *Dillenkofer*, *infra*, Chapter IX, **9.EC.7.** and Note (3) thereafter. See also *supra*, Chapter II, 2.4.1., Introductory Note under b).

The significance of liability not based on conduct

As mentioned at the outset of this Chapter and in the excerpts from legal writers,[194] the rise of liability not based on conduct throughout the 20th century can be linked with a number of circumstances that were present in all legal systems under study. The main ones are briefly recalled here. First of all, the theoretical model of liability for wrongful conduct reached its limits. It is true that, as seen in Chapter III,[195] wrongfulness was becoming increasingly objective, through reliance on an abstract notion of unlawfulness coupled with the progressive disappearance of culpability as a general condition for liability to arise. Nevertheless, in the case of accidents involving technical devices (cars, industrial products, etc.), even a strongly objectivized concept of wrongfulness loses relevance in the face of injury caused by mechanical failures or brief human lapses that could not truly be characterized as wrongful.[196] Secondly, liability for wrongful conduct was in practice increasingly tipped against victims, who were simply not in a position to establish wrongful conduct on the part of the defendant (and causation) where the relevant facts were within the sphere of control of the defendant. Thirdly, the insurance sector was developing and expanding in such a way as to offer affordable loss-spreading techniques: given the availability of liability insurance, it made sense to move away from loss-shifting (i.e. asking if it is justified to shift the loss onto the defendant) towards loss-spreading (i.e. seeking to channel the loss upon the person best placed to insure against it).

As a consequence, a number of regimes of liability not based on conduct appeared in each of the legal systems under study, as surveyed in the excerpts from legal writing.[197] The overall picture is quite varied. In some areas, EC legislation or international conventions have led to the introduction of relatively similar regimes in every system: such is the case for product liability,[198] liability for injury resulting from air transport accidents,[199] and liability arising from accidents at nuclear installations.[200] Besides these areas, there is no overlap between the three legal systems studied here, with the exception of liability for animals.[201] Under German law, a limited number of risk-based liability (*Gefährdungshaftung*) regimes have been introduced through specific legislation, covering vast areas

[194] *Supra*, **6.G.2.**, **6.F.4.**, and **6.E.9.**

[195] See *supra*, Chapter III, 3.2.2. (on unlawfulness) and 3.2.3. (on culpability).

[196] Unless one is willing to go as far as to consider the very fact of using such technical devices as unlawful in and of itself: as E. Deutsch points out *supra*, **6.G.2.**, liability not based on conduct covers fields of endeavour that are in and of themselves lawful, but which give rise to a risk of injury that cannot be ignored.

[197] See *supra*, **6.G.2.** (E. Deutsch on German law), **6.F.4.** (G. Viney on French law) and **6.E.9.** (M.R. Brazier on English law).

[198] With Directive 85/374, *infra*, **6.EC.33.** The implementation of that Directive is reviewed *infra*, 6.3.3.A. (German law), 6.3.3.B. (French law) and 6.3.3.C. (English law), from which it appears that the regimes resulting from the respective national implementations of the Directive are not necessarily as similar as one would have thought.

[199] Through the Warsaw Convention for the Unification of Certain Rules relating to International Carriage by Air of 12 October 1929, 137 LNTS 11 and its subsequent amendments, as well as Regulation 2027/97 of 9 October 1997 [1997] OJ L 185/1. See *infra*, 6.2.2.

[200] Through the Paris Convention on Third-Party Liability in the Field of Nuclear Energy of 29 July 1960, JO, 11 February 1969, the Brussels Convention supplementing the Paris Convention of 31 January 1963 (1963) 2 ILM 685, the Brussels Convention relating to Civil Liability in the Field of Maritime Carriage of Nuclear Material of 17 December 1971, JO, 3 August 1975, and subsequent protocols applicable to these conventions. See *infra*, 6.4.2. under e).

[201] See *infra*, 6.2.2.

such as road traffic accidents[202] or environmental liability.[203] These regimes have received a fair amount of attention from legal writers, and a general theory of risk-based liability has emerged as a result. In French law, the legislature has created a large number of more circumscribed regimes of liability "by virtue of law" (*de plein droit*), which have not attracted much attention,[204] with the exception of the *Loi Badinter* concerning road traffic accidents.[205] Rather, the distinctive feature of French law is the general regime of liability for injury caused by things under one's *garde*, which arose out of a far-reaching interpretation of Article 1384(1) C.civ. in the case law of the Cour de cassation.[206] As for English law, its fragmented structure makes it less necessary to develop a general theory of "strict liability". Alongside a small number of relatively ancient strict liability torts (including trespass to land, the rule in *Rylands* v. *Fletcher*[207] or defamation), one finds a few legislative interventions (concerning liability for animals[208] or defective products[209]) and breach of statutory duty, a tort that can impose strict liability if the underlying statute does not require fault.[210] Of the three systems studied here, English law is the one where liability not based on conduct is the least widespread.

The relationship between liability for wrongful conduct and liability not based on conduct

Regimes of liability not based on conduct differ from existing regimes of liability based on wrongful conduct in many respects. Accordingly, the legal systems under study here have faced the issue of how these two realms relate to one another.[211]

Under English and German law, the fault principle is well-established, so that regimes of liability not based on wrongful conduct must be seen as an exception. What is more, under both systems, courts have concluded that liability not based on conduct must actually be introduced by the legislature. Under German law, the BGH has thus held that there is no risk-based liability (*Gefährdungshaftung*) outside of the legislative regimes which expressly provide for it. In support of this conclusion, the BGH invoked legal certainty.[212] The position of the BGH is criticized in legal writing, however.[213] The English common law contains a number of strict liability torts that were created by the courts before the 20th century, first and foremost among them the rule in *Rylands* v. *Fletcher*.[214] However, the rise of the tort of negligence—which is based on wrongful conduct—in the 20th century has influenced the whole law of tort, and by now English courts are unwill-

---

[202] See *infra*, 6.2.1.A.

[203] See *infra*, **6.G.40.**

[204] They are enumerated in the excerpt from G. Viney, *supra*, **6.F.4.**

[205] *Infra*, **6.F.16.**

[206] The main features of that regime are examined *supra*, **6.F.5.** (foundations), **6.F.6.–7.** (concept of behaviour of the thing or *fait de la chose*) and **6.F.8.** (concept of keeper or *gardien*).

[207] See *supra*, Chapter II, 2.3.1.

[208] See *infra*, 6.2.2.

[209] See the Consumer Protection Act 1987, *infra*, **6.E.38.**, implementing Directive 85/374, *infra*, **6.EC.33.** in the United Kingdom.

[210] See *supra*, **6.E.11.**

[211] For a broader comparative perspective on this issue, see von Bar II at 378 ff., para. 348 ff.

[212] See *supra*, **6.G.1.**

[213] Ibid., Note (3).

[214] See *supra*, Chapter II, 2.3.1., Introductory Note under a).

ing to extend the range of strict liability on their own motion, relying instead on Parliament to introduce new strict liability torts.[215]

French law has taken another course. Already, in the late 19th century, the Cour de cassation was re-interpreting Article 1384(1) C.civ., which until then had been seen as little more than a declaratory provision, to turn it into an autonomous regime of liability for injury caused by things.[216] With its celebrated *Jand'heur* decision of 13 February 1930,[217] the Cour de cassation established the regime of liability for things under one's *garde* as a regime of liability without fault, and dismissed every suggestion made in legal writing to restrict its scope.[218] Evidently, French courts consider that they can create new regimes of liability without fault if that appears warranted, as they have recently done again with respect to liability for others.[219] Nevertheless, a closer look at the regime of liability for things at Article 1384(1) C.civ. shows that considerations pertaining to liability for fault are still present. For instance, as regards the requirement that some "behaviour of the thing" (*fait de la chose*) must have been involved, in cases where the thing in question was not in motion when the injury occurred or did not come in contact with the victim, the victim must show that the thing behaved "abnormally", was "abnormally" positioned or suffered from an "internal defect".[220] That comes close to showing that someone breached a standard of care in relation to the thing.[221] Similarly, in determining who is the keeper (*gardien*), courts have focussed on the *factual* (as opposed to legal) power over the thing, so that for instance the owner of a car ceases to be its keeper as soon as the car is stolen.[222] The keeper will thus be the person who should in fact have prevented the injurious incident from occurring.[223] Accordingly, while French courts have taken it upon themselves to create regimes of liability not based on fault, they have nevertheless not completely left aside considerations pertaining to fault.

The general structure of liability not based on conduct

At the theoretical level, it is generally agreed in all three systems studied here that the creation of an exceptional risk or danger provides the justification for imposing liability not based on wrongful conduct.[224] In all the regimes examined throughout this Chapter, some activity or installation exposes the general population to increased danger, be it driving a car, keeping an animal, manufacturing industrial products, operating nuclear or power installations, etc. Indeed, on the basis of a thorough comparative study, Schamps

---

[215] See *supra*, **6.E.10.**
[216] Cass. civ., 18 June 1896, *Teffaine*, S 1897.I.17, D 1897.I.433.
[217] *Supra*, **6.F.5.**
[218] See ibid. and Notes (3) to (6). The Cour de cassation refused to restrict the scope of Article 1384(1) C.civ. along any of the lines that had been put forward in legal writing, including moveable, autonomous, defective or dangerous things.
[219] See *supra*, Chapter V, **5.F.24.** (liability for children) and **5.F.25.** (general regime of liability for others).
[220] See *supra*, **6.F.6.–7.** and notes thereafter.
[221] See von Bar II at 338–9 and 345–6, para. 311 and 316.
[222] As found in the leading decision of 2 December 1941, *Connot v. Franck, supra,* **6.F.8.**
[223] Ibid., Note (4).
[224] See *supra*, **6.G.2.** and Note (2) thereafter, **6.F.4.** and Note (1) thereafter as well as **6.E.9.** and Note (2) thereafter.

was able to conclude that the creation of danger constituted a basic foundation for civil liability.[225]

Beyond that agreement on the theoretical foundations of the regime, when it comes to the actual structure of regimes of liability not based on conduct, a distinction can be made between French and English law,[226] on the one hand, and German law, on the other.

This distinction is already reflected in the terminology used in the various systems. Under French law, the regimes surveyed in this Chapter are called "liability without fault" (*responsabilité sans faute*) and "liability by virtue of the law" (*responsabilité de plein droit*). Irrespective of the designation, the underlying idea is the same: the requirement that the defendant behaved wrongfully is removed.[227] The same idea is conveyed by the expression "strict liability" under English law.[228] In contrast, under German law, the regimes examined in this Chapter all fall under the broad heading of "risk-based liability" (*Gefährdungshaftung*). The basic idea behind risk-based liability is not only that the requirement of wrongful conduct is removed (as under the French and English understanding), but also that it is replaced as the basis for liability by another concept, namely risk. Given that distinction, this Chapter was entitled "Liability not based on conduct" in order to emphasize the common features between the three systems while not using the terminology of one particular system.

Under the German approach, therefore, the specific risk which justifies the creation of a regime of risk-based liability (*Gefährdungshaftung*) is integrated throughout the general structure of the regime. Nowhere is that made clearer than in the assessment of causation. In its leading decision of 27 January 1981,[229] the BGH held that the adequacy theory of causation did not apply to risk-based liability regimes.[230] Rather, the "scope of rule" (*Schutzzweck der Norm*) theory of causation is decisive.[231] The key consideration is whether the injury for which the victim is seeking compensation represents a specific manifestation of the risk against which the liability regime is meant to protect the general public.[232] As pointed out by E. Deutsch, not all risk-based liability regimes follow that approach very closely; product liability under the German *Produkthaftungsgesetz*,[233] for instance, tends to come closer to the French approach outlined below than to the German general approach.[234]

---

[225] See Schamps at 843–51, concluding in the light of a study of the law of Italy, the Netherlands, Switzerland, England, the United States, Belgium and France.

[226] Given the limited number of strict liability regimes under English law, it is difficult to reach a conclusion on the point under discussion here. Strict liability torts that were introduced by legislation, as well as the rule in *Rylands* v. *Fletcher* and other older strict liability torts, would appear to follow the French model, according to which a given state of facts acts as the triggering factor for liability to arise (without necessarily reflecting the underlying risk). However, to the extent it is sometimes a strict liability tort, the tort of breach of statutory duty would tend to follow the German model, since the "scope of the rule" theory is generally used when it is applied: see *supra*, Chapter IV, **4.E.6.**

[227] See *supra*, **6.F.4.** and Note (5) thereafter.

[228] See *supra*, **6.E.9.** and Note (2) thereafter.

[229] *Supra*, **6.G.3.**

[230] That theory is discussed *supra*, Chapter IV, Introductory Note under c) as well as **4.G.1.** and notes thereafter.

[231] That theory is discussed *supra*, Chapter IV, Introductory Note under d) as well as **4.G.2.** and notes thereafter.

[232] For another case applying that principle, see *supra*, Chapter IV, **4.G.3.**

[233] See *infra*, **6.G.34.**

[234] See *supra*, **6.G.2.** and Note (5) thereafter. E. Deutsch calls that regime "enlarged risk-based liability" (*erweiterte Gefährdungshaftung*).

In contrast, under French and English law, the specific risk which serves as a justification for liability by virtue of law (*responsabilité de plein droit*) or strict liability, respectively, is not necessarily carried through in the general structure of the liability regime.[235] Nevertheless, some device must be used to define—and, by the same token, limit—the scope of application of the liability regime.[236] Under French law, that device is usually called the "triggering factor" (*fait générateur*),[237] i.e. a state of fact that must be present for the liability regime to apply. However, the triggering factor is usually defined in a fairly objective and concrete fashion, which does not necessarily coincide with the underlying risk. In the case of the general regime of liability for things, the triggering factor is the "behaviour of the thing" (*fait de la chose*). For instance, if the thing in question was in motion and came in contact with the victim, the *fait de la chose* is made out, without more.[238] As mentioned above, if the thing either did not move or did not touch the victim, then it must be shown that it behaved abnormally, was abnormally placed or suffered from an internal defect.[239] These latter criteria might come closer to circumscribing the risk associated with the use of a thing, but they are usually rather seen as an application of the explanatory/adequacy theory of causation.[240] As will be seen below, the same approach is followed under the *Loi Badinter*, where the concept of "traffic accident", which delineates its scope of application, is construed in a very concrete fashion, without reference to the underlying risk.[241]

In the end, the significance of these differences in the general approach to liability not based on conduct should not be exaggerated, since in practice the scope of application of the risk-based liability regimes under German law and the corresponding regimes under French or English law (as the case may be) will largely overlap.

Beyond these differences, the regimes of liability not based on conduct share a number of basic concepts, which will be explored in greater detail when examining specific areas in the following subsections.

First of all, the concepts of keeper, *Halter* and *gardien* are used to identify the person upon whose shoulders liability will rest. These concepts are very similar from one system to the other, and they always hinge upon the control over the source of risk that is covered by the regime in question, be it an installation, an activity, a product, etc.[242]

Secondly, as many authors point out,[243] the borderline between liability based on wrongful conduct and liability not based on conduct is sometimes very thin, the difference between the two being more a matter of degree than kind. That can best be observed when it comes to the grounds of defence open to the defendant. In most regimes of

---

[235] See the discussion of the general regime of liability for things under French law, *supra*, **6.F.5.** and Note (7) thereafter, including the excerpt where Bénac-Schmidt/Larroumet argue that, once a regime of liability by virtue of law is set up, it would be unfair to victims to limit its application to cases which would somehow be connected with the underlying risk, while excluding other cases which are analogous in fact.

[236] Otherwise, one is dealing with a regime of liability based on causation alone (*Kausalhaftung*), which is foreign to all the legal systems studied here.

[237] In a broader theoretical perspective, wrongful conduct can be seen as one triggering factor for liability among others, as done in Viney and Jourdain, *Conditions*.

[238] See *supra*, **6.F.6.–7.**, Note (2).

[239] See *supra*, **6.F.6.** (no contact) and **6.F.7.** (no movement) and Notes (3) and (4).

[240] Ibid. at Note (5).

[241] See *infra*, **6.F.17.**

[242] von Bar II at 357–62, para. 325–8.

[243] See E. Deutsch, *supra*, **6.G.2.**; M.R. Brazier, *supra*, **6.E.9.** as well as von Bar II at 341- 4, para. 313–4.

liability not based on conduct, the defendant can avoid liability by showing that some "extraneous cause"[244] was at the source of the injury.[245] That involves proving that the injury was indeed caused by an event over which the defendant had no control and which he or she could neither foresee nor avoid. In that case, the defendant must actually identify the cause of the injury, so that a defence of "extraneous cause" amounts to showing that the defendant did not cause the injury.[246] Consequently, under regimes of liability not based on conduct, it should not be open to the defendant to show that he or she actually took all the requisite care and that the injury nonetheless happened, without actually identifying a "extraneous cause" for the injury: that would amount to claiming that the defendant did not behave wrongfully and should escape liability. Nonetheless, as will be seen below when dealing with road traffic accidents[247] and product liability,[248] the distinction is not always easy to make.

6.2. LIABILITY FOR ACCIDENTS

This section is concerned with "accidents", that is to say those cases where injury—often, but not exclusively, severe bodily harm—is caused without intent to do so, in the course of typical social relationships, for instance work or transportation. Accidents occur almost inevitably once mechanized means of production or transportation are used, and in most cases they cannot be attributed to anybody's fault or negligence. As was mentioned many times in the previous section, the rise of accidents in the course of industrialization in the 19th century was one of the main reasons why, in the various legal systems under study here, alternatives to fault as the basis for liability were sought.[249]

Given that work-related accidents have generally been taken out of the realm of liability altogether and regulated on a first-party insurance basis, road traffic accidents remain the main category of accidents still covered by the law of torts.[250] In the majority of legal systems, road traffic accidents have been put under a specific regime of liability not based on fault, and accordingly the bulk of this section is dedicated to these well-established and well-developed regimes, where some useful comparisons can be made.

Other liability regimes concerning accidents—including the regime of liability for injury caused by animals, which could be seen as a historical forerunner of modern

[244] Sometimes called *cas fortuit, force majeure*, Act of God, *höhere Gewalt*, etc. See von Bar II at 347–54, para. 318–22. Some regimes do not allow the defendant even to argue "extraneous cause" as a defence, including, amongst those studied in this Chapter, the *Loi Badinter, infra*, **6.F.16.**

[245] The same can also be done under regimes of liability for wrongful conduct: see *supra*, Chapter III, 3.2.3.

[246] See on this point, for French law, *supra*, Chapter IV, **4.F.38.–39.** and Notes (1) to (3) thereafter.

[247] See the discussion of the concepts of "inexcusable fault" (*faute inexcusable*) under the *Loi Badinter, infra*, **6.F.20.** and "unavoidable event" (*unabwendbares Ereignis*) under § 7(2) StVG, *infra*, **6.G.15.**

[248] See the discussion of the "product development risk" defence, *supra*, 6.3., throughout the section.

[249] See *supra*, for German law, **6.G.2.** and Notes (1) and (2) thereafter and for French law, **6.F.4.** and Note (1) thereafter.

[250] In Germany, for instance, G. Kirchhoff, "Der Verkehrsunfall im Zivilprozeß" MDR 1997, 901 notes that in 1995, road traffic accident cases represent the third largest group of cases before civil courts, after sale and lease matters, accounting for some 10% of the case load. What is more, those road traffic accident cases that actually come before courts make up a mere 4% of all road traffic accident cases, the rest being settled without judicial proceedings.

regimes of liability for accidents—are dealt with in the second subsection, and a comparative overview completes the section.

Furthermore, the topics of the next two sections—product liability and environmental liability—could also be seen as accident cases, broadly speaking. However, they present certain peculiarities which justify their being covered in a separate section.

6.2.1. ROAD TRAFFIC ACCIDENTS

This subsection concerns liability for road traffic accidents, especially the two regimes of liability not based on fault which have been put in place in Germany (at §§ 7–20 of the *Straßenverkehrsgesetz* (StVG)[251]) and in France (through the Act of 5 July 1985, also known as the *Loi Badinter*[252]). Under English law, road traffic accidents are not dealt with under any specific regime, and therefore generally fall to be decided under the tort of negligence;[253] accordingly, less attention is devoted to English law under this heading.

6.2.1.A. GERMAN LAW

Introductory Note

It did not take long for the German legislature to become convinced that the general fault-based grounds of liability of §§ 823(1), 823(2) and 826 BGB were inadequate in the context of road traffic accidents; risk-based liability (*Gefährdungshaftung*) was introduced as early as 1909.[254] The currently applicable legislation, the *Straßenverkehrsgesetz* (StVG), dates from 1952, and has been amended many times since. The second chapter of the *Straßenverkehrsgesetz*, comprising §§ 7–20, deals more specifically with liability. Its most relevant parts are reproduced below. Cases have been included on the main elements of liability pursuant to § 7 StVG, namely the concepts of "operation of a motor vehicle" (*Betrieb eines Kraftfahrzeuges*), keeper (*Halter*) of a motor vehicle and exoneration on account of an "unavoidable event" (*unabwendbares Ereignis*), which refers to the standard of the "ideal driver" (*Idealfahrer*).

Straßenverkehrsgesetz of 19 December 1952[255]   **6.G.12.**

"§ 7.   (1) If in the course of the operation of a motor vehicle a person is killed, the body or the health of a person is injured or an object is damaged, the keeper of the motor vehicle is obliged to compensate the injured party for the damage resulting therefrom.

(2) The duty to compensate is excluded if the accident was caused by an unavoidable event which is not due to a defect in the construction of the vehicle or to the failure of its mechanism. An event is deemed to be unavoidable in particular if it is due to the conduct of the

---

[251] *Infra*, **6.G.12.**
[252] *Infra*, **6.F.16.**
[253] See *supra*, Chapter III, **3.E.17.**
[254] With the *Gesetz über Verkehr mit Kraftfahrzeugen* (Motor Vehicle Act) of 3 May 1909.
[255] As amended, BGBl.I.837, BGBl.III.9231–1. English translation by K. Lipstein and B. Markesinis in Markesinis at 813 ff. (with some terminological changes).

injured party, of a third party who is not an employee or of an animal and if both the keeper and the driver of the vehicle have applied that care which is required in the light of the circumstances.

(3) If somebody uses the vehicle without the knowledge and consent of the keeper of the vehicle that person is liable to pay compensation for the damage in the place of the keeper; in addition the keeper himself remains liable to pay compensation if the use of the motor vehicle was facilitated by his negligence. The first sentence of this paragraph does not apply if the person using the vehicle was employed by the keeper for the purpose of operating the vehicle of if he was entrusted with the vehicle by the keeper.

§ 8.   The provisions of § 7 do not apply . . . if the injured person was operating the motor vehicle.

§ 8a. (1) If a passenger in a motor vehicle has been killed or injured, the keeper of the vehicle is only liable in accordance with § 7 if a commercial transport of passengers for remuneration is involved . . .

§ 12. (1) The person who is bound to pay compensation is liable to pay:

   1. Where one person was killed or injured a lump sum of up to DEM 500,000 and no more or periodic payments up to DEM 30,000 per annum;
   2. Where several persons were killed or injured in the same event, notwithstanding the limits laid down in 1., a total lump sum of DEM 750,000 and no more or periodical payments of DEM 45,000 . . .
   3. Where an object was damaged, up to an amount of DEM 100,000 even if several objects were damaged in the same accident.

   (2) If the damages to be paid to several claimants involved in the same event exceed in total the maximum amount enumerated in . . . 2. or in 3., the damages payable to each individual are reduced in proportion of the total in relation to the maximum amount . . .

§ 16. Any provisions of federal law are unaffected according to which the keeper of a motor vehicle is more extensively liable for damage caused by the vehicle than according to the provisions of the present law, or according to which another person is liable . . .

§ 18. (1) In the circumstances covered by § 7(1), the driver of the motor vehicle is also liable to pay compensation in accordance with the provisions of §§ 8 to 15. No liability exists if the damage was not caused by the culpable conduct of the driver."

Note

(1) The *Straßenverkehrsgesetz* imposes risk-based liability (*Gefährdungshaftung*) on the keeper (*Halter*) of a motor vehicle. As G. Müller puts it: "[This liability] is incurred on the basis of social responsibility by the keeper of a motor vehicle . . . because of the operation of such motor vehicle. It is the price to pay for the authorization to create a source of danger by operating a motor vehicle."[256]

(2) The main conditions for liability under § 7 StVG to arise are:

- The victim must have suffered the kind of injury that comes under the scope of protection of § 7 StVG: like most other provisions concerning risk-based liability under German law, it builds on the approach of § 823(1) BGB, where the protected interests (*Rechtsgüter*) are enumerated.[257] § 7 StVG covers death, injury to the body, to health as well as damage to property. Unlike § 823(1) BGB, § 7 StVG *does not mention* freedom (of action) or "other rights"—an expression which has been used to extend the

---

[256] G. Müller, "Besonderheiten der Gefährdungshaftung nach dem StVG" (1995) 46 VersR 489.
[257] See *supra*, Chapter I, 1.4.3.

protection of § 823(1) BGB to the general *Persönlichkeitsrecht*[258] and the *Recht am Gewerbebetrieb*.[259] These *Rechtsgüter* are accordingly not protected by § 7 StVG.

- The injury must have been caused by the "operation of a motor vehicle" (*Betrieb eines Kraftfahrzeuges*). The interpretation given to that expression by German courts is reviewed further below under the next case.
- There must be a causal link between the injury and the operation of the motor vehicle. Not only must the operation of the motor vehicle be the *conditio sine qua non* ("but for" test) of the injury, but, under the *Schutzzweck der Norm* theory as applied to risk-based liability, the injury must represent a specific manifestation of the very risk against which § 7 StVG provides protection.[260] A good example of the assessment of causation under § 7 StVG can be found in the decision of the BGH of 2 July 1991, in a case where the noise caused by a collision had caused panic amongst the pigs in a nearby intensive farming installation.[261] Many pigs were killed or injured. There the BGH found that the damage to the pigs was a manifestation of the risks inherent in intensive farming (which makes the animals ultra-sensitive) and not of the risks of motor vehicle traffic.
- The defendant must have been the keeper (*Halter*) of the motor vehicle, the operation of which caused the injury. That element is discussed in greater detail in the second next case below.

(3) One of the peculiarities of the regime of § 7 ff. StVG lies in the possibility of exoneration because of an "unavoidable event" (*unabwendbares Ereignis*) at § 7(2) StVG. According to the general theory of risk-based liability (*Gefährdungshaftung*) under German law, only the presence of *force majeure* (*höhere Gewalt*) should be able to defeat liability; in fact, *force majeure* would indicate that the source of the injury lay outside of the scope of the risk against which the liability regime aims to provide protection. Depending on how the term "unavoidable event" is interpreted, an element of fault (an "impurity" in a risk-based regime) could be introduced into the regime of §§ 7 ff. StVG; the interpretation of that term is studied at greater length in connection with the third next case reproduced below.

(4) Some persons are excluded from the scope of protection of § 7 StVG. First, as provided in § 8 StVG, persons who were in fact involved in the "operation of the motor vehicle" cannot benefit from § 7 StVG; they are then left with the possibility of recourse only under the general fault-based regimes of the BGB (§§ 823, 826, 839).[262] The class of excluded persons, which is to be construed narrowly, comprises the driver of the car (when he or she is not the keeper thereof) and also, for example, persons who were examining the car for possible defects or who were helping to pull the car out of a snow bank.[263] Secondly, § 8a StVG by implication deprives passengers from the benefit of § 7

---

[258] See *supra*, Chapter I, 1.4.3., Introductory Note under b), as well as Chapter II, 2.2.1.

[259] See *supra*, Chapter I, 1.4.3., Introductory Note under b), as well as Chapter II, 2.3.2., Introductory Note under d), **2.G.37.** and **2.G.38.**

[260] On causation under German law in general, see *infra*, Chapter IV, 4.1.1. On the specific application of the *Schutzzweck der Norm* theory in the context of *Gefährdungshaftung*, see *supra*, **6.G.3.** and notes thereafter.

[261] *Supra*, Chapter IV, **4.G.3.**

[262] G. Müller, "Besonderheiten der Gefährdungshaftung nach dem StVG" (1995) 46 VersR 489 at 491–2. § 8 StVG also provides that § 7 StVG does not apply to vehicles whose maximum speed does not exceed 20 km/h.

[263] See G. Müller, ibid.; Larenz/Canaris at 623.

StVG as against the keeper of the motor vehicle that they were in, unless they were transported for consideration and on a commercial basis;[264] many authors question the fairness of the rule in § 8a StVG, since the danger created by the use of motor vehicles concerns equally all passengers.[265]

(5) The regime of §§ 7 ff. StVG also differs from the fault-based regimes of the BGB in the rules concerning the damages to be awarded. First, the rules of §§ 842–845 BGB concerning damages in cases of death and injury are replaced by those of §§ 10–11 StVG, which are in some respects broader, in others narrower. Secondly, in the absence of a specific provision enabling the recovery of *Schmerzensgeld*, it is excluded pursuant to the general rule of § 253 BGB; the exclusion of *Schmerzensgeld* is generally perceived as a questionable gap (*Lücke*) in the regime of §§ 7 ff. StVG.[266] Thirdly and most importantly, § 12 StVG provides for a maximum sum in damages to be awarded, depending on the nature of the injury, the number of victims and the nature of the relief (lump-sum payment or rent). Such maximal sum is generally less than could have been awarded under a fault-based regime such as § 823(1) BGB. The limitation is generally justified by the need to keep the risk insurable.[267]

(6) The StVG contains its own rules for the sharing of liability between parties.[268] First, § 9 StVG concerns contributory fault (*Mitverschulden*) on the part of the victim:[269] the general rules of § 254 BGB apply, under which compensation can be reduced or even excluded because of the contributory fault of the victim. Furthermore, § 17(1) StVG governs cases where two or more keepers are liable to a third party under § 7 StVG for the same injury: here liability will be apportioned as between the keepers on the basis of the causal significance of their respective contribution to the injury.[270] The second sentence of § 17(1) StVG extends the rule of § 254 BGB and § 9 StVG in the context of risk-based liability: indeed if the victim was himself or herself the keeper of one of the motor vehicles involved in the accident, the amount to be received from the keepers of the other vehicles will be reduced in proportion to the causal significance of the victim's involvement—or even extinguished altogether—irrespective of whether the victim was at fault or not.

(7) § 18 StVG also provides for liability on the part of the driver, but, unlike the liability of the keeper, such liability is fault-based. § 16 StVG also provides that the regime of § 7 StVG is not exclusive of the general fault-based liability regimes of the BGB (§§ 823, 826, 839), so that the victim can base a claim against a keeper on both regimes. While §§ 7 ff. StVG are more favourable to the victim than the fault-based regimes of the BGB so far as the establishment of liability is concerned, the latter are more favourable to the victim than §§ 7 ff. StVG so far as the amount of recoverable compensation is concerned

---

[264] Similarly, the second sentence of § 8a limits the liability for damage to things which were in a motor vehicle to those things which commercial passengers for value were carrying or bringing with them.

[265] See G. Müller, "Besonderheiten der Gefährdungshaftung nach dem StVG" (1995) 46 VersR 489 at 492.

[266] Ibid. at 493–4.

[267] Ibid. at 492–3.

[268] Ibid. at 490–1. These rules are also discussed, in the context of contributory fault, *infra*, Chapter VII, **7.G.8.**, where §§ 9 and 17 StVG are reproduced.

[269] On *Mitverschulden* under German law in general, see *infra*, Chapter VII, 7.1.2.

[270] These keepers remain liable jointly and severally (as *Gesamtschuldner*) towards the victim, according to the general rules of German tort law: see *infra*, Chapter IV, **4.F.38.–39.**, Note (4).

since they do not limit the amount which can be recovered by way of damages, and they allow for the recovery of *Vermögensschaden*.

The following cases can be found (with notes) at <http://www.rechten.unimaas. nl/casebook>:

6.G.13. BGH, 19 April 1988. Fall from bicycle without contact.
6.G.14. BGH, 26 November 1996. Scirocco never came back.
6.G.15. BGH, 17 April 1992. Porsche at over 130 km/h.

6.2.1.B. FRENCH LAW

Introductory Note

Under French law, a specific statute has also been enacted to cover liability for motor vehicle accidents, namely the *Loi 85–677 tendant à l'amélioration de la situation des victimes d'accidents de la circulation et à l'accélération des procédures d'indemnisation* of 5 July 1985, also known as the *Loi Badinter*. That statute is presented below, with four cases touching upon the main issues arising under it.

While the first German statute on that topic was enacted in 1908,[271] it would be a mistake to conclude that it took almost 80 more years for France to address the fate of the victims of motor vehicle accidents. In fact, at the beginning of the century, the "newly discovered" regime of liability without fault for things pursuant to Article 1384(1) C.civ. was rapidly extended to injury caused by motor vehicles;[272] the famous *Jand'heur* decision,[273] which put that regime on solid foundations, concerned a traffic accident, as did most of the leading cases under Article 1384(1) C.civ.

Act 85–677 of 5 July 1985[274]   **6.F.16.**

LOI BADINTER

"Chapter 1—Compensation for victims of road traffic accidents
   Article 1—The provisions of this Chapter shall apply to victims of a road traffic accident, including when they are being conveyed pursuant to a contract, in which a land surface motor vehicle is involved, together with its trailers or semi-trailers, if any, with the exception of trains and trams operating on their own tracks.
   Section I—Provisions governing the right to compensation
   Article 2—The driver or holder (*gardien*) of a vehicle mentioned in Article 1 may not, as against victims, including drivers, plead force majeure or act of a third party.

---

[271] *Supra*, 6.2.1.A., Introductory Note.
[272] On that regime, see *supra*, 6.1.2.
[273] Cass. Ch. réun., 13 February 1930, *supra*, **6.F.5.**
[274] Loi 85–677 tendant à l'amélioration de la situation des victimes d'accidents de la circulation et à l'accélération des procédures d'indemnisation (Act aiming at the improvement of the position of victims of traffic accidents and the acceleration of compensation procedures) of 5 July 1985, JO, 6 July 1985, D 1985. Lég. 371. Translation by N. Sims.

Article 3—Victims, apart from the drivers of land surface motor vehicles, shall be compensated for the damage resulting from personal injury suffered by them and their own fault on their part may not be pleaded against them, save where inexcusable fault on their part was the sole cause of the accident.

When the victims referred to in the preceding subparagraph are under the age of 16 years or over the age of 70 years or where, irrespective of their age, they are, at the time of an accident, holders of a certificate attesting a degree of permanent incapacity or invalidity of at least 80%, they shall in all cases be compensated for the damage resulting from the personal injuries that they have suffered.

Nevertheless, in the cases mentioned in the two preceding subparagraphs, the victim shall not be compensated by the person who caused the accident for the damage resulting from personal injuries where that person intentionally sought the damage suffered.

Article 4—Fault on the part of the driver of the land surface motor vehicle shall have the effect of limiting or excluding compensation for the damage suffered by him.

Article 5—Fault on the part of the victim shall have the effect of limiting or excluding compensation for damage to property suffered by the victim. However, the victim shall be entitled to compensation for supplies and equipment obtained on medical prescription according to the rules applicable to compensation for personal injury.

Where the driver of a land surface motor vehicle is not the owner of it, the driver's fault may be pleaded against the owner as regards compensation for damage caused to his vehicle. The owner shall have a right of action against the driver.

Article 6—Loss suffered by a third party owing to damage caused to the immediate victim of a road traffic accident shall be made good, regard being had to the limitations or exclusions applicable to the compensation of such damage [*i.e.* the damage caused to the immediate victim] . . ."

Notes

(1) Following a long and difficult process,[275] the *Loi Badinter* was enacted in part to correct certain deficiencies of the regime of liability for things under Article 1384(1) C.civ. as it had been developed by courts. It builds on that regime, and in fact it cannot be understood without prior knowledge of the case law under Article 1384(1) C.civ.

In its Chapter I, dealing with compensation for victims of traffic accidents, the *Loi Badinter* contains not only provisions that reform civil liability at Section I but also significant provisions concerning motor vehicle insurance at Sections II and III. As a result, Article L. 211–1 of the *Code des assurances* was modified to extend the compulsory motor vehicle insurance (to be taken out by the person in whose name a vehicle is registered) so as to cover all injury to third parties suffered in accidents in which the motor vehicle was involved, and irrespective of who was the keeper (*gardien*) of the vehicle or was driving the vehicle at the time of the accident. Furthermore, pursuant to Articles L. 211–8 ff. of the *Code des assurances* (added by the *Loi Badinter*), the insurer of a motor vehicle involved in an accident is bound to make an offer of compensation for personal injury to the victims of the accident no later than eight months following the accident. An offer of compensation for damage to property must be made within eight months of a claim being filed. A series of provisions have the object of enabling victims to assess the adequacy of the offer and decide on it, and to deter insurers from making insufficient offers.[276]

---

[275] See Viney and Jourdain, *Conditions* at 1089–95, para. 963–7.
[276] That process is studied by Le Tourneau and Cadiet at 929 ff., para. 3863 ff.

Moreover, Articles 421–1 ff. of the *Code des assurances* (also introduced by the *Loi Badinter*) provide for the establishment of an industry-wide guarantee fund to step in when, for various reasons, victims do not receive a compensation offer.[277]

The liability regime of Articles 2 to 6 of the *Loi Badinter* is therefore essentially concerned with defining the scope of the compensation to be paid to the victim by the insurer. The focus of the inquiry is moved from the liability of the defendant to the compensation to be received by the victim.

(2) Following some discussion on this point,[278] it is now established that the *Loi Badinter* creates an autonomous regime of liability, separate from, and independent of, Article 1384(1) C.civ. in particular, even though some elements of that regime must be seen in light of the case law under Article 1384(1) C.civ. Accordingly, *if and to the extent* that the regime of the *Loi Badinter* applies, other regimes, such as those of Articles 1382–3 or 1384(1) C.civ., are excluded.[279]

Compensation under the *Loi Badinter* will be payable if the following conditions are satisfied:

– The plaintiff must have suffered **injury**. Here as elsewhere, French law does not limit or hierarchize *a priori* the rights and interests which are protected. Injury to the person, damage to property as well as economic loss are thus recoverable.[280]

– A **traffic accident** occurred. The first case below deals with that element.

– The insured motor vehicle was **involved** (*impliqué*) in that accident. The second case below touches upon that element, one of the innovative (but controversial) aspects of the *Loi Badinter*.

– There must be a **causal link between the accident and the injury**. A key point in the *Loi Badinter* is the replacement of the traditional causation test, whereby the "triggering factor" (*fait générateur*) is linked to the injury, with two distinct steps: first, the involvement of the vehicle in the accident, and secondly, causation in the traditional sense between that accident and the injury. The implementation of that two-step scheme in practice has been one of the main difficulties in the application of the *Loi Badinter*, as illustrated in the third case below.

– The person whose liability is sought (through the insurer) was the **keeper** (*gardien*) or **driver** of the vehicle in question. The concept of keeper used under the *Loi Badinter* is the same as under liability for things in general pursuant to Article 1384(1) C.civ.[281] The definition of "driver" is discussed below. Persons other than the keeper or driver of the vehicles involved in the accident cannot be made liable under the *Loi Badinter*, and hence any liability on their part falls to be settled according to the other liability regimes (usually Articles 1382–1383 C.civ.).[282]

---

[277] For instance, the identity of the other party to the accident remains unknown, the other party was in breach of its obligation to be insured or the insurer of the other party is insolvent.

[278] See Viney and Jourdain, *Conditions* at 1100–4, para. 974–6; Le Tourneau and Cadiet at 905–6, para. 3787.

[279] If the regime of the *Loi Badinter* does not apply for one reason or another (e.g. one of the elements is not present), the other regimes become available again.

[280] Viney and Jourdain, *Conditions* at 1147–8 and 1167–8, para. 1016–7 and 1031. On the absence of limitation or hierarchization under French tort law in general, see *supra*, Chapter I, 1.4.2.

[281] Viney and Jourdain, *Conditions* at 1135, para. 1004. On the concept of *gardien* under Article 1384(1) C.civ., see *supra*, **6.F.8.** and notes thereafter.

[282] Viney and Jourdain, *Conditions* at 1136–8, para. 1005–6.

The *Loi Badinter* is therefore a regime of liability without fault, since the conduct of the driver or *gardien* of the vehicle (and its wrongful character) is not relevant, either as an element to be proven by the plaintiff or as a possible defence (absence of fault). Once the elements mentioned above are established, the victim has a *right to compensation*.[283]

(3) One of the aims of the *Loi Badinter* was to limit the grounds available to the defendant (and his or her insurer) on which to seek a reduction of, or exoneration from, liability. Indeed, once compensation for the victim becomes central, with a system of compulsory third-party liability insurance, any reduction of liability means that the loss would fall not on the insurer of the defendant (in practice) but on the victim. Since first-party insurance is not compulsory, the chances are that in many cases the victim would himself or herself bear such loss.

The *Loi Badinter* is clear on one point, at Article 2: *force majeure* and the conduct of a third-party cannot be invoked against the victim.[284]

The only defence left to the keeper or driver is thus the fault of the victim.[285] The *Loi Badinter* does not attach any significance to the conduct of the victim if it did not constitute a fault, thus emphasizing the punitive character of a reduction in or elimination of compensation on account of the fault of the victim.[286] The *Loi Badinter* puts the use of that defence in a fairly complex framework (at Articles 3–6), which is summed up in the following table:

Victims	Immediate victims				Indirect victims
Injury	Personal injury			Property damage	
	All victims, except drivers		Victims who were also drivers		
	Young, old, invalid	All others			
Available grounds		Inexcusable fault as exclusive cause	Fault	Fault	Same as applicable to immediate victim, as well as fault of indirect victim
	Voluntary infliction of injury				
Impact	No compensation (All-or-nothing)		Compensation reduced or excluded		Same as for immediate victim

[283] See Viney and Jourdain, *Conditions* at 1143, para. 1011.

[284] See Viney and Jourdain, *Conditions* at 1144–7, para. 1013–5; Le Tourneau and Cadiet at 924, para. 3849.

[285] It will be recalled that, under the main regimes of liability under the *Code civil* (Art. 1382–3, Art. 1384(1) as applied to things), the fault of the victim can lead to complete exoneration if it qualifies as an extraneous cause (irresistible, unforeseeable, external to the defendant); otherwise, it can be invoked to obtain a reduction in liability. See *supra*, Chapter III, 3.2.3. and Chapter IV, **4.F.38.–39.**, Note (2) as well as *infra*, Chapter VII, 7.1.1.

[286] See Viney and Jourdain, *Conditions* at 1148, para. 1018; Le Tourneau and Cadiet at 919, para. 3829.

The availability of the defence therefore depends on a series of factors:

(i) for **immediate victims**, as regards **personal injury** (including its economic consequences), three groups must be distinguished:

    (A) victims who were also **drivers**, against whom fault (in general) can be pleaded
(Article 4), in order to *reduce or eliminate* compensation;

    (B) non-driving victims who are young (less than 16), old (more than 70) or invalid
(more than 80% incapacity), against whom only the voluntary self-infliction of
injury (e.g. suicide) can be pleaded (Article 3, second and third paragraphs), in
order to *eliminate* compensation altogether ("all-or-nothing");

    (C) all other non-driving victims, against whom, in addition to voluntary self-
infliction of injury, "inexcusable fault" (*faute inexcusable*) can be pleaded, as
long as the inexcusable fault was the "exclusive cause" of the accident, in order
to *eliminate* compensation altogether ("all-or-nothing"). The fourth case below
deals with the concept of inexcusable fault (Article 3, first and third paragraphs),
which hitherto had been used only in the context of work accidents;

(ii) for **immediate victims**, as regards **damage to property**,[287] the defendant's insurer can
invoke the fault of the victim as a defence (Articles 4 and 5, paragraph 1) in order to
reduce or eliminate compensation. Furthermore, the fault of the driver can be
pleaded against the owner of the vehicle (Article 5, paragraph 2);

(iii) for **indirect victims**, the defendant's insurer can raise the defences available against the
immediate victim, taking into account the group to which the immediate victim
belongs (Article 6). By implication, case law has concluded that no other defences
can be raised against an indirect victim, with the exception of the fault of the indirect victim himself or herself.[288]

The scheme of Articles 3 to 6 of the *Loi Badinter* has faced criticism from legal writers.[289]
At the systemic level, it distorts the regime of liability without fault of the *Loi Badinter*
by introducing fault considerations (even if they pertain to the victim and not to the
defendant).[290] At the policy level, the scheme clearly "sacrificed" drivers, since contributory fault can be raised against them;[291] it can be argued that the *Loi Badinter* actually
put them in a worse position.[292] At the practical level, the scheme of Articles 3 to 6 is difficult to apply, as the following example shows.

---

[287] With the exception of the loss resulting from the need to purchase medical apparatus (prosthetic aids, etc.)
which is treated as a consequence of personal injury.

[288] See Le Tourneau and Cadiet at 929, para. 3862; Viney and Jourdain, *Conditions* at 1170–4, para. 1034–6.

[289] It is covered in detail by Viney and Jourdain, *Conditions* at 1147 ff., para. 1016 ff. and Le Tourneau and
Cadiet at 917 ff., para. 3820 ff.

[290] See Le Tourneau and Cadiet at 905–6, para. 3787.

[291] See Viney and Jourdain, *Conditions* at 1157–8, para. 1024; Le Tourneau and Cadiet at 918–9, para. 3826.
It seems that the complex system put in place at Articles 3 to 6, including the introduction of inexcusable fault
as a defence and the "sacrifice" of drivers, resulted from a political compromise required to ensure the passing
of the statute: see A. Tunc, "Traffic Accident Compensation" in A. Hartkamp et al., (eds.), *Towards a European
Civil Code*, 2nd edn. (Nijmegen: Ars Aequi Libri, 1998) 461 at 464–6.

[292] Indeed, at the time when the *Loi Badinter* was enacted, the Cour de cassation had not yet gone back on
its *Desmares* decision (Cass. civ. 2e, 21 July 1982, JCP 1982.II.19861, D 1982.Jur.449, Gaz.Pal. 1982.Jur.391), in
which the court had held that the fault of the victim (when it did not qualify as *force majeure*) could not
partially exonerate the defendant under Article 1384(1) C.civ. Commentators generally think that the *Desmares*
decision was taken in order to prompt the legislature into action. Once that was done, at least in relation to

In the case of the driver (the claimant driver) who claims for his or her loss against the driver/keeper of another car involved in the accident (the other driver), the other driver (or presumably his or her insurer) can invoke the fault of the claimant driver against the claim.[293] If the claimant driver was indeed at fault and the other driver was not (but nevertheless remains liable, since the *Loi Badinter* contains a regime of liability without fault), how is the liability of the other driver affected? If only fault is taken into account, the other driver should be exonerated, but that would run against the very principle of liability without fault which underpins the *Loi Badinter*. If instead liability is reduced in proportion to the causal significance of the faulty conduct of the claimant driver—which is more consistent with liability without fault—then why should the *Loi Badinter* attach any significance to whether the conduct of the claimant driver was faulty or not? The issue gave rise to considerable debate in the case law and in legal writing,[294] and finally the Cour de cassation pragmatically settled for the second approach: the claimant driver is entitled to compensation, and his or her fault will exonerate the other driver fully only if such fault is the *exclusive cause* of the accident (a requirement that was not explicitly set out in Article 4 of the *Loi Badinter*).[295] Otherwise, compensation is reduced proportionally to the causal significance of the fault of the claimant driver.[296]

(4) A key element in the framework of the *Loi Badinter* is the concept of driver: the driver can be made liable, and different compensation rules apply to the victim who was a driver. Case law has generally taken a restrictive approach to the definition of "driver", in order to minimize the impact of the less favourable compensation rules applicable to them.[297] Accordingly, the driver is the person who commands of the vehicle at the time when the accident occurred, irrespective of whether the vehicle itself was actually in operation. A person who was outside the car, was getting into it or leaving it cannot (or no longer) be its driver. Furthermore, case law will presume that victims were not driving the car in which they were; it is up to the defendant to show that the claimant was in fact driving and should thus be put under the less favourable regime applicable to drivers.[298]

The following cases can be found (with notes) at <http://www.rechten.unimaas.nl/casebook>:

6.F.17. Cass. civ. 2e, 5 January 1994, *Caisse mutuelle d'assurance et de prévoyance* v. *Caneiro*. Shredder.

6.F.18. Cass. civ. 2e, 20 January 1993, *Morizet* v. *Cathelin*. Surprised pedestrian falls over.

---

traffic accidents, with the *Loi Badinter*, the Cour de cassation reversed its *Desmares* case law and returned to the orthodox approach, under which the fault of the victim leads to the partial exoneration of the defendant: Cass. civ. 2e, 6 April 1987, *infra*, Chapter VII, **7.F.4**. See Viney and Jourdain, *Conditions* at 289–91, para. 428.

[293] *Loi Badinter*, Art. 4.

[294] See Viney and Jourdain, *Conditions* at 1162–7, para. 1029; Le Tourneau and Cadiet at 919–20, para. 3832–3.

[295] Cass. Ch. mixte, 28 March 1997, Bull.civ. 1997.Ch.mixte. 1, D 1997.Jur.294.

[296] The principles applicable to the apportionment between the victim and the defendant in cases of contributory fault are discussed further *infra*, Chapter VII, 7.1.1.

[297] See Viney and Jourdain, *Conditions* at 1158–61, para. 1025–7; Le Tourneau and Cadiet at 917–8, para. 3822–4.

[298] As a result, it is conceivable that, where the evidence is not conclusive, a vehicle could have been without a driver for the purposes of the *Loi Badinter*!

6.F.19. Cass. civ. 2e, 19 February 1997, *Die Bundesknappschaft* v. *Sté Rhône-Loire consultant*. Cardiac arrest following accident.

6.F.20. Cass. Ass. plén., 10 November 1995, *Larher* v. *Sté Harscoat*. In the middle of the street at night.

6.2.1.C. ENGLISH LAW

Unlike what has happened in Germany and France, the legislature has not intervened to establish a specific liability regime for motor vehicle accidents under English law. The considerable number of claims and amount of litigation arising from such accidents—which are no less numerous in England than elsewhere—has thus been left to the general principles of the law of torts, and in practice essentially to the law of negligence. Accordingly, a large body of the case law relating to negligence concerns road traffic accidents, and in some respects it contains specific developments relating to such accidents, which are briefly surveyed below.[299]

As regards the **duty of care**, few specific problems arise in relation to traffic accidents. Indeed, it is beyond doubt that drivers owe a duty of care to other road users;[300] as with other types of cases falling under the law of negligence, the existence of a duty of care is questioned only in cases involving psychological injury (or "nervous shock" as it is often called) to a primary or a secondary victim.[301] Similarly, **causation and remoteness of damage** are assessed much as in other cases of negligence, even if that sometimes creates difficulties, given that road traffic accidents can be complex and hard to reconstruct.[302]

On the other hand, road traffic accident cases show some specificity when it comes to the **standard of care** for negligence, which is notably stricter there.[303] A number of factors explain this. First, the Road Traffic Act makes it a criminal offence for a person to use, or to permit another person to use a motor vehicle on a road unless the user is covered by insurance (which may be taken out by the owner of the vehicle, by the user himself or herself or by someone else, such as the user's employer). The insurance in question must be issued by a statutorily authorized insurer and must cover, in particular, liability in tort in respect of personal injury and (up to at least GBP 250,000) damage to property other than the vehicle itself.[304] Even if courts rarely admit it, compulsory liability insurance affects the balance between plaintiff and defendant, since the issue is no longer whether the defendant "deserves" to be made liable for the victim's loss, but rather whether the case is such that the victim should bear the loss instead of the defendant's insurer, which

---

[299] See also *supra*, Chapter II, 2.1.2., Introductory Note under c).

[300] See *supra*, Chapter I, **1.E.22.** and Note (3) thereafter.

[301] One of the leading cases on that issue is a traffic accident case, *Page* v. *Smith*, *supra*, Chapter II, **2.E.9.** See also *supra*, Chapter II, **2.E.8.–9.** and notes.

[302] Markesinis and Deakin at 302. See, for instance, *Fitzgerald* v. *Lane*, *supra*, Chapter IV, **4.E.40.**, where the plaintiff pedestrian was hit by two cars in rapid succession. Since it was impossible to determine which car had caused which part of the injury, both drivers were held jointly and severally liable for their part (there was also contributory negligence on the part of the plaintiff).

[303] On the standard of care for negligence in general, see *supra*, Chapter III, 3.2.2.C.

[304] See Road Traffic Act 1988 (c. 52), ss. 143 and 145.

ultimately spreads it over all insurance policyholders.[305] Secondly, the Highway Code contains a series of relatively concrete rules of conduct relating to traffic. While it is true that those rules provide nothing more than evidence that a party was negligent or not, so that compliance with them does not exclude negligence,[306] it is tempting to bring the standard of care close to these relatively mechanical rules.[307] As a consequence, the assessment of negligence in road traffic accident cases has become more objective and stricter than elsewhere. In the words of Markesinis and Deakin:[308]

> "[I]n road traffic cases the law appears to go further: not only does it take no account of individual frailty, but it also takes no account of human frailty generally . . . Should an error, often unavoidable, . . . result in disaster, it will be accounted negligent. For, once the error has been isolated for legal purposes as being 'the cause', the objective approach requires us to say that the mythical 'reasonable man' would not have made that particular error. Momentary inattention and distractions are not morally blameworthy, but the point is that in this area the law has chosen not to distinguish between 'error' and 'fault'."

The system of compulsory third-party insurance under the Road Traffic Act has been complemented by an agreement between the UK Government and the insurers who are authorized to issue the compulsory insurance, whereby the latter have founded the Motor Insurers Bureau, which is responsible for ensuring that victims receive compensation where (i) the tortfeasor is uninsured (in violation of the Road Traffic Act), (ii) the insurer of the tortfeasor is not bound to compensate the victim because the insurance policy is invalid or (iii) the identity of the tortfeasor is unknown.[309]

Even if compulsory liability insurance, a stricter standard of care and the setting up of the Motor Insurers Bureau go some way towards alleviating the weaknesses of tort law as regards traffic accidents, many authors, including P.S. Atiyah, favour replacing tort law with no-fault insurance schemes on the model of certain North American jurisdictions,[310] though such proposals have been made as much to reduce the legal costs associated with claims by victims as to improve their chances of recovering compensation. Already by the 1970s, the Royal Commission on Civil Liability and Compensation for Personal Injury (the Pearson Commission) had recommended such a system for road traffic accidents,[311] but its recommendation was not taken up by Parliament. More recently, the Lord Chancellor's Department released a Consultation Paper on compensation for road traffic accidents, with a proposal for a no-fault scheme for less serious

---

[305] In a rare occurrence, Lord Denning MR expressly acknowledged how compulsory insurance affected the reasoning of the courts in *Nettleship* v. *Weston* [1971] 2 QB 691, 3 All ER 581, CA, quoted *supra*, Chapter III, **3.E.17.**, Note (1).

[306] *Clerk & Lindsell on Torts* at 351, para. 7–140; Markesinis and Deakin at 298–9.

[307] In *Clerk & Lindsell on Torts* at 351–5, para. 7–141 to 7–143, a survey is made of the considerable case law dealing with matters such as speed, braking, driving in the wrong lane and crossing a line of stationary traffic, crossroads, pedestrian crossings and level crossings.

[308] At 299. For a classical example of this tendency, see *Roberts* v. *Ramsbottom* [1980] 1 WLR 823, discussed *supra*, Chapter III, **3.E.17.**, and notes thereafter. See however the recent case of *Mansfield* v. *Weetabix Ltd.*, ibid.

[309] See *Clerk & Lindsell on Torts* at 356–7, para. 7–145; Markesinis and Deakin at 302–4.

[310] See for instance P.S. Atiyah, *The Damages Lottery* (Oxford: Hart Publishing, 1997), in particular 173 ff. See also the critical assessment of the current law in Markesinis and Deakin at 300–2.

[311] The Commission was appointed in 1974 and filed its Report, *On Civil Liability and Compensation for Personal Injury* (Cmnd. 7054) in 1978. It is discussed in Rogers at 43–6.

injuries (claims below GBP 2,500).[312] At this point in time, however, the issue does not seem to be very high on the political agenda in the UK.

6.2.1.D. EUROPEAN LAW

The following legislative instruments can be found (with notes) at <http://www. rechten.unimaas.nl/casebook>:

6.EC.21. Directive 72/166 of 24 April 1972.
6.EC.22. Directive 84/5 of 30 December 1983.
6.EC.23. Directive 90/232 of 14 May 1990

6.2.2. OTHER ACCIDENTS

This subsection briefly reviews other regimes of liability not based on fault which apply to accidents, namely liability for animals and for injury caused by transportation means other than motor vehicles.

Liability for animals

This heading can be found at <http://www.rechten.unimaas.nl/casebook>.

Liability for injury caused by means of transportation other than motor vehicles

---

This heading can be found at <http://www.rechten.unimaas.nl/casebook>.

6.2.3. COMPARATIVE OVERVIEW

This section was concerned with liability regimes applicable to accidents. In practice, road traffic accidents form the most relevant area for a comparative study. Liability for animals was briefly surveyed; it is imposed upon the keeper irrespective of his or her conduct under the laws of France, Germany and England.[313] In addition, specific liability regimes also exist for accidents caused by means of transportation other than motor vehicles: the Warsaw Convention dealing with liability of airlines has been implemented in all the systems surveyed here,[314] and moreover Germany also has a specific risk-based liability regime for injury arising in the course of transport by rail.[315]

Both Germany and France have introduced specific liability regimes for road traffic accidents, through the *Straßenverkehrsgesetz* of 19 December 1952[316] and the *Loi*

---

[312] Lord Chancellor's Department, *Compensation for Road Accidents: A Consultation Paper* (1991), discussed in Markesinis and Deakin at 304–8.
[313] *Supra*, 6.2.2.
[314] Ibid.
[315] Ibid.
[316] *Supra*, **6.G.12.**

Badinter of 5 July 1985[317] respectively. Both those regimes are not based on the wrongful conduct of the defendant. In contrast, under English law there are no specific provisions dealing with liability for road traffic accidents; such accidents are dealt with under the general rules of tort law, in particular the tort of negligence.[318] Nevertheless, the presence of a compulsory insurance scheme, pursuant to the Road Traffic Act, has had an influence on the reasoning of English courts, which tend to be harsher on defendants in negligence claims arising from car accidents.[319]

Given that basic difference between French and German law, on the one hand, and English law, on the other hand, it may be thought that the scope for the emergence of a converged *ius commune* in the area of liability for road traffic accidents is very limited. Nevertheless, that area has been given a European dimension through the enactment of a series of directives concerning liability insurance for motor vehicle accidents.[320] While the prime purpose of these directives is to harmonize the provisions regarding insurance cover in order to ensure the free movement of persons (with their vehicles), they also have an impact on the substance of the law of civil liability,[321] if only because the law of civil liability will tend to evolve in step with compulsory insurance coverage, as was mentioned in the previous paragraph with reference to English law. For instance, the compulsory insurance cover (the "green card") must extend to damage to property and personal injuries, up to a certain amount; it cannot exclude unauthorized use of the vehicle; it must extend to passengers other than the driver, etc. Beyond those provisions, however, the actual coverage of the compulsory insurance, and more fundamentally the scope and nature of liability for road traffic accidents, remains for the Member States to decide.

In this section, the German *Straßenverkehrsgesetz* and the French *Loi Badinter* were examined in greater detail. While each is the product of the specific approach to liability not based on conduct which prevails in its respective system, they nevertheless harbour a very similar basic structure.

The StVG follows the general model for risk-based liability (*Gefährdungshaftung*) under German law, as outlined in the previous section.[322] Accordingly, it contains a exhaustive list of protected interests (limited to life, health and property), on the model of § 823(1) BGB,[323] and liability is limited to a maximum amount.[324] In contrast, the *Loi Badinter* builds upon the principles of general regime of liability for things at Article 1384(1) C.civ.,[325] which it modifies in a few significant respects to create a new liability regime.[326] Hence, in comparison with the StVG, it contains neither an exhaustive list of protected interests nor a ceiling amount on liability. On the basis of the grounds of

---

[317] *Supra*, **6.F.16.**
[318] *Supra*, 6.1.3.
[319] Ibid.
[320] Directive 72/196, *supra*, **6.EC.21.**; Directive 84/5, *supra*, **6.EC.22.**; Directive 90/232, *supra*, **6.EC.23.**, to which a fourth Directive will be added shortly.
[321] See for instance ECJ, Judgment of 28 March 1996, Case C–129/94, *Ruiz-Bernaldez* [1996] ECR I–1829, discussed *supra*, **6.EC.21.–23.**, Note (2).
[322] See *supra*, 6.1.1.
[323] § 7(1) StVG, *supra*, **6.G.12.** and Note (2) thereafter.
[324] § 12 StVG, ibid.
[325] See *supra*, 6.1.2.
[326] See *supra*, **6.F.16.**, Note (2).

defence that remain available to the defendant, however, it provides less protection to property and economic interests than to life and bodily integrity.[327]

When it comes to the scope of application of the liability regime, the StVG and the *Loi Badinter* operate differently. On the one hand, the scope of application of the StVG was interpreted in line with the general approach outlined by the BGH, which rests on the "scope of rule" (*Schutzzweck der Norm*) theory.[328] Accordingly, the application of the StVG is very closely linked to the assessment of causation. An injury occurs in the "operation of a motor vehicle" within the meaning of § 7(1) StVG—and therefore comes within the scope of application of the StVG—as soon as the motor vehicle played a role in the occurrence of the injury and the injury represents a specific manifestation of the very risk associated with the operation of motor vehicles.[329] On the other hand, the *Loi Badinter*, like Article 1384(1) C.civ., differs from German law in that it does not rely on any notion of risk that would underlie the liability regime and at the same time limit its scope of application. Rather, case law under the *Loi Badinter* relies on more concrete and operational criteria. Accordingly, the *Loi Badinter* will apply whenever there is a "traffic accident", which is broadly defined by the Cour de cassation as any accident where a vehicle was in motion, even if the injury resulted from the operation of a part of the vehicle (e.g. machinery on a trailer) that is not related to its motion.[330] Similarly, causation is not dealt with by reference to risk: the *Loi Badinter* contains a complex two-stage process to relieve the victim of evidentiary difficulties. In a first step, the victim must show that the car of the defendant was involved (*impliqué*) in the accident: the car will be involved if it either came in contact with the victim or was a necessary condition ("but for" test) for the accident.[331] Once involvement in the accident is shown, then the injury is presumed to result from the accident, unless the defendant proves that his or her car played no role in the occurrence of the injury.[332] In the end, while it can be assumed that the respective scope of application of the StVG and the *Loi Badinter* will broadly coincide, the assessment proceeds along fairly different lines.

Beyond these differences, the StVG and the *Loi Badinter* are broadly similar in their general structure.

First of all, they both attach liability to the keeper of the motor vehicle. Under the *Loi Badinter*, the concept of "keeper" (*gardien*) is taken directly from the case law under Article 1384(1) C.civ.[333] Under the StVG, "keeper" (*Halter*) is construed slightly differently: as it has been construed in the case law of the BGH, it is more stable than the French "keeper" (*gardien*). Under the StVG, for a person to lose his or her quality as "keeper" of a motor car, that person must have lost the power to dispose of the vehicle for a prolonged period.[334]

---

[327] The *Loi Badinter* does not reduce the range of defences available against claims for damage to property: see ibid, Art. 4 and 5, as well as Note (3) thereafter.

[328] See BGH, 27 January 1981, *supra*, **6.G.3.**

[329] See how the BGH defined "operation of a motor vehicle", *supra*, **6.G.13.** For a case turning around whether the injury constituted a specific manifestation of the risk associated with motor vehicles, see *supra*, Chapter IV, **4.G.3.**

[330] See *supra*, **6.F.17.**

[331] See *supra*, **6.F.18.** and notes thereafter.

[332] See *supra*, **6.F.19.** and notes thereafter.

[333] See *supra*, **6.F.8.** and notes thereafter.

[334] See *supra*, **6.G.14.** and notes thereafter. In comparison, under French law, the mere fact of dispossession, e.g. when a car is stolen, will usually suffice to transfer the *garde* of the car: see *supra*, **6.F.8.**

Secondly, both the *Loi Badinter* and the StVG limit the range of defences available to the defendant,[335] although the *Loi Badinter* is stricter than the StVG. Under the StVG, in line with the general theory of risk-based liability under German law, the defendant can invoke *force majeure* (*höhere Gewalt*) to defeat liability.[336] In addition, § 7(2) StVG enables the defendant to avoid liability by showing that the injury was due to an "unavoidable event" (*unabwendbares Ereignis*). While that might appear to re-introduce fault elements in the risk-based liability regime of the StVG, the concept of "unavoidable event" has been interpreted very narrowly in the case law, by using the "ideal driver" as a point of reference: only those events which would have been unavoidable for that ideal driver will qualify for the purpose of § 7(2) StVG.[337] The practical impact of § 7(2) StVG is accordingly limited. Under French law, the main modification brought about by the *Loi Badinter* was precisely to restrict the grounds of defence available to the defendant. The *Loi Badinter* creates a fairly complex system, which depends on the class of victim and the type of injury:[338] by way of summary, for most victims of personal injury (except those who were also driving one of the cars involved in the accident), the defendant will only be able to avoid liability by showing that the inexcusable fault (*faute inexcusable*) of the victim was the exclusive cause of the injury or that the victim voluntarily brought about the injury upon himself or herself.[339] In its case law, the Cour de cassation has given a narrow interpretation to inexcusable fault: it consists in conduct that is exceptionally grave and intentional, so as to expose the victim to a danger of which he or she should have been aware.[340]

Thirdly, both the StVG and the *Loi Badinter* put the car driver in a far worse position than other victims of road traffic accidents. Under § 8 StVG, the driver is deprived of the benefit of the liability regime of the StVG, so that he or she is typically left with his or her claims under § 823, 826 or 839 BGB, as the case may be.[341] Similarly, it was said that drivers were "sacrificed" when the *Loi Badinter* was enacted: while they can bring claims for compensation under the *Loi Badinter* if they are injured in a road traffic accident, the defendant can answer by raising the contributory fault of the driver, so that the liability of the defendant towards the injured driver will be reduced or even extinguished.[342]

6.3. PRODUCT LIABILITY

Product liability is probably the best area in which to study how liability for wrongful conduct and liability not based on conduct relate to one another and how difficult it can be in practice to draw a clear line between the two.

---

[335] Defences are discussed at greater length *infra*, Chapter VII. See in particular the discussion of the interplay between the principles of contributory fault and the regimes of the *Loi Badinter* and the StVG at **7.F.1.–3.** and notes thereafter and **7.F.6.** (for the *Loi Badinter*) as well as **7.G.7.** and **7.G.8.** (for the StVG).

[336] *Supra*, **6.G.12.**, Note (3).

[337] *Supra*, **6.G.15.** and notes thereafter.

[338] See *supra*, **6.F.16.** and Note (3) thereafter.

[339] Where the victim is a young child (less than 16 years old), an older person (more than 70 years old) or an invalid, the defendant can only invoke the voluntary infliction of injury as a defence: ibid.

[340] *Supra*, **6.F.20.** and notes thereafter.

[341] *Supra*, **6.G.12.**, Note (4).

[342] *Supra*, **6.F.16.**, Note (3).

Injuries caused by products began to give rise to serious policy concerns in the second half of the 20th century, when the combined effect of increasingly sophisticated consumer products—from household equipment to pharmaceutical products —, automated large-scale production processes and modern distribution chains left the end-user in a difficult position. The end-user was purchasing a product not from the manufacturer directly, but from a retailer who might stand a number of steps away from the manufacturer in the distribution chain. The complex processes of product development and manufacture were internal to the manufacturer and thus unknown to the end-user and probably to the retailer as well. If the end-user suffered physical injury or damage to property due to the product, the traditional liability systems offered him or her some form of contractual recourse (typically based on warranty) against the retailer, and perhaps also a delictual or tortious recourse against the manufacturer. While the contractual liability of the retailer might be easier to establish—assuming that warranties had not been excluded —, such liability might be limited, and in any event the retailer usually did not have the financial resources required to meet substantial claims by the victim. As regards the manufacturer, the victim faced an uphill battle in trying to demonstrate fault or negligence, as the case may be.

While it is generally agreed that the law should be modified in order to redress the obvious disadvantages of the traditional liability system and give the victim better recourse against the manufacturer that put the product on the market, a number of solutions are possible:

– Some of them involve modifying the regime of tort liability applicable to the manufacturer: at the opposite extreme from traditional fault-based liability would be a regime where the manufacturer would be liable for all injury caused by the products that it has placed on the market. While such a regime would undoubtedly square with the theories of risk-based liability[343] and improve the position of victims, most consider that it would overburden producers and have a "chilling effect" on innovation. Accordingly, some form of balance has been sought and, as shown below, in most systems the striking of the balance involves introducing concepts such as "defect", "security", etc. to delineate the scope of the manufacturer's liability.

– Other solutions involve an erosion of the principles of "privity" or "relativity" of contract, so as to enable the end-user to benefit from the contractual remedies which the first buyer would have had against the manufacturer if the product had injured the first buyer.

This section begins with a survey of the national laws concerning product liability. The survey shows that Germany and England have anchored product liability within tort law. While officially retaining fault as the basis for liability, both these systems have minimized the significance and impact of the requirement of fault by developing certain rules related to the burden of proof. France, on the other hand, has blurred the boundary between contract and delict to a greater extent, and has followed a different approach to the topic.

---

[343] The manufacturer would bear the burden of the risk that it had created by putting on the market sophisticated products the advantages of which for end-users are counterbalanced by an increased danger of injury. See for instance the theoretical foundations of *Gefährdungshaftung* under German law, *supra*, **6.G.2.** and Note (2) thereafter, the theory of risk under French law, *supra*, **6.F.4.** and notes thereafter as well as the justification for strict liability under English law, *supra*, **6.E.9.** and Note (2) thereafter.

Differences between the legal systems of the Member States led the European Community to attempt to harmonize the law of product liability with Directive 85/374 of 25 July 1985 on the approximation of the laws, regulations and administrative provisions of the Member States concerning liability for defective products.[344] However, the Directive did not affect existing law, but merely supplemented it with a new harmonized regime.[345] The second subsection surveys how the Directive has been implemented in the legal systems under study, and the difficulties to which it has given rise.

6.3.1. NATIONAL LAWS

6.3.1.A. GERMAN LAW

Introductory Note

a) Under German law, apart from (i) provisions concerning pharmaceutical products in the *Arzneimittelgesetz*[346] and (ii) the *Produkthaftungsgesetz*, which implemented Directive 85/374,[347] both of which are discussed further below, there is no specific provision dealing with product liability; this should not be taken to mean that before Directive 85/374 injury caused by industrial products was of no concern to German law. In the 1960s, German academics realized that the general framework of tort law as it had evolved until then could not adequately deal with cases where a customer suffers injury to the person or damage to property because of an industrial product, for the reasons outlined above in the introduction to this section.

A number of propositions were put forward by academics as to how to adapt the law of civil liability, involving changes in the law of contract, in the law of tort or even the creation of a new autonomous liability regime. In a landmark decision on 26 November 1968, reproduced below, the BGH took stock of the academic literature and ultimately chose to follow the course of applying the law of delict, i.e. § 823 BGB.

b) Nonetheless, in that decision, the BGH articulated a specific set of rules applicable to the liability of the manufacturer for its products, so that product liability has become a fairly self-contained sub-set of liability pursuant to § 823(1) BGB. The concept of *Verkehrspflicht* has been used extensively in the German law of product liability in order to concretize the rules of conduct applicable to manufacturers: a breach of one of these *Verkehrspflichten* resulting in injury to one of the protected interests (*Rechtsgüter*) enumerated at § 823(1) BGB, combined with fault on behalf of the producer (which, as seen below, is presumed once the breach is established), suffices to engage the liability of the producer under § 823(1) BGB.

Case law has developed a number of broad categories of *Verkehrspflichten* applicable to manufacturers, concerning the avoidance of manufacturing defects (*Fabrikationsfehler*), design defects (*Konstruktionsfehler*) and instruction defects (*Instruktionsfehler*).

---

[344] *Infra*, **6.EC.33.**

[345] Ibid., Art. 13.

[346] AMG, Drug Act of 24 August 1976, BGBl.I.2445, §§ 84 ff. These provisions create a regime of risk-based liability (*Gefährdungshaftung*) for defects in pharmaceutical products. See *infra*, **6.G.34.**, Note (4).

[347] *Infra*, **6.G.34.**

The landmark case of 26 November 1968, reproduced below, concerned a manufacturing defect. A case concerning a design defect and one concerning an instruction defect have also been included.

c) There is also a temporal dimension to product liability under German law, in that case law has established that manufacturers are under a duty to monitor their products (*Produktbeobachtungspflicht*) after they have been put on the market. The fourth case below concerns that duty, which plays a significant role in the treatment of the so-called "product development risks" under German law.

BGH, 26 November 1968[348] **6.G.24.**

LIABILITY FOR DEFECTIVE PRODUCTS
MANUFACTURING DEFECT (*FABRIKATIONSFEHLER*)

Fowl pest

Once the victim shows that he or she has suffered injury to one of the Rechtsgüter *of § 823(1) BGB as a result of a defect in a product, it is presumed that the manufacturer of that product violated a* Verkehrspflicht, *that it was at fault and that such fault caused the defect; the manufacturer then bears the burden of exonerating itself.*

Facts: The plaintiff's chickens were vaccinated against fowl pest by Dr. H., a veterinary surgeon, who used a vaccine produced by the defendant. Nevertheless, a few days later the pest broke out amongst the chickens. The plaintiff lost over 4000 chickens. The vaccine used by Dr. H. had been bought directly from the defendant, in half-litre bottles. The production batch from which the vaccine came had been analyzed and approved by an independent research institute; thereafter it had been bottled. The standard procedure is for half-litre bottles to be vacuum-sealed. Bottles from this batch were sent to research institutes for inquiry; it was found that the bottles were not sterile and contained the virus responsible for fowl pest. Other poultry farms experienced the same difficulties with vaccine coming from the same batch. Dr. H. assigned to the plaintiff all his rights against the defendant. The plaintiff sued the defendant (with whom it had no contractual relationship) on the ground that the vaccine had not been properly produced (*Fabrikationsfehler*).

Held: The court of first instance and the court of appeal allowed the claim, on the basis that the defendant was contractually liable to Dr. H. for the injury suffered by the plaintiff. The BGH upheld the decision of the court of appeal, for other reasons.

Judgment: "[SOLUTIONS ARISING OUT OF THE CONTRACT BETWEEN THE MANUFACTURER AND DR. H.]

I. The principles concerning the *recovery of sums on account of damage sustained by third parties* [*Drittschadensliquidation*] cannot be applied in the present case [emphasis in original].

1. . . . In principle, on the basis of a contract only he who sustains the damage and who legally bears the damage can claim its redress. If a third party sustains the damage, then the wrongdoer . . . is only liable to him in tort law . . . The case law has only allowed for exceptions in special cases, namely when the interests protected by the contract between the creditor under the contract and the holder of the interest are shifted to a third party as a result of a special legal relationship, so that in law the damage is to be sustained by him and not the creditor . . .

Such an exceptional case is not present here . . .

2. The court of appeal also found that a duty of care on the manufacturer for the benefit of the third party arose from the aim and purpose of the contract [between the manufacturer and Dr. H.].

---

[348] BGHZ 51, 91. Translation by Y.P. Salmon.

It could be thought the court of appeal thereby wished to grant the plaintiff a claim for compensation arising from *a contract with protective effect for a third party* [emphasis in original]. This cannot be accepted.

a) . . . It is not open to any third party who suffered damage as a consequence of the breach of a contractual obligation to derive his own claim for compensation from the contract [reference omitted] . . . That can only be accepted if the creditor [of the obligation that was breached] is co-responsible so to say for the 'good and ill' of the third party, when damage to the latter also affects him, because [the creditor] is under a duty towards the third party for his protection and care. This relationship between the creditor of the contractual obligation and a third party, characterized in every respect by a personal relationship, leads to the protective effect for the benefit of the third party, and not the relationship between the creditor and his contractual partner. Such a relationship does not exist at all in a contract of sale or contract for services . . .

[SOLUTIONS ARISING OUT OF A SPECIAL OR QUASI-CONTRACTUAL RELATIONSHIP BETWEEN PLAINTIFF AND DEFENDANT]

II. If therefore the contested judgment cannot be justified by the reasoning expounded therein, it is to be examined whether it can be upheld on another ground. The plaintiff . . . also referred to §§ 823ff. BGB. Moreover, he pleaded . . . the direct liability of the manufacturer towards the end user ('*producer liability*') [emphasis in original, references omitted].

1 . . . [The proponents of a more extensive liability of the producer] wish to afford the end-user his own claim for damages, which should be directly aimed at the manufacturer as an '*action directe*' [in French in the original]—such as the claim afforded by law under §§ 823 ff. BGB—and independent of the contract between the vendor and the manufacturer . . .

a) The claim would be recognized without more, if the view supported by Diederichsen (Die Haftung des Warenherstellers, 1967) were followed, to the effect that the manufacturer must assume responsibility for all kinds of product defects regardless of fault, just as with risk-based or even 'strict liability' [in English in the original] . . . In any case liability without fault is incompatible with the principles of the law of liability as they currently stand . . .

b) Neither is it possible . . . in law to afford the end-user a direct claim by assuming the conclusion of a direct, albeit tacit, guarantee contract (*Garantievertrag*) between him and the producer (see in this way, Müller, AcP 1965, 311). The fact that the producer distributes his products under his brand does not generally imply a willingness to assume liability towards the user for diligence in manufacture . . . [references omitted]. In any case, even the advertising of branded products . . . cannot be construed as an acceptation of liability for any defect in the product [reference omitted] . . .

c) It is also excluded that the end-user could be afforded a claim for reparation on the sole basis of a breach of a duty of care that would arise from 'social contact' (compare Lorenz in the Festschrift für Nattorp, 1961 at 83; Soergel-Schmidt Vor § 275 at para. 5) . . . While some relationship is undoubtedly present from a sociological perspective, it does not in law carry such weight that it could lead to claims in liability on the basis of a special legal relationship.

2. According to a view that deserves peculiar consideration, a quasi-contractual special legal relationship (*Sonderrechtbeziehung*) between end-user and producer should be recognized in law, based on reliance (*Vertrauensgedanke*). Indeed, the relationship between the purchaser of a injurious product and its manufacturer, as it already exists before the occurrence of the damage, could be closer than any relationship arising between the manufacturer and 'someone' when—and only when—the latter incurs damage because of a product of the manufacturer . . . In view of the claims for damages of the purchaser, however, it could be thought that they should remain based on contract even if the purchaser did not buy the goods directly from the manufacturer, but from a trader . . .

The present case does not concern a series of legally independent contracts of sale that are in fact linked to one another in a 'distribution chain' where, indeed, the vendor has often become merely the 'distributor' of the manufacturer and where, as a consequence, a 'direct recourse' appears sensible . . .

[SOLUTIONS ARISING OUT OF THE LAW OF DELICT]
III. On the basis of the facts as found by the court of appeal the conditions of § 823 BGB are fulfilled. The vaccine supplied by the defendant was defective and caused the chickens' illness. Even if . . . contract law is not applicable here, the starting point must still remain that the defendant is liable for his own fault. *If someone, while making use of an industrial product in accordance with its purpose, suffers injury to one of the* Rechtsgüter *protected by § 823(1) BGB because the product was defectively manufactured, it is up to the manufacturer to explain how the defect came about and so to demonstrate that it was not at fault* [emphasis added].

1. In cases of 'producer liability' the victim must still prove that the damage was caused by a defect in the product. Here the plaintiff must thus prove that the fowl pest broke out amongst its chickens because the vaccine came from the defendant and contained active viruses when it was delivered . . .

3 . . . It is indeed correct that the court of appeal found that no fault on the part of the defendant was established . . . That does not necessarily mean that the case must be remitted to the trial judge, for it was up to the defendant to exonerate himself . . .

aa) This results from the mere fact that the claim of the plaintiff is also founded on § 823(2) BGB. [Indeed, the defendant had breached § 6 AMG by putting on the market a vaccine with injurious effects.] If . . . an infringement of a protective statute is proven, then it is presumed to have happened culpably . . .

bb) However, this rule on the burden of proof would also apply if the plaintiff could only base his claim on § 823(1) BGB. It would then also be up to the defendant to exonerate himself.

In any case the plaintiff who relies on § 823(1) BGB must in fact show—and prove if necessary—not only the existence of a causal link between the damage suffered and the behaviour of the tortfeasor, but also the fault of the tortfeasor (BGHZ 24, 21 at 29). However, the proof of those elements significantly depends on the extent to which the plaintiff can explain the objective course of events in detail. That becomes particularly difficult when the course of events in question took place in a plant, during the manufacture of the [defective] product. Case law has for some time already come to the aid of the victim, in that it considered as sufficient the proof of a causal chain which according to experience points towards a 'fault in the organization' (*Organisationsverschulden*) on the part of the manufacturer. However, this will not suffice when it comes to claims based on 'producer liability'. All too often the factory owner will plead that the product defect could also have been caused in a manner that does not support a finding of fault on his part—an allegation which the plaintiff cannot easily rebut, since it brings one back to occurrences in the tortfeasor's plant. Consequently, when the injury arises from the sphere of risk associated to the plant of a manufacturer, it cannot be accepted that the manufacturer would be exonerated simply by bringing up possible explanations for the presence of a defect in the product which would be compatible with an absence of fault on its part. In the case of producer liability, this conclusion is dictated by the legitimate interests of the injured party—irrespective of whether the injured party was an end-user, a user or a third party. On the other hand, the legitimate interests of the producer do not forbid requiring it to prove that it was not at fault.

Admittedly, this rule of proof intervenes only if the injured party has proved that the damage found its origin within the sphere of organization and risk (*Organisations- und Gefahrenbereich*) controlled by the manufacturer, and more specifically through an objective defect or impropriety for circulation . . . Once the plaintiff satisfies this burden of proof, the producer is 'in a better position' to explain the course of events and bear the consequences of the lack of proof. It overlooks production, determines and organizes the manufacturing process and the delivery of the finished products . . . [The victim] cannot explain the course of events in such a way as to allow the court to make a reliable finding on whether [the defective product is to be traced to] an omission for which management is to be blamed or whether [i] it is attributable to a manufacturing defect for which a worker is responsible, [ii] it was the 'odd unit' which always props up from time to time or [iii] it relates to a 'development defect' which was unforeseeable according to the state of the art in technology and science at the time. Thus if the reason why the course of events cannot be explained [by the victim] lies within the realm of the producer, it must also belong to his sphere of risk. It is accordingly proper and reasonable that the producer would bear the consequences of the risk of being unable to prove the absence of fault on its part . . .

It will always . . . depend on the situation of the interests at hand in the respective case. It is left open whether the owner of a smaller factory, whose manufacturing process is transparent and can be reviewed . . ., should also be expected to assume the risk that evidence would be inconclusive. As regards cases such as the present one, in any event, it falls on the manufacturer to exonerate himself.

4. The defendant failed to bring forward this exonerating proof."

Notes

(1) The above case marks the beginning of product liability as a specific branch of German law. Its significance can hardly be overstated; thirty years later, it is still often referred to. The factual situation was simple, and yet it brought to the fore the key difficulties surrounding product liability: the plaintiff's contractual relationship was with the veterinary surgeon, Dr. H., not with the defendant, yet a contractual claim against Dr. H. was not suitable. In addition, Dr. H. had assigned all his claims against the manufacturer to the plaintiff, so that the plaintiff could also attempt to recover from the manufacturer any damages to which Dr. H would have been entitled.

In dealing with the plaintiff's claim against the manufacturer, the BGH went through all possible avenues.

(2) First, the BGH examined (under I.) whether the plaintiff could recover his losses under the contract between the defendant and Dr. H., as the court of appeal had found. The plaintiff had invoked the two main doctrines used to extend the protective scope of a contract under German law, namely the recovery of sums on account of damage sustained by third parties (*Drittschadensliquidation*) and the protective effect of contracts in relation to third parties (*Vertrag mit Schutzwirkung zugunsten Dritter*). Both those doctrines have been used, for instance, in order to broaden the scope of contractual liability for others pursuant to § 278 BGB, and thus provide make good the perceived deficiencies of delictual liability for others pursuant to § 831 BGB.[349]

With respect to *Drittenschadensliquidation*, the plaintiff invoked the rights of Dr. H. against the defendant, which had been assigned to him, arguing in substance that Dr. H. would have been able to recover from the defendant for the loss suffered by the plaintiff. The BGH took the position that the doctrine of *Drittschadensliquidation* should be applied restrictively, since it constitutes an exception to the distinction between contractual and delictual liability. The relationship between Dr. H. and the plaintiff, as supplier and acquiror of the vaccine, was not such that one could say that it was almost by chance that the plaintiff rather than Dr. H. suffered the loss.

[349] See *supra*, Chapter V, 5.1.3. under g). See also *supra*, Chapter II, **2.E.48.**, **2.G.52.** and notes thereafter.

The doctrine of *Vertrag mit Schutzwirkung zugunsten Dritter* was similarly inapplicable, since the relationship between Dr. H. and the plaintiff—a standard supplier/acquiror relationship—did not come within the category of those where the "good or ill" (*Wohl und Wehe*) of a third party is entrusted to one of the parties to the contract.

The BGH thus rejected a solution based on contract such as had been adopted by the court of appeal; in so doing the BGH may have felt that, in what was clearly going to be a leading decision, it was preferable to put the law of product liability onto a more "universal" basis than contract law, where it would have been dependent on the fulfilment in any given case of the conditions of the special doctrines of *Drittschadensliquidation* (which would in any event require an assignment of claims, as in the annotated case) or *Vertrag mit Schutzwirkung zugunsten Dritter*.[350]

(3) In the years preceding the BGH judgment in the annotated case, a number of distinguished writers had made the more adventurous suggestion of granting victims a direct remedy against the manufacturer, based on a specific liability regime arising out of a special or quasi-contractual relationship between end-user and manufacturer.

The BGH came to the conclusion that those suggestions could not be followed:

- The proposal of U. Diederichsen to put in place a regime of liability not based on fault for product defects was not consistent with the fault principle as understood by the BGH, since it was for the legislature to introduce regimes not based on fault (under II.1.a));[351]
- K. Müller had suggested that a "warranty contract" could be implied from the representations made by the manufacturer to the end-user through trademarks and advertising; the BGH rejected that conclusion (under II.1.b));
- W. Lorenz had suggested that, from a sociological perspective, the relationship between manufacturer and end-user should give rise to certain legal obligations on the part of the former. Here again, the BGH rejected the suggestion, since it did not think that it was appropriate to give legal effect to these social relationships (under II.1.c));
- The same idea was behind a proposal from C.-W. Canaris that the law should recognize a form of "quasi-contractual relationship" between the two ends of a chain of contracts, the manufacturer and end-user, the intensity of which would lie somewhere between a contractual relationship and the typical "happenstance" delictual relationship which arises when someone injures another by accident. That quasi-contractual relationship could be developed by analogy with the pre-contractual relationship, which has given rise to a specific set of liability rules (so-called *culpa in contrahendo*). The BGH did not reject that proposal, but instead pointed out that the annotated case was not a "chain of contracts" case as the proponents of this option had in mind (under II.2.). In the aftermath of the annotated case, where the BGH decisively opted for the delictual route, the idea of quasi-contractual liability has not been taken up further in the case law.[352]

---

[350] See Münchener-Mertens, § 823 at 1547, para. 271.
[351] See *supra*, **6.G.1.** and notes thereafter.
[352] Although legal writers have continued to develop it: see Münchener-Mertens, § 823 at 1547, para. 272.

(4) The only avenue left to the plaintiff, according to the BGH, was thus the law of delict (under III.). The BGH established the basis of the German law of product liability under § 823(1) BGB in the following sentence:

"If someone, while making use of an industrial product in accordance with its purpose, suffers injury to one of the *Rechtsgüter* protected by § 823(1) BGB because the product was defectively manufactured, it is up to the manufacturer to explain how the defect came about and so to demonstrate that it was not at fault."

It can be seen from that statement and from the reasoning that follows that product liability is guided by the following principles:

– The concept of "defect" (*Fehler*) plays a central role in the definition of the applicable *Verkehrspflicht*. Indeed industrial products, even if properly conceived, built and operated, often create a certain risk of injury, as is the case with cars, production tools, etc. That risk of injury is part of the risks to which everyone is exposed in the course of everyday life (*allgemeines Lebensrisiko*), and the manufacturer should not be made answerable for it. Defective products, however, create an increased risk of injury, and hence a manufacturer is under a duty to do all that is necessary (*erforderlich*) and reasonable (*zumutbar*) not to put into circulation defective products;[353] the content of that *Verkehrspflicht* is discussed below in relation to the next case. Accordingly, the victim must show that the product was defective; alternatively, the victim can show that the product failed to comply with the provisions of a protective enactment (*Schutznorm*) within the meaning of § 823(2) BGB.[354] As the BGH recalled, the victim must also establish injury, as usual, as well as causation between that injury and the defect in the product in question. Causation is not presumed, but the victim can rely on *prima facie* evidence (*Anscheinsbeweis*) in demonstrating it.[355]
– Once the victim has shown the above, it is presumed that (i) the manufacturer infringed a *Verkehrspflicht*, so acting wrongfully (*rechtswidrig*) (ii) the manufacturer was at fault (*Verschulden*) in doing so, and (iii) the fault of the manufacturer was the cause of the defect.[356] The burden of proof then falls on the manufacturer to exonerate itself in respect of those elements. The BGH explained that these presumptions would arise not only in cases where the manufacturer infringed a protective enactment (*Schutznorm*) within the meaning of § 823(2) BGB, but also where the *Verkehrspflicht* not to put defective products on the market was infringed (§ 823(1) BGB). As the BGH stated, the victim is not in a position to set out the course of events that led to the defect, so as to establish all the conditions of liability as regards the manufacturer; the burden of putting that evidence forward should therefore fall on the manufacturer, who oversees the production process. Accordingly, wrongfulness and fault of the manufacturer may be presumed once it has been shown that a product was defective, and hence the risk that the course of events leading to the defect cannot be reconstructed (*Unaufklärbarkeitsrisiko*) falls on the manufacturer.

[353] See T. Wieckhorst, "Vom Produzentenfehler zum Produktfehler des § 3 ProdHaftG" (1995) 46 VersR 1005 at 1006.
[354] As underlined in Münchener-Mertens, § 823 at 1564 ff, para. 306 ff, many statutes contain such protective norms, for instance with regard to food, motor vehicles, medical products or product safety.
[355] See BGH, 12 November 1991, in a part of the judgment not reproduced *infra*, **6.G.26.** The rules relating to the burden of proof as regards causation under German law (including *prima facie* evidence) are reviewed *infra*, Chapter IV, **4.G.19.** and notes thereafter.
[356] Münchener-Mertens, § 823 at 1562, para. 299.

(5) The annotated case provides a typical example of a manufacturing defect (*Fabrikationsfehler*), where a mistake was made in manufacturing the actual product unit that caused the injury. The manufacturer is under a duty (*Verkehrspflicht*) to organize production in such a way as to prevent manufacturing defects from arising, including through quality controls at the various stages of production and after it has been completed.[357]

(6) While the presumptions "discovered" by the BGH in the annotated case go a long way towards improving the position of the victim, product liability under German law ultimately remains fault-based, and it is conceivable that a manufacturer will succeed in discharging the burden put upon it. Towards the end of the excerpt, the BGH surveys the various possible explanations for a product defect:

– There was a mistake at management level in the manufacturer's organization, for which the manufacturer is liable under § 823(1) BGB;[358]
– One of the workers in the production chain was at fault. In practice, this corresponds to a case of liability for employees (*Verrichtungsgehilfe*) pursuant to § 831 BGB. As has been shown earlier in this work,[359] case law in relation to § 831 BGB (in particular the doctrine of decentralized exoneration) has made it easier for employers to rebut the presumption of fault contained in § 831. In the annotated case, the BGH left it open whether that case law applies where product liability is in issue. In a subsequent decision, however, the BGH held that the doctrine of decentralized exoneration does not apply in product liability cases: "[In such cases,] the manufacturer must allege and prove that the production process was not susceptible to being influenced by the individual mistakes of the employees . . . Should the [manufacturer] not come forward with [that] evidence, then it must identify the employees who worked on the production of the actual product that led to the injury and put forward, in respect of each and everyone of them, exonerating evidence relating to selection and supervision, in accordance with the second sentence of § 831(1) BGB."[360] In fact, exoneration pursuant to § 831 BGB is thus close to impossible in product liability cases;
– The defective product was the "odd unit" (*Ausreißer*) which, despite all the precautions taken by the manufacturer in accordance with the applicable *Verkehrspflichten*, still ended up defective. Indeed, the *Verkehrspflicht* incumbent upon the manufacturer is not to prevent any and all defects in its products, but rather to take all *necessary* (*erforderlich*) and *reasonable* (*zumutbar*) measures to prevent such defects from arising, in accordance with the fault-based nature of product liability under § 823 BGB.[361] Accordingly, it is conceivable that the "odd unit" might still suffer from a defect even if the manufacturer has complied with its *Verkehrspflichten*: if the manufacturer succeeds in demonstrating that such was the case, no liability will arise;
– Finally, the BGH also envisaged the possibility that the defect may have been caused by a "product development defect" (*Entwicklungsfehler*), that is to say by a defect that

---

[357] Münchener-Mertens, § 823 at 1556, para. 287.
[358] This type of mistake is similar in nature to the *Organisationsverschulden* as it is used to circumvent the limitations of § 831 BGB with respect to liability for employees: see *supra*, Chapter V, 5.1.3. under i).
[359] See *supra*, Chapter V, 5.1.3. under d) to f).
[360] BGH, 19 June 1973, NJW 1973, 1602 at 1603, VersR 1973, 862 at 863.
[361] *Supra*, Chapter III, 3.2.1. and 3.2.2.B.

was not foreseeable in the light of the state of scientific and technical knowledge as it existed at the time. Here again, it is consistent with the fault-based nature of the liability regime and with the *Verkehrspflicht* incumbent upon the manufacturer to free the manufacturer from liability if the defect could not have been foreseen at the time when the product was put on the market. That issue is discussed at greater length in the third next case below.[362]

In the end, the manufacturer has, broadly speaking, two lines of argument open to it in order to rebut the presumption of fault: either the product was the "odd unit" (*Ausreißer*) or the defect could not have been foreseen in the light of scientific and technical knowledge at the time. It will be seen below in connection with other types of product defects that these two lines of argument are not always open. Under the product liability regime pursuant to § 823 BGB which the BGH developed in the annotated case, the presumptions against the manufacturer are therefore relatively difficult to rebut,[363] and hence the regime, while remaining fault-based in theory, moves far away from traditional fault-based liability in practice.

(7) The interplay between tort law and the law of sale (where pursuant to §§ 459 ff. BGB, the vendor guarantees the buyer against defects) has been one of the most vexed problems arising out of the regime of liability for product defects under § 823 BGB, as it was set out by the BGH in the annotated case.[364] If, for instance, someone buys a table a leg of which turns out to be defective and breaks, the buyer has a recourse against the seller under the law of sale, since the table suffered from a defect; pursuant to § 462 BGB, the buyer can then obtain either the rescission of the sale (*Wandelung*) or a reduction of the sale price (*Minderung*). There is no recourse pursuant to § 823(1) BGB, since no infringement of ownership as such has occurred, given that the table was defective as from the moment it was bought. Accordingly, the substance of the acquired property—a defective table—was not affected by the defect, and any damage to the buyer would be more in the nature of a *reiner Vermögensschaden*. On the other hand, if the table was laid with valuable china tableware when its leg failed, the buyer of the table would have a claim against the manufacturer under § 823 BGB for any resulting damage to the china,[365] since the breakage represents a violation of the substance of other property of the buyer, which was caused by a defect in the table.

Problems arise in the case of more complex objects, when a defective part—often a very small one—causes damage to the whole object; in Germany, the expression "creeping damage" (*Weiterfresserschaden*) has been coined to illustrate the phenomenon. In a case decided by the BGH on 24 November 1976, an industrial cleaning installation used chemical vapours, which were produced by heating a chemical liquid in a container with heating elements (like an electric kettle); a small switch activated by a floater (*Schwimmschalter*) ensured that the heating elements would be turned off should they cease to be fully immersed.[366] The small switch was defective and as a result the whole

---

[362] *Infra*, **6.G.27.**

[363] Münchener-Mertens, § 823 at 1562, para. 299.

[364] In general, it is possible under German law to elect between remedies under tort or contract law when both are available (*Anspruchkonkurrenz*): see *supra*, Chapter I, 1.3.1.

[365] Unless the manufacturer can prove that it was not at fault, as seen in the preceding note.

[366] (*Schwimmschalter*—floating switch), BGHZ 67, 359.

installation was destroyed by fire. The BGH broke away from its traditional position and allowed the owner of the cleaning installation to claim the full amount of the damage to the installation from the manufacturer, as a species of product liability under § 823(1) BGB. The rationale of the BGH was fully exposed in a subsequent decision of 18 January 1983, dealing with a claim to recover the damages caused to a car as a result of an accident caused by a defective accelerator pedal.[367] As the BGH explained:[368]

"a) Contrary to the obligation of guarantee [imposed upon the seller] under the law of sale, *Verkehrspflichten* arising under the law of delict do not have as their object the protection of contractual expectations that the acquired property will be free from defects, in particular expectations relating to the use or value of the property (use interest (*Nutzungsinteresse*) or value interest (*Äquivalenzinteresse*)) [reference omitted]. They relate rather to the interest . . . in not suffering infringements of one's ownership or possession through the things put into circulation by the manufacturer (integrity interest (*Integritätsinteresse*)). Yet the manufacturer is under a delictual duty to avoid its products, because of a . . . defect, damaging or destroying not only other property of the acquiror, but also the products themselves. *As a matter of principle, the interest of the acquiror in preventing damage to, or destruction of, the acquired property is no less worthy of protection than the integrity interest in his or her other property* [emphasis added; reference omitted] . . . If damage to or destruction of the acquired property represents the injury that the manufacturer had to prevent pursuant to a delictual *Verkehrspflicht*, in view of the integrity interest of the [acquiror], then the latter can recover compensation for that injury from the manufacturer under the law of delict.

b) These cases must be distinguished from those where the injury represents the loss in value of the [acquired] property as a result of a defect, in view of the use or value interest of the acquiror . . . That loss of value, as a result of a defect, already affected the property at the time of acquisition; if the alleged injury is identical to that loss of value, then it must be attributed to unmet contractual expectations, thereby leaving no room for claims to damages under the law of delict [reference omitted]. Where, on the other hand, the injury is not identical (*stoffgleich*) to that loss of value, the injury may—also—reflect an infringement of the integrity interest of the [acquiror]; in principle, it can then also be covered by the liability of the producer under the law of delict, even when there is a concurrence with contractual guarantee [claims] [reference omitted]. It is indeed acknowledged that the law of delict cannot be excluded by the law of contract or *vice versa*; liability under each body of law follows its own rules."

In its decision in the case in question, the BGH has acknowledged that it would be difficult to distinguish between cases where the injury is identical to the loss in value protected solely by contractual recourse and those where it goes beyond it and can thus be recovered under the law of delict as well.[369] In general, the issue must be examined from a natural or economic point of view: if the defective part cannot be removed from the rest of the property or if the defect in that part cannot economically be cured, then the whole property was already irremediably affected when it was bought; hence the injury is identical to the loss in value and the claimant can proceed against the seller only under the law of contract.[370] In a subsequent case, a compressor motor had been damaged after it ran out of oil because of a defective oil conduit; there the BGH completed its reasoning by adding that when a defect in a part of a product could have been remedied, so that the value of the whole product was not affected from the very beginning, and the defective part later caused damage to the whole of the product, then the damage can be recovered from the manufacturer under the law of delict, since it is not identical with the initial loss in value (which affected the defective part only).[371] Whether the acquiror should have

[367] (*Gaszug*—accelerator pedal), BGHZ 86, 256.
[368] Ibid. at 258–60.
[369] For more details, see the explanation given by E. Steffen (who as a judge at the BGH played a role in the evolution of that line of case law), "Die Bedeutung der 'Stoffgleichheit' mit dem 'Mangelunwert' für die Herstellerhaftung aus Weiterfresserschaden" (1988) 39 VersR 977.
[370] Ibid. at 262.
[371] BGH, 14 May 1985 (*Kompressor*—Compressor), NJW 1985, 2420.

been able to detect the defect before the whole product was damaged is irrelevant to the claim under the law of delict.[372]

More recently, the BGH has added a further dimension to its case law by focusing on the rest of the product (the non-defective parts), as opposed to the product as a whole. In a decision of 12 February 1992, it found that, when the defective part was connected to the rest of the product in such a way that the non-defective parts were damaged in the course of remedying the defect, the integrity interest of the acquiror *in the non-defective parts* was affected and a claim under § 823(1) BGB was open for the damage to the non-defective parts.[373] Again, in a decision of 31 March 1998 in a case where defective transistors had been welded to the board of an electronic car lock system, so that they could not economically be removed without damaging the other components, the BGH found that the integrity interest of the acquiror *in the non-defective parts* had been infringed because those parts had been rendered useless (and worthless) when they were inextricably connected to the defective transistors.[374] The decision of 31 March 1998 marks a further expansion of the law of delict to cover cases which would have been excluded under the reasoning of the decision of 18 January 1983 mentioned in the previous paragraph.[375]

In general, the BGH case law on "creeping damage" has not been well received by legal writers, who generally argue that the BGH is undermining the well thought-out and balanced regime of the law of sale (§§ 459 ff. BGB) by allowing the law of delict to apply, even in cases where the claimant bought directly from the manufacturer.[376]

OLG Düsseldorf, 29 November 1996[377]   **6.G.25.**

Design defect (*Konstruktionsfehler*)

Quick-release bicycle wheel

A manufacturer is under a duty to take all necessary and reasonable measures to avoid danger. The required level of safety is to be assessed in the light of the average expectations of the target consumer group, within limits reflecting the state of the art (the upper limit) and established technical knowledge (the lower limit). Compliance with product standards provides evidence that the manufacturer has complied with its duty, but is not conclusive.

Facts: The plaintiff bought a mountain bicycle which can also lawfully be used on the public highway, since it complied with the applicable regulations.[378] The front wheel was attached to the fork with a quick-release hub, which allowed the wheel to be fitted or removed by moving a lever on the side of the hub. Less than one month after having bought the bicycle, the plaintiff was seriously injured in an accident which he alleged was due to

---

[372] BGH, 24 March 1992 (*Nockenwellensteuerrad*—Camschaft steering wheel), NJW 1992, 1678.

[373] (*Kondensator*—Condensator), BGHZ 117, 183.

[374] (*Transistor*), NJW 1998, 1942, MDR 1998, 842.

[375] See F. Graf von Westphalen, "Neue Aspekte der Produzentenhaftung" (1998) 52 MDR 805 and M. Franzen, "Deliktische Haftung für Produktionsschäden" JZ 1999, 702.

[376] See the review made by C. Katzenmeier, "Produkthaftung und Gewährleistung des Herstellers teilmangelhafter Sachen" (1997) 50 NJW 486.

[377] NJW 1997, 2333. Translation by Y.P. Salmon.

[378] The *Straßenverkehrs-Zulassungs-Ordnung* (Road Traffic Licensing Ordinance, StVZO), in the version promulgated on 28 September 1988, BGBl.I.1793.

the front wheel coming off the fork while he was riding. He sued the defendant, the manufacturer of the bicycle, under § 823 BGB, on the basis of a defect in the design (*Konstruktionsfehler*) of the bicycle.

Held: The court of first instance allowed the claim in part. The Oberlandesgericht varied the judgment of the court of first instance as regards *Schmerzensgeld*, but otherwise upheld it, albeit for different reasons. No further appeal was lodged with the BGH.

Judgment: "When someone is injured because of a defective product, the mere fact that the product was defective does not suffice to establish that the manufacturer caused the injury unlawfully and culpably. Rather, for the manufacturer to be liable under § 823(1) BGB, it must be shown that, under the circumstances of the case, the manufacturer, in manufacturing the product or in putting it into circulation, infringed the objective standard of care and thus violated a duty to take care (*Verkehrspflicht*) incumbent upon him [references omitted]. The duty to take care incumbent upon the manufacturer requires that such measures be taken during the production as are necessary and reasonable in the given case in order to avoid danger [reference omitted]. In that regard, when assessing the content of the duty to take care as regards products (*Produktsicherungspflicht*), the average expectation of the user for whom the product is destined is of primary importance. In addition, regard must be had to the level of safety that is possible and reasonable according to the current state of scientific and technical knowledge (*Erkenntnisstand von Wissenschaft und Technik*). That level of safety generally denotes the upper boundary of the safety requirements, while established technical knowledge (*anerkannte Regeln der Technik*) represents the lower boundary, the minimum to be expected. Failure to respect established technical knowledge usually implies that a duty to take care was breached [references omitted].

[The Oberlandesgericht then found that the bicycle model met the DIN 79 100 standard applicable to bicycles to be used on public roads.]

Compliance with DIN standards does not however suffice to discharge the duty to take care incumbent on the producer, if progress has superseded the standard [reference omitted] or if, in the course of using technical equipment, dangers became known which are not yet reflected in the DIN standard [reference omitted]. However the present case does not fall within one of these situations . . ."

Notes

(1) The annotated case concerns another type of product defect, namely a defect in the design of a product (*Konstruktionsfehler*). In its judgment, the OLG reviewed the case law on the content of the *Verkehrspflicht* incumbent upon the manufacturer, and in particular the definition of defect in the context of the design of a product.

In general, as the OLG noted, the manufacturer will be liable if it has not exercised the care objectively warranted in the circumstances of the case, thus infringing a duty to take care (*Verkehrspflicht*). That duty, as mentioned above, consists in taking such measures to prevent danger as are necessary (*erforderlich*) and reasonable (*zumutbar*) in the circumstances of the case.

As regards necessity, the primary focus is on consumers' safety and security expectations. The relevant expectations are not those of the actual claimant, but rather the average expectations of the target group of consumers of the product in question, as the OLG recalled. However, technical considerations complement consumers' expectations by setting both upper and lower limits to the level of security which it is necessary for the producer to achieve. An upper limit is found in the state of the art in science and technology (*Stand von Wissenschaft und Technik*): manufacturers are not bound to achieve a level of product safety in excess of what can be achieved in the current state of the art in science and technology, even if consumers' expectations may be higher. It follows that manufacturers will not incur liability if the product defect could not be foreseen (and prevented) in the light of scientific and technical knowledge at the time; that is the so-called exception for "product development risks" (*Entwicklungsfehler*). At the other end of the spectrum, irrespective of consumer expectations, manufacturers must comply with established technical knowledge (*anerkannte Regeln der Technik*). A failure to do so is evidence of a breach of duty. The overall picture is thus that the necessary safety level is determined by consumer expectations, these being however constrained by the state of the art in science and technology (upper limit) and the recognized technical knowledge (lower limit).[379]

The criterion of reasonableness, the second branch of the test for the *Verkehrspflicht* of the manufacturer, is meant to reflect economic realities. In any event, manufacturers are bound to respect minimum safety requirements (established technical knowledge); in addition, the more significant the danger, the more manufacturers are expected to take all necessary precautions against it, regardless of economic considerations. Nonetheless, to the extent that minimum requirements are met and the danger is less significant, economic considerations can come into play: manufacturers cannot be expected to offer the same level of product safety in a low-priced product as in a much more expensive model, but they are expected to respect the minimal safety requirements (established technical knowledge) even in their cheapest models.[380] Cars provide a good example of how the level of safety (beyond minimum requirements) which can reasonably be expected from a product may vary with price.

(2) When it comes to design defects (*Konstruktionsfehler*), as in the annotated case, the *Verkehrspflicht* incumbent upon the manufacturer translates into a duty to design products which do not create danger in the course of the use for which they are designed. The manufacturer must make provision for likely instances of misuse of the product, ensuring even when so misused, the product will present no danger to the user.[381]

In the case of design defects, the manufacturer has only a small chance of rebutting the various presumptions (wrongfulness, fault, causation between fault and product defect) that arise once the plaintiff has demonstrated that the product was defective. It is not possible to argue that the defective product was the odd defective unit (*Ausreißer*) which escaped all due precautions, since a design defect affects all units of the product in question.[382] The only possibility left is then to argue that the defect was not foreseeable on the basis of scientific and technical knowledge as it stood at the time. For design defects even more than for manufacturing defects, liability under § 823(1) BGB is, therefore, fairly stringent for the manufacturer.

(3) As the annotated case shows, product standards play a central role in assessing whether the manufacturer has complied with its *Verkehrspflicht* in the design of its product. In the annotated case, the bicycle was equipped with a quick-release hub on the front wheel. In a part of the case not reproduced above, the plaintiff argued that the manufac-

---

[379] On the issue as a whole, see T. Wieckhorst, "Vom Produzentenfehler zum Produktfehler des § 3 ProdHaftG" (1995) 46 VersR 1005 at 1006 and Münchener-Mertens, § 823 at 1553–4, para. 286.
[380] See T. Wieckhorst, ibid. at 1007.
[381] Ibid., and Münchener-Mertens, § 823 at 1554, para. 283.
[382] Münchener-Mertens, § 823 at 1558, para. 291.

turer should have added some mechanism to retain the wheel if the bicycle was ridden with the hub released. The OLG rejected that argument, essentially on the basis that the DIN standard applicable to bicycles did not require such a mechanism when quick-release hubs were used (since it can easily be seen from the position of the lever whether the hub is released). The OLG then inquired into possible grounds for requiring safety mechanisms going beyond the DIN standard, such as subsequent developments showing that the standard was insufficient or instances of dangers which were not taken into account when the standard was formulated. Since none of these were present, the OLG concluded that the product was not affected by any design defect.

(4) In the annotated case, while there was no design defect, the manufacturer was nonetheless found liable on account of an instruction defect, since the instructions merely showed how to operate the quick-release hub, without mentioning that danger would arise if the hub was not securely fastened to the wheel. The reasoning of the OLG was essentially based on the following case, which is the leading case as concerns instruction defects.

BGH, 12 November 1991[383]   **6.G.26.**

Instruction defect (*Instruktionsfehler*)

Children's tea

A manufacturer is under a duty to provide users with instructions that warn them against dangers arising in the course of using its products. In the case of dangers to health, the warning must be given separately from other product information and enable the user also to appreciate why the product can be dangerous.

Facts: The defendant was a manufacturer of children's herbal tea, which it sold in the form of a powder to be mixed with water. If mixed according to instructions, the resulting herbal tea had a sugar content of 9,6%. The tea was suitable to use as a drink for babies and small children and to calm them when they went to bed. The defendant also sold plastic bottles for children's tea, in 52 and 120 ml formats, which were fitted with an ortho-pedic teat, the specially formed tip of which brought the liquid further behind the child's teeth than the tradi-tional teat.

In September 1981, a scientific journal for dentistry published an article showing that "prolonged sucking" (*Dauernückeln*) of children's tea, such as occurred when the bottle was left with the baby or child for the night, was liable to cause severe decay of milk teeth, a phenomenon which became known as the "baby-bottle syn-drome" or "nursing-bottle syndrome". Acting on that information, the defendant added the following sentence to the "Instructions for preparation" printed on the packaging of the tea, as of November 1981:

Hold the bottle yourself and do not leave it with the child as a "sucking bottle" (*Nückelfläschchen*); frequent or lasting con-tact with the teeth, for instance before sleep, can lead to tooth decay.

A sticker containing a similar message was stuck on packages that had already been produced but were still in stock at the time. As of December 1982, the above sentence was taken out of the "Instructions for prepara-tion" and printed in a separate box entitled "Important information", circled in black, together with the weight of the package and the ingredients.

It appeared from evidence submitted by the plaintiff that nursing-bottle syndrome was already known in sci-entific circles as early as 1971.

The plaintiff was born in 1979 and was given children's tea manufactured by the defendant from November 1979 until June 1983, in order to help him fall asleep and sleep through the night. The 120 ml bottle sold by the defendant was left with him for that purpose, and he drank on average 1200 ml of tea a day. When he was

[383] BGHZ 116, 60. Translation by Y.P. Salmon.

between 18 and 24 months old, his parents noted that his teeth showed signs of decay. As it turned out, six of his teeth were decayed, and three had to be removed.

The plaintiff sued the defendant for the pain and inconvenience resulting from the damage to his teeth, on the ground that the defendant was liable under § 823(1) BGB in relation to the instructions given with its tea product.

Held: The court of first instance rejected the claim. The court of appeal reversed and allowed the claim in part. The BGH upheld the judgment of the court of appeal.

Judgment: "1 . . .a) The court of appeal rightly held that the manufacturer of an industrial product is under a duty to warn the user of the dangers which could arise from the use of the product [reference omitted], insofar as the use remains within the parameters of the general purpose of the product [reference omitted]. Under some circumstances, the warning must even extend to likely misuses of the product [reference omitted]. The manufacturer is relieved from the duty to warn only if, and insofar as, he can presume that his product will only fall into the hands of persons who are familiar with its dangers [reference omitted]. This also applies to the warnings against improper use [references omitted] . . .

[Under b), the BGH found that the baby-bottle syndrome arose in the course of the general purpose of the tea and the bottle, so that the defendant was under a duty to take care (*Verkehrspflicht*) to warn users of the dangers associated with the prolonged contact of the product with teeth.]

c) The court of appeal rightly held that the defendant failed to fulfil its duty to warn.

aa) That applies of course for the time until the end of November 1981, because until that time neither the packaging of the children's tea product nor the nursing bottle bore relevant warnings.

bb) Moreover, the [BGH] also agrees with the court of appeal that the packaging labels used as of November 1981 . . . did not meet the formal and substantive requirements of an adequate warning. The court of appeal rightly emphasized that, if the use of a product gives rise to considerable danger for human health, the duty to inform and warn is particularly stringent. In such cases, according to the case law of the [BGH], important notices about the dangers of the product and its use must appear clearly. They cannot for example be hidden among other bits of information about dosage, advertising claims and so on [reference omitted]. In substance, the notices should read in such a way that the user comprehends and appreciates the existing dangers. That can only be achieved if the nature of the danger is clearly emphasized, so that the user of the product can fully appreciate it, without having to reflect upon the warning or to make deductions on the basis of it [reference omitted]. The justification for the warning must be understood: in the cases where considerable injury to the body or health can result from an improper use of the product, the warning must explain the workings of the product, so that it can be seen why the product is dangerous [reference omitted].

Such a clear warning is particularly necessary where advertising counters the idea that the product could be dangerous when used in a given manner . . .

dd) As regards the parents of the plaintiff, the defendant did not fulfil its duty to warn either with the box text which was first put into circulation with the print date of December 1982 . . . The court of appeal rightly points out that, in any case for the user who is familiar with the product, no significant changes would be apparent such as would bring him to examine the entire packaging text anew . . .

2. The court of appeal rightly held that the defendant was at fault (*Verschulden*).

a) . . . It need not be considered whether the children's tea manufacturer is under a duty to secure speedy access to all reports in dentistry journals . . . about the results of clinical trials and research concerning tooth decay . . .

In its quality as manufacturer of children's tea products which contain sugar, the defendant should have taken it upon itself to investigate the dangers for the teeth of children which might arise through the consumption of its products; indeed it had recommended that its product be used in the 'little tea bottle' and it could not have failed to notice that modern teats allowed the drink to flow behind the upper front teeth. Furthermore, the defendant recommended the tea 'as a good-night drink before going to sleep', and it had emphasized that its tea was beneficial and ensured that the child would sleep satisfied through the night. It must have been evident to the responsible persons in the defendant company that the tea would be given to children in the evening even after they had brushed their teeth, and would also be left with them for sucking during the evening and night time. Had the defendant taken into account this use of the tea in its tests, then as a specialist business for infant food it should have noticed the dangers before the dental profession became aware of the baby-bottle syndrome . . .

b) Even in the absence of those concrete grounds for finding that the defendant behaved culpably, the court of appeal could have assumed that the defendant was negligent on account of its having breached its duty to warn.

In the present case it is established that the defendant put its product into circulation with defective instructions . . . In product liability cases, it can at once be assumed that such an insufficiency in the instructions accompanying the product arose because the defendant was at fault (*Verschulden*), unless the defendant succeeds in proving that he committed no fault. This reversal of the burden of proof was introduced by the [BGH] for the specific case of manufacturing defects (*Fabrikationsfehler*) (BGHZ 51, 91 [Fowl pest][384]). In subsequent case law, the application of those principles was extended to design defects (*Konstruktionsfehler*) [reference omitted] . . .

There is no reason to adopt a different solution for instruction defects (*Instruktionsfehler*) when a product is put into circulation. By analogy with manufacturing and design defects, the plaintiff simply must prove that it was necessary to provide instructions to the user [on the danger in question]. It then falls to the manufacturer to present the relevant facts and to prove that he committed no fault because he was not able to ascertain the dangers [references omitted]. The defendant was unable to adduce this evidence."

Notes

(1) In addition to duties relating to the design and the production of industrial products, discussed in connection with the two previous cases, the *Verkehrspflicht* incumbent upon the manufacturer under German law also encompasses a duty in respect of the information provided with the product.[385]

Indeed, a great part of the risk of injury created by manufactured products arises from improper use. In accordance with the manufacturer's *Verkehrspflicht* to take all necessary (*erforderlich*) and reasonable (*zumutbar*) measures to prevent dangers created by its products, the manufacturer must provide instructions that enable users to avoid danger.[386] Under 1.a) of the annotated judgment, the BGH set out the main elements of that duty: the manufacturer must warn the user of the dangers which may arise from any use of the product for its normal purpose, and even from likely misuses. The instructions must take into account not only prospective buyers of the product, but also other prospective users (e.g. children).[387] Only if the users can be assumed to be familiar with the dangers of the product is the manufacturer freed from that duty.

---

[384] *Supra*, **6.G.24.**

[385] See Münchener-Mertens, § 823 at 1554–5, para. 284–5.

[386] See T. Wieckhorst, "Vom Produzentenfehler zum Produktfehler des § 3 ProdHaftG" (1995) 66 VersR 1005 at 1008.

[387] See in this respect BGH, 9 June 1998 (*Feuerwerkskörpern*—Fireworks), BGHZ 139, 79, NJW 1998, 2905, where the BGH held that a manufacturer of fireworks had to take into account that children would be using its

(2) Under 1.c), it is worth noting how stringent German law can be as regards the content and appearance of the warnings, especially when health risks are involved.[388] The first warning introduced by the defendant in November 1981 was deemed insufficient both in form and substance (under 1.c)bb)). As regards form, it was not sufficiently isolated from the other instructions found on the packaging, and in substance it did not explain why the product could be dangerous for the child's health, so that the danger was not immediately apparent to the user. The BGH found that the "weakness" of the warning was compounded by the publicity made by the defendant, advocating the virtues of its product for small children. Even when, in December 1982, the defendant separated the warning from the rest of the instructions for use and put it in a box with the title "Important information", the defendant still had not fulfilled its duty to inform users, since according to the BGH, the overall graphic design of the packaging had not been sufficiently changed to bring the *pre-existing* user to re-examine it and take note of the warning (under 1.c)dd)).

(3) The BGH was equally severe when it came to the assessment of fault (*Verschulden*). The parties had argued over the extent to which the defendant had to keep abreast of scientific research concerning tooth decay. The BGH found that, irrespective of that issue, the defendant should of its own motion have conducted research into the safety of leaving children's tea bottles with children overnight, since it must have known that that was a likely use of its product. Had such research been conducted, the defendant would have known earlier of the risk of tooth decay.

In any event, the BGH added that, as with manufacturing defects (*Fabrikationsfehler*) and design defects (*Konstruktionsfehler*), the fault of the manufacturer is to be presumed as soon as the plaintiff shows that the product was put on the market with inadequate instructions (i.e. that it suffered from an instruction defect or *Instruktionsfehler*). Given that, as for design defects, the defence that the defective product was an "odd unit" is not available in the case of instruction defects, the possibilities of exoneration are fairly limited: the only avenue open to the manufacturer is more or less to challenge that there was any defect (i.e. to show that the instructions were adequate).[389] In the annotated case, the manufacturer had not been able to bring forward exonerating evidence in this respect.

(4) The "baby-bottle syndrome" continued to keep German courts busy after the annotated case. In 1994, the BGH reaffirmed the annotated judgment in a second "children's tea" decision.[390] In 1995, the BGH found that the warning, as it was put on the packaging as of December 1982, was sufficient for *new* consumers, who had begun to use the children's tea only after December 1982.[391] The 1995 decision was followed by the lower courts in other children's tea cases, one of which was even brought, unsuccessfully, before the Bundesverfassungsgericht on the ground that the BGH case law violated the constitutional rights of the plaintiffs.[392]

products, and would even have to include warnings to retailers not to resell its products to children who would not use them under adult supervision.

[388] See also Münchener-Mertens, § 823 at 1555–6, para. 286.

[389] Münchener-Mertens, § 823 at 1558, para. 291.

[390] BGH, 11 January 1994 (*Kindertee*—Children's tea), NJW 1994, 932. That decision centred upon problems relating to the apportionment of liability when the plaintiff had used products coming from two manufacturers, pursuant to the second sentence of § 830(1) BGB: on this issue, see *infra*, Chapter IV, **4.F.38.–39.**, Note (4).

[391] BGH, 31 January 1995 (*Kindertee*—Children's tea), NJW 1995, 1286. In a recent case, however, the BGH found that a warning put on a slip of paper included in the package of a baby bottle was not sufficient: BGH, 2 March 1999, DB 1999, 891.

[392] BVerfG, 16 October 1996, NJW 1997, 249.

BGH, 17 March 1981[393]   **6.G.27.**

OBLIGATION TO MONITOR PRODUCTS

Apple scab

Once a product has been put into circulation, a manufacturer is under a duty to keep abreast of new information concerning danger relating to the use of the product, and to take appropriate action to prevent any danger thus coming to its attention.

Facts: The plaintiff operated a large orchard, where a fungicide manufactured by the defendant was used to combat apple scab. In 1974, the fungicide was not effective, since a strain of pesticide-resistant scab fungi that had originally been insignificant had become dominant. Apple scab attacked the plaintiff's apple trees, and as a result he suffered severe losses. The same phenomenon occurred in other orchards in the region. He sued the defendant under § 823(1) BGB, alleging, among other things, that the defendant had failed in its duty to monitor its product after the product had been put on the market.

Held: The court of first instance and the court of appeal dismissed the plaintiff's claim. The BGH upheld the judgment of the court of appeal.

Judgment: "A manufacturer can also infringe his duties to take care (*Verkehrspflichten*) because he does not sufficiently monitor the use of his product in practice. His duties to take care do not end when he puts his products into circulation [reference omitted] . . . [A] manufacturer who discovers that his product may pose dangers only after having put it into circulation [is] obliged to do everything which can reasonably be expected of him under the circumstances to ward off those dangers [references omitted] . . . The manufacturer cannot simply trust that he will become aware of such dangers more or less by chance . . . In particular as regards mass-produced and mass-distributed products, the manufacturer is . . . also under a duty towards the general public both to monitor his products for any dangers that would become known and to keep informed of any uses of his products that create a potential danger [references omitted]. He is bound to stay abreast of the course of development of science and technology in the relevant field [reference omitted]. For firms of the size of the defendant, which sell their products all over the world, that [duty] also extends to following the outcomes of scientific congresses and conferences as well as analyzing the entire international specialized literature [reference omitted].

However, in the present case, the defendant fulfilled that duty to monitor products . . .

c) The only issue in the present case is therefore whether, in 1974, the defendant . . . should already have given certain express *warnings* regarding the use of 'B.' in pomaceous fruit cultures, on the basis of its monitoring of the product . . . [The BGH was of the opinion that in fact there was no sufficient basis for the defendant to conclude that a danger was present and thus that it was under no duty to warn customers]".

Notes

(1) The annotated case concerns a fourth aspect of the *Verkehrspflicht* incumbent upon a manufacturer, namely the obligation to monitor its products after they have been put on the market. As the BGH stated, the duties of the manufacturer do not end when its products are put into circulation. The duty to monitor products comprises both the

---

[393] BGHZ 80, 199. Translation by Y.P. Salmon.

proper monitoring of developments occurring after a product has been put on the market as well as reacting appropriately if a new problem surfaces.

(2) As concerns the monitoring of the product, the BGH made it clear that the duty requires the manufacturer actively to seek information about the behaviour and impact of its products when they are used, as well as keeping up with scientific and technological development. That obligation has been given quite a wide reach: for instance, a motorcycle manufacturer is bound to keep track of accessories supplied by *third parties* for use with its motorcycles, and to warn customers against using accessories (such as a handlebar cover) which may affect the safety of the motorcycle.[394]

In the annotated case, the BGH was of the opinion that, on the facts, the defendant had met that part of the duty.

(3) The duty to monitor products is of course not discharged merely by monitoring. If and when the manufacturer identifies a new danger relating to its product, it is bound, pursuant to the *Verkehrspflicht* discussed in relation to the previous three cases, to change its production methods, review its product design or modify the product instructions, as the case may be; if the new danger cannot be prevented, then the manufacturer will have to discontinue supply of the product.[395] As regards units which are already on the market, the manufacturer may, depending on the circumstances, be under a duty to issue a warning to its customers or even to recall its products (including the assumption of replacement or repair costs).[396] In the annotated case, the plaintiff had argued that the defendant, once it saw that its product might be ineffective—also a form of danger for customers—was under a duty to warn its customers; the BGH found, however, that there was no sufficient basis for the manufacturer to conclude that a new danger was present.

(4) The duty to monitor products differs in one major respect from the other aspects of the *Verkehrspflicht* incumbent upon manufacturers (avoidance of defects in production or design, and the duty to provide adequate information): as the BGH held in a part of the annotated case not reproduced above, and also in a sister case,[397] the presumptions set out for the benefit of the plaintiff in its leading decision of 26 November 1968[398] *do not apply* in the case of the duty to monitor products. The plaintiff therefore bears the full burden of proof on all issues (including wrongfulness, fault and causation) given that the relevant factors to be established (evolution of scientific and technical knowledge, etc.) are not exclusively within the "sphere of knowledge" of the defendant.

(5) The main role of the duty to monitor products in the overall system of product liability under § 823 BGB is to fill the gap in protection that would otherwise potentially be left open when the defendant invokes the defence that the defect was not foreseeable in the light of scientific and technical knowledge at the time the product was put on the market (*Entwicklungsfehler*).[399] Accordingly, while the defendant will escape liability for injury which may be caused by defects that are not reasonably detectable on the basis of scientific and technical knowledge, the duty to monitor products ensures that the manu-

---

[394] See BGH, 9 December 1986 (*Lenkerverkleidung*—Handlebar cover), BGHZ 99, 167.
[395] See Münchener-Mertens, § 823 at 1557, para. 289.
[396] Ibid.
[397] BGH, 17 March 1981 (*Apfelschorf*—Apple scab), BGHZ 80, 186.
[398] *Supra*, **6.G.24.**
[399] See T. Wieckhorst, "Vom Produzentenfehler zum Produktfehler des § 3 ProdHaftG" (1995) 66 VersR 1005 at 1008.

facturer will be deprived of the benefit of the *Entwicklungsfehler* argument as soon as scientific and technical knowledge reaches the point where the defect becomes known and foreseeable. Furthermore, the duty to monitor products has effects both *ex ante* and *ex post*: not only must the manufacturer make changes for future production, but it must also issue a warning or recall products already into circulation.

(6) Accordingly, in the end, the German regime of product liability under § 823 BGB, as it has been developed in BGH case law, leaves the manufacturer with precious few means of escaping liability, once the plaintiff has shown that the injurious product was defective, be it a production, design or instruction defect. In general, the manufacturer can claim that the defect was not foreseeable in light of scientific and technical knowledge at the time, but the scope of that claim is limited by the duty to monitor products. With respect to manufacturing defects in particular, it is also possible for the manufacturer to escape liability if it can prove that the defective product was an "odd unit" (*Außreiser*) that escaped all precautions taken in pursuance of the applicable *Verkehrspflicht*.

6.3.1.B. FRENCH LAW

Introductory Note

a) Under French law, product liability has generally not been treated as a distinct problem, for which specific solutions needed to be developed. Accordingly, a number of liability regimes can be applied to injuries arising from the use of manufactured products, of which the main ones are reviewed in the following paragraphs. Depending on the facts, one or more of those regimes may apply.

As may be seen from the annotated case below and the examination of the implementation of Directive 85/374 in France,[400] one of the applicable regimes developed by case law over recent years, namely that involving an implicit contractual obligation not to endanger the safety of users of the product (*obligation de sécurité*), comes close to a specific product liability regime as it is known under German law, for instance. However, the implications of such a contractual obligation has not yet become firmly established, and the recent implementation of Directive 85/374 in French law has cast a shadow over its future.

b) First of all, it may be that the victim is injured by a product that was under the *garde* of another person. The general regime of liability for things under one's *garde*, pursuant to Article 1384(1) C.civ.,[401] would then provide a basis for a claim against the keeper (*gardien*) of the thing, provided that it can be established that the injury was due to the behaviour of a thing (*fait de la chose*) of which the defendant was the keeper. The notion of "product defect" does not play a central role in liability under Article 1384(1) C.civ.;[402] such liability arises without fault, which puts the victim in a favourable position. But the keeper may not have the financial means to compensate the victim (if the keeper were a

---

[400] See *infra*, 6.3.3.B.
[401] That regime has been studied *supra*, 6.1.2.
[402] Although for things that were not in motion, the requirement of abnormality can be satisfied, among others, by showing that the thing that caused the damage had an internal defect.

neighbour or a friend, for instance). Furthermore, in a large number of cases of injury arising from manufactured products, the victim was himself or herself the keeper of the injurious product, so that the number of "product liability" cases where Article 1384(1) C.civ. can be used is limited.

c) Moreover, in accordance with the prohibition imposed by French law on *option*,[403] the regime of Article 1384(1) C.civ. is not available when the victim was in a contractual relationship with the *gardien* of the thing that did the damage, for instance if a house-owner suffers injury because of a defect in a tool that was used by a worker conducting repairs in the house.[404] Some writers have questioned the appropriateness of depriving victims of the benefits of Article 1384(1) C.civ. in such cases, but the prohibition of *option* nonetheless continues to apply.[405] As a result, efforts have been made to find a way, within French contract law, to give such victims a position comparable to the one that they would enjoy under Article 1384(1) C.civ. if there had been no contractual relationship:

– One solution involved implying an *obligation de sécurité* (duty to ensure safety) into the defendant's contract with the victim. Such an obligation, however, generally remains an *obligation de moyens* (i.e. it binds the debtor to nothing more than use of best efforts and accordingly involves an examination of the debtor's conduct), and therefore puts the victim in a less favourable position than under the regime of liability without fault that is established by Article 1384(1) C.civ.[406]
– Secondly, in many cases, especially those involving professionals, case law has made the contractual debtor liable for defects in the tools and instruments used in the execution of the contract: for example, physicians and surgeons are responsible for the quality of the materials and instruments which they use in discharging their obligation to treat the patient.[407] This is an *obligation de résultat*: the debtor is liable for the injury resulting from those tools and instruments, unless it was due to an extraneous cause (*cause étrangère*).[408]
– A third possibility is to create, within the contractual realm, a regime of liability for things similar to that of Article 1384(1) C.civ. While that approach has generally been dismissed by legal writers, it seems to have been recognized by the Cour de cassation in the first annotated case below, and is discussed at greater length in the notes thereafter.

d) The preceding paragraphs covered the situation where the victim is injured by a manufactured product under the *garde* of another. As previously mentioned, in most cases in which manufactured products cause injury they do so to the person who had them under his or her *garde* or who was otherwise using or consuming them (as in the case of consumables, including foods and medicines).

[403] If the defendant's relationship with the plaintiff is governed by a contract, the plaintiff is not allowed to sue the defendant in tort and is confined to his or her contractual rights: see *supra*, Chapter I, 1.3.1.
[404] See Viney and Jourdain, *Conditions* at 698–701, para. 742; Le Tourneau and Cadiet at 470, para. 1586.
[405] See Le Tourneau and Cadiet at 471, para. 1588 and the authors there cited.
[406] See Viney and Jourdain, *Conditions* at 476–87 and 701–2, para. 550–4 and 743; Le Tourneau and Cadiet at 460–1, para. 1556–8. One exception to this general trend is the *obligation de sécurité* incumbent upon manufacturers and trade sellers as regards the products that they put into circulation, which remains an *obligation de résultat*, as is seen below.
[407] See *supra*, Chapter III, **3.F.10.**, Note (4).
[408] See Viney and Jourdain, *Conditions* at 703–4, para. 744; Le Tourneau and Cadiet at 502, para. 1715–7.

In many cases, the victim will have bought the injurious product, and will thus be linked to another person through a contractual relationship (usually a sale) relating to the product in question. The victim may then be able to sue the counterparty for breach of contract.

The first basis on which a claim may be made is the warranty against latent defects (*garantie des vices cachés*), which is expressly provided by the *Code civil* as regards sale (Art. 1641 ff. C.civ.), lease of things (*louage de choses*, Art. 1721 C.civ.) or loan of non-consumable things (*prêt à usage*, Art. 1891 C.civ.) and has been extended by case law to other contracts relating to property.[409] For the sake of simplicity, the discussion will be carried out by reference to the warranty as it is implied into a contract of sale. The extent of that warranty has been construed broadly in the case law:

– According to Article 1641 C.civ., the warranty extends to defects (*vices* or *défauts*) "which make the property unfit for the use for which it was intended or lessen the usefulness of the property to such an extent that the buyer would not have bought the property, or would have bought it at a lesser price, had he known of the defects". Case law has hesitated between various interpretations of the concept of "defect", but it is now settled that property is defective if it lacks its "normal characteristics" or cannot fulfil its "normal purpose".[410]
– The warranty covers latent or hidden defects (*vices cachés*) only. Apparent defects, which the buyer could see upon inspection before the purchase, are excluded from the warranty. Case law expects trade or professional buyers to be more thorough in their inspection than consumers.[411]
– Pursuant to Article 1644 C.civ., the buyer can choose between **rescission of the sale** (in which case the property is returned to the seller and the purchase price repaid to the buyer) or a **reduction in the sale price**; case law has added a third option, the **repair or replacement** of the defective property.[412] Furthermore, according to Articles 1645–6 C.civ., the seller may also be liable for **damage caused as a result of the defect** (i.e. personal injury or damage to other property) if the seller knew of the defect. French case law has come to presume that manufacturers and trade sellers know or should have known of the defect. Accordingly when a manufacturer or trader sells a defective product, it is liable to the buyer for all personal injury or damage to other property arising from the defect, pursuant to an *obligation de résultat*.[413] It follows that the manufacturer or trader cannot plead by way of defence that the defect could not have been discovered on the basis of the state of scientific or technical knowledge at the time; the notion of "product development risk" finds no application in the context of the warranty against latent defects.[414]
– The warranty was meant to benefit the buyer. However, with the advent of complex distribution chains, French case law has established that the benefit of the warranty is

---

[409] Viney and Jourdain, *Conditions* at 712–4, para. 749.
[410] See Cass. civ. 1re, 27 October 1993, Bull.civ. 1993.I.302 and subsequent case law. See also Viney and Jourdain, *Conditions* at 717–21, para. 751 to 754–1 and Le Tourneau and Cadiet at 718–9, para. 2872–7.
[411] See Le Tourneau and Cadiet at 719–20, para. 2878–83.
[412] Le Tourneau and Cadiet at 723, para. 2895.
[413] See Viney and Jourdain, *Conditions* at 725–7, para. 758; Le Tourneau and Cadiet at 723–4, para. 2896–9.
[414] Ibid.

passed down the chain to the next buyer, together with title to the property. As a result, the last buyer (the end-user) can bring a claim based on the warranty against not only the last seller (usually a retailer), but also any and all intermediaries in the distribution chain, up to and including the manufacturer (the so-called *action directe*).[415]

The main drawback of the warranty against latent defects, however, is the brief and imprecise limitation period provided for by Article 1648 C.civ.: an action must be brought "within a short time" (*dans un bref délai*) after the defect has been discovered.

e) A second possibility to recover for injury caused by a manufactured product not under the *garde* of another person is to invoke, against the contracting party who provided the product, a breach of the obligation to deliver a product that complies with the contractual description (*obligation de délivrance d'un produit conforme*), as found generally in the contracts involving transfer of a piece of property (in the case of sale, at Articles 1603–4 C.civ.).[416] Much like the warranty against latent defects, that obligation is passed down the contractual chain and can thus be relied upon by the consumer directly against the manufacturer.[417] However, as the Cour de cassation has held, that obligation covers the contractual expectations of the parties, and it is not necessarily applicable in all cases where products cause injury. Furthermore, where a claim is possible on the basis of the warranty against latent defects, an action based on the obligation to deliver a product that complies with the contractual description is in principle excluded.[418]

f) In order, amongst other things, to circumvent the short limitation period of the warranty against latent defects, case law has elaborated a series of general obligations incumbent upon contractual parties, comprising the obligation to inform and warn the other contractual party (*obligation d'information et de mise en garde*) and not to endanger the safety of the other party (*obligation de sécurité*). Those obligations are deemed to be an ancillary part of a large number of contractual relationships, and they are also transmitted through the distribution chain, thus giving the consumer a direct recourse against the manufacturer and any intermediaries.[419]

The **obligation to inform** implies that the user of a product must receive all the information required in order to use the product in accordance with its purpose and without injury; it is a relatively strict obligation, although from time to time the Cour de cassation characterizes it as *obligation de moyens* only.[420]

According to the Cour de cassation, the **obligation relating to safety**, as it applies to manufacturers and trade sellers with respect to the products that they put into circulation, means that "the trade seller is bound to deliver products that are free from any defect

---

[415] Viney and Jourdain, *Conditions* at 714–7, para. 750; Le Tourneau and Cadiet at 724–5, para. 2901–4.
[416] Viney and Jourdain, *Conditions* at 736–8, para. 763–3; Le Tourneau and Cadiet at 709–11, para. 2836–43.
[417] Le Tourneau and Cadiet at 714, para. 2856.
[418] Viney and Jourdain, *Conditions* at 738–43, para. 763–4 to 763–6; Le Tourneau and Cadiet at 711, para. 2844.
[419] Viney and Jourdain, *Conditions* at 750–1, para. 764.
[420] Viney and Jourdain, *Conditions* at 425–9 and 743–5, para. 509–11 and 763–7. See also Le Tourneau and Cadiet at 462–8, para. 1563–80.

which could create a risk for persons or property".[421] While in general that obligation tends to be an *obligation de moyens* only,[422] the obligation imposed on manufacturers and trade sellers concerning the *safety* of their products is an *obligation de résultat*: it is established, in particular, that "product development risks" (i.e. risks arising from defects that could not be detected in the state of scientific and technical knowledge at the time) cannot be invoked as a defence.[423] The obligation relating to safety is discussed at greater length in the notes under the first annotated case below and under the third document (decision of 9 July 1996).

g) The above paragraphs surveyed the contractual actions open to those who suffer loss or injury as a result of the acquisition or use of a manufactured product where they had acquired the product pursuant to a contractual relationship (sale, lease, loan, etc.). As mentioned before, this is a fairly typical situation in product liability cases. However, the product in question may well also cause injury to another person (a relative, friend, guest or even bystander) who is not part of a contractual chain leading up to the manufacturer (a "third-party victim"). In principle, the third party victim cannot benefit from the contractual obligations outlined above (warranty against latent defects, obligation to deliver a product that complies with the contractual description, obligation to inform, obligation not to endanger safety) and must therefore base his or her claim in delict.

Under the French law of delict, the third-party victim can bring an action based on Article 1384(1) C.civ. against the person who was the keeper of the thing, but in the situation under study here such an action may well be either unrealistic (the keeper is a relative or close friend) or illusory (the keeper is not insured and does not have enough assets to provide full compensation).

As has previously been mentioned,[424] in order to provide a basis for a claim against the manufacturer of the injurious product, an attempt was made to split the *garde* pursuant to Article 1384(1) C.civ. in two, between structural *garde* (*garde de structure*) and behavioural *garde* (*garde de comportement*). The underlying idea was that, for more sophisticated industrial objects, it was only appropriate to attribute the *garde* of the "structure"—i.e. the design and construction—to the person who actually influenced it, namely the manufacturer, since those structural elements were outside the control of the person who actually controlled the thing at the time when the injury was caused. In that way, third-party victims could have used Article 1384(1) C.civ. against the manufacturer directly. The suggestion that the *garde* could be split in that way was not well received in legal writing and has since been almost abandoned in the case law as well.

The third-party victim was therefore left with the general fault-based regime of Articles 1382–3 C.civ.; in the application of that regime, there is some case law of the Cour de cassation to the effect that putting a defective product on the market is evidence of fault on

---

[421] Cass. civ. 1re, 20 March 1989, D 1989.Jur.381. That phrase has been taken up again repeatedly in subsequent cases, including the annotated case below. See also Viney and Jourdain, *Conditions* at 745–8, para. 763–8; Le Tourneau and Cadiet at 457–60, para. 1549–54.

[422] Viney and Jourdain, *Conditions* at 476–87, para. 550–4; Le Tourneau and Cadiet at 460- 1, para. 1556–8.

[423] See for instance Cass. civ. 1re, 9 July 1996, *infra*, **6.F.30.**, where a blood transfusion centre was found liable for the injury caused by HIV-infected blood, even if it was not possible to detect the infection at the time. See also Viney and Jourdain, *Conditions* at 748, para. 763–8.

[424] See *supra*, **6.F.8.**, Note (6).

the part of the manufacturer.[425] Nevertheless, there was a feeling that it was hardly justifiable from a policy point of view to leave the third-party victim to prove fault while the victim who can rely on a contractual relationship to get at the manufacturer can rely on an *obligation de résultat*. Accordingly, French law has apparently loosened the strict division between contract and tort law by extending to third parties the benefit of the contractual obligation not to endanger the safety of product users, thereby in fact creating a new liability regime for product defects. That recent development took place in the case reproduced next. It remains to be seen whether the new regime is firmly established.

h) In the case of contamined blood products, the legislature intervened, with the Act 91–1406 of 31 December 1991, to create a specific compensation mechanism in addition to the general regimes applicable to product liability, as described above. The Act is reproduced below, followed by a case where its relationship to the general regimes of civil liability is discussed.

Cass. civ. 1re, 17 January 1995[426]   **6.F.28.**
Sté Planet Wattohm v. *Caisse populaire d'assurance-maladie du Morbihan*

CONTRACTUAL LIABILITY FOR THINGS
BENEFICIARIES OF THE CONTRACTUAL OBLIGATION DE SÉCURITÉ

Hoop

*The trade seller is bound, towards not only the other contracting party but also third parties, to deliver products that are free from any defect which could create a risk for persons or property. A party to a contract is liable to the other party for damage resulting from the behaviour of a thing (*fait de la chose*) used in the execution of the contract.*

Facts: The plaintiffs' four-year old child was injured while playing with a hoop in the course of physical exercise classes at her private school. The injury was due to a defect in the hoop, which had been purchased by the school from Sté Armand Colin et Bourrelier, a specialist vendor of school materials, and had been manufactured by Sté Planet Wattohm. The plaintiffs sued the school for breach of contract and sued the vendor and the manufacturer on the basis of Article 1382 C.civ.

Held: The court of appeal found that the vendor and the manufacturer were liable *in solidum* towards the victim, and dismissed the claim against the school. The Cour de cassation upheld the decision of the court of appeal as regards the vendor and the manufacturer, and annulled it as regards the school.

Judgment: "[ON THE CLAIM AGAINST THE VENDOR]
The court of appeal found that Armand Colin et Bourrelier was liable for the consequences of the accident of the young [child], which was due to a production defect in the hoop. Against that judgment, Armand Colin and Bourrelier argues that, in its quality as distributor of a hoop which had been approved by the National Centre of Educational Materials . . ., it could not be considered at fault for not having submitted the hoop to a thorough technical examination, given that the defect—which is imputable solely to the manufacturer—was not obvious . . .

However, the trade seller is bound to deliver products that are free from any defect . . . which could create a risk for persons or property. It is bound as much to third parties as to the purchaser.

---

[425] See Cass. civ. 3e, 18 April 1972, Bull.civ. 1972.II.233 and Cass. civ. 3e, 5 December 1972, D 1973.Jur.401.
[426] Bull.civ. 1995.I.43, D 1995.Jur.350, with note by P. Jourdain. Translation by Y.P. Salmon.

Within its sovereign realm, the court of appeal found as a fact that the hoops presented, by their very design, a risk of accident. That sole ground sufficed to provide a legal justification for its decision . . .

[ON THE CLAIM AGAINST THE MANUFACTURER]

Against the judgment that ordered it to indemnify Armand Colin et Bourrelier against the damages to be paid as a result of the decision in the present case, Planet Wattohm argues that . . . a person who is condemned *in solidum* with another has a recourse against that other person only for part of the said condemnation. If the two persons were at fault, the definitive apportionment of the damages [as between them] relates to the seriousness of their respective faults . . .

However, the court of appeal found that the defect in the hoop, which caused the injury suffered by [the child], was entirely imputable to Planet Wattohm, which conceived and manufactured itself that product. The court of appeal correctly concluded that, since Planet Wattohm had to sell hoops free from any production defect which could create a danger for persons or property, it had to bear the entirety of the damages awarded against it in reparation of the injury caused to [the child] . . .

[ON THE CLAIM AGAINST THE SCHOOL]

An educational establishment is contractually liable to ensure the safety of the pupils with which it is entrusted. It is liable for the injury caused to them not only because of its fault, but also because of the 'behaviour of things' which it uses in the fulfilment of its contractual obligations.

In order to conclude that the . . . school is not liable, the court of appeal states that it is not proven that the accident resulted from a fault of the establishment in the course of fulfilling its contractual obligations.

In ruling as it did, the court of appeal infringed [Articles 1135 and 1147 C.civ.]."

Notes

(1) The annotated case essentially maps out the main tenets of the French law of product liability. Most of the major grounds of liability were discussed in the judgment, and the Cour de cassation introduced significant new developments in the law.

The facts were simple: the victim had been injured because of a hoop the design of which was defective. Her parents sued the manufacturer of the hoop and the specialized distributor on the basis of Article 1382 C.civ. and they sued the school which bought the hoop and used it in the course of education on the basis of contract.

(2) The Cour de cassation first dealt with the claim against the vendor of the hoop, which was a trade seller of school materials. Up to the Cour de cassation, that claim had been based on Article 1382 C.civ. The seller argued—not without merit—that it was not at fault, since the hoop had been certified by the administration, the defect was not apparent and it was not reasonable to expect a distributor to conduct such an in-depth examination of the product as would have revealed the hidden defect. If the seller was going to be liable at all then, it would have to be on the basis of a regime of liability without fault.

The Cour de cassation found the seller liable on the basis of the obligation not to endanger the safety of persons and property (*obligation de sécurité*), as it applies to trade sellers and manufacturers. Yet, as seen above, the *obligation de sécurité* is an ancillary contractual obligation, read into certain contracts by case law. It was first set out by the Cour de cassation in a decision of 20 March 1989,[427] and has been reiterated many times since.[428]

In the annotated case, the victim was not a party to any contract (or chain of contracts) with the seller, whose contract had been with the school. Nevertheless, the Cour de cassation found that the *obligation de sécurité* also applied for the benefit of third parties who were injured by a defective product. In his comment on the annotated case, P. Jourdain explained the decision of the Cour de cassation by a concern to put all victims under similar conditions, whether they were in a contractual relationship with the seller or not; indeed, the risks presented by manufactured products are the same for all victims.[429] In short, the Cour de cassation is turning the contractual *obligation de sécurité* into a new regime of extra-contractual liability, without much of a basis in the *Code civil*; as P. Jourdain points out, this is not without precedent.[430] Still it is worth noting how effortlessly the Cour de cassation flew over the relatively strict division between contract and tort under French law: this had led Le Tourneau and Cadiet, for instance, to characterize the decision as a "legal error".[431] The Cour de cassation has subsequently confirmed the annotated case.[432]

(3) According to the Cour de cassation, fault was irrelevant to the *obligation de sécurité* as it applies to trade vendors and manufacturers. The key element is the presence of a "defect which could create a risk for persons or property". As the Court held, as soon as the hoop was found to be defective, in that it presented a risk of accident due to its very design, the breach of the *obligation de sécurité* was made out. The Court thus reaffirmed the principle that the *obligation de sécurité* incumbent on trade vendors and manufacturers is an obligation of result (*obligation de résultat*). As P. Jourdain remarked, from the moment the Cour de cassation took that obligation out of the contractual realm to extend its benefit to all persons, it might have been more appropriate to leave the contractual terminology behind and instead speak of a regime of liability without fault for defective products; after all, this is the result of the decision of the Cour de cassation in the annotated case.[433]

(4) Even if the Cour de cassation did not provide a full outline of that new liability regime, it can be seen, as P. Jourdain notes, that it bears some similarity to Directive 85/374 on product liability:[434] under the new regime, no distinction is made between contracting parties and third parties, and the concept of product defect plays a central role in triggering liability.[435] It could be said that, with this case, the Cour de cassation was in fact attempting to make up for France's failure to implement Directive 85/374 by inter-

---

[427] Cass. civ. 1re, 20 March 1989, D 1989.Jur.381.

[428] See Viney and Jourdain, *Conditions* at 747–9, para. 763–8; Le Tourneau and Cadiet at 717, para. 2867.

[429] P. Jourdain, Note, D 1995.Jur.350 at 352.

[430] Indeed the regime of liability without fault for inconveniences between neighbours (*troubles de voisinage*, see *supra*, Chapter II, 2.3.3., Introductory Note under c) and *infra*, 6.4.1. under b)) has no foundation in the *Code civil*, and the general regimes of liability without fault for things (see *supra*, 6.1.2.) and for others (see *supra*, Chapter V, **5.F.23.** and notes thereafter), while formally resting on Article 1384(1) C.civ., are essentially judicial creations: Jourdain, ibid. at 353.

[431] Le Tourneau and Cadiet at 717, para. 2868.

[432] See for instance Cass. civ. 1re, 3 March 1998, *infra*, **6.F.36.**

[433] P. Jourdain, Note, D 1995.Jur.350 at 353; Le Tourneau and Cadiet at 458, para. 1549.

[434] See *infra*, **6.EC.33.**

[435] P. Jourdain, Note, D 1995.Jur.350 at 352–3.

preting French law in the light of that Directive, in line with the principle that national law should be construed so as to conform with EC law.[436] The link between this new regime and Directive 85/374 was made even more explicit in two decisions of 3 March 1998, reproduced below, and 28 April 1998 respectively.[437]

(5) Under the new regime, both the manufacturer and the trade seller are liable to the victim *in solidum* for the full amount of the injury.[438] In the second part of the judgment, the Cour de cassation ruled on the apportionment of liability as between the trade seller and the manufacturer. It found that, since the product defect was attributable to the manufacturer, it alone should bear the full burden of liability. Through the apportionment rules, therefore, liability will thus ultimately rest on to the manufacturer.

(6) The third part of the judgment in the annotated case was equally innovative. There, for the first time, the Cour de cassation acknowledged that there could be a contractual regime of liability for things, probably modelled on Article 1384(1) C.civ., but within the contractual realm. As the Cour de cassation held, within the framework of its contractual obligations, the contracting party is liable not just for *faulty* conduct, but also, in the absence of fault, for breaches caused by the behaviour of the things (*fait de la chose*) used in the course of discharging the contract.

When applied to the case at bar, the reasoning of the court becomes fairly complex. The private school was bound by contract to conduct an educational programme for children at the school, including physical education. As an ancillary obligation to that contract, it was also bound by an *obligation de sécurité* to ensure the safety of the children; that obligation was an obligation of means (*obligation de moyens*), in accordance with the general trend under French law.[439] In the course of discharging its principal obligation by providing, amongst other things, physical education, the school made use of the hoop, which turned out to present a danger to children who used it because it was defective. Before the annotated case, the school would not have been liable for a breach of its ancillary *obligation de sécurité*, since it was not at fault in creating that danger to the children. But the Cour de cassation in the annotated case found that the school was liable for the conduct of the thing irrespective of any fault on its part: in practical terms, this means that the distinction between obligations of means and of result becomes pointless when the injury is caused by the behaviour of a thing (*fait de la chose*) used in the course of executing a contract, since a regime of contractual liability without fault applies, presumably on the model of Article 1384(1) C.civ.[440]

The annotated case could therefore have a wide impact on the law of contractual liability: the Cour de cassation, however, apparently wanted to restrict the scope of this regime of contractual liability for things to *defective* things only, where a *danger for*

---

[436] See Viney and Jourdain, *Conditions* at 789, para. 785–1. On the principle of conform interpretation, see *infra*, **6.F.29.–30.**, Note (4).

[437] Cass. civ. 1re, 3 March 1998, *infra*, **6.F.36.**; Cass. civ. 1re, 28 April 1998, JCP 1998.II.10088. In that latter case, the Cour de cassation ruled on the basis of "Articles 1147 and 1384(1) C.civ., interpreted in light of Directive 85/374".

[438] On liability *in solidum*, see *infra*, Chapter IV, **4.F.38.–39.** and Notes (1) to (3) thereafter.

[439] For manufacturers and trade sellers, the *obligation de sécurité* regarding the products that they put into circulation is an *obligation de résultat*, as seen above. By now, this has become the exception; in most contractual relationships where an *obligation de sécurité* is implied, it is in the nature of an *obligation de moyens*: see Le Tourneau and Cadiet at 460–1, para. 1556–8; Viney and Jourdain, *Conditions* at 476–87, para. 550–4.

[440] See the comment of P. Jourdain, D 1995.Jur.350 at 354.

personal safety arises.[441] In any event, the new regime has not yet become firmly established.[442] Most authors have criticized the artificiality of the reasoning of the Cour de cassation: instead of bridging the contract/tort divide as it did in the same decision as regards the *obligation de sécurité* of the manufacturer and trade seller, the court refused simply to extend the application of Article 1384(1) C.civ. to contractual relationships and created a parallel regime of contractual liability for things.[443] It might indeed be more appropriate to apply the law of delict to cases where personal injury occurs in the course of executing a contract, since the risk related to the use of industrial products is not specific to contractual relationships.[444]

(7) The annotated case therefore provides a good overview of the regimes applicable to cases of damage caused by manufactured products under French law:

- On the one hand, the regime of Article 1384(1) C.civ. continues to apply to put the victim in a fairly good position when the injury has been caused by a product under the *garde* of another person with whom the victim is not under a contractual relationship, and that irrespective of whether the product was defective or not. A parallel regime of contractual liability for things used to discharge a contractual obligation—apparently limited to defective things only—could provide some form of protection in the contractual realm as well, although it is not yet firmly established. In the annotated case, the victim could accordingly recover its damages from the private school.
- On the other hand, manufacturers and trade sellers are under an *obligation de sécurité* (meaning that products should not be defective) in the nature of an obligation of result (*obligation de résultat*) towards all contracting parties down the chain to the consumer and, following the annotated case, under a regime of liability without fault towards third party victims for defective products. The situation should be similar as regards the obligation to inform users of the product (*obligation d'information et de mise en garde*). This whole regime is not yet very firmly established, and its continuing existence is now called into question by the recent implementation of Directive 85/374 in French law.[445] In the annotated case, the victim used the new regime to recover damages from the manufacturer and the distributor of educational products.

In addition, the warranty against latent defects and the contractual obligation to deliver a product complying with the contractual description can also provide some protection against injury from manufactured products, but only to victims who find themselves in a contractual relationship concerning the product in question.

---

[441] See P. Jourdain, ibid. and Viney and Jourdain, *Conditions* at 706, para. 745.
[442] See the review of subsequent case law in Viney and Jourdain, *Conditions* at 707–9, para. 745.
[443] P. Jourdain, Note, D 1995.Jur.350 at 354–5; Viney and Jourdain, *Conditions* at 709–10, para. 745–1; Le Tourneau and Cadiet at 470–1, para. 1587–8.
[444] Ibid.
[445] See *infra*, 6.3.3.B.

Act 91–1406 of 31 December 1991[446]   6.F.29.–30.
and
Cass. civ. 1re, 9 July 1996[447]
X. v. GAN incendie accidents

LIABILITY FOR CONTAMINATED BLOOD PRODUCTS

Under the Act of 31 December 1991, a Fund is in charge of compensating the victims of infection by HIV following a blood transfusion. The Act does not extinguish civil liability claims. Blood transfusion centres are under an obligation of result as regards the safety of their products. Private hospitals are under an obligation of result as regards the safety of blood products prepared within their organization, and under an obligation of means as regards the safety of blood products prepared elsewhere.

A. Act 91–1406 of 31 December 1991   6.F.29.

"Article 47—I. The victims of damage resulting from infection by the human immunodeficiency virus caused by a transfusion of blood products or an injection of products derived from blood carried out on the territory of the French Republic shall be compensated under the conditions set out below . . .

III. Full compensation for the damage defined at para. I shall be assured by an indemnity fund with legal personality, presided over by a president of a chamber or a councillor of the Cour de cassation, whether in office or having honorary status, and shall be administered by an indemnity committee.

A council comprising representatives of the associations concerned shall assist the president of the Fund.

IV. In their claim for compensation, the victims or their successors in title must establish infection by HIV by transfusions of blood products or injections from products derived from blood . . .

V. The Fund shall be required to present any victim mentioned in para. I with a compensation offer within a period to be determined by decree but not exceeding 6 months from the date on which the Fund receives complete documentation in support of the alleged damage. This provision shall also apply in the event of aggravation of damage already covered under para. I.

The offer shall state the assessment made by the Fund in regard to each head of damage, notwithstanding the absence of stabilisation, and in particular in regard to the fact of seropositivity together with the amount of compensation to be awarded to the victim, regard being had to the benefits set out in Art. 29 of Act 85–677 of 5 July 1985 and of compensation of any kind received or to be received from other persons liable in respect of the same damage . . .

VIII. The victim shall have a right of action before the courts against the Compensation Fund only if his claim for compensation has been rejected, if no offer has been made to him within the period mentioned in the first subparagraph of para. V or if he has not accepted the offer made to him. That legal action must be brought before the Cour d'appel de Paris.

IX. The Fund shall have a right of subrogation in the amount of the sum paid in pursuance of the rights of the victim against the person responsible for the damage and against the persons

---

[446] Loi 91–1406 portant diverses dispositions d'ordre social (Social Law (Amendment) Act) of 31 December 1991, JO, 4 January 1992, 178, D 1992.Lég.96. Translation by N. Sims.
[447] D 1996.Jur.610 (published with other decisions of the same date, all annotated by Y. Lambert-Faivre). Translation by N. Sims.

required on any ground to ensure reparation, in whole or in part, within the limit of the amount of benefits provided to the victim. However, the Fund may bring an action by way of this right of subrogation only when the damage is attributable to a fault (*faute*) . . .”

B. Cass. civ. 1re, 9 July 1996   **6.F.30.**

Contaminated blood transfusion

Facts: Sylvain X died of AIDS as a result of a contaminated blood transfusion during an operation. His heirs brought an action in damages on the basis of Art. 1147 ff. C.civ. against the blood transfusion centre which had supplied the blood. The blood transfusion centre raised two defences: first, that the action was inadmissible since Act 91–1406 of 31 December 1991 (which set up the indemnity fund) allegedly excluded ordinary civil actions; and secondly that the contamination of the blood was undetectable and therefore the loss arose by *force majeure* for which the blood transfusion centre was not liable. The centre also relied on Directive 85/374 as relieving it from liability for the risk in question as a product development risk.

Held: The court of appeal rejected all the pleas raised by the blood transfusion centre and confirmed the judgment of the court of first instance insofar as it held the defendant liable to the heirs of the deceased, but revised the quantum of damages. The *Cour de cassation* upheld the decision of the court of appeal in all respects.

Judgment: “As to the first plea: . . . the judgment appealed against considered that it followed from the Act of 31 December 1991 and from the obligation on victims to provide information to either the indemnity fund or the court, in any case in which one or the other of them was seized of the matter, that neither the law nor its implementing decree made the scheme which it introduced mandatory, thus prohibiting victims from bringing an action before the ordinary courts. The court of appeal, before which it was not alleged that the damage suffered by the victims was fully made good by the compensation offered by the Fund, correctly inferred therefrom that their action was admissible. The plea is therefore unfounded.

On the second plea . . . the court of appeal correctly considered that the contract for the supply of blood or its derivatives by the transfusion centre required the latter body to supply products free of defects without exemption from liability otherwise than for *force majeure*, and that an inherent defect in the product, even if undetectable, did not constitute for the supplying body a case of *force majeure*. The judgment is therefore justified in law and none of the pleas on appeal is well-founded . . .

It is alleged that the judgment appealed against declined to take into account the Directive [85/374] of 25 July 1985 whereas, according to the plea, the national court deciding a case the subject-matter of which comes within the scope of the Directive is obliged to interpret its national law in the light of the directive and its purpose . . .

However, although the national court, deciding a case whose subject-matter comes within the scope of a directive, is required to interpret its domestic law in the light of the wording and objectives of that directive, such obligation is conditional on the directive being mandatory for the Member State and leaving it no option in adapting its national law to Community law. Art. 15 (1)(c) of Directive 85/374 of 25 July 1985 on liability for defective products leaves Member States with the option, with regard to liability for defective products, to introduce the so-called exception for product development risks into their national law. It follows that the plea, which invokes provisions of the directive which refer to national law, cannot be upheld.

On those grounds the appeals are dismissed . . .”

Notes

(1) Because of the immensity and complexity of the problem of infection with HIV through contaminated blood products,[448] legislative intervention was needed, in order to coordinate the use of public and private funds to compensate the large number of HIV victims. This was done by Art. 47 of Act 91–1406 of 31 December 1991, which provides for the creation of a Fund to ensure the full compensation of all material and non-material damage sustained by the direct and indirect victims of contaminated blood transfusions made in France.[449] Three-quarters of the compensation is payable upon HIV infection occurring, and one-quarter at Stage IV of the illness, provided that the development of full-blown AIDS is proved.[450] The Fund can obtain reimbursement of the compensation paid to the victims from those responsible for the causing the infection if they were at fault (see Art. 47(IX) of the Act).

The Fund created by Art. 47 of Act 91–1406 aims to provide full compensation, as appears from the way in which it defines damage:

"Personal non-material damage from HIV infection covers all the disturbances in living conditions resulting from seropositivity and the advent of illness. The prejudice thus includes, from the stage of seropositivity onwards, all psychological disturbances flowing from HIV infection: reduction in life expectancy, uncertainty with regard to the future, fear of physical and moral suffering, isolation, interference with family and social life, sexual and, as the case may be, reproductive prejudice. It also includes all non-material damage that appeared or will appear when the illness follows, such as suffering, aesthetic prejudice and attendant loss of amenity".[451]

This broad definition has been taken over in a somewhat amended form by the Cour de cassation in a judgment of 2 April 1996.[452] For injury suffered as a consequence of a blood transfusion contaminated with Hepatitis C (for which there is no special legislation), the Cour de cassation has allowed compensation on account of anxiety as a head of damage.[453]

---

[448] R. Errera describes the situation in "Recent Decisions of the French Conseil d'État" [1993] Pub L 537 as follows: "During the mid–1980s, around 1,200 haemophiliacs (that is, about half of those registered) have been infected with HIV following blood transfusions. Two hundred and fifty have died . . . [A]ll avenues of the law have been and are being used: a former Prime Minister and two other ministers may be indicted and tried by a special court set up under the Constitution; the former head of the National Transfusion Centre, a physician, and several other doctors and civil servants have been sentenced to imprisonment by a criminal court in Paris. Several victims have sued local transfusion centres and have obtained damages . . . Other victims have sued the state in the administrative courts, and one of these actions led to a judgment of the European Court of Human Rights finding that there had been unreasonable delay causing a breach of Art. 6(1) ECHR (*X* v. *France*, 23 March 1993, 14 EHRR 483, JCP 1992.II.21896, note Apostolodis, D 1992.Somm.334, note Renucci)." See also, later on, Cass. crim., 22 June 1994, JCP 1994.II.22310, English translation at [1995] ECC 346.

[449] For a thorough examination, see Y. Lambert-Faivre, "L'indemnisation des victimes post-transfusionnelles du SIDA: hier, aujourd'hui et demain . . ." (1993) 92 RTDciv. 17, as well as Y. Lambert-Faivre, "Principes d'indemnisation des victimes post-transfusionnelles du SIDA" D 1993.Chron.67, dealing with 20 decisions of the Cour d'appel de Paris of 27 November 1992 (see also Gaz.Pal. 1992.Jur.727) concerning issues of interpretation of the Act 91–1406, such as: the rebuttable presumption of causation between the blood transfusion and the HIV contamination (Art. 47(IV)), the notion of damage specifically related to HIV infection, recovery of material losses due to the closing of the sick person's enterprise, non-splitting of the compensation payable upon the occurrence of the infection, non-material damage (chronic depression, anxiety) of close relatives and of a partner living with the sick person in a stable relationship and the kind of damage for which compensation can be obtained.

[450] Cass. civ. 2e, 20 July 1993, D 1993.Jur.526, annotated by Y. Chartier.

[451] Quoted by P. Jourdain, Chronique (1995) 94 RTDciv. 627.

[452] Bull.civ. 1996.II.88. See G. Viney, Chronique, JCP 1996.I.3985.

[453] Cass. civ. 1re, 9 July 1996, Bull.civ. 1996.I.306.

(2) Instead of availing themselves of the Act 91–1406, victims may opt for other remedies.[454] Many have done so in order to obtain compensation for losses that are not covered by the Fund or if they have not requested payment by the Fund at all.[455]

The judgment of 9 July 1996 reproduced above raises several interesting issues. The first is the relationship between the special compensation mechanism under the Act 91–1406 and ordinary civil liability. In a judgment of the same date, the Cour de cassation decided that, when a victim of HIV infection accepts an offer from the Fund for *full* compensation, the victim is prevented from seeking further indemnity for the same injury (in that case non-material injury).[456] The judgment reproduced above lays down, however, that victims are not prevented from turning to the ordinary courts when their injury has not been fully compensated by the sum awarded by the Fund. Following those decisions of the Cour de cassation, it would seem that French law is now sufficiently clear to address the objections formulated by the ECtHR in a judgment of 4 December 1995, *Bellet* v. *France*, as to the ambiguous character of Art. 47(VIII) of the Act 91-1406 in the light of Art. 6(1) ECHR.[457]

(3) The judgment also raises a second issue, this time of substantive law, concerning the liability of *blood transfusion centres* (which hold a monopoly over the conservation and supply of blood). In the annotated judgment and in another judgment of the same date, the Cour de cassation, on the basis of Art. 1147 C.civ. (relating to contractual liability), imposes a regime of liability without fault on those centres: it is not possible for them to invoke in defence a defect in the product supplied to the centre (even if the defect could not be detected by the centre). The judgment of 9 July 1996 confirms in this respect two earlier judgments of the Cour de cassation given in 1995.[458]

As regards the liability of *hospitals* for the blood products they use in the course of their operations, the Cour de cassation held in *Dupuy*, the second of the two 1995 judgments, that the liability (again contractual) of a *private hospital* was based on "a mere obligation of prudence and care in the provision of blood products supplied by a transfusion centre".[459] P. Jourdain, in his comment on *Dupuy*, criticized the fact that the Cour de cassation did not impose the heavier burden of liability without fault of the transfusion centres on hospitals as well.[460]

The liability of *public hospitals* falls to be decided by the Conseil d'État, which came to the same result as the Cour de cassation. In three judgments of 26 May 1995, the Conseil d'État distinguished between the situation where the blood products come from a transfusion centre that is part of the same legal entity as the hospital, and those where they

[454] R. Errera, "Recent Decisions of the French Conseil d'État" [1993] Pub L 535 at 539.

[455] See Art. 47(VIII) of the Act 91–1406: under certain circumstances, a special procedure before the Cour d'appel de Paris can be initiated to review the fund's decision or failure to act. In another judgment of 9 July 1996, the Cour de cassation held that this special jurisdictional provision does not prevent plaintiffs who have not accepted the fund's offer from continuing the action which they had already instituted before the courts normally competent for such matters.

[456] Cass. civ. 1re, 9 July 1996, D 1996.Jur.611.

[457] Ser. A No. 333-B, D 1996.Jur.357, annotated by M. Collin-Demumieux. For other ECtHR decisions relating to the French system of compensation for persons infected with HIV, see J. Moreau, Annotation, JCP 1995.II.22468.

[458] Cass. civ. 1re, 12 April 1995, JCP 1995.II.22467, annotated by P. Jourdain.

[459] See also, in respect of blood contaminated with hepatitis C, Cass. civ. 1re, 13 November 1996, D 1996.IR.268.

[460] P. Jourdain, Note, JCP 1995.II.22467.

come from an outside centre.[461] In the first situation, the Conseil d'État held that the legal entity regrouping the hospital and the transfusion centre was liable on a no-fault basis for injury resulting from the infected nature of the blood supplied by the centre, although its reasoning is not based on the interpretation of the *Code civil*, but rather on the general principle of no-fault liability of public authorities for dangerous activities.[462] However, where the hospital received contaminated blood products from an outside transfusion centre that belongs to another legal entity, the hospital was held to be liable only for *faute de service ou d'organisation* (negligence in the provision or organization of services).[463] J. Moreau, in his comment on those decisions, considers that the distinction made by the Conseil d'État may have been motivated by the need to ensure that in any event the victim has a recourse against the blood transfusion centre under a favourable liability regime: where the centre is in the same legal entity as the hospital, the victim can recover under the no-fault liability regime applicable to public authorities, as in *N'Guyen* and *Jouan*, while where the centre is independent from the hospital, as in *Pavan*, the victim has a recourse before the civil courts, where the independent centre is under an obligation of result (*obligation de résultat*), as mentioned above; in that case it may be appropriate to leave the liability of the hospital to be assessed on a fault basis.[464]

(4) The judgment of the Cour de cassation of 9 July 1996 reproduced above raises a third issue relating to the application of Directive 85/374 on liability for defective products.[465]

Directive 85/374 on its face applies to blood products just as it does to other products. Art. 7(e) of the Directive provides that the "producer" (in the sense of Art. 3 of the Directive) of a defective product can escape liability if he can prove that the defect in question could not be detected given the state of scientific knowledge at the time when the product was put on the market (the so-called "exception for product development risks"). Art. 15(1)(b) of the Directive,[466] however, enables Member States not to introduce in their national law the exception for product development risks allowed by Art. 7(e) and accordingly to hold manufacturers liable even if the defects could not have been detected with the scientific means available at the time. At the time of the judgment, France had not yet implemented Directive 85/734.[467]

In the case that gave rise to the judgment of 9 July 1996, the transfusion centre argued that the court of appeal should have interpreted French law in conformity with the provisions of Directive 85/374, and in particular that it should have read into French law the exception for product development risks of Art. 7(e). The Cour de cassation rejected that argument. It found that Art. 7(e) of the Directive was "not binding on Member States",

---

[461] CÉ, 26 May 1995, *N'Guyen*, *Jouan* and *Pavan*, JCP 1995.II.22468, annotated by J. Moreau.

[462] *N'Guyen* and *Jouan* cases, ibid. See *supra*, Chapter III., 3.3.3.B., and in particular **3.F.43.** and notes thereafter.

[463] CÉ, 26 May 1995, *Pavan*, JCP 1995.II.22468.

[464] JCP 1995.II.22468. See also, on these three judgments, the critical comments of J.-H. Stahl and D. Chauvaux, "Chronique générale de jurisprudence administrative française" AJDA 1995, 496 at 508–16, where the liability of the State, the transfusion centres and the hospitals is placed in the general context of the case law of the Conseil d'État on medical liability.

[465] *Infra*, **6.EC.33.**

[466] The Cour de cassation mistakenly refers to it as Art. 15(1)(c).

[467] Directive 85/374 was implemented with the Act 98–389 of 19 May 1998, introducing Art. 1386–1 to 1386–18 in the *Code civil*, *supra*, **6.F.37.**

on grounds that "Art. 15(1)(c) [sic] of Directive 85/374 . . . leaves Member States with the option to introduce the [liability] exception for product development risks into their national law". The reasoning of the Cour de cassation is not entirely satisfactory. In the French national courts, the blood transfusion centre sought to rely on Art. 7(e) of the Directive as in effect conferring on the centre an immunity from civil liability in respect of product development risks. But:

(i) under the case law of the ECJ as it currently stands, provisions of a directive—assuming that they are sufficiently clear, as seems to be the case with Art. 7(e)—cannot themselves have direct effect in the national courts except against the Member States and other public bodies; therefore, if only for that reason, the blood transfusion centre (whether it itself was a public or private body) could not rely directly on Art. 7(e) of Directive 85/374 against a private individual who had been infected by contaminated blood;[468]

(ii) secondly, in the event that the blood transfusion centre could have relied on Art. 7(3) of the Directive against a private individual, the latter could have invoked Art. 13 of the Directive, which expressly provides that the Directive "shall not affect any rights which an injured person may have according to the rules of the law of contractual or non-contractual liability or a special liability system existing at the moment when this Directive is notified". Since, at the time when the Directive came into force, French law put blood transfusion centres under a regime of liability without fault, without an exception for product development risks,[469] Art. 13 preserves the rights of the injured person notwithstanding the exemption from liability which Art. 7(e) of the Directive creates.

There were therefore good reasons why the blood transfusion centre should not have been able to rely on the potential exception for product development risks provided for in Art. 7(e) of Directive 85/374, as giving it an exemption against strict liability. But instead the Cour de cassation, following the line of argument of the blood transfusion centre, which had relied on the ECJ case-law to the effect that national law is whenever possible to be interpreted so as to make it conform to Community law (in this case Art. 7(e) of the Directive), rejected that argument on the ground that Art. 7(e) was not binding because of the freedom left to Member States by Art. 15(1)(b) not to introduce the exception for product development risks. Yet France had *not* exercised that freedom; it had done something quite different: at the time of the judgment, it had not implemented the Directive at all even though the deadline implementation had long passed.[470]

---

[468] If the blood transfusion centre were a public body, it could certainly not rely on a directly effective provision against a private individual. See on this aspect of direct effect, called "inverse vertical direct effect", S. Prechal, *Directives in European Community Law* (Oxford: Oxford University Press, 1995) at 304–5.

[469] See P. Jourdain, JCP 1995.II.22467.

[470] A better argument could have been that the obligations for a national court to interpret its national law in accordance with an unimplemented directive should not in effect either impose a specific obligation upon or—one might add—take away a specific right to compensation from a private individual: see ECJ, Judgment of 26 September 1996, Case C–168/95, Arcaro [1996] ECR I–4705.

6.3.1.C. ENGLISH LAW

Introductory Note

a) English law has not experienced significant doctrinal or theoretical developments concerning product liability, contrary to other common law jurisdictions, such as the states of the USA. Injuries arising from the use of manufactured products have been dealt with under the general rules of English law, of which the most relevant are those relating to the sale of goods and to the tort of negligence.

b) As regards the law of sale, the relevant parts of the common law have been superseded by the Sale of Goods Act,[471] with almost identical provisions covering the other types of contract involving the supply of goods or services.[472] Pursuant to s. 13(1) of the Act, it is an implied term in every sale by description that the goods sold correspond to their description. The scope of this condition for product liability is limited: a sale by description occurs whenever goods are sold not individually, but rather as goods of a certain description (the most obvious example being bulk sales). Not all features qualify as part of the description of a good, however; the description is limited to the essential characteristics of the goods or the purpose of the sale.[473]

In addition, two further contractual terms are implied in every sale that takes place "in the course of a business" (thus excluding sales made outside of a profession or business, e.g. sale of a second-hand car by its private owner, etc.):[474]

–   The goods are of "satisfactory quality" (s. 14(2) of the Act), that is to say, they meet the quality expectations of a reasonable person. Accordingly, supply of a defective product will usually constitute a breach of this contractual term.[475]
–   The goods are fit for the purpose(s) which the buyer explicitly or implicitly made known to the seller, unless the buyer did not rely on the skill and judgment of the seller in that respect (s. 14 (3) of the Act). That condition has been interpreted liberally, so that it is always implied that the goods are at least fit for the use to which they are ordinarily put, and the burden of proof is on the seller to show absence of reliance.[476]

Under English law, these three contractual terms cannot be excluded from *consumer* transactions, and their exclusion is subject to a reasonableness test in *other* transactions.[477]

A contractual claim based on one of these terms is advantageous, since there is no need to prove fault on the part of anyone; it suffices to show that the goods did not comply with one of the terms above.[478] Furthermore, the claimant can—in addition to other

---

[471] Originally, the Sale of Goods Act 1893, 56 & 57 Vict. c. 71. The relevant provisions are now to be found in the Sale of Goods Act 1979, c. 54.
[472] See, for the contract of hire purchase, the Supply of Goods (Implied Terms) Act 1973, c.13 and for other contracts, the Supply of Goods and Services Act 1982, c. 29.
[473] See Howells at 53–6; *Clerk & Lindsell on Torts* at 487, para. 9–05.
[474] See Howells at 56–7.
[475] *Clerk & Lindsell on Torts* at 487, para. 9–06.
[476] See Howells at 61–3; *Clerk & Lindsell on Torts* at 487–8, para. 9–07.
[477] See Howells at 65 as well as Stapleton at 39–41.
[478] *Clerk & Lindsell on Torts* at 488, para. 9–08.

contractual remedies—request compensation not only for the reduction in value of the goods in question, but also for consequential damage, both to the person and to property.[479]

English law, however, has firmly clung to the doctrine of privity of contract to this day; not only is the law of sale of no avail to third parties who were not in a contractual relationship with the seller concerning the injurious product, but the consumer is not able to go up the contractual chain and sue the manufacturer directly: he or she can only make a claim based on contract against the seller.[480]

c) Accordingly, in the typical case of injury caused by a manufactured product sold through a modern distribution chain, the sole recourse of the consumer against the manufacturer will lie in tort. In that respect, the famous case of *Donoghue* v. *Stevenson*, probably the single most significant decision in the English law of negligence,[481] dealt more specifically with a problem of product liability, in that a decomposed snail was allegedly present in a bottle of ginger-beer, as a result of some mistake in the bottling process. Before the decision of the House of Lords, the manufacturer was shielded even from tort claims, on the basis that, unless the product was dangerous, no duty of care in tort arose in the absence of a contractual relationship between manufacturer and consumer.[482] With his celebrated "neighbour principle", Lord Atkin in *Donoghue* v. *Stevenson* established that a duty of care could arise as a general matter whenever certain conditions were met;[483] in relation to the manufacturer in particular, he wrote:

> "A manufacturer of products which he sells in such a form as to show that he intends them to reach the ultimate consumer in the form in which they left him with no reasonable possibility of intermediate examination, and with the knowledge that the absence of reasonable care in the preparation or putting up of the products will result in an injury to the consumer's life or property, owes a duty to the consumer to take reasonable care."

Following *Donoghue* v. *Stevenson*, therefore, the victim became able to sue the manufacturer for the tort of negligence in product liability cases. The Privy Council's opinion in *Grant* v. *Australian Knitting Mills*, reproduced below, confirmed *Donoghue* v. *Stevenson* and set out more fully the applicable principles.

d) The tort of negligence offers a somewhat more limited scope of protection than an action for breach of contract. It was seen earlier that, as a general rule, negligence does not enable the recovery of pure economic loss, that is economic loss not consequential upon any personal injury or property damage.[484] When a product turns out to be defective, its value decreases; that loss in value, however, represents a form of pure economic

---

[479] Rogers at 326.

[480] See *Clerk & Lindsell on Torts* at 488, para. 9–08; Stapleton at 41; Howells at 64; Rogers at 327. In some limited cases, however, it has been found that the representations made by the manufacturer to the ultimate buyer, either directly (in response to a query) or through advertising, gave rise to a collateral warranty from the manufacturer to the ultimate buyer directly, thus enabling the buyer to sue the manufacturer in contract: Howells, ibid.; Stapleton at 38.

[481] It is reproduced *supra*, Chapter I, **1.E.23.** and discussed there for its relevance to the law of negligence in general.

[482] Rogers at 327; Howells at 69–70.

[483] In the current state of the common law, these conditions are that harm was reasonably foreseeable, the defendant and plaintiff stood in a proximity relationship and it is fair, just and reasonable to impose a duty of care: see *supra*, Chapter I, 1.4.1.B.

[484] See *supra*, Chapter II, **2.E.36.** and notes thereafter.

loss, and as such it cannot be recovered in an action for the tort of negligence.[485] By contrast, any personal injury or damage to other property which results from the product defect is clearly recoverable. Difficulties arise when the defective product causes physical damage to itself: such damage is generally seen as a direct consequence of the failure of the product to meet contractual expectations, and as such is then only recoverable under contract.[486]

Like German law, English law was faced with the problem of component parts causing damage to the whole of a product: is the product as a whole to be seen as an item of property different from the component part, so that recovery for the damage to the whole product could be sought in tort? English courts generally take a fairly prudent attitude: in *D&F Estates* v. *Church Commissioners for England*, a case dealing with a building, the House of Lords had seemed to put forward a theory of "complex structures" whereby the other parts of a complex building would be deemed to constitute other property in relation to the defective part.[487] That theory might have also applied to defective products, but in any event it was expressly disavowed by the House of Lords in its subsequent decision in *Murphy* v. *Brentwood District Council*.[488] In the end, therefore, recovery would only be possible in the clearest cases, where the component was functionally distinct and could be detached from the whole product, because for instance the plaintiff bought it as a separate part and installed it himself or herself or the component was not an integral part of what the plaintiff bought.[489]

The defect may also be detected before the product could cause any damage, so that costs are incurred in curing the defect so as to make the product safe. In both *D&F Estates* v. *Church Commissioners of England* and *Murphy* v. *Brentwood District Council*, the House of Lords denied that the owner of the product could recover such costs in tort: any such claim must be contractual.[490]

e) Two main criticisms have been levelled against the use of negligence as the main basis for product liability claims under English tort law.[491] First, it has been argued that the tort of negligence imposes too heavy a burden of proof on the plaintiff, who has to establish—beyond the existence of a duty of care between manufacturer and user,[492] which is generally self-evident—that the manufacturer was negligent,[493] that such negligence caused loss or injury to the plaintiff and that such loss or injury was not too remote a consequence of the negligence.[494]

---

[485] See Rogers at 335; *Clerk & Lindsell on Torts* at 494, para. 9–18. It should be pointed out that, in *Junior Books* v. *Veitchi Co. Ltd.* [1983] 1 AC 520, HL, the plaintiff was able to recover in tort for the loss in value resulting from defective flooring; that decision, however, was the high point of the post-*Anns* period, and it is doubtful whether it would still hold beyond its narrow facts in the light of the position taken by the House of Lords in *Murphy* v. *Brentwood DC* [1991] 1 AC 398: see *supra*, Chapter I, 1.4.1.B.

[486] Ibid.

[487] *D&F Estates* v. *Church Commissioners for England* [1989] AC 177, HL.

[488] [1991] 1 AC 398, HL.

[489] See *Clerk & Lindsell on Torts* at 494–5, para. 9–19 and 9–20; Rogers at 335–7; Howells at 84–5.

[490] See Rogers at 337.

[491] See Stapleton at 43–4.

[492] On the concept of duty of care in general and its application to the various types of injury, see *supra*, Chapter I, 1.4.1.B.

[493] On the standard of care required under the tort of negligence, see *supra*, Chapter III, 3.2.1. and 3.2.2.C.

[494] The issues of causation and remoteness of damage are discussed *supra*, Chapter IV.

English law has not provided a very strong response to that criticism. As the next two cases show, English courts have adopted a "common sense" approach to the assessment of the facts in product liability cases, allowing the plaintiff to make the best of the evidence which he or she can bring before the court. Nevertheless, English courts have always declined to formulate this approach in legal terms; in the next two annotated cases, dating from 1935 and 1998 respectively, the court simply assessed the evidence and refused to apply the maxim *res ipsa loquitur* (presumption of fact). By contrast with German law, therefore, no elaborate body of rules relating to evidence and the burden of proof in product liability cases has emerged in English law.

f) The second criticism is more fundamental: it puts in question the appropriateness of dealing with product liability cases on a fault basis, suggesting instead that cases involving personal injury be dealt with under a strict liability regime.[495] Despite considerable efforts, English law was not reformed in that direction in the 1970s.[496]

Many English jurists were also keeping an eye on developments in the USA as a possible inspiration for the evolution of the common law of England. It is beyond the scope of this work to provide a detailed exposition of US product liability law, but it is worth drawing the attention of the reader to the activity of the American Law Institute (ALI) in the area.[497] Developments in the case law of many US states in the early 1960s led the ALI to propose in 1965 a new regime for product liability at s. 402A of the *Restatement (Second) of Torts*:[498]

"(1) One who sells any product in a defective condition unreasonably dangerous to the user or consumer or to his property is subject to liability for physical harm thereby caused to the ultimate user or consumer, or to his property, if
(a) the seller is engaged in the business of selling such a product, and
(b) it is expected to and does not reach the user or consumer without substantial change in the condition in which it is sold.
(2) The rule stated in Subsection (1) applies although
(a) the seller has exercised all possible care in the preparation and sale of his product, and
(b) the user or consumer has not bought the product from or entered into any contractual relation with the seller."

S. 402A has been introduced in the law of most US states, by statute or through case law. Even if s. 402A, as formulated in 1965, appeared to constitute a strict liability regime, it seems that in many cases the reality of court practice was otherwise. The growing importance of product liability in the USA and the perceived gap between s. 402A and reality prompted the ALI to revisit the topic and issue a separate *Restatement (Third) of Torts:*

---

[495] See, among the best known proponents of such a solution, T.G. Ison, *The Forensic Lottery* (London: Staples Press, 1967) and P. Atiyah, *Accidents, Compensation and the Law* (London: Weidenfeld & Nicholson, 1970), now in its 5th edition (P. Cane, *Atiyah's Accidents, Compensation and the Law*, 5th edn. (London: Butterworths, 1993)).

[496] Stapleton at 45–6.

[497] Founded in 1923, the ALI is a private institution whose membership is made up of practising lawyers, judges and academics who have been elected by their peers. The ALI aims to contribute to the clarification, simplification and improvement of the common law of America, and one of its main endeavours in that respect is the preparation of Restatements of various fields of law. Those restatements are highly regarded, and they are often either adopted in a statute or taken up in the case law of US states. See the ALI home page at <http://www.ali.org>.

[498] See Markesinis and Deakin at 565–9; Stapleton at 23–36.

Product Liability in 1998, the key provisions of which are the first three sections of Chapter 1, Topic 1 ("Liability Rules Applicable to Products Generally"):[499]

"1. One engaged in the business of selling or otherwise distributing products who sells or distributes a defective product is subject to liability for harm to persons or property caused by the defect.

2. A product is defective when, at the time of sale or distribution, it contains a manufacturing defect, is defective in design, or is defective because of inadequate instructions or warnings. A product:

(a) contains a manufacturing defect when the product departs from its intended design even though all possible care was exercised in the preparation and marketing of the product;

(b) is defective in design when the foreseeable risks of harm posed by the product could have been reduced or avoided by the adoption of a reasonable alternative design by the seller or other distributor, or a predecessor in the commercial chain of distribution, and the omission of the alternative design renders the product not reasonably safe;

(c) is defective because of inadequate instructions or warnings when the foreseeable risks of harm posed by the product could have been reduced or avoided by the provision of reasonable instructions or warnings by the seller or other distributor, or a predecessor in the commercial chain of distribution, and the omission of the instructions or warnings renders the product not reasonably safe.

3. It may be inferred that the harm sustained by the plaintiff was caused by a product defect existing at the time of sale or distribution, without proof of a specific defect, when the incident that harmed the plaintiff:

(a) was of a kind that ordinarily occurs as a result of product defect; and

(b) was not, in the particular case, solely the result of causes other than product defect existing at the time of sale or distribution."

This new Restatement aims to reflect the state of product liability law in the US by drawing at the outset a distinction between manufacturing defects, on the one hand, and design and instruction defects, on the other. The first are left under a strict liability regime, while the latter two categories are placed under a regime which comes close to negligence.[500] The plaintiff is helped by the evidentiary rule of s. 3, however.

Privy Council[501]   **6.E.31.**
Grant v. *Australian Knitting Mills*

LIABILITY OF MANUFACTURER IN NEGLIGENCE
BURDEN OF PROOF

Defective underwear

A duty of care within the meaning of Donoghue v. Stevenson *arises between the victim of injury due to a defective product and the manufacturer whenever the victim came within the class of intended users of the product. The burden of proof falls upon the plaintiff for all elements of the tort of negligence, but the court may make inferences from the facts evidenced by the plaintiff in order to establish the fault of the manufacturer.*

Facts: The plaintiff bought underwear manufactured by the defendants from a retailer. The plaintiff subsequently suffered from dermatitis which, as it turned out, had been caused by a reaction with sulphites present in the underwear. Sulphites are a by-product of the chemicals used in treating the wool from which the underwear was made and they should normally have been removed in the course of the treatment. The plaintiff sued the retailer from whom he had bought the underwear as well as the manufacturer.

---

[499] On the new Restatement and the process leading up to it, see D.G. Owen, "American Products Liability Law Restated" (1998) 6 Cons LJ 161.

[500] See *Restatement (Third) of Torts: Products Liability* (1998), Comments under s. 1.

[501] [1935] AC 85.

Held: The court of first instance allowed the claim against both defendants. The court of appeal reversed that decision and dismissed the claim. The Privy Council restored the judgment of the court of first instance.

Judgment: LORD WRIGHT:[502] "[Lord Wright first reviewed the evidence and found that the court of first instance had correctly assessed it.] That conclusion means that the disease contracted, and the damage suffered by the [plaintiff], were caused by the defective condition of the garments which the retailers sold to him, and which the manufacturers made and put forth for retail and indiscriminate sale . . . The liability of each [defendant] depends on a different cause of action, though it is for the same damage. [Lord Wright then dealt with the liability of the retailer, finding that it was established on the basis of a breach of implied terms relating to fitness for purpose and merchantable quality.]

But when the position of the manufacturers is considered, different questions arise: there is no privity of contract between the appellant and the manufacturers: between them the liability, if any, must be in tort, and the gist of the cause of action is negligence. The facts . . . show . . . negligence in manufacture. According to the evidence, the method of manufacture was correct: the danger of excess sulphites being left was recognized and was guarded against: the process was intended to be fool proof. If excess sulphites were left in the garment, that could only be because some one was at fault. The [plaintiff] is not required to lay his finger on the exact person in all the chain who was responsible, or to specify what he did wrong. Negligence is found as a matter of inference from the existence of the defects taken in connection with all the known circumstances: even if the manufacturers could by apt evidence have rebutted that inference they have not done so.

On this basis, the damage suffered by the appellant was caused in fact . . . by the negligent or improper way in which the manufacturers made the garments. But this mere sequence of cause and effect is not enough in law to constitute a cause of action in negligence, which is a complex concept, involving a duty as between the parties to take care, as well as a breach of that duty and resulting damage . . .

[The argument of the defendant] was based on the contention that the present case fell outside the decision of the House of Lords in *Donoghue* v. *Stevenson* [1932] AC 562.[503] [Lord Wright reviewed that case and quoted from the opinion of Lord Atkin.]

It is clear that [*Donoghue* v. *Stevenson*] treats negligence, where there is a duty to take care, as a specific tort in itself, and not simply as an element in some more complex relationship or in some specialized breach of duty, and still less as having any dependence on contract. All that is necessary as a step to establish the tort of . . . negligence is to define the precise relationship from which the duty to take care is to be deduced. It is, however, essential in English law that the duty should be established: the mere fact that a man is injured by another's act gives in itself no cause of action . . . In *Donoghue* v. *Stevenson*, the duty was deduced simply from the facts relied on—namely, that the injured party was one of a class for whose use, in the contemplation and intention of the makers, the article was issued to the world, and the article was used by that party in the state in which it was prepared and issued without it being changed in any way and without there being any warning of, or means of detecting, the hidden danger; there was, it is true, no personal intercourse between the maker and the user; but though the duty is personal, because it is inter partes, it needs no interchange of words, spoken or written, or signs of offer or assent; it is thus different in character from any contractual relationship . . .

One further point may be noted. The principle of *Donoghue* v. *Stevenson* can only be applied where the defect is hidden and unknown to the consumer, otherwise the directness of cause and effect is absent . . .

---

[502] Viscount Hailsham LC, Lord Blanesburgh, Lord Macmillan and Sir Lancelot Sanderson concurring.
[503] *Supra*, Chapter I, **1.E.23.**

If the foregoing are the essential features of *Donoghue* v. *Stevenson*, they are also to be found
. . . in the present case. The presence of the deleterious chemical in the pants, due to negligence in
manufacture, was a hidden and latent defect, just as much as were the remains of the snail in the
opaque bottle: it could not be detected by any examination that could reasonably be made. Nothing
happened between the making of the garments and their being worn to change their condition. The
garments were made by the manufacturers for the purpose of being worn exactly as they were worn
in fact by the [plaintiff] . . .

[The defendant] sought to distinguish *Donoghue* v. *Stevenson* from the present [case] on the
ground that in the former the makers of the ginger-beer had retained 'control' over it in the sense
that they had placed it in stoppered and sealed bottles, so that it would not be tampered with until
it was opened to be drunk . . . [Here] there was no 'control' because nothing was done by the manufacturers to exclude the possibility of any tampering while the goods were on their way to the user.
Their Lordships do not accept that contention. The decision in *Donoghue* v. *Stevenson* did not
depend on the bottle being stoppered and sealed: the essential point in this regard was that the article should reach the consumer or user subject to the same defect as it had when it left the manufacturer . . .

[The defendant] further contended . . . that if the decision in *Donoghue* v. *Stevenson* were
extended even a hair's-breadth, no line could be drawn, and a manufacturer's liability would be
extended indefinitely . . .

In their Lordships' opinion it is enough for them to decide this case on its actual facts.

No doubt many difficult problems will arise before the precise limits of the principle are defined:
many qualifying conditions and many complications of fact may in the future come before the
Courts for decision. It is enough now to say that their Lordships hold the present case to come
within the principle of *Donoghue* v. *Stevenson* . . ."

Notes

(1) The annotated case has become a leading case in English product liability law
because of its discussion of both the burden of establishing negligence and the confirmation of *Donoghue* v. *Stevenson* in respect of the duty of care between manufacturer and
user. In the annotated case, the victim had sued in contract the retailer from which he had
bought his underwear, and in tort the manufacturer of such underwear. The retailer was
liable in contract, under the South Australian Sale of Goods Act in force at the time,[504]
because of a breach of implied terms relating to fitness for purpose and merchantable
quality (now replaced by "satisfactory quality").

As regards the claim in tort against the manufacturer, the plaintiff was able to establish
that his condition (dermatitis) resulted from the presence of sulphites in the underwear
which he had purchased. The defendant was in fact caught by its own evidence:[505] since
it had shown that its process was "fool proof", as the Privy Council noted, the defect in
the underwear must have been attributable to the fault of an employee of the defendant,
whom the plaintiff did not have to identify in order to engage the liability of the defendant.[506] The Privy Council added that "negligence is found as a matter of inference" from
the facts.

---

[504] Sales of Goods Act 1895, 58 & 59 Vict. No. 630, s. 14.
[505] As Howells notes at 72.
[506] See *supra*, Chapter V, 5.1.1.B.

Indeed, in cases involving manufacturing defects, English courts are quite willing to come to the help of the plaintiff by inferring negligence from the evidence that the product was defectively manufactured.[507] The next case explores this issue in greater detail.

(2) In cases of design defects or failures to warn, however, inferences of fact are usually of little help to the plaintiff.

As for design defects, the plaintiff must show that the risk of injury was foreseeable at the time when the product was put into circulation by the manufacturer; accordingly, the manufacturer will be exonerated under English law if a defect was such as to constitute a "product development risk"—i.e. a defect which could not be foreseen in the state of scientific and technical knowledge at the time. Even if the defect and the ensuing risk of injury were foreseeable, the defendant might still be exonerated if the plaintiff cannot show that the risk in question was such that it outweighed the benefits to be derived from putting the product into circulation.[508] In other words, certain products, such as for example matches or pharmaceutical products, are inherently dangerous, but their usefulness justifies putting them on the market nonetheless—provided that appropriate safety measures have been taken. Furthermore, compliance with applicable standards is generally seen as evidence that the manufacturer took the requisite safety measures.[509]

(3) Similarly, when the injury follows from a failure on the part of the manufacturer to give appropriate warning to consumers through labelling or instructions, the plaintiff bears the burden of proving that, in view of the risk, the defendant ought to have given a warning to the consumer (or a different one from the one that was actually provided).[510] Manufacturers do not have to warn of obvious risks which the user must be assumed to know, but English courts do not readily assume such knowledge.[511] The warnings must cover not only the dangers arising from normal use, but also those linked with foreseeable misuse of the product.[512]

It should be noted that the duty to warn also extends to dangers even if they come to the attention of the manufacturer only after the product has been put into circulation; if the danger is serious, the manufacturer may be bound to issue a warning to existing customers or even recall its product.[513]

(4) As is usual in negligence cases, the plaintiff must also prove causation between the fault of the defendant and the injury, which may be quite a difficult task, especially when many causes could have intervened in bringing about the damage.[514] That issue has played a large role in English law, in part because of the remark by Lord Atkin in *Donoghue* v. *Stevenson* that the liability of the manufacturer is engaged if the goods were sold so as to leave resellers and consumers with "no reasonable possibility of intermediate examination".[515] That statement took on a life of its own but, as authors acknowl-

---

[507] Howells at 73; *Clerk & Lindsell on Torts* at 495–6, para. 9–21; Rogers at 334–5.
[508] *Clerk & Lindsell on Torts* at 496–7, para. 9–22; Howells at 73–5.
[509] Howells at 75–6.
[510] See *Clerk & Lindsell on Torts* at 497–8, para. 9–23.
[511] Howells at 77.
[512] Howells, ibid.; *Clerk & Linsell on Torts* at 501–2, para. 9–32.
[513] See *Clerk & Lindsell on Torts* at 498, para. 9–24; Howells at 79–80.
[514] See Howells at 81–4; *Clerk & Lindsell on Torts* at 498, para. 9–25 and 9–26; Rogers at 331–2.
[515] See *supra*, Chapter I, **1.E.23.**

edge, it is in fact linked with causation:[516] if the victim could have inspected the product but did not, or if he or she still used the product after an inspection had revealed a defect, then the chain of causation between manufacturer and victim was broken;[517] as the Privy Council noted in the annotated case, *Donoghue* v. *Stevenson* applies only if the defect was hidden and not reasonably observable or known to the victim. Similarly, the manufacturer will be exonerated if the plaintiff cannot prove that the defect was already present at the time when the product was released by the manufacturer;[518] as the Privy Council put it in the annotated case, "the article should reach the consumer or user subject to the same defect as it had when it left the manufacturer".

(5) The annotated case is also significant with respect to the duty of care, in that it confirmed *Donoghue* v. *Stevenson* as it pertains to defective products. In an attempt to restrict its scope, the manufacturer had argued that *Donoghue* should be limited to its facts. The Privy Council disagreed and stated unequivocally that the rationale of *Donoghue* applied whenever the facts enabled the existence of a duty of care to be established, irrespective of any relationship (or its lack) between plaintiff and defendant: it suffices that the victim comes within the class of persons for whom the product was put into circulation (i.e. prospective users). Just as in *Donoghue*, that condition was met in the annotated case. The court also dismissed the "floodgates" argument brought forward by the manufacturer, finding that any problems that might arise in the course of applying *Donoghue* v. *Stevenson* should be solved as they arose in other cases.

The following case can be found (with notes) at <http://www.rechten.unimaas.nl/casebook>:

6.E.32. Court of Appeal, *Carroll* v. *Fearon*. Defective tyre.

6.3.2. DIRECTIVE 85/374

Introductory Note

Consumer protection became an element of Community policy in 1975, when the Council adopted a Resolution on a preliminary programme for a consumer protection and information policy,[519] followed in 1981 by a second programme[520] and in 1989 by a new three-year programme for the years 1990–1992.[521] In 1986, the Single European Act added Art. 95 [then 100a] to the EC Treaty, in order to provide a more flexible framework for legislative measures aimed at the attainment of the internal market. Art. 95(3) provides that the Commission, in its proposals under Art. 95 concerning among other things,

[516] Howells at 80–1; *Clerk & Lindsell on Torts* at 499, para. 9–27. The possibility of intermediate inspection—which subsequent case law has reframed as a probability of inspection—also has a bearing on the duty of care, as those authors and Rogers at 332–3 point out: if it is to be expected that an intermediary will inspect the goods, there may not be sufficient proximity between manufacturer and consumer for a duty of care to arise.

[517] See Howells at 81; *Clerk & Lindsell on Torts* at 500–1, para. 9–29 and 9–30. On interventions by the victim or a third party in the chain of causation, see *infra*, Chapter IV, 4.3.

[518] *Clerk & Lindsell on Torts* at 501, para. 9–31.

[519] [1975] OJ C 92/2.

[520] Council Resolution of 19 May 1981 on a second programme of the European Economic Community for a consumer protection and information policy [1981] OJ C 133/1.

[521] Three year action plan of consumer policy in the EEC (1990–1992), COM(90)98final.

consumer protection, is to take as a base a high level of protection. In 1992, the Treaty on European Union introduced into the EC Treaty a general provision on consumer protection, Art. 153 [then 129a], whereby the Community institutions "shall contribute to the attainment of a high level of consumer protection", through, among other things, harmonization measures adopted pursuant to Art. 95 EC.

Most of the legislative measures taken by the Community within the above framework relate to the area of contract law; the most important so far are Directive 93/13 of 5 April 1993 on unfair terms in consumer contracts and Directive 1999/44 on certain aspects of the sale of consumer goods and associated guarantees.[522]

Some of the consumer protection directives, and more particularly Directive 93/13 on unfair terms in consumer contracts (Art. 7(2)), already obliged Member States to allow persons or organisations that have a legitimate interest in consumer protection under national law to take action before courts or competent administrative bodies in order to prevent conduct prohibited by the directive in question. In addition, Directive 98/27 of 19 May 1998 on injunctions for the protection of consumers' interests[523] harmonized national rules relating to actions for an injunction aimed at the protection of the collective interests of consumers included in some of the consumer protection Directives listed in the Annex (amongst which is included Directive 93/13 on unfair terms in consumer contracts, but not Directive 85/374 on liability for defective products[524]). The directive is intended to facilitate injunctions in cross-border situations, that is in the event of infringements which have effects in other Member States. It allows a public body and/or consumer or entrepreneurial association to be designated as a "competent authority" to bring actions for injunctions.[525] It binds each Member State to allow designated consumer organizations from another Member State to bring actions before its courts against infringements falling within the scope of the Directives listed in the Annex, which would originate from the first Member State but have an impact on consumers in the second Member State.[526] Directive 98/27 does not cover actions for monetary compensation, however.[527]

Some directives have also affected tort law, most importantly Directive 85/374 of 25 July 1985 on liability for defective products.[528] In 1990, the Commission also proposed a Directive on the liability of suppliers of services which, unlike the Directive 85/374, rested on fault-based liability (but established a rebuttable presumption of fault), but that proposal was withdrawn in the face of the considerable opposition it encountered.[529]

The Council of Europe has also invested time and effort in relation to the issue of common rules on product liability. In 1976, at approximately the same time as the European Commission put forward its proposal for what would become Directive 85/374, the European Convention on Products Liability in regard to Personal Injury and Death was opened for signature.[530] Since this was in many respects similar to the Commission proposal as it unfolded, it became superfluous for the Member States of the EU, which have not signed or ratified it.[531]

---

[522] [1993] OJ L 95/29 and [1999] OJ L 171/12 respectively.

[523] Directive 98/27 of 19 May 1998 on injunctions for the protection of consumers' interests [1998] OJ L 166/51.

[524] *Infra*, **6.EC.33.**

[525] Directive 98/27 of 19 May 1998 on injunctions for the protection of consumers' interests [1998] OJ L 166/51, Art. 3.

[526] Ibid., Art. 4(1).

[527] Ibid., Art. 2(1).

[528] *Infra*, **6.EC.33.**

[529] Proposal for a Council Directive on the liability of suppliers of services [1990] OJ C 12/8.

[530] European Convention on Products Liability in regard to Personal Injury and Death of 27 January 1977, ETS No. 91.

[531] See also the Convention on the Law Applicable to Products Liability (1972), Actes et documents de la Douzième session, Vol. III, 246, which is a product of the Hague Conference on Private International Law.

Directive 85/374 of 25 July 1985[532]   **6.EC.33.**
on the approximation of the laws, regulations and
administrative provisions of the Member States
concerning liability for defective products

"*Article 1*. The producer shall be liable for damage caused by a defect in his product.

Article 2. For the purpose of this Directive 'product' means all movables, even if incorporated into another movable or into an immovable. 'Product' includes electricity.

Article 3. 1. 'Producer' means the manufacturer of a finished product, the producer of any raw material or the manufacturer of a component part and any person who, by putting his name, trade mark or other distinguishing feature on the product presents himself as its producer.

2. Without prejudice to the liability of the producer, any person who imports into the Community a product for sale, hire, leasing or any form of distribution in the course of his business shall be deemed to be a producer within the meaning of this Directive and shall be responsible as a producer.

3. Where the producer of the product cannot be identified, each supplier of the product shall be treated as its producer unless he informs the injured person, within a reasonable time, of the identity of the producer or of the person who supplied him with the product. The same shall apply, in the case of an imported product, if this product does not indicate the identity of the importer referred to in paragraph 2, even if the name of the producer is indicated.

Article 4. The injured person shall be required to prove the damage, the defect and the causal relationship between defect and damage.

Article 5. Where, as a result of the provisions of this Directive, two or more persons are liable for the same damage, they shall be liable jointly and severally, without prejudice to the provisions of national law concerning the rights of contribution or recourse.

Article 6. 1. A product is defective when it does not provide the safety which a person is entitled to expect, taking all circumstances into account, including:

(a) the presentation of the product;

(b) the use to which it could reasonably be expected that the product would be put;

(c) the time when the product was put into circulation.

2. A product shall not be considered defective for the sole reason that a better product is subsequently put into circulation.

Article 7. The producer shall not be liable as a result of this Directive if he proves:

(a) that he did not put the product into circulation; or

(b) that, having regard to the circumstances, it is probable that the defect which caused the damage did not exist at the time when the product was put into circulation by him or that this defect came into being afterwards; or

(c) that the product was neither manufactured by him for sale or any form of distribution for economic purpose nor manufactured or distributed by him in the course of his business; or

(d) that the defect is due to compliance of the product with mandatory regulations issued by the public authorities; or

(e) that the state of scientific and technical knowledge at the time when he put the product into circulation was not such as to enable the existence of the defect to be discovered; or

(f) in the case of a manufacturer of a component, that the defect is attributable to the design of the product in which the component has been fitted or to the instructions given by the manufacturer of the product.

[532] [1985] OJ L 210/29, as modified by Directive 1999/34 of 10 May 1999 [1999] OJ L 141/20. Directive 1999/34 removed the possibility that Member States could exclude primary agricultural products and game from the scope of their national legislation implementing Directive 85/374.

Article 8. 1. Without prejudice to the provisions of national law concerning the right of contribution or recourse, the liability of the producer shall not be reduced when the damage is caused
both by a defect in product and by the act or omission of a third party.

2. The liability of the producer may be reduced or disallowed when, having regard to all the circumstances, the damage is caused both by a defect in the product and by the fault of the injured
person or any person for whom the injured person is responsible.

Article 9. For the purpose of Article 1, 'damage' means:

(a) damage caused by death or by personal injuries;

(b) damage to, or destruction of, any item of property other than the defective product itself,
     with a lower threshold of 500 ECU, provided that the item of property:

   (i) is of a type ordinarily intended for private use or consumption, and

   (ii) was used by the injured person mainly for his own private use or consumption.

This Article shall be without prejudice to national provisions relating to non-material damage.

Article 10. 1. Member States shall provide in their legislation that a limitation period of three
years shall apply to proceedings for the recovery of damages as provided for in this Directive. The
limitation period shall begin to run from the day on which the plaintiff became aware, or should
reasonably have become aware, of the damage, the defect and the identity of the producer . . .

Article 11. Member States shall provide in their legislation that the rights conferred upon the
injured person pursuant to this Directive shall be extinguished upon the expiry of a period of 10
years from the date on which the producer put into circulation the actual product which caused the
damage, unless the injured person has in the meantime instituted proceedings against the producer.

Article 12. The liability of the producer arising from this Directive may not, in relation to the
injured person, be limited or excluded by a provision limiting his liability or exempting him from
liability.

Article 13. This Directive shall not affect any rights which an injured person may have according
to the rules of the law of contractual or non-contractual liability or a special liability system existing at the moment when this Directive is notified . . .

Article 15. 1. Each Member State may:

(a) [deleted by Directive 1999/34];

(b) by way of derogation from Article 7 (e), maintain or, subject to the procedure set out in para-
     graph 2 of this Article, provide in this legislation that the producer shall be liable even if he
     proves that the state of scientific and technical knowledge at the time when he put the prod-
     uct into circulation was not such as to enable the existence of a defect to be discovered . . .

Article 16. 1. Any Member State may provide that a producer's total liability for damage resulting from a death or personal injury and caused by identical items with the same defect shall be limited to an amount which may not be less than 70 million ECU . . ."

Notes

(1) The following are the core provisions of Directive 85/374, so far as liability is concerned:

- Article 1, which makes the producer (as defined in Article 3(1)), as well as the importer
  and eventually each supplier (Article 3(2) and (3)) liable for damage caused by a defect
  in its product (as defined in Article 2);
- Article 4, which states that the injured person must prove damage, a defect (as defined
  in Article 6) and the causal link between both;
- Article 5, which provides for joint and several liability where two or more persons are
  liable for the same damage;

- Article 8, which precludes reduction of the liability of the producer if the damage is also caused by the act or omission of a third party (but permits reduction of that liability in the event of contributory negligence of the victim); and
- Article 12, which prohibits limitation and exclusion clauses.

As appears from Article 1, the Directive aims to introduce liability not based on wrongful conduct for defective products, subject, however, to many restrictions. For instance, by implication from Article 2, the Directive does not cover immovable property.[533] Furthermore, Article 7 of the Directive sets out various defences, the most controversal of which is the "state of the art" or "development risk" defence provided for by Article 7(e).[534] Finally, limitation periods and periods for the extinction of rights are provided for in Article 10 and 11.

The Directive covers damage caused by death or personal injury (subject to the potential limitation permitted by Article 16); it also covers damage to property, within the boundaries of Article 9(b). The issue of compensation for non-material damage is left to the national laws.

(2) Directive 85/374 can be seen as a reflection of common trends and principles present in many, if not all, legal systems of the Member States. As G. Howells points out, even though, at the time when the Directive was adopted, "no European country had a liability regime which was specifically designed to cover all products, the idea of a distinct product liability regime was not unknown in Europe".[535] As was seen in the previous subsection dealing with national laws on product liability, Howells further notes that "many European legal systems were already developing their laws" in the direction taken in the Directive "to trace responsibility back to the producer"; that is "perhaps most clearly seen in countries such as France, Belgium and Luxembourg by the creation of an *action directe* between the consumer-purchaser and higher links in the distribution chain and in Austria by the notion of contracts having protective effects for third parties".[536] In other countries, such as in Germany, the same objective was pursued through the strengthening of tort law, i.e. through the introduction of a reversal of the burden of proof for cases of product defects.[537] With Directive 85/374, the Community apparently opted for tort rather than contract law as a means of resolving product liability disputes, although it is left to the Member States how to transpose the rules into their legal system.[538]

---

[533] Blood and blood products, when separated from the human body, fall within the scope of Art. 2. See L. Dommering-Van Rongen, *Produktenaansprakelijkheid* (Deventer: Kluwer, 1991) at 86–9. See also *supra*, **6.F.30.** and Note (4) thereunder.

[534] Art. 15(1)(b) permits Member States not to maintain or introduce that defence in their national law.

[535] G. Howells, "Product Liability" in A.S. Hartkamp et al., eds., *Towards a European Civil Code* (Nijmegen: Ars Aequi Libri, 1994) 313 at 316–17.

[536] Ibid., footnotes omitted.

[537] Ibid. at 318, with reference to BGH case law. See *supra*, 6.3.1.A.

[538] As will be seen *infra*, **6.F.37.**, Directive 85/374 has been implemented under French law through a liability regime that does not fall under either tort/delict or contract law. Under Art. 5 of the Brussels Convention on jurisdiction and the enforcement of judgments in civil and commercial matters of 27 September 1968 [1972] OJ L 299/32, the qualification of a rule as contractual or tortious is of importance to define the jurisdiction of a national court: for a case relating precisely to product liability, see ECJ, Judgment of 17 June 1992, Case C–26/91, *Jakob Handte & Co. GmbH* v. *Traitements mécano-chimiques des surfaces SA* [1992] ECR I–3967, and the conclusions of Advocate-General Jacobs at I–3977.

In any event, regardless of whether the various national laws opted for contract or tort law, the trend towards stricter product liability was already present in many of the national laws, to the point where one might even say that, when compared to those national laws, "the directive does not seem to have adopted [a] strong version of liability", a conclusion which is supported by the provisions of the Directive concerning the level of safety to be expected of a product, which is to be judged at "the time when the product was put into circulation" (Article 6(1)(c)), and the permissible defence of development risk (Article 7(e)), even if the producer then bears the burden of proof.[539]

(3) Directive 85/374 offers a good example of how the EC legislative process can help to harmonize, not unify, crucial parts of national tort laws by building on "the general principles common to the laws of the Member States", to use the words of Article 288 EC.[540] That harmonization is brought about (i) in respect of issues which have not yet, or not uniformly, been settled in the national laws (ii) by adopting solutions which, if not totally in line with trends observed in the national laws, at least do not contradict those trends, and (iii) by leaving some choice to the Member States as to the form and method of implementation, thanks to the use of a Directive.[541]

The enactment of Directive 85/374 by no means closed the chapter on the harmonization of national rules, as will be seen below when examining its implementation in German, French and English law.[542] Not only has the implementation of the Directive in the Member States given rise to debates on how to implement it and how to use the options left by the Directive, but in some countries the Directive also led to a reconsideration (by the legislature) or a re-interpretation (by the courts) of rules of national law not affected by it, with a view to making national law as homogeneous as possible and avoiding the introduction, as a result of the implementation of the Directive, of distinctions which were not present before.[543] Furthermore, even after it has been implemented in national law, the Directive may still play a role, because national courts must (or may, in areas not covered by the Directive) interpret their national laws in conformity with Community law, regardless of whether they have actually been seized of the issue by the parties.[544]

(4) Article 13 of Directive 85/374 provides that the Directive shall not affect the rights of the victim pursuant to national law as it existed at the moment when the Directive is notified. The victim of injury from a defective product may thus enjoy protection that

---

[539] G. Howells, "Product Liability" in A.S. Hartkamp et al., (eds.), *Towards a European Civil Code* (Nijmegen: Ars Aequi Libri, 1994) 313 at 319, with further details and references.

[540] The judicial process can play a similar role: see *infra*, Chapter IX, **9.EC.6.**

[541] Art. 249(3) EC. See G. Howells, "Product Liability" in A.S. Hartkamp et al., (eds.), *Towards a European Civil Code* (Nijmegen: Ars Aequi Libri, 1994) 313. For a thorough investigation of the Directive in the UK and US legal context, see J. Stapleton, *Product Liability* (London: Butterworths, 1994). At 342–3 and 346, the author indicates that the Directive does not provide conclusive evidence (it rather does the contrary) that its limited no-fault regime should serve as a model for similar situations, since it over-emphasizes the "supply-side" element in product-related injuries, to the exclusion of other factors.

[542] *Infra*, 6.3.3.A., 6.3.3.B. and 6.3.3.C. respectively.

[543] See for instance, BGH, 9 May 1995, *infra*, **6.G.35.** On this "reflex" (or "spill-over") effect of the Directive, see L. Dommering-Van Rongen, *Produktenaansprakelijkheid* (Deventer: Kluwer, 1991) at 67–8, who emphasizes that that effect may also lead to a lessening of consumer protection for the sake of harmonisation, when national laws provide more protection than the Directive.

[544] That issue was emphasized by the ECJ when it rejected the action brought by the Commission against the UK implementation of Directive 85/374: see *infra*, **6.EC.39.**

goes beyond that which is provided in the Directive, a point which might explain, for instance, why the ProdHaftG, which implements the Directive in German law, does not appear to have been used very often, since the national law is in some respects more advantageous than the Directive.[545]

(5) On 28 July 1999, the Commission issued a Green Paper on Liability for Defective Products,[546] as it had undertaken to do in the course of the debates on Directive 1999/34.[547] This Green Paper essentially aims to gather information on the workings and impact of Directive 85/374 in the Member States and to prepare the launch of a discussion on a revision of the Directive. In particular, the Commission wants to examine whether a revision of the Directive is justified on the following points:

- what the Commission terms the "balance" of the Directive, i.e. the main principles of "objective" liability, "relative" liability (availability of defences such as product development risk), limitation in time and public order nature of the liability regime;
- changing the rules of proof, especially as regards the proof of causation, the standard of proof, the availability of information from the producer and the preparation of expert reports;
- introducing mechanisms for apportioning liability between many producers (e.g. market share liability);
- changing or removing the "product development risk" defence;
- modifying the financial limits on liability;
- modifying the limitation period;
- requiring producers to take insurance;
- creating reporting and publication mechanisms to increase transparency;
- extending the scope of the Directive to real/immoveable property;
- extending the coverage of the Directive to non-material damage and damage to goods put to professional use;
- improving access to justice through injunctions and collective actions (as is the case with consumer protection directives[548]).

6.3.3. IMPLEMENTATION OF DIRECTIVE 85/374

The implementation of Directive 85/374 throughout the EU was completed when France adopted the Act 98–389 of 19 May 1998, more than 10 years after the deadline set in the Directive for its implementation. The present subsection surveys the implementation of the Directive in Germany, France and the UK, in the light of statutory enactments and cases.

---

[545] See *infra*, **6.G.34.**, Note (3).
[546] Green Paper on Liability for Defective Products, COM(1999)396final.
[547] Directive 1999/34 of 10 May 1999 [1999] OJ L 141/20.
[548] See *supra*, 6.3.2., Introductory Note.

6.3.3.A. GERMAN LAW

Introductory Note

a) According to Howells, Germany followed a "minimalist approach" to the implementation of Directive 85/374, with the aim of avoiding major changes to its law.[549] As he mentions, "it is with regard to Germany that a knowledge of pre-directive law is most essential".[550] The comments below on the *Produkthaftungsgesetz* (ProdHaftG) of 15 December 1989, which implemented the Directive in German law, point out how Germany used its leeway under the Directive, and survey the differences between the ProdHaftG and product liability law under § 823 BGB.[551]

b) One of the striking features of the ProdHaftG is how little it seems to have been used since its enactment. Nonetheless, the BGH, in its first major decision under the ProdHaftG, interpreted it (as well as the Directive itself) in a most notable fashion; excerpts from that decision are reproduced below.

Produkthaftungsgesetz[552]   **6.G.34.**

"**§ 1. Liability.** (1) If, as a result of a product defect, a person is killed, is injured or affected in his health, or a thing is damaged, the producer is obliged to compensate the person who suffered the damage for the ensuing harm. In the case of damage to property this rule applies only if an object other than the defective product is damaged and if this object is normally intended for private use of consumption and has been used by the injured party primarily for that purpose.

(2) The obligation to pay damages is excluded if:

1. the producer did not put the product into circulation;

2. it is to be assumed, having regard to the circumstances, that the product was not yet defective when it was put into circulation;

3. the producer has neither manufactured the product for sale or for any other form of commercial distribution nor has manufactured or distributed it in the course of his professional activities;

4. the defect is due to the fact that at the time when the producer put the product into circulation it complied with mandatory legal provisions;

5. the defect could not yet be discerned, having regard to the state of the art in science and technology at the time when the producer put the product concerned into circulation.

(3) In addition, the manufacturer of a part of the product is exempt from the obligation to pay compensation if the defect was caused by the construction of the product into which the part was inserted or by the instructions of the producer of the product. The first sentence applies *mutatis mutandis* to a producer of a basic substance (*Grundstoff*).

(4) The person who has suffered the harm bears the burden of proving the defect and its causal connection with the harm. In a dispute as to whether the obligation to pay compensation is excluded according to sub-paragraphs (2) or (3), the producer bears the burden of proof.

---

[549] Howells at 141.

[550] Howells at 123.

[551] The application of § 823 BGB in product liability cases is surveyed *supra*, 6.3.1.A.

[552] ProdHaftG, Product Liability Act of 15 December 1989, BGBl.I.2198, as amended by Act of 25 October 1994, BGBl.I.3082. English translation by K. Lipstein in Markesinis at 542 ff. (with some terminological changes).

§ 2. **Product.** Product in the meaning of this Act includes every moveable object, even if it forms part of another moveable or of an immoveable, as well as electricity . . .

§ 3. **Defect.** (1) A product is defective if it does not provide that degree of safety which can be justifiably expected, having regard to all the circumstances, in particular

a) its presentation;

b) its use which may be reasonably expected;

c) the time when it was put into circulation.

(2) A product is not defective for the sole reason that later on an improved product was put into circulation . . .

§ 7. **Extent of damages in case of death.** (1) In case of death, the expenses incurred in an attempt to restore health must be compensated together with the material loss suffered by the deceased in consequence of the loss or reduction of his earning capacity or of his increased needs. Damages also include the funeral expenses parable to the person who incurred them.

(2) If at the time of injury the deceased was connected with a third party by a relationship which rendered him, actually or potentially, liable by law to maintain that person, and if the third party lost his right to maintenance in consequence of the death, he is entitled to damages in so far as the deceased during the period of his life expectancy would have been liable to maintain him. This liability arises also if the third party was conceived at the time of death but not yet born.

§ 8. **Extent of damages in case of injury to the person.** If injury was caused to the body or to health, the expenses incurred in restoring health must be compensated together with the pecuniary loss suffered by the injured party resulting from the temporary or permanent loss or reduction of his earning capacity or from his increased needs.

§9. **Damages by way of periodical payments.** (1) Damage arising in the future as a result of the total or partial loss of earning capacity and of increased needs together with the damages payable to a third party in accordance with § 7(2) is to be compensated by periodical payments.

(2) § 843(2) to (4) apply.

§ 10. **Maximum rate of damages.** (1) If death or injury to the person has been caused by a product or by products of the same kind affected by the same defect, the liability to pay damages is limited to a maximum of DEM 160 million.

(2) If the damages payable to several injured parties exceed the maximum rate set out in sub-paragraph (1), the individual damages are reduced in proportion of their total to the maximum rate allowable.

§11. **Extent of compensation in case of damage to goods.** Where goods are damages, the person who suffered the damage has to bear the loss up to DEM 1125 . . .

§15. **Liability for drugs; liability according to other legal provisions.** (1) The provisions of the *Produkthaftungsgesetz* do not apply if, due to the use of a pharmaceutical product destined for human use and sold to the customer within the scope of application of the *Arzneimittelgesetz* (Drug Act) . . . a person is killed or his body or health otherwise affected.

(2) Liability in accordance with other provisions remains unaffected."

Notes

(1) In general, Germany tracked Directive 85/374 relatively closely in the ProdHaftG. In particular, the provisions of the Directive relating to the definition of "producer",[553]

---

[553] Art. 3 of Directive 85/374, which is implemented through § 4 ProdHaftG. The "reasonable time" to be given to the supplier to inform the victim of the identity of the producer at Art. 3(3) of Directive 85/374, has been translated by § 4(3) ProdHaftG into a one-month time limit.

joint and several liability,[554] intervention of a third party or of the victim,[555] limitation,[556] extinction of claims[557] and exclusion clauses[558] have been taken over almost word for word in the ProdHaftG, and accordingly they are not reproduced above. Germany made use of the choices expressly offered by the Directive as follows:

- At § 1(2)5. ProdHaftG, Germany provided for the "development risk" defence, which it could have excluded pursuant to Article 15(1)(b) of Directive 85/374.
- At § 10 ProdHaftG, Germany availed itself of Article 16 of Directive 85/374 and introduced a ceiling on liability for injury to persons, fixed at the minimum required by the Directive (DEM 160 million, now somewhat more than EUR 70 million).

Germany has thus used all those possibilities to limit the ambit of the Directive.

(2) In other ways, Germany also sought to anchor the ProdHaftG within the general system of German tort law, and in particular within the general theory of risk-based liability (*Gefährdungshaftung*):[559]

- The Directive was implemented in a separate statute, and not by amendment of the BGB itself, in accordance with the general principle that fault-based liability is the rule, as reflected in the BGB, and that liability not based on fault is an exception that must be introduced through special legislation (to be construed narrowly).[560]
- § 1(1) ProdHaftG is formulated using an enumerative list of protected *Rechtsgüter*, on the model of § 823(1) BGB.[561]
- By virtue of § 253 BGB and in the absence of an enabling provision in the ProdHaftG, non-material damage cannot be recovered, in accordance with the general practice as regards risk-based liability under German law.[562] The Directive is without prejudice to national law regarding non-material damage.[563]
- At §§ 7–9 ProdHaftG, the scope and mode of compensation for cases of death or personal injury are set out in detail, as is customary in risk-based liability regimes. These provisions are not mandated or forbidden by the Directive; they stand in direct relation to §§ 842–845 BGB.[564] The ProdHaftG is more generous than the BGB, since in the case of death it allows for recovery of the costs of attempted medical treatment as well as the loss of earnings or earning power suffered by the deceased before his or her death. As for cases of physical injury, § 8 ProdHaftG corresponds to the case law under the BGB.

---

[554] Art. 5 of Directive 85/374, which is implemented through § 5 ProdHaftG.

[555] Art. 8 of Directive 85/374, which is implemented through § 6 ProdHaftG.

[556] Art. 10 of Directive 85/374, which is implemented through § 12 ProdHaftG.

[557] Art. 11 of Directive 85/374, which is implemented through § 13 ProdHaftG.

[558] Art. 12 of Directive 85/374, which is implemented through § 14 ProdHaftG.

[559] The general approach of German law as regards liability not based on conduct, including the principles relating to *Gefährdungshaftung*, is outlined *supra*, 6.1.1.

[560] See *supra*, **6.G.1.** and notes thereafter.

[561] The exhaustive list technique is discussed *supra*, Chapter I, **1.G.26.–27.** and notes thereafter.

[562] See *supra*, **6.G.2.**, Note (2).

[563] Art. 9 *in fine* of Directive 85/374.

[564] On these provisions, see *supra*, Chapter II, 2.1.1., Introductory Note under b), as well as *infra*, Chapter VIII, 8.5.1.

(3) The regime of the ProdHaftG differs from product liability pursuant to § 823 BGB in a number of significant respects:[565]

-   The main difference lies of course in the basis for liability. The specific regime developed in the BGH case law for product liability under § 823 remains ultimately based on fault. By contrast, the ProdHaftG creates a risk-based regime (*Gefährdungshaftung*), under which the fault of the manufacturer or the violation of a *Verkehrspflicht* are not relevant; the precise nature of liability under the ProdHaftG is still disputed, however, as is seen under the case below, dealing with "product development risk" (*Entwicklungsfehler*).[566]
-   The definition of "defect" at § 3 ProdHaftG is broadly co-terminous with the concept of defect which underpins the *Verkehrspflicht* incumbent upon the manufacturer pursuant to § 823(1) BGB,[567] with one exception. While the wording § 3 ProdHaftG encompasses manufacturing defects (*Fabrikationsfehler*),[568] design defects (*Konstruktionsfehler*)[569] and instruction defects (*Instruktionsfehler*),[570] it does not extend to breaches of the duty to monitor products (*Produktbeobachtungspflicht*) once they have been released on the market.[571] Indeed, pursuant to § 3(1)(c) ProdHaftG, the time when the product was put on the market is relevant in order to determine if there was a defect, and accordingly shortcomings which appear only later, in the light of additional knowledge or experience, are excluded from the definition.
-   The ProdHaftG provides a narrower scope of protection, since it does not extend to the "other rights" mentioned in § 823 BGB, and in particular to the *Recht am Gewerbebetrieb*.[572]
-   A ceiling is put on recovery of personal injury under the ProdHaftG, whereas there is no ceiling under § 823 BGB.
-   Non-material damage cannot be recovered (*Schmerzensgeld*) under the ProdHaftG, contrary to § 823 BGB.[573]
-   For damage to property, there is a deductible of DEM 1125 at § 11 ProdHaftG, whereas there is no deductible under § 823 BGB.

---

[565] See in general Staudinger-Oechsler, Intro ProdHaftG at 267–8, para. 51–3; P. Marburger, "Grundsatzfragen des Haftungsrechts unter dem Einfluß der gesetzlichen Regelungen zur Produzenten- und zur Umwelthaftung" (1992) 192 AcP 1 at 5–6.

[566] See the discussion of the various positions in Larenz/Canaris at 643–4; Marburger, ibid. at 10–2; Münchener-Cahn, § 1 ProdHaftG at 2135–6, para. 2–3.

[567] See T. Wieckhorst, "Vom Produzentenfehler zum Produktfehler des § 3 ProdHaftG" (1995) 66 VersR 1005.

[568] For an instance of manufacturing defect, see *supra*, **6.G.24.**

[569] For an instance of design defect, see *supra*, **6.G.25.**

[570] For an instance of instruction defect, see *supra*, **6.G.26.**

[571] See P. Marburger, "Grundsatzfragen des Haftungsrechts unter dem Einfluß der gesetzlichen Regelungen zur Produzenten- und zur Umwelthaftung" (1992) 192 AcP 1 at 4. The duty is discussed *supra*, **6.G.27.**

[572] See Münchener-Cahn, § 1 ProdHaftG at 2137–8, para. 6. On the "other rights", see *supra*, Chapter I, 1.4.3., Introductory Note under b). On the *Recht am Gewerbebetrieb*, see *supra*, Chapter II, 2.3.2., Introductory Note under d) as well as **2.G.37.** and notes thereafter.

[573] See Staudinger-Oechsler, § 1 ProdHaftG at 301, para. 36–7.

– At § 1 ProdHaftG, unlike § 823 BGB, the range of protected property is restricted, since it is limited to property used or consumed for private purposes.[574]

– § 1 ProdHaftG also excludes from the scope of protection of the Act damage to the defective product itself. It will be recalled that, pursuant to a controversial line of BGH case law on "creeping damage" (*Weiterfresserschaden*), damage caused by a component to a defective product can be recovered under § 823 BGB, provided that the damage is not identical with the loss in value flowing from the defect in the component (*Mangelunwert*).[575] German authors disagree as to whether such "creeping damages" are excluded from the scope of the ProdHaftG.[576] On the one hand, it appears that it was the intention of the Member States to ensure that "creeping damage" cases were excluded from Directive 85/374; on the other hand, since a component is a product in and of itself, pursuant to Article 1 of Directive 85/374 and § 2 ProdHaftG, it could be argued that the rest of the product in which a component has been incorporated constitutes "another product" relative to that component.

In the light of the above, even if the ProdHaftG is meant to offer better protection to the victim in doing away with the notion of fault, it can be seen that in practice it suffers from a fair number of gaps by comparison with § 823 BGB. It will accordingly come as no surprise that the ProdHaftG has not been widely used since its coming into force in 1990, and that claims under § 1 ProdHaftG have generally been combined with claims under § 823 BGB in order to attempt to recover as much as possible.

(4) Pursuant to § 15(1) ProdHaftG, an important product category is left outside the field of application of the ProdHaftG, namely pharmaceutical products.[577] They are in fact covered by another, more specific product liability regime at §§ 84 ff. of the *Arzneimittelgesetz* (AMG).[578] The AMG, although enacted in 1976, is broadly similar to the ProdHaftG, except as regards the treatment of product development risks.

According to § 84(1) AMG, the drug manufacturer is liable for physical damage resulting from "such injurious effects as may arise in the course of normal use of pharmaceutical products, which are unjustifiable in the light of medical knowledge and which find their source in the development or manufacture" of the drug. That provision covers the categories of manufacture (*Fabrikationsfehler*) and design (*Konstruktionsfehler*) defects. For liability to arise, the victim must prove that the injurious effects of the product were excessive, when balanced against its purpose: thus it is to be expected that medication

---

[574] See Münchener-Cahn, § 1 ProdHaftG at 2140–1, para. 11–6; Staudinger-Oechsler, § 1 ProdHaftG at 298–300, para. 21–31.

[575] See *supra*, **6.G.24.**, Note (7).

[576] See Larenz/Canaris at 646–7; Münchener-Cahn, § 1 ProdHaftG at 2138–9, para. 9–10; Staudinger-Oechsler, § 1 ProdHaftG at 294, para. 9–20; P. Marburger, "Grundsatzfragen des Haftungsrechts unter dem Einfluß der gesetzlichen Regelungen zur Produzenten- und zur Umwelthaftung" (1992) 192 AcP 1 at 6–10.

[577] At Art. 14, Directive 85/374 specifically mentions that it applies without prejudice to other "special liability systems" which may have existed at the time when it was enacted. This did not mean that Member States could exclude the application of the Directive where such "special liability systems" apply. Accordingly, it must be assumed that § 84 AMG constitutes the German implementation of the Directive as regards pharmaceutical products. As to whether that represents a correct implementation of Directive 85/374, see Howells at 142 and D. Vogel, *Die Produkthaftung des Arzneimittelherstellers nach schweizerischem und deutschem Recht mit zusätzlichen Berücksichtigung der EG-Produkthaftungs-Richtlinie und weiterer Rechtsordnungen* (Zürich: Schulthess, 1991) at 113–6.

[578] Drug Act of 24 August 1976, BGBl.I.2995.

used in e.g. cancer treatments will have side-effects which could not be accepted for pain-killers that are available over the shop counter.

§ 84(2) AMG concerns instruction defects (*Instruktionsfehler*): the drug manufacturer is also liable for physical damage resulting from "labelling, instructions for use or instructions to professionals which did not correspond to medical knowledge".

No indication is given in either § 84(1) or (2) AMG as to the moment in time when medical knowledge must be ascertained: it could be either the time when the product was put into circulation or a later point in time, such as the time when a claim was put forward under the AMG. If the relevant point in time is the former, the manufacturer is not liable for product development risks; if the relevant point in time is the latter, it is. German authors are not unanimous on that point, but most authors would make the manufacturer liable for product development risks, especially as the Contergan tragedy,[579] in response to which the AMG was enacted, was precisely a case where the injurious side-effects of the product were not known or foreseeable when the products were put into circulation.[580] If the AMG makes the drug manufacturer liable for product development risks, in contrast with other manufacturers whose situation is governed by the ProdHaftG, a question could arise as to whether such a targeted restriction on the availability of the product development risk defence is compatible with Directive 85/374.

BGH, 9 May 1995[581]   **6.G.35.**

PRODUCT DEVELOPMENT RISK

Mineral water bottle explodes

*The "product development risk"defence at Article 7(e) of Directive 85/374 and § 1(2)5 ProdHaftG applies only to design defects (*Konstruktionsfehler*). The manufacturer cannot be exonerated under the ProdHaftG even if the defective product was the "odd unit" affected by a manufacturing defect despite all reasonable precautions.*

Facts: The defendant was a bottler of sparkling mineral water. The water was distributed in reusable glass bottles. When the bottles were brought back to the bottler, they were first examined visually by workers (while they were still in plastic cases), to eliminate damaged or foreign bottles. They were then mechanically taken out of the case, and taken through the washing equipment. Afterwards, they were visually examined again by other workers as they moved along a conveyor belt, and then passed through an "electronic inspector", a machine which electronically examined the bottom and the neck of the bottle to detect any damage to the glass. Two further visual inspections followed before the bottles were brought to the filling installation. Prior to filling, the bottles were tested by pressurizing them up to 5 bar, i.e. 1,7 bar higher than the pressure normally resulting from sparkling mineral water. Two further visual inspections occurred after the bottles had been filled.

The nine-year old plaintiff suffered serious eye injury when a mineral water bottle exploded as she was carrying it. It appeared from the evidence that the explosion resulted from the presence of a 4 mm chip in the bottle.

The plaintiff sued the defendant, both under § 1 ProdHaftG and (in order to obtain *Schmerzensgeld*) under § 823 BGB.

---

[579] Contergan was the German trademark for thalidomide.

[580] See Larenz/Canaris at 649 as well as E. Deutsch, "Arzneimittelschaden: Gefährdungshaftung, Verschuldenshaftung, Staatshaftung" in *Festschrift für Karl Larenz* (München: Beck, 1983) 111 at 115.

[581] BGHZ 129, 353. Translation by Y.P. Salmon.

Held: The court of first instance and the court of appeal dismissed the claim. The BGH reversed the decision of the court of appeal and remitted the case for further consideration.

Judgment: "a) If the bottle exploded because of the chip, then the defendant is liable to the plaintiff for her material damage, under the first sentence of §1(1) ProdHaftG . . .

b) However, even if the mineral water bottle did not burst because of the chip, but rather because of a hairline crack in another area . . ., then the claim under the first sentence of § 1(1) ProdHaftG would still not be defeated because the defect could not be detected under the state of science and technology [at the time], contrary to what the court of appeal held.

aa) The court of appeal rightly took as a starting point that a product is to be considered defective, within the meaning of § 3(1) ProdHaftG, if it does not afford the safety which may justifiably be expected under the circumstances. The court of appeal correctly went on to find that a consumer expects a bottle of sparkling mineral water to be free from damage, including hairline cracks and microfissures, which could provoke an explosion . . . If a bottle presents such a fissure . . ., it suffers from a so-called manufacturing defect (*Fabrikationsfehler*), even if it was conceivably the 'odd unit' that slipped through the controls (*Ausreißer*) [references omitted].

bb) Even if the production of such an 'odd unit' cannot be avoided despite all reasonable precautions, it still does not fall within the class of defects that could not have been detected in the light of the state of the art in science and technology at the time, within the meaning of Art. 7(e) of Directive 85/374 or of § 1(2)5 ProdHaftG, which implements the Directive in German law.

Both these provisions aim to exclude liability in cases involving so-called development risks (*Entwicklungsrisiken*) [references omitted], namely cases where the dangerous property of the product that led to the injury could not be discovered at the time the product was put into circulation, even with all the means at the disposal of science and technology [references omitted]. The liability without fault of the manufacturer [under the ProdHaftG] reaches no further than what was objectively feasible, using the knowledge about risks that was available at the time the product was put into circulation [references omitted]. Accordingly, the concept of 'development risks' extends only to those risks which are inherent in the design of the product and which could not be avoided given the state of the art in technology at the time [references omitted]; it does not include unavoidable manufacturing defects. During the preparation of Directive 85/374, it was agreed that the conditions of Art. 7(e) would only be fulfilled by a so-called design defect (*Konstruktionsfehler*), and not by a manufacturing defect (*Fabrikationsfehler*). Similarly, the German legislature wanted to exclude from the scope of the ProdHaftG only those dangers . . . which could not be detected at the development and design phase despite all reasonable care . . .

However, the risks associated with employing re-usable glass bottles for carbonated beverages have been known for a long time . . . If the filling process causes defects . . . to appear . . . in the re-useable bottles or if pre-existing hairline cracks remain undetected, we are not facing development defects incurred at the design stage. Liability for such so-called 'odd units' cannot be defeated by § 1(2)5 ProdHaftG . . .

c) There is no need to make a preliminary reference to the ECJ in this matter . . .

The present case . . . is not about the interpretation of the concept of the state of the scientific knowledge. Rather it concerns whether and how far the German legislature made use of the possibility which it had, pursuant to Art. 15(1)(b) of Directive 85/374, to make exceptions from Art. 7(b) of the Directive and thus allow the manufacturer to be held liable [for product development risks]. This is a question for the national courts alone. But even if the interpretation of a term used in a Community Directive is at stake, a reference to the ECJ is only required if the point of interpretation is controversial in case law or legal writing [reference omitted], or if the court wishes to depart from the case law of the ECJ on a point material to the case [reference omitted]. The present case does not fulfil either of these conditions."

Notes

(1) The annotated case, in addition to being the most significant case on the ProdHaftG, is noteworthy in many respects.

The case touches upon the very nature of liability under the ProdHaftG. It concerned a manufacturing defect (*Fabrikationsfehler*), in that the particular bottle that caused the injury was somehow damaged during the refilling process. The manufacturer had alleged that the defective bottle was the "odd unit" (*Ausreißer*) which suffered from a manufacturing defect despite all the precautions taken in the re-filling process. Under § 823 BGB, the manufacturer is not liable for the injury caused by such an "odd unit".[582] The manufacturer argued that it should be exonerated under the ProdHaftG as well, pursuant to § 1(2)5, which implements in German law the "product development risk" defence found at Article 7(e) of Directive 85/374.

In dealing with that argument, the BGH proceeded to interpret § 1(2)5 ProdHaftG in the light of the established categories of product liability under § 823 BGB. The reasoning of the BGH was as follows. The "odd units" are those which end up defective despite all reasonable precautions: while they could fall under the wording of Article 7(e) of Directive 85/374 or § 1(2)5 ProdHaftG, it was the intention of the institutions that enacted those provisions that they should apply only to design defects (*Konstruktionsfehler*) and not to manufacturing defects such as here affected the "odd" bottle. Accordingly, the manufacturer could not invoke § 1(2)5 ProdHaftG in defence, and was therefore liable pursuant to § 1(1) ProdHaftG, since the conditions for liability were met (injury, defect and causation).

While they agree with the BGH as to the result, legal writers have criticized the reasoning of the BGH on the ground that it superimposes upon Article 7(e) of Directive 85/374 and § 1(2)5 ProdHaftG the categories of defects developed under § 823 BGB, whereas neither the Directive nor the ProdHaftG appears to be structured along those lines.[583] Furthermore, there is no reason why the applicability of the "product development risk" should be excluded *a priori* for manufacturing defects: even if such a case should be rare, it is conceivable that a deficiency in the manufacturing process could not have been discovered in the state of scientific and technical knowledge at the time of manufacture (e.g. it was not known that such a mishap in the manufacturing process could happen), thus constituting a "product development" defect within the meaning of Article 7(e) of Directive 85/374 or § 1(2)5 ProdHaftG.[584] It might have been preferable for the BGH to have avoided the discussion of the various types of defects altogether and instead simply to have found that the "odd unit" problem is not a case of "development risk" at all, since the risk is usually known, even if it is unavoidable.[585]

---

[582] See *supra*, **6.G.24.**, Note (6). In the annotated case, the victim had also pleaded § 823 BGB. In its ruling, the BGH dealt with that claim as well, and it actually held that the defective bottle was not an "odd unit" since, on the facts, the production controls of the manufacturer were not sufficient.

[583] See Staudinger-Oechsler, § 1 ProdHaftG at 321, para. 118–20 and U. Foerste, Comment, (1995) 50 JZ 1063. But see Münchener-Cahn, § 1 ProdHaftG at 2149–52, para. 47–53.

[584] Foerste, ibid. See also *Clerk & Lindsell on Torts* at 506, para. 9–42, who conclude that the Directive and the UK Consumer Protection Act 1987 make it difficult for manufacturers to escape liability for manufacturing defects, although "the 'development risks' defence . . . may on occasion be relevant".

[585] It will be recalled that in the *Fowl pest* case, *supra*, **6.G.24.**, the BGH seemed to have considered that the "odd unit" (*Ausreißer*) defence was distinct from the "development risk" defence (see Note (6) thereunder).

(2) In the light of the above, it is interesting to compare the means of defence available to the manufacturer under § 823 BGB and under the ProdHaftG. Under § 823 BGB, the manufacturer essentially has two possible defences, namely that the defect—irrespective of its nature—could not be foreseen given the state of scientific and technical knowledge at the time (*Entwicklungsfehler*) and, in the case of manufacturing defects (*Fabrikations-fehler*) only, that the defective product was the "odd unit" (*Ausreißer*) which escaped all reasonable precautions in the manufacturing process.[586] It is clear from the annotated case that the *Ausreißer* defence is not available under the ProdHaftG, and that the "product development risk" defence is available only for design defects (*Konstruktionsfehler*) and probably also for instruction defects (*Instruktionsfehler*).[587]

In the end, therefore, it seems beyond question that under the ProdHaftG, liability for manufacturing defects is not dependent on fault and is truly risk-based (*Gefährdungshaftung*).[588]

As for liability for design and instruction defects, the situation is less clear, since the availability of the "product development risk" defence turns the conduct of the manu-facturer into an issue: was the risk of injury foreseeable for the manufacturer or not? On the one hand, certain commentators argue that the difference from § 823 BGB is then fairly limited, and that the ProdHaftG is not much stricter than fault-based liability.[589] On the other hand, other commentators would restrict the ambit of the "product devel-opment risk" defence in the same way as the "unavoidable event" defence of § 7(2) StVG:[590] only risks which were not foreseeable by the "ideal manufacturer" should lead to exoneration.[591] The judgment of the ECJ in *Commission* v. *UK* would seem to give weight to the latter opinion.[592]

(3) In the annotated case, the BGH also declined to make a preliminary reference to the ECJ (under c). The BGH argued that it was not interpreting Directive 85/374, but rather assessing how far the German legislature had made use of the possibility, created by Article 15(1)(b) of Directive 85/374, of not providing a "product development risk" defence. Yet there is no evidence in the ProdHaftG that the German legislature intended to use Article 15(1)(b) of the Directive. Quite to the contrary, § 1(2)5 is almost identical with Article 7(e) of the Directive.[593]

The BGH also held that it was not bound to make a reference to the ECJ, on the rather surprising grounds that there would be no disagreement in case law or literature on the

---

[586] See *supra*, 6.3.1.A.

[587] In the annotated case, the BGH seems to imply that the "product development risk" defence would not apply to instruction defects (*Instruktionsfehler*), which does not appear to be correct, since it is often the case, especially with pharmaceutical products, that the danger against which the user should have been warned was not known in the state of scientific and technical knowledge at the time when the product was put on the market.

[588] See Staudinger-Oechsler, Intro ProdHaftG at 261–2, para. 37.

[589] See Staudinger-Oechsler, Intro ProdHaftG at 262–3, para. 38–42.

[590] See *supra*, **6.G.12.**, Note (3) as well as **6.G.15.** and notes thereafter.

[591] See Larenz/Canaris at 645–6. See also P. Marburger, "Grundsatzfragen des Haftungsrechts unter dem Einfluß der gesetzlichen Regelungen zur Produzenten- und zur Umwelthaftung" (1992) 192 AcP 1 at 12–4.

[592] See *infra*, **6.EC.39.**

[593] It is interesting to note that the Cour de cassation, in a decision of 9 July 1996, also made a questionable use of Article 15(1)(b) of Directive 85/374 in order to dismiss an argument that the injury had resulted from the realization of a product development risk: *supra*, **6.F.30.** and Note (4) thereafter.

issue and that it did not intend to deviate from the case law of the ECJ (there was none at the time).

The decision of the BGH in the annotated case had a bearing on the interpretation of Directive 85/374, even if only indirectly. It is certainly sensible in its result, even if its reasoning is open to criticism. Nonetheless, it is not widely known outside Germany, and as such it is not impossible that, if courts in other Member States are not aware of the decision or disagree with the BGH, the interpretation of such a central concept in Directive 85/374 as the "product development risk" may differ from one Member State to another.[594] It is regrettable that the matter was not referred to the ECJ so as to ensure that the issue would be authoritatively settled for the whole of the EC.

6.3.3.B. FRENCH LAW

Introductory Note

France was the last EU Member State to implement Directive 85/374. With the Act 98–389 of 19 May 1998, reproduced and reviewed below, a new liability regime was introduced at Articles 1386–1 to 1386–18 of the *Code civil*.

It would be inaccurate, however, to state that France had remained idle between the adoption of Directive 85/374 by the Council of the European Union in 1985 and its implementation by France in 1998. In view of the difficulties encountered with the implementation process,[595] French courts, under the lead of the Cour de cassation, took it upon themselves to interpret French law in such a way as to introduce Directive 85/374 in the case law. The development of the contractual *obligation de sécurité* incumbent upon the manufacturer and trade seller, which was extended beyond the contractual realm to third-party victims of defective products, is directly attributable to the willingness of French courts to construe French law in the light of the Directive.[596] The case reproduced below provides a clear example of that willingness.[597]

---

[594] See G. Howells, "Product Liability" in A.S. Hartkamp et al., (eds.), *Towards a European Civil Code*, 2nd ed. (Nijmegen: Ars Aequi Libri, 1998) 449 at 459–60.

[595] A first draft bill was prepared by a committee headed by J. Ghestin and presented in 1987. It was very ambitious, since it would have not only implemented Directive 85/374, but also completely modified the liability rules of manufacturers and trade sellers. The proposal was watered down when it was sent to the French National Assembly, but nonetheless the issue of product development risks proved a major stumbling block. The proposal was withdrawn in 1992. Another bill was presented in 1993 but failed to be adopted before the Assembly was dissolved in 1997. Since, in the meantime, the ECJ had condemned France, the threat of a procedure under Article 171 EC Treaty (with fines) prompted the French National Assembly finally to enact implementing legislation in 1998. See Viney and Jourdain, *Conditions* at 787–8, para. 785.

[596] See *supra*, 6.3.1.B., Introductory Note under f) and g) as well as **6.F.28.** and notes thereafter.

[597] For another example where French product liability law was construed in the light of Directive 85/374, see *supra*, **6.F.30.**

INTERPRETATION OF NATIONAL LAW IN LIGHT OF DIRECTIVE 85/374

Slow release tablets

A product is defective when it does not provide the safety which a person is entitled to expect.

Facts: The defendant, a manufacturer of pharmaceutical products, marketed under the name "Kaléorid" a product containing potassium chloride, which was formulated not as a conventional capsule, but rather as a slow release tablet. Such a tablet is not dissolved in the stomach; instead it passes through to the intestine, thereby ensuring that the medication is released for the duration of the digestion process. The plaintiff was pre-scribed Kaléorid in June 1988. In October 1988, he had to undergo emergency surgery following severe inflam-mation of the lower abdomen. Surgery revealed that the inflammation was caused by a Kaléorid tablet that became stuck in the plaintiff's appendix. The plaintiff sued the defendant under Article 1147 C.civ.

Held: The court of first instance dismissed the claim. The court of appeal reversed the judgment of the court of first instance and allowed the claim. The Cour de cassation upheld the decision of the court of appeal.

Judgment: "Against the judgment of the court of appeal which found it . . . liable, the [defendant] argues that the obligation not to endanger safety (*obligation de sécurité*) imposed upon a pharma-ceutical producer ceases with the delivery of a product whose therapeutic effect is in accordance with established scientific knowledge and which does not normally present for the user any incon-venience or danger exceeding the expected therapeutic effect. That obligation does not automati-cally reach so far as to cover all injury which could result from the use of the pharmaceutical product. Thus, when it adopted the expert report without finding that the product was defective, the court of appeal infringed Article 1147 C.civ.

However, the producer must deliver products that are free from any defect which could create a risk for persons or property, that is to say a product which provides the safety which a person is enti-tled to expect. It is evident from the findings of the court of appeal that the harm suffered by [the plaintiff] is imputable to the very characteristics of the tablet's indigestible capsule which, when it remained in the victim's intestine, caused the inflammation and its consequences. These findings established that the product was defective, and the court of appeal thus provided a legal justifica-tion for its decision."

Notes

(1) As has already been seen,[599] in a line of case law starting with the decision of 20 March 1989[600] and confirmed in the decision of 17 January 1995,[601] the Cour de cassa-tion has imposed on the manufacturer and the trade seller an *obligation de sécurité* in respect of their products, namely a duty to "deliver products that are free from any defect which could create a risk for persons or property".

At issue in the annotated case was the definition of "defect" for the purposes of that duty. The victim had been injured because a slow release tablet had become trapped in his appendix. He argued that the tablet was defective. The manufacturer replied that the

[598] JCP 1998.II.10049, D 1998.IR.96. Translation by Y.P. Salmon.
[599] See *supra*, 6.3.1.B., Introductory Note under f) and g).
[600] Cass. civ. 1re, 20 March 1989, D 1989.Jur.381.
[601] *Supra*, **6.F.28.**

tablet, which contained potassium chloride, produced therapeutic effects in line with established scientific and technical knowledge, and that any disadvantages which might result from its use did not exceed those therapeutical benefits. On the basis of this balancing of risks and benefits, the manufacturer concluded that the product was not "defective". It is worth noting that such a balancing analysis is now being put forward as representing the state of product liability law in the US in the *Restatement (Third) on Torts: Product Liability*.[602]

Dismissing the argument, the Cour de cassation decided to apply a consumer expectation test, taken directly from Directive 85/374: a product is defective when it does not "provide the safety which a person is entitled to expect". The report of the *conseiller rapporteur* makes it very clear that in deciding as it did, the Cour de cassation would keep the *obligation de sécurité* in line with Directive 85/374. When consumer expectations (instead of a risk-benefit analysis) are taken as the criterion, it can hardly be denied that pharmaceutical products that can remain trapped in the appendix and cause severe complications are defective. Since the victim had succeeded in establishing that his injury was caused by the tablet, the liability of the manufacturer was thus engaged.

(2) The link between the French regimes of liability for defective products as they may arise in contract or tort and Directive 85/374 was made even more explicit in a further decision of 28 April 1998 concerning HIV-infected blood products, where the Cour de cassation began its reasoning as follows: "Having regard to Articles 1147 and 1384(1) C.civ., interpreted in the light of Directive 85/374".[603] In that decision, the Cour de cassation confirmed its previous decision of 17 January 1995 whereby the liability of the manufacturer for defective products applies irrespective of whether the victim is party to a contract with—or a contract chain leading to—the manufacturer.

Code civil[604]   **6.F.37.**

"Title IVbis—Liability for defective products
Art. 1386–1. The producer shall be liable for the injury caused by a defect in his product, irrespective of whether he is contractually bound to the victim or not.
Art. 1386–2. The provisions of this Title shall apply to compensation for injury arising from an interference with a person or with property other than the defective product itself.
Art. 1386–3. 'Product' means every moveable property, even if incorporated in an immoveable property . . . Electricity shall be deemed to be a product.
Art. 1386–4. A product is defective within the meaning of this Title when it does not provide the safety which a person is entitled to expect.
    In ascertaining the safety which a person is entitled to expect, all circumstances shall be taken into account, including the presentation of the product, the use to which one could reasonably expect that it would be put and the time when it was put into circulation.

---

[602] See *supra*, 6.3.1.C., Introductory Note under f). The annotated case would fall under § 2(b) of the *Restatement* (design defect). See also D. Owen, "American Products Liability Law Restated" (1998) 6 Cons LJ 161 at 173–7.
[603] Cass. civ. 1re, 28 April 1998, JCP 1998.II.10088.
[604] Articles added by the Loi 98–389 relative à la responsabilité du fait des produits défectueux of 19 May 1998, JO, 21 May 1998, D 1998.Lég.184.

A product shall not be considered defective for the sole reason that another better product was subsequently put into circulation.

Art. 1386–5.   A product is put into circulation when the producer voluntarily releases it from its possession.

A product can only be put into circulation once.

Art. 1386–6.   'Producer' shall mean, when acting in the course of a business, the manufacturer of a finished product, the producer of any raw material or the manufacturer of a component part.

Any person shall be deemed to be a producer if he acts in the course of a business and:

(1) by putting his name, trade mark or other distinguishing feature on the product, presents himself as its producer;

(2) imports into the Community a product for sale, hire (with or without a promise to sell) or any other form of distribution . . .

Art. 1386–7.   Any person who sells, hires (with the exception of leasing and hires that can be assimilated to leasing) or otherwise supplies a product in the course of a business shall be liable for product defects as if he were the producer.

The contributory recourse of the supplier against the producer shall follow the same rules as the claim of the direct victim. However, the supplier must act within a year from the filing of the claim against him.

Art. 1386–9.   The plaintiff shall be required to prove the damage, the defect and the causal relationship between defect and damage.

Art. 1386–10.   The producer may be held liable for the defect even if the product was manufactured according to established knowledge or existing norms, or was approved by the Administration.

Art. 1386–11.   The producer shall be liable by virtue of the law (*responsable de plein droit*) unless he proves:

(1) that he did not put the product into circulation; or

(2) that, having regard to the circumstances, it is probable that the defect which caused the damage did not exist at the time when the product was put into circulation by him or that this defect came into being afterwards; or

(3) that the product was not destined to be sold or otherwise distributed;

(4) that the state of scientific and technical knowledge at the time when he put the product into circulation was not such as to enable the existence of the defect to be discovered; or

(5) that the defect is due to compliance of the product with mandatory legislation or regulation.

The producer of a component part shall not be liable either if he proves that the defect is attributable to the design of the product in which the component has been fitted or to the instructions given by the producer of the product.

Art. 1386–12   The means of exoneration provided for at Article 1386–11(4) shall not be available to the producer if the injury was caused by a part of the human body or products taken from the human body.

The means of exoneration provided for at Article 1386–11(4) and (5) shall not be available to the producer if he did not take appropriate measures to prevent the injurious consequences of a defect which became apparent within 10 years after the product was put into circulation . . .

Art. 1386–15.   Contractual clauses which aim to exclude or limit liability for defective products are prohibited and deemed not to have been included in the contract.

However, clauses included in a contract between traders are valid to the extent that they concern damage to property which the victim does not use mainly for private use or consumption.

Art. 1386–16. Save where the producer was at fault, the liability of the producer under this Title shall be extinguished 10 years after the date on which the producer put into circulation the actual product which caused the damage, unless the victim has in the meantime instituted court proceedings . . .

Art. 1386–18. The provisions of this Title are without prejudice to the rights which the victim of injury may hold under the law of contractual or extra-contractual liability or under a specific liability regime.

The producer shall remain liable for the consequences of his own fault and that of persons for whom he is responsible."

Notes

(1) With the introduction of Title IVbis (Articles 1386–1 to 1386–18) in the *Code civil*, the French National Assembly implemented Directive 85/374 in French law. In general, these Articles track the corresponding provisions of the Directive; accordingly, the provisions dealing with joint and several liability,[605] intervening acts of the victim,[606] intervening acts of third parties[607] and limitation[608] have not been reproduced above, since they are for all intents and purposes identical to the text of Directive 85/374. France has made use of the options given in the Directive as follows:

– at Article 1386–11(4), France did not exclude the defence of "product development risk", as it could have done pursuant to Article 15(1)(b) of Directive 85/374;[609]
– no ceiling amount was set on liability for personal injury (see Article 16 of Directive 85/374).

(2) On a number of points, however, Title IVbis differs from or adds to Directive 85/374, generally in such a way as to improve the position of the victim. The main ones are:

– Article 1386–2 C.civ. defines the scope of protection more generally than Article 9 of the Directive. In particular, there is no deductible for property damage, as provided for at Article 9(b) of the Directive.[610] Furthermore, liability for property damage is not limited to property used or consumed for private purposes, as provided for by Article 9(b)(i) and (ii) of the Directive. Instead, liability under Title IVbis is extended to all damage to property other than the product itself, but under Article 1386–15(2),

---

[605] Art. 1386–8 C.civ., implementing Art. 5 of Directive 85/374. Art. 1386–8 only mentions the manufacturer of a defective component and the manufacturer of the whole product, but it is thought that, in line with the general principles of French tort law, all other defendants would also be liable *in solidum*: see C. Larroumet, "La responsabilité du fait des produits défectueux après la loi du 19 mai 1998" D 1998.Chron.311 at 312–3. On liability *in solidum*, see *infra*, Chapter IV, **4.F.38.–39.** and Notes (1) to (3) thereafter.

[606] Art. 1386–13 C.civ., implementing Art. 8(2) of Directive 85/374.

[607] Art. 1386–14 C.civ., implementing Art. 8(1) of Directive 85/374.

[608] Art. 1386–17 C.civ., implementing Art. 10 of Directive 85/374.

[609] On the discussions surrounding that issue, see P. Jourdain, "Commentaire de la loi n° 98–389 du 19 mai 1998 sur la responsabilité du fait des produits défectueux" JCP(E) 1998.1204 at 1211–2.

[610] See Viney and Jourdain, *Conditions* at 803, para. 787–7; Jourdain, ibid. at 1207.

undertakings are allowed to exclude liability for damage to "non-private" property *as between themselves.*[611]

– The range of persons potentially liable under Title IVbis is broader than contemplated in the Directive. While Article 1386–6 C.civ. is more or less co-terminous with Article 3(1) of the Directive, Article 1386–7 C.civ. differs from Article 3(3) of the Directive in that, instead of being able to escape liability if they direct the victim to the producer, suppliers remain liable but can look to the producer for indemnity. Commentators have argued that Article 1386–7 C.civ. is more consistent with French law, whereby all the members of the distribution chain remain liable to the victim.[612]

– At Article 1386–12(2), the French legislature has sought to introduce into French law an obligation to monitor products, on the model of the German *Produktbeobachtungspflicht,*[613] by depriving manufacturers of the "product development risk" and "mandatory rule" defences if they fail to remedy defects which appear within 10 years after the product is put into circulation.[614]

– "Putting the product into circulation" is defined at Article 1386–5 C.civ., since the notion was not used in French law.[615]

– Because of concerns arising from the contaminated blood scandal, Article 1386–12(1) C.civ. excludes the "product development risk" defence in the case of products coming or derived from the human body.[616]

– If the producer was at fault, Article 1386–16 provides that claims under Title IVbis are not extinguished 10 years after the product has been put into circulation.[617]

While Article 13 of the Directive expressly preserves *existing* liability regimes which may apply to product liability, nowhere in the Directive is there any indication that it would constitute a *minimum* harmonization measure, which Member States could implement more favourably for the consumer.[618] The Commission has taken France before the ECJ for incorrect implementation of Directive 85/374 with respect to the first three points listed above.[619]

---

[611] See C. Larroumet, "La responsabilité du fait des produits défectueux après la loi du 19 mai 1998" D 1998.Chron.311 at 313, 314; Jourdain, ibid.

[612] See Larroumet, ibid. at 313. See also Viney and Jourdain, *Conditions* at 797, para. 786–8; Jourdain, ibid. at 1208.

[613] See *supra,* **6.G.27.** and notes thereafter.

[614] See Viney and Jourdain, *Conditions* at 802–3, para. 787–6; C. Larroumet, "La responsabilité du fait des produits défectueux après la loi du 19 mai 1998" D 1998.Chron.311 at 315–6; P. Jourdain, "Commentaire de la loi n° 98–389 du 19 mai 1998 sur la responsabilité du fait des produits défectueux" JCP(E) 1998.1204 at 1213.

[615] See Viney and Jourdain, *Conditions* at 794, para. 786–4; Larroumet, ibid. at 314–5; Jourdain, ibid. at 1209.

[616] See Viney and Jourdain, *Conditions* at 801–2, para. 785–5; Larroumet, ibid. at 315–6; Jourdain, ibid. at 1212–3; A. Laude, "La responsabilité des produits de santé" D 1999.Chron.189. A similar differentiation of treatment between manufacturers is present in German law, with pharmaceutical companies having to bear product development risks pursuant to § 84 AMG, while other manufacturers are relieved of them under the ProdHaftG: see *supra,* **6.G.34.**, Note (4).

[617] See Viney and Jourdain, *Conditions* at 795, para. 786–6; Jourdain, ibid. at 1214.

[618] With the exception of those issues where Member States were left with a choice, at Articles 15 and 16 of the Directive.

[619] See "Defective products: Commission decides to take Greece and France to Court of Justice over failure to implement Directive correctly" Press Release IP 00/24 (13 January 2000).

(3) The regime of Title IVbis takes a special place in relation to the existing product liability regimes under contract or tort law.[620]

First, Title IVbis is an autonomous title of Book Three of the *Code civil*, on the same footing as Title III on contracts in general (including contractual liability) and Title IV on delictual liability; it does not therefore fall on either side of the contract/tort divide under French law. In line with that treatment, Article 1386–1 C.civ. specifies that liability under Title IVbis arises irrespective of the presence of any contractual relationship. Because Title IVbis is so detached from the traditional liability regimes under the *Code civil*, some commentators[621] are of the opinion that Directive 85/374 should rather have been implemented in a separate statute (as is the case for most specific liability regimes in France, including the *Loi Badinter*[622]).

Secondly, the French legislature clearly intended Title IVbis to constitute a head of liability without fault, as can be seen from Article 1386–11 C.civ., which states that the manufacturer is liable "by virtue of the law" (*de plein droit*), and not because of any fault.[623] It remains to be seen how that statement can be reconciled with the "product development risk" defence at Article 1386–11 C.civ., since so far that defence had not been present under French law precisely because the applicable regimes were not based on fault.[624]

(4) Article 1386–18 C.civ., mirroring Article 13 of Directive 85/374, provides that the regime introduced pursuant to the Directive is without prejudice to the existing liability regimes which may apply in product liability cases.

In cases where the injurious product is under the *garde* of a person other than the victim, the victim may invoke liability for things pursuant to Article 1384(1) C.civ. or the new contractual liability for things, enunciated in the decision of 17 January 1995[625] but, in all likelihood, against some person other than the manufacturer.

If the manufacturer stood in a contractual relationship—either direct or through a chain of contracts—with the victim, the manufacturer may be liable for a breach of the warranty against defects (such as that of Article 1641 ff. C.civ. for sale), a breach of the obligation to deliver a product in conformity with contractual expectations or a breach of the implied obligation to inform the consumer (*obligation de renseignement*) or not to endanger his or her safety (*obligation de sécurité*). In practice, the latter two obligations are the most relevant in typical product liability cases. The decision of 17 January 1995 establishes that the *obligation de sécurité*—and presumably the *obligation de renseignement* as well—actually benefit third parties, so that there need have been no contractual relationship between the manufacturer and the victim.[626]

The *obligation de renseignement* and the *obligation de sécurité* have been shaped by French courts in line with Directive 85/374, given the prolonged absence of implementing legislation, as discussed under the previous case. Nevertheless, both obligations are

---

[620] These regimes are surveyed, *supra*, 6.3.1.B.

[621] P. Jourdain, "Commentaire de la loi n° 98–389 du 19 mai 1998 sur la responsabilité du fait des produits défectueux" JCP(E) 1998.1204 at 1205.

[622] Act 85–677 of 5 July 1985, *supra*, **6.F.16.**

[623] Viney and Jourdain, *Conditions* at 790–1, para. 785–2.

[624] See C. Larroumet, "La responsabilité du fait des produits défectueux après la loi du 19 mai 1998" D 1998.Chron.311 at 315.

[625] *Supra*, **6.F.28.**

[626] Ibid.

obligations of result (*obligations de résultat*),[627] with the consequence that where the victim relies on either of them, the "product development risk" cannot be raised as a defence. French courts have held that their duty to interpret French law in the light of the Directive did not go so far as to require the introduction of a "product development risk" defence.[628]

Given the strong parallelism between those obligations as they have been developed by French courts and the new Title IVbis, the introduction by the French legislature of the "product development risk" defence in French law at Article 1386–11(5) C.civ. has led commentators[629] to predict that the defence will be recognized in cases based on the *obligation de renseignement* or the *obligation de sécurité*, or even that those obligations will be overshadowed by the new regime of Title IVbis.

If the liability regimes developed around the *obligation de renseignement* and *obligation de sécurité* and extended to third parties are not modified in the wake of the implementation of the Directive, the chances are that they will tend to be preferred to the regime of Title IVbis, since the "product development risk" defence remains excluded from them.[630]

6.3.3.C. ENGLISH LAW

Introductory Note

The UK was among the few Member States that actually implemented Directive 85/374 within the deadline of three years given at Article 19(1). Moreover, for the first time apparently, the UK implemented a piece of EC legislation not through an Order under the European Communities Act 1972,[631] but rather through an Act of Parliament. The Consumer Protection Act 1987, whose first part (ss. 1–9) purported to transpose Directive 85/374 into UK law, is reproduced and commented upon below.

The most controversial provision of Part I of the Consumer Protection Act 1987 was certainly the product development risk defence at s. 4(1)(e) of the Act. As in other countries, that issue was the subject of fairly lively discussion in the UK, and it was argued that s. 4(1)(e) was not a proper implementation of Art. 7(e) of Directive 85/374. The European Commission agreed with the argument and brought the UK before the ECJ pursuant to Article 226 EC on that very issue. The judgment of the ECJ sheds some light on the construction of the "product development risk" defence under Directive 85/374, and it is reproduced below.

---

[627] That conclusion is less firm as regards the *obligation de renseignement*, which is sometimes characterized as an obligation of means (*obligation de moyens*).

[628] In Cass. civ. 1re, 9 July 1996, *supra*, **6.F.30.**, the Cour de cassation even invoked Article 15(1)(b) of Directive 85/374 in support of its position: see Note (4) thereafter.

[629] See C. Larroumet, "La responsabilité du fait des produits défectueux après la loi du 19 mai 1998" D 1998.Chron.311 at 316; G. Viney, "L'introduction en droit français de la directive européenne du 25 juillet 1985 relative à la responsabilité du fait des produits défectueux" D 1998.Chron.291 at 298–9. Contra: P. Jourdain, "Commentaire de la loi n° 98–389 du 19 mai 1998 sur la responsabilité du fait des produits défectueux" JCP(E) 1998.1204 at 1214–5.

[630] Viney and Jourdain, ibid.; Jourdain, ibid. at 1215.

[631] European Communities Act 1972 (c. 68).

Consumer Protection Act 1987[632] **6.E.38.**

"1. **Purpose and construction . . .** (1) This [Act] shall have effect for the purpose of making such provision as is necessary in order to comply with the [Directive 85/374] and shall be construed accordingly.

(2) In this [Act], except in so far as the context otherwise requires— . . .

'product' means any goods or electricity and (subject to subsection (3) below) includes a product which is comprised in another product, whether by virtue of being a component part or raw material or otherwise; . . .

(3) For the purposes of this [Act] a person who supplies any product in which products are comprised, whether by virtue of being component parts or raw materials or otherwise, shall not be treated by reason only of his supply as supplying any of the products so comprised.

2. **Liability for defective products.** (1) Subject to the following provisions of this [Act], where any damage is caused wholly or partly by a defect in a product, every person to whom subsection (2) below applies shall be liable for the damage.

(2) This subsection applies to—

(a) the producer of the product;

(b) any person who, by putting his name on the product or using a trade mark or other distinguishing mark in relation to the product, has held himself out to be the producer of the product;

(c) any person who has imported the product into a member State from a place outside the member States in order, in the course of any business of his, to supply it to another . . .

(5) Where two or more persons are liable by virtue of this [Act] for the same damage, their liability shall be joint and several.

(6) This section shall be without prejudice to any liability arising otherwise than by virtue of this [Act].

3. **Meaning of 'defect'.** (1) Subject to the following provisions of this section, there is a defect in a product for the purposes of this [Act] if the safety of the product is not such as persons generally are entitled to expect; and for those purposes 'safety', in relation to a product, shall include safety with respect to products comprised in that product and safety in the context of risks of damage to property, as well as in the context of risks of death or personal injury.

(2) In determining for the purposes of subsection (1) above what persons generally are entitled to expect in relation to a product all the circumstances shall be taken into account, including—

(a) the manner in which, and purposes for which, the product has been marketed, its get-up, the use of any mark in relation to the product and any instructions for, or warnings with respect to, doing or refraining from doing anything with or in relation to the product;

(b) what might reasonably be expected to be done with or in relation to the product; and

(c) the time when the product was supplied by its producer to another;

and nothing in this section shall require a defect to be inferred from the fact alone that the safety of a product which is supplied after that time is greater than the safety of the product in question.

4. **Defences.** (1) In any civil proceedings by virtue of this [Act] against any person ('the person proceeded against') in respect of a defect in a product it shall be a defence for him to show—

(a) that the defect is attributable to compliance with any requirement imposed by or under any enactment or with any Community obligation; or

(b) that the person proceeded against did not at any time supply the product to another; or

(c) that the following conditions are satisfied, that is to say—

---

[632] c. 43.

(i) that the only supply of the product to another by the person proceeded against was otherwise than in the course of a business of that person's; and

(ii) that section 2(2) above does not apply to that person or applies to him by virtue only of things done otherwise than with a view to profit; or

(d) that the defect did not exist in the product at the relevant time; or

(e) that the state of scientific and technical knowledge at the relevant time was not such that a producer of products of the same description as the product in question might be expected to have discovered the defect if it had existed in his products while they were under his control; or

(f) that the defect—

(i) constituted a defect in a product ('subsequent product') in which the product in question had been comprised; and

(ii) was wholly attributable to the design of the subsequent product or to compliance by the producer of the product in question with instructions given by the producer of the subsequent product.

(2) In this section 'the relevant time', in relation to electricity, means the time at which it was generated, being a time before it was transmitted or distributed, and in relation to any other product, means—

(a) if the person proceeded against is a person to whom subsection (2) of section 2 above applies in relation to the product, the time when he supplied the product to another;

(b) if that subsection does not apply to that person in relation to the product, the time when the product was last supplied by a person to whom that subsection does apply in relation to the product.

5. **Damage giving rise to liability.** (1) Subject to the following provisions of this section, in this [Act] damage means death or personal injury or any loss of or damage to any property (including land).

(2) A person shall not be liable under section 2 above in respect of any defect in a product for the loss of or any damage to the whole or any part of any product which has been supplied with the product in question comprised in it.

(3) A person shall not be liable under section 2 above for any loss of or damage to any property which, at the time it is lost or damaged, is not—

(a) of a description of property ordinarily intended for private use, occupation or consumption; and

(b) intended by the person suffering the loss or damage mainly for his own private use, occupation or consumption.

(4) No damages shall be awarded to any person by virtue of this Part in respect of any loss of or damage to any property if the amount which would fall to be so awarded to that person, apart from this subsection and any liability for interest, does not exceed GBP 275 . . .

6. **Application of certain enactments etc . . .** (7) It is hereby declared that liability by virtue of this [Act] is to be treated as liability in tort for the purposes of any enactment conferring jurisdiction on any court with respect to any matter . . ."

Notes

(1) If the peculiarities of the British legislative drafting style are set aside,[633] the Consumer Protection Act 1987 probably represents the truest implementation of

---

[633] From a stylistic point of view, it is interesting to compare the English version of Directive 85/374 with the Consumer Protection Act 1987, for instance Article 1 of the Directive with its equivalent at s. 2(1) of the Act. It shows that the relationship between languages and legal systems is not as exclusive as one might suppose, since while both documents are in the same language, some form of translation was nonetheless needed between the

Directive 85/374 among the legal systems considered here. The provisions of the Act on the liability of suppliers,[634] the prohibition on exclusions from liability[635] and limitation and extinction periods,[636] which follow Directive 85/374 in substance, have not been reproduced above. The UK has exercised the options provided for in the Directive as follows:

- As s. 4(1)(e), the "product development risk" defence is included, whereas the UK could have excluded it pursuant to Article 15(1)(b) of the Directive.
- The UK did not subject liability under the Act to any ceiling as regards personal injury, as was permissible by virtue of Article 16 of the Directive.

(2) The Act adds to Directive 85/374 in certain respects:

- S. 1(3) of the Act specifically provides that suppliers of finished products are not to be considered as suppliers of the components or raw materials that were used in the production of those finished products. The supplier of a car fitted with a defective tyre therefore cannot be sued as the supplier of defective tyre. That provision appears merely as a clarification, which does not depart from the Directive.
- The second half of s. 3(1) further defines "safety" by stating that it applies to the product and its components, and that it includes safety in relation both to personal injury and property damage. Here again, the provision appears to be a mere clarification.
- The "product development risk" defence at s. 4(1)(e) refers to whether the defect could be discovered by "a producer of products of the same description", unlike Art. 7(e) of the Directive where no such reference is made. That is the main difference between the Act and the Directive, and it is considered in greater detail in the next annotated case.
- The second phrase of s. 5(2) of the Act explicitly excludes any liability for damage caused by a defective component to any other part of the product in which it is comprised, a point not dealt with so clearly in the Directive. Thus, although the purchaser of a new car can sue the manufacturer of a defective tyre which was fitted to the car at the time of its purchase, he or she cannot recover compensation for damage to the car itself, resulting from the defect in the tyre.[637] Accordingly, there is no room under the Act for a theory of "complex structures" such as once was mooted in the UK,[638] and far less for a body of case law on "creeping damage" (*Weiterfresserschaden*) as in Germany;[639] that appears to be a reasonable construction of Directive 85/374.

In s. 5(4) of the Act, the figure of GBP 275 is not a deductible for property damage (as in the equivalent German provision, § 11 ProdHaftG), but rather a threshold figure, i.e. no

Directive, the style of which was rather typical of Continental drafting, and the Act, which is written in the traditional style of UK legislation.

[634] S. 2(3) of the Act, implementing Art. 3(3) of the Directive.

[635] S. 7 of the Act, implementing Art. 12 of the Directive.

[636] S. 6(6) of the Act, bringing modifications to the Limitation Act 1980 (c. 58) and the Prescription and Limitation (Scotland) Act 1973 (c. 52) so as to implement Art. 10 and 11 of the Directive.

[637] *Clerk & Lindsell on Torts* at 514–5, para. 9–61. The limitation of liability created by s. 5(2) applies only if the defective component was *supplied to the consumer* as part of a product: the person who buys a defective tyre and fits it upon his or her car can sue the tyre manufacturer for damage which may be caused to the car by the defective tyre.

[638] See *supra*, 6.3.1.C., Introductory Note under d).

[639] See *supra*, **6.G.24.**, Note (7).

compensation will be awarded if the damage does not exceed GBP 275, but once it does exceed that figure, the whole of the damage will be recoverable. This difference with § 11 ProdHaftG is due to a discrepancy between the German and English language versions of Article 9(b) of Directive 85/374.[640]

(3) Compared with French and German law, there are fewer difficulties with integrating the regime of the Act within the rest of English tort law, given the fragmented structure of English tort law.[641] As stated in s. 6(7), the Act is to be treated as establishing tort liability for the jurisdictional purposes. Indeed, the Act can be seen as creating a specific and autonomous tort—in principle involving strict liability—which is added to the English law of torts.[642] The conditions for liability are defined at s. 2 of the Act, so that the presence or absence of a contractual relationship between the victim and the manufacturer, or the presence or absence of a duty of care for the purposes of liability in negligence, is not relevant. Conversely, pursuant to s. 2(6) of the Act, other heads of liability, whether for breach of contract[643] or under the tort of negligence,[644] remain unaffected by the Act.

It has been suggested that the application of the Act will involve building upon the distinction between manufacturing defects, design defects and failures to warn, which was already known in the law of negligence.[645]

The Act appears to be no less generous towards the victim than the common law, but it is not clear that it confers on consumers much by way of advantage over the common law.[646] The Act has now been in force for more than a decade, but it seems that it has given rise to no major decision so far. Some commentators would not see that as a sign that the Act is not useful, pointing out that the vast majority of liability claims are settled out of court, and that evidence would seem to indicate that the Act plays a role in such settlements.[647]

ECJ, 29 May 1997[648]   **6.EC.39.**
Commission v. *UK*

IMPLEMENTATION OF DIRECTIVE 85/374 IN ENGLISH LAW

Product development risk

Under Article 7(e) of Directive 85/374, the manufacturer must prove that the objective state of scientific and technical knowledge, including the most advanced level of such knowledge,

---

[640] It will be recalled that France chose not to implement that part of Directive 85/374: *supra*, **6.F.37.**, Note (2). The French version of Article 9(b) of Directive 85/374 corresponds to the German version.

[641] See *supra*, Chapter I, **1.E.20.** and **1.E.21.**

[642] *Clerk & Lindsell on Torts* at 503–4, para. 9–37. Rogers at 340 would reserve judgment as to whether the Act truly introduces a strict liability tort.

[643] See *supra*, 6.3.1.C., Introductory Note under b).

[644] See *supra*, 6.3.1.C., Introductory Note under c), d) as well as **6.E.31.** and **6.E.32.**

[645] See *Clerk & Lindsell on Torts* at 506–7, para. 9–42 to 9–44; Rogers at 343–6.

[646] See *Clerk & Lindsell on Torts* at 503–4, para. 9–37; Rogers at 351–2; Markesinis and Deakin at 598–9; Howells at 96–7. On the use of inferences of fact under the common law, see *supra*, **6.E.31.** and **6.E.32.**

[647] See M. Mildred, "The Impact of the Directive in the United Kingdom" in *Directive 85/374/EEC on Product Liability: Ten Years After* (Louvain-la-Neuve: Centre de droit de la consommation, 1996) 41 at 49–56.

[648] Case C–300/95 [1997] ECR I–2649.

without any restriction as to the industrial sector concerned, did not enable the existence of the defect to be discovered. The knowledge to be taken into account is limited to knowledge that was accessible at the time when the product was put into circulation.

Facts: The Commission brought an action against the United Kingdom before the ECJ pursuant to Article 226 EC, arguing that the UK had not properly implemented Directive 85/374 in UK law, and in particular that the defence of "product development risk" at s. 4(1)(e) of the Consumer Protection Act 1987 did not correspond to Article 7(e) of Directive 85/374.

Held: The ECJ dismissed the Commission's application.

Judgment: "16. In its application, the Commission argues that the United Kingdom legislature has broadened the defence under Article 7(e) of the Directive to a considerable degree and converted the strict liability imposed by Article 1 of the Directive into mere liability for negligence . . .

23. In order to determine whether the national implementing provision at issue is clearly contrary to Article 7(e) as the Commission argues, the scope of the Community provision which it purports to implement must first be considered.

24. In order for a producer to incur liability for defective products under Article 4 of the Directive, the victim must prove the damage, the defect and the causal relationship between defect and damage, but not that the producer was at fault. However, in accordance with the principle of fair apportionment of risk between the injured person and the producer set forth in the seventh recital in the preamble to the Directive, Article 7 provides that the producer has a defence if he can prove certain facts exonerating him from liability, including 'that the state of scientific and technical knowledge at the time when he put the product into circulation was not such as to enable the existence of the defect to be discovered' (Article 7(e)).

25. Several observations can be made as to the wording of Article 7(e) of the Directive.

26. First . . ., since that provision refers to 'scientific and technical knowledge at the time when [the producer] put the product into circulation', Article 7(e) is not specifically directed at the practices and safety standards in use in the industrial sector in which the producer is operating, but, unreservedly, at the state of scientific and technical knowledge, including the most advanced level of such knowledge, at the time when the product in question was put into circulation.

27. Second, the clause providing for the defence in question does not contemplate the state of knowledge of which the producer in question actually or subjectively was or could have been apprised, but the objective state of scientific and technical knowledge of which the producer is presumed to have been informed.

28. However, it is implicit in the wording of Article 7(e) that the relevant scientific and technical knowledge must have been accessible at the time when the product in question was put into circulation.

29. It follows that, in order to have a defence under Article 7(e) of the Directive, the producer of a defective product must prove that the objective state of scientific and technical knowledge, including the most advanced level of such knowledge, at the time when the product in question was put into circulation was not such as to enable the existence of the defect to be discovered. Further, in order for the relevant scientific and technical knowledge to be successfully pleaded as against the producer, that knowledge must have been accessible at the time when the product in question was put into circulation. On this last point, Article 7(e) of the Directive, contrary to what the Commission seems to consider, raises difficulties of interpretation which, in the event of litigation, the national courts will have to resolve, having recourse, if necessary, to Article [234 EC].

30. For the present, it is the heads of claim raised by the Commission in support of its application that have to be considered . . .

32. The Commission takes the view that inasmuch as section 4(1)(e) of the Act refers to what may be expected of a producer of products of the same description as the product in question, its wording clearly conflicts with Article 7(e) of the Directive in that it permits account to be taken of the subjective knowledge of a producer taking reasonable care, having regard to the standard precautions taken in the industrial sector in question.

33. That argument must be rejected in so far as it selectively stresses particular terms used in section 4(1)(e) without demonstrating that the general legal context of the provision at issue fails effectively to secure full application of the Directive. Taking that context into account, the Commission has failed to make out its claim that the result intended by Article 7(e) of the Directive would clearly not be achieved in the domestic legal order.

34. First, section 4(1)(e) of the Act places the burden of proof on the producer wishing to rely on the defence, as Article 7 of the Directive requires.

35. Second, section 4(1)(e) places no restriction on the state and degree of scientific and technical knowledge at the material time which is to be taken into account.

36. Third, its wording as such does not suggest, as the Commission alleges, that the availability of the defence depends on the subjective knowledge of a producer taking reasonable care, having regard to the standard precautions taken in the industrial sector in question.

37. Fourth, the Court has consistently held that the scope of national laws, regulations or administrative provisions must be assessed in the light of the interpretation given to them by national courts [reference omitted]. Yet in this case the Commission has not referred in support of its application to any national judicial decision which, in its view, interprets the domestic provision at issue inconsistently with the Directive.

38. Lastly, there is nothing in the material produced to the Court to suggest that the courts in the United Kingdom, if called upon to interpret section 4(1)(e), would not do so in the light of the wording and the purpose of the Directive so as to achieve the result which it has in view and thereby comply with the third paragraph of Article [249 EC] [reference omitted]. Moreover, section 1(1) of the Act expressly imposes such an obligation on the national courts."

Note

The annotated case concerned the nature of the regime of liability created by Directive 85/374 and the interpretation of one of the key elements in that respect, namely the "product development risk" defence provided for at Article 7(e) of the Directive and introduced in the legal systems under study here.[649]

The position of the Commission was that, since Directive 85/374 was intended to introduce a liability regime where the fault of the producer would not be relevant, the "product development risk" defence at Article 7(e) of the Directive should not involve any examination of the conduct of the manufacturer, the only issue being whether the state of scientific and technical knowledge was such as would have enabled the defect to be discovered.[650] The United Kingdom responded that its implementation was not inconsistent with the Directive, and that, especially in view of Article 1(1) of the Act, UK courts would be bound to interpret the Act so as to implement the Directive fully; in any event, in the absence of case law indicating that the interpretation given to Article 4(1)(e) of the Act

---

[649] See § 1(2)5 ProdHaftG, *supra*, **6.G.34.**; Art. 1386–11(4) C.civ., *supra*, **6.F.37.**; s. 4(1)(e) of the Consumer Protection Act 1987, *supra*, **6.E.38.** Of all the Member States, only Luxembourg and Finland have chosen to use the possibility offered by Art. 15(1)(b) of the Directive and generally to extend the liability of the manufacturer to development risks as well.

[650] See para. 16–8 of the judgment in the annotated case (not reproduced here).

would not be consistent with the Directive, it was premature to bring the UK before the Court of Justice for breach of the EC Treaty.

In considering those arguments, the ECJ needed to put forward its own interpretation of the expression "state of scientific and technical knowledge at the time when [the producer] put the product into circulation" at Article 7(e) of the Directive. Beyond the narrow question of construction, the underlying issue was the "fair apportionment of the risks inherent in modern technological production" between manufacturer and consumer, to use the terms of the second recital of Directive 85/374.[651] The more difficult it is for the manufacturer to show that a defect could not have been discovered, the more the manufacturer will have to conduct research and testing before releasing a product on the market and obtain extensive insurance coverage. Conversely, the less the burden on the manufacturer, established by Article 7(e) of the Directive, the likelier it is that victims themselves will have to bear the consequences of product risks.

Here the ECJ treated of Article 7(e) as raising two issues: the level of knowledge to be taken into consideration and the accessibility of such knowledge. On the first issue, the ECJ found that Article 7(e) creates quite a considerable hurdle: the defect must have been impossible to detect not only for the industrial branch of which the manufacturer was part, but also in general, given *the most advanced level of scientific and technical knowledge*. That issue is thus to be settled objectively, without regard to the situation of the manufacturer or even of the industrial branch in question: this would mean, for instance, that the veterinary product industry would have to keep abreast of scientific and technical knowledge in other sectors as well, such as the pharmaceutical industry. On the second issue (accessibility), however, the ECJ was content to leave the door open by finding that the knowledge "must have been accessible at the time", without more. In the eyes of the ECJ, Article 7(e) of the Directive was not unequivocal as regards the test for accessibility and there was no need to clarify the issue in the annotated case; the Advocate-General had proposed a "reasonableness" test for accessibility, whereby information that was not reasonably accessible (e.g. an article published in Chinese in a local Chinese journal) would not count towards establishing the state of accessible knowledge.[652] There is therefore some room for considerations relating to the behaviour of persons in the position of the manufacturer in the application of Article 7(e) of Directive 85/374.

The ECJ concluded that the Commission had not put forward sufficient evidence to show that Article 4(1)(e) of the Act would be construed by the UK courts differently from Article 7(e) of the Directive.

In the end, while the ECJ dismissed the Commission's application, it still interpreted the defence of Article 7(e) of Directive 85/374 fairly restrictively, leaving open however the issue of "accessibility". The judgment of the ECJ in the annotated case was criticized for failing to bring clarity to the interpretation of Article 7(e) of Directive 85/374,[653] which has led some commentators to renew their call for the abolition of the "product development risk" defence which is allowable by the Directive.[654]

---

[651] See C. Hodges, "Development Risks: Unanswered Questions" (1998) 61 Mod LR 560 at 561–3.

[652] ECJ, Opinion of the Advocate General of 23 January 1997, Case C–300/95, *Commission* v. *United Kingdom* [1997] ECR I–2649 at 2660.

[653] See C. Hodges, "Development Risks: Unanswered Questions" (1998) 61 Mod LR 560 at 569–70.

[654] M. Mildred and G. Howells, "Comment on 'Development Risks: Unanswered Questions'" (1998) 61 Mod LR 570.

6.3.4. COMPARATIVE OVERVIEW

Product liability provides a prime example of how closely liability not based on conduct is related to liability for wrongful conduct and how difficult it can become to distinguish between the two. In addition, it also provides a good illustration of the interaction between Member State and Community laws, in light of the enactment and implementation of Directive 85/374 on product liability, which sought to create a harmonized product liability framework throughout the EC.

Member State product liability laws

Even if the second recital of Directive 85/374 states that "liability without fault on the part of the producer is the sole means of adequately solving the problem" of injury caused by defective products, none of the systems under study here (England, France, Germany) had actually abandoned fault as the basis for the liability of the producer for injury caused by its products.

Among the systems studied here, German law is certainly the most developed. The German law of product liability[655] moves away from traditional fault-based liability in that the victim is helped by a series of presumptions, including a presumption of fault, once it is shown that the product was defective; the producer has few means of exoneration at its disposal. Yet in theory German product liability law remains firmly anchored on fault. The central element of that regime, the duty of safety (*Verkehrspflicht*) relating to product defects, refers to the conduct of the producer with its elements of necessity and reasonableness.[656] Risk-based liability (*Gefährdungshaftung*) under German law, as exemplified by § 7 StVG (Road Traffic Act),[657] obeys a different theoretical framework, where no *Verkehrspflicht* comes into play and the central element is the specific risk created by the activity or installation for which liability is imposed.

Product liability became a specific sector of the German law of civil liability more than 30 years ago in the wake of a decision of the BGH of 26 November 1968 in the *Fowl pest* (*Hühnerpest*) case.[658] In its judgment, the BGH surveyed all possible ways of dealing with the challenges of injury caused by products (short of legislative intervention), namely contractual liability, liability on the basis of a quasi-contractual or *sui generis* relationship and tortious/delictual liability. The BGH chose the third option and issued the following statement of principle:

"If someone, while making use of an industrial product in accordance with its purpose, suffers injury to one of the legal interests (*Rechtsgüter*) protected by § 823(1) BGB because that product was defectively manufactured, it is up to the manufacturer to explain how that defect came to happen and so to demonstrate that he was not at fault."

Liability for injury caused by products in Germany thus hinges around the notion of product *defect*, which serves both to limit the liability of the producer (no liability will

---

[655] Or "producer liability" (*Produzentenhaftung*), as it was originally called, in order to emphasize that liability was still based on the fault of the producer.

[656] See *supra*, **6.G.24.**, Note (4).

[657] See *supra*, 6.2.1.A.

[658] *Supra*, **6.G.24.**

ensue for damage caused by products that were free of defects) and to delineate the respective evidentiary burdens of the producer and victim (based on their respective spheres of control). The duty of safety or *Verkehrspflicht* at issue in product liability cases was framed as the duty to do all that is necessary (*erforderlich*) and reasonable (*zumutbar*) in order not to put in circulation defective products.[659] Accordingly, the victim must show that (i) he or she suffered injury to a protected interest under § 823(1) BGB, (ii) that such injury was caused by a product manufactured by the producer and (iii) that the product in question was defective. Once that is shown, it is presumed that (i) the producer breached its *Verkehrspflicht* and acted wrongfully, (ii) the producer was at fault and (iii) that such fault caused the product to be defective. The liability of the producer under § 823(1) BGB is therefore engaged, unless the producer succeeds in rebutting one of those presumptions.

The concept of product defect has been further developed in the case law, so that three major categories of defects are now recognized, namely manufacturing defects (*Fabrikationsfehler*),[660] design defects (*Konstruktionsfehler*)[661] and instruction defects (*Instruktionsfehler*).[662] For all three categories, the only means of exoneration open to the producer in practice (in addition to the "odd unit" or *Ausreißer* argument available in manufacturing defect cases[663]) is to show that the danger or risk that materialized was not foreseeable at the time when the product was manufactured, so that there was no duty to prevent it. Such a risk is called a development risk (*Entwicklungsrisiko*) under German law.

It can be noted *in passim* that the general framework described above comes very close to the US law of product liability, as it has recently been restated in the *Restatement (Third) of Torts: Product Liability* (1998).[664] This supports one of the general observations made throughout this casebook, namely that in practice the alleged abyss between the civil law and the common law is not as significant as it is often made out to be; on product liability as in other areas, German law, both in the underlying policy considerations and in the actual law, is close to the common law, while French law follows another course.[665] In some other situations, French and English law are close while German law stands out.[666]

Under German product liability law, in addition to the above, there is a further category of *Verkehrspflicht* relating to product defects called the duty to monitor products (*Produktbeobachtungspflicht*).[667] Indeed the duties of the producer are not extinguished once the product is put into circulation: the producer must watch both reports arising

---

[659] See T. Wieckhorst, "Vom Produzentenfehler zum Produktfehler des § 3 ProdHaftG" [1995] VersR 1005.

[660] A typical example is the *Fowl pest* case itself, where a vaccine against fowl pest was not properly manufactured and remained contaminated with active viruses: *supra*, **6.G.24.**

[661] See OLG Düsseldorf, 29 November 1996 (*Quick release bicycle wheel*), *supra*, **6.G.25.**

[662] See the line of BGH cases dealing with the instructions given with child tea preparations, the main case being BGH, 12 November 1991, *supra*, **6.G.26.**

[663] The "odd unit" (*Ausreißer*) defence consists in arguing that the defective product was the odd defective unit that will always be produced, despite all the precautions taken to control production.

[664] The main difference being that, under US law as restated, it is not possible to invoke the "odd unit" (*Ausreißer*) defence for manufacturing defects: see *Restatement (3rd) of Torts: Products Liability* (1998), s. 1.

[665] For another area where the same tendency can be observed, see the treatment of pure economic loss (or *reiner Vermögensschaden*), discussed *supra*, Chapter II, 2.3.

[666] For instance, as concerns liability for injury caused by employees: see *supra*, Chapter V, 5.1.1.

[667] On this duty, see BGH, 17 March 1981 (*Apple scab*), *supra*, **6.G.27.**

from the use of the product as well as scientific developments in order to detect any new danger relating to its product that may become known. Once such a danger is identified, appropriate steps must be taken (from the issuance of warnings to product withdrawals and recalls).

In contrast to German law where product liability was put under a particular regime of delictual liability more than 30 years ago, French law has not until recently conceived of product liability as a specific problem of civil liability, leaving it to be dealt with within the general regime of liability. In this respect, it must be kept in mind that French law is distinguished by the prohibition against *cumul*, i.e. the use of delictual liability rules in a situation that should be governed by contractual rules.[668]

If the product causing the injury was being kept (*garde*) by another person (the *gardien*) than the victim, then the victim has a recourse against the keeper (*gardien*) (not necessarily the producer) pursuant to the general regime of liability for things under Article 1384(1) C.civ. That regime is not based on fault, and the keeper will thus be liable for any injury caused by the behaviour of the product in question (*fait de la chose*), irrespective of whether the product was defective or not.[669] If perchance the victim was in a contractual relationship with the keeper (i.e. the product was used in the course of executing a contract involving the victim and the keeper), then Article 1384(1) C.civ. cannot apply. While in that situation contractual recourses used to be less favourable, since they rested on a breach of an implied obligation to ensure the safety of the victim (*obligation de sécurité*), recent case law of the Cour de cassation appears to have recognized a contractual regime of liability for things along the same lines as Article 1384(1) C.civ., so that the prohibition on *cumul* would make no substantive difference in such a case.[670]

In most cases, however, Article 1384(1) C.civ. or its contractual equivalent will not apply; usually, in product liability cases, the victim himself or herself was the *gardien* of the product.[671] If the victim bought the injurious product, French law will then allow contractual recourses to go up the distribution chain to the actual producer, so that he or she could invoke the traditional contractual recourses against the producer directly, including the warranty against latent defects, the obligation to deliver a product in conformity with the other party's contractual expectations, which may not cover all cases of product defects, and implied contractual obligations to inform and warn the other contractual party (*obligation d'information et de mise en garde*) and not to endanger the safety of the other party (*obligation de sécurité*). The latter obligation, in particular, has been interpreted in the past 15 years to imply that the producer must "deliver products that are free of any defect which would create a risk for persons or property".[672] In the case of the producer, that obligation is one of result (*obligation de résultat*), meaning that the pro-

---

[668] See *supra*, Chapter I, 1.3.1.

[669] See *supra*, 6.1.2.

[670] See Cass. civ. 1re, 17 January 1995, *supra*, **6.F.28.**

[671] At some time, a theoretical construct was put forward, whereby *garde* would be split in two, between its structural (*garde de structure*) and behavioural (*garde de comportement*) aspects. The structural garde of a product would have been left with the manufacturer, so that liability for product defects (i.e. defects in the inner structure of the product) could have been attached to the manufacturer through Article 1384(1) C.civ. This theory, while it was accepted in some cases, generally met with resistance and has now become obsolete: see *supra*, **6.F.8.**, Note (5).

[672] Cass. civ. 1re, 20 March 1989, D 1989.Jur.381.

ducer is bound to achieve the results (deliver products free of defects), without regard to its conduct. Accordingly, liability arises if that result is not achieved, even if there was no fault. More specifically, the *obligation de sécurité* applicable to the manufacturer excludes any "product development risk" defence.

If the victim could not somehow benefit from Article 1384(1) C.civ. or from those contractual recourses, however (e.g. the victim is a third-party bystander), he or she used to be left with the general fault-based delictual liability regime of Art. 1382–1383 C.civ. At the beginning of the 1970s, the Cour de cassation held that a producer was at fault if it put a defective product in circulation, thereby putting the victim in a better position to succeed in a claim under Art. 1382–1383 C.civ.[673] Since a key judgment of 17 January 1995, however, the implied *obligation de sécurité* mentioned above is available not only to the other contracting parties, but also to third parties as well.[674] That decision, while it puts third parties in the same favourable position as contracting parties vis-à-vis the producer, is not easy to reconcile with the general framework of French civil law, in particular the prohibition on *cumul*.

Recent developments under French law, in particular the rise of the implied contractual *obligation de sécurité* and the extension of its benefit to third parties, took place against the background of Directive 85/374 and its long-delayed implementation in French law, so that it is difficult to predict how French law would have evolved if that Directive had not been enacted. Nevertheless, it can be said that French law chose as much as possible not to turn product liability into a separate liability regime. Indeed, the general regime of delictual liability for things, pursuant to Article 1384(1) C.civ., was already well-established before the problems related to injury caused by products started to draw attention. Furthermore, in contrast with German law, French law has tended to prefer the contractual route in order to supplement its law of civil liability to the extent needed to deal with those problems.

Much like French law, English law did not turn product liability into a specific field of law, leaving cases to be dealt with under general liability rules. English law stands here in contrast with other common law jurisdictions, such as the states of the USA, where specific product liability regimes were developed over many decades.

A range of contractual recourses are available to the victim of injury caused by a product. In the main types of contract involving the supply of goods, applicable legislation intervenes to imply certain terms, including that the goods correspond to the description given and (in transactions made in the course of a business) that the goods are of satisfactory quality and fit for their ordinary or stated purpose.[675] Since under English law the doctrine of privity of contract remains strong, however, these recourses are only available against the immediate contracting party, and cannot be used against parties further up the contractual chain (contrary to the situation in French law).

In most cases, therefore, the victim will look to tort law for a remedy. One of central cases in English tort law, *Donoghue* v. *Stevenson*, dealt precisely with a product liability situation, where a lady became ill after finding a decomposed snail at the bottom of her

---

[673] See Viney and Jourdain, *Conditions* at 345, para. 459-1.
[674] See Cass. civ. 1re, 17 January 1995, *supra*, **6.F.28.**
[675] See for instance, for the contract of sale, the Sale of Goods Act 1973, s. 13 and 14.

bottled drink.[676] The House of Lords held that the producer was under a duty of care to the ultimate consumer of the product, thereby enabling the victim of product injury to direct a tort claim against the producer. *Donoghue* v. *Stevenson* was confirmed in a subsequent case, *Grant* v. *Australian Knitting Mills*.[677] There the Privy Council also set out the evidentiary approach for product liability cases: the courts will not depart from the basic substantive principles of negligence, whereby the plaintiff must discharge the burden of proof regarding injury, a duty of care, breach of that duty, causation and remoteness of damage. However, courts will adopt a robust common sense approach to the appreciation of evidence, drawing inferences of fact to the benefit of the victim. In *Grant*, the Privy Council found that the unexplained presence of residue chemicals in underwear supported an inference of negligence.[678] That common sense approach to the assessment of evidence has remained informal to this day, and courts have refused to turn it into hard and fast rules (unlike what happened under German law).[679] While such an approach may be adequate for manufacturing defects, it is more difficult to apply in cases involving design or instruction defects, where inferences of fact are harder to draw; the victim is then left with a relatively heavy burden of proof.

Directive 85/374

Seen against that background, Article 1 of Directive 85/374,[680] whereby "[t]he producer shall be liable for damage caused by a defect in his product" may sound very innovative, given that at the time none of the systems surveyed here had broken away from fault-based liability in relation to injury caused by products.[681] The rest of the Directive, however, somewhat fails to live up to the ideal of Article 1.

The most controversial provision of the Directive, and the one that most squarely contradicts Article 1, remains the "product development risk" defence, included at Article 7(e), pursuant to which the producer can be exonerated if it proves "that the state of scientific and technical knowledge at the time when [it] put the product into circulation was not such as to enable the existence of the defect to be discovered". That provision appears clearly related to a similar defence under German law, but it must be recalled that German law is fault-based. The ECJ, in its judgment over the UK implementation of Article 7(e), reduced the danger that Article 7(e) would bring the regime of Directive 85/374 back to a fault basis.[682]

---

[676] See *supra*, Chapter I, **1.E.23.**

[677] *Supra*, **6.E.31.**

[678] It is interesting to note that the Privy Council took the opposite direction from the BGH. In *Grant*, the manufacturing process was shown to be "fool proof"; in that light, the presence of residue chemicals was interpreted by the court as a sign that some fault must have been committed somewhere along the production chain. In Germany, evidence that the producer took all reasonable care in its manufacturing process would rather lead to the conclusion that the defective product was the "odd unit" (*Ausreißer*) that escapes quality control, and the producer would be exonerated.

[679] See the recent Court of Appeal decision in *Carroll* v. *Fearon*, *supra*, **6.E.32.**

[680] *Supra*, **6.EC.33.**

[681] French law was on its way to develop a regime of product liability not based on fault, but the decisive developments surrounding the *obligation de sécurité* imposed on the producer for the benefit of contracting parties as well as third parties occurred after the adoption of Directive 85/374.

[682] See *supra*, **6.EC.39.** and note thereafter.

Other elements of the Directive also indicate a desire to limit its scope, such as the focus on the time of putting into circulation for the definition of defect and the exclusion of liability (Articles 6(1)(c), 6(2), 7(b), 7(e)), the limitation of allowable property damage (Article 9(b)), the absence of provisions on non-material damage (Article 9), the limitation and sunset periods (Articles 10 and 11) and the ability to put a ceiling on personal injury claims (Article 16). In this respect, while some of those limitations may appear arbitrary to the comparatist, they might also reflect the tensions inherent in the legislative process at the EC level. While product liability experts from the various Member States certainly exerted an influence on the Directive, "horizontal" forces affecting the whole of EC law also came into play. First of all, the Directive is based on Article 94 EC (requiring unanimity), and accordingly it was meant to harmonize the laws of the Member States, and not necessarily to restate them in a coherent way. Community institutions are very apt at making EC law progress by producing compromises that are acceptable to all interested parties, even if they may not be as perfect as one would desire. Secondly, a number of actors, including lobby groups, try to further their interests at the EC level, irrespective of the situation in the Member States. For instance, the position of industrial and consumer groups on the product development risk defence depended not on the law of their respective Member State, but on their own interests.

One important weakness of the Directive is the combination of a full harmonization approach with a harmonized regime that does not replace or exclude existing national laws. Indeed, only Articles 15 and 16 allow Member States to deviate from the provisions of the Directive on certain points. Otherwise, they are bound to implement it as is, and cannot for instance (as is usual in EC environmental law directives) include in their implementation statutes any provision that would provide more consumer protection than the Directive. Against that, Article 13 leaves national rules concerning product liability untouched, so that the regime created by the Directive will run in parallel to existing national law. As a result, it would be expected that national law will be preferred to the regime created by the Directive wherever it remains on balance more favourable to the plaintiff.

Implementation of Directive 85/374

In Germany, Directive 85/374 was implemented with the *Produkthaftungsgesetz* (ProdHaftG) of 15 December 1989.[683] The ProdHaftG is in general fairly true to the Directive, although Germany has used all the possibilities to limit the ambit of the new liability regime.

Beyond that, however, the German legislature sought to "harmonize" the ProdHaftG with the rest of German liability law, and in particular with the general principles applicable to risk-based liability (*Gefährdungshaftung*).[684] This has further limited the scope of the ProdHaftG.[685] For one, the Directive was implemented in a separate statute, the ProdHaftG, and not in the BGB, in line with the prevailing view according to which risk-based liability is foreign to the general regime of the BGB and must be enacted outside of

---

[683] *Supra*, **6.G.34.**
[684] These principles are discussed in detail *supra*, 6.1.1.
[685] See *supra*, **6.G.34.**, Note (3).

it.[686] Furthermore, the ProdHaftG is formulated by reference to a list of protected inter-ests (*Rechtsgüter*), in accordance with the general approach of German tort law, but as in other risk-based liability regimes, "other rights" such as the general *Persönlichkeitsrecht* or the right to an established and active business (*Recht am eingerichteten und ausgeübten Betrieb*) are excluded from its coverage.

According to the general theory of risk-based liability under German law, these restric-tions on the scope of recoverable injury under risk-based liability regimes, in comparison with the fault-based regimes of §§ 823(1), 823(2) and 826 BGB, constitute a form of coun-terpart for a loosening of the substantive conditions of liability, since the need to prove fault and wrongfulness disappears. In the case of the ProdHaftG, however, the inclusion of the product development risk defence at § 1(2)5., means that the substantive difference with the regime of fault-based liability developed under § 823(1) BGB is slight. In essence, when compared with that regime, the ProdHaftG marks an improvement only insofar as the "odd unit" (*Ausreißer*) defence is no longer available in manufacturing defect cases.[687] In addition, the concept of "defect" at § 3 ProdHaftG does not include the duty to mon-itor products (*Produktbeobachtungspflicht*) after their being put into circulation, contrary to the regime of § 823(1) BGB. It will accordingly come as no surprise that the ProdHaftG has been only sparsely used in the almost ten years since its enactment.

In what appears still to be the only major case involving the ProdHaftG to have reached the BGH, some interesting issues are raised in relation to the "post-implementation" phase of Community directives.[688] That case involved a mineral water bottle that had exploded; the defendant raised the "odd unit" (*Ausreißer*) defence and argued that such defence was covered by the product development risk defence at § 1(2)5 ProdHaftG. Instead of finding that the "odd unit" defence was distinct from the product development risk defence and thus not available under the ProdHaftG, the BGH went on to rule that, under Directive 85/374 and the ProdHaftG, the product development risk defence in any event did not apply to manufacturing defects (*Fabrikationsfehler*), but only to design (*Konstruktionsfehler*) defects. Yet neither the Directive nor the ProdHaftG makes any dis-tinction between the three types of defects. Furthermore, the BGH found that there was no need to refer the issue to the ECJ, since the BGH was merely deciding on how far Germany had made use of the derogation provided for at Art. 15(1)(b) of Directive 85/374 for the product development risk defence. That case shows that, firstly, in dealing with a directive or with its implementing legislation, national courts are bound to try to fit it within the general framework of their national law, so that the harmonization impulse given by the enactment of a directive can be followed by a "centrifugal" effect when national courts begin to consider implementing legislation (and through it the directive). Secondly, that effect is compounded if national courts fail to refer cases to the ECJ; this creates the risk that a court in another Member State would come to a different conclusion if faced with the same question, so that a central element of Directive 85/374 would not be interpreted in the same fashion throughout the EU.

---

[686] See *supra*, **6.G.1.** and notes therafter.
[687] See *supra*, **6.G.35.**, Note (2).
[688] BGH, 9 May 1995, *supra*, **6.G.35.**

In France, given that Directive 85/374 has been implemented only last year, with the Act 98–389 of 19 May 1998,[689] courts had previously undertaken, in accordance with the principle that national law should be interpreted in conformity with EC directives, to bring French law in line with Directive 85/374. As mentioned before, the rise of the implied contractual obligations to inform and warn users (*obligation de renseignement*) and not to endanger their safety (*obligation de sécurité*), and their extension beyond the scope of the contract to the benefit of third parties,[690] took place against the background of Directive 85/374. In recent cases, the Cour de cassation has expressly referred to Directive 85/374 in the interpretation of French law, or adopted the wording of the Directive in its grounds for judgment.[691] As regards product development risks, however, the Cour de cassation had taken it upon itself to use the derogation provided for at Article 15(1)(b) of Directive 85/374, so as to conclude that the product development risk defence is not available under French law.[692] In the end, therefore, French courts have to a great extent aligned French law with Directive 85/374, while not introducing the product development risk.

The implementing legislation, Act 98–389 of 19 May 1998, added a new Title IVbis to the French *Code civil*, at Art. 1386–1 to 1386–18. Liability under that title does not belong with either contractual or delictual rules; the legislature thus reached the same conclusion as the Cour de cassation, which in its judgment of 17 January 1995 ignored the contract/tort divide when it extended the *obligation de sécurité* to third parties.[693] Liability under Title IVbis is intended to create liability "by virtue of the law" (*de plein droit*), as is expressly stated at Article 1386–11 C.civ.. However, the French legislature, after intense debate, decided not to use the derogation of Article 15(1)(b) of Directive 85/374, and thus to include the product development risk defence at Article 1386–11(4) C.civ. (except for blood products).

One of the most striking features of Title IVbis is that it deviates from the Directive, in favour of victims, on many points where the Directive did not apparently allow any derogation.[694] These derogations are open to question from the point of view of Community law.[695]

It is still to early to foresee what impact Title IVbis will have on French law. It could induce courts to introduce the product development risk defence in the general rules of civil liability as well, in which case it would mark a setback for French victims of product-related injuries. If on the other hand French courts continue to refuse that defence under the general rules of civil liability, those rules would remain at least in that respect more favourable than Title IVbis, and thus that title would be used as little as its counterpart in Germany.

---

[689] See *supra*, **6.F.37.**

[690] No decision has yet extended the *obligation de renseignement* to the benefit of third parties, but commentators generally agree that, in light Cass. civ. 1re, 17 January 1995, *supra*, **6.F.28.**, such an extension should take place once the issue arises before a court.

[691] See Cass. civ. 1re, 3 March 1998, *supra*, **6.F.36.** as well as Cass. civ. 1re, 28 April 1998, JCP 1998.II.10088.

[692] See Cass. civ. 1re, 9 July 1996, *supra*, **6.F.30.**

[693] See Cass. civ. 1re, 17 January 1995, *supra*, **6.F.28.**

[694] *Supra*, **6.F.37.**, Note (2).

[695] Indeed, the Commission begun proceedings under Article 226 EC against France for incorrect implementation of the Directive: see "Defective products: Commission decides to take Greece and France to Court of Justice over failure to implement Directive correctly" Press Release IP/00/24 (13 January 2000).

Finally, among the systems studied here, England appears to have implemented Directive 85/374 with the most accuracy and expediency. Even if Part I of the Consumer Protection Act 1987 bears little resemblance with Directive 85/374 on its face, in substance it is fairly faithful to the Directive.[696] Given the less integrated structure of English tort law when compared to the German or French law of civil liability, it was also easier to introduce Directive 85/374 in the common law, in the form of a new strict liability tort.

On one central point, however, the Commission took the UK to the ECJ for failure to implement Directive 85/374 properly, namely the product development risk defence.[697] In its judgment, the ECJ set out a relatively strict interpretation of the product development risk defence at Article 7(1)(e) of Directive 85/374. For the ECJ, that defence must be assessed in light of the most advanced level of knowledge at the time of putting the product into circulation (irrespective of the situation of the producer), provided that such knowledge was accessible. In the light of the ECJ decision, the chances that the product development risk defence would open a back door to fault within the framework of Directive 85/374 are reduced.[698]

Impact of harmonization through Directives on the convergence of legal systems

In light of the above, it can be seen that the difference between liability for wrongful conduct and liability not based on conduct can be very slight. With respect to product liability, once the burden of proof is reassigned so as to relieve the victim from the need to show facts that are within the control of the producer,[699] it comes down to two defences open to the manufacturer, namely the "odd unit" (*Ausreißer*) and product development risk defences. If those defences are entertained, as is the case under German and English law, then the regime remains fault-based; if they are removed, as is the case under French law—at least when the regimes of Article 1384(1) C.civ, or the implied *obligation de sécurité* are relied upon—then the regime is not based on wrongful conduct anymore. The key problem with Directive 85/374 in that respect is that, while it professes to create a regime not based on wrongful conduct at Article 1, it makes room for the product development risk defence at Article 7(1)(e), so that its true nature remains unclear. If the ECJ judgment in *Commission* v. *UK* is followed by national courts, then Directive 85/374 and its implementing legislations will move towards "true" liability not based on wrongful conduct.

Product liability also provides an excellent case-study of the interaction between Community and national laws. Against the background of fairly different national laws (at least in the systems under study), Directive 85/374 purported to create a harmonized regime, whose coherency was however affected by the specific dynamics of Community law-making, including the need to compromise. Its implementation nevertheless shows how quickly a harmonized text can start to be "disharmonized" again. Firstly, the various implementing legislations vary in significant respects. Secondly, as shown by the BGH

---

[696] *Supra*, **6.E.38.**

[697] See *Commission* v. *UK*, *supra*, **6.EC.39.**

[698] In fact, the defence might in the end resemble the "ideal driver" defence of § 7(2) StVG (Road Traffic Act) in Germany, which is seen not as a fault element, but as a means of delineating the sphere of risk attributable to the producer. See *supra*, 6.2.1.A., and in particular **6.G.15.**

[699] That is done under all systems, whether formally (under German law), as a matter of common sense (under English law) or as a result of the substance of the law (under French law, when Article 1384(1) C.civ. or the implied *obligation de sécurité* is relied upon).

decision discussed above, there is a significant risk that national courts will interpret the implementing legislation without regard for its Community dimension and will thus produce diverging bodies of national case law.

Directive 85/374 dealt with a subset of civil liability, a century-old field of law that is well developed in all Member States. Given that, for each Member State, implementing legislation is bound to try to bridge the gap between the harmonized text and the rest of the law of civil liability, one could venture that a harmonizing effort such as Directive 85/374 is unlikely to result in a higher degree of harmonization than generally exists between the civil liability laws of the Member States. In that respect, Directive 85/374 shows the limits of piecemeal harmonization, and more particularly how it may result in jeopardizing the overall internal consistency of national laws in an area where consistency is required because of the similarily of the issues raised.

6.4. FROM LIABILITY BETWEEN NEIGHBOURS TO ENVIRONMENTAL LIABILITY

Whereas regimes of liability not based on conduct have been introduced as regards traffic accidents (in France and Germany)[700] and product liability (with Directive 85/374),[701] environmental liability has been evolving more slowly.

The first two subsections cover smaller areas within what could broadly be called environmental liability. All the systems under study here apply some form of regime of liability not based on wrongful conduct in relations between neighbours, which have already been described at greater length;[702] they are briefly reviewed in the first subsection. In addition, a number of regimes attach liability on a basis other than wrongful conduct in cases of injury caused by certain buildings or installations; those regimes are covered in the second subsection.

Among the jurisdictions surveyed here, only Germany has gone as far as to introduce some form of liability not based on conduct on a broad basis in the environment sector, through the *Umwelthaftungsgesetz* (UHG) of 10 December 1990, which is examined in the third subsection.

6.4.1. LIABILITY REGIMES APPLICABLE BETWEEN NEIGHBOURS

This heading can be found at <http://www.rechten.unimaas.nl/casebook>.

---

[700] See *supra*, 6.2.1. for German law and 6.2.2. for French law.
[701] Directive 85/374 is reproduced *supra*, **6.EC.33.** For a discussion of the implementation of Directive 85/374, see *supra*, 6.3.3.A. (Germany), 6.3.3.B. (France) and 6.3.3.C. (UK).
[702] See in general *supra*, Chapter II, 2.3.

6.4.2. LIABILITY FOR BUILDINGS, NETWORKS AND NUCLEAR INSTALLATIONS

This heading can be found at <http://www.rechten.unimaas.nl/casebook>.

6.4.3. ENVIRONMENTAL LIABILITY

The following materials can be found (with notes) at <http://www.rechten.unimaas.nl/casebook>:

6.G.40. Umwelthaftungsgesetz.

6.CE.41. Convention on Civil Liability for Damage resulting from Activities Dangerous to the Environment of 21 June 1993.

6.4.4. COMPARATIVE OVERVIEW

At this point in time, the emergence of a European *ius commune* as concerns environmental liability appears to be further away than in the two other areas previously surveyed, namely accidents (in particular road traffic accidents) and product liability. However, just as in those two areas, the impetus for convergence at the European level is strong: as the Commission mentioned in its recent White Paper, it is well-established that the protection of the environment has a transnational dimension, and a harmonized liability regime would strengthen existing EC environmental legislation.[703] Furthermore, according to the Commission, Member States are reluctant to impose a heavier environmental liability regime on their firms for fear of impairing their competitiveness, so that such a regime would have to be adopted at the European level if it is not to affect competitiveness.[704] Accordingly, it is conceivable that a Directive containing a harmonized regime of environmental liability would be adopted at the EC level within the next few years, with a degree of harmonization that would perhaps compare with, if not exceed, that of Directive 85/374 on product liability. The convergence of the various legal systems would then make a great step forward, provided that the implementation of the Directive and the application of the resulting national laws does not unwind the convergence brought about through the Directive.[705]

In any event, there is a firm historical basis for convergence, in that the legal systems surveyed here all contain fairly similar liability regimes which are specifically applicable as between neighbours. Under German law, that regime is found at § 906 BGB,[706] whose content has also been applied by analogy to disputes which fall under § 823 BGB but proceed from the same factual basis (emissions from a piece of land).[707] Under French law, case law has developed a specific regime concerning inconveniences between neighbours

---

[703] White Paper on Environmental Liability, COM(2000)66final (9 February 2000) at 12, 27.

[704] Ibid. at 13.

[705] See on that problem the examination of the implementation of Directive 85/374, *supra*, 6.3.3.

[706] *Supra*, 6.4.1. under a) and Chapter II, 2.3.2., Introductory Note under f).

[707] See *supra*, Chapter II, **2.G.39.** and notes thereafter.

(*troubles de voisinage*).[708] Under English law, the tort of nuisance and the rule in *Rylands* v. *Fletcher* apply specifically to disputes between neighbours.[709] All those regimes are distinct from the general liability regime in that liability does not depend on wrongful conduct on the part of the defendant, but rather on an assessment of the inconvenience complained of. An objective balancing of the interests of the plaintiff and the defendant then takes place. In general, in order for liability to arise, the inconvenience must exceed the bounds of what is normal or reasonable at the location in question.

In addition to those regimes, the legal systems under study here contain other regimes applicable to buildings, networks and nuclear installations. French and German law have inherited from Roman law provisions concerning the liability of the owner (under French law) or occupant (under German law) for injury caused by the collapse of a building that was not properly built or maintained; while the German regime remains based on wrongful conduct (albeit with a presumption against the occupant),[710] the French regime is not based on conduct.[711] German law imposed risk-based liability (*Gefährdungshaftung*) on the operators of energy and water distribution networks.[712] Finally, Germany, France and the UK have implemented in their respective legal orders the international conventions creating a regime of liability not based on conduct for nuclear installations.[713]

Nevertheless, those regimes are not suitable for modern "environmental damage" problems.[714] Environmental damage goes beyond the classical protected interests (life, health, property) to include damage to nature or biodiversity (i.e. diffuse collective interests). It is not always accidental and can often arise progressively ("chronic damage" or *Allmählichkeitschaden*). It arises beyond neighbouring pieces of land to broader areas, often going across national borders. Frequently, the sums at stake are immense. Finally, victims face huge problems of proof, given that the events at the origin of the damage occurred within the sphere of control of the defendant and causation is rarely clear (often, a number of circumstances play a role in the occurrence of injury).

It is generally agreed that, in order to address those problems, a broad-based liability regime is required, which would break new ground in many respects: not only would it have to apply irrespective of the conduct of the defendant (if problems of proof and transaction costs are to be avoided), but it would also have to cover new heads of damage going beyond the traditional protected interests. Furthermore, given the stakes, such a regime cannot be conceived without a close coordination with legislation concerning environmental standards and insurance.

In view of the Directive which is likely to come in the following years, this section surveyed two of the most advanced pieces of legislation concerning environmental

---

[708] *Supra*, 6.4.1. under b) and Chapter II, 2.3.3., Introductory Note under c).

[709] *Supra*, 6.4.1. under c) and Chapter II, 2.3.1., Introductory Note under a) as well as **2.E.35.** and notes thereafter.

[710] *Supra*, 6.4.2. under b).

[711] *Supra*, 6.4.2. under c).

[712] *Supra*, 6.4.2. under d).

[713] *Supra*, 6.4.2. under e).

[714] See *supra*, 6.4.3., Introductory Note under a).

liability put forward in Europe in recent years, namely the German *Umwelthaftungsgesetz* (UHG) of 10 December 1990[715] and the Lugano Convention of 21 June 1993.[716]

The UHG builds upon the general theory of risk-based liability (*Gefährdungshaftung*) under German law,[717] and in this respect it is less innovative than more specific pieces of German legislation such as the *Wasserhaushaltsgesetz*[718] or the *Gentechnikgesetz*.[719] Indeed, the UHG imposes liability for damage to the legal interests traditionally protected under German law (life, health, property)[720] arising from an "impact on the environment"[721] coming from one of a long list of industrial installations enumerated in annex to the UHG.[722] The UHG does not therefore cover "environmental damage" that would arise independently of any infringement of a traditional protected interest. Its most innovative feature remains the presumption of causation at § 6(1) UHG: if the victim proves that an installation such as that of the defendant could typically cause the injury, then it will be presumed that the installation of the defendant indeed caused the injury.[723] However, strangely enough in a regime that is meant to be based on risk and not on wrongful conduct, the defendant can rebut that presumption by showing that the installation was operated in conformity with all relevant legal obligations.[724]

When compared to the moderate and incremental advances of the UHG, the Lugano Convention might appear revolutionary. It applies generally to activities involving dangerous substances or waste (without reference to a list of installations).[725] It covers "environmental damage" arising beyond infringements to traditional protected interests.[726] Like the UHG, it imposes liability independently of the conduct of the operator of the installation.[727] It contains provisions directing the court to take into account the dangerousness of the activity in the assessment of causation, without going so far as to introduce a presumption of causation.[728] It also deals with jurisdictional issues, which are bound to be central to cross-border cases; between the Member States of the EU, however, the provisions of the Brussels Convention will have precedence.[729]

In its White Paper on Environmental Liability, the Commission notes that a number of Member States consider that the Lugano Convention is too far-reaching.[730] Accordingly,

---

[715] Environmental Liability Act, *supra*, **6.G.40.**

[716] Convention on Civil Liability for Damage resulting from Activities Dangerous to the Environment, *supra*, **6.CE.41.**

[717] *Supra*, 6.1.1.

[718] WHG, Water Resources Act, see *supra*, 6.4.3., Introductory Note under d).

[719] GenTG, Genetic Engineering Act, see *supra*, 6.4.3., Introductory Note under e).

[720] *Supra*, **6.G.40.**, Notes (1) and (3).

[721] Consisting in the "spread of materials, shocks, odours, pressure, radiation, gases, vapours, heat or other phenomena through ground, air or water": ibid., Note (4).

[722] Ibid., Note (2).

[723] Ibid., Note (5).

[724] Ibid., Note (6).

[725] *Supra*, **6.CE.41.**, Art. 2(1).

[726] Ibid., Art. 2(7).

[727] Ibid., Art. 6.

[728] Ibid., Art. 10.

[729] Ibid., Notes (4) and (5). The Brussels Convention will soon be replaced by a Regulation adopted on the basis of the new Article 65 EC (as added by the Treaty of Amsterdam).

[730] White Paper on Environmental Liability, COM(2000)66final (9 February 2000) at 24-5.

it is likely that the Directive that could be adopted within a few years will go further than the UHG[731] in imposing liability on the industry, but not as far as the Lugano Convention.

[731] Since, as explained above, concerns for the competitiveness of national firms, which might play a role in preventing the imposition of heavier liability regimes at national level, are not as crucial at Community level.

CHAPTER SEVEN
DEFENCES

The defences discussed in this chapter are defences to an action in tort, the existence of which would otherwise have been established. In other words, this chapter does not deal with defences which the defendant may invoke to show that one of the elements needed to establish a tort (such as a duty of care, wrongful conduct, causation or damage) is missing, as these have been previously examined or mentioned in other chapters.[1] The only defences which are considered here are those which the defendant is able to invoke because of conduct of the plaintiff, or which are otherwise imputable to the plaintiff. Such defences are mainly: (i) contributory fault or negligence, (ii) assumption of risk and implied consent, without dealing therefore with express exemption clauses (dealt with in the Contracts casebook) and (iii) illegality. Other concepts which are sometimes presented as defences, such as force majeure, mistake, legitimate defence, necessity, legal duty, statutory authority as well as limitation or prescription will not be examined here.

The defences dealt with will be examined mainly in connection with the general rules on liability for one's own conduct, but also, where relevant, in connection with liability regimes not based on one's own conduct.

7.1. CONTRIBUTORY FAULT

Introductory Note

In the common law the term "contributory negligence" is traditionally used whereas in continental legal systems the broader term 'contributory fault' (including both negligent and intentional conduct) is more familiar. The terms are used hereinafter as synonyms.[2]

The French *Code civil* does not contain any provision dealing specifically with the problems of apportionment of liability due to the contributory fault of the victim. These problems are solved by the case law of the Cour de cassation.

By contrast, the German BGB contains general rules in § 254, for all kinds of obligations. The first paragraph of § 254 reads as follows:[3]

[1] For a discussion of some of these defences in English law, see Rogers at 872–82 and Markesinis & Deakin at 711–22; in French law, Viney and Jourdain, *Conditions* at 491–514, para. 556–71; in German law, Larenz/Canaris at 363. For a comparative analysis of the laws of all the EU Member States, see von Bar II at 504–97, para. 485–561: the defences examined herein are dealt with at 533–75, para. 504–39. See also, J. Limpens, "Liability for one's own act" in A. Tunc, ed., *International Encyclopedia of Comparative Law—Vol. XI: Torts* (Tübingen: Mohr, 1979) at 81 ff., para. 2–165 ff.

[2] For a discussion of the defence under other legal systems of EU Members States than those discussed hereafter, especially the laws of Austria, Belgium, Greece, Italy and Spain, see von Bar II at 549–75, para. 517–39. For a discussion of economic aspects of the defence of contributory negligence, see P. Newman, ed., *The New Palgrave Dictionary of Economics and the Law* (London: Macmillan, 1998), under the entries "Comparative negligence", "Contributory and comparative negligence", "Due care" and "Last clear chance".

[3] For the second paragraph and related provisions, see *infra*, 7.1.2, Introductory Note.

"If a fault of the injured party has contributed to the occurrence of the damage, the duty to compensate and the extent of the compensation to be made depend upon the circumstances, especially upon how far the injury has been caused predominantly by one of the other party."

Under English law, the principle of apportionment of liability in case of contributory negligence is laid down in the Law Reform (Contributory Negligence) Act 1945:[4]

"Where any person suffers damage as the result partly of his own fault and partly of the fault of any other person or persons, a claim in respect of that damage shall not be defeated by reason of the fault of the person suffering the damage, but the damages recoverable in respect thereof shall be reduced to such extent as the court thinks just and equitable having regard to the claimant's share in the responsibility, for the damage . . ."

7.1.1. FRENCH LAW

Cass. civ., 28 February 1910[5]　　　　　　　　**7.F.1.–3.**
Nourrigat v. *Pech*
and
Cass. civ. 2e, 16 July 1953[6]
Suter v. *Sté Le Berry*
and
Cass. Ass. plén., 9 May 1984[7]
Lemaire v. *Declerq*

THE APPORTIONMENT PRINCIPLE

A fault committed by the victim of an accident cannot fully (but only partially) exonerate the defendant from liability (unless it qualifies as cause étrangère*). A contributory fault can be held against a child of thirteen without the court having to decide whether the child was capable of understanding the consequences of his or her actions.*

1. Cass. civ., 28 February 1910　　　　　　　　**7.F.1.**

Loss of fingers

Facts: The plaintiff Nourrigat, a farmhand, was employed by the defendant Pech at his farm. He drove a machine for treating vines with sulphur, the gear wheels of which were not covered by any protective device. He stopped to give explanations to the farm manager. Another employee of the defendant, who was responsible for the team, suddenly made the horses drawing the machine move off. In attempting to get back hold of the reins, which had slipped out of his grip, the plaintiff's right hand became caught in the gear wheels and he lost three fingers.

---

[4] *Infra*, **7.E.11.**, s. 1(1).
[5] DP 1913.I.43, S 1911.I.329, annotated by G. Appert. Translation by R. Bray.
[6] JCP 1954.II.7792, annotated by R. Rodière. Translation by A. Dumas-Eymard.
[7] D 1984.Jur.525, with opinion of AG Cabannes and note by F. Chabas, JCP 1984.II.20255, with note by P. Jourdain, (1984) RTDciv. 508, with note by J. Huet. Translation by R. Bray.

Held: An action for damages brought by the plaintiff was dismissed at first instance and on appeal on the ground that the plaintiff had himself been negligent. The Cour de cassation quashed the judgment of the court of appeal.

Judgment: ". . . Having regard to Articles 1382 and 1384 C.civ., although the courts at first instance have sole jurisdiction to make findings of fact, it is for the Cour de cassation to determine whether the facts as found have the legal characteristics of fault as laid down by law, and result in the perpetrators incurring liability. . . The court of appeal dismissed the claim for damages and interest on the ground that Nourrigat was the victim of his own lack of care. Yet it is implicit in the findings set out above that Pech was guilty of fault which contributed to the occurrence of the accident, and the victim's carelessness could not exonerate Pech from all responsibility. Consequently, in ruling as it did, the contested judgment failed to take account of the legal consequences of the facts as found in it and, for that reason, infringed the provisions cited above. On those grounds, the Court quashes [the decision of the court of appeal]."

2. Cass. civ. 2e, 16 July 1953   **7.F.2.**

Insufficiently guarded trap door

Facts: The plaintiff, Suter, entered the café run by the defendant, Le Berry, early one morning; making his way to a table, he fell through a concealed trap door and was severely injured in consequence.

Held: The court of appeal apportioned liability equally, on the ground of concurring fault on the part of the defendant's employees and of the plaintiff. The Cour de cassation quashed the judgment of the court of appeal and remitted the case for consideration.

Judgment: "Having regard to Articles 1382 and 1383 C.civ.
   While it is for the trial judges to determine once and for all the facts from which they infer definitively (*souverainement*) the existence of . . . fault, the legal characterization of that fault may be controlled by the Cour de cassation. It follows from the [judgment of the court of appeal] that Suter, after entering the café Le Berry . . . as he made his way towards a table, moved a chair in order to sit in it. This chair, in combination with an armchair, hid an open hatch, into which Suter fell seven meters, thereby suffering serious injuries. In order to apportion liability for this accident half and half between Société Le Berry and the plaintiff, the [court of appeal] relies exclusively on the concurring faults imputed both to the employees of the said company and the victim himself. It states, on the one hand, that Le Berry committed a fault in failing to take any effective safety measures around the hatch to the cellar, left open in the middle of the central aisle, which constituted the ordinary and only path from the entrance to the tables. On the other hand, [the court of appeal] holds against Suter a fault for not having paid sufficient attention to the layout of the café. However, while the [court of appeal] could infer from those findings that Société Le Berry was at fault, it does not in any way follow that, in moving the obstacle abnormally situated in a point where the café's customers would naturally need to have free passage—when this obstacle, rather than indicating danger, in fact hid it—Suter lacked the care that one is entitled to require, in similar circumstances, from any man gifted with ordinary care. Therefore, it follows that in so deciding, the court of appeal failed to give its decision a correct legal basis."

3. Cass. Ass. plén., 9 May 1984   7.F.3.

Electrocution of child

Facts: As a result of a mistake made by the an electrician, Lemaire, in assembling a light socket, a thirteen-year old child, D. Leclerq, was electrocuted when he screwed in a light bulb. The parents brought a claim for damages against the electrician. It appeared from the evidence that in order to carry out that operation safely, the circuit-breaker should have been disengaged.

Held: The court of appeal found the electrician liable, but held that the child was responsible for fifty per cent of the damage, so that the parents were only awarded half of the amount of damages sought. The Cour de cassation dismissed the appeal.

Judgment: "The [parents] complain that the judgment held [the electrician] responsible for only one half of the consequences of the accident which killed their child by electrocution as a result of defective electrical work on their farm. The ground of appeal is that the court was not entitled to hold a thirteen-year old child guilty of fault contributing to the occurrence of the injury that he suffered, without considering whether he had sufficient ability to understand the consequences of his negligent act. Since it is found in the judgment [of the court of appeal] that the position of the rotating switch did not give any indication [as to its state], D. Leclercq should have turned off the electricity supply by operating the circuit-breaker before screwing in the bulb. In view of those findings, the court of appeal, which was not under a duty to determine whether the minor was capable of understanding the consequences of his act, was entitled to consider on the basis of Article 1382 C.civ. that the victim committed a fault which contributed, together with that of [the electrician], to the occurrence of the damage to such extent as was definitively determined by the court. Hence the ground of appeal is unfounded."

Notes

(1) The three annotated judgments[8] confirm a well-established solution, albeit that its legal basis remains controversial:[9] the plaintiff is not entitled to full compensation if he or she contributed to the damage through his or her own fault. However, as a general rule, the victim's contributory fault will not completely exonerate the defendant from the consequences of his or her own wrongdoing; that would be the case though if the victim's conduct qualifies as *cause étrangère* (extraneous cause), i.e. if it was unforeseeable (*imprévisible*) and unavoidable (*irrésistible*) for the defendant, and could be shown to constitute the sole cause of harm.[10] The proportion of damages that the defendant should bear despite the fault of the victim is determined along the same lines as the apportionment of liability between joint tortfeasors, and the solution is the same: the court must take into consideration the seriousness of the fault shown on both sides.[11] However, regard may be had to other circumstances, in particular the respective causal impact of the conduct of the parties;[12] and the defendant may even be completely exonerated in exceptional cases, such as when the victim committed an intentional fault or provoked the tortfeasor.

[8] The first and the third are reproduced with commentary in *Les grands arrêts* at 488 and 493.

[9] Viney and Jourdain, *Conditions* at 285–7, para. 426. The most plausible explanation appears to be the wish to "punish" the guilty victim: S. Carval, *La responsabilité civile dans sa fonction de peine privée* (Paris: LGDJ, 1995) at para. 278 ff.

[10] Viney and Jourdain, *Conditions* at 246, para. 402. On *cause étrangère*, see *supra*, Chapter III, 3.2.3. and Chapter IV, 4.1.3.

[11] See also *supra*, Chapter IV, 4.2.

[12] See Viney and Jourdain, *Conditions* at 295–6, para. 432; *Les grands arrêts* at 491–2.

The three excerpted judgments also show that the Cour de cassation is willing, in this area at least, to interpret its power to quash the decision of the trier of fact in an extensive way.[13] That appears especially from the second judgment, where apportionment to the detriment of the victim was refused by the Cour de cassation, and the judgment of the court of appeal quashed, because that court had misconstrued its findings of fact to infer fault on the part of the victim. In the first judgment as well, the Cour de cassation reviewed the findings of fact made by lower courts, this time to hold the defendant partially liable for an act of his employee.

(2) Whilst the Conseil d'État has confirmed that the principle of partial exoneration leading to apportionment applies also in administrative law,[14] criminal courts refused for some time to apportion civil liability between tortfeasor and victim[15] (except where the victim had participated in the crime[16]). They changed their view after a decision of the full Cour de cassation of 28 January 1972,[17] but then only for injury sustained as a result of crimes against the person, and for damage resulting from crimes against property, e.g. theft or fraud. Apportionment is excluded for such crimes because it would in practice allow the defendant to retain part of the illicit profit resulting from his or her crime.[18]

(3) In earlier case law of the Cour de cassation,[19] the principle of partial exoneration was understood to cover also situations where the *liability of the defendant* arose not on account of his or her conduct (Articles 1382–1383 C.civ.) but on account of *conduct of others*—as exemplified in the first and the second annotated judgments (liability for employees)—or of the behaviour of *things* (Articles 1384(1) and 1385 C.civ.) or *animals* (Article 1386 C.civ.). This broad understanding was subsequently curtailed, in respect of liability for *things*, first by the *Desmares* judgment[20] and then (subject to certain conditions) by the *Loi Badinter*, as explained further below. But, in a later judgment of 6 April 1987[21], the *Desmares* judgment was overturned. Accordingly, with the exception of car accidents falling under the regime of the *Loi Badinter*, the fault of the plaintiff can again be invoked as a ground of partial exoneration even when the defendant is liable on account of the conduct of other persons or the behaviour of things.

Reciprocally, the "*fault of the victim*" leading to apportionment is also construed broadly. In order to limit his or her liability, the defendant may also rely on acts of persons for whom the victim is responsible.[22] At one time, the Cour de cassation even held that a non-negligent course of conduct could also be held against the victim to reduce the

---

[13] In France, the court of appeal is also empowered to make findings of fact, on the same footing as the court of first instance.

[14] See in particular CÉ, 4 December 1970, JCP 1970.II.16764, with note by D. Ruzié.

[15] For reasons of criminal procedure, Viney and Jourdain, *Conditions* at 288–9, para. 427. As to civil claims before criminal courts in France (the so-called *action civile*), see *supra*, Chapter II, 2.5.1, Introductory Note under a).

[16] Cass. crim., 24 January 1962, Bull.crim. 1962.58.

[17] Cass. Ch. mixte, 28 January 1972, JCP 1972.II.17050, with the conclusions of A.G. Lindon, (1972) RTDciv. 405, with note by G. Durry.

[18] Viney and Jourdain, *Conditions* at 293, para. 430; *Les grands arrêts* at 492.

[19] Cass. Req., 13 April 1934, S 1934.I.313, with the report of Gazeau, annotated by H. Mazeaud, D 1934.I.41, annotated by R. Savatier.

[20] Cass. civ. 2e, 21 July 1982, D 1982.Jur.449, with opinion of Charbonnier and annotation by C. Larroumet.

[21] *Infra*, **7.F.4.**

[22] See the case law quoted by Viney and Jourdain, *Conditions* at 288–9, para. 427 who point out that this case law leads to the victim being held liable for part of his or her loss even without fault on the part of the victim.

defendant's liability.[23] However, the Cour de cassation has never accepted that assumption of risk by the plaintiff as such constituted a reason for apportionment, except when it amounts to fault.[24]

(4) As the third annotated judgment shows, the tendancy to take a broad view of the victim's fault culminated in the finding that even the "fault" (seen objectively) of a child who lacked the ability to appreciate the consequences of his actions (*discernement*) sufficed to lead to a reduction of compensation because of contributory fault.

Prior to that judgment, the Cour de cassation had held that no apportionment could take place in the absence of a subjective fault on the part of the child.[25] The annotated judgment was one of five given on the same date in which the Assemblée plénière of the Cour de cassation defined the scope of liability of minors and their parents,[26] holding that it was irrelevant whether the minor was subjectively capable of discerning the consequences of his actions; the basic concept of fault was thus to be defined objectively in order to assess the conduct of *both* the defendant and the plaintiff.[27]

(5) Some commentators have criticized the solution set out above, whereby the defendant can be partially exonerated on account of a broadly construed concept of fault as applied to the conduct of the victim. The concept of *faute* as it is found in Articles 1382–1383 C.civ. originally related to the defendant. The courts gave it a broad objective interpretation because they were concerned that the victim should enjoy greater protection.[28] For those critics, when the Cour de cassation simply applied that broad concept, through a mirror effect, to contributory fault, it overemphasized rationality at the expense of the basic purposes of civil liability.[29] Indeed, the liberal intent behind the broad objective construction of fault backfires when that construction is applied to contributory fault, since it is bound to deprive the plaintiff of full compensation in the same measure as—when applied to the defendant—it increased the protection of the plaintiff by extending the range of cases where the defendant will be liable. The case law of the Cour de cassation led to severe consequences for the victim, since it has meant that compensation was reduced not only when the victim infringed a rule of conduct imposed by law, but also when the victim breached the "general duty to look after oneself" (*obligation générale de veiller à sa propre sécurité*) or even when its "contributory fault" actually arose from the conduct of persons, or the behaviour of things, for whom/which the victim must answer. Moreover, the apparent symmetry between plaintiff and defendant is warped by the play of third-party or liability insurance to the benefit of the defendant, so

---

[23] Cass. civ. 2e, 17 December 1963, D 1964.Jur.569, annotated by A. Tunc, JCP 1965.II.14075, annotated by N. Dejean de la Bâtie. See further Viney and Jourdain, *Conditions* at 291–3, para. 429; see also *infra*, **7.F.4**, Note (1).

[24] Viney and Jourdain, *Conditions* at 296–8, para. 433. See *infra*, 7.2.3.

[25] Cass. civ. 2e, 11 June 1980, Bull. civ. 1980.II.140, D 1981.IR.323.

[26] See *supra*, Chapter III, **3.F.19** and notes thereafter.

[27] As for the defendant's conduct, the Cour de cassation thus harmonized the rules relating to acts of a minor and the rules on acts of mentally handicapped persons within the meaning of Article 489–2 C.civ.: see *supra*, **3.F.18** and **3.F.19** and Note (3). It is more than probable that the Cour de cassation will also want to harmonize these situations with regard to other victims: Viney and Jourdain, *Conditions* at 298–9, para. 433–1.

[28] See *supra*, Chapter III, 3.2.2.A.

[29] The application of the broad concept of fault to this situation as well has been criticized for not taking into account the particularity of the victim's act which, in the majority of cases, is only an unfortunate reaction to the tortfeasor's act: C. Lapoyade-Deschamps, *La responsabilité de la victime* (Bordeaux, 1977) at 33–49, referred to by Viney and Jourdain, *Conditions* at 285–7 and 299, para. 426 and 433–2.

that the only person who ultimately "pays" for his or her fault is often the victim. It has therefore been proposed that—at least until the system of compensation is entirely over-hauled—only serious or inexcusable fault should be held against the plaintiff; a simple fault (i.e. according to the objective standard used to assess the conduct of the defendant) would leave the victim's right to compensation intact, at least where the liability of the defendant is covered by insurance.[30] The *Loi Badinter* marked a clear step in that direction, as regards the compensation of victims of motor vehicle accidents.[31]

(6) What the legislature did for traffic accidents still remains to be done, however, for other risks to which children are exposed daily. The Cour de cassation, far from following in the footsteps of the *Loi Badinter* for these other risks, has shown surprising severity in its case law. It characterized as *"fautif"* behaviour which one could argue is typical of a child, thereby reducing the compensation awarded to that child.[32] In any event, those decisions stand in manifest contradiction to the aim of protecting the victims of bodily harm, which is one of the dominant tendencies of French tort law today.[33]

Cass. civ. 2e, 6 April 1987[34]   **7.F.4.**
Bardèche v. Jonier

CONTRIBUTORY FAULT IN THE CONTEXT OF LIABILITY WITHOUT FAULT

Falling branch

*The keeper (*gardien*) of a thing within the meaning of Article 1384 (1) C.civ. (other than a vehicle) will be exonerated in part if he or she proves that the victim's fault contributed to the occurrence of the damage caused by the thing.*

Facts: Bardèche entered the property of Jonier, where the latter was felling trees. Although he had been asked several times to leave the property because of the danger of falling branches, he stayed and was injured by a branch which Jonier had cut from a tree with a chain saw. Bardèche brought an action against Jonier, the keeper (*gardien*) of the chain saw within the meaning of Article 1384 (1) C.civ.

Held: The court of appeal held that Bardèche's fault was not unforeseeable or unavoidable for Jonier and that therefore Jonier was entirely responsible for the damage caused. The Cour de cassation quashed the judgment of the court of appeal.

---

[30] See A. Tunc, "Les causes d'exonération de la responsabilité de plein droit de l'art. 1384, al. 1er" D 1975.Chron.83; G. Viney, "La faute de la victime d'un accident corporel: le présent et l'avenir" JCP 1984.I.3155; Viney and Jourdain, *Conditions* at 299, para. 433–2.

[31] See *infra*, **7.F.5.–6.** The *Loi Badinter* is discussed in greater detail *supra*, Chapter VI, 6.2.1.B. See Viney and Jourdain, *Conditions* at 293–4, para. 431. Following the enactment of the *Loi Badinter*, another judgment of the Cour de cassation rendered on the same day as the third annotated judgment, Cass. Ass. plén., 9 May 1984, *Derguini v. Tidu*, JCP 1984.II.20256, is no longer good law, since it concerned a traffic accident.

[32] See Starck, Roland and Boyer at para. 991; also Cass. civ. 2e, 28 February 1996, Bull.civ. 1996.II.54, D 1996.Jur.602, with note by F. Duquesne, (1996) RTDciv. 628, with note by P. Jourdain (an 8-year old child running towards a friend who was carrying a saucepan constituted a *'faute'*); Cass. civ. 2e, 19 February 1997, Bull. civ. 1997.II.53, Resp.Ass. 1997.Com.154 (a young child approaching a moving see-saw constituted a *'faute'* as well).

[33] *Supra*, Chapter II, 2.1.3. and 2.1.5.

[34] Bull.civ. 1987.II.86, D 1988.Jur.32, with note by C. Mouly, JCP 1987.II.20828, with note by F. Chabas, (1987) RTDciv. 767, with note by J. Huet. Also reproduced with commentary in *Les grands arrêts* at 560. Translation by R. Bray.

Judgment: "Having regard to Article 1384(1) C.civ., the keeper of the thing which was the instrument causing the damage will be exonerated in part from his liability if he proves that the victim's fault contributed to the occurrence of the damage . . . The [court of appeal] found that Bardèche, who had been asked several times to go away in view of the danger from falling branches, was guilty of fault when he remained on the site. It found, however, that that fault was neither unforeseeable (*imprévisible*) nor unavoidable (*irrésistible*) so far as Jonier was concerned, and it proceeded to hold Jonier entirely responsible for the damage in his capacity as keeper. In so ruling, the appeal court did not infer the proper legal consequences from its findings of fact, and it thus infringed the aforementioned provision."

Notes

(1) The annotated judgment, one of three delivered on the same date,[35] re-introduced the principle that the defendant would be partially exonerated as a result of the victim's fault in cases where the defendant is liable under the regime of liability for things (Article 1384(1) C.civ.), i.e. in the context of liability not based on conduct.[36] With that judgment, the case law on contributory fault in the context of liability not based on conduct has come full circle, as appears from the following and Note (2).

At first the courts left little room for the fault of the victim within the framework of liability under Article 1384(1) C.civ., since it could be taken into account only if it amounted to a *cause étrangère* for the defendant (i.e. it was unavoidable and unforeseeable), so that the defendant would be *entirely* exonerated.[37] That approach was in line with the key ruling of the Cour de cassation in *Jand'heur*, according to which only *cause étrangère* could fully exonerate the defendant from liability under Article 1384(1) C.civ.[38] In a subsequent judgment of 13 April 1934, the Cour de cassation took a more balanced approach, however, by holding that the liability of the defendant *can be reduced* in proportion to the degree of fault of the victim.[39] Accordingly, it became possible, in the context of liability under Article 1384(1) C.civ., to apportion liability between a plaintiff whose fault contributed to the occurrence of the damage and the keeper of the injurious thing, who is presumed to be responsible for part of the damage. In the wake of that judgment, courts became very generous for the keeper, who was partly exonerated even where no fault on the part of the victim could be proven.[40]

However, in the *Desmares* ruling of 21 July 1982,[41] the Cour de cassation returned to the "all-or-nothing" approach laid down in *Jand'heur* by ruling that "only an event constituting *force majeure*

---

[35] Another of the judgments, Cass. civ. 2e, 6 April 1987, *Waeterinckx*, D 1988.Jur.32 is reproduced in French, and in English translation, in M. Vranken, *Fundamentals of European Civil Law* (London: Blackstone Press, 1997) at 249.

[36] For a thorough discussion of the regime of Article 1384(1) C.civ., see *supra*, Chapter VI, 6.1.2. The annotated judgment has been confirmed many times since: Cass. civ. 2e, 8 June 1994, D 1994.IR.181, JCP 1994.IV.2012; Cass. civ. 2e, 8 March 1995, D 1995.Somm.232, Resp.Ass. 1995.Com.196; Cass. civ. 2e, 22 March 1995, D 1995.IR.99, JCP 1995.IV.1265, Resp.Ass. 1995.Com.195; Cass. civ. 2e, 18 December 1995, D 1996.IR.35, JCP 1996.IV.380.

[37] *Supra*, **7.F.3.**, Note (1). On *cause étrangère*, see *supra*, Chapter III, 3.2.3: if the victim's fault amounts to *cause étrangère* the defendant is not liable at all. See, for example, the Cass. civ., 8 February 1938, *Taponier* v. *Bernheim*, DH 1938.194, S 1938.I.136, Gaz.Pal. 1938.I.558, reproduced in *Les grands arrêts* at 557–8.

[38] Cass. Ch. réun., 13 February 1930, *supra*, Chapter VI, **6.F.6**, more specifically Note (2) thereunder.

[39] Cass. Req., 13 April 1934, D 1934.I.41, with report by Gazeau and annotation by R. Savatier, S 1934.I.313, with annotation by H. Mazeaud.

[40] For instance, where a pedestrian is involved in a road traffic accident. Cass. civ. 2e, 17 December 1963, D 1964.Jur.569, with note by A. Tunc, JCP 1965.II.14075, with note by N. Dejean de la Bâtie; Cass. civ. 2e, 6 April 1965, JCP 1966.II.14485, with note by P. Esmein; Cass. civ. 2e, 12 May 1971, JCP 1972.II.17086, with note by J. Boré; Cass. civ. 2e, 4 October 1972, JCP 1973.II.17450, with note by B. Starck.

[41] Cass. civ. 2e, 21 July 1982, D 1982.Jur.449, with opinion by Charbonnier and note by C. Larroumet, JCP 1982.II.19861, with note by F. Chabas; see *Les grands arrêts* at 558.

[or *cause étrangère*] will exonerate the keeper (*gardien*)... from liability under Article 1384(1) C.civ.; if the conduct of the victim was not unforeseeable (*imprévisible*) and unavoidable (*irrésistible*) for the keeper, he or she cannot be exonerated from liability, even in part." As a result, the fault of the victim, however serious, could not have any impact on the liability of the keeper (*gardien*) unless it qualified as *cause étrangère* for the keeper, in which case the defendant was fully exonerated. *Desmares* was followed by the Criminal Chamber and was extended by the Civil Chamber to liability for animals under Art. 1385(1) C.civ.[42] Its application was however limited to these liability regimes; the general regime of liability for one's own conduct (Articles 1382–3 C.civ.) was excluded from its scope.[43]

(2) Many observers saw *Desmares* as a call by the judiciary for legislative reform. It became indeed a catalyst for legislative intervention:[44] it was followed fairly quickly with the enactment of the *Loi Badinter* on 5 July 1985, whose special regime of compensation for motor vehicle accidents included provisions relating to contributory fault. Following that reform, the Cour de cassation, in the annotated judgment, reinstated the principle of apportionment between the keeper (*gardien*) of a thing and a victim who was at fault as regards cases not coming under the *Loi Badinter*. From a policy perspective, such a reinstatement is acceptable in areas where, as in the annotated judgment, no system of compulsory insurance exists. There it is, indeed, easier to accept that the liability of the defendant—who is not insured—should be reduced at the expense of the victim who was at fault. And, of course, the liability of the defendant will even be excluded altogether if the conduct of the plaintiff qualified as *cause étrangère* for the defendant.[45]

(3) As mentioned above, the *Loi Badinter*[46] was enacted in the wake of the *Desmares* controversy, in order to introduce an improved system of compensation for the victims of accidents involving one or more motor vehicles; it will be recalled that third-party insurance against claims arising from motor vehicle accidents is compulsory.[47] Article 2 provides that the keeper (*gardien*) of a vehicle can no longer be exonerated from liability towards victims, including drivers,[48] not even because of *force majeure* or the conduct of a third party. The only remaining defence is the contributory fault of the victim, subject however to several limitations contained at Articles 3 to 6. In this regard, the precise effect

---

[42] Cass. civ. 2e, 18 January 1984, Gaz.Pal. 1984.Pan.140, JCP 1984.IV.96, (1984) RTDciv. 724, with note by J. Huet: here also it was held that only an event having the character of a *force majeure* could exonerate the *gardien* of an animal, and that, accordingly, the conduct of the victim, if it was not unforeseeable and irresistible, could not exonerate the *gardien*.

[43] See Cass. civ. 2e, 21 July 1982, *Guillaume*, Gaz.Pal. 1982.Somm.317, with note by F. Chabas; Cass. civ. 2e, 8 December 1982, JCP 1983.IV.67; Cass. crim., 25 January 1983, Bull.crim. 1983.28.

[44] See J.-L. Aubert, "L'arrêt *Desmares*: une provocation à quelles réformes?" D 1983.Chron.1. See further F. Terré, P. Simler and Y. Lequette, *Droit civil—Les obligations* (Paris: Dalloz, 1996) at para. 771–2 and 887–942.

[45] Cass. civ. 2e, 2 April 1997, Bull.civ. 1997.II.109; Cass. civ. 1re, 6 October 1998, Bull.civ. 1998.I.269; Cass. civ. 2e, 27 May 1999, Bull.civ. 1999.II.104. See Viney and Jourdain, *Conditions* at 249, para. 403 where the difference in meaning of this complete exoneration is discussed in the case of fault liability as compared to liability without fault.

[46] *Supra*, Chapter VI, **6.F.18.**

[47] C. Larroumet, "L'indemnisation des victimes d'accidents de la circulation: l'amalgame de la responsabilité civile et de l'indemnisation automatique" D 1985.Chron.237; for a description of the settlement procedures, see T. Antony Downes, "French Lessons on Motor Accident Compensation" in R. White and B. Smythe, (eds.), *Current Issues in European and International Law* (London: Sweet & Maxwell, 1990).

[48] In that respect the *Loi Badinter* surpasses the *Desmares* ruling.

of the *Loi Badinter* depends largely on the status of the victim and on the kind of damage.[49] Whilst it remains, or rather resurfaces,[50] as a defence as regards damage to property, little room is left for contributory fault as against injury to the person.[51]

Cass. Ass. plén., 19 June 1981[52] **7.F.5.–6.**
Mandin v. *Foubert*
and
Cass. civ. 2e, 10 October 1985[53]
Coulon v. *Gleize*

Relevance of the victim's fault against "reflex" harm (*dommage par ricochet*)

The fault of the direct victim can be relied on by the defendant to reduce the compensation recoverable by the dependents of the direct victim in respect of the harm that they suffered as a result of the injury to the direct victim.[54]

1. Cass. Ass. plén., 19 June 1981 **7.F.5.**

Surviving dependants

Facts: Mr. Foubert was travelling in his car with his wife and minor daughter Florence. He died as a result of a collision between the car and a lorry driven by Mandin. Mrs. Foubert (acting for herself and her daughter) and her adult son, Didier, brought claims for compensation against Mandin. Mrs. Foubert claimed for the injuries that were inflicted to her and her daughter in the collision, as well as for the harm that they had both suffered as a result of Mr. Foubert's death. Didier claimed for pain and suffering as a result of his father's death.

Held: The court of appeal held that, in the absence of personal fault on the part of the claimants, no apportionment of liability could be made by reason of the fault committed by Mr. Foubert. The Cour de cassation quashed the decision of the court of appeal insofar as it concerned the harm that the three claimants had sustained as a result of Mr. Foubert's death, but not as regards the injury that Mrs. Foubert and her daughter had sustained personally.

---

[49] Further details were provided on the *Loi Badinter* and its application, *supra*, Chapter VI, 6.2.1.B. For a short summary, see Viney and Jourdain, *Conditions* at 293–4, para. 431; F. Terré, P. Simler and Y. Lequette, *Droit civil—Les obligations* (Paris: Dalloz, 1996) at para. 919–55.

[50] That is, as compared with the *Desmares* judgment which had eliminated the defence in general terms with regard to liability of the keeper (*gardien*) within the meaning of Art. 1384(1) C.civ.

[51] As for the effect of the defence of contributory fault on the claim of a "reflex" victim (*victime par ricochet*), see *infra*, **7.F.5.–6.**, Note (1).

[52] D 1982.Jur.85, with opinion of A.G. Cabannes and note by F. Chabas, JCP 1982.II.19712, with report of A. Ponsard, Gaz.Pal. 1981.Jur.529, with note by J. Boré, (1981) RTDciv. 857, with note by G. Durry; *Les grands arrêts* at 119. Translation by R. Bray.

[53] Bull.civ. 1985.II.152. Translation by R. Bray.

[54] Where, however, the claim of the dependent of direct victim (who was a driver) is for loss or damage that he or she has suffered in his or her own right, rather than in his or her capacity as a dependent, fault on the part of the driver victim is irrelevant. Moreover, if the dependents were passengers, they will now receive compensation for their personal injury, even when they committed a fault for which, depending on the category of victims they belong to, they are not accountable.

698

Judgment: "Having regard to Article 1382 C.civ.

The person whose fault caused the damage . . . is partly exonerated from liability if he proves that the fault of the victim contributed towards the occurrence of the damage. That rule applies not only where the claim for compensation is brought by the victim himself, but also where it is brought by a third party who, acting on his own account, seeks compensation for the personal harm which he suffered as a result of the death of or bodily injury sustained by the victim. Although the third party's claim is distinct in purpose from that which the victim would have been able to assert (even where the third party is also the victim's successor), it nevertheless results from the same originating event considered in all the circumstances . . .

[T]he [court of appeal] held that, in the absence of fault on the part of the [claimants], no apportionment of liability could be made to their detriment by reason of any fault on the part of Mr. Foubert. Although that decision is justified as regards compensation for the damage sustained by Mrs. Foubert and Florence as a result of the injuries that they received, harm for which they were entitled to claim compensation in full . . ., the decision was not justified as regards the harm which both they and Didier suffered as a result of Mr. Foubert's death. By disregarding any fault on the part of Mr. Foubert when the [claimants] sought damages for the harm caused to them by the latter's death, the court of appeal infringed the aforementioned provision.

On those grounds, the Court quashes the judgment given by the court of appeal, but only as regards compensation for the harm suffered by the [claimants] as a result of the death of Mr. Foubert, insofar as it declared that any fault on the part of Mr. Foubert could not be relied on as against the [claimants]."

2. Cass. civ. 2e, 10 October 1985 7.F.6.

Surviving dependants

Facts: In a collision between two cars, one driven by Mrs. Coulon, the other by Gleize, Mrs. Coulon was fatally injured. She had not been using a seatbelt, which constitutes faulty conduct. Mr. Coulon brought a claim, on behalf of himself and his minor daughter, for damages sustained as a result of Mrs. Coulon's death.

Held: The court of appeal reduced the damages awarded to Mr. Coulon on account of Mrs. Coulon's fault. The Cour de cassation dismissed the appeal.

Judgment: "Under Articles 4 and 6 of the *Loi Badinter* . . ., fault committed by the driver of a motor vehicle has the effect of limiting or excluding compensation for the damage sustained by him and for the harm caused by that damage to third parties.

Having found that Mrs. Coulon had omitted to fasten her seatbelt, the [court of appeal] held that the only injuries which she sustained were to her face and were caused when, as a result of the impact, her head violently struck the windscreen.

The court of appeal was entitled to infer from those findings that the victim contributed to the damage for which compensation was sought, to an extent which it had sole jurisdiction to determine."

Notes

(1) The first annotated judgment, one of two concerning indirect victims given on the same day, marks the end of a period of uncertainty and experimentation, and confirms a solution already adopted by the full Cour de cassation seventeen years earlier.[55] Under

[55] Cass. Ch. réun., 25 November 1964, D 1964.Jur.733, with the conclusions of A.G. Aydalot, JCP 1964.II.13972, with note by P. Esmein; *Les grands arrêts* at 505. See also F. Terré, P. Simler & Y. Lequette, *Droit civil—Les obligations* (Paris: P. Dalloz, 1996) at para. 844 and 935.

the so-called "opposability rule", the victim's own fault can be relied on by the defendant, not only against the victim who claims damage for harm sustained personally, but also against "reflex victims" (*victimes par ricochet*) who sustained harm as a result of the direct victim's death or bodily injury.

The second Civil Chamber followed this ruling,[56] as did the Criminal Chamber,[57] and it has achieved general acceptance. In the area of road traffic accidents, the *Loi Badinter* also adopted this solution as a matter of principle (but see Note (2)). It states in Article 6 that "loss suffered by a third party owing to damage caused to the immediate victim of a road traffic accident shall be made good, regard being had to the limitations or exclusions applicable to the compensation of such damage".[58] Article 6 is applied in the second annotated judgment.

The rationale behind the "opposability" rule is that even though the claim of an indirect victim is distinct, in term of its purpose, from that of the immediate victim, it nevertheless results from the same originating event. While there is a duality of damage, there is a unity of the original occurrence.[59]

(2) After the *Loi Badinter*, the first annotated judgment remains good law for all areas of tort law other than road traffic accidents. And also in the area of road traffic accidents, it remains useful as an expression of the general rule of "opposability" which underlies the solution retained in Article 6 of the *Loi Badinter* as regards the contributory fault of direct victims who were drivers of a vehicle, as the second annotated judgment shows. However, as for the fault of other victims (i.e. those who were not drivers), Article 6 contains severe limitations, in that it can be relied on by the defendant against the indirect victims whose "reflex injury" (*dommage par ricochet*) arose from the injury to such a direct victim, only in so far as permitted by Article 3. And indeed, that provision grants far-reaching protection to certain classes of victims (as long as they were not drivers) of a road traffic accident, since they will be held contributory negligent only under limited conditions; by the same token, "reflex victims" (*victimes par ricochet*) will not see their claims reduced on account of contributory negligence of such a direct victim.

Under Article 6 of the *Loi Badinter*, the fault of "reflex victims" (*victimes par ricochet*) themselves will normally not be taken into account. However, that can lead to shocking consequences in cases where a driver was himself or herself a "reflex victim", for instance where the spouse of the driver was a passenger and died as a consequence of the accident. In such a case, if the driver was himself or herself at fault, he or she would then be treated more favourably as an indirect or "reflex victim" than as a direct victim. In a judgment of 15 March 1995, the Cour de cassation put an end to this anomaly:[60] Article 4 of the *Loi*

---

[56] Cass. civ. 2e, 6 January 1982, Gaz.Pal. 1982.Pan.174, with note by F. Chabas.; Cass. civ. 1re, 11 January 1983, Gaz.Pal. 1983.Pan.141, with note by F. Chabas.

[57] Cass. crim., 26 January 1982, Bull.crim. 1982.30, Gaz.Pal. 1982.Somm.235.; Cass. crim., 2 May 1983, Bull.crim. 1983.277.

[58] See *supra*, **6.F.18** and, for comment, Starck, Roland and Boyer at para. 185–7; Viney and Jourdain, *Conditions* at 1170, para. 1034 ff.

[59] "*S'il y a dualité de dommages, il y a unité du fait générateur*": Starck, Roland and Boyer at para. 184. Before the first annotated judgment, there had been a considerable debate as to the legal basis in favour of the theory of opposability, but that seems now to belong to the past. See Viney and Jourdain, *Conditions* at 305–6, para. 435 ff.

[60] Cass. crim., 15 March 1995, Bull.crim. 1995.103, JCP 1995.IV.1558, D 1996.Somm.119, with note by D. Mazeaud, (1995) RTDciv. 642, with note by P. Jourdain. That judgment was later confirmed by the Joined Chambers of the Cour de cassation: Cass. Ch. mixte, 28 March 1997, Bull.civ. 1997.Ch.mixte.1, D 1997.Jur.294, with note by H. Groutel, (1997) RTDciv. 681, with note by P. Jourdain.

Badinter, whereby the contributory fault of a driver can be raised as a defence against a claim from the driver, now takes precedence over Article 6.[61]

7.1.2. GERMAN LAW

Under German law, the apportionment principle is contained in § 254 BGB:

§ 254. (1) If a fault of the injured party has contributed to the occurrence of the damage, the duty to compensate and the extent of the compensation to be made depend upon the circumstances, especially upon how far the injury has been caused predominantly by the one or the other party.

(2) This applies also if the fault of the injured party was limited to omission to call the attention of the debtor to the danger of unusual serious damage, of which the debtor neither knew nor ought to have known, or to an omission to avert or mitigate the damage. § 278 applies *mutatis mutandis*.[62]

The apportionment principle contained in § 254 BGB is also incorporated in a number of specific regimes of risk-based liability (*Gefährdungshaftung*), for example at § 9 of the *Straßenverkehrsgesetz* (StVG) of 29 December 1952.[63] The StVG also regulates, at § 17, the apportionment between drivers of motor vehicles as amongst themselves and towards third parties:

§ 9. [Contributory negligence of the injured party]
If the injured party contributed to the damage by his negligence, § 254 BGB applies with the proviso that if property is damaged, negligence on the part of the person exercising factual control over the property is treated as equivalent to negligence on the part of the injured party.

§ 17. [Contribution among several persons liable to pay compensation]
(1) If damage is caused by several motor vehicles and if the custodians of the vehicles involved are bound by law to pay compensation to a third party, the custodians' liability to pay compensation and the extent of the compensation to be paid as between themselves depends upon the circumstances, especially whether the damage has been caused predominantly by one or the other of the parties. The same applies to the liability of one of the custodians if the damage was caused to another custodian of a vehicle involved in the accident.

(2) The provisions of para. (1) apply by way of analogy if the damage is caused by a motor vehicle and an animal or by a motor vehicle and a railway trail.

---

[61] See Cass. civ. 2e, 18 March 1998, Bull.civ. 1998.II.85; Cass. cur. 2e, 5 November 1998, Bull.civ. 1998.II.254. See further Viney and Jourdain, *Conditions* at 1172, para 1036.

[62] § 278 BGB provides: "The debtor [of a contractual obligation] shall answer for the negligence of his legal representative and of the persons that he uses for the fulfilment of his obligation under the same conditions as for his own negligence. § 276(2) does not apply". § 276(2) BGB provides: "There can be no exoneration in advance from liability for intentional conduct".

[63] *Supra*, Chapter VI, **6.G.12**. Before then, the Act was called *Gesetz über den Verkehr mit Kraftfahrzeugen.*

CONTRIBUTORY NEGLIGENCE OF A MINOR

Child knocked down

*A five-year old child (exempt from liability pursuant to § 828(1) BGB) is liable to have his or her contributory "fault" (*Mitverschulden*) set against him or her only exceptionally, where fairness requires it, by analogy with § 829 BGB. That will not be the case where the tortfeasor was obliged to be insured against third-party liability.*

Facts: The first defendant was driving his car in the offside lane of a dual carriage way road, the carriageways being divided by a cultivated central reservation. A child, aged 5, walked from the central reservation in front of the first defendant's car, which struck the child, causing her serious and lasting injuries. The second defendant was the third-party liability insurer of the first defendant. The plaintiff was the social insurance organisation by whom the child was covered through her father. The plaintiff claimed restitution of the social insurance benefits against both defendants, by way of subrogation. The defendants argued that the plaintiff could not require restitution of the amount claimed, since the child substantially contributed to the occurrence of the accident.

Held: The plaintiff's claim was upheld by the court of first instance and by the court of appeal. The BGH dismissed the appeal from the court of appeal.

Judgment: "2. . . . . The court of appeal reduced the defendants' liability pursuant to § 9 StVG and § 254 BGB, by applying § 829 BGB *mutatis mutandis*, on account of the contribution made to the accident by the child, who was deemed to be incapable of fault . . .

3. The appeal against that judgment is unsuccessful . . .

(a) According to the principles formulated by this Chamber, the exceptional nature of § 829 BGB is to be taken into account even where it is applied *mutatis mutandis* in relation to § 254 BGB [references omitted]. The basic principle enshrined in the law must be respected: persons incapable of fault are neither liable to pay compensation nor have to relieve tortfeasors of the duty to pay compensation, where those persons contributed to the occurrence of an accident. [That principle] may not be replaced by apportionment of damage on grounds of fairness. In addition, the rule set out in § 829 BGB was enacted for a different situation and hence may not be directly applied in connection with § 254 BGB; accordingly, particular restraint must be exercised in applying that provision in the context of § 254 BGB. It must not be forgotten that, under § 829 BGB, it is permissible to modify the application of the principles of liability only where this is not only *justified* by fairness (*Billigkeit*) but also *necessary* in the light of all the circumstances of the case; the rule of fairness [laid down in § 829] retains an exceptional character as against the exemption, in principle, of persons incapable of fault from contributory liability for damage.

(b) In assessing and weighing the personal circumstances of the injured party and the circumstances which led to the accident . . ., the court of appeal proceeded in accordance with those rules.

[I]n assessing whether the economic circumstances necessitate a reduction in liability on the part of the tortfeasor on grounds of fairness, it is of decisive importance to know whether the tortfeasor had to be compulsorily insured against third-party liability. [Where he had to be so insured] there is, as a general rule, no justification for any modification [on grounds of fairness under § 829] of the principle that a contributory fault on the part of an injured party who is incapable of fault [under § 828(1) BGB] will not reduce the liability of the tortfeasor. This does not elevate the existence of insurance cover against third-party liability on the part of the torfeasor to being a ground

[64] NJW 1973, 1795. Translation by R. Bray.

for liability, nor does this force upon the third-party liability insurer the tasks of an indemnity insurer . . .

The fact that the consequences of the damage as far as the injured child is concerned are covered by social security does not lead to a different legal assessment . . .

(c) Likewise a different assessment concerning the relationship between the share of the blame for the road accident attributable to the first defendant and that attributable to the injured child is not necessary. In assessing the respective contributions towards the causation of the accident, the appeal court did not . . . apply an incorrect criterion. The fact that the first defendant was not guilty of any fault in respect of the road accident, but instead has to answer 'only' for the danger posed by his vehicle, does not mean as a matter of course, in the face of significant contributory 'fault' on the part of the child who is incapable of fault, that there exists a justification to differentiate between contributions as required for the application of § 829 BGB."

Notes

(1) Before the enactment of the BGB, in the event of *Mitverschulden* or contributory fault of the plaintiff, compensation was denied unless the defendant had acted intentionally. This all-or-nothing rule, known as *Culpakompensation,* was abolished[65] by § 254(1) BGB, which is part of the first section of the second book of the BGB relating to legal obligations in general, and is therefore applicable to the law of contract and delict. Contributory fault of the plaintiff now constitutes an exception to the principle of full compensation.

As appears from § 254(2), contributory fault may also consist in an omission "to call [someone's] attention to the danger of unusual serious damage" or an omission "to avert or mitigate the damage" and may thus occur *after* as well as *before* the occurrence of the actual harm. Issues arising under § 254(2) are dealt with in the chapter on remedies.[66]

For § 254 BGB to be applicable, (i) the victim must have acted unlawfully, i.e. he or she must have infringed a duty of care, either intentionally or negligently (§ 276(1) BGB), (ii) his or her conduct must be imputable to him or her[67] and (iii) there must be a causal link between his or her conduct and the injury.[68] When the conditions of § 254 are fulfilled, the compensation which the defendant is bound to pay may be reduced (or even negated altogether), depending upon the circumstances of the case—i.e. especially the seriousness of the respective faults of the parties and the extent to which each fault caused the damage.[69] Furthermore, as will be seen later,[70] special provisions have enlarged the scope of the victim's contributory "fault" in the context of risk-based liability (*Gefährdungshaftung*) to include sources of risk for which he or she is held to be responsible.

(2) As mentioned, for apportionment to occur under § 254 BGB, it must be proved that the victim infringed a duty of care (*Sorgfaltsverletzung*). Often the victim will have infringed a duty imposed by law or a contractual obligation.[71] However, the infringement

---

[65] See Staudinger-Schiemann, § 254 at para. 1; E. Deutsch, "Einschränkung des Mitverschuldens aus sozialen Gründen?" ZRP 1983, 137.
[66] See *infra,* Chapter VIII, 8.2.2.
[67] Which is not so if the victim falls within the classes of persons referred to in §§ 827, 828 BGB.
[68] See Münchener-Grunsky, § 254 at 498–501, para. 19–21a.
[69] Larenz at 549–50.
[70] *Infra,* **7.G.8**, Note (1).
[71] D. Medicus, *Schuldrecht—Vol. 1: Allgemeiner Teil,* 10th edn. (München: Beck, 1998) at para. 674.

may also consist in an omission by the victim to take the precautions which a reasonable person would have taken to protect his or her own legal interests (*Rechtsgüter*). Contributory fault may therefore also arise when the victim did not properly speaking commit a "fault" as against another person, but was simply not sufficiently cautious (intentionally or negligently) as to avoid being harmed. The concept of "contributory fault" (*Mitverschulden*) in the context of § 254 is therefore controversial.[72] It is generally considered not to have the exact same meaning as the concept of "fault" under § 823(1) BGB. Indeed, someone who endangers himself is not necessarily considered to have behaved in an "unlawful", or even "blameworthy" fashion, in contradistinction with someone who did not behave towards others in accordance with the general standards of conduct as required by law.[73]

The question is indeed to what extent a legal system is willing to punish the carelessness of the victim towards himself or herself. If A gets into a car with B whom A knows to be drunk, A infringes no legal duty merely by travelling with B. But if A suffers harm while riding with B and brings a claim against B who behaved in a blameworthy way, then A must be held accountable for his own careless behaviour in putting himself in a position such that the conduct of B may lead to injury to him.[74] The concept of "*Verschulden*" in § 254 (1) BGB must therefore be understood to encompass both unlawful behaviour against someone else—which can qualify as "fault" (*Verschulden*) within the meaning of § 823(1) BGB—and failure to take appropriate action to protect one's own interests against harm.[75] Such "fault" towards oneself (*Verschulden gegen sich selbst*) is then defined as an infringement of an *Obliegenheit*, that is a duty "of a lesser intensity, the observance of which cannot be enforced, but can nonetheless have legal consequences".[76] For indeed, "[a]lthough the law does not command one to take reasonable care of one's own interests, it does refuse to let another be burdened with the consequences of a failure to do so".[77] However, framing the duty to oneself as an *Obliegenheit* is criticized by some commentators because it would require a pre-existing legal relationship between the parties;[78] those commentators would prefer to define the issue as a question of distribution of risks. Another possibility is to see § 254 BGB as an emanation of the principle of good faith (*Treu und Glauben*) laid down in § 242 BGB: the victim does not act wrongly in neglecting his or her own interests, but it would not be consistent with good faith for him or her to demand full compensation if these interests are injured.[79]

(3) The victim's "contributory fault" (*Mitverschulden*) must have contributed in some way to the damage. So, when the passenger of a drunken motorcyclist was injured in a traffic accident caused by a car that did not respect the motorcycle's right of way, drunkenness is not taken into account if it neither contributed to the accident nor aggravated its consequences.[80] Moreover, the contributory fault must also be of sufficient causal impact when compared with the defendant's conduct. For instance, in cases of intentional

---

[72] Kötz at para. 552 ff.

[73] Larenz at 539–40.

[74] For examples in the case law differentiating concrete situations, see Lange at 640 ff.

[75] See R. Greger, "Mitverschulden und Schadensminderungspflicht—Treu und Glauben im Haftungsrecht?" NJW 1985, 1130 at 1132–33.

[76] Lange at 552; Staudinger-Schiemann, § 254 at para. 30–1.

[77] Lange at 553–4; see also *infra*, Chapter VIII, 8.2.2. in relation with the duty to mitigate harm.

[78] J. Esser and E. Schmidt, *Schuldrecht: ein Lehrbuch*, Vol. 1, Pt. 2, 7th edn. (Heidelberg: Müller, 1993) at 258–9.

[79] See H. Stoll, *Das Handeln auf Eigene Gefahr* (Tübingen: Mohr, 1961) at 315 ff.; Munchener-Grunsky, § 254 at para. 2. See also *infra*, **7.G.10.** and Note thereafter.

[80] BGH, 2 February 1960, VersR 1960, 479.

or malicious conduct on the part of the defendant, the contributory fault of the victim (if it consisted in a slight carelessness) will probably not be given any weight.

As for *causation*, the plaintiff's "fault" under § 254 will be assessed—like the conduct of the defendant—in the light of the prevalent theories of causation under German law, namely the adequacy and "scope of rule" (*Schutzzweck der Norm*),[81] both of which aim to correct the shortcomings of the equivalency theory. With regard to adequacy, harm brought about by the plaintiff's fault must have been reasonably foreseeable.[82] As for the "scope of rule" theory, it dictates that compensation should be reduced on account of *Mitverschulden* only for such injury as the legal duty or *Obliegenheit* infringed by the victim aimed to prevent.[83]

The significance of causation in the application of § 254 BGB is further highlighted by the broad interpretation of the notion of *Mitverschulden* which, departing from the strict wording of § 254 BGB, is deemed to include contributory *Betriebsgefahr* on an equal footing with contributory fault (*Mitverschulden*).[84] This move away from contributory fault as such (*Mitverschulden*), towards a broader concept of contribution to causation (*Mitverursachung*), became even more apparent in the risk-based liability (*Gefährdungshaftung*) regimes enacted by special legislation, which speak only in terms of causation. For instance, in § 17(1) StVG, apportionment is made between two parties who are both liable on the basis of a creation of risk (*Gefährdung*), by reference to how far the injury "has been *caused predominantly* by one or the other of the parties".[85]

(4) The concept of contributory fault (*Mitverschulden*) at § 254(1) BGB implies that, regardless of whether the victim's conduct consists in a wrong against another or a breach of an *Obliegenheit* concerning the victim himself or herself, it can be held against the victim, because of intentional or negligent conduct within the meaning of § 276(1) BGB.[86] § 276(1) BGB refers in this context to §§ 827 and 828 BGB relating to the elimination or reduction of liability of the defendant on the ground of unconsciousness or mental illness (§ 827 BGB)[87] or because of young age, a distinction being drawn between those who are seven years of age or less (§ 828 (1) BGB) and those who are older than seven years but less than eighteen (§ 828(2) BGB).[88]

It nevertheless remains controversial under what precise conditions the claim for compensation of a minor will be reduced on account of *Mitverschulden*.[89] It is clear from the case law that a minor's *Mitverschulden* will be taken into account only if he was capable of committing a fault under § 828(2) BGB. So, when a child of between 7 and 18 years of age should have been able to appreciate the consequences of his or her actions, the child will have his or her *Mitverschulden* set against his or her claim. Some argue that the child's

---

[81] Münchener-Grunsky, § 254 at 499–500, para. 20. For a general discussion of the theories of causation under German law, see *supra*, Chapter IV, 4.1.1.

[82] D. Medicus, *Schuldrecht—Vol. 1: Allgemeiner Teil*, 10th edn. (München: Beck, 1998) at para. 678.

[83] Ibid.

[84] BGH, 23 June 1952, *infra*, **7.G.8.**

[85] Ibid, Notes (1) and (3).

[86] *Supra*, Chapter III, 3.2.1., under b).

[87] But not where the person involved has brought himself or herself in such a situation by drinking alcohol or the like: second sentence of § 827 BGB.

[88] Those provisions are dealt with *supra*, Chapter III, 3.2.3.B.

[89] See Staudinger-Schiemann, § 254 at para. 42.

Mitverschulden should affect the claim also where the child was incapable of recognizing the danger that his or her action posed to himself or herself.[90]

(5) The annotated judgment concerned the contributory negligence of a child of five years for injury caused to her in a traffic accident, to which § 254 BGB applies by virtue of § 9 StVG.[91] The question to be resolved was whether the child, who pursuant to § 828(1) BGB is incapable of committing a fault (because she is less than 7 years old), must nevertheless see her claim for damages reduced on the basis of a "mirror" application of § 829 BGB. It will be recalled that § 829 BGB provides that persons who are not liable in tort by virtue of §§ 827 or 828 BGB must pay compensation for damage caused by them insofar as fairness (*Billigkeit*) dictates, under the circumstances (and insofar as compensation cannot be claimed from a person responsible for them).[92] The case law of the BGH made it clear that § 829 BGB may also be applied within the framework of § 254 BGB, provided that the exceptional character of § 829 is properly taken into account. That means that § 829 should be applied in a "mirror" fashion in the context of § 254 only when fairness *requires* it (and not merely *justifies* it) under the relevant circumstances.[93] Amongst those circumstances, § 829 refers in particular to "the relative positions of the parties" which, according to the annotated judgment, includes the fact that the first defendant, the driver of the car, was obliged by law to be insured against third-party liability (here under a policy with the second defendant). Where such insurance is taken there is normally no reason to apply § 829 BGB in a context where the victim was a minor who is incapable of fault and whose conduct contributed to the occurrence of damage. In such a situation, fairness does not require the minor to see his or her compensation reduced. According to the BGH, that conclusion is not affected by the fact that the minor had obtained certain social security benefits in respect of the harm sustained by her as a consequence of the accident. Nor did it matter, interestingly enough, that the tortfeasor (the first defendant) "was not guilty of any fault . . . but, instead, has to answer 'only' for the danger posed by his vehicle" under § 7 StVG.[94]

(6) One of the interesting issues arising with respect to § 254 BGB is whether and under what circumstances the conduct of other persons can be imputed to the plaintiff as *Mitverschulden*, so as to reduce the liability of the defendant. It could be thought that the answer is provided by the second sentence of § 254(2) BGB, from which it results, through the reference to § 278 BGB,[95] that the fault of the injured person's "legal representative and of the persons that he uses for the fulfilment of his obligation" also gives rise to an apportionment of liability under § 254. Yet that provision raises as many issues as it

---

[90] See J. Esser and E. Schmidt, *Schuldrecht: ein Lehrbuch*, Vol. 1, Pt. 2, 7th edn. (Heidelberg: Müller, 1993) at 266–7; but see among others Kötz at para. 559, who argues on policy grounds that such an approach would contradict the very rationale behind § 254 BGB, which is arguably to encourage the individual to modify his or her own behaviour in order to reduce the possibility of accidents occurring.

[91] *Infra*, **7.G.8.**

[92] *Supra*, Chapter III, 3.2.3.B.

[93] Staudinger-Schiemann, § 254 at para. 44. In an earlier decision of 10 April 1962, BGHZ 37, 102, NJW 1962, 1199, which was referred to in the annotated judgment, the application of § 829 BGB in the context of § 254 BGB was accepted, but only in order to allow a reduction of future damages in the event that the relative positions of the parties were to change.

[94] The application of § 254 BGB (or equivalent) in the context of risk-based liability (*Gefährdungshaftung*) is discussed in the next annotated case.

[95] The operation of § 278 BGB is explained in greater detail *supra*, Chapter V, 5.1.1.C. under g).

answers. First of all, the second sentence of § 254(2) applies on its face to § 254(2) only, but it is well established that it applies also to § 254(1) BGB.[96]

Secondly, the effect of the second sentence of § 254(2) would be to make § 278 BGB applicable through a "mirror" effect: A would see his or her claim for compensation reduced on account of the contributory fault of a person for whom—in the case of a claim where A would be the defendant—A would have to answer under § 278 BGB. However, § 278 cannot so easily be turned around, and its application in the context of § 254 remains controversial.[97] The main problem is that § 278 BGB requires a pre-existing contractual relationship: its function is to ensure that contracting parties are liable for the third parties which they bring in for the execution of their contractual obligations (the "execution assistants"or *Erfüllungsgehilfe*). When § 278 BGB is applied in the context of § 254 BGB, a pre-existing contractual relationship between the victim and the wrongdoer would therefore be required before the conduct of the third party could be imputed to the victim by way of *Mitverschulden*. That is the position defended by the BGH in its case law, on the ground that the application of § 278 BGB should not put the victim in a worse situation than when § 278 BGB is used against a defendant.[98] Some legal writers argue, however, that the conduct of the legal representative of the victim should be imputed to the victim as *Mitverschulden*, irrespective of whether there was a contractual relationship with the defendant, since otherwise the victim could end up deriving an advantage from dealing through a legal representative.[99] In any event, the case law is generous in recognizing contractual relationships for the purpose of applying § 278 BGB in the context of § 254 BGB; "something that resembles an obligation" (*etwas einer Verbindlichkeit ähnliches*) will suffice.[100]

In addition, despite the absence of any wording to that effect, it is well established in case law that, under § 254 BGB, the conduct of corporate organs will be imputed to the victim, if it is a corporation (by a reciprocal application of § 31 BGB), and the conduct of employees (*Verrichtungsgehilfe*) will be imputed to their employer (by reciprocal application of § 831 BGB).[101]

The main practical consequence of the position taken by the BGH in its case law regarding the application of § 278 BGB in the context of § 254 BGB is that, when a child claims for compensation for injury he or she has suffered, any fault on the part of the parents, who are the legal representatives of the child, will not be held as contributory fault (*Mitverschulden*) against the child (unless there was a contractual relationship between the child and the defendant, which is usually not the case).[102]

[96] Kötz at para. 569; D. Medicus, *Schuldrecht—Vol. 1: Allgemeiner Teil*, 10th edn. (München: Beck, 1998) at para. 679.

[97] See in greater detail Staudinger-Schiemann, § 254 at para. 95–109. J. Esser and E. Schmidt, *Schuldrecht: ein Lehrbuch*, Vol. 1, Pt. 2, 7th edn. (Heidelberg: Müller, 1993) at 265–7; B. Kleindienst, "Die entsprechende Anwendung des § 278 BGB bei mitwirkendem Verschulden" NJW 1960, 2026.

[98] See BGH, 12 November 1991, BGHZ 116, 60 at 74 (reproduced in part, *supra*, Chapter VI, **6.G.26**). If it were otherwise (no pre-existing relationship would be required when § 278 BGB is applied in the context of § 254 BGB), a much larger range of conduct by third parties (e.g. legal representative, etc.) would be imputed to the victim.

[99] See for instance Lange at 603 ff, and the authors mentioned by Münchener-Grunsky, § 254 at 525, para. 77.

[100] See Lange at 376 and Münchener-Grunsky, § 254 at 525–6, para. 78–81.

[101] See Münchener-Grunsky, § 254 at 527, para. 83–4. If the conduct of the employee is imputed to the employer by way of *Mitverschulden*, it is open to the employer to show that he or she was not at fault (within the framework of § 831 BGB: see *supra*, Chapter V, 5.1.1.C. under d) to f)).

[102] See on this point, in a comparative perspective, von Bar II at 550–1, para. 532.

BGH, 23 June 1952[103]   7.G.8.

CONTRIBUTORY NEGLIGENCE IN ROAD TRAFFIC ACCIDENTS

Motor cars collide

*Under § 254 BGB and by reference to § 17 (1) StVG, a defendant who is liable for a fatal car accident pursuant to § 823 BGB may raise as a defence the contribution (*Mitverantwortlichkeit*) of the victim* qua *keeper of a motor car within the meaning of § 7 StVG, even if the victim was not at fault.*

Facts: The husband of the plaintiff was driving his motorcar. The defendant drove his lorry into the car. The husband of the plaintiff sustained fatal injuries.

Held: The court of first instance dismissed the claim for damages. The court of appeal reversed the judgment of the court of first instance. The BGH upheld the judgment of the court of appeal.

Judgment: "[The BGH first established that the defendant was equally liable according to § 823 BGB, but that the husband of the plaintiff was not at fault.]

The court of appeal obviously assumed that no apportionment is necessary since the husband of the plaintiff was without blame for the accident and therefore § 254 BGB could not be set against him—and thereby against the plaintiff. This opinion does not seem to be justified.

According to the case law, § 254 BGB is to be applied even if the plaintiff was without fault—and this in spite of the wording of § 254 BGB which requires contributory fault (*Verschulden*) in the occurrence of the damage—that is where he would be liable for the damage caused by virtue of a statutory [risk-based liability] regime [reference omitted] . . .

The *first sentence* of § 17 [StVG] concerns first of all the case in which an injured third party can claim damages from several keepers (*Halter*) of the vehicles who are liable as a result of the involvement of their vehicles in the occurrence of the damage [emphasis added]. No distinction can be made between such third-party claims according to whether some of the keepers are liable only because of the operational risk (*Betriebsgefahr*) they created and some also because of fault. The apportionment between the keepers of the vehicles involved in that situation depends exclusively upon causal impact. Consequently, it has never been in doubt that, when it comes to the apportionment, one keeper cannot deny his liability as with the other keepers (*Innenverhältnis*), solely on the ground that his liability *vis-à-vis* the victim is merely based on an operational risk for which he has to answer according to § 7 [StVG], as compared with another of the keepers who would also be liable on the basis of fault pursuant to § 823 BGB. This fault might be relevant for the calculation of apportionment only in so far as it had a causal impact on damage which has arisen.

The *second sentence* of § 17(1) [StVG] governs, in direct connection with the first sentence, the case where the damage was caused to another keeper of a vehicle involved in the accident [emphasis added]. It provides that the same [solution as in the first sentence] is to apply regarding the liability of keepers as between themselves. Hence the interpretation should prevail according to which in such situations the operational risk created by the victim must also be taken into account in the process of weighing up factors of causation. This applies even if fault can be imputed only to the [defendant] but not to the victim. As the Chamber held [with regard to] § 1 [HaftpflG] (BGHZ 2, 355 at 358), weighing up contributory factors of causation under § 254 BGB in cases of liability without fault corresponds to mainstream legal thinking. It leads in such case to the result that the risk-based liability (*Gefährdungshaftung*) of the [defendant] is not completely excluded by a con-

[103] BGHZ 6, 319, NJW 1952, 1015. Translation by I. Wendt and M. Jelbert.

tributary fault of the victim. In the present case, it is consistent with this result if the risk-based liability of the victim is not completely disregarded in view of the fault of the [defendant], thus leading here again to weighing up factors of causation.

This result cannot be rejected on the grounds that it would be unfair or was not wanted by the legislature. If the legislature introduced a regime of liability without fault which in its effects, in relation to the causation of the damage, is put in the same category as negligent behaviour, it is also a matter of fairness to take the liability of the keeper under that regime into account also when it benefits a defendant who was at fault . . .

These considerations conclusively lead to setting against the injured keeper, and thus also against the plaintiff, the causal risk (*Betriebsgefahr*), irrespective of the ground of liability on the part of the defendant . . ."

Notes

(1) Read literally, § 254(1) BGB does not allow apportionment to the detriment of a victim who has not committed a contributory *fault*. However, specific statutory regimes of risk-based liability (*Gefährdungshaftung*) have provided for apportionment in cases where two parties were involved, both of whom were held liable under that regime for the creation of risk (*Gefährdung*). The second sentence of § 17(1) StVG provides an example.[104]

Despite the restrictive wording of § 254(1) BGB, the case law of the RG, and subsequently of the BGH, came gradually to acknowledge the principle of apportionment as a general rule, regardless of whether the victim's share was derived from fault or arose by reason of the creation of risk (*Gefährdung*). In its early case law, for reasons of fairness, the RG held that the applicability of risk-based liability regimes on the plaintiff's side had to be disregarded when the defendant's liability was based on risk only (i.e. when the defendant was not at fault). Subsequently, and starting with the annotated judgment, the BGH, noting the inconsistency to which the case law of the RG had led, began to view apportionment as a question of weighing causal elements (*Abwägung der Ursächlichkeit*), regardless of whether those causal elements were based on fault or risk.

To come to that conclusion, the BGH took as a starting point the reasoning underlying § 17(1) StVG. The first sentence of § 17(1) StVG deals with the apportionment of liability *between* the respective keepers of several vehicles involved in the same traffic accident, as *against the victim*. For that purposes, that provision takes account of "whether the damage has been caused predominantly by one or the other of the parties". Therefore it is not the degree of fault, if any, but the causal impact that is decisive to effect apportionment. The second sentence of § 17(1) StVG goes on to say that the same holds true for determining "the liability of *one of the keepers* if the damage was caused *to the keeper* of another vehicle involved in the accident" [emphasis added]. On that basis, the BGH concluded that, where apportionment under § 254(1) BGB is to be determined, causal impact of the factors generating liability is the decisive criterion, regardless (for all parties, defendants and plaintiffs) of whether such factors are based on considerations of fault or risk (*Gefährdung*).[105]

---

[104] For more details on the risk-based liability regime of § 7 ff. StVG, see *supra*, Chapter VI, 6.2.1.A. An overview of the risk-based regimes under German law is given in Chapter VI, **6.G.2.** and notes thereafter.

[105] Münchener-Grunsky, § 254 at 495–6, para. 10.

(2) In a later judgment of 13 April 1956,[106] the BGH re-affirmed that conclusion and applied it to a claim in damages for pain and suffering brought by the keeper of one of the vehicles involved. In that judgment, like in the annotated judgment, § 254 BGB was applied to a claim brought by a person who was not only keeper but also driver of a motor vehicle. However, if the keeper and the driver of a vehicle are *not* the same person, a claim by the keeper for compensation for damage to his or her car may be reduced under § 254 BGB, because of the risk created by the operation of the vehicle (*Betriebsgefahr*) of the vehicle *and* because of negligence on the part of the driver.[107] By contrast, the claim of a driver will be reduced, according to § 254 BGB, only because of the driver's own negligence and not because of the operational risk, which affects exclusively the position of the keeper[108] who has created a potential danger by putting the vehicle into operation (*Betrieb*).

(3) Reference to § 254 BGB is made predominantly in the context of road traffic accidents,[109] for which § 7 StVG imposes risk-based liability on the keeper of a motor vehicle.[110]

Again in the context of road traffic accidents, apportionment because of—true—contributory *fault* arises when the victim, whether a driver or a passenger, omitted to use a seatbelt or, in the case of a motorcycle, to wear a helmet. Even before the imposition of a legal obligation to use seatbelts or to wear helmets,[111] the BGH had held that such an omission may lead to a reduction in compensation for the victim on the grounds of contributory negligence under § 254 BGB *if* a normal, intelligent person would have considered it prudent to use a seatbelt, or wear a helmet, in the circumstances.[112] After the use of seatbelts (and helmets) was made compulsory, the BGH confirmed its earlier case law without any reservations: not using a seatbelt, in violation of the law, constitutes contributory fault (*Mitverschulden*) within the meaning of § 254(1) BGB.[113] It emphasized, however, that the failure to use a seatbelt leads to reduction of compensation for *those* injuries the existence or gravity of which is causally related to the failure.[114] But this does not preclude trial courts from applying a uniform scale of reduction for injuries affected by failure to use a seatbelt or helmet, even though the actual effect of that failure may vary from one case to the other. A uniform scale is consistent with the global assessment (*Gesamtbetrachtung*) as to compensation for damage under § 254(1) BGB, and it is practical.[115]

---

[106] BGHZ 20, 259. English translation by T. Weir in Markesinis at 841.

[107] BGH, 20 January 1954, BGHZ 12, 124.

[108] BGH, VersR 1963, 380. The keeper has created a risk (*Gefährdung*) by taking a machine (car) in operation (*Betrieb*).

[109] Cf § 9 StVG. See further the overview in Münchener-Grunsky, § 254 at 501–7, para. 23–33.

[110] See further *supra*, Chapter VI, 6.2.1.A.

[111] At § 21a(1) of the Straßenverkehrsordnung (StVO, Road Traffic Regulations) of 16 November 1970, BGBl.I.1565.

[112] BGH, 20 March 1979, NJW 1979, 1363. In that case the BGH reduced the defendant's liability by 20 percent because of the victim did not use a seatbelt (or rather had not fitted seatbelts in his car). The BGH took the view that failure to fit, or use, seatbelts may constitute fault but, because of the absence of a strong general conviction amongst drivers, at the time of the accident, of the need to fit seatbelts to their cars, the BGH regarded the fault in this case as only slight. See, in similar terms, BGH, 30 January 1979, NJW 1979, 980 in respect of wearing a helmet.

[113] Staudinger-Schiemann, § 254 at para. 50–1.

[114] BGH, 1 April 1980, NJW 1980, 2125.

[115] Ibid.

An interesting point in the case law is whether the obligation to use seatbelts or to wear helmets is compatible with the basic freedom of the individual laid down in Article 2 GG. The BVerfG[116] and the BGH[117] have consistently taken the position that the obligation does not infringe Article 2 GG; the European Commission of Human Rights has taken the same position in relation to Article 8 ECHR.[118]

BGH, 6 July 1976[119]   **7.G.9.**

EXCLUSION OF LIABILITY FOR ANIMALS

Dog in heat

*Under § 833 BGB, the keeper of an animal (*Tierhalter*) is liable for all damage falling within the scope of the risk created by the unpredictable conduct of the animal, but liability can be reduced, or even extinguished, within the framework of § 254 BGB, in proportion with the danger created by the animal of another keeper or the contributory fault of the latter.*

Facts: The plaintiff was the owner of a pedigree chow breeding bitch. The defendant was the keeper of a mongrel dog. In December 1973, the plaintiff was walking her dog (on heat at that time) on a lead when they met the defendant's dog which was not on a lead. The plaintiff's attempts to separate the animals were unsuccessful and they mated. The plaintiff claimed damages from the defendant for the costs of veterinary care she had incurred for her dog, i.e. an abortion and the treatment of resulting uterine inflammation, as well as for her loss of income because she was prevented from obtaining and selling a litter of purebred chows.

Held: The court of first instance and the court of appeal dismissed the claim. The appeal to the BGH was to no avail.

Judgment: "1. The court of appeal takes an appropriate starting point, [namely] that the mere connection between the existence of an animal and some damage is not sufficient to impose liability for animals on the basis of the regime of liability for animals under § 833 BGB [reference omitted]. The first sentence of § 833 BGB concerns a case of risk-based liability (*Gefährdungshaftung*), i.e. liability for damages resulting from dangers and risks which cannot fully be kept under control [references omitted] . . . Therefore, in addition to examining the causal connection between the behaviour of an animal and the injury, both the RG and the BGH always examined whether the injury is to be attributed to a 'specific' danger characteristic of the animal [reference omitted] or to an 'actual' or 'typical' danger of the animal [reference omitted]. Obviously, it would be inconsistent with the purpose of [§ 833 BGB]—as it was just outlined—if the keeper of an animal were to be held liable for any damage in which the animal was involved in one way or another (e.g. as a mere projectile).

2. The Chamber is not able to follow the court of appeal where the latter considers that mating is not the realisation of a risk related to the keeping of an animal . . .

b)The conclusion of court of appeal . . . does not accord with the protective scope (*Schutzzweck*) of the first sentence of § 833 BGB . . .

bb) A definition that correctly delineates the scope of the risk related to the keeping of animals must follow from the object and purpose of the statutory provision. Since the reason for the

---

[116] EuGRZ 1976, 283.
[117] BGH, 1 April 1980, NJW 1980, 2125, with further reference to BGH, 20 March 1979, BGHZ 74, 25 and BGH, 10 April 1979, NJW 1979, 1367.
[118] Opinion of 13 December 1979 in *X* v. *Belgium*, EuGRZ 1980, 170.
[119] NJW 1976, 2130. Translation by I. Wendt.

specific regime of liability of the keeper of animals lies in the unpredictability of the behaviour of an animal and the resulting danger for life, health and the property of third persons [reference omitted] the keeper of the animal must be held liable for any damage resulting from such unpredictability. That definition is also compatible contemporary scientific knowledge

cc) Accordingly, once the risk emanating from the animal is held to comprise exclusively such animal behaviour as is unpredictable for the keeper, at least every mating without the knowledge and consent of the keeper must be seen as a realization of that risk . . .

3. Despite this error of law, the judgment of the court of appeal stands . . .

a) Contrary to the view of the court of appeal, the plaintiff did indeed suffer an economic disadvantage from the mating of her dog, which can be considered as damage. Legally speaking, the act of mating constitutes damage to property within the meaning of § 833 BGB. Because of the insemination, the plaintiff was not able to use her bitch as she intended, namely (as she alleged) to bring the bitch to Holland shortly afterwards for mating with a selected pedigree chow and thus to raise young animals to be sold. The ability to use the bitch for [breeding] influences its value, so that depriving [the owner] of that ability can lead to damage [reference omitted].

b) However, the defendant's risk-based liability is excluded in the present case, because of the risk-based liability of the plaintiff and her own contributory negligence (*Mitverschulden*) (§ 254 BGB).

aa) The damage which the plaintiff suffers from the mating of her bitch is partly caused by the animal itself so that § 254 BGB must be applied by analogy. Until now, case law already applied § 254 BGB by analogy in cases where a legal interest (*Rechtsgut*), other than that in the keeper's own animal, was injured through both the keeper's animal and another animal. The same should also be done where the animals of different keepers injure each other [reference omitted], or where only one of the animals is 'injured', but where the risk related to the keeping of that animal was a contributory factor. Recent statutes creating risk-based liability regimes take the same approach (see § 17(2) StVG; the second sentence of § 41(1) LuftVG; the second sentence of § 34(1) AtomG). In the present case, the compensation owed by the defendant is further reduced because of the plaintiff's contributory negligence. According to her own submissions, she knew that her bitch was on heat. As every keeper knows, or at least should know, this is a difficult period because a bitch on heat attracts dogs from all around. So, if the bitch is taken for a walk in the short period when it is 'on heat', its keeper is not only expected not to let it run around freely . . . but also, if he takes it for a walk at all, to take further protective measures [reference omitted], or to take the animal somewhere where other dogs are not to be expected. It is not sufficient to keep the bitch on a lead, as the plaintiff did.

bb) Since the risk that damage can occur from mating emanates—at least with dogs—from the female and [since] the plaintiff was guilty of contributory negligence, the apportionment leads to the conclusion that the defendant is exonerated and hence that the plaintiff must bear her own damage. Consequently, the outcome of the judgment of the court of appeal turns out to be correct."

Notes

(1) The excerpted judgment is interesting for several reasons. First, it illustrates the application of § 254 BGB in a field other than road traffic accidents. Second, it illustrates how § 254 is applied in respect of all risk-based liability regimes (*Gefährdungshaftung*). Third, it demonstrates how, in the BGH's view, several contributory elements of fault (*Mitverschulden*) or causation (*Mitverursachung*) attributable to the injured party (here the keeper of the bitch) tend to reduce, or even exclude, the liability of the defendant (here the keeper of the mongrel dog) for the injury caused by his animal. In this respect the BGH draws an analogy with the provisions concerning contributory "conduct" in other risk-based liability regimes, notably § 17(2) StVG, dealt with above in connection with the

preceding case. Weighing the various causal elements, the court comes to the conclusion, in the annotated judgment, that there is no liability on the part of the defendant dog-keeper, since the causal impact of the plaintiff's contributory fault *and* of the risk related to the animal kept by the plaintiff accounted for the whole injury.

(2) The last point mentioned deserves further attention. It relates to the apportionment between causal elements of a different nature, namely fault (*Verschulden*) and risk (*Betriebsgefahr* or operational danger), to determine the existence, and the extent, of the liability of the defendant within the framework of § 254 BGB and corresponding provisions under risk-based liability regimes. Where objects for which risk-based liability exists (vehicles, animals, etc.) are involved on the side of both plaintiff and defendant, a number of factors must be taken into consideration. Some are related to fault (the respective faults of the two sides), and others to risk (the impact of the risk related to the vehicles or the animals held by each party).[120] As H. Kötz noted,[121] although an apportionment between fault (*Verschulden*) and risk (*Gefährdung*) may seem like comparing apples with pears, the case law seems to reach just and fair results.[122]

BGH, 11 May 1971[123]   **7.G.10.**

Mitverschulden as against secondary victim

Suffering widow

*A claim made by an indirect victim (here the widow of the direct victim of an accident) under § 823(1) BGB for injury suffered in her own right (psychological injury), while not coming within the scope of application of § 846 BGB, will nevertheless be reduced on account of the contributory fault (*Mitverschulden*) of the direct victim, on the basis of an analogy with § 254 BGB and the principle of good faith (§ 242 BGB), because there is a causal link between the injury to the direct victim and to the indirect victim.*

Facts: The plaintiff's husband, aged sixty-four, was killed in an accident caused by the defendant. The plaintiff claimed compensation for injury to her health which she allegedly suffered as a result of her husband's accidental death.

Held: The court of first instance allowed the claim entirely. The court of appeal allowed the claim, but only in part. The BGH quashed the judgment of the court of appeal and remitted the case for further consideration.

Judgment: "A . . . The judgment of the court of appeal is, in the first place, vitiated insofar as it is premised on the plaintiff having suffered genuine injury to health as a result of being informed of the accident [references omitted].

---

[120] To measure that risk (*Betriebsgefahr*) in a given case, the factors to be considered include, to take liability for motor vehicle accidents under § 7 StVG as an example, the actual speed of the object, the power of the engine, the weight of the vehicle, etc.: see Lange at 614–6.

[121] Kötz at 562, with reference to BGH case law, and at 563, where a concrete example is discussed involving two drivers and one pedestrian (all of them contributory negligent, and the first two being keepers of their respective vehicle).

[122] See for further examples, J. Esser and E. Schmidt, *Schuldrecht: ein Lehrbuch*, Vol. 1, Pt. 2, 7th edn. (Heidelberg: Müller, 1993) at 267–70.

[123] BGHZ 56, 163. Translation by I. Wendt.

713

The law as it stands refuses damages for inflicted pain . . . insofar as it does not result from injury to [one's] body or [one's] health. It is however compatible with that legislative decision that an autonomous claim for compensation could be brought by a person who suffers genuine injury to physical or intellectual/mental health as a result of an exceptional "traumatic" impact brought about by experiencing, or being informed of, an accident . . .

On the other hand, one must be aware of the fact that, as is well known and shown by experience, a strongly negative event that provokes sensations of pain, grief and fright frequently results in severe disturbance of physiological processes and mental functions. To recognize such disturbance as an injury to health within the meaning of § 823(1) BGB would not be compatible with the legislative intent . . .

B. I. Should the court of appeal, on reconsideration of the case, again conclude that a valid claim exists, then it may not disregard the contributory negligence of the deceased husband.

1. The court of appeal is right in so far as it rejects the analogous application of § 846 BGB to cases like the present . . . Claims of [dependants] based on §§ 844 and 845 BGB find their origin in . . . conduct that was directed against the direct victim [reference omitted]. That is why § 846 BGB states that the negligence of the [direct] victim, which has contributed to the occurrence of damage to a third party [i.e. the dependent], must be set off against claims based on §§ 844 and 845 BGB. That makes sense within the framework of §§ 844 and 845 BGB, but it is not appropriate in the case of an autonomous claim brought by a third party [i.e. the indirect victim] on the basis of § 823 (1) BGB . . .

2. Nevertheless, at least for cases such as the present, one has to agree with the . . . view that the contributory negligence of the deceased husband may not be left out of consideration in assessing the wife's claim for compensation of the injury to her own health that she indirectly sustained. This follows from an analogous application of the provisions in § 254 BGB, which reflect the general legal principle embodied in § 242 BGB [reference omitted].

(a) This is beyond doubt in relation to the *claim* relating to *pain and suffering* (§ 847 BGB) which is to be assessed in equity. The case law of the BGH [reference omitted] recognizes that for such claim, in contradistinction to the rules applicable to pecuniary loss, the peculiar susceptibility of the victim to injury, as a result of his or her specific physical and mental condition, may be taken into account to reduce his or her claim. In respect of damages for pain and suffering, the direct victim's *own* contributory negligence—which is not at issue here—also constitutes no more than one factor for the assessment of equitable compensation under the circumstances [reference omitted]. The same must hold true for other causal factors which are personal to the claimant, such as, in the present case, the family relationship with the person who was injured or killed.

b) However, in respect of injury to health resulting from the so-called "long-range" effect (*Fernwirkung*), [it] is also correct that, with regard to *pecuniary* loss, the contributory negligence of the direct victim of an accident must be taken into account against the relative who indirectly suffers damage to his or her own health. For indeed, a causal link between the injury to health alleged by the plaintiff and the accidental death of her husband would arise only because there is a personal relationship between the person suffering an impairment of health due to mental shock [i.e. the indirect victim] and the direct victim of the accident, whereby the former, so to speak, appropriates the latter's misfortune as her own. It is inconceivable that the mere news of the accidental death of another person with whom the plaintiff was *not* in a close relationship would have the same effect; this would at least be so unusual that in such a case injury to health would not be foreseeable and, accordingly, that the damage could no longer be reasonably imputed to the defendant.

Where the personal relationship is so decisive for the occurrence of injury to the plaintiff's health, the husband's contributory negligence in respect of the accident must then also affect the plaintiff's claim against the defendant for the compensation of pecuniary loss. In such a case, it is appropriate to apply by analogy the basic principle embodied in § 254 BGB, which operates as a bar to claims to the extent that an other essential cause of damage [in addition to the defendant's conduct] stems from the plaintiff's own sphere of responsibility."

Note
§ 846 BGB states: "If, in the cases provided for by §§ 844 and 845, a fault of the injured party has contributed to the occurrence of the harm which the third party has suffered, the provisions of § 254 apply to the claim of the third party". As a result of that provision, the contributory negligence of a person who was injured or killed in an accident reduces the damages recoverable by his or her dependents, insofar as they are entitled to obtain compensation under the restrictive conditions of §§ 844 and 845.[124] In the excerpted judgment the widow, although not directly involved in her husband's fatal accident (i.e. not a direct victim), claimed that she had suffered a severe nervous shock upon hearing of the death of her husband. If her condition qualifies as a psychological illness,[125] she would be able to obtain compensation for interference with her own health under § 823 (1) BGB.[126] She would then not come within the category of dependents, at least not for that type of injury, but would qualify as a victim in her own right—albeit an indirect one—to whom § 846 does not apply.

Nothwitstanding that finding, the BGH decided in the annotated judgment that the deceased's own contributory fault (*Mitverschulden*) is to be taken into account in the calculation of damages for pecuniary loss, and a fortiori of damages for pain and suffering (*Schmerzengeld*),[127] on the basis of the general principle of good faith (*Treu und Glauben*) laid down in § 242 BGB. The reason given for that conclusion is that any psychological injury to the widow would essentially be a consequence of her close personal relationship to the primary victim.[128]

---

[124] See *supra*, Chapter II, 2.1.1., Introductory Note and *infra*, Chapter VIII, 8.5.1., Introductory Note.

[125] In the case at issue, the BGH did not acknowledge, on the basis of the expert opinion submitted to the court of appeal, that such development had already taken place. It did not exclude that possibility, however, and addressed the question of the possible application of § 254 BGB if such development were to take place in the future.

[126] See *supra*, Chapter II, **2.G.4**, for a judgment referring explicitly to the above excerpted judgment as the basis of its decision not to grant compensation, in that case, for mere natural grief and psychological disturbance *not* qualifying as injury to health.

[127] See the reasons given in the annotated judgment, under B.I.2 a).

[128] See the excerpted judgment under B.I.2.b). For criticism of the reasoning, see K. Deubner, Comment, NJW 1985, 1392. But see Larenz at 548, who finds the result acceptable despite some criticism because, as seen from the perspective of the defendant, any shock suffered by the plaintiff is a further consequence of the accident to the occurrence of which the deceased contributed.

7.1.3. ENGLISH LAW

Law Reform (Contributory Negligence) Act 1945[129]   **7.E.11.–12.**
and
Court of Appeal[130]
Davies v. *Swan Motor Co. (Swansea) Ltd.*

CONTRIBUTORY NEGLIGENCE
THE APPORTIONMENT PRINCIPLE; THE STANDARD OF CARE THE VICTIM OWES TO HIMSELF

A finding of contributory negligence on the part of the victim does not require the existence of a duty of care towards the defendant; it is sufficient to show a lack of reasonable care on the part of the plaintiff for his own safety.

1. Law Reform (Contributory Negligence) Act 1945   7.E.11.

"**1.** (1) Where any person suffers damage as the result partly of his own fault and partly of the fault of any other person or persons, a claim in respect of that damage shall not be defeated by reason of the fault of the person suffering the damage, but the damages recoverable in respect thereof shall be reduced to such extent as the court thinks just and equitable having regard to the claimant's share in the responsibility for the damage . . .

(2) Where damages are recoverable by any person by virtue of the foregoing subsection subject to such reduction as is therein mentioned, the court shall find and record the total damages which would have been recoverable if the claimant had not been at fault . . .

4. The following expressions have the meanings hereby respectively assigned to them, that is to say . . . 'damage' includes loss of life and personal injury; . . .

'fault' means negligence, breach of statutory duty or other act or omission which gives rise to a liability in tort or would, apart from this Act, give rise to the defence of contributory negligence;"

2. *Davies* v. *Swan Motor Co. (Swansea) Ltd.*   7.E.12.

Dust-cart collision

Facts: The plaintiff's husband, a dustman employed by the Swansea Corporation, was standing on the steps on the offside of a dust-cart operated by the Corporation. The defendant's bus, while overtaking the dust-cart, collided with it and, in so doing, caused fatal injuries to the plaintiff's husband.

Held: The Court of Appeal allowed the claim, but found that the deceased contributed to his injuries to an extent that the plaintiff's damages should be reduced by one-fifth.

Judgment: DENNING LJ:[131] "The legal effect of the Act of 1945 is simple enough. If the plaintiff's negligence was one of the causes of his damage, he is no longer defeated altogether. He gets reduced damages. But the practical effect of the Act is wider than its legal effect. Previously, in order to mitigate the harshness of the doctrine of contributory negligence, the courts in practice sought to select, from a number of competing causes, which was *the* cause—the effective or predominant cause—of the damage and to reject the rest. Now the courts have regard to all the causes and apportion the damages accordingly. This is not a change in the law as to what constitutes contributory

---

[129] 8 & 9 Geo. 6 (c. 28).
[130] [1949] 2 KB 291, [1949] 1 All ER 620, CA.
[131] All three members of the court (Bucknill, Evershed and Denning LJJ) concurred in separate opinions.

negligence. The search in theory was always for all the causes. But it is a change in the practical application of it. . . .

. . . It has sometimes been suggested that an injured plaintiff is not guilty of contributory negligence unless he is under a duty of care towards the defendant . . . In my opinion, [that] is not a correct approach. When a man steps into the road he owes a duty to himself to take care for his own safety, but he does not owe any duty to a motorist who is going at an excessive speed to avoid being run down. Nevertheless, if he does not keep a good lookout, he is guilty of contributory negligence. The real question is not whether the plaintiff was neglecting some legal duty, but whether he was acting as a reasonable man and with reasonable care . . ."

Notes

(1) The common law rule which entirely excluded the claim of a plaintiff who had been guilty of contributory negligence,[132] was abolished by the Law Reform (Contributory Negligence) Act 1945.[133] Instead of leaving contributory negligence to operate as a complete defence, it introduced in its place a regime of apportionment: the plaintiff's claim is not defeated entirely by reason of his contributory negligence. Apart from the doctrine of mitigation of damage,[134] the Act thus provides the only means for the defendant of avoiding to be liable for the full amount of damages in cases of tort.

The old common law rule was difficult to justify in terms of causation since, as soon as any causal weight could be attributed to the plaintiff's fault, the defendant's fault was treated as irrelevant and the loss was said to "lie where it fell".[135] In an attempt to mitigate the potential injustices arising out of the rule, the law became fraught with complications in order to attribute causation entirely to the defendant. In particular, the courts developed the "last opportunity" rule (according to G. Williams a mere "palliative for the crude common-law rule"[136]), which provided that the party who had the "last clear chance" of avoiding the accident in question—that is very often the defendant—was to be deemed solely responsible for the resulting damage.[137] A decision of the Privy Council in 1916[138] further complicated the issue by establishing the principle of "constructive last opportunity", the effect of which was that responsibility fell on the party who *but for* his prior negligence, *would have had* the last chance of avoiding the accident.[139]

In the case excerpted above, Denning LJ considered the last opportunity rule to be "dead before the Act",[140] and he subsequently declared the rule "obsolete".[141] Since then no court has seen fit to revive it.[142] However, the issue of who had the last opportunity may be relevant where the later negligence of the defendant eclipses the prior carelessness of the plaintiff entirely.[143] Moreover, it may

---

[132] See *Butterfield* v. *Forrester* (1809) 11 East 60.

[133] The principle of apportionment for losses caused by maritime collisions was recognized in admiralty law before the more general adoption of the principle in the Act of 1945. See the Maritime Conventions Act 1911, 1 & 2 Geo. 5 (c. 57), s. 1.

[134] See for example *Darbishire* v. *Warran*, *infra*, Chapter VIII, **8.E.8.**

[135] G. Williams, *Joint Torts and Contributory Negligence* (Stevens: London, 1951) at 247.

[136] Ibid.

[137] *Davies* v. *Mann* (1842) 10 M & W 546.

[138] *British Columbia Electric Railway* v. *Loach* [1916] 1 AC 719.

[139] See G. Williams, *Joint Torts and Contributory Negligence* (Stevens: London, 1951) at 244–5.

[140] [1949] 2 KB 291 at 323, not reproduced above. See also the opinion of Evershed LJ at 318 (not reproduced), where he states that the Act "has rendered it no longer necessary to resort to devices of that kind".

[141] *Jones* v. *Livox Quarries Ltd.* [1952] 2 QB 608 at 616, CA.

[142] Markesinis and Deakin at 683.

[143] [1949] 2 KB 291 at 323 per Denning LJ.

be taken into consideration when considering the relative blameworthiness of the parties, once contributory negligence has been established.[144]

The power to apportion damages under the Act has meant that the courts have been liberated from some of the pretences of the old law, and there is no longer the same inclination to avoid finding a small element of contributory negligence on the part of the plaintiff and in that way to find the defendant solely liable.[145] Apportionment is now the rule, from which it also follows that any finding that, given the degree of *contributory* negligence, the plaintiff's damages should be reduced by 100 per cent, must be illogical.[146] It is nonetheless possible for the conclusion to be reached that, as a matter of causation, the plaintiff's own fault was so overwhelming that it was the sole effective cause of the relevant damage, so as to exclude liability of the defendant. That may be particularly so in the event of a second accident, where the defendant is exonerated on the ground that the plaintiff's conduct has amounted to a *novus actus interveniens*.[147]

(2) The very essence of contributory negligence is that the damage should have resulted partly from the plaintiff's fault and partly from that of the defendant. As pointed out by Denning LJ in the excerpted judgment, the plaintiff's contributory negligence does not imply necessarily that the plaintiff "is under a duty of care towards the defendant". The real question is whether the plaintiff "was acting as a responsible man and with reasonable care"[148] or, as Viscount Simon said in *Nance* v. *British Columbia Electric Railways Co. Ltd.*,[149] whether the plaintiff "did not in his own interest take reasonable care of himself and contributed, by his want of care, to his own injury".

Under Section 4 of the Act reproduced above, "fault" is defined as "negligence, breach of statutory duty or other act or omission which gives rise to liability in tort or would, apart from this Act, give rise to the defence of contributory negligence". It has been suggested that the first part of this definition refers to both the defendant's and the plaintiff's fault and that the second part refers to the plaintiff's lack of care (including instances where the plaintiff does not act in breach of a duty towards the defendant).[150] The second part would then mean that the defence of contributory negligence is "available to *any* action in tort (save where expressly excluded by statute) and in any other case where at common law such a defence defeated the plaintiff's claim".[151]

"Contributory negligence is set up as a shield"[152] against the plaintiff's claim: it does not constitute an action in its own right but its result is that the plaintiff "cannot call on the other party to compensate him in full".[153] Where the defendant suffers damage, however, a counterclaim may be brought.[154]

---

[144] See *Cakebread* v. *Hopping Bros. (Whetstone) Ltd.* [1947] KB 641; *Clerk and Lindsell on Torts* at para. 3–12.

[145] [1949] 2 KB 291 at 310, per Bucknill LJ and at 322, per Denning LJ.

[146] *Pitts* v. *Hunt* [1991] 1 QB 24 at 28, per Balcombe LJ. See also *infra*, **7.E.28.**

[147] See also *supra*, Chapter IV, 4.3.2.

[148] Per Lord Denning in the annotated judgment.

[149] *Nance* v. *British Columbia Electric Railways* [1951] AC 601 at 611, PC.

[150] G. Williams, *Joint Torts and Contributory Negligence* (Stevens: London, 1951) at 318- 9 and Markesinis and Deakin at 689; *Forsikringsaktieselskapet Vesta* v. *Butcher* [1988] 3 WLR 565 at 573, per O'Connor LJ (decision of the Court of Appeal affirmed by the House of Lords at [1989] AC 852); Rogers at 234.

[151] *Clerk & Lindsell on Torts* at para. 3–14.

[152] *Nance* v. *British Columbia Electric Railway Co. Ltd.* [1951] AC 601 at 611, PC per Viscount Simon.

[153] Ibid.

[154] Markesinis and Deakin at 685.

(3) In considering whether the plaintiff exercised sufficient care towards the defendant or in his own interest, the standard applied to the plaintiff in contributory negligence is the same as that of the "reasonable person" for the purposes of establishing liability for negligence generally.[155] However, while a reasonable person may be expected to take precautions against the possible negligence of others in certain situations "when experience shows such negligence to be common",[156] there is no duty to anticipate the negligence of others.[157]

As already seen[158] the legislature has not intervened to establish a specific liability regime for motor vehicle accidents under English law, and it has been left to the general principles of the law of torts, that is essentially to the law of negligence, to solve the considerable amount of litigation arising from such accidents. That is obviously also the case for the application of the defence of contributory negligence.[159] Judgments concerning contributory negligence in traffic cases are notable, it has been observed,[160] for their flexible assessment of the particular facts in issue and their rejection of "rules of law", such as the "rule" that a person who collides with an unlit vehicle at night *must* be contributorily negligent, or that a driver who collides with a pedestrian on a pedestrian crossing *cannot* plead contributory negligence, or that a driver who crosses a junction controlled by lights with the lights in his favour *is not* negligent if he collides with another vehicle which has entered the crossing against the lights. In each case, the question is one of fact, not law.[161]

(4) Any contributory negligence on the part of the plaintiff, however imprudent his behaviour, must be shown to be a cause of the relevant damage.[162] As Lord Atkin stated: "If the plaintiff were negligent but his negligence was not a cause operating to produce the damage there would be no defence. I find it impossible to divorce any theory of contributory negligence from the concept of causation".[163] The principles applicable to determine whether the plaintiff's own fault contributed to his injury are the same as those governing whether the defendant caused those injuries.[164] It matters not whether the operative fault of the plaintiff is prior, or subsequent to the defendant's wrongdoing.[165]

Under Section 4 of the Act, 'damage' is defined to *include* 'loss of life and personal injury' and is therefore not confined to those two categories. The Act also covers damage to property and there is no reason why it should not apply to pure economic loss.[166]

---

[155] See *supra*, Chapter III, 3.2.2.C.

[156] *Grant* v. *Sun Shipping Co* [1948] AC 549 at 567, HL per Lord Du Parcq.

[157] See *Westwood* v. *Post Office* [1974] AC 1, HL in which it was held to be reasonable for a workman to assume that his employer had complied with his statutory duties. See also *Clerk and Lindsell on Torts* at para. 3–23, who point out that a lesser degree of circumspection may be required of the plaintiff "where he has been thrown off his guard by the conduct of the defendant".

[158] *Supra*, Chapter VI, 6.2.1.C.

[159] That is illustrated by the judgment excerpted above and by the judgments reproduced *infra*, **7.E.13** and **7.E.15.**

[160] *Clerk and Lindsell on Torts* at para. 3–26.

[161] For the cases, see *Clerk and Lindsell on Torts* at para. 3–26.

[162] Rather than of the accident itself, see *Froom* v. *Butcher*, *infra*, **7.E.14.**

[163] *Caswell* v. *Powell Duffryn Associated Collieries Ltd.* [1940] AC 152 at 165, HL.

[164] *Clerk and Lindsell on Torts* at para. 3–13. See for these principles *supra*, Chapter IV, 4.1.2.

[165] Ibid. See *Admiralty Commissioners* v. *SS Volute* [1922] 1 AC 129, HL (decided under the Maritime Conventions Act 1911, 1 & 2 Geo. 5 (c. 57)).

[166] Markesinis and Deakin at 689 who point out however, that its application to such cases will be limited. See also T. Dugdale, "Contributory Negligence applied to Economic Loss: *Platform Home Loans* and *Fancy and Jackson*" (1999) 62 Mod LR 281 and the cases discussed therein.

(5) The question arises whether it is possible for the contributory negligence of the direct victim to be held against the claim of a secondary victim. Section 5 of the Fatal Accidents Act 1976[167] states that:

"where any person dies as a result partly of his own fault and partly of the fault of any other person or persons, and accordingly if an action were brought for the benefit of the estate under the Law Reform (Miscellaneous Provisions) Act 1934 the damages recoverable would be reduced under section 1(1) of the Law Reform (Contributory Negligence) Act 1945, any damages recoverable in an action under this Act shall be reduced to a proportionate extent."

To understand this convoluted provision, it should be recalled that, until the Law Reform (Miscellaneous Provisions) Act 1934,[168] the general rule at common law was that the death of either party extinguished any existing cause of action in tort by one against the other.[169] That rule was abolished by the Act of 1934 as a result of which, generally, causes of action subsisting against or vested in any person on his death now survive against or, as the case may be, for the benefit of his estate. That cause of action is the one to which the first limb of section 5 of the Fatal Accidents Act 1976 refers as being subject to the apportionment rule for contributory negligence. The Act of 1934 did not, however, create any new cause of action, e.g. for the dependents not acting on behalf of the estate. Such a cause of action had already been created by the Fatal Accidents Act 1864, now the Fatal Accidents Act 1976,[170] and the second limb of section 5 of that Act refers to the effect of the deceased's contributory negligence on the claims of dependents.

While the Act is silent on the point, authors believe that the contributory negligence of a dependent is also relevant.[171] In such a case the damages recoverable by a dependent who was guilty of contributory negligence should be reduced, under section 1(1) of the Act of 1945,[172] while other innocent dependents should receive their damages in full[173] (the remedy under the Fatal Accidents Act 1976 being granted to dependents individually).

Another statutory example of the rule that a third party (an heir or a dependent) is "identified" with the negligence of another is to be found in section 1(7) of the Congenital Disabilities (Civil Liability) Act 1976,[174] which identifies a child with the contributory negligence of one of its parents, where the parent's carelessness caused the child to be born disabled. The damages are reduced to such extent as the court thinks just and equitable having regard to the extent of the parent's responsibility.

Apart from those statutory provisions where third persons are identified, for purposes of contributory negligence, with the plaintiff, there are other applications of the "doctrine of identification", as it was called, albeit that the tendency of the law has been to move away from identification rather than towards it.[175] A prime example is, in the context of vicarious liability, where the plaintiff is identified with any person for whom he is

---

[167] 1976 (c. 30), s. 5, as amended by section 3(2) of the Administration of Justice Act 1982 (c. 53).
[168] 24 & 25 Geo. 5 (c. 41).
[169] Rogers at 801.
[170] *Supra*, Chapter II, **2.E.10**, note (1).
[171] See Rogers at 816.
[172] See *Mulholland* v. *McCrea* [1961] NI 135.
[173] See *Dodds* v. *Dodds* [1978] QB 543.
[174] 1976 (c. 28). See *supra*, Chapter II, **2.E.5.**
[175] *Clerk and Lindsell on Torts* at para. 3–31.

vicariously responsible.[176] However, the contributory negligence of an independent contractor for whom the plaintiff is not responsible does not affect his claim.[177] Nor is the child in the charge of an adult identified with the latter's negligence.[178]

(6) The application of the defence of contributory negligence to torts other than negligence is not always clear. Before the Law Reform (Contributory Negligence) Act 1945, case law had established that such a defence was available in actions for nuisance on the highway and breach of statutory duty.[179] There was only scant authority for a more general application to other torts,[180] undoubtedly because of the fact that before the Act the defence operated as a complete, all-or-nothing, defence at common law.[181] The introduction of apportionment through the Act probably led to a greater readiness by the judiciary to allow pleas of contributory negligence in other torts as well,[182] even though the wording of section 4 of the Act was not very clear in that respect.

The issue of whether mere negligence should be a defence to deliberate, and so arguably more blameworthy, conduct arises when considering the status of the defence with regard to intentional torts, such as trespass to the person. The relative culpability of the parties is, however, merely one element to be taken into consideration when apportioning damages, alongside the relative causal impact of the parties' actions. In *Murphy* v. *Culhane*,[183] where the plaintiff initiated a criminal affray which resulted in his death, Lord Denning MR (at 98–99) suggested that his contributory negligence would lead to the reduction of any compensation awarded to his widow.[184] However, in *Lane* v. *Holloway*,[185] the court rejected the argument that the fact that a victim had provoked an attack established contributory negligence. The test would appear to be whether the conduct of the victim was of sufficient gravity when weighed against that of the tortfeasor.

The application of the defence of contributory negligence to strict liability torts is controversial. As Markesinis and Deakin have noted: "If the defence does not apply, it could be said that a defendant who has not been at fault would be worse off than if he had been negligent, when the defence would clearly be relevant. To apply the defence, however, would mean that, questions of causation aside, the standard set by law would then be somewhat less than strict".[186] In the context of strict liability torts imposed by statute, the Consumer Protection Act 1987[187] admits the application of the defence,[188] as does the Animals Act 1971.[189]

There are some instances where the defence is expressly excluded. The Torts (Interference with Goods) Act 1977, thus provides that "[c]ontributory negligence is no defence in proceedings

---

[176] See Rogers at 242; Salmond and Heuston at 497; on vicarious liability, see *supra*, Chapter V, 5.1.1.B.

[177] See Rogers at 242.

[178] But see the Fatal Accidents Act 1976, *supra*, **2.E.10.**, s. 1(7) and *Ducharme* v. *Davies* (1984) 1 WWR 699.

[179] As for nuisance on the highway, see *Butterfield* v. *Forrester* (1809) 11 East 60 and, since the 1945 Act, *Trevett* v. *Lee* [1955] 1 WLR 113 at 122, CA. As for breach of statutory duty, see *Caswell* v. *Powell Duffryn Associated Collieries Ltd.* [1940] AC 152, HL.

[180] There is some authority to suggest that the defence is available under the rule in *Rylands* v. *Fletcher*: see *PMG* v. *Liverpool Corporation* [1923] AC 587, HL.

[181] *Clerk and Lindsell on Torts* at para. 3–14.

[182] Ibid.

[183] [1977] QB 94.

[184] Ultimately the claim failed on grounds of consent and *ex turpi causa*, see *infra*, 7.2. and 7.3; see Hudson, "Contributory Negligence as a Defence to Battery" (1984) 4 Legal Studies 332.

[185] [1968] 1 QB 379.

[186] See Markesinis and Deakin at 690. See also *infra*, **7.E.13**, Note (4).

[187] 1987 (c. 43), s. 6(4).

[188] As permitted by Directive 85/374, Art. 8(2): see *supra*, Chapter VI, **6.EC.35.**

[189] 1971 (c. 22), s. 10.

founded on conversion, or on intentional trespass to goods."[190] Under common law, contributory negligence did not operate as a defence to deceit either and this position appears to be unchanged,[191] albeit that contributory negligence can be relied on by a defendant to a claim under the Misrepresentation Act 1967.[192]

While the defence of contributory negligence was not available in contract before the annotated Act, the Court of Appeal has ruled that, where the liability of the defendant in contract is concurrent with an identical liability in tort, the defence of contributory negligence is available to the defendant.[193]

Court of Appeal[194]
Gough v. *Thorne*

7.E.13.

STANDARD OF CARE FOR CHILDREN AND DISABLED

Bubble car collision

A very young child may not be held guilty of contributory negligence. An older child may but it depends on the circumstances: regard must be had as to whether he or she is of such an age as reasonably to be expected to take precautions for his or her own safety.

Facts: The plaintiff, a 13-year old girl, was waiting on the pavement to cross the road, with her two brothers, one of 17 and one of 10 years of age, when she was waved across by the driver of a lorry which stopped for her. Whilst crossing she was hit and injured by a "bubble" car (a small transparent domed car), driven by the defendant, that came through the space between the front of the lorry and a bollard.

Held: The court of first instance found the plaintiff guilty of contributory negligence and reduced her damages by one-third. The court of appeal allowed the appeal and granted the plaintiff the full amount of her claim.

Judgment: LORD DENNING MR:[195] "The judge has found that the defendant driver was negligent. He said that the 'bubble' car was going too fast in the circumstances, and that the driver did not keep a proper look-out because he ought to have seen the lorry driver's signal and he did not see it. He found, therefore, that the defendant, the driver of the 'bubble' car, was to blame and negligent. Then there came the question whether the little girl, the plaintiff, was herself guilty of contributory negligence. As to that, the judge found that she was one-third to blame for this accident. I will read what the judge said about it. 'Was there contributory negligence?' he asked. He answered:

> 'I think that there was. I think that the plaintiff was careless in advancing past the lorry into the open road without pausing to see whether there was any traffic coming from her right. I do not think that her responsibility was very great. After all, the lorry driver had beckoned her on. She might have thought it unlikely that any traffic would try to come through the gap. She might have thought that if there were any traffic coming from that direction, it would wait until the lorry started to move or gave the all clear. She was, after all, only thirteen years old. I assess her degree of responsibility at one-third.'

I am afraid that I cannot agree with the judge. A very young child cannot be guilty of contributory negligence. An older child may be; but it depends on the circumstances. A judge should only find a

---

[190] 1977 (c. 32), s. 11(1).
[191] Markesinis and Deakin at 690; *Clerk and Lindsell on Torts* at para. 3–19.
[192] 1967 (c. 7), s. 2. See *Gran Gelato Ltd.* v. *Richcliff (Group) Ltd.* [1992] Ch 560.
[193] In *Forsikringsaktieselskapet Vesta* v. *Butcher* [1989] AC 852, HL.
[194] [1966] 3 All ER 398, [1966] 1 WLR 1387.
[195] Danckwerts LJ concurring.

child guilty of contributory negligence if he or she is of such an age as reasonably to be expected to take precautions for his or her own safety: and then he or she is only to be found guilty if blame should be attached to him or her. A child has not the road sense or the experience of his or her elders. He or she is not to be found guilty unless he or she is blameworthy.

In this particular case I have no doubt that there was no blameworthiness to be attributed to the plaintiff at all. Here she was with her elder brother crossing a road. They had been beckoned on by the lorry driver. What more could you expect the child to do than to cross in pursuance of the beckoning? It is said by the judge that she ought to have leant forward and looked to see whether anything was coming. That indeed might be reasonably expected of a grown-up person with a fully developed road sense, but not of a child of 13½.

I am clearly of opinion that the judge was wrong in attributing any contributory negligence to the plaintiff, aged 13½; and I would allow the appeal accordingly."

SALMON LJ: "I entirely agree . . . The question as to whether the plaintiff can be said to have been guilty of contributory negligence depends on whether any ordinary child of 13½ could be expected to have done any more than this child did. I say, 'any ordinary child'. I do not mean a paragon of prudence; nor do I mean a scatter-brained child; but the ordinary girl of 13½."

Notes

(1) The standard of care imposed in contributory negligence cases is broadly the same as that in respect of negligence in general, and while it is thus objective and impersonal, as with other aspects of the law of negligence it may nonetheless be modified to take into account the circumstances of the case.[196] The defendant bears the burden of proving contributory negligence on the part of the plaintiff, but "this may be inferred from the plaintiff's own evidence, or on a balance of probabilities from the facts".[197]

As is evident from the excerpted case, *children* may be held to a lower standard of self-protection.[198] As Salmon LJ indicates, the standard is that of "any ordinary child of 13½ [. . . by which] I do not mean a paragon of prudence; nor do I mean a scatter-brained child; but the ordinary girl of 13½". This does not necessarily mean that children will never be held guilty of contributory negligence. It depends on the age of the child, the circumstances of the case and the knowledge by the particular child of perils to which the defendant's negligence has exposed him.[199] Thus in *Morales* v. *Ecclestone*,[200] an 11-year-old boy who was injured after he ran out on to a busy road without looking was held to be 75 per cent to blame for his injuries.

While the courts are unwilling to find a very young child guilty of contributory negligence, *Clerk & Lindsell on Torts* express the view, contrary to that of Lord Denning in the excerpted judgment, "there is no age below which a child *cannot* be guilty of contributory negligence".[201] The Pearson Commission recommended however that it should not be possible to raise the defence of contributory negligence against a child under 12 years.[202]

[196] See further *supra*, Chapter III, 3.2.2.C. See also *supra*, **3.E.25** on the liability of children in general and **3.E.24** on the liability of persons of unsound mind.

[197] *Clerk and Lindsell on Torts* at para. 3–32 with references to case law.

[198] The Occupier's Liability Act 1957 (5 & 6 Eliz. 2, c. 31), s. 2(3)(a) warns expressly that "an occupier must be prepared for children to be less careful than adults".

[199] *Clerk and Lindsell on Torts* at para. 3–24 suggest that Lord Denning's insistence, in the excerpted judgment, on "blameworthiness" of the child's conduct takes subjectivity too far.

[200] *Morales* v. *Ecclestone* [1991] RTR 151, CA.

[201] *Clerk and Lindsell on Torts* at para. 3–24.

[202] *The Royal Commission on Civil Liability and Compensation for Personal Injury*, Vol. 1 Cmnd 7054 (1978), at para. 1077.

Not only children but also *disabled* persons may be held liable for contributory negligence, albeit in a varying degree. Whilst normally the standard of care expected of a defendant is based on the assumption that others possess normal faculties,[203] when it is known that the person to whom a duty is owed has a physical defect e.g. only one eye,[204] a higher standard of care is owed on the part of the defendant. When considering contributory negligence on the part of such persons, e.g. the elderly, reference must be made to their "individual circumstances and infirmities".[205]

(2) Even a normal plaintiff's ability to act prudently may be affected by the need, in an *emergency* produced by the defendant's negligence, to decide in the "agony of the moment", on a course of action without time for full consideration.[206] So, provided that the plaintiff acted in a reasonable apprehension of the danger and that the means chosen to avoid it were reasonable, he or she cannot be met by a plea of contributory negligence. In *Jones* v. *Boyce*,[207] the plaintiff was a passenger on a coach who upon seeing the coach go out of control due to the defendant's negligence, believed (mistakenly) that it was in imminent danger of overturning, jumped and broke his leg. Lord Ellenborough CJ held that if misconduct on the part of the defendant had placed the plaintiff "in such a situation as obliged him to adopt the alternative of a dangerous leap, or to remain at certain peril" so as "to render what he did a prudent precaution for the purpose of self-presentation", his claim should succeed (as it did). However, where action is taken to avoid a mere personal inconvenience, one may not run a considerable risk to be rid of it.[208]

(3) A *passenger* who travels in a vehicle driven by a person whom he knows to be drunk is likely to have his damages reduced on account of his contributory negligence if he suffers injury in an accident caused to some extent by the driver's impaired capacity to drive carefully; and the courts are reluctant to modify the plaintiff's standard of self-care when his own judgment is diminished through drunkenness. In *Owens* v. *Brimmell*,[209] the court held that the plaintiff's damages should be reduced by 20% for his contributory negligence in travelling with a driver whom he knew to be drunk. According to Tasker Watkins J,[210]

"a passenger may be guilty of contributory negligence if he rides with the driver of a car whom he knows has consumed alcohol in such quantity as is likely to impair to a dangerous degree that driver's capacity to drive properly and safely. So, also, may a passenger be guilty of contributory negligence if he, knowing that he is going to be driven in a car by his companion later, accompanies him upon a bout of drinking which has the effect, eventually, of robbing the passenger of clear thought and perception and diminishes the driver's capacity to drive properly and carefully".

[203] *Bourhill* v. *Young* [1943] AC 92 at 109, HL per Lord Wright.
[204] *Paris* v. *Stepney Borough Council* [1951] AC 367, HL; for a discussion of the "egg-shell skull" cases, see *supra*, Chapter IV, 4.3.1.
[205] *Clerk & Lindsell on Torts* at para. 3–25. See also *supra*, Chapter III, **3.E.17** as regards liability in negligence of disabled persons in general.
[206] G. Williams, *Joint Torts and Contributory Negligence* (London: Stevens, 1951) at 360–4.
[207] *Jones* v. *Boyce* (1816) 1 Starkie 493.
[208] See *Sayers* v. *Harlow Urban District Council* [1958] 1 WLR 623, CA where the plaintiff's course of action in attempting to escape from a lavatory cubicle in which she had been trapped was held to have amounted to contributory negligence; see Rogers at 240.
[209] [1977] QB 859, [1976] 3 All ER 765, QBD.
[210] Ibid. at 866–7 (QB), 771 (All ER).

(4) *Employees* are not, as a group, held to any different standard from other potential plaintiffs. However, as held in *Staveley Iron and Chemical Co. Ltd.* v. *Jones*,[211]

> "there may be cases, such as those involving breach of statutory duty, where an employer who is in breach of his duty cannot be heard as against his own servant who has been injured thereby to say that some risky act due to familiarity with the work or some inattention resulting from noise of strain amounts to contributory negligence [though it may amount to negligence as against a fellow employee who has been injured by it] . . .
>
> [In] Factory Act cases the purpose of imposing the absolute obligation is to protect the workmen against those very acts of inattention which are sometimes relied upon as constituting contributory negligence so that too strict a standard would defeat the object of the statute."

Similarly while a person must take into account the possibility of others being careless and may be guilty of contributory negligence if he fails to do so,[212] an employee's claim against his employer for breach of statutory duty can generally not be met by a plea of contributory negligence on the ground that the employee should have taken into account the possibility of the employer's breach of statutory duty;[213] indeed in a breach of statutory duty case a plea of contributory negligence will always be difficult to establish.[214]

(5) The courts are unwilling to find *rescuers* guilty of contributory negligence, and they can generally recover fully in respect of any damage sustained,[215] in the course of the actual rescue,[216] providing that they acted reasonably in the circumstances.[217]

Court of Appeal[218]   **7.E.14.**
Froom v. *Butcher*

CAUSATION. APPORTIONMENT

Failure to wear seatbelt

Contributory negligence is established not only where the plaintiff's negligence contributed to the occurrence of the damaging incident itself but also where it contributed to the extent of his resulting injuries.

Facts: The plaintiff sustained injuries largely to his head and chest when his car collided with that of the defendant due to the latter's negligent driving. The plaintiff was not wearing a seatbelt and was thrown against the windscreen by the impact of the collision.

---

[211] *Staveley Iron and Chemical Co. Ltd.* v. *Jones* [1956] AC 627 at 648, HL per Lord Tucker. And see Markesinis and Deakin at 687 and Rogers at 241–2.

[212] *Jones* v. *Livox Quarries Ltd.* [1952] 2 QB 608, CA per Denning LJ.

[213] *Westwood* v. *Post Office* [1974] AC 1 at 16, HL per Lord Kilbrandon; see *Clerk & Lindsell on Torts* at para. 3–22.

[214] Ibid.

[215] *Brandon* v. *Osborne Garrett & Co. Ltd.* [1924] 1 KB 548, and see *Baker* v. *Hopkins (T.E.) & Son Ltd.*, *infra*, **7.E.15.**

[216] *Harrison* v. *British Railways Board* [1981] 3 All ER 679 provides an example of a case where the plaintiff's contributory negligence did not relate to anything done in the course of the actual rescue but consisted of the failure of the plaintiff (a guard on a passenger train), as the man in authority, to reduce the danger by doing what he was duty-bound to do. In consequence, his damages were reduced by 20 per cent.

[217] On rescuers, see also *supra*, Chapter IV, **4.E.36.** and notes thereafter.

[218] [1976] QB 286 at 291.

Held: The Court of Appeal found that the plaintiff was contributorily negligent and his damages were reduced accordingly.

Judgment: LORD DENNING MR:[219] "*Contributory negligence*

Negligence depends on a breach of duty, whereas contributory negligence does not. Negligence is a man's carelessness in breach of duty to *others*. Contributory negligence is a man's carelessness in looking after *his own* safety. He is guilty of *contributory* negligence if he ought reasonably to have foreseen that, if he did not act as a reasonable prudent man, he might be hurt himself: see *Jones* v. *Livox Quarries Ltd.* [1952] 2 QB 608 . . .

The cause of the damage

In these seatbelt cases, the injured plaintiff is in no way to blame for the accident itself. Sometimes he is an innocent passenger sitting beside a negligent driver who goes off the road. At other times he is an innocent driver of one car which is run into by the bad driving of another car which pulls out on to its wrong side of the road. It may well be asked: why should the injured plaintiff have his damages reduced? The accident was solely caused by the negligent driving by the defendant. Sometimes outrageously bad driving. It should not lie in his mouth to say: 'You ought to have been wearing a seatbelt.' That point of view was strongly expressed in *Smith* v. *Blackburn* [1974] RTR 533, 536 by O'Connor J:

> '. . . the idea that the insurers of a grossly negligent driver should be relieved in any degree from paying what is proper compensation for injuries is an idea that offends ordinary decency. Until I am forced to do so by higher authority, I will not so rule.'

I do not think that is the correct approach. The question is not what was the cause of the accident. It is rather what was the cause of the damage. In most accidents on the road the bad driving, which causes the accident, also causes the ensuing damage. But in seatbelt cases the cause of the accident is one thing. The cause of the damage is another. The *accident* is caused by the bad driving. The *damage* is caused in part by the bad driving of the defendant, and in part by the failure of the plaintiff to wear a seatbelt. If the plaintiff was to blame in not wearing a seatbelt, the damage is in part the result of his own fault. He must bear some share in the responsibility for the damage: and his damages fall to be reduced to such extent as the court thinks just and equitable . . . In a leading case in this court, under the [Law Reform (Contributory Negligence) Act 1945], we looked to the cause of the *damage*: see *Davies* v. *Swan Motor Co. (Swansea) Ltd.* [1949] 2 KB 291, 326. In the crash helmet cases this court also looked at the causes of the damage: see *O'Connell* v. *Jackson* [1972] 1 QB 270. So also we should in seatbelt cases . . .

The share of responsibility

Whenever there is an accident, the negligent driver must bear by far the greater share of responsibility. It was his negligence which caused the accident. It was also a prime cause of the whole of the damage. But in so far as the damage might have been avoided or lessened by wearing a seatbelt, the injured person must bear some share. But how much should this be? Is it proper to enquire whether the driver was grossly negligent or only slightly negligent? Or whether the failure to wear a seatbelt was entirely inexcusable or almost forgivable? If such an inquiry could easily be undertaken, it might be as well to do it. In *Davies* v. *Swan Motor Co.*, the court said that consideration should be given not only to the causative potency of a particular factor, but also its blameworthiness. But we live in a practical world. In most of these cases the liability of the driver is admitted, the failure to

---

[219] Lawton and Scarman LJJ concurring.

wear a seatbelt is admitted, the only question is: what damages should be payable? This question should not be prolonged by an expensive inquiry into the degree of blameworthiness on either side, which would be hotly disputed. Suffice it to assess a share of responsibility which will be just and equitable in the great majority of cases . . ."

Notes

(1) Any contributory negligence on the part of the plaintiff, however imprudent his action, must be shown to be *a* cause of the relevant damage. The causal link runs from fault to damage, and not necessarily to the accident as such. The effect of this rule becomes clear when the defendant is solely responsible for the accident in which the plaintiff suffers injury, while the negligence of the plaintiff contributed to the extent or nature of the ensuing injuries. In *Capps* v. *Miller*,[220] a motorcyclist's failure to secure a crash helmet did not contribute to the accident at all, which was caused entirely by the defendant's fault. The Court of Appeal overturned the ruling of the judge at first instance who had considered only the link between the plaintiff's contributory negligence and the accident rather than the harm sustained. It must be shown that if the plaintiff had taken the relevant precautions, his or her injuries would have been reduced; so, the plaintiff's damages will not be reduced if his or her negligence in omitting to wear a seatbelt had no link to the injury.[221]

(2) To establish contributory negligence on the part of the plaintiff, the test is whether the plaintiff acted reasonably, that is whether he or she took sufficient care in looking after his or her own safety. The fact that legislation makes it compulsory in general for seatbelts and crash helmets to be worn by road users[222] is a useful indicator of what is reasonable, but it is not conclusive: it is not only the unlawfulness of the conduct but also the failure to behave in a reasonably prudent manner which underlies a claim of contributory negligence.[223]

So, although the plaintiff's personal opinion as to the efficacy of seatbelts will normally be disregarded,[224] the failure of a plaintiff to wear a seatbelt (or crash helmet) may be held to be "reasonable" in certain circumstances, such as where a medical condition should make it more dangerous to wear the seatbelt than risk the consequences of not so doing.[225]

(3) When apportioning damages under the Law Reform (Contributory Negligence) Act 1945, once contributory negligence is established and it is proved that the plaintiff's negligence was a cause operating to produce the damage, "the damages recoverable in respect thereof shall be reduced to such extent as the court thinks just and equitable having regard to the claimant's share in the responsibility for the damage . . .".[226] As Lord

---

[220] *Capps* v. *Miller* [1989] 1 WLR 839, [1989] 2 All ER 333, CA.

[221] See *Lertora* v. *Finzi* [1973] RTR 161, County Court.

[222] See Road Traffic Act 1988 (c. 54), s. 15.

[223] See Weir at 257.

[224] Lord Denning in an unexcerpted part of the annotated judgment.

[225] *McKay* v. *Borthwick* [1982] SLT Rep. 265, Outer House, where the plaintiff was held not to be contributorily negligent in not wearing a belt on a short journey as she suffered from a hiatus hernia on which the belt would have pressed. See also *Condon* v. *Condon* [1978] RTR 483 in which it was held that, if it could be medically established that the plaintiff's use of a seatbelt would trigger her claustrophobia, her omission to wear one would not constitute contributory negligence.

[226] *Supra*, **7.E.11.**, s. 1(1).

Denning states in the excerpted judgment, recalling his earlier judgment in *Davies v. Swan Motor Co. (Swansea) Ltd.*,[227] "both the degree of blameworthiness and causative potency of the plaintiff's lack of care should be considered when apportioning damages". Or, in the words of T. Weir: "In determining the proportion by which the plaintiff's damages are to be reduced, attention must be paid to the respective blameworthiness of the parties as well as to the causative potency of their acts or omissions: if attention were not paid to causative potency, a careless plaintiff would recover nothing from a defendant who was free from fault but strictly liable".[228] The latter point is reminiscent of the position taken by German courts as regards contributory fault (*Mitverschulden*) in cases involving risk-based liability (*Gefährdungshaftung*) regimes, which however are more numerous under German law (and under French law), including among others liability of car keepers for car accidents.[229]

In an unexcerpted part of the annotated judgment, Lord Denning suggested standard reductions for failure to wear a seatbelt if the defendant can show that it made a difference: 15 per cent if the injuries would have been less serious, 25 per cent if they would have been avoided.

7.2. ASSUMPTION OF RISK

7.2.1. ENGLISH LAW

The following cases can be found (with notes) at <http://www.rechten.unimaas.nl/casebook>:

7.E.15. Court of Appeal, *Baker* v. *T.E. Hopkins & Son Ltd.* Rescuer overcome by fumes.

7.E.16. Court of Appeal, *Nettleship* v. *Weston.* Learner-driver injures instructor.

7.E.17. Court of Appeal, *Morris* v. *Murray.* Drunken pilot.

7.E.18. Court of Appeal, *Condon* v. *Basi.* Serious leg injury.

7.2.2. GERMAN LAW

The following cases can be found (with notes) at <http://www.rechten.unimaas.nl/casebook>:

7.G.19. BGH, 14 March 1961. Young driver.

7.G.20. BGH, 5 November 1974. Unlucky football player.

7.G.21. BGH, 13 November 1973. Vanity does not pay.

---

[227] *Supra,* **7.E.12.**
[228] Weir at 256.
[229] *Supra,* **7.G.8.** and notes thereafter, **7.G.9.** and notes thereafter; see also *supra,* **7.F.4.** and notes thereafter.

7.2.3. FRENCH LAW

The following cases can be found (with notes) at <http://www.rechten.unimaas.nl/casebook>:

7.F.22. Cass. crim., 25 June 1969, *St-Jean*. Unfortunate rescuer.
7.F.23. Cass. civ. 2e, 28 January 1987, *Malherbe* v. *Amar*. A game of squash.
7.F.24. Cass. civ. 2e, 8 March 1995, *Bizouard* v. *AGF*. Capsized yacht.

7.3. ILLEGALITY

7.3.1. FRENCH LAW

The following case can be found (with notes) at <http://www.rechten.unimaas.nl/casebook>:

7.F.25. Cass. civ. 1re, 17 November 1993. *Groupe Drouot* v. *Rumeau*. Injured thief.

7.3.2. GERMAN LAW

The following cases can be found (with notes) at <http://www.rechten.unimaas.nl/casebook>:

7.G.26. BGH, 25 September 1952. Abortion requested.
7.G.27. BGH, 6 July 1976. Unemployed prostitute.

7.3.3. ENGLISH LAW

The following case can be found (with notes) at <http://www.rechten.unimaas.nl/casebook>:

7.E.28. Court of Appeal, *Pitts* v. *Hunt*. Irresponsible passenger.

7.4. COMPARATIVE OVERVIEW

Contributory fault

There are three possibilities to account for the impact of a contributory fault (whether intentional or by negligence) of the plaintiff on the liability of the defendant. Firstly, it can be argued that contributory fault should have no impact at all, on the ground that after all the injury was caused in the first place by the defendant's conduct (or by a person or thing for which the defendant is responsible), which is enough to hold the defendant fully liable. The second possibility is the opposite: the fault of the plaintiff entirely exonerates the defendant from liability, since a person who has caused injury to himself or herself must bear the full consequences of that injury. The third possibility is to let the victim and the tortfeasor each bear part of the consequences of the injury.[230] Whereas the first solution was apparently retained in early French law and the second, in German law and in English law (before the Law Reform (Contributory Negligence) Act 1945),[231] the third solution is now generally preferred. In Germany and England (at least for the tort of negligence) it is even enshrined in a statutory provision (§ 254 BGB and the 1945 Act),[232] whereas in France it is based on the case law of the Cour de cassation.[233]

It is common ground that "fault" is to be understood differently in the context of contributory fault than it is generally in the context of liability for one's own conduct. In the latter context, fault—mainly negligence—generally consists in the breach of a duty towards other persons, whereas in the context of contributory fault, the concept of "fault" will also encompass a shortcoming in taking due care of one's own rights or interests, e.g. one's own safety.[234]

Whatever the difference between the defence of contributory fault and the general regime of liability for one's own conduct, in both cases the concept of "fault" means that one did not behave as a reasonable person and with reasonable care, as regards one's own interests or the interests of a third party respectively. As a consequence, fault is construed in the same fashion in both contexts,[235] as can be seen, in the three legal systems studied here, when looking at contributory fault on the part of children. On that issue, French law is especially harsh, since it allows contributory fault to be held against young children (infants) who have no discernment. While it is in line with the "objectivization" of fault under the general regime of Articles 1382–1383 C.civ., that position was criticized as overly rational, at the expense of justice.[236] Under English and German law, where the general concept of fault leaves more room for a more concrete standard of assessment,[237] children can also be contributorily negligent, depending on the circumstances. Under English law, that will be the case when the child "is of such an age as reasonably to be expected to take precaution for his or her own safety".[238] Under German law, minors between 7 and 18 years can be made liable if they are capable of understanding that they are responsible for the consequences which their conduct may have on third parties (§ 828(1) BGB) or, in the case of contributory fault, on themselves. If they do not possess that understanding (or if they are younger than 7, § 828(1) BGB), they cannot be held liable and by the same token contributory fault cannot be held against them; however, the liability of the defendant may exceptionally be reduced, through an analogous application of § 829 BGB, if fairness *requires* it.[239]

Under all three legal systems, difficult issues arise when "contributory fault" is applied in the context of a liability regime not based on one's own conduct, such as those that

---

[230] Called comparative negligence in the USA.
[231] *Supra*, **7.E.11.**, Note (1).
[232] See *supra*, 7.1., Introductory Note.
[233] *Supra*, **7.F.1.–3.**
[234] *Supra*, **7.G.7.**, Note (2) and **7.E.12.**, Note (2).
[235] See in particular *supra*, **7.E.13.**, Notes (3) to (5).
[236] *Supra*, **7.F.3**, Notes (4) and (5).
[237] *Supra*, Chapter III, **3.E.15** and Notes thereafter, as well as **3.G.12**, Note (1).
[238] Lord Denning in *Gough* v. *Thorne, supra,* **7.E.13.**
[239] For an application, see *supra*, **7.G.7** and Note (5) thereafter..

were surveyed in the preceding two Chapters. If the principles of contributory fault are applied, so that the defendant's liability under one of these regimes is diminished, or even excluded, on account of some fault of the victim, such liability may be deprived of its content—at least partly—or of its force, which is why under English law the application of contributory negligence to other torts than negligence remains controversial.[240] In legal systems where, as in Germany, liability not based on conduct (risk-based liability or *Gefährdungshaftung*) arises only as a result of specific legislative enactments, the issue will normally be solved by the legislature itself in the enactment in question. Where the defendant is obliged by law to take out insurance for the relevant activity or installation—as it is frequently the case—it is considered unfair to let the plaintiff bear part of his or her injury because of contributory fault, as he or she will often be uninsured. Still, case law must intervene to determine how these regimes will interact, for instance where a conflict occurs between the general regime of liability for one's own conduct (§ 823ff. BGB) and a regime of risk-based liability.[241]

In countries where regimes of liability not based on conduct have been introduced by the courts alone, as in France, equity considerations may affect the application of contributory fault. Thus, under the general regime of liability for things at Article 1384(1) C.civ.,[242] the fault of the victim can lead to a reduction of the liability of the defendant (or even to exoneration, if the fault of the victim qualifies as a *cause étrangère*, namely if it was unforeseeable and unavoidable).[243] The Cour de cassation had adopted a different position (no reduction of liability on account of the victim's fault unless it was a *cause étrangère*) for some time in the 1980s, with its *Desmares* judgment of 1982, but the original position was re-instated in 1987,[244] after the enactment of the *Loi Badinter* of 5 July 1985.

The *Loi Badinter*, dealing with car accidents, represents the most significant exception made by a legislature to the general rules on contributory fault.[245] It abolishes the defence of contributory negligence in respect of certain classes of victims who were not drivers: as regards injury to the person, only inexcusable fault that was the "sole cause" of the injury can be argued against them (and narrower still, only intentional fault can be argued against persons below the age of 16 or over 70 or persons suffering from serious incapacity or invalidity).[246] Under English law, there are no specific rules on contributory negligence in cases of road traffic accidents,[247] whereas in Germany the special rules on "contributory fault" at §§ 9, 17 StVG are analogous to the general provisions of § 254 BGB.[248] The provisions of the *Loi Badinter* may seem drastic when compared to German and English law, but it must be seen that children were far more affected by the

---

[240] *Supra*, **7.E.12.**, Note (6).

[241] See for instance *supra*, **7.G.8.**, where the defendant was liable under § 823(1) BGB and sought a reduction because the victim was the keeper of a motor car (to which risk-based liability is attached pursuant to § 7 StVG) and **7.G.9.**, where the defendant, liable under § 833 BGB as the keeper of his dog, argued that his liability should be reduced on account of the contributory negligence of the plaintiff.

[242] That regime is presented in greater detail *supra*, Chapter VI, 6.1.2.

[243] On this development in the case law of the Cour de cassation, see *supra*, **7.F.4.**, Note (1).

[244] Ibid.

[245] On the *Loi Badinter*, see *supra*, Chapter VI, 6.2.1.B.

[246] At Art. 3 of the *Loi Badinter*: see *supra*, **7.F.4.**, Note (3).

[247] *Supra*, **7.E.12.**, Note (3).

[248] § 9 StVG, *supra*, 7.1.1., Introductory Note.

application of contributory negligence in France, given the very objective interpretation of "fault" in the case of young children, and the lack of specific "fairness" provisions concerning minors in the Code civil, such as § 828 BGB under German law. With respect to product liability, mention must be made of Directive 85/374 which allows, "having regard to all the circumstances", the liability of the producer to be reduced or lifted altogether because of contributory fault for which the victim must answer.[249] The English and the German implementing legislation simply refer to the general rules on contributory negligence,[250] whereas under French law that provision was implemented in the Code civil.[251]

Whenever contributory fault can be raised as a defence against the direct victim, it is generally recognized that the contributory fault of the direct victim can be argued as well against dependants of the direct victim, or "reflex victims" (*victimes par ricochet*), in cases of death or bodily injury. In France, that rule emerged from the case law of the Cour de cassation;[252] with respect to road traffic accidents, it is found in Article 6 of the *Loi Badinter* but is mainly applicable to the contributory fault of direct victims who were drivers.[253] In Germany, that rule is contained in § 846 BGB. In England it is set out in section 5 of the Fatal Accidents Act 1976.[254] It is interesting to note that the rule has not always been uncontroversial in either France[255] or England.[256]

The rules concerning contributory fault, as they now prevail in the legal systems examined here, will result in an apportionment of liability, i.e. liability will be divided, and therefore the damage shared, between defendant and plaintiff in accordance with, and in proportion to, the elements that contributed to the occurrence of the damage. Contributing to the damage does not necessarily mean the same as contributing to the accident, however: failing to wear a seatbelt or a helmet may contribute to injury, without causing the accident.[257] The elements which may be taken into account include, in the first place, the respective faults of the wrongdoer and the victim. In addition other elements are relevant, where they trigger liability under the legal system in question, for instance if a party was the keeper of a car or animal that contributed to the damage,[258] or if a party was responsible for the conduct of a third person.[259] Furthermore, unlawful conduct which might not lead to liability in the absence of subjective fault might regarded as a relevant element, as is exemplified by the application of § 829 BGB in the context of § 254 BGB.[260] In order to weigh these elements against one another, all of the systems reviewed here consider both the degree of fault and the causal impact. Under English and

[249] Directive 85/374, Art. 8(2), *supra*, Chapter VI, **6.EC.35.**

[250] As contained in the Law Reform (Contributory Negligence) Act of 1945, *supra*, **7.E.11.** and in § 254 BGB respectively.

[251] Article 1386–13, *supra*, Chapter VI, **6.F.39.**

[252] *Supra*, **7.F.5** and **7.F.6.**

[253] As regards the contributory fault of other direct victims, Art. 3 of the *Loi Badinter* allows the defence only exceptionally: see Art. 6 referred to above and *supra*, **7.F.6.**, Note (2).

[254] *Supra*, **7.E.12.**, Note (5).

[255] At least before the judgment of the Cour de cassation in 1981, which settled the matter: *supra*, **7.F.5.** Controversy continued to exist until recently with regard to the fault of a "reflex victim" (*victime par ricochet*) who was also a driver: see *supra*, **7.F.5.–6.**, Note (2).

[256] Where the common law was to the contrary before it was changed by statute.

[257] *Supra*, **7.E.14.**; see also *supra*, **7.G.8.**, Note (3).

[258] *Supra*, **7.G.8.** and **7.G.9.**

[259] *Supra*, **7.F.1.–3.** and Note (3) thereafter (defendant's liability), **7.G.7.**, Note (6) and **7.E.11.–12.**, Note (5) (plaintiff's liability).

[260] *Supra*, **7.G.10.**

German law, priority seems to be given to the causal impact,[261] whereas under French law the degree of the fault seems to be the predominant factor.[262]

None of the three major legal systems has openly gone so far yet as to include, amongst the relevant elements, events other than faulty behaviour or events that trigger liability under regimes not based on one's conduct. The new Dutch BW has taken that step; Article 6:101 BW allows courts to take into consideration, for the apportionment of liability, all circumstances which can be imputed to the victim (e.g. the fact that the defendant and/or the plaintiff is insured) in view of reducing the defendant's liability.[263] That provision also gives some guidance to the court as to how the different elements are to be weighed against one another or given precedence.[264]

Assumption of risk

Assumption of risk, *volenti non fit injuria* and implied consent are, broadly speaking, synonyms to refer to a defence which the defendant raises against a plaintiff who has accepted the risk of injury knowingly—but without fault, because otherwise the defence of contributory negligence would be more appropriate.[265] That defence typically arises in three categories of cases: rescue cases, cases involving a drunken or inexperienced driver or pilot and cases concerning sports, mainly competitive ones. Generally speaking, each of the three systems examined herein tends to treat each category in a similar fashion: rescuers are rescued in turn by the courts which tend to be sympathetic towards their claims; reckless or very negligent persons accompanying inebriated drivers or pilots are not treated kindly,[266] whereas those riding with inexperienced drivers are better off; participants in competitive sport are left in the cold in that their claims for compensation will be allowed only when serious mistakes were made.

Under English law claims brought by a *rescuer* who suffered injuries due to his benevolent intervention raise several questions related to (i) the existence of a duty of care, (ii) causation (*novus actus interveniens*),[267] (iii) assumption of risk (*volenti non fit injuria*) and (iv) contributory negligence.[268] Only the third is considered here: it appears that the rescuer does not normally fall under the maxim *volenti non fit injuria*, since he or she acted in response to a situation of peril without having assumed the risk beforehand; moreover, the rescuer is under a moral, if not legal, duty to intervene and thus cannot be seen as a "volunteer".[269] Under German law, the same issue is seen not so much from the point of view of assumption of risk as from that of causation between the conduct of the tortfeasor action and the harm sustained by the victim.[270] Causation is not necessarily broken

---

[261] *Supra*, **7.E.14.**, Note (3) and **7.G.7.**, Notes (1) and (3).

[262] *Supra*, **7.F.1.–3.**, Note (1).

[263] Compare with German law, where insurance may be considered as one of the relevant circumstances in deciding whether to grant compensation on grounds of fairness under § 829 BGB. See *supra*, **7.G.7.**, Note (5).

[264] Asser-Hartkamp 4-III, 10th edn. (Deventer: Tjeenk Willink, 1998) at 30, para. 25.

[265] See further *supra*, 7.2., Introductory Note.

[266] To the point even that their claim against the driver (or his insurer) would be met by a defence of illegality or contributory negligence.

[267] See *supra*, Chapter IV, 4.3.3.

[268] *Supra*, **7.E.15.** and Note (1) thereafter.

[269] Ibid, Note (2).

[270] The "invitation" (*Herausforderung*) criterion is used to assess causation in such cases: see *supra*, Chapter IV, 4.3.3. and in particular **4.G.37.**

because the rescuer freely decides to intervene, unless the conduct of the rescuer was not justifiable under the circumstances.[271] Under French law, only serious fault on the part of the rescuer can lead to a partial exoneration of the defendant; where the rescuer did not commit any serious fault, "his awareness of the danger to which he exposed himself with a sense of duty cannot have as consequence a discharge, even partial, of the liability of the defendant."[272] French law will even compensate the rescuer for injury sustained, even if the defendant was not at fault, if the conditions of *negotiorum gestio* (*gestion d'affaires*) are fulfilled or a valid "rescue agreement" (*convention d'assistance*) can be inferred from the circumstances.[273] Accordingly, none of the legal systems reviewed considers that the decision of the rescuer to intervene can in and of itself provide a defence that would eliminate or even reduce the liability of the defendant; serious negligence or unjustifiable conduct on the part of the rescuer is required for that.[274]

Leaving aside special statutory provisions such as s. 149 of the Road Traffic Act 1988[275] or Article 3 of the *Loi Badinter*,[276] the *inexperienced or drunken driver* or pilot will rarely be able to argue in defence, as a ground for complete exoneration, that the victim voluntarily accepted to be carried as a passenger by him or her (*volenti non fit injuria*); rather, he or she might achieve partial exoneration under the defence of contributory negligence. *Morris* v. *Murray*[277] illustrates the exceptional character of the defence of *volenti non fit injuria*: there the claim of the plaintiff was rejected on the basis of *volenti non fit injuria*, since he had knowingly accepted to board the light aircraft of the defendant, even though the weather conditions were poor, the aircraft would have to take off downwind and uphill, and the two parties had been drinking heavily. In *Nettleship* v. *Weston*,[278] however, the claim of the plaintiff, who was teaching a friend to drive, was not rejected on the ground of an alleged waiver of liability (which could not be inferred under the circumstances); still the claim was reduced because of contributory negligence. As for German and French law,[279] flying with an obviously drunken pilot could hardly be construed as an implicit agreement to waive the liability of the defendant entirely. Leaving aside special statutory provisions, it would seem more probable that, in such a case, the liability of the defendant would rather be reduced or even eliminated on account of contributory negligence.

There is a risk inherent in almost any *sport*, not only where participants are competing against one another,[280] but also where they merely play together without competition. Such risk may play a role in determining (i) whether and to what extent there is a duty of care, (ii) if so, whether a breach of duty (or fault) occurs, and (iii) if these questions are

[271] See OLG Stuttgart, 24 November 1964, NJW 1965, 112 (English version in Markesinis at 629–32.)

[272] *Supra*, **7.F.22.** and Note (1) thereafter. Nor can it relieve the keeper of a thing from liability under Art. 1384(1) C.civ.: Cass. civ. 2e, 11 July 1962, D 1963.Jur.40.

[273] *Supra*, **7.F.22.**, Note (2).

[274] Under French law, the decision made by the plaintiff to come to the rescue is not a defence either under the regime of liability for things of Art. 1384(1) C.civ.: Cass. civ. 2e, 11 July 1962, D 1963.Jur.40.

[275] Reproduced *supra*, **7.E.28.**, Note (3). The reference in Beldam LJ's judgment is to s. 148(3) of the earlier Road Traffic Act 1972 (c. 20).

[276] *Supra*, 7.2.3., Introductory Note under d).

[277] *Supra*, **7.E.17.**

[278] *Supra*, **7.E.16.**

[279] *Supra*, **7.G.19.**, Note (1) and **7.G.20.**, Note (1). See also *supra*, 7.2.3., Introductory Note under d).

[280] Either as direct opponents, as in boxing, football or tennis or as competitors to win a contest, as in horse racing or ice-skating.

answered in the affirmative, whether and to what extent liability is to be reduced or even eliminated because of assumption of risk.

Only the last question was examined in this chapter. All three legal systems take the same attitude with respect to participating in a sport which is *intrinsically dangerous* either because participants intend to hurt the adversary physically and consent in advance to be hurt—as in boxing—or because they make use of dangerous vehicles or equipment—as in car racing. The three systems agree that participating in such sports or games is tantamount to a mutual agreement to exonerate each another, which does not relieve players, however, from observing the rules of the game. The same position is taken as regards spectators who choose to watch the game at a particularly dangerous spot, and who may also be deemed to have waived liability in advance for any harm suffered through the conduct of a participant.[281] In other words, except for special circumstances, a participant in an intrinsically dangerous sport will normally be relieved from liability on the ground that the victim *consented a priori*.

As regards other competitions where physical contact between the players is not contemplated and must be avoided as much as possible, the three legal systems take a similar view. Here, however, the basis is not consent *a priori*, but rather some kind of assumption of risk. English law accepts that a participant or a spectator in such a competition assumes the risk that injury might be inflicted upon him or her in the course of the competition,[282] unless the conduct of the defendant is such that it displays a reckless disregard for the other's safety.[283] The fact that the harmful conduct did not comply with the rules or conventions of the game is not decisive as such, but it is relevant to assess the reckless character of the act. French law comes to the same result through a distinction between normal risks and abnormal risks. As for the former, the victim is deemed to have accepted that a player will not commit a fault in the sense of Articles 1382–1383 C.civ. when he or she simply made a "fault in the course of the game" (*faute de jeu*), that is when he or she breached a technical rule of the game. However, when a player intentionally or manifestly broke the rules of the game, he or she committed a "fault against the game" (*faute contre le jeu*);[284] that is an abnormal risk which the victim cannot be held to have accepted, and for which the defendant remains liable under Articles 1382–1383 C.civ. The distinction between normal and abnormal risks is also applied where the defendant is liable as the keeper (*gardien*) of a thing pursuant to Article 1384(1) C.civ.[285] For instance, a yacht owner and skipper could not argue that the members of his crew had assumed the risk of death, because it cannot obviously be seen as a normal risk, although it occurred in the course of a normal sport event.[286]

Broadly speaking, German law reaches similar results in practice but follows a distinct, and rather peculiar, type of reasoning. Since the BGH judgment of 14 March 1961,[287]

---

[281] *Supra*, **7.E.18.**, Note (1), **7.F.23.**, Note (2) and **7.G.20.**, Note (1).

[282] That assumption is directed not so much at the risk of injury itself, but at the lack of reasonable care on the part of the defendant that may lead to injury.

[283] Diplock LJ in *Wooldridge* v. *Sumner* [1963] 2 QB 43, CA in the case of a spectator. See *supra*, **7.E.18.**, Note (2).

[284] *Supra*, **7.F.23.**

[285] But see for car accidents *supra*, 7.2.3., Introductory Note under c).

[286] *Supra*, **7.F.24.**

[287] *Supra*, **7.G.19.**

consent—i.e. the will of the victim—can justify relief from liability only in exceptional cases, namely in combat sports such as boxing, as stated above. In other cases, the defendant can argue in defence that the victim was "acting at his own risk", but the basis of that defence is to be found not in consent, but in the general principle of good faith (*Treu und Glauben*) of § 242 BGB. Good faith forbids someone from acting inconsistently with prior behaviour (*venire contra factum proprium*); the application of that maxim leads to an apportionment between plaintiff and defendant, as provided in § 254 BGB.[288] Indeed, § 254 BGB constitutes a specific application of good faith (*Treu und Glauben*) to the law of damages: according to the BGH, it is "wrong for a victim to invoke the liability of the defendant without taking account of the fact that he himself consciously created or helped to create [a] dangerous situation".[289] In later case law,[290] however, the BGH gave a specific meaning to the maxim *venire contra factum proprium* in cases of *competitive sports which are not inherently dangerous*, such as football, where all players may potentially injure one another even when they comply with the rules of the game. In those cases, the maxim was understood to imply that the mere fact that a player brings a claim against another player already runs against *venire contra factum proprium*. In other words, in those cases, the maxim is applied so as to lead to a *complete* exoneration from liability, leaving no room for apportionment under § 254 BGB. The end result is thus a distinction between three categories:

- combat sports where players intend to hurt one another, where consent (*Einwilligung*) provides a basis for complete exoneration;[291]
- competitive sports where players are in a position potentially to injure one another, where the defendant can also be completely exonerated (at least so long as the rules of the game are observed), but this time on a different basis. Here it would be against good faith (*Treu und Glauben*) to bring a claim against another player;
- sports where players play with, but not against, one another, where partial exoneration may occur depending on the circumstances, which are to be weighed in accordance with § 254 BGB.

Illegality

As exposed in the Introductory Note,[292] the defence of illegality will be raised only exceptionally—mainly when contributory negligence is, for one or another reason, not available—where the victim voluntarily participated in the illegal conduct which caused harm to him or her. The defence will lead to a complete exoneration, because of *ex turpi causa non oritur actio* or, in other words, *nemo auditur propriam turpitudinem allegans*.

In French law, the defence used to be raised mainly against claims for "reflex damage" (*dommage par ricochet*) brought by concubines of the direct victim; however, the Cour de cassation changed its case law and the defence of illegality is no longer admissible in such cases.[293] Nowadays, the defence will be available only where compensation would lead in

---

[288] See *supra*, 7.1.2.
[289] *Supra*, **7.G.19.** (under IV) in the case of an inexperienced young driver and his companion.
[290] BGH, 5 November 1974, *supra*, **7.G.20.**
[291] Eventually also in cases of risk-based liability (*Gefährdungshaftung*): *supra*, **7.G.21.**
[292] *Supra*, 7.3., Introductory Note.
[293] *Supra*, 7.3.1., Introductory Note under a) and more particularly *supra*, Chapter II, **2.F.19.**, Note (1).

itself to an illicit or immoral result.[294] In German law, while the BGB contains special provisions prohibiting acting *contra bonos mores* in the area of contracts and restitution, in tort law there is only § 826 BGB, which is a head of liability. There is no distinct provision which would conversely allow for a defence of illegality against a plaintiff who acted *contra bonos mores*. In such cases, the plaintiff will be held to have committed contributory negligence, which may lead to apportionment of liability under § 254(1) BGB.[295] In English law, the defence of *ex turpi causa* may be successful, under the tort of negligence, in situations where compensation would be an affront to "public conscience". More specifically, it will be used where the plaintiff's conduct makes it impossible for the court to set the appropriate standard of care.[296] The defence will be raised foremost in situations where the plaintiff is involved in criminal activity, with the defendant or alone, but it may also apply where the conduct of the plaintiff was reprehensible, while not constituting a criminal offence.[297] For the defence to apply, the plaintiff's own wrongdoing must be connected with the injury of which he or she complains.[298]

Illegality is sometimes used as a defence against a claim for lost income which the plaintiff derives from unlawful or immoral activity, e.g. where a prostitute sues the wrongdoer for lost income as a result of injury. Under French law, in order for the defendant to be exonerated on account of illegality, compensation must in itself lead to an illicit or immoral result.[299] Under German law, compensation was granted in one case, but up to the level of minimum subsistence only.[300] There seems to be no clear authority on this point under English law.[301]

---

[294] *Supra*, 7.3.1., Introductory Note and **7.F.25.**
[295] *Supra*, **7.G.26.**
[296] *Supra*, **7.E.28.** where both propositions are used, be it in different judgments.
[297] *Supra*, 7.3.3., Introductory Note under b).
[298] *Supra*, **7.E.28.**, Note (2).
[299] *Supra*, 7.3.1., Introductory Note under a).
[300] *Supra*, **7.G.27.**
[301] *Supra*, 7.3.3., Introductory Note under b).

CHAPTER EIGHT
REMEDIES

No branch of the law can live without remedies, i.e. legal actions which can be brought before a court of law to enforce the rights which individuals or collectivities derive, or believe that they can derive, from the rules of that branch of the law. In this Chapter we will examine the remedies which the legal systems analysed herein put at the disposal of plaintiffs seeking to enforce their right to reparation for harm to legal interests which, in the legal system concerned, are protected by the law of tort.

The foregoing may give the impression that the notions of remedies and of rights can neatly be distinguished. That is not correct, however, since many of the subjects dealt with in this Chapter concern as much the definition of the right to reparation itself as the procedural rules to enforce that right in a court of law.

Tort law, as mentioned repeatedly before, is mainly about reparation of harm, but not exclusively, however, as will be emphasized in Section 1 of this Chapter. There other functions of tort law are highlighted, namely judicial recognition of the plaintiff's legally protected interests, prevention of future harm, punishment and prevention of unjust enrichment. In that context attention will be drawn primarily to the distinction between compensation, satisfaction, punishment and restitution.

In Sections 2 and 3 the principle of full reparation will be discussed, starting first in Section 2 with the general principles governing the nature and extent of reparation and foremost with the rule of restitution in integrum, or full reparation. It may be understood either as restitution in kind, i.e. *restoration* of the situation in which the plaintiff would have been if he had not sustained the injury, or as compensation, i.e. the grant of an *equivalent* for the harm suffered. The principle of full reparation by the defendant is qualified by the duty of the plaintiff to mitigate harm, which we have chosen here to put in terms of the definition of recoverable harm, rather than in terms of causation.

A major issue which arises particularly in personal injury cases relates to the compensation of harm which may be subject to future developments. The question with which all legal systems are confronted is whether such compensation should consist of a once-and-for all award, or whether the compensation should be reviewable. A closely related issue is whether the damages should take the form of a capital sum or of periodical payments. When a legal system opts for a once-and-for-all award, mostly in the form of a capital sum, a further question is whether damages are to be assessed in a rough-and-ready way, or rather as exactly as possible. Where it chooses for reviewable compensation, the legal system must provide for flexible procedural machinery. All these issues and questions are examined in Section 3.

Sections 4 and 5 then apply the general principles set out in the preceding sections to loss of or damage to property and to personal injury and death, respectively. As for loss of or damage to property, the main issues are the appropriate measure of damages in respect of physical damage to property and the recoverability of damage resulting from the loss of use of property. It is in this respect that the concept of damage, that is to say the basis on which damages are to be assessed, becomes concrete: is that basis the cost of restoring the state of affairs (i.e. of the assets involved), either by repairing or by replacing the damaged property, *or* is it the difference in the owner's financial position after the wrongdoing, when compared with what it would have been if the wrongdoing would not have occurred. As for injury to the person, comparing the plaintiff's financial position after the wrongdoing with the situation where that wrongdoing would not have occurred become even more difficult and the importance of policy reasons will have to be recognized in that respect. The section will more particularly deal with the issue of collateral benefits.

Finally, in Section 6 other remedies than damages, mainly injunctive relief, will be briefly discussed.

8.1. THE PURPOSES OF AN AWARD IN TORT

Introductory Note

The plurality of purposes which tort law and the available remedies have to fulfil is recognized by many, but not all, legal systems. It is essential to discern those purposes because they may exercise considerable influence on the rules governing redress for injury.[1]

To make reparation for harm that has been inflicted is without doubt a prime function of tort law in any legal system and is generally achieved through monetary *compensation,* when reparation in kind is impossible or inappropriate.[2] The French legal system expressly recognizes this function only but, as will be seen later, even in France remedies are occasionally called upon to fulfil other roles, albeit covertly so as not to conflict with the accepted approach.

Another widely recognized function is that of the *judicial recognition* of the plaintiff's right or legally protected interest: the *declaration of rights.* Indeed this role underlies tort law in general: every judgment which holds a wrongdoer liable affirms the infringed right or interest of the victim. The mere recognition of another's right or interest may predominate, either because the violation of the plaintiff's right caused no appreciable harm (as in an award of *nominal damages* in English law or the *franc symbolique* in French law), or because the plaintiff attaches greater importance to the recognition of his right than to effective compensation for the harm. Thus, for example, in the case of injury to non-material interests, the plaintiff is often satisfied by merely symbolic compensation.

The special issues posed by the redress of non-material harm leads some legal systems, for example the German, to differentiate between *compensation* for material harm and *satisfaction* for non-material harm. That differentiation may influence the rules governing assessment of damages, particularly because of the importance attached to certain cir-

---

[1] On the purposes underlying liability see H. Stoll, "Consequences of liability: remedies" in *International Encyclopedia of Comparative Law—Volume XI/8: Torts* (Tübingen: Mohr, 1986) at para. 1–154.
[2] See *infra,* 8.2.

cumstances, for example the degree of culpability or the financial position of plaintiff and wrongdoer, which are not relevant in a purely compensatory analysis.

Some tort law remedies have as their goal the *prevention* of future harm. Specific remedies of tort law may have a directly preventive function, e.g. injunctive relief, which may even be granted where the tortious wrong has not yet occurred but appears to be imminent. Where a wrong has effected a state of affairs which is the source of continuing harm, the prevention of future harm may also be achieved by the concrete restoration of the *status quo ante*, so that it may be difficult to distinguish between reparation and prevention.[3]

The idea of prevention is of course not foreign to tort law in general, with the threat of liability in tort itself possibly exercising a deterrent effect on potential wrongdoers. This preventive function may be bolstered if the emphasis is shifted away from the compensatory idea, the remedies instead having as their aim the *punishment* and *prevention of unjust enrichment* of the wrongdoer. When punishment is the sole aim of the remedy, the compensatory principle is completely absent. Punitive damages are openly accepted only in English law, albeit in a restrictive way. This does not mean that the idea of punishment is unknown in other legal systems.[4] Similarly, the aim of *prevention of the wrongdoer's enrichment* is not compatible with the compensatory approach as such. When stressing that the wrongdoer may not be enriched by his tortious conduct, the emphasis is no longer on compensation for the harm inflicted, since the harm will not necessarily correspond with the wrongdoer's enrichment. As will be shown, the prevention of enrichment plays a role in the assessment of damages in certain cases.

In the examination which follows, the varied aims of remedies recognized by different legal systems, and their impact on the assessment of damages, will be discussed. In this section, attention will be drawn primarily to the distinction between compensation, satisfaction and punishment.

8.1.1. ENGLISH LAW

Introductory Note[5]

Generally speaking, the object of an award in tort is to make good the harm sustained by the plaintiff. However, in some cases reparation, more particularly a damages award, is not the single, or even main, function of an award in tort.[6]

Thus, damages may be *nominal*. Lord Halsbury gave the following definition in *The Mediana*:[7]

---

[3] See *infra*, 8.6.
[4] See *inter alia* H. Stoll, "Schadensersatz und Strafe. Eine rechtsvergleichende Skizze" in E. von Caemmerer, S. Mentschikoff and K. Zweigert, (eds.), *Ius privatum gentium. Festschrift für Max Rheinstein zum 70. Geburtstag*, II (Tübingen: Mohr, 1969) at 569 and "Penal Purposes in the Law of Tort" (1970) 18 AJCL 3; A.T. Bolt and J.A.W. Lensing, *Privaatrechtelijke boete* (Deventer: Kluwer, 1993).
[5] For an outline of the object of an award of damages in English law, see H. McGregor, *McGregor on Damages*, 16th edn. (London: Sweet & Maxwell, 1997) at para. 9–18.
[6] For an analysis of the ethical underpinnings of the law of damages see P. Cane, *The Anatomy of Tort Law* (Oxford: Hart Publishing, 1997) at 115–9.
[7] [1900] AC 113, HL at 116.

"'Nominal damages' is a technical phrase which means that you have negatived anything like real damage, but that you are affirming by your nominal damages that there is an infraction of a legal right which, though it gives you no right to any real damages at all, yet gives you a right to the verdict or judgment because your legal right has been infringed".

Historically, a plaintiff whose right was infringed could (at common law) claim only a judgment awarding a sum of money[8]; in the absence of actual damage, that sum was fixed at a symbolic amount. Nominal damages are mainly awarded for torts actionable *per se*, that is those giving rise to liability without a need to show real damage. It is clear that the object of the award of nominal damages is not compensation for damage but the *judicial recognition* of the infringed right.[9] Such a recognition may prevent future wrongdoing, albeit that that function has been taken over, to a large extent, by the equitable remedy of injunction.[10]

Damages may be *punitive* or *exemplary*, the object then being to punish the wrongdoer. Their role, their interrelationship with compensatory damages (especially for non-material harm), and the conditions for making an exemplary award are discussed in two decisions of the House of Lords reproduced below: *Rookes* v. *Barnard*[11] and *Cassell & Co. Ltd.* v. *Broome*.[12]

The issue of whether the tortfeasor may be obliged to make restitution for an *unjust enrichment* is problematic. As will be seen, the consideration of prevention of unjust enrichment is, in many cases, not absent from an award of exemplary damages and, for some torts, may be decisive for the proper measure of damages.[13]

---

[8] H. McGregor, *McGregor on Damages*, 16th edn. (London: Sweet & Maxwell, 1997) at para. 420.

[9] "Nominal damages may also be awarded where the fact of loss is shown but the necessary evidence as to its amount is not given": H. McGregor, ibid. at para. 423. An award of nominal damages may also be a means to condemn the defendant to pay the plaintiff's legal costs; however, the award of costs is today left to the discretion of the court: H. McGregor, ibid. at para. 428–429. See also H. Stoll, "Consequences of liability: remedies" in *International Encyclopedia of Comparative Law—Volume XI/8: Torts* (Tübingen: Mohr, 1986) at para. 84.

[10] H. McGregor, ibid. at para. 427; H. Stoll at para. 84. See *infra* 8.6.

[11] **8.E.1.**

[12] **8.E.2.**

[13] See *infra* 8.2.

House of Lords[14]   **8.E.1.–2.**
Rookes v. *Barnard*
and
House of Lords[15]
Cassell & Co. Ltd. v. *Broome*

APPLICABILITY OF EXEMPLARY DAMAGES

1. *Rookes* v. *Barnard*   **8.E.1.**

Dismissal resulting from intimidation of employee

Apart from cases where exemplary damages are expressly authorized by statute, such awards are limited to cases of oppressive, arbitrary or unconstitutional action by civil servants and to cases of conduct calculated to make a profit exceeding the compensation payable to the plaintiff.

Facts: The plaintiff resigned his membership of a trade union. Upon the plaintiff's refusal to rejoin the trade union, the defendants, officials of the union, informed the plaintiff's employers, that if the plaintiff was not removed from office, the rest of the workforce, as union members, would withdraw their labour. The plaintiff was dismissed.

Held: The court of first instance held that the threats to strike (in breach of an agreement) were unlawful acts constituting intimidation; the jury, directed by the trial judge that they could award exemplary damages, awarded the plaintiff GBP 7,500. The court of appeal reversed the decision, holding that a threat to break a contract did not fall within the tort of intimidation. The House of Lords, allowing the plaintiff's appeal, held that the defendants had committed the tort of intimidation and, allowing the defendants' cross-appeal, that the facts disclosed in the trial judge's summing-up showed no case for exemplary damages. A new trial on the question of damages was ordered.

Judgment: LORD DEVLIN: "Exemplary damages are essentially different from ordinary damages. The object of damages in the usual sense of the term is to compensate. The object of exemplary damages is to punish and deter. It may well be thought that this confuses the civil and criminal functions of the law; and indeed, so far as I know, the idea of exemplary damages is peculiar to English law. There is not any decision of this House approving an award of exemplary damages and your Lordships therefore have to consider whether it is open to the House to remove an anomaly from the law of England.

It must be remembered that in many cases of tort damages are at large, that is to say, the award is not limited to the pecuniary loss that can be specifically proved. In the present case, for example, and leaving aside any question of exemplary or aggravated damages, the appellant's damages would not necessarily be confined to those which he would obtain in an action for wrongful dismissal. He can invite the jury to look at all the circumstances, the inconveniences caused to him by the change of job and the unhappiness maybe by a change of livelihood. In such a case as this, it is quite proper without any departure from the compensatory principle to award a round sum based on the pecuniary loss proved.

Moreover, it is very well established that in cases where the damages are at large the jury (or the judge if the award is left to him) can take into account the motives and conduct of the defendant

---

[14] [1964] AC 1129, [1964] 2 WLR 269, [1964] 1 All ER 367, [1964] 1 Lloyd's Rep. 28, HL.
[15] [1972] AC 1027, [1972] 2 WLR 645, [1972] 1 All ER 801, HL.

where they aggravate the injury done to the plaintiff. There may be malevolence or spite or the manner of committing the wrong may be such as to injure the plaintiff's proper feelings of dignity and pride. These are matters which the jury can take into account in assessing the appropriate compensation. Indeed, when one examines the cases in which large damages have been awarded for conduct of this sort, it is not at all easy to say whether the idea of compensation or the idea of punishment has prevailed.

But there are also cases in the books where the awards given cannot be explained as compensatory, and I propose therefore to begin by examining the authorities in order to see how far and in what sort of cases the exemplary principle has been recognised . . .

These authorities convince me of two things. First, that your Lordships could not, without a complete disregard of precedent, and indeed of statute, now arrive at a determination that refused altogether to recognise the exemplary principle. Secondly, that there are certain categories of cases in which an award of exemplary damages can serve a useful purpose in vindicating the strength of the law and thus affording a practical justification for admitting into the civil law a principle which ought logically to belong to the criminal. I propose to state what these two categories are; and I propose also to state three general considerations which, in my opinion, should always be borne in mind when awards of exemplary damages are being made . . .

The first category is *oppressive, arbitrary or unconstitutional action by the servants of the government* [emphasis added]. I should not extend this category—I say this with particular reference to the facts of this case—to oppressive action by private corporations or individuals. Where one man is more powerful than another, it is inevitable that he will try to use his power to gain his ends; and if his power is much greater than the other's, he might, perhaps, be said to be using it oppressively. If he uses his power illegally, he must of course pay for his illegality in the ordinary way; but he is not to be punished simply because he is the more powerful. In the case of the government it is different, for the servants of the government are also the servants of the people and the use of their power must always be subordinate to their duty of service. It is true that there is something repugnant about a big man bullying a small man and, very likely, the bullying will be a source of humiliation that makes the case one for aggravated damages, but it is not, in my opinion, punishable by damages.

Cases in the second category are those in which *the defendant's conduct has been calculated by him to make a profit for himself which may well exceed the compensation payable to the plaintiff* [emphasis added] . . . It is a factor also that is taken into account in damages for libel; one man should not be allowed to sell another man's reputation for profit. Where a defendant with a cynical disregard for a plaintiff's rights has calculated that the money to be made out of his wrongdoing will probably exceed the damages at risk, it is necessary for the law to show that it cannot be broken with impunity. This category is not confined to moneymaking in the strict sense. It extends to cases in which the defendant is seeking to gain at the expense of the plaintiff some object—perhaps some property which he covets—which either he could not obtain at all or not obtain except at a price greater than he wants to put down. Exemplary damages can properly be awarded whenever it is necessary to teach a wrongdoer that tort does not pay.

To these two categories which are established as part of the common law there must of course be added any category in which exemplary damages are *expressly authorised by statute* [emphasis added].

I wish now to express three considerations which I think should always be borne in mind when awards of exemplary damages are being considered. First, the plaintiff cannot recover exemplary damages unless he is the victim of the punishable behaviour. The anomaly inherent in exemplary damages would become an absurdity if a plaintiff totally unaffected by some oppressive conduct which the jury wished to punish obtained a windfall in consequence.

Secondly, the power to award exemplary damages constitutes a weapon that, while it can be used in defence of liberty . . . can also be used against liberty. Some of the awards that juries have made in the past seem to me to amount to a greater punishment than would be likely to be incurred if the conduct were criminal; and, moreover, a punishment imposed without the safeguard which the criminal law gives to an offender. I should not allow the respect which is traditionally paid to an assessment of damages by a jury to prevent me from seeing that the weapon is used with restraint . . .

Thirdly, the means of parties, irrelevant in the assessment of compensation, are material in the assessment of exemplary damages. Everything which aggravates or mitigates the defendant's conduct is relevant."

2. *Cassell & Co. Ltd.* v. *Broome* **8.E.2.**

Defamation concerning naval disaster

Exemplary damages are reluctantly awarded as an exception to the general rule of restitutio in integrum, notwithstanding the many objections against their award and in spite of the fact that compensatory damages, especially in actions for defamation, may already have a highly subjective element.

Facts: The plaintiff, a distinguished retired naval officer, brought actions for libel against the publishers and the author of a book in which he was held responsible for a great naval disaster in the Second World War. He claimed exemplary damages.

Held: At first instance, the jury awarded the plaintiff GBP 15,000 compensatory and GBP 25,000 exemplary damages. The court of appeal dismissed the defendants' appeal and its decision was upheld by the House of Lords.

Judgment: LORD HAILSHAM OF ST. MARYLEBONE L.C. : "In almost all actions for breach of contract, and in many actions for tort, the principle of restitutio in integrum is an adequate and fairly easy guide to the estimation of damage, because the damage suffered can be estimated by relation to some material loss. It is true that where loss includes a pre-estimate of future losses, or an estimate of past losses which cannot in the nature of things be exactly computed, some subjective element must enter in. But the estimate is in things commensurable with one another, and convertible at least in principle to the English currency in which all sums of damages must ultimately be expressed.

In many torts, however, the subjective element is more difficult. The pain and suffering endured, and the future loss of amenity, in a personal injuries case are not in the nature of things convertible into legal tender . . . Nor so far as I can judge, is there any purely rational test by which a judge can calculate what sum, greater or smaller, is appropriate. What is surprising is not that there is difference of opinion about such matters, but that in most cases professional opinion gravitates so closely to a conventional scale. Nevertheless in all actions in which damages, purely compensatory in character, are awarded for suffering, from the purely pecuniary point of view the plaintiff may be better off. The principle of restitutio in integrum, which compels the use of money as its sole instrument for restoring the status quo, necessarily involves a factor larger than any pecuniary loss.

In actions of defamation and in any other actions where damages for loss of reputation are involved, the principle of restitutio in integrum has necessarily an even more highly subjective element [emphasis added]. Such actions involve a money award which may put the plaintiff in a purely financial sense in a much stronger position than he was before the wrong. Not merely can he recover the estimated sum of his past and future losses, but, in case the libel, driven underground, emerges from its lurking place at some future date, he must be able to point to a sum awarded by a jury sufficient to convince a bystander of the baselessness of the charge. As Windeyer J. well said in *Uren v. John Fairfax & Sons Pty. Ltd.*, 117 CLR 115, 150:

"It seems to me that, properly speaking, a man defamed does not get compensation *for* his damaged reputation. He gets damages *because* he was injured in his reputation, that is simply because he was publicly defamed. For this reason, compensation by damages operates in two ways—as a vindication of the plaintiff to the public and as consolation to him for a wrong done. Compensation is here a solatium rather than a monetary recompense for harm measurable in money" [emphasis in original].

This is why it is not necessarily fair to compare awards of damages in this field with damages for personal injuries. Quite obviously, the award must include factors for injury to the feelings, the anxiety and uncertainty undergone in the litigation, the absence of apology, or the reaffirmation of the truth of the matters complained of, or the malice of the defendant. The bad conduct of the plaintiff himself may also enter into the matter, where he has provoked the libel, or where perhaps he has libelled the defendant in reply. What is awarded is thus a figure which cannot be arrived at by any purely objective computation. This is what is meant when the damages in defamation are described as being "at large". In a sense, too, these damages are of their nature punitive or exemplary in the loose sense in which the terms were used before 1964 [i.e. before *Rookes* v. *Barnard, supra*], because they inflict an added burden on the defendant proportionate to his conduct, just as they can be reduced if the defendant has behaved well—as for instance by a handsome apology—or the plaintiff badly, as for instance by provoking the defendant, or defaming him in return . . .

It is this too which explains the almost indiscriminate use of "at large", "aggravated", "exemplary" and "punitive" before *Rookes* v. *Barnard* . . . My own view is that in no English case, and perhaps even in no statute, where the word "exemplary" or "punitive" or "aggravated" occurs before 1964 can one be absolutely sure that there is no element of confusion between the two elements in damages. It was not until Lord Devlin's speech in *Rookes* v. *Barnard* that the expressions "aggravated", on the one hand, and "punitive" or "exemplary", on the other, acquired separate and mutually exclusive meanings as terms of art in English law.

. . .

The true explanation of *Rookes* v. *Barnard* is to be found in the fact that, where damages for loss of reputation are concerned, or where a simple outrage to the individual or to property is concerned, *aggravated damages* in the sense I have explained can, and should in every case lying outside the categories, take care of the exemplary element, and the jury should neither be encouraged nor allowed to look beyond as generous a solatium as is required for the injuria simply in order to give effect to feelings of indignation [emphasis added]. It is not that the exemplary element is excluded in such cases. *It is precisely because in the nature of things it is, and should be, included in every such case that the jury should neither be encouraged nor allowed to look for it outside the solatium and then to add to the sum awarded another sum by way of penalty additional to the solatium* [emphasis added]. To do so would be to inflict a double penalty for the same offence.

The surprising thing about *Rookes* v. *Barnard* is not that Lord Devlin restricted the award of *exemplary damages* viewed as an addition to or substitution for damages by way of solatium to the three so-called categories, *but that he allowed the three so-called categories to exist by way of exception to the general rule* [emphasis added]. That he did this is due at least in part to the fact that he felt himself bound by authority to do so, but partly also because he thought that there were cases where, over and above the figure awarded for loss of reputation, for injured feelings, for outraged morality, and to enable a plaintiff to protect himself against future calumny or outrage of a similar kind, an additional sum was needed to vindicate the strength of the law and act as a supplement to its strictly penal provisions [references omitted]."

LORD REID: "I must now deal with those parts of Lord Devlin's speech which have given rise to difficulties. He set out two categories of cases which in our opinion comprised all or virtually all the reported cases in which it was clear that the court had approved of an award of a larger sum of damages than could be justified as compensatory. Critics appear to have thought that he was inventing something new. That was not my understanding. We were confronted with an undesirable anomaly. We could not abolish it. We had to choose between confining it strictly to classes of cases where it was firmly established, although that produced an illogical result, or permitting it to be extended so as to produce a logical result. In my view it is better in such cases to be content with an illogical result than to allow any extension.

It will be seen that I do not agree with Lord Devlin's view that in certain classes of case exemplary damages serve a useful purpose *in vindicating the strength of the law* . . . [emphasis added]

I think that the objections to allowing juries to go beyond compensatory damages are overwhelming. To allow pure punishment in this way contravenes almost every principle which has been evolved for the protection of offenders. There is no definition of the offence except that the conduct punished must be oppressive, high-handed, malicious, wanton or its like—terms far too vague to be admitted to any criminal code worthy of the name. There is no limit to the punishment except that it must not be unreasonable. The punishment is not inflicted by a judge who has experience and at least tries not to be influenced by emotion: it is inflicted by a jury without experience of law or punishment and often swayed by considerations which every judge would put out of his mind. And there is no effective appeal against sentence. All that a reviewing court can do is to quash the jury's decision if it thinks the punishment awarded is more than any twelve reasonable men could award. The court cannot substitute its own award. The punishment must then be decided by another jury and if they too award heavy punishment the court is virtually powerless. It is no excuse to say that we need not waste sympathy on people who behave outrageously. Are we wasting sympathy on vicious criminals when we insist on proper legal safeguards for them?"

LORD DIPLOCK: "My Lords, had I been party to the decision in *Rookes* v. *Barnard* I doubt I should have considered it still necessary to retain the first category [abuse of power by public officials] . . .

I have no similar doubts about the retention of the second category. It too may be a blunt instrument to prevent unjust enrichment by unlawful acts. But to restrict the damages recoverable to the actual gain made by the defendant if it exceeded the loss caused to the plaintiff, would leave a defendant contemplating an unlawful act with the certainty that he had nothing to lose to balance against the chance that the plaintiff might never sue him or, if he did, might fall in the hazards of litigation. It is only if there is a prospect that the damages may exceed the defendant's gain that the social purpose of this category is achieved—to teach a wrong-doer that tort does not pay.

To bring a case within this category it must be proved that the defendant, at the time that he committed the tortious act, knew that it was unlawful or suspecting it be unlawful deliberately refrained from taking obvious steps which, if taken, would have turned suspicion into certainty. While, of course, it is not necessary to prove that the defendant made an arithmetical calculation of the pecuniary profit he would make from the tortious act and of the compensatory damages and costs to which he would render himself liable, with appropriate discount for the chances that he might get away with it without being sued or might settle the action for some lower figure, it must be a reasonable inference from the evidence that he did direct his mind to the material advantages to be gained by committing the tort and came to the conclusion that they were worth the risk of having to compensate the plaintiff if he should bring an action."

Notes

(1) In *Rookes* v. *Barnard* the House of Lords considered for the first time the status of an award of exemplary damages and the basis for such an award.[16] This subject was dealt with by Lord Devlin, the other Law Lords concurring. The question had to be reconsidered by the House of Lords eight years later in *Cassell & Co. Ltd.* v. *Broome* due to the

---

[16] *Rookes* v. *Barnard, supra*, at 1196 per Lord Evershed.

opposition of the Court of Appeal[17] which, mirroring the cool reception *Rookes* v. *Barnard* received in the Commonwealth, had judged it to be wrongly decided, unworkable and not binding on the Court of Appeal.[18] In the House of Lords, it was claimed that, as Lord Devlin was the only member of the House whose speech dealt with the question of exemplary damages, it had resulted in "an unduly fundamentalist approach to the actual language employed",[19] "treating sentences and phrases in a single speech as if they were provisions in an Act of Parliament"[20] so that Lord Devlin's exposition had been misinterpreted. In *Cassell & Co. Ltd.* v. *Broome* seven Law Lords expressed their sometimes considerably diverging opinions, demonstrating that in English law the idea of punishment of a tortfeasor is far from uncontroversial.

(2) The distinction between compensatory and exemplary damages is at first glance clear: the object of compensatory damages is to compensate; the object of exemplary damages to punish and deter.[21] However, this distinction loses its sharpness when the difficulties faced in giving adequate compensation for injury to non-material interests, by definition not calculable in money terms, are recognized. Lord Hailsham called this "the subjective element in damages". This subjective element means that in many cases damages are "at large", i.e. that "the award is not limited to the pecuniary loss that can be specifically proved",[22] it is "a figure which cannot be arrived at by any purely objective computation".[23] In assessing damages "at large", the motives and conduct of the defendant where they exacerbate the injury done to the plaintiff, can be taken into account, with such an award known as *aggravated damages*,[24] albeit that they are still within the compensatory framework. Lord Hailsham recognized that such damages are in a broad sense "punitive or exemplary", because "they inflict an added burden on the defendant proportionate to his conduct".[25] As Lord Devlin stated, "aggravated damages . . . can do most, if not all, of the work that could be done by exemplary damages",[26] a view which has been reiterated in subsequent cases.[27] Thus, the difference between aggravated damages remaining within the compensatory framework, in which the exemplary element is not excluded however, and exemplary damages, which have for object to punish and deter in the sense given by Lord Devlin in *Rookes* v. *Barnard*, is apparently not a matter of principle but of quantity: exemplary damages include "an additional sum needed to vindicate

---

[17] [1971] 2 QB 354, [1971] 2 WLR 853, [1971] 2 All ER 187, CA, sub nom. *Broome* v. *Cassell & Co. Ltd.* The Court of Appeal's attitude was sharply criticized in *Cassell & Co. Ltd.* v. *Broome, supra*, by Lord Hailsham at 1053–1055 and Lord Reid at 1084.

[18] *Cassell & Co. Ltd.* v. *Broome, supra*, at 1052–3 and 1067–8 per Lord Hailsham.

[19] *Cassell & Co. Ltd.* v. *Broome, supra*, at 1068 per Lord Hailsham.

[20] *Cassell & Co. Ltd.* v. *Broome, supra*, at 1085 per Lord Reid.

[21] *Rookes* v. *Barnard, supra*, at 1221 per Lord Devlin.

[22] Ibid.

[23] *Cassell & Co. Ltd.* v. *Broome, supra*, at 1071 per Lord Hailsham. Lord Hailsham calls a compensation for injured feelings "at large" a "solatium", to be distinguished from compensation in the strict sense of the word. See also German law, *infra*, **8.G.3.**, where the distinction is also drawn.

[24] *Rookes* v. *Barnard, supra*, at 1221. See also Lord Diplock's exposition on damages "at large", aggravated damages and punitive damages in *Cassell & Co. Ltd.* v. *Broome, supra*, at 1124–5.

[25] *Cassell & Co. Ltd.* v. *Broome, supra*, at 1071, see also at 1076.

[26] *Rookes* v. *Barnard, supra*, at 1230.

[27] See *Thompson* v. *Commissioner of Police of the Metropolis* [1997] 3 WLR 403, CA at 413, referring to the Law Commission's Consultation Paper No. 132 *Aggravated, Exemplary and Restitutionary Damages* (1993), in which it is pointed out that the award of aggravated damages may have a penal element.

the strength of the law, acting as a supplement to its strictly penal provisions".[28] Thus, as Lord Devlin put it, "a jury should be directed that *if, but only if,* the sum which they have in mind to award as compensation . . . is inadequate to punish [the defendant] for his outrageous conduct, to mark their disapproval of such conduct and to deter him from repeating it, then it can award some larger sum [emphasis added].",[29] a direction which has henceforth been called the "if but only if" test and to which subsequent cases refer.

(3) Lord Devlin recognizes two categories of cases at common law[30] in which exemplary damages may be awarded. His description of those categories has been clarified in subsequent cases.

(a) The first category is, in Lord Devlin's words, "oppressive, arbitrary or unconstitutional action by the servants of the government".[31] It has been stressed that the term "government" may have a wide application. This category can apply to "all those who by common law or statute are exercising functions of a governmental character".[32] However, awards of exemplary damages falling within this category are rare.[33] It has been decided that the powers and duties of a nationalized body engaged in the commercial supply of water, should not be considered to be the exercise of executive power derived from government.[34]

Recently, in *Thompson* v. *Commissioner of Police of the Metropolis*,[35] the Court of Appeal has stressed some particularities of awards by way of exemplary damages in cases of false imprisonment and malicious prosecution, when compared with cases of the second category referred to under (b) below, which make consistency in the amount of damages more likely. The existence of a profit motive on the part of the wrongdoer, a factor justifying the award in cases of the second category and affecting its quantum, is absent in cases of false imprisonment and malicious prosecution. In addition, as the defendant is usually a chief police officer, exemplary damages should play a lesser role since it is more difficult to justify an award of exemplary damages where the defendant is not the wrongdoer but his "employer". The Court also refers to the fact that, in that category of cases, damages are paid out of public funds. These considerations have led the Court of Appeal to formulate very detailed guidance, including the appropriate level of the award, for juries in such cases. Contrary to the traditional view,[36] the Court considers it conducive to greater transparency if a separate award is made for each category of damages ("ordinary" compensatory damages—called "basic" damages—, aggravated damages—though compensatory and not intended as a punishment, in fact containing a penal element—and exemplary damages).[37] It also emphasized the nature of the injury in these cases to be analogous to that in personal injury cases, especially pain

---

[28] *Cassell & Co. Ltd.* v. *Broome, supra,* at 1077.

[29] *Rookes* v. *Barnard, supra,* at 1228.

[30] I.e. apart from instances where the award of damages is authorized by statute. But it is doubtful whether any statutory provision authorizes such an award. In *Rookes* and *Cassell*, two Acts are referred to (the Reserve and Auxiliary Forces (Protection of Civil Interests) Act 1951, 14 & 15 Geo. 6, c. 65, and the Copyright Act 1956, 4 & 5 Eliz. 2, c. 74) but the question as to whether the awards for which those statutes provide are exemplary has remained open or has been answered in the negative; see H. McGregor, *McGregor on Damages*, 16th edn. (London: Sweet & Maxwell, 1997) at 304–6, para. 458–60.

[31] *Rookes* v. *Barnard, supra,* at 1226.

[32] *Cassell & Co. Ltd.* v. *Broome, supra,* at 1088 per Lord Reid, see also at 1077–8 per Lord Hailsham.

[33] H. McGregor, *McGregor on Damages*, 16th edn. (London: Sweet & Maxwell, 1997) at para. 446.

[34] *A.B. and Others* v. *South West Water Services Ltd.* [1993] QB 507, [1993] 2 WLR 507, [1993] 1 All ER 609, CA.

[35] [1997] 3 WLR 403, CA at 413–4.

[36] Expressed by Lord Hailsham in *Cassell & Co. Ltd.* v. *Broome, supra,* at 1072.

[37] *Thompson* v. *Commissioner of Police of the Metropolis* [1997] 3 WLR 403, CA at 417.

and suffering, so that "there is no justification for two tariffs".[38] These considerations express the growing concern of judges for consistency in awards across the various categories of cases, including, as is evident from *John* v. *MGN Ltd.,*[39] cases of defamation.

(b) The second category was described by Lord Devlin as containing cases where "the defendant's conduct has been calculated by him to make a profit for himself which may well exceed the compensation payable to the plaintiff". The description is "not intended to be limited to the kind of mathematical calculations to be found on a balance sheet".[40] Lord Hailsham examined in detail the application of the category to publishers in libel cases,[41] and Lord Reid considered the potential impact on the publishers' freedom to conduct their business.[42]

Lord Diplock doubted the necessity of the first category, but accepted exemplary damages for the second category on the basis that, although such an award may be a blunt instrument to prevent unjust enrichment by unlawful acts, it would not be right to restrict the damages recoverable to the actual gain, as the mere loss of profits may not be sufficiently dissuasive.[43] It has been observed however, that "the awarding of exemplary damages is a somewhat makeshift and arbitrary method of preventing a tortfeasor's unjust enrichment. For on this rationale all tortfeasors should be required to give up their profits whether they have acted in such a way as to merit punishment or not".[44]

(4) In *Rookes* v. *Barnard*, Lord Devlin viewed the concept of exemplary damages as an "anomaly" confusing the civil and criminal functions of the law.[45] He considered the House to be unable, by force of authority, to refuse to recognize the exemplary principle but found that limits could be imposed upon it.[46]

In *Cassell & Co. Ltd.* Viscount Dilhorne expressed the view that the award of exemplary damages could not be restricted to the categories expounded by Lord Devlin.[47] He criticized the fact that, through the restriction of the award of exemplary damages, other anomalies and illogicalities are created. Why should only a servant of government be liable to exemplary damages, and why should conduct not inspired by the profit motive but similar to it not lead to such an award?[48] Lord Reid recognized the illogicalities which would arise but he preferred this lack of logic, which he regarded

---

[38] *Thompson* v. *Commissioner of Police of the Metropolis* [1997] 3 WLR 403, CA at 413.

[39] [1997] QB 586, [1996] 3 WLR 593, [1996] 2 All ER 35, CA.

[40] *Cassell & Co. Ltd.* v. *Broome, supra,* at 1079 per Lord Hailsham, also at 1101 per Viscount Dilhorne and at 1130 per Lord Diplock.

[41] *Cassell & Co. Ltd.* v. *Broome, supra,* at 1079.

[42] *Cassell & Co. Ltd.* v. *Broome, supra,* at 1089.

[43] *Cassell & Co. Ltd.* v. *Broome, supra,* at 1130, see also at 1129: "This would seem to be analogous to the civil law concept of enrichessement indue subject to a similar limitation that the act resulting in enrichment must be tortious".

[44] H. McGregor, *McGregor on Damages,* 16th edn. (London: Sweet & Maxwell, 1997) at para. 457.

[45] See for a discussion of the arguments for and against exemplary damages A. Burrows, "Reforming Exemplary Damages: Expansion or Abolition?" and N. J. McBride, "Punitive Damages" in P. Birks, (ed.), *Wrongs and Remedies in the Twenty-First Century* (Oxford: Clarendon Press, 1996) 153 and 175 respectively.

[46] *Rookes* v. *Barnard, supra,* at 1126.

[47] *Cassell & Co. Ltd.* v. *Broome, supra,* at 1107–9 (dissenting).

[48] The Court of Appeal had expressed the same criticisms: see *Broome* v. *Cassell & Co. Ltd.* [1971] 2 QB 354 at 381 per Lord Denning MR, at 386–7 per Salmon LJ and at 397–8 per Phillimore LJ. See also Law Commission Report No. 247, *Aggravated, Exemplary and Restitutionary Damages* (1997), proposing a detailed legislative scheme under which punitive damages would be available for any tort or equitable wrong (Draft Bill clause 3(3)), if the defendant has "deliberately and outrageously" disregarded the plaintiff's rights (Draft Bill clause 3(6)).

as the inevitable result of recognizing only those categories supported by "firmly established authority", rather than a widening of the concept.[49]

The scope of cases in which exemplary damages may be awarded, has been restricted accordingly by the Court of Appeal. In *A.B. and Others* v. *South West Water Services Ltd.*,[50] the Court held that exemplary damages are not available in respect of those causes of action for which such damages were not awarded prior to 1964, the year in which *Rookes* v. *Barnard* was decided, a state of affairs which has been described as unfortunate "because it commits the law to an irrational position in which the result depends not on principle but upon the accidents of litigation (or even of law reporting) before 1964, at a time, moreover, when the distinction between exemplary and aggravated damages was by no means so clearly drawn as it is now".[51]

(5) Jury trial remains for defamation actions, and juries play a particular role in awarding exemplary damages in such cases. As explained in *John* v. *MGN Ltd.*:[52]

"Respect for the constitutional role of the jury in such actions, and judicial reluctance to intrude into the area of decision-making reserved to the jury, have traditionally led judges presiding over defamation trials with juries to confine their jury directions to a statement of general principles, eschewing any specific guidance on the appropriate level of general damages in the particular case".

This state of affairs resulted in a tendency towards excessive jury awards of both compensatory and exemplary damages, showing the need for more substantial guidance.

While at first it was considered that juries should be guided only in terms which assist them to appreciate the real value of large sums, inviting them to consider the purchasing power of the award,[53] the opinion that the jury should be referred to awards made in other cases gained more and more ground. Meanwhile, under the Courts and Legal Services Act 1990[54] the Court of Appeal was empowered, upon finding a jury award to be excessive, "to substitute for the sum awarded by the jury such sum as appears to the court to be proper" in place of ordering a new trial. Thus, in *Rantzen* v. *Mirror Group Newspapers (1986) Ltd.*,[55] while it was acknowledged that due to the lack of guidance in the past, no reference to previous cases could be made, the hope was expressed that awards for defamation claims, substituted by the Court of Appeal, could establish guidelines as to proper awards. However, it was still considered that awards in actions for damages in personal injury cases could not be used to provide guidance for an award in an action for defamation.[56] This final objection was overcome in *John* v. *MGN Ltd.*:[57]

---

[49] *Cassell & Co. Ltd.* v. *Broome, supra,* at 1088.

[50] [1993] QB 507, [1993] 2 WLR 507, [1993] 1 All ER 609, CA (a claim in public nuisance).

[51] Rogers at 746.

[52] [1996] 3 WLR 593, CA at 608.

[53] See *Sutcliffe* v. *Pressdram Ltd.* [1991] 1 QB 153, [1990] 2 WLR 271, [1990] 1 All ER 269, CA at 290 and *Rantzen* v. *Mirror Group Newspapers (1986) Ltd.* [1994] QB 670, CA at 696.

[54] C. 41.

[55] [1994] QB 670, CA. In that case, the Court of Appeal substituted GBP 100,000 for the jury award of GBP 250,000 to a television presenter, who was the victim of libellous articles about her work for sexually abused children.

[56] *Rantzen* v. *Mirror Group Newspapers (1986) Ltd.* [1994] QB 670, CA at 694–5.

[57] [1996] 3 WLR 593, CA at 614 per Sir Thomas Bingham MR. In this case of libel against a well-known musician, the jury had made an award of GBP 75,000 by way of compensatory damages and of GBP 275,000 by way of exemplary damages. The Court of Appeal reduced the awards to GBP 25,000 and GBP 50,000 respectively.

"It is in our view offensive to public opinion, and rightly so, that a defamation plaintiff should recover damages for injury to reputation greater, perhaps by a significant factor, than if that same plaintiff had been rendered a helpless cripple or an insensate vegetable. The time has in our view come when judges, and counsel, should be free to draw the attention of juries to these comparisons."

(6) The existence of exemplary damages as a special category of damages award under English law raises questions in the context of European law. That is particularly the case of Article 10 ECHR.[58]

In *Rantzen* v. *Mirror Group Newspapers (1986) Ltd.*,[59] the court concluded that the term "excessive" under s. 8(1) of the Courts and Legal Services Act 1990[60] had to be interpreted in accordance with Art. 10 ECHR. It considered that the grant of an almost limitless discretion to a jury failed to provide a satisfactory measurement for deciding what is a necessary restriction in a democratic society on the exercise of the right to freedom of expression to protect the reputation of others and considered therefore that the common law required the courts to subject large awards of damages to a more searching scrutiny than had been customary in the past.[61] Later, in *Tolstoy Miloslavsky* v. *United Kingdom*,[62] the European Court of Human Rights, having endorsed the observations of the Court of Appeal in *Rantzen*, found that the size of the award[63] in conjunction with the lack of adequate and effective safeguards (prior to the entry into force of the Courts and Legal Services Act 1990) violated Art. 10 of the Convention. In *John* v. *MGN Ltd.*,[64] the Court of Appeal referred to Art. 10, albeit only to reinforce the conclusions that it had reached independently of the Convention, stating that an appropriate award of exemplary damages "should never exceed the minimum sum to meet the public purpose underlying such damages, that of punishing the defendant, showing that tort does not pay and deterring others".

As for EC law, the issue of exemplary damages was raised in the ECJ's judgment in *Brasserie du Pêcheur and Factortame,*[65] in connection with conduct of public authorities in breach of Art. 43 EC alleged to constitute oppressive, arbitrary or unconstitutional behaviour.[66] The Court held that "in so far as such conduct may constitute or aggravate a breach of Community law, an award of exemplary damages . . . cannot be ruled out if such damages could be awarded pursuant to a similar claim founded on domestic law".[67] The English High Court has now decided that the plaintiffs in *Factortame* had no right to exemplary damages under English law.[68]

---

[58] Art. 10: "1. Everyone has the right of freedom of expression . . . 2. The exercise of these freedoms, since it carries with it duties and responsibilities, may be subject to such formalities, conditions, restrictions or penalties as are prescribed by law and are necessary in a democratic society . . . for the protection of the reputation or rights of others . . ."

[59] [1994] QB 670, CA.

[60] *Supra*, Note (5).

[61] *Rantzen* v. *Mirror Group Newspapers Ltd.* [1994] QB 670, CA at 692.

[62] ECtHR, *Tolstoy Miloslavsky* v. *United Kingdom*, 13 July 1995, Ser. A No. 316-B: see *infra*, Chapter IX, 9.2. Introductory Note under c).

[63] GBP 1,500,000 by way of *compensatory* damages!

[64] [1996] 3 WLR 593, CA at 619.

[65] *Infra*, Chapter IX, **9.EC.6.**

[66] Ibid., Note (3)(a).

[67] Ibid., para. 89.

[68] [1997] EuLR 475; see J. Steiner, "The Limits of State Liability for Breach of European Community Law" European Public Law 1998, 79. The issue of exemplary damages was not argued on the appeal to the Court of

8.1.2. GERMAN LAW

Introductory Note[69]

In German law, the compensatory principle (*Ausgleichsprinzip, Ausgleichsgedanke*[70]) is enunciated in the first sentence of § 249 BGB:

> "A person who is obliged to make reparation for harm must restore the situation which would have existed if the circumstances giving rise to the obligation to make reparation had not occurred."

The prevailing view in legal textbooks is that this principle is fundamental to the German law of damages. Any other purposes that the law of damages may fulfil are considered to be a mere side upon effect of reparation. Thus, it is recognized that tort law may have a preventive effect upon potential wrongdoers (*Präventionsgedanke*).[71] It is also stressed that the redress of harm contributes to the assertion of subjective rights: the injured right lives on in a claim for damages (*Rechtsfortsetzungsgedanke*), which is entirely in keeping with the compensatory principle.[72] Despite the prevailing academic view that any punitive element (*Pönalgedanke*) is foreign to the law of damages,[73] an examination of the case law shows that the level of awards may not always be easily reconciled with a purely compensatory approach. A functional analysis highlights the overlapping of compensatory and punitive purposes.[74]

It was the issue of redress for non-material harm which initially led the BGH to distinguish between redress (*Ausgleich*) and satisfaction (*Genugtuung*).[75] In a later judgment denying the enforceability in Germany of an award of punitive damages made by a US court, the BGH examined the nature and functions of an award of damages under German law compared with punitive damages.[76] However the BGH's case law is still in a state of evolution as its case law concerning unconscious victims shows.[77] Moreover, an analysis of BGH case law on the protection of personality rights reveals that the ideas of

---

Appeal [1998] ELRev 456 at 478–9, nor was it pursued before the House of Lords [1999] 3 WLR 1062, [1999] All ER 906.

[69] See for an outline of the "functions" of redress for injury in German law, from a comparative view, H. Stoll, *Haftungsfolgen im bürgerlichen Recht. Eine Darstellung auf rechtsvergleichender Grundlage* (Heidelberg: Müller, 1993) at 147–235.

[70] Lange at 9; Larenz at 424.

[71] At least in so far as it concerns liability based on fault: the preventive function of the risk of liability is conceivable only if the liable person can take precautionary measures. Any preventive effect may be diminished by liability insurance: Lange at 10–1; Larenz at 423.

[72] Lange at 11–2; Larenz at 424–5.

[73] Lange at 12; Larenz at 423.

[74] H. Stoll, *Haftungsfolgen im bürgerlichen Recht. Eine Darstellung auf rechtsvergleichender Grundlage* (Heidelberg: Müller, 1993) at 67.

[75] **8.G.3.**

[76] **8.G.4.** As a matter of English law, it would seem that the enforcement of a foreign judgment for exemplary or punitive damages is not contrary to public policy: L. Collins (gen. ed.), *Dicey & Morris on the Conflict of Laws*, 13th edn. (London: Sweet and Maxwell, 2000) at 526; but foreign judgments for multiple damages, e.g. treble damages under U.S. antitrust law, and certain other similarly oriented awards are rendered statutorily unenforceable by section 5 of the U.K. Protection of Trading Interests Act 1980 ,c.11.

[77] *Supra*, Chapter II, 2.1.1.

deterrence and prevention of unjust enrichment are not entirely absent from German law.[78]

Despite these considerations, the reparatory principle remains the basic principle of the German law of damages. For, indeed, the reparation of harm (*Naturalrestitution* and *Kompensation*) is the only independent function of the law of damages, with the other functions dependent upon it, as they are not decisive of an award of damages.[79] The importance of such secondary functions as satisfaction, punishment, deterrence and prevention of unjust enrichment now fall to be considered.

BGH, 6 July 1955[80] **8.G.3.**

Assessing *Schmerzensgeld*

Compensation and satisfaction

The award of damages for non-material harm has a double function: compensation and satisfaction. In assessing damages all circumstances relating to both parties may be taken into account.

Facts: Unknown.

Held: At the request of the Sixth Civil Chamber—in a decision the facts of which are not revealed—the Great Civil Chamber held that all circumstances, such as the degree of culpability of the defendant, and the financial position of both defendant and plaintiff, including, in this respect, the fact that the defendant was insured, should be taken into account when assessing damages for non-material harm (*Schmerzensgeld*) under § 847 BGB.

Judgment: "I.3. . . . . The award of *Schmerzensgeld* has a dual function in law. It should provide the injured party with adequate redress (*Ausgleich*) for non-material harm. At the same time it is intended to indicate that the wrongdoer owes the victim satisfaction (*Genugtuung*) for what he has done to him.

Of these two functions, that of reparation (*Entschädigung*) or redress (*Ausgleich*) is at the fore. The purpose of the claim is redress for the harm sustained. However the latter eludes arithmetical assessment. The underlying idea may perhaps be formulated as follows: the wrongdoer, who has not only inflicted material harm upon the injured party but also gravely affected his life, is to aid the latter to ease his burden as far as possible, through his payments. With respect to this purpose of *Schmerzensgeld*, the seriousness, severity, and duration of the pain, disfigurement and suffering constitute the main basis for an assessment of fair compensation (*billige Entschädigung*). Therefore the award required to give such redress primarily depends upon the extent of the harm. . . . [A]s the Code requires *fair* compensation . . . the level of damages cannot be determined by the purpose of redress in isolation, in particular since that purpose is inadequate by itself to fix the level of award with any degree of accuracy [emphasis in original].

Bearing in mind the foregoing, however, even if damages claims in tort, including damages for non-material harm, no longer have any direct penal character, nevertheless today the purpose of

---

[78] **8.G.5.** The prevention of unjust enrichment also plays a role in the assessment of damages in certain cases discussed *infra*, 8.2.

[79] H. Stoll, *Haftungsfolgen im bürgerlichen Recht. Eine Darstellung auf rechtsvergleichender Grundlage* (Heidelberg: C.F. Müller Juristischer Verlag, 1993) at 151 and at 184–235.

[80] BGHZ 18, 149. Translation by Y. P. Salmon.

redress (*Ausgleichsgedanken*) still has associations with its former function as a fine or, to use the appropriate terminology of the corresponding Swiss legal concept, as satisfaction (*Genugtuung*). It is evident from legal history that damages for non-material harm developed from criminal law . . .

It is true that the action for *Schmerzensgeld* under § 847 has been formally interpreted by the legislature as a claim for damages in civil law. In substance, however, it does not bear the character of a usual claim of this kind, i.e. to redress material harm. Its purpose to make good harm (*Wiederherstellungsfunktion*) cannot be realized by reparation in kind (*Naturalherstellung*) as when harm is material. To that extent there is no true making good (*Wiedergutmachung*). Certainly an attempt to redress the harm (*Ausgleich*) is to be made, but the award cannot be fixed arithmetically. It is impossible to concentrate on the notion of redress (*Ausgleich*) alone, because non-material harm can never be expressed in money terms, and the possibilities for redress (*Ausgleich*) by means of money payments are only very limited . . . [N]on-material harm concerns 'interests (*Güter*) not assessable in money terms'. The monetary award necessary to achieve redress (*Ausgleich*) cannot be determined by 'so to speak, offsetting pain with pleasures which are intended to erase the victim's sufferings from his memory'. Even where it is possible to redress physical and mental suffering to a certain extent by pleasures and amenities, widely differing possibilities almost always exist as to how redress (*Ausgleich*) is to be effected without a sufficient basis being found in redress as the sole purpose of damages. The purpose of redress alone provides only a very rough standard for the assessment of damages, especially for more serious levels of non-material harm. This is particularly apparent if the non-material harm is so extensive that redress is hardly imaginable, as for instance in those cases in which the victim's body has been so badly injured that redress is hardly attainable. This becomes most evident where, as a consequence of the specific nature of some non-material harm, redress is completely impossible, as is often the case, for example, for psychological disturbances . . . In the case of psychological disturbance in particular, . . . it will often be impossible to redress feelings of unhappiness since the injured party himself is not conscious of the harm. Nevertheless, it is right to award damages for non-material harm even in this case. While it is indeed true that the award of money damages under § 847 BGB, serves to redress non-material harm, the achievement of this aim is not however a prerequisite for such an award. Incidentally, a similar case would arise if the injured party's financial situation is such that no amount of money could induce a sense of happiness to redress the non-material harm that he has sustained.

The function of satisfaction (*Genugtuung*), which cannot be disassociated from the law of damages for non-material harm, acquires special significance with regard to these classes of case of non-material harm. The satisfaction function recognizes the existence of a definite personal relationship, between the wrongdoer and the victim, arising from the harmful act, which, by its nature, requires that, in the assessment of the damages award, *all* of the circumstances of the case are taken into account . . . [emphasis in original].

II. It follows from the preceding observations, that in the assessment of *Schmerzensgeld* the severity and extent of the impairment of the way of life (*Lebensbeeinträchtigung*) must be given prime consideration. This aspect is to be given the most weight. However, all circumstances which characterize the particular harmful act may also be taken into account.

I. One such circumstance is the *degree of culpability* of the wrongdoer. The seriousness of the wrong . . . is not only to be considered . . . with regard to its effect upon the injured party: the fact that the harm was caused by the wrongdoer's reckless or even intentional behaviour, may certainly have left the injured party embittered, while he may be more disposed to accept as his fate harm caused by slight negligence. But apart from the reaction of the injured party, it may be in keeping with fairness (*Billigkeit*) and the notion of satisfaction (*Genugtuung*) if, in fixing damages under § 847 BGB in the individual case, intention and recklessness count against the wrongdoer, while particularly slight negligence counts in his favour [emphasis in original]. . . .

2. The economic circumstances of the injured party may also possibly influence the assessment of damages on grounds of fairness.

The economic circumstances (*Vermögensverhältnisse*) of the victim may sometimes affect the notion of redress (*Ausgleich*) inasmuch as the function of redress (*Ausgleichsfunktion*) is less significant if, for example, the injured party is in such an advantageous economic position that sums of money paid by the wrongdoer can hardly offer any redress (*Ausgleich*) for the non-material harm suffered by him. In such cases the satisfaction function of damages comes to the fore. On the other hand, if the victim is accustomed to a higher standard of living, the award of higher levels of *Schmerzensgeld*, in individual cases, does not appear to be precluded.

3. Finally the economic circumstances of the wrongdoer may also be taken into account in the assessment of damages (*Entschädigung*) under § 847 BGB.

(a) From the perspective of fairness, i.e. taking into consideration the circumstances of both parties, the idea of redress (*Ausgleich*) should not in general result in the serious and lasting impoverishment of the wrongdoer. Certainly here too, the need to offer satisfaction and to redress the harm is of prime importance. The wrongdoer's unfortunate economic situation will have greater or lesser weight according to the cause of the harmful event, and particularly the seriousness of the wrong. Particularly reprehensible behaviour on the part of the wrongdoer, such as inconsiderate recklessness or even intentional acts may temper considerably any concern to preserve him from economic distress. On the other hand, if the wrongdoer is in a particularly advantaged economic position, it may appear fair to award higher damages in the exercise of the court's discretion. . . .

(e) It has been much disputed . . . whether the wrongdoer's liability insurance is relevant to the consideration of his economic circumstances.

The view was formerly expressed . . . that the entitlement of the wrongdoer to liability insurance indemnities could not be taken into account since the purpose of liability insurance is to indemnify the insured party in respect of payments which fall due by virtue of his liability and that this has first to be established. However, that view concentrates solely on the relationship between the wrongdoer and his insurer, while in reality it begs the question whether and to what extent the wrongdoer's liability insurance can affect his liability towards the injured party. In this respect the following consideration applies quite generally to awards made under § 847 BGB: a wrongdoer who is liberated from liability through insurance, to the extent of the sum insured, is in a more advantageous economic position than a wrongdoer who must bear the harm resulting from a tortious act alone . . ."

Notes

(1) The redress of non-material harm is provided for in § 847(1) BGB:

"In the case of injury to body or health, or in the case of deprivation of liberty, the injured party may also demand a fair compensation in money for non-material harm."

The BGH's predecessor, the *Reichsgericht*, had already decided that an award for non-material harm had to be "fair" and "reasonable" (*billig*) in respect of all the circumstances of the case, including not only the extent and duration of the pain, disfigurement and suffering, but also the financial position of *both* parties, the degree of culpability and the circumstances which led to the damage. Another view at that time was that the award had only to be fair with reference to its purpose, namely compensation for non-material harm, and according to that view, only the plaintiff's circumstances were to be considered.[81] The

---

[81] Thus, e.g. BGH, 29 September 1952, BGHZ 7, 223, where it was held that the wrongdoer's financial position should not be taken into account.

question was finally put to the Great Civil Chamber of the BGH. In a part of the annotated judgment not excerpted,[82] the Great Civil Chamber referred to the general structure of the BGB (*Gesamtaufbau*). Analysing some provisions of the BGB referring to the concept of a fair assessment (*nach billigem Ermessen*), it came to the conclusion that fair assessment requires all relevant circumstances to be taken into account. The Great Civil Chamber went on to hold that the same conclusion follows from the legal concept (*rechtliche Sinn*) of *Schmerzensgeld*[83] and its dual function : not only compensation (*Ausgleich*) but also satisfaction (*Genugtuung*). Indeed, *Genugtuung* reflects a definite personal relationship, arising from the injurious act, between the wrongdoer and the victim which, by its nature, requires all the circumstances of the case to be taken into account.[84] Fair assessment is held by the Great Civil Chamber to contain a reference to the situation of both parties, in that, for instance, compensation may not place the defendant in a position of serious poverty.[85]

(2) In the annotated judgment, the BGH found that, by its very nature, an award of *Schmerzensgeld* cannot be fixed on a purely compensatory basis. Non-material harm is not arithmetically convertible into money. According to the BGH, without the idea of *Genugtuung*—an expression borrowed from Swiss law[86]—an outright justification for the award of *Schmerzensgeld* cannot be given. This is particularly clear in cases where it is impossible to consider the "pleasures and amenities" which the plaintiff may obtain by means of the award, to be a real compensation, for example where the plaintiff is gravely injured. In such instances, *Schmerzensgeld* is meant not only to compensate but also to "indicate that the wrongdoer owes the victim satisfaction for what he has done to him".

The annotated judgment has been criticized for recalling unnecessarily the penal element with which the award of damages for non-material harm has had associations in the past.[87] It is considered that the fact that, by its very nature, non-material harm is not assessable in money terms, is sufficient to explain the inability of a precise assessment of monetary relief and that § 847(1) BGB takes this sufficiently into account by providing that the award must be "fair", which permits circumstances to be considered which are otherwise irrelevant in a merely compensatory approach.

(3) Recent case-law dealing with unconscious victims, on the one hand, and the effect of a criminal prosecution on the quantum of damages, on the other hand, evidences the repudiation by the BGH of any element of punishment in the assessment of *Schmerzensgeld*.[88]

---

[82] Under I.2.

[83] On the meaning of *Schmerzensgeld*, a term not used in § 847 BGB, see *supra*, Chapter II, 2.1.1 Introductory Note, under b).

[84] See annotated judgment at I.3., last paragraph.

[85] Under II.3.a) of the excerpt.

[86] But it is not credited with the same meaning: H. Stoll, *Haftungsfolgen im bürgerlichen Recht. Eine Darstellung auf rechtsvergleichender Grundlage* (Heidelberg: Müller, 1993) at 203; Larenz at 476. In Swiss law, *Genugtuung* merely refers to monetary compensation for non-material harm.

[87] Larenz at 476–7; Lange at 438; H. Stoll, ibid. at 202–3. See also the well-documented contribution of B.R. Kern, "Die Genugtuungsfunktion des Schmerzensgeldes—ein pönales Element im Schadensrecht ?" AcP 1991, 247.

[88] Compare Lange at 437.

(a) In the case of an unconscious victim, the BGH initially took the position that the award of *Schmerzensgeld* cannot have a compensatory function since the victim is unable to feel any pain and suffering and the award can in no way relieve his affliction, and that the victim can likewise gain no satisfaction as he is not in a position to appreciate the injury and its relationship to the defendant's wrongdoing.[89] In such a case the award can only have a symbolic function (without necessarily amounting to a merely symbolic sum[90]) as a way of atonement (*zeichenhafte Wiedergutmachung, Sühnefunktion*), inflicting a sacrifice (*fühlbares Opfer*) on the wrongdoer. However, in its judgment of 13 October 1992,[91] the BGH decided that the very interference with one's personality (*Zerstörung der Persönlichkeit*) entitles the victim to *compensation*, independent of the subjective perception of the victim, clearly abandoning the concept of atonement (*Gedanke der Sühne*) or punishment as a basis of the award.[92]

(b) In its judgment of 29 November 1994[93] relating to non-material damage suffered by the plaintiff as a result of being threatened by a bank robber, the BGH decided that the civil law concept of *Genugtuung* is not an aspect of punishment or fine, but rather an additional factor to consider in the assessment of damages, and stressed that an award of *Schmerzensgeld* is not a private law penalty (*Privatstrafe*) but is merely compensation. It seems that by this the BGH intended to refine the *Genugtuungsfunktion* and to embed it in the reparatory principle.[94] In accordance with its new emphasis, the BGH stated that the amount of *Schmerzensgeld* cannot be influenced by the fact that the wrongdoer is criminally prosecuted and that the victim may draw satisfaction from a resulting conviction.[95] Moreover, the indivisible character of an award of *Schmerzensgeld* is emphasized in this judgment: a claim for *Schmerzensgeld* cannot be divided into a part representing the *Ausgleichsfunktion* (reparatory function) and another part representing the *Genugtuungsfunktion* (satisfaction function).[96] Moreover, the BGH doubted whether *Genugtuung* could play a role in cases of harm resulting from mere negligence.[97]

---

[89] BGH, 16 December 1975, NJW 1976, 1147, see comments of J. Niemeyer and H. Hupfer, NJW 1976, 1792, VersR 1976, 660; BGH, 22 June 1982, NJW 1982, 2123, VersR 1982, 880.

[90] In the judgment of BGH, 16 December 1975, NJW 1976, 1147, an award of DEM 30,000 was upheld.

[91] BGHZ 120, 1, NJW 1993, 781, annotated by E. Deutsch, JZ 1993, 516, annotated by D. Giesen. See also F. J. Nieper, "Schmerzensgeld bei Empfindungsunfähigkeit: Entschädigung für objektiven immateriellen Schaden" (1996) 4 Eur. R Priv. L. 223 at 225, and in a comparative context, the other contributions in the same issue at 221 *et seq*. The BGH reaffirmed its new position in a judgment of 16 February 1993, NJW 1993, 1531. That judgment has brought German law into line with French and English law: *supra*, Chapter II, 2.1.

[92] BGH, 13 October 1992, BGHZ 120, 1 at 6: ". . . It [is of lesser] importance in tort and damages law . . . the non-material harm sustained is of much greater relevance . . .".

[93] BGHZ 128, 117, NJW 1995, 781. The BGH reaffirmed this position in a judgment of 16 January 1996, NJW 1996, 1591.

[94] See E. Steffen, "Schmerzensgeld bei Persönlichkeitsverletzung durch Medien. Ein Plädoyer gegen formelhafte Berechnungsmethoden bei der Geldentschädigung" NJW 1997, 10 at 12. E. Steffen is a former president of the BGH.

[95] Compare H. Stoll, *Haftungsfolgen im bürgerlichen Recht. Eine Darstellung auf rechtsvergleichender Grundlage* (Heidelberg: Müller, 1993) at 208. See, concerning exemplary damages in English law, the case *Archer* v. *Brown* [1985] QB 401, QBD which decided (at 423) that where the defendant has already been sentenced for the conduct for which damages were claimed, no exemplary award should be made. *Thompson* v. *Commissioner of Police of the Metropolis* [1997] 3 WLR 403, CA decided (at 418–9) that the jury should be invited to take into account future disciplinary procedures against the defendant only "where there is clear evidence that such proceedings are intended to be taken in the event of liability being established and that there is at least a strong possibility of the proceedings succeeding".

[96] The court of appeal had assessed the normal award of *Schmerzensgeld* at DEM 8,000 and had then reduced it by half on account of the fact that, as a consequence of the wrongdoer's criminal prosecution, the *Genugtuungsfunktion* was absent. The BGH found that division itself to be contrary to § 847 BGB.

[97] As for the specific meaning of *Genugtuung* in the context of infringements of personality rights, see *infra*, **8.G.5.**

(4) In the original version of § 847(1) BGB[98] the claim for *Schmerzensgeld* was in principle neither inheritable nor transferable. The law was changed in 1990 however, and there are no longer any specific conditions to be met to inherit or transfer a claim for *Schmerzensgeld*.[99]

BGH, 4 June 1992[100]   **8.G.4.**

ENFORCEABILITY OF US JUDGMENT AWARDING PUNITIVE DAMAGES

Sexual abuse

Punitive damages which pursue various objectives under US law are inconsistent with German ordre public *rules in the area of tort law; such rules only allow for compensation of the plaintiff's harm, and not his enrichment.*

Facts: The plaintiff seeks enforcement (*Vollstreckbarerklärung*) in Germany of a judgment of the Superior Court of the State of California, granting an award of USD 750,260 for a finding of sexual abuse. This amount is made up of an award of USD 260 for past medical costs and USD 100,000 for future medical costs, USD 50,000 for accommodation, USD 200,000 for "anxiety, pain, suffering and general damages of that nature" and USD 400,000 by way of "exemplary and punitive damages".

Held : The action was allowed by the court of first instance which granted the full sum plus interest, and was partially upheld by the court of appeal, which awarded USD 275,325. The BGH declined to enforce the Californian judgment in so far as that judgment awarded USD 400,000 by way of exemplary and punitive damages.

Judgment: "According to the law of most states of the USA 'punitive or exemplary damages' . . . are granted as a sum supplementary to purely compensatory damages, if the wrongdoer is found liable for intentional, malicious or reckless conduct as an aggravating circumstance of the tortious conduct [references omitted]. As of late, a consciously negligent, blatant disregard of the general public's security interests may be enough [references omitted]. The award is always at the unfettered discretion of the court. With such an order up to four main purposes are pursued [references omitted]: the wrongdoer should be punished for his brutal behaviour, meaning moreover that possible acts of revenge by the victim become superfluous. The wrongdoer and the general public should be deterred from behaviour which is harmful to society, insofar as the mere risk of a duty to compensate does not guarantee a sufficient behavioural control. The injured party should be rewarded for his efforts in enforcing the law and thus his contribution towards the strengthening of the legal order in general. Finally the victim should receive a supplement to reparation felt to be inadequate, which may among other things act as a substitute for the absence of social security protection [references omitted]; in this way, the plaintiff's out-of-court expenses which are not independently recoverable may be taken into consideration . . .

---

[98] Second sentence of § 847(1) BGB: "The claim is not transferable and does not pass to the heirs, unless it is established by contract or if a legal action has been commenced" (*rechtshängig geworden ist*).

[99] See Lange at 446–7 and BGH, 6 December 1994, NJW 1995, 783.

[100] BGHZ 118, 312, JZ 1993, 261, annotated by E. Deutsch, NJW 1992, 3096, annotated by H. Koch, "Ausländischer Schadensersatz vor deutschen Gerichten" NJW 1992, 3073, RIW 1993, 132, annotated by A. Schütze, ZZP 1993, 79, annotated by H. Schack, IPRax 1993, 310, annotated by H. Koch and J. Zekoll, "Zweimal amerikanische 'punitive damages' vor deutschen Gerichten" IPRax 1993, 288. Translation by Y. P. Salmon. See also J. Rosengarten, "Der Präventionsgedanke im deutschen Zivilrecht. Höheres Schmerzensgeld, aber keine Anerkennung und Vollstreckung US-amerikanischer punitive damages?" NJW 1996, 1935.

3. The enforceability of the US judgment, awarding 'punitive damages', fails on grounds of *ordre public* . . . [references omitted].

a) The modern German civil law system envisages the redress (*Ausgleich*) of harm (§§ 249 ff. BGB) as the only consequence of a tortious act, not the enrichment of the victim [references omitted] . . . That is independent of whether the claim to make good harm is brought before the civil court or before the criminal court in an ancillary procedure [references omitted]. Punishment and—according to the seriousness of the wrong—deterrence are possible goals of criminal sanctions [references omitted], in the form of money penalties received by the State, they are not goals of the civil law.

Likewise the consideration of allowing the victim as plaintiff to receive a reward finds its explanation in an understanding of private law as a social system with a general preventive effect [references omitted]. In place of the State, the individual appears as a "private" attorney for the State (*privater Staatsanwalt*) [references omitted]. According to the German concept of law (*Rechtsauffassung*), that is incompatible with the State monopoly in the field of punishment and the special procedural guarantees that are provided in that context . . . In particular, the US concept of 'punitive damages', justified by the public interest functions of punishment and deterrence, cannot be compared with the satisfaction function (*Genugtuungsfunktion*) which, according to general principles of German law, is to be considered when assessing *Schmerzensgeld* according to § 847 BGB and for infringements of the general personality right [references omitted]. In the first place, in the assessment of *Schmerzensgeld* [references omitted], prime consideration is to be given to the severity and extent of the impairment of the [victim's] way of life (*Lebensbeeinträchtigung*) (the seriousness and duration of the pain, suffering and disfigurement) rather than his satisfaction (*Genugtuungsfunktion*), while the importance of the other circumstances is to be determined by reference to the specific case [references omitted]. In the second place, the satisfaction function (*Genugtuungsfunktion*) does not establish that an award of *Schmerzensgeld* has a direct penal character [references omitted]. . . .

e) Taking as a starting point that [the concept of US punitive damages is shaped by considerations of punishment and deterrence], it is blatantly irreconcilable with fundamental principles of German law to admit the domestic enforceability of an overall award of punitive damages (*Strafschadensersatz*) of a not insignificant level."

Notes

(1) In the excerpted part of the judgment,[101] the BGH recalls the purposes for which punitive damages may be awarded in the USA: punishment, deterrence, a reward for maintaining the legal order and an additional allowance where compensation is felt to be incomplete. The BGH considers all but the last of these functions to be inconsistent with the German legal system as expressed in § 328(4) of the Code of Civil Procedure, according to which a foreign judgment is not enforceable if "the application of foreign law contradicts the basic principles of German rules and the principles of justice underpinning them to such an extent that it is intolerable according to domestic principles". According to the BGH, the only legitimate purpose of an award of damages is redress, to the exclusion of private law penalties. The BGH affirms that the *Genugtuungsfunktion* cannot be compared with a penalty: *Genugtuung* is tied to the reparatory function of an award for

---

[101] On the context of this decision, and subsequent issues, from a private international law perspective, see J. Pirrung, "The German Federal Constitutional Court Confronted with Punitive Damages and Child Abduction" in A. Borras et al eds, *Liber Amicorum Georges A. L. Droz, On the Progressive Unification of Private International Law* (The Hague: Martinus Nijhoff Publishers, 1996).

non-material harm.[102] The only purpose of punitive damages which the BGH considers to be in keeping with German law is that of additional reparation: thus the BGH objects neither to an award which aims to prevent the wrongdoer's enrichment (*Gewinnabschöpfung*), nor the compensation of judicial costs.

In a part of the judgment not reproduced, it is noted that when a German judge is unable to break down the foreign award into its functional components, the judge must nevertheless consider the aims which characterize the indivisible award.[103] As such an award is characterized by the purposes of punishment and deterrence, the award is unenforceable.[104]

(2) In a part of the judgment not excerpted, the BGH did not object to the fact that the judgment allowed plaintiff's counsel 40 per cent of the overall award granted to the plaintiff. It also allowed enforcement of the award of USD 200,000 for "anxiety, pain, suffering and general damages of that nature", even if such an award exceeded the awards commonly granted by German judges. Therefore, the annotated judgment is considered by legal writers to favour enforceability.[105]

E. Deutsch warns against excessive tolerance of foreign awards for non-material harm: "The way from compensation of non-material harm to punitive damages is a short one".[106] He considers it to be unimportant whether the foreign judgment identifies the award for non-material harm as compensatory or punitive, the decisive question being whether the award is proportionate to that which would be granted under German law.

BGH, 15 November 1994[107]   **8.G.5.**

NON-MATERIAL HARM RESULTING FROM THE PROFIT-DRIVEN INFRINGEMENT OF THE
GENERAL PERSONALITY RIGHT

Caroline of Monaco insulted

Where there is a reckless commercialization of the plaintiff's personality, the profits gained from the violation of the law are to be considered in the assessment of damages, which must have a genuine inhibiting effect.

Facts: The plaintiff, Princess Caroline of Monaco, claimed money damages of at least DEM 100,000 for the non-material harm sustained by the infringement of her personality rights through the publication in two weekly magazines of an invented "exclusive" interview, "paparazzi" photographs and untrue allegations concerning her mental state and personal life.

---

[102] As has been noted (*supra*, **8.G.3.**, Note (3)(b)) this was also emphasized in the BGH's judgment of 29 November 1994, BGHZ 128, 117, NJW 1995, 781. In the annotated judgment, the BGH refers to its case law concerning a symbolic award for non-material harm. As has been indicated, the BGH changed its position (*supra*, Note (3)(a) under **8.G.3.**).

[103] See annotated judgment under 3. d), not excerpted.

[104] See annotated judgment under 3. e) aa), not excerpted.

[105] *Inter alia* H. Koch, "Ausländischer Schadensersatz vor deutschen Gerichten" NJW 1992, 3073 at 3075; H. Schack, note below BGH, 4 June 1992, ZZP 1993, 104 at 104 and 108.

[106] E. Deutsch, note below BGH, 4 June 1992, JZ 1992 at 267.

[107] BGHZ 128, 1, NJW 1995, 861, *JZ* 1995, 360, annotated by P. Schlechtriem. Translation by Y. P. Salmon. See comment on the case of H. P. Westermann (1997) 5 Eur. R Priv. L. 237 and F.W. Grosheide (1997) 5 Eur. R Priv. L. 252 who examines the case from a comparative perspective in the context of recent Dutch case law.

Held: The court of first instance awarded the plaintiff DEM 30,000 damages for non-material harm (*Schmerzensgeld*). The court of appeal confirmed that judgment. The BGH quashed the court of appeal's judgment insofar as it had dismissed the plaintiff's claim for more substantial damages.

Judgment: "The award of damages for a violation of the general personality right does not constitute compensation for non-material harm (*Schmerzensgeld*)under § 847 BGB *stricto sensu*, but is a legal remedy (*Rechtsbehelf*) which finds its basis in the protective function of Art. 1 and 2(1) GG [references omitted]. The making of a money award is based on the belief that without such an entitlement, violations of human dignity and honour would frequently remain without sanction with the result that the legal protection of the personality right would wither away. By contrast to a claim for *Schmerzensgeld*, in a claim for money compensation for an infringement of the general personality right, the satisfaction (*Genugtuung*) of the victim is a prime consideration [references omitted]; the Chamber adheres to this view despite reservations expressed in the literature [references omitted]. Furthermore, the legal remedy should serve a preventive function [references omitted].

The reasoning in the judgment of the court of appeal with regard to the disputed level of award in this case does not accord with the specific purpose of the claim for monetary compensation for infringement of the personality right. In the opinion of the court of appeal, the fact that the defendant infringed the personality right in order to make a profit must, like the idea of prevention, be omitted from consideration in the assessment of damages. In the opinion of the Chamber, that conclusion can be seen to be too narrow in a case such as this. The case is characterized by the fact that the defendant deliberately infringed the personality right of the plaintiff as a means of increasing the circulation of his publication, and therefore in the pursuit of his own commercial interests. Without monetary compensation which is significant to the defendant, the plaintiff would, to a large extent, be left without protection against such an irresponsible unauthorized commercial exploitation of her personality; orders to retract and correct may achieve only an inadequate protection of the plaintiff since, as shown, such an order can succeed only if the rights of the defendants to press freedom are observed. However, an order to pay monetary compensation is adequate to achieve the preventive aim also required by the personality right only if the award is of a level corresponding to the level of profit for which the personality right was infringed. That does not mean that a complete "restitution of profits" (*Gewinnabschöpfung*) is to be carried out in such cases of reckless commercial exploitation of the personality, but rather that the receipt of profits from the infringement is to be included as a factor in the assessment of the level of damages due. Therefore, a genuinely deterrent effect must result . . . The gravity of the infringement of the personality right may be considered as a further factor in the assessment . . . Furthermore, it has to be borne in mind that the monetary compensation may not reach such a level that press freedom is limited disproportionately. However, there can be no talk of this if the press is to be prevented from such a reckless commercial exploitation of the personality, as in the case at hand . . ."

Notes

(1) This judgment—followed by a similar judgment in a case brought by the same plaintiff[108]—is in line with case-law regarding assessment of damages for non-material harm in the case of infringement of the general personality right, as established by the well-known BGH judgments in the *Herrenreiter* and *Ginseng* cases.[109] In *Herrenreiter*, the BGH decided that the constitutional protection of the general personality right (Art. 1

[108] BGH, 5 December 1995, NJW 1996, 984 ("*Caroline von Monaco II*") on similar facts, in which untrue statements were published in two weekly magazines alleging that she was fighting breast cancer.

[109] See *supra*, Chapter II, **2.G.26.**, Note (3). BGH, 14 February 1958, *Herrenreiter*, BGHZ 26, 349, NJW 1958, 827, annotated by K. Larenz; BGH, 19 September 1961, *Ginseng*, BGHZ 35, 363, NJW 1961, 2059.

and 2 GG) would be ineffective without the possibility of an award of damages for non-material harm. In that case, the BGH held that the award was based on § 847 BGB by way of analogy. However, in the *Ginseng* case, the BGH founded the award directly on Art. 1 and 2 GG and by doing so, it went beyond the restrictive provisions of § 253 and 847 BGB without compromising the system of the BGB.[110]

In the *Soraya* case, the Federal Constitutional Court held that the approach of the BGH was in conformity with the Constitution.[111] One of the objections advanced against the BGH jurisprudence was that a judge, who is bound by statute (*Gesetz*), could not grant an award for non-material damages not provided for by statute law. The Federal Constitutional Court stressed that the judge is bound by *legislation and law* ("*Gesetz und Recht*"), the latter not being confined to statutory provisions, so allowing creative jurisprudence (*schöpferische Rechtsfindung*). It drew attention to the distance between codification and modern society, characterized by the growing impact of mass media, and having pointed out that other modern legal systems allow awards for non-material harm in the case of an infringement of the general personality right, asked whether the judge himself could fill the legislative lacuna. It came to the conclusion that the BGH "has merely developed further the principles originating from the constitutionally legitimated legal order by means inherent in the system [references omitted]. The legal proposition so established is therefore a legitimate component part of the legal order and, as a "general law" in the meaning of Art. 5(2) GG, forms a justifiable limit on press freedom".[112]

Therefore, the award of damages for non-material harm in the case of an infringement of the general personality right is not *Schmerzensgeld* within the meaning of § 847 BGB. Rather, it constitutes a remedy (*Rechtsbehelf*) founded on the imperatives expressed in Art. 1 and 2 GG. That remedy is close to *Schmerzensgeld*, to be sure, as would appear from the recognition of the *Genugtuungsfunktion* but is however distinct from it because, as decided in the *Ginseng* case, "the satisfaction function predominates over the compensatory principle".[113] It is not surprising that, as a consequence, this case law in particular has given rise to the question to what extent civil law remedies may aim at punishment and deterrence.

(2) In the *Caroline of Monaco* case, in openly recognizing the purpose of prevention for the first time, the BGH stated that the assessment of damages must take into account the profit motive underlying the infringement of the personality right so that the award may have a genuine inhibitive effect (*Hemmungseffekt*). However, the BGH's decision was not entirely innovative. In the *Ginseng* case, the BGH had decided that "dishonest profit-seeking can be tackled effectively only if it is backed up with the risk of a marked material loss"[114] and the BVerfG affirmed that the BGH's jurisprudence "serves the development and effective protection of a legally protected interest (*Rechtsgut*)".[115]

In this respect the annotated judgment gives rise to the intriguing question of the extent to which the profit motive is to be taken into account. The BGH considered that the profit motive is a circumstance which may increase the award, although it should not lead to an outright restitution of

---

[110] German legal doctrine is sceptical about this jurisprudential solution: see Lange at 450–1 and references.
[111] BVerfG, 14 February 1973, NJW 1973, 1221. This decision is severely criticized by Larenz/Canaris at 496.
[112] Ibid. at 1226.
[113] BGH, 19 September 1961, BGHZ 35, 363 at 369.
[114] Ibid.
[115] BVerfG, 14 February 1973, NJW 1973, 1221 at 1226.

the enrichment (*Gewinnabschöpfung*), as provided for in § 687 (2) BGB.[116] The court to which the case was remitted decided, in accordance with this consideration, that it was not correct to assess damages on the basis of the concrete profit realized by the publisher. It regarded an award of DEM 180,000 to be adequate.[117] It is noteworthy however that the court was prepared to consider that in future cases, larger sums of damages might be awarded if publishers did not change their practices and that the award of DEM 180,000 went far beyond the level of awards commonly granted at that time.[118]

(3) The annotated case highlights the similarity of the approach of the German courts to the award of damages for infringement of the personality right to the approach of the English courts to the award of exemplary damages. Indeed, before an English court it is likely that this case would have given rise to an award of exemplary damages. Similarly, the considerations of the BGH concerning the predominance of *Genugtuung*, the importance of the purpose of prevention and the relevance of the profit motive in assessing damages, parallel the "public purpose underlying [exemplary] damages, that of punishing the defendant, showing that tort does not pay and deterring others".[119] It is not surprising that an annotator of the case promptly qualified the award as a private law penalty (*Strafschadensersatz*).[120]

8.1.3. FRENCH LAW

Introductory Note

Besides the prevention of a permanent or threatened wrong, the reparation of harm is the sole purpose of an award of damages in French law, and the harm sustained is the sole criterion to be considered in the assessment of damages.[121] Notwithstanding this rule, French legal doctrine has acknowledged the existence of some concept of private law penalty (*peine privée*), be it overt or covert.

The exclusive character of the compensatory principle and the respect of the Cour de cassation for the sovereign power of the trial judge means that the abundance of English and German case law on the purposes of damages awards is not mirrored in French law. The recognition of the functions of prevention, punishment and deterrence in everyday French legal practice is largely due to the influence of French academic legal literature.[122] For instance, the award of symbolic damages cannot be reconciled with a pure compensatory approach. Likewise, a judgment which orders publication of the decision, which is

---

[116] As to whether a claim for restitution can be based on the law of unjust enrichment (§ 812 BGB) or *negotiorum gestio* (§ 687 (2)), see *infra*, **8.G.15.**, Note (4).

[117] OLG Hamburg, 25 July 1996, NJW 1996, 2870.

[118] E. Steffen, "Schmerzensgeld bei Persönlichkeitsverletzung durch Medien. Ein Plädoyer gegen formelhafte Berechnungsmethoden bei der Geldentschädigung" NJW 1997, 10 at 12; see also interview with E. Steffen, "Das Schmerzensgeld soll den Verleger ruhig schmerzen" ZRP 1996, 366.

[119] *John* v. *MGN Ltd.* [1996] 3 WLR 593, CA at 619. Even the levels of award are comparable (GBP 75,000 in *John* v. *MGN Ltd.*; DEM 180,000).

[120] W. Seitz, "Prinz und die Prinzessin—Wandlungen des Deliktsrechts durch Zwangskommerzialisierung der Persönlichkeit" NJW 1996, 2848.

[121] **8.F.6.**

[122] See on the functions of tort law in general also A. Tunc, *La responsabilité civile*, 2nd edn. (Paris: Economica, 1989) at 133 ff., para. 160 ff.

quite common in cases of infringement of personality rights,[123] is also said to be compensatory, but it may be questioned whether this kind of remedy can be explained on the basis of the compensatory principle alone.

Cass. civ. 2e., 8 May 1964[124]   **8.F.6.**
Harang-Martin v. *Bonneau*

IRRELEVANCY OF DEGREE OF CULPABILITY

Insulting neighbour

When assessing damages, the degree of culpability may not be taken into account.

Facts: The plaintiff was insulted by her neighbour, the defendant, who had already been found liable for a similar offence.

Held: The Cour de cassation quashed the judgment of the court of first instance ordering the defendant to pay substantial damages to the plaintiff, on the ground that in assessing damages he had taken the defendant's previous liability into consideration.

Judgment: "The damages necessary to compensate for the harm sustained must be calculated according to the level of harm suffered; the seriousness of the wrong has no influence upon the level of those damages.

The widow Bonneau, who contends that she was insulted by Mrs. Harang, her neighbour, brought an action against her to remedy the harm she sustained.

Having proceeded to an investigation, the court upheld the claim. In so ruling, the court of first instance stated merely that there were grounds for accepting the statements of three of the witnesses and ordering the defendants to pay considerable damages, as it was not the first time that Mrs. Harang had so acted and she had already been found liable previously for a similar act.

When ruling on the *action civile* for compensation for damage caused by the commission of a criminal offence, the judgment which established the wrong should not take into consideration the seriousness of the wrong in assessing the level of damages. The judgment needed to ascertain only whether the alleged harm was real and that there was a causal connection between it and the wrong and then to measure the extent of the harm, all points on which explanation was omitted. The decision is thus not legally justified."

Notes

(1) This judgment makes it clear that, even in assessing damages for non-material harm, the degree of culpability may not be taken into account: the judge may consider only the seriousness of the harm, not the seriousness of the wrong. In proclaiming the rule that the judge has to "measure" the extent of the harm, the undeniable incommensurability of non-material harm to money is ignored. This position differs from that taken in English and German case law, as has been highlighted.

It may be noted that the facts of the case are not entirely clear: it is unknown whether the defendant had previously insulted others or the plaintiff herself. In the latter situation

---

[123] **8.F.7.**
[124] JCP 1965.II.14140, annotated by P. Esmein. Translation by Y. P. Salmon.

the judge might have considered her recidivism to aggravate the *harm* and, on that basis, increase the award.

(2) French legal writing defines an award of damages as a *peine privée* when the size of the award does not correspond to the amount of harm but is determined by the degree of culpability and aims at the repression of wrongful conduct rather than the compensation of the plaintiff.[125] By excluding the consideration of the degree of culpability, the Cour de cassation has implicitly rejected the *peine privée*.

It has however been stressed in legal writing that the judge's sovereign power (*pouvoir souverain*) to assess damage results in an almost unrestricted liberty to evaluate the level of award, so that the judge may take into account circumstances which are foreign to the compensatory approach, e.g. the degree of culpability, without any risk of interference by the Cour de cassation if the judge does not articulate such considerations in his judgment.[126]

Cour d'appel de Paris, 26 April 1983[127]   **8.F.7.**

S.A. Cogedipresse v. *C.*

PUBLICATION OF JUDGMENT AS COMPENSATION

Deathbed photograph

An order to publish the judgment has a compensatory rather than a punitive aim.

Facts: *Paris-Match*, a weekly magazine published by Société Cogedipresse, the defendant, printed a "paparazzi" photograph of J.-M. C., a well-known singer-songwriter on his deathbed following a fatal road traffic accident. The photograph, taken despite the fact that his widow, Patricia C., had taken all possible steps to secure the room in which his mortal remains lay, was published with an accompanying text in honour of the memory of the musician. In the action against the publishers his widow, the plaintiff, claimed damages for herself and her and the deceased's children.

Held: The court of first instance ordered the defendant to pay FRF 50,000 to the widow and FRF 25,000 to each of their two children and furthermore ordered the publication of the judgment in *Paris-Match* and three newspapers. The court of appeal upheld the judgment of the lower court.

Judgment:"The Soc. Cogedipresse, as at first instance, recognizes that the disputed publication was made without the authorization and even against the will of Patricia C and points out that the appeal relates only to the assessment of the damage. While it admits liability, it maintains that the publication of the face of a dead man accompanied as in this case by a commentary 'to the glory' of the subject, does not have the scandalous character which was attributed to it. In addition it maintains that the method of assessment of the damage should respect certain principles and in particular should not take into account any circumstance external to the damage, such as the seriousness of the wrong or the situation of the parties . . . It adds that orders requiring publication are

---

[125] F. Givord, *La réparation du préjudice moral* (Paris: Dalloz, 1938) at 110 who quotes from L. Hugueney, *L'idée de peine privée en droit contemporain* (thèse Dijon, 1904).
[126] Starck, Roland and Boyer at 534, para. 1333–4; Viney, *Effets* at 8–9, para. 6; G. Viney and B. Markesinis, *La réparation du dommage corporel. Essai de comparaison des droits anglais et français* (Paris: Economica, 1985) at 54–6, para. 33.
[127] D 1983.Jur.376, annotated by R. Lindon. Translation by Y. P. Salmon.

not, as the judgment described them, a remedy complementary to damages, but appear to the weekly magazine to be in reality a sanction, which is contrary to the principles governing the assessment of damage. On these grounds it requests that the disputed decision be quashed.

Patricia C. . . . requests confirmation of the judgment in that it has recognized, as a principle, that 'no one may, without the assent of the family, reproduce and circulate with publicity the face of a person on his deathbed, regardless of the celebrity of the deceased' and in that it decided that the Soc. Cogedipresse 'should have been fully aware of having carried out a serious attack on the sanctity of private life for a purely commercial goal.'

. . .

On this:

The Court considers that, on the basis of relevant grounds, the court of first instance correctly noted the wrongful character of the publication in issue, which is not disputed by the Soc. Cogedipresse.

Damages are intended to make good the harm sustained, and should not vary according to the gravity of the wrong committed. In this case, the court precisely evaluated the harm sustained by Patricia C. and her children. The decision must also be confirmed on this point.

The Soc. Cogedipresse wrongly claims that the ordered publication would have a purely punitive result. In fact the order requiring publication, which must be confirmed . . ., contributes to the making good of harm as it allows public acknowledgement of the fact that Patricia C. neither wanted nor even tolerated the publication of photographs of the mortal remains of her husband.

It was fair to award Patricia C on behalf of herself and her children the sum of FRF 5000 pursuant to Art. 700 New Code of Civil Procedure for the legal costs incurred."

Notes

(1) The annotated judgment first recalls that the degree of blameworthiness should not be taken into account in the assessment of damages. In an oft-quoted note on this judgment, R. Lindon stresses that however correct that affirmation may be, it gives rise to a serious problem because it results in a disproportion between the awards granted to plaintiffs and the substantial profits realized by publishers, so that publishers are unlikely to be dissuaded from future infringements by the threat of a claim for damages. He suggests that the amount of harm could be determined by the number of readers, so that the level of damages would be set on the basis of the circulation of the newspaper or magazine. In this way, the award would be proportionate to the publisher's profit. It is clear that that suggestion, even if it can be reconciled with the compensatory approach, has in fact a preventive aim: publishers are consequently dissuaded from infringing personality rights because such infringements "do not pay". The suggestion has been received favourably,[128] although the question remains whether it would not be preferable to recognize explicitly the deterrent function of such an award. In the *Le grand secret* case,[129] the circulation of a book was taken into account in the assessment of damages and a total award of FRF 340,000 was granted to the four plaintiffs, together with an injunction to prevent distribution of the book.

[128] See *inter alia* Starck, Roland and Boyer at 534–5, para. 1335–7, deploring the fact that the judge cannot take the profit-driven nature of the tortious act ("*faute lucrative*") into account. See also S. Carval, *La responsabilité civile dans sa fonction de peine privée* (Paris: LGDJ, 1995) at para. 33.

[129] Paris, 27 May 1997, JCP 1997.II.22894 annotated by E. Derieux, upholding TGI Paris, 23 October 1996, JCP 1997.II.22844, annotated by E. Derieux; see *supra*, Chapter II, **2.F.29.** See also, but granting a very moderate award, TGI Paris, 26 February 1975, D 1975.Jur.322, annotated by R. Lindon, and referring to a limited circulation: TGI Paris, 27 February 1974, D 1974.Jur.530, annotated by R. Lindon.

There now seems to be a tendency to grant larger awards in cases of injury to the plaintiff's right to privacy, albeit that the level of French awards remains lower than comparable sums awarded in Germany or England.[130]

(2) In the annotated case the court affirmed the compensatory nature of an order to publish a judgment. Recently, in a case in which the plaintiffs' interests as consumers were infringed, the Cour de cassation affirmed that publication of the judgment may be ordered only by way of reparation of harm, so that Art. 1382 C.civ. is infringed when it is evident from the reasons given that the judge ordered publication for the good of the collective consumer interest.[131]

It has been noted that while the publication of the judgment may contribute to redress especially in cases of defamation—the public is then informed of the defamatory character of the allegations and the victim's honour is duly rehabilitated—this may be of doubtful value in cases of infringement of privacy because the publication of the judgment may actually enlarge the circulation of the revelations.[132] But even in these cases, such an order may contribute indirectly to redress because it allows public knowledge of the plaintiff's lack of consent.[133] That view was stated by the Cour d'appel de Paris,[134] in a later judgment in which it held that:

> "The court need not have verified whether the publicity given to its decision was appropriate to the nature of the detrimental act and did not create the risk of aggravating the damage, since the measure claimed and ordered was proportionate to the harm sustained; . . . in the case at hand [the plaintiff], who alone is entitled to decide whether this form of reparation is satisfactory for her, has an interest in making known, in the situation in which she finds herself, that the dissemination of the contested photograph was made against her will and in contravention of her rights and that she intends to vindicate the respect of her private life judicially."

That has not prevented some authors stressing that publication may have a punitive character, because of the publicity which is given to the condemnation of the defendant's conduct and the financial cost which publication necessarily entails.[135]

(3) A symbolic award (*franc symbolique*) is common in French legal practice. The award may be granted when the judge finds the defendant liable but where there is no appreciable harm. This award corresponds to an award of *nominal damages* in English law.[136] A judgment of this kind does not aim at compensation, but is merely the judicial declaration of the infringed right, from which the plaintiff may draw satisfaction, and which may also have a preventive effect, especially when publication of the judgment is ordered.

---

[130] S. Carval, *La responsabilité civile dans sa fonction de peine privée* (Paris: LGDJ, 1995) at para. 30; P. Kayzer, *La protection de la vie privée par le droit. Protection du secret de la vie privée*, 3rd edn. (Marseille-Paris: Presses Universitaires d'Aix-Marseille-Economica, 1995) at para. 202.

[131] Cass. civ. 1re, 14 May 1992, Bull.civ. 1992.I.138; see on earlier case law of lower courts Viney, *Effets* at 63, para. 45. See also Cass. crim. 4 February 1986, Bull.crim. 1986.107 in which it was affirmed that publication of a criminal judgment may be ordered at the request of the plaintiff by way of compensation but not by way of additional punishment and Viney, *Effets* at 36, para. 24.

[132] See, for example, Paris, 14 May 1975, D 1976.Jur.291.

[133] P. Kayzer, *La protection de la vie privée par le droit. Protection du secret de la vie privée*, 3rd edn. (Marseille-Paris: Presses Universitaires d'Aix-Marseille-Economica, 1995) at 375, para. 205.

[134] Paris, 28 November 1988, D 1989.Jur.410, annotated by J. L. Aubert.

[135] S. Carval, *La responsabilité civile dans sa fonction de peine privée* (Paris: LGDJ, 1995) at para. 31.

[136] G. Viney and B. Markesinis, *La réparation du dommage corporel. Essai de comparaison des droits anglais et français* (Paris: Economica, 1985) at 57, para. 35.

Frequently, a plaintiff claims the *franc symbolique* when he attaches more importance to the recognition of his or her right than to effective compensation for harm and is satisfied by the condemnation of the defendant's wrongful conduct. Such a claim may be inspired by the plaintiff's concern that he or she should not be suspected of money-making motives—a suspicion that may also be refuted by a request for the court officially to affirm in the judgment that the plaintiff will donate the award to a charity, albeit that such a request is not always allowed.[137] The sovereign power of the judge to assess damages does not however permit him to make a symbolic award (even when the award exceeds FRF 1) on the basis that pain and suffering are in fact not susceptible to compensation. This would contravene the rule of full compensation which applies without distinction to both material and non-material harm.[138]

An example of an award of a *franc symbolique* is given by the judgment of the Cour d'appel de Paris in the *Benetton* case[139] in which an association defending the interests of AIDS patients, and some AIDS patients themselves, claimed damages because of Benetton's publicity referring to AIDS, which was claimed to abuse the freedom of expression and opinion. The court of appeal awarded the *franc symbolique* both to the association, which claimed that symbolic award, and to the other plaintiffs, whereas the court of first instance had granted FRF 50,000 to each of the individual plaintiffs on the basis of reasons which would have allowed every AIDS patient to claim the same award. As illustrated by the *Benetton* case, the fact that associations for the protection of collective interests may sue when such an interest is endangered, enlarges the ambit in which the law of damages may pursue the functions of punishment and deterrence.[140]

(4) Plaintiffs may be encouraged to bring an action against a wrongdoer because the French law of civil procedure[141] provides that the judge may condemn the unsuccessful defendant to pay the plaintiff's costs, in particular the advocate's fee, which are not included in the "legal expenses" proper, a provision which was applied in the annotated judgment.

(5) Finally, it should be borne in mind that Art. 9 C.civ. provides for specific remedies in cases of infringement of privacy, after a summary procedure (*en référé*). The enforceability of a judgment which orders publication of a decision, is strengthened when an *astreinte*, a penalty imposed e.g., on a daily basis, for non-compliance with an order, is granted.[142]

---

[137] On the *franc symbolique* see P. Kayzer, *La protection de la vie privée par le droit. Protection du secret de la vie privée*, 3rd edn. (Marseille-Paris: Presses Universitaires d'Aix-Marseille-Economica, 1995) at 367–9, para. 198–200 and S. Carval, *La responsabilité civile dans sa fonction de peine privée* (Paris: LGDJ, 1995) at para. 28 and 34.

[138] Cass. crim., 15 May 1957, D 1957.Jur.530; Cass. civ. 2e, 28 November 1962, D 1963.Jur.77. Compare with Cass. crim., 16 May 1974, D 1974.Jur.513, report by Dauvergne, approving an award of FRF 1 to the owner of a supermarket as compensation for inconvenience and the costs of prevention and detection of shoplifting in a case in which the culprit was caught *in flagrante delicto* because, "in the established circumstances of the case, the court of appeal could, without contradiction, fix the amount of the aforesaid damage at this figure".

[139] Paris, 28 May 1996, D 1996.Jur.617, annotated by B. Edelman, reversing TGI Paris, 1 February 1995, D 1995.Jur.569, annotated by B. Edelman; see *supra*, Chapter II, 2.2.2, Introductory Note under c).

[140] Viney, *Effets* at 9, para. 6. See also *supra*, Chapter II, **2.F.61.**, Note (3).

[141] Art. 700 New Code of Civil Procedure (Nouv. C. Pr. Civ.), as modified by Decree 91–1266 of 19 December 1991.

[142] See in the context of infringements of personality rights S. Carval, *La responsabilité civile dans sa fonction de peine privée* (Paris: LGDJ, 1995) at 39–43.

8.2. THE PRINCIPLE OF FULL REPARATION

Introductory Note

The victim of a wrong must be compensated for his or her loss and damage. The principles governing the scope of protection and recoverable harm are presented in Chapter II. In the present chapter, after having dealt in the preceding section with the purposes of an award in tort, we will discuss the rules governing the nature and extent of reparation, starting in this section with the general principles.

The most general principle is the rule of *restitutio in integrum* or full reparation, which may be understood either as *restitution in kind*, i.e. restoration of the *status quo ante*, more exactly restoration of the situation in which the plaintiff would have been if he had not sustained the injury, or as *compensation*, i.e. the grant of an equivalent in kind or in money for the harm suffered.[143] While this principle is expressed in very similar terms in French and English case law and in the German BGB, the implementation of the principle may differ from one legal system to another, as will be seen in this section and Sections 3, 4 and 5, which deal with the rules for trial courts to follow in assessing damages for material and non-material harm. Where a wrong has effected a state of affairs which is the source of continuing harm, the restoration of the *status quo ante* eliminates the source of harm and consequently prevents recurrent, future harm. This will be examined in Section 6, dealing with injunctive relief, as in some instances it may be difficult, especially from a comparative view, to distinguish between reparation and prevention of harm.

The principle of full reparation by the defendant is qualified by the so-called duty on the part of the plaintiff to mitigate damage. This may be put in terms of causation or in terms of the definition of recoverable harm. We have chosen to deal with the principles governing mitigation of damage in this section whilst certain issues surrounding its application will be discussed later in the chapter.

In this section the question will also be examined whether in some instances the award may have as its purpose not only the compensation of the plaintiff's loss, but also the recovery of benefits gained by the defendant as a consequence of the injurious act, i.e. to prevent unjust enrichment, a question which has been extensively examined in English and German law.

---

[143] H. Stoll, "Consequences of liability: remedies" in *International Encyclopedia of Comparative Law—Vol. XII/8: Torts*, A. Tunc, (ed.) (Tübingen: Mohr, 1986) at 8–9, para. 9, at 11, para. 12, at 41–2, para. 39 and at 61 ff., para. 63 ff. It may be noted that there is no uniform terminology. The distinction made in the text between the two forms of reparation: *restitution in kind* and *compensation* (in money) emphasizes the *object* of the remedy (restoration of the *status quo ante* versus delivery of an equivalent).

8.2.1. ENGLISH LAW

Introductory Note

Damages are "the pecuniary compensation, obtainable by success in an action, for a wrong which is either a tort or a breach of contract".[144] Compensation is always given as a sum of money. The remedies which may achieve restitution in kind will be examined in Section 6.

The principle of full compensation is a general rule "from which one must always start in resolving a problem as to the measure of damages".[145] It must be seen in conjunction with the plaintiff's duty to mitigate the loss which exists both in cases of property damage[146] and in cases of personal injury.[147]

For reasons of the assessability, uniformity and predictability of awards, in cases of grave injury the award is basically fixed at a conventional figure. As a consequence the assessment of harm in a personal injury case is only exceptionally now left to a jury.[148]

It is a matter of current debate whether damages may be *restitutionary*: with regard to some torts, it is argued that damages should be assessed not on the basis of the loss suffered by the plaintiff, but on the basis of the benefit gained by the defendant.[149]

Court of Appeal[150]   **8.E.8.**
Darbishire v. *Warran*

FULL COMPENSATION AND DUTY TO MITIGATE DAMAGE

Damaged shooting-brake

A plaintiff is entitled to receive such a sum of money in damages as will place him in the position he would have been in but for the tortious event; he is debarred from claiming damages for harm sustained due to his neglect to take reasonable steps to mitigate loss.

Facts: In 1958 the plaintiff bought a used car—a Lea Francis 1951 shooting-brake—for about GBP 330. In 1962, the car was seriously damaged in a collision caused by the defendant's negligence. The cost of repairing the car was GBP 192; the market value of the car was assessed at between GBP 80 and GBP 85.

Held: The court of first instance awarded damages on the basis of the cost of repairs. The Court of Appeal reversed this judgment and fixed the level of damages at the market value.

Judgment: PEARSON LJ[151]: "There is no complete definition of the expression 'market value' in the evidence or the judgment, but I understand it as meaning standard replacement market value, that

---

[144] H. McGregor, *McGregor on Damages*, 16th edn. (London: Sweet & Maxwell, 1997) at 3, para. 1.
[145] Ibid. at 9, para. 10.
[146] **8.E.8.**
[147] **8.E.9.**
[148] **8.E.10.**
[149] **8.E.11.**
[150] [1963] 1 WLR 1067, [1963] 3 All ER 310.
[151] Harman LJ and Pennycuick J delivered concurring judgments with regard to the appropriate measure of damages. However, Pearson LJ was in the minority with regard to the specific question of whether allowance should be made, in the level of damages, for the good condition of the damaged car; see *infra*, Note (2).

is to say, the retail price which a customer would have to pay in July, 1962, on a purchase of an average vehicle of the same make, type and age or a comparable vehicle. It is not the price for a sale to a dealer or between dealers. It appears from a passage in the judgment that the "market value" does not include any allowance for the good maintenance and reliability of the plaintiff's vehicle.

What are the principles applicable? The first and main principle is that the plaintiff is entitled to receive as damages such a sum of money as will place him in as good a position as he would have been in if the accident had not occurred. In *Liesbosch Dredger* v. *Edison S.S. (Owners)*[152] Lord Wright said:

'It is not questioned that when a vessel is lost by collision due to the sole negligence of the wrongdoing vessel the owners of the former vessel are entitled to what is called *restitutio in integrum*, which means that *they should recover such a sum as will replace them, so far as can be done by compensation in money, in the same position as if the loss had not been inflicted on them, subject to the rules of law as to remoteness of damage* [emphasis added].'

Now, but for the accident, the plaintiff would have continued to have the use of his existing motor-car, the 1951 Lea Francis shooting brake, undamaged. The accident deprived him of it. To be restored to substantially the same position, he needed such sum of money as would enable him to provide himself with an equivalent vehicle either by having the existing damaged vehicle repaired or by finding and acquiring another vehicle equally good.

There is, however, a second principle [references omitted]:

'The fundamental basis is thus compensation for pecuniary loss flowing from the breach; but this first principle is qualified by a second, which imposes on a plaintiff the duty of taking all reasonable steps to mitigate the loss consequent on the breach, and debars him from claiming any part of the damage which is due to his neglect to take such steps. In the words of James LJ [references omitted] 'The person who has broken the contract is not to be exposed to additional cost by reason of the plaintiffs not doing what they ought to have done as reasonable men, and the plaintiffs not being under any obligation to do anything otherwise than in the ordinary course of business'.'

For the purposes of the present case it is important to appreciate the true nature of the so-called 'duty to mitigate the loss' or 'duty to minimise the damage.' The plaintiff is not under any actual obligation to adopt the cheaper method: if he wishes to adopt the more expensive method, he is at liberty to do so and by doing so he commits no wrong against the defendant or anyone else. The true meaning is that the plaintiff is not entitled to charge the defendant by way of damages with any greater sum than that which he reasonably needs to expend for the purpose of making good the loss. In short, he is fully entitled to be as extravagant as he pleases but not at the expense of the defendant.

Now did the plaintiff in this case take all reasonable steps to mitigate the loss consequent on the breach? He knew from his dealings with the insurance company that they assessed the replacement market value at £85, and he accepted payment from them on that basis. The insurance company advised against repairs. He was told, at one time at any rate, by the repairers that it was uneconomic to have the vehicle repaired. He had estimates of the cost and there is no evidence of the estimates being inaccurate. After spending about £180, he would have a vehicle worth only about £85. And yet he made no attempt to find another car . . .

In my view it is impossible to find from the evidence that the plaintiff took all reasonable steps to mitigate the loss, or did all that he reasonably could do to keep down the cost . . .

It is vital, for the purpose of assessing damages fairly between the plaintiff and the defendant, to consider whether the plaintiff's course of action was economic or uneconomic, and if it was uneconomic it cannot (at any rate in the absence of special circumstances, of which there is no evidence in this case) form a proper basis for assessment of damages. The question has to be considered from

---

[152] [1933] AC 449 at 459, excerpted *supra*, Chapter IV, **4.E.27.**

the point of view of a business man. It seems to me the practical business view is that if the cost of repairing your damaged vehicle is greatly in excess of the market price, you must look around for a replacement and you would expect to find one at a cost not far removed from the market price, although unless you were lucky you might have to pay something more than the standard market price to obtain a true equivalent of a well-maintained and reliable vehicle.

In my view the defendant succeeds on the issue of principle. The assessment should be based on the market price and not on the much higher cost of repairing the damaged vehicle, and therefore the judge's assessment was made on a wrong basis and should be reduced.

In considering what reduction should be made, it may not be appropriate to take the exact figure of the market price, which I understand to be the standard market price of an average vehicle of the make, type and age of the plaintiff's vehicle. There should be an element of flexibility in the assessment of damages to achieve a result which is fair and just as between the parties in the particular case . . . Although I am not able to agree with the learned judge that . . . the cost of repair, can be regarded as a reasonable figure as between the parties, I do agree with him that the bare market value seems too low, as he accepted the plaintiff's evidence as to good maintenance and reliability . . ."

Notes

(1) The way in which the principle of full reparation or compensation is qualified by the so-called duty to mitigate damage is clearly demonstrated in this case.[153] In accordance with that duty, "the plaintiff must take all reasonable steps to mitigate the loss to him consequent upon the defendant's wrong and cannot recover damages for any such loss which he could have avoided but has failed, through unreasonable action or inaction, to avoid".[154]

Although the expression is in common usage, the expression "duty to mitigate the loss" is inaccurate: a plaintiff cannot owe a duty to himself, i.e. to mitigate his own damage. As Pearson LJ states, the true meaning is that the plaintiff, though not under any actual obligation to adopt the cheaper method, is "not entitled to charge the defendant by way of damages with any greater sum than that which he reasonably needs to expend for the purpose of making good the loss". As a consequence, the duty to mitigate the loss or minimize the damage limits the expenses that the plaintiff may claim, and introduces a normative element: only those expenses which a *reasonable* plaintiff should incur are recoverable. The requirement of *reasonableness* is also recognized in the concurring opinions of Harman LJ and Pennycuick J.[155]

In the excerpted case the duty to mitigate damage arose after the injury had occurred, that is when the plaintiff considered which method of reparation (replacing or repairing the car) he wished to adopt to make good the harm sustained. Although the underlying idea is the same, this case may be distinguished from those cases in which the plaintiff's failure to mitigate the damage affects the extent of the harm itself as where the plaintiff refuses to undergo surgery, as will be seen in the next case.[156]

[153] On the principle of full compensation, see also *Livingstone* v. *Rawyards Coal Company* (1880) 5 App.Cas. 25, HL at 39 per Lord Blackburn.

[154] H. McGregor, *McGregor on Damages*, 16th edn. (London: Sweet & Maxwell, 1997) at 185–6, para. 285. The duty to mitigate a loss applies in contract and tort. See the overview of tort cases, ibid. at 206–8, para. 319–21.

[155] *Darbishire* v. *Warran, supra*, per Harman LJ at [1963] 1 WLR 1071 and Pennycuick J at [1963] 1 WLR 1078.

[156] Compare with German law, *infra*, **8.G.12.**, Note (2)(c).

(2) The Court of Appeal set the level of damages at the "market value" of the damaged car. Pearson LJ understood this to mean the "standard replacement market value", that is to say the retail price which a customer would have to pay on a purchase of an average vehicle of the same make, type and age or a comparable vehicle. He noted that this "market value" does not include any allowance for the good maintenance and reliability of the damaged car. Accordingly, he fixed the car's value at GBP 105, allowing for good maintenance and reliability, whereas a car of the same make, type and age was valued at GBP 80 in a trade guide and at GBP 85 by the insurance company.[157] That view was shared neither by Harman LJ, who considered that there were no exceptional circumstances allowing a departure from the market value in this case, [158] nor by Pennycuick J, who considered that, in reaching the market value of the car, the hypothetical valuer must be regarded as having taken into account all its relevant attributes; Pennycuick J. therefore came to the conclusion that "it cannot be legitimate to take the market value and then make an addition for good condition. To do so is to bring the same factor into account twice over".[159] Moreover, the plaintiff's interest in being able to keep his own preferred car is not taken into account; the "correct test of pecuniary interest" excludes the consideration of "the personal convenience of the plaintiff".[160]

Privy Council[161]   **8.E.9.**
Selvanayagam v. *University of the West Indies*

DUTY TO MITIGATE DAMAGE. PERSONAL INJURY

Diabetic refusing surgery

A plaintiff who rejected surgery contrary to a medical recommendation must show that he acted reasonably.

Facts: The plaintiff, a professor of civil engineering at the defendant university, fell into a trench on the university campus. He sustained a severe neck injury for which a consultant surgeon recommended surgery. The plaintiff suffered from diabetes which could have led to surgical complications, and he refused to have the operation.

Held: The court of appeal, reversing the judgment of the court of first instance, held that the plaintiff had unreasonably refused surgery and assessed damages on the basis that, had the plaintiff acted reasonably, he was likely to have completely recovered his earning capacity within six months of the accident. That judgment was reversed by the Privy Council.

Judgment: LORD SCARMAN: "Was the Court of Appeal right to reverse the judge's finding that the plaintiff acted reasonably in refusing an operation to his neck? . . .
Dr. Ghouralal [a consultant neuro-surgeon] believed that surgical therapy to the neck would help. If there was no operation, the neck would get worse, in his opinion. It would be a major operation but "not very risky" . . . Chances of success would be "quite good" . . . He, therefore, did recom-

---

[157] *Darbishire* v. *Warran, supra*, at [1963] 1 WLR 1077.
[158] Ibid. at 1073.
[159] Ibid. at 1079.
[160] Ibid. Compare the approach of German law, *infra*, **8.G.12.**, Note (2)(d).
[161] [1983] 1 WLR 585, [1983] 1 All ER 824.

mend in 1975 an operation, and was of the opinion that some six months later the plaintiff would have been fit to resume his professional work. At the very end of his evidence . . . Dr. Ghouralal added that the plaintiff knew of the risks of infection which a diabetic would run and that "it is for the patient to decide on whether he should have the operation or not".
. . .

Their Lordships do not doubt that the burden of proving reasonableness was upon the plaintiff. It always is, in a case in which it is suggested that, had a plaintiff made a different decision, his loss would have been less than it actually was . . . Their Lordships would add a further comment on the law, well established though it is. *The rule that a plaintiff who rejects a medical recommendation in favour of surgery must show that he acted reasonably is based upon the principle that a plaintiff is under a duty to act reasonably so as to mitigate his damage . . . The question is one of fact . . .* [emphasis added]. In *Richardson* v. *Redpath, Brown & Co. Ltd.* [1944] AC 62, 68, Viscount Simon L.C. said that the material question is "whether the workman" (i.e. the plaintiff) "who refuses to be operated upon is acting reasonably in view of the advice he has received." Their Lordships would, with respect, put the question in more general terms. Though the advice received will almost always be a major factor for consideration, the true question is whether in all the circumstances, including particularly the medical advice received, the plaintiff acted reasonably in refusing surgery . . . For these reasons, their Lordships are of the opinion that the Court of Appeal was wrong to reverse the judge. . ."

Notes

(1) The excerpted opinion confirms that the rule of mitigation of damage is well-established in the context of an unreasonable refusal of medical treatment.[162] The rule raises difficult issues of law and policy—whether there is a need to mitigate—particularly in relation to personal injuries. However, what is unreasonable or reasonable is a question of fact in each case,[163] as the excerpted opinion also shows: "the true question is whether in all the circumstances including particularly the medical advice received, the plaintiff acted reasonably in refusing surgery . . .".[164] There is, moreover, divergent case-law with regard to whether the reasonableness of the plaintiff's decision is to be considered against a subjective or objective standard.[165]

(2) It has been suggested[166] that in the annotated case the decision concerning the burden of proof was arrived at *per incuriam*. In *Steele* v. *Robert George*[167] and in *Richardson* v. *Redpath, Brown & Co. Ltd.*,[168] the onus of proving the unreasonableness of a workman's refusal to undergo an operation was regarded to be on the defendant employer.

---

[162] The principles were set out in two cases concerning workmen's compensation claims, decided by the House of Lords, in which the relative importance of medical advice was discussed: *Steele* v. *Robert George* [1942] AC 497, HL and *Richardson* v. *Redpath, Brown & Co. Ltd.* [1944] AC 62, HL. For further comments see A.H. Hudson and H. McGregor, "Mitigation and Refusal of Medical Treatment: Reasonableness and Onus of Proof" (1983) 46 Mod LR 754.

[163] H. McGregor, *McGregor on Damages*, 16th edn. (London: Sweet & Maxwell, 1997) at para. 300; Rogers at 758.

[164] *Selvanayagam* v. *University of the West Indies, supra*, at 589 per Lord Scarman.

[165] See A.H. Hudson and H. McGregor, "Mitigation and Refusal of Medical Treatment: Reasonableness and Onus of Proof" (1983) 46 Mod LR 754 at 754–6.

[166] See ibid. at 758–759.

[167] [1942] AC 497, HL.

[168] [1944] AC 62, HL.

(3) It is a matter of debate whether the question of mitigation, for instance in cases of refusal of medical treatment, may be put in causation terms.[169] In *Emeh* v. *Kensington and Chelsea and Westminster Area Health Authority*,[170] the question was posed both in terms of mitigation of damage and in terms of a *novus actus interveniens* breaking the chain of causation, showing that different approaches may reach the same solution.[171] In that case, a mother who might lawfully have had an abortion was still able to claim for the expense of bringing up a child conceived owing to the negligent failure of a sterilisation operation.

Court of Appeal[172]   **8.E.10.**
Ward v. *James*

CONVENTIONAL MEASURE OF DAMAGES

Quadriplegic plaintiff

In cases of grave injury to the person where it is difficult to assess a fair compensation in money, the award must basically be a conventional figure derived from experience and awards in comparable cases, thus also achieving some measure of uniformity and predictability in awards. None of this is achieved when the damages are left at large to the jury.

Facts: The plaintiff became a permanent quadriplegic following an accident in which he was the passenger in a car driven by the defendant, when it overturned. He brought an action for damages for personal injuries against the driver alleging the accident to have been caused by his negligence. On the application of the plaintiff, trial by jury was ordered.

Held: The Court of Appeal did not interfere with the order which was in line with the considerations current at that time but laid down new guidelines for the future.

Judgment: LORD DENNING MR[173]: "For many years . . ., it has been said that serious injuries afford a good reason for ordering trial by jury . . . Recent experience has led to some doubts being held on this score. It begins to look as if a jury is an unsuitable tribunal to assess damages for grave injuries, at any rate in those cases where a man is greatly reduced in his activities. He is deprived of much that makes life worthwhile. No money can compensate for the loss. Yet compensation has to be given in money. The problem is insoluble. To meet it, the judges have evolved a conventional measure. They go by their experience in comparable cases. But the juries have nothing to go by. Let me illustrate this from the cases:

. . . [There follows an overview of cases of quadriplegia, loss of a limb, loss of expectation of life and unconsciousness.]

Lessons of Recent Cases. These recent cases show the desirability of three things: First, *assessability* : In cases of grave injury, where the body is wrecked or the brain destroyed, it is very difficult to assess a fair compensation in money, so difficult that the award must basically be a conventional

---

[169] See A.H. Hudson and H. McGregor "Mitigation and Refusal of Medical Treatment: Reasonableness and Onus of Proof" (1983) 46 Mod LR 754 at 757.

[170] [1985] 1 QB 1012, [1985] 2 WLR 233, [1984] 3 All ER 1044, CA; see also *supra*, Chapter II, **2.E.6.** and notes thereafter. On *novus actus intervenious*, see *supra*, Chapter IV, 4.3.3.

[171] [1985] 1 QB 1012, CA at 1018–19 per Waller LJ and at 1025 per Slade LJ.

[172] [1966] 1 QB 273, CA.

[173] Sellers, Pearson, Davies and Diplock LJJ concurred with the judgment of Lord Denning.

figure, derived from experience or from awards in comparable cases. Secondly, *uniformity*: There should be some measure of uniformity in awards so that similar decisions are given in similar cases; otherwise there will be great dissatisfaction in the community, and much criticism of the administration of justice. Thirdly, *predictability*: Parties should be able to predict with some measure of accuracy the sum which is likely to be awarded in a particular case, for by this means cases can be settled peaceably and not brought to court, a thing very much to the public good. None of these three is achieved when the damages are left at large to the jury. Under the present practice the judge does not give them any help at all to assess the figure. The result is that awards may vary greatly, from being much too high to much too low. There is no uniformity and no predictability [emphasis in original].

. . . [There follows a discussion of the possibility of correcting an award of juries, the possibility of giving more guidance to juries by allowing counsel or judge to refer to awards in comparable cases or to conventional figures.]

Conclusion: The result of it all is this: We have come in recent years to realise that the award of damages in personal injury cases is basically a conventional figure derived from experience and from awards in comparable cases. Yet the jury are not allowed to know what that conventional figure is. The judge knows it, but the jury do not. This is a most material consideration which a judge must bear in mind when deciding whether or not to order trial by jury. So important is it that the judge ought not, in a personal injury case, to order trial by jury save in exceptional circumstances."

Notes

(1) In this extract, Lord Denning MR recognized the judicial evolution towards a conventional scale for damages in cases of serious personal injury. In such cases, there is an unavoidable tension between the harm sustained and the available remedy, in that compensation may only be given in money, whereas the nature of the harm makes money compensation often inadequate: "No one of us would suffer it [loss of expectation of life] for all the gold in the Bank of England".[174]

As explained by Lord Denning (in a part of the judgment not reproduced),[175] counsel has been allowed to inform *the judge* of the level of awards in previous cases only since 1951. However, it was considered that there were overwhelming objections against *the jury* being referred to comparable cases or conventional figures: "the proceedings would be in danger of developing into an auction".[176] As a consequence, trial by jury for a personal injury claim was considered to be inappropriate and to be ordered only in exceptional circumstances, as recommended in the annotated judgment.

Since the annotated judgment, trial by jury has virtually disappeared for personal injury cases.[177] The policy stated in *Ward* v. *James* was affirmed in *H.* v. *Ministry of*

---

[174] *Ward* v. *James*, *supra*, at 297.

[175] *Ward* v. *James*, *supra*, at 297 and 302.

[176] *Ward* v. *James*, *supra*, at 302. As has been indicated *supra*, **8.E.1.–2.**, Note (5), legal practice has changed; see *John* v. *MGN Ltd.* [1996] 3 WLR 593, CA at 615 per Thomas Bingham MR: "Indeed, far from developing into an auction . . . the process of mentioning figures would in our view induce a mood of realism on both sides".

[177] A *right* to jury trial is available only in cases of fraud, libel, slander, malicious prosecution or false imprisonment. In other cases, trial is without jury, though there is a *discretion* to order trial with a jury. The rules governing the mode of trial (as modified by the Supreme Court Act 1981, c. 54) are discussed in *H.* v. *Ministry of Defence* [1991] 2 QB 103, CA in which it is noted that since *Ward* v. *James*, there is only one reported instance of an order for trial of a personal injury case with a jury (*H.* v. *Ministry of Defence* [1991] 2 QB 103, CA at 109). However, jury trial remains quite common in Scotland and Northern Ireland: H. McGregor, *McGregor on Damages*, 16th edn. (London: Sweet & Maxwell, 1997) at 1361, para. 2090.

Defence,[178] emphasizing the need for consistency as a touchstone of justice, although the Court of Appeal considered that trial by jury might be appropriate in a personal injury case, if there was a claim for exemplary damages.[179]

(2) As has been already mentioned,[180] judges are now concerned with consistency in awards across the various categories of cases, including cases of defamation, malicious prosecution and false imprisonment. The reticence towards giving more guidance to the jury, which is still evident in *Ward* v. *James*, has now vanished.[181]

Court of Appeal[182]   **8.E.11.**
Strand Electric and Engineering Co. Ltd. v. *Brisford Entertainments Ltd.*

RESTITUTIONARY DAMAGES

Wrongfully detained switchboards

The owner of goods wrongfully detained is entitled to damages equivalent to a reasonable hire charge, which is not based on the loss to the plaintiff but on the fact that the defendant has used the goods for his own purposes.

Facts: The defendants, negotiating for the purchase of a theatre, were permitted to go into possession before completion of the purchase. The plaintiffs, as part of their business, had hired out portable switchboards to the previous owners of the theatre. The defendants, having taken possession of the theatre, refused to return them. The plaintiffs claimed the return of the switchboards and damages for the period of detention.

Held: The court of first instance ordered the return of the switchboards and in assessing damages, made allowance for the possibility that, if the switchboards had been returned to the plaintiffs, some of them might not have been hired out by them for the whole period or might have been accidentally destroyed. The Court of Appeal allowed the plaintiffs nonetheless to recover damages equivalent to the full market rate of hire for the whole period of detention.

Judgment: DENNING LJ: "In assessing damages, whether for a breach of contract or for a tort, the general rule is that the plaintiff recovers the loss he has suffered, no more and no less. This rule is, however, often departed from. Thus in cases where the damage claimed is too remote in law the plaintiff recovers less than his real loss [references omitted]. In other cases the plaintiff may get more than his real loss. Thus, where the damage suffered by the plaintiff is recouped or lessened owing to some reason with which the defendant is not concerned, the plaintiff gets full damages without any deduction on that account [references omitted]. Again, in cases where the defendant has obtained a benefit from his wrongdoing he is often made liable to account for it, even though the plaintiff has lost nothing and suffered no damage [references omitted].

The question in this case is: What is the proper measure of damages for the wrongful detention of goods? Does it fall within the general rule that the plaintiff only recovers for the loss he has suffered or within some other, and if so what, rule? It is strange that there is no authority upon this point in English law; but there is plenty on the analogous case of detention of land. The rule there is that a wrongdoer, who keeps the owner out of his land, must pay a fair rental value for it, even

---

[178] [1991] 2 QB 103, CA.
[179] Ibid. at 112.
[180] See *supra*, **8.E.1.–2.**, Note (5).
[181] See *Thompson* v. *Commissioner of Police of the Metropolis* [1997] 3 WLR 403, CA and *John* v. *MGN Ltd.* [1997] QB 586, CA, discussed *supra*, **8.E.1.–2.**, Notes (3)(a) and (5).
[182] [1952] 2 QB 246, [1952] 1 All ER 796.

though the owner would not have been able to use it himself or to let it to anyone else. So also a wrongdoer who uses land for his own purposes without the owner's consent, as, for instance, for a fair ground, or as a wayleave, must pay a reasonable hire for it, even though he has done no damage to the land at all: *Whitwham* v. *Westminster Brymbo Coal Company*.[183] I see no reason why the same principle should not apply to detention of goods.

If a wrongdoer has made use of goods for his own purposes, then he must pay a reasonable hire for them, even though the owner has in fact suffered no loss. It may be that the owner would not have used the goods himself, or that he had a substitute readily available, which he used without extra cost to himself. Nevertheless the owner is entitled to a reasonable hire. If the wrongdoer had asked the owner for permission to use the goods, the owner would be entitled to ask for a reasonable remuneration as the price of his permission. The wrongdoer cannot be better off because he did not ask permission. He cannot be better off by doing wrong than he would be by doing right. He must therefore pay a reasonable hire. This will cover, of course, the wear and tear which is ordinarily included in a hiring charge; but for any further damage the wrongdoer must pay extra. I do not mean to suggest that an owner who has suffered greater loss will not be able to recover it. Suppose that a man used a car in his business, and owing to its detention he had to hire a substitute at an increased cost, he would clearly be able to recover the cost of the substitute. In such cases the plaintiff recovers his actual loss. I am not concerned with those cases.

I am here concerned with the cases where the owner has in fact suffered no loss, or less loss than is represented by a hiring charge. In such cases if the wrongdoer has in fact used the goods he must pay a reasonable hire for them . . . The claim for a hiring charge is therefore not based on the loss to the plaintiff, but on the fact that the defendant has used the goods for his own purposes. It is an action against him because he has had the benefit of the goods. It resembles, therefore, an action for restitution rather than an action of tort . . ."

ROMER LJ: "In my judgment the three salient facts on which the assessment of damages in this case depends are, first, that the equipment of the plaintiffs which the defendants detained was profit-earning property; secondly, that the plaintiffs normally hired out the equipment in the course of their business; and, thirdly, that the defendants during the period of wrongful detention applied the property to the furtherance of their own ends . . .

The fundamental aim in awarding damages is in general to compensate the party aggrieved. The inquiry is: What loss has the plaintiff suffered by reason of the defendants' wrongful act? In determining the answer to this inquiry the question of quantifying the profit or benefit which the defendant has derived from his wrongful act does not arise; for there is no necessary relation between the plaintiffs' loss and the defendants' gain. It follows that in assessing the plaintiffs' loss in the present case one is not troubled by any need to evaluate the actual benefit which resulted to the defendants by having the plaintiffs' equipment at their disposal.

That element then being out of the way, the only substantial reason put forward by the defendants why the plaintiffs should not receive the full hiring value of the equipment during the period of detention is that the plaintiffs might not have been able to find a hirer. In my judgment, however, a defendant who has wrongfully detained and profited from the property of someone else cannot avail himself of a hypothesis such as this. It does not lie in the mouth of such a defendant to suggest that the owner might not have found a hirer; for in using the property he showed that he wanted it and he cannot complain if it is assumed against him that he himself would have preferred to become the hirer rather than not have had the use of it at all."

SOMERVELL LJ also delivered a judgment allowing the appeal.

[183] [1896] 2 Ch 538.

Notes

(1) This case deals with *restitutionary* damages, that is to say the borderland between damages and restitution.[184] "Restitution" is "that branch of law dealing with unjust enrichment and part of that is concerned with restitution of benefits obtained through wrongs".[185] Damages are called *restitutionary* when the measure of damages is the benefit obtained by the defendant through the wrong, rather than the loss to the plaintiff. The difference between a strict compensatory approach and a restitutionary approach may be considerable when the wrong did not inflict a perceptible loss on the plaintiff, but allowed the defendant to make a gain. This is the case, for instance, when the defendant misappropriated a chattel for a period in which the plaintiff would not have utilized it, hired it out or disposed of it in any way. The plaintiff lost nothing, but the defendant made a gain by saving the cost of hire. The distinction between a compensatory and restitutionary analysis may become blurred if the plaintiff is compensated for the loss of opportunity to use his property as such, regardless of whether the plaintiff would have let the property or would have used it or not.[186] Thus the question arises as to whether in that case, the real scope of damages is not the restitution of the profit obtained by the defendant by saving the cost of hire rather than the compensation of the plaintiff.[187]

The annotated case, dealing with *interference with goods*,[188] provides an illustration of the tension between the compensatory and the restitutionary approaches. Denning LJ considered the plaintiffs' claim as being actually a "claim for hiring charge . . . not based on the loss to the plaintiff"; "an action against [the defendant] because he had the benefit of the goods", and an action which "resembles, therefore, an action for restitution rather than an action of tort". On the other hand, Romer LJ considered the key question to be the loss suffered by the plaintiff. However, in that respect, it was not, he said, for the defendant who had wrongfully profited from the property, to avail himself of a hypothe-

---

[184] Debate surrounds restitutionary damages. One of the main issues is the question whether "restitutionary damages" are still "damages" or belong exclusively to the law of restitution. Conditions for the existence of a restitutionary duty and their scope are also questioned. The law of restitution and restitutionary damages have undergone considerable developments; consequently it is not surprising that the views in this field diverge considerably. See and compare *inter alia*: J. Sharpe and S.M. Waddams, "Damages for lost opportunity to bargain" (1982) 2 OJLS 290; P. Birks, *An Introduction to the Law of Restitution*, 2nd edn. (Oxford: Clarendon Press, 1989) at 313–57; M. Jackman, "Restitution for wrongs" (1989) 48 Camb LJ 302; A. Burrows, *The Law of Restitution* (London: Butterworths, 1993), in particular at 376–419; Lord Goff and G. Jones, *The Law of Restitution*, 4th edn. (London: Sweet & Maxwell, 1993) at 714–34; A. Burrows, *Remedies for Torts and Breach of Contract*, 2nd edn. (London: Butterworths, 1994) at 286–314; E. Cooke, "Trespass, Mesne Profits and Restitution" (1994) 110 LQR 420; N.J. McBride and P. McGrath, "The Nature of Restitution" (1995) 15 OJLS 33; H. McGregor, "Restitutionary Damages" in P. Birks (ed.), *Wrongs and Remedies in the Twenty-First Century* (Oxford: Clarendon Press, 1996) at 203.

[185] Rogers at 750.

[186] Rogers at 752.

[187] It was Denning LJ's opinion in the annotated case that a plaintiff is not required to prove the defendant to have gained a positive benefit; the saving of an expense, i.e. a negative benefit, is also an enrichment. This seems to have been controversial in the old case of *Philipps* v. *Homfray* (1883) 24 ChD 439, CA. See also A. Burrows, *Remedies for Torts and Breach of Contract*, 2nd edn. (London: Butterworths, 1994) at 291; H. McGregor, "Restitutionary Damages" in P. Birks, (ed.), *Wrongs and Remedies in the Twenty-First Century* (Oxford: Clarendon Press, 1996) at 216.

[188] The case deals with the tort of detinue, abolished by the Torts (Interference with Goods) Act 1977 (c. 32). Detinue was primarily an action for the return of the goods, a broader remedy than that available where the cause of action relied on by the plaintiff was conversion, for which, before the 1977 Act, the only remedy was damages. See Rogers at 613–14; H. McGregor, *McGregor on Damages*, 16th edn. (London: Sweet & Maxwell, 1997) at 906–7, para. 1375–8. See also *supra*, Chapter I, **1.E.21.**

sis that during the period of detention the plaintiffs might not have been able to find a hirer. Somervell LJ confined his judgment (which is not reproduced) to the facts of the case.[189] As for the measure of damages, it should be noted that both Somervell and Romer LJJ considered the *actual benefit* which the defendants had obtained to be irrelevant.[190]

(2) Until now, the restitutionary approach has also been applied—or it is contended that this approach prevails or should prevail—in the following classes of case.

(a) *Interference with land*. The plaintiff who has been wrongfully deprived of his land may claim damages for the loss arising from the period of wrongful occupation by the defendant. Such damages are recoverable in the so-called *action for mesne profits*,[191] in the annotated case regarded by both Denning LJ and Somervell LJ to be the nearest analogy to the case before the court.[192] In such an *action for mesne profits*, the normal measure of damages is the ordinary letting value of the property. Here too, the question arose as to whether the plaintiff is entitled to damages regardless of whether or not he could show that he would have let the property to anybody else and whether or not he would have used the property himself. That question was answered in the affirmative in *Swordheath Properties Ltd.* v. *Tabet*,[193] which was cited recently by the Privy Council in *Inverugie Investments Ltd.* v. *Hackett*,[194] which also displays the reluctance of the Privy Council to depart outright from the compensatory principle:[195]

"It is sometimes said that these cases are an exception to the rule that damages in tort are compensatory. But this is not necessarily so. It depends how widely one defines the 'loss' which the plaintiff has suffered. As the Earl of Halsbury LC pointed out in *Mediana* [references omitted] it is no answer for a wrongdoer who has deprived the plaintiff of his chair to point out that he does not usually sit in it or that he has plenty of other chairs in the room."

The reasoning in *The Mediana*,[196] permits the conclusion that in cases of wrongful user, the measure of damages is based on the acknowledgement of a notional (abstract) loss.[197] As E. Cooke notes, "the benefit to the defendant will often in fact be the same as the loss to the plaintiff, or the notional loss where the plaintiff would not in fact have let the land. Thus the compensatory and restitutionary analysis may yield the same results . . .".[198]

---

[189] *Strand Electric and Engineering Co. Ltd.* v. *Brisford Entertainments Ltd, supra*, at 252: "I do not wish in this so far uncharted field to go beyond the facts of the case".

[190] Ibid. at 252 per Somervell LJ and at 256 per Romer LJ.

[191] The plaintiff can recover the land itself by the action for the recovery of the land (formerly known as the action of ejectment). The action for mesne profits was formerly brought after judgment in ejectment but may now be joined with the action for recovery of the land itself: H. McGregor, *McGregor on Damages*, 16th edn. (London: Sweet & Maxwell, 1997) at 878, para. 1417; Rogers at 488–9.

[192] Denning LJ referred to the old case of *Whitwham* v. *Westminster Brymbo Coal Company* [1896] 2 Ch 538, CA.

[193] *Swordheath Properties Ltd.* v. *Tabet* [1979] 1 WLR 285, CA at 288, [1979] 1 All ER 240, CA at 242. For more details on previous case law, see H. McGregor, *McGregor on Damages*, 16th edn. (London: Sweet & Maxwell, 1997) at 985–6, para. 1504.

[194] [1995] 1 WLR 713, [1995] 3 All ER 841, PC.

[195] Ibid. at 717–18.

[196] [1900] AC 113, HL; *infra*, **8.E.35.**

[197] *Infra*, **8.G.15.**, Note (2)(b) and thereafter.

[198] E. Cooke, "Trespass, Mesne Profits and Restitution" (1994) 110 LQR 420 at 427. Compare the opinion of Nicholls LJ stating that the law has reached this conclusion "*by giving to the concept of loss or damage in such*

However, two recent (and factually similar) cases, *Ministry of Defence* v. *Ashman*[199] and *Ministry of Defence* v. *Thompson*,[200] gave cause for new consideration to the inter-relationship between the compensatory and restitutionary approaches.

The facts of the first case were as follows. Mrs Ashman had to leave the house rented from the Ministry of Defence after her husband, a sergeant in the army, left her. The rent (GBP 95 per month) was at a "concessionary" rate of about one fifth of the market rent on the open market (GBP 472 per month). Mrs Ashman could leave the house only after having received alternative housing from the local authority (at GBP 33 per week). The Ministry of Defence claimed damages at the market rent and not at the concessionary rent. Hoffmann LJ[201] said:

> "A person entitled to possession of land can make a claim against a person who has been in occupation without his consent on two alternative bases. The first is *for the loss which he has suffered in consequence of the defendant's trespass*. This is the *normal measure of damages in the law of tort*. The second is *the value of the benefit which the occupier has received.* This is *a claim for restitution* [emphasis added]. The two bases of claim are mutually exclusive . . . It is true that in the earlier cases it has not been expressly stated that a claim for mesne profits for trespass can be a claim for restitution. Nowadays I do not see why we should not call a spade a spade."

After having accepted that the Ministry's claim was a claim for restitution, Hoffmann LJ considered that evidence of what the Ministry would have done with the house was irrelevant and that the only question which was left was how to value the benefit which the defendant had received. In that respect, he emphasized that a benefit may not be worth as much to the defendant as to someone else. In the circumstances of that case, it was held that the value of the occupation to Mrs Ashman amounted to the rent she would have had to pay for suitable local authority housing (that is to say, more or less GBP 33 per week). Finally, he said that if the plaintiff has suffered greater loss, for example because the house would have been re-let at the market value, it was always open to him to elect for the alternative measure of damages in tort.

These cases raise the question as to whether the plaintiff is only entitled either to *compensation in tort* for the concrete loss which must be shown or to *restitution of the benefit* which the individual defendant gained and, thus, whether therefore there is no longer room for compensation on the basis of a notional loss. It seems that this is not the state of the law.[202] Indeed, it appears from *Inverugie Investments Ltd.* v. *Hackett,* referred to above, that damages for mesne profits[203] may indeed be assessed on the basis of a notional loss.

a case a wider meaning [emphasis added] than merely financial loss calculated by comparing the property owner's financial position after the wrongdoing with what it would have been had the wrongdoing never occurred": *Stoke-on-Trent City Council* v. *W. & J. Wass Ltd.* [1988] 1 WLR 1406, CA at 1416.

[199] [1993] 2 EGLR 102, (1993) 25 HLR 513, CA. For a thorough discussion of this case, see E. Cooke, "Trespass, Mesne Profits and Restitution" (1994) 110 LQR 420 at 425 and conclusions at 430.

[200] [1993] 2 EGLR 107, (1993) 25 HLR 552, CA. Here, the Court of Appeal was differently constituted; Sir John Megaw and Glidewell LJ agreed with the opinion of Hoffmann LJ in this case, Hoffmann LJ summarized the principles of *Ministry of Defence* v. *Ashman.*

[201] With whom Kennedy LJ concurred, saying that the approach "may be somewhat analogous to quasi-contractual restitution". Lloyd LJ disagreed; according to him, a claim for restitution was not pleaded and it was doubtful whether such a claim was available in the case of wrongful occupation of land. Thus, he assessed damages on the basis of the concessionary rent because the Ministry could not show that the house, if vacated at time, would have been let at the market rent.

[202] See H. McGregor, *McGregor on Damages*, 16th edn. (London: Sweet & Maxwell, 1997) at 988–9, para. 1508.

[203] The Privy Council emphasized that the plaintiff claimed damages for mesne profits and was not asserting a restitutionary claim as an independent cause of action, so that the point which divided the Court of Appeal in *Ministry of Defence* v. *Ashman* did not arise for decision: *Inverugie Investments Ltd.* v. *Hackett* [1995] 1 WLR 713, [1995] 3 All ER 841, PC at 843.

In that case, the defendants were the owners of a hotel in The Bahamas, consisting of 164 apartments, 30 of which they had leased for 99 years to the plaintiff. The defendants had wrongfully occupied the plaintiff's 30 apartments. In the period of trespass, the hotel had an occupancy rate of about 35 per cent and was running at a loss. It was debated whether the defendants had to pay a reasonable rent for the occupation of 30 apartments for the period of their trespass. It was decided that the correct principle was that:[205]

> "The plaintiff may not have suffered any *actual* loss by being deprived of the use of his property. But under the user principle[204] he is entitled to recover a reasonable rent for the wrongful use of his property by the trespasser. Similarly, the trespasser may not have derived any *actual* benefit from the use of the property. But under the user principle he is obliged to pay a reasonable rent for the use which he has enjoyed. The principle need not be characterised as exclusively compensatory, or exclusively restitutionary; it combines elements of both." [emphasis in original].

As a consequence, it was decided that the defendants had to pay the reasonable rent even though they had been unable to derive any actual benefit from the use of the apartments (the hotel running at a loss) and even though the plaintiff would not have been able to let all of the apartments to tour operators for the entire period.

(b) The restitutionary analysis may also be relevant in cases of interference with land in which *damages* are awarded *in lieu of injunction*. The leading case here is *Wrotham Park Estate Co. Ltd.* v. *Parkside Homes Ltd.*,[206] a case of breach of contract the relevant principles of which are also applicable to tort.[207] In that case, the defendant had built houses in breach of a covenant. The plaintiffs claimed a mandatory injunction[208] for the demolition of the buildings. The injunction was refused but the court awarded damages. It was conceded that the value of the plaintiff's estate was not diminished in consequence of the breach; nonetheless, substantial rather than nominal damages were awarded. The court cited the leading authorities on restitutionary damages, *inter alia* the annotated case. Applying the general rule in contract to calculate a sum of damages which would place the plaintiffs in the same position as if the covenant had not been broken, it was decided that a just substitute for a mandatory injunction would be such a sum of money as might reasonably have been demanded by the plaintiffs as a *quid pro quo* for relaxing the covenants (fixed at 5 per cent of the anticipated profit). Although the judge found that the plaintiffs would not have granted any relaxation, on the facts of the case, the judge felt bound "for present purposes [to] assume that [the plaintiffs] would have been induced to do so".[209]

This approach is called the "hypothetical bargain approach", as it is based on the hypothesis that the plaintiff would have agreed to bargain.[210] It is said that the damages

---

[204] The denomination "user principle" was introduced by Nicholls LJ in *Stoke-on-Trent City Council* v. *W. & J. Wass Ltd.* [1988] 1 WLR 1406, CA at 1416 for the rule that the wrongdoer is liable to pay, as damages, a reasonable sum for the wrongful use he has made of another's property.

[205] *Inverugie Investments Ltd.* v. *Hackett* [1995] 1 WLR 713, [1995] 3 All ER 841, PC at 845.

[206] [1974] 1 WLR 798, [1974] 2 All ER 321, ChD.

[207] *Bracewell* v. *Appleby* [1975] Ch 408, [1975] 2 WLR 282, [1975] 1 All ER 993, ChD; *Carr-Saunders* v. *Dick McNeil Associates Ltd.* [1986] 1 WLR 922, [1986] 2 All ER 888, ChD.

[208] See *infra*, 8.6.

[209] *Wrotham Park Estate Co. Ltd.* v. *Parkside Homes Ltd.* [1974] 1 WLR 798 at 815, [1974] 2 All ER 321 at 341.

[210] A. Burrows, *Remedies for Torts and Breach of Contract*, 2nd edn. (London: Butterworths, 1994) at 298–9.

do not compensate any loss to the plaintiffs, but are best viewed as restitutionary damages.[211] There is, however, an opposite view:[212]

> "I cannot, however, accept that [the] assessment of damages in *Wrotham Park* was based on other than compensatory principles. . . . [The judge] had to assess the damages necessary to compensate the plaintiffs for this continuing invasion of their right. He paid attention to the profits earned by the defendants, as it seems to me, not in order to strip the defendants of their unjust gains, but because of the obvious relationship between the profits earned by the defendants and the sum which the defendants would reasonably have been willing to pay to secure release from the covenant".

(c) The restitutionary approach, or more precisely the hypothetical bargain approach, is also evident in cases of *infringement of an intellectual property right*, e.g. a patent. Where the plaintiff exploits the invention himself, the measure of damages will normally be the profit which would have been realized by the plaintiff if the sales, which he lost due to the infringement, had been made by him. Where the patent is exploited through the granting of a licence for royalty payments, the measure of damages will be the sums which the infringer would have paid by way of royalty if he had acted lawfully.[213] Here also the question arises whether, at common law, the plaintiff is entitled to damages even where he can show no loss, e.g. because he would not have sold patented products in the area where the defendant has sold them. In *Watson Laidlaw & Co. v. Pott, Cassells & Williamson*[214] it was said:

> "There remains that class of business which the respondents would not have done; and in such cases it appears to me that the correct and full measure is only reached by adding that a patentee is also entitled, on the principle of price or hire, to a royalty for the unauthorised sale or use of every one of the infringing machines in a market which the [patentee], if left to himself, might not have reached"

It has been pointed out that this approach aims at the reversal of the defendant's unjust enrichment rather than compensation.[215]

It must be stressed that, in addition to common law damages, an equitable remedy is available *inter alia* for torts involving an infringement of intellectual property rights.[216] This remedy, called an "account of profits", requires the defendant to draw up an account of, and then to pay, the amount of the net profits that he has acquired by the wrongful conduct. This equitable remedy is confined to those torts which have their roots in equity.

---

[211] Burrows, ibid. at 313. This was also the view of Steyn LJ in *Surrey County Council and another v. Bredero Homes Ltd.* [1993] 3 All ER 705 at 714, CA.

[212] *Jaggard v. Sawyer* [1995] 1 WLR 269, CA at 281–2, [1995] 2 All ER 189, CA at 202, per Sir Thomas Bingham MR.

[213] *General Tire and Rubber Co. v. Firestone Tyre and Rubber Co. Ltd.* [1975] 1 WLR 819, HL at 824, [1975] 2 All ER 173, HL at 177–8 per Lord Wilberforce.

[214] (1914) 31 RPC 104, HL at 120 per Lord Shaw; cited in H. McGregor, *McGregor on Damages*, 16th edn. (London: Sweet & Maxwell, 1997) at 1269–70, para. 1958; see also A. Burrows, *Remedies for Torts and Breach of Contract*, 2nd edn. (London: Butterworths, 1994) at 180.

[215] Ibid.

[216] Infringement of a patent, copyright, design right or trademark. This remedy is also available for passing off and breach of confidence: A. Burrows, ibid. at 300.

It has been noted that "this is not a policy justification and it can be argued that the role of an account of profits should be expanded to reverse gains by any deliberate tort".[217]

(3) It is a matter of current debate whether restitutionary damages are available for all torts. In *Stoke-on-Trent City Council* v. *W. & J. Wass Ltd.*,[218] the Court of Appeal refused to grant restitutionary damages in a case of *nuisance*.

In this case, the defendants operated a market without permission from the plaintiff City Council. The Council held markets itself and obtained an injunction restraining the defendant from holding the market. The plaintiff Council could not prove any loss during the period before obtaining the injunction but was entitled, according to the judgment of the court of first instance, to an award of damages calculated by reference to the licence fee that the defendants could reasonably have been required to pay. That judgment was reversed by the Court of Appeal, entitling the plaintiffs only to an award of nominal damages. The reasons for this solution amount to the absence of a sound analogy between the case of infringement of a market right on the one hand and the case of infringement of a patent or a trespass on the other. Nourse LJ[219] was unwilling to innovate in this field of law (an opinion which has, however, been called "particularly unfortunate"[220]):

> "Although I would accept that there may be a logical difficulty in making a distinction between the present case and the way-leave cases, I think that if the user principle were to be applied here there would be an equal difficulty in distinguishing other cases of more common occurrence, particularly in nuisance. . . . And yet the application of that principle to such cases would not only give a right to substantial damages where no loss had been suffered but would revolutionise the tort of nuisance by making it unnecessary to prove loss. . . . It is possible that the English law of tort, more especially of the so-called "proprietary torts", will in due course make a more deliberate move towards recovery based not on loss suffered by the plaintiff but on the unjust enrichment of the defendant: see *Goff and Jones, The Law of Restitution*, 3rd ed. (1986), pp. 612–614. But I do not think that that process can begin in this case and I doubt whether it can begin at all at this level of decision."

Apart from the so-called "proprietary wrongs", the question as to whether and for which torts restitutionary damages are available remains open.[221] However, in a recent report the Law Commission expresses a reserved opinion.[222]

---

[217] Burrows, ibid. See also H. McGregor, "Restitutionary Damages" in P. Birks, (ed.), *Wrongs and Remedies in the Twenty-First Century* (Oxford: Clarendon Press, 1996) at 209 for a discussion of the requirement of deliberate conduct. Rogers at 752: "In any event, we operate perfectly happily with the remedy of account of profits in areas like breach of copyright or breach of confidence and while those wrongs are not commonly regarded as falling squarely into torts that is because of a combination of history and convenience"; and E. Cooke, "Trespass, Mesne Profits and Restitution" (1994) 110 LQR 420 at 430: "More work is needed to show why, if restitution is available as a remedy for trespass to land, that does not in general entitle the plaintiff to an account of profits".

[218] [1988] 1 WLR 1406, CA.

[219] Ibid. at 1415.

[220] See H. McGregor, "Restitutionary Damages" in P. Birks, (ed.), *Wrongs and Remedies in the Twenty-First Century* (Oxford: Clarendon Press, 1996) at 208 and references.

[221] According to McGregor, restitutionary damages should not be restricted to torts which can be classified as proprietary because the essential justification for them is that they ensure that a person is not permitted to profit from his wrong. This result may be achieved by a "rationalisation of the exemplary damages profit exception" which *Rookes* v. *Barnard* allows: H. McGregor, ibid. at 208–9. In a comparable way: A. Burrows, *Remedies for Torts and Breach of Contract*, 2nd edn. (London: Butterworths, 1994) at 306. Conversely, denying that "restitution for wrongs" exists in English law and arguing that the restitutionary duty should arise only in response to proprietary wrongs which involve the user of another's property: N.J. McBride and P. McGrath, "The Nature of Restitution" (1995) 15 OJLS 33 at 45.

[222] See Law Commission Report No. 247, *Aggravated, Exemplary and Restitutionary Damages* (1997) on the availability of restitution for proprietary torts, Part III, section 2(1)(a) and for non-proprietary wrongs, section 2(1)(c). The report concludes that the development of the law on restitution for wrongs is in general best left to

8.2.2. GERMAN LAW

Introductory Note

General provisions relating to the reparation of harm, regardless of the legal foundation of the duty to make good the harm, are found in §§ 249–254 BGB; provisions dealing specifically with tortious liability are laid down in §§ 842 ff. A survey of the general principles of the German law of damages found in §§ 249 ff. will be undertaken in this section. First the principle of *restitutio in integrum* or full reparation will be explored.[223] German law adheres to the primacy of *Naturalrestitution*, which is broadly interpreted in the case-law and includes the restoration of the *status quo ante* through a monetary award. The plaintiff's duty to mitigate damage, under § 254(2) BGB, will then be discussed in connection with a plaintiff's refusal to undergo surgery.[224]

The assessment of *Schmerzensgeld* (damages for non-material loss) is not left entirely to the discretion of the trial judge and is subject to review by the BGH, especially with regard to the judge's duty to give reasons for deviating from awards granted in comparable cases.[225]

Finally, the issue of the extent to which the prevention of unjust enrichment can be reconciled with the compensatory principle will be considered.[226]

BGH, 15 October 1991[227]   **8.G.12.**

REPARATION IN KIND (§ 249 BGB) IN THE CASE OF A DAMAGED CAR

Damaged Porsche

The restoration of damage to a motor vehicle through repair or through the purchase of a replacement car are both forms of reparation in kind under § 249 BGB. It is inherent in the second sentence of § 249 BGB, that in order to be recoverable, the cost of repair must remain within the limits of what is regarded as expedient (zweckmäßig) *and appropriate* (angemessen).

Facts: The plaintiff's car was damaged in an accident caused by the defendant's negligence. The plaintiff had the car repaired in the repairshop of the garage that he himself owned. According to an expert's assessment, the cost of repairs (*Reparaturkosten*) amounted to DEM 93,396.30. As a result of the damage and despite the repairs, the market value of the car was reduced by an estimated DEM 5,000 (*Wertmindering*). The market value of an equivalent car (*Wiederbeschaffungswert*) was DEM 105,000 and the salvage value of the wrecked car (*Restwert*) was DEM 30,000; the net cost to the plaintiff of purchasing a replacement car (*Wiederbeschaffungsaufwand*) would therefore have amounted to DEM 75,000.

the courts (Part III, section 3(1), para. 3.38–3.47, and recommendations (4)–(6)), while the desire is expressed to move towards a single restitutionary remedy for wrongs (para. 3.82–3.84 and recommendation (14)), which should be available where exemplary damages could be awarded (para. 3.48–3.53, recommendations (7)–(8)).

[223] **8.G.12.**
[224] **8.G.13.**
[225] **8.G.14.**
[226] **8.G.15.**
[227] BGHZ 115, 364, NJW 1992, 302, JZ 1992, 480 annotated by H. Lange. Translation by Y. P. Salmon.

Held: The court of appeal awarded the plaintiff only the net cost of buying a replacement car (DEM 75,000) on the ground that the cost of repairs plus the depreciation in value (DEM 98,396.30) exceeded *the cost of replacement* by more than 30 per cent. The judgment was reversed by the BGH on the ground that the cost of repairs and the reduction in value claimed did not exceed *the market value of a replacement car* (DEM 105,000).

Judgment: "II. . . . 1. It was wrong of the court of appeal to fix damages for the plaintiff's damaged car on the basis of the cost of replacement (*Ersatzbeschaffung*) according to § 287(1) ZPO at only DEM 75,000. The plaintiff can claim the repair cost of DEM 93,396 plus the depreciation in value (*Wertminderung*) of DEM 5000 because that expenditure proves to be economically viable when compared with the costs of providing a replacement car.

a) Under the second sentence of § 249 BGB the injured party who takes it into his own hands to restore the original situation, is entitled to claim the requisite sum of money from the wrongdoer. The wrongdoer may give a money compensation for the loss of value sustained only if and insofar as restoration (*Herstellung*) is impossible, is insufficient to remedy the harm (*Entschädigung*) (§ 251(1) BGB) or requires disproportionate levels of expenditure (first sentence of § 251(2) BGB). If *Naturalrestitution* is possible, disproportionality thus sets the limit beyond which the plaintiff is no longer entitled to claim repair (*Naturalrestitution*), but may claim only money compensation for the depreciation in value of his *Vermögen* (*Kompensation*). To that extent, *Naturalrestitution* has priority over monetary compensation.

b) However it is not to be inferred from the scheme of damages law that in the case of damage to a motor vehicle, the plaintiff may always have his car repaired at the expense of the wrongdoer up to the limit of disproportionality. The comparison between cost of restoration (*Restitutionskosten*), on the one hand, and the value of the damaged object as an item of the plaintiff's assets (*als Posten in der Vermögensbilanz*), on the other, is indeed of importance for the setting of the ceiling expressed in the first sentence of § 251(2) BGB up to which the wrongdoer must bear the costs of restoration (*Herstellung*) instead of the plaintiff [references omitted]. However, the decisive question here— whether and, if so, at what level of expenditure the plaintiff may have his car repaired at the expense of the wrongdoer if he can obtain a replacement car of equal value at a lower cost—does not concern the distinction between *Restitution* and *Kompensation*, as will be elaborated below. Indeed the limit on repair costs is not set just by the ceiling of disproportionality expressed in the first sentence of § 251(2) BGB but is already set [without proportionality coming into play] by the purpose of restoration (*Herstellung*) in the first sentence of § 249 BGB and the condition in the second sentence of § 249 BGB that such restoration be requisite (*Erforderlichkeit*).

aa) The plaintiff who takes the restoration of the damage to his motor vehicle into his own hands [as the second sentence of § 249 BGB allows him to do] normally has two means at his disposal: he can have his car repaired or he can acquire a replacement car (of the same value). *As the Chamber has repeatedly stated and affirms once more, the latter form of redress* (Schadensbeseitigung) *is also a form of* Naturalrestitution [references omitted; emphasis added]. For indeed, the objective of restoration (*Restitution*) is not confined just to repair (*(Wieder) Herstellung*) of the damaged *object*; it consists more comprehensively, in accordance with the first sentence of § 249 BGB, in restoring the *situation* which, from an economic perspective would have existed had the harmful event not occurred [emphasis in original; references omitted].

bb) *If there is more than one possible means of achieving redress by way of* Naturalrestitution, *the plaintiff must choose the one which demands the lowest expenditure* [emphasis added]. This principle of economic efficiency (*Wirtschaftlichkeitspostulat*) has also been emphasized many times by the Chamber. It finds its legal embodiment in the requirement, contained in the second sentence of § 249 BGB, that the repair be requisite (*Erforderlichkeit*), but it actually arises from the very concept of harm. For indeed, the injured party's loss . . . *is no greater than the amount which needs to be spent to restore the* Vermögen . . . *in a reasonable way to a condition which is equivalent to the original one* [emphasis added].

The requirement that damage is to be restored in an economically reasonable way does not however mean that the plaintiff has to save money for the benefit of the wrongdoer nor to behave as if he himself has to bear the damage [references omitted]. Nonetheless, the latter standpoint may be of relevance for the question of whether the plaintiff kept the expenditure within reasonable limits [references omitted], *since under the second sentence of § 249 BGB, the wrongdoer is liable to bear only those costs which would appear expedient* (zweckmässig) *and appropriate* (angemessen) *to put right the damage from the standpoint of a sensible, economically-minded person in the position of the injured party* [references omitted; emphasis added]. Certainly, when examining whether the injured party conformed to that course of action, consideration should be given to his particular situation, in particular his individual knowledge and personal means of action as well as the possible particular difficulties facing him, since the second sentence of § 249 BGB postulates the injured party managing the situation himself. However this subject-oriented assessment of damages (*subjektbezogene Schadensbetrachtung*) does not mean that expenditure is to be considered to be inappropriate only from the viewpoint of the duty to mitigate damage as required by § 254(2) BGB: from the outset the duty to give redress (*Schadensersatzpflicht*) already covers only those expenses which remain within the limits of economic reasonableness [references omitted].

cc) Bearing in mind the most economically reasonable way for the plaintiff to effect the repair which he has taken into his own hands, an answer is required to the question whether, and if so to what extent, the repair costs may exceed the costs of acquisition of a replacement vehicle, without exceeding the defendant's duty to pay damages under the second sentence of § 249 BGB. In answering that question, it cannot be objected that, if repairs are actually effected, the economic efficiency of the repair becomes irrelevant . . . This [objection] gives insufficient weight to the fact that replacement, as well as repair, is also a form of *Naturalrestitution* . . .

ee) Above all it must also be borne in mind, that the repair of the plaintiff's trusted car is usually better able to satisfy his interest in preserving the physical condition of his assets (*Integritätsinteresse*) than replacement [references omitted]. *Therefore it is in accordance with the principles of damages law that the plaintiff who decides to effect repair and also provably undertakes it, be awarded the costs of repair* (Instandsetzung) *which exceed, within limits, the cost of replacement* [emphasis added]. . . . As to the extent of this range of tolerance, trial judges have in practice granted an additional 30 per cent at their discretion in accordance with § 287(1) ZPO, and the present Chamber has repeatedly approved that practice [references omitted]. However in the case law of the lower courts and in the literature it is disputed how this range of tolerance is to be calculated: according to one view, in the comparative assessment the (anticipated) costs of repair plus the vehicle's possible further depreciation are to be compared with its replacement *value* (*Wiederbeschaffungswert*), i.e. the full costs of replacement; according to the other view, the comparison is merely to be made with the *out-of-pocket expense* of replacement (*Wiederbeschaffungsaufwand*) i.e. the replacement value minus the salvage value of the damaged vehicle [references omitted; emphasis in original].

The present Chamber has not hitherto needed to answer the question at issue; it falls to be decided now. In so doing the Chamber [takes] the view that in those cases, in which—as here—the plaintiff really effects repair, when comparing repair with replacement, the salvage value (*Restwert*) need not be deducted from the replacement value."

Notes

(1) Unlike English and French law,[228] a clear distinction is drawn in German law between *Naturalrestitution* (reparation in kind or restoration of the *status quo ante*) dealt with in § 249 BGB, and *Kompensation* (compensation in money) dealt with in § 251 BGB.[229]

(a) The defendant's duty to make reparation in kind (*Naturalrestitution*), or restoration, is expressed in the first sentence of § 249 BGB:

> A person who is obliged to make reparation for harm (*Schadensersatz*) must restore the situation which would have existed if the circumstance giving rise to the obligation to make reparation had not occurred.

In principle, the wrongdoer must restore, or procure the restoration of, the *status quo ante*. However, so far as injury to the person and damage to property are concerned, the second sentence of § 249 BGB allows the plaintiff to take restoration into his own hands by entitling him to claim from the wrongdoer the sum of money required for the purpose of restoration (the requisite sum):

> If redress is to be made for injury to a person or damage to property (*Beschädigung einer Sache*), the claimant may demand, in place of restoration, the sum of money required to effect such restoration.

Thus, the plaintiff is not obliged to leave restoration to the defendant: the second sentence of § 249 empowers the plaintiff to choose how restoration is to be achieved (*Ersetzungsbefugnis*),[230] thereby avoiding discussions as to whether the defendant has properly carried out repairs and whether he, the plaintiff, is obliged to accept them.[231] In cases of injury to the person, the plaintiff will obviously want to take his fate into his own hands and will claim the sum of money required to cover the cost of doing so; similarly in cases of damage to property, actual practice is reflected in the second rather than the first sentence of § 249.

The plaintiff is allowed to claim, *from the outset*, the sum of money required to effect restoration only in case of personal injury or damage to property. In other cases, § 250 BGB provides that the plaintiff must set the defendant an adequate time limit (*Fristsetzung*) within which to effect restoration, accompanied by a declaration that he will refuse such restoration if it is not effected within that period, in which case the plaintiff can claim only monetary compensation.[232]

A claim based on § 249 is a claim for restoration (*Herstellungsanspruch*) irrespective of whether the plaintiff claims actual restoration by the defendant under the first sentence or a sum of money for restoration to be effected by himself or herself under the second sentence. In other words, the fact that the second sentence of § 249 allows the plaintiff to claim a sum of money does not alter the purpose of the claim which is to restore the plaintiff's health and property (*Integritätsinteresse* or *Herstellungsinteresse*).

[228] For further comparative material, see von Bar II at para. 131–6.
[229] See annotated judgment at II.1.a).
[230] And even to leave the damaged property unrepaired (*Dispositionsfreiheit, infra* 8.4).
[231] BGH, 29 October 1974, BGHZ 63, 182 at 184.
[232] It is questionable whether such monetary compensation is the requisite sum of money mentioned in the second sentence of § 249 or rather the compensation in money mentioned in § 251. See Lange at 231–3; Larenz at 473; Münchener-Grunsky, § 250 at para. 2.

§ 249 is also understood to safeguard the plaintiff's *non-material interests*: § 253 BGB, which provides that money compensation (*Entschädigung in Geld*) for non-material harm is available *only* in cases determined by statute, is held to cover only money compensation in the sense of § 251 (*Kompensation*) and not restoration or the sum of money required for the purpose of restoration under either the first or the second sentence of § 249.[233]

In case of *personal injury, Naturalrestitution* may consist e.g. in medical treatment to enable the victim to recover, or to mitigate suffering, including costs incurred by relatives in visiting the injured person, or in measures to improve the injured person's condition (nursing, prosthesis, . . .). Under § 249 BGB, the plaintiff can claim also the cost of rehabilitation or retraining to recover his earning capacity.[234] In case of *loss of* or *damage to property, Naturalrestitution* consists in repair or replacement.[235] Examples of reparation in kind of *non-material harm* are the retraction of defamatory allegations and the return of all copies of a handwritten letter unlawfully obtained.[236]

(b) § 251(1) BGB deals with compensation in money (*Kompensation*). It states:

When restoration is impossible or insufficient to make good the harm suffered by the creditor, the person obliged to make reparation must indemnify the creditor in money

to which the first sentence of § 251(2) adds that:

Where restoration is possible only at a disproportionate cost, the person obliged to make reparation may indemnify the creditor through compensation in money.[237]

A claim under § 251 is called a *Kompensationsanspruch* and as the name suggests, its aim is not restoration (*Naturalrestitution*) but compensation (*Kompensation*). The award is intended to safeguard the plaintiff's interest in *the value* of his assets (*Wertinteresse* or *Summeninteresse*) and is therefore assessed on the basis of the depreciation of the plaintiff's estate (*Vermögen*).[238] As already mentioned, in contradistinction to *Naturalrestitution* (§ 249), money compensation in the sense of § 251 is available for *non-material harm* only where there is a statutory provision to that effect (§ 253).

In providing that compensation in money (*Kompensation*) is to be paid when restoration (*Naturalrestitution*) is impossible or insufficient, § 251(1) BGB takes into consideration *the plaintiff's interest* in not being left without compensation. Conversely, § 251(2) takes into consideration *the defendant's interest* in not being burdened with restoration when, though possible, it is achievable only at disproportionate cost.[239]

(c) It follows from §§ 249 and 251 (1) and (2) BGB that the plaintiff is primarily entitled to the restoration of the *status quo ante* (*Naturalrestitution*)—as to the form restoration may take, see Note (2)—and that the plaintiff must be satisfied with money compensation (*Kompensation*) only if, and insofar as, restoration is impossible or insuffi-

---

[233] Lange at 212–13; Münchener-Grunsky, § 249 at para. 2 and 13a.
[234] Lange at 308–10; Münchener-Grunsky, § 249 at para. 6. When those costs are *recurrent*, they also fall under § 843(1) BGB, dealing specifically with tortious liability: see *infra*, **8.G.41.**, Note (3).
[235] Münchener-Grunsky, § 249 at para. 7 and *infra*, Note (2)(a).
[236] Lange at 217.
[237] In 1990, § 251(2) BGB was amended so as to add: "Expenses incurred in the treatment of an injured animal are not disproportionate merely because they considerably exceed the animal's value".
[238] For the notion of *Vermögen*, see *supra*, Chapter I, **1.G.26.–27.**, Note (1).
[239] Münchener-Grunsky, § 251 at para. 1.

cient to remedy the harm,[240] or requires disproportionate expenditure. By giving priority to *Naturalrestitution*, the German law of damages aims to safeguard in full both the plaintiff's material *and* non-material interests (*Integritätsinteresse*), irrespective of whether the injury has actually caused a reduction in the plaintiff's estate (*Vermögen*). So for example, a claim for restoration is available for bodily harm even where the plaintiff's income or prospects of advancement are not affected by it.[241] But, if the plaintiff is to be satisfied with money compensation (*Kompensation*), then the measure of damages lies in the depreciation in value of the plaintiff's estate (*Wertinteresse*); in that case, non-material harm is also recoverable, though *only* in cases where there is a statutory provision to that effect (§ 253 BGB).

Although both the second sentence of § 249 and § 251 provide for monetary awards, they have, as stated above, different aims (which also explains the considerable differences in the size of awards in some instances).[242] §§ 249 and 251 BGB may be combined. For instance, where the value of a piece of property is reduced despite the repairs, the plaintiff may claim, in addition to the cost of repairs under § 249, money compensation for the depreciation in value under § 251 BGB.

(d) As recalled in the annotated judgment,[243] where restoration, though possible, is achievable only at disproportionate cost, the proportionality rule laid down in § 251(2) operates as a limit to *Naturalrestitution* provided in § 249, from where *Kompensation* under § 251 enters into effect.

The distinction between *Naturalrestitution* and *Kompensation*, the ensuing differences in the size of the awards and the application of the proportionality rule are reflected in the following examples.

A judgment of the BGH of 13 May 1975[244] concerned an environmentally valuable tree that had been tortiously destroyed; the BGH held that the owner of the land on which the tree stood could claim the cost of restoration[245]—consisting in planting a tree of (nearly) the same age (which was possible, although very expensive)—only if, having regard to the kind, status and function of the tree, a sensible, economically-minded (*wirtschaftlich vernünftig*), person would have done so. In that case, the cost of planting a forty-year-old chestnut tree would have amounted to about DEM 16,000. The BGH upheld the judgment entitling the plaintiff to claim only, by way of partial restoration (*Teilwiederherstellung*), the cost of planting a five-year-old tree (DEM 420) and, by way of money compensation (*Kompensation*), damages amounting to the resulting decrease in value of the plot of land (the case being sent to another court for final assessment of the award).

In a judgment of 8 December 1987, [246] relating to a house that has been burnt down,[247] the

---

[240] Insufficient restoration within the meaning of § 251(1) BGB is of little importance. Where restoration is only partially possible, the plaintiff may claim additional compensation in money. An example of a possible, though insufficient, restoration is where restoration would take an unreasonably long period of time: Münchener-Grunsky, § 251 at para. 5.

[241] Lange at 211.

[242] Ibid. at 213 and *infra*, Note (1)(d).

[243] At II.1.b).

[244] VersR 1975, 1047.

[245] The BGH held that *Naturalrestitution* of a destroyed tree (which is not fungible) remains possible. The tree is only a part of the plot of land and it is the plot of land which must be restored.

[246] BGHZ 102, 322.

[247] In such a case, the only possible means of redress by way of *Naturalrestitution* is repair. As in the case of the destroyed tree mentioned in the text, the BGH held that *Naturalrestitution* remains possible even when the house has been completely destroyed since it is the plot of land including the house (and not the house as such)

question of disproportion was answered by comparing the cost of restoration (reduced on account of the advantage of getting new for old) with the pre-existing market value of the damaged property (*Verkehrswert, Wiederbeschaffungswert*). However, in deciding whether restoration requires disproportionate expenditure, the plaintiff's non-material interest in being enabled to go on living at the same place will also be taken into account.[248]

In case of personal injury, there is an inherent difficulty in carrying out an economic weighing of the plaintiff's non-material interest in his health against the material interests of the defendant, but that does not mean that the proportionality rule laid down in § 251(2) does not apply. But the defendant's material interest will only exceptionally outweigh the plaintiff's *Integritätsinteresse*. In a case decided by the BGH,[249] the court dismissed, on the ground of disproportionality, a claim by a plaintiff for the cost of cosmetic surgery (DEM 2950) to remove a small scar, to which he would have been entitled under § 249 BGB.[250] As a consequence, the plaintiff was entitled to only an award of money compensation for his non-material harm (§§ 253 and 847 BGB) of DEM 400.

(e) Finally, it must be noted that the principles of the German law of damages, as formulated in §§ 249, 251 and 253 BGB, are expressed or implemented in other provisions.

By virtue of § 252(1) BGB, the plaintiff is entitled to claim compensation for *lost profits*. That rule is considered to be a mere application of the *Differenzmethode* according to which recoverable material damage amounts to the difference between the plaintiff's financial position after the harmful event and that which would have existed had the harmful event not occurred.[251] Thus, the owner of a car which is used for the provision of commercial services, e.g. a taxi, may claim, in addition to the cost of repairs of the damaged car (§ 249), compensation for profits lost during the period needed for repair (§ 252). §§ 842–843(1) implement the same principle in the context of loss of income. The second sentence of § 252 BGB lessens the onus of proof regarding the extent of harm by providing that lost profits are those which could *probably* have been expected in the ordinary course of things or in the light of the special circumstances of the case.[252]

With regard to non-material harm, § 847 BGB provides that the injured person is entitled to compensation in money in cases of injury to body or health or deprivation of liberty.

(2) (a) The annotated case deals with restoration (*Naturalrestitution*) in cases of damage to a motor vehicle. It relates more specifically to the relationship between two means of restoration that are available to the plaintiff, namely repair of the damaged car and replacement by a car of the same value: the BGH regards both as forms of *Naturalrestitution*. For, indeed, § 249 BGB does not require restoration of the damaged *object* as such but requires a restoration of the *situation* which would have existed had the harmful event not occurred.[253]

which must be "restored". However, the *BGH* draws a distinction between a reconstruction of the house (*Wiederaufbau*) falling within *Naturalrestitution* and the building of a new house (*Neubau*), falling outside the scope of *Naturalrestitution* (BGHZ 102, 322 at 328–9).

[248] Lange at 418; see also BGHZ 102, 322 at 327.

[249] BGH, 3 December 1974, BGHZ 63, 295.

[250] For a discussion of the circumstances which are to be taken into account, see ibid.at 300–1.

[251] Compare Larenz at 492; Münchener-Grunsky, § 252 at para. 1; H. Kötz, *Deliktsrecht*, 7th edn. (Neuwied: Luchterhand, 1996) at 206, para. 530. See also *infra*, **8.G.32.**, Note (1).

[252] See *infra*, **8.G.42.**, Note (2).

[253] At II.1.b) aa). In the same way, the earlier judgment BGH, 20 June 1972, *NJW* 1972, 1800. See Münchener-Grunksy, § 251 at para. 4: Grunsky criticizes the analysis described in the text, emphasizing that only in the case of fungible goods (*vertretbare Sachen*) can restoration of the *status quo ante* be achieved by replacing the damaged object by another object of the same description; such treatment cannot be extended to used motor-cars since a complete equivalence can never be achieved. When *Naturalrestitution* includes

(b) As the BGH emphasized, its judgment deals with the choice between two means of *Naturalrestitution*, and not with the distinction between *Naturalrestitution* and *Kompensation*,[254] but that does not mean that it is not necessary, here too, to consider the issue of disproportionate expense. In that case however, it is the principle of economic efficiency (*Wirtschaftlichkeitspostulat*) which requires the plaintiff "if there is more than one possible means of achieving redress by way of *Naturalrestitution* . . . to choose the one which demands the lowest expenditure".[255] It finds its legal embodiment "in the requirement, contained in the second sentence of §249 BGB, that the repair be requisite but it actually arises from the very concept of harm".[256]

(c) The concept of economic appropriateness (*Wirtschaftlichkeit*) introduces a normative (and restrictive) element into the concept of damage, making it unnecessary to invoke the duty to mitigate damage[257] as a device to restrict the defendant's duty to restore the *status quo ante*, by holding that "*from the outset* the duty to give redress covers only those expenses which remain within the limits of economic reasonableness [emphasis added]".[258] It is obvious, however, that the normative approach and the duty to mitigate damage express the same rationale, i.e. that the plaintiff is not allowed to burden the defendant with the reimbursement of unreasonable (and thus presumably avoidable) expenses.

In a judgment of 23 March 1976,[259] the BGH stressed that the duty to choose the most economic means of redress (*die Pflicht zur Auswahl des wirtschaftlichsten Wegs*) is not founded on the plaintiff's duty to mitigate damage under § 254(2) BGB. Whilst the duty to mitigate damage deals with limiting the harm itself, the duty to choose the most cost-effective means of redress deals with the question of what expenses are to be recognized as reasonably required for the purpose of redress in the circumstances of the case.[260] However, in a judgment of 7 May 1996[261], when considering whether the cost of hire of a substitute car during repair was "requisite", the BGH recognized the similarity between the normative approach and the duty to mitigate damage.

Such a normative approach does not however result in an assessment of damages which excludes consideration of the individual characteristics of the plaintiff and the circumstances under which he acts.[262] The *subjektbezogene Schadensbetrachtung* (subject-oriented assessment of damage), as it is called in the annotated judgment,[263] is held to be inherent in the provision of the second sentence of § 249 dealing with a plaintiff

---

replacement of destroyed property by similar property of the same value, the question arises whether the plaintiff is still entitled to claim the requisite sum of money under the second sentence of § 249 which, indeed, refers only to injury to a person or *damage* to a thing (*Beschädigung einer Sache*) and *not* to a total loss (*Zerstörung*): H. Lange, note to the annotated judgment, JZ 1992, 480. This question is explicitly left open in BGH, 10 July 1984, BGHZ 92, 84 at 87–8, JZ 1985, 39, annotated by D. Medicus.

[254] At II.1.b).
[255] At II.1.b) bb).
[256] Ibid.
[257] See *infra*, **8.G.13.**
[258] Annotated judgment under II.1.b) bb) *in fine*.
[259] BGHZ, 66, 239 at 248.
[260] The same wording as in the annotated judgment can be found in BGH, 24 April 1990, BGHZ 111, 168 at 178.
[261] BGH, 7 May 1996, JZ 1996, 1075 at 1076.
[262] BGH, 29 October 1974, BGHZ 63, 182 at 184.
[263] At II.1.b) bb).

managing the situation himself. This *subjektbezogene Schadensbetrachtung* is rightly considered to be a prerequisite for the realization of full reparation for the plaintiff.[264]

(d) Weighing the elements which may help a plaintiff to choose between two available means of redress by way of *Naturalrestitution*, the BGH further observes, in the annotated judgment, that repairing the car frequently amounts to a more effective safeguard of the plaintiff's *Integritätsinteresse* than the purchase of a substitute. It therefore accepts that the cost of repairs may exceed the replacement value (*Wiederbeschaffungswert*), albeit within a limit of no more than 30 per cent, as acknowledged in the BGH case law.[265]

In gauging whether repair rather than replacement is "reasonable", it is not necessary to take the salvage value of the car into account.[266] In justifying this solution, the BGH, in a part of the judgment not reproduced, notes the importance of a simple and practicable yardstick to cope with the "mass phenomenon of road traffic accidents".[267]

The plaintiff is entitled to such an authorized excess, called the "*Integritätszuschlag*", only when two conditions are met. First, the car must actually be repaired[268] and secondly, the cost of repair must not exceed the replacement value by more than 30 per cent. As a consequence, a plaintiff who has his car repaired at a cost that exceeds by more than 30 per cent the cost of replacement, is entitled to recover only a sum equivalent to the cost of replacement,[269] since in such a case repairs are no longer "economically meaningful" and the defendant is not to be burdened with a cost which is not requisite (*erforderlich*). W. Grunsky[270] questions the need of the *Integritätszuschlag*, suggesting that such an award may signify the protection of a mere sentimental interest (*bloßes Affektionsinteresse*) which has no place in the law of damages.[271]

---

[264] BGH, 7 May 1996, JZ 1996, 1075 at 1076.

[265] At II.1.b) ee).

[266] Ibid. See also H. Lange, comment on BGH, 15 October 1991, JZ 1992, 480 at 481.

[267] See BGH, 15 October 1991, NJW 1992, 302 at 304; BGH, 15 October 1991, NJW 1992, 305 at 306. It may be noted that the cost of hiring a substitute during repairs may be taken into account in comparing the cost of repairs and the cost of replacement (BGH, 15 October 1991, NJW 1992, 302 at 305). If the damaged car is not repaired, the salvage value is to be taken into account in the computation of the (final) cost of replacement.

[268] BGH, 5 March 1985, NJW 1985, 2469.

[269] BGH, 15 October 1991, NJW 1992, 305, JZ 1992, 481, annotated by H. Lange, BGHZ 115, 375. Where the cost of repair cannot be recovered, the plaintiff is entitled to the actual cost of replacement only, that is the full cost of replacement less the salvage value of the damaged car.

[270] W. Grunsky, comment on BGH, 17 March 1992, JZ 1992, 806 at 807. The BGH decision concerns the plaintiff who carries out repairs himself; such a plaintiff is also entitled to the "*Integritätszuschlag*" on the estimated cost of repairs which would have been paid had repairs been carried out in a garage. W. Grunsky's annotation gives an overview of the settled and unresolved issues surrounding the "*Integritätszuschlag*".

[271] Compare Pennycuick J's *dictum* in *Darbishire v. Warran, supra,* **8.E.8.**, Note (2)

BGH, 13 May 1953[272] **8.G.13.**

Surgery or retraining

A plaintiff is under a duty to undergo surgery "if it is simple and safe, not connected with exceptional pain, and offers the certain prospect of cure or substantial improvement". A plaintiff who is not under a duty to undergo surgery, may nonetheless be under a duty to retrain in order to exercise a suitable profession.

Facts: The plaintiff was severely injured in a car accident and could no longer exercise his profession as a car-fitter. The defendants contended that the plaintiff had to undergo surgery or at least retrain to regain his capacity for work. The plaintiff claimed to be entitled to refuse this.

Held: The court of appeal found that the plaintiff was entitled to refuse both surgery and retraining. The BGH partially reversed the judgment with regard to the refusal to be retrained.

Judgment: "I. With respect to the preconditions under which an injured person is to be expected to undergo medical surgery, the court of appeal follows the established case law of the *Reichsgericht*, which is not disputed by the appellant. Likewise this Chamber sees no reason to depart from that case law. Accordingly, the plaintiff can be expected to undergo medical surgery only if it is simple and safe, not connected with exceptional pain, and offers the certain prospect of cure or substantial improvement.

In the case at hand, the court of appeal found that there was not a certain prospect of substantial improvement. It is possible to assess the chances of success of the surgery only in the light of its desired aim. Here, the amputation would be intended to improve the plaintiff's ability to walk, so that he could offset or reduce his loss of earnings by learning to become an office machine mechanic. However, since the court of appeal doubts . . . whether any significant reduction of the damage is possible, an appraisal which is left to the trial court, it was entitled to conclude, without error in law, that there was no certain prospect of success. But in the absence [of such prospects of success] it was correct in law to hold that the plaintiff cannot be expected to undergo an above-the-knee leg amputation, more particularly for the subjective reasons explained below. . . .

II. However, the court of appeal did not take into account the fact that the defendants suggested to the plaintiff not only post-operative retraining, but also retraining *without* any medical intervention [emphasis in original]. Clearly, the offer to provide the plaintiff, following retraining as an office machine mechanic, with the necessary tools to exercise that occupation from home also extended to retraining without surgery. *Insofar as the defendants demand that the plaintiff submit to retraining without amputation, different principles apply to those which would apply had they demanded a fundamental interference with his physical integrity.* In principle, the victim is obliged to make profitable use of any capacity to work that he may possess. He cannot require the wrongdoer to pay him lifelong periodical payments on account of the accident, if he does not make use of his capacity to work, as it exists or may be restored with a reasonable effort. Rather, the victim must make serious endeavours to avert loss as far as possible, which includes if necessary undertaking a change of occupation with or without retraining. The victim must discharge this duty in good faith (*nach Treu und Glauben*) [references omitted] . . . In order to determine what can be expected of the victim, account should be taken of his personal circumstances and the need for family members to

---

[272] BGHZ 10, 18. Translation by Y. P. Salmon.

take care of him, as well as his chances of being able to mitigate at least part of the loss through the new occupation [references omitted; emphasis added].

When it comes to the mitigation of damage (*Pflicht zur Schadensminderung*), the duty to undergo surgery differs from the duty to submit to retraining in one important respect, namely that the victim is to be expected to retrain as soon as any chance of success exists. Nonetheless, the chances of success may influence the demands on the injured party in the case of the duty to retrain as well. The less the prospect that the loss would be mitigated, according to the type of possible retraining and the expected situation on the labour market, the less also the duty on the part of the victim to prepare himself to pursue a new occupation. In this context, the age of the victim, his marital status and the type of injury may also be significant. However, the victim can in principle be required to leave his family for a shorter or longer period in order to take part in retraining, especially if it remains possible for him to visit his family on occasion and if the wrongdoer is willing to bear the related costs."

Notes

(1) The plaintiff's duty to mitigate damage is expressly stated in § 254(2) BGB where it is presented as an application of the general rule, laid down in § 254(1) concerning the legal consequences of *Mitverschulden* (contributory fault), on the duty to make reparation.[273] The excerpted judgment deals with the duty to undergo surgery and the duty to retrain; the scope of that duty has been examined in various cases.[274]

It may be noted that, as in English law, there has been discussion of the question whether it is appropriate to consider the plaintiff's failure to mitigate damage as a "*Verschulden*", a breach of "duty". German academic legal writers have proposed various theoretical explanations: "*Verschulden*" towards the defendant, "*Verschulden*" of the plaintiff towards himself ("*Verschulden gegen sich selbst*") and breach of an "*Obliegenheit*".[275] According to H. Lange's formulation, it would appear that English and German law take a similar approach to the underlying principle and its practical consequences: "Although the law does not command one to take reasonable care of one's own interests, it does however refuse to allow the consequences of a failure to do so to fall to the expense of another".[276]

(2) In a judgment of 15 March 1994,[277] the BGH confirmed the approach taken in the annotated judgment, and ruled that a plaintiff may not be held to be under a duty to minimize the damage by undergoing an operation on the basis of medical opinion alone.

---

[273] See *supra*, Chapter VII, 7.1.

[274] See for a discussion of case law with regard to other duties to mitigate damage: Lange at 577–90.

[275] See Lange at 549–53. *Obliegenheiten* are defined as "Duties of a lesser intensity, observance of which cannot be enforced, but of which neglect nonetheless has legal consequences": Lange at 552, see also *supra*, Chapter VII.

[276] Lange at 553–4; compare *supra*, **8.E.8.**, Note (1).

[277] NJW 1994, 1592.

ASSESSMENT OF *SCHMERZENSGELD*

Youngster permanently injured

Though the assessment of Schmerzensgeld *is basically a matter for the trier of fact, his or her assessment is subject to review by the BGH, especially with regard to his or her duty to give reasons for deviating from awards granted in comparable cases.*

Facts: The plaintiff, who was a passenger in a car, suffered serious and permanent injury in an accident in which the driver of the vehicle was killed. The plaintiff, who was fifteen years old at the time of the accident, claimed *Schmerzensgeld* amounting to a lump sum of at least DEM 20,000 and monthly periodical payments of DEM 150, from the deceased driver's insurance company.

Held: Both the court of first instance and the court of appeal awarded a lump sum of DEM 30,000 and a monthly periodical payment of DEM 300. The BGH reversed the judgment of the court of appeal.

Judgment: "II. . . . 1. Certainly this court must exert particular restraint when reviewing the assessment of *Schmerzensgeld*, essentially because 'it cannot as such be determined whether [the level of] compensation for non-material harm is reasonable or not, given that such harm is not directly assessable in monetary terms' [references omitted].

The measure of fair compensation (*billige Entschädigung*) within the meaning of § 847 BGB must thus be assessed anew in the light of the circumstances of each individual case, taking into account the function of such compensation, namely redress (*Ausgleich*) and satisfaction. In so doing, the tension between the interests of the victim and the economic capacity of the wrongdoer—seen also from a macro-economic perspective—is to be taken into consideration as well. Consequently, it is in principle in the province of the trier of fact to assess the amount and type of *Schmerzensgeld* to be awarded, and for that purpose he is specifically released from [the general rules on evidence and on the burden of proof by] § 287 ZPO. [279] As a matter of principle, his award cannot be challenged for the mere reason that it appears insufficient or, as is the case here, excessive. In this respect, the BGH cannot substitute its assessment for that of the trier of fact.

Nevertheless, the discretion of the trier of fact is not boundless; he is not allowed to make an arbitrary determination of Schmerzensgeld, *but rather he must indicate how he endeavoured to award adequate compensation in the light of the harmful event* [emphasis added]. He must give complete consideration to all the circumstances that are relevant to the level of the *Schmerzensgeld*, and his reasoning must not violate rules of law, logic or experience [references omitted]. Certainly, he is not precluded from awarding lower or higher sums than those hitherto granted in similar cases if it appears necessary to him in the circumstances—particularly in view of economic developments or changing general values. But then the trial judge must give reasons for it and, in so doing, he must not lose sight of the economic interests of the liable party; in particular, he must make clear that he [references omitted] also took into consideration within sensible limits, to the victim's advantage, any liability insurance on the part of the wrongdoer, while not forgetting that in the end the burden of expansive damages awards falls to be borne by the community of insurance policyholders . . .

2. . . . c) The capitalized periodical payments award fixed by the court of appeal . . . amounts to a payment of . . . DEM 67,676. Altogether, [the plaintiff] has thus been awarded a *Schmerzensgeld*

---

[278] VersR 1976, 967. Translation by Y. P. Salmon.

[279] First sentence of Art. 287(1) ZPO: "If the existence or extent of the harm or the interest to be restored is disputed by the parties, the court will decide freely on the matter, by an assessment of all the circumstances of the case."

of almost DEM 100,000. Such amounts have generally hitherto been granted only in cases of [injuries having] very serious and continuing consequences. The court of appeal rightly stressed that the injuries suffered by the plaintiff qualify as grave injuries, especially in view of the loss of her senses of smell and taste, the change in her personality and her young age, meaning that she must permanently bear such a considerable limitation in her world of experience (*Erlebenssphäre*). Nevertheless, as this Chamber is qualified to say on the basis of a decade-long experience in cases concerning *Schmerzensgeld*, in terms of seriousness the fate of this plaintiff cannot be classified in the uppermost category of non-material harm . . .

The court of appeal also had to come to grips with such considerations as required by the principles of legal certainty and equal treatment, which despite the diversity of cases must come to bear in the assessment of *Schmerzensgeld* as well."

Notes

(1) This judgment echoes a concern seen in English case law for consistency in awards for non-material harm.[280] Thus, the BGH while recognizing the role of the trial judge, reserves the right to review the assessment of *Schmerzensgeld* to some extent, emphasizing the duty of the trial judge to give reasons for an assessment which departs from those in comparable cases. Such an assessment must also take account of the interests of the defendant and the defendant's insurer, that is, indirectly, of the community of insurance policyholders (*Versicherten-Gemeinschaft*) which ultimately carries the burden of damages awards.

(2) In the annotated judgment, the BGH disapproved of the assessment of the trial judge on various grounds, in sharp contrast to the restrictive powers which the French Cour de cassation reserves to itself.[281] These reasons are explored in the excerpt. Moreover, in a part of the judgment not reproduced here, the BGH requires that, when the judge grants both a lump sum (in this case for the first period of one and a half years) and periodical payments (in this case for the period thereafter) by way of *Schmerzensgeld*, the two awards should be harmonized (*ein angemessenes Verhältnis*). In the annotated case, that requirement was not met, according to the BGH.

BGH, 8 October 1971[282] **8.G.15.**

ABSTRACT ASSESSMENT OF DAMAGES IN CASE OF SLAVISH IMITATION

Electrical wall sockets

The infringement of certain intellectual property rights may lead to an assessment of damages not only on the basis of actual harm, including the loss of profits suffered by the plaintiff, but also on the basis of an appropriate licence fee or the profits realized by the wrongdoer. Due to the similarities between slavish imitation and an infringement of intellectual property rights, damages may be assessed on the basis of a reasonable licence fee also in cases of slavish imitation.

---

[280] See *supra*, **8.E.10.**
[281] See *infra*, **8.F.19.**, Note.
[282] BGHZ 57, 116. Translation by Y. P. Salmon.

Facts: The defendant was found liable for the slavish imitation (*sklavischer Nachahmung*) of electrical wall sockets manufactured by the plaintiff. The plaintiff claimed damages amounting to an appropriate licence fee (*Lizenzgebühr*).

Held: The court of appeal awarded the plaintiff damages assessed as an appropriate licence fee, at 2.5 per cent of the net returns (*Nettoverkaufserlös*) realized by the defendant. The BGH upheld that judgment.

Judgment: "II. 1. According to a constant line of authorities of the *Reichsgericht* [references omitted] which has been followed by the BGH . . . [references omitted], the harm caused by the wrongful infringement of another's copyright, patent, utility model or ornamental design rights, may be calculated in three ways: as the plaintiff's actual loss, including the lost profit (§§ 249, 252 BGB); alternatively as a lost appropriate licence fee, or, yet again, the wrongdoer's gain (*Verletzergewinn*) can be claimed. As has been repeatedly emphasized in the aforementioned case-law (see further BGHZ 20, 345, 353—Paul Dahlke; 44, 372, 374—Meßmer Tee II) these are particular methods of assessing damages and not independent causes of action.

. . .

The reasons which led to the recognition that assessment of damages (*Schadensberechnung*) for [infringement of] the exclusive industrial property rights mentioned above should use as a basis the lost licence fee and the wrongdoer's gain, result from the character of these industrial property rights with their particular vulnerability and the injured party's resulting special need for protection [references omitted]. Because of the incorporeal nature of the protected legal interests—by contrast with physical objects—the holder of the right cannot take precautions against infringements; furthermore he can often ascertain the infringements only with difficulty and finally proof of a certain lost profit frequently poses particular difficulties for him, since the hypothetical course of events ([which would have occurred] but for the intervention of the wrongdoer) cannot be reconstructed so easily. However, a fairly sure basis for this [assessment] results from the fact that the industrial property rights, which reserve certain forms of exploitation exclusively to the holder of the right and exclude all others from this exploitation, are also intrinsically and usually exploitable by way of the grant of a royalty-bearing licence (*Lizenzvergabe*)—apart from or instead of direct exploitation; hence the licence [fee] saved by the wrongdoer represents the lost profits (*Gewinnentgang*) of the holder of the right. Furthermore, due to the exclusive character of an industrial property right it can be assumed, on the basis of common experience of life that, in exploitation of his own right, the holder of the right would have received what the wrongdoer obtained through the use of the other's industrial property right.

This case law supplement to the general rules of the law relating to damages for the assessment of loss in cases of infringement of copyright, patent, utility model and ornamental design rights thereby meets a practical need which arises because of the nature of the particular interest [that has been infringed] and the consideration that, as a matter of fairness, no one is to be placed in a better position through an infringement of such rights, than if he had sought and been given the permission of the holder of the right. The same position with regard to the interest [that has been infringed] may also be present in relation to other non-physical exclusive proprietary rights . . .

This legal viewpoint is to be adhered to.

2. By contrast, the case at hand concerns the wider question of whether an assessment of damages on the basis of the lost licence fee is also possible in cases in which the injured party had no (exclusive) industrial property right, and it was only his competitive position that was unlawfully infringed [references omitted].

. . . [The BGH summarizes the view of the court of appeal on the similarities and dissimilarities between a position protected merely by the law of unfair competition (*eine nur wettbewerbsrechtlich geschützten Position*) and industrial property rights (*Immaterialgüterrechten*)]

799

The difference in the protected interests militates against a general, indiscriminate transfer of the principles of industrial property law into the law of unfair competition. This also holds true for the principles of assessment of damages which were developed for infringements of exclusive industrial property rights due to their special nature and to accommodate the holder of the right's special need for protection. A breach of the law relating to unfair competition cannot be directly equated with an infringement of such an exclusive right . . . [references omitted].

Nevertheless, a position analogous to an industrial property right can also arise in the law relating to unfair competition, if the imitation of the product of another's intellectual effort is not only legally prohibited in relation to one particular competitor who commits an act of unfair competition but, because of the special value to be attributed to protection (*Schutzwert*) of the copied product, is also forbidden to all others under the law relating to unfair competition. In such a case, that is where the product of the other's intellectual effort merits protection in its concrete form because of its specific nature and may not be exploited by the wrongdoer or a third party, a similar protection is granted as in the case of an industrial property right despite the absence of an exclusive right. For this reason, licensing is also usual for the exploitation of the other's product and is recognized by the legal order [references omitted], since a legal position [*Rechtsposition*] can be granted to the licensee, from which any third party is excluded. Thus, slavish imitation [*sklavischen Nachahmung*] which is forbidden to all under the law relating to unfair competition because of the value to be attributed to protection (*Schutzwert*) of the copied product, also results in a position with regard to the protected interests similar to that which arises from an infringement of industrial property rights. The entitled person has a legal position in respect of the product of his intellectual effort, which is protected against others (even if only by virtue of the law of unfair competition), and must be valued in the same way as the position of the holder of an industrial property right regarding its increased vulnerability and the difficulties faced in proving damage. This congruity on the basis of the position with regard to the protected interests in such cases governed by the law of unfair competition, justifies the adoption of the methods of assessment of damages on the basis of the lost licence fee that is recognized for infringements of industrial property rights."

Notes

(1) The excerpted case ranks among numerous others dealing mainly with exclusive rights, in particular intellectual and industrial property rights. Such case-law turns around the same issues as those English cases concerning "proprietary wrongs".[283] May damages be assessed on the basis of the profit which the defendant obtained by the wrong, assuming that that profit corresponds to the plaintiff's loss (even when that is a mere assumption)? Is such a method of assessment of damages still in line with the fundamental principle of reparation, or does it reflect another purpose, namely the prevention of unjust enrichment?

The annotated judgment states that in cases of infringement of copyright, patents and utility model and ornamental design rights (*Patent-, Gebrauchsmuster-, Geschmacksmuster- und Urheberrechte*) there are three ways of assessing damages: 1) on

---

[283] See *supra*, **8.E.11.**, Notes. It may be noted that, under German law, this discussion concerns only intellectual property rights and certain analogous cases. In German law, a case such as *Strand Electric and Engineering Co. Ltd.* falls under the law of unjust enrichment (see Larenz/Canaris at 172–3; E. von Caemmerer, "Bereicherung und unerlaubte Handlung" in *Festschrift für Ernst Rabel*, I (Tübingen: Mohr, 1954), 333 at 358). Leaving the industrial property cases aside, there is no room for a concept of notional damage in the German law of damages (see *infra*, 8.4).

the basis the plaintiff's actual loss (*konkreter Schaden*) including loss of profits; 2) by reference to a reasonable licence fee; and 3) on the basis of the profits realized by the wrong-doer. The latter two methods, deemed acceptable by the BGH because of the specific characteristics of industrial property rights,[284] are "abstract" in that damages are assessed without reference to the "concrete" circumstances of the case, i.e. without the need to prove actual loss.[285] As the excerpt shows, the measure of damages is founded largely on general assumptions based on "common experience of life" ("*nach der Lebenser-fahrung*").[286] In the case of an infringement of an industrial property right it is assumed that, had the defendant acted lawfully, he would have had to pay a licence fee, or that the plaintiff himself, rather than the defendant, would have realized the profit from the exploitation of the right. It would be unfair to place the wrongdoer in a better position than someone who had obtained a licence from the owner of the right[287] (thus also Denning LJ in *Strand Electric and Engineering*: "The wrongdoer cannot be better off because he did not ask permission. He cannot be better off by doing wrong than he would be by doing right"[288]).

(2) The method of abstract assessment of damages adopted for the industrial property rights referred to above, has been extended to cases in which other exclusive rights are infringed.

In the *Paul Dahlke* case,[289] in which an actor's image was used for publicity purposes without his permission, the BGH held that such permission is usually given only for a considerable sum and that the defendant's conduct constituted "an inadmissible infringement of another's exclusive *valuable* (*vermögenswertes*) right" [emphasis in original] to which the rule with regard to infringement of intellectual property rights applies. The BGH allowed damages for *material* harm (whereas it was not prepared, at the time, to grant damages for *non-material* harm).[290] However, such an award for material damage, assessed on the basis of a licence fee, cannot be granted if the plaintiff would have refused to authorize the use of his name or image,[291] although this does not preclude a claim for non-material harm.[292]

The same approach was adopted in *Meßmer-Tee II*,[293] dealing with the infringement of a trade-mark—even though, as noted in a part of the annotated judgment not reproduced, "no true grant

---

[284] See excerpt at II.1., second paragraph, where the characteristics are enumerated.

[285] See for a definition of abstract assessment of damages (*abstrakte Schadensberechnung*) Lange at 354 (and see also at 345). The concept is also used in connection with the second sentence of § 252 BGB which allows an assessment of lost profits "which would have been expected with probability in the ordinary course of events, or in the specific circumstances, specifically taking account of arrangements made and precautions taken". However, the second sentence of § 252 BGB merely provides a mitigation of the onus of proof with regard to the extent of actual harm and an assessment on the basis of § 252 is therefore not "abstract" in the meaning as defined in the text above (Lange at 345 ff. and 356).

[286] Reference to the "*Lebenserfahrung*" is also found in e.g. BGH, 18 February 1977, NJW 1977, 1062.

[287] The requirement of fairness (*Billigkeit*) already appears in the *Paul Dahlke* case: BGH, 8 May 1956, BGHZ 20, 345 at 353; see also the *Miss Petite* case: BGH, 16 February 1973, BGHZ 60, 206.

[288] [1952] 2 QB 246 at 254, *supra*, **8.E.11.**

[289] BGH, 8 May 1956, BGHZ 20, 345.

[290] Such award was allowed for the first time in the *Herrenreiter* case: BGH, 14 February 1958, BGHZ 26, 349, NJW 1958, 827, annotated by K. Larenz. See *supra*, Chapter II, **2.G.26.**, Note (3).

[291] *BGH*, 18 March 1959, BGHZ 30, 7 at 16–17.

[292] *Herrenreiter*, BGH, 14 February 1958, BGHZ 26, 349, NJW 1958, 827, annotated by K. Larenz. See *supra*, Chapter II, **2.G.26.**, Note (3).

[293] BGH, 12 January 1966, BGHZ 44, 375. The similarities and differences between a *Warenzeichen* and the mentioned intellectual property rights are discussed at 376–7.

of a licence was in question and no exclusive position was transferred"—and in *Miss Petite*,[294] a case dealing with the infringement of the right to protection of one's name or commercial denomination (*Namens-oder Firmenrecht*).

As is shown by the annotated judgment, an abstract assessment of damages has also been upheld by the BGH in cases where the plaintiff has no exclusive right whatsoever, but where similar circumstances prevail. So in the case of slavish imitation, which constitutes an act of unfair competition towards any, rather than one specific, competitor, the BGH found that the plaintiff was entitled to a reasonable licence fee.[295]

(3) It is clear that an abstract assessment of damages (*abstrakte Schadensberechnung*) involves a concept of notional damage.[296] That is particularly striking when the plaintiff would not have granted a licence to the defendant at all, as was argued by the defendant in *Meßmer-Tee II*.[297] The BGH accepted that the assessment of damages was based on a fiction (*Fiktion eines Lizenzvertrages*),[298] and the Court's analysis resembles the "hypothetical bargain approach" found in English law.[299]

In line with the abstract assessment of damages, the quantum of damages is determined on an objective, but hypothetical basis of a license fee, as would have been negotiated between a reasonable licensor and an equally reasonable licensee.[300]

(4) As in English law, it has been questioned whether the assessment of a reasonable licence fee or of profits made by the defendant is still compatible with the concept of compensatory damages. Some authors have stressed that such an "abstract" approach falls outside the realm of the law of damages:[301] while the claim for a reasonable licence fee would then belong to the law of unjust enrichment (*ungerechtfertigte Bereicherung*, § 812(1) BGB), the claim for profits made by the defendant would be governed by the rules on *negotiorum gestio:* (*Geschäftsführung ohne Auftrag*, § 687(2) BGB).[302] And indeed, the BGH has recognized that such claims may be founded upon those rules.

---

[294] BGH, 16 February 1973, BGHZ 60, 206. The protection of a name or commercial denomination is comparable to the protection of a trademark (*Warenzeichen*). See for a discussion of similarities and differences between a right to name or commercial denomination and the intellectual property rights mentioned above: Ibid. at 208–9.

[295] See excerpt at II.2. The same conclusion was reached in a case of use of a trade secret (*Betriebsgeheimnis*): BGH, 18 February 1977, NJW 1977, 1062.

[296] Lange at 356–7, referring to E. Steindorff, "Abstrakte und konkrete Schadensberechnung" (1959) 158 AcP 431. See note 283, last sentence, *supra.*

[297] BGH, 12 January 1966, BGHZ 44, 372.

[298] Ibid. at 379.

[299] See ibid. at 380–1, and *supra*, **8.E.11.**, Notes (2) and (3). For further examples see the BGH judgments in *Miss Petite*, BGH, 16 February 1973, BGHZ 60, 206 at 211 and *Tolbutamid*, BGH, 6 March 1980, BGHZ 77, 16 at 25 (infringement of patent).

[300] BGH, 12 January 1966, BGHZ 44, 372 at 380–1; see also BGH, 6 March 1980, BGHZ 77, 16 at 25. Compare E. Steindorff, "Abstrakte und konkrete Schadensberechnung" (1959) 158 AcP 431 at 453–4.

[301] E. von Caemmerer, "Bereicherung und unerlaubte Handlung" in *Festschrift für Ernst Rabel*, I, 333 at 354; in the same way, while recognizing that such claims are related to the law of damages, Lange at 363–4. Compare Larenz at 515–516, E. Deutsch, *Haftungsrecht, I, Allgemeine Lehren* (Köln: Carl Heymanns, 1976) at 445 and H. Stoll, "Consequences in liability: remedies in *International Encyclopedia of Comparative Law—Vol. XI/8: Torts* (Tübingen: Mohr, 1986), at 47. For a comparative overview, see D. König, "Gewinnhaftung" in *Festschrift für Ernst von Caemmerer* (Tübingen: Mohr, 1954) at 179.

[302] See further Larenz/Canaris at 173 and 278–9. See also H. Stoll, ibid. at 225–35.

In *Vitusulfal*,[303] the BGH upheld an award of the restitution of benefits obtained by the defendant through the infringement of a trademark, on the basis of § 687(2) BGB.[304] In the *Paul Dahlke*[305] and *Carrera* judgments,[306] both concerning infringements of personality rights, the BGH confirmed that an award of a reasonable licence fee can be based on § 812(1) BGB. In *Meßmer-Tee II* [307] the Court also referred to §§ 812ff. to justify the award of a reasonable licence fee in the case of infringement of a trademark.[308] A claim for restitution of profits on the basis of § 687(2) and a claim for a licence fee on the basis of § 812 BGB are to be distinguished in that § 687(2), unlike § 812, requires the defendant to have acted knowingly.[309]

The BGH's reasoning in *Carerra*[310] shows that application of the law of unjust enrichment reaches the same conclusion as application of the law of damages; and, moreover, that the idea of prevention of unjust enrichment also underlies the solution based on tort rules.[311] The relationship between a claim for damages and a claim for the restitution of an unjust enrichment has been affirmed by the BGH.[312]

8.2.3. FRENCH LAW

Introductory Note

The French *Code civil* contains no specific provisions on compensation for tortious harm. Art. 1382 C.civ. states only that the tortfeasor is obliged to make good (*réparer*) the damage. Nor does the French *Code civil*, unlike the German BGB, lay down rules applying to both contractual and tortious liability (although some provisions concerning contractual liability are applicable in tort[313]). The rules concerning the notion of damage and the means and extent of reparation are almost entirely the product of case law.

[303] BGH, 24 February 1961, BGHZ 34, 320.

[304] The benefits subject to restitution are limited to those which the defendant gained by using the plaintiff's trademark and do not include benefits that are the result of his own efforts, the use of industrial equipment and so on: see BGHZ 34, 320 at 323 4. See also E. von Caemmerer, "Bereicherung und unerlaubte Handlung" in *Festschrift für Ernst Rabel*, Vol. I (Tübingen: Mohr, 1954) 333 at 356. Compare H. McGregor, "Restitutionary Damages" in P. Birks, (ed.), *Wrongs and Remedies in the Twenty-First Century* at 216.

[305] BGH, 8 May 1956, BGHZ 20, 345.

[306] BGH, 26 June 1981, BGHZ 81, 75.

[307] BGH, 12 January 1966, BGHZ 44, 372.

[308] Ibid. at 380; see also BGH, 18 December 1986, BGHZ 99, 244.

[309] See *Kunststoffhohlprofil II*, BGH, 24 November 1981, BGHZ 82, 299 at 309. See, from a comparative perspective, E. von Caemmerer, "Bereicherung und unerlaubte Handlung" in *Festschrift für Ernst Rabel*, Vol. I (Tübingen: Mohr, 1954) 333 at 359–60. In English law it is also suggested that an account of profits may be ordered only in cases of deliberate conduct. See *supra*, **8.E.11.**, Note (2)(c).

[310] BGH, 26 June 1981, BGHZ 81, 75.

[311] Ibid. at 81–2. The defendant is not permitted to argue that he would not have used the plaintiff's image or name if he had known that the plaintiff would have demanded a licence fee (compare Romer LJ in *Strand Electric and Engineering* [1952] 2 QB 246, *supra*, **8.E.11.**): "It does not lie in the mouth of such a defendant to suggest that the owner might not have found a hirer; for in using the property he showed that he wanted it and he cannot complain if it is assumed against him that he himself would have preferred to become the hirer rather than not have had the use of it at all" at 257.

[312] *Kunstoffhohlprofil I*, BGH, 30 November 1976, BGHZ 68, 90 at 94; *Tolbutamid*, BGH, 6 March 1980, BGHZ 77, 16 at 25.

[313] Art. 1142–1145 C.civ. deal with the obligation to act or to refrain from acting (*obligation de faire ou de ne pas faire*) and contain some provisions (the interpretation of which is the subject of much discussion) which are also relied on in tort cases (see *infra*, **8.F.17.**, Notes). Art. 1146–1155 C.civ. lay down provisions concerning damages in case of non-performance of an obligation. Some of those provisions are considered to be an expression of general principles and therefore also applicable in tort law.

While the notion of damage has not been greatly elaborated in French case law or the academic legal literature,[314] the requirements that damage must meet to be recoverable are clearly expressed: it has to be legitimate, certain,[315] and personal to the plaintiff.[316] The requirement of certainty is of particular relevance when considering future damage and loss of a chance.[317]

The principle of *restitutio in integrum* is well-established in French law,[318] and it may be realized either by non-pecuniary reparation or by compensation in money. The trial judge is empowered under French law to choose the most appropriate form of redress,[319] albeit in some instances reparation in money may not be ordered when the plaintiff seeks reparation in kind.[320]

While little attention is paid to the issue of mitigation of damage in general, the matter has been examined in the context of a plaintiff's refusal to undergo surgery or other medical treatment, without however receiving a clear answer, it would appear.[321]

It must be emphasized that French tort law is largely characterized by the recognition of the sovereign power (*pouvoir souverain*) of the triers of fact (those are the courts of first instance *and* the courts of appeal[322]), the exercise of which is not subject to review by the Cour de cassation, to assess the existence and extent of damage in concreto, that is on the basis of the concrete elements of the case.[323] The reluctance of the Cour de cassation to submit the assessment of damages to review, based on the proposition that it is a matter of fact and not of law, explains the relative lack of elaboration of French damages law when compared with English and German law.

Finally, the status of the idea of the prevention of unjust enrichment in French law will be considered in the context of unauthorized infringements of privacy and personality rights by analogy with industrial property rights.[324]

Cass. civ. 2e., 4 February 1982[325] **8.F.16.**
Babin v. Cie La Union et le Phénix espagnol

RESTITUTIO IN INTEGRUM IN CASE OF DAMAGE TO PROPERTY.

Car damaged by lorry

It follows from the principle of restitutio in integrum *that the victim of damage to property should be able to claim in full either the expenses incurred to repair the damaged property or*

---

[314] *Supra*, Chapter I, 1.4.2, Introductory Note.

[315] Ibid. On certainty of damage, see *supra*, Chapter IV, 4.1.3.and **4.F.8.**

[316] Ibid.

[317] *Infra*, 8.5. See also, with regard to the loss of a chance, *supra*, Chapter II, **2.F.11**, Note (2) and Chapter IV, 4.2.2.

[318] **8.F.16.**

[319] **8.F.17.**

[320] See *infra*, **8.F.17.**, Note (3).

[321] **8.F.18.** and Notes (1), (2) and (3) below it.

[322] Both the court of first instance and the court of appeal enjoy the same discretion and there are therefore no limits as to the court of appeal's power to change the court of first instance's exercise of discretion.

[323] **8.F.19.**

[324] **8.F.20.**

[325] JCP 1982.II.19849, annotated by J.-F. Barbieri. Translation by Y.P. Salmon.

*its replacement value, and that the risks inherent in the sale of the damaged property should
be borne by the tortfeasor.*

Facts: The plaintiff's car was damaged by a lorry. The plaintiff had received from her insurer compensation amounting to the car's sale value [before the accident] (*valeur vénale*), minus the value of the wrecked car. She then sued the owner of the lorry and its insurer for additional compensation, on the basis that she was entitled to the full value of her car before the accident and that it was for the defendants to realize whatever they could for the wrecked vehicle.

Held: The Cour de cassation quashed the judgment of the trial judge who had refused to award additional compensation.

Judgment: "The characteristic purpose of civil liability is to restore as exactly as possible the balance destroyed by the harm, and to return the victim to the situation in which he would have been if the harmful event had not occurred, at the expense of the liable person. Consequently, full reparation (*réparation intégrale*) for damage caused to an object can be effected only by refunding the costs incurred to repair the object or by paying a sum of money amounting to its replacement value.

The victim of harm who is entitled to full reparation does not have to bear the risk of the sale of the wreck, which, except where both parties agree on this point, should be borne by the liable party.

[The plaintiff], whose car had been damaged by a truck of the *La Haye* company, claimed from that company, which was liable for the harm, and its insurer . . . the balance of compensation of the damage already partially compensated by her mutual benefit insurance.

In rejecting [the plaintiff's] claim, the disputed judgment, final as to the facts, stated only that for want of proof of her outlays, the appellant's claim could not succeed.

However, since [the plaintiff] had submitted that her insurer had compensated her only on the basis of the sale value [before the accident] (*valeur vénale*) of her vehicle, minus the salvage value of the wreck, the court, in so ruling, failed to apply [Art. 1382 C. civ.] correctly. On those grounds the judgment must be set aside."

Note

The annotated judgment confirms the well-established principle of *restitutio in integrum* or full reparation.[326] Although not laid down in any legislative provision of tort law,[327] the principle has never been questioned, and its formulation is very close to that found in German and English law. It is however no more than a principle which may justify divergent solutions, as will be illustrated in Section 4. It may suffice here to mention that a case such as that considered in the annotated judgment may give rise to three types of question: (1) What is the measure of damages (the cost of repairs, the purchase price of a replacement car, or the sale value of the car before it was damaged) to be applied under the circumstances (e.g. when repair of the car is more expensive than replacement; or when it can be neither repaired nor replaced)? (2) Is the level of damages affected by the fact that the plaintiff did not spend any money to repair or replace the car, and does not intend to undertake such restoration? (3) Is it incumbent on the defendant or on the plaintiff to undertake the sale of the wrecked car, and to bear the risk inherent in such sale (in the annotated judgment the risk is imposed upon the defendant)? These questions, which will be dealt with in Section 4, are the subject of much uncertainty.

---

[326] For details of further case law on the issue, see Viney, *Effets* at 81.
[327] The principle of full compensation in contract law is laid down in Art. 1149 C.civ.

THE *POUVOIR SOUVERAIN* OF THE TRIER OF FACT
TO CHOOSE THE APPROPRIATE FORM OF REDRESS

House damaged by subsidence

The trier of fact is deemed to have ordered reparation in kind when he orders the defendant to pay an advance to the plaintiff and allows the plaintiff to have repairs to his house carried out by a contractor of his own choice, under the supervision of an expert designated by the court to assess the amount of damages at the time that the works, both foreseeable and unforeseeable, were carried out.

Facts: The plaintiff's house was damaged by subterranean works undertaken in the defendant's coal mine.

Held: The Cour de cassation upheld the court of appeal's decision that the plaintiff was entitled to have repairs carried out by a contractor of his choice and, in anticipation of a final decision as to the amount of damage, was entitled to receive an advance payment from the defendant, holding that such a decision was part of the court of appeal's *pouvoir souverain* to order reparation in kind at the defendant's expense.

Judgment: "The contested judgment, ruling on the compensation for damage caused to [the plaintiff's] house by subsidence attributable to work carried out in galleries of the [defendant] colliery, required [the defendant] to make an advance payment (*provision*) to [the plaintiff] in anticipation of having his house put back into good order by a contractor of his choice under the supervision of an expert. The expert was to be engaged to verify the final cost of the work, both foreseen and unforeseen, to certify the successful completion of the work and to assess the loss caused by the carrying out of the work and the depreciation of the building and then to lodge his report with the Tribunal de grande instance . . .

The court of appeal is criticized for having deferred the assessment of damages to be awarded as compensation in money (*réparation par équivalent*) for the sole purpose of both updating the assessment of damages on the date of completion of the work and taking into account possible further loss, whereas damages payable by a party who is liable in tort ought to be determined definitively on the day of the judgment which sets those damages, on the basis of the certain loss caused by the harmful event.

However, the court of appeal decided that the rebuilding would be effected by [the plaintiff] who, being the owner, would both choose the contractor, charged with the carrying out of the work, and be the person to whom the work would be handed over on completion. The court of appeal, in the exercise of its sovereign power of appraisal, thus chose to award [the plaintiff] reparation in kind (en nature) *and not compensation in money* (par équivalent pécuniaire) [emphasis added]. The ground of appeal therefore fails."

Notes

(1) In the annotated judgment, the Cour de cassation affirmed the court of appeal's sovereign power, i.e. not subject to review by the Cour de cassation, to choose reparation in kind (*en nature*), instead of in money (*par équivalent pécuniaire*), as the appropriate form of reparation. The state of law on this point is rather uncertain. First, there is no

[328] Gaz.Pal. 1982.Jur.109, annotated by F. Chabas. Translation by Y. P. Salmon.

unequivocal definition of reparation "in kind" or "in money".[329] Secondly, it is not clear whether the trial judge may in every instance choose freely between reparation "in kind" and compensation in money.[330]

(2) The annotated judgment shows that the term reparation "in kind" may be given a broad meaning. Indeed, the court of appeal had ordered the defendant to pay an advance to the plaintiff, and permitted the plaintiff to have the repairs carried out by a contractor at the defendant's expense, the amount of which was to be assessed by an independent expert and determined by the court. Such reparation is nonetheless qualified by the annotated judgment as reparation in kind, as opposed to compensation in money (*par équivalent pécuniaire*). However, it is clear that the order upheld by the annotated judgment was of a *pecuniary* nature, the defendant being ordered to pay a sum of money rather than itself to undertake the restoration of the damaged house.

It may be noted that, in legal writing, reparation *en nature* and reparation *par équivalent* are distinguished in various ways. The distinguishing criterion may be the *nature of the court's order*; "*en nature*" is then equated with non-pecuniary reparation (e.g. an order to pull down a house which has been illegally erected, a judgment that includes an order for its publication), and "*par équivalent*" is equated with pecuniary reparation (*dommages et intérêts*, money compensation).[331] Other authors refer to the *effect of the court's order*: in a case of reparation in kind (*en nature*), the plaintiff is restored to the identical situation in which he or she would have been if he or she had not been harmed (e.g. an order to return the stolen object) whereas equivalent reparation (*équivalent*) does not restore the *status quo ante* but gives an equivalent to the plaintiff which may be pecuniary or non-pecuniary (e.g. the publication of the judgment in a case of defamation, the delivery of a substitute for a damaged or stolen object).[332]

It would seem that the difference between the two methods of reparation in this case related to the question of who was to bear the risk as to the actual cost of the required repairs. Reparation by way of compensation in money would have consisted here in the defendant being ordered to pay the cost of repairs assessed at the time of judgment, as established by a prior estimate and without reference to the cost of the repairs that were subsequently found to be necessary and were carried out, which would have meant that the risk of an insufficient estimate of the repair cost would have been borne by the plaintiff. Conversely, when the cost of repair is assessed after completion of the repairs, it is the defendant who bears that risk. That is the reason why the defendant claimed that the appeal judgment should have assessed damages at the time of its judgment and not upon the completion of the repairs,[333] charging the expert with the reassessment of the cost of foreseen and unforeseen repairs. The Cour de cassation rejected that argument on the ground that the order constituted reparation in kind, and not in money. As F. Chabas observes in his commentary to the annotated judgment, the court of appeal's decision to

---

[329] See *infra* Note (2).

[330] See *infra* Note (3).

[331] This distinction is made by Viney, *Effets* at 22 ff., para. 14 ff. Compare Starck, Roland and Boyer at 517–18, para. 1284–5 and 522, para. 1300–1.

[332] H. L. J. Mazeaud and F. Chabas, *Traité théorique et pratique de la responsabilité civile délictuelle et contractuelle*, III, 6th edn. (Paris: Montchrestien, 1978) at 614 ff., para. 2302 ff.

[333] Y. Chartier, *La réparation du préjudice dans la responsabilité civile* (Paris: Dalloz, 1983) at 497. See also F. Chabas, Comment on the annotated judgment, Gaz.Pal.1982.Jur.109 at 109.

order reparation in kind (by a third party), at the defendant's expense, can be considered to be an application by analogy of the contractual provisions laid down in Art. 1143–1144 C.civ.[334]

The reparation in kind which was ordered by the court of appeal combines elements of both of the two meanings given to "reparation in kind" (*Naturalherstellung*) in German law, i.e. referring to both a restoration of the *status quo ante* to be performed by the wrongdoer or on his behalf (first sentence of § 249 BGB) and the payment of a sum of money requisite for the purpose of restoration (second sentence of § 249 BGB). Indeed, the order effects a restoration of the *status quo ante*, but that restoration is not effected by the defendant (or on his behalf) but is effected at his expense. However, such an order is not to be equated with an award under the second sentence of § 249 BGB, since the latter is final and is not an advance to be adjusted following the repair.[335]

(3) As to the question of whether a trial judge may choose freely between the two forms of reparation, in cases of buildings which were erected in breach of a property right (*droit réel*), including an easement (*servitude légale*), or in breach of urban development rules, the Cour de cassation has held that, subject to certain restrictions, the judge may not award compensation in money when the plaintiff claims reparation in kind, i.e. demolition of the building.[336] The Cour de cassation enunciated this rule in connection with Art. 1143 C.civ.[337] which forms part of French contract law, but is apparently also applicable in tort.[338]

Legal writers have tried to formulate rules which should govern the choice between reparation in kind and equivalent reparation. H. L. J. Mazeaud and F. Chabas have taken the position that the judge cannot, generally, impose equivalent reparation when the plaintiff claims reparation in kind and such reparation is possible.[339] Likewise, the judge may not order equivalent reparation in favour of the plaintiff when reparation in kind is offered by the defendant (unless it exposes the plaintiff to risks or has other drawbacks attached to it). Conversely, the judge may order reparation in kind when the plaintiff claims equivalent reparation or when equivalent reparation is offered by the defendant. In other words, only when equivalent reparation is claimed, can the judge freely decide the form of reparation. That view has gained support in legal writing[340] but the Cour de cassation has never adopted these rules. Another view has been taken by M. E. Roujou de Boubée, who emphasizes that the effect of some awards "in kind" is not reparation for harm already inflicted but the elimination of an unlawful situation, which is an ongoing source of harm, and thus intended to prevent future damage.[341] According to M.E. Roujou de Boubée, the

---

[334] Art. 1143 C.civ.: ". . . the creditor has the right to demand destruction of whatever has been done in violation of an undertaking; he may obtain authorization to destroy it himself at the expense of the debtor without payment of damages, in such a case".

Art. 1144 C.civ.: "The creditor may also, in case of non-performance, be authorized to perform the obligation himself at the expense of the debtor." The *Loi n° 91–650 portant réforme des procédures civiles d'inexécution* of 9 July 1991, JO, 14 July 1991, D 1991.Lég.317, added a second paragraph which reads as follows: "[The debtor] may also be ordered to pay, in advance, the sums required for such performance".

[335] BGH, 25 October 1996, NJW 1997, 520.

[336] Viney, *Effets* at 72–4, para. 52.

[337] Quoted above.

[338] See Cass. civ. 3e, 22 May 1997, Bull.civ. 1997.III.75 and the comment of G. Viney, Chronique, JCP 1997.4070 at 518, para. 26–7.

[339] H. L. J. Mazeaud and F. Chabas, *Traité théorique et pratique de la responsabilité civile délictuelle et contractuelle*, III, 6th edn. (Paris: Montchrestien, 1978) at 615, para. 2303 ff. and 633, para. 2318.

[340] Viney, *Effets* at 60, para. 43.

[341] M.E. Roujou de Boubée, *Essai sur la notion de réparation* (Paris: LGDJ, 1974) at 209–17.

judge's freedom to decide the means of reparation is not applicable when the plaintiff seeks the termination of a wrong.[342]

Due to the parallels between such reparation in kind and injunctive relief, the case law will be further examined in Section 6.

Cass. crim., 3 July 1969[343]   8.F.18.
Pourpour v. Reynaud

PLAINTIFF'S DUTY TO MITIGATE DAMAGE BY UNDERGOING MEDICAL TREATMENT

Injured plaintiff refusing surgery

It is within the judge's pouvoir souverain *to decide whether, on the basis of all the available evidence and not only a medical report, the plaintiff may refuse surgery without reducing the damages to which he or she is entitled. If so, it would be contrary to the principle of full compensation for the judge to reduce the amount of compensation because of the plaintiff's refusal.*

Facts: The plaintiff was the victim of an accident caused by the defendant. He refused surgery which, according to expert opinion, would have improved his condition.

Held: The Cour de cassation upheld the court of appeal's decision that the surgery was not without real risk for the plaintiff and that therefore the amount of damages could not be reduced.

Judgment: "The disputed judgment fixed the level of damages due to [the claimant], following a road traffic accident for which, in an earlier definitive decision, [the defendant] was declared entirely liable. [The defendant], asserting that the victim's partial permanent disability (*incapacité permanente partielle*) could be mitigated by a surgical operation, requested that the judgment be deferred and that the experts be engaged again in order to determine the level of incapacity which [the claimant] would continue to suffer after that operation if it was carried out. That request was rejected by the court of appeal on the ground that the victim justifiably refused to subject himself to the surgery which presented some real risks for him.

This appreciation of the facts concerned the sovereign powers of the triers of fact. The expert report constituted but one element subjected to the examination of the court, which was not bound by the opinions expressed in that report [emphasis added]. The judges have the right and the duty to supplement and rectify, where necessary, the opinion of the experts in view of the documents filed in the procedure subject to appeal.

In addition, the judges are unable to impose an operation on the victim which he refuses to undergo; consequently they could not reduce the damages allowed on the basis of that refusal without infringing the principle according to which the harm suffered by the victim should be redressed in full [intégralement réparé]. *The appeal is therefore dismissed* [emphasis added]."

Notes

(1) The court of appeal had decided, on the facts of the case, that the victim was entitled to refuse the operation because of its material risks. In the annotated judgment the

---

[342] Ibid. at 218–53. G. Viney largely adheres to this view, see Viney, *Effets* at 59 ff., para. 43 and at 70 ff., para. 50 ff.
[343] JCP 1970.II.16447 annotated by R. Savatier. Translation by Y. P. Salmon.

criminal chamber of the Cour de cassation considered that it was for the trier of fact to take that decision freely on the basis, not only of a non-binding expert opinion, but also of the other documents that were before the court. The Cour de cassation further stated that "the judges are unable to impose an operation on the victim which he refuses to undergo", and that the judge may not "consequently . . . reduce the damages allowed on the basis of that refusal without infringing the principle according to which the harm suffered by the victim should be redressed in full." If those statements were to be taken literally, rather than confined to the facts of the case before the court, it would appear that a victim could never be under a duty to mitigate damage by undergoing surgery.[344]

(2) The position was clarified five years later when, on 30 October 1974, the criminal chamber, again, of the Cour de cassation handed down a judgment[345] in a case where the victim had refused a blood transfusion on religious grounds and subsequently died. The court of first instance had reduced the damages award because, although it was uncertain that the victim would have survived if he had accepted the blood transfusion, it was considered that the victim had nonetheless reduced his chances of survival through his own fault. The court of appeal refused, however, to consider whether the victim's decision constituted a fault or not; the victim's refusal should be taken into account only if it was certain that it had contributed to the result, which was not the case according to the court of appeal. The Cour de cassation disagreed because the court of appeal

> "failed to ascertain whether the victim, by his fault, had deprived himself of a chance of improvement or survival, by knowingly not accepting the care that his condition required; such a fault must be taken into account when quantifying the damages for the loss sustained if refusal contributed to the eventuation of the damage."

Accordingly, it would seem that an unreasonable refusal by the plaintiff to undergo medical treatment constitutes a fault which reduces the damages award; the court to which the case was sent for final determination held so.[346] The judgment was followed by other courts;[347] it was also specified that the reasonableness of the victim's decision should be considered against subjective criteria, according to the circumstances in which the victim found himself or herself at the time.[348]

(3) However, in 1994 the Code civil was amended by the insertion of Article 16–3 Code civil,[349] which provides:

> "The integrity of the human body may be infringed only in the event of therapeutic necessity for the individual. The consent of the interested party must be obtained in advance, unless the con-

---

[344] Such is the interpretation of the judgment by e.g. P. J. Doll, "Des conséquences pécuniaires du refus par la victime d'un accident de se soumettre à une opération chirurgicale améliorante après consolidation des blessures" JCP 1970.I.2351 at para. 15.

[345] Cass. crim., 30 October 1974, JCP 1975.II.18038, annotated by L. Mourgeon, D 1975.Jur.178, annotated by R. Savatier. See also P. J. Doll, "Convient-il de tenir compte du refus délibéré de la victime de se priver d'une chance d'amélioration de son état ou de survie dans le calcul des dommages-intérêts revendiqués par ses ayants cause?" Gaz.Pal. 1975.Doct.331.

[346] Lyon, 6 June 1975, JCP 1976.II.18 322, annotated by L.M., D 1976.Jur.415 annotated by R. Savatier.

[347] See Viney, *Effets* at 169–70, para. 123; Starck, Roland and Boyer at 538–40, para. 1346–8. See also TGI Laval, 13 February 1967, D 1968.Jur.39, annotated by M. Le Roy.

[348] TGI Paris, 13 May 1981, JCP 1982.II.19887, annotated by F. Chabas. See also Cass. civ. 2e, 13 January 1966, Gaz.Pal. 1966.Jur.375.

[349] Inserted by *Loi n° 94–653 relative au respect du corps humain* of 29 July 1994, JO, 30 July 1994, D 1994.Lég.406.

dition of the [interested party] requires a medical intervention to which he is not in a position to consent".

In a judgment of 19 March 1997,[350] the Second civil chamber of the Cour de cassation decided that as a consequence of Art. 16–3 C.civ. a plaintiff could be obliged to undergo medical treatment only in instances provided for by law.[351] The defendants objected to the award of a lump sum to the plaintiff who had refused to undergo surgery to fit a prosthesis which would have mitigated his disability. They argued, on the one hand, that the award of a lump sum, which was assessed without taking into account the beneficial consequences of medical treatment, precluded a reassessment of damages in the case of improvement of the plaintiff's disability and, on the other hand, that the defendant should not bear the pecuniary consequences of the plaintiff's refusal. Referring to the plaintiff's freedom to refuse surgery, the Cour de cassation held that the court of appeal had rightly decided that the plaintiff was not bound to have a prosthesis fitted and that it was within the free discretion of the trial court to award a lump sum. G. Viney points out that in referring to Art. 16–3 C.civ., the court seems to preclude *any* challenge to the victim's decision and that the difficulties faced in distinguishing the "trivial" from the "serious" medical intervention may explain this position.[352]

(4) Apart from the issue of a refusal to undergo medical treatment, little attention has been paid to the existence of a duty to mitigate damage.[353]

Cass. crim., 26 June 1984[354]   **8.F.19.**
Guimber v. *Aaron*

POUVOIR SOUVERAIN OF THE TRIER OF FACT

Medical disability scale

Damages have to be assessed in concreto, *though that does not preclude a reference to a medical disability scale. In assessing damages, the judge has a* pouvoir souverain *that cannot be the subject of review by the Cour de cassation.*

Facts: The plaintiff claimed damages for injury sustained in a traffic accident, which had necessitated a splenectomy. An expert had estimated the plaintiff's permanent disability at 5 per cent, adding however that the disability could fall within a bracket of between 5 per cent and 30 per cent.

Held: The court of first instance assessed damages on the basis of a disability of 30 per cent. The court of appeal fixed the plaintiff's disability at 10 per cent by reference to a medical disability scale. The Cour de cassation upheld the judgment of the court of appeal.

---

[350] Cass. civ. 2e, 19 March 1997, Bull.civ. 1997.II.48.

[351] There are only a few legal exceptions to the principle of inviolability of the human body; see Viney, *Effets* at 169, footnote 87 and P. J. Doll, "Des conséquences pécuniaires du refus par la victime d'un accident de se soumettre à une opération chirurgicale améliorante après consolidation des blessures" JCP 1970.I.2351 at para. 16.

[352] G. Viney, Chronique, JCP 1997.I.4070 at 519–20, para. 29–30. G. Viney refers to cases of contaminated blood transfusion which have shown that even a blood transfusion, considered to be a trivial medical intervention, may not be without serious risk.

[353] See Starck, Roland and Boyer at para. 1345–50.

[354] Bull.crim. 1984.648. Translation by Y. P. Salmon.

811

Judgment: "The disputed judgment [of the court of appeal], had set the level of partial permanent disability (*incapacité permanente partielle*) at 10 per cent and thus set the damages for the total amount of her personal injury at FRF 64,887 in place of that of FRF 191,887 granted by the judge of first instance (partial permanent disability of 30 per cent); [the court of appeal held] "that it appears from an 'indicative scale of functional disability in civil law', such as is to be found in the *Concours médical* of 19 June 1982, that the partial permanent disability resulting from a splenectomy without complications, as in the case at hand, may be assessed at 10 per cent; and that it is appropriate to apply this level"; [that finding] is criticized [by the plaintiff] on the ground that the trial judges, sovereign to assess the extent of the harm, must rule on this point '*in concreto*' and not according to a general or predetermined rule; and that in this case the judges of the court [of appeal], who fixed the level of [the plaintiff's] partial permanent disability on the sole ground referred to above, founded their assessment of the harm sustained by the victim on essentially general and abstract elements and therefore did not give legal foundation to the decision in view of the aforementioned provisions.

[The Cour de cassation held:] To determine the [plaintiff's] partial permanent disability . . . the court of appeal, after having analyzed the conclusions of the medical report in which the designated expert fixed the disability at 5 per cent, notes that that [expert], interpreting his conclusions made in a letter addressed to the president of the Tribunal de Police, indicates that "the reparation of harm in civil law and industrial injury have different bases, partial permanent disability being capable of assessment within a bracket of 5 per cent and 30 per cent".

The same court [of appeal] then states "in adopting the most favourable rate to the plaintiff, i.e. 30 per cent, the court of first instance did not provide facts to justify its assessment. As appears from the 'indicative scale of functional disability in civil law', such as appeared in the *Concours médical* of 19 June 1982, the partial permanent disability resulting from a splenectomy with no complications, such as arose in this case, may be assessed at 10 per cent; it is appropriate to apply that rate". . . .

In so proceeding *the court of appeal did not rule* in abstracto *by way of a general rule* (par voie de disposition générale et réglementaire), *but rather, on the contrary, took account of the concrete circumstances of the case to which it made express reference. In addition, the assessment of harm suffered by the plaintiff was within the sovereignty [of the court of appeal], and so escapes review by the Cour de cassation* [emphasis added].

On those grounds the appeal is dismissed."

Notes

(1) The annotated judgment illustrates two basic principles of the French law on damages: (1) the assessment of damages must be made *in concreto* by the trier of fact (court of first instance or court of appeal); (2) the sovereign power (*pouvoir souverain*) of the trier of fact in assessing damages is not subject to review by the Cour de cassation.

That the assessment should be made *in concreto* means that the judge has to take into account all the concrete elements of the case which may influence the amount of damages: each case is unique and demands an individualized assessment. The amount cannot be assessed *in abstracto* on the basis of a previously fixed scale of damages ("*par voie de disposition générale et réglementaire*").[355] However, that does not preclude the trier of fact

---

[355] This is a reference to Article 5 C.civ. which provides: "Judges are forbidden to decide the cases submitted to them by way of a general and rule-making (*réglementaire*) decision". This provision has its roots in the French Revolution and was intended as a reaction against the judiciary claiming legislative power, as was the case in the *Ancien Régime*.

from taking into account a medical disability scale or comparisons with other awards, provided that they are not treated as determinative.[356]

The judge's sovereign power is very extensive. The judge is not obliged to specify the elements which have been taken into account in the assessment of damages;[357] he is not bound by any model; he is not obliged to follow the method used by plaintiff or defendant; he can allow one global amount for all the harm sustained (*toutes causes de préjudice confondues*), or he can split the award.[358] The Cour de cassation permits little review, as it considers the assessment of damages to be largely a matter of fact and not of law: it will censure a judgment only when it infringes a principle of law, e.g. when damages were assessed *in abstracto*, or the quantum was influenced by irrelevant considerations (e.g. the degree of culpability), or when full compensation was not given, e.g. by refusing damages for a specific kind of damage.[359] The Cour de cassation is even more reluctant to subject the reasons given to review.[360]

(2) The necessity of making similar awards in comparable cases has also been recognized by the French lower courts which, in practice, take their usual level of damages into account albeit usually covertly.[361] However, lower courts refrain from giving comprehensive justification for their assessments of the amount of damages and do not justify their awards by comparison with other awards. Therefore, awards of damages in comparable cases may diverge considerably, without being subjected to review by the Cour de cassation.

The *Loi Badinter*[362] has somewhat improved this situation. Art. 26 provides for a publication of damages assessed in judgments and settlements out of court, and the resulting publication of awards has contributed to greater uniformity in damages awards made by the courts of appeal.[363] However, the assessment of damages in comparable cases seems to diverge and legal practice is described as being "uncertain".[364]

---

[356] Compare Cass. crim., 3 November 1955, D 1956.Jur.557, annotated by R. Savatier and Cass. crim., 13 April 1976, D 1976.IR.141. See, in greater detail, Viney, *Effets* at 93–4, para. 64.

[357] E.g. Cass. crim., 9 February 1982, JCP 1982.IV.153.

[358] However, the recourse which is available to tiers payeurs (mainly social security institutions), forces the judge to make a distinction between harm for which the tiers payeurs can recoup their expenditures and harm for which they cannot recoup it. *Infra*, 8.5. See in greater detail Viney, *Effets* at 90–2, para. 62.

[359] See, in greater detail, Viney, *Effets* at 93–6, para. 64.

[360] See for further details Viney, *Effets* at 96–9, para. 65–6. See, for instance, Cass. comm., 5 December 1989, Bull.civ. 1989.IV.307.

[361] See R. Savatier in his annotation to the *Cornet* judgment, D 1956.Jur.557 at 557–8.

[362] *Supra* Chapter VI, **6.F.16.**

[363] G. Viney, *L'indemnisation des victimes d'accidents de la circulation* (Paris: LGDJ, 1992) at 121.

[364] M. Quenillet-Bourrié, "L'évaluation monétaire du préjudice corporel: pratique judiciaire et données transactionnelles" JCP 1995.I.3818 at para. 1.

Cass. civ. 1re, 17 November 1987[365]   **8.F.20.**
Delon v. S.A. "Ici Paris"

PLAINTIFF'S INJURY V. DEFENDANT'S PROFIT

Unauthorized publication

The quantum of the plaintiff's material harm may not be assessed as a function of the profits realized by the defendant as a result of the unauthorized publication.

Facts: The weekly magazine *Ici Paris* published an article on the private life of the plaintiff, a well-known film actor, accompanied by a photograph, without his consent. He claimed damages for material and non-material harm.

Held: The Cour de cassation upheld the court of appeal's judgment dismissing the plaintiff's claim for damages for material harm.

Judgment: "Following the publication in April 1984 of an article in the weekly magazine *Ici Paris* entitled 'Alain Delon undergoes surgery in Cuba', illustrated by a photograph of the actor, the latter claimed from the company *Ici Paris* payment of various sums by way of damages and the publication of an official statement in several daily newspapers and weekly magazines.
    . . .
    Mr Alain Delon appeals from the judgment [of the court of appeal] which rejected his damages claim "for the illegitimate exploitation of his image and private life for commercial and publicity purposes"; the grounds of the appeal are that, on the one hand, the court of appeal ignored his submissions that, by these acts, the company *Ici Paris* realized an illegitimate benefit of which he was deprived and which caused him a loss of income constituting, by its very nature damage of a commercial character, and that, on the other hand, in limiting itself in such a way to the moral harm and damage to the artist's reputation and career, the court of appeal failed to apply Art.1382 C. civ. correctly.
    However, in support of its sovereign assessment of the nature and extent of the recoverable harm (*dommage réparable*) the court of appeal, in response to the submissions, held that the extent of the harm sustained by Mr Delon was not a function of the profit realized by the company *Ici Paris*. It follows that the appeal must be dismissed."

Notes

(1) The plaintiff claimed that he had suffered non-material and material harm as a result of an unauthorized publication, for commercial reasons, of an article concerning his private life accompanied by a photograph. He claimed, *inter alia,* damages for material harm, by reference to the profit gained by the publisher. It may be assumed—but it is not explicit in the judgment—that the plaintiff argued that the publisher would have had to pay for the publication if his permission had been asked and obtained. The court of appeal dismissed the claim, holding that the plaintiff suffered merely non-material harm and that damages for material harm could not be granted as a function of the defendant's profit. The Cour de cassation upheld that judgment, referring to the judge's sovereign power to assess the nature and extent of the harm. The annotated judgment illustrates once again the reluctance of the Cour de cassation to give guidance regarding the appropriate measure of damages.

[365] Bull.civ. 1987.I.301. Translation by Y. P. Salmon.

(2) The Cour de cassation has shown the same reluctance regarding the award of damages in cases of infringement of patent rights,[366] an area which is not without analogy with the infringement of privacy and personality rights.[367]

In French case-law relating to the infringement of industrial property rights, rules comparable to those found in English and German law are applied; but the French courts have given no explicit consideration to the propriety of setting damages equal to a notional licence fee without reference to the concrete circumstances of the case and, in particular, whether the plaintiff would actually have granted a licence and if so, on what terms. In the case law a distinction is drawn between the manufacturing plaintiff and the licensing plaintiff. The damage suffered by the manufacturing plaintiff is assessed either on the basis of the net profits made by the defendant, or on the basis of the profits that the plaintiff would have made. A licensing plaintiff is entitled to damages amounting to the unpaid licence fee.[368]

Many authors have expressed their unease about this case law. The assessment of damages on the basis of the profits made by the defendant may entitle the plaintiff to more than the harm that he has suffered; it is therefore argued that the defendant should be allowed to prove that the plaintiff's loss was less.[369] The assessment of damage suffered by a licensing plaintiff gives rise to the objection that such a measure of damages has no deterrent effect: the defendant is no worse off than if he had sought a licence legitimately.[370] Once again, there is a tension between the formally absolute strict compensatory approach, and the purposes of prevention of unjust enrichment and punishment and deterrence.

(3) The purposes of prevention of unjust enrichment and punishment and deterrence have been more openly acknowledged in certain judgments.

In a case concerning the infringement of a well-known trademark, the Paris court of appeal held:[371]

> "that for the assessment of the sums . . . to compensate for [the] damage which is at the same time non-material and material . . . it is advisable to take account primarily of the incidence which the use of the Rotschild name could have in the enrichment which Helmut Rotschild and his companies [the defendants] have obtained and in the appreciation of the value of business capital exploited by them . . .".

This judgment has been considered to conform to the orthodox compensatory approach (the defendants' enrichment being only a presumption of fact to assess the plaintiffs' damage),[372] but has also been considered to grant an "exemplary" award.[373]

---

[366] J. Azéma, Annotation on Paris, 2 March 1971, D 1972.Jur.48 at 48.

[367] See *supra*, Chapter II, 2.2.2.

[368] J. Azéma, Annotation on Paris, 2 March 1971, D 1972.Jur.48 at 49. See also Y. Chartier, *La réparation du préjudice dans la responsabilité civile* (Paris: Dalloz, 1983) at 643–8.

[369] J. Azéma, ibid.; Y. Chartier, ibid. at 645.

[370] J. Azéma, ibid. at 49–50; Y. Chartier, ibid. at 647.

[371] Paris, 10 July 1986, JCP 1986.II.20712, annotated by E. Agostini.

[372] E. Agostini, ibid. E. Agostini subsequently changed his opinion ("Les agissements parasitaires en droit comparé, le cas Helmut Rotschild" JCP 1987.I.3284): "If it is *a priori* unusual that harm is assessed in the person of its author and not in that of its victim, one should not lose sight of the fact that such parasitism renders all resultant gains suspect and justifies the imposition of a private law penalty of a real deterrent nature, preventing the repetition of such an imitation." (quoted by S. Carval, *La responsabilité civile dans sa fonction de peine privée* (Paris: LGDJ, 1995) at 138).

[373] S. Carval, *La responsabilité civile dans sa fonction de peine privée* (Paris: L.G.D.J., 1995) at 138. In Paris, 1 July 1986 and TGI Paris, 4 March 1987, D 1988.Somm.350, annotated by J.M. Mousseron and J. Schmidt, it

In a later judgment of 12 November 1991,[374] the Paris court of appeal was even more categorical and precise. It held:

> "According to practice, the compensatory rate of royalty is determined by reference to the rate that the patentee could impose in the framework of a licence granted freely to a third party operating in similar conditions, and is increased to take into account the fact that the infringer is not a contractual licensee who has freely negotiated the rate which would be applied, and that he is not in a position to refuse the conditions imposed upon him."

Such judgments are met with understanding and sympathy, but at the same time they are criticized due to the difficulty of reconciling them with a strict compensatory approach.[375]

(4) In contrast to German and English law, in French law it is not possible to rely on rules of unjust enrichment to sustain jurisprudential solutions. The French rules on the restitution of unjust enrichment, giving rise to a claim called *actio de in rem verso*, play only a subsidiary role, as the action is available only in the absence of any other remedy. Consequently, when the defendant incurs tortious liability, the *actio de in rem verso* is not available. Thus it has recently been suggested that the role of *peine privée* should be recognized in the field of industrial property rights and law of unfair competition, and that the scope of application of the *actio de in rem verso* should be enlarged by legislative intervention.[376]

8.3. FORM OF COMPENSATION AND ASSESSMENT OF FUTURE DAMAGE.

Introductory Note

a) In personal injury cases in particular, certain questions arise relating to compensation for harm which may be subject to future developments. The major issue is whether such compensation should consist of a *once-and-for-all award*—that is without possibility of revision if the injury turns out to be more or less serious than foreseen or if other circumstances (e.g. changes in the level of wages) produce changes for better or worse—or whether the compensation should be *revisable*. Another issue is what form damages should take: a *capital sum* (*capital* in French; *Kapital* in German, *lump sum* in common law terms) or *periodical payments* (*rente* in French; *(Geld)rente* in German).[377] Both issues are often—but not necessarily—interrelated: a damages award by way of a capital sum involves in principle a once-and-for-all assessment, excluding any review of the cap-

was held: "The compensation of infringement of copyright has a dual function, reparatory and deterrent; the level of the award may be greater than the harm sustained by the patentee." The statement is followed by an overview of case law in which the same idea is expressed.

[374] Paris, 12 November 1991, D 1993.Somm.378, annotated by J.M. Mousseron and J. Schmidt.

[375] J.M. Mousseron and J. Schmidt, Annotation, D 1993.Somm.378.

[376] S. Carval, *La responsabilité civile dans sa fonction de peine privée* (Paris: LGDJ, 1995) at 156–63.

[377] Periodical payments are sometimes called annuities. "Annuity" is also used to refer to the contract by which the insurance company (a life office) contracts to make payments during the plaintiff's life. The same term is also used in the context of calculation of the damages for future loss: see *infra*, **8.E.23.**, Note (2).

ital sum, whilst a damages award by way of periodical payments involves in principle a revisable assessment. As will be seen in this section, English law essentially provides for payments of a lump sum on a once-and-for-all basis whilst German law adheres in principle to revisable periodical payments, without excluding the possibility of a non-revisable capital award. But, as French law shows, an award of damages may (to some extent) be open to revision irrespective of whether a capital sum or periodical payments were awarded.

The advantages and disadvantages of a non-revisable lump sum award compared with a revisable periodical payments award are well known.[378] A non-revisable lump sum puts an end to the dispute between plaintiff and defendant once-and-for-all. The defendant (or rather, more commonly, his insurer) does not have to make arrangements for continuing payments. The plaintiff has free disposition of the lump sum: e.g. he may buy an annuity which gives him a periodical income or decide to invest in a business of his own. It is said that a lump sum encourages the plaintiff to overcome the restrictions imposed by his disability and that it may prevent the development of compensation neurosis. Finally, the plaintiff does not bear the risk of the defendant's insolvency.

The main objection to the lump sum award is that, while the plaintiff has lost a periodical income, a lump sum burdens him with the trouble and risks of investing the capital. Conversely, a periodical payments scheme protects the plaintiff against the premature dissipation of the capital. The unforeseeable impact of future uncertainties is counterbalanced where the periodical payments award is revisable. Moreover, as periodical payments are awarded for the duration of the plainitff's life where he has suffered a permanent disability, with resulting loss, it is unnecessary to estimate the victim's life expectancy. Conversely, lump sum awards may greatly over-compensate or greatly under-compensate the plaintiff because of the impossibility of predicting the plaintiff's actual lifetime.

b) Obviously, the approach of a revisable award is more consistent with the principle of full compensation which implies that, at the end of the day, damage and compensation accord. However, the principle of full compensation is not the only concern which comes into play, as is shown by the above enumeration of advantages and disadvantages of both approaches from which it appears that a once-and-for-all award, without possibility of revision, may be in the interest of the plaintiff and/or the defendant. Moreover, the possibility of unrestricted revision demands flexible procedural machinery, and it may be felt that this would not be in the public interest.

c) A non-revisable award of damages compels the judge to take into account many uncertainties as regards future damage. That gives rise to the question whether damages are to be assessed in a *rough-and-ready* way or *as exactly as possible*, in other words whether the courts should resign themselves to the inevitable inaccuracy of the assessment or whether, rather, they should arithmetically calculate the award on the basis of explicit assumptions about e.g. life expectancy, future rates of earnings and future inflation.

---

[378] *Inter alia* Rogers at 765–76; Salmond and Heuston at 531. A thorough and balanced discussion is given in H. McGregor, "Personal injury and death" in *International Encyclopedia of Comparative Law—Vol. XI/9: Torts* (Tübingen: Mohr, 1986) at para. 53–9.

8.3.1. ENGLISH LAW

Introductory Note

The English law of damages is based on the long-standing principle of a lump sum awarded on a once-and-for-all basis. The scope of the once-and-for-all rule is discussed in *Brunsden v. Humphrey*.[379] The inherent limitations of such an approach have long been recognized,[380] and indeed, modifications have been made to the system. Thus, the court may postpone the issue of the quantum of damages until after the hearing on liability and, in the meantime, grant *interim payments* to the plaintiff.[381] Furthermore, the courts have been enabled by the Supreme Court Act 1981[382] to award *provisional damages*[383] and, more recently, following the practice of *structured settlements*,[384] the Damages Act 1996[385] has allowed them to award *periodical payments* if plaintiff and defendant consent to such an award.[386] In spite of these changes, English law is still characterized by the lump sum principle and, until recently, also by the "rough and ready" assessment of future damage which, however, has now been abandoned and replaced by the principle that the court must calculate the lump sum as accurately as possible.[387]

Court of Appeal[388]   **8.E.21.–22.**
Brunsden v. *Humphrey*
and
House of Lords[389]
Lim Poh Choo v. *Camden and Islington Area Health Authority*

THE LUMP SUM AWARD "ONCE-AND-FOR-ALL"

1. *Brunsden* v. *Humphrey*   **8.E.21.**

Injured coachman

Although damage to goods and injury to the person have been occasioned by one and the same wrongful act, they give rise to distinct causes of action and, therefore, the recovery in an action for compensation for damage to the goods is no bar to a subsequent action for personal injury.

Facts: The plaintiff sustained personal injury and his cab was damaged in an accident due to the negligence of the defendant's servant. After having brought an action for damage to the cab, the plaintiff brought a second

---

[379] **8.E.21.**
[380] **8.E.22.**
[381] *Infra,* **8.E.21–22.**, Note (4)(i).
[382] C. 54.
[383] *Infra,* **8.E.21–22.**, Note (4)(ii).
[384] *Infra,* **8.E.21–22.**, Note (4)(iii).
[385] C. 48.
[386] *Infra,* **8.E.21–22.**, Note (4)(iv).
[387] **8.E.23.**
[388] (1884) 14 QBD 141.
[389] [1980] AC 174, HL.

action claiming damages for personal injury, alleging that he had been ignorant of the seriousness and the extent of the injuries at the time of the first proceedings.

Held: Reversing the judgment of the court of first instance, the Court of Appeal held that the second action was not barred by the previous proceedings.

Judgment: BOWEN LJ:[390] ". . . [T]he question to be decided is whether the damage done by the negligent driving of the defendant's servant to the plaintiff's cab is in substance the same cause of action as the damage caused by such negligence to the plaintiff's person. *Nobody can doubt that if the plaintiff had recovered any damages for injuries to his person, he could not have maintained a further action for fresh bodily injuries caused by the same act of negligence, merely because they had been discovered or developed subsequently, see Fetter v. Beale* [emphasis added]. "The jury," says the Court in that case, "have in the former action considered the nature of the wound and given damages for all the damage that it had done to the plaintiff." This authority however leaves still open the point I now have to determine, whether the cause of action arising from damage to the plaintiff's cab is in substance identical with that which accrues in consequence of the damage caused to his person.
. . . One wrong was done as soon as the plaintiff's enjoyment of his property was substantially interfered with. A further wrong arose as soon as the driving also caused injury to the plaintiff's person. Both causes of action, in *one* sense, may be said to be founded upon one act of the defendant's servant, but they are not on that account identical causes of action . . . It may be said that it would be convenient to force persons to sue for all their grievances at once and not to split their demands; but there is no positive law . . . against splitting demands which are essentially separable [references omitted] . . . In the present case the plaintiff's particulars in the county court were confined to the damage done to his cab; the injury to his person, therefore, was neither litigated nor considered in the county court. The real test is not, I think, whether the plaintiff had the opportunity of recovering in the first action what he claims to recover in the second [references omitted]."

2. *Lim Poh Choo* v. *Camden and Islington Area Health Authority*   8.E.22.

Plaintiff suffering irremediable disability

The award of a lump sum is final and not susceptible to review.

Facts: The plaintiff, aged 36, was admitted to hospital for minor surgery. Due to the negligence of a member of the defendant health authority hospital's staff, she suffered extensive and irremediable brain damage. She claimed damages for, among other things, the cost of future care and for loss of future earnings.

Held: The court of first instance and the court of appeal made allowance for inflation in the multiplier for future losses. The House of Lords disagreed.

Judgment: LORD SCARMAN:[391] "The course of the litigation illustrates, with devastating clarity, the insuperable problems implicit in a system of compensation for personal injuries which (unless the parties agree otherwise) can yield only a lump sum assessed by the court at the time of judgment. Sooner or later—and too often later rather than sooner—if the parties do not settle, a court (once liability is admitted or proved) has to make an award of damages. *The award which covers past, present and future injury and loss must, under our law, be of a lump sum assessed at the conclusion of the legal process. The award is final; it is not susceptible to review as the future unfolds, substituting fact for estimate* [emphasis added]. Knowledge of the future being denied to mankind, so much of the

---

[390] Brett MR concurring, Coleridge LCJ dissenting.
[391] With whom Lord Diplock, Viscount Dilhorne and Lord Simon of Glaisdale concurred.

award as is to be attributed to future loss and suffering—in many cases the major part of the award—will almost surely be wrong. There is really only one certainty: the future will prove the award to be either too high or too low. . . .

. . . *Lump sum compensation cannot be a perfect compensation for the future* [emphasis added]. An attempt to build into it a protection against future inflation is seeking after a perfection which is beyond the inherent limitations of the system."

Notes

(1) Under the once-and-for-all rule, damages *resulting from one and the same cause of action* must be assessed and recovered once-and-for-all, i.e. without possibility of revision. This rule was laid down in the old case of *Fetter* v. *Beale*,[392] to which the first annotated judgment refers. It applies irrespective of the question of future damage as it makes no difference whether all the harm has arisen at the time of proceedings or whether injury has been sustained at that time but will accrue in the future to a foreseeable extent, or whether the harm in question was neither foreseen nor foreseeable so that no compensation was sought for it. In the last case, the refusal of a second action may cause considerable hardship.[393]

The once-and-for-all rule has been said to be based on the legal proverbs *interest republicae ut sit finis litium* (it is in the public interest that there should be an end to litigation) and *nemo debet bis vexari pro una et eadem causa* (no one can be called to account twice for one and the same cause of action). It has been noted that those reasons are rather unconvincing.[394]

(2) In the first annotated case, the once-and-for-all rule was qualified in that it was held by a majority of the Court of Appeal that when two *distinct rights* are violated, the plaintiff may bring successive actions in respect of each of those rights.[395] To justify two actions, it is not enough that the same act amounts to two *distinct violations of the same right*.[396] As a consequence, the recoverability of damage after previous proceedings depends on the question whether that damage results from the violation of a right which is distinct from the right underlying the loss for which compensation was given in the first proceedings.[397] Thus, the mere fact that the plaintiff claims for a harm which was not taken into account when the first award was assessed, does not entitle him to claim additional damages for further loss that the plaintiff has sustained as a result of the violation of the right originally relied on.

---

[392] (1701) 1 Ld.Raym. 339, 692 or *Fitter* v. *Veal* (1701) 12 Mod. 542 (see Rogers at 740).

[393] H. McGregor, *McGregor on Damages*, 16th edn. (London: Sweet & Maxwell, 1997) at 275, para. 414.

[394] Rogers at 740. These proverbs are also cited in *Brunsden* v. *Humphrey, supra*, at 147. At 145, Brett MR expressed his doubts about the desirability of the rule.

[395] For a discussion of whether successive actions may be brought in other classes of case, see Rogers at 741–2.

[396] Salmond and Heuston at 551, where some arguments for and against the rule in *Brunsden* v. *Humphrey* are presented.

[397] But see the criticism of Coleridge LCJ: ". . . [I]t seems to me a subtlety not warranted by law to hold that a man cannot bring two actions, if he is injured in his arm and in his leg, but can bring two, if besides his arm and leg being injured his trousers which contain his leg, and his coat-sleeve which contains his arm, have been torn. The consequences of holding this are so serious, and may be very probably so oppressive, that I at least must respectfully dissent from a judgment which establishes it": *Brunsden* v. *Humphrey, supra*, at 153.

In *Talbot* v. *Berkshire County Council*,[398] the ruling in *Brunsden* v. *Humphrey* was criticized for having ignored the general rule of *res judicata*[399] which precludes a party from raising a matter in a subsequent action which could, with reasonable diligence, have been raised in earlier proceedings. Indeed, in *Brunsden* v. *Humphrey*, the plaintiff could reasonably have been expected to have claimed damages for damage to the goods and for personal injury in the same proceedings. As a consequence, the rule of *res judicata* may bar a plaintiff from claiming compensation for harm which has not yet been compensated. In other words, the principle of full compensation may be qualified by procedural considerations.

(3) The second annotated judgment expresses the common law principle that damages may be awarded only by way of a lump sum on an "once-and-for-all" basis, that is without possibility of review, and underlines the inherent limitations of such system. Thus, in the case of personal injury (as in the case of death) the assessment of future damage will inevitably depend on many imponderables: the period, extent and evolution of the plaintiff's disability, the impact on the plaintiff's earning capacity, the evolution in the plaintiff's earnings (e.g. chances of promotion), the risk of unemployment, the need for and the cost of future care, the impact of inflation and so on.

(4) Over the years the limitations resulting from an unrestricted application of the lump sum system have been attenuated.

(*i*) *Postponed trial* and *interim payments*. The issue of the quantum of damages may be *postponed* until after the hearing on liability.[400] In the meantime, the court may award the plaintiff, under certain conditions,[401] *interim payments* (a single payment or instalments) to enable him or her to cope with the loss already sustained. The award of interim payments is not an award of damages: the payments are subject to repayment if it turns out that sums received exceed the amount of damages to be awarded.

(*ii*) *Provisional damages*. S. 32A of the Supreme Court Act 1981 and s. 51 of the County Courts Act 1984 have enabled the courts to make an award of *provisional damages* in a claim for personal injuries. Such award can be made where it is proved or admitted that there is a chance that at some time in the future the injured person will, as a result of the act or omission which gave rise to the cause of action, develop some serious disease or suffer some serious deterioration in his physical or mental condition.[402] The injured person is entitled to apply for further damages at a future date if he or she develops the disease or suffers the deterioration but, subject thereto, the award of provisional damages is final.

Willson v. *Ministry of Defence*[403] is one of the rare reported cases in which a claim for provisional damages was made. The judgment interprets the provisions of s. 32A of the Supreme Court Act 1981 as requiring "a clear and severable risk rather than continuing deterioration" before an award

---

[398] [1994] QB 290, CA at 301.

[399] In a loose sense, based upon the public policy interest in preventing a multiplicity of actions.

[400] The general powers conferred on the English courts by the new Civil Procedure Rules 1998 in the interest of improved "case-management" by the courts (see Part 1 of the Rules) include the power to direct a trial of any issue and to decide the order in which issues are to be tried (see rule 3.1 of the Rules). Those powers are effectively in substitution for, *inter alia*, the more specific powers previously conferred by Rules of the Supreme Court ("RSC"), Order 33 which provided for the order of separate trials of issues of liability and damages.

[401] Civil Procedure Rules 1998, r. 25.1 and r. 25.6–25.9. These rules effectively replace RSC, Order 29, r. 9.

[402] See also Part 41 of the Civil Procedure Rules 1998.

[403] [1991] 1 All ER 638.

of provisional damages can be made. The chance of subsequent epilepsy in cases of cranial injuries[404] or perhaps the development of full-blown AIDS following HIV infection[405] have been raised as possible examples of such a risk; by contrast, in *Willson* v. *Ministry of Defence* the development of arthritis following orthopaedic injury was held to constitute "continuing deterioration". For some, this restrictive interpretation "is justifiable because an extension to gradual deterioration would vastly increase the number of cases in which provisional awards could be made and introduce a serious measure of uncertainty into the system";[406] for others the judgment reveals the conservatism of the courts, which results in damages awards which are too low if the risk materializes and too high if it does not.[407] It has been claimed "that the obstacles to using the procedure will ensure that it remains a backwater of personal injury litigation despite, the [Damages] Act 1996".[408]

(iii) Structured settlements. In an effort to attain some of the advantages of periodical payments within the framework of a once-and-for-all approach, the practice of structured settlements was developed in the late 1980s.[409]

A structured settlement operates as follows:

"The defendant's insurer, usually after having informally agreed a lump sum figure with the plaintiff, will agree to convert part of the damages into a series of periodic payments. To fund the arrangement the insurer purchases an annuity on the plaintiff's life. The payments are 'structured' to meet the individual's needs and are free of tax in the plaintiff's hands. This is because the Revenue [the UK tax authority] have accepted that they may be considered instalments of capital rather than income. In return for making this arrangement the insurer will bargain for a discount on the conventional lump sum figure."[410]

Under a structured settlement, the plaintiff benefits from some of the advantages of periodical payments.[411] The settlement can offer protection against inflation by linking the payments to rises in the Retail Prices Index. The payments can be arranged to last for as long as the plaintiff lives. The plaintiff does not bear the risk of making the necessary investments and is protected from premature dissipation of the capital. Moreover, the set-

---

[404] Markesinis and Deakin at 745.

[405] Rogers at 768.

[406] Ibid.

[407] Markesinis and Deakin at 745–6.

[408] R. Lewis, "Lobbying and the Damages Act 1996: 'Whispering in Appropriate Ears' " (1997) 60 Mod LR 230 at 237. Under s. 3 of the Damages Act 1996 (c. 48), where a plaintiff is awarded provisional damages and subsequently dies as a result of the anticipated condition, dependents will not be prevented from recovering the losses that they sustain from the death: Ibid.

[409] See for a detailed analysis, see R. Lewis, "The Merits of a Structured Settlement: The Plaintiff's Perspective" (1993) 13 OJLS 530, where it is said that the development of the structured settlement represents "the most important change to our damages system in almost half a century" and R. Lewis, "Legal Limits on the Structured Settlement of Damages" (1993) 52 Camb LJ 470. See further Chapter 6A of Kemp & Kemp, *The Quantum of Damages*. It must be noted that structured settlements are considered only when the plaintiff is entitled to at least about half a million pounds (see R. Lewis, "Lobbying and the Damages Act 1996: 'Whispering in Appropriate Ears'" (1997) 60 Mod LR 230 at 235). Recent legislation provides full protection in the event of the insurer's insolvency: Ibid. at 235–6.

[410] R. Lewis (1993) 13 OJLS 530 at 530. These settlements have been made possible because of the tax benefit. Indeed, while the income from a traditional lump sum payment is taxed, the payments made under a structured settlement are not. So the plaintiff would have to invest a larger sum to obtain the same amount which is paid to him under the settlement. This tax benefit allows the insurer to negotiate a discount on the lump sum figure. See also Rogers at 766–7; Markesinis and Deakin at 747–50.

[411] For an enumeration, see Introductory Note, under (a).

tlement can be tailored to meet the needs of the plaintiff, e.g. by providing for larger sums at various dates. However, a structured settlement still operates within the framework of a once-and-for-all approach. It is based on the lump sum which the court would have awarded and it cannot be revised, e.g. in the case of an alteration in the plaintiff's condition or in the case of an increased living standard. Finally, a structured settlement (a) cannot be judicially imposed and (b) cannot be implemented after a judgment for a money sum has been given or the plaintiff has received his or her award of damages.[412]

(*iv*) *Periodical payments award.* The limitation just mentioned at (b) above has been somewhat mitigated by the fact that section 2(1) of the Damages Act 1996[413] now empowers a court awarding damages in an action for personal injury to order that the damages are wholly or partly to take the form of periodical payments. However, here again, such award can be made only with the consent of both parties.[414]

House of Lords[415]   **8.E.23.**
Wells v. *Wells*

THE CALCULATION OF ONCE-AND-FOR-ALL AWARDS

Serious brain damage

The award of a lump sum should be calculated as precisely as possible, in order to provide, by its capital and income, periodical sums equal to the plaintiff's estimated periodical loss.

Facts: In each of three joined cases the defendants had admitted liability for causing serious personal injury. In the first case, a part-time nurse, aged nearly 58, suffered serious brain damage in a traffic accident. As a consequence she was no longer capable of working or caring for herself or her family. In the second case the plaintiff, six years old at the date of trial, was injured before birth by the maladministration of a drug intended to induce labour and became very severely handicapped. In the third case, the plaintiff, then aged 24, suffered serious brain damage when, while he was working in a steel mill, a white-hot steel bar buckled and struck him on the head.

Held: (1) In awarding damages in the form of a lump sum the court has to calculate as best it can the sum that would be adequate, by its capital and income, to provide periodical sums equal to the plaintiff's estimated periodical loss over the period during which that loss is likely to continue. In calculating that sum, a discount must be applied which has, as its purpose, to eliminate over-compensation arising from the award of a lump sum that will earn interest during the years of future loss and expenses. (2) The injured plaintiffs were not in the same position as an ordinary prudent investor and were entitled to the greater security achieved by investment in index-linked government securities ("gilts"), which currently yielded a net return of 3 per cent (instead of the conventional basis of the annual return of 5 per cent that a prudent investor could obtain from a mixture of equities and ordinary gilts). (3) Where the judge has accepted medical evidence as to the plaintiff's life expectancy, there is no justification for any discount in respect of "the contingencies of life".

---

[412] R. Lewis, "Legal Limits on the Structured Settlement of Damages" (1993) 52 Camb LJ 470 at 473 and 478–9.
[413] C. 48, Section 2(1).
[414] See Rogers at 767.
[415] [1999] 1 AC 345, [1998] 3 WLR 329.

Judgment: LORD HOPE OF CRAIGHEAD:[416] *"It has often been said that the assessment of damages is not an exact science—that all the law can do is to work out as best it can, in a rough and ready way, the sum to be paid to the plaintiff as compensation for the loss and injury* [emphasis added]. There remains much truth in these statements, despite the important advances which have been made in the search for greater accuracy. The amount of the award to be made for pain, suffering and loss of amenity cannot be precisely calculated. All that can be done is to award such sum, within the broad criterion of what is reasonable and in line with similar awards in comparable cases, as represents the court's best estimate of the plaintiff's general damages. Nor can the accuracy which can usually be achieved in the assessment of past loss of wages and of other past losses and expense which fall under the broad heading of special damages be matched when it comes to the future. *The court cannot say precisely what will happen. It can only proceed by means of assumptions. The calculations which it then makes will involve the use of arithmetic as the multiplier is applied to the multiplicand. To that extent the exercise will give the impression of accuracy. But the accuracy of the result achieved by arithmetic will depend on the assumptions on which it has been based* [emphasis added]. In making these assumptions the court must do the best it can on the available evidence.

Nevertheless the object of the award of damages for future expenditure is to place the injured party as nearly as possible in the same financial position as he or she would have been in but for the accident. The aim is to award such a sum of money as will amount to no more, and at the same time no less, than the net loss. As Lord Oliver of Aylmerton said in *Hodgson* v. *Trapp* [1989] AC 807, 826:

> "Essentially what the court has to do is to calculate as best it can the sum of money which will on the one hand be adequate, by its capital and income, to provide annually for the injured person a sum equal to his estimated annual loss over the whole of the period during which that loss is likely to continue, but which, on the other hand, will not, at the end of that period, leave him in a better financial position than he would have been apart from the accident. Hence the conventional approach is to assess the amount notionally required to be laid out in the purchase of an annuity which will provide the annual amount needed for the whole period of loss."

The annuity approach requires that, *once the necessary assumptions have been made, the calculation of the award will result in an amount which matches as accurately as possible the sum required over the entire period of the assumed loss* [emphasis added]."

Lord STEYN:[417] ". . . The Court of Appeal have assumed that the same investment policy would be suitable for all investors, regardless of any special needs. *The premise that plaintiffs, who have perhaps been very seriously injured, are in the same position as ordinary investors is not one that I can accept* [emphasis added]. Such plaintiffs have not chosen to invest: the tort and its consequences compel them to do so. For plaintiffs an investment in equities is inherently risky, notably in regard to the timing of the investment. The annuity method contemplates sales of capital from time to time. With equities there is the risk that planned sales of capital will have to be made during a slump, thereby eroding the capital and depleting the fund . . . Typically, by investing in equities an ordinary investor takes a calculated risk which he can bear in order to improve his financial position. On the other hand, the typical plaintiff requires the return from an award of damages to provide the necessities of life. For such a plaintiff it is not possible to cut back on medical and nursing care as well as other essential services. His objective must be to ensure that the damages awarded do not run out. It is money that he cannot afford to lose. The ordinary investor does not have the same concerns. It is therefore unrealistic to treat such a plaintiff as an ordinary investor. It seems to me entirely reasonable for such a plaintiff to be cautious and conservative. He does not have the freedom of choice available to the ordinary investor. If a comparison is to be made . . . the position of plaintiffs is much closer to that of elderly, retired individuals who have limited savings which they

---

[416] [1998] 3 WLR 329 at 356–7. Lord Clyde and Lord Hutton delivered speeches to the same effect as those of Lord Hope of Craighead, Lord Lloyd of Berwick and Lord Steyn (see below).
[417] [1998] 3 WLR 329 at 353–4.

want to invest safely to provide for their declining years. Such individuals would generally not invest in equities. But for the plaintiffs the need for safety may often be more compelling. In any event, it seems to me difficult to say that an investment in index-linked securities would be *unreasonable* [emphasis in original]."

LORD LLOYD OF BERWICK:[418] "*It is of the nature of a lump sum payment that it may, in respect of future pecuniary loss, prove to be either too little or too much* [emphasis added]. So far as the multiplier is concerned, the plaintiff may die the next day, or he may live beyond his normal life expectation of life. So far as the multiplicand is concerned, the cost of future care may exceed everyone's best estimate. Or a new cure or less expensive form of treatment may be discovered. But these uncertainties do not affect the basic principle. *The purpose of the award is to put the plaintiff in the same position, financially, as if he had not been injured. The sum should be calculated as accurately as possible, making just allowance, where this is appropriate, for contingencies* [emphasis added]. But once the calculation is done, there is no justification for imposing an artificial cap on the multiplier. There is no room for a judicial scaling down. . . .

[In] *Thomas* v. *Brighton Authority* [the] agreed medical evidence was that the plaintiff has a life expectancy to the age of 60. [The trial judge] held [reference omitted], however, that he ought to reduce the arithmetical multiplier by about 20 per cent. "to cater for hazards of life in such cases". In the result he took a multiplier of 23. The Court of Appeal agreed with the judge's approach but started from a different starting-point. With a 4.5 per cent. discount rate the arithmetical multiplier came to 20. Reduced by 15 per cent., rather than 20 per cent., they arrived at a multiplier of 17.

Was it correct for the judge and the Court of Appeal to reduce the arithmetical multiplier, and therefore, in effect, override the expectation of life agreed by the doctors?. . .

. . . [T]he inevitable result of reducing the multiplier to 17 . . . will be that the plaintiff's damages will run out when he is 39 . . .

There is no purpose in the courts making as accurate a prediction as they can of the plaintiff's future needs if the resulting sum is arbitrarily reduced for no better reason than that the prediction might be wrong. A prediction remains a prediction. Contingencies should be taken into account where they work in one direction, but not where they cancel out. There is no more logic or justice in reducing the whole life multiplier by 15 per cent. or 20 per cent. on an agreed expectation of life than there would be in increasing it by the same amount.

. . .

. . . I do not suggest that the judge should be a slave to the tables. There may well be special factors in particular cases. But the tables should now be regarded as the starting-point, rather than a check. A judge should be slow to depart from the relevant actuarial multiplier on impressionistic grounds, or by reference to "a spread of multipliers in comparable cases" especially when the multipliers were fixed before actuarial tables were widely used."

Notes

(1) The annotated judgment puts an end to the rough-and-ready assessment of damages for future loss caused by personal injury. Until the annotated judgment, as Lord Hope states, "it has often been said that the assessment of damages is not an exact science—that all the law can do is to work out as best it can, in a rough and ready way, the sum to be paid to the plaintiff as compensation for the loss and injury".[419] This rough-and-ready approach was applied in several respects and resulted, in particular, in future inflation being taken into account in only a rough-and-ready way and the courts being

---

[418] [1998] 3 WLR 329 at 332–3 and 345–7.
[419] See e.g. *Hodgson* v. *Trapp* [1989] 1 AC 807, HL at 826 per Lord Oliver of Aylmerton and *Hunt* v. *Severs* [1994] 2 AC 350, HL at 365 per Lord Bridge of Harwich.

somewhat opposed to use of actuarial tables. Under the new approach, in Lord Hope's words, "once the necessary assumptions have been made, the calculation of the award will result in an amount which matches as accurately as possible the sum required over the entire period of the assumed loss". Of course, in Lord Lloyd's words, "it is of the nature of a lump sum payment that it may, in respect of future pecuniary loss, prove to be either too little or too much" since the court cannot say precisely what will happen in the future. But this very wisdom does not justify the calculation of the award not being made as accurately as possible, once the court has made assumptions about life expectancy, future rate of earning and so on, in order to provide, by its capital and income, periodical sums equal to the plaintiff's estimated periodical loss.

The general basis for the calculation of such a lump sum is mentioned in the speech of Lord Hope and will be discussed in Note (2). In calculating the lump sum, a discount must be applied for acceleration of payment. The assumptions upon which the appropriate rate for such discount is selected, as explained in Lord Steyn's speech, and the impact of the new view on the importance of actuarial calculations, as expressed by Lord Lloyd, will be discussed in Notes (3) and (4), and Note (5) respectively.

(2) The conventional approach of assessing the lump sum in the case of personal injury is called the "multiplier method", by which the net annual loss (the multiplicand) is multiplied by a figure (the multiplier) which is based upon the number of years during which the loss will last, taking into account the fact that a lump sum is given to compensate for continuing, periodical loss (see *infra*). This method is also applied in the case of fatal accidents, although, of course, the multiplicand and multiplier are then determined on different bases.

Indeed, in case of *death*, the loss suffered by dependents consists in the loss of that part of the deceased's income which would have been spent for their benefit. Consequently, the multiplicand is assessed at the annual wages earned by the deceased from which the amount of the deceased's own living expenses is deducted; the multiplier is determined on the basis of the number of years from the date of death during which the dependents would have been benefited from the deceased, which means that both the deceased's and the dependents' prospects must be taken into account and that the period of dependency of each of the dependents may vary for indeed, a child's dependency ceases at an earlier stage than that of a spouse. In cases of *personal injury*, of course, such considerations do not arise, and only the plaintiff's working life expectancy needs to be determined.

In calculating the multiplier, account must be taken of the fact that the lump sum is given to compensate for successive instalments of future loss and that the damages in respect of each successive instalment of the loss that has yet to occur will be earning interest in the meanwhile. Any rational award of damages must therefore allow for the advantage to the plaintiff of this "acceleration" of payment. As a consequence, a discount must be applied and, as stated by Lord Oliver in the quotation to which Lord Hope refers, the objective is to arrive at "a sum of money which will . . . be adequate, by its capital and income, to provide annually for the injured person a sum equal to his estimated annual loss over the whole of the period during which that loss is likely to continue".[420]

---

[420] This method is known as the "annuity" approach or method: see Lord Lloyd in the annotated judgment [1998] 3 WLR 329 at 333 and Lord Steyn at 353. With a lump sum award, the damages are calculated on the assumption that at the end of the relevant period the fund will be exhausted; this might occur because of

(3) To select the multiplier, the appropriate interest rate representing the discount for acceleration of payment must be chosen. Until the annotated judgment, and for a long time, the multipliers that were used by the judges, were appropriate to interest rates of 4 per cent to 5 per cent,[421] i.e. the rate of interest which could be obtained on the lump sum during periods of stable currency.[422] In modern times however, money has not retained its value.[423] Accordingly, the question arose as to whether, in the calculation of the lump sum, account must be taken of the fact that, by the time when the expected loss occurs, the currency will, by reason of inflation, be worth less than it was at the time of the award.[424]

Initially, the English courts assumed that plaintiffs could protect themselves by investment of the money received in fixed interest securities. Since in time of inflation, the rate of interest tends to be higher, it was assumed that what the plaintiff lost by inflation, was roughly equivalent to what the plaintiff gained by the higher rate of interest. As Lord Diplock stated in *Cookson* v. *Knowles*,[425] "inflation is taken care of in a rough and ready way by the higher rates of interest obtainable as one of the consequences of it". However, the interest on fixed interest securities did not adequately compensate for the erosion in their real value due to inflation and, in addition, the whole of the interest was taxed as income even though it also contained compensation for the decline in the value of money.[426]

An alternative investment strategy was to invest the fund in equities (ordinary shares in industrial and commercial companies) and the courts assumed that the plaintiff could take care of future inflation by investing the lump sum sensibly in a mixed "basket" of equities and gilts.[427] A prudent investor is assumed to be able to obtain an average a return of 4 to 5 per cent, provided that he or she could leave the capital invested for a substantial period of time without the risk of having to make significant withdrawals at a time when capital values are depressed because of falls in the stock market.[428]

---

draw-down of capital over the period or because an annuity (which is referred to by Lord Oliver in *Hodgson* v. *Trapp* [1989] AC 807 at 826, to which Lord Hope refers) was purchased for the period in question. How the plaintiff chooses in fact to proceed is, in the case of a lump sum award, entirely a matter for him or her.

[421] This was so "[w]hether the judges using them were conscious of this or not": Lord Diplock, in *Cookson* v. *Knowles* [1978] 2 WLR 978, HL at 986. See also at 991 per Lord Fraser of Tullybelton.

[422] This rate was probably related to the rates of interest which were currently available in the market for depositing the money in a bank: Lord Hope in the annotated judgment: [1998] 3 WLR 329 at 358.

[423] So far as *past* inflation is concerned, it has long been recognized that awards of damages should reflect the value of the currency at the date of the award: see *Mitchell* v. *Mulholland and another (No. 2)* [1972] 1 QB 65, CA at 83. Therefore, when looking at previous awards in comparable cases, the courts have recognized the need to take account of the decline in the value of the currency since the date of the previous award: see Kemp & Kemp, *The Quantum of Damages* (London: Sweet & Maxwell) at para. 1–016, 1–017 and 7.007.

[424] For a detailed analysis, see D. Kemp, "Discounting compensation for future loss" (1985) 101 LQR 556.

[425] Lord Diplock in *Cookson* v. *Knowles* [1979] AC 556, HL at 571–2.

[426] Even disregarding the effect of tax, the "real interest rate" (price inflation minus the nominal interest rate) on 20-year British Government securities averaged only 1.52 per cent over the years 1970–1990 (Kemp and Kemp, *The Quantum of Damages* (London: Sweet & Maxwell) at para. 0–141) and in years when inflation was running at a rate in excess of 10 per cent the real interest rate was generally negative.

[427] Lord Lloyd in the annotated judgment [1998] 3 WLR 329 at 333.

[428] The average annual return net of tax on a 20-year investment in *equities* over the period 1960 to 1997, without reinvesting the income, was about 4 per cent. However, it was not until 1989 that equity prices regained their old pre–1972 level in real terms: see Lord Lloyd in the annotated judgment [1998] 3 WLR 329 at 335. A detailed discussion of investments and their return can also be found in the decision of the Court of Appeal in the annotated case [1997] 1 WLR 652 at 666–72.

As a result of these views on how a "prudent investor" is deemed to act, the courts held that plaintiffs in personal injury cases, like ordinary investors, were able to adopt a prudent investment strategy, including investment of a substantial portion of the fund in equities. As a consequence, the Court of Appeal[429] in the case under review believed that the conventional discount rate of 4.5 per cent should apply (contrary to what the first instance judges held who, in a brave departure from precedent, had applied a rate of 2.5 per cent).

(4) In the annotated judgments, their Lordships, as illustrated by Lord Steyn's speech, no longer subscribed to the view that a plaintiff in a personal injury case must be regarded as an "ordinary investor". Such a plaintiff cannot leave the capital invested for a substantial period of time without the need to make significant withdrawals, since he or she "requires the return from an award of damages to provide the necessities of life". Accordingly, he or she is not able to defer selling equities when the equity market suffers a fall, and should therefore not be required to invest the lump sum awarded in equities but should instead be entitled to a secure investment which offers protection against inflation.

Such an investment has been made available by the introduction, in 1981, of *Index Linked Government Securities* ("ILGS"). ILGS are secure because they are issued by the British Government and both capital and income are protected against inflation. In addition, as a range of such stocks, with different redemption dates, became available, they offered a solution to the problem facing the plaintiff who was awarded damages on account of future loss.

However, the problem with this kind of investment is that it generally carries interest at a rate of only 3 per cent. For, indeed, applying the lower discount rate makes a substantial difference. In the example of an average annual cost of care of GBP 10,000 on a life expectancy of 20 years, use of a discount rate of 5 per cent results in an award of GBP 124,600 whereas use of a discount rate of 3 per cent results in an award of GBP 148,800.[430] However, this has not prevented the House of Lords accepting the lower rate, which from now on, subject to section 1 of the Damages Act 1996, should be the new guideline rate for general use.[431]

(5) Besides the choice of the appropriate interest rate in order to calculate the discount for acceleration of payment, the selection of the correct multiplier also requires an assessment of the plaintiff's life expectancy. On the basis of these two figures (interest rate and life expectancy), the multiplier can be calculated arithmetically. However, until the annotated case, the English courts preferred the "haphazard approach of making a somewhat arbitrary reduction in the number of years of loss to arrive at the multiplier".[432] That was because the courts were traditionally opposed to use of actuarial tables and used them only "as a check on assessments arrived at by the familiar conventional methods".[433] That position was explained by the view that actuarial calculations deal with the average

---

[429] [1997] 1 WLR 652. See on the Court of Appeal judgment D. Kemp, "Discounting damages for future loss" (1997) 113 LQR 195.

[430] Example given by Lord Lloyd at 333.

[431] Section 1 (1) of the Damages Act 1996 provides that in determining the return to be expected from the investment of a sum awarded as damages for future pecuniary loss in an action for personal injury, the court shall take into account the rate of return which may from time to time be prescribed by an order made by the Lord Chancellor. Subsection (2) provides that subsection (1) shall not however prevent the court from taking a different rate of return into account if any party shows that it is more appropriate in the case in question.

[432] H. McGregor, *McGregor on Damages*, 16th edn. (London: Sweet & Maxwell, 1997) at 1024, para. 1567.

[433] *Hunt* v. *Severs* [1994] 2 AC 350, HL at 365 per Lord Bridge of Harwich; see also *infra* **8.E.52.**

case rather than the individual plaintiff.[434] They would introduce into the assessment of damages "a false appearance of accuracy and precision in a sphere where conjectural estimates have to play a large part".[435]

The above view was subjected to attack. In addition, suitable actuarial tables were produced by a working party (the "Ogden Tables") and, following the recommendation of the Law Commission,[436] their use was sanctioned by the Civil Evidence Act 1995[437] which provides in section 10(1):

"The actuarial tables (together with explanatory notes) for use in personal injury and fatal accident cases issued from time to time by the Government Actuary's Department are admissible in evidence for the purpose of assessing, in an action for personal injury,[438] the sum to be awarded as general damages for future pecuniary loss."

Nevertheless, in the annotated case, the Court of Appeal held that the Ogden Tables were not to be applied without adjustment, and referring to *Hunt* v. *Severs*, went on to say[439]:

". . . [T]he suggestion that, in fixing the multiplier, the court is making a judgment which is little more than a mathematical exercise is erroneous . . . Furthermore . . . the probabilities come into play in order to arrive at the appropriate discount when fixing . . . a 'fair' multiplier. In the process of assessing this discount the court must take into account not only financial considerations such as the accelerated payment and the availability of capital as well as income to meet future expenses, but also, bearing in mind life's manifold contingencies, the degree of likelihood that the particular plaintiff may not live out his full expectation of life; and, in the case of future loss of earnings that he might not have continued to work throughout his full working span, or (in the case of a child) that he might never have become an earner [references omitted]. These factors are of course helpfully addressed with a considerable degree of sophistication in the second edition of the Ogden Tables which will no doubt be of considerable assistance in the future; but they cannot of course cater for every relevant circumstance, affecting the individual plaintiff, which will enter into the final assessment."[440]

It is clear from the speech of Lord Lloyd of Berwick that the House of Lords firmly disagreed and that once the judge has, as in the annotated case, assessed the plaintiff's life expectancy, there is no justification for any discount in respect of the contingencies of life. As a consequence, the House of Lords held that the multiplier was assessed at too low a level both at first instance and on appeal, and that the appropriate multiplier was 26.58, as against the 17 used by the judge at first instance and the 23 used by the Court of Appeal.[441]

---

[434] This view is explained in *Mitchell v. Mulholland (No 2)* [1972] 1 QB 65, CA at 76 ff.

[435] *Taylor v. O'Connor* [1971] AC 115, HL at 140 per Lord Pearson.

[436] See for more details H. McGregor, *McGregor on Damages*, 16th edn. (London: Sweet & Maxwell, 1997), 1024 at para. 1568.

[437] C. 38.

[438] Section 10(3)(b) states that, for the purpose of that section, 'action for personal injury' includes an action brought by virtue of the Fatal Accidents Act 1976, *supra*, Chapter II, **2.E.10.**

[439] [1994] 2 AC 350, HL.

[440] [1997] 1 WLR 652, CA at 676.

[441] Lord Lloyd in the annotated judgment [1998] 3 WLR 329 at 347. In practice judges had imposed a limit of 18 years in fixing a multiplier: see Lord Steyn in the annotated judgment at 350.

8.3.2. GERMAN LAW

Introductory Note

In contrast to English law, German law favours revisable awards of periodical payments: § 843(1) BGB allows the award of periodical payments in case of loss of earnings or increased costs as a result of impairment of body or health; § 844(2) BGB grants the award to dependents of the victim upon his death (see also § 845[442]). The periodical payments award is characterized by an almost unlimited possibility of revision, at the request of either party, when substantial changes occur in the circumstances which were decisive in the making of the award.[443] By and large, the German procedural framework is so flexible that, to a considerable extent, the plaintiff is allowed to obtain full compensation— or is precluded from being enriched –however the damage develops in the future.[444]

Sometimes, a capital sum may be more advantageous for the plaintiff than periodical payments. In the presence of a serious reason (*ein wichtiger Grund*), § 843(3) BGB—to which §§ 844 and 845 refer—allows the plaintiff to claim a capital sum instead of periodical payments. Unlike the periodical payments award, such a capital sum is not revisable, and consequently the court's assessment should accommodate potential future changes as far as possible.[445] Capital payments on the basis of § 843(3) BGB are rarely ordered by the courts. However, parties may settle for a capital sum out of court even in the absence of a serious reason.

BGH, 20 December 1960[446]   **8.G.24.**

Revision of a periodical payments award

Totally invalidated 25 years later

An action for variation (Abänderungsklage; § 323 ZPO) *of a periodical payments award can be brought when there is a change in the plaintiff's earning capacity, as when changes in economic circumstances are reflected in wage increases.*

Facts: The plaintiff, aged 22, was the victim of a car accident in 1930. The court of first instance had granted him an annuity until the age of 65 on the basis of a reduction in earning capacity of 50 per cent and a salary of 1690 *Reichsmark* per annum. The plaintiff became a total invalid in 1954 and brought an *Abänderungsklage* to increase the annuity. An increase was finally granted, in the amount of DEM 936 quarterly, by a judgment by the Stuttgart Court of Appeal on 8 October 1958. On 5 December 1958, the plaintiff also sought a declaration (*Feststellungsklage*; § 256 ZPO) that the defendant was obliged to make good all further future harm resulting from the 1930 accident, arguing, on the one hand, that further wage and price increases were possible and his condition might deteriorate, and on the other, that without such declaration, a new claim for additional compensation might be at risk of extinction by prescription.

---

[442] See *infra*, 8.5.1., Introductory Note.
[443] **8.G.24.** and Note (1) below it.
[444] See *infra*, **8.G.24.**, Note (2); for a general discussion see M. Schultz, "Schadensfortentwicklung und Prozeßrecht" (1991) 191 AcP 433.
[445] **8.G.25.**
[446] BGHZ 34, 110. Translation by Y. P. Salmon.

Held: The *Feststellungsklage* was allowed by the court of first instance. The court of appeal reversed the judgment of the court of first instance on the ground that an *Abänderungsklage* remained available to the plaintiff. The BGH upheld the decision of the court of appeal.

Judgment: "The court of appeal rejected the claim on the ground that the plaintiff does not have a legal interest in obtaining the desired declaration (*Feststellungsklage*) (§ 256 ZPO). That is not open to legal objection.

1. By a judgment of the court of appeal of Stuttgart of 8 October 1958, the plaintiff was awarded a quarterly periodical payment of DEM 936 until the completion of his sixty-fifth year of life for his full loss of wages which he had claimed from the defendant. By the present action [the plaintiff] wishes to safeguard future claims in respect of changed wage and price conditions, by a judgment which would legally establish the defendant's duty to compensate [the plaintiff] for [his] loss (*Schadensersatzpflicht*). That claim would be well-founded if the plaintiff could [then] achieve an increase in the periodical payment not through an action for variation (*Abänderungsklage*) under § 323 ZPO, but through a simple supplementary claim [for recurrent performance] (*Nachforderungs-* or *Zusatzklage*) on the basis of § 258 ZPO, as suggested in recent literature. Since, according to that literature, under the latter procedure . . . the question whether the plaintiff has any claim to damages would have to be examined anew, he would have a legal interest that the defendant's duty to compensate him be legally established already. The BGH cannot however follow the view that the periodical payments can be increased by such [supplementary claim for recurrent performance] under § 258 ZPO, without the need for the conditions of § 323 ZPO being met. . . .

Rather, it is closer to the wording of the law and also in keeping with its spirit and purpose that, through the introduction of § 323 ZPO, the legislator provided a specific procedure for use in all cases where substantial changes in circumstances that were decisive for a judgment ordering recurrent performance necessitate variation of the judgment. *Claims for recurrent performance [by the defendant]—above all for the payment of maintenance under family law and for the payment of damages under §§ 843, 844(2) and § 845 BGB—have the special feature that their award, level and duration depend on future and often changing circumstances* [emphasis added]. Since the development of circumstances often cannot be foreseen, in many cases the judge cannot adapt his judgment to this supposed future state of affairs. *This uncertainty in the assessment of future developments is taken into account in § 323 ZPO by allowing variation for changed circumstances where there is a substantial change in some circumstance on which the judgment was based* [emphasis added]. Therefore, § 323 ZPO contains an application in the field of procedure, of the principle *rebus sic stantibus* [according to which contracts become inoperative if conditions have changed fundamentally] . . . [and] at the same time provides the procedure by which variations can be implemented in relation to prior judicial decisions.

. . .

To be sure, a definite obstacle is present for the plaintiff who seeks, pursuant to § 323 ZPO, an increase in the awarded periodical payments, as the law requires a *substantial* change in the circumstances that were decisive for the assessment of the periodical payments award as a prerequisite for increasing the level of the award [emphasis in original] . . . *Changes in economic conditions could and should be regarded today as substantial in the sense of § 323 ZPO, if they lead to a change in the wages and salaries of civil servants and employees* [emphasis added]. In this way the interests of the plaintiff who is able to rely only on an action for variation of an earlier judgment (*Abänderungsklage*) are sufficiently protected . . .

2. Likewise, the plaintiff cannot claim to have a legal interest in bringing [the] action for a declaration (*Feststellungsklage*) on the ground that he needs to be protected against an extinction of rights by prescription in the event of a subsequent change in circumstances (§ 323 ZPO). Whether a claim for variation of an earlier judgment (*Abänderungsanspruch*) under § 323 ZPO can be

extinguished by prescription at all need not be considered. If prescription is possible, time could begin to run only after the occurrence of the changes that legally justify the variation of the judgment . . .

3. In so far as the plaintiff relied on possible changes in his state of health to justify his claim, the court of appeal denied his interest in obtaining a declaratory judgment.

On appeal [to the BGH], the plaintiff seeks to derive his interest to legal protection [i.e. his interest in obtaining a declaratory judgment] from the fact that the defendant could nonetheless plead extinctive prescription in the following case: if, in the future, light sedentary work is arranged for the plaintiff, then it is probable that his entitlement to periodical payments would partially fall away. But, it is also possible that his state of health might then deteriorate in such a way that he was no longer able to perform even light sedentary work. If the plaintiff were then again to claim his full periodical payments award, the defendant could be expected to plead extinctive prescription and argue that he should have brought an action for a declaration (*Feststellungsklage*) earlier.

These objections raised on [the present] appeal are unjustified. The decisive factor is that the plaintiff already possesses a judgment for performance (*Leistungsurteil*), which grants him, in the form of periodical payments, full compensation for his loss of wages. He cannot then further secure that definitively established entitlement through an action for a declaration (*Feststellungsklage*) . . . However, later modifications are possible. But they can be claimed through the action for variation (*Abänderungsklage*) under § 323 ZPO, in so far as they [the changes in circumstances] are 'substantial'. If the plaintiff should desire an increase of the periodical payments award after a successful action for variation has been brought by the defendant, then the same conditions apply for the extinctive prescription of [the plaintiff's] claim, as those already stated [under 2]."

Notes

(1) The annotated judgment deals with the revision of a periodical payments award. In this context, three kinds of action are discussed in the judgment: the claim for recurrent performance (*Klage auf wiederkehrende Leistungen*) under § 258 ZPO,[447] the action for variation (*Abänderungsklage*) (§ 323 ZPO)[448] and the action for declaration (*Feststellungsklage*) (§ 256 ZPO).[449]

The *Klage auf wiederkehrende Leistungen* referred to in § 258 ZPO is an action to obtain *recurrent performance*, for instance periodical payments by way of damages under §§ 843 BGB ff. (the so-called *Haftpflichtrenten*).

Through this action, the plaintiff claims a "performance" (*Leistung*) which is why the action is called *Leistungsklage*, a denomination for actions to obtain an order requiring a defendant to perform an act or an obligation (in contrast with other kinds of actions, e.g. an action to obtain a declaratory judgment (see below)). A *Leistungsklage*, e.g. a claim for recurrent performance (*Wiederkehrende Leistung*), which is brought in subsequent proceedings in respect of harm which was not subject of the earlier proceedings, is called more specifically a *Nachforderungs-* or *Zusatzklage* (supplementary demand or claim).

[447] § 258 ZPO: "In case of recurrent performance, a claim for future payment may also be made for performance which falls due only after the handing down of the judgment".
[448] § 323(1) ZPO: "When an award for recurrent performance has been made and a substantial change occurs in the circumstances which were decisive in the making of the award, or in the determination of the level of the award or in the duration of the payments, each party is entitled to bring a claim for a corresponding variation of the judgment."
[449] § 256(1) ZPO: "In order to determine the existence or non-existence of a legal relationship, . . . a claim may be brought if the plaintiff has a legal interest in an immediate judicial decision establishing whether the legal relationship exists".

Under § 323 ZPO, a judgment ordering recurrent performance may always be "varied" when a substantial change occurs in the circumstances which were decisive in the making of the award, the determination of the level of the award or the duration of the payments. A claim to obtain such a variation, which may be brought by both the plaintiff and the defendant, is called an *Abänderungsklage*.

A *Feststellungsklage*, provided for in § 256 ZPO, is an action not to obtain performance (*Leistung*) of something but to obtain a declaratory judgment as to the existence or non-existence of a legal relationship (*Rechtsverhältnis*), such as the existence of the defendant's liability.

(2) In the annotated case the question arose whether the plaintiff had a legal interest in bringing a *Feststellungsklage* for a judgment declaring the defendant liable to make good all further damage that the plaintiff might suffer in future as a result of the accident that had occurred nearly 30 years earlier. The BGH answered that question in the negative, as this was not a case where it was appropriate for the plaintiff to introduce a *Leistungsklage* (that is, in the present case, by way of a *Nachforderungs-* or *Zusatzklage*[450]). Rather the plaintiff's appropriate course was to bring an *Abänderungsklage* for variation of the original judgment by reason of the occurrence of a substantial change in the relevant circumstances, the expression "substantial change" being given a wide interpretation by the BGH in that altered economic circumstances are deemed to constitute a substantial change when they lead to a change in a wage levels.[451] Finally, the BGH held that, *if* the *Abänderungsklage* is capable of being extinguished by prescription, time does not begin to run until the eventuation of the developments that give rise to the claim for variation.[452]

Indeed, the *Abänderungsklage* allows the reassessment of damages however the damage develops in the future. Even though in the course of an action to obtain periodical payments the court is bound to take into account future developments,[453] those predictions are not irreversible. The annotated judgment shows that an award of periodical payments may also be revised when there is an alteration in the plaintiff's earning capacity[454] as when a change in economic circumstances is reflected in an increase in wage levels.[455]

(3) The claim for a declaratory judgment, the *Feststellungsklage* (§ 256 ZPO) (which was not allowed in the annotated case) provides another illustration of the flexible German procedural framework to allow the plaintiff to obtain full compensation for future damage. Subject to there being a legal interest, such a claim can be relied on when

---

[450] As was stated in a part of the annotated judgment not reproduced, BGH, 20 December 1960, BGHZ 34, 110 at 118–19: "A *Nachforderungsklage* is permissible, if the plaintiff brought only a partial claim in the first proceedings, for example when he only claimed a part of his loss of earnings or initially only claimed an annuity for a short period of time. Then the bringing of a further claim does not fall under the scope of § 323 ZPO to adapt the earlier judgment to the altered circumstances, but, as is generally recognized, constitutes a genuine additional claim (*Nachforderung*) that is to be brought under § 258 ZPO."

[451] See under 1.

[452] See under 2 and 3.

[453] Lange at 46; Palandt-Thomas, § 843 at para. 17. But as a consequence of the annotated judgment, courts do no longer predict the future economic circumstances as the *Abänderungsklage* is available: see BGH, 8 January 1981, *infra*, **8.G.24.**

[454] See under 3. This circumstance also led to an increase of the periodical payments award as decided by the Stuttgart Court of Appeal on 8 October 1958, as referred to in the annotated case.

[455] See under 1.

damage may arise in the future but has not yet materialized or when its future development is unpredictable. After having obtained a declaration, the plaintiff can claim compensation when damage actually materializes and is therefore more precisely assessable.

A judgment of the BGH of 3 December 1951[456] provides an example of a *Feststellungsklage* brought by a plaintiff, aged 47, after the death of his 12 year old daughter in a traffic accident. By virtue of § 844(2), a person may be entitled to damages for the death of a person bound by law to maintain the plaintiff (*unterhaltspflichtig*). In this case, the plaintiff, who was not in need at the time of the accident, was not in good physical health so that the need for future care could not be ruled out. Even though no damage had been sustained by the plaintiff, there was a material likelihood that he would need support in the future which the deceased person would have been able to provide. Since a very short limitation period was running against the plaintiff, the BGH recognized the latter's interest in establishing his legal relationship with the defendant, and therefore his legal interest in bringing a *Feststellungsklage* to preclude extinctive prescription.

BGH, 8 January 1981[457]   **8.G.25.**

ONCE-AND-FOR-ALL ASSESSMENT OF A CAPITAL SUM

Beetle and Porsche collide

The plaintiff cannot claim the revision of an award of a capital sum, which means that the court, in assessing the capital sum, must take future developments into account.

Facts: The plaintiff was severely injured in a car accident when his Volkswagen Beetle was in collision with the defendant's Porsche. In consequence, he was left unable to work for the rest of his life and he claimed damages in the form of a capital sum.

Held: The court of first instance awarded the plaintiff DEM 826,040.98 for his loss of earnings. The court of appeal rejected the plaintiff's claim that the court of first instance should have awarded further damages to allow for future increases in the level of wages. The BGH reversed the judgment of the court of appeal.

Judgment: "1. As a rule, if and insofar as the plaintiff has been rendered unable to work through bodily injury caused by the defendant which gives rise to the duty to pay compensation, § 843(1) BGB entitles the plaintiff to claim an award of periodical payments which should serve to make good (*Ausgleich*) the plaintiff's loss of income (*Erwerbsschaden*). If wages or income that he would have earned but for his injury are lost, the defendant must pay him the amount that he would have earned but for the harmful event. In order to ensure that result, the periodical payments must be 'dynamic', i.e. must take into account the future wage or salary level that is the basis for the hypothetical calculation. However, it is not the practice of the courts to provide . . . [in an original order for periodical payments] for such 'dynamism' on the basis of a consideration of future changes in price and wage structures; instead, the adjustment is essentially left to be made by later variation, under the conditions laid down by § 323 ZPO, of future periodical payments having regard to changes in general economic circumstances (see in particular the fundamental decision of the Chamber BGHZ 34, 110ff.).[458]

---

[456] BGHZ 4, 133.
[457] BGHZ 79, 187. Translation by Y. P. Salmon.
[458] *Supra*, **8.G.24.**

2. The capital sum (*Kapitalabfindung*) that the court can award the plaintiff under the conditions laid down by § 843(3), is intended to provide compensation for this loss of future earnings definitively by a one-off payment. Its assessment is based on the following theoretical model: the plaintiff is to receive the capital sum which,—according to his individual circumstances—is sufficient, together with the interest on the capital, to pay him the periodical payments due for the period of time for which the periodical payments are expected to be required [references omitted]. The specific factors in the calculation are to be assessed according to the particular features of the case, so that the trial court must necessarily venture prognoses on the future developments of the circumstances of the plaintiff's life and economic data. As still remains to be discussed in detail in the case at hand, it is in the nature of things that the longer the periods concerned, the greater the uncertainties affecting such prognoses. Nevertheless, they must be weighed in the consideration of 'for' and 'against'. *The risk of error accompanies the calculation of every capital sum; it is inherent not only in the capital sum negotiated by the parties by way of settlement, but also in the capital sum that is determined by the court* [references omitted]. *Someone who claims a capital sum instead of recurrent periodical payments consciously undertakes this risk, because he counts on receiving advantages from it* [emphasis added]. In law the payment of a capital award is not automatically imposed on the defendant [references omitted], but is ordered only under particular circumstances; however the defendant will not infrequently himself have an interest in the payment of a capital sum to settle the case once and for all, which above all applies to liability insurers.

. . . [There follows a discussion of the use of mortality tables and the need to take into account "individual circumstances in so far as they deviate from the statistical averages".]

3. The obviously quite substantial uncertainties of a prognosis of the future development of the personal and, above all, economic circumstances of the plaintiff, mean that in individual cases a substantial change in the bases of the assessment of the capital sum to the benefit and also to the detriment of the plaintiff is to be expected; this has led in the literature to the suggestion that, by analogous application of § 323 ZPO in the event of substantial changes in the circumstances relevant for the calculation of the capital sum, an action for the variation (*Abänderung*) of the amount of the judicially awarded capital sum is permitted.

In favour of this is the consideration that the capital award is to a large extent no different from the cash value of the periodical payments due, and that therefore the possibility of variation of those payments for changed circumstances [the 'dynamism' referred to above] should logically also be extended to the capital granted in their place; moreover the possibility of a later adjustment because of changed circumstances would operate in the interest of fair compensation for the plaintiff, which should be neither more nor less than that which was lost [references omitted].

However, the Chamber is not able to follow that view, which overlooks the fact that a capital award (as under § 843(3) BGB) is more than a mere arithmetical total of future payments. . . . It is in the nature of a capital payment that it contains elements of a settlement (*Vergleich*), even if judicially ordered. As already emphasized, someone who opts for compensation by a capital payment instead of by periodical payments, takes the risk that the factors determining its calculation are based on estimations and uncertain prognoses; it is for that reason that the law will not force, at the request of the defendant, a capital award on the plaintiff who is entitled to a periodical payments award. If [the plaintiff] nonetheless opts for the capital sum, it is because, when the risks are weighed up, it appears to him, for whatever reasons, to be more advantageous. However, with that he relinquishes any [subsequent] reconsideration of future developments of his personal and economic conditions. *The wrongdoer will wish, and is entitled to be sure, that if he must pay a capital sum, with such payment the case is settled for him once and for all. The uncertainties of future developments also present for him have been taken into account when calculating the capital sum. This element of bringing peace [between the parties] by weighing uncertain future possibilities, precludes the*

835

variation of the capital sum by analogous application of § 323 ZPO [references omitted; emphasis added].

4. *If for these reasons a later variation of the capital sum because of substantially changed circumstances is not possible, then this makes the function of the trial court particularly clear, i.e. to consider in their assessment possible future developments of the factors that are determinative of the amount* [references omitted; emphasis added]. The reasons for the court of appeal's basic objection to consideration of possible future alterations of the pay structure, whether due to increases in real income or only to allow for inflation, are therefore substantially unsustainable on legal grounds.

. . .

d) Likewise the view of the court of appeal . . . that it had already favoured the plaintiff so much in other ways that possible future changes to pay levels were already sufficiently accommodated in its assessment, cannot be followed. . . .

e) Finally the court of appeal rejected the consideration of future increases in income in the determination of the capital sum because their occurrence and scope are not certain and even a merely approximate calculation is not possible. Likewise, that cannot be approved as a principle.

Despite all these considerations [viz. the impossibility of making a certain prognosis of future wages and rates of return in the long term], *the future development of wages and salaries cannot remain completely unconsidered in determining the capital award. It belongs to the function of the trial court to consider all relevant circumstances in the context of § 287 ZPO* [emphasis added]. [The court] always has to rely on more or less uncertain prognoses and will have to be content with mere probabilities again and again. Therefore it falls within the proper exercise of its discretion to make such forecasts about probable future nominal and real increases in wages and salaries, despite all uncertainties, and according to its assessment to base the calculation of the capital sum on factors tending to increase or reduce, or to correct the mathematically obtained result by deductions or additions [references omitted]. Admittedly, as the appellant contends, from today's standpoint, a simple extrapolation of past data expressing a constant economic growth over a long time [references omitted] is obviously not sufficient, as the changed economic situation shows."

Notes

(1) According to § 843(3) BGB, if there is serious reason for so doing, a plaintiff may claim a capital sum (*Kapitalabfindung*) instead of periodical payments, e.g. when the plaintiff wishes to make a new start in life, or when a capital payment would have beneficial effects on his condition, or the solvency of an uninsured defendant is doubtful. A periodical payments award may be combined with a partial capital payment; a capital payment may also be claimed subsequent to a periodical award. A capital sum may be requested only by the plaintiff, and likewise only the plaintiff may subsequently demand the conversion of periodical payments into a capital sum.[459]

The fact that the plaintiff and the defendant ask for a capital award does not in itself constitute a serious reason, within the meaning of § 843(3) BGB, for the making of such an award and the court will not for that reason only order a capital payment. That, however, does not prevent the plaintiff and the defendant from agreeing a capital sum out of court, which has become general practice.

Most frequently damages are not claimed by the plaintiff but by his social security insurer, to whom the claim for damages for loss of earnings has been assigned; likewise

---

[459] See in more detail Münchener-Stein, § 843 at para. 47–9.

the damages are paid by the defendant's liability insurer. It is generally in the interest of both insurers to "close their books" by agreeing a capital sum.[460]

(2) As held in the annotated judgment, a capital award, unlike a periodical payments award, is never open to subsequent variation. This holds true not only when the economic circumstances upon which the assessment of damages was based appear to have been wrongly assessed, but also when the personal situation of the plaintiff, e.g. his health or earning capacity, has been misjudged.

The BGH views a capital award as a settlement (*Vergleich*) which by its very nature cannot be revised. Since the plaintiff is free to opt for compensation by way of a capital sum, e.g. because he expects it to be the most advantageous alternative, he must also bear the risks inherent in an assessment based upon estimates and uncertain predictions.[461] This solution has been harshly criticized by academic writers.[462] Although they accept that a capital payment, based as it is upon a prognosis of uncertainties, may not be questioned whenever the prognosis proves to be incorrect, they argue that subsequent variation should be possible if the actual development is so different that it falls completely outside the range of expectations (*Prognosespektrum*).[463]

(3) The annotated judgment shows that the BGH is very much aware of the unavoidable inaccuracy of assessing future damage but that does not mean that courts may make "rough-and-ready" assessments. Precisely because of the unavailability of subsequent variation, it is the duty of the courts to make a full prognosis of the plaintiff's life expectancy and health, of his future wages and the return on the capital (as possibly influenced by taxation), and to fix the capital sum on the basis of explicit assumptions. As was held in the annotated judgment, future wage increases have to be taken into account even when no certain forecast is possible[464] and it would be inconsistent not to do so on the ground that other assumptions may in the future prove to have been unduly favourable to the plaintiff.[465]

8.3.3. FRENCH LAW

Introductory Note

While French law requires damage to be *certain* in order to be recoverable,[466] that requirement does not preclude the compensation of *future damage*. In a well-known judgment of 1 June 1932, the Cour de cassation held that "if it is not possible to allow damages for purely potential harm, it is otherwise when the harm, while future, appears to the trial

---

[460] H. Kötz, *Deliktsrecht*, 7th edn. (Neuwied: Luchterhand, 1996) at 207, para. 534; H. McGregor, "Personal injury and death" in *International Encyclopedia of Comparative Law—Vol. XI/9: Torts* (Tübingen: Mohr, 1986) at para. 61–2; Markesinis at 919–20; J. Nehls, "Kapitalisierung von Schadensersatzrenten" VersR 1981, 407 at 412.

[461] Under 2 and 3 of the annotated judgment.

[462] Münchener-Stein, § 843 at para. 49.

[463] Münchener-Stein, § 843 at para. 62.

[464] Under 4 e) of the annotated judgment.

[465] See also the annotated judgment under 4 d).

[466] *Supra*, Chapter I, 1.4.2, Introductory Note under b). See also *supra*, Chapter IV, 4.1.3.

judge to be the certain and direct result of a current state of affairs and capable of imme-diate assessment".[467] Such conditions often exist in personal injury claims.

The French *Code civil* is silent on the mode of compensation, which is therefore left to be determined by the trier of fact, who, by virtue of his *pouvoir souverain*, is free to choose between a capital or periodical payments award.[468]

The only limitation on the revision of both capital and periodical payments awards is to be found in the rule of *res judicata*, albeit that it is not as far-reaching as the once-and-for-all rule in English law. As a consequence, and unlike German law,[469] the form of the award is not decisive for the issue of revision: both kinds of award may be subject to revi-sion, albeit only insofar as it is advantageous to the plaintiff.[470] Whether periodical pay-ments are revisable has been considered particularly with regard to changes in the value of money, and the question has been resolved in the affirmative.[471]

As a further consequence of the *pouvoir souverain* of the trier of fact in French law, the question whether the court must assess future damage as exactly as possible, or whether it may resort to a rough-and-ready estimate has never as such arisen. Hence there are no detailed rules governing the assessment of damages, particularly important in cases of personal injury, and the assumptions on which the calculation of damages is based are most frequently not expressed.[472]

Cass. civ. 2e, 29 April 1994[473]   **8.F.26.**
Groupement français d'assurances v. *Marcellus*

METHOD OF COMPENSATION AT THE JUDGE'S FREE CHOICE

Periodical payments award

It is for the trier of fact to decide whether compensation for the damage shall be by way of an award of periodical payments, even if it has not been requested by the parties.

Facts: The plaintiff sustained personal injury in a road traffic accident, caused by the driver of the vehicle in which he was a passenger. The plaintiff claimed damages for the cost of future care by a third party.

Held: The court of appeal allowed a periodical payments award although neither the plaintiff nor the defendant had claimed such an award. The Cour de cassation upheld the judgment of the court of appeal.

Judgment: "The judgment is criticized for having ordered [the defendant] and [his insurer] to com-pensate [the plaintiff] under the head of third-party assistance in the form of a periodical payment on the ground that, as a result of Arts. 4 and 5 of the New Code of Civil Procedure, the judge may rule only on that which is claimed. [It is argued that] in deciding that the compensation for the third party assistance should be paid in the form of periodical payments, which none of the parties had claimed, the court of appeal ruled *ultra petita* and infringed the provisions cited.

[467] Cass. Req., 1 June 1932, D 1932.I.102, report by Pilon.
[468] **8.F.26.** and see *supra*, **8.F.19.**
[469] *Supra*, **8.G.25.**
[470] **8.F.28–29.**
[471] **8.F.27.**
[472] **8.F.26.**; also *infra*, 8.5.
[473] Resp.Ass. 1994. Com.243. Translation by Y. P. Salmon.

It was in the exercise of its sovereign power to determine the means of redress of harm that the court of appeal, which was not bound to explain itself on the methods of assessment of damages, awarded the victim periodical payments to cover the cost of the third-party assistance.

Hence the appeal is not well founded."

Notes

(1) In the annotated judgment the Cour de cassation leaves it to the lower courts, as judges of fact, to use their *pouvoir souverain* to grant compensation in the form of periodical payments, even when none of the parties had requested such a form of compensation, or even when they had agreed that the award should be of a capital sum.[474] The Cour de cassation has recognized the absoluteness of this *pouvoir souverain* in another case, where the plaintiff had claimed a capital award; the lower court, referring to a supposed principle that compensation by way of a capital award should prevail, had held that it could not make a periodical payments award. The Cour de cassation held that in so finding, the lower court, as trier of fact, had "misinterpreted the extent of his powers".[475]

It has been stated, by reference to a judgment of the Cour de cassation of 21 June 1989,[476] that the trier of fact is not always free to choose between the two forms of compensation.[477] However, in that case the Cour de cassation quashed a judgment of the court of appeal on account of the failure of the court of appeal to deal with a party's pleadings, as it is bound to do, and more particularly to deal with the defendant's argument that the very poor state of health of the plaintiff excluded any calculation based upon life expectancy and, consequently, excluded the award of a capital sum.

It has been observed that the judge's *pouvoir souverain* is restricted only by the rule of full compensation.[478] However, that rule does not restrict the judge's freedom to choose between a periodical payments award and a capital sum, since both forms of compensation enable the judge to award full compensation for the harm suffered.

(2) The *Loi Badinter*[479] has introduced a new rule into French law by providing that, in the case of damages to redress harm resulting from an accident, the court may, at the plaintiff's request, convert a previous award of periodical payments into an award of a capital payment when the conversion is warranted by the plaintiff's personal situation.[480] The rule applies irrespective of whether the periodical payments were agreed on extrajudicially or awarded by judgment. It has been noted that this provision should facilitate claims by the plaintiffs, and awards by courts, of periodical payments.[481]

---

[474] See for a discussion of the case law with regard to the choice between a capital and a periodical payments award: Starck, Roland and Boyer at 522–4, para. 1302–5; Viney, *Effets* at 180–5, para. 132–34.

[475] Cass. civ. 2e, 21 November 1973, JCP 1974.II.17897, annotated by S. Brousseau.

[476] Cass. civ. 2e, 21 June 1989, Bull.civ. 1989.II.133.

[477] Starck, Roland and Boyer at 523, para. 1303.

[478] Viney, *Effets* at 181, para. 133.

[479] See *supra*, Chapter VI, **6.F.16**.

[480] Art. 44 *Loi Badinter*, ibid.: "In all cases where an annuity has been awarded, whether contractually or judicially, to redress harm resulting from an accident, the beneficiary (*créditrentier*) may, when his personal situation justifies it, ask the judge to order that the periodical payments falling due in the future (*arrérages à échoir*) be replaced entirely or in part by a capital sum, according to a conversion table fixed by law." As this provision (unlike Art. 43, *infra*, **8.F.27.**, Note (2)) deals with personal injury resulting from "an accident", its application is not limited to victims of *traffic* accidents: see Viney, *Effets* at 185, para. 134.

[481] See also **8.F.27.**, Note (2). Viney, *Effets* at 185, para. 134. But under Art. 44 *Loi Badinter*, ibid., periodical payments are capitalized on the basis of an outdated table: see Y. Lambert-Faivre, *Droit du dommage corporel. Systèmes d'indemnisation*, 3rd edn. (Paris: Dalloz, 1996) at 187.

Cass. Ch. Mixte, 6 November 1974[482]

8.F.27.

Sourdonnier v. *Gallien*

INDEX-LINKED PERIODICAL PAYMENTS

Disabled mason

It is not inconsistent with the conclusive nature of a judicial decision to index-link the periodical payments awarded under it nor is it contrary to law for the judge to award part of the damages in the form of such periodical payments.

Facts: The plaintiff, a 21-year old stonemason, was severely injured in a road traffic accident for which the defendant was declared entirely responsible. The plaintiff became a total and incurable invalid, with a very limited life expectancy.

Held: The court of first instance had assessed the damages at FRF 981,266.59. On appeal by both defendant and plaintiff, the court of appeal[483] assessed the damages at FRF 1,126,266.59 and *suo motu* converted a part of the damages award (FRF 605,000) into index-linked periodical payments. The Cour de cassation upheld the appeal judgment.

Judgment: "Ruling on a claim by [the plaintiff] for compensation for the consequences of an accident not covered by social security, for which, pursuant to Art. 1384 (1) C. civ., [the defendant] had been declared entirely liable, the contested judgment ordered [the defendant] and her insurer . . . to pay the plaintiff a capital sum and index-linked periodical payments . . .;

The judgment is criticized for having ordered the linking of the periodical payments award to wage levels, first on the ground that such an indexation had not been requested by [the plaintiff] and the judgment granted him the entirety of his claims, so that the court of appeal ruled *ultra petita* [adjudicated on something which was not sought], and further on the ground that compensation is [to be] fixed definitively on the day of judgment and no legal provision permits judges to index-link periodical payments in the area of road traffic accidents.

However, by virtue of Arts. 1382 and 1384 C. civ., the trial judges are bound to ensure that the victim is fully compensated for the harm that he has sustained; *they do not infringe the definitive character of their decision by measures which they consider necessary to compensate someone who has become a permanent invalid in an equitable and adequate way at every point of time, however the economic circumstances evolve* [emphasis added].

The court of appeal stated that because of the accident [the plaintiff], a stonemason aged 25, had been rendered a bedridden invalid which would preclude him from engaging in any remunerative activity and excluded all hope of anything other than extremely diminished life, and that his definitive and total invalidity would necessitate the constant assistance of a third party. Without failing to apply correctly the provisions relied on on appeal [before the Cour de cassation], the court of appeal converted a part of the . . . award into an annuity [*rente viagère*] index-linked to the "All France quarterly index of wages of all professions" ["*indice trimestriel des salaires toutes activités, série France entière*"], and specified the methods of adjustment of this periodical payment award [*rente*].

Furthermore, in this case, the court of appeal, which was not precluded from so doing by any legislative provision, has assessed the appropriateness of converting a part of the sum claimed by [the

---

[482] JCP 1975.II.17978, with the Opinion of First Advocate-General Gégout, annotated by R. Savatier; *Les grands arrêts* at 483. Translation by Y. P. Salmon.
[483] Poitiers, 17 January 1973, JCP 1973.II.17393, annotated by R. Savatier.

plaintiff] into index-linked periodical payments, the level of which [the court of appeal] assessed within the limits of the claim.

Thus the decision is legally justified."

Notes

(1) Whether a periodical payments award can be *index-linked*, that is to say automatically revised because of monetary fluctuations, has been a matter of long-standing controversy. In French law, this question is distinguished from the issue of whether an award may be revised because of an alteration in the plaintiff's condition.[484] Whilst the latter concerns a change related to the damage itself, the former concerns a change related to the pecuniary expression of the indemnity. In the annotated judgment, the Cour de cassation endorsed for the first time the making of an index-linked periodical payments award.[485] The potential effects of a decline in purchasing power following on a periodical payments award had previously rendered it an unattractive option. An Act of 1951,[486] followed by numerous others in successive years, provided for once-only increases of judicially awarded periodical payments, albeit that such readjustments were not entirely sufficient to offset the effects of inflation.[487]

Before the annotated judgment, a major objection to indexation was that the award had to be final at the moment of the judgment and that future economic circumstances, influencing the purchasing power of the currency, were not related to either the defendant's fault or the resulting damage. A revision was deemed possible only in case of an alteration in the victim's condition whilst the extension of the possibility of revision to take account of inflation was held to be inconsistent with the rule of *res judicata*. Ultimately, legislative measures were considered the only appropriate means to allow for the effects of inflation.[488] In his Opinion in the annotated case, the Advocate-General pointed out that there was no legal provision whatsoever that prohibited the indexation of periodical payments awards. Moreover, contractual indexation clauses were valid and, since 1972, the legislature had allowed index-linked maintenance allowances in the field of family law. A further argument was that an index-linked periodical payments award did not conflict with the rule that damage has to be assessed at the moment of the judgment since the indexation does not relate to the assessment of the injury sustained (*évaluation du dommage*) but relates to its compensation (*réparation*). Finally, the Advocate-General was not convinced by the argument that index-linked periodical payments would cause serious problems for insurers. The Cour de cassation followed the Advocate-General's Opinion, stressing the basic rule of full compensation and affirming that it is not inconsistent with the final character of the judicial decision to take measures enabling the compensation to be full at every moment of time.

Another illustration of the variability of a periodical payments award is provided by a judgment of the Cour de cassation[489] by which the defendant was ordered to pay to the hospital the costs of the plaintiff's treatment, the payments to be made monthly

---

[484] *Infra*, **8.F.28–29.**

[485] It may be noted that, in French law, the rule that the award must take into account the effects of inflation *before* judgment, had already been established by a judgment of the Cour de cassation in 1942: Cass. civ., 23 March 1942, Gaz.Pal. 1942.I.135, D 1942.Jur.118; see Viney, *Effets* at 116, para. 82.

[486] *Loi 51–695 portant majoration de certaines rentes viagères et pensions* of 24 May 1951, JO, 5 June 1951, JCP 1951.III.16169.

[487] See Viney, *Effets* at 119, para. 83; *Les grands arrêts* at 486.

[488] E.g. Cass. Soc., 2 May 1952, D 1952.Jur.413, annotated by R. Savatier.

[489] Cass. civ. 2e, 17 April 1975, D 1976.Jur.152, annotated by A. Sharaf Eldine.

according to the variable daily costs incurred in respect of the plaintiff's stay in hospital and treatment. The reasons given are identical to those in the annotated judgment: the judge may take all appropriate measures to ensure that the victim is fully compensated for his injury at every point of time.

(2) An Act of 27 December 1974,[490] as amended by Art. 43 of the *Loi Badinter*,[491] has provided for the automatic (*de plein droit*) indexation of previously awarded periodical payments, whether settled out of court or judicially awarded, when they concern compensation for damage resulting from a *traffic* accident, even when the indexation of payments has been provided for neither judicially nor by contract.

Cass. Req., 30 December 1946[492]   **8.F.28.–29.**
Établissements Brun d'Arre v. *Menard*
and
Cass. civ. 2e, 12 October 1972[493]
Deletang v. *Préfet d'Ille-et-Vilaine et Adam*

NO REVISION IN CASE OF IMPROVEMENT IN THE INJURED PERSON'S CONDITION

An improvement in the injured person's condition does not justify the revision of a periodical payments award or a capital award.

1. Cass. Req., 30 December 1946   **8.F.28.**

Plaintiff improving after judgment (1)

Facts: The plaintiff was compensated for personal injury by a judgment that awarded him a capital sum. In subsequent proceedings, the defendant, arguing that the plaintiff's health had subsequently improved, claimed partial reimbursement of the damages.

Held: The court of appeal dismissed the claim. The Cour de cassation upheld the appeal judgment.

Judgment: "The reasons given in the contested judgment no less than those given in the previous judgment that established the liability of the [defendant and assessed damages] show that the court, at the time, assessed the totality of the compensation for harm in the form of the payment of a capital award to the victim, *without reserving to itself any subsequent right of review or revocation. The capital award itself has, in civil law, the characteristic of a final lump sum (caractère forfaitaire et*

---

[490] *Loi n° 74–1118 relative à la revalorisation de certaines rentes allouées en réparation du préjudice causé par un véhicule terrestre à moteur et portant diverses dispositions d'ordre civil* of 27 December 1974, JO, 28 December 1974, JCP 1975.III.42362. Art. 1 of *Loi n° 74–1118* states: "Annuities granted, whether contractually or judicially, to a victim, or in case of death, to his dependants, to make good harm caused by a road traffic accident shall be increased *ipso jure*, according to the revalorization indices laid down in Article L. 455 of the Social Security Code." On the issue of index-linked periodical payments and on the legislator's intervention, see further Viney, *Effets* at 116–25, para. 82–5.

[491] *Supra*, Chapter VI, **6.F.16.**, The *Loi Badinter* removed a restriction contained in the Act of 1974 to instances of at least 75 per cent disability.

[492] D 1947.Jur.178. Translation by Y. P. Salmon.

[493] D 1974.Jur.536, annotated by P. Malaurie, JCP 1974.II.17609, annotated by S. Brousseau. Translation by Y. P. Salmon.

définitif); the mere reservation made by the defendant as recorded in the previous judgment [to claim partial reimbursement of the damages paid in case of a significant improvement in the plaintiff's condition], cannot have the effect of securing for the defendant an action for revision for which no basis can be found in any legal principle [emphasis added].

Consequently, in stating that [the defendant] had no right to reclaim part of the sum awarded against it by a final legal decision, and in declaring its action for the revision of damages inadmissible, the contested judgment, which is properly reasoned, did not infringe any of the aforementioned provisions [*inter alia* Arts. 1350, 1383, 1384 C. civ.] and founded its decision on a correct legal basis."

2. Cass. civ. 2e, 12 October 1972   **8.F.29.**

Plaintiff improving after judgment (2)

Facts: [The plaintiff], having obtained compensation for personal injury by an award of periodical payments, underwent surgery which considerably reduced her disability. The costs were paid by her employer, the préfet d'Ille-et-Vilaine, who claimed reimbursement from the tortfeasor, who in turn claimed a reduction of the periodical payments award because of the improvement in the plaintiff's health, her level of disability having been reduced from 80 to 40 per cent.

Held: The court of appeal allowed the claim of the victim's employer and dismissed the tortfeasor's claim. The Cour de cassation reversed the judgment only with regard to the claim of the employer.

Judgment: "As to the . . . plea [relating to the torfeasor's claim that the amount of the periodical payments should be reduced]:

. . . The judgment [of the court of appeal] is criticized for having held that the rule of *res judicata* precluded the revision of the award of periodical payments. However, the court of appeal observes that the rule of *res judicata* precludes the revision of the award because of the improvement of [the plaintiff's] state of health [emphasis added], . . . since the [initial] judgment [establishing liability] did not foresee any variation in the harm, which was then considered to be unalterable, and did not expressly reserve the possibility of reassessing it. In view of those observations, the court of appeal was legally justified in reaching the decision that it did, without violating the rule of *res judicata*.

As to the same plea . . . [but relating to the employer's claim that the cost of surgery should be reimbursed]:

The principle of *res judicata* is applied with regard to the subject-matter of the judgment, on condition that the thing claimed is the same, and that the claim, founded on the same cause of action, is between the same parties, acting in the same capacity.

The harm is fixed definitively at the date on which the judge hands down his decision; *a new claim for damages for the same wrong may be brought subsequently only in the event of a deterioration in the victim's condition.* [emphasis added]

The contested judgment states that the operation was not that which was previously foreseen, but that, thanks to scientific progress, it had resulted in an improvement in the victim's condition, which had been considered to be unalterable in 1959. [The operation] was not effected because of a deterioration in [the plaintiff's] condition, and consequently it did not concern a new recoverable harm. Thus there was no new harm by reason of a deterioration in [the plaintiff's] state of health but, rather, there was, on the contrary, an improvement in her condition; on those facts, the court of appeal, in ordering [the tortfeasor] to reimburse the préfet d'Ille-et-Vilaine, failed to apply [Arts. 1351 and 1382 C. civ.] correctly."

Notes

(1) Both judgments show that, *in principle*, a *tortfeasor* cannot claim the revision of a damages award because of an *improvement* in the injured person's condition, irrespective of whether compensation was granted by way of a capital or a periodical payments award. In the second annotated judgment, concerning a *periodical payments award*, that result was based upon the rule of *res judicata* (Art. 1351 C.civ.), while in the first annotated judgment, with regard to a *capital award*, the impossibility of revision resulted from the very nature of the capital award which has by definition "the characteristic of a final lump sum" (*caractère forfaitaire et définitif*).[494]

However, as can be deduced from the second annotated judgment (relating to the tort-feasor's claim for a reduction in the periodical payments), a court may reserve the right to revise a *periodical payments award* because of an improvement in the victim's condition. Such reservation (*réserve*), which has to be made explicitly by the court itself,[495] makes the rule of *res judicata* inoperative with regard to the subject-matter of the reservation.

It remains doubtful whether such reservation can also be made in the case of a *capital award*. The uncertainty as to whether a reservation can be validly made for a capital award results from the fact that, in that case, the reason for excluding revision consists in the fact that a capital award is by def-inition a *final* lump sum (and does not result, as in the case of periodical payments awards, from the rule of *res judicata*). For, indeed, as some authors point out,[496] it is contradictory to proclaim a cap-ital award to be final and, at the same time, to leave open the possibility of a revision. Others dis-agree for which they find support in the explicit reference in the first annotated judgment that the contested judgment did mention the absence, in that case, of a reservation as to a possible and sub-sequent right of review (which it seemed, therefore, to regard as possible).[497]

(2) Whilst the defendant cannot claim the revision of a damages award because of an improvement in the plaintiff's condition, it is open to *the plaintiff* to claim additional damages in case of a *deterioration* in his or her condition irrespective of whether com-pensation was granted by way of a capital or a periodical payments award.[498]

Indeed, the rule of *res judicata* does not bar a later claim for additional damages. That is because that rule is applicable only when both the cause of action and *the subject-matter of the claim* (*chose demandée*) in the subsequent proceedings (between the same parties acting in the same capacity) are identical to those in the earlier proceedings. Damage resulting from a deterioration in the victim's condition is deemed to be new recoverable harm which is not within the subject-matter of the first claim, which is also

[494] It would appear, however, that if the rule of *res judicata* bars the defendant's claim for a reduction of the periodical payments, a claim for partial reimbursement of the capital sum must encounter the same objection. Compare Y. Lambert-Faivre, *Droit du dommage corporel. Systèmes d'indemnisation*, 3rd edn. (Paris: Dalloz, 1996) at 236; Y. Chartier, *La réparation du préjudice dans la responsabilité civile* (Paris: Dalloz, 1983) at 884.

[495] It appears that a reservation of the right to reduce the periodical payments award is not made very often: Viney, *Effets* at 109, para. 75.

[496] Y. Lambert-Faivre, *Droit du dommage corporel. Systèmes d'indemnisation*, 3rd edn. (Paris: Dalloz, 1996) at 235–6, para. 224; Y. Chartier, *La réparation du préjudice dans la responsabilité civile* (Paris: Dalloz, 1983) at 883–5, para. 745; S. Brousseau, Note under Cass. civ. 2e, 12 October 1972, JCP 1974.II.17609; compare Viney, *Effets* at 108, para. 75.

[497] Note under Cass. Req., 30 December 1946, D 1947.Jur.178; M.E. Roujou de Boubée, *Essai sur la notion de réparation* (Paris: LGDJ, 1974) at 392 (but see also at 389); P. Malaurie, Note under Cass. civ. 2e, 12 October 1972, D 1974.Jur.537.

[498] On the effect of subsequent events that would worsen the situation of the victim, see *supra*, Chapter IV, **4.F.32.**

why it is not necessary (although possible) for the court to reserve the right to grant additional damages in case of deterioration.[499]

The case-law allowing a claim for additional damages on account of a deterioration in the victim's condition has been confirmed, with regard to victims of traffic accidents, by Art. 22 of the *Loi Badinter*.[500] But, of course, that case-law does not allow the court to re-assess harm for which compensation was recovered in the first judgment since only additional harm may be compensated in subsequent proceedings.[501]

(3) It is apparent from the foregoing that the *res judicata* rule is not unfavourable for the plaintiff, in that it does not preclude a claim for additional damages if his or her condition deteriorates, irrespective of whether the award is for periodical payments or for a capital sum. Conversely, the plaintiff generally need not fear a reduction if his or her situation improves, as a reservation of the right to revise the award, although valid for periodical payments awards, is only reluctantly, and exceptionally, made by the courts.

However, the Cour de cassation's case-law remains controversial, in that some authors believe the distinction drawn between improvement and deterioration in the victim's condition to be irrelevant,[502] whilst others believe it to be justifiable only for policy reasons[503]—admitting at the same time that the courts should make more frequent use of the reservation of the right to revise periodical payments awards when the victim's condition improves.[504]

8.4. LOSS OF OR DAMAGE TO PROPERTY

8.4.1. GERMAN LAW

The following cases can be found at <http://www.rechten.unimaas.nl/casebook>:
8.G.30. BGH, 23 March 1976. Unrepaired car sold.
8.G.31. BGH, 24 March 1959. New for old.
8.G.32. BGH, 9 July 1986. Use of house prohibited by city council.

8.4.2. ENGLISH LAW

The following cases can be found at <http://www.rechten.unimaas.nl/casebook>:
8.E.33. Court of Appeal, *Dominion Mosaics and Tile Co* v. *Trafalgar Trucking Co.* Paternoster machines.

---

[499] Viney, ibid. at 111–13, makes, in that respect, no distinction as to the form of the award.

[500] *Supra*, Chapter VI, **6.F.16.** Art. 22: "The victim may, within the period of time laid down in Article 2270–1 C.civ., claim from the insurer who paid the damages [under the original judgment] compensation for the worsening of harm which he has suffered.

[501] E.g. Cass. civ. 2e, 7 July 1993, Bull.civ. 1993.II.250.

[502] P. Malaurie, Note under Cass. civ. 2e, 12 October 1972, D 1974.Jur.537 and references.

[503] Y. Chartier, *La réparation du préjudice dans la responsabilité civile* (Paris: Dalloz, 1983) at 886–7, para. 747.

[504] Viney, *Effets* at 116, para. 81.

8.E.34. Court of Appeal, *The London Corporation.* Unrepaired ship sold.

8.E.35. Court of Appeal, *Harbutt's "Plasticine" Ltd.* v. *Wayne Tank and Pump Co. Ltd.* Plasticine factory destroyed by fire.

8.E.36. House of Lords, *The Mediana.* Standby lightship.

8.4.3. FRENCH LAW

The following cases can be found at <http://www.rechten.unimaas.nl/casebook>:

8.F.37. Cass. crim., 17 December 1969, *Amey.* Damaged car (1).

8.F.38. Cass. civ. 2e, 31 March 1993, *Thévenin* v. *Les Cars bleus Brossard.* Damaged car (2).

8.F.39. Cass. civ. 2e, 9 May 1972, *Société Bonneau* v. *Ponce.* Collapse of wall.

8.F.40. Cass. civ. 2e, 23 November 1988, *SMAC Acieroïd* v. *Perrot.* Buildings irreparably damaged by mining.

8.F.41. Cass. crim., 6 December 1983, *SNCF* v. *Hubert.* Damaged turbo-train.

8.5. COMPENSATION: PERSONAL INJURY AND DEATH

8.5.1. GERMAN LAW

The following cases can be found at <http://www.rechten.unimaas.nl/casebook>:

8.G.42. BGH, 5 May 1970. Qualified chemist.

8.G.43. BGH, 16 February 1970. Remarriage of widower.

8.5.2. FRENCH LAW

The following cases can be found at <http://www.rechten.unimaas.nl/casebook>:

8.F.44. Cass. civ. 2e, 3 June 1955, *Établ. Cabour* v. *Lecat.* Injured employee.

8.F.45. Cass. crim., 7 July 1966, *Desombres* v. *Pocreau.* Young widow.

8.F.46. Cass. civ. 2e, 14 October 1992, *Schmitt* v. *Laporte.* Mother taking care of injured child.

8.F.47. Cass. civ. 2e, 3 October 1990, *Compagnie General Accident* v. *Bauthéas.* Management of husband's firm by his widow after his death (1).

8.F.48. Cass. civ. 2e, 2 November 1994, *Compagnie General Accident* v. *Bauthéas.* Management of husband's firm by his widow after his death (2).

8.5.3. ENGLISH LAW

The following cases can be found at <http://www.rechten.unimaas.nl/casebook>:

8.E.49. Court of Appeal, *Moeliker* v. *A. Reyrolle and Co.* Injured craftsman.

8.E.50. House of Lords, *Hunt* v. *Severs*. Tortfeasor taking care of the plaintiff.

8.6. OTHER REMEDIES

8.6.1. ENGLISH LAW

Introductory Note

In addition to damages, several other, more or less specific remedies are available under English law. Some of them are confined to a specific tort; others have their roots in equity. They can be subdivided into two categories: remedies for torts are either *judicial*, by way of an action in law, or *extra-judicial*, by way of self-help.[505]

The latter category deals with situations where the plaintiff is entitled to redress the wrong himself.[506] Remedies of self-help may have a very narrow scope of application; thus, for instance, the so-called "right of distress damage feasant" allows an owner of land to detain chattels that are unlawfully on his land and cause damage, as a means of compelling the owner of the chattels to pay damages.[507] Other remedies may be more widely used; thus, for instance, the so-called "abatement of nuisance" allows the victim of a nuisance to remove the trouble at source.[508] However, it has been said that the law does not favour the remedy of abatement, and indeed, this form of self-redress has been confined to clear and simple cases which would not justify the expense of legal proceedings, and to urgent cases which require an immediate remedy.[509] Moreover, the exercise of the right is subject to many conditions.[510]

The judicial remedies for torts are damages, injunctions and orders for specific restitution of property.[511] Orders for specific restitution are available in case of possession of another's property[512] and will not be discussed here.[513] This section will deal with the remedy of injunction, which is an order by the court restraining the commission or continuance of a tort.

An injunction is called *prohibitory* when it orders the defendant not to do something, that is to say to desist from wrongful conduct[514] whereas it is called *mandatory* when the defendant is ordered to do something, namely, in the field of tort, to take positive

---

[505] Salmond and Heuston at 501.

[506] See for a detailed overview *Clerk & Lindsell on Torts* at 1539 ff.

[507] Rogers at 675; *Clerk & Lindsell on Torts* at 1553 ff., para. 29 ff.

[508] Rogers at 675–6; *Clerk & Lindsell on Torts* at 1549 ff., para. 29–22 ff.

[509] *Burton* v. *Winters* [1993] 1 WLR 1077, CA at 1081–2, relating to a case in which the question arose as to whether a victim of an encroachment on her land by half of a garage wall was entitled to exercise a right of abatement. The question was answered in the negative; it was emphasized that self-redress, resulting in the demolition of the garage wall, would have been out of all proportion to the damage suffered by the plaintiff.

[510] See Rogers at 792–3; *Clerk & Lindsell on Torts* at 1549–51, para. 29–23.

[511] Salmond and Heuston at 501.

[512] For instance the so-called action of ejectment, referred to *supra*, **8.E.11.**, Note (2)(a).

[513] See Rogers at 485 ff., 613–14 and 800.

[514] A. Burrows, *Remedies for Torts and Breach of Contract*, 2nd edn. (London: Butterworths, 1994) at 388; Rogers at 794; Salmond and Heuston at 554.

action to rectify the consequences of what he has already done.[515] As A. Burrows underlines—

> "the distinction [between prohibitory and mandatory injunctions] is one of substance and not one of form so that, for example, an injunction ordering the defendant not to allow a particular building to remain standing on his land is a mandatory injunction, since in substance the defendant is being ordered to knock the building down."[516]

It is obvious that in the case of a mandatory injunction, the remedy of injunction can achieve restitution in kind or, more exactly, the elimination of an unlawful situation to prevent future damage. An injunction is called *quia timet*[517] when the plaintiff brings the action to prevent the commission of a tort in the future.[518]

A further distinction is made between *final* (or *perpetual*) injunctions and *interlocutory* injunctions. An interlocutory injunction is issued "provisionally before the hearing of an action, in order to prevent the commission or continuance of an alleged injury in the meantime, pending an inquiry into the case and a final determination of the right of the plaintiff to a perpetual injunction".[519]

It may be noted that, in civil proceedings, as a matter of domestic English law, an injunction cannot be directly ordered against the Crown.[520] Whether this restriction is compatible with Community law is open to doubt in so far as domestic rules must afford adequate protection to the individual concerned for the rights which he derives from Community Law.[521]

It is important to note that injunctive relief is an equitable remedy—i.e. originally belonging exclusively to the jurisdiction of the Court of Chancery[522]—so that its award lies within the discretion of the judge. The two cases, relating to the remedies of a mandatory injunction[523] and to an award of damages in lieu of injunction,[524] will be discussed especially from the point of view of the circumstances and conflicting interests which are weighed up in deciding whether an injunction will be issued or not.

---

[515] Burrows, ibid. at 388; Rogers at 797; Salmond and Heuston at 554.

[516] Burrows, ibid. at 388.

[517] This means "since he fears": Burrows, ibid. at 389.

[518] Salmond and Heuston at 555; Rogers at 798.

[519] Salmond and Heuston at 554. See on the principles on which interlocutory injunctions are to be granted *American Cyanamid Co.* v. *Ethicon Ltd.* [1975] AC 396, HL, and in actions for defamation *Herbage* v. *Pressdram Ltd.* [1984] 1 WLR 1160, CA. See also Rogers at 795–7. A plaintiff to whom an interlocutory injunction is granted is required, as the "price of the injunction", to give to the court a "cross-undertaking in damages" to the effect that it will compensate the defendant for any loss sustained by reason of the injunction if it subsequently transpires that it ought not to have been granted: see further the *Supreme Court Practice* 1999 at para. 29/L/23.

[520] *Clerk & Lindsell on Torts* at 1537, para. 28–35 referring to the Crown Proceedings Act 1947, s. 21, and to the leading case of *M* v. *Home Office* [1994] 1 AC 377, HL, in which it was decided that injunctions can, however, be granted against an officer of the Crown when sued in his personal capacity and, in judicial review proceedings (to which s. 21 does not apply), when sued in his official capacity. In the Court of Appeal, Lord Donaldson MR described the absence of a power to grant injunctive relief against central government (except to protect rights under Community law) as "anomalous and in any judgment wrong in principle": [1992] QB 244 at 306.

[521] See further M. Brealey and M. Hoskins, *Remedies in EC Law*, 2nd edn. (London: Sweet & Maxwell, 1998) at 153–4.

[522] Rogers at 793.

[523] **8.E.51.**

[524] **8.E.52.**

House of Lords[525]
Redland Bricks Ltd. v. Morris

8.E.51.

MANDATORY INJUNCTION

Land slip

The grant of a mandatory injunction is entirely discretionary. General principles for its application are (i) a very strong probability that grave damage will accrue in the future; (ii) damages will not be a sufficient or adequate remedy; (iii) the cost to the defendant to do the works may be taken into account when the defendant has not acted unreasonably; (iv) the defendant must be informed precisely what he is ordered to do.

Facts: The defendants, a brick company, excavated earth and clay and a large pit was left on their land. As a result, part of the plaintiffs' land began to slip and a small part of it slipped onto the defendants' land. Remedial work had been undertaken but was of no effect. The plaintiffs claimed damages and injunctive relief. It was accepted that further slipping of one acre of the plaintiffs' land was likely to occur and that the only way to prevent this was by back-filling the clay-pit up to the plaintiffs' boundary. The cost of doing that might be GBP 35,000 whereas the present value of one acre of the land was between GBP 1,500 and 1,600.

Held: The court of first instance had given damages in the sum of GBP 325 for the damage which had already been incurred and ordered the defendants to "take all necessary steps to restore the support" to the plaintiffs' land. The court of appeal dismissed the defendants' appeal. The House of Lords reversed the appeal judgment.

Judgment: LORD UPJOHN[526]: ". . . [I]f a person withdraws support from his neighbour's land that gives no right of action at law to that neighbour until damage to his land has thereby been suffered; damage is the gist of the action. When such damage occurs the neighbour is entitled to sue for the damage suffered to his land and equity comes to the aid of the common law by granting an injunction to restrain the continuance or recurrence of any acts which may lead to a further withdrawal of support in the future.

The neighbour may not be entitled as of a right to such an injunction, for the granting of an injunction is in its nature a discretionary remedy, but he is entitled to it "as of course" which comes to much the same thing and at this stage an argument on behalf of the tortfeasor, who has been withdrawing support that this will be very costly to him, perhaps by rendering him liable for heavy damages for breach of contract for failing to supply e.g., clay or gravel, receives scant, if any, respect. A similar case arises when injunctions are granted in the negative form where local authorities or statutory undertakers are enjoined from polluting rivers; in practice the most they can hope for is a suspension of the injunction while they have to take, perhaps, the most expensive steps to prevent further pollution.

But the granting of an injunction to prevent further tortious acts and the award of compensation for damage to the land already suffered exhausts the remedies [to] which at law and (under this heading) in equity the owner of the land is entitled. He is not prejudiced at law for if, as a result of the previous withdrawal of support, some further slip of his land occurs he can bring a fresh action for this new damage and ask for damages and injunctions.

---

[525] [1970] AC 652.
[526] [1970] AC at 664–7, Lord Reid, Lord Morris of Borth-y-Gest, Lord Hodson and Lord Diplock concurring.

But to prevent the jurisdiction of the courts being stultified equity has invented the quia timet action, that is an action for an injunction to prevent an apprehended legal wrong, though none has occurred at present, and the suppliant for such an injunction is without any remedy at law.

. . .

My Lords, quia timet actions are broadly applicable to two types of cases: first, where the defendant has as yet done no hurt to the plaintiff but is threatening and intending (so the plaintiff alleges) to do works which will render irreparable harm to him or his property if carried to completion . . . [T]hose cases are normally, though not exclusively, concerned with negative injunctions. Secondly, the type of case where the plaintiff has been fully recompensed both at law and in equity for damage he has suffered but where he alleges that the earlier actions of the defendant may lead to future causes of action. In practice this means the case of which that which is before your Lordships' House is typical, where the defendant has withdrawn support from his neighbour's land or where he has so acted in depositing his soil from his mining operations as to constitute a menace to the plaintiff's land. It is in this field that the undoubted jurisdiction of equity to grant a mandatory injunction, that is an injunction ordering the defendant to carry out positive works, finds its main expression, though of course it is equally applicable to many other cases. Thus, to take the simplest example, if the defendant, the owner of a land, including a metalled road over which the plaintiff has a right of way, ploughs up that land so that it is no longer usable, no doubt a mandatory injunction will go to restore it; damages are not a sufficient remedy, for the plaintiff has no right to go upon the defendant's land to remake his right of way.

. . . The grant of a mandatory injunction is, of course, entirely discretionary and unlike a negative injunction can never be "as of course". Every case must depend essentially upon its own particular circumstances. Any general principles for its application can only be laid down in the most general terms:

1. A mandatory injunction can only be granted where the plaintiff shows a very strong probability upon the facts that grave damage will accrue to him in the future . . . It is a jurisdiction to be exercised sparingly and with caution but in the proper case unhesitatingly.

2. Damages will not be a sufficient or adequate remedy if such damage does happen. This is only the application of a general principle of equity; it has nothing to do with Lord Cairns' Act or *Shelfer's* case [1895] 1 Ch 287.

3. Unlike the case where a negative injunction is granted to prevent the continuance or recurrence of a wrongful act the question of the cost to the defendant to do works to prevent or lessen the likelihood of a future apprehended wrong must be an element to be taken into account:

(a) where the defendant has acted without regard to his neighbour's rights, or has tried to steal a march on him or has tried to evade the jurisdiction of the court or, to sum it up, has acted wantonly and quite unreasonably in relation to his neighbour he may be ordered to repair his wanton and unreasonable acts by doing positive work to restore the status quo ante even if the expense to him is out of all proportion to the advantage thereby accruing to the plaintiff . . .

(b) but where the defendant has acted reasonably, though in the event wrongly, the cost of remedying by positive action his earlier activities is most important for two reasons. First, because no legal wrong has yet occurred (for which he has not been recompensed at law and in equity) and, in spite of gloomy expert opinion, may never occur or possibly only upon a much smaller scale than anticipated. Secondly, because if ultimately heavy damage does occur the plaintiff is in no way prejudiced for he has his action at law and all his consequential remedies in equity.

So the amount to be expended under a mandatory order by the defendant must be balanced with these considerations in mind against the anticipated possible damage to the plaintiff and if, on such balance, it seems unreasonable to inflict such expenditure upon one who for this purpose is no more than a potential wrongdoer then the court must exercise its jurisdiction accordingly . . .

4. If in the exercise of its discretion the court decides that it is a proper case to grant a manda-

tory injunction, then the court must be careful to see that the defendant knows exactly in fact what he has to do and this means not as a matter of law but as a matter of fact, so that in carrying out an order he can give his contractors the proper instructions. . . .

My Lords, I shall apply these principles or conditions to this case, and I can do so very shortly.
. . .

4. . . . The terms of the order imposed upon the [defendants] an absolutely unqualified obligation upon them to restore support without giving them any indication of what was to be done. The judge might have ordered the [defendants] to carry out the remedial works described by the [plaintiffs'] expert in his evidence though it would have to be set out in great detail. I could have understood that, but as it was thought to cost GBP 30,000 that would have been most unreasonable and would have offended principle 3, but the order in fact imposed went much further; it imposed an unlimited and unqualified obligation upon the [defendants], and I do not know how they could have attempted to comply with it . . .".

Notes

(1) In this excerpt, Lord Upjohn discusses the interrelationship between the *common law* remedy of *damages*, compensating for loss resulting from torts which have actually been committed, and the *equitable* remedy of *injunction*, preventing either a threatened tort or the continuance or repetition of a tort, so preventing the realization of future harm. In this context, different kinds of injunctions are discussed: prohibitory (negative) injunctions and mandatory injunctions; injunctions when a tort has already been committed and injunctions *quia timet*.

The *quia timet* character of the mandatory injunction granted at first instance in the annotated case seems to have depended on the fact that further *damage* threatened, though it was not entirely certain. The classification of the injunction as *quia timet* in such a case has been criticized. Indeed, a *quia timet* action is generally considered to be, as Lord Upjohn also states, "an action for an injunction to prevent an apprehended legal wrong, *though none has occurred at present* [emphasis added]",[527] in other words, where no complete cause of action yet exists, so for instance in a case where damage is the gist of the action, before damage has actually occurred.[528] In the annotated case however, the wrongful withdrawal of support from the plaintiff's land had already been committed and some damage had already occurred, though further damage was apprehended. Moreover, the plaintiff had been granted a prohibitory injunction, restraining the defendants from further withdrawal of support. Thus, the mandatory injunction clearly did not relate to future acts of the defendants. As Lord Upjohn explains, in this case, where the plaintiff has been fully recompensed both at law and in equity, the *quia timet* injunction is ordered to *prevent future causes of action as a consequence of earlier actions of the defendant*. Indeed, in such a case the plaintiff has a new cause of action each time that new damage occurs[529] but this circumstance cannot as such sufficiently explain why the

[527] A statement by D that he intends to act in a way which, as P claims, will constitute a tort in relation to P or other clear evidence of such intention will support a *quia timet* action by P against D.

[528] See Salmond and Heuston at 555; *Clerk & Lindsell on Torts* at 1513–4, para. 28–10; Rogers at 798; Markesinis and Deakin at 783.

[529] This is a case of continuing injury in which successive actions may be brought; see Section 3, footnote 395. This exception is a consequence of the fact that prospective damages cannot be claimed, however probable the occurrence of future damage may be. See for instance *Hooper v. Rogers* [1975] Ch 43, CA, at 47, confirming that damages cannot be awarded at common law in a case of probable or even certain future

injunction is *quia timet* since, for instance, prohibitory injunctions restraining the defendant from a future withdrawal of support (or from other continuing or recurrent torts) are never considered to be *quia timet*.[530] Also the fact that the plaintiff has recovered redress for damage which he has already suffered may not explain the characterization of the injunction as *quia timet* because then, in the field of torts, almost every mandatory injunction would be *quia timet*.[531] Actually, the fact that future damage is threatened, that is to say that the occurrence and extent of damage are not certain, is the salient fact which justifies the characterization of the injunction as *quia timet*.

(2) Lord Upjohn emphasizes the distinction between prohibitory (or negative) injunctions and mandatory injunctions. Although both remedies are equitable, and thus discretionary, the grant of a mandatory injunction is subject to more conditions. Whilst a plaintiff is generally entitled to a prohibitory injunction "as of course" and will be deprived of that remedy only if special circumstances exist, as follows from the following case, a mandatory injunction can never be "as of course". In the annotated case, Lord Upjohn lays down the general principles for the grant of such an injunction and in his view, a notable point of difference between prohibitory and mandatory injunctions is that only when the court orders a mandatory injunction, the financial implications for the defendant should be taken into account provided that the defendant has acted reasonably, though in the event wrongly. However, since the order of a prohibitory injunction may also depend on the magnitude of the injury, the defendant's conduct and the financial implications for him, as follows from the next case, this point of difference may not be as clear as Lord Upjohn suggests.[532]

(3) It is obvious that a mandatory injunction may lead to a restoration of the state of affairs in which the plaintiff would have been if he had not sustained the injury, that is to say that injunctive relief, when it removes the source of permanent harm, achieves restitution in kind.

physical damage to the land or buildings from loss of support based upon a present decline in the market value of the land due to such probable or certain future physical damage.

[530] See A. Burrows, *Remedies for Torts and Breach of Contract*, 2nd edn. (London: Butterworths, 1994) at 389–90.

[531] *Clerk & Lindsell on Torts* at 1515, para. 28–12. Compare Rogers at 798.

[532] It may be noted that in the excerpted case, before the Court of Appeal ([1967] 1 WLR 967, [1967] 3 All ER 1), it was accepted that the principles of *Shelfer's* case (see **8.E.52.**) were applicable and an injunction was granted. It has been suggested that the reasons in the annotated case for the rejection of application of *Shelfer's* case are unclear and unconvincing: see Hanbury & Martin, *Modern Equity*, 14th edn. (London: Sweet & Maxwell, 1993) at 765. On the other hand, the "economic efficiency" of remedies has attracted much attention from writers in the field of Law and Economics: see for example the entries in *The New Palgrave Dictionary of Economics and the Law*, P. Newman, (ed.), (Basingstoke: MacMillan Reference Limited, 1998), on *Coase theorem* (in relation to the tort of nuisance) and *specific performance* (the equivalent of a mandatory injunction to remedy a breach of contract). See also *supra*, Chapter I, **1.E.3.**, Note (3) and **1.US.10.** and **1.US.11**.

Court of Appeal[533]   **8.E.52.**
Shelfer v. *City of London Electric Lighting Co.*

DAMAGES IN LIEU OF INJUNCTION

Nuisance by electricity company

Damages in substitution for an injunction may be given only if (i) the injury to the plaintiff's right is small, and (ii) is one which is capable of being estimated in money, and (iii) is one which can be adequately compensated by a small money payment, and (iv) the case is one in which it would be oppressive to the defendant to grant an injunction. The public interest is not a sufficient reason for refusing to protect by injunction an individual whose rights are being persistently infringed.

Facts: The vibration, noise and steam caused by the operations of the engines of the defendant electricity company, built next to a pub, caused a nuisance to the lessee of the pub. The plaintiff sought relief by way of injunction.

Held: The court at first instance refused injunctive relief and awarded damages. That decision was unanimously reversed by the Court of Appeal.

Judgment: LINDLEY LJ:[534] "[E]ver since *Lord Cairns' Act* was passed the Court of Chancery has repudiated the notion that the Legislature intended to turn that Court into a tribunal for legalizing wrongful acts; or in other words, the Court has always protested against the notion that it ought to allow a wrong to continue simply because the wrongdoer is able and willing to pay for the injury he may inflict. Neither has the circumstance that the wrongdoer is in some sense a public benefactor (*e.g.* a gas or water company or a sewer authority) ever been considered a sufficient reason for refusing to protect by injunction an individual whose rights are being persistently infringed."

A.L. SMITH LJ:[535] "Many Judges have stated and I emphatically agree with them, that a person by committing a wrongful act (whether it be a public company for public purposes or a private individual) is not thereby entitled to ask the Court to sanction his doing so by purchasing his neighbour's rights, by assessing damages in that behalf, leaving his neighbour with the nuisance, or his lights [the light entering the windows of his house] dimmed, as the case may be.

In such cases the well-known rule is not to accede to the application, but to grant the injunction sought, for the plaintiff's legal right has been invaded, and he is *prima facie* entitled to an injunction.

There are, however, cases in which this rule may be relaxed, and in which damages may be awarded in substitution for an injunction as authorized by [section 2 of Lord Cairns' Act].

In any instance in which a case for an injunction has been made out, if the plaintiff by his acts or laches [delay] has disentitled himself to an injunction the Court may award damages in its place. So again, whether the case be for a mandatory injunction or to restrain a continuing nuisance, the appropriate remedy may be damages in lieu of an injunction, assuming a case for an injunction to be made out.

In my opinion, it may be stated as a good working rule that :—

(1.) If the injury to the plaintiff's legal right is small,

(2.) And is one which is capable of being estimated in money,

---

[533] [1895] 1 Ch 287.
[534] [1895] 1 Ch at 315–6.
[535] [1895] 1 Ch at 322–3.

(3.) And is one which can be adequately compensated by a small money payment,

(4.) And the case is one in which it would be oppressive to the defendant to grant an injunction:— then damages in substitution for an injunction may be given.

There may be also cases in which, though the four above-mentioned requirements exist, the defendant by his conduct, as, for instance, hurrying up his buildings so as if possible to avoid an injunction, or otherwise acting with a reckless disregard to the plaintiff's rights, has disentitled himself from asking that damages may be assessed in substitution for an injunction.

It is impossible to lay down any rule as to what, under the differing circumstances of each case, constitutes either a small injury, or one that can be estimated in money, or what is a small money payment, or an adequate compensation, or what would be oppressive to the defendant. This must be left to the good sense of the tribunal which deals with each case as it comes up for adjudication."

Notes

(1) The annotated case shows that, although the plaintiff is considered to be *prima facie* entitled to a prohibitory injunction to prevent a continuing or recurrent wrong, the court may exceptionally grant damages "in lieu of an injunction". The power to award such damages was originally contained in the Chancery Amendment Act 1858,[536] called Lord Cairns' Act, and is now contained in section 50 of the Supreme Court Act 1981.[537]

As explained in the preceding annotated judgment, historically, common law courts could grant damages as compensation for past wrongs but could not grant injunctions to restrain e.g. continued commission of the wrong in the future whereas courts of equity could grant such injunctive relief but not damages. The Common Law Procedure Act 1854[538] gave courts of common law a limited power to grant equitable relief whilst the Chancery Amendment Act 1858 ("Lord Cairns' Act"), gave the Court of Chancery the power to award damages in lieu of or in addition to an injunction.[539] Section 2 of Lord Cairns' Act provided:

> "In all cases in which the Court of Chancery has jurisdiction to entertain an application for an injunction . . . against the commission or continuance of any wrongful act . . . it shall be lawful for the same Court, if it shall think fit, to award damages to the party injured, either in addition to or in substitution for such injunction . . . and such damages may be assessed in such manner as the Court shall direct".

That provision enabled the Chancery Court to award an injunction to restrain unlawful conduct in the future and damages for unlawful conduct in the past. In addition, the Chancery Court could award damages instead of granting an injunction to restrain unlawful conduct in the future and in this respect, the damages compensate the plaintiff for future unlawful conduct.[540] Lord Cairns' Act has been repealed and replaced by subsequent Acts; the power to award damages in addition to or in substitution for an injunction is now contained in section 50 of the Supreme Court Act 1981, which provides: "Where the Court of Appeal or the High Court has jurisdiction to entertain an

---

[536] 21 & 22 Vict. c. 27.

[537] C. 54.

[538] 17 & 18 Vict. c. 125. Subsequently, the Judicature Acts 1873–1875 brought about the concurrent jurisdiction of law and equity in all civil causes and matters in *all* civil courts and did so on the basis that in any matter where there is a conflict or variance between the rules of equity and the rules of common law, the rules of equity shall prevail. See now Supreme Court Act 1981, s. 49(1). The High Court and the Court of Appeal together constitute the Supreme Court of Judicature (from which appeals lie, by leave, to the House of Lords).

[539] The jurisdiction to grant an injunction now applies to the High Court (Supreme Court Act 1981, s. 37(1)) and, subject to exceptions, to the County Courts. See for more details Hanbury & Martin, *Modern Equity*, 14th edn. (London: Sweet & Maxwell, 1993) at 708–9, 718 ff. and 763 ff.

[540] See the overview given by Sir Thomas Bingham MR in *Jaggard* v. *Sawyer*, [1995] 2 All ER 189, CA at 196–7.

application for an injunction or specific performance, it may award damages in addition to, or in substitution for, an injunction or specific performance".

Damages in substitution for an injunction are different from common law damages because they are available where no legal wrong has yet occurred or where loss may continue in the future whereas no common law damages in respect of damage that has not yet occurred may be claimed.[541]

(2) The award of damages in lieu of an injunction has been controversial since the result of such an award could amount to the legalization of the commission of a tort by a defendant who is able and willing to pay damages. As clearly appears from the annotated case, the award of damages is not meant to amount to a purchase of the defendant's rights[542] and as a general rule, a plaintiff whose legal right is or will be violated, is *prima facie* entitled to the grant of an injunction. Nevertheless, under the conditions mentioned in the annotated case, an injunction may not be the appropriate remedy and damages will be awarded.

It may be noted that the principles set out in the judgments in the annotated case are somewhat similar to the principles laid down in *Redland Bricks*, though in *Shelfer*, the conditions were framed as those under which the court can *refrain from imposing a prohibitory injunction*, whilst in *Redland Bricks* the conditions were framed as those needing to be satisfied before a court can *issue a mandatory injunction*. Indeed, both cases refer to: (1) the magnitude of injury: in *Shelfer*'s case only a small injury[543] (e.g. a very temporary injury) allows the court to depart from the general rule of restraining an injury by a prohibitory injunction whilst the issue of a mandatory injunction is allowed only where grave injury will probably accrue in the future; (2) the adequacy of money compensation; (3) the defendant's conduct: wanton, reckless or unreasonable disregard of the plaintiff's right disentitles a defendant from asking that damages may be assessed in substitution for an injunction (*Shelfer*) or that the court should take the cost of remedial works into account (*Redland Bricks*). Perhaps, the only difference is not of principle but of application: in *Shelfer*, as has been recently emphasized, "the test is one of *oppression*, and the court should not slide into application of a general balance of convenience test [emphasis added]".[544]

(3) The annotated case also gives rise to the question as to whether the public interest may prevail over the plaintiff's private interest in refusing protection by injunction, a question which is answered in the negative. A case which raised a doubt about this issue was *Miller* v. *Jackson*,[545] relating to nuisance caused by the activities of an old-established

---

[541] Hanbury & Martin, *Modern Equity*, 14th edn. (London: Sweet & Maxwell, 1993) at 763; for a case dealing with equitable damages for future injury, see *Hooper* v. *Rogers* [1975] Ch 43, CA, referred to in footnote 529.

[542] On this point see also *Leeds Industrial Co-operative Society Ltd.* v. *Slack* [1924] AC 851, HL at 860–1 per Viscount Finlay. In that case, it was decided, by a majority of three to two, that under Lord Cairns' Act damages could be awarded in substitution for an injunction *quia timet* where injury was threatened but had not yet been sustained. In that case, the defendant had started to erect a building which, when completed, would cause a wrongful obstruction to the plaintiff's lights; however, the interference would be small and adequately compensable by damages.

[543] See for more details A. Burrows, *Remedies for Torts and Breach of Contract* 12th edn. (London: Butterworths, 1994) at 393 ff.

[544] *Jaggard* v. *Sawyer* [1995] 2 All ER 189, CA at 203, per Sir Thomas Bingham MR.

[545] [1977] QB 966, [1977] 3 All ER 338, CA.

cricket club, resulting in cricket balls landing in the garden of a newly built house that the plaintiff had recently bought. The view of Lord Denning MR that the public interest should prevail over the private interest, was not shared by the Court of Appeal in *Kennaway* v. *Thompson*,[546] in which the plaintiff's house stood alongside a lake on which racing and water skiing activities were organized and which caused a nuisance. After having applied the *Shelfer* principles, the court granted a very detailed injunction limiting the activities of the motor boat racing club to prevent inconvenience beyond that which other occupiers in the neighbourhood could be expected to bear.

(4) It may be remembered that where damages are awarded in lieu of an injunction, the question may arise as to whether damages may be "restitutionary".[547]

8.6.2. GERMAN LAW

Introductory Note

German law draws a distinction between claims for reparation under tort law (*deliktischer Schadensersatzansprüche*) and claims to bring to an end, or prevent the occurrence of, unlawful interference (*Abwehransprüche*). The latter claims are called either *Beseitigungsanspruch* or *Unterlassungsanspruch*.[548] In bringing a *Beseitigungsanspruch*, which may be freely translated as a claim for demolition, the plaintiff claims that a present unlawful interference, which has continuing effects, should be brought to an end.[549] An *Unterlassungsanspruch*, which may be translated as a claim for a prohibitory injunction, is intended to prevent the imminent commission of an unlawful act.[550]

The BGB contains no general provision providing for such claims which are only covered in specific provisions, for instance, to mention the most important ones, in the case of unlawful infringement of name (§ 12)[551] and ownership (§ 1004).[552] The general legal principle (*allgemeiner Rechtsgedanke*) underlying these provisions has led to recognition of the availability of general injunctive relief in every instance of infringement and threatened infringement of not only other absolute rights within the meaning of § 823(1) BGB but also of every protected right or interest.[553]

---

[546] [1981] QB 88.

[547] See *supra*, **8.E.11.**, Note (2)(c).

[548] See for a concise but clear explanation: W. Fikentscher, *Schuldrecht*, 8th edn. (Berlin: Walter de Gruyter, 1992) at 809, para. 1359.

[549] **8.G.53.**

[550] **8.G.54.**

[551] § 12 BGB: "If the right of the person entitled (*Berechtigter*) to use a name is disputed by a third party, or if the interest of the authorized person is injured by the fact that a third party uses the same name without authorization, then the entitled person may require the third party to discontinue the infringement. If further infringements are to be apprehended, he may claim an injunction."

[552] § 1004(1) BGB: "If ownership (*Eigentum*) is interfered with in a way otherwise than by dispossession or the withholding of possession, the owner may bring an action against the person guilty of the disturbance for its discontinuance. If further infringements are to be apprehended, the owner may claim an injunction."

[553] See W. Fikentscher, *Schuldrecht*, 8th edn. (Berlin: Walter de Gruyten, 1992) at para. 1360–1; Larenz/Canaris at 673–4; Palandt-Thomas, Introduction to § 823 at para. 16; Palandt-Bassenge, § 1004 at para. 2. For a discussion of injunctive relief in the case of the threatened infringement of a 'duty of safety': C. von Bar, "Vorbeugender Rechtsschutz vor Verkehrspflichtverletzungen" Karlsruher Forum, Supplement VersR 1983, 80.

Whereas culpability (*Verschulden*) is a prerequisite for a claim for reparation, it is not a prerequisite for the availability of these *Abwehransprüche*: an unlawful (*widerrechtlich*) infringement suffices. For the *Unterlassungsklage*, in line with the wording of the second sentence of § 1004(1) BGB, subsequent infringements in the future must be feared (*Wiederholungsgefahr*). However, that condition has been relaxed so that the claim is also available upon the initial threat of infringement.[554] A *Beseitigungsklage* is available only where an unlawful infringement of a right or interest continues to interfere with the plaintiff's rights.[555]

The distinction between *Beseitigungsklage* and *Unterlassungsklage* consists in the fact that the former is directed to the *removal of a source of interference* resulting from an unlawful act whereas the latter aims to *prevent a future unlawful act*. The *Beseitigungsklage* is akin to a claim for reparation (*Schadensersatzanspruch*) since a common characteristic is that both are brought *after* the injurious event, whereas the *Unterlassungsklage* is brought *before* an unlawful act and in order to prevent it. However, the *Beseitigungsklage* and *Schadensersatzanspruch* differ in that, whereas the *Beseitigungsklage* effects the removal of the source of interference in order to prevent future harm, a *Schadensersatzanspruch* is directed to the restoration of the *status quo ante* by repairing, in kind or in money, the realized harmful effects of the wrong.[556] Of course, this distinction is not always obvious and may give rise to discussion.[557] *Beseitigungsklage* and *Schadensersatzanspruch* are also different in that culpability is not needed for the availability of a *Beseitigungsklage*. In that respect, the *Beseitigungsklage* is similar to the *Unterlassungsklage* since the enforcement of legally protected rights and interests as such is the central point of both claims.

It may be noted that the *Reichsgericht* initially considered both claims to be a specific means of *Schadensersatz* (compensation for damage) within the meaning of § 249 BGB. Subsequently, both claims have been founded on an analogous application of § 1004 BGB, providing for what was called in Roman law the *actio negatoria*.[558] The claim on the basis of § 1004 BGB is therefore also called a *negatorischer* or *quasi-negatorischer Anspruch*.[559]

A judgment which admits a *Beseitigungs-* or *Unterlassungsklage* is final. In urgent cases, the plaintiff may request an interim order, called an *einstweilige Verfügung*.

Finally, it may be noted that self-help (*Selbsthilfe*) is not unknown in German law. Besides some specific provisions allowing the plaintiff to take justice into his own hands,[560] §§ 229–231 BGB deal with the conditions under which *Selbsthilfe* is lawful, and the consequences of its unlawful exercise.

---

[554] W. Fikentscher, ibid. at 1363.

[555] See W. Fikentscher, ibid. at para. 1362; Palandt-Bassenge, § 1004 at para. 22.

[556] E. Deutsch, *Unerlaubte Handlungen und Schadensersatz. Ein Grundriß* (Bonn-München: Heymann, 1987) at 227, para. 459.

[557] *Supra*, **8.G.53.**, Note (2).

[558] H. Kötz, *Deliktsrecht*, 7th edn. (Neunsied Luchterhand, 1996) at 247–8, para. 647. Under Roman law the *actio negatoria* "was given to an owner who wished to assert the freedom of his land from an easement": see Markesinis at 26.

[559] There is no unequivocal terminology; see Palandt-Bassenge, § 1004 at para. 2. Legal history shows that the scope of application of that claim has been widened starting with absolute rights such as that of ownership and ending with every legally protected right or interest. See, from a comparative viewpoint, H. Kötz, "Vorbeugender Rechtsschutz im Zivilrecht" (1974) 174 AcP 145.

[560] See Münchener-von Feldmann, § 229 at para. 1. For instance § 910(1) BGB: "The owner of land can cut off and retain the roots of a tree or a bush, which encroach from an adjoining property . . ."

The two cases discussed below, show that the principle of proportionality (*Verhältnis-mäßigkeit*) is to be taken into account when deciding whether an *Unterlassungs-* or *Beseitigungsklage* may be granted.

BGH, 24 April 1970[561]   **8.G.53.**

PROPORTIONALITY OF A DEMOLITION ORDER

Illegally erected extensions

Where a defendant has built deliberately in breach of urban development rules and without planning permission, the owners of neighbouring property are entitled to an order requiring the defendant to pull down the illegally erected building, even if that is possible only at a disproportionate cost.

Facts: The defendant had built extensions (a two-storey building and a 43 metre long wall), without planning permission and in breach of urban development rules which prohibited building within a certain distance of the border between his and the plaintiffs' land. The plaintiffs claimed principally the demolition of the extensions, with a subsidiary claim for damages for the diminution in value of their land.

Held: The court of first instance dismissed the claim for demolition and granted damages. That judgment was reversed by the court of appeal, which ordered demolition, and the judgment of the court of appeal was upheld by the BGH.

Judgment: "Contrary to the contention of the [defendant], the removal of the buildings erected without planning permission is not precluded by § 251(2) BGB, which provides that a defendant may compensate in money if the restoration of the original condition is possible only through disproportionate expenditure. Since that provision is a result of the principle of good faith [*Treu und Glauben*], the question of disproportionality is a matter going to the reasonableness of both parties [references omitted]. Therefore the application of § 251 (2) BGB [in favour of the defendant] is precluded by the fact that the defendant . . . acted in breach of the ban on building and without having a building permit, which had been refused to him because of his failure to observe the requirement that a certain distance be left between buildings, with the result that he deliberately exceeded the land development boundaries. Given this state of affairs the plaintiffs do not act against good faith [*Treu und Glauben*], if they claim the removal of the buildings which were erected without planning permission."

Notes

(1) The annotated case makes it clear first that the principle of proportionality, contained in § 251(2) BGB, is applicable to a claim for demolition of an unlawfully erected building and secondly that, as under English law, the defendant's conduct, in this case the deliberate infringement of urban development rules, may disentitle him from asking the court to take account of the cost of remedial works when deciding whether to order demolition.[562]

In earlier case-law, the BGH had already decided that the principle of proportionality contained in § 251(2) BGB was also applicable to the *Beseitigungsanspruch*, since a plain-

---

[561] NJW 1970, 1180. Translation by Y. P. Salmon.
[562] This has been questioned in legal writing: see Lange at 237–8.

tiff should not be entitled to a remedy for which (as said above[563] and repeated below in Note (2)) culpable conduct is not required, and which is more far-reaching therefore than the remedy of *Schadensersatz* (§ 249 BGB) for which culpable conduct is required and to which § 251(2) does apply. In the annotated case, the BGH justified the application of the principle of proportionality on the basis of the general principle of good faith (*Treu und Glauben*) of which the proportionality rule is a specific application.[564]

(2) In a part of the annotated case not reproduced, the BGH decided that the planning regulation, which prohibited building within a certain distance of the border, constituted a protective statute (*Schutzgesetz*) within the meaning of § 823(2) BGB, so that the plaintiff was entitled to claim not only compensation but also the "termination of the unlawful situation created by the defendant", in this case demolition of the extension and wall that had been unlawfully erected. In this respect, the BGH referred to § 249 BGB, providing for *Naturalrestitution*.[565]

This gives rise to the question how to distinguish between *Naturalrestitution* by application of § 249 BGB and *Beseitigung* by application of § 1004 BGB.[566] The question is of considerable practical importance because *Beseitigung* within the meaning of § 1004 BGB does not require culpability whereas *Naturalrestitution* within the meaning of § 249 BGB, does require it. If *Beseitigung* within the meaning of § 1004 BGB were given a broad meaning, so as to include *Naturalrestitution,* a defendant would also be liable for reparation of harm caused by conduct which is not culpable, and this could result in a form of risk-based liability (*Gefährdungshaftung*) not expressly provided by statute.[567] In the annotated case the BGH was not concerned with the distinction between *Naturalrestitution* (§ 249 BGB) and *Beseitigung* (§ 1004 BGB) since it was there indisputable that the defendant had acted not only unlawfully but also culpably. According to the general view, § 1004 BGB entitles the plaintiff to claim only that the defendant shall cease to continue an unlawful interference, or that a permanent *source of interference* caused by past conduct, be removed; a claim for removal of harmful *consequences* that have already arisen (*bereits eingetretenen Einwirkungsfolgen*) as a result of past wrongful interference, cannot be claimed on the basis of § 1004 BGB but constitutes a claim for reparation of harm (*Schadensersatz*).

The difficulties faced in distinguishing between the removal of effects that have already occurred as a result of past interference, on the one hand, and cessation of continuing interference or removal of a permanent source of interference, on the other hand,[568] are illustrated by a recent judgment,[569] in which the BGH decided that a plaintiff was entitled to claim removal of soil contamination (*Beseitigung der Bodenkontaminierung*) on the basis of § 1004 BGB, regardless of the fact that the defendant no longer operated his business. Indeed, the contaminating products continued

---

[563] See *supra*, 8.6.2. Introductory Note.

[564] See further Larenz/Canaris at 702.

[565] See *supra*, **8.G.12** and Notes following.

[566] For the debate on this issue, see in general Larenz/Canaris at 700; Soergel-Mühl, § 1004 at para. 112–13. For references to the annotated case, see Lange at 237–8 (according to H. Lange, the annotated case concerns a claim for *Naturalrestitution*); Palandt-Bassenge, § 1004 at para. 38 and Soergel-Mühl, § 1004 at para.114 (both referring to the annotated case in the context of a claim for *Beseitigung*).

[567] Larenz/Canaris at 674, 700 and 703–4. On the general approach to risk-based liability under German law, see *supra*, Chapter VI, 6.1.1. and in particular **6.G.1.**

[568] See *inter alia* F. Baur, "Der Beseitigungsanspruch nach § 1004 BGB" (1961) AcP 160, 465 at 487 ff.

[569] BGH, 1 December 1995, NJW 1996, 845.

to interfere with the plaintiff's property or, in other words, constituted a permanent source of interference (*Quelle der Eigentumsstörung*) as long as they were not removed. The BGH confirmed that the borderline between the *negatorischen Beseitigungsanspruch* and the *deliktsrechtlichen Schadensersatzanspruch* is an unresolved problem and went on to admit that to a certain extent *Beseitigung* and *Schadensersatz* may have the same reparatory effect. The BGH referred to the classic textbook example of a window which is broken by a stone thrown onto the plaintiff's property, which gives rise to the question whether not only removal of the stone but also repair of the window constitutes *Beseitigung*.[570] However the BGH found that the removal of substances which contaminated the plaintiff's soil was comparable with the removal of the stone in the classic example (and not with repair of the window) although some legal commentators took the view that oil which had penetrated the plaintiff's soil,[571] unlike the stone in the classic example, could not be removed by way of a claim for *Beseitigung*. Finally, the BGH held that the fact that the removal of the contaminating oil which had penetrated the plaintiff's soil necessarily involved removal of the contaminated soil (that is removal of effects, which, in principle, constitutes *Schadensersatz*) did not preclude the plaintiff from obtaining *Beseitigung*.

In conclusion, it seems that the demolition of an illegally erected building may be claimed on the basis of § 1004 BGB since it may be considered that there is an unlawful interference with the plaintiff's rights as long as the building stands.

(3) The *Beseitigungsanspruch* finds a specific application in the field of defamation and other infringements of personality rights and has been developed into the independent claim of *Widerruf* (retraction by the defendant of the untrue allegation).[572]

BGH, 26 February 1993[573]   **8.G.54.**

PROHIBITORY INJUNCTION (*UNTERLASSUNG*) IN THE CASE OF CONTRAVENTION
OF A PROTECTIVE STATUTORY RULE (*SCHUTZNORM*)

Noisy ballet school

The plaintiff may claim a prohibitory injunction on the basis of §§ 823(2) and 1004(1) BGB when the defendant does not comply with the obligations contained in a planning permit which provide for limitation of noise nuisance, even when the conditions for applying § 906 BGB are not fulfilled.

Facts: The plaintiff was tenant of a plot of land neighbouring that of the defendant. The patio of the plaintiff's house was situated on the border with the defendant's land. The defendant ran a ballet school. The planning permits, which the defendant had needed to convert the basement of his house into a ballet room, stipulated that certain sound limits should not be exceeded and that the windows must be closed when music was played. The defendant did not comply with those obligations and the plaintiff claimed that the defendant be ordered to do so.

[570] This example is also mentioned *inter alia* by F. Baur, "Der Beseitigungsanspruch nach § 1004 BGB" (1961) AcP 160, 465 at 488 and by H.-G. Mertens, "Zum Inhalt des Beseitigungsanspruchs aus § 1004 BGB" NJW 1972, 1783 at 1784–5.
[571] For numerous references, see BGH, 1 December 1995, NJW 1996, 845 at 846–7.
[572] See further Larenz/Canaris at 707 ff.; Soergel-Mühl, § 1004 at para. 120 ff.
[573] BGHZ 122, 1, NJW 1993, 1580. Translation by Y. P. Salmon.

Held: At first instance, the claim was dismissed. On appeal, the plaintiff's claim to order the defendant to keep the windows closed was only partially granted in that the defendant was ordered to keep the windows closed after 7 a.m. The judgment of the court of appeal was quashed by the BGH.

Judgment: "3. . . . It is indeed correct that in the relations between neighbouring property owners the special provisions of §§ 906 ff. BGB determine whether emissions from the other property constitute a lawful or unlawful interference. To this extent, the conflict between the property rights of the owners, each of whom may basically do as he wishes with his property and can exclude others from any interference with it (§ 903 BGB), is regulated in only a general way by these provisions which limit the owners' powers directly. However these provisions do not preclude the application of more particular regulation under a protective statutory rule (*Schutznorm*) and so do not apply to a prohibitory injunction (*Unterlassungsanspruch*) granted on the basis of a protective statute (*Schutzgesetz*) (§ 823(2) BGB). The violation of the *Schutzgesetz* establishes the unlawfulness (*Rechtswidrigkeit*) of the conduct. Where an applicable legal rule of conduct (*Verhaltensanordnung*) is issued by an administrative body (*Verwaltungsbehörde*), a [form of] risk-based liability (*Gefährdungstatbestand*) is established, which places the protection of neighbours in the forefront, without the need to establish actual harm. Through this specific legal protection (*Rechtsschutz*), the legal interests (*Rechtsgüter*) of the neighbour (in his property, health) are particularly effectively protected, albeit only indirectly. This additional legal protection granted to the plaintiff can be claimed through a prohibitory injunction (*Unterlassungsklage*), because it is only in keeping with the purpose of a mandatory rule of conduct (*Verhaltensgebot*) imposed on the defendant if it is enforceable regardless of its effects in the particular individual case.

. . .

4. . . . Likewise, the defendant cannot oppose the plaintiff's claim on grounds of good faith (*Treu und Glauben*). The action for a prohibitory injunction (*Unterlassunsanspruch*) is based solely on objective unlawfulness (*Rechtswidrigkeit*) under § 823(2) BGB, for instance because of the infringement of land development regulations which protect neighbours; the Chamber has already expressed the view that an *Unterlassungsanspruch* may go no further than a damages claim based on the wrongful violation of a protective law. The legal principle of proportionality must always be borne in mind (§ 251(2) BGB) [references omitted]. However, there are no indications in the case at hand that the observance of the provisions [of the planning permit] affects the defendant in an unreasonable way."

Notes

(1) The annotated case provides an illustration of an *Unterlassungsklage* where the plaintiff relied exclusively on a *Schutznorm* within the meaning of § 823(2) BGB.[574] It shows that the *Unterlassungsklage* is a very efficient remedy as it prevents future unlawful conduct and *a fortiori* future harm and that, in line with the preceding case, the principle of proportionality applies to the *Unterlassungsklage*.[575]

It may be noted that the protective statute enlarged the protection of the plaintiff's interests since the provisions of the planning permission contained more stringent obligations than the obligations which would have resulted from § 906 ff. BGB which deals with the general obligations that subsist as between neighbours.[576] The court of appeal took the view that the provisions of the planning permission could not impose

---

[574] On the *Unterlassungsklage* in the case of defamation and infringements of personality rights, see Larenz/Canaris at 707 ff.

[575] See also Larenz/Canaris at 706.

[576] See *supra*, Chapter II, 2.3.2., in particular **2.G.39.**

more stringent obligations on the defendant and decided therefore that the defendant was only obliged to close the windows after 7 a.m. However, the BGH reversed that decision.

(2) An *Unterlassungsklage* is available, according to the wording of § 1004 BGB, only where there is a risk of continued or repeated infringement (*Wiederholungsgefahr*) but it has been recognized in the case law that the claim is also available in the case of a threat of infringement where no infringement has yet occurred, in which case the claim is called a *vorbeugende Unterlassungsklage*.[577] A *Wiederholungsgefahr* is generally presumed from an earlier infringement; the conclusion that there was a *Wiederholungsgefahr* in the annotated case did not give rise to difficulties.

8.6.3. FRENCH LAW

Introductory Note

Unlike English and German law, French case law does not draw a clear distinction between reparation (in kind or in money) for harm and removal of the source of harm in order to prevent future harm. The latter is also considered to be reparation, notably reparation *in kind*.[578] However, it has already been explained that in legal writing the view has been taken that the distinction must be made[579] and indeed the case law shows that, especially in cases of infringement of property rights, enforcement in kind of the infringed right is more imperative than compensation in money, even to the extent that there is no longer room for the trial court's *pouvoir souverain*.[580]

As in German and English law, French law also offers the plaintiff the possibility of claiming interim relief in urgent cases ("*ordonnance de référé*").[581]

Under French law, some specific provisions outside the law of tort provide for a remedy of self-help[582] but it is stated by way of a general rule that a plaintiff cannot take justice into his own hands.[583]

---

[577] Soergel-Mühl, § 1004 at para. 168. See for instance BGH, 6 July 1954, BGHZ 14, 163. Compare the English *quia timet* injunction, *supra*, **8.E.51.**, Note (1).

[578] **8.F.55.**

[579] See *supra*, **8.F.17.**

[580] **8.F.56.**

[581] Art. 808 New Code of Civil Procedure: "In all urgent cases, the President of the *tribunal de grande instance* may prescribe by interim order any measures which will not imperil the final determination of any important issue (*contestation sérieuse*) or one which is required by the existence of a dispute".

Art. 809(1): "The President may always make an interim order prescribing measures of conservation or of restoration which are required either to prevent imminent damage or to terminate manifestly unlawful interference [with the plaintiff's rights]."

[582] See, for instance, Art. 673 C.civ. providing for an occupier's right to trim overhanging branches or encroaching roots of trees on his neighbour's property.

[583] See J. Ghestin and G. Goubeaux, *Traité de droit civil– Introduction générale*, 3rd edn. (Paris: LGDJ, 1990) at 463.

Paris, 24 June 1980[584]   **8.F.55.**
Consorts Citroën v. *Éditions Olivier Orban*

Car manufacturer's widow insulted

The court can order by way of reparation in kind the seizure and destruction of all the copies of a book containing personally offensive passages and enjoin the defendant from their future publication.

Facts: A biography of A. Citroën, a famous French car manufacturer, was published in 1954. In 1956, after proceedings in which the court found that the book contained personally offensive passages, the author, and the Citroën family came to a settlement in which the author undertook not to include those passages in new editions of the book. A new edition was published in 1977, containing most of the passages objected to. The Citroën family claimed (1) publication of the judgment, (2) destruction of the copies of the unsold books and (3) an order restraining publication of a new edition, coupled with the imposition of an *astreinte* (penalty payment in the event of breach of the order) from both the author and the publisher, who was not a contracting party to the 1956 settlement.

Held: The court of first instance condemned the author to pay damages and ordered the publication of the judgment. It dismissed the claim against the publisher on the ground that the publisher was not a contracting party to the 1956 settlement and was not a party to the breach of contract so that the court could not order the destruction of the unsold books and the claimed injunctive order. The court of appeal reversed the judgment of the court of first instance, holding that the publisher should have known that the book contained passages which were not allowed to be published, and granted the claims, coupling the prohibitory injunction with the imposition of an *astreinte* of FRF 1,000 per breach of the order.

Judgment: "On the compensation of the harm [*réparation du préjudice*] sustained by the Citroën family:

The reproduction of passages in the book . . . which [the author] had undertaken to remove by settlement of 30 October 1956, caused serious harm to the Citroën family which can be fully compensated only by the suppression of those passages.

However, with regard to the volumes already published, the passages cannot simply be deleted or excised because of their multiplicity, their length and their distribution throughout the work.

Therefore the seizure and destruction of all volumes which contain the offending passages still to date in the publisher's possession are ordered.

It is moreover appropriate to prohibit [the publisher] and [the author] from any publication of new editions of the work containing the passages in question and from any transfer of their rights [to publish them] to others.

. . .

Furthermore it is appropriate to order the publication of the operative part of the present judgment (*dispositif*) in five daily newspapers and five weekly or monthly magazines at the choice of the Citroën family and at the expense of [the author] and the [publisher]."

Notes

(1) The annotated case shows that under French law, injunctive orders—which find parallels with mandatory and prohibitory injunctions under English law and orders of *Beseitigung* and *Unterlassung* under German law—may be granted to remedy harm. In

---

[584] D 1980.Jur.583, annotated by R. Lindon. Translation by Y. P. Salmon.

fact, when the publisher was ordered to destroy the unsold copies of the book containing the offensive passages, he was ordered to take positive action to correct the consequences of what he had unlawfully done in order to prevent harmful effects in the future (mandatory injunction; *Beseitigung*) and when he was ordered to refrain from publication in the future (prohibitory injunction *quia timet*; grant of *vorbeugende Unterlassungsklage*), future unlawful acts were prevented.

(2) As a result of the view that injunctive orders may be issued by way of reparation, until recently little attention has been paid to the distinction between reparation, on the one hand, and prevention of future harm by elimination of the source of harm, on the other. However, the distinction between reparation and injunctive relief is not unknown in French law. Thus, Art. 9(2) C.civ. relating to interference with the right to privacy,[585] provides:

> "Judges may, *without prejudice to reparation* for the injury sustained, prescribe all measures, such as sequestration, seizure and others, appropriate *to prevent or terminate an infringement of privacy*; such measures may, in appropriate cases, be taken by interim order [emphasis added]."

It has been stated that the remedies which are contained in this provision are intended to safeguard the plaintiff's subjective right as such.[586] The view that the plaintiff is entitled to protection of the right itself, has led to the view that the trier of fact does not have a *pouvoir souverain* where the plaintiff claims the elimination of an unlawful situation which is an ongoing source of harmful interference with the plaintiff's right.[587] This issue will be discussed in the Notes under the next case.

Cass. civ. 1re, 1 March 1965[588]   **8.F.56.**
Cliquet v. Cousin

R<small>EPARATION IN KIND</small>

Illegally erected garage

The court may not dismiss the claim for demolition of an illegally erected building when such demolition is possible on the ground that demolition would be disproportionate to the purpose in hand.

Facts: The defendant erected a garage directly abutting onto the perimeter wall of the plaintiff's villa without complying with the urban development rule that prohibits the erection of buildings within a certain distance of the border between neighbouring properties. The plaintiff claimed demolition of the garage.

Held: The court of appeal dismissed the claim and granted damages on the grounds, first, that the plaintiff did not show the nature and extent of harm caused by the erection of the garage and, secondly, that demolition would effect a harsh result. The Cour de cassation quashed the judgment of the court of appeal.

---

[585] On the right to privacy under French law, see *supra*, Chapter II, 2.2.2.
[586] J. Ravanas, in *Juris-Classeur Civil*, v° "Art. 9", Fasc. 2 at para. 60 ff.
[587] *Supra*, Note (3) under **8.F.17.**
[588] JCP 1965.II.14134. Translation by Y. P. Salmon.

Judgment: "Having regard to Art. 1143 C. civ.:

The judgment states that [the defendant] had erected, on the edge of his land, a garage which he built in such a way that it derived structural support from the perimeter wall [*mur de clôture*] of the neighbouring villa belonging to [the plaintiff], in violation of the planning provisions of the town of Nice, which reserve a three-metre wide zone of *non aedificandi* [area subject to a building ban] around the border of each plot of land.

The trial judges were requested to order the demolition of the wrongfully erected construction and to award damages

In allowing [the plaintiff] only monetary compensation, the appeal judges held that he had specified neither the nature nor the extent of the prejudice that he pleaded, not having sustained any inconvenience, and that the 'rigorous application of the legal rule would only have the effect of resulting in a barbarous solution'.

Having recognized the existence of the town planning infringement and the possibility of the performance of the claimed reparation in kind [*condamnation en nature*], the court of appeal, in refusing to grant such reparation because it would present 'disadvantages . . . disproportionate to the goal aimed at', failed to apply [Art. 1143 C.civ.] correctly [omission in original]."

Notes

(1) In the annotated case concerning a *violation of town planning regulations*, the Cour de cassation held that the court was precluded from imposing reparation in money where the plaintiff asked for condemnation in kind (*condamnation en nature*) requiring the defendant to demolish the garage that he had illegally erected, even if the prejudicial consequences of such a condemnation were disproportionate to the purpose in hand.

Before the annotated case, it had been doubted whether a neighbour could rely on provisions of planning regulations or permits to claim either damages or the demolition of a building which was erected in breach of such provisions.[589] The annotated case confirms that a plaintiff is entitled to claim demolition of a building that has been erected in contravention of such provisions. Since the annotated case, that solution has been confirmed many times.[590] It must be noted, however, that in later cases, unlike in the annotated case, it has been emphasized that the plaintiff is entitled to claim demolition only if he can prove that he has been personally prejudiced as a consequence of the contravention, e.g. by obstruction of the plaintiff's view; but subject to that restriction, the court, as before, may not to refuse reparation in kind where the existence of the town-planning infringement is established and the reparation in kind is possible.[591]

In the annotated case the Cour de cassation applied Art. 1143 C.civ. to justify the imperative character of reparation in kind. Art. 1143 C.civ. is a provision of contract law[592] under which the obligee

---

[589] See M.-E. Roujou de Boubée, *Essai sur la notion de réparation* (Paris: LGDJ, 1974) at 221.

[590] It may be noted that, after the annotated judgment, an Act of 31 December 1976 on urban development has somehow restricted the availability of the claim for demolition: see Viney, *Effets* at 55–6, para. 39 and at 74, para. 52.

[591] Cass. civ. 3e, 15 March 1977, Bull. civ. 1977.III.122, cited by Y. Chartier, *La réparation du préjudice dans la responsabiliti civile* (Paris: Dalloz, 1983) at 494; Cass. civ. 3e, 1 February 1978, Bull.civ. 1978.III.70; Cass. civ. 3e, 7 June 1979, JCP 1980.II.19415, annotated by J. Ghestin. Compare M.-E. Roujou de Boubée, *Essai sur la notion de réparation* (Paris: LGDJ, 1974) at 222. Compare the older case Cass. civ. 3e, 10 December 1969, D 1970.Jur.323, with report of *conseiller* Frank, in which the Cour de cassation upheld the judgment of the court of appeal which had appreciated, in the exercise of its *pouvoir souverain*, the "methods and extent of the repair of the damage and the possibility of the execution in kind of the judgment solicited".

[592] As has already been said, in principle the rules of contract law does not apply to actions in tort. See Chapter I, **1.F.13.**

865

has the right to demand reversal of whatever has been done in violation of a covenant. The application of Art. 1143 C.civ. in the annotated case has been criticized for ignoring the distinction between obligations resulting from a servitude which has been agreed on a contractual basis, on the one hand, and "urban development servitudes", on the other.[593] Nonetheless, the applicability of Art. 1143 C.civ. in cases of the kind under consideration is firmly established in case-law and has recently been confirmed.[594]

(2) Also in cases of *infringement of property rights* (including servitudes) and therefore outside the scope of tort law,[595] the court, notwithstanding its *pouvoir souverain*, may be precluded from granting monetary compensation where the plaintiff who has been prejudiced by the situation claims reparation in kind, regardless of the proportion between the plaintiff's prejudice and the financial implications of the order for the defendant.

Thus, in a case in which a block of flats had been built to an excessive height, in breach of a servitude,[596] as a result of which the neighbours suffered prejudice (obstruction of their view, overshadowing, increase of the humidity level), the Cour de cassation quashed the judgment of the court of appeal which had refused to order the defendant to demolish the offending part, because of the prejudice caused to the purchasers of the upper flats.[597]

Where the defendant put up a building that encroaches onto his neighbour's land, the neighbour is entitled to claim demolition of the building to safeguard the integrity of his own property right.[598] By a judgment of 11 July 1969, the Cour de cassation held that the plaintiff was entitled to enforce that right regardless of the fact that only a very small strip of the plaintiff's land had been built on, rejecting the defendant's argument that the cost of demolition was disproportionate to the value of the occupied strip of the plaintiff's land.[599]

[593] Y. Chartier, *La réparation du préjudice dans la responsabiliti civile* (Paris: Dalloz, 1983) at 494, referring to R. Savatier, "Propriété immobilière et contraintes d'urbanisme; la condamnation à démolir" D 1974.Chron.59 at para. 18. See for obligations or servitudes resulting from the conditions of a *lotissement* e.g. Cass. civ. 1e, 3 December 1962, D 1963.Jur.302; Cass. civ. 3e, 6 November 1969, JCP 1969.II.16286, annotated by G.G.

[594] Cass. civ. 3e, 22 May 1997, Bull. civ. 1997.III.113 and the comment of G. Viney, "Chronique", JCP 1997.I.4070 at 518, para. 26–7.

[595] See for a very detailed and recent overview R. Mevoungou Nsana, "Le préjudice causé par un ouvrage immobilier: réparation en nature ou par équivalent", RTDciv. (1995), 733. The author distinguishes harm resulting from "*empiètement*", consisting in either building across a borderline (*usurpation d'un terrain*) or interference with a servitude (*entrave à l'exercice d'une servitude*) and harm resulting from "*nuisances*", consisting of *troubles de voisinage* (e.g. nuisance by noise, nuisance by smell) and *nuisances fautives* (e.g. non-compliance with planning regulations).

[596] Where a building is erected in breach of a servitude which has been contractually agreed, the imperative character of the demolition is based on Art. 701 C.civ. or Art. 1143 C.civ; for more details see M.-E. Roujou de Boubée, *Essai sur la notion de réparation* (Paris: LGDJ, 1974) at 226 ff.

[597] Cass. civ. 1re, 30 November 1965, *JCP* 1966.II.14481.

[598] See M.-E. Roujou de Boubée, *Essai sur la notion de réparation*, at 225–6.

[599] Cass. civ. 3e, 11 July 1969, JCP 1971.II.16658, annotated by A. Plancqueel. It has been argued that the plaintiff's claim should be dismissed if it constitutes an *abus de droit* (abuse of a legal right): see Viney, *Effets* at 72 and 75. On this basis, the Belgian Cour de cassation has dismissed a claim for demolition and granted damages only: Cass., 10 September 1971, RCJB 1976, 300, annotated by P. Van Ommeslaghe. Likewise, the BGH has dismissed a *Beseitigungsklage* on the basis of the general principle of proportionality: the claim for demolition was there considered to be an abuse of the legal right in question (*rechtsmißbräuchlich*): BGH, 21 June 1974, BGHZ 62, 388. Under Dutch law too, the plaintiff cannot claim demolition where it would harm the defendant disproportionately (*onevenredig veel zwaarder*); in such a case, a servitude entitling the defendant to occupy the plaintiff's land is granted or the parcel of land is transferred against payment, provided that the defendant has not acted deliberately (*kwade trouw*) or with gross fault (*grove schuld*): Art. 5:54 NBW. See also, prior to the enactment of the NBW: Hoge Raad, 17 April 1970, NJ 1971, 89. Unless the violation of the plaintiff's right is trivial, an English court would probably arrive at the same solution as that reached by the Cour de cassation in its judgment of 11 July 1969 on the ground that otherwise a person could, in effect, compulsorily acquire his neighbour's property, an argument which is also mentioned in the judgment of 11 July 1969. *Clerk & Lindsell on Torts* at para. 28–06.

(3) Case law dealing with *interference with* the plaintiff's *quiet enjoyment of his property* resulting from escapes of noise, smell etc. from neighbouring property (*troubles de voisinage*) is less stringent, in that the trial judge's *pouvoir souverain* is recognized.[600] It is beyond doubt that the courts may order the defendant to carry out remedial works in order to prevent or lessen the interference and eventually to order the defendant to refrain from the interfering activity, as in a case in which the plaintiffs, living in a flat on the ground floor, obtained an order that the defendant was to refrain from operating a noisy bakery on the first floor, although he had carried out works, suggested by an expert but actually ineffectual to prevent a nuisance by noise.[601]

But the making of such an order is discretionary: the lower court enjoys its normal *pouvoir souverain* in choosing between compensation in money and measures to restrain the interference,[602] so that it is doubtful that French law contains a general principle that a plaintiff is entitled, as of right, to obtain an order requiring the elimination of interferences in order to prevent future prejudice.[603] The case law has been criticized because it would make possible the continuance, against payment, of a situation regarded to be unpermissible.[604] Conversely, G. Viney emphasizes that liability for *troubles de voisinage* is a no-fault liability regime that applies even when the defendant was not at fault in such cases, it must be possible for the court to allow, against payment of damages, the continuance of an activity which constitutes a nuisance for the neighbours but is beneficial to society as a whole.[605]

(4) The availability of injunctive relief—reparation in kind—is of course dependent on its feasibility, as the annotated case confirms. More far-reaching are the restrictions resulting from the respect which the judge must give to *administrative prerogatives*.[606] Thus, the court cannot order measures which are contrary to the provisions of an administrative permit nor can it directly or indirectly order the defendant to refrain from the authorized activity. In such a case, the court is only allowed to impose additional conditions to prevent or to lessen the harmful interferences. In addition, administrative courts are extremely reluctant to grant injunctive relief against the Administration[607] and a plaintiff is not allowed to claim reparation in kind where he suffers harm as a consequence of public works that infringe his property rights or constitute *troubles de voisinage*.[608]

---

[600] See also R. Mevoungou Nsana, "Le préjudice causé par un ouvrage immobilier: réparation en nature ou par équivalent" RTDciv. 1995, 733 at 765–6, para. 49 and at 771–2, para. 54–6. On *troubles de voisinage*, see *supra*, Chapter II, 2.3.3., Introductory Note under c) as well as Chapter VI, 6.4.1. under b).

[601] Cass. civ. 2e, 30 May 1969, JCP 1969.II.16069, annotated by L. Mourgeon.

[602] Viney, *Effets* at 75; Cass. civ. 2e, 8 December 1977, Bull.civ. 1977.II.236.

[603] Compare M.-E. Roujou de Boubée, *Essai sur la notion de réparation* (Paris: LGDJ, 1974) at 248, who argues that such a general principle should be recognized but affirms that case law dealing with *troubles de voisinage* imposes limits on this principle.

[604] See *inter alia* Roujou de Boubée, ibid. at 243; this argument has also been met in *Shelfer's* case, *supra* **8.E.52.**

[605] Viney, *Effets* at 76.

[606] M.-E. Roujou de Boubée, *Essai sur la notion de réparation* (Paris: LGDJ, 1974) at 249 ff.; Y. Chartier, *La réparation du préjudice dans la responsabilité civile* (Paris: Dalloz, 1983) at 479, para. 381; Viney, *Effets* at 52–8, para. 37–41; R. Mevoungou Nsana, "Le préjudice causé par un ouvrage immobilier: réparation en nature ou par équivalent" (1995) RTDciv., 733 at 773 ff.

[607] Viney, *Effets* at 56–7, para. 40.

[608] Ibid. at 57–8, para. 41.

8.7. COMPARATIVE OVERVIEW

The ultimate purpose of an action in tort is to obtain a *remedy*. The tort laws of each legal system provide for various remedies, fulfilling different purposes[609]. Those purposes are, to a large extent, found in each legal system and it is not surprising that as a consequence the general principles of the law of remedies of each legal system are very similar, although, of course, the concrete implementation of the principles may differ. The general principles and lines of thought will be emphasized in the discussion which follows, respectively dealing with (1) the classification of remedies, (2) the purposes of redress for injury and the general principles of assessment of damages, (3) the effect of the form of compensation and procedural rules on the implementation of the principle of full reparation, (4) the implementation of the principle of full reparation (a) in the case of loss of or damage to property and (b) in the case of personal injury and death.

Classification of remedies

a) It is not easy to make a clear classification of remedies which is accurate for each legal system. Indeed, the legal systems do not distinguish the various kinds of remedies on the basis of the same criteria and in addition, there may be difficulties in making the distinction within each legal system. Leaving the particularities of each legal system aside, a fruitful distinction can be drawn on the basis of two criteria: (1) the *judicial* or *extra-judicial* character of the remedy and (2) the effect of the remedy: does it give *redress* for injury, that is to say does it seek to make good the realized harmful consequences of a tort or is it intended to *obviate* injury, either by removing an ongoing source of harm or by preventing the commission of the unlawful act as such?

Extra-judicial remedies are of only limited importance. Whilst English law provides for various remedies of self-help[610] and German law has worked out general rules on *Selbsthilfe*,[611] French law is not acquainted with the remedy of self-help, although, of course, the idea of *"justice privée"* is not unknown.[612] It may be stated as a general rule that a remedy of self-help is available only in specific, exceptional cases and is subject to rigid conditions.[613]

b) (i) The classification of remedies into those that seek to *make good* an injury that *has* occurred and those that are intended *to obviate injury* (injunctive relief) is reflected, in English law, in the distinction made between the remedy of damages, on the one hand, which always consists in the payment of a sum of money,[614] and injunctive relief on the other. In German law, the divide runs between *Schadensersatz* (§§ 249 ff. BGB) and

---

[609] See also *supra*, Chapter I, 1.2.1. to 1.2.4.

[610] See *supra*, 8.6.1., Introductory Note.

[611] See *supra*, 8.6.2., Introductory Note.

[612] See *supra*, 8.6.3., Introductory Note.

[613] For an overview relating to the law of all EU Member States, of the defence of self-help and the related defences of self defence (*Notwehr, défense légitime*) and necessity (*Notstand, état de nécessité*), see von Bar II at 515 ff., 517 ff. and 526 ff. See also *supra*, Chapter III, 3.2.4.

[614] *Supra*, 8.2.1., Introductory Note.

Abwehransprüche (*Beseitigungsanspruch* or *Unterlassungsanspruch*).[615] French tort law does not draw this distinction clearly so that a defendant may be condemned by way of "reparation" to do or refrain from doing something to obviate future damage.[616]

(ii) *Redress for injury and injunctive relief may have the same effect* where the removal of a permanent source of harm caused by a past unlawful act (e.g. the obstruction of light by an illegaly erected construction), which removal is regarded in some legal systems (as in France) as reparation in kind, obviates the occurrence of future harm at the same time and has therefore the same effect as injunctive relief would take in other legal systems (as in England).

That helps to acknowledge the relative character of, on the one hand, English law, where *redress* for injury is always said to be given by way of a sum of money, and, on the other hand, German law, which puts the principle of *Naturalrestitution* first, and French law, which also recognizes the possibility of *réparation en nature* in the sense of restorative steps to be taken by the defendant. And, indeed leaving aside the cases in which the defendant is ordered to correct what he has done or has omitted to do (for which under English law a mandatory injunction is available as well) and cases in which the defendant is ordered to return goods which are wrongfully in his possession (for which also under English law an order may be available[617]) or to deliver substitutes for goods of the plaintiff in relation to which the defendant has committed a tort,[618] there are hardly cases in German and French law where a defendant is allowed or ordered to effect the reparation himself or herself.

(iii) Provided that there is a recoverable harm according to the rules of law, the court has no discretion to award redress or not. Conversely, with regard to ordering injunctive relief the position of each legal system as to *the exercise of discretion by the court* is basically different.

In English law, the remedy of injunction, being an equitable remedy, is said to be a discretionary remedy by nature.[619] In French law, the choice between a monetary award and injunctive relief lies in principle within the judge's discretion, although in some classes of case a "condemnation in kind" (*condemnation en nature*), where possible and claimed by the plaintiff, is obligatory.[620] Conversely, in German law both the choice between *Naturalrestitution* (including restoration by the defendant or on his initiative) and *Kompensation* and the choice between the award of injunctive relief (*Abwehransprüche*) and the award of redress are governed by the same principle laid down in § 251(2) BGB so that there is no difference as to the judge's discretion.

Despite these differences, there are *common lines of thought*, especially in German and English law. A first common line of thought is that *injunctive relief protects the plaintiff's right more satisfactorily than an award of damages* against unlawful interferences.

---

[615] *Supra*, 8.6.2., Introductory Note.

[616] *Supra*, **8.F.55.** and **8.F.56.**

[617] See Rogers at 614.

[618] In Germany and France, in the years following the Second World War defendants were condemned to deliver substitute goods; see Larenz at 467 and A. Tunc, "Comment réparer, dans une économie de taxation et de rationnement, le préjudice de la perte d'un bien?" D 1946.Chron.57.

[619] *Supra*, 8.6.1., Introductory Note and **8.E.51.**

[620] *Supra*, **8.F.56.** and Notes.

This is particularly clear in German law which does not require culpability as a pre-requisite for the availability of injunctive relief.[621] The preference for the protection of the plaintiff's right as such also explains why in English law the plaintiff is entitled to a pro-hibitory injunction "as of course", notwithstanding the discretionary nature of injunc-tive relief: an injunction may be refused only where the interference with the plaintiff's right is trivial[622] or on the ground that, in line with equitable principles generally, the plaintiff's conduct has debarred him.[623] To be sure, English law is much more reticent than German law to grant injunctive relief where the defendant is ordered to take posi-tive action to rectify the consequences of what he has already done. Indeed, the grant of a mandatory injunction is never "as of course" and, provided that no grave damage will accrue to the plaintiff in the future and that damages are a sufficient or adequate remedy, English law shows a clear preference for the remedy of damages.[624]

Secondly, in both English and German law, *the appropriateness of injunctive relief is dependent on accompanying circumstances* such as the conduct of plaintiff and defendant and the cost of remedial works: a preference for the protection of the plaintiff's right as such against unlawful interferences may not have *unreasonable* consequences.

In English law, both the *Shelfer* principles and the principles for the application of a (*quia timet*) mandatory injunction are intended to achieve a fair balance between the interests of plaintiff and defendant. In German law, this balance is sought on the basis of the principle of proportionality (*Verhältnismäßigkeit*), being a matter of reasonableness on the side of plaintiff and defendant (*Zumutbarkeit auf beide Seiten*).[625] Not only the principle as such, but also its concrete application may be very similar in German and English law, as is evident from the case in which the defendant was disentitled from argu-ing that injunctive relief would be unreasonable, where his conduct was deliberate.[626]

French law takes *a less clear and less satisfactory position with regard to the judge's dis-cretion in ordering injunctive relief or granting damages.* First, generally applicable guide-lines governing the judge's choice between a monetary award and injunctive relief have not been elaborated in the case law. Indeed, both kinds of remedy are not always distin-guished and are considered to be two branches of one and the same "remedy", namely reparation of harm. Secondly, in the classes of case in which the judge cannot impose a monetary award where the plaintiff claims a condemnation in kind, the trial judge is not allowed to appeal to principles of reasonableness or proportionality, although legal writ-ing argues in favour of application of those principles.[627] It may be hypothesized that in this respect, French law may see innovations. It is notable that the distinction between a

---

[621] *Supra*, 8.6.2., Introductory Note.

[622] Damages may only be awarded in lieu of an injunction under the conditions mentioned in *Shelfer*, *supra*, **8.E.52.**

[623] See A. Burrows, *Remedies for Torts and Breach of Contract*, 2nd edn. (London: Butterworths, 1994) at 393 and 446 ff., e.g. where the plaintiff, with knowledge of his rights, has acquiesced in the act complained of, so that it would be dishonest or unconscionable for the plaintiff to seek to enforce his right: *Shaw* v. *Applegate* [1978] 1 All ER 123, CA.

[624] *Supra*, **8.E.51.**

[625] *Supra*, **8.G.53.** and **8.G.54.**

[626] *Supra*, **8.E.51.**, **8.E.52.**, Note (2) and **8.G.53**. Under both legal systems the criterion is therefore "reason-ableness" and not "disproportionaility" which as such is not sufficient to deprive a plaintiff of his right to injunctive relief.

[627] *Supra*, **8.F.56.** and Notes (1) and (3) thereunder.

monetary award and injunctive relief has been expressly recognized in legal writing and is also clearly considered in case law relating to infringement of property rights[628] and in the legal provision dealing with the right to privacy (Art. 9(2) C.civ.).[629] This is perhaps not coincidental since the BGB also expressly provides for *Abwehransprüche* in the case of unlawful infringement of ownership (§ 1004 BGB) and name (§ 12 BGB), which is a specific personality right. Accordingly, there is a primary need to protect the plaintiff's absolute rights such as property or personality rights.[630] However that is, an unequivocal recognition, in French law, of the specificities of the remedy of reparation of harm, on the one hand, and injunctive relief, on the other, may lead to more explicit rules governing the judge's choice between a monetary award and injunctive relief.

c) Finally, it may be noted that in civil procedures injunctive relief against public authorities is excluded or limited by the different legal systems to a varying degree,[631] a variety which may be reduced however by the harmonizing effect of the ECJ's case-law in respect of interim relief,[632] at least in areas of the national law that are affected by EC law.

The purposes of redress for injury and the general principles of assessment of damages

In distinguishing the different purposes of redress for injury, it is fruitful to emphasize both the distinction between *material* and *non-material* harm and the *particularities of some classes of case.*

a) (i) Each legal system adheres to the principle that, where an actionable tort has been committed against the plaintiff, he or she is entitled to full reparation for *material damage* suffered by him or her.[633] As has been explained, such reparation is generally achieved through monetary relief and where German and French law advocate the principle of reparation in kind, this principle must be principally understood as a guideline to assess the monetary award, as will be explained below.

Moreover, each legal system recognizes the qualification of the principle of full reparation by the so-called *duty to mitigate damage.* That principle plays a more pronounced role in English and German than in French law.[634] In French law the duty to mitigate damage has been discussed only in the case of refusal to undergo medical treatment;[635] by contrast, in English and German law the duty to mitigate[636] is discussed in the case law in connection with situations of every description, where it is used to determine for which

---

[628] *Supra,* **8.F.56.**

[629] *Supra,* **8.F.55.,** Note (2).

[630] In respect of personality rights, it has been argued that the remedies for which Art. 9(2) C.civ. provides, neither require tortious liability nor need to "repair" harm: they are only intended to protect the infringed right as such: J. Ravanas in *Juris-Classeur civil*, v° "Art. 9", Fasc. 2 at para. 60 ff.

[631] *Supra,* Section 6.1., Introductory Note and **8.F.56.**, Note (5). See with regard to German law, Lange at 222–4.

[632] See M. Brealy and M. Hoskins, *Remedies in EC Law*, 2nd edn. (London, Sweet & Maxwell, 1998) at 152–64; W. van Gerven, "Of Rights, Remedies and Procedures" (2000), 37 CMLRev. at 501–36. See more generally, *infra*, Chapter IX, 9.1 and 9.4.

[633] *Supra,* **8.E.8., 8.G.12.** and **8.F.16.**

[634] It plays also a role in areas of the national laws affected by the case law of the ECJ with regard to compensation for breaches of Community law: see *infra*, **9.EC.3**, para. 33 (dealing with the liability of the Community).

[635] *Supra,* **8.F.18.**

[636] Or, in German law, the underlying idea also expressed by the so-called *Wirtschaftlichkeitspostulat*: see **8.G.12.,** Note (2)(b).

harmful consequences redress can be given (for instance in the case of a plaintiff refusing particular medical treatment)[637] but also to contribute to the establishment of the measure of damages (for instance in the case of a damaged car giving rise to the question as to whether damages are to be assessed on the basis of the cost of repair or the cost of replacement).[638]

(ii) The principle of full reparation may take on a particular meaning in cases where *the defendant has made profits by the wrongdoing*. This raises the question of "restitutionary" damages, the borderland between the *law of damages* and the *law of unjust enrichment*. Although the question as to whether damages may be assessed on the basis of the profits made by the defendant in such a case is controversial in each legal system, the fact that the defendant has been enriched by his wrongdoing will often affect the assessment of damages.

This is particularly clear in cases dealing with *infringement of intellectual property rights*, where the relevance of the defendant's enrichment is recognized, albeit with varying degrees of candour. In France, which adheres exclusively to the principle of strict equivalence between harm and damages, the defendant's enrichment can be taken into account only as a presumption of fact to assess the amount of harm suffered by the plaintiff.[639] However, due to his *pouvoir souverain* and the absence of a requirement to give reasons for the assessment of the damages, the trier of fact (court of first instance or court of appeal) is able to go beyond this provided that he does not confess to being influenced by considerations which are not reconcilable with a strict compensatory approach. In English law—leaving the equitable remedy of account of profits aside—damages are assessed in cases of infringement of an intellectual property right on the basis of the hypothesis that the plaintiff would have agreed to let his right. This approach, however hypothetical it may be, is considered to be in line with the compensatory approach. German law openly recognizes that the law of damages may reach the same conclusions as the law of unjust enrichment, a solution which is based upon practical considerations, especially the particular vulnerability of these rights.[640] As has been explained, the idea of "restitutionary" damages also plays a prominent role in English law in cases of *proprietary wrongs*.[641] In German law, damages for material harm are assessed on the same basis in cases of *infringement of personality rights*, provided that the plaintiff would have agreed to authorize the use of his name or image, for example.[642]

b) (i) The case of *infringement of a personality right* where the plaintiff would not have authorized the use of his name or image, raises the question of the assessment of *non-material damage* and the importance of the penal element in the law of damages. As in the case of assessment of damages for material harm resulting from the infringement of intellectual property rights, the defendant's enrichment may be taken into account, not only from the perspective of prevention of unjust enrichment but also from the perspective of deterrence and/or punishment.

---

[637] *Supra*, **8.E.9.** and **8.G.13.** See also **8.G.43.**, Note (3) dealing with the duty incumbent on the widow or widower to mitigate the damage by seeking employment after the spouse's death.

[638] *Supra*, **8.E.8.** and **8.G.12.**

[639] *Supra*, **8.F.20.**, Notes (2) and (3).

[640] *Supra*, **8.G.15.** and notes thereafter.

[641] *Supra*, **8.E.11.** and notes thereafter.

[642] *Supra*, **8.G.15.**, Note (2). See for a similar case in France: Paris, 9 November 1982, D. 1984.Jur.30.

The aim of punishment and deterrence through the award of damages against tortfeasors is openly accepted, albeit subject to severe restrictions, only in English law, as is shown in *Rookes* v. *Barnard*[643] and *Cassell & Co. Ltd.* v. *Broome*.[644] Prevention of a tortfeasor's unjust enrichment is one of the considerations which play a role in the assessment of exemplary damages.[645] Punitive damages cannot be awarded in German law.[646] However, in assessing the award of damages for non-material harm in the case of an infringement of the general personality right, the profit motive underlying the infringement of the personality right has to be taken into account and the purpose of prevention is openly recognized. As a consequence, the award is quite similar to an award of exemplary damages under English law.[647] In accordance with the formally absolute, strict compensatory approach in French law, considerations other than the extent of harm, e.g. the profit motive, are not supposed to play a role in the assessment of damages[648] but, here again, the trier of fact can go beyond this strict compensatory approach without any risk of interference by the Cour de cassation if he or she does not confess to having taken such considerations into account.

(ii) Leaving aside the case of infringement of personality rights, the *specificity of redress for non-material harm* explains some other qualifications to the principle of full reparation. The fact that non-material harm is not arithmetically convertible into money is fully recognized in English and German law. Therefore, in English law damages for non-material harm, such as pain and suffering, are considered to be "at large": they are still considered to be compensatory but are at the same time different; they are a solatium rather than a monetary recompense for harm.[649] This analysis is echoed in the dual function of an award for non-material damage (*Schmerzensgeld*) in German law: compensation (*Ausgleich*) and satisfaction (*Genugtuung*).[650] As a consequence, both legal systems recognize that, besides the objective severity of the injury, other circumstances such as the degree of culpability may, in certain circumstances and within limits, be taken into account. The question whether this view involves a penal element in the law of damages seems in this respect largely theoretical.[651] Conversely, French law purports to apply a strict compensatory principle in assessing damages for non-material harm: the degree of culpability is not supposed to be taken into account. But again, the *pouvoir souverain* of the trier of fact casts some doubt upon the concrete implementation of this principle in practice.[652]

(iii) The impossibility of an exact assessment of non-material harm raises the question of *how arbitrary assessment can be avoided*. In this respect, English and German law are again very similar.

---

[643] *Supra*, **8.E.1.**
[644] *Supra*, **8.E.2.**
[645] *Supra*, **8.E.1.–2.**, Note (3)(b).
[646] *Supra*, **8.G.4.**
[647] *Supra*, **8.G.5.** and notes thereafter.
[648] *Supra*, **8.F.7.**, Note (1) and **8.F.20.**
[649] *Supra*, **8.E.2.** and Note thereafter. See also *supra*, Chapter I, **1.E.4.**
[650] *Supra*, **8.G.3.**
[651] Compare the view of Lord Hailsham of St. Marylebone LC, *supra*, **8.E.2.** with the evolution of the BGH's case law, *supra*, **8.G.3.** and Note (3) thereafter.
[652] *Supra*, **8.F.6.** and notes thereafter.

In England, the need for consistency in awards has been realized in the field of personal injury by virtually excluding trial by jury. In *Ward* v. *James*,[653] it was considered that assessability of non-material damage means that the award must be a conventional figure, derived from awards in comparable cases, giving a certain uniformity and predictability to the awards. Also in the classes of case in which trial by jury has survived (defamation, malicious prosecution or false imprisonment), the same need for consistency has (very recently) led to the giving of detailed guidance to the jury[654] and to the recognition of the possibility of drawing the attention of the jury to previous awards, across the categories of personal injury, defamation or malicious prosecution.[655] In Germany, the lower court's assessment of *Schmerzensgeld* is subject to review by the BGH, emphasizing the need for consistency. The BGH puts stringent requirements on the lower court's duty to give reasons: the court must give reasons for an assessment which departs from those in comparable cases,[656] but the mere conformity of an award with those granted in comparable cases does not as such justify the assessment.[657] The French approach to assessment *in concreto*, the *pouvoir souverain* of the trier of fact (lower court) and the absence of any requirement for the trial judge to give reasons for an assessment have impeded the development of guidelines with regard to the assessment of damages. Although the trier of fact may now take account of awards in comparable cases (provided that such reference does not constitute the decisive argument) and recent legislation is intended to contribute to more uniformity, legal practice seems nonetheless to remain unable to guarantee equal treatment for injured plaintiffs.[658]

c) Finally, the idea of actual redress for injury seems to fade where the mere recognition of the plaintiff's right or interest predominates (nominal damages under English law and the *franc symbolique* under French law).[659]

The effect of the form of compensation and procedural rules on the implementation of the principle of full reparation

a) It is difficult to implement the principle of full reparation or, in other words, the principle of strict equivalence between harm and redress, when the harm continues to produce effects in the future, which will, or may, be subject to change, as personal injury cases show. Especially where the question of reparation for future loss arises,[660] the principle of full reparation is balanced with other considerations, mainly the public policy interest in preventing a multiplicity of actions. The differences between the English, German and

[653] *Supra,* **8.E.10.**
[654] *Thompson* v. *Commissioner of Police of the Metropolis, supra,* **8.E.1.–2.,** Note (3)(a).
[655] *John* v. *MGN Ltd., supra,* **8.E.1.–2.,** Note (5).
[656] *Supra,* **8.G.14.**
[657] BGH, 24 May 1988, NJW 1989, 773.
[658] *Supra,* **8.F.19.** and notes thereafter.
[659] *Supra,* 8.1.1., Introductory Note.
[660] But not only in that case. Indeed, this question is also raised in the case where the plaintiff claims by a subsequent action compensation for harm which already existed at the moment of the earlier proceedings. See, in this respect, the doubts about the correctness of *Brunsden* v. *Humphrey* (*supra,* **8.E.21.**) expressed in *Talbot* v. *Berkshire County Council* and based on the view that the rule of *res judicata* precludes a party from raising a matter which could, with reasonable diligence, have been raised in earlier proceedings (*supra,* **8.E.21–22.**) Note (2); a meaning to which the earlier opinion under French law on *res judicata* corresponded but which has been abandoned in favour of the opinion that, besides identity and quality of the parties, only the identity of the subject-matter of the claim is decisive (Cass. Ass. plén., 9 June 1978, Gaz.Pal. 1978. Jun, 1957). Nor are subsequent claims relating to a different subject-matter prohibited under German law (*Zusatz-* or *Nachforderungsklage, supra,* **8.G.24.,** Notes (1) and (2).

French legal systems are in this respect considerable, although in practice the differences may be considered to be attenuated.

Originally, English law provided a very rigid framework, requiring damages resulting from one and the same cause of action to be assessed and recovered once-and-for-all,[661] excluding any review of the lump sum award.[662] Conversely, the starting point in German law is the award of periodical payments, revisable at any moment in the future as far as a substantial change occurs in the circumstances which were decisive in the granting of the award.[663] In French law, the form of the award is left to be determined by the trier of fact (court of first instance or court of appeal) who is free to choose between a capital or periodical payments award;[664] revision of the award is possible without restriction in the case of a deterioration in the plaintiff's condition, regardless of whether a capital sum or periodical payments were awarded.[665]

The initial position of English law caused considerable hardship in cases where the plaintiff suffered a deterioration for which the previous, unrevisable award had not allowed. This position has been attenuated to some extent. A *provisional damages award*, not precluding further damages,[666] may be claimed. However, the conditions allowing a provisional damages award have been restrictively construed so that in practice such an award seems to provide no valuable alternative for the once-and-for-all approach. A practical solution for the difficulty of providing compensation during the period in which the plaintiff's physical condition is not sufficiently settled to make the assessment of damages possible is the award of *interim payments*, pending the final assessment of damages.[667] Whilst interim payments may relieve the plaintiff's immediate financial situation, they do not affect the unrevisability of the final once-and-for-all award. The same holds true for *structured settlements*, developed by legal practice and encouraged by recent legislation, that provide for periodical payments. They have the advantage of offering protection against inflation and are designed to meet the continuing needs of the plaintiff, so far as those needs are foreseen at the date of the settlement and irrespective of how long the plaintiff lives thereafter. However, they remain a conversion of a lump sum. Moreover, such settlements are not available as of right to a plaintiff.[668] Finally, recent legislation empowers the courts to award *periodical payments*, albeit with no possibility of revision and subject to the consent of the parties.[669]

Likewise, the position of German law must be put into perspective. The appearance of liability and social security insurers has meant that the extra-judicial settlement of a capital sum has become general practice.[670] It is noteworthy that where a capital sum is

---

[661] *Supra,* **8.E.21.**

[662] *Supra,* **8.E.22.**

[663] Supra, **8.G.24.**

[664] *Supra,* **8.F.26.** However, periodical payments awards have become attractive only since 1974 when the Cour de cassation accepted that the award may be index-linked: *supra,* **8.F.27.**

[665] The possibility of revision of the award in case of improvement in the victim's condition is discussed further in the text.

[666] *Supra,* **8.E.21–22.,** Note (4)(ii).

[667] *Supra,* **8.E.21–22.,** Note (4)(i).

[668] *Supra,* **8.E.21–22.,** Note (4)(iii).

[669] *Supra,* **8.E.21–22.,** Note (4)(iv).

[670] *Supra,* **8.G.25.,** Note (1).

awarded, the award is never open to revision.[671] In other words, in German law, the very nature of the capital award also involves a once-and-for-all assessment.

The idea that a capital award involves a once-and-for-all assessment has also been expressed in French case law in the case of a plaintiff whose condition unexpectedly improves after the judgment:[672] revision is possible only if the court made a reservation of the right to revise the award but such reservation is never (or cannot be) made where a capital award has been made.[673] However, that idea does not receive unqualified application since it does not apply in the case of a deterioration in the plaintiff's condition. In conclusion, French law attaches greater importance to the distinction between deterioration and improvement in the victim's condition from the point of view of the rule of *res judicata* than to the form of the award. Finally, it must be noted that the possibility of revision of the award is recognized only in the case of a change in the plaintiff's *physical condition*. Altered economic circumstances are not taken into account (apart from index-linked periodical payments awards) as such alteration is regarded as being connected with the monetary assessment of damages only and to review that assessment would be contrary to the rule of *res judicata*.[674]

b) A once-and-for-all assessment of future damage, especially in cases of personal injury or fatal accident, raises *the question of the accuracy of the assessment*. It would hardly be a satisfactory solution if trial courts did not aim at an assessment which is as accurate as possible, including for future damage which is by definition uncertain. If that damage is to be assessed once-and-for-all, the assessment must be based on a reasonable prognosis of the future without which it would be an unacceptable guess and an unjustifiable departure from the principle of full reparation. The need for accuracy in the assessment of future damage has been emphasized in German case law[675] and, very recently, also in English case law.[676] Conversely, due to the *pouvoir souverain* of the trier of fact, the need for an accurate assessment of future damage is not clearly expressed in French case law.[677]

c) The possibility of adjustment of the award to accommodate future changes may influence *the notion of recoverable damage*. If a once-and-for-all assessment of future damage is required, it must inevitably involve an estimate as to the chances of a particular event happening in the future, where its occurrence is not certain at the moment of the trial but at the same time cannot be ruled out. If the once-and-for-all assessment did not take that probable circumstance into account, it would be unduly disadvantageous to the plaintiff. This holds true not only for situations which influence the financial expression of the amount of harm—e.g. the prospect of promotion, influencing the amount of loss of income—but also for circumstances relating to the existence of the harm itself—i.e. the question as to whether the plaintiff will actually suffer a loss of income. A comparison of German, English and French case law on *loss of earning capacity*[678] shows that the diffi-

---

[671] *Supra,* **8.G.25.**
[672] *Supra,* **8.F.28.**
[673] *Supra,* **8.F.28–29.,** Note (1).
[674] Y. Chartier, *La réparation du préjudice dans la responsabilité civile* (Paris: Dalloz, 1983) at 869–70.
[675] *Supra,* **8.G.25.**
[676] *Supra,* **8.E.23.**
[677] *Supra,* 8.3.3., Introductory Note.
[678] *Supra,* **8.G.42., 8.F.44.** and **8.E.49.**

culties caused by uncertain future circumstances in the once-and-for-all assessment may indeed be overcome by enlarging the notion of recoverable harm.

Perhaps not by coincidence, the English law of damages, based on a once-and-for-all assessment, recognizes the loss of earning capacity as an autonomous recoverable head of damage where the plaintiff has not yet suffered any concrete loss of income. Indeed, such an assessment compels the English courts to consider the risk that a plaintiff will at some future time suffer financial damage because of his disadvantage in the labour market, to be an existing recoverable head of damage.[679] Conversely, the German law of damages is opposed to such a head of damage and grants compensation only if the "abstract" loss of earning capacity involves a concrete loss of earnings.[680] This requirement of a concrete loss is not disadvantageous to the plaintiff since German law always enables the plaintiff to claim compensation *when* he suffers that loss and *to the concrete extent* of that loss. The opposition of loss of earning capacity (as such, regardless of the loss of income) to concrete loss of income has not clearly been explored in French case law and legal writing.[681] However, it may be considered that the notion of *incapacité permanente partielle*, the methods of its assessment[682] and the emphasis which French law lays on physical disability regardless of its concrete financial consequences,[683] show that the core of the French law of damages also consists in an assessment once-and-for-all, overcoming the difficulties of assessing an award for future damage by adopting a large and rather indefinite notion of recoverable harm.

The implementation of the principle of full reparation in the case of loss of or damage to property

A comparison of German, English and French case-law on reparation of damage to property highlights the basic (and interrelated) questions with regard to the implementation of the principle of full reparation. The basic question is on which basis are damages to be assessed: on the basis of the cost of restoring the state of affairs (i.e. of the assets involved) which would have existed but for the tortious event *or* by comparing the property owner's financial position (i.e. the value of his or her estate) after the wrongdoing with what it would have been had the wrongdoing not occurred? And, furthermore, where restoration is chosen as a basis, restoration by which means: by repairing or by replacing the damaged property, or by another reasonable means of redress? Those questions are examined hereafter under a) for each of the three legal systems. The analysis leads to a common principle (see under b) (i)) which is taken as a starting point to examine related questions under b) (ii)–(iv).

---

[679] *Supra*, **8.E.49.**

[680] *Supra*, **8.G.42.**

[681] Legal writing has paid attention to the distinction between *préjudice physiologique* and *préjudice économique* (*supra*, **8.F.43–44.** Note (2)); however both the concrete loss of income and the loss of earning capacity as such are considered to be *préjudice économique* (compare Viney at 164–5, para.118, Y. Chartier, *La réparation du préjudice dans la responsabilité civile* (Paris: Dalloz, 1983) at 221–4, para. 172–3 and Y. Lambert-Faivre, *Droit du dammage corporel Systèmes d'indemnisation*, 3rd edn. (Paris: Dalloz, 1996) at 182–3, para. 117).

[682] *Supra*, Note (4) under **8.F.43–44.**

[683] As is also shown by case law on revision of a capital or periodical payments award, only considering the improvement or deterioration in the plaintiff's *physical* condition to be an attenuation or aggravation of the damage.

Those related questions are:

- Does the plaintiff's decision as to whether restoration is to be carried out affect the applicable measure of damages?
- Does the kind of property involved, more particularly the difference between moveables and real estate, play a role?
- To what extent is the concrete situation of the particular plaintiff to be taken into account in the assessment of damages?
- Is the assessment of damages considered to be a matter of fact or a matter of law?

a) (i) German law draws the distinction between *Naturalrestitution* (§ 249 BGB) and *Kompensation* (§ 251 BGB).[684] *Naturalrestitution*, i.e. restoration of the *status quo ante* to preserve the physical condition of the plaintiff's assets, is in principle to be performed by the wrongdoer (rarely possible) or on his initiative (§ 249, first sentence, BGB). However, the second sentence of § 249 BGB includes in the concept of *Naturalrestitution* a monetary award, as it entitles the plaintiff to claim the sum of money requisite for the purpose of restoration. Thus linking the monetary award under § 249 BGB to the purpose of restoration explains why such an award ceases to be available where restoration is "impossible" (or "insufficient" to repair the harm) (§ 251(1) BGB). Moreover, the plaintiff is not allowed to achieve restoration at any price and, therefore, the award under § 249 BGB is not available where restoration is possible only at a disproportionate cost (§ 251(2) BGB). In such cases, *Kompensation*, which is (necessarily) compensation in money, takes the place of *Naturalrestitution* and since *Kompensation* purports to preserve the value of the assets, the award is then assessed on the basis of the difference between the plaintiff's financial position after the wrongdoing with what it would have been had the wrongdoing not occurred. It is to be remembered that an award under § 249 BGB (that is by way of *Naturalrestitution*) takes also into account the plaintiff's non-economic interest in preserving the physical condition of his assets[685] whilst in the case of an award under § 251 BGB (that is *Kompensation*), non-material harm can according to § 253 BGB be compensated in money only when that is authorized by statute.

Where restoration of the *status quo ante* (*Naturalrestitution*) can be achieved by either effecting repair works or replacing the damaged object, e.g. in the case of damage to fungible goods, the choice between both forms of *Naturalrestitution* is governed by the so-called *Wirtschaftlichkeitspostulat*, that is the principle of economic efficiency requiring that, if there is more than one possible means of restoration, the plaintiff must choose the one which appears expedient and appropriate from the standpoint of a reasonable, economically-minded person.[686] In fact, this postulate inherent to § 249 BGB and the proportionality rule which is used in § 251(2) BGB to draw the line between *Naturalrestitution* and *Kompensation*, are the expression of the same principle,[687] namely that the plaintiff is entitled to reparation for harm but within the limits of reasonableness,

---

[684] *Supra*, **8.G.12.** and notes thereafter.

[685] E.g. in the case of a damaged house: BGH, 8 December 1987, BGHZ 102, 323 at 326–7.

[686] *Supra*, **8.G.12.** and Note (2)(b) thereafter. In respect of motorcars, this requirement has resulted in a fixed rule, making a standardized assessment of damages possible: see **8.G.12.**, Note (2)(d).

[687] See for an example of application of the proportionality rule, which is very similar to the *Wirtschaftlichkeitspostulat*, the case of a completely burnt-down house, which is not a fungible good and for which as a consequence replacement cannot be a form of *Naturalrestitution*: *supra*, **8.G.12.**, Note (1)(d). In both cases a comparison is made between the cost of repair and the market (replacement) value, be it as

taking into account the defendant's interest and finally the public interest that defendants are not to be unreasonably burdened.

The distinction between *Naturalrestitution* and *Kompensation* with regard to loss of or damage to property becomes important where the cost of repair exceeds the decrease of value, that is when preserving the physical condition of the asset is more costly than preserving the value of the plaintiff's estate. The application of the principles of *Wirtschaftlichkeit* and proportionality shows which considerations must then be borne in mind when balancing the conflicting interests of plaintiff and defendant.[688]

However important the distinction between *Naturalrestitution* and *Kompensation* may be on the theoretical level, as a practical matter it does not necessarily involve a difference in the size of the award. Indeed, in the case of *loss* of property, the decrease of value of the plaintiff's estate (i.e. *Kompensation*) is assessed on the basis of the *market value* (*Verkehrswert*) of the property of which the plaintiff has been deprived, which in turn is generally equated with its replacement cost (*Wiederbeschaffungswert*),[689] i.e. the sum to be paid when buying an equivalent (as in the case of replacement by way of *Naturalrestitution*) and thus not on the basis of what the plaintiff would have received if he had sold the property immediately before the tort (*Zeitwert*, which is equivalent to the French "*valeur vénale*").[690] The only difference in such case between an award of money by way of *Kompensation* under § 251 BGB and an award made as *Naturalrestitution* under § 249 BGB seems to be that the latter is only possible where replacement, as in German law, is defined as a means of *Naturalrestitution*, which is a matter of terminology rather than of substance. In the case of *damage* to property, the award under § 251 BGB may be less than the cost of repair[691] but the BGH stated nonetheless that the award may then also be assessed having regard to the cost of repair.[692]

As a final note on *Naturalrestitution*, it should be recalled that, when the value of the property after its repair is increased when compared to its value at the time of the damaging event, the increase is deducted from the recoverable cost of repair.[693] That shows that the principle of *Naturalrestitution* which implies that the plaintiff's interest in preserving the physical condition of his assets may not be curtailed by an unavoidable increase in value, is nevertheless qualified by considerations relating to the consequences of the repair on the plaintiff's financial position, and thus relating to the criterion of preservation of value which is characteristic for *Kompensation*.

measure of damages by way of *Naturalrestitution* (in the case of a motorcar) or by way of *Kompensation* (in the case of the house).

[688] A BGH judgment on damage to an ecologically valuable tree is very instructive in this respect, see *supra*, **8.G.12.**, Note (1)(d).

[689] BGH, 10 July 1984, BGHZ 92, 84 at 90–1.

[690] See also Münchener Grunsky, § 251 at para. 8; Palandt-Heinrichs, § 251, mentioning that the profit margin, and thus the difference between *Zeitwert* and *Wiederbeschaffungswert*, with regard to motor cars amounts about 20 per cent. See also for a very detailed and clear discussion of the concepts *Zeitwert* and *Wiederbeschaffungswert* in connection with *Naturalrestitution* and *Kompensation*: D. Giesen, "Kraftfahrzeug-Totalschaden und Haftpflichtrecht" NJW 1979, 2065.

[691] As is shown in the case of the damaged house which was sold before the claim for *Naturalrestitution* was granted: BGH, 2 October 1981, BGHZ 81, 385; *supra*, **8.G.30.**, Note (2). As explained, this circumstance precluded the plaintiff to obtain the award under § 249 BGB. In that case, the plaintiff was entitled to only the difference between the market value of the house in an undamaged state and the price at which it was sold.

[692] BGH, 5 March 1993, NJW 1993, 1793; *supra*, **8.G.30.**, Note (2).

[693] *Supra*, **8.G.31.**

Whatever the significance, in German law, of the distinction between *Naturalrestitution* and *Kompensation* on the theoretical level, on the practical level the basic rules with regard to loss of or damage to property, may be summarized as follows. In the case of loss of property, the plaintiff is entitled to the replacement cost. In the case of damage to property, the plaintiff is entitled to the cost of repair, provided that repair is possible and not unreasonable; if it is impossible or unreasonable, the plaintiff is entitled to the cost of replacement. The requirement of reasonableness thus governs the choice between repair and replacement,[694] as it also governs the choice between repair and diminution in value of the damaged property.[695]

(ii) The distinction drawn in German law between assessing damages on the basis of the cost of restoration of the assets, and assessing them on the basis of the diminution in value, is also drawn in English law. The distinction is more important though in cases of *damage to land and buildings* than in cases of *damage to goods*. Indeed, in cases of damage to goods, the diminution in value of the damaged chattel and the cost of repair (as long as it is reasonable for the plaintiff to effect the repair) are equated with each other,[696] whilst in the case of damage to land and buildings both "measures of damages" (cost of repair and diminution in value) are expressly distinguished and lead to divergent awards. In the latter case (damage to land and buildings), the reasonableness of the plaintiff's course of action is a decisive factor as to whether the plaintiff is entitled to claim the cost of restoration or the cost of another reasonable means of redress (such as purchasing or leasing other property). Moreover, reinstatement may be inappropriate where the expenditure for any of them would be out of all proportion as compared to the diminution in value.[697] In the case of *loss of goods*, the normal measure of damages is the purchase value of the destroyed chattels.[698] except where it would be unreasonable for the plaintiff to demand an exact replacement.[699]

The choice between repair or replacement as alternative means of redress is also governed by the requirement that the plaintiff's course of action should be reasonable: repair will not be granted where the cost of repair exceeds the purchase value of the damaged goods (significantly), that is to say where repair would be *uneconomic*.[700]

In English law, the award of damages assessed on the basis of actual restoration of the damaged property is not to be corrected, as under German law (see before under (i)), by reference to the assessment of damages on the basis of a decrease in value, as the issue of "new for old" shows. Where in such a situation betterment cannot be avoided, the plaintiff remains entitled to the full cost of reparation, regardless of the benefit of getting new for old, and therefore of an increase in value.[701]

It appears from the foregoing that by and large the basic scheme in English law is similar to that of German law. In the case of loss of property, the plaintiff is entitled to the

---

[694] That is between the two alternatives of *Naturalrestitution*, e.g. in the case of motorcars, *supra*, **8.G.12.**
[695] That is to say the choice between *Naturalrestitution* and *Kompensation*.
[696] *Supra*, **8.E.34.** and Note (1) thereafter.
[697] *Supra*, **8.E.35.** and Notes (1) and (2) thereafter.
[698] *Supra*, **8.E.33.**, Note (1).
[699] *Supra*, **8.E.33.**, Note (3).
[700] *Supra*, **8.E.8.** and **8.E.35.**, Note (2) dealing in that case with damage to land and buildings.
[701] *Supra*, **8.E.35.** and Note (3) thereafter.

replacement cost. In the case of damage to property, the plaintiff is entitled to the cost of repair, provided that repair is possible and not unreasonable. As in German law the requirement of reasonableness governs the choice between cost of repair and cost of replacement as well as the choice between repair and diminution in value.

(iii) French law clearly adheres to the rule that damages must enable the plaintiff to restore the state of affairs that would have existed but for the tortious event.[702] On the basis of that rule, the plaintiff is entitled either to the cost of repair or to the cost of replacement.[703] This also explains why the Cour de cassation has finally rejected the view that the sale value (*valeur vénale*), i.e. the price at which the object could have been sold before the tortious event, provides an appropriate measure of damages.[704] As to the choice between the two means of reparation, the case law of the Cour de cassation gives no clear answer: the second civil chamber considers that the plaintiff is entitled to claim only the less onerous of repair or replacement; the criminal chamber sees no objection to an award of the cost of repair that exceeds the replacement cost, provided that the plaintiff has actually effected the repair.[705]

Unlike German and English law, in French law the distinction between the measure of damage consisting in the cost of restoration of the assets involved and the measure of damage consisting in the diminution in value has not clearly or generally been made. Which may explain why the question of reasonableness has not arisen either with regard to the choice between cost of repair and cost of replacement, even more so because French law does not generally tend to appeal to the concept of reasonableness to balance conflicting interests.[706]

Like English law, French law entitles the plaintiff to keep the full cost of restoration where a complete repair unavoidably involves betterment, thus showing that the principle of *restitutio in integrum* is primarily intended to enable the plaintiff to actually restore the damage at the tortfeasor's expense rather than to compensate for the decrease in value.[707]

b) (i) From the above comparison of German, English and French law, it may be stated as a *starting point* that in the case of loss of property, the plaintiff is entitled to the replacement cost whilst in the case of damage to property, the plaintiff is essentially entitled to choose for a monetary award enabling him to achieve a restoration of the state of affairs which would have existed but for the tortious event, either by repairing or replacing the damaged property, provided that restoration, as compared with damages assessed on the basis of diminution in value, and the choice for either repair or replacement do not appear to be *unreasonable*.

Notwithstanding this starting point which the legal systems have in common, the *solution finally reached* by each legal system will depend on some other factors which are discussed hereafter.

---

[702] *Supra*, **8.F.16.**
[703] *Supra*, **8.F.16.** in the case of a damaged car and **8.F.39–40** in the case of damage to land and buildings. See also **8.F.17.** in which case the final monetary award was to be assessed after completion of the repairs.
[704] *Supra*, **8.F.38.** in the case of a damaged car and **8.F.40.** in the case of damage to land and buildings.
[705] *Supra*, **8.F.16, 8.F.37.** and **8.F.37–38.**, Note (2).
[706] As is illustrated as well by the lesser role played by the concept of mitigation of damage in French law and by the absence of a general principle governing the choice between an award of damages and injunctive relief.
[707] *Supra*, **8.F.39.** and **8.F.39.–40.**, Note (2).

(ii) A first category of factors on which the final outcome may depend is *whether the plaintiff decides to effect restoration or not and what kind of property* (goods or buildings) is involved. In the case of damage to goods, when a legal system recognizes the plaintiff's interest in having the damaged object repaired rather than replaced, the plaintiff is entitled to claim the more expensive cost of repair only when repair is actually effected.[708] In contrast, in some instances the plaintiff is entitled to claim the cost of restoration (repair or replacement, whichever is lower), regardless whether the plaintiff decides to effect restoration or not. In those instances, the plaintiff is free to do whatever he wishes with the award.[709] The application of that principle clearly differs according to the kind of damaged property.

In German law, the principle of *Dispositionsfreiheit* applies in the case of damage to goods and damage to buildings, *provided that reparation in kind is still possible*. However, that possibility of reparation is given a different meaning; whilst the sale of a damaged car does not disentitle the plaintiff to claim the cost of repair under § 249 BGB, the sale of a damaged house reduces the plaintiff's entitlement to an award under § 251 BGB.[710] In English law, a distinction is also made. The fact that the plaintiff does not replace the lost chattel[711] or does not effect repairs and sells the damaged chattel, does not affect the applicable measure of damages. In the case of damage to buildings however, the plaintiff's future intentions as to the use of property are taken into account in deciding what is the appropriate measure of damages.[712] Finally, it may be noted that in adopting a more flexible rule for moveables, considerations of practicability and certainty have been decisive both in German law[713] and in English law.[714]

(iii) The elaboration of the aforementioned starting point depends also on *the extent to which the concrete situation of the particular plaintiff is to be taken into account*.

In German law, the readiness to take account of the concrete situation of the particular plaintiff is expressed by the principle of *Subjektbezogenheit* which applies when assessing the sum requisite for the purpose of reparation referred to in the second sentence of § 249.[715] English law also pays attention to the specific circumstances in which the plaintiff finds himself, as *Dodd Properties Ltd.* v. *Canterbury City Council*[716] shows. In that case, the principle that damages are normally assessed at the date of the wrong was not applied and the plaintiffs were entitled to the much higher cost of repair eight years later, since, having regard to all the relevant circumstances, it was *reasonable* to have the repairs carried out then. In French law, the requirement of an assessment *in concreto* is clearly considered to be a general rule of the law of damages. It is however difficult to evaluate

---

[708] In that way German law, *supra*, **8.G.12.**, Note (2)(d) (*"Integritätszuschlag"*) and French law, *supra*, **8.F.37–38.**, Note (1) (case law of the criminal chamber of the Cour de cassation).

[709] See for German law the principle of *Dispositionsfreiheit*, allowing in the case of damaged motorcars the so-called *"Ersatz fiktiver Reparaturkosten"*, *supra*, **8.G.30.** For English law: *supra*, **8.E.33.** (loss of chattel) and **8.E.34.** (damage to chattel) and for French law: *supra*, **8.F.38.** (motorcar).

[710] *Supra*, **8.G.30.**, Note (2)

[711] *Supra*, **8.E.33.**

[712] *Supra*, **8.E.35.**, Note (1).

[713] *Supra*, **8.G.30.**, Note (2) with regard to motor cars.

[714] *Supra*, **8.E.34.** referring to the desirability of a measure of damages which can be easily and definitely established.

[715] *Supra*, **8.G.12.** and Note (2)(c) thereafter, **8.G.30.** and Note (1) thereafter.

[716] [1980] 1 WLR 433, CA.

the practical meaning of this rule for the assessment of damage to property, as a consequence of the traditional austerity of the reasons which judges give for the evaluation of damages.

(iv) A last factor to be considered here concerns the question as to *whether the assessment of damages is considered to be a matter of fact or a matter of law*. German law clearly considers questions of the assessment of damages to be largely a matter of law, a view which means that the assessment of damages is based upon careful and comprehensive reasons so that the German law of damages offers a structured framework—perhaps sometimes too complex—of general principles and their applications to specific cases. Likewise English law considers the assessment of damages largely to be a matter of law: although damages may be a question of fact, they must be measured as the law requires[717] and as a consequence, the circumstances which are relevant to the choice and application of the appropriate "measure of damages" are clearly discussed in case law. Conversely, French law considers the assessment of damage to be largely a matter of fact. However, this view does not preclude the Cour de cassation, in some classes of cases—especially cases of damage to property—, from reviewing whether the principle of full reparation, expressed by the appropriate "measure of damages", has been applied.[718]

This distinction between English and German law on the one hand, and French law on the other, is also illustrated by case law on the issue of *loss of use*. In German law, since material damage is in principle assessed on the basis of the *Differenzmethode* and loss of use, in the absence of lost profits or incurred expenses, is not reflected in a difference between two financial positions, the BGH has been led to resort to a normative concept of recoverable damage which also involves a "measure" of damages.[719] As a consequence, the absence of a *prima facie* difference between the plaintiff's financial position after the wrongdoing with what it would have been if the wrongdoing had not occurred, does not lead to an unreasoned assessment of damages. In English law too, the absence of the impossibility of an exact pecuniary assessment of loss of use where the plaintiff does not hire a substitute, has not precluded the development of technical rules governing the quantification of the damages to be awarded.[720] Conversely, in French law, there is hardly any reported case-law on this issue and the assessment of damages seems to be "*ex aequo et bono*", in fact unreasoned.[721]

The implementation of the principle of full reparation in the case of personal injury and death

Also in the case of personal injury and death, the principle of full reparation is not as such sufficient to determine the award of damages in cases where there is some difficulty

---

[717] *Admiralty Commissioners* v. *S.S. Chekiang* [1926] AC 637, HL at 643 per Lord Sumner, concurring with Viscount Dunedin, who referred to his speech in *Admiralty Commissioners* v. *S.S. Susquehanna* [1926] AC 655, HL at 659 ff., in "thinking that the time has come, when your Lordships may . . . devote some short time to the rules applicable to the measure of damages in collision actions".

[718] Thus, it will quash a judgment on the ground, for example, that it assessed the damages on the basis of the sale value: *supra*, **8.F.15.** and **8.F.37.**

[719] *Supra*, **8.G.32.** and Notes thereafter.

[720] *Supra*, **8.E.36.** and Note (2) thereafter.

[721] *Supra*, **8.F.41.** and Notes thereafter.

in comparing the plaintiff's financial position after the wrongdoing with what his situation would have been if the wrongdoing had not occurred. The cases which have been discussed in Section 5 provide illustrations of such difficulties and of the methods of overcoming these difficulties by each legal system. In this respect, the importance of policy reasons must be recognized: a merely technical view on the rule of full compensation cannot lead to satisfying solutions, a conclusion which also emerges from cases in which the issue of collateral benefits arises.

a) A first case is *the loss of earning capacity* which is not reflected in a pecuniary loss, e.g. because the disability does not affect the plaintiff's income. In this case, German law adheres to a pure application of the *Differenzmethode*, equating material damage with an arithmetically assessable pecuniary loss.[722] Conversely, English[723] and French law[724] recognize the existence of loss of earning capacity as a recoverable head of damage. It has been explained above, under the heading discussing the impact of procedural rules (under c)), that this marked contrast is possibly to be explained by an opposite starting point with regard to the possibility of subsequent adjustment of the award to take account of future changes. It goes without saying that, in such cases, since the award under English and French law is not related to a concrete pecuniary loss, its calculation cannot be other than rough-and-ready and based on a judicial, conventional appraisal for which no arithmetical justification can be given.

b) A second case is *the loss of housekeeping capacity* in all cases in which the cost of employing a domestic help is not incurred, that is to say where the reduced capacity to carry out household work is overcome by additional efforts by the injured person or by relatives, or where the injured person is simply left with an inferior level of housekeeping as a consequence. A variant is the case in which the injured person's spouse gives up his employment, or shortens his or her hours of paid work, in order to render assistance and as a consequence suffers a loss of income. This case raises three (interrelated) questions:

- Who is entitled to damages ?
- How is the award to be assessed ?
- Is the assessment affected by the fact that a third person benevolently renders assistance ?

(i) The question of who is entitled to damages is raised where a third person renders assistance or suffers a loss of income.

Since both English and German law as a rule entitle only the injured person to damages, the third person as such is not allowed to recover the value of his services or the loss of income. In addition, both legal systems have abandoned the view that the husband is entitled to damages for the loss of his wife's domestic services.[725] As a consequence, compensation can be granted only to the plaintiff herself (or himself—albeit reported caselaw does not yet reveal exceptions to the traditional gender roles).

---

[722] *Supra*, **8.G.42.**
[723] *Supra*, **8.E.49.**
[724] *Supra*, **8.F.44.**
[725] Both in German and English law, the husband was able to recover for the loss of his wife's domestic services; see **8.G.42.**, Note (5) and H. McGregor, *McGregor on Damages*, 16th edn. (London: Sweet & Maxwell, 1997) at 912, para. 1464, footnote 14.

(ii) As to the question how a housewife's entitlement to damages for loss of house-keeping capacity is to be assessed, there are two grounds on which such entitlement can be based, each providing for a measure of damages.

It may be considered, as in German law,[726] that housekeeping is in principle to be equated with employment so that the housewife is entitled to damages amounting to the value of the services she can render no longer, on the same footing as an employee who is entitled to damages for loss of income as a consequence of no longer being able to work as she did before the tortious event. It may also be considered, as in English law,[727] that the housewife, even if she does not in fact employ a home help, is entitled to a sum equal to the cost of employing such a help to cope with the loss of her housekeeping capacity, as the housewife is free to use the money received as she wishes. Both considerations may lead to a largely similar result if the value of the services of the housewife is assessed on the basis of the cost of employing a home help. However, under English law, the house-wife cannot recover damages under this head in respect of the period before trial save to the extent that a home help has actually been employed and costs thereby incurred.[728] That difference between the treatment of past and future loss is perhaps to be explained by the fact that a once-and-for-all approach must entitle the plaintiff to such an award to enable the plaintiff to cope with the loss whatever may happen in the future. Here again, German law shows the advantage of allowing the review of an earlier assessment.[729] As has been said, in France the issue of loss of housekeeping capacity has not resulted in a significant body of reported case law but legal writing has drawn attention to the basic questions discussed.[730]

(iii) The third question as to the issue of collateral benefits arises where a third person benevolently renders assistance.

German law applies the legal principle, underlying § 843(4) BGB, that the assistance benevolently rendered does not relieve the defendant of liability to pay damages.[731] In English law, this question has been dealt with in *Hunt* v. *Severs*,[732] a case of nursing care benevolently rendered by a third person which will be discussed now.

c) In cases where *nursing care or domestic assistance is gratuitously rendered to the injured person*, the injured person does not suffer a *prima facie* assessable loss. As a consequence of their limitative approach with regard to protected interests,[733] both English and German law are faced with a difficulty: the person who renders services (and possibly suffers a loss of income as a consequence) has "no cause of action" in English law,[734] nor is he entitled under German law to damages for *reiner Vermögensschaden*.[735]

---

[726] *Supra*, **8.G.42.**, Note (5).

[727] *Supra*, **8.E.49.**, Note (3).

[728] *Daly* v. *General Steam Navigation Co. Ltd, supra*, **8.E.49.**, Note (3).

[729] BGH, 8 February 1983, BGHZ 86, 372.

[730] Y. Chartier, *La réparation du préjudice dans la responsabilité civile* (Paris: Dalloz, 1983) at 664, para. 536, doubting whether the award, based on an assimilation of a housewife to a home help, is justified where the housewife does not use home help, and whether the loss is suffered by the injured housewife or by the members of the family.

[731] *Supra*, **8.G.42.**, Note (5).

[732] *Supra*, **8.E.50.**

[733] *Supra*, General Introduction and in greater detail, Chapter II, 2.1.

[734] *Supra*, **8.E.50.**

[735] *Supra*, Larenz/Canaris at 586.

In addition, the allocation of the loss to the injured person seems to be more problematical than in the case of loss of housekeeping capacity since, unlike in the latter case, the plaintiff's need for care does not consist in an inability on the part of the plaintiff to render services which may be valued in terms of money.

German law solves the problem by applying § 843(1) BGB which provides for a claim for *vermehrte Bedürfnisse*, equating the need itself to recoverable damage, so that damages are recoverable regardless of whether the plaintiff spends the sum of money for the purpose in respect of which it is granted.[736] It may be noted that this position is considered to be inherent to § 843(1) BGB and is not based on the second sentence of § 249 BGB, although it resembles the principle of *Dispositionsfreiheit*. In English law, this approach was also valid under *Donelly* v. *Joyce*[737] but has recently been abandoned in *Hunt* v. *Severs*[738] which has emphasized the objective of compensating the voluntary carer and, as a consequence, has decided that the injured plaintiff should hold the damages on trust for the voluntary carer. The idea that the award is finally intended to compensate the voluntary carer, is also expressed in German legal writing[739] and it may be thought that the making of the award to the injured person is simply a judicial fiction to prevent an important loss, worthy of recovery, remaining uncompensated because of restrictive rules, the application of which is not, in the circumstances, expedient. One might have expected that French law would entitle the *voluntary carer* to obtain damages directly from the wrongdoer since the general clause of Art. 1382 C.civ. offers full protection to all kinds of legitimate interests and does not contain any *a priori* limitation as to the class of protected persons.[740] Although, in earlier case law,[741] the Cour de cassation had held that the injured person's spouse was entitled to claim damages, the prevailing view now is that *the injured person himself or herself* is entitled to damages, regardless of whether relatives benevolently render assistance and whether expenses are actually incurred.[742] The reasons on the basis of which the Cour de cassation has reached this solution, are not clearly expressed. If the award is assessed once-and-for-all, an explanation may be that the plaintiff must be enabled to cope with the loss whatever may happen in the future[743] or, as the criminal chamber of the Cour de cassation stated, the voluntary assistance is an uncertain fact, foreign to the victim[744], and when it is terminated, the plaintiff must have the necessary funds at his disposal to bear the cost of professional assistance. Another explanation may be the application of the rule dealing with gratuitous payments and collateral benefits. Indeed, in French law, as in English[745] and German[746] law, gratuitous

---

[736] *Supra*, **8.G.1.**, Note (3).
[737] *Supra*, **8.E.50.**, Note (2).
[738] *Supra*, **8.E.50.**
[739] Larenz/Canaris at 586.
[740] *Supra*, Chapter I, Section 1.4.2.
[741] *Supra*, **8.F.46.**, Note (1).
[742] *Supra*, **8.F.46.**
[743] See the explanation for the different assessment of past and future damage resulting from the loss of housekeeping capacity in *Daly* v. *General Steam Navigation C. Ltd.* (*supra*, **8.E.49.**, Note (3)) put forward in this Comparative Overview.
[744] *Supra*, **8.F.46.**, Note (1).
[745] *Supra*, **8.E.50.** and Note (1) thereafter.
[746] *Supra*, **8.G.42.**, Note (4).

payments are generally ignored on account of the policy reason that the defendant may not be released from liability for damages because of a third person's benevolence.[747]

d) Finally, it must be noted that in many of the cases referred to above[748] *the plaintiff's freedom to use the money received*—a principle which is also applicable in cases of loss of or damage to property, as has been mentioned earlier—appears to be an important argument to justify the assessment of damages in cases where the plaintiff's financial position is affected neither by incurred expenses nor by lost income.

In conclusion

A comparison of the German, English and French legal systems shows that the attitude of a legal system towards the assessment of damage depends to a large extent on the answer given to two interrelated questions: *Are damages to be assessed as accurately as possible? Is the assessment of damages, basically, a matter of law or a matter of fact?* In this respect, the French legal system where the assessment of damages is essentially a matter of fact to be decided by the trier of fact (court of first instance and court of appeal) which have a very extensive *pouvoir souverain*, is the least stringent one. In sharp contrast, the German legal system which requires any divergence from the *Differenzmethode* to be justified by the courts, seems to be the most stringent. English law lies in between: it is elaborated less dogmatically than German law but this does not preclude most questions on the assessment of damages receiving a reasoned justification, thus allowing a further working out of general principles and specific applications. Obviously, the more a legal system requires the assessment of harm and damages to be well-founded in law, the more the assessment of damages will meet the ultimate goals of predictability, equality and legal certainty.

---

[747] As to the assessment of damages, compare the solutions under German (*supra*, **8.G.42.**, Note (5)), French (*supra*, **8.F.46.**) and English law (*Housecroft* v. *Burnett*, *supra*, **8.E.50.**, Note (3) and *Daly* v. *General Steam navigation Co. Ltd.*, *supra*, **8.E.49.**, Note (3)).

[748] Compare e.g. German (*supra*, **8.G.42.**, Note (3)), French (*supra*, **8.F.46.**), and English law (*Daly* v. *General Steam navigation Co Ltd.*, *supra*, **8.E.49.**, Note (3)).

CHAPTER NINE
IMPACT OF SUPRANATIONAL AND INTERNATIONAL LAW

The first section of this Chapter discusses the case law of the ECJ regarding the extra-contractual liability of both the Community and its Member States. The second section deals with the case law of the ECtHR on Article 41 ECHR, as well as with the recent case of *Osman* v. *UK*, which shows how the ECHR could have an impact on the domestic laws of civil liability in Europe. The third section touches upon the case law of international courts and arbitral tribunals. Finally, a fourth section is concerned with the impact of international law and supranational law on the domestic legal systems.

9.1. CASE LAW OF THE EUROPEAN COURT OF JUSTICE

Introductory Note

a) The European Community is the main part of the first (by far the most important) pillar of the European Union. Its law comprises two regimes of extra-contractual liability—or tortious liability,[1] as we will call it hereafter—for breaches of Community law.

The first regime governs the liability of **Community institutions**[2] and their servants in the performance of their duties. It finds its source in Article 288(2) EC, which reads: "In the case of non-contractual liability, the Community shall, in accordance with the general principles common to the laws of the Member States, make good any damage caused by its institutions or by its servants in the performance of their duties".[3] That provision is applied by the Court of Justice of the European Communities (ECJ) pursuant to Article 235 EC, which confers upon the ECJ "jurisdiction in disputes relating to compensation for damage" under Article 288(2) EC.[4]

The second regime relates to the tortious liability of **Member States** for breaches of Community law. It finds its origins exclusively in the case law of the ECJ—essentially

---

[1] The question of whether liability can arise as a consequence of lawful legislative or administrative acts is left aside here. The position of the ECJ, as one author points out, is still at an embryonic stage: see H.J. Bronkhorst, "The valid legislative act as a cause of liability of the Communities" in Heukels and McDonnell 153, with references to national laws.

[2] According to Art. 7 EC, the Community institutions comprise the European Parliament, the Council of the European Union, the European Commission, the Court of Justice of the European Communities, the Court of Auditors, the Economic and Social Committee and the Committee of Regions.

[3] The European Coal and Steel Community (ECSC) and the Euratom treaties (the two other parts of the first pillar of the EU) contain similar or identical provisions at Art. 40 ECSC Treaty and Art. 188 Euratom Treaty. They will not be further discussed here.

[4] Including the Court of First Instance (CFI) "attached to the Court of Justice" (Art. 225 EC), which now has jurisdiction over actions for damages pursuant to Art. 288(2) EC, subject to appeal on matters of law to the ECJ.

preliminary rulings pursuant to Article 234 EC, at the request of national courts—in conjunction with the case law of national courts applying ECJ precedents in litigation before them. Indeed, in contrast to the first regime, not only does the EC Treaty fail to attribute jurisdiction—let alone exclusive jurisdiction—to the ECJ over disputes relating to the tortious liability of Member States for breaches of Community law, but it does not even contain any provision establishing that liability in principle or outlining the conditions for it.

The **principle** of liability on the part of Member States for breaches of Community law was laid down by the ECJ in its famous *Francovich* judgment, where the ECJ replied to preliminary questions submitted by two Italian courts that "it is a principle of Community law that the Member States are obliged to make good loss and damage caused to individuals by breaches of Community law for which they can be held responsible".[5] The Court stated that that principle is "inherent in the system of the Treaty".[6]

In *Francovich* and subsequent judgments, the ECJ has progressively established the principle of liability on the part of Member States and has elaborated the conditions that give rise to it. As for the principle, the ECJ has held in *Brasserie du Pêcheur* that such liability extends to all breaches of Community law, "irrespective of whether the breach which gave rise to the damage is attributable to the legislature, the judiciary or the executive".[7] In order to come to these conclusions, the Court relied on "generally accepted methods of interpretation, in particular by reference to the fundamental principles of the Community legal system and, where necessary, general principles common to the legal systems of the Member States".[8] The Court referred more specifically to Article 288(2) EC, which "is simply an expression of [a] general principle familiar to the legal systems of the Member States" and to international law.[9]

As for the **conditions** that give rise to liability on the part of Member States for breaches of Community law, the ECJ had said in *Francovich* that "they depend on the nature of the breach of Community law giving rise to the loss and damage".[10] In *Brasserie du Pêcheur*, the Court added that, in the absence of written rules, it "draws inspiration" from the same "general principles common to the laws of the Member States" to which Article 288(2) refers.[11] Indeed, since the protection of individuals "cannot vary depending on whether a national authority or a Community authority is responsible for the damage", the conditions for the liability of the Community (under Article 288(2) EC) and of Member States to arise must be the same.[12]

Beyond the principle of and the conditions for liability on the part of Member States, the ECJ turned in *Brasserie du Pêcheur* to the **duty** and the **extent of reparation.** In respect of both these issues, the Court referred to the domestic legal system of each Member State, provided that "the conditions for reparation" and "the criteria for determining the extent of reparation must not be less favourable than those relating to similar domestic

---

[5] Judgment of 19 November 1991, Cases C-6/90 and 9/90, *Francovich* v. *Italy* [1991] ECR I-5357 at para. 37.
[6] Ibid. at para. 35.
[7] *Infra*, **9.EC.6.** at para. 34.
[8] Ibid. at para. 27.
[9] Ibid. at para. 28–9, 34.
[10] Ibid. at para. 38.
[11] Ibid. at para. 41.
[12] Ibid. at para. 42.

claims and must not be such as in practice to make it impossible or excessively difficult to obtain reparation".[13]

b) Article 288(2) EC is part of the range of remedies open to individuals against wrongful acts or omissions of the Community institutions and their civil servants. Under certain circumstances, individuals can ask the CFI to review the legality of binding Community acts (Article 230 EC) or to condemn failures to act on the part of Community institutions (Article 232 EC). Proceedings for compensation, brought before the Community courts pursuant to Article 235 EC, are a normal corollary thereof.[14] For such proceedings to succeed, the claimant must establish (i) the existence of a wrongful act or omission on the part of the institution (*faute de service*) or its servants (*faute personnelle*),[15] (ii) damage suffered by the claimant and (iii) a causal link between the two.[16]

The tortious liability of the Community can be engaged both by purely "factual" acts and by "legal" acts, either of an individual nature (e.g. a decision) or a normative nature (e.g. a regulation). For the purposes of this study, factual acts and individual legal acts will be considered together.[17] They will be submitted to the "classic" test of reasonableness, i.e. whether the Community institution concerned acted as a reasonable public authority would have acted under the circumstances of the case.

Instances of the third category, namely liability for legal acts of a normative nature ("legislative acts") have attracted far more attention. In order to assess whether the Community institution concerned has committed a wrongful act or omission, the ECJ has developed the so-called *Schöppenstedt* test which was formulated as follows:[18]

> "Where legislative action involving measures of economic policy is concerned, the Community does not incur non-contractual liability for damage suffered by individuals as a consequence of that action . . . unless a sufficiently flagrant [or serious] violation of a superior rule of law for the protection of the individual has occurred".

The test applies not only to actions involving measures of economic policy, but also to other legislative action involving measures of political or legislative policy characterized by a wide discretion.[19]

---

[13] Ibid. at para. 67 and, with slight differences, para. 83. Compare with Judgment of 19 November 1991, Cases C-6/90 and 9/90, *Francovich* v. *Italy* [1991] ECR I-5357 at para. 42–3.

[14] However, it has been made clear by the ECJ, Judgment of 2 December 1971, Case 5/71, *Aktien-Zuckerfabrik Schöppenstedt* v. *Council* [1971] ECR 975, that prior annulment of the impugned Community act is not a pre-condition for the success of proceedings for compensation under Art. 288 EC.

[15] As to the condition that the servant must have acted in the performance of his duties, see ECJ, Judgment of 10 July 1969, Case 9/69, *Sayag* v. *Leduc* [1969] ECR 329, discussed in P. Craig and G. de Burca, *EC Law—Text, Cases & Materials* (Oxford: Oxford University Press, 1995) at 511–14.

[16] On these conditions, see *infra*, **9.EC.1.–2.**

[17] See *infra*, **9.EC.1.–2.** In the case of factual acts and individual legal acts, the Community institutions may also be liable towards their respective civil servants. The CFI has exclusive jurisdiction over proceedings brought by civil servants against the institution by which they are employed, pursuant to Art. 236 EC. Even if Community liability towards its civil servants is more of a contractual than tortious nature, cases brought before the Community Courts pursuant to Art. 236 EC will be considered here to the extent that the Courts apply the same principles to them as to Art. 288(2) EC cases: see *Brummelhuis-Leussink*, *infra*, **9.EC.1.**, where a civil servant's claim under the Staff Regulations and Art. 236 EC was dealt with concurrently with a third party claim under Arts. 235 and 288(2).

[18] Judgment of 2 December 1971, Case 5/71, *Aktien-Zuckerfabrik Schöppenstedt* v. *Council* [1971] ECR 975 at para. 11.

[19] See Judgment of 18 April 1991, Case C-63/89, *Assurances du crédit SA* v. *Council* [1991] ECR I-1799 at

As appears from the Court's judgment in *Schöppenstedt*, the test comprises three elements: (i) a sufficiently serious breach, (ii) of a superior rule of law, (iii) that has as an object the protection of the individual (plaintiff). Liability for legislative acts not characterized by the exercise of wide discretion is to be assessed, like acts of the first two categories mentioned above, under the "classic" test of liability, namely whether the defendant institution acted reasonably.[20] Three recent judgments applying the test of reasonableness are reproduced below.[21]

In *Brasserie du Pêcheur*,[22] the Court explained the rationale for the *Schöppenstedt* test as follows: "where the legality of measures is subject to judicial review, exercise of the legislative function must not be hindered by the prospect of actions for damages whenever the general interest of the Community requires legislative measures to be adopted which may adversely affect individual interests". That is why, "in a legislative context characterized by the exercise of a wide discretion . . . the Community cannot incur liability unless the institution concerned has manifestly and gravely disregarded the limits on the exercise of its powers".[23]

c) Whereas in *Francovich* the ECJ chose not to take into account its case law under Article 288(2) EC when outlining the conditions for liability on the part of Member States,[24] it did so in a most explicit way in *Brasserie du Pêcheur*, as already stated. The Court drew a parallel between the two regimes because it wanted to apply the *Schöppenstedt* test also to Member State liability for breaches of Community law in situations where "a Member State acts in a field where it has a wide discretion, comparable to that of the Community institutions in implementing Community policies".[25] Before "applying"[26] that test in the two cases before the Court in *Brasserie du Pêcheur*,[27] the ECJ held that indeed the Member States enjoyed wide discretion in both cases.[28] The Court then stated (with regard to the "serious breach" condition) that in such a situation "the decisive test for finding that a breach of Community law is sufficiently serious is whether the Member State or the Community institution concerned manifestly and gravely disre-

---

para. 11, where the Court acknowledged that the competent Community institutions enjoyed "a discretion in relation to the stages in which harmonization is to take place".

[20] See M.H. van der Woude, "Liability for Administrative Acts under Art. 215(2) EC" in Heukels and McDonnell 109 at 114.

[21] *Infra*, **9.EC.3.–5.** For a summary of ECJ case law on liability for legislative acts, see A. Arnull, "Liability for legislative acts under Art. 215(2) EC" in Heukels and McDonnell 129 at 139 ff.

[22] Where the ECJ applied the *Schöppenstedt* test to liability on the part of Member States.

[23] *Infra*, **9.EC.6.** at para. 45.

[24] Although Advocate-General Mischo had recommended that it do so: see his Opinion, [1991] ECR I-5000 at para. 71.

[25] *Infra*, **9.EC.6.** at para. 47.

[26] "Applying" is not the correct term. In preliminary ruling procedures, it is for the national court to apply in the instant case the answer given by the ECJ to the preliminary questions that the national court submitted to the ECJ. But, as is widely known, the ECJ as a matter of fact very often itself applies the answer to the facts of the case, or at least assesses the factual situation. See an explicit example in ECJ, Judgment of 26 March 1996, Case C-392/93, *R.* v. *H.M. Treasury, ex p. British Telecommunications* [1996] ECR I-1631 at para. 41 (as compared with *Brasserie du Pêcheur*, **9.EC.6.** at para. 58).

[27] i.e. the German *Biersteuergesetz* (Beer Duty Act) of 14 March 1952, BGBl.I.149, version promulgated on 14 December 1976 BGBl.I.3341 and the UK Merchant Shipping Act 1988 (c. 12).

[28] *Infra*, **9.EC.6.** at para. 48 and 49.

garded the limits on its discretion", after which it enumerated the "factors which the competent court may take into consideration":[29]

Although the analogy drawn between the two regimes of tortious liability for breaches of Community law is to be approved in principle, one may question whether it is correct to put on the same footing the discretion of the Member States concerned in both cases and the wide discretion of the Community institutions in implementing Community policies. Indeed, the scope of Member States' discretion under Community law normally extends to the interpretation of Community legal provisions and eventually the implementation of existing policies. It would seem that the scope of that discretion is less than that of Community institutions, particularly the Council, when they take policy decisions.[30] That is particularly so in instances where, as in *British Telecommunications*, the discretion left to the national legislature was of an 'interpretative' nature only.[31]

In the light of the *Schöppenstedt* test, as it now applies to liability on the part of Member States for breaches of Community law, the ECJ distinguishes between situations where the Member State concerned (i) as in *Francovich*, had no discretion whatsoever and simply failed in its duty to implement a Community directive in national law within the prescribed period of time (*carence*) and (ii) as in *British Telecommunications*, implemented the directive in all good faith but did so incorrectly. Whereas in the former case the Member State has committed a sufficiently serious breach in the exercise of its legislative power to become liable in tort,[32] in the latter case the Member State will ordinarily not be liable.[33] In *Brasserie du Pêcheur*, the good faith criterion was also used, with regard to breaches of EC Treaty provisions by the national legislature concerned.[34] Subsequently, in *Dillenkofer*, the Court reviewed its case law, holding that where there is no or very little discretion involved, as when a Member State altogether fails to implement a directive (*Francovich* and *Dillenkofer*) or an administrative authority contravenes a directly applicable EC Treaty provision (*Hedley Lomas*), the mere infringement of Community law in and of itself constitutes a sufficiently serious breach.[35]

d) At the end of this overview, we come to the question whether the two regimes of tortious liability for breaches of Community law impose any restrictions on the scope of protection in terms of either protected rights or interests or of protected persons.

(i) As for restrictions based on **protected interests**, in the current state of the case law, the question must be answered in the negative under both systems. Since Community law is primarily concerned with economic matters, breaches of Community law will typically result in economic losses, more often than not even in "pure" economic losses (i.e. unaccompanied by any physical or property damage). If tortious liability for breaches of Community law is to have any meaning, such losses must be eligible for compensation. In

---

[29] Ibid. at para. 55 and 56.

[30] See further W. van Gerven, "Bridging the unbridgeable: Community and National tort laws after *Francovich* and *Brasserie*" (1996) 45 ICLQ 507 at 517–19; but see P.P. Craig, "Once more unto the breach: the Community, the State and Damages Liability" (1997) 113 LQR 67 at 79 ff.

[31] Judgment of 26 March 1996, Case C-392/93, *R. v. H.M. Treasury, ex p. British Telecommunications* [1996] ECR I-1631.

[32] *Brasserie du Pêcheur, infra*, **9.EC.6.** at para. 46.

[33] Judgment of 26 March 1996, Case C-392/93, *R. v. H.M. Treasury, ex p. British Telecommunications* [1996] ECR I-1631 at para. 45.

[34] *Infra*, **9.EC.6.** at para. 59 and 63.

[35] *Infra*, **9.EC.7.**

respect of Member State liability, this conclusion has been explicitly confirmed by the ECJ in *Brasserie du Pêcheur* in as many words:[36]

> "Total exclusion of loss of profit as a head of damage for which reparation may be awarded in the case of a breach of Community law cannot be accepted. Especially in the context of economic or commercial litigation, such a total exclusion of loss of profit would be such as to make reparation of damage practically impossible".

As appears from this ruling, the principle of full reparation is not necessarily part of Community law on State liability: in *Brasserie du Pêcheur*, where the ECJ speaks of "reparation . . . commensurate with the loss or damage sustained" and states that "*total exclusion of loss of profit as a head of damage . . . cannot be accepted* [emphasis added]".[37] The conclusion that economic losses, including pure economic losses, are recoverable also holds true for the liability of Community institutions under Article 288(2) EC. Even more so, it would seem that for this type of liability, the principle of full reparation will be applied,[38] subject only to certain defences, such as contributory negligence[39] or that "the damage alleged does not exceed the limits of the economic risks inherent in operating in the sector concerned".[40] With respect to other protected interests, the ECJ has so far given no indication that any head of damage, e.g. for non-material injury, would be excluded; in fact, the *Leussink-Brummelhuis* case shows that claims may be brought under Article 288 for non-material injury by primary victims.[41]

(ii) Conversely, an affirmative answer should be given to the second half of the question, dealing with restrictions on the basis of **protected persons.** Under both tortious liability regimes, a *Schutznorm* concept seems to operate, according to which the plaintiff can recover compensation only when he or she belongs to a group of persons which the Community law provision which was infringed was intended to protect. As regards Community liability under Article 288(2) EC, the ECJ has held explicitly in *Schöppenstedt*, above, that there must be a "violation of a superior rule of law for the protection of the individual".[42] In *Leussink-Brummelhuis*, the Court held that while primary victims could recover compensation under Article 288 for non-material injury, dependants could not do so.[43] As for liability on the part of Member States, both for violations of the duty to implement a directive and for other breaches of the EC Treaty, the terminology used by the Court points in the same direction, since the first condition for liability to arise is that the infringed provision was intended to confer rights on individuals.[44]

---

[36] *Infra*, **9.EC.6.** at para. 87.

[37] *Ibid.*, at para. 82 and 87.

[38] On the question whether that includes interest, at which rate and from when, see A. Van Casteren, "Art. 215(2) EC and the question of interest" in Heukels and McDonnell 199.

[39] Judgment of 7 November 1985, Case 53/84, *Adams v. Commission* [1985] ECR 3539.

[40] Judgment of 6 December 1984, Case 59/83, *Biovilac NV v. Community* [1984] ECR 4057 at 4080–1.

[41] *Infra*, **9.EC.1.** and notes. See further A.G. Toth, "The concepts of damage and causality as elements of non-contractual liability" in Heukels and McDonnell 179 at 190.

[42] For a case where that condition was not fulfilled, see Judgment of 13 March 1992, Case 282/90, *Vreugdenhil BV v. Commission* (*Vreugdenhil II*) [1992] ECR I-1937 at para. 20–1.

[43] See *infra*, **9.EC.1.**

[44] See *Brasserie du Pêcheur*, *infra*, **9.EC.6.** at para. 54 and *Dillenkofer*, *infra*, **9.EC.7.** at para. 22, repeating Judgment of 19 November 1991, Cases C-6/90 and 9/90, *Francovich v. Italy* [1991] ECR I-5357 at para. 40.

e) All of the foregoing relates to liability in tort of public bodies and authorities as well as their servants, at the level of both the Community and the Member States. In view of ECJ case law, the national tort laws of the Member States will have to be adapted to the extent that they make it impossible for individuals to safeguard fully the rights which they derive from Community law against public authorities.

It is still an open issue whether it is also an inherent principle of Community law that individuals must be entitled under the national law of Member States to compensation for harm suffered as a consequence of *other individuals* having infringed Community law. Under the laws of the Member States, a right to compensation is generally acknowledged in cases of breach of a Community law provision which imposes direct obligations upon individuals, such as Articles 81 and 82 EC or other Treaty provisions having *horizontal* direct effect. It is our view that the principle of individual tortious liability for breaches of Community law is also inherent in the Treaty, for the same reasons as the principle of State liability, i.e. full effectiveness of Community law and full protection of the rights which Community law grant to individuals.[45]

Should the principle of individual tortious liability for breaches of Community law be accepted, the ECJ should accordingly indicate the substantive conditions under which such liability arises, as it has done for the principle of State liability, and national rules contrary thereto should be set aside. As a further consequence, ECJ case law would induce a certain harmonization of private tort law.

9.1.1. TORTIOUS LIABILITY OF THE COMMUNITY FOR FACTUAL ACTS AND FOR INDIVIDUAL LEGAL ACTS

ECJ, 8 October 1986[46]   **9.EC.1.**
Cases 169/83 and 136/84, Leussink-Brummelhuis v. Commission

COMMUNITY LIABILITY FOR FACTUAL ACTS. COMPENSATION FOR NON-MATERIAL INJURY

Crash with official car

The European Community is liable on the basis of Article 288(2) EC for non-material damage resulting from a breach of a duty of care against one of its civil servants.

Facts: On 7 April 1978 Mr. Leussink, a Commission official on Commission business, was being driven by another Commission official on a German motorway in a car belonging to the Commission, when the vehicle went out of control, rolled over several times and stopped against a signpost beside the motorway. He suffered very serious injuries including several fractures of the skull and of his ribs, bruising to the abdomen and lungs with consequential infection, the loss of his right eye and injury to his left eye, loss of his senses of smell and taste, loss of strength in his left arm and loss of six square centimetres of tissue from his skull. He was in coma for three months.

[45] *Francovich*, ibid., at para. 33. See further, W. van Gerven, "Bridging the unbridgeable: Community and National tort laws after *Francovich* and *Brasserie*" (1996) 45 ICLQ 507 at 530–2 and the Opinion in Case C-128/92, *H.J. Banks & Co. v. British Coal Corporation* [1994] ECR I-1209 at para. 36 (delivered before the judgment of the ECJ in *Brasserie du Pêcheur*).
[46] [1986] ECR 2801.

In Case 136/84, Mr. Leussink requested the annulment of the implicit Commission decision rejecting his claim for non-material damage and on the basis of Article 236 EC sought BEF 5,000,000 in compensation for such damage. In Case 169/83, Mr. Leussink's wife and four children respectively asked for BEF 3,000,000 and 1,000,000 (per child) in compensation for their non-material damage, on the basis of Articles 235 and 288(2) EC. The two cases were joined for decision.

Held: Mr. Leussink's claim was granted for an amount of BEF 2 million. The claims of his spouse and children were dismissed because their damage was indirect.

Opinion of Advocate-General Sir Gordon SLYNN (excerpts): [In Case 136/84:] "The issues are therefore whether any unlawful conduct on the part of the Commission is shown and whether [the applicant's] damage was caused by that conduct.

In my opinion the Commission owed a duty of reasonable care to its officials in the provision of the car used for official purposes; it would be liable if it could be shown that that care had not been taken in the selection and maintenance of the car or its constituent parts or if it was driven negligently by a servant of the Commission.

The German authorities found that the accident was due to the thread coming off the rear tyre which led to the air escaping so that the car, which was then travelling at about 140 kilometres an hour, skidded and rolled over . . .

That does not normally happen if due care is taken in the selection and inspection and maintenance of the tyre. I accept the applicant's argument that there is a *prima facie* case of a breach of duty of care, that the probability is that proper inspection would have revealed that there was a defect in the tread of the tyre and that this would have been discovered by proper inspection earlier than the date of the accident, even if it would not have been noticed by the driver whilst actually driving the car. The Commission has produced no evidence to rebut this *prima facie* case, which was to my mind clearly raised against it in the written pleadings . . .

The physical damage suffered is accepted to have resulted from the accident. It is said, however, that the psychological harm and the loss of enjoyment of life did not result from the accident. Reliance is placed on brief references in the medical report to problems between Mr. Leussink and his superior and his wife prior to the accident. I do not regard these as sufficient to establish the kind of personality traits now shown by Mr. Leussink. In any event it seems to me plain beyond argument that those traits, even if not caused, were aggravated seriously, by the accident. In my opinion the causal link between the lack of care and the injury relied on is clearly established . . .

The assessment of quantum in this sort of case is never easy, especially as there is no body of earlier decisions in Community law. I would accept that some of the items in the 75 per cent (e.g. loss of an eye, disorders of the sense of smell and taste) include an element falling within the *'préjudice moral'* relied on by the applicant, quite apart from the 10 per cent 'psychological and non-material injury'. On the other hand, the break-up of his family life, the general loss of enjoyment of life, and of work, and the other psychological and personal disturbances relied on (which are described in the file and which I do not think it necessary or desirable to set out in detail in this Opinion) seem to me to be serious . . ."

[In Case 169/83:] "Unlike Mr. Leussink's claim, it seems to me that this claim was correctly put under Articles [235] and [288] of the Treaty, since the claim is for the independent loss of the family and is not a dispute between an official and his institution . . .

I accept that the family have suffered the disruption of family life and the psychological and schooling problems which they allege. There is nothing to suggest that this is exaggerated. It is also clear that their problems flow from the effect on Mr. Leussink of the accident, itself due to a breach of duty of care on the part of the defendant. On the other hand, it does not seem to me that Community law recognizes, or should recognize, that all consequences which can be said indirectly to result from a wrongful act are compensable in damages. Albeit that direct and immediate consequences may be so compensable, what are in effect the consequences of such consequences are not in the same position. A line has to be drawn where the responsibility of the defendant ceases. Beyond that line the consequences are too remote. Here the loss claimed by the family did not result from the breach of duty or the accident. It followed the effect of that accident on Mr. Leussink. I do not consider that the damage alleged is of a kind which gives rise to non-contractual liability under Articles [235] and [288] of the Treaty. It is in my view too remote. I would accordingly dismiss this claim as unfounded."

Judgment: "The matter which must therefore be examined next is whether the Commission must be held liable for the accident and, if so, . . . whether the existence of a causal link is sufficiently proved.

THE COMMISSION'S LIABILITY

[The accident] was . . . an accident at work and the question to be considered is whether the Commission failed to exercise the diligence required of it *qua* employer as regards the inspection, maintenance and use of the official car.

According to a technical expert's report drawn up at the request of the German Public Prosecutor's Office, the accident occurred because the tread came away from a tyre. The report mentions a number of possible causes, some of which could be attributable to poor maintenance or inadequate inspection of the vehicle or to negligent use. The Commission has not furnished any evidence enabling the Court to establish to which of those factors the detachment of the tread must be attributed.

As the Commission was best placed to provide evidence in that respect, such uncertainty must be construed against it. The applicants' contention that the accident was due to negligence for which the Commission is liable must therefore be accepted.

THE INJURY SUFFERED AND THE CAUSAL LINK

The information provided to the Court justifies the finding that the extremely serious injuries sustained by Mr. Leussink have had consequences which were not only economic, particularly as far as his family and social relationships are concerned. Such consequences constitute non-material damage giving rise to entitlement to compensation. None of the documents laid before the Court cast doubt on the existence of a causal link between the accident and that injury . . .

As the Court has held in its judgment of 2 October 1979 in Case 152/77 *Miss B* v. *Commission* [1979] ECR 2819, psychological and non-physical consequences must be taken into account when determining the rate of invalidity under the insurance scheme provided for by the Staff Regulations. A breakdown of the rate of invalidity (75 per cent) shows that this was indeed done in this case. Besides the percentages adopted for the impairment of Mr. Leussink's hearing, sense of smell and sense of taste, a rate of 10 per cent was fixed for psychological and non-physical injury. That rate corresponds to compensation of almost BEF 1,000,000.

However, in view of the extreme gravity of the non-economic consequences which the accident has had for Mr. Leussink, the Court considers it equitable to award him additional compensation of BEF 2,000,000 together with interest thereon at the rate of 8 per cent per annum from the commencement of the action on 23 May 1984.

As regards the claims by Mr. Leussink's wife and children for compensation for the effects of the accident on their family life, it must be recognized that the family, too, has suffered on account of the accident and its sequelae, particularly of a psychological nature, for Mr. Leussink . . .

Although there can be no doubt about the reality of those effects or about the existence of a link with the accident, they are nevertheless the indirect result of the injury suffered by Mr. Leussink and do not constitute part of the harm for which the Commission may be held liable in its capacity as employer. This is borne out by the fact that the legal systems of most Member States make no provision for compensating such effects.

It follows that the application lodged by Mrs Brummelhuis and Monica, Mirjam, Mechteld and Maud Leussink must be dismissed."

Notes

(1) In the case above, the Community was found liable on the basis of a wrongful act or omission by a Commission employee, giving rise to a motor accident. In the absence of any explanation to the contrary, it was reasonable to infer that the accident would not have occurred but for some negligence on the part of the employees with responsibility for the vehicle; and the Commission could not demonstrate that the accident was not due to a faulty inspection or a failure to inspect the vehicle in question. For factual acts of Community institutions, the ECJ case law does not impose any particular degree of wrongfulness in order to find liability, as illustrated by the above case.[47] It will be seen below that, as a consequence of the *Schöppenstedt* decision, liability for legislative action characterized by the exercise of a wide discretion (where it involves measures of economic policy) requires a "sufficiently serious violation" of "a superior rule of law for the protection of the individual".

While the analysis of the ECJ in the case above may on the surface seem to be inspired by French law (fault, causation, damage), it must be noted that the Court nonetheless took due care to establish the existence of a duty between the plaintiff and the Commission, in that it held the Commission, as employer, to be under a duty to inspect and maintain the cars that it put at the disposal of its officials.[48] A certain element of the common law duty of care analysis is therefore present in the reasoning of the Court (and explicit in the Opinion of Advocate-General Slynn).

(2) The annotated judgment illustrates very well the absence of any *a priori* limits on tortious liability in Community law as regards primary victims. Following the Opinion of Advocate-General Slynn, the ECJ awarded damages for non-material prejudice of various kinds, including family break-up, loss of amenity and other disturbances. Much as under French law, the judgment evidences little concern with the systematization of non-material damage and the avoidance of overlaps.

On the other hand, the attitude of the ECJ towards the claims of Mr Leussink's dependants was remarkably strict. The Court summarily dismissed those claims as indirect, and stated that the laws of most Member States would also not allow compensation in such a case. At the very least, that assertion is not accurate for the French legal tradition, where the claims of dependants—even for non-material damage, as in *Brummelhuis-Leussink*—are broadly admitted.[49] Under the common law of England, as *Alcock* v. *Chief Constable of South Yorkshire Police* demonstrates, recovery of non-material damage by secondary victims is not *a priori* excluded, although the legal hurdles are considerable.[50] Only under

---

[47] The same is true for legislative acts not characterized by a wide discretion: *infra*, **9.EC.2.**

[48] For another example, see the tragic case dealt with in ECJ, Judgment of 7 November 1985, Case 53/84, *Adams* v. *Commission* [1985] ECR 353 where the Court found that Adams' express request for confidentiality had put the Commission under a duty towards Adams. The Court also found, however, that the applicant himself contributed significantly to the damage which he suffered and that therefore the damage had to be apportioned equally between the two parties. Also in respect of the applicant the Court did not apply a particular test of wrongfulness.

[49] See *supra*, Chapter II, 2.1.3., Introductory Note and notes Chapter II, **2.F.19.**

[50] *Supra*, Chapter II, **2.E.8.** and notes.

German law, in fact, is there such a clear refusal of claims for non-material damage by secondary victims.[51]

ECJ, 28 May 1970[52]   **9.EC.2.**

Cases 19, 20, 25 and 30/69, Richez-Parise v. Commission

LIABILITY FOR INDIVIDUAL LEGAL ACTS. ECONOMIC LOSS

Misinformed civil servants

While the inaccurate interpretation of a legal provision does not in itself constitute a wrongful act, delay on the part of the authority in correcting that interpretation can lead to liability for ensuing economic loss.

Facts: In the course of implementing the Treaty establishing a single Council and a single Commission of the European Communities,[53] the Commission was empowered by Regulation 259/68 to reduce its staff to reflect a reduction in the number of posts. On 5 March 1968, the applicants (Commission officials) received a circular from the Commission inviting them to take advantage of the special financial provisions designed to induce officials voluntarily to terminate their service. The applicants were directed to contact the competent Commission departments to obtain information on how these special provisions would apply in their individual case. The information that the applicants received led them to believe that Article 5(7) of Regulation 259/68 would entitle them to receive their full pension rights as of their 55th birthday. They submitted a request to terminate their service before the deadline of 18 April 1968. In April 1968, the Commission reached the view that the interpretation that it had given to Article 5(7) of Regulation 259/68 was erroneous and issued a warning to its staff in general terms to the effect that the information given by its departments was not binding. The Commission terminated the service of the applicants in June 1968. A few months later, the applicants received an official statement with respect to their pension entitlement; in it the Commission followed its revised interpretation of Article 5(7) of Regulation 259/68 and stated that the full pension rights of the applicants would come into effect as of their 60th birthday. In the meanwhile, the applicants did not exercise their right to choose between their pension entitlement or a lump-sum payment in lieu (Article 6 of Regulation 259/68). After the time for so doing had expired, the applicants brought claims before the ECJ, requesting the Court to uphold the Commission's original interpretation of Regulation 259/68 or, in the alternative, to award them damages.

Held: The ECJ found that the Commission was at fault for not warning the applicants earlier that its original interpretation of the Regulation was incorrect. Instead of the remedies requested by the applicants, however, the ECJ ordered that the time period given to them to choose between their pension entitlement and a lump-sum payment be re-opened.

Judgment: "31. For the application to be well founded it must be established that the defendant is liable for a wrongful act or omission which caused the applicants a still subsisting injury.

32. It is not contested that the appropriate departments supplied the applicants with incorrect information concerning the rights which they would be able to assert in the event of termination of their service.

33. Nor is it contested that this information was supplied as a consequence of the request by the Commission to the officials concerned to contact the competent departments in order to obtain information on the rights which they would have should Article 4 of Regulation No 259/68 be applied. . . .

36. Apart from the exceptional instance, the adoption of an incorrect interpretation does not constitute in itself a wrongful act.

[51] See *supra*, Chapter II, **2.G.4.** and notes.
[52] [1970] ECR 325.
[53] [1967] OJ 152.

37. Even the fact that the authorities request those concerned to obtain information from the competent departments does not necessarily involve those authorities in an obligation to guarantee the correctness of information supplied and does not therefore make them liable for any injury which may be occasioned by incorrect information.

38. However, whilst it may be possible to doubt the existence of a wrongful act concerning the supply of incorrect information, the same cannot be said of the departments' delay in rectifying the information . . .

41. A correction made shortly before or after 16 April, that is to say, before the time when those concerned had to make their decision, would have certainly enabled the defendant to avoid all liability for the consequences of the wrong information.

42. The failure to make such a correction is, on the other hand, a matter of such a nature as to render the Communities liable.

43. The applicants have failed, however, to adduce sufficient evidence to establish that their requests for termination of service were based on the wrong information supplied to them and not corrected in good time. . . .

45. On the other hand it would be reasonable to assume that, under the impression that they would receive a full pension from the age of 55, the applicants did not take into consideration the possibility of renouncing their pension rights under Article 6 of Regulation No 259/68 in order to benefit from the grant provided for by that article.

48. As compensation for the injury which they have suffered, it is therefore appropriate to allow them a fresh limitation period and to rule that for them the period laid down in Article 6 shall be deemed to run from the date of this judgment."

Notes

(1) The above judgment appears to concern what French administrative law would characterize as a *faute de service*, i.e. a wrong committed by the institution itself, here giving inaccurate information on the pension rights of civil servants. *Faute de service* is generally contrasted with *faute personnelle*, namely the wrong committed by an individual civil servant in the course of performing his or her duty.[54] The distinction between these two types of cases, however, is not made as sharply in Community law as in French administrative law.[55]

In *Richez-Parise*, the ECJ restricted the potential scope of *faute de service* in the context of wrongful interpretation of provisions of Community law by Community institutions by ruling that "apart from the exceptional instance, the adoption of an incorrect interpretation does not constitute in itself a wrongful act". The Court chose instead to attach liability to a more concrete element, i.e. the undue delay in rectifying the inaccurate interpretation given to the applicants in the first instance. In *Kohll*[56], the Court held that there was no *faute de service*, on the basis that the "incorrect interpretation was supplied in reply to a hypothetical question [and] . . . the relevant texts were available to the applicant who was thus in a position to inform himself as to the correct interpretation".

---

[54] As was the case in *Brummelhuis-Leussink, supra*, **9.EC.1.**

[55] Note however that the concept of *faute de service* (in the English version, "wrongful act or omission in the performance of its functions") is found at Article 40 of the ECSC Treaty. It is not mentioned in the EC Treaty.

[56] Judgment of 11 July 1980, Case 137/79, *Kohll* v. *Commission* [1980] ECR 2601, at para. 15. In the judgment of 13 July 1972, Case 79/71 *Heinemann* v. *Commission* [1972] ECR 579, a case dealing with the same wrongful interpretation as *Richez-Parise*, the Court reached the same conclusion.

In *Compagnie Continentale*, the Council had failed to express some reservations as to applicability of a legal provision in a resolution aiming at giving information and guidance to economic operators. Here the Court found that such an omission "was likely to distort the task of informing which the Council had assumed and was such as to make it liable".[57]

It appears from the above that whether the misinterpretation of Community law leads to a *faute de service* will depend on whether under the circumstances of the case the Community institution in question has "acted negligently and without due care and circumspection", as formulated by Advocate-General Trabucchi in *Roquette*.[58] In that case, the Advocate-General was of the opinion that "[bearing] in mind the undoubted complexity of the legislation in question, I consider it reasonable to rule out the possibility that, given the conditions under which it took place, a mistake in interpreting the law can create liability". The Court decided the case on other grounds.[59]

As appears from the above case and the previous one (*Brummelhuis-Leussink*), in the case of acts not characterized by a wide discretion the Court seems to apply a classic liability test, that is of whether the public authority concerned was acting reasonably, i.e. as a reasonable public authority would have acted under the circumstances of the case.[60]

(2) In the annotated judgment, the ECJ understandably insists on the need to demonstrate the causal link between wrong and damage. It will be seen below that the causal link becomes even more important in legislative act cases.

The Court thus finds that applicants had not established that their decision to leave the service was caused by the inaccurate interpretation given to them, and the Court accordingly held that the applicants' loss was limited to the loss of the opportunity to choose a lump-sum payment instead of pension rights. It will be noted that the Court required the Commission to make good that damage suffered by the applicants by crafting an innovative remedy, namely the re-opening of the period given to them to make the choice between a lump sum and pension rights.

In contrast, in the *Heinemann* judgment referred to above, the Court concluded that there was a causal link between the wrongful interpretation and the decision of the applicants to leave the Commission's service. It accordingly ordered the Commission to pay the applicant monthly compensation from the age of 55 to 60.

---

[57] Judgment of 4 February 1975, Case 169/73, *Compagnie Continentale* v. *Council* [1975] ECR 117 at para. 21.

[58] Case 26/74, *Société Roquette Frères* v. *Commission* [1976] ECR 677 at 693.

[59] See further J.V. Louis et al., *Commentaire Mégret: Le droit de la CEE: 10—La Cour de Justice. Les Actes des institutions*, 2nd edn., (Bruxelles: Éd. de l'Univ. de Bruxelles, 1993) at 293 ff.

[60] See also M.H. Van der Woude, "Liability for Administrative Acts under Art. 215(2) EC" in Heukels and McDonnell 109 at 118.

9.1.2. LIABILITY OF THE COMMUNITY FOR LEGISLATIVE ACTS CHARACTERIZED BY A WIDE DISCRETION

ECJ, 19 May 1992[61]   **9.EC.3.**
Joined Cases C-104/89 and C-37/90, Mulder v. Council

LIABILITY FOR LEGISLATIVE ACTS. ECONOMIC LOSS

Milk levies

The Community is liable on the basis of Article 288(2) EC to make good the damage suffered as a result of a regulation which constituted a serious breach of the principle of protection of legitimate expectations.

Facts: Due to excessive milk production, an additional levy due on milk deliveries in excess of a reference quantity was introduced.[62] The reference quantity was due to be fixed according to deliveries during a reference year (in the case of the applicants, 1983). The applicants were farmers who pursuant to Regulation 1078/77 had undertaken not to produce milk or dairy products for a five-year period including 1983, and accordingly they had made no deliveries during the reference year. Pursuant to the implementing Council Regulation 857/84 and Commission Regulation 1371/84, persons in the position of the applicants were not to be granted any reference quantity, and would have had to pay the additional levy on the whole of their deliveries upon resuming production after the end of the five-year period. The applicants challenged the regulations before the ECJ. In judgments of 28 April 1988,[63] the Court found that Regulations 857/84 and 1371/84 infringed the principle of the protection of legitimate expectations, in so far as they made no provision for the allocation of a reference quantity to producers in the situation of the applicants. Subsequently, Council Regulation 764/89 introduced for such producers a reference quantity equal to 60 per cent of deliveries made by them in the last year before the beginning of the five-year period. Regulation 764/89 was also declared invalid by judgments of 11 December 1990.[64] The applicants brought an action for compensation for the damage suffered as a result of the application of the Council and Commission Regulations referred to above.[65]

Held: The action succeeded in respect of damage resulting from the application of Regulation 857/84 but was dismissed in respect of damage resulting from the application of Regulation 764/89. The parties were ordered to inform the Court within 12 months of their agreement on the quantum of damages.

Judgment: **"(a) The basis for liability**

12. The second paragraph of Article [288] of the Treaty provides that, in the case of non-contractual liability, the Community, in accordance with the general principles common to the laws of the Member States, is to make good any damage caused by its institutions in the performance of their duties. The scope of that provision has been specified in the sense that the Community does not incur liability on account of a legislative measure involving choices of economic policy unless a sufficiently serious breach of a superior rule of law for the protection of the individual has

---

[61] [1992] ECR I-3061.

[62] Through Regulation 856/84 of 31 March 1984, adding an Art. 5c to Regulation 804/68 on the Common organisation of the market in milk and milk products [1984] OJ L 90/10.

[63] Case 120/86, *Mulder* v. *Minister van Landbouw en Visserij* [1988] ECR 2321 and Case 170/86, *von Deetzen* v. *Hauptzollamt Hamburg-Jonas* [1988] ECR 2355.

[64] Case C-189/89, *Spagl* v. *Hauptzollamt Rosenheim* [1990] ECR I-4539 and Case C-217/89, *Pastätter* v. *Hauptzollamt Bad Reichenhall* [1990] ECR I-4585.

[65] Following the 1990 judgments, a new regulation, Regulation 1639/91 [1991] OJ L 150/35 was adopted to deal with the matter. It also led to a preliminary ruling of the ECJ, Judgment of 5 May 1994, Case C-21/92, *Kamp* v. *Hauptzollamt Wuppertal* [1994] ECR I-1619, whereby the Court found no reasons to hold Regulation 1639/91 invalid.

occurred (see, in particular, the judgment in Joined Cases 83 and 94/76, 4, 15 and 40/77 *HNL* v. *Council and Commission* [1978] ECR 1209, paragraphs 4, 5 and 6). More specifically, in a legislative field such as the one in question, which is characterized by the exercise of a wide discretion essential for the implementation of the Common Agricultural Policy, the Community cannot incur liability unless the institution concerned has manifestly and gravely disregarded the limits on the exercise of its powers (see in particular the judgment in *HNL* v. *Commission and Council*, paragraph 6).

13. The Court has also consistently held that, in order for the Community to incur non-contractual liability, the damage alleged must go beyond the bounds of the normal economic risks inherent in the activities in the sector concerned [references omitted].

14. Those conditions are fulfilled in the case of Regulation No 857/84 as supplemented by Regulation No 1371/84.

15. In this regard, it must be recalled in the first place that, as the Court held in the judgments of 28 April 1988 in *Mulder* and *von Deetzen*, . . . those regulations were adopted in breach of the principle of the protection of legitimate expectations, which is a general and superior principle of Community law for the protection of the individual.

16. Secondly, it must be held that, in so far as it failed completely, without invoking any higher public interest, to take account of the specific situation of a clearly defined group of economic agents, that is to say, producers who, pursuant to an undertaking given under Regulation No 1078/77, delivered no milk during the reference year, the Community legislature manifestly and gravely disregarded the limits of its discretionary power, thereby committing a sufficiently serious breach of a superior rule of law.

17. That breach is all the more obvious because the total and permanent exclusion of the producers concerned from the allocation of a reference quantity, which in fact prevented them from resuming the marketing of milk when their non-marketing or conversion undertaking expired, cannot be regarded as being foreseeable or as falling within the bounds of the normal economic risks inherent in the activities of a milk producer.

18. In contrast, contrary to the applicants' assertions, the Community cannot incur liability on account of the fact that Regulation No 764/89 introduced the 60 per cent rule.

19. Admittedly, that rule also infringes the legitimate expectation of the producers concerned with regard to the limited nature of their non-marketing or conversion undertaking, as the Court held in the judgments in *Spagl* and *Pastätter*, cited above. However, the breach of the principle of the protection of legitimate expectations which was held to exist cannot be described as being sufficiently serious within the meaning of the case-law on the non-contractual liability of the Community.

20. In that regard, it must be borne in mind first that, unlike the 1984 rules, which made it impossible for the producers concerned to market milk, the 60 per cent rule enabled those traders to resume their activities as milk producers. Consequently, in the amending regulation, Regulation No 764/89, the Council did not fail to take the situation of the producers concerned into account.

21. Secondly, it must be observed that, by adopting Regulation No 764/89 following the judgments of 28 April 1988 in *Mulder* and *von Deetzen*, . . . the Community legislature made an economic policy choice with regard to the manner in which it was necessary to implement the principles set out in those judgments. That was based, on the one hand, on the 'overriding necessity of not jeopardizing the fragile stability that currently obtains in the milk products sector' (fifth recital in the preamble to Regulation No 764/89) and, on the other, on the need to strike a balance between the interests of the producers concerned and the interests of the other producers subject to the scheme. The Council made that choice in such a way as to maintain the level of other producers' reference quantities unchanged while increasing the Community reserve by 600,000 tonnes, or 60 per cent of aggregate foreseeable applications for the allocation of special reference quantities,

which, in its view, was the highest quantity compatible with the aims of the scheme. Accordingly, the Council took account of a higher public interest, without gravely and manifestly disregarding the limits of its discretionary power in this area.

22. In the light of the foregoing, it must therefore be held that the Community is bound to make good the damage suffered by the applicants as a result of the application of Regulation No 857/84, as supplemented by Regulation No 1371/84 . . . but not the damage resulting from the application of Regulation No 764/89 . . .

(b) The damage

23. With regard to the evaluation of the damage which must be regarded as resulting from the application of the 1984 rules, it must be stated *in limine* that all the applicants in the two cases applied for the allocation of a reference quantity under the additional levy scheme before their non-marketing undertakings expired, and resumed the marketing of milk at the latest immediately after they were granted a special reference quantity under Regulation No 764/89. Accordingly, they manifested, in an appropriate manner, their intention to resume milk production, with the result that the loss of income from milk deliveries cannot be regarded as being the consequence of the applicants' freely deciding to give up milk production . . .

26. As regards the extent of the damage which the Community should make good, in the absence of particular circumstances warranting a different assessment, account should be taken of the loss of earnings consisting in the difference between, on the one hand, the income which the applicants would have obtained in the normal course of events from the milk deliveries which they would have made if, during the period between 1 April 1984 (the date of entry into force of Regulation No 857/84) and 29 March 1989 (the date of entry into force of Regulation No 764/89), they had obtained the reference quantities to which they were entitled and, on the other hand, the income which they actually obtained from milk deliveries made during that period in the absence of any reference quantity, plus any income which they obtained, or could have obtained, during that period from any replacement activities . . .

32. The basis which should be taken for calculating the income which the applicants would have received in the normal course of events if they had made milk deliveries corresponding to the reference quantities to which they were entitled is the profitability of a farm representative of the type of farm run by each of the applicants, it being understood that account can be taken in that regard of the reduced profitability generally shown by such a farm during the period when milk production is started up.

33. As regards income from any replacement activities which is to be deducted from the hypothetical income referred to above, it must be noted that that income must be taken to include not only that which the applicants actually obtained from replacement activities, but also that income which they could have obtained had they reasonably engaged in such activities. This conclusion must be reached in the light of a general principle common to the legal systems of the Member States to the effect that the injured party must show reasonable diligence in limiting the extent of his loss or risk having to bear the damage himself. Any operating losses incurred by the applicants in carrying out such a replacement activity cannot be attributed to the Community, since the origin of such losses does not lie in the effects of the Community rules.

34. It follows that the amount of compensation payable by the Community should correspond to the damage which it caused."

Notes

(1) The above case is remarkable in many respects. First of all, it is one of the few cases where an applicant has obtained damages under Article 288(2) EC for a legislative act. In *Mulder* the ECJ combines the notion of "sufficiently serious breach" with the criterion of

"manifest and grave disregard by a Community institution of the limits on the exercise of its powers", making it clear with the terms "more specifically" at para. 12 that the second expression clarifies the first, as proposed by the Advocate-General in his Opinion.

(2) Secondly, it shows that the Community liability regime for legislative acts is not excessively restrictive at least on one issue, namely the need to show exceptional damage affecting the plaintiff above and beyond other persons. In *Mulder*, the ECJ accepted that the claim of the plaintiff was not defeated by the mere fact that he was merely a member of a large class especially affected by the legislative acts. In earlier case law, the Court had insisted that liability would arise only if the illegality affected a limited, well-defined group of enterprises. In *Mulder*, where only five producers were involved in the Court proceedings but many more were concerned, the Court was content to find that the plaintiff were part of "a clearly defined group of economic agents" (at para. 16).

(3) Thirdly, *Mulder* provides a prime example of the impact of the *Schöppenstedt* test. On the one hand, the failure in Regulations 857/84 and 1371/84 to give any reference quantity to producers participating in the cessation of production programme established by Regulation 1078/77 was found to represent a *sufficiently serious breach* to give rise to liability. On the other hand, even though the reference quantity of 60 per cent of their previous production granted to those producers by Regulation 764/89 was also held to be invalid,[66] Regulation 764/89 did *not* constitute a sufficiently serious breach and no Community liability was incurred. In *Mulder*, the ECJ conducted a balancing test between the "higher public interest" pursued by the Community institutions and the interests of the producers in order to see if there had been a sufficiently serious breach. In the case of Regulation 764/89, the higher public interest in reducing milk production was held to outweigh the legitimate expectations of the producers, since the affected producers were not totally penalized by having to pay an additional levy on the whole of their deliveries upon resuming production. Yet a breach of those legitimate expectations had led the ECJ to annul Regulation 764/89 in *Spagl*; one could conclude that the ECJ case law is more stringent when it comes to Community *liability* than with respect to the *legality* of Community acts.

(4) Fourthly, in *Mulder* the ECJ did not hesitate to award compensation for what could be characterized as pure economic loss (under English law) or *reiner Vermögensschaden* (under German law), and hence in principle not eligible for compensation in those two legal systems.[67] The ECJ was however careful to set limits to the recovery of such losses, by insisting for instance that (i) as formulated in earlier case law, "in order for the Community to incur non-contractual liability, the damage alleged must go beyond the bounds of the normal economic risks inherent on the activities in the sector concerned" (at para. 13 with references), (ii) income derived from replacement activities which "the applicants would have received in the normal course of events" must be taken into account (para. 32), and (iii) the award must be reduced by deducting potential income from replacement activities which the applicants should reasonably have engaged in,

---

[66] Judgments of 11 December 1990, Case C-189/89, *Spagl* v. *Hauptzollamt Rosenheim* [1990] ECR I-4539 and Case C-217/89, *Pastätter* v. *Hauptzollamt Bad Reichenhall* [1990] ECR I-4585.

[67] Although an argument could be made under German law that the *Recht am Gewerbebetrieb* is violated: see *supra*, Chapter II, 2.3.2.

because of the general principle "that the injured party must show reasonable diligence in limiting the extent of his loss or risk having to bear the damage himself " (para. 33).[68]

(5) The annotated judgment required the parties to negotiate on the quantum of damages, in line of those principles. The parties could not agree on all points, and the matter went back before the ECJ for a final judgment on the issues where no agreement had been reached.[69]

In that judgment the Court set out the principles governing the calculation of the loss of earnings actually suffered by each of the applicants during the period in respect of which compensation is to be paid. Such loss of earnings "consists in the difference between, on the one hand, the income which the applicants would have obtained in the normal course of events from the milk deliveries which they would have made if, during [that] period. . . they had obtained the reference quantities to which they were entitled (the hypothetical income) and, on the other hand, the income which they actually obtained from milk deliveries made during that period in the absence of any reference quantity, plus any income which they obtained, or could have obtained, during that period from any replacement activities (the alternative income)".[70] The Court added that such "loss of earnings must be assessed, so far as possible, on the basis of the individual data and figures reflecting the actual situation of each applicant and of his farm", but found that "[i]n the present case, however, such an assessment based on individual, factual data runs up against structural and material obstacles concerning both the hypothetical income and the alternative income".[71]

The Court then considered the points on which the parties had reached agreement as well as the expert report which it had ordered, concerning the determination of the hypothetical receipts and the alternative income.[72] As parties had not fully agreed on the value of statistical data in combination with actual figures of loss, the Court concluded on that point that "like a national court, it therefore has a broad discretion as to both the figures and the statistical data to be chosen and also, above all, as to the way in which they are to be used to calculate and evaluate the damage."[73] It also gave precise indications as to which party bears the burden of proof with respect to the constituent elements and the scope of the loss.[74] The Court then applied those principles to the concrete cases brought forward by the applicants.

---

[68] For a thorough examination of the concept of damage, proof of damage, assessment of damage and quantum of damage, as well as of the concept of causality, see A.G. Toth, "The Concepts of Damage and Causality as elements of non-contractual Liability" in Heukels and McDonnell 179.

[69] ECJ, Judgment of 27 January 2000, Cases C–104/89 and C–37/90, *Mulder* v. *Commission* (not yet reported).

[70] Ibid. at para. 60.

[71] Ibid. at para. 63 and 64.

[72] Ibid. at para. 67–72.

[73] Ibid. at para. 79.

[74] Ibid. at para. 82–4.

CFI, 18 September 1995[75]   **9.EC.4–5.**
Case T-167/94, Nölle v. Council
and
CFI, 18 September 1995[76]
Case T-168/94, Blackspur DIY Ltd. v. Council

LIABILITY FOR LEGISLATIVE ACTS

Anti-dumping determinations constitute legislative acts for which the Community is not liable unless there is a sufficiently serious breach of a superior rule of law protecting the individual and a clear causal link is present.

1. CFI, 18 September 1995, Nölle   **9.EC.4.**

Paint brushes

Facts: The applicant was an importer of paint brushes. Following the adoption of Regulation 3052/88 imposing a provisional anti-dumping duty on those products, the applicant was required to post security in order to cover provisionally the amount of duty which could be imposed. The duties were to be collected pursuant to Regulation 725/89, but the applicant challenged the validity of that Regulation, and the ECJ annulled it on 22 October 1991.[77] In the present proceedings, the applicant claimed compensation for the amount it had to pay to finance the posting of security under Regulation 3052/88 until the amount of the security was returned to it following the annulment of Regulation 725/89.

Held: The CFI rejected the applicant's claim.

Judgment: "44. The applicant draws a distinction between Community measures that are legislative and those that are administrative, and takes the view that, although adopted in the form of a regulation, anti-dumping measures lie in fact somewhere between those two categories. According to the applicant, a similar distinction also ought to be drawn in respect of the origin of the Community's liability arising from the adoption of unlawful anti-dumping measures. Thus, the applicant contends that where the illegality of an anti-dumping regulation is attributable to a breach of the rules inherent in the assessment of complex economic facts, the stricter conditions as to Community liability, that is to say those governing liability by reason of legislative measures, will apply. In contrast, where the illegality is attributable to a breach of procedural rules or rules of an administrative nature, so-called "simple" conditions will apply. In the opinion of the applicant, this case comes in principle within the second category. The Commission's fault lay in its breach of the procedural rule set out in Article 2(5)(a) of the Basic Regulation concerning determination of the reference country . . .

50. The Court notes that the applicant is seeking compensation for the damage which it claims to have suffered by reason of the adoption of Regulation No 725/89, declared invalid by the Court of Justice.

51. It should be borne in mind in this regard, as the Court of Justice held in its judgment in *Epicheiriseon Metalleftikon Viomichanikon kai Naftiliakon* [Judgment of 28 November 1989, Case C-122/86 [1989] ECR 3959] that measures of the Council and Commission in connection with a proceeding relating to the possible adoption of anti-dumping measures constitute legislative action

---

[75] [1995] ECR II-2589.
[76] [1995] ECR II-2627.
[77] Case C-16/90, *Nölle* v. *Hauptzollamt Bremen-Freihafen* [1991] ECR I-5163.

involving choices of economic policy and that, in accordance with settled case-law, Community liability can be incurred by virtue of such measures only if there has been a sufficiently serious breach of a superior rule of law for the protection of individuals (judgments of the Court of Justice in *Zuckerfabrik Schöppenstedt* [other references omitted]).

52. In those circumstances, the Court takes the view that the opinion expressed by the applicant to the effect that Community liability ought in this case to be determined on the basis of the nature of the alleged breach (breach of procedural rules) and not on the basis of the Community measure at the origin of the alleged damage is unfounded and that it is for that reason necessary to consider whether the defendant institutions committed a sufficiently serious breach of a superior rule of law for the protection of individuals . . .

[The CFI then considered whether the Community institutions were at fault. The applicant had raised four arguments in this respect. The CFI dismissed the first three, but found that the Community institutions did not respect the principles of care and proper administration when they chose Sri Lanka rather than Taiwan as the reference country for the purposes of the anti-dumping investigation. The next question was whether that fault constituted a sufficiently serious breach.]
. . .

85. The Court points to settled case-law establishing that the requirement of a sufficiently serious breach of a provision means, in a legislative field such as that in the present case, where the exercise of a wide discretion is essential for the implementation of the common commercial policy, that the Community cannot incur liability unless the institution concerned has manifestly and gravely disregarded the limits on the exercise of its powers (see the judgments in *HNL*, cited above, in *Mulder* [reproduced above], cited above, and in *Campo Ebro*, cited above).

86. In its judgment in *Nölle*, the Court of Justice found that 'Nölle has produced sufficient factors, already known to the Commission and the Council during the anti-dumping proceeding, to raise doubts as to whether the choice of Sri Lanka as a reference country was appropriate and not unreasonable' and that 'although the institutions are not required to consider every reference country suggested by the parties during an anti-dumping proceeding, the doubts which arose in this case with regard to the choice of Sri Lanka ought to have led the Commission to examine the proposal made by the plaintiff in greater depth' (paragraphs 30 and 32 of the judgment).

87. It must accordingly be held, as is clear from the grounds set out in *Nölle*, that the Court of Justice did not hold that the choice of Sri Lanka as the reference country was inherently wrong, but simply took the view that, in the light of the doubts raised by the applicant, the Commission ought to have carried out a more detailed investigation in order to determine whether, as the applicant had argued, Taiwan might be a more appropriate choice. As the Commission has also quite correctly pointed out, that which is doubtful is far from being manifest and arbitrary.

88. It should be noted in this connection that when the applicant raised doubts as to the appropriateness of Sri Lanka as the reference country, the Commission did not wholly fail to consider whether Taiwan might be a more appropriate reference country—conduct which, in the circumstances, might well have constituted a serious failure to meet its obligations of proper administration *vis-à-vis* the parties involved in the proceeding—but rather it did not make a serious and sufficient effort to that end. This is clear from paragraph 34 of the *Nölle* judgment, in which the Court of Justice found that the letter which the Commission had addressed to the two main producers in Taiwan when determining the reference country could not be regarded as a sufficient attempt to obtain information in view of the wording of that letter and the extremely short period allowed for a reply, which made it practically impossible for the producers in question to cooperate.

89. It follows that, in so far as the Community institutions did not fail completely in the duty of care and proper administration which they owed to the applicant but simply failed properly to appreciate the extent of their obligations under that principle, the breach of the principle of care

cannot in this case be regarded as a sufficiently serious breach or a manifest and grave breach, as defined in the case-law of the Court of Justice [references omitted].

90. In any event, it must be added that even if the Commission had carried out a more serious investigation as to whether Taiwan might be an appropriate reference country, there could be nothing to prevent Sri Lanka, at the conclusion of such an investigation, from proving to be an appropriate and reasonable choice for the purposes of Article 2(5)(a) of the basic regulation.

91. Consequently, in the absence of a sufficiently serious breach of a rule of law protecting the applicant, and without there being any need to examine whether the other conditions for Community liability have been satisfied in this case, the application must be dismissed as being unfounded."

2. CFI, 18 September 1995, *Blackspur*   **9.EC.5.**

Paint brushes

Facts: The applicant was a retailer of tools for amateur home repair ("Do-it-yourself"). Following the adoption of Regulations 3052/88 and 725/89, the applicant was required to pay anti-dumping duties on a shipment of paint brushes which it had ordered before the imposition of duties. Regulation 725/89 was annulled by the ECJ on 22 October 1991.[78] The applicant went bankrupt a few months after it had paid anti-dumping duties on the brushes, and it brought a claim before the CFI for the losses incurred due to the imposition of those duties.

Held: The CFI rejected the claim of the applicant.

Judgment: "40. The Court notes in this regard that, according to the case-law of the Court of Justice, there is a causal link for the purposes of the second paragraph of Article [288] of the Treaty where there is a direct causal link between the fault committed by the institution concerned and the injury pleaded, the burden of proof of which rests on the applicants [references omitted] . . .

46. It is . . . clear from the documents in the case that Blackspur was not engaged in importing brushes from China prior to the imposition of the contested anti-dumping duty and that Blackspur's assertion that imports of brushes from China accounted for half of its turnover during the period prior to the imposition of the anti-dumping duty is uncorroborated by any evidence. In those circumstances, it cannot be accepted that the alleged loss of the commercial outlet represented by the sales of brushes from China was the principal cause of the poor financial results that led to Blackspur's being wound up . . .

48. It follows from the foregoing that, even if it could have had the effect of reducing the turnover achieved on Chinese brushes during the financial year 1989/1990, the alleged loss of the commercial outlet represented by the sale of such brushes did not in fact in any way prevent Blackspur from continuing with its commercial activities and even considerably increasing its turnover during the financial year 1989/1990, the period immediately preceding the institution of the proceedings which led to its liquidation . . . Consequently . . ., it cannot be accepted that Blackspur' s liquidation was attributable to poor financial results occasioned by the discontinuance of its sales of Chinese brushes, depriving it of profits estimated by the applicants to be [GBP] 586 000, following the imposition of an anti-dumping duty on those brushes, and, even less so, to the allegedly unlawful conduct of the defendant institutions in connection with the imposition of that duty . . .

50. For that reason, the Court takes the view that the liquidation of Blackspur and the damage which may have resulted from this cannot be linked causally to the imposition of an anti-dumping duty on brushes originating in China or to the various unlawful acts which, according to the

---

[78] Ibid.

applicants, were committed by the defendant institutions in connection with the anti-dumping proceeding in question. Consequently, in the manifest absence of a causal link demonstrated by the applicants between the damage alleged and the ostensibly unlawful conduct of the Community institutions, the application for compensation brought by Blackspur must be dismissed."

Notes

(1) These two cases have been chosen for inclusion here because they provide a clear application, by the CFI, of the case law of the Court of Justice on liability for legislative acts under Article 288(2) EC.

In *Nölle*, the CFI first inquired whether there was a fault on the part of the Community institutions. That inquiry involved revisiting the ECJ judgment that had annulled Regulation 725/89.[79] It will be recalled that that judgment was rendered in the course of a preliminary ruling under Article 234 EC, following a reference by a German court before which Nölle was sued for payment of the anti-dumping duties. Within the framework of Article 234, the ECJ was concerned with answering the questions of the German court on the validity of Regulation 725/89, and not with the position of Nölle *vis-à-vis* the Community institutions. In the action for damages under Article 288 EC, the CFI therefore had to see whether the mistake made by the Community institutions, as found by the ECJ in the preliminary ruling, also constituted a fault, actionable at the suit of the applicant Nölle. That mistake had consisted in the failure properly to consider the evidence in relation to the choice of the reference country for the purposes of the anti-dumping investigation.[80] Here again, the notion of duty of care underpins the reasoning of the Court. The Court rejected the arguments based on Article 253 EC (duty to give reasons), the right to a fair hearing or misuse of powers. It found however that the mistake made by the Community institutions in the determination of the reference country constituted a breach of the principle of care and proper administration.

Having found a breach, the CFI then moved to the next stage, namely whether the breach was sufficiently serious, and applied the standard of "manifest and grave disregard for the limits of the powers of the Community institution" in question. The CFI has no difficulty in finding that the breach fell short of constituting such disregard.

The CFI did not need to examine the other conditions of the *Schöppenstedt* test, namely whether the right that was infringed was a superior rule of law for the protection of the individual.[81]

In *Blackspur*, the CFI dismissed the action on the issue of causation alone (i.e. without examining the nature of the breach). It is worth comparing *Blackspur* with *Brummelhuis-Leussink*[82] on this point. In the latter case, the burden of proof in relation to the cause of the accident was held to lie on the Commission, since the relevant facts were primarily within its knowledge and an explanation for the accident was required. By contrast, in *Blackspur*, the CFI held that it was for the applicant to present clear evidence of a causal

---

[79] Case C-16/90, *Nölle v. Hauptzollamt Bremen-Freihafen* [1991] ECR I-5163.

[80] In cases where the country of origin is not a market-economy country, the reference country is used to establish the normal value against which the export price is compared to see if there has been dumping. See Art. 2.A.7 of Regulation 384/96 on protection against dumped imports from countries not members of the European Community, [1996] OJ L 56/1.

[81] See *supra*, 9.1., Introductory Note under b).

[82] *Supra*, **9.EC.1.**

link between the legislative act and the damage that the applicant had suffered. It seems that on the evidence in *Blackspur*, no causal link could be established. *Blackspur* thus examplifies the difficulty likely to be encountered by an applicant who, on the basis of Article 288 EC, seeks compensation from the Community for the loss that the applicant claims to have suffered because of improper legislative action by a Community institution: in most such cases, the complexity of the economic policy decisions underlying the legislative action will make it difficult for the applicant to establish the necessary degree of fault on the part of the Community institution; and in addition the complexity of the economic situation, in the context of which the applicant's loss occurred, will make it difficult for the applicant to establish, as is needed, the causal link between the legislative action and the applicant's loss.

(2) The applicant in *Nölle* proposed an improvement on the "bright line" test in *Schöppenstedt*, whereby the mere fact that a decision involved economic policy considerations suffices to raise the fault standard to "a sufficiently serious breach". It insisted on the particular nature of anti-dumping proceedings, where on the one hand complex economic factors come into play, but on the other hand the interests of individual parties are so intimately concerned[83] that a fairly developed set of procedural rules has been put in place to protect their respective rights.[84] The applicant proposed not to apply the *Schöppenstedt* standard and instead to use the "normal" standard when the alleged violation stems from a breach of a procedural or administrative rule (right of defence, etc.), as opposed to a breach occurring in the economic assessment. The CFI did not, however, accept this refinement on *Schöppenstedt*.

9.1.3. LIABILITY ON THE PART OF MEMBER STATES FOR BREACHES OF COMMUNITY LAW

ECJ, 5 March 1996[85] **9.EC.6.**
Joined Cases C-46/93 and C-48/93, Brasserie du Pêcheur SA v. Germany,
R. v. Secretary of State for Transport, ex p. Factortame

SCOPE AND CONDITIONS OF LIABILITY ON THE PART OF MEMBER STATES FOR BREACHES OF COMMUNITY LAW

German beer law. UK shipping law

Liability on the part of Member States for breaches of Community law is an inherent principle of Community law, applicable to breaches of all descriptions. In areas where the

---

[83] This can be seen in the fact that even if anti-dumping determinations take the form of regulations, in general all parties involved in the proceedings will have standing to challenge the determination: CFI, Judgment of 11 July 1996, Case T-161/94, *Sinochem Heilongjiang v. Council* [1996] ECR II-695.

[84] Following the WTO Agreement of 1994, the procedural framework has been greatly expanded and formalized: see Regulation 384/96 on protection against dumped imports from countries not members of the European Community, [1996] OJ L 56/1.

[85] [1996] ECR I-1029.

Member States enjoy legislative discretion, the conditions for liability are (i) the infringed provision of Community law was intended to confer rights on individuals, (ii) the breach is sufficiently serious and (iii) there is a causal link between the breach and the damage suffered.

Facts: Case C-46/93: A French brewery, Brasserie du Pêcheur, was forced to cease exporting beer to Germany because its beer did not comply with the *Reinheitsgebot* (purity requirement) of the *Biersteuergesetz* (German Beer Law), although it complied with French legal requirements. The Commission acted on this and brought infringement proceedings against Germany. In a judgment of 12 March 1987, the ECJ condemned Germany for having contravened Article 28 EC (prohibition of quantitative restrictions on imports and measures having equivalent effect).[86] Brasserie du Pêcheur then brought proceedings in the German courts, claiming damages from the German government to compensate it for the loss suffered due to the breach of the EC Treaty; in the course of the proceedings, the BGH requested from the ECJ a preliminary ruling on the liability of Member States for breaches of Community law.

Case C-48/93: Factortame, a United Kingdom company owned by Spanish shareholders, was prevented from registering its fishing vessels (and hence from fishing under the United Kingdom flag) because the Merchant Shipping Act 1988 imposed conditions on registration relating to the nationality, residence and domicile of the owners of the vessels. In infringement proceedings brought by the Commission, the ECJ found that the impugned provisions of the Act were contrary to Article 43 EC (prohibition on restrictions to freedom of establishment).[87] Factortame brought proceedings against the British Government in the English courts, claiming both compensatory and exemplary damages. The Divisional Court referred preliminary questions to the ECJ.

Held: The principle of State liability for breaches of Community law enunciated in the case law of the ECJ is applicable where the breach originates in an action taken by a national legislature. Even in a field where Member States enjoy wide discretion, individuals suffering loss are entitled to reparation if (i) the Community rule which was infringed is intended to confer rights upon them, (ii) the breach is sufficiently serious and (iii) there is a causal link between breach and damage. If the three conditions are satisfied, reparation of the damage must be made by the Member State and must be commensurate with the loss or damage sustained.

Judgment: **"State liability for acts and omissions of the national legislature contrary to Community law.**

16. By their first questions, each of the two national courts essentially seeks to establish whether the principle that Member States are obliged to make good damage caused to individuals by breaches of Community law attributable to the State is applicable where the national legislature was responsible for the infringement in question.

17. In Joined Cases C-6/90 and C-9/90 *Francovich and others* [1991] ECR I-5357, paragraph 37, the Court held that it is a principle of Community law that Member States are obliged to make good loss and damage caused to individuals by breaches of Community law for which they can be held responsible . . .

20. The Court has consistently held that the right of individuals to rely on the directly effective provisions of the Treaty before national courts is only a minimum guarantee and is not sufficient in itself to ensure the full and complete implementation of the Treaty [references omitted]. The purpose of that right is to ensure that provisions of Community law prevail over national provisions. It cannot, in every case, secure for individuals the benefit of the rights conferred on them by Community law and, in particular, avoid their sustaining damage as a result of a breach of Community law attributable to a Member State. As appears from paragraph 33 of the judgment in *Francovich and others*, the full effectiveness of Community law would be impaired if individuals were unable to obtain redress when their rights were infringed by a breach of Community law.

21. This will be so where an individual who is a victim of the non-transposition of a directive and is precluded from relying on certain of its provisions directly before the national court because

---

[86] Case 178/84, *Commission v. Germany* [1987] ECR 1227.

[87] ECJ, Judgment of 25 July 1991, Case C-221/89, *R. v. Secretary of State for Transport, ex parte Factortame Ltd. a.o.* [1991] ECR I-3905; also ECJ, Judgment of 4 October 1991, Case C-246/89, *Commission v. United Kingdom* [1991] ECR I-4585.

they are insufficiently precise and unconditional, brings an action for damages against the defaulting Member State for breach of the third paragraph of Article [249] of the Treaty. In such circumstances, which obtained in the case of *Francovich and others*, the purpose of reparation is to redress the injurious consequences of a Member State's failure to transpose a directive as far as beneficiaries of that directive are concerned.

22. It is all the more so in the event of infringement of a right directly conferred by a Community provision upon which individuals are entitled to rely before the national courts. In that event, the right to reparation is the necessary corollary of the direct effect of the Community provision whose breach caused the damage sustained.

23. In this case, it is undisputed that the Community provisions at issue, namely Article [28] of the Treaty in Case C-46/93 and Article [43] in Case C-48/93, have direct effect in the sense that they confer on individuals rights upon which they are entitled to rely directly before the national courts. Breach of such provisions may give rise to reparation . . .

29. The principle of the non-contractual liability of the Community expressly laid down in Article [288] of the Treaty is simply an expression of the general principle familiar to the legal systems of the Member States that an unlawful act or omission gives rise to an obligation to make good the damage caused. That provision also reflects the obligation on public authorities to make good damage caused in the performance of their duties . . .

31. In view of the foregoing considerations, the Court held in *Francovich and others*, at paragraph 35, that the principle of State liability for loss and damage caused to individuals as a result of breaches of Community law for which it can be held responsible is inherent in the system of the Treaty.

32. It follows that that principle holds good for any case in which a Member State breaches Community law, whatever be the organ of the State whose act or omission was responsible for the breach.

33. In addition, in view of the fundamental requirement of the Community legal order that Community law be uniformly applied (see, in particular, Joined Cases C-143/88 and C-92/89 *Zuckerfabrik Süderdithmarschen and Zuckerfabrik Soest* [1991] ECR I-415, paragraph 26), the obligation to make good damage caused to individuals by breaches of Community law cannot depend on domestic rules as to the division of powers between constitutional authorities.

34. As the Advocate General points out in paragraph 38 of his Opinion, in international law a State whose liability for breach of an international commitment is in issue will be viewed as a single entity, irrespective of whether the breach which gave rise to the damage is attributable to the legislature, the judiciary or the executive. This must apply *a fortiori* in the Community legal order since all State authorities, including the legislature, are bound in performing their tasks to comply with the rules laid down by Community law directly governing the situation of individuals.

35. The fact that, according to national rules, the breach complained of is attributable to the legislature cannot affect the requirements inherent in the protection of the rights of individuals who rely on Community law and, in this instance, the right to obtain redress in the national courts for damage caused by that breach.

36. Consequently, the reply to the national courts must be that the principle that Member States are obliged to make good damage caused to individuals by breaches of Community law attributable to the State is applicable where the national legislature was responsible for the breach in question.

Conditions under which the State may incur liability for acts and omissions of the national legislature contrary to Community law

37. By these questions, the national courts ask the Court to specify the conditions under which a right to reparation of loss or damage caused to individuals by breaches of Community law

attributable to a Member State is, in the particular circumstances, guaranteed by Community law.

38. Although Community law imposes State liability, the conditions under which that liability gives rise to a right to reparation depend on the nature of the breach of Community law giving rise to the loss and damage (*Francovich and others*, paragraph 38).

39. In order to determine those conditions, account should first be taken of the principles inherent in the Community legal order which form the basis for State liability, namely, first, the full effectiveness of Community rules and the effective protection of the rights which they confer and, second, the obligation to cooperate imposed on Member States by Article [10] of the Treaty (*Francovich and others*, paragraphs 31 to 36).

40. In addition, as the Commission and the several governments which submitted observations have emphasized, it is pertinent to refer to the Court's case-law on non-contractual liability on the part of the Community.

41. First, the second paragraph of Article [288] of the Treaty refers, as regards the non-contractual liability of the Community, to the general principles common to the laws of the Member States, from which, in the absence of written rules, the Court also draws inspiration in other areas of Community law.

42. Second, the conditions under which the State may incur liability for damage caused to individuals by a breach of Community law cannot, in the absence of particular justification, differ from those governing the liability of the Community in like circumstances. The protection of the rights which individuals derive from Community law cannot vary depending on whether a national authority or a Community authority is responsible for the damage.

43. The system of rules which the Court has worked out with regard to Article [288] of the Treaty, particularly in relation to liability for legislative measures, takes into account, inter alia, the complexity of the situations to be regulated, difficulties in the application or interpretation of the texts and, more particularly, the margin of discretion available to the author of the act in question.

44. Thus, in developing its case-law on the non-contractual liability of the Community, in particular as regards legislative measures involving choices of economic policy, the Court has had regard to the wide discretion available to the institutions in implementing Community policies.

45. The strict approach taken towards the liability of the Community in the exercise of its legislative activities is due to two considerations. First, even where the legality of measures is subject to judicial review, exercise of the legislative function must not be hindered by the prospect of actions for damages whenever the general interest of the Community requires legislative measures to be adopted which may adversely affect individual interests. Second, in a legislative context characterized by the exercise of a wide discretion, which is essential for implementing a Community policy, the Community cannot incur liability unless the institution concerned has manifestly and gravely disregarded the limits on the exercise of its powers (Joined Cases 83/76, 94/76, 4/77, 15/77 and 40/77 *HNL and others* v *Council and Commission* [1978] ECR 1209, paragraphs 5 and 6).

46. That said, the national legislature—like the Community institutions—does not systematically have a wide discretion when it acts in a field governed by Community law. Community law may impose upon it obligations to achieve a particular result or obligations to act or refrain from acting which reduce its margin of discretion, sometimes to a considerable degree. This is so, for instance, where, as in the circumstances to which the judgment in *Francovich and others* relates, Article [249] of the Treaty places the Member State under an obligation to take, within a given period, all the measures needed in order to achieve the result required by a directive. In such a case, the fact that it is for the national legislature to take the necessary measures has no bearing on the Member State's liability for failing to transpose the directive.

47. In contrast, where a Member State acts in a field where it has a wide discretion, comparable

to that of the Community institutions in implementing Community policies, the conditions under which it may incur liability must, in principle, be the same as those under which the Community institutions incur liability in a comparable situation.

48. In the case which gave rise to the reference in Case C-46/93, the German legislature had legislated in the field of foodstuffs, specifically beer. In the absence of Community harmonization, the national legislature had a wide discretion in that sphere in laying down rules on the quality of beer put on the market.

49. As regards the facts of Case C-48/93, the United Kingdom legislature also had a wide discretion. The legislation at issue was concerned, first, with the registration of vessels, a field which, in view of the state of development of Community law, falls within the jurisdiction of the Member States and, secondly, with regulating fishing, a sector in which implementation of the common fisheries policy leaves a margin of discretion to the Member States.

50. Consequently, in each case the German and United Kingdom legislatures were faced with situations involving choices comparable to those made by the Community institutions when they adopt legislative measures pursuant to a Community policy.

51. In such circumstances, Community law confers a right to reparation where three conditions are met: the rule of law infringed must be intended to confer rights on individuals; the breach must be sufficiently serious; and there must be a direct causal link between the breach of the obligation resting on the State and the damage sustained by the injured parties.

52. Firstly, those conditions satisfy the requirements of the full effectiveness of the rules of Community law and of the effective protection of the rights which those rules confer.

53. Secondly, those conditions correspond in substance to those defined by the Court in relation to Article [288] in its case-law on liability of the Community for damage caused to individuals by unlawful legislative measures adopted by its institutions.

54. The first condition is manifestly satisfied in the case of Article [28] of the Treaty, the relevant provision in Case C-46/93, and in the case of Article [43], the relevant provision in Case C-48/93. Whilst Article [28] imposes a prohibition on Member States, it nevertheless gives rise to rights for individuals which the national courts must protect [reference omitted]. Likewise, the essence of Article [43] is to confer rights on individuals [reference omitted].

55. As to the second condition, as regards both Community liability under Article [288] and Member State liability for breaches of Community law, the decisive test for finding that a breach of Community law is sufficiently serious is whether the Member State or the Community institution concerned manifestly and gravely disregarded the limits on its discretion.

56. The factors which the competent court may take into consideration include the clarity and precision of the rule breached, the measure of discretion left by that rule to the national or Community authorities, whether the infringement and the damage caused was intentional or involuntary, whether any error of law was excusable or inexcusable, the fact that the position taken by a Community institution may have contributed towards the omission, and the adoption or retention of national measures or practices contrary to Community law.

57. On any view, a breach of Community law will clearly be sufficiently serious if it has persisted despite a judgment finding the infringement in question to be established, or a preliminary ruling or settled case-law of the Court on the matter from which it is clear that the conduct in question constituted an infringement.

[The ECJ then applies these criteria to the two cases at bar and goes on to discuss the third condition for liability on the part of Member States.] . . .

65. As for the third condition, it is for the national courts to determine whether there is a direct causal link between the breach of the obligation borne by the State and the damage sustained by the injured parties.

66. The aforementioned three conditions are necessary and sufficient to found a right in

individuals to obtain redress, although this does not mean that the State cannot incur liability under less strict conditions on the basis of national law.

67. As appears from paragraphs 41, 42 and 43 of *Francovich and others*, cited above, subject to the right to reparation which flows directly from Community law where the conditions referred to in the preceding paragraph are satisfied, the State must make reparation for the consequences of the loss and damage caused in accordance with the domestic rules on liability, provided that the conditions for reparation of loss and damage laid down by national law must not be less favourable than those relating to similar domestic claims and must not be such as in practice to make it impossible or excessively difficult to obtain reparation (see also Case 199/82 *Amministrazione delle Finanze dello Stato* v *San Giorgio* [1983] ECR 3595).

68. In that regard, restrictions that exist in domestic legal systems as to the non-contractual liability of the State in the exercise of its legislative function may be such as to make it impossible in practice or excessively difficult for individuals to exercise their right to reparation, as guaranteed by Community law, of loss or damage resulting from the breach of Community law.

69. In Case C-46/93 the national court asks in particular whether national law may subject any right to compensation to the same restrictions as apply where a law is in breach of higher-ranking national provisions, for instance, where an ordinary Federal law infringes the *Grundgesetz* of the Federal Republic of Germany.

70. While the imposition of such restrictions may be consistent with the requirement that the conditions laid down should not be less favourable than those relating to similar domestic claims, it is still to be considered whether such restrictions are not such as in practice to make it impossible or excessively difficult to obtain reparation.

71. The condition imposed by German law where a law is in breach of higher-ranking national provisions, which makes reparation dependent upon the legislature's act or omission being referable to an individual situation, would in practice make it impossible or extremely difficult to obtain effective reparation for loss or damage resulting from a breach of Community law, since the tasks falling to the national legislature relate, in principle, to the public at large and not to identifiable persons or classes of person.

72. Since such a condition stands in the way of the obligation on national courts to ensure the full effectiveness of Community law by guaranteeing effective protection for the rights of individuals, it must be set aside where an infringement of Community law is attributable to the national legislature.

73. Likewise, any condition that may be imposed by English law on State liability requiring proof of misfeasance in public office, such an abuse of power being inconceivable in the case of the legislature, is also such as in practice to make it impossible or extremely difficult to obtain effective reparation for loss or damage resulting from a breach of Community law where the breach is attributable to the national legislature.

74. Accordingly, the reply to the questions from the national courts must be that, where a breach of Community law by a Member State is attributable to the national legislature acting in a field in which it has a wide discretion to make legislative choices, individuals suffering loss or injury thereby are entitled to reparation where the rule of Community law breached is intended to confer rights upon them, the breach is sufficiently serious and there is a direct causal link between the breach and the damage sustained by the individuals. Subject to that reservation, the State must make good the consequences of the loss or damage caused by the breach of Community law attributable to it, in accordance with its national law on liability. However, the conditions laid down by the applicable national laws must not be less favourable than those relating to similar domestic claims or framed in such a way as in practice to make it impossible or excessively difficult to obtain reparation.

The possibility of making reparation conditional upon the existence of fault

75. By its third question, the Bundesgerichtshof essentially seeks to establish whether, pursuant to the national legislation which it applies, the national court is entitled to make reparation conditional upon the existence of fault (whether intentional or negligent) on the part of the organ of the State to which the infringement is attributable.

76. ... [T]he concept of fault does not have the same content in the various legal systems.

77. Next, it follows from the reply to the preceding question that, where a breach of Community law is attributable to a Member State acting in a field in which it has a wide discretion to make legislative choices, a finding of a right to reparation on the basis of Community law will be conditional, *inter alia*, upon the breach having been sufficiently serious.

78. So, certain objective and subjective factors connected with the concept of fault under a national legal system may well be relevant for the purpose of determining whether or not a given breach of Community law is serious (see the factors mentioned in paragraphs 56 and 57 above).

79. The obligation to make reparation for loss or damage caused to individuals cannot, however, depend upon a condition based on any concept of fault going beyond that of a sufficiently serious breach of Community law. Imposition of such a supplementary condition would be tantamount to calling in question the right to reparation founded on the Community legal order.

80. Accordingly, the reply to the question from the national court must be that, pursuant to the national legislation which it applies, reparation of loss or damage cannot be made conditional upon fault (intentional or negligent) on the part of the organ of the State responsible for the breach, going beyond that of a sufficiently serious breach of Community law.

The actual extent of the reparation

81. By these questions, the national courts essentially ask the Court to identify the criteria for determination of the extent of the reparation due by the Member State responsible for the breach.

82. Reparation for loss or damage caused to individuals as a result of breaches of Community law must be commensurate with the loss or damage sustained so as to ensure the effective protection for their rights.

83. In the absence of relevant Community provisions, it is for the domestic legal system of each Member State to set the criteria for determining the extent of reparation. However, those criteria must not be less favourable than those applying to similar claims based on domestic law and must not be such as in practice to make it impossible or excessively difficult to obtain reparation.

84. In particular, in order to determine the loss or damage for which reparation may be granted, the national court may inquire whether the injured person showed reasonable diligence in order to avoid the loss or damage or limit its extent and whether, in particular, he availed himself in time of all the legal remedies available to him.

85. Indeed, it is a general principle common to the legal systems of the Member States that the injured party must show reasonable diligence in limiting the extent of the loss or damage, or risk having to bear the damage himself (Joined Cases C-104/89 and C-37/90 *Mulder and others* v *Council and Commission* [1992] ECR I-3061, paragraph 33).

86. The Bundesgerichtshof asks whether national legislation may generally limit the obligation to make reparation to damage done to certain, specifically protected individual interests, for example property, or whether it should also cover loss of profit by the claimants. It states that the opportunity to market products from other Member States is not regarded in German law as forming part of the protected assets of the undertaking.

87. Total exclusion of loss of profit as a head of damage for which reparation may be awarded in the case of a breach of Community law cannot be accepted. Especially in the context of economic or commercial litigation, such a total exclusion of loss of profit would be such as to make reparation of damage practically impossible.

88. As for the various heads of damage referred to in the Divisional Court's second question, Community law imposes no specific criteria. It is for the national court to rule on those heads of damage in accordance with the domestic law which it applies, subject to the requirements set out in paragraph 83 above.

89. As regards in particular the award of exemplary damages, such damages are based under domestic law, as the Divisional Court explains, on the finding that the public authorities concerned acted oppressively, arbitrarily or unconstitutionally. In so far as such conduct may constitute or aggravate a breach of Community law, an award of exemplary damages pursuant to a claim or an action founded on Community law cannot be ruled out if such damages could be awarded pursuant to a similar claim or action founded on domestic law.

90. Accordingly, the reply to the national courts must be that reparation by Member States of loss or damage which they have caused to individuals as a result of breaches of Community law must be commensurate with the loss or damage sustained. In the absence of relevant Community provisions, it is for the domestic legal system of each Member State to set the criteria for determining the extent of reparation. However, those criteria must not be less favourable than those applying to similar claims or actions based on domestic law and must not be such as in practice to make it impossible or excessively difficult to obtain reparation. National legislation which generally limits the damage for which reparation may be granted to damage done to certain, specifically protected individual interests not including loss of profit by individuals is not compatible with Community law. Moreover, it must be possible to award specific damages, such as the exemplary damages provided for by English law, pursuant to claims or actions founded on Community law, if such damages may be awarded pursuant to similar claims or actions founded on domestic law."

Notes

(1) The significance of the *Brasserie du Pêcheur* judgment, not only as regards liability on the part of Member States for breaches of Community law, but also with respect to the development of a common law of Europe, cannot be overstated.[88]

In the judgment, the Court decided or clarified many issues relating to the Community tort law regime for liability on the part of Member States.

First, following *Francovich* in 1991, a debate arose as to the role and significance of the principle of liability on the part of Member States within the overall framework of judicial protection in Community law. Some were of the opinion that *Francovich* in fact created a sort of subsidiary or residual recourse in cases where the doctrine of direct effect could not be used by an individual to derive the benefits which he or she would have obtained from a proper and timely implementation of a directive; in other cases, Community law would simply leave the issue of liability to the laws of the various Member States. That position was defended by the German, Irish and Netherlands Governments before the ECJ in *Brasserie du Pêcheur*. The ECJ explicitly took the opposite position at paragraphs 20 to 22 above. According to the ECJ, the principle of liability of the part of Member States for breaches of Community law is a general principle applicable to all cases where a Member State infringes Community law, whether the breach concerns a provision of the EC Treaty or of a regulation or the implementation of a directive.[89] *Francovich* is thus but a special case of a more general principle, which in

---

[88] To name but one comment on *Brasserie du Pêcheur* and several subsequent judgments, P. Oliver "A Court of Justice" (1997) 34 CMLRev 635.

[89] Governed by Art. 249(3) EC Treaty.

Brasserie du Pêcheur is applied for the first time by the ECJ to a different situation, namely a breach of a directly effective provision of the EC Treaty.[90]

(2) In *Brasserie du Pêcheur*, the Court also addresses the argument advanced by Germany, among others, that a broad Community principle of liability on the part of Member States for breaches of Community law would be incompatible with the constitutional orders of the Member States, which often do not provide for, or severely limit, the liability of the legislature (and often also the judiciary). It is interesting to note that, in order to refute that argument, the ECJ draws on international law, where the State is liable internationally for the actions of all its organs without exception and without distinction.[91] The ECJ could also have invoked its long-standing case law under Article 226 EC, according to which a Member State cannot oppose the provisions of its internal legal order to justify its failure to comply with Community law.

(3) A key element in *Brasserie du Pêcheur*, as mentioned above, is the relationship between liability of the part of Member States under the *Francovich* principle and Community liability under Article 288(2) EC.[92] In his Opinion in *Brasserie du Pêcheur*, Advocate General Tesauro discussed the issue at length and reviewed the arguments raised on both sides.[93] As was seen above, the Community tortious liability regime of Article 288(2) EC can properly be characterized as fairly restrictive: the criteria for Community liability, in particular the *Schöppenstedt* test as it applies to the broadly defined class of "economic policy" measures, make it very difficult for applicants to succeed.[94] Advocate General Tesauro himself recognized this, and expressed dissatisfaction with the current state of the case law of Article 288(2) EC, which he links to an overly deferential attitude towards the legislature. He stated that "the application of [the *Schöppenstedt*] approach, however, in a good few cases had made for perplexity".[95] Yet in the end Advocate-General Tesauro ventured the opinion that it is more important that the conditions for liability on the part of the Community and Member States be harmonized. Any other result would hardly be reconcilable with the rule of law, since the compensation which an individual could obtain for a breach of Community law would then depend on whether the Community or a Member State committed the breach. Nonetheless, Advocate-General Tesauro advocated a more subtle application of the Article 288(2) case law, whereby the ECJ would recognize that the *Schöppenstedt* test had been too widely applied to the Community in situations where it was arguable that the

---

[90] Art. 28 EC in *Brasserie du Pêcheur* and Art. 43 EC in *Factortame*, in that case.

[91] Similarly, in a federation, the federal State cannot plead its internal constitutional provision to escape liability for breaches committed by the local entities. However, this does not mean that the federal State must necessarily pay compensation for the breaches committed by those entities, if those entities are already liable for the consequences of their own breaches of Community law. See ECJ, Judgment of 1 June 1999, Case C–302/97, *Konle v. Austria* [1999] ECR I–3099. See *infra*, the discussion of international law, in particular the *Diplomatic and Consular Staff in Tehran* case, **9.INT.11.**

[92] See *supra*, 9.2., Introductory Note under c).

[93] See Opinion of Advocate-General Tesauro, 28 November 1995, Joined Cases C-46/93 and C-48/93 [1996] ECR I-1029.

[94] *Supra*, **9.EC.1.–5.**

[95] Opinion of Advocate-General Tesauro, 28 November 1995, Joined Cases C-46/93 and C-48/93 [1996] ECR I-1029 at para. 64. In this context, Advocate General Tesauro picks up with apparent approval the argument raised by the applicants in *Nölle*, *supra*, **9.EC.4.**, Note (2) that the application of the *Schöppenstedt* test should depend not only on the nature of the decision made but also on the nature of the breach.

Community action involved the kind of legislative discretion contemplated in *Schöppenstedt* and that Member States often have less discretion than the Community when they act under Community law.

The ECJ did not completely follow the suggestions of its Advocate-General. At para. 45, the Court acknowledged that the conditions of liability of the part of the Community and Member States could not be different. Yet it merely restated the rationale behind the *Schöppenstedt* test (the prospect of liability could hinder the exercise of legislative power in the general interest and the legislative organs enjoy wide discretion). Then the Court at paras. 46–7 finds that Member States may have a lesser margin of discretion, but it barely mentions that in certain instances this may apply to Community institutions as well. The seeds of an about-turn on the extensive application of the *Schöppenstedt* test to Community institutions may have been sown, but they have not yet ostensibly matured in *Brasserie du Pêcheur*. Furthermore, in applying its statements to the facts of the two cases before it, the ECJ at paras. 48 and 49 concluded that Germany and the United Kingdom both enjoyed considerable discretion in their action. The Court relied for that conclusion on the absence of harmonization at Community level in the fields concerned. On the other hand, it could have been argued that the provisions of the EC Treaty which were infringed[96] were so clear that they left little room for appreciation by the Member States.

(4) From a practical perspective, the most interesting part of the judgment is where the ECJ lays down the conditions for liability on the part of Member States. They are (i) the rule of law infringed must be intended to confer rights on individuals, (ii) the breach must be sufficiently serious[97] and (iii) there must be a causal link between the breach and the damage. It will be recalled that the Court found that in the two instant cases, the Member States in question (Germany and the United Kingdom respectively) enjoyed considerable discretion. As will be seen below, there are instances where the Member State was found to have less or no discretion.[98]

(i) The Court quickly found that the first condition was fulfilled in the case of Articles 28 and 43 EC. The first condition was discussed at greater length in *Dillenkofer*.[99]

(ii) As for the second condition, the Court provides a list of factors which may be examined in order to see whether the breach was sufficiently serious. A detailed analysis of each of these factors would be too lengthy here, and in fact they remain to be further developed by subsequent case law. It can be noted, however, that the Court specifically emphasizes one of these factors at para. 57 of the judgment: a persisting breach following an adverse judgment of the Court in and of itself constitutes a sufficiently serious breach; it must be added that, if the Member State is found to be in breach of its obligations pursuant to Article 227 EC, Article 228 EC provides for the possibility of fines as well.[100]

---

[96] Arts. 28 and 43 EC.

[97] The term "sufficiently serious" in English does not precisely correspond to the terms used in the other languages: see for instance *suffisamment caractérisé* in French or *hinreichend qualifiziert* in German.

[98] *Infra*, **9.EC.7.**, Note (1).

[99] *Infra*, **9.EC.7.**, Notes (3) and (4).

[100] The first proceedings under Art. 228(2) EC have been instituted by the Commission: see among others Cases C-121/97 and 122/97, *Commission v. Germany*.

Even if *Brasserie du Pêcheur* is a preliminary ruling—where the Court, as it recognizes explicitly at para. 58, cannot substitute its assessment for that of the national courts[101]—the ECJ nonetheless applied the factors outlined at para. 56 to the cases at bar. It found that, in Case C-46/93 (German Beer Law), in view of Article 28 EC and ECJ case law, Germany could hardly justify a prohibition on the use in Germany of the designation *"Bier"* for beers lawfully produced in other Member States. On the other hand, the German prohibition on certain additives in beer was less of a clear-cut case, at least until the ECJ ruled on the issue in 1987.[102] After the preliminary ruling of the ECJ, the BGH proceeded to decide the case on the basis of the ECJ judgment.[103] The BGH relied on the distinction made by the ECJ. It found that the action in damages by Brasserie du Pêcheur against Germany relied primarily on the refusal by German authorities to authorize the marketing of its products because of the additives that they contained. That being so, the BGH recalled that the ECJ had acknowledged that Germany enjoyed a wide measure of discretion. Accordingly, the BGH came to the conclusion that Germany had not committed a sufficiently serious breach of Community law in the period leading up to the judgment of the ECJ in 1987 for its liability to be engaged.

As far as Case C-48/93 is concerned, the ECJ found that the provisions of the United Kingdom Merchant Shipping Act 1988 which imposed restrictions on the ability to register vessels should be assessed differently depending on whether the restrictions related to nationality (a clear violation of Article 43 EC) or to residence and domicile (where there was more room to argue that the restrictions came within the exercise of legislative discretion). The case was considered by the English courts in light of the decision of the ECJ. In *Factortame (No. 5)*,[104] the House of Lords decided that the UK had committed a sufficiently serious breach within the meaning given by the ECJ with respect to the conditions relating to nationality, residence and domicile. The issue of causation was left open for later. The House of Lords accordingly did not distinguish between the conditions relating to nationality, on the one hand, and those relating to residence or domicile, on the other hand, even though the ECJ had hinted at such a distinction. In his speech, Lord Slynn of Hadley referred to the case law of the ECJ under 288(2) EC. In concluding that the breach was sufficiently serious, Lord Slynn emphasized that the provision at issue (Art. 28 EC) was clear and fundamental, that the UK government was not acting inadvertently and that the UK government had been warned by its own officials (and by the Commission) that the legislation would probably be contrary to EC law. Lord Hope of Craighead put forward three reasons why the breach was sufficiently serious: it concerned a central provision of the Treaty itself, there was a potential for obvious and immediate damage and the UK government used methods of achieving its policy which provided little protection to the interests of the claimants.

In *British Telecommunications*, the ECJ applied the factors listed in *Brasserie du Pêcheur*, and found that a good faith implementation of a directive which turned out to

---

101 Compare with ECJ, Judgment of 26 March 1996, Case C-392/93, *R. v. H.M. Treasury, ex p. British Telecommunications* [1996] ECR I-1631 at para. 41.
102 ECJ, Judgment of 12 March 1987, Case 178/84, *Commission v. Germany* [1987] ECR 1227.
103 BGH, 24 October 1996, EuZW 1996, 761, ZIP 1996, 2022.
104 *R. v. Secretary of State for Transport, ex p. Factortame (No. 5)* [1999] 3 WLR 1062, HL.

be incorrect did not constitute a sufficiently serious breach of Community law.[105] In support of that conclusion it stated that Article 8(1) of Directive 90/531 (at stake in that case) is "imprecisely worded and was reasonably capable of bearing, as well as the construction applied to it by the Court in this judgment, the interpretation given to it by the United Kingdom in good faith and on the basis of arguments which are not entirely devoid of substance . . . That interpretation, which was also shared by other Member States, was not manifestly contrary to the wording of the directive or to the objective pursued by it".[106] Indeed, one of the factors listed in *Brasserie du Pêcheur* is the clarity and precision of the infringed rule.

(iii) The Court expressly refers to national courts on the issue of causation, specifying only that the causal link must be "direct". Causation may in fact act as an important hurdle to the applicants.[107] In the BGH case concluding Case C-46/93, discussed above, the BGH relied on causation to dismiss the claims of Brasserie du Pêcheur for damage suffered after the ECJ had found in 1987 that the German law on additives in beer violated Article 28 EC, in the form of lower turnover, etc. The BGH took note that Brasserie du Pêcheur took all appropriate measures to ensure that German authorities complied with the 1987 ECJ judgment, and it reasoned then that any damage Brasserie du Pêcheur may have suffered after that judgment was due to the need to (re-)build a distribution network in Germany. It could not be linked to any breach by Germany after the judgment of the ECJ. Compensation for losses suffered after the judgment was accordingly denied.

In *R. v. Secretary of State for the Home Department, ex p. Gallagher*,[108] the Court of Appeal was dealing with a damages claim by Mr Gallagher in the aftermath of a preliminary ruling by the ECJ in Mr Gallagher's favour against the United Kingdom.[109] The Court of Appeal found that the breach committed by the United Kingdom in not implementing the relevant directive was sufficiently serious. The fate of the case turned on the issue of causation. Gallagher's argument was that the breach committed by the United Kingdom had deprived him of the chance to obtain a favourable decision on his stay in the United Kingdom.[110] The Court of Appeal found that in all likelihood the decision taken by the United Kingdom authorities would have been the same if the relevant directive had been correctly implemented, and denied any causal link.

Now that the House of Lords has decided, further to the annotated judgment, that the UK committed a sufficiently serious breach of Community law, it remains to be seen whether English courts will also decide that there was a direct causal link between those breaches and the damage sustained by the applicants. As stated above, that is a matter for the national courts to decide. It is noteworthy, however, that in two recent judgments, the ECJ proceeded to make a direct finding in respect of causation. In *Brinkmann*,[111] the ECJ held, on the basis of the information available to it, that there was no direct causal link,

---

[105] ECJ, Judgment of 26 March 1996, Case C-392/93, *R. v. H.M. Treasury, ex p. British Telecommunications* [1996] ECR I-1631.

[106] Ibid. at para. 43.

[107] For an examination of the problems related to causation from the perspective of English law, see F. Smith and L. Woods, "Causation in *Francovich*: The Neglected Problem" (1997) 46 ICLQ 925.

[108] [1996] 2 CMLRep 951, CA.

[109] ECJ, Judgment of 30 November 1995, Case C-175/94, [1995] ECR I-4253.

[110] Note the use of a "loss of a chance" type of argument in English law: see *supra*, **2.E.49.**

[111] ECJ, Judgment of 24 September 1998, Case C–319/96, *Brinkmann Tabakfabriken GmbH* v. *Skattenministeriet* [1998] ECR I–5255.

In *Rechberger*,[112] the ECJ held that, once the national court had found that there was a direct causal link between the breach committed by a Member State and the injury suffered by the claimant (as was the case), the liability of the Member State was not excluded by the act of a third party or the occurrence of exceptional or unforeseeable events which, if the directive concerned had been duly implemented by the Member State concerned, would not have hindered effective consumer protection under the directive.

(5) As mentioned at the outset, *Brasserie du Pêcheur* is also significant for the emergence of a common law of Europe. Indeed the ECJ articulates the relationship between national law and Community law in a way that opens many possibilities for mutual influence. Community liability under Article 288(2) EC is a matter exclusively for Community law, where the "general principles common to the laws of the Member States" serve as a background for what are ultimately rules of Community law.

The liability of Member States for breaches of Community law appears to involve an even subtler balance between Community law and national law.

Procedurally, this liability regime is applied not by the ECJ, but by the national courts, at the occasion of the application of preliminary rulings of the ECJ, according to the established cooperation framework of Article 234 EC.

Substantively, liability of the part of Member States for breaches of Community law is a Community law matter since *Francovich* at the latest. *Brasserie du Pêcheur* dispels any lingering doubts on the primacy of Community law in this area, as seen above. Yet the ECJ seems to want to limit the Community law rules on liability on the part of Member States to the minimum, and leave the matter to be settled according to national law to the greatest extent possible.[113] There is a clear parallel here with the "new approach" harmonization endeavours under Article 95 EC.[114] At para. 66 of the judgment, the Court concludes its review of the conditions for liability on the part of Member States by stating that liability must follow from the fulfilment of these conditions, but that national law can of course lead to liability for breaches of Community law under less stringent conditions. As laid out there, national law otherwise governs, as long as breaches of Community law are treated at least as favourably as breaches of national law and the effectiveness of Community law is not hindered.

Throughout its judgment, the ECJ dismisses the application of many rules of national law which it finds are likely to prevent individuals from deriving the full benefits of the Community law regime for liability on the part of Member States. Such is the case for:

- the German rule that compensation is allowable only if the legislative body was under a duty to the plaintiff or an identifiable group of which the plaintiff is a member (paras. 71–2);[115]
- the English rule requiring a proof akin to abuse of power for the tort of misfeasance of public office to be made out (para. 73);

---

[112] ECJ, Judgment of 15 June 1999, Case C–140/97, *Rechberger* v. *Austria* [1999] ECR I–3499.

[113] See for a clear example, ECJ, Judgment of 22 April 1997, Case C-66/95, *R.* v. *Secretary of State for Social Security, ex p. Sutton*, [1997] ECR I–2163.

[114] Especially since the advent of subsidiarity under Art. 5 (ex 3b) EC in 1993.

[115] *Drittbezogenheit*; see BGH, 29 March 1971, *supra*, Chapter III, **3.G.35.**

– the German hierarchy of protected interests at § 823 BGB, which generally leads to the exclusion of recovery for *Vermögensschaden* (paras. 87–8).[116]

On the other hand, the ECJ accepts that the award of exemplary damages under English law is compatible with the Community law regime for liability on the part of Member States, but it does not make it compulsory on other national laws to offer such a possibility (para. 89). If exemplary damages are possible for breaches of national law, however, they must also be allowable for breaches of Community law.

(6) That latter point leads to a last issue, namely whether *Brasserie du Pêcheur* will also contribute to the emergence of a common law of Europe through the feedback into national law of the principles developed in the Community law liability regimes. For instance, it is not inconceivable that, as a result of *Brasserie du Pêcheur*, Member States where acts or omissions of the legislature do not give rise to liability could contemplate introducing such liability for breaches of higher rules or principles of national law as well. Similarly, if German courts must abandon the system of protected interests at § 823 BGB (or if English courts must abandon their reluctance to compensate pure economic losses) in cases of liability for breaches of Community law, discussion may arise on the need to retain these restrictions for the liability of public authorities for violations of German law (or English law). The impact of Community liability rules on national liability regimes need not always lead to a potentially increased liability of public authorities. For example, it may well be that national courts or legislatures draw inspiration from Community law and adopt the criterion of sufficiently serious breach when reviewing the conduct of public authorities in certain areas.

(7) In *Brasserie du Pêcheur* the impact of Community law relating to liability of Member States upon the national legal systems concerned the application of rules of a substantive nature, i.e. the conditions for liability to arise. The impact of Community law is also apparent in respect of national rules of a procedural nature, such as e.g. national limitation periods. In this respect, as seen above, the ECJ also favours the approach that the matter should be settled according to national law to the greatest extent possible subject, however, to the requirement that rules applicable to Community cases cannot be less favourable than those relating to similar actions of a domestic nature, and that the rules applied cannot make it impossible in practice to exercise the relevant community rights.[117]

---

[116] *Supra*, Chapter I, **1.G.27.**, and Chapter II, 2.3.2.

[117] For a general overview, see M. Hoskins, "Tilting the Balance: Supremacy and National Procedural Rules" (1996) 21 ELRev 365. For a recent application relating to State liability, see three ECJ judgments of 10 July 1997 in Case C-261/95, *Palmisani* v. *INPS* [1997] ECR I-4025 at para. 23 ff., Cases C-94/95 and 95/95, *Bonifaci* v. *INPS* [1997] ECR I-3969 at para. 45 ff. and Case C-373/95, *Maso* v. *INPS* [1997] ECR I-4051 at para. 33 ff.

ECJ, 8 October 1996[118]   **9.EC.7.**
Joined Cases C-178, C-179, C-188, C-189 and C-190/94, Dillenkofer v. Germany

LEGISLATIVE DISCRETION OF MEMBER STATES. CONFERRING RIGHTS ON INDIVIDUALS

Stranded travellers

Failure to do anything to implement a directive constitutes a sufficiently serious breach of Community law. The intention to confer rights on individuals is to be assessed from the whole of the provision in question, both in letter and in spirit.

Facts: Directive 90/314 required Member States to introduce in their national laws by 31 December 1992 a requirement for organizers and retailers of travel packages to constitute security for the refund of money paid by customers and for their repatriation in case of insolvency.[119] Germany implemented the Directive through the Act of 24 June 1994 with effect as of 1 July 1994.[120] Dillenkofer and the other plaintiffs in the case lost their advance payments or had to pay for repatriation following the bankruptcy of two tour operators in 1993. They brought actions for damages against Germany for breach of Community law in failing to implement Directive 90/314 on time. The court of first instance in Germany referred preliminary questions to the ECJ.

Held: Failure to take any measure to transpose a directive in order to achieve the result it prescribes within the period laid down for that purpose constitutes per se a serious breach of Community law and consequently gives rise to a right of reparation for individuals suffering injury if the result prescribed by the directive entails the grant to individuals of rights whose content is identifiable and a causal link exists between the breach of the State's obligation and the loss and damage suffered.

The result prescribed by Article 7 of Council Directive 90/314/EEC of 13 June 1990 on package travel, package holidays and package tours entails the grant to package travellers of rights guaranteeing a refund of money paid over and their repatriation in the event of the organizer's insolvency; the content of those rights is sufficiently identifiable.

Judgment: **"Conditions under which a Member State incurs liability**

16. The crux of these questions is whether a failure to transpose a directive within the prescribed period is sufficient per se to afford individuals who have suffered injury a right to reparation or whether other conditions must also be taken into consideration . . .

20. The Court has held that the principle of State liability for loss and damage caused to individuals as a result of breaches of Community law for which the State can be held responsible is inherent in the system of the Treaty (*Francovich*, paragraph 35; Joined Cases C-46/93 and C-48/93 *Brasserie du Pêcheur and Factortame* [1996] ECR I-1029, paragraph 31; Case C-392/93 *British Telecommunications* [1996] ECR I-1631, paragraph 38; and Case C-5/94 *Hedley Lomas* [1996] ECR I-2553, paragraph 24). Furthermore, the Court has held that the conditions under which State liability gives rise to a right to reparation depend on the nature of the breach of Community law giving rise to the loss and damage (*Francovich*, paragraph 38; *Brasserie du Pêcheur and Factortame*, paragraph 38, and *Hedley Lomas*, paragraph 24).

21. In *Brasserie du Pêcheur and Factortame*, at paragraphs 50 and 51, *British Telecommunications*, at paragraphs 39 and 40, and *Hedley Lomas*, at paragraphs 25 and 26, the Court, having regard to the circumstances of the case, held that individuals who have suffered damage have a right to reparation where three conditions are met: the rule of law infringed must have been intended to confer rights on individuals; the breach must be sufficiently serious; and there must be a direct causal link between the breach of the obligation resting on the State and the damage sustained by the injured parties.

[118] [1996] ECR I-4845.
[119] Directive 90/314 of 13 June 1990 on package travel, package holidays and package tours [1990] OJ L 158/59.
[120] BGBl.I.1322.

22. Moreover, it is clear from the *Francovich* case which, like these cases, concerned non-transposition of a directive within the prescribed period, that the full effectiveness of the third paragraph of Article [249] of the Treaty requires that there should be a right to reparation where the result prescribed by the directive entails the grant of rights to individuals, the content of those rights is identifiable on the basis of the provisions of the directive and a causal link exists between the breach of the State's obligation and the loss and damage suffered by the injured parties.

23. In substance, the conditions laid down in that group of judgments are the same, since the condition that there should be a sufficiently serious breach, although not expressly mentioned in *Francovich*, was nevertheless evident from the circumstances of that case.

24. When the Court held that the conditions under which State liability gives rise to a right to reparation depended on the nature of the breach of Community law causing the damage, that meant that those conditions are to be applied according to each type of situation.

25. On the one hand, a breach of Community law is sufficiently serious if a Community institution or a Member State, in the exercise of its rule-making powers, manifestly and gravely disregards the limits on those powers (see Joined Cases 83/76, 94/76, 4/77, 15/77 and 40/77 *HNL and others* v. *Council and Commission* [1978] ECR 1209, paragraph 6; *Brasserie du Pêcheur and Factortame*, paragraph 55; and *British Telecommunications*, paragraph 42). On the other hand, if, at the time when it committed the infringement, the Member State in question was not called upon to make any legislative choices and had only considerably reduced, or even no, discretion, the mere infringement of Community law may be sufficient to establish the existence of a sufficiently serious breach (see *Hedley Lomas*, paragraph 28).

26. So where, as in *Francovich*, a Member State fails, in breach of the third paragraph of Article [249] of the Treaty, to take any of the measures necessary to achieve the result prescribed by a directive within the period it lays down, that Member State manifestly and gravely disregards the limits on its discretion.

27. Consequently, such a breach gives rise to a right to reparation on the part of individuals if the result prescribed by the directive entails the grant of rights to them, the content of those rights is identifiable on the basis of the provisions of the directive and a causal link exists between the breach of the State's obligation and the loss and damage suffered by the injured parties: no other conditions need be taken into consideration.

28. In particular, reparation of that loss and damage cannot depend on a prior finding by the Court of an infringement of Community law attributable to the State (see *Brasserie du Pêcheur*, paragraphs 94 to 96), nor on the existence of intentional fault or negligence on the part of the organ of the State to which the infringement is attributable (see paragraphs 75 to 80 of the same judgment).

29. The reply to Questions 8, 9, 10, 11 and 12 must therefore be that failure to take any measure to transpose a directive in order to achieve the result it prescribes within the period laid down for that purpose constitutes per se a serious breach of Community law and consequently gives rise to a right of reparation for individuals suffering injury if the result prescribed by the directive entails the grant to individuals of rights whose content is identifiable and a causal link exists between the breach of the State's obligation and the loss and damage suffered.

Grant to individuals of rights whose content is sufficiently identifiable

30. By its first two questions, the national court asks whether the result prescribed by Article 7 of the Directive entails the grant to package travellers of rights guaranteeing the refund of money paid over and repatriation in the event of the insolvency of the travel organizer and/or the retailer party to the contract (hereinafter 'the organizer'), and whether the content of those rights can be sufficiently identified . . .

33. The question whether the result prescribed by Article 7 of the Directive entails the grant of rights to individuals must be examined first.

34. According to the actual wording of Article 7, this provision prescribes, as the result of its implementation, an obligation for the organizer to have sufficient security for the refund of money paid over and for the repatriation of the consumer in the event of insolvency.

35. Since the purpose of such security is to protect consumers against the financial risks arising from the insolvency of package travel organizers, the Community legislature has placed operators under an obligation to offer sufficient evidence of such security in order to protect consumers against those risks.

36. The purpose of Article 7 is accordingly to protect consumers, who thus have the right to be reimbursed or repatriated in the event of the insolvency of the organizer from whom they purchased the package travel. Any other interpretation would be illogical, since the purpose of the security which organizers must offer under Article 7 of the Directive is to enable consumers to obtain a refund of money paid over or to be repatriated.

37. That result is, moreover, confirmed by the penultimate recital in the preamble to the Directive, according to which both the consumer and the package travel industry would benefit if organizers were placed under an obligation to provide sufficient evidence of security in the event of insolvency.

38. In that connection, the German and United Kingdom Governments' argument that the Directive, which is based on Article [95] of the Treaty, is aimed essentially at ensuring freedom to provide services and, more generally, freedom of competition cannot be valid.

39. First, the recitals in the preamble to the Directive repeatedly refer to the purpose of protecting consumers. Secondly, the fact that the Directive is intended to assure other objectives cannot preclude its provisions from also having the aim of protecting consumers. Indeed, according to Article [95(3)] of the Treaty, the Commission, in its proposals submitted pursuant to that article, concerning *inter alia* consumer protection, must take as a base a high level of protection.

40. Similarly, the German and United Kingdom Governments' argument that the actual wording of Article 7 shows that this provision simply requires package travel organizers to provide sufficient evidence of security and that its lack of reference to any right of consumers to such security indicates that such a right is only an indirect and derived right must be rejected.

41. In this regard, it suffices to point out that the obligation to offer sufficient evidence of security necessarily implies that those having that obligation must actually take out such security. Indeed, the obligation laid down in Article 7 would be pointless in the absence of security actually enabling money paid over to be refunded or the consumer to be repatriated, should occasion arise.

42. Consequently, it must be concluded that the result prescribed by Article 7 of the Directive entails the grant to package travellers of rights guaranteeing the refund of money that they have paid over and their repatriation in the event of the organizer's insolvency.

43. The next point to be examined is whether the content of the rights in question are identifiable on the basis of the provisions of the Directive alone.

44. The persons having rights under Article 7 are sufficiently identified as consumers, as defined by Article 2 of the Directive. The same holds true of the content of those rights. As explained above, those rights consist in a guarantee that money paid over by purchasers of package travel will be refunded and a guarantee that they will be repatriated in the event of the insolvency of the organizer. In those circumstances, the purpose of Article 7 of the Directive must be to grant to individuals rights whose content is determinable with sufficient precision.

45. That conclusion is not affected by the fact that, as the German Government points out, the Directive leaves the Member States considerable latitude as regards the choice of means for achieving the result it seeks. The fact that States may choose between a wide variety of means for achieving the result prescribed by a directive is of no importance if the purpose of the directive is to grant to individuals rights whose content is determinable with sufficient precision.

46. The reply to the first two questions must therefore be that the result prescribed by Article 7 of the Directive entails the grant to package travellers of rights guaranteeing a refund of money paid over and their repatriation in the event of the organizer's insolvency; the content of those rights is sufficiently identifiable."

Notes

(1) In *Dillenkofer*, the ECJ examines in greater depth two of the key issues of *Brasserie du Pêcheur*, namely the characterization of the breach and the assessment of the provision which has allegedly been breached.

As regards the first issue, it will be recalled that in *Brasserie du Pêcheur*, the Court reaffirmed that "the conditions under which [Member State] liability gives rise to a right to reparation depend on the nature of the breach of Community law giving rise to loss and damage".[121] Having found that in *Brasserie du Pêcheur* the Member States enjoyed considerable legislative discretion, the ECJ proceeded to outline the three conditions for liability. In view of the above statement, the question then arose whether the three conditions would be different in cases where a Member State would not enjoy such discretion.

In *Dillenkofer* at para. 24, the ECJ explains that the above statement in *Brasserie du Pêcheur* "meant that those conditions are to be applied according to each type of situation". Consequently, the three conditions laid out in *Brasserie du Pêcheur* are applicable irrespective of whether Member States had much discretion or not in a given case. The degree of discretion then has an impact on the assessment of whether the breach was sufficiently serious. In *Dillenkofer* as in *Francovich*, the breach consisted in the failure to carry out the implementation of a directive on time.[122] At para. 26, the ECJ concludes that such a failure constitutes as such a sufficiently serious breach of Community law. In *Hedley Lomas*, which turned around the liability of a Member State, the United Kingdom, for having refused to issue an export licence, i.e. an administrative decision, contrary to Article 29 EC, the ECJ found that "where . . . the Member State in question was not called upon to make any legislative choices and had only considerably reduced, or even no, discretion, the mere infringement of Community law may be sufficient to establish the existence of a sufficiently serious breach".[123] Future cases will likely indicate how the ECJ deals with breaches of Community regulations (for instance in the field of commercial policy, if a Member State fails to respect certain measures concerning products from third countries) or decisions (for example in the field of State aids). In both these cases, the Member State has in fact little or no discretion.

(2) In *Dillenkofer*, there was debate before the ECJ as to whether Germany had implemented the directive in time: Germany submitted first that the German legislature had put in place the legislative framework for imposing the obligations prescribed by the directive within the prescribed implementation period, and secondly that the case law of

[121] *Supra*, **9.EC.6.** at para. 38.

[122] A subsequent case before the ECJ, *Rechberger* v. *Austria*, Judgment of 15 June 1999, Case C–140/97 [1999] ECR I–3499 also involved the implementation of Article 7 of Directive 90/314. There, Austria had limited the application of that Article to trips taken on a date later than the time-limit prescribed for transposition of the Directive (1 May 1995 in the case of Austria). In the absence of any basis for such a restriction in the wording of Directive 90/314, the ECJ found that such a defective implementation would constitute a sufficiently serious breach of Community law.

[123] ECJ, Judgment of 23 May 1996, Case C-5/94, *R.* v. *Ministry of Agriculture, ex p. Hedley Lomas (Ireland) Ltd.* [1996] ECR I-2553 at para. 28.

the BGH provided some protection to package travellers. The Court gave these arguments short shrift, holding in respect of the first that Member States are required to adopt *all* measures necessary to implement the directive (para. 49) and in respect of the second that the BGH case law in question did not fulfil the purpose of the directive (para. 57 ff.). Moreover, according to settled case law of the ECJ, a directive must be implemented with unquestionable binding force and with the specificity, precision and clarity required in order to satisfy the requirement of legal certainty (para. 48). That result is not achieved by issuing a legal framework only or relying on case law (para. 67).

The refusal of the ECJ in *Dillenkofer* to entertain arguments that Germany was in good faith in trying to implement Directive 90/314 is in stark contrast, it would seem, with the leniency of the Court in *British Telecommunications*[124] and in *Denkavit*,[125] where the ECJ accepted that a Member State was in good faith when it implemented the Directive but in an incorrect way, as appeared later.[126]

(3) In the above case, the ECJ also examines further the first condition for liability on the part of Member States, namely that the provision that was breached was intended to confer rights on individuals. In the case of directives, the ECJ adds at para. 27, the content of these rights must be identifiable from the directive itself.

The Directive at issue in *Dillenkofer*, Directive 90/314, merely provided at Article 7 that "the organizer and/or retailer party to the contract shall provide sufficient evidence of security for the refund of money paid over and for the repatriation of the consumer in the event of insolvency". There is no explicit mention of a right to recover lost money or be repatriated. Nonetheless, according to the Court, it is an inescapable conclusion that Directive 90/314 thereby intended to confer rights on individual customers of the tour operators and travel agencies. The Court relies for this on the objective of customer protection stated in the preamble of Directive 90/314 and mandated by Article 95(3) EC. Furthermore, the Court finds that it would be illogical to require tour operators and travel agents to furnish evidence of their having taken the requisite measures to protect customers if it was not thereby intended that customers would indeed be protected.

(4) It remains to be seen how the ECJ will elaborate the concept of "rights granted to an individual" by a Community law provision. Until now, the Court had in mind rather specific rights which relate (in Hohfeldian terms) to:[127] (i) **claims** for unpaid wages,[128] or for refunds or repatriation in case of insolvency of the travel organizer,[129] (ii) **powers** to

---

[124] ECJ, Judgment of 26 March 1996, Case C-392/93, *R. v. H.M. Treasury, ex p. British Telecommunications* [1996] ECR I-1631.

[125] ECJ, Judgment of 17 October 1996, Joined Cases C-283/94, C-291/94 and C-292/94 *Denkavit Internationaal BV* v. *Bundesamt für Finanzen* [1996] ECR I-5063.

[126] That is even clearer, it would seem, in light of ECJ, Judgment of 16 December 1993, Case C-334/92, *Wagner Miret* v. *Fondo de Garantía Salarial* [1993] ECR I-6911, where the Court, in an early application of *Francovich* (in respect of the same directive), did not entertain for a moment the possibility that the Spanish government in that case could have been in good faith in believing that the directive did not apply to a certain category of employees.

[127] For a broader analysis of ECJ case law in Hohfeldian terms, see C. Hilson and T. Downes, "Making Sense of Rights: Community Rights in EC Law" (1999) 24 ELRev 121.

[128] As in ECJ, Judgment of 19 November 1991, Cases C-6/90 and C-9/90, *Francovich* v. *Italy* [1991] ECR I-5357, and *Wagner Miret* v. *Fondo de Garantía Salarial* [1993] ECR I–6911.

[129] As in *Dillenkofer* itself.

terminate a contract[130] or to bring a court action against a company financing a consumer contract,[131] or (iii) **immunities** from the rules on public procurement[132] or to income tax for parent companies.[133] Yet other parts of Community legislation, such as directives on environmental law, to name but these,[133A] do not normally intend to grant specific rights to a special class of individuals, even though the often precise obligations which they impose on Member States (for instance on the quality of ground water, bathing water or water for human consumption) may ultimately aim at the preservation of the health of citizens generally.[134] The question is whether a general aim such as that would be enough to fulfil the "granting rights" condition. In his Opinion in Case C-237/90, *Commission* v. *Germany*, Advocate-General Jacobs acknowledged that compensation would be possible for incorrect implementation of Article 10(1) of Directive 80/1778 (water for human consumption).[135] He was of the opinion that the Directive granted rights to individuals to the extent that it intended to protect public health, as was acknowledged by the Court in its previous judgment in Case 58/89, *Commission* v. *Germany*.[136]

---

[130] As in ECJ, Judgment of 14 July 1994, Case C-91/92, *Faccini Dori* v. *Recreb SRL* [1994] ECR I-3325, where the ECJ mentioned the possibility of seeking compensation on the basis of *Francovich*.

[131] As in ECJ, Judgment of 7 March 1996, Case C-192/94, *El Corte Inglés* v. *Blázquez Rivero* [1996] ECR I-1281, where the ECJ also mentioned the possibility of asking compensation.

[132] As in ECJ, Judgment of 26 March 1996, Case C-392/93, *R.* v. *H.M. Treasury, ex p. British Telecommunications* [1996] ECR I-1631.

[133] As in ECJ, Judgment of 17 October 1996, Joined Cases C-283/94, C-291/94 and C-292/94, *Denkavit Internationaal BV* v. *Bundesamt für Finanzen* [1996] ECR I-5063.

[133A] In *Three Rivers District Council* v. *Governor and Company of the Bank of England* [1999] 4 All ER 800, CA, a majority of the Court of Appeal denied that depositors who had lost money in the collapse of a bank could derive rights from the First Banking Directive of 12 December 1977 [1977] OJ L 322/30; accordingly, they could not rely on that Directive to claim damages against the supervisory authority, the Bank of England. The Court of Appeal held that, although "it is reasonably clear that the 1977 Directive does confer enforceable rights on credit institutions which are to be supervised under its provisions . . . [t]here is not . . . any sufficient clarity or certainty in the position of depositors (or other customers of credit institutions). The fact that the Directive is in general terms for the benefit of depositors cannot be conclusive." It added nonetheless that "[h]ad intended rights been precisely and unconditionally defined, the large size and indefinite character of the class benefited would not have been conclusive against the conferment of enforceable rights". The House of Lords dismissed the subsequent appeal, holding that it is not possible to discover in the Directive provisions which entail the granting of rights to individuals ([2000] 2 WLR 1220, *per* Lord Hope of Craighead). The House of Lords found that this matter was *acte clair*, so that it was not appropriate to make a preliminary reference to the ECJ.

[134] In *Dillenkofer, supra,* **9.EC.7.** at para. 39, the Court indicates that the fact that a directive is intended to assure other objectives (of a general nature) "cannot preclude its provisions from also having the aim of protecting consumers".

[135] ECJ, Judgment of 24 November 1992, Case C-237/90, *Commission* v. *Germany* [1992] ECR I-5973, Opinion of Advocate-General Jacobs at I-6005.

[136] ECJ, Judgment of 17 October 1991, Case C-58/89, *Commission* v. *Germany* [1991] ECR I-4983. See also the Opinion of Advocate-General Lenz in ECJ, Case C-337/89, *Commission* v. *United Kingdom* [1992] ECR I-6103 at I-6132 and the later judgment of 12 December 1996, Case C-298/95, *Commission* v. *Germany* [1996] ECR I-6739. In *Three Rivers District Council* v. *Governor and Company of the Bank of England* [2000] 2 WLR 1220, HL, the House of Lords acknowledged in *obiter dictum* that the previously mentioned ECJ judgments "demonstrate that the potential width of the class of persons granted rights does not militate against the conclusion that the relevant provisions of these [environmental] Directives were intended to create rights."

9.2. CASE LAW OF THE EUROPEAN COURT OF HUMAN RIGHTS

Introductory Note

a) The European Convention for the Protection of Human Rights and Fundamental Freedoms (ECHR), signed first in 1950, is in force in the—ever growing number of—member countries of the Council of Europe, and the Protocols to the ECHR apply in a varying number of these countries.[137] Thirteen Articles of the ECHR, together with three in the First Protocol, contain the rights which the Contracting Parties undertake to secure for everyone within their jurisdiction. Four further rights are included in the Fourth Protocol to the ECHR. By and large the ECHR covers "the individual's personal life and the need to live life to the full, according to personal wishes, together with those rights which are involved in instance of conflict with the authorities and the law".[138] In the context of this book, the important provisions of the ECHR are those concerning the rights to life (Article 2), liberty and security of person (Article 5), a fair and public hearing within a reasonable time by an independent and impartial tribunal (Article 6) in combination with an effective remedy before a national authority (Article 13), respect for private and family life (Article 8), freedom of thought, conscience and religion (Article 9), freedom of expression (Article 10), freedom of assembly and association (Article 11), marrying and founding a family (Article 12), peaceful enjoyment of one's possessions (Article 1 of the First Protocol).

The ECHR established a European Commission for Human Rights and a European Court for Human Rights (ECtHR). By virtue of the Eleventh Protocol to the ECHR these bodies were replaced by one single permanent Court.[139] Even then, there remain striking differences between the nature and function of the ECtHR in Strasbourg and the ECJ in Luxembourg. One is "that one of the main tasks of the [ECJ] is to safeguard the uniform interpretation, and consequently application, of Community law. It is the exclusive duty of the [ECtHR], on the other hand, to establish whether a Contracting State has violated a specific Convention provision in a particular case".[140] Despite those differences, it can be said from the work of the ECtHR in applying the ECHR that "a case law is slowly and gradually emerging in which authoritative judgments form a system which will ultimately result in some uniformity of application within the legal orders of the Contracting States", not unlike what happens with EC law as interpreted by the ECJ.[141]

As the European Union has not—yet—adhered to the ECHR,[142] there are no institutional links between the ECJ and the ECtHR. But the ECJ as a Community institution

---

[137] ETS No. 5.

[138] R. Beddard, *Human Rights and Europe*, 3rd edn. (Cambridge: Grotius Publications, 1993) at 2.

[139] The Protocol entered into force on 1 November 1998. See on the Protocol H.G. Schermers, "Adoption of the 11th Protocol to the European Convention on Human Rights" (1995) 20 ELRev 559.

[140] A.W. Heringa, "The 'consensus principle'. The role of 'common law' in the ECHR case law" (1996) 3 MJ 108 at 140–1.

[141] Ibid.

[142] See ECJ, Opinion 2/94 of 28 March 1996, Accession of the Community to the ECHR [1996] ECR I-1759, in which the ECJ held that as Community law now stands, the Community has no competence to accede. On the options open to the EU following the Opinion of the ECJ, see A.G. Toth, "The European Union and

931

must, as required by Article 6(2) EU (which is, itself, a reflection of earlier ECJ case law), "respect fundamental rights, as guaranteed by the [ECHR] and as they result from the constitutional traditions common to the Member States, as general principles of Community law".[143]

b) The ECHR and the case law of the ECtHR hereunder make a contribution to the emergence of a common European tort law in two respects. First, the Convention created an autonomous compensation regime for persons whose rights and freedoms have been violated, at Article 41 (ex 50) ECHR, which reads:[144]

> "If the Court finds that there has been a violation of the Convention or the protocols thereto, and if the internal law of the High Contracting Party allows only partial reparation to be made, the Court shall, if necessary, afford just satisfaction to the injured party".

The judgment of 31 October 1995 in *Papamichalopoulos* v. *Greece* illustrates how Article 41 is applied by the ECtHR: before discussing and establishing the amount of damages for which the Greek government was liable, the ECtHR described the obligation of ECHR members to pay damages if they violate the ECHR as follows:[145]

> "The Court points out that by Article [46(1)] of the Convention the High Contracting Parties undertook to abide by the decision of the Court in any case to which they were parties; furthermore, Article [46(2)] provides that the judgment of the Court shall be transmitted to the Committee of Ministers which shall supervise its execution. It follows that a judgment in which the Court finds a breach imposes on the respondent State a legal obligation to put an end to the breach and make reparation for its consequences in such a way as to restore as far as possible the situation existing before the breach".

The ECtHR then added:

> "The Contracting States that are parties to a case are in principle free to choose the means whereby they will comply with a judgment in which the Court has found a breach. This discretion as to the manner of execution of a judgment reflects the freedom of choice attaching to the primary obligation of the Contracting States under the Convention to secure the rights and freedoms guaranteed (Article 1). If the nature of the breach allows of *restitutio in integrum*, it is for the respondent State to effect it, the Court having neither the power nor the practical possibility of doing so itself. If, on the other hand, national law does not allow—or allows only partial— reparation to be made for the consequences of the breach, Article [41] empowers the Court to afford the injured party such satisfaction as appears to it to be appropriate . . .".

Human Rights: the way forward" (1997) 34 CMLRev 491. See further B. de Witte, "The past and future role of the European Court of Justice in the protection of Human Rights" in Ph. Alston, (ed.), *The EU and Human Rights* (Oxford: OUP, 1999) 859.

[143] For a summarizing statement of the present state of the "general principles" doctrine developed by the ECJ, see ECJ, Judgment of 29 May 1997, Case C–299/95, *Kremzow* v. *Austria* [1997] ECR I–2629 at para. 14–5. Even after the Human Rights 1998 (c. 42, to enter into force on 1 October 2000), which "incorporates" part of the ECHR into UK law, EC law may in certain areas offer more beneficial remedies in the UK than the ECHR: see J. Wadham and H. Mountfield, *Blackstone's Guide to the Human Rights Act 1998* (London: Blackstone, 1999) at 56–7.

[144] Article 41 ECHR replaced (and simplified) the former Art. 50 ECHR. For a thorough examination of the former Art 50 ECHR, see G. Dannemann, *Schadensersatz bei Verletzung der Europäischen Menschenrechtskonvention* (Köln: Heymanns, 1994) with an extensive summary in English at 453–76. See also J. Fr. Flauss, "La réparation due en cas de violation de la Convention européenne des droits de l'homme" (1996) J T Droit Européen, 8.

[145] *Infra*, **9.ECHR.8.** at para. 34.

c) The case law of the ECtHR plays a second, and seemingly more decisive, role in the emergence of common European tort law rules through its findings that certain legislative, administrative or judicial measures taken by a ECHR Contracting State concerning tortious liability under its national law violate one of the rights guaranteed by the ECHR or its Protocols. These measures would typically affect whether, to what extent and under which conditions compensation is available to individuals (for instance, the exclusion of any compensation for damage flowing from a certain type of accident).

Recent ECtHR judgments offer good examples of such measures. For instance, in *Tolstoy Miloslavsky* v. *UK*, the application of United Kingdom law was found to violate the ECHR because it led to excessive compensation.[146] The Court considered that an especially large amount of damages in respect of defamation was disproportionate and would breach the right to freedom of expression under Article 10 ECHR. The damage award in that case was approximately three times larger than the highest amount previously awarded by any English jury in libel cases. Similarly, in *Pressos Compania Naviera SA* v. *Belgium*, the applicable Belgian law prevented the award of full compensation for an expropriation.[147] The ECtHR found there a violation of the ECHR. In *Osman* v. *UK*, the ECHR also found that an English court had breached Article 6 ECHR when it rejected a claim in negligence against a public authority at a preliminary stage.[148]

ECtHR, 31 October 1995[149]   **9.ECHR.8.**
Papamichalopoulos v. *Greece*

UNLAWFUL DISPOSSESSION. FULL COMPENSATION

Expropriation by Navy

A Contracting State which violated Article 1 of the First Protocol to the ECHR by reason of an unlawful dispossession is bound to pay compensation for material and non-material damage.

Facts: In 1967, the Greek navy occupied the land of the applicants to use it as a base and a holiday resort for naval officers. Subsequently, the Greek Government failed to act on court decisions in favour of the applicants and on its own promises to correct that injustice. In a Judgment of 24 June 1993 ("the principal judgment"),[150] the ECtHR found that the occupation without compensation and the failure of subsequent attempts to remedy the situation resulted for the applicants in a loss of the ability to dispose of their property, amounting to a de facto expropriation of the applicants' land, as such incompatible with the applicants' right to the peaceful enjoyment of their possessions, guaranteed in Article 1 of the First Protocol to the ECHR. As the issue of the application of Article 50 (now 41) ECHR was not ready for decision then, the Court invited the Government and the applicants to submit, within two months, the names of experts for the purpose of valuing the disputed land and to inform the Court of any friendly settlement they might reach. Two of the three experts filed their report on 19 December 1994, but the third expert did not contribute to the report.

Held: The unexplained fact that only two of the three experts took part in writing the report did not affect its validity. Greece was required to return the land and buildings in issue or pay a specific amount in respect of material damage; and also to pay a specific sum for non-material damage.

146 Judgment of 13 July 1995, Ser. A No. 376-B.
147 Judgment of 20 November 1995, *infra*, **9.ECHR.9.**
148 Judgment of 28 October 1998, *infra*, **9.ECHR.10.**
149 Ser. A No. 330-B.
150 Ser. A No. 260-B.

Judgment: "36. The act of the Greek Government which the Court held to be contrary to the Convention was not an expropriation that would have been legitimate but for the failure to pay fair compensation; it was a taking by the State of land belonging to private individuals, which has lasted 28 years, the authorities ignoring the decisions of national courts and their own promises to the applicants to redress the injustice committed in 1967 by the dictatorial regime.

The unlawfulness of such a dispossession inevitably affects the criteria to be used for determining the reparation owed by the respondent State, since the pecuniary consequences of a lawful expropriation cannot be assimilated to those of an unlawful dispossession. In this connection, international case-law, of courts or arbitration tribunals, affords the Court a precious source of inspiration; although that case-law concerns more particularly the expropriation of industrial and commercial undertakings, the principles identified in that field are valid for situations such as the one in the instant case.

In particular, the Permanent Court of International Justice held as follows in its judgment of 13 September 1928 in the case concerning the factory at Chorzów:

'reparation must, as far as possible, wipe out all the consequences of the illegal act and reestablish the situation which would, in all probability, have existed if that act had not been committed. Restitution in kind, or, if this is not possible, payment of a sum corresponding to the value which a restitution in kind would bear; the award, if need be, of damages for loss sustained which would not be covered by restitution in kind or payment in place of it—such are the principles which should serve to determine the amount of compensation due for an act contrary to international law.' (Collection of Judgments, Series A no. 17, p. 47)

37. In the present case the compensation to be awarded to the applicants is not limited to the value of their properties at the date on which the Navy occupied them. In the principal judgment the Court took as its basis for assessing the impugned interference the length of the occupation and the authorities' inability for years on end to allot the applicants the land promised in exchange. For that reason it requested the experts to estimate also the current value of the land in issue; that value does not depend on hypothetical conditions, as it would if the land was in the same state today as in 1967. It is clear from the expert report that since then the land and its immediate vicinity—which by virtue of its situation had potential for development for tourism—has undergone development in the form of buildings which serve as a leisure centre for naval officers and related infrastructure works. Nor does the Court overlook that the applicants themselves at the time had a scheme for the economic development of their properties, on which work had already begun (see paragraph 31 above).

38. Consequently, the Court considers that the return of the land in issue . . . would put the applicants as far as possible in a situation equivalent to the one in which they would have been if there had not been a breach of Article 1 of Protocol No. 1; the award of the existing buildings would then fully compensate them for the consequences of the alleged loss of enjoyment . . .

39. If the respondent State does not make such restitution within six months from the delivery of this judgment, the Court holds that it is to pay the applicants, for damage and loss of enjoyment since the authorities took possession of the land in 1967, the current value of the land, increased by the appreciation brought about by the existence of the buildings, and the construction costs of the latter. As to the determination of the amount of this compensation, and having regard to the considerable divergence between the methods of calculation employed for the purpose by the parties to the dispute, the Court adopts the findings in the expert report for the assessment of the damage sustained. The amount therefore comes to GRD 4,200,000,000 for the land and GRD 1,351,000,000 for the buildings, plus interest at 6 per cent from the expiry of the aforementioned period of six months until payment is actually made.

40. More particularly, as regards the buildings, the Court cannot accept the Government's submission that awarding compensation under this head is a matter coming exclusively within the jurisdiction of the national courts as it requires prior interpretation of national law and complete clarification of the circumstances of the case; the applicants, they said, had available to them in the

national legal system effective remedies to satisfy their excessive demands. The Court considers, firstly, that the buildings form part of the *restitutio in integrum* (see paragraph 38 above). It points out, secondly, that it has declared the applicants to be the victims of a breach of Protocol No. 1; requiring them to exhaust domestic remedies in order to be able to obtain just satisfaction from the Court would prolong the procedure instituted by the Convention in a manner scarcely in keeping with the idea of the effective protection of human rights . . .

41. The applicants also sought GRD 6,000 million in respect of the non-pecuniary damage they had allegedly sustained as a result of the 'extraordinary suffering' and the 'intolerable mockery' of which they had been the victims during the three decades that their dispute with the State had lasted.

42. The Government found that amount 'quite absurd' as it was almost twice as much as the value of the land as assessed by the experts. The non-pecuniary damage alleged by the applicants was attributable exclusively to their own conduct, because they had dropped all the proceedings they had brought in the national courts although those proceedings had not been wholly without prospects of success.

43. The Court considers that the breach of the Convention caused the applicants definite non-pecuniary damage arising from the feeling of helplessness and frustration in the face, firstly, of the Navy's and successive governments' refusal to comply with the decisions of the Greek judicial and administrative authorities (see paragraphs 7–12 of the principal judgment) and, secondly, of the failure of the attempt to recover land of equal value in exchange (see paragraphs 14–22 and 26–27 of the principal judgment).

The Court awards each of the applicants GRD 450,000 under this head, in other words GRD 6,300,000 in all . . .

For these reasons, the Court unanimously:

1. *Holds* that the expert report is valid;

2. *Holds* that the respondent State is to return to the applicants, within six months, the land in issue of an area of 104,018 sq.m. including the buildings on it;

3. *Holds* that, failing such restitution, the respondent State is to pay the applicants, within six months, GRD 5,551,000,000 (five thousand five hundred and fifty-one million) in respect of pecuniary damage, plus non-capitalisable interest at 6 per cent from the expiry of the six-month period (point 2 of the operative provisions) until payment;

4. *Holds* that the respondent State is to pay the applicants, within three months, GRD 6,300,000 (six million three hundred thousand) in respect of non-pecuniary damage."

Notes

(1) The *quantum* of damages for material losses imposed in the annotated case by the ECtHR on the basis of Article 41 (ex 50) ECHR is quite substantial. Note, however, that those damages must only be paid if Greece fails to return the premises. Because of the illegal character of the expropriation and the disregard of national court decisions and promises to redress the injustice, the Court wanted to wipe out, as far as possible, all the consequences of the illegal act, and it stuck to the principle of *restitutio in integrum* strictly.[151] The ECtHR cited in authority for its reasoning the judgment of the Permanent Court of International Justice in the *Chorzów Factory* case, another case of unlawful expropriation.[152] If the measure involved had been legitimate but for the failure to pay fair compensation, the ECtHR award would have been less—Article 41 only requires just

[151] According to J. McBride, "The right to property" (1996) 21 ELRev 40 at 50.
[152] *Infra*, **9.INT.15.**

satisfaction—since, as the ECtHR writes, "the pecuniary consequences of a lawful expropriation cannot be assimilated to those of an unlawful dispossession".

(2) It follows from the wording of Article 41 ECHR that a Contracting State is only liable when the Court has found that it has violated the applicant's rights under the ECHR. Only the applicant is entitled to compensation. Therefore, compensation will extend only to damage suffered by a person whose rights have been violated and who at the same time is an applicant before the ECtHR.[153]

According to Article 41 ECHR, the Court will only award damages if compensation is not or not fully possible under domestic law; accordingly, applicants must first exhaust domestic remedies. It appears from paragraph 40 of the above judgment that the ECtHR interprets this requirement "in keeping with the idea of the effective protection of human rights".

ECtHR, 20 November 1995[154]   9.ECHR.9.
Pressos Compania Naviera S.A. v. Belgium

RETROACTIVE IMMUNITY FROM LIABILITY. INTERFERENCE WITH "POSSESSION"

Damage caused by harbour pilots

An act granting to the State immunity against tort claims from individuals with retroactive effect violates Article 1 of the First Protocol to the ECHR and gives rise to compensation.

Facts: In a judgment of 15 December 1983, the Belgian Court of Cassation reversed its case law on Article 251 of the Belgian Shipping Act.[155] Formerly, harbour pilots (*loods*) were regarded as "servants" of either the captain, the owner or the charterer of the vessel within the meaning of Article 1384(3) of the Civil Code. Accordingly, one of the latter was liable under Article 1384(3) of the Civil Code if, in the event of a collision, harm was caused to a third party. With the judgment of 15 December 1983, liability for the acts of the pilot was shifted over to the State which had organized the service to which the pilot belonged. In reaction to that judgment and in order for the State to avoid that liability, the Act of 30 August 1988 was enacted, whereby the Act of 3 November 1967 on the piloting of sea-going vessels was amended to grant immunity to the State against tort claims from third parties resulting from the acts of pilots, with retroactive effect to 15 December 1983.[156] Twenty-four shipowners involved in accidents in Belgian and Dutch territorial waters (and their insurers) applied to the Belgian Arbitration Court to have the Act of 30 August 1988 declared void. The Arbitration Court dismissed their application on 5 July 1990. The applicants then went before the European Commission for Human Rights, which on 4 July 1994 expressed the opinion that Belgium breached Article 6(1) of the ECHR, but not Article 1 of the First Protocol to the ECHR. The case was brought before the ECtHR.

Held: Article 1 of the First Protocol was breached, and accordingly it is not necessary to discuss Article 6(1) ECHR. The application of Article 50 (now 41) ECHR was reserved.

Judgment: "Article 1 of Protocol No. 1:

[The Court first had to decide whether the Act of 30 August 1988 interfered with the 'possession' of the applicants. It found that, in light of the established rules of Belgian law making the tortious liability of the State subject to the general tortious liability regime, the applicants could argue that

---

[153] G. Dannemann, *Schadensersatz bei Verletzung der Europäischen Menschenrechtskonvention* (Köln: Heymanns, 1994) at 457 (English summary) discusses many other issues, such as compensation for loss of a chance, future damages, material and non-material damage and particularly causation. See also J. Fr. Flauss. *supra*, n. 144, at 13–15.

[154] Ser. A No. 332. See also P. Lambert, "L'épilogue européen des accidents de pilotage des bateaux dans l'estuaire de l'Escaut" (1996) 115 JT 794.

[155] Book II, Title II, Commercial Code.

[156] Act of 30 August 1988, amending the Act on Harbour Pilots.

they had a 'legitimate expectation' that their damage claims, which all occurred before entry into force of the 1988 Act, would be recognized. The damage claims of the applicants which were set aside by the Act of 30 August 1988 constituted an asset and therefore amounted to possession within meaning of the first sentence of Article 1.[157]

The ECtHR then concluded that the Act of 30 August 1988 constituted interference with these "possessions". The next stage was to examine whether this interference was justified. After having assessed whether the Act of 30 August 1988 was in the public interest, the Court moved on to the issue of proportionality.]

(b) Proportionality of the interference

38. An interference with the peaceful enjoyment of possessions must strike a 'fair balance' between the demands of the general interest of the community and the requirements of the protection of the individual's fundamental rights. The concern to achieve this balance is reflected in the structure of Article 1 as a whole, including therefore the second sentence, which is to be read in the light of the general principle enunciated in the first sentence (see paragraph 33 above). In particular, there must be a reasonable relationship of proportionality between the means employed and the aim sought to be realised by any measure depriving a person of his possessions.

Compensation terms under the relevant legislation are material to the assessment whether the contested measure respects the requisite fair balance and, notably, whether it imposes a disproportionate burden on the applicants. In this connection, the taking of property without payment of an amount reasonably related to its value will normally constitute a disproportionate interference and a total lack of compensation can be considered justifiable under Article 1 only in exceptional circumstances . . .

39. In the present case the 1988 Act quite simply extinguished, with retrospective effect going back 30 years and without compensation, claims for very high damages that the victims of the pilot accidents could have pursued against the Belgian State or against the private companies concerned, and in some cases even in proceedings that were already pending.

40. The Government invoked the financial implications, which were both enormous and unforeseeable, of the Court of Cassation's judgment of 15 December 1983. During preparatory work on the 1988 Act, the financial impact of the actions then pending against the Belgian State had been assessed at BEF 3.5 thousand million . . .

[Finally] the Government contended that the 1988 Act was also intended to bring the Belgian legislation into line with that of neighbouring countries . . .

42. The Court recalls that the Court of Cassation had recognised in its 'La Flandria' judgment of 5 November 1920 that the State and the other public-law bodies were subject to the general law of tort . . .

Since then the Court of Cassation had admittedly not had occasion to hear cases relating to the State's liability concerning pilot services, but it was certainly not unforeseeable that it would apply to this type of case, at the first opportunity, the principles that it had defined in general terms in the judgment of 1920 . . .

43. The financial considerations cited by the Government and their concern to bring Belgian law into line with the law of neighbouring countries could warrant prospective legislation in this area to derogate from the general law of tort.

Such considerations could not justify legislating with retrospective effect with the aim and consequence of depriving the applicants of their claims for compensation.

Such a fundamental interference with the applicants' rights is inconsistent with preserving a fair balance between the interests at stake.

---

[157] Prepared on the basis of the summary prepared by the ECtHR registry but not binding on the Court.

44. It follows that in so far as the 1988 Act concerned events prior to 17 September 1988, the date of its publication and its entry into force, it breached Article 1 of Protocol No. 1.”

Notes

(1) The annotated judgment shows the impact which ECtHR case law can have on the tort law of a Contracting State. In this instance, an Act limiting the tortious liability of the State was found to violate the ECHR to the extent it had retroactive effect. The Act in issue had been enacted by Parliament to set aside a judgment of the Court of Cassation, which decided that harbour pilots were to be regarded as “servants” of the State within the meaning of Article 1384(3) of the Belgian Civil Code (vicarious liability), and accordingly that the State was liable under the general rules of tort for the acts of harbour pilots. The Court of Cassation judgment was in line with well established case law whereby the tortious liability of the State and public authorities falls under the general tort regime also applicable to private persons.[158] However, nineteenth-century case law of the Court of Cassation, rendered well before the *Flandria* judgment, had denied State liability for pilots, and in that respect the Court reversed its earlier case law. Yet as the ECtHR found, one cannot speak of a turnabout in the case law (*renversement de jurisprudence*), since the *Flandria* line of case law was so well established that it was foreseeable that the earlier case law on State liability for pilots would be reversed as soon as the issue came before the Court of Cassation again, which it only did with the judgment of 15 December 1983.

(2) A striking feature of the above judgment is the broad interpretation given to the term “possessions” (*biens* in the French version) in Article 1 of the First Protocol to the ECHR.[159] The Court also applies the proportionality test in a way that could have far-reaching consequences, holding that retroactivity could not be justified by the severe financial implications which the Court of cassation judgment would have for the national budget (allegedly BEF 3.500 millions). It remains to be seen, of course, how large a sum the Court would award on the basis of Article 41 ECHR if no agreement could be reached between the parties.[159A] As seen above, the Court is more lenient when a lawful expropriation has taken place and litigation bears more on the amount of the fair compensation, as opposed to cases of unlawful dispossession.[160] In the above case the Act of 30 August 1988 retroactively annihilated the tort claims of the applicants for past events; while this seems to be a dispossession, it could well be that it is found in good faith, given that the above judgments made a novel and rather broad interpretation of the term “possessions”.[161]

(3) In a subsequent case, the ECtHR was faced with a modification of the UK tax regime, which had the effect of changing the treatment of building societies retrospec-

[158] Since Court of cassation, 5 November 1920, *La Flandria*, Pas. 1920.I.193.

[159] See J. McBride, “The Right to Property” (1996) 21 ELRev 41 and P. Lambert, “L’épilogue européen des accidents de pilotage des bateaux dans l’estuaire de l’Escaut” (1996) 115 JT 794 at 798–9.

[159A] In a subsequent decision of 3 July 1997, *Pressos Compania Naviera SA* v. *Belgium*, Rep. 1997–IV the ECtHR struck out 24 of the 25 cases, since they were pending before Belgian courts (which would rule in the light of the decision in the annotated case) and awarded to the 25th applicant (against which a final court decision dismissing the claim had already been rendered), under Art 50 (now 41) ECHR, one-half of the amount for which it had been found liable towards third parties, thus apportioning liability on an equitable basis

[160] *Supra*, **9.ECHR.8.**, Note (1).

[161] See also P. Lambert, “L’épilogue européen des accidents de pilotage des bateaux dans l’estuaire de l’Escaut” (1996) 115 JT 794 at 800.

tively.[162] The building societies were arguing that the transitional measures surrounding that modification infringed their rights under Article 1 of the First Protocol to the ECHR. In its judgment, the ECtHR refused to rule on whether the tax claims under the ancient regime constituted "possessions" within the meaning of that provision.[163] On the assumption that they were indeed possessions, the Court found that the UK legislation did not in any event infringe Article 1 of the First Protocol.[164]

ECtHR, 28 October 1998[165]   **9.ECHR.10.**
Osman v. UK

LIABILITY OF PUBLIC AUTHORITIES

Harassing teacher

Article 6(1) ECHR is infringed by a rule whereby claims in negligence against the police force will be rejected at a preliminary stage, without consideration of their merits, because it is generally not fair, just and reasonable to impose a duty of care on the police force.

Facts: A teacher became attached to a 15-year-old schoolboy, and started to harass him with allegations relating to certain sexual practices. After being dismissed from the school in the middle of 1987, he kept harassing the schoolboy. Those facts were known to the police, who had even received a statement by the teacher that he might commit a crime. In December 1987, the teacher provoked an accident with a car in which the schoolboy was a passenger. The police inquired into the matter but did not pursue it further. In March of 1988, the teacher shot and injured the schoolboy and killed his father. The boy and his mother claimed in negligence against the police force. On the preliminary issue of whether there was a duty of care, the Court of Appeal dismissed the claim, finding that, while there was a very close degree of proximity amounting to a special relationship between the plaintiffs' family and the investigating police officers, it would be against public policy to impose a duty of care.

Held: The judgment of the Court of Appeal violated Article 6(1) EHCR (unanimous decision).

Judgment: "APPLICABILITY OF ARTICLE 6(1) ECHR
    136. The Court recalls at the outset that Article 6(1) secures to everyone the right to have any claim relating to his civil rights and obligations brought before a court or tribunal. In this way the Article embodies the "right to a court", of which the right of access, that is the right to institute proceedings before courts in civil matters constitutes one aspect only [reference omitted]. . .
    138. The Court would observe that the common law of the respondent State has long accorded a plaintiff the right to submit to a court a claim in negligence against a defendant and to request that court to find that the facts of the case disclose a breach of a duty of care owed by the defendant to the plaintiff which has caused harm to the latter. The domestic court's enquiry is directed at determining whether the constituent elements of a duty of care have been satisfied, namely: whether the damage is foreseeable; whether there exists a relationship of proximity between the parties; and whether it is fair, just and reasonable to impose a duty of care in the circumstances. . .
    Although the applicants have argued in terms which suggest that the exclusionary rule operates as an absolute immunity to negligence actions against the police in the context at issue, the Court

---

[162] ECtHR, 23 October 1997, *National & Provincial Building Society v. UK*, Rep. 1997-VII, 2325, (1997) 25 EHRR 127.
[163] Ibid. at 2350–1, para. 69–70.
[164] Ibid. at 2353–55, para. 80–3.
[165] Rep. 1998-VIII.

accepts. . . that the rule does not automatically doom to failure such a civil action from the outset but in principle allows a domestic court to make a considered assessment on the basis of the arguments before it as to whether a particular case is or is not suitable for the application of the rule. . .

139. On that understanding the Court considers that the applicants must be taken to have had a right, derived from the law of negligence, to seek an adjudication on the admissibility and merits of an arguable claim that they were in a relationship of proximity to the police, that the harm caused was foreseeable and that in the circumstances it was fair, just and reasonable not to apply the exclusionary rule outlined in the Hill case. In the view of the Court the assertion of that right by the applicants is in itself sufficient to ensure the applicability of Article 6(1) of the Convention. . .

Compliance with Article 6(1) ECHR

147. The Court recalls that Article 6(1) embodies the 'right to a court', of which the right of access, that is, the right to institute proceedings before a court in civil matters, constitutes one aspect.

However, this right is not absolute, but may be subject to limitations; these are permitted by implication since the right of access by its very nature calls for regulation by the State. In this respect, the Contracting States enjoy a certain margin of appreciation, although the final decision as to the observance of the Convention's requirements rests with the Court. It must be satisfied that the limitations applied do not restrict or reduce the access left to the individual in such a way or to such an extent that the very essence of the right is impaired. Furthermore, a limitation will not be compatible with Article 6(1) if it does not pursue a legitimate aim and if there is not a reasonable relationship of proportionality between the means employed and the aim sought to be achieved [reference omitted]. . .

148. Against that background the Court notes that the applicants' claim never fully proceeded to trial in that there was never any determination on its merits or on the facts on which it was based. The decision of the Court of Appeal striking out their statement of claim was given in the context of interlocutory proceedings initiated by the Metropolitan Police Commissioner and that court assumed for the purposes of those proceedings that the facts as pleaded in the applicants' statement of claim were true. The applicants' claim was rejected since it was found to fall squarely within the scope of the exclusionary rule formulated by the House of Lords in the Hill case.

149. The reasons which led the House of Lords in the Hill case to lay down an exclusionary rule to protect the police from negligence actions in the context at issue are based on the view that the interests of the community as a whole are best served by a police service whose efficiency and effectiveness in the battle against crime are not jeopardised by the constant risk of exposure to tortious liability for policy and operational decisions.

150. Although the aim of such a rule may be accepted as legitimate in terms of the Convention, as being directed to the maintenance of the effectiveness of the police service and hence to the prevention of disorder or crime, the Court must nevertheless, in turning to the issue of proportionality, have particular regard to its scope and especially its application in the case at issue. While the Government have contended that the exclusionary rule of liability is not of an absolute nature. . . and that its application may yield to other public-policy considerations, it would appear to the Court that in the instant case the Court of Appeal proceeded on the basis that the rule provided a watertight defence to the police and that it was impossible to prise open an immunity which the police enjoy from civil suit in respect of their acts and omissions in the investigation and suppression of crime.

151. The Court would observe that the application of the rule in this manner without further enquiry into the existence of competing public-interest considerations only serves to confer a blanket immunity on the police for their acts and omissions during the investigation and suppression of crime and amounts to an unjustifiable restriction on an applicant's right to have a determination on the merits of his or her claim against the police in deserving cases.

In its view, it must be open to a domestic court to have regard to the presence of other public-interest considerations which pull in the opposite direction to the application of the rule. Failing this, there will be no distinction made between degrees of negligence or of harm suffered or any consideration of the justice of a particular case. It is to be noted that in the instant case Lord Justice McCowan. . . appeared to be satisfied that the applicants, unlike the plaintiff Hill, had complied with the proximity test, a threshold requirement which is in itself sufficiently rigid to narrow considerably the number of negligence cases against the police which can proceed to trial. Furthermore, the applicants' case involved the alleged failure to protect the life of a child and their view that that failure was the result of a catalogue of acts and omissions which amounted to grave negligence as opposed to minor acts of incompetence. The applicants also claimed that the police had assumed responsibility for their safety. Finally, the harm sustained was of the most serious nature.

152. For the Court, these are considerations which must be examined on the merits and not automatically excluded by the application of a rule which amounts to the grant of an immunity to the police. . .

154. For the above reasons, the Court concludes that the application of the exclusionary rule in the instant case constituted a disproportionate restriction on the applicants' right of access to a court. There has accordingly been a violation of Article 6(1) of the Convention."

Notes

(1) In the annotated case, the applicants before the ECtHR were not attacking an act of the executive power (as in *Papamichalopoulos* v. *Greece*[166]) or a legislative act (as in *Pressos Compania Naviera* v. *Belgium*[167]), but rather an act of the English judiciary, namely the decision of the Court of Appeal in *Osman* v. *Ferguson*, whereby their claim was rejected.[168] Indeed, as is generally the case with international treaties, the obligations incumbent upon the parties to the ECHR are binding upon the State as a whole, including the judiciary.[169]

(2) In *Osman* v. *Ferguson*, as in many other English cases concerning the liability of public authorities,[170] the plaintiff's claim was rejected at a preliminary stage—on an application from the defendant for the court to strike out the claim[171]—on the basis that the claim was bound to fail, since even if all the alleged facts were true, there was no duty of care on the part of the police and thus no liability in negligence could arise. The Court of Appeal had assessed the case in the light of the *Caparo* test, with its three branches: a duty of care will arise if (i) the harm was *reasonably foreseeable,* (ii) the relationship between defendant and plaintiff was sufficiently *proximate* and (iii) it is *fair, just and reasonable* to impose a duty of care upon the defendant.[172]

[166] *Supra,* **9.ECHR.8.**
[167] *Supra,* **9.ECHR.9.**
[168] *Osman* v. *Ferguson* [1993] 4 All ER 344, CA. See in that respect s. 6(3)(a) of the Human Rights Act 1998, (c. 42) where courts or tribunals are explicitly brought under the term "public authority". The House of Lords acting in its judicial capacity is also included through s. 6(4).
[169] See *infra,* **9.INT.12.** and Note (2) thereafter. On that point, the regime of liability of Member States for breaches of Community law, as it was developed by the ECJ (see *supra,* 9.1.3.) follows the model of international law, since Member States can be liable irrespective of whether the breach was committed by the executive, legislative or judiciary branch: see *supra,* **9.EC.6.** at para. 34.
[170] See *supra,* Chapter III, 3.3.1.
[171] The powers of the court to strike out claims are set out in Rule 3.4 of the Civil Procedure Rules. See the discussion *supra,* Chapter III, **3.E.32.**, Note (2).
[172] The *Caparo* test is discussed *supra,* Chapter I, 1.4.1.B. Excerpts from *Caparo Industries plc* v. *Dickman* can be found *supra,* Chapter II, **2.E.47.**

In its reasoning, the Court of Appeal relied heavily on the House of Lords decision in *Hill* v. *Chief Constable of West Yorkshire*.[173] In that case, the House of Lords was faced with a claim by the mother of the last victim of the "Yorkshire Ripper" against the police. The claimant alleged that the police had failed to issue sufficient warnings to potential victims of that serial killer. The House of Lords dismissed the claim on the ground that there was no proximity (second branch of the *Caparo* test), since the victim was one of a large number of young women living in the area where previous crimes had occurred. In addition, the House of Lords stated that it would not be fair, just and reasonable to impose a duty of care on the police authorities (third branch of the *Caparo* test):[174]

> "Potential existence of such liability may in many instances be in the general public interest, as tending towards the observance of a higher standard of care in the carrying on of various different types of activity. I do not, however, consider that this can be said of police activities. The general sense of public duty which motivates police forces is unlikely to be appreciably reinforced by the imposition of such liability so far as concerns their function in the investigation and suppression of crime. From time to time they make mistakes in the exercise of that function, but it is not to be doubted that they apply their best endeavours to the performance of it. In some instances the imposition of liability may lead to the exercise of a function being carried on in a detrimentally defensive frame of mind. The possibility of this happening in relation to the investigative operations of the police cannot be excluded. . . The manner of conduct of such an investigation must necessarily involve a variety of decisions to be made on matters of policy and discretion, for example as to which particular line of inquiry is most advantageously to be pursued and what is the most advantageous way to deploy the available resources. Many such decisions would not be regarded by the courts as appropriate to be called in question, yet elaborate investigation of the facts might be necessary to ascertain whether or not this was so. A great deal of police time, trouble and expense might be expected to have to be put into the preparation of the defence to the action and the attendance of witnesses at the trial. The result would be significant diversion of police manpower and attention from their most important function, that of the suppression of crime. Closed investigations would require to be reopened and retraversed, not with the object of bringing any criminal to justice but to ascertain whether or not they had been competently conducted."

In *Osman* v. *Ferguson*, the Court of Appeal was of the opinion that, contrary to the situation in *Hill*, there was a relationship of proximity between the defendants and the plaintiff (second branch of the *Caparo* test). However, it felt compelled by the generality of the reasoning in *Hill* to reject the claim on the ground that it would not be fair, just and reasonable to impose a duty of care upon the defendant (third branch of the *Caparo* test).

Osman v. *Ferguson* therefore involved the combination of a procedural device (application to strike out at a preliminary stage) with the application of a substantive rule (the third branch of the *Caparo* test), which resulted in the plaintiff's claim being rejected without any significant examination of its facts or its merits.

On the face of *Osman* v. *Ferguson*, it would therefore seem that the reasoning of *Hill* is of such general scope that it will work so as to exclude any duty of care on the part of the police force. That led the ECtHR, in *Osman* v. *UK*, to use the term "exclusionary rule" to

---

[173] *Hill* v. *Chief Constable of West Yorkshire* [1989] AC 53, HL.
[174] Ibid. per Lord Keith. That passage is mentioned in the annotated judgment at para. 91 (in the restatement of English law).

describe the effect of the *Hill* decision as it was construed by the Court of Appeal in *Osman* v. *Ferguson*.

(3) For the ECtHR in the annotated case, the rights of the Osmans under Article 6(1) ECHR were at stake (admissibility), and the UK had violated them through the decision of the Court of Appeal (substance of the case).

With respect to admissibility, the main difficulty, when proceeding under Article 6(1) ECHR, is that it is meant to protect the right of access to courts, and not substantive rights. At para. 139, the Court framed the right in question as "the right. . . to seek an adjudication on the admissibility and the merits of an arguable claim that they were in a relationship of proximity to the police, that the harm caused was foreseeable and that in the circumstances it was fair, just and reasonable not to apply the exclusionary rule outlined in the Hill case." The ECtHR thus remains within the realm of Article 6(1) ECHR: it is dealing with the right to present a claim in negligence before English courts, and in particular to argue that there was a duty of care. But while the ECtHR reiterates the three branches of the *Caparo* test, the third branch is turned around: instead of the traditional formulation ("whether it is fair, just and reasonable to impose a duty of care on the defendant"), the Court sees it as a matter of making an exception to the "exclusionary rule" outlined in *Hill* v. *Chief Constable of West Yorkshire*.[175] That "exclusionary rule" can however be seen as the conclusion reached by the House of Lords in *Hill* that, as a general matter, it would not be fair, just and reasonable to impose a duty of care on the police force. The key factor, perhaps, that led the ECtHR to formulate the right under Art. 6(1) ECHR as set out above was *Swinney* v. *Chief Constable of Northumbria*,[176] the one case where the Court of Appeal found that there were countervailing public policy factors which made it fair, just and reasonable to impose a duty of care.[177] In the eyes of the ECtHR, the "exclusionary rule" of *Hill* was therefore not as absolute as it was made out to be.[178]

By framing the right under Art. 6(1) ECHR in such terms at the admissibility stage, the ECtHR was able to conclude, when it came to the substance of the case, that there has been a violation of Article 6 (1) ECHR. At that stage, the ECtHR also took into account the procedural dimension of the case before the UK courts, since the claim had been "struck out" on a preliminary basis without any examination of the merits (para. 148). The ECtHR found that the Court of Appeal should not have struck out the claim without examining competing public policy considerations which might have counterbalanced those enumerated in *Hill*, so that a duty of care could have arisen. In so doing, the Court of Appeal had restricted the right of the Osmans to see their claim decided on its merits in a way that was disproportionate.

(4) The annotated judgment has already been heavily criticized by some English commentators. In a conference, Lord Hoffmann stated that the decision "fills [him] with

---

[175] [1989] 1 AC 53, [1988] 2 All ER 238.

[176] [1997] QB 464, CA. In that case, a policeman had negligently allowed the name of an informant to become public, even though the police had undertaken to keep it secret. The Court of Appeal found that the interest of the general public in a proper treatment of confidential matters by the police counterweighed the public policy grounds set out in *Hill*.

[177] See L.C.H. Hoyano, "Policing Flawed Police Investigations: Unravelling the Blanket" (1999) 26 Mod LR 912 at 917–20.

[178] Indeed at para. 151, the ECtHR stated that the rule cannot be absolute.

apprehension".[179] He suggested that the ECtHR in fact ventured into an examination of the substantive rights of litigants, and "ignore[d] one of the principal reasons for the present doctrine, which is to avoid a trial altogether, to avoid the waste of public resources involved in a judicial investigation, usually on legal aid, as to whether the public authority should reasonably have provided the benefit or not."[180] In his speech in *Barrett* v. *Enfield London Borough Council*,[181] Lord Browne-Wilkinson said: "I confess that I find the decision of the Strasbourg court extremely difficult to understand". For him as well, the ECtHR misconstrued the nature of the "fair, just and reasonable" test: it is a prerequisite for a duty of care to arise at all, not an "immunity", and once it has been found as a matter of law that it is not fair, just and reasonable to impose a duty of care in a given case, then the same conclusion will follow in other similar cases.

(5) It is too early to assess the consequences of the annotated judgment on English law.[182] As seen previously, the judgment of the ECtHR might have played a role in the change of approach to the liability of public authorities evidenced in *Barrett* v. *Enfield London Borough Council*, although the leading speeches of Lord Slynn and Lord Hutton do not refer to it.

Nevertheless, it seems difficult to envisage how the striking-out power could still be used to dismiss claims at a preliminary stage on the ground that, irrespective of the other two branches of the *Caparo* test, it would not be fair, just and reasonable to impose a duty on the defendant.[183] The third branch of the *Caparo* test could thus no longer be invoked at a preliminary stage, without an examination on the merits. It remains open to discussion whether a claim can still be struck out on the ground that there is no relationship of proximity between the plaintiff and the defendant (second branch of the *Caparo* test). At para. 151, the ECtHR apparently left that door open, and at least one decision has taken the view that striking out for lack of proximity was still permissible after *Osman* v. *UK*.[184]

As mentioned before, the combined effect of the annotated judgment and *Barrett* v. *Enfield London Borough Council*[185] could very well be that all the public policy factors that intervened to lead to the dismissal of claims in negligence against public authorities at a preliminary stage, for lack of a duty of care, will now be discussed on the merits of the case, in relation to the issue of whether the duty of care was breached.[186]

(6) In a broader perspective, a comparison could be made between the impact of the annotated judgment and that of the case law of the ECJ on the liability of Member States

---

[179] Lord Hoffmann, "Human Rights and the House of Lords" (1999) Mod LR 159 at 164.

[180] Ibid. See also the similar criticism made by T. Weir, "Down Hill—All the Way?" (1999) Camb LJ 4.

[181] *Supra*, Chapter III, **3.E.32.**

[182] With the entry into force of the Human Rights Act 1998 (c. 42), most of the rights guaranteed by the ECHR, amongst which the right to a fair trial laid down in Article 6 (but not the right to an effective remedy laid down in Article 13), and by its protocols, amongst which the right to peaceful enjoyment of property, laid down in Protocol 1, have now been incorporated into English law, so that courts should take it upon themselves to construe the common law in light of ECtHR judgments such as *Osman* v. *UK*. (see s. 2 of the Act and 8 of the Act). On the Human Rights Act 1998, see J. Wadham and H. Mountfield, *Blackstone's Guide to the Human Rights Act 1998* (London: Blackstone, 1999) and S. Greer, "A Guide to the Human Rights Act 1998" (1999) 24 ELRev 3.

[183] See M. Vranken, "Duty of care, public policy, and the European Convention on Human Rights: *Osman* v. *United Kingdom*" (1999) 7 Torts Law Journal 40 at 45.

[184] *Palmer* v. *Tees Health Authority* [1999] Lloyd's Rep Med 351, CA.

[185] *Supra*, Chapter III, **3.E.32.**

[186] See *supra*, Chapter III, **3.E.32**, Note (4), relying on P. Craig and D. Fairgrieve, "*Barrett*, Negligence and Discretionary Powers" [1999] Pub L 626.

for breaches of Community law, as exemplified by *Brasserie du Pêcheur*.[187] In both cases, the European courts, when they considered provisions of national law, ultimately found against *a priori* limitations on the scope of protection of civil liability. In the annotated judgment, the ECtHR held that an absolute exclusion of liability of public authorities in negligence—because there would be no duty of care on public policy grounds—would breach Article 6(1) ECHR. In *Brasserie du Pêcheur*, the ECJ concluded that the principle of effective protection of rights granted under Community law dictated that the general exclusion of recovery for pure economic loss (*reiner Vermögensschaden*) under German law be set aside in cases of State liability for breaches of Community law.[188] In both cases, the European courts could refer to the law of comparable European States to ascertain that the fears that justified those *a priori* limitations had not materialized or could be addressed with less drastic means than an *a priori* limitation.[189] On that basis, it might be thought—although further evidence will be needed before any conclusion can be reached—that European jurisdictions are likely to take an unfavourable stance towards *a priori* limitations of liability which operate at a preliminary stage without consideration of the merits of the case.

(7) It should be mentioned that another major case on the liability of public authorities in the past decade, *X.* v. *Bedfordshire County Council*,[190] has also been brought before the institutions of the ECHR. In its Reports[191] on the cases, the European Commission of Human Rights (as it still existed then) followed the reasoning of the ECtHR in *Osman* v. *UK* and held that Article 6 ECHR had been violated when claims in damages were rejected on an application to strike out, on the ground that public policy factors militated against the imposition of a duty of care on the public authorities.[192] The cases are now pending before the ECtHR.

9.3. CASE LAW OF INTERNATIONAL COURTS AND ARBITRAL TRIBUNALS

The following materials can be found (with notes) at <http://www.rechten. unimaas.nl/casebook>:

9.INT.11. ICJ, 24 May 1980, *United States Diplomatic and Consular Staff in Tehran* (*USA* v. *Iran*). Hostage crisis.

9.INT.12. UN International Law Commission, *Draft Articles on State Responsibility* (excerpts).

---

[187] *Supra*, **9.EC.6.**

[188] Ibid. at para. 86–7. See also Note (5) thereafter.

[189] For instance, the liability of public authorities can be kept within bounds through a requirement that the breach of duty be particularly severe. Similarly, liability for pure economic loss can be limited through the general criteria of liability (causation, etc.).

[190] [1995] 2 AC 633, [1995] 3 WLR 152, [1995] 3 All ER 353, HL. The decision of the House of Lords in that case has been largely superseded by *Barrett* v. *Enfield London Borough Council*, *supra*, **3.E.32.** (see also the notes thereafter).

[191] The decision of the House of Lords joined a number of cases, which were brought separately before the European Commission of Human Rights.

[192] See European Commission of Human Rights, Report of 10 September 1999, *T.P.* v. *UK* and Report of 10 September 1999, *Z* v. *UK*.

9.INT.13. ICJ, 9 April 1949, *Corfu Channel case (Merits)* (*UK* v. *Albania*). Corfu Channel.

9.INT.14. UN International Law Commission, *Draft Articles on State Responsibility* (excerpts).

9.INT.15. PCIJ, Judgment No. 13, 13 September 1928, *Factory at Chorzów (Merits)* (*Germany* v. *Poland*). Chorzów Factory.

9.INT.16. UN International Law Commission, *Draft Articles on State Responsibility* (excerpts).

9.4. IMPACT OF SUPRANATIONAL AND INTERNATIONAL TORT LAW ON DOMESTIC LAWS

The impact of European Community law on domestic legal systems

The changes brought by supranational and international law to domestic law in general, and domestic tort law in particular, are most apparent in the case of the *law of the European Community* (EC), the most significant pillar of the European Union. For indeed, although the EC is limited in scope by the objectives and competences which the Member States have assigned to it in Articles 2 and 3 EC Treaty, it is intended primarily to establish an internal market, that is to effect market integration in the widest sense of the word.[193] In legal terms, this broad objective implies that all domestic rules and measures which run counter to that objective must be set aside—irrespective of the area of law or of the rank or nature of those rules and measures. Changes in domestic legal systems result first and foremost from the provisions of the EC Treaty, in particular those relating to the four freedoms on which the concept of market integration is based, namely freedom of movement of goods, persons, services and capital;[194] in the second place, they also follow from Community measures laid down in secondary legislation, mainly directives, which implement the provisions of the EC Treaty in instances where differences between national laws could affect the functioning or the establishment of the internal market.

Given that the objectives and the competences of the EC are limited in scope, and that the purpose of the EC is market integration and not unification of the law, harmonization of national laws through the EC comes into question only to the extent that it is needed for the establishment and functioning of the internal market. That means that Community law has a fragmented impact on national laws: its perspective remains slanted by the need to achieve market integration.[195] For that same reason, EC law also disrupts the unity and equilibrium of the legal system of each Member State, since it has

---

[193] The objective of the EC is therefore not to establish a single legal system, but to bring about market integration between the Member States. See further P.J. Slot, "Harmonisation" (1996) 21 ELRev 378.

[194] Arts. 7a, 30, 48, 52, 59 and 73b EC Treaty.

[195] See further W. van Gerven, "Community and national legislators, regulators, judges, academics and practitioners: living together apart" in B.S. Markesinis, (ed.), *Law Making, Law Shaping, Law Finding: The Clifford Chance Lectures*, vol. II (New York: Oxford University Press, 1997) 13.

an impact only on national rules that hinder market integration whilst leaving untouched national rules which are unrelated to market integration but otherwise pursue, at national level, a similar purpose to the rules affected by Community law.[196]

The ECJ judgment of 28 March 1996 in *Ruiz Bernáldez*,[197] gives a typical example of the fragmentation effect which directives may have. In that case the directives related to insurance against civil liability for motor vehicle accidents.[198] In its judgment, the ECJ, relying on the aim of the directives, held that statutory provisions or contractual clauses in insurance policies cannot exclude compensation to third parties who are victims of an accident caused by drunken driving. It was of no concern to the ECJ whether its ruling was in accordance with prevailing doctrine in each Member State as regards exemption clauses or with the defences legally available to defendants in road traffic accidents. It is for the national legislature and judiciary to find ways to fit the ECJ ruling into their own legal system and, as the case may be, to reconcile it with other conflicting or diverging rules. A further example of the invasive and disruptive effect of directives is that a further directive may compel Member States to give victims a direct right of action against insurers.[199] Member States will then have to provide for such a right of action (if they do not already do so) in their national law relating to contractual or tortious liability, which could eventually lead them to revisit the treatment of third party rights under contract law, and in particular the principle of privity or relativity of contract.

The foregoing should not lead one to conclude that harmonization produces only disruptive effects on national legal systems. As set out above, Directive 85/374 on product liability obviously brings the legal systems of the Member States closer to each other in the specific field of liability for defective products.[200] Built as it is on rules and principles common to the Member States, or at least on emerging common trends, the Directive marks a further step in completing national liability regimes, as it may help national lawmakers to solve open questions for which no clear solution had yet been found, against a background of harmonization with other legal systems.[201] Such interplay between Community and national laws can be fruitful, however, only if the Community makes a deliberate effort to look for common principles, or at least emerging common trends, in the course of preparing the directive.[202] By the same token, national authorities, including national courts, must be prepared to develop their national laws with a view not only to preserving the overall consistency in the application of their respective legal system, but also to maintaining the co-ordination with the legal systems of the Member States in the application of Community law.[202A] This should be the case not only in areas that are directly affected by Community law, but also in other areas closely related to those affected areas.

---

[196] Harmonization through directives in not in itself a uniform concept, as different methods have been developed to address different areas of the law: P.J. Slot, "Harmonisation" (1996) 21 ELRev 378, distinguishes between harmonization to define law and policy at Community level, total harmonization, optional harmonization, partial harmonization, minimum harmonization, alternative harmonization and mutual recognition of national rules and controls. Obviously, the disruptive effect of a directive is commensurate with its harmonizing effect, in the sense that total harmonization is at the top of both the harmonization and the disruption column. As Slot emphasizes at 383, total harmonization fell out of favour with the Member States because it gave them insufficient flexibility.

[197] *Supra*, Chapter VI, **6.EC.23.–25.**, Note (2).

[198] Ibid.

[199] Ibid., Note (3).

[200] *Supra*, Chapter VI, **6.EC.35.**, and notes thereafter.

[201] See in particular ibid., Note (3).

[202] As was the case for Directive 85/374, ibid.

[202A] The implementation of Directive 85/374 on liability for defective products, *supra*, Chapter VI, **6.EC.33.**, in the laws of the Member States illustrates that harmonization can be significantly impaired if Member States do not attempt to achieve uniformity in the application of the implemented Community legislation as well: see *supra*, Chapter VI, 6.3.3.

Remedies to enforce rights under Community law

So far as judicial protection of the rights which persons can derive from Community law ("Community rights") is concerned, the prime driver for the harmonization of national remedies is the case law of the European Court of Justice, as it interprets basic principles of Community law and provisions of the EC Treaty. Since the EC Treaty can only be amended as a result of an Intergovernmental Conference of the Member States, the interpretation given to the EC Treaty by the ECJ in its case law is virtually definitive.

The case law of the ECJ on the judicial protection of Community rights finds its origin in the ECJ's own doctrine of direct effect, which concerns provisions of the EC Treaty (to which both vertical and horizontal direct effect are given) and of directives (to which only vertical direct effect is given), provided in both cases that the provision in question is sufficiently precise and unconditional. Persons wishing to enforce the rights derived from those provisions against conflicting measures taken by national authorities (and where the provisions have horizontal direct effect, against private individuals), may do so directly before national courts. Even if a provision in a directive has no direct effect, it will nevertheless have an impact on domestic laws because of the duty imposed on all public bodies (including in the first place national courts) to construe national law in conformity with Community law. Furthermore, since the judgments of the ECJ in *Francovich*[203] and subsequently in *Brasserie du Pêcheur*,[204] it has become clear that Member States may be held liable before national courts for serious breaches of Community law which have resulted in injury (including pure economic loss), regardless of the State organ (legislature, executive, judiciary) which is responsible for the breach.

Compensation for injury caused by breaches of Community law on the part of Member States, as laid down in the aforementioned judgments, is only one of the judicial remedies which the ECJ has required Member States to put in place in order to ensure that European citizens can effectively enforce their Community rights.[205] Other remedies include restitution[206] and interim relief.[207] Whilst the Court was at the outset rather reluctant to compel domestic courts to create new remedies, since that conflicts with the principle of procedural autonomy of the Member States, such reluctance became less

---

[203] Discussed *supra*, 9.1., Introductory Note under a).

[204] *Supra*, **9.EC.6.**

[205] See E. Szyszczak, "Making Europe more relevant to its citizens: effective judicial process" (1996) 21 ELRev 351.

[206] For restitution cases relating to the recovery of charges imposed by national authorities contrary to Community law: see ECJ, Judgment of 16 December 1976, Case 33/76, *Rewe-Zentralfinanz e.G.* v. *Landwirtschaftskammer für das Saarland* [1976] ECR 1989; ECJ, Judgment of 16 December 1976, Case 45/76, *Comet BV* v. *Produktschap voor Siergewassen* [1976] ECR 2043; ECJ, Judgment of 9 November 1983, Case 199/82, *Amministrazione delle Finanze dello Stato* v. *SpA San Giorgio* [1983] ECR 3595; ECJ, Judgment of 27 February 1980, Case 68/79, *Hans Just I/S* v. *Danish Ministry for Fiscal Affairs* [1980] ECR 501; ECJ, Judgment of 14 January 1997. Joined Cases C–192/95 et al., *Société Comateb* v. *Directeur général des douanes et droits indirects* [1997] ECR I–165; ECJ, Judgment of 2 December 1997, Case C–188/95, *Fantask A/S* v. *Industrieministeriet* [1997] ECR I–6783.

[207] For interim relief cases see ECJ, Judgment of 19 June 1990, Case C-213/89, *R.* v. *Secretary of State for Transport, ex p. Factortame* [1990] ECR I-2433; ECJ, Judgment of 21 February 1991, Joined Cases C-143/88 and C-92/89, *Zückerfabrik Süderdithmarschen AG* v. *Hauptzollamt Paderborn* [1991] ECR I-415; ECJ, Judgment of 9 November 1995, Case C-465/93, *Atlanta Fruchthandelsgesellschaft MbH* v. *Bundesamt für Ernährung und Forstwirtschaft* [1995] ECR I-3761; ECJ, Judgment of 26 November 1996, Case C–68/95, *T. Port GmbH & Co KG* v. *Bundesanstalt für Landwirtschaft und Ernährung* [1996] ECR I–6065.

apparent in subsequent judgments.[208] It has never disappeared, however, as shown by the court's case law relating to whether national procedural rules, including limitation periods, are permissible where they limit the effectiveness of Community law.[209]

To answer this question, the ECJ must strike a sensible balance between the need to assure that rules of substantive Community law remain uniform in their application and the need to rely on national procedural rules to ensure their enforcement by national authorities.

The ECJ has expressed that balancing process in what has by now become a sort of classic formula: "In the absence of harmonised Community rules of procedure, it is for the national courts to apply their own national rules of procedure in claims involving matters of Community law, save that: (a) the rules applied to Community cases cannot be less favourable than those relating to similar actions of a domestic nature, and (b) the rules applied cannot make it impossible in practice to exercise the relevant Community rights".[210] This formula is also used in connection with compensation for breaches of Community law on the part of Member States, as recognized in *Francovich* and *Brasserie du Pêcheur*, where the ECJ had to define the right to, and the extent of, reparation.[211]

A dual system of tort liability for breaches of Community law waiting for harmonization

As set out above, EC law comprises two regimes of extra-contractual liability for breaches of Community law.[212] The first concerns the liability of Community institutions and their officials, and it is set out in Article 288(2) EC and the related case law of the ECJ. The second relates to the liability of Member States, their organs and officials, and it is based on a principle that is "inherent in the system of the Treaty", according to the ECJ in *Francovich*. Under the first regime, plaintiffs who have sustained damage can bring suit before the Community courts (CFI and ECJ), while under the second one, plaintiffs who have suffered damage must bring their claim before a national court (which may ask the ECJ for a preliminary ruling on the interpretation of Community law). In *Brasserie du Pêcheur*, the ECJ:[213]

- extended liability on the part of Member States to all breaches of Community law (and not merely to breaches consisting in a failure to transpose a directive within the prescribed time period, as was the case in *Francovich*);
- elaborated the substantive conditions for liability to arise, adding that it would draw inspiration for that purpose, in the absence of written rules, from the general principles common to the laws of the Member States; and
- outlined its approach on the duty and the extent of compensation.

It was in connection with the third of those elements that the ECJ restated its aforementioned "classic formula" concerning remedies.

---

[208] See W. van Gerven, "Of Rights, Remedies and Procedures" (2000) 37 CMLR 501.

[209] See G.C. Rodriguez Iglesias and J.P. Keppenne, "L'incidence du droit communautaire sur le droit national" in *Mélanges Michel Waelbroeck* (Brussels: Bruylant, 1999) 517 at 535–41.

[210] Thus formulated for the first time in ECJ, Judgment of 16 December 1976, Case 33/76, *Rewe-Zentralfinanz e.G. v. Landwirtschaftskammer für das Saarland* [1976] ECR 1989 at para. 13.

[211] See *Brasserie du Pêcheur, supra*, **9.EC.6.** at para. 67 and 83.

[212] *Supra*, 9.1., Introductory Note.

[213] See further on each of these three points, *supra*, 9.2., Introductory Note under a).

[214] *Supra*, **9.EC.1–5.**

Article 288(2) EC refers to the general principles common to the laws of the Member States in connection with the non-contractual liability of the Community; and the ECJ has expressed the intention to develop the regime of liability on the part of Member States for breaches of Community law on the basis of those general principles (second point above). The case law of the ECJ may therefore be taken as providing a guideline to the tortious liability of Member States for breach of EC law. Accordingly, judgments of the ECJ and CFI under Article 288(2) EC have been included and discussed here.[214] To date, the Court has applied its Article 288 case law, in the area of State liability, only in respect of legislative acts which are characterized by a wide discretion. According to its judgment in *Schöppenstedt* (rendered under Article 288),[215] for liability to occur in the exercise of a wide discretion, there must be "a sufficiently flagrant violation of a superior rule of law for the protection of the individual".[216] In *Mulder*, the ECJ refined that test,[217] whilst in recent judgments, the CFI has clarified the conditions of "serious breach"[218] and direct causal link.[219]

In applying the *Schöppenstedt* test also where Community law has been infringed *by a Member State*, the ECJ has taken a very broad view of what can be regarded as a national legislative act characterized by a wide discretion.[220] Moreover, until now the ECJ has found that only a total failure to implement a directive in time constitutes a serious breach when wide discretion is involved; in failing to implement a directive, the Court said, the Member State concerned has "manifestly and gravely disregard[ed] the limits on its discretion".[221] In that judgment, the ECJ also attempted to clarify the requirement that the directive must entail the grant to individuals of rights which are sufficiently identified in order for liability to arise as a result of a failure to implement it.[222]

It has been argued that the ECJ gave too wide an ambit to the *Schöppenstedt* test under Article 288(2) EC by applying it to situations where it was questionable that the Community action at issue involved the kind of wide legislative discretion which the test presupposes. As a consequence, the ECJ has also been applying the test too widely in cases of liability on the part of Member States.[223] In line therewith, it is submitted that the case law of the ECJ on the regime of liability of Member States for breaches of Community law would gain in depth if the Court, in elaborating that regime, were to take the whole of its case law on Article 288(2) EC into consideration, that is to say its case law as it relates not only to the exercise of wide discretion by public authorities (the *Schöppenstedt* line of cases), but also to instances of wrongful interpretation of Community law by Community institutions in areas which do not involve the exercise of wide discretion. The latter instances can be compared with the situation in *British Telecommunications*, where a Member State had acted upon a wrong interpretation of Community law. In order to illustrate the entire body of ECJ case law under Article 288(2) EC, two judgments have been included where negligent driving by a Community official and wrongful interpretation of Community law by Community institutions were at stake.[224]

---

[215] ECJ, Judgment of 2 December 1971, Case 5/71, *Aktien-Zuckerfabrik Schöppenstedt v. Council* [1971] ECR 975.

[216] The so-called "serious breach" test: *supra*, 9.2., Introductory Note under b).

[217] *Supra*, **9.EC.3.** at para. 12–13 and 15–16. In a subsequent judgment, the ECJ set out the principles governing the calculation of loss of earnings and of alternative income: ibid., Note (5).

[218] In *Nölle*, *supra*, **9.EC.4.**

[219] In *Blackspur*, *supra*, **9.EC.5.**

[220] Besides *Brasserie du Pêcheur*, *supra*, **9.EC.6.** at para. 45–50, see also *British Telecommnications*, *supra*, **9.EC.6.**, Note (4) under (ii).

[221] See *Dillenkofer*, *supra*, **9.EC.7.** and Notes (1) and (2).

[222] Ibid. at para. 30–46. See also Notes (3) and (4).

[223] See the Opinion of Advocate-General Tesauro in *Brasserie du Pêcheur*, *supra*, **9.EC.116.**, Note (3).

[224] *Supra*, **9.EC.1.–2.** See further W. van Gerven, "Taking Article 215 EC seriously", in J. Beatson and T. Tridimas, (eds.), *New Directions in European Public Law* (Oxford: Hart Publishing, 1998).

It is to be hoped that, on the basis of its case law under Article 288(2) EC, to which it referred in *Brasserie du Pêcheur*, the ECJ will also flesh out the other conditions that give rise to liability on the part of Member States, namely a direct causal link between the breach and the loss suffered[225] and the existence of damage, and that it will develop principles regarding the nature and extent of compensation. It is further to be hoped that in doing so, the ECJ will systematically look for principles common to the legal systems of the Member States, on which it can build its case law both for the liability of Community institutions under Article 288(2) EC and for the liability of Member States under the *Francovich* principle. By the same token, the ECJ will be in a position to harmonize those two regimes of liability for breaches of Community law, as well as those regimes and the tortious liability regimes otherwise applicable in the Member States.

The influence of Community law on national tort laws: the Communitarization of national laws

Under the impetus of the full effect doctrine developed by the ECJ and of secondary legislation enacted by the Community institutions, Community law has invaded vast areas of national law, including some where one would not have expected to find it.

Brasserie du Pêcheur illustrates how the influence of Community law is felt in the area of tort liability on the part of the State, its organs, subdivisions and officials. Throughout the judgment, the ECJ dismisses the application of many rules of national law which it finds would prevent individuals from deriving full benefits from Community law. That is the case, in particular, for national rules that exclude compensation for legislative acts or omissions—or that allow it only if the legislative body was under a duty towards the plaintiff or an identifiable group to which the plaintiff belongs;[226] for national rules requiring proof of misfeasance in public office for liability to arise, such misfeasance being inconceivable in the case of the legislature;[227] for national rules precluding compensation for *reiner Vermögensschaden* or pure economic loss.[228]

The impact of Community law on national laws is not limited to changes which are the direct consequence of the case law of the ECJ or of secondary legislation.[229] It is not unlikely that changes mandated by Community law will in turn provoke further change in national law, because of the necessity to maintain harmony between areas of national law affected by Community law and areas not so affected.[230] That should not necessarily lead to increased liability on the part of public authorities. In those Member States where public authorities are subject to a severe liability regime, it may be that the influence of Community law will bring about a loosening of that liability regime, for example if the "serious breach" criterion is also applied for the liability of public authorities for breaches of national law.[231]

The impact of the case law of the ECJ has been limited so far to the tortious liability of public bodies, in the first place the State. That may change if and when the ECJ

225 See *supra*, **9.EC.6.**, Note (4)(iii).
226 Compare with *supra*, **8.G.100.** and **8.F.103.**
227 See *supra*, Chapter III, 3.3.1.
228 See *supra*, **9.EC.6.**, Note (5).
229 As in the case of Directive 85/374, *supra*, Chapter VI, **6.EC.35.**
230 See *supra*, **9.EC.6.**, Note (6) and ibid., Note (3).
231 *Supra*, **9.EC.6.**, Note (6).

were to decide that, as a matter of Community law, individuals should also be liable for breaches of Community law, where Community law imposes a direct obligation upon them. Such is already the case for breaches of Articles 81 and 82 EC and also for provisions which are considered to have not only vertical but also horizontal direct effect.[232] An extension of the principle of tortious liability for breaches of Community law, as articulated in *Francovich*, to cover breaches committed by individuals as well, should follow in our view from the reasoning of the ECJ in *Francovich*: if the principle of liability on the part of Member States for breaches of Community law is inherent in the Treaty, since it is necessary to give full effect to directly applicable Treaty provisions and, to secure full legal protection for those deriving rights from those provisions, the same should be true for the liability of individuals.[233] If the ECJ were to acknowledge that principle in the context of tort litigation between individuals, it should at the same time set out the conditions that may give rise to liability.[234]

Influence, back and forth: the Europeanization of Community law

In our view, the prospects for further harmonization, either through secondary legislation or case law of the ECJ, depend on whether such harmonization takes place on the basis of the "principles common to the legal systems of the Member States", as they are called in Article 288(2) EC. As explained elsewhere,[235] if the ECJ—or the Commission for that matter—wishes to pursue harmoniously, that is with the support of the Member States, its creative task of developing Community law and promoting its uniform application, it must look for common ground in the national legal systems on which to build its efforts. That is the only way to preserve homogeneity between Community law and national laws, while not jeopardizing consistency between the different areas of Community law, and to respect Article 151 EC, whereby the Community must "contribute to the flowering of the cultures of the Member States, while respecting their national and regional diversity and at the same time bringing the common cultural heritage to the fore". Similarities and differences between the national legal systems are part of that cultural heritage.

In the area of extra-contractual liability, the quest for consistency between the two liability regimes under Community law has now become imperative, as a consequence of the ruling of the ECJ in *Brasserie du Pêcheur*, according to which "in the absence of particular justification . . . [t]he protection of the rights which individuals derive from Community law cannot vary depending on whether a national authority or a Community authority is responsible for the damage".[236] In that same area, homogeneity between those Community regimes and the Member States' liability regimes is desirable because of the requirement of uniform application of Community law throughout the Community. For the reasons mentioned above, if a sufficiently high level of uniform application of Community law is to be readily accepted by the Member States, it must be based on the general principles common to the laws of the Member States.

---

[232] Such as Arts. 28, 39, 43, 49 and 141 EC.

[233] See further the Opinion of the Advocate-General in Case C-128/92, *H.J. Banks & Co. v. British Coal Corporation* [1994] ECR I-1209 at para. 36.

[234] *Supra*, 9.1., Introductory Note under c).

[235] W. van Gerven, "Taking Article 215 EC seriously" in J. Beatson and T. Tridimas, (eds.), *New Directions in European Public Law* (Oxford: Hart Publishing, 1998) 35.

[236] *Supra*, **9.EC.6.** at para. 42.

Accordingly, the ECJ may wish to develop or re-examine concepts used in its case law on extra-contractual liability in the light of similar concepts found in the laws of the Member States concerning the liability of public authorities, namely:

- sufficiently serious breach (*violation suffisamment caractérisée*);
- a superior rule of law "for the protection of the individual"[237] or "intended to confer rights on individuals".[238] The ECJ seems to regard both expressions as synonymous. They may be seen as references to the *Schutznorm* concept in German law, the *relativiteit* rule in Dutch law or the "neighbour principle" in English law;
- "direct causation" between breach and loss, which seems to contain a requirement of directness in respect of causation;[239]
- "damage sustained by the injured parties",[240] which raises the question what conditions damage must fulfil in order to be recoverable;
- "the actual extent of reparation",[241] which leads to the question whether full or only adequate compensation is required[242] and the question what measure of "reasonable diligence" the injured person must exercise in avoiding or mitigating loss.[243]

To develop these concepts harmoniously, comparative law research is of strategic importance[244] (hence the present casebooks). Among other issues, comparative research is needed in particular to gain a proper understanding of the basic concept of fault, about which the ECJ states that it "does not have the same content in the various legal systems", while mentioning that "certain objective and subjective factors connected with the concept of fault under a national legal system may well be relevant for the purpose of determining whether or not a given breach of Community law is serious".[245] Those objective and subjective factors (relating to illegality and imputability respectively) must be studied in the perspective not only of State liability but also of liability of individuals.[246] In any event, the notion of "fault" will unavoidably have to be examined in the context of both State liability and individual liability, since many legal systems do not generally treat public authorities any differently from individuals under tort law: see for instance the law of England, Scotland, Ireland, Belgium or the Netherlands.[247]

[237] As in the *Schöppenstedt* test, see *supra*, **9.EC.3.** at para. 12.

[238] As in *Dillenkofer*, for instance, *supra*, **9.EC.7.** at para. 21.

[239] As used in the case law of the ECJ under Art. 288(2) EC, see *Blackspur*, *supra*, **9.EC.115.** at para. 40 and *Dillenkofer*, ibid. at para. 21.

[240] *Brasserie du Pêcheur*, *supra*, **9.EC.6.** at para. 65 and *Dillenkofer*, ibid. at para. 17.

[241] *Brasserie du Pêcheur*, ibid., heading preceding para. 81.

[242] In *Brasserie du Pêcheur*, ibid., the ECJ states at para. 82 that "reparation . . . must be *commensurate* with the loss or damage sustained so as to ensure the effective protection for the rights [of individuals]" (emphasis added).

[243] Ibid. at para. 84 ff.

[244] W. van Gerven, "Bridging the unbridgeable: Community and National Tort laws after *Francovich* and *Brasserie*" (1996) 45 ICLQ 539.

[245] *Brasserie du Pêcheur*, *supra*, **9.EC.6.** at para. 76 and 78.

[246] All the more if the Court were to acknowledge that the liability of individuals for breaches of Community law is also an inherent principle in the system created by the EC Treaty: cf. *supra*, 9.1., Introductory Note under e).

[247] As a result of the present case law of the Court, which requires that breaches of Community law and similar breaches of national law be treated equally (see *Brasserie du Pêcheur*, *supra*, **9.EC.6.** at para.74), the "classic" criteria of illegality and imputability must be used to assess the liability of the public authorities for breaches of Community law in Member States where those criteria are normally used under tort

The impact of the law of the Council of Europe and the ECHR on national legal systems

There is not much to be said about the impact of legal instruments prepared within the framework of the Council of Europe, such as the Convention on Civil Liability for Damage to the Environment.[248] In all likelihood, the Convention will never come into force for lack of a sufficient number of ratifications.[249] That being so, it may nevertheless serve as an example for legislative work to be carried out elsewhere regarding civil liability for environmental harm.[250] Since damage to the environment often gives rise to cross-border litigation, the present work gives some information on the interpretation of Article 5(3) of the Brussels Convention setting forth a special ground of jurisdiction in matters relating to tort, delict or quasi-delict.[251]

ECHR law exerts some influence on national legal systems, albeit less than EC law, because of important differences between the respective objectives of those supranational legal orders. Whilst the purpose of the EC is to achieve market integration between the Member States, the ECHR purports to protect the fundamental freedoms and human rights of persons. The main tasks of the ECJ are therefore to supervise the legality of Community actions (including the respect of the fundamental freedoms and human rights embodied in the ECHR), to examine the compatibility of Member State measures with Community law as well as to preserve the uniform application of Community law in the Member States. In comparison, the functions of the ECtHR are more limited, consisting solely in establishing whether a Contracting State[252] has violated a specific provision of the ECHR in a particular case.[253] Nevertheless, as a result of the activity of the ECtHR, "a case law is slowly and gradually emerging in which authoritative judgments form a system which will ultimately result in some uniformity of application within the legal orders of the Contracting States".[254]

Given these differences, the ECtHR contributes to the emergence of a common law of Europe in the area of tort liability in two respects. First, the ECtHR applies Article 41 ECHR,[255] whereby it can provide for just satisfaction to an injured person, if a violation of the ECHR by a Contracting State has been established *and* if the internal law of that State allows only partial reparation or no reparation at all.[256] Although the case law of the ECtHR under Article 41 ECHR cannot influence domestic law directly and can only

---

law to gauge the behaviour of private individuals and public authorities alike. That means that public authorities having committed a "Euro-tort" are worse off in those Member States than in the other Member States where a less rigorous tortious liability regime (based on *faute grave*, for instance) generally applies to public authorities.

[248] *Supra*, Chapter VI, **6.CE.43.**

[249] Even if the Convention were to come into effect, it would apply in the relationships between Member States of the EU only to the extent that no Community rule governed the area in question: Ibid., Art. 25(2).

[250] See ibid., Notes (1) to (3).

[251] See ibid., Notes (4) to (6).

[252] As to whether the ECtHR has jurisdiction to establish that actions of EC institutions are infringing the ECHR, see W.P.J. Wils, "La compatibilité des procédures communautaires en matière de concurrence avec la Convention européenne des droits de l'homme" (1996) 32 CDE 329.

[253] A.W. Heringa, "The 'Consensus principle'. The role of common law in the ECHR case law" (1996) 3 MJ 108.

[254] Ibid.

[255] Art. 41 ECHR was formerly Art. 50, before the entry into force of Protocol No. 11.

[256] See *supra*, 9.2, Introductory Note under a) and *Papamichalopoulos, supra*, **9.ECHR.8.** with notes.

lead to the creation of an independent tort regime under the ECHR, it will contribute to the emergence of harmonized liability rules in Europe.

The second way in which the case law of the ECtHR can help in the emergence of a common European tort law, this time directly, is when the ECtHR rules on infringement proceedings brought against a specific rule of the tort law of a Contracting State or a measure based thereon,[257] including rules and measures that try to exclude the application of tort law to certain cases, as was the case in *Pressos Compania Naviera*[258] In that case an Act of the Belgian legislature granted immunity to the Belgian State against a new application of tortious liability which had arisen as a result of the case law of the Belgian Court of Cassation; the Act was found by the ECtHR to violate Article 1 of Protocol 1 of the ECHR to the extent that the Act had retrospective effect.

Besides having a direct impact on Belgian tort law, that judgment may also indirectly influence the laws of the other Contracting States, in that it regards a damage claim as a "possession" (*bien*) within the meaning of the first sentence of Article 1 of Protocol 1 to the ECHR. That interpretation will no doubt have repercussions in all Contracting States, as it relates to a basic concept of any legal system.

The potential influence of the ECHR on domestic tort laws was also evident in *Osman* v. *UK*,[259] where the ECtHR found that the judgment of the English Court of Appeal in *Osman* v. *Ferguson*[260] breached Art. 6 ECHR. In that case, the Court of Appeal had dismissed a claim against the police force at the preliminary stage, on the ground that, as a matter of public policy, no duty of care could be imposed on the police force towards citizens (even though there was a relationship of proximity). According to the ECtHR, the claimants had a right to be heard on the merits as to whether there were not countervailing public policy considerations that would have justified the imposition of a duty of care, and therefore their right to access to a civil court (under Article 6 ECHR) had been violated. In light of that judgment, it could be that broad *a priori* rules that exclude (or limit) the liability of certain categories of defendants, or the compensation for certain types of damages, might face closer scrutiny under human rights instruments.

The impact of international law

Public international law, insofar as it relates to State responsibility, cannot influence domestic legal systems to the same extent as EC law or even ECHR law. State responsibility remains a matter of inter-State relationships, and as such it operates separately from the domestic law of tort. Nonetheless, the frontier between those two realms is becoming increasing porous; in the current context of economic globalization, transborder litigation concerning for instance breaches of contract or violations of international trade or public procurement norms will increasingly be pursued at both the domestic level (by the aggrieved party before the courts of the State of the other party) and the international level (between the State of the aggrieved party and the State of the other party). Some form of "dialogue" between domestic tort laws and the law of State responsibility is likely

---

[257] See for instance the judgment in *Tolstoy Miloslavsky*, *supra*, 9.2, Introductory note under c).

[258] *Supra*, **9.ECHR.9.**

[259] *Supra*, **9.INT.11.** This regime is laid out in greater detail in the Draft Articles on State Responsibility, *supra*, **9.INT.12., 9.INT.14.** and **9.INT.16.**

[260] *Supra*, **9.INT.13.**

to ensue. With that in mind, some key features of the scope of protection under the law of State responsibility were surveyed in section 3.

The case of the *United States Diplomatic and Consular Staff in Tehran*, for instance, illustrates the workings of the law of State responsibility as an inter-State regime.[261] Even if the hostage crisis was triggered by the action of a group of people who apparently had no link to the Iranian State, the failure of Iran to intervene to put an end to the hostage-taking was considered by the ICJ to be a breach of international law. The State responsibility of Iran could then be invoked.

The most striking difference between the law of State responsbility and domestic tort laws in general lies in the so-called *secondary* nature of State responsibility, which means that there is no unifying set of conditions that give rise to State responsibility; everything is left to the content of the international law obligations themselves. State responsibility occurs when a norm of international law has been infringed (unlawfulness) through conduct which can be attributed to the State. Whether some form of fault or the causation of damage is required depends on the international norm the breach of which is alleged. In the *Corfu Channel* case, for instance, the ICJ found that the international norm at stake required Albania not knowingly to allow its territory to be used for acts detrimental to other States.[262] An element of knowledge therefore had to be proved by the claimant, the United Kingdom.

Finally, the judgment of the PCIJ in the *Factory at Chorzów* case[263] and the related Draft Articles on State Responsibility[264] show that State responsibility contains no limitation on the scope of protection according to the type of interest which was infringed, with the possible exception of loss of profit (*lucrum cessans*), the recovery of which is not yet firmly established.

---

[261] *Supra*, **9.INT.15.**
[262] *Supra*, **9.INT.16.**
[263] *Supra*, **9.ECHR.10.**
[264] *Osman* v. *Ferguson* [1993] 4 All ER 344, CA.

Index

This index only covers the contents of this book. Materials placed on the Website of the Ius Commune Casebooks (<http://www.rechten.unimaas.nl/casebook>) have not been indexed here. A number of the topics mentioned in this index are dealt with at greater length in the materials made available electronically.

Numbers refer to pages.

Page references in italics indicate a short note or explanation on the meaning of the word or expression (usually in a foreign language).

Page references in bold indicate a discussion of the subject-matter in one of the excerpted materials.

There is no general entry for references to English, French or German law, since these appear from the table of contents.